The Longman Anthology of World Literature

VOLUME F

THE TWENTIETH CENTURY

David Damrosch
COLUMBIA UNIVERSITY
The Ancient Near East; Mesoamerica

April Alliston
PRINCETON UNIVERSITY
The Age of the Enlightenment

Marshall Brown
UNIVERSITY OF WASHINGTON
The Nineteenth Century

Page duBois
UNIVERSITY OF CALIFORNIA, SAN DIEGO
Classical Greece

Sabry Hafez
UNIVERSITY OF LONDON
Arabic and Islamic Literature

Ursula K. Heise
COLUMBIA UNIVERSITY
The Twentieth Century

Djelal Kadir
PENNSYLVANIA STATE UNIVERSITY
The Twentieth Century

David L. Pike
AMERICAN UNIVERSITY
Rome and the Roman Empire; Medieval Europe

Sheldon Pollock
UNIVERSITY OF CHICAGO
South Asia

Bruce Robbins
COLUMBIA UNIVERSITY
The Nineteenth Century

Haruo Shirane
COLUMBIA UNIVERSITY
Japan

Jane Tylus
NEW YORK UNIVERSITY
Early Modern Europe

Pauline Yu
AMERICAN COUNCIL OF LEARNED SOCIETIES
China

The Longman Anthology of World Literature

David Damrosch

General Editor

VOLUME F

THE TWENTIETH CENTURY

Djelal Kadir

Ursula K. Heise

with contributions by

David Damrosch, Sabry Hafez, and Pauline Yu

PEARSON

Longman

New York   San Francisco   Boston
London   Toronto   Sydney   Tokyo   Singapore   Madrid
Mexico City   Munich   Paris   Cape Town   Hong Kong   Montreal

Vice President and Editor-in-Chief: *Joseph Terry*
Development Manager: *Janet Lanphier*
Development Editor: *Adam Beroud*
Senior Marketing Manager: *Melanie Craig*
Senior Supplements Editor: *Donna Campion*
Media Supplements Editor: *Nancy Garcia*
Production Manager: *Douglas Bell*
Project Coordination, Text Design, and Page Makeup: *Elm Street Publishing Services, Inc.*
Senior Design Manager/Cover Designer: *Nancy Danahy*
On the Cover: Detail from *Dream of a Sunday Afternoon in the Alameda,* 1947–1948, mural,
    Hotel del Prado, by Diego Rivera (1866–1957). 4.8 × 15m, 15¾ × 49¼ ft. Copyright ©
    Schalkwijk/Art Resource, New York.
Photo Research: *Photosearch, Inc.*
Manufacturing Buyer: *Lucy Hebard*
Printer and Binder: *Quebecor-World/Taunton*
Cover Printer: *The Lehigh Press, Inc.*

For permission to use copyrighted material, grateful acknowledgment is made to the copyright holders on pages 1149–1154, which are hereby made part of this copyright page.

Library of Congress Cataloging-in-Publication Data

The Longman anthology of world literature / David Damrosch, general editor.—1st ed.
     v.   cm.
   Includes bibliographical references and index.
   Contents: v. A. The ancient world—v. B. The medieval era—v. C. The early
modern period—v. D. The seventeenth and eighteenth centuries—v. E. The
nineteenth century—v. F. The twentieth century.
   ISBN 0-321-05533-0 (v. A).—ISBN 0-321-16978-6 (v. B).— 0-321-16979-4
(v. C).— 0-321-16980-8 (v. D).— 0-321-17306-6 (v. E).— 0-321-05536-5 (v. F).
   1. Literature—Collections.   2. Literature—History and criticism.
I. Damrosch, David.
PN6013.L66 2004

                                     2003061890

Please visit us at http://www.ablongman.com/damrosch.

To place your order, please use the following ISBN numbers:

ISBN Volume One Package *The Ancient World to The Early Modern Period*
(includes Volumes A, B, and C): **0-321-20238-4**

ISBN Volume Two Package *The Seventeenth Century to The Twentieth Century*
(includes Volumes D, E, and F): **0-321-20237-6**

Or, to order individual volumes, please use the following ISBN numbers:

ISBN Volume A, *The Ancient World:* 0-321-05533-0
ISBN Volume B, *The Medieval Era:* 0-321-16978-6
ISBN Volume C, *The Early Modern Period:* 0-321-16979-4
ISBN Volume D, *The Seventeenth and Eighteenth Centuries:* 0-321-16980-8
ISBN Volume E, *The Nineteenth Century:* 0-321-17306-6
ISBN Volume F, *The Twentieth Century:* 0-321-05536-5

1 2 3 4 5 6 7 8 9 10—QWT—06 05 04 03

CONTENTS

BERTOLT BRECHT (1898–1956)   354

PRIMO LEVI (1919–1987)   405

⇒ PERSPECTIVES ⇐
Echoes of War   419

LIST OF ILLUSTRATIONS

Color Plates

following page 6

Black-and-White Images

Maps

On the Cover

Detail from *Dream of a Sunday Afternoon in the Alameda,* 1947–1948. The great Mexican painter Diego Rivera (1886–1957) made this huge mural for a hotel in downtown Mexico City near the Alameda Central Park. Some fifty feet long by fifteen feet high, the full mural (shown on the back cover of this volume) presents a historical panorama from pre-Conquest times up through Mexico's modern revolutionary struggles. In the front cover's detail from the center of the mural, Diego Rivera himself appears as a child escorted by a strange pair of parents. The "father" here is a founder of Mexican historical painting, José Guadalupe Posada, while the "mother" is a famous image created by Posada, "La Calavera Catrina" (Dressed-up Death's head) based on the skeleton figures popular in Mexican folk art; she wears a feathered serpent, emblem of the Aztec god Quetzalcoatl. Behind young Diego stands his future wife, the painter Frieda Kahlo, holding an oriental yin-yang symbol, while beside her stands the Cuban revolutionary poet José Marti. The scarlet lady next to young Diego is said to be a portrait of one of his mistresses. Both realistic and highly symbolic, Rivera's "Dream" is a multiple allegory of Mexican history, of the artist's own life, and of art itself.

PREFACE

Our world today is both expanding and growing smaller at the same time. Expanding, through a tremendous increase in the range of cultures that actively engage with each other; and yet growing smaller as well, as people and products surge across borders in the process known as globalization. This double movement creates remarkable opportunities for cross-cultural understanding, as well as new kinds of tensions, miscommunications, and uncertainties. Both the opportunities and the uncertainties are amply illustrated in the changing shape of world literature. A generation ago, when the term "world literature" was used in North America, it largely meant masterworks by European writers from Homer onward, together with a few favored North American writers, heirs to the Europeans. Today, however, it is generally recognized that Europe is only part of the story of the world's literatures, and only part of the story of North America's cultural heritage. An extraordinary range of exciting material is now in view, from the earliest Sumerian lyrics inscribed on clay tablets to the latest Kashmiri poetry circulated on the Internet. Many new worlds—and newly visible *older* worlds of classical traditions around the globe—await us today.

How can we best approach such varied materials from so many cultures? Can we deal with this embarrassment of riches without being overwhelmed by it, and without merely giving a glancing regard to less familiar traditions? This anthology has been designed to help readers successfully navigate "the sea of stories"—as Salman Rushdie has described the world's literary heritage. This preface will outline the ways we've gone about this challenging, fascinating task.

CONNECTING DISTINCTIVE TRADITIONS

Works of world literature engage in a double conversation: with their culture of origin and with the varied contexts into which they travel away from home. To look broadly at world literature is therefore to see patterns of difference as well as points of contact and commonality. The world's disparate traditions have developed very distinct kinds of literature, even very different ideas as to what should be called "literature" at all. This anthology uses a variety of means to showcase what is most distinctive and also what is commonly shared among the world's literatures. Throughout the anthology, we employ three kinds of grouping:

☞ **CROSSCURRENTS: A major grouping at the beginning of each volume, bringing together literary responses to worldwide developments.**

☞ **PERSPECTIVES: Groupings that provide cultural context for major works, illuminating issues of broad importance.**

☞ **RESONANCES: Sources for a specific text or responses to it, often from a different time and place.**

The "Crosscurrents" sections that open our six volumes highlight overarching issues or developments that many cultures have faced, often in conversation with neighboring cultures and more distant ones too. "Creation Myths and Social Realities" in antiquity, for example, brings together creation stories that circulated throughout the ancient Near East, westward to Greece, and eastward to India. "The Folk and Their Tales" in the nineteenth century shows the interplay of folk traditions between India and Europe, Africa and the Americas, Native Americans and Euro-Americans.

Regional divisions predominate in our Volumes A through C, reflecting the distinctive development of the world's major literary traditions over the centuries before the modern period. For each of these volumes, the Crosscurrents provide an initial, cross-cutting overview of a major issue, giving a reminder that there have been important contacts across cultures as far back as we know—and showing too how different cultures can independently address matters of common human concern. In our more globally organized later volumes D through F (mid-seventeenth century to the present), the Crosscurrents demonstrate the increasing interconnectedness of the world's literary traditions.

Throughout the anthology, our many "Perspectives" sections provide cultural context for the major works around them, giving insight into such issues as the representation of death and immortality (in the ancient Near East); the meeting of Christians, Muslims, and Jews in medieval Iberia; the idea of the national poet in the nineteenth century; and "modernist memory" in the twentieth. Perspectives sections also provide an opportunity for focused regional groupings within our globally structured later volumes, with "Other Americas" in the nineteenth century, for example, and "Modernism and Revolution in Russia" in the twentieth. Perspectives sections give a range of voices and views, strategies and styles, in highly readable textual groupings. The Perspectives groupings serve a major pedagogical as well as intellectual purpose in making these selections accessible and useful within the time constraints of a survey course.

Finally, our "Resonances" perform the crucial function of linking works across time as well as space. For Homer's *Iliad,* a Resonance shows oral composition as it is still practiced today north of Greece, while for the *Odyssey* we have Resonances giving modern responses to Homer by Franz Kafka, Derek Walcott, and the Greek poet George Seferis. Accompanying the traditional Navajo "Story of the Emergence" (Volume E) is an extended selection from *Black Elk Speaks* which shows how ancient imagery infused the dream visions of the Sioux healer and warrior Nicholas Black Elk, helping him deal with the crises of lost land and independence that his people were facing. Resonances for Conrad's *Heart of Darkness* (Volume F) give selections from Conrad's diary of his own journey upriver in the Congo, and a speech by Henry Morton Stanley, the explorer-journalist who was serving as publicist for King Leopold's exploitation of his colony in the years just before Conrad went there. Stanley's surreal speech—in which he calculates how much money the Manchester weavers can make providing wedding dresses and burial clothes for the Congolese—gives a vivid instance of the outlook, and the rhetoric, that Conrad grimly parodies in Mr. Kurtz and his associates.

PRINCIPLES OF SELECTION

Beyond our immediate groupings, our overall selections have been made with an eye to fostering connections across time and space: a Perspectives section on "Courtly Women" in medieval Japan (Volume B) introduces themes that can be followed up in

"Court Culture and Female Authorship" in Enlightenment-era Europe (Volume D), while the ancient Mediterranean and South Asian creation myths at the start of Volume A find echoes in later cosmic-creation narratives from Iceland (Volume B), Mesoamerica (Volume C), and indigenous peoples today (Volume E). Altogether, we have worked to create an exceptionally coherent and well-integrated presentation of an extraordinary variety of works from around the globe, from the dawn of writing to the present.

Recognizing that different sorts of works have counted as literature in differing times and places, we take an inclusive approach, centering on poems, plays, and fictional narratives but also including selections from rich historical, religious, and philosophical texts like Plato's *Republic* and the Qur'an that have been important for much later literary work, even though they weren't conceived as literature themselves. We present many complete masterworks, including *The Epic of Gilgamesh* (in a beautiful verse translation), Homer's *Odyssey*, Dante's *Inferno*, and Chinua Achebe's *Things Fall Apart*, and we have extensive, teachable selections from such long works as *The Tale of Genji, Don Quixote*, and both parts of Goethe's *Faust*.

Along with these major selections we present a great array of shorter works, some of which have been known only to specialists and only now are entering into world literature. It is our experience as readers and as teachers that the established classics themselves can best be understood when they're set in a varied literary landscape. Nothing is included here, though, simply to make a point: whether world-renowned or recently rediscovered, these are compelling works to read. Throughout our work on this book, we've tried to be highly inclusive in principle and yet carefully selective in practice, avoiding tokenism and also its inverse, the piling up of an unmanageable array of heterogeneous material. If we've succeeded as we hope, the result will be coherent as well as capacious, substantive as well as stimulating.

LITERATURE, ART, AND MUSIC

One important way to understand literary works in context is to read them in conjunction with the broader social and artistic culture in which they were created. Literature has often had a particularly close relation to visual art and to music. Different as the arts are in their specific resources and techniques, a culture's artistic expressions often share certain family resemblances, common traits that can be seen across different media—and that may even come out more clearly in visual or musical form than in translations of literature itself. This anthology includes dozens of black-and-white illustrations and a suite of color illustrations in each volume, chosen to work in close conjunction with our literary selections. Some of these images directly illustrate literary works, while others show important aspects of a culture's aesthetic sensibility. Often, writing actually appears on paintings and sculptures, with represented people and places sharing the space with beautifully rendered Mayan hieroglyphs, Arabic calligraphy, or Chinese brushstrokes.

Music too has been a close companion of literary creation and performance. Our very term "lyric" refers to the lyres or harps with which the Greeks accompanied poems as they were sung. In China, the first major literary work is the *Book of Songs*. In Europe too, until quite recent times poetry was often sung and even prose was usually read aloud. We have created two audio CDs to accompany the anthology, one for Volumes A through C and one for volumes D through F. These CDs give a wealth of poetry and music from the cultures we feature in the anthology; they are both a valuable teaching resource and also a pure pleasure to listen to.

AIDS TO UNDERSTANDING

A major emphasis of our work has been to introduce each culture and each work to best effect. Each major period and section of the anthology, each grouping of works, and each individual author has an introduction by a member of our editorial team. Our goal has been to write introductions informed by deep knowledge worn lightly. Neither talking down to our readers nor overwhelming them with masses of unassimilable information, our introductions don't seek to "cover" the material but instead try to uncover it, to provide ways in and connections outward. Similarly, our footnotes and glosses are concise and informative, rather than massive or interpretive. Time lines for each volume, and maps and pronunciation guides throughout the anthology, all aim to foster an informed and pleasurable reading of the works.

GOING FURTHER

The Longman Anthology of World Literature makes connections beyond its covers as well as within them. Bibliographies at the end of each volume point the way to historical and critical readings for students wishing to go into greater depth for term papers. The Companion Website we've developed for the course (www.ablongman.com/worldlit) gives a wealth of links to excellent Web resources on all our major texts and many related historical and cultural movements and events. The Web site includes an audio version of our printed pronunciation guides: you can simply click on a name to hear it pronounced. Finally, the Web site includes readings of works in the original and in translation, with accompanying texts, giving extensive exposure to the aural dimension of many of the languages represented in the anthology.

For instructors, we have also created an extensive, two-volume instructor's manual, *Teaching World Literature*—written directly by the editors themselves, drawing on our years of experience in teaching these materials.

TRANSLATION ACROSS CULTURES

The circulation of world literature is always an exercise in cultural translation, and one way to define works of world literature is that they are the works that gain in translation. Some great texts remain so intimately tied to their point of origin that they never read well abroad; they may have an abiding importance at home, but don't play a role in the wider world. Other works, though, gain in resonance as they move out into new contexts, new conjunctions. Edgar Allan Poe found his first really serious readers in France, rather than in the United States. *The Thousand and One Nights,* long a marginal work in Arabic traditions oriented toward poetry rather than popular prose, gained new readers and new influence abroad, and Scheherazade's intricately nested tales now help us in turn to read the European tales of Boccaccio and Marguerite de Navarre with new attention and appreciation. A Perspectives section on *"The Thousand and One Nights* in the Twentieth Century" (Volume F) brings together a range of Arab, European, and American writers who have continued to plumb its riches to this day.

As important as cultural translation in general is the issue of actual translation from one language to another. We have sought out compelling translations for all our foreign-language works, and periodically we offer our readers the opportunity to think directly about the issue of translation. Sometimes we offer distinctively different translations of differing works from a single author or source: for the Bible, for example, we give Genesis 1–11 in Robert Alter's lively, oral-style translation, while we give selected psalms in the magnificent King James Version and the Joseph story in the lucid New International Version. Our selections from Homer's *Iliad* appear in Richmond Lattimore's stately older translation, while Homer's *Odyssey* is given in Robert Fagles's eloquent new version.

At other times, we give alternative translations of a single work. So we have Chinese lyrics translated by the modernist poet Ezra Pound, by the scholar-aesthete Arthur Waley, and by the contemporary poet and novelist Vikram Seth; and we have Petrarch sonnets translated by the Renaissance English poet Thomas Wyatt and also by contemporary translators. These juxtapositions can show some of the varied ways in which translators over the centuries have sought to carry works over from one time and place to another—not so much by mirroring and reflecting an unchanged meaning, as by refracting it, in a prismatic process that can add new highlights and reveal new facets in a classic text. At times, when we haven't found a translation that really satisfies us, we've translated the work ourselves—an activity we recommend to all who wish to come to know a work from the inside.

We hope that the results of our years of work on this project will be as enjoyable to use as the book has been to create. We welcome you now inside our pages.

David Damrosch

ACKNOWLEDGMENTS

In the extended process of planning and preparing this anthology, the editors have been fortunate to have the support, advice, and assistance of many people. Our editor, Joe Terry, and our publisher, Roth Wilkovsky, have supported our project in every possible way and some seemingly impossible ones as well, helping us produce the best possible book despite all challenges to budgets and well-laid plans in a rapidly evolving field. Their associates Janet Lanphier and Melanie Craig have shown unwavering enthusiasm and constant creativity in developing the book and its related Web site and audio CDs and in introducing the results to the world. Our development editors, first Mark Getlein and then Adam Beroud, have shown a compelling blend of literary acuity and quiet diplomacy in guiding thirteen far-flung editors through the many stages of work. Peter Meyers brought great energy and creativity to work on our CDs. Donna Campion and Dianne Hall worked diligently to complete the instructor's manual. Celeste Parker-Bates cleared hundreds and hundreds of text permissions from publishers in many countries, and Sherri Zuckerman at Photosearch, Inc., cleared our many photo permissions.

Once the manuscript was complete, Doug Bell, the production manager, oversaw the simultaneous production of six massive books on a tight and shifting schedule. Valerie Zaborski, managing editor in production, also helped and, along the way, developed a taste for the good-humored fatalism of Icelandic literature. Our lead copyeditor, Stephanie Magean, and her associates Martha Beyerlein, Elizabeth Jahaske, and Marcia LaBrenz marvelously integrated everyone's writing, and then Amber Allen and her colleagues at Elm Street Publishing Services worked overtime to produce beautiful books accurate down to the last exotic accent.

We are specifically grateful for the guidance of the many reviewers who advised us on the creation of this book: Roberta Adams (Fitchburg State College); Adetutu Abatan (Floyd College); Magda al-Nowaihi (Columbia University); Nancy Applegate (Floyd College); Susan Atefat-Peckham (Georgia College and State University); Evan Balkan (CCBC-Catonsville); Michelle Barnett (University of Alabama, Birmingham); Colonel Bedell (Virginia Military Institute); Thomas Beebee (Pennsylvania State University); Paula Berggren (Baruch College); Mark Bernier (Blinn College); Ronald Bogue (University of Georgia); Terre Burton (Dixie State College); Patricia Cearley (South Plains College); Raj Chekuri (Laredo Community College); Sandra Clark (University of Wyoming); Thomas F. Connolly (Suffolk University); Vilashini Cooppan (Yale University); Bradford Crain (College of the Ozarks); Robert W. Croft (Gainesville College); Frank Day (Clemson University); Michael Delahoyde (Washington State University); Elizabeth Otten Delmonico (Truman State University); Jo Devine (University of Alaska Southeast); Gene Doty (University of Missouri—Rolla); James Earle (University of Oregon); R. Steve Eberly (Western Carolina University); Walter Evans (Augusta State University); Fidel Fajardo-Acosta (Creighton University); Mike Felker (South Plains College); Janice Gable (Valley Forge Christian College); Stanley Galloway (Bridgewater College); Doris Gardenshire (Trinity Valley Community College); Jonathan Glenn (University of Central Arkansas); Dean Hall (Kansas State University); Dorothy Hardman (Fort Valley State University); Elissa Heil (University of the Ozarks); David Hesla (Emory University);

Susan Hillabold (Purdue University North Central); Karen Hodges (Texas Wesleyan); David Hoegberg (Indiana University-Purdue University—Indianapolis); Sheri Hoem (Xavier University); Michael Hutcheson (Landmark College); Mary Anne Hutchinson (Utica College); Raymond Ide (Lancaster Bible College); James Ivory (Appalachian State University); Craig Kallendorf (Texas A & M University); Bridget Keegan (Creighton University); Steven Kellman (University of Texas—San Antonio); Roxanne Kent-Drury (Northern Kentucky University); Susan Kroeg (Eastern Kentucky University); Tamara Kuzmenkov (Tacoma Community College); Robert Lorenzi (Camden County College—Blackwood); Mark Mazzone (Tennessee State University); David McCracken (Coker College); George Mitrenski (Auburn University); James Nicholl (Western Carolina University); Roger Osterholm (Embry-Riddle University); Joe Pellegrino (Eastern Kentucky University); Linda Lang-Peralta (Metropolitan State College of Denver); Sandra Petree (University of Arkansas); David E. Phillips (Charleston Southern University); Terry Reilly (University of Alaska); Constance Relihan (Auburn University); Nelljean Rice (Coastal Carolina University); Colleen Richmond (George Fox University); Gretchen Ronnow (Wayne State University); John Rothfork (West Texas A & M University); Elise Salem-Manganaro (Fairleigh Dickinson University); Asha Sen (University of Wisconsin Eau Claire); Richard Sha (American University); Edward Shaw (University of Central Florida); Jack Shreve (Allegany College of Maryland); Jimmy Dean Smith (Union College); Floyd C. Stuart (Norwich University); Eleanor Sumpter-Latham (Central Oregon Community College); Ron Swigger (Albuquerque Technical Vocational Institute); Barry Tharaud (Mesa State College); Theresa Thompson (Valdosta State College); Teresa Thonney (Columbia Basin College); Charles Tita (Shaw University); Scott D. Vander Ploeg (Madisonville Community College); Marian Wernicke (Pensacola Junior College); Sallie Wolf (Arapahoe Community College); and Dede Yow (Kennesaw State University).

We also wish to express our gratitude to the reviewers who gave us additional advice on the book's companion Web site: Nancy Applegate (Floyd College); James Earl (University of Oregon); David McCracken (Coker College); Linda Lang-Peralta (Metropolitan State College of Denver); Asha Sen (University of Wisconsin—Eau Claire); Jimmy Dean Smith (Union College); Floyd Stuart (Norwich University); and Marian Wernicke (Pensacola Junior College).

The editors were assisted in tracking down texts and information by wonderfully able research assistants: Kerry Bystrom, Julie Lapiski, Katalin Lovasz, Joseph Ortiz, Laura B. Sayre, and Lauren Simonetti. April Alliston wishes to thank Brandon Lafving for his invaluable comments on her drafts and Gregory Maertz for his knowledge and support. Marshall Brown would like to thank his research assistant Françoise Belot for her help and Jane K. Brown for writing the Goethe introduction. Sheldon Pollock would like to thank Whitney Cox, Rajeev Kinra, Susanne Mrozik, and Guriqbal Sahota for their assistance and Haruo Shirane thanks Michael Brownstein for writing the introduction to Hozumi Ikan, and Akiko Takeuchi for writing the introductions to the Noh drama.

It has been a great pleasure to work with all these colleagues both at Longman and at schools around the country. This book exists for its readers, whose reactions and suggestions we warmly welcome, as *The Longman Anthology of World Literature* moves out into the world.

ABOUT THE EDITORS

David Damrosch (Columbia University). His books include *The Narrative Covenant: Transformations of Genre in the Growth of Biblical Literature* (1987), *Meetings of the Mind* (2000), and *What Is World Literature?* (2003). He has been president of the American Comparative Literature Association (2001–2003) and is general editor of *The Longman Anthology of British Literature* (1998; second edition, 2002).

April Alliston (Princeton University). Author of *Virtue's Faults: Correspondence in Eighteenth-Century British and French Women's Fiction* (1996), and editor of Sophia Lee's *The Recess* (2000). Her book on concepts of character, gender, and plausibility in Enlightenment historical narratives is forthcoming.

Marshall Brown (University of Washington). Author of *The Shape of German Romanticism* (1979), *Preromanticism* (1991), *Turning Points: Essays in the History of Cultural Expressions* (1997), and, forthcoming, *The Gothic Text.* Editor of *Modern Language Quarterly: A Journal of Literary History,* and the *Cambridge History of Literary Criticism,* Vol. 5: Romanticism.

Page duBois (University of California, San Diego). Her books include *Centaurs and Amazons* (1982), *Sowing the Body* (1988), *Torture and Truth* (1991), *Sappho Is Burning* (1995), *Trojan Horses* (2001), and *Slaves and Other Objects* (2003).

Sabry Hafez (University of London). His books include *The Genesis of Arabic Narrative Discourse* (1993) and the edited volumes *A Reader of Modern Arabic Short Stories* and *Mahmoud Darwish.*

Ursula K. Heise (Columbia University). Author of *Chronoschisms: Time, Narrative, and Postmodernism* (1997) and of the forthcoming *World Wide Webs: Global Ecology and the Cultural Imagination.*

Djelal Kadir (Pennsylvania State University). His books include *Columbus and the Ends of the Earth* (1992), *The Other Writing: Postcolonial Essays in Latin America's Writing Culture* (1993), and *Other Modernisms in an Age of Globalizations* (2002). He served in the 1990s as editor of *World Literature Today* and is coeditor of the *Comparative History of Latin America's Literary Cultures* (2004). He is the founding president of the International American Studies Association.

David L. Pike (American University). Author of *Passage Through Hell: Modernist Descents, Medieval Underworlds* (1997) and *Subterranean Cities: Subways, Sewers, Cemeteries and the Culture of Paris and London* (forthcoming), and of articles on topics ranging from medieval otherworlds and underground Paris, London, and New York to Canadian cinema.

Sheldon Pollock (University of Chicago). His books include *The Ramayana of Valmiki* Volume 3 (1991) and *The Language of the Gods in the World of Men* (forthcoming). He recently edited *Literary Cultures in History: Reconstructions from South Asia* (2003), and (with Homi Bhabha et al.) *Cosmopolitanism* (2002).

Bruce Robbins (Columbia University). His books include *The Servant's Hand: English Fiction from Below* (1986), *Secular Vocations* (1993), *Feeling Global: Internationalism in Distress* (1999), and a forthcoming study of upward mobility narratives in the nineteenth and twentieth centuries. Edited volumes include *Cosmopolitics: Thinking and Feeling Beyond the Nation* (1998).

Haruo Shirane (Columbia University). Author of *The Bridge of Dreams: A Poetics of "The Tale of Genji"* (1987) and of *Traces of Dreams: Landscape, Cultural Memory, and the Poetry of Bashō* (1998). He is coeditor of *Inventing the Classics: Modernity, National Identity, and Japanese Literature* (2000) and has recently edited *Early Modern Japanese Literature: An Anthology 1600–1900*.

Jane Tylus (New York University). Author of *Writing and Vulnerability in the Late Renaissance* (1993), coeditor of *Epic Traditions in the Contemporary World* (1999), and editor and translator of Lucrezia Tornabuoni de' Medici's *Sacred Narratives* (2001). Her study on late medieval female spirituality and the origins of humanism is forthcoming.

Pauline Yu (American Council of Learned Societies). President of the American Council of Learned Societies, she is the author of *The Poetry of Wang Wei* and *The Reading of Imagery in the Chinese Poetic Tradition*, the editor of *Voices of the Song Lyric in China*, and coeditor of *Culture and State in Chinese History* and *Ways with Words: Writing about Reading Texts from Early China*.

Umberto Boccioni's *Unique Forms of Continuity in Space,* 1913, is the Futurist Manifesto in Bronze. More than the suggested human form that is contained in the aerodynamic wrappings, Boccioni is praising technology and speed. His sculpture evokes the declaration of the Manifesto that "the roaring automobile is more beautiful than the Winged Victory" (the *Nike of Samothrace*). By the middle of the twentieth century, automobile design would indeed take on the winged fenders of Boccioni's sculpture. One year after the 1909 Futurist Manifesto of Marinetti (page 22), Boccioni was one of the signers of a Futurist painting manifesto, and author of "Manifesto of Futurist Sculpture" (1912).

The Twentieth Century

A CENTURY OF WAR AND REVOLUTIONS

Human history is principally a record of strife. Few centuries in the history of humanity, though, can rival the magnitude, efficiency, and lethal intensity of the twentieth
century's conflicts. No decade, and few individual years in the course of the century,
have been free of war, revolutions, uprisings, or military and civil confrontation. The
most advanced century in terms of its technological and scientific know-how has also
been marked by deadly results: two world wars, with a combined human death toll of
over ninety million; numerous revolutions, at least a handful of which changed the
course of history beyond their particular contexts—the Mexican Revolution of 1910,
the Russian Revolution of 1917, the Chinese Revolutions between 1924 and 1949, the
Cuban Revolution of 1959; wars of emancipation from colonial regimes that culminated in as many as seventeen new nation-states in a single year (1960) in Africa
alone; the use of the deadliest weapon ever devised and deployed by humankind—the
atomic bombs dropped on Hiroshima and Nagasaki in August 1945 by the United
States; and then a so-called "Cold War" under the constant threat of worldwide
nuclear conflagration for more than half of the twentieth century, during which 149
localized proxy wars on behalf of the rival ideologies of the superpowers killed more
than twenty-three million people. By the end of the century, no part of the earth and
no culture in it remained untouched by some external political and military force, cultural influence, or economic intrusion.

THE ART OF STRIFE

Like any art form, literature is neither immune to historical conflict nor is it simply
symptomatic or reflective of strife that surrounds it. Art itself serves as instrument
and as occasion for engagement, contestation, and struggle. And these struggles intensified in the early twentieth century with the eclipse of nineteenth-century ideals of
historical progress and rational explanations of motives and wants. The twentieth century upended that orderliness and rationality in its pursuit of the underside of things
and the far side of reason. The "real" no longer sufficed. Twentieth-century art and
science were bent on divulging reality's hidden faces, its surrealist para-realities. And
while the nineteenth century may have privileged the role of the individual writer and
originality of genius in the creation of science, art, and literature, in the twentieth century, the cult of novelty and individuality placed a premium on disruption. Thus the
order of continuity was first subjected to the disorder of rupture, breakage, destruction, and eradication before a new generation of artists or writers, or a new school or
mode of art, could feel that they attained cultural legitimacy. And so it was that the
twentieth century entered history with the greatest human upheaval, the Great War of
1914–1918. It would be dubbed the First World War in retrospect, when it proved a
mere rehearsal in the magnitude of its destruction that left a whole continent in ruins,

over forty million human casualties, and a modern humanity pondering the destructive potential of its technological and scientific advancements. The literature that ushered in and succeeded that conflagration would always be marked by an obsessive concern for the underside of reason and the darker side of human ingenuity. All subsequent literature to the end of the century would carry the signs of this ambivalence and equivocation, to the point where such ambiguity in the culture of the twentieth century and its legacy came to be prized as the mark of accomplished literature.

The language of war becomes also the language of artistic and aesthetic advancement and self-affirmation. The eruption of twentieth-century modernity becomes synonymous with the self-designation of "avant-garde," a military term for the frontline deployment of shock troops. And the self-announcement of a literary movement's arrival invariably is through the shrill proclamation of a "manifesto," or some other form of self-assertive declaration whose shock value spells more an interruption of one's antecedents than an affirmation of one's own program. "Revolution" paradoxically becomes pattern, a repetition as much as a rupture, often couched in a descriptive language that revels in self-contradiction. Hence, paradoxical assertions like "the tradition of the new" would be proclaimed by more than one poet and by an even greater number of historians and critics of art and literature. If rational evolution was the progressive cause of eighteenth-century enlightenment and of the science of the nineteenth century, then interruptive revolution was the explanatory method of twentieth-century scientific and artistic processes, especially so in the art of literature.

MODERNITY, MODERNISM, MODERNIZATION

Modulation and conformity, then, are not attributes one could associate with the twentieth century. In characteristic fashion, rather, the century elevated modernism, modernization, and modernity to a privileged status as the ultimate mode to which all human activity was destined to advance. Failure to attain to this mode of modes in art, literature, technology, science, or governance pegged a culture as underdeveloped, the opposite of progressive, or, at best, euphemistically designated as in the process of developing. Often judged by criteria of outwardly measurable material achievement, modernity came to be synonymous with the value of what made such material progress possible—namely, modernization. Modernization moved with and beyond modernism in the arts to designate advancements in technology and industry, especially the scientific harnessing, ordering, and exploitation of natural resources and native populations, with "natural" being rooted in the same etymology as "native." The legacy of late nineteenth-century colonization in Africa and Asia, along with recolonization in Latin America, neatly divided the world between the civilizing modern colonialist and the premodern native, who depended on the colonist for entry into the course of modern human history. Modernism in the arts was most often consonant and complicit with this newly global world order, thus consolidating the division between the modern and the modernizing, the developed and the developing, the arrived and the aspiring but not-yet-accomplished.

David Alfaro Siqueiros, *Echo of a Scream,* 1937.

Decolonization / Recolonization

The emancipatory movements of decolonization starting at the mid-twentieth century aggravated the contest between the principal ideologies of the century—namely, the Marxist East and the Capitalist West. The newly independent nations were transformed into the testing ground—and often the battleground—of the two systems that competed to bring about the salvation and guarantee the future redemption of those new nations in the annals of history. This competition was often largely a test of the loyalty of those nations' leaders to one or the other of these ideologies, and the people themselves generally were deemed expendable. The people were to be governed, and, even when democratic principles were the ostensible goal of their emancipation, the new nations were considered foremost as client states rather than truly independent national cultures. And while rule by and for the people was the ideal that the rhetoric of contesting ideologies proclaimed most frequently, popular movements were often seen as inconvenient and troublesome impediments to the overarching goals of the superpowers. Truly emancipatory changes were likewise troublesome to the local "comprador class," or governing surrogates. These were usually military and well armed, and they had responsibility for keeping the rabble in line and in docile conformity to

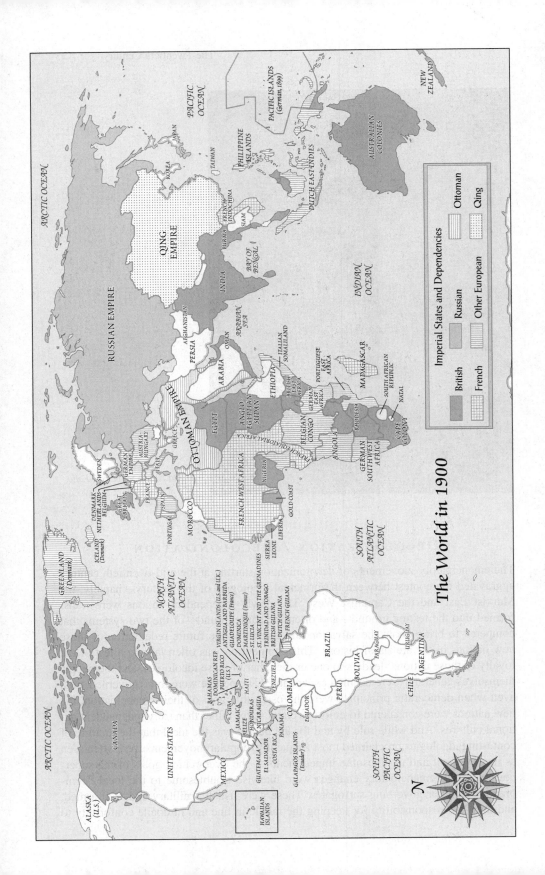

The World in 1900

Imperial States and Dependencies

British	Ottoman
French	Qing
Russian	
Other European	

the more exalted interests of a better world and a greater cause, usually those that suited the economic and ideological purposes of the superpowers. Those interests usually came cloaked in a multitude of rhetorical vestments such as liberation, democracy, progress, modernization, and development.

The competition between the Marxist and capitalist systems and their geopolitical interests, often articulated through this shared vocabulary, came to be the dynamic that propelled history in the twentieth century, leading some capitalist thinkers to declare the end of history when the Soviet system collapsed in 1989. The first U.S. President George Bush was to declare a "New World Order," one that no longer required the separate designations of First, Second, and Third Worlds, since by the last decade of the century there was only one world and a common global interest for all.

The place and space of national literature and literary culture in the course of the twentieth century thus emerged as a problem, since the notion of nation itself came under question. In the Marxist system, the world was viewed as a transnational culture without frontiers, a world order in which humanity would transcend local divisions and produce a world literature infinitely more meaningful than the bourgeois and parochial. The triumphant capitalist system, for its part, deemed its own cultural paradigm as the point of reference and standard for all world culture, with free capital moving unimpeded in a world without economic borders. Since it is in the perverse nature of things to have opposites converge, the internationalism of the Marxist/Soviet East came to coincide perfectly well with the transnationalism and multiculturalism of the capitalist West. Literature in both instances would be deemed of greater value in proportion to its universal appeal and the capacity of the local and of the particular to project the universal from within it unto the world stage and the higher order of humanity's shared cultural heritage.

These were cultural and economic forms of globalization before the term "globalization" itself attained global currency. The idea of a racial culture and a national literature were the twentieth century's inheritance from German Romanticism and, specifically, a legacy of Johann Gottfried von Herder, the German founder of the systematic study of language and race, what specialists would designate as philology and ethnology. Herder's notions of language, race, and nation came into question by the second half of the twentieth century, just when an even greater number of nations began to emerge as a result of decolonization in the hitherto colonized parts of the world. Colonialism had held governability at a premium, and certainly at a higher priority than the actual demographic and cultural distribution of the governed peoples in the lands of their ancestors. Now, the nation itself as a political and cultural formation came into dispute principally as a result of the rupture in those convenient or expedient national borders that were imposed by colonial powers for the sake of colonial governance.

National literature itself, in turn, would become a subject of debate, as would the language in which literatures would be written and read, since geography, language, culture, and nation did not necessarily coincide as they were arrayed by colonial powers. And while the emergence of such postcolonial studies sought to disentangle such pesky questions, studies themselves became potential and actual case studies in the very intricacies of colonialism, decolonization, and recolonization. And when nation, religion, race, ethnicity, and geography would be expediently and forcefully constructed as overlapping—secular and scientific history notwithstanding—colonialism and occupation would overflow from the twentieth into the twenty-first century in

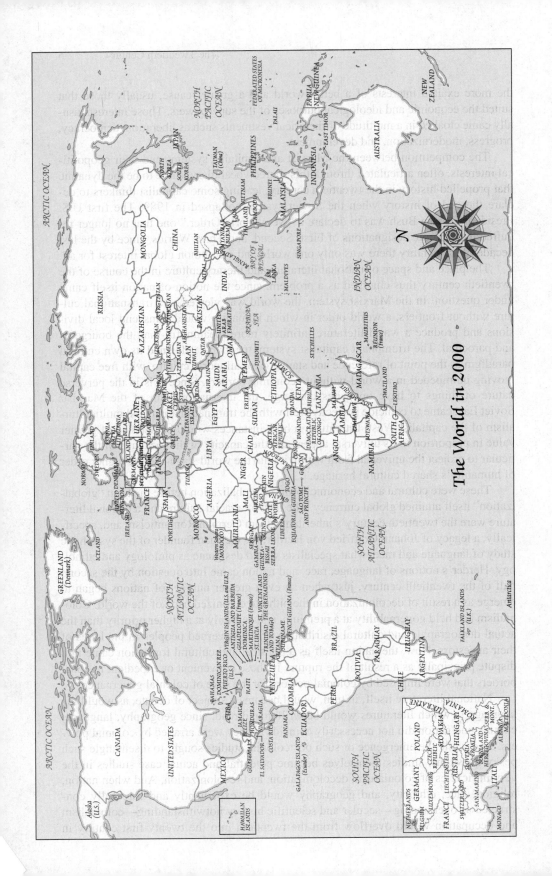

The World in 2000

Plate 1 Gustav Klimt, *The Kiss,* Austria, 1907–1908. Gustav Klimt's *The Kiss* is part of a mural frieze that wraps around the dining room of the Palais Stoclet, a building in the Art Nouveau style in Brussels, Belgium. Art Nouveau was a transitional movement between late nineteenth-century Symbolism and the more concrete and geometric modernist forms such as Cubism, foreshadowed here in the intense patterning of the clothing and the flattening out of the figures. The Viennese Klimt captures the eternal theme of Genesis in this richly colored work that bridges painting and decorative art. The Romanian sculptor Constantin Brancusi portrays the same scene in a stone sculpture with the same title one year later (1909). *(Erich Lessing / Art Resource, New York.)*

Plate 2 Belgian mining magnate and African chauffeur, Congo Free State, early 1900s. Even while Joseph Conrad and Pablo Picasso were imaginatively exploring Africa and its cultures, African artists were in turn exploring the new arrivals. This wooden sculpture portrays a Belgian industrialist and his imported automobile, adapting both to traditional modes of representation. The automobile is decorated in patterns used in African cloth and basketry, while the industrialist differs from his native driver only in the detail of his goatee. The driver guides the car with serene confidence, not so much steering the wheel as holding it like a votive offering to the gods. *(Werner Forman / Art Resource, New York.)*

Plate 3 Pablo Picasso, *Les Demoiselles d'Avignon,* France, 1907. A groundbreaking work that signaled the advent of modernism in the visual arts, the scandalous subject matter—prostitutes at a brothel—was also highly innovative in its technique. Neither the interior space of the brothel nor the still life of fruit on a table in the foreground nor the women's bodies are constructed according to the rules of perspectival painting. Instead, they combine what would normally be views from different angles in an attempt to convey a new sense of reality as a shifting construct from multiple perspectives rather than a solid bedrock of perception. The African masks that take the place of two of the women's faces exemplify many modernist artists' interest in "primitive" art and its expressive potential. *(Copyright © 2005 Estate of Pablo Picasso / Artists Rights Society [ARS], New York. Les Demoiselles d'Avignon, 1907. Acquired through the Lille P. Bliss Bequest. Digital image © The Museum of Modern Art / Licensed by SCALA / Art Resource, New York. The Museum of Modern Art, New York.)*

Plate 4 Salvador Dali, *The Persistence of Memory (Soft Watches),* Spain, 1931. Dali's classic painting portrays watches—icons of modern timekeeping and of mechanical, public and normative time—in soft melting shapes that would make it technically impossible for them to indicate time correctly. Locating these watches in a barren, dreamlike landscape that prominently features a strange object that might be part of a face or a limb or perhaps a carcass, Dali points to a subjective, psychological temporality that cannot be measured by mechanical means and whose workings many modernist artists and writers sought to explore. *(Copyright © 2005 Salvador Dali, Gaia-Salvador Dali Foundation / Artists Rights Society [ARS], New York. The Persistence of Memory, 1931. Given anonymously. Digital image © The Museum of Modern Art / Licensed by SCALA / Art Resource, New York. The Museum of Modern Art, New York.)*

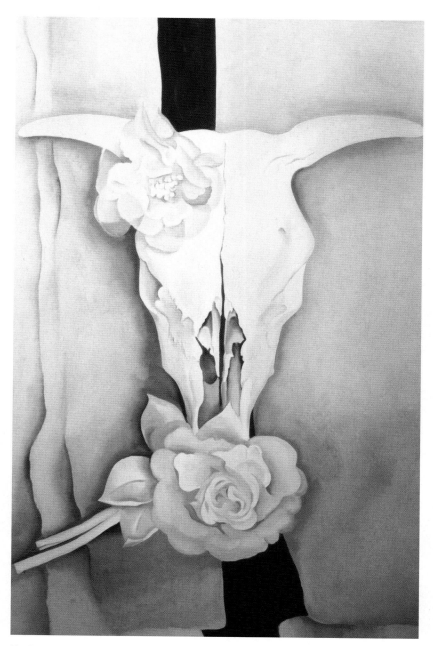

Plate 5   Georgia O'Keeffe, *Cow's Skull with Calico Roses,* United States, 1932. Juxtaposing the fragility of the rose with the hardness of a desert-cured bone, this painting serves as a counterpoint to the abstract art of European modernism. The still-life of the European tradition becomes metamorphosed into the shock of these American contrasts. O'Keeffe claimed to find something keenly alive in the dead objects of the vast American desert. *(Copyright © 2005 The Georgia O'Keeffe Foundation / Artists Rights Society [ARS], New York. Art Institute of Chicago, IL / The Bridgeman Art Library.)*

Plate 6   Poster of Mao Zedong, China, 1966. This image symbolizes the Cultural Revolution of the 1960s, a radical re-education of the Chinese people and China's intellectuals, many of whom were either sent to the countryside for "re-education," imprisoned, exiled, or killed. Among his other endeavors, Mao was also a poet, whose verses were memorized by all Chinese schoolchildren. His criteria for what constitutes legitimate literature have defined the shape of China's literary culture and education. The assembled masses are all studying Mao's "Red Book" of saying and precepts, which became the handbook of every Chinese man, woman, and child. *(Sovfoto / Eastfoto.)*

Plate 7 Bhupen Khakhar, *Ghost City Night,* India, 1992. Khakhar poignantly portrays the social isolation of homosexual couples, who meet at night far outside the confines of the city and are separated
from it by a vast empty surface in fiery colors. Shadowy embraces in grey and black erase almost all individuality from the gay men, whose individual features cannot be recognized for the most part; ghostlike figures, they are only partially real to the residents of the city and carefully kept out of the light of
daytime. *(Courtesy Gallery Chemould, Bombay, India.)*

Plate 8 Frank Gehry, Guggenheim Museum, Bilbao, Spain, 1993–1997. Gehry's quintessentially post-modern work of architecture combines a steel frame and titanium-sheathed surface with curved and asymmetrical shapes that do not follow any predictable layout. This interweaving of metallic material usually associated with machinery and industry, and forms that look as if they had grown organically, makes for the distinctive character of a museum that helped to revitalize a decaying industrial district along the Nervión river in this northern Spanish city. *(Stéphane Pons / Photos12.com.)*

territorial and cultural struggles from southern Mexico to East Timor in Indonesia to Palestine and Israel, thereby enacting, yet again, the same traumas of history, ironically enough, perpetrated by those whose ethnic history in previous centuries had redefined historical trauma as holocaust.

HISTORY, MEMORY, AND TRAUMA

Memory has always been a human obsession and an instrument of political, economic, and territorial definition. In the twentieth century, it has been of intense cultural interest. Remembering and forgetting are selective activities that often serve specific social, cultural, and political interests. Philosophy and psychoanalysis in the early twentieth century explored individual experiences of time and memory, even as technology, labor management, and political ideology forged ways to universalize and standardize such experiences. A unified time measuring system was introduced for the entire globe; the invention of the assembly line and new models of efficiency reshaped factory work; and wireless communication tied continents together without significant time delay. Somewhat later, the Bolshevik Revolution in Russia and fascist movements in Western Europe and Asia imposed ideologically based models of historical time that simultaneously sought a complete break from the past and selectively idealized particular earlier periods of history.

Early twentieth-century notions of time greatly influenced the literature written up until World War II, and these ideas were profoundly ambivalent and at times even paradoxical. In the economic sphere, pressures toward efficiency and standardization imposed increasing temporal homogeneity and speed. Countries that consisted of many different local time zones saw themselves forced to adopt a national standard to ensure reliable railway traffic, and international communication and commerce led to the creation of global time zones and the Greenwich mean time (GMT) standard. The American efficiency expert Frederick Taylor discovered that industrial work could be sped up and made more efficient by breaking down complex processes into simpler ones, and distributing them over different workers who would perform one and the same task over and over again. This mode of work was complemented by Henry Ford's introduction, in 1913, of the assembly line in his Highland Park car factory.

But this tendency toward ever-greater speed and standardization in industry and commerce was counterbalanced in the cultural sphere by in-depth inquiries into the complexity of individual time experience. Sigmund Freud's psychoanalytical theories introduced complexity into the simple notion of remembering. Philosophers William James and Henri Bergson explored the ways in which time is experienced in individual consciousness, as opposed to the regular progression of clock time and the institutional regularities of public time. While one set of social developments tended to streamline, homogenize, objectify, and speed up time, another emphasized the irreducible idiosyncrasies of memory and expectation as they are actually experienced by individuals.

Einstein's relativity theory, which deals precisely with abstract and objective time, questioned time as an absolute measure as it was known from Newtonian mechanics. Einstein's theory was often misinterpreted as a parallel to attempts in the humanities and arts to represent the "relativity" of subjective time, even though Einstein was revising the laws of physics, not those of psychology. Conversely, some artists and writers drew their inspiration not from psychological insights but precisely from the hard mechanics of new technologies: the Italian Futurists, for example, exulted in speed and simultaneity, which became their inspiration for inventing innovative types of poetry and performance. Similarly, the Dadaists and Surrealists were fascinated with the technological possibilities of photography and film, which for them became new ways of exploring the workings of memory and vision. The modernist period, then, opened up a variety of ways of thinking about time and memory, which different thinkers and artists appropriated in diverse ways.

If it was common for avant-gardists of all stripes to call for a complete break with the past, cataclysmic political events made violent rupture come real in the historical arena. To many contemporaries, World War I appeared as the end of an era: the slaughter of millions, carried out by means of innovative technologies that superseded face-to-face confrontation, seemed to signal the end of a nineteenth-century vision of "civilized" human society. Many of the violent political upheavals of the time echoed the rhetorical proclamations of a historical ground zero: the Mexican Revolution, the Russian Revolution, and the rising fascist movements of Italy, Germany, and Japan, in their own ways, all aimed to wipe the slate of historical time clean and start the future anew. That such complete historical breaks were impossible in practice soon became obvious to those who lived under the new regimes, though the political structures often persisted long after the utopian impulse had vanished.

After World War II, as the rhetoric of historical rupture shifted to those nations that aimed to break away from colonial rule, literature became an important means of working through the history of colonialism and recuperating indigenous myths and memories. In the industrialized world, in the meantime, enormous technological innovations generated new waves of accelerated socioeconomic cycles that spread commodification and consumerism into art, information technologies, and scientific knowledge. Since commercialism in combination with new media such as television and the computer seemed to direct people's thinking mostly toward the present, some observers worried that historical thinking might become impossible in the nanosecond culture of the late twentieth century. This weakening of historical sense came to be regarded as a hallmark of "postmodernism."

History, however, never ceased to be a central cultural concern, as communities and nations around the globe sought to come to terms with legacies of violence, oppression, and discrimination, and attempted to develop forms of historical discourse that would incorporate a plurality of voices. In Western Europe and the United States, the Holocaust became the main paradigm in debates over how to write and rewrite history, especially as eyewitness testimony progressively succumbed to time's passage. In Spain and Latin America, memories of brutal dictatorial regimes, censorship, death squads, torture, and "disappeared" prisoners came into focus. In Eastern Europe and across the former Soviet Union, the collapse of communist and socialist governments raised a myriad of questions on how to deal with a historical legacy whose relevance to the present was suddenly uncertain. Questions of collaboration and resistance, of historical continuity and rupture emerged in this context in very different guises than in the West.

In countries such as Australia founded as settler colonies, violent controversies erupted over the history of white dominance and discrimination against aboriginals, reaching their peak in open discussions of the "lost generation" of aborigines who had been taken away from their parents. Histories of racial oppression also occupied center stage in the United States, which attempted to come to terms with the legal and cultural revindications of those who were not Americans of European descent. Similar questions became focal concerns in much of what was formerly called the "Third World"; the South African Truth and Reconciliation Commission, a forum for working through the atrocities committed under white apartheid rule, was one of the most visible manifestations of such attempts to make heard the voices of those who had been formerly silenced, and to make their perspectives part of "official" history. In all of these struggles over what and how to remember historically, literary texts played a crucial role as articulate means of conveying the perspective of those whose viewpoint had long been ignored, and for preserving the memories of communities that no longer exist.

In such contexts, the psychological notion of "trauma" has helped communities cope with the memory of painful and violent events. Literary texts, with their dual ability to make remote events come close to the reader and yet to preserve a sense of distance through their fictionalization, proved to be one way in which such traumatic histories could be worked through. But recent literature that focuses on the recuperation of history by no means always aims at its darker sides. Quite often, its purpose is simply to draw the reader's attention to individuals and communities that never occupied center stage in world history but that nevertheless deserve to be remembered as part of a much more abundantly varied cultural legacy than textbook versions of history can convey. In the midst of what some call the "information glut" of the late twentieth and early twenty-first centuries, literature has remained a vital medium for embodying the memories, both individual and collective, that make for a rich and long-range sense of history, even in an era sometimes called posthistorical.

POSTS: POSTMODERN AND POSTCOLONIAL

The shifting definitions of culture, nation, history, and literature complicated the universal claims of modernism and the emancipatory principles of decolonization that were the driving force during the first two-thirds of the twentieth century. Both the aesthetic program of modernism and the economic and technical ambitions of modernization had relied upon a unified and coherent world view that fractured as the century progressed. A new era seemed to be emerging beyond such programmatic and salvationist master schemes. This novelty was signaled by the prefix "post," a prefix attached to any number of movements, schools, cultural phenomena, and even to history itself, in the last quarter of the century. While postmodernism and postcolonialism would become commonplace terms, from this side of our new century's threshold these usages now often appear as extensions, or even as reinforcements of what they supposedly succeeded or superseded.

Thus postmodernism sought to disrupt the overarching, universalist schemes of modernism by focusing on the particular, the contextually specific, and the individually differentiated. In fact, it ended up blurring the particularity of specific cultures in the process of questioning its own implausible position as a metanarrative, or a narrative about a narrative, capable of negotiating between the specific and the general, the particular and the universal, the local and the global. Postmodernism emerged, then, as a symptom of its own impossibility, yet another case of an explanatory scheme that couldn't comprehend the world phenomena it took as object of its reflections. And while elaborate critical and historical schemes of explanation have been devised for the unreachable, the incomprehensible, and the fragmented, the wistful or ironic admission of such impossibility became an implicit admission of a belief in what can no longer be whole or wholly comprehended. Indirectly, then, postmodernism reiterates the persistence of the modernist ideal, just as postcolonialism destines emancipated cultures to a perpetual colonial fate that is pegged to their supposedly overcome colonial histories.

CULTURES IN MOTION:
MIGRATION, TRAVEL, AND DISPLACEMENT

In 1990, the anthropologist James Clifford called on ethnographers to shift their focus of study from traditional villages, conceived of as self-contained spatial and cultural entities, to the ways in which premodern as well as modern and postmodern cultures traverse space. It was an apt moment for such a call, at the end of a century of unprecedented population movements around the planet. From millions of people displaced by war or political oppression and migrant workers in search of a livelihood to the millions of leisure travelers who seasonally move between countries and continents, the 1900s were a century on the move.

Political upheaval was a major force behind the uprooting of large numbers of people throughout the century. The military conflicts and geopolitical restructuring of Europe during World War II created nearly a million displaced persons. In the decades since then, the flood of refugees has never stopped: hundreds of thousands fled from Communist oppression in Eastern Europe and from colonial violence in Northern Africa. Palestinians were dislocated by the creation of Israel in 1948 and the Six-day War of 1967, even as the establishment of the state of Israel created a haven for Jews who had been persecuted both in fascist Western Europe and Communist Eastern Europe. "Boat people" took to the oceans to escape from political oppression and reprisals in Vietnam, Cuba, and Haiti. Millions of Afghans fled from Soviet occupation in the 1980s, and over two million people were displaced in Central America during the civil wars of the same decade. Ethnic conflicts and civil wars in sub-Saharan Africa generated an unending stream of internally displaced people and cross-border refugees. The 1990s brought eerie reminiscences of World War II with televised footage of populations on the run in Kosovo, and in the early twenty-first century, the United Nations High Commissioner for Refugees still reports upward of twenty million refugees worldwide. Throughout the twentieth century, then, political circumstances created waves of displacement. In many cases, the refugees were not able to return to their homes, or could do so only after long intervals. In the meantime, they carried their cultural legacies with them and often recreated them far away from home, sometimes triggering significant cultural changes in their host environments.

But such "diaspora" cultures weren't created only by adverse political circumstances. The search for better educational or economic opportunities has likewise taken populations around the globe. Sometimes these populations followed the routes

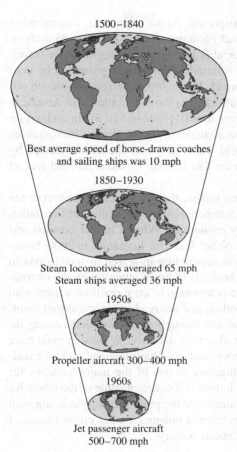

1500–1840

Best average speed of horse-drawn coaches
and sailing ships was 10 mph

1850–1930

Steam locomotives averaged 65 mph
Steam ships averaged 36 mph

1950s

Propeller aircraft 300–400 mph

1960s

Jet passenger aircraft
500–700 mph

Global shrinkage: the effect of changing transport
technologies on "real" distance.

established by colonialism, migrating from the former colonies to the colonist metropolis, as in the case of Arab minorities in France, and Indian and Caribbean emi-
grants to Britain. The arts in general, and literature in particular, have reflected this
multiplication of cultural identities in an abundance of themes, genres, and styles that
can no longer be attributed to a single national tradition.

But if literature has been greatly enhanced and expanded by what were originally circumstances of dire human necessity, it has also benefited from those travelers who sought out different cultural settings by choice. Throughout the twentieth
century, artists and writers have traveled—sometimes temporarily, sometimes permanently—to places that they thought would better suit their imaginations. American poets and novelists traveled to London and Paris in the 1910s and 1920s, becoming part of avant-garde movements. In the 1950s and 1960s, they journeyed to
India and Japan in search of innovative and perhaps more authentic forms of spiritual inspiration and literary expression. From the 1930s to the 1960s Latin American
writers were drawn to Paris, bridging European literary aesthetics with those of their
home countries. Such migrations increased as international communication and
transportation became more easily accessible in the second half of the century, and

cultural identities became likewise more dispersed. At the same time, a burgeoning global literary market has made international literature more available even to those readers and writers who are not willing or able to engage in long-distance travel. Cultural products create their own global itineraries, sometimes prompted by censorship at home, sometimes by success abroad. James Joyce's *Ulysses*—judged obscene in Ireland and England—was first published in Paris, and the Latin American "boom" novels of the 1960s and 1970s were mostly published in Spain and avidly read by both European and Latin American audiences. Today, Hindi film romances are wildly successful across the Arab world, Brazilian soap operas are viewed by millions in Europe, and the novels of a writer like Salman Rushdie are read around the world.

The heady excitement of global culture traffic, though, should not obscure the fact that the work of many writers remains hampered by the difficulties of translation in book markets that are driven mostly by economics. When Chinese novelist and playwright Gao Xinjiang was awarded the Nobel Prize for Literature in 2000, booksellers in Europe and the United States went scrambling in search of translations to offer their readers, since his work had not been given much attention by the international book market. By the same token, the celebration of cosmopolitan writers who live in one place, publish their work in another, and are read in several dozen countries should not let us forget that for many writers throughout the twentieth century international migration was a sad necessity rather than a choice. Writers in exile have left their mark on the course of literary history, and exile has remained no less a reality for twentieth-century writers. While literature is one of the major vehicles for twentieth-century cultures in motion, then, it does still confront some of the obstacles that literature had to overcome in earlier centuries. In the process of surmounting such political, economic, and cultural difficulties, human imagination has created some of the greatest literary masterpieces of the twentieth-century.

SCIENCE, TECHNOLOGY, AND PROGRESS

Few forces have transformed societies around the globe as much as science and technology in the twentieth century. The existence of the so-called "industrialized nations" and, indeed, the life of almost all societies at the beginning of the third millennium are deeply dependent on science and technology. For many, this increasing dependence is intimately associated with the notion of progress in material, social, and intellectual terms, just as it was at the beginnings of the Industrial Revolution and throughout much of the nineteenth century. But while the twentieth century gave rise to an unprecedented number of scientific insights and technological innovations, science and technology also came to be questioned with a new intensity, both in terms of their intrinsic nature and in terms of their effects on human societies. This uneasy dependence on science and technology has significant consequences for many dimensions of cultural life, and particularly for literature. At the turn of the millennium, literary creativity is redefining itself both in relation to new media that don't rely on printed text, and in relation to techno-scientific kinds of knowledge and imagination that were conventionally considered the antithesis of literary invention.

Science and technology themselves were transformed by numerous changes in theory and practice over the course of the twentieth century. For the cultural imagination, three changes have held particular significance: the shift in public scientific interest from physics in the early twentieth century to biology more recently, the emergence of new media of communication, and the fusion of information and communication technology that took place during the "digital revolution" in the last quarter of the century. Developments in physical theory between the turn of the century and World War II not only profoundly changed the discipline itself but exerted an almost magical attraction for the educated public as well as for artists and writers. The public imagination was engaged by concepts such as "relativity theory," "quantum mechanics," or the "uncertainty principle," even though their exact meaning and mathematical bases were often poorly understood. They led people to wonder what it might mean to live in a world ruled not by certain "laws of nature" but by statistical probabilities, where time and space were no longer the self-evident and self-identical foundations of experience that they appeared to be.

Physics continued to hold public interest in the aftermath of World War II, as the invention of the atomic bomb and the civilian production of nuclear energy demonstrated its enormous power. But its unprecedented destructiveness in the attacks on Hiroshima and Nagasaki, as well as the long-term dangers associated with nuclear power plants, also aroused skepticism as to the desirability of such "progress," and led to public opposition that reached its peak in the student unrest of the 1960s. In the meantime, however, biology began to attract public attention with the widely publicized discovery of DNA in the 1950s, which promised a completely new understanding of life and reproduction. By the 1990s, the specters of the Nuclear Age had receded from public discussion, even though they occasionally continued to make their presence felt. Instead, public concerns began to focus on genetically modified foods and the implications of genetic cloning in some species, including humans. If radioactivity had long become associated with gothic images of deformed or oversized bodies, such images now shifted to the realm of biotechnology. The possibility of artificially created humans in particular called up echoes of literary and cultural motifs with deep roots in history, from Ovid's Pygmalion and the Jewish legend of the Golem to Mary Shelley's *Frankenstein* and the androids, replicants, and cyborgs of much twentieth-century science fiction. As so often in the history of technology, important innovations were accompanied by utopian hopes as well as fears of disaster that represent the latest technologies through age-old cultural templates.

Along with fundamental changes in scientific theory, a whole array of technological inventions transformed twentieth-century societies, from the mass production of automobiles to the invention of plastics, the vacuum tube, and the contraceptive pill. But it was the emergence of new media that proved particularly momentous for the cultural imagination in general and literary production in particular. The invention of the telephone, radio, motion picture, television, the long-playing record, and eventually the computer and the Internet all contributed to change the ways in which we imagine space and time. Along with new transportation technologies, the media contributed to shortening distances across the globe and to speeding up the pace at which goods and services could be exchanged. Each new medium also subtly altered the ways in which already existing media functioned. If families in the 1930s would gather around the radio, they would assemble in front of the TV in the 1970s and may now disperse to use an ever-increasing variety of electronic devices conveying stories, images, and games. Film and television compete with each other as well as with literary forms for some cultural functions of storytelling, and the significance of letter writing has changed with the introduction of the telephone and, yet again, with that of electronic mail. The older media are for the most part not extinguished by the arrival of newer ones but change their cultural functions and relevance. This fact is of crucial importance for understanding the ways in which literature changed between the beginning of the twentieth century and its close. For while more literary texts are produced and distributed at the turn of the third millennium than ever before, the social role of literature has changed, since in many literate societies it no longer stands alone as the crucial conveyor of cultural and human values.

But new media also open up new possibilities for literary creation broadly understood, as the digital revolution in particular has demonstrated. The invention of computers—especially of the personal computer—and the rise of the Internet have become the latest icons of techno-scientific progress. These have given rise to utopian hopes for a better connected, better informed, more democratic, and more tolerant world society, not unlike the hopes expressed when the radio was first invented. While concerns about privacy, surveillance, and commercialism have somewhat dampened the excitement that accompanied the burgeoning computer culture of the late 1980s and early 1990s, the computer continues to attract those who think of technological innovation as a means for improved human futures. More subtly, the personal computer and the Internet seem to put in question the very meaning of the word "technology" as it was understood in the modern age, when it was mostly associated in the popular imagination with machines and heavy industry. Computers, which increase in power and connectivity even as they shrink in size and communicate by more and more invisible means, seem to defy conventional notions of the "machine," and appear better described by the metaphor of a new "environment." This new medium with its ability to merge text, image, sound, and touch is already beginning to reshape possibilities for storytelling, lyrical expression, and theatrical performance.

But new scientific insights and technological artifacts have by no means led to uniform cultural optimism regarding the role of science and technology in human societies. On the contrary, from about the middle of the twentieth century, enthusiasm for techno-scientific progress was increasingly countered by moods of distrust and skepticism. Two technologically sophisticated world wars and the forty-year Cold War threat of nuclear annihilation convinced many that science and technology do not necessarily lead to a better world, as they are often deployed in ways that harm rather than help the welfare of ordinary people—especially those who do not have the privilege of living in the most scientifically advanced societies.

In the 1960s, this skepticism toward technology acquired even deeper resonance with the increasingly widespread perception that science and technology were contributing to the rapid despoliation of the natural environment. As the environmental movement gained visibility and some cultural and political power, it pointed out that technology-based lifestyles were increasingly leading to the destruction of habitats; the extinction of species; the pollution of air, water, and soil; and the rapid consumption of nonrenewable resources. In the former Communist bloc, such perceptions are compounded by the realization that even regimes that explicitly claimed to be acting on behalf of the common people wreaked havoc on nature. In the so-called Third World, environmentalist concerns form an explosive mix with resistance to the economic domination of Western chemical, pharmaceutical, and energy corporations. In all of these contexts, the notion that science and technology are associated with progress in any but the most superficial and material sense has come under intense scrutiny, and in some cases has been replaced by a nostalgia for what were thought to be the simple, harmonious, and nature-based cultures of premodern civilizations. While such views hardly constitute a majority view in any society, they have given rise to generalized cultural unease and ambivalence toward unchecked techno-scientific progress.

In academic and intellectual circles, this skepticism manifested itself from the 1970s on in sustained criticism of science and of techno-scientific rationality in such disciplines as philosophy, history, sociology, anthropology, and literary or cultural studies. In this perspective, it was not only the uses of science and technology that were suspect, but more fundamentally the theoretical assumptions and methodological procedures they use to obtain their insights. Are scientific researchers really "objective" when they carry out their work, or do their underlying values shape the procedures and outcomes of their research? Is the exclusion of women and nonwhite races from scientific research a historical accident, or is science in some respects inherently sexist and racist? Does scientific knowledge differ from other types of knowledge only in the social power it is granted, or does it have a special status with regard to the natural world? Whose interests does scientific research serve? What should its relation to liberatory political projects be? These and similar questions were amply debated, and the skeptical questioning of science was at times met with outrage and indignation on the part of scientists. This debate is an important symptom of changes in cultural attitudes toward science and technology. In many ways, it harkens back to the anti-Enlightenment skepticism that surged up during the Romantic era, even as the Industrial Revolution was transforming European societies.

In the Romantic period, literature played an important part in formulating concerns over the Enlightenment emphasis on the rational faculties of humans and the ways in which science and technology were affecting minds, bodies, and communities. To this day, literature—and poetry in particular—has often been defined as the medium that best embodies the intuitive and affective faculties that science and technology seem to leave out of consideration. Yet the encounter between literature, science, and technology is a good deal more complicated today than it was at the turn of the nineteenth century. Much of "world literature" has not evolved out of the Western Romantic tradition and defines its relation to techno-scientific modernization quite differently. Even within the Western tradition, resistance to technological dehumanization competes with literary enthusiasm for technology, from the Italian Futurists' celebration of technological speed all the way to the digital enthusiasm of the science fiction genre that has become known as "cyberpunk." Literature is in the process redefining itself in an altered media landscape that sometimes limits the reach of literary expression and sometimes opens up new venues for it. Science, technology, media, and our ambivalence toward them make up part of the force field that shapes literary creation at the turn of a new millennium.

THE TWENTIETH CENTURY

YEAR	THE WORLD	LITERATURE
1890		
		1899, 1902 Joseph Conrad, *Heart of Darkness*
1900		
	1900 Boxer Rebellion: nationalist forces rebel in China; suppressed by an international force	
	1901 Queen Victoria dies. Edward VII becomes king (to 1910)	**1901** Tomas Mann, *Buddenbrooks*
	1904 Belgian commission investigates atrocities in Congo	**1904** Alfred Jarry, *Ubu the King*
	1904–1905 Russo-Japanese War over rivalry in Korea and Manchuria, won by Japan	
	1906 Persian Shah Nasir ud-Din grants constitution	**1907** August Strindberg, *Ghost Sonata*
		1907 Premchand publishes first volume of stories, banned by the British as
	1908–1913 Kamal Ataturk leads revolution establishing modernizing government in Turkey	subversive
1910		**1909** F. I. Marinetti, *Futurist Manifesto*
	1911–1912 Manchu dynasty overthrown in China; Sun Yat-sen elected president of Republic of China	**1911–1923** Rainer Maria Rilke, *Duino Elegies*
	1913 War in Balkans over Serbian claims to Macedonia	**1913** Rabindranath Tagore awarded Nobel Prize in Literature
		1913–1927 Marcel Proust, *A la recherche du temps perdu*
	1914–1918 World War I	**1914** James Joyce, *Dubliners*
		1915 Rupert Brooke, *1914 and Other Poems*
		1915 Virginia Woolf, *The Voyage Out*
		1916 Franz Kafka, *The Metamorphosis*
	1917–1922 Russian Revolution leads to establishment of Soviet Union	**1916** W. B. Yeats, *Easter 1916* and other poems on the Irish Rebellion
		1918 Lu Xun, "A Madman's Diary"
		1918 Tristan Tzara, *Dada Manifesto*
	1919 League of Nations formed	**1919–1931** Vicente Huidobro, *Altazor*
	1919 Mahatma Gandhi begins campaign of nonviolent resistance against British rule in India	
	1919–1922 Irish rebellion leads to formation of independent Republic of Ireland, with Northern Ireland remaining British	
1920		
	1922 Fascist leader Benito Mussolini becomes Italian prime minister	**1922** César Vallejo, *Trilce*
		1922 James Joyce, *Ulysses*
	1922 Egypt achieves independence from Britain	**1922** T. S. Eliot, *The Waste Land*
		1922 Osip Mandelstam, *Tristia*
	1924 Vladimir Lenin dies; Joseph Stalin becomes Soviet leader	**1924** André Breton, *First Surrealist Manifesto*
		1925 Virginia Woolf, *Mrs Dalloway*
	1927 Charles Lindbergh completes first solo flight across the Atlantic	**1928** Mário de Andrade, *Macunaíma: The Hero Without Any Character*
	1929–mid-1930s Wall Street stock market crashes; worldwide depression follows	**1929** William Faulkner, *The Sound and the Fury*
	1929 First airplane flight over South Pole	

YEAR	THE WORLD	LITERATURE
1930		
	1933 Adolf Hitler becomes chancellor of Germany; Nazi party wins elections	
	1935–1949 Mao Zedong's Communist Party gains ascendancy in China	
	1936–1939 Spanish Civil War, won by fascist General Francisco Franco against the constitutional government	**1938** Jean-Paul Sartre, *Nausea*
		1939–1941 Bertolt Brecht, *Mother Courage and Her Children*
	1936 Italy takes over Ethiopia	**1939, 1954** Aimé Césaire, *Notebook of a Return to the Native Land*
	1939–1945 World War II	
1940		
	1940 Germany, Japan, and Italy form Axis alliance	**1940** Richard Wright, *Native Son*
		1940 Federico García Lorca, *Poet in New York*
		1942 Albert Camus, *The Stranger*
		1943 T. S. Eliot, *Four Quartets*
	1945 United States drops atomic bombs on Hiroshima and Nagasaki	**1944** Jorge Luis Borges, *Fictions*
	1945 United Nations established	
	1947 India achieves independence from England; Pakistan splits off as separate country	**1947** Thomas Mann, *Doktor Faustus*
	1947–1948 Partition of Palestine, creating State of Israel	**1948** Léopold Sédar Senghor, *Anthologie de la nouvelle poésie nègre et malgache*
	1948–1949 Soviets blockade West Berlin. U.S. and Western European nations form NATO to oppose Soviet expansion	**1948** T. S. Eliot awarded Nobel Prize in literature
	1949 Apartheid established as South African government policy	**1949** George Orwell, *1984*
		1949 Bertolt Brecht founds Berliner Ensemble in East Berlin
1950		
	1950–1953 Korean War, resulting in standoff between North and South Korea	
	1951 Chemist Carl Djerassi invents the birth control pill	
	1953 Stalin dies	**1952, 1957** Samuel Beckett, *Waiting for Godot* and *Endgame*
	1953 Watson and Crick discover DNA	
	1954–1962 Algerian War of Independence from France	**1955** Vladimir Nabokov, *Lolita*
		1955 Juan Rulfo, *Pedro Páramo*
	1956 Suez Crisis; Egypt defeats French and English efforts to maintain control of Suez Canal	**1956–1957** Naguib Mahfouz, *Cairo Trilogy*
	1956 Hungary's attempt to withdraw from the Warsaw Pact is ended through Soviet military intervention	
	1957 European Economic Community founded, creates the beginnings of a common market in Western Europe	**1957** Boris Pasternak, *Doctor Zhivago*
		1958 Primo Levi, *Survival in Auschwitz*
		1958 Chinua Achebe, *Things Fall Apart*
	1959 Fidel Castro overthrows Fulgencio Batista and ascends to power in Cuba	**1959** Günter Grass, *The Tin Drum*
1960		
	1960 Seventeen African colonies achieve independence from Europe	**1960** Clarice Lispector, *Family Ties*
	1960 Senghor becomes president of Senegal (through 1980)	
	1961 Russian Yuri Gagarin becomes first astronaut in space	**1961** Joseph Heller, *Catch-22*
		1961 V. S. Naipaul, *A House for Mr. Biswas*
	1961 Berlin Wall built, dividing East and West Berlin	

YEAR	THE WORLD	LITERATURE
	1962 Cuban missile crisis leads to the brink of nuclear confrontation between the United States and USSR	**1962** Derek Walcott, *In a Green Night*
	1962 Publication of Rachel Carson's *Silent Spring;* beginnings of the environmentalist movement	
	1963 U.S. President John F. Kennedy is assassinated	**1963** Anna Akhmatova, *Requiem*
		1963 Alain Robbe-Grillet, *Towards a New Novel*
	1965–1975 Vietnam War, won by Soviet-supported North against U.S.-supported South	**1963** Julio Cortázar, *Hopscotch*
	1967 Six-day War between Israel and Arab neighbors	**1967** Gabriel García Márquez, *A Hundred Years of Solitude*
	1968 Martin Luther King Jr. and Robert Kennedy are assassinated	
	1968 Soviet Union crushes the "Prague Spring" reformist movement	
	1968 Leftist student revolts in Paris, Berlin, and Mexico City; Tet offensive in Vietnam	
	1969 Civil unrest in Ireland leads to the intervention of British troops	**1969** Samuel Beckett awarded Nobel Prize in literature
	1969 American astronauts land on the moon	
1970		
		1972 Italo Calvino, *Invisible Cities*
	1973 Socialist government of Chilean president Salvador Allende overthrown through military coup backed by U.S.	**1973** Thomas Pynchon, *Gravity's Rainbow*
	1974 Personal computers begin to be marketed	**1974** Emile Habiby, *The Secret Life of Saeed the Pessoptimist*
	1974–1990 Military dictatorship of Augusto Pinochet in Chile	
	1975 General Franco dies; constitutional monarchy established in Spain	**1975** Wole Soyinka, *Death and the King's Horseman*
	1976 Mao Zedong dies in China	
	1978 The first "test-tube baby," Louise Brown, born in Britain	
	1979 Nicaraguan dictator Anastasio Somoza Debayle overthrown by Sandinistas	**1979** Nadine Gordimer, *Burger's Daughter*
		1979 Mariama Bâ, *So Long a Letter*
	1979 Shah of Iran deposed	
1980		
		1980 Mahasweta Devi, *Breast-Giver*
		1981 Salman Rushdie, *Midnight's Children*
		1981 Leslie Marmon Silko, *The Storyteller*
	1984 Bishop Desmond Tutu of South Africa awarded Nobel Peace Prize	**1982** Isabel Allende, *The House of the Spirits*
	1986 Philippine dictator Ferdinand Marcos overthrown	**1986** Ngugi wa Thiong'o, *Decolonizing the Mind*
	1989 Iran's Ayatollah Khomenei issues a decree of death against Salman Rushdie for *Satanic Verses*	**1988** Toni Morrison, *Beloved*
	1989 Eastern European nations begin to break free from Soviet bloc	
	1989 Fall of Berlin Wall; pro-democracy demonstration in Tiananmen Square, Beijing, ends in students' deaths	

YEAR	THE WORLD	LITERATURE
1990		
	1990 East Germany and West Germany reunified	**1990** Derek Walcott, *Omeros*
	1990 Iraq invades Kuwait, is repelled by U.S.-led coalition	
	1991 Breakup of Soviet Union	**1991** Nadine Gordimer awarded Nobel Prize in literature
	1992 Earth Summit convened in Rio de Janeiro to discuss global environment	**1992** Derek Walcott awarded Nobel Prize in literature
	1992 Signing of Maastricht Treaty creates European Union	
	1993 World Wide Web becomes accessible to broad public	
	1994 Civil War in Rwanda between Hutu and Tutsi; a half-million casualties	**1994** Salman Rushdie, *East, West*
	1994 Nelson Mandela elected first black president of South Africa	
	1996 Cloning of the sheep Dolly	**1995** José Saramago, *Blinders*
	1997 British rule ends in Hong Kong, which becomes part of China	
	1999 Adoption of the Euro as common currency by the European Union	**1999** Carlos Fuentes, *The Years with Laura Díaz*
2000		
		2000 Nobel Prize in literature awarded to Gao Xingjian, first Chinese recipient

⌘ CROSSCURRENTS ⌘
The Art of the Manifesto

Perhaps more than any previous age, the twentieth century saw its own beginning as the start of a new and unprecedented turn in human history. In many respects, those early pronouncements have been borne out. Technology and war were among the preeminent subjects with which European artists and writers declared their arrival on the historical scene. As one of the first such declarations, the Futurist Manifesto of 1909 was unmistakable in this regard. From the praise of speed and technological marvels to the fascism of its high priest Filippo Marinetti, Futurism proved an exemplary prophecy of Europe's historic destiny in the first half of the century. The other manifestos gathered here proved no less prophetic. True prophecy foresees the inevitable, and the realities of literary and sociopolitical history of the recently concluded twentieth century corroborate just how accurately the destiny of the century was manifested to the writers and artists who proclaimed its future in these manifestos.

What are manifestos, anyway? The specimens gathered here indicate that a manifesto is a cry emanating from a speaker who turns back and forward in time and in history, declaring a break with what was, diagnosing how things are, and proclaiming what should be. It's an urgent call with resolute conviction that censors and rejects but that also offers an alternative program and a new direction. Manifestos have their origins in the nineteenth century and are basically political (for example, Marx and Engels's *Communist Manifesto*). With the first decades of the twentieth century, they expand from the political into the aesthetic sphere of engaged literature and art. While they view their task as critical of the past and of the status quo, they are also resolutely convinced of their constructive mission and redemptive role for the future. They critique with reasoned persuasion or with irony and with ridicule. They see themselves as principled and uncompromising, even if they actually embody a historical compromise in the principles they espouse and the program they prescribe. They often consider their own stance as primal and outside of causality, even if in fact they are the symptomatic effect of causes they condemn. They see themselves as beginning anew, but they are deaf to the echoes of what they rejected—what is not new—that still resonates in their voice. In this sense, manifestos are historic documents, even when they reject history. As such, they are instructive, and they are just as revealing as they are prophetic. It's important, then, to begin reading a century by reading how it declared itself, what it saw as its own future, what its most resonant voices proclaimed as cultural program for its place in human history.

Such determination, conviction, and commitment inevitably raise the decibel level and tend to focus vision. The tone of manifestos, then, tends to be rather shrill and the sight partial. In this regard, these manifestos not only proclaim what was to be the future of the twentieth century but also foreshadow what the century would wreak upon itself. They can thus be read not only for what they proclaim but also for what they signify. As programs for the future, they might be considered in the light of what they represent as symptoms of their time. Now that we can look back on their proclamations and recipes for human endeavors in the arts and in literature that were to save the century from the past, we might assess their significance in the light of what became of the future they foresaw.

Filippo Tommaso Marinetti
1876–1944

Born in Alexandria, Egypt, Marinetti studied literature at the Sorbonne and launched his career, and that of Futurism, with his manifesto in the Paris daily *Le Figaro* on February 20, 1909.

Writing in French and in Italian, Marinetti portrayed the dynamic movement of the machine age, praised its instruments (the automobile, aviation, telecommunications) and highlighted the dangers and beauty of the technology of war with which the twentieth century began. The movement itself, in the literary and in the visual arts, flourished for a decade following the publication of the Futurist Manifesto, with a 1912 exhibition in Paris as the high point of Futurist art. The influence of Futurism, along with Cubism in painting, with which it coincided, would be felt in a number of other modernist movements in the early part of the century, most notably Russian constructivism. Marinetti returned to Italy and received a degree in law. His writings would turn decidedly political and his ideological bent would gravitate to fascism, the dominant political strain at the time in the Italy of Marinetti.

The Foundation and Manifesto of Futurism[1]

We had been up all night, my friends and I, under the Oriental lamps with their pierced copper domes starred like our souls—for from them too burst the trapped lightning of an electric heart. We had tramped out at length on the luxurious carpets from the East our inherited sloth, disputing beyond the extremes of logic and blackening much paper with frenzied writing.

An immense pride swelled our chests because we felt ourselves alone at that hour, alert and upright like magnificent beacons and advance guard posts confronting the army of enemy stars staring down from their heavenly encampments. Alone with the stokers working before the infernal fires of the great ships; alone with the black phantoms that poke into the red-hot bellies of locomotives launched at mad speed; alone with the drunks reeling with their uncertain flapping of wings around the city walls.

Suddenly we started at the formidable sound of the enormous double-decked trams that jolted past, magnificent in multicolored lights like villages at holiday time that the flooded Po[2] has suddenly rocked and wrenched from their foundations to carry over the cascades and through the whirlpools of a flood, down to the sea.

Then the silence became profound. But while we were listening to the interminable mumbled praying of the old canal and the creaking bones of the moribund palaces on their mossy, dank foundations, we suddenly heard automobiles roaring voraciously beneath our windows.

"Let's go!" I said, "Let's go, friends! Let's go out. Mythology and the Mystic Ideal are finally overcome. We are about to witness the birth of the centaur and soon we shall see the first angels fly! . . . The doors of life must be shaken to test the hinges and bolts! . . . Let's take off! Behold the very first dawn on earth! There is nothing to equal the splendor of the sun's rose-colored sword as it duels for the first time in our thousand-year darkness! . . ."

We went up to the three snorting beasts to pat lovingly their torrid breasts. I stretched out on my machine like a corpse on a bier; but I revived at once under the steering wheel, a guillotine blade that menaced my stomach.

The furious sweep of madness took us out of ourselves and hurled us through streets as rough and deep as stream beds. Here and there a sick lamp in a window taught us to mistrust the fallacious mathematics of our wasted eyes.

I cried, "The scent! The scent is enough for the beasts! . . ."

---

1. Translated by Joshua C. Taylor. 2. River that runs through the city of Turin, where the Futurist Manifesto was proclaimed.

And we like young lions pursued Death with his black pelt spotted with pale crosses, streaking across the violet sky so alive and vibrant.

Yet we had no ideal lover reaching her sublime face to the clouds, nor a cruel queen to whom to offer our bodies, twisted in the forms of Byzantine rings! Nothing to die for except the desire to free ourselves at last from our too exigent courage!

And we sped on, squashing the watchdogs on their doorsteps who curled up under our scorching tires like starched collars under a flat-iron. Death, domesticated, overtook me at every turn to graciously offer me her paw, and from time to time she would stretch out on the ground with the sound of grinding teeth to cast up soft caressing glances from every puddle.

"Let's break away from rationality as out of a horrible husk and throw ourselves like pride-spiced fruit into the immense distorted mouth of the wind! Let's give ourselves up to the unknown, not out of desperation but to plumb the deep pits of the absurd!"

I had hardly spoken these words when suddenly I spun around with a drunken lurch like a dog trying to bite his tail, and there all at once coming towards me were two cyclists, wavering in front of me like two equally persuasive but contradictory arguments. Their stupid dilemma was being disputed right in my way. . . . What a nuisance! Auff! . . . I stopped short and—disgusting—was hurled, wheels in the air, into a ditch. . . .

"Oh! maternal ditch, almost to the top with muddy water! Fair factory drainage ditch! I avidly savored your nourishing muck, remembering the holy black breast of my Sudanese nurse. . . . When I got out from under the upturned car—torn, filthy, and stinking—I felt the red hot iron of joy pass over my heart!

A crowd of fishermen armed with their poles, and some gouty naturalists were already crowding around the wonder. With patient and meticulous care they put up a high framework and enormous iron nets to fish out my automobile like a great beached shark. The machine emerged slowly, shedding at the bottom like scales its heavy body so sound, and its soft upholstery so comfortable.

They thought it was dead, my fine shark, but the stroke of my hand was enough to restore it to life, and there it was living again, speeding along once more on its powerful fins.

So, with face smeared in good waste from the factories—a plaster of metal slag, useless sweat, and celestial soot—bruised, arms bandaged, but undaunted, we declare our primary intentions to all *living* men of the earth:

Manifesto of Futurism

1. We intend to glorify the love of danger, the custom of energy, the strength of daring.
2. The essential elements of our poetry will be courage, audacity, and revolt.
3. Literature having up to now glorified thoughtful immobility, ecstasy, and slumber, we wish to exalt the aggressive movement, the feverish insomnia, running, the perilous leap, the cuff, and the blow.
4. We declare that the splendor of the world has been enriched with a new form of beauty, the beauty of speed. A race-automobile adorned with great pipes like serpents with explosive breath . . . a race-automobile which seems to rush over exploding powder is more beautiful than the *Victory of Samothrace*.[3]

---

3. A Greek island in the northern Aegean Sea, where the statue of Nike ("Victory") was excavated in 1863. Created around 200 B.C.E., the Victory of Samothrace is now housed in the Louvre Museum in Paris.

5. We will sing the praises of man holding the flywheel of which the ideal steering-post traverses the earth impelled itself around the circuit of its own orbit.

6. The poet must spend himself with warmth, brilliancy, and prodigality to augment the fervor of the primordial elements.

7. There is no more beauty except in struggle. No masterpiece without the stamp of aggressiveness. Poetry should be a violent assault against unknown forces to summon them to lie down at the feet of man.

8. We are on the extreme promontory of ages! Why look back since we must break down the mysterious doors of Impossibility? Time and Space died yesterday. We already live in the Absolute for we have already created the omnipresent eternal speed.

9. We will glorify war—the only true hygiene of the world—militarism, patriotism, the destructive gesture of anarchists, the beautiful Ideas which kill, and the scorn of woman.

10. We will destroy museums, libraries, and fight against moralism, feminism, and all utilitarian cowardice.

11. We will sing the great masses agitated by work, pleasure, or revolt; we will sing the multicolored and polyphonic surf of revolutions in modern capitals; the nocturnal vibration of arsenals and docks beneath their glaring electric moons; greedy stations devouring smoking serpents; factories hanging from the clouds by the threads of their smoke; bridges like giant gymnasts stepping over sunny rivers sparkling like diabolical cutlery; adventurous steamers scenting the horizon; large-breasted locomotives bridled with long tubes, and the slippery flight of airplanes whose propellers have flaglike flutterings and applauses of enthusiastic crowds.

It is in Italy that we hurl this overthrowing and inflammatory declaration, with which today we found Futurism, for we will free Italy from her numberless museums which cover her with countless cemeteries.

Museums, cemeteries! . . . Identical truly, in the sinister promiscuousness of so many objects unknown to each other. Public dormitories, where one is forever slumbering beside hated or unknown beings. Reciprocal ferocity of painters and sculptors murdering each other with blows of form and color in the same museum.

That a yearly visit be paid there as one visits the grave of dead relatives, once a year! . . . We are ready to grant it! . . . That an annual offering of flowers be laid at the feet of the *Gioconda,*[4] we conceive it! . . . But to take for a daily walk through the museums our spleen, lack of courage, and morbid restlessness, we will not grant it! . . . Why will you poison yourselves? Why will you decay?

What can one see in an old picture except the artist's laborious contortions, struggling to overcome the insuperable barriers ever resisting his desire to express his entire dream?

To admire an old picture is to pour our sentiment into a funeral urn instead of hurling it forth in violent gushes of action and productiveness. Will you thus consume your best strength in this useless admiration of the past from which you will forcibly come out exhausted, lessened, and trampled?

In truth, this daily frequenting of museums, libraries, and academies (those graveyards of vain efforts, those Mount Calvaries[5] of crucified dreams, those registers

---

4. Painting by Leonardo da Vinci from 1506, commonly known as the Mona Lisa.   5. The place of Jesus' crucifixion.

of broken-down springs! . . .) is to the artist as the too-prolonged government of parents for intelligent young people, inebriated with their talent and ambitious will.

For the dying, invalids, and prisoners, let it pass. Perhaps the admirable past acts as a salve on their wounds, as they are forever debarred from the future. . . . But we will have none of it, we the young, the strong, the living futurists! . . .

Therefore welcome the kindly incendiarists with the carbon fingers! . . . Here they are! . . . Here! . . . Away and set fire to the bookshelves! . . . Turn the canals and flood the vaults of museums! . . . Oh! Let the glorious old pictures float adrift! Seize pickax and hammer! Sap the foundations of the venerable towns!

The oldest among us are thirty; we have thus at least ten years in which to accomplish our task. When we are forty, let others—younger and more daring men— throw us into the wastepaper basket like useless manuscripts! . . . They will come against us from far away, from everywhere, leaping on the cadence of their first poems, clawing the air with crooked fingers and scenting at the academy gates the good smell of our decaying minds already promised to the catacombs of libraries.

But we shall not be there. They will find us at last, on a winter's night, in the open country, in a sad, iron shed pitter-pattered by the monotonous rain, huddled round our trepidating airplanes, warming our hands at the miserable fire made with our present-day books flickering merrily in the sparkling flight of their images.

They will mutiny around us, panting with anguish and spite, exasperated one and all by our proud dauntless courage, they will rush to kill us, their hatred so much the stronger as their hearts will be overwhelmed with love and admiration for us! And powerful and healthsome Injustice will then burst radiantly in their eyes. For art can only be violence, cruelty, and injustice.

The oldest among us are thirty, yet we have already squandered treasures, treasures of strength, love, daring, and eager will, hastily, raving, without reckoning, never stopping, breathlessly. Look at us! We are not exhausted. . . . Our heart is not in the least weary! For it has been nourished on fire, hatred, and speed! . . . You are astonished? It is because you do not even remember living! . . .

Erect on the pinnacle of the world, we once more hurl forth our defiance to the stars.

Your objections? Enough! Enough! I know them! I quite understand what our splendid and mendacious intelligence asserts. We are, it says, but the result and continuation of our ancestors.—Perhaps! Be it so! . . . What of that? But we will not listen! Beware of repeating such infamous words! Rather hold your head up!

Erect on the pinnacle of the world we hurl forth once more our defiance to the stars! . . .

Tristan Tzara
1896–1963

Tristan Tzara, whose real name was Samuel Rosenstock, was born in Romania in 1896. After cofounding the review *Simbolul* with a friend in 1912 and studying mathematics and philosophy at the University of Bucharest, he went to Zurich in the fall of 1915. He became one of the founders and major figures of the Dadaist movement, first in Zurich, and then in Paris, propagating Dada with extraordinary energy and passion as a force designed to do away with outdated traditions and conventional artistic forms. Protesting against the bourgeois societies that brought about mass slaughter in World War I, the Dadaists attempted to take art outside the confines of cultural institutions and to bring it back into immediate contact with life practice. In his *Unpretentious Proclamation,* which was first read in Zurich at a Dada soirée in 1919, Tzara tries to shake up his audience both through his critique of "art" and through his aggressively unorthodox typography. His proclamation is only one of a series of manifestos and lectures in which Tzara outlines the spirit of Dadaism.

The Dadaist movement in Paris lost force in the early 1920s but was succeeded by other avant-garde impulses. Tzara joined André Breton's Surrealist movement in 1929 and wrote poetry that is more inspired by Surrealist explorations of the unconscious than the Dadaist play on nonsensical language. He took an active interest in the Spanish Civil War and, once World War II broke out, joined the French resistance. After the end of the war, he published several more volumes of poetry, in which a more conventional view of the human condition emerges. His earlier work has remained a lasting influence on twentieth-century literature and art. His *Seven Dada Manifestos* (1924) have become classics of avant-garde writing, and his instructions on how to write a Dadaist poem, by cutting up a newspaper, mixing up the clippings and pasting them back together in random order, inspired many later attempts to make revolutionary art out of everyday objects and to create innovative literature by scrambling linguistic order through "cut-up" methods.

Unpretentious Proclamation[1]

Art is putting itself to sleep to bring about the birth of the new world **"ART"** — *a parrot word* — replaced by **DADA**, PLESIOSAURUS, or handkerchief

The talent THAT CAN BE LEARNT *turns the poet into an ironmonger*
TODAY *criticism balances doesn't throw up any resemblances*

Hypertrophic painters hyperaestheticised and hypnotised by the hyacinths of the muezzins of hypocritical appearance

CONSOLIDATE THE EXACT HARVEST OF CALCULATION

HYPODROME OF IMMORTAL GUARANTEES: *There is no importance there is neither transparence nor appearance*

MUSICIANS SMASH YOUR BLIND INSTRUMENTS on the stage

The BAZOOKA is only for my understanding. **I write because it's natural like I piss like I'm ill**

---

1. Translated by Barbara Wright.

Art needs an operation

Art is a *PRETENSION* heated at the **TIMIDITY** of the urinary basin, hysteria born in the **studio**

We are looking for a **straightforward pure sober unique** force.we are looking for **NOTHING** we affirm the **VITALITY** of every **instant** the the **anti-philosophy of** spontaneous **acrobatics**

At this moment I hate the man who whispers before the interval—eau de cologne—sour theatre. SWEET WIND.

IF EVERYONE SAYS THE OPPOSITE IT'S BECAUSE HE'S RIGHT

Prepare the action of the geyser of our blood—the submarine formation of transchromatic aeroplanes, metals with cells and ciphered in the upsurge of images

above the rules of the

Beautiful and of its inspection

It isn't for those abortions who still worship their own navels

—◄◆►—

André Breton
1896–1966

André Breton's lifelong dedication to rebellion against tradition notwithstanding, his rebellious youth in Paris was spent in the shadow of the greatest bulwarks of the French tradition. The Surrealist Manifesto (1924) was composed and signed by Breton and his nonconformist colleagues across the street from the Panthéon, that monumental structure erected to the sanctity of the French intellectual tradition, the resting place of Voltaire, Rousseau, and Zola, a temple of culture that was born an anachronism, its windows boarded up in 1789, the year in which it was completed. It was there, in the Hotel des Grands Hommes, that Breton used to hole up in his room to brood over the decadence of grandeur. Surrealism shifts the focus from cause and effect to paradox and the happenstance, and these circumstances of Surrealism's own genesis may be as paradoxical as "the absolute nonconformity" to causal reality proclaimed in the manifesto. Breton began studying medicine in 1913, serving as a physician's assistant during World War I and in a psychiatric hospital starting in 1915. These experiences gave him a fascination with neuropsychology and parareality, which led to Surrealism and its preoccupation with dreams, automatic writing, and hypnotic states. His first book, *Magnetic Fields* (1921), co-authored with Philippe Soupault, dealt with automatic writing. Called the "Pope of Surrealism," Breton devoted his life to the international promotion of the movement through two additional manifestos, numerous lectures and books, and several periodical reviews founded expressly for this purpose.

from The Surrealist Manifesto[1]

* * *

We are still living under the reign of logic, but the logical processes of our time apply only to the solution of problems of secondary interest. The absolute rationalism which remains in fashion allows for the consideration of only those facts narrowly relevant to our experience. Logical conclusions, on the other hand, escape us. Needless to say, boundaries have been assigned even to experience. It revolves in a cage from which release is becoming increasingly difficult. It too depends upon immediate utility and is guarded by common sense. In the guise of civilization, under the pretext of progress, we have succeeded in dismissing from our minds anything that, rightly or wrongly, could be regarded as superstition or myth; and we have proscribed every way of seeking the truth which does not conform to convention. It would appear that it is by sheer chance that an aspect of intellectual life—and by far the most important in my opinion—about which no one was supposed to be concerned any longer has, recently, been brought back to light. Credit for this must go to Freud.[2] On the evidence of his discoveries a current of opinion is at last developing which will enable the explorer of the human mind to extend his investigations, since he will be empowered to deal with more than merely summary realities. Perhaps the imagination is on the verge of recovering its rights. If the depths of our minds conceal strange forces capable of augmenting or conquering those on the surface, it is in our greatest interest to capture them; first to capture them and later to submit them, should the occasion arise, to the control of reason. The analysts themselves can only gain by this. But it is important to note that there is no method fixed a priori for the execution of this enterprise, that until the new order it can be considered the province of poets as well as scholars, and that its success does not depend upon the more or less capricious routes which will be followed.

It was only fitting that Freud should appear with his critique on the dream. In fact, it is incredible that this important part of psychic activity has still attracted so little attention. (For, at least from man's birth to his death, thought presents no solution of continuity; the sum of dreaming moments—even taking into consideration pure dream alone, that of sleep—is from the point of view of time no less than the sum of moments of reality, which we shall confine to waking moments.) I have always been astounded by the extreme disproportion in the importance and seriousness assigned to events of the waking moments and to those of sleep by the ordinary observer. Man, when he ceases to sleep, is above all at the mercy of his memory, and the memory normally delights in feebly retracing the circumstance of the dream for him, depriving

---

1. Translated by Patrick Waldberg.
2. Sigmund Freud (1856–1939), founder of modern psychology and psychiatry. His theories on dreams and the unconscious were influential for modern literature and its manifestos.

it of all actual consequence and obliterating the only *determinant* from the point at which he thinks he abandoned this constant hope, this anxiety, a few hours earlier. He has the illusion of continuing something worthwhile. The dream finds itself relegated to a parenthesis, like the night. And in general it gives no more counsel than the night. This singular state of affairs seems to invite a few reflections:

1. **Within the limits** to which its performance is restricted (or what passes for performance), *the dream,* according to all outward appearances, is continuous and bears traces of organization. Only memory claims the right to edit it, to suppress transitions and present us with a series of dreams rather than the dream. Similarly, at no given instant do we have more than a distinct representation of realities whose co-ordination is a matter of will. It is important to note that nothing leads to a greater dissipation of the constituent elements of the dream. I regret discussing this according to a formula which in principle excludes the dream. For how long, sleeping logicians, philosophers? I would like to sleep in order to enable myself to surrender to sleepers, as I surrender to those who read me with their eyes open, in order to stop the conscious rhythm of my thought from prevailing over this material. Perhaps my dream of last night was a continuation of the preceding night's, and will be continued tonight with an admirable precision. It could be, as they say. And as it is in no way proven that, in such a case, the "reality" with which I am concerned even exists in the dream state, or that it does not sink into the immemorial, then why should I not concede to the dream what I sometimes refuse to reality—that weight of self-assurance which by its own terms is not exposed to my denial? Why should I not expect more of the dream sign than I do of a daily increasing degree of consciousness? Could not the dreams as well be applied to the solution of life's fundamental problems? Are these problems the same in one case as in the other, and do they already exist in the dream? Is the dream less oppressed by sanctions than the rest? I am growing old and, perhaps more than this reality to which I believe myself confined, it is the dream, and the detachment that I owe to it, which is ageing me.

2. **I return to the waking state.** I am obliged to retain it as a phenomenon of interference. Not only does the mind show a strange tendency to disorientation under these conditions (this is the clue to slips of the tongue and lapses of all kinds whose secret is just beginning to be surrendered to us), but when functioning normally the mind still seems to obey none other than those suggestions which rise from that deep night I am commending. Sound as it may be, its equilibrium is relative. The mind hardly dares express itself and, when it does, is limited to stating that this idea or that woman has an effect on it. What effect it cannot say; thus it gives the measure of its subjectivism and nothing more. The idea, the woman, disturbs it, disposes it to less severity. Their role is to isolate one second of its disappearance and remove it to the sky in that glorious acceleration that it can be, that it is. Then, as a last resort, the mind invokes chance—a more obscure divinity than the others—to whom it attributes all its aberrations. Who says that the angle from which that idea is presented which affects the mind, as well as what the mind loves in that woman's eye, is not precisely the same thing that attracts the mind to its dream and reunites it with data lost through its own error? And if things were otherwise, of what might the mind not be capable? I should like to present it with the key to that passage.

3. **The mind of the dreaming man** is fully satisfied with whatever happens to it. The agonizing question of possibility does not arise. Kill, plunder more quickly, love as much as you wish. And if you die, are you not sure of being roused from the dead?

Let yourself be led. Events will not tolerate deferment. You have no name. Everything is inestimably easy.

What power, I wonder, what power so much more generous than others confers this natural aspect upon the dream and makes me welcome unreservedly a throng of episodes whose strangeness would overwhelm me if they were happening as I write this? And yet I can believe it with my own eyes, my own ears. That great day has come, that beast has spoken.

If man's awakening is harsher, if he breaks the spell too well, it is because he has been led to form a poor idea of expiation.

4. **When the time comes** when we can submit the dream to a methodical examination, when by methods yet to be determined we succeed in realizing the dream in its entirety (and that implies a memory discipline measurable in generations, but we can still begin by recording salient facts), when the dream's curve is developed with an unequalled breadth and regularity, then we can hope that mysteries which are not really mysteries will give way to the great Mystery. I believe in the future resolution of these two states—outwardly so contradictory—which are dream and reality, into a sort of absolute reality, a surreality, so to speak, I am aiming for its conquest, certain that I myself shall not attain it, but too indifferent to my death not to calculate the joys of such possession.

They say that not long ago, just before he went to sleep, Saint-Pol-Roux[3] placed a placard on the door of his manor at Camaret which read: THE POET WORKS.

There is still a great deal to say, but I did want to touch lightly, in passing, upon a subject which in itself would require a very long exposition with a different precision. I shall return to it. For the time being my intention has been to see that justice was done to that hatred of the marvellous which rages in certain men, that ridicule under which they would like to crush it. Let us resolve, therefore: the Marvellous is always beautiful, everything marvellous is beautiful. Nothing but the Marvellous is beautiful.

* * * One night, before falling asleep, I became aware of a most bizarre sentence, clearly articulated to the point where it was impossible to change a word of it, but still separate from the sound of any voice. It came to me bearing no trace of the events with which I was involved at that time, at least to my conscious knowledge. It seemed to me a highly insistent sentence—a sentence, I might say, which knocked at the window. I quickly took note of it and was prepared to disregard it when something about its whole character held me back. The sentence truly astounded me. Unfortunately I still cannot remember the exact words to this day, but it was something like: "A man is cut in half by the window"; but it can only suffer from ambiguity, accompanied as it was by the feeble visual representation of a walking man cut in half by a window perpendicular to the axis of his body. It was probably a simple matter of a man leaning on the window and then straightening up. But the window followed the movements of the man, and I realized that I was dealing with a very rare type of image. Immediately I had the idea of incorporating it into my poetic material, but no sooner had I invested it with poetic form than it went on to give way to a scarcely intermittent succession of sentences which surprised me no less than the first and gave me the impression of such a free gift that the control which I had had over myself up to that point seemed illusory and I no longer thought of anything but how to put an end to the interminable quarrel which was taking place within me.

3. Paul Roux (1861–1940), French Symbolist poet whose celebration by the Surrealists at a brazenly scandalous banquet on May 9, 1925, caused great indignation among decent folk and the intervention of the police.

Totally involved as I was at the time with Freud, and familiar with his methods of examination which I had had some occasion to practise on the sick during the war, I resolved to obtain from myself what one seeks to obtain from a patient—a spoken monologue uttered as rapidly as possible, over which the critical faculty of the subject has no control, unencumbered by any reticence, which is spoken thought as far as such a thing is possible. It seemed to me, and still does—the manner in which the sentence about the man cut in two came to me proves it—that the speed of thought is no greater than that of words, and that it does not necessarily defy language or the moving pen. It was with this in mind that Philippe Soupault[4] (with whom I had shared these first conclusions) and I undertook to cover some paper with writing, with a laudable contempt for what might result in terms of literature. The ease of realization did the rest. At the end of the first day we were able to read to each other around fifty pages obtained by this method, and began to compare our results. Altogether, those of Soupault and my own presented a remarkable similarity, even including the same faults in construction: in both cases there was the illusion of an extraordinary verve, a great deal of emotion, a considerable assortment of images of a quality such as we would never have been capable of achieving in ordinary writing, a very vivid graphic quality, and here and there an acutely comic passage. The only difference between our texts seemed to me essentially due to our respective natures (Soupault's is less static than mine) and, if I may hazard a slight criticism, due to the fact that he had made the mistake of distributing a few words in the way of titles at the head of certain pages—no doubt in the spirit of mystification. On the other hand, I must give him credit for maintaining his steadfast opposition to the slightest alteration in the course of any passage which seemed to me rather badly put. He was completely right on this point, of course. In fact it is very difficult to appreciate the full value of the various elements when confronted by them. It can even be said to be impossible to appreciate them at the first reading. These elements are outwardly *as strange to you who have written them as to anyone else,* and you are naturally distrustful of them. Poetically speaking, they are especially endowed with a very high degree of *immediate absurdity.* The peculiarity of this absurdity, on closer examination, comes from their capitulation to everything—both inadmissible and legitimate—in the world, to produce a revelation of a certain number of premises and facts generally no less objective than any others.

In homage to Guillaume Apollinaire[5]—who died recently, and who appears to have consistently obeyed a similar impulse to ours without ever really sacrificing mediocre literary means—Soupault and I used the name SURREALISM to designate the new mode of pure expression which we had at our disposal and with which we were anxious to benefit our friends. Today I do not believe anything more need be said about this word. The meaning which we have given it has generally prevailed over Apollinaire's meaning. With even more justification we could have used SUPERNATURALISM, employed by Gerard de Nerval[6] in the dedication of *Filles de Feu.* In fact, Nerval appears to have possessed to an admirable extent the spirit to which we refer. Apollinaire, on the other hand, possessed only the letter of surrealism

---

4. Philippe Soupault (1897–1990), French poet and early collaborator of André Breton in the Surrealist movement.
5. Guillaume Apollinaire (1880–1918), born Wilhelm Apollinaire de Kostrowitzky in Rome, coined the term "sur-realism," with a hyphen, in the May 18, 1917, program notes for the premiere of the ballet *Parade* by another Surrealist, Jean Cocteau.
6. Pen name of Gérard Labrunie (1808–1855), who was adopted by the Surrealists as forerunner because of his exploration of frontiers between reality and illusion. He suffered from madness and committed suicide.

(which was still imperfect) and showed himself powerless to give it the theoretical insight that engages us. Here are two passages by Nerval which appear most significant in this regard:

"I will explain to you, my dear Dumas, the phenomenon of which you spoke above. As you know, there are certain story-tellers who cannot invent without identifying themselves with the characters from their imagination. You know with what conviction our old friend Nodier told how he had had the misfortune to be guillotined at the time of the Revolution; one became so convinced that one wondered how he had managed to stick his head back on."

". . . And since you have had the imprudence to cite one of the sonnets composed in this state of SUPERNATURALIST reverie, as the Germans would say, you must hear all of them. You will find them at the end of the volume. They are hardly more obscure than Hegel's[7] metaphysics or Swedenborg's[8] MEMO-RABLES, and would lose their charm in explication, if such a thing were possible, so concede me at least the merit of their expression . . ."

It would be dishonest to dispute our right to employ the word SURREALISM in the very particular sense in which we intend it, for it is clear that before we came along this word amounted to nothing. Thus I shall define it once and for all:

SURREALISM, noun, masc., Pure psychic automatism by which it is intended to express, either verbally or in writing, the true function of thought. Thought dictated in the absence of all control exerted by reason, and outside all aesthetic or moral preoccupations.

ENCYCL. Philos. Surrealism is based on the belief in the superior reality of certain forms of association heretofore neglected, in the omnipotence of the dream, and in the disinterested play of thought. It leads to the permanent destruction of all other psychic mechanisms and to its substitution for them in the solution of the principal problems of life.

* * *

The Declaration of January 27, 1925[1]

[A SURREALIST MANIFESTO]

With regard to a false interpretation of our enterprise, stupidly circulated among the public, We declare as follows to the entire braying literary, dramatic, philosophical, exegetical and even theological body of contemporary criticism:

We have nothing to do with literature; But we are quite capable, when necessary, of making use of it like anyone else.

Surrealism is not a new means of expression, or an easier one, nor even a metaphysic of poetry. It is a means of total liberation of the mind and of all that resembles it.

---

7. Georg Wilhelm Friedrich Hegel (1770–1831). One of the most systematic of German philosophers, Hegel sought to give a logical explanation to history, its origin, and its ultimate ends.

8. Emanuel Swedenborg (1688–1772), Swedish scientist, philosopher, and visionary theologian, who proclaimed a "new spiritual era" in his time.
1. Translated by Maurice Nadeau.

We are determined to make a Revolution.

We have joined the word surrealism to the word revolution solely to show the disinterested, detached, and even entirely desperate character of this revolution.

We make no claim to change the mores of mankind, but we intend to show the fragility of thought, and on what shifting foundations, what caverns we have built our trembling houses.

We hurl this formal warning to Society; Beware of your deviations and faux-pas,[2] we shall not miss a single one.

At each turn of its thought, Society will find us waiting.

We are specialists in Revolt. There is no means of action which we are not capable, when necessary, of employing.

We say in particular to the Western world: surrealism exists. And what is this new ism that is fastened to us? Surrealism is not a poetic form. It is a cry of the mind turning back on itself, and it is determined to break apart its fetters, even if it must be by material hammers!

Bureau de Recherches Surréalistes,
15, Rue de Grenelle

Signed: Louis Aragon, Antonin Artaud, Jacques Baron, Joë Bousquet, J.-A. Boiffard, André Breton, Jean Carrive, René Crevel, Robert Desnos, Paul Éluard, Max Ernst, et al.

Mina Loy
1882–1966

For much of the twentieth century, Mina Loy was remembered mostly as a friend and contemporary of many of the most important writers and artists of the 1910s and 1920s. In their biographies, she is mentioned as a glamorous presence on the major avant-garde scenes in Europe and the United States—witty, talented, self-confident, and beautiful. Fresh assessments in recent years have turned her into an established figure in her own right, as an innovative artist, poet, designer, and feminist thinker.

Mina Gertrude Lowy was born in London in 1882. Her cosmopolitan nomadism began in 1899, when she was sent to art school in Munich; for the next three and a half decades, she moved back and forth from London and Paris to Florence and New York. In 1903, she married fellow art student Stephen Haweis in Paris, and instead of adopting his name, changed her own to "Loy." In Florence, where she lived for almost a decade, she became acquainted with the Italian Futurists. Futurism made a deep impact on her thought and writing, and is clearly visible in the structure and typography of the "Feminist Manifesto," which are strongly reminiscent of the manifestos of Marinetti, whom Loy knew; yet her focus on the condition of women differs radically from Marinetti's often disdainful comments about femininity. In 1915, a group of her poems entitled "Love Songs" was published in the inaugural issue of *Others* magazine. They gave rise to heated controversy because of their explicit references to women's sexuality, childbirth, and marital difficulties. More of her poetry was published between 1917 and 1923, and won the recognition of eminent modernist poets such as William Carlos Williams, Ezra Pound,

2. Missteps.

and T. S. Eliot. Her subsequent work continued to include writing, but focused more centrally on art projects, such as assemblages from found objects. She lived in New York from 1936 to 1953, and then moved to Aspen, Colorado, to join her daughters, where she remained until her death in 1966.

Feminist Manifesto

The feminist movement as at present instituted is Inadequate

Women if you want to realise yourselves—you are on the eve of a devastating psychological upheaval—all your pet illusions must be unmasked—the lies of centuries have got to go—are you prepared for the Wrench—? There is no half-measure—NO scratching on the surface of the rubbish heap of tradition, will bring about Reform, the only method is Absolute Demolition

Cease to place your confidence in economic legislation, vice-crusades & uniform education—you are glossing over Reality.
Professional & commercial careers are opening up for you—
Is that all you want ?

And if you honestly desire to find your level without prejudice—be Brave & deny at the outset—that pathetic clap-trap war cry Woman is the equal of man—

for

She is NOT!

The man who lives a life in which his activities conform to a social code which is a protectorate of the feminine element—is no longer masculine
The women who adapt themselves to a theoretical valuation of their sex as a relative impersonality, are not yet Feminine
Leave off looking to men to find out what you are not—seek within yourselves to find out what you are
As conditions are at present constituted—you have the choice between Parasitism, & Prostitution—or Negation

Men & women are enemies, with the enmity of the exploited for the parasite, the parasite for the exploited—at present they are at the mercy of the advantage that each can take of the others sexual dependence—. The only point at which the interests of the sexes merge—is the sexual embrace.

The first illusion it is to your interest to demolish is the division of women into two classes   the mistress, & the mother every well-balanced & developed woman knows that is not true, Nature has endowed the complete woman with a faculty for expressing herself through <u>all</u> her functions—there are <u>no</u> <u>restrictions</u> the woman who is so incompletely evolved as to be un-self-conscious in sex, will prove a restrictive influence on the temperamental expansion of the next generation; the woman who is a poor mistress will be an incompetent mother—an inferior mentality—& will enjoy an inadequate apprehension of Life.

To obtain results you must make sacrifices & the first & greatest sacrifice you have to make is of your "<u>virtue</u>" The fictitious value of woman as identified with her physical purity—is too easy a stand-by—rendering her lethargic in the acquisition of intrinsic merits of character by which she could obtain a concrete value—therefore, the first self-enforced law for the female sex, as a protection against the man made bogey of virtue—which is the principal instrument of her subjection, would be the <u>unconditional</u> surgical <u>destruction of virginity</u> through-out the female population at puberty—.

The value of man is assessed entirely according to his use or interest to the community, the value of woman, depends entirely on <u>chance</u>, her success or insuccess in manoeuvering a man into taking the life-long responsibility of her— The advantages of marriage are too ridiculously ample—compared to all other trades—for under modern conditions a woman can accept preposterously luxurious support from a man (with-out return of any sort—even offspring)—as a thank offering for her virginity
The woman who has not succeeded in striking that advantageous bargain—is prohibited from any but surreptitious re-action to Life-stimuli—& <u>entirely</u> <u>debarred</u> maternity.
Every woman has a right to maternity—
Every woman of superior intelligence should realize her race-responsibility, in producing children in adequate proportion to the unfit or degenerate members of her sex—

Each child of a superior woman should be the result of a definite period of psychic development in her life—& not necessarily of a possibly irksome & outworn continuance of an alliance—spontaneously adapted for vital creation in the beginning but not necessarily harmoniously balanced as the parties to it—follow their individual lines of personal evolution—
For the harmony of the race, each individual should be the expression of an easy & ample interpenetration of the male & female temperaments—free of stress
Woman must become more responsible for the child than man—
Women must destroy in themselves, the desire to be loved—
The feeling that it is a personal insult when a man transfers his attentions from her to another woman
The desire for comfortable protection instead of an intelligent curiosity & courage in meeting & resisting the pressure of life sex or so called love must be reduced to its initial element, honour, grief, sentimentality, pride & consequently jealousy must be detached from it.

Woman for her happiness must retain her deceptive fragility of appearance, combined with indomitable will, irreducible courage, & abundant health the outcome of sound nerves—
Another great illusion that woman must use all her introspective clear-sightedness & unbiassed bravery to destroy—for the sake of her self respect is the impurity of sex the realisation in defiance of superstition that there is nothing impure in sex—except in the mental attitude to it—will constitute an incalculable & wider social regeneration than it is possible for our generation to imagine.

⊶ ⋙⋘ ⊷

Yokomitsu Riichi
1898–1947

Yokomitsu Riichi, the son of a civil engineer, started writing after he entered Waseda University in Tokyo in 1916, where he also established his first contacts with other young writers. (His last name appears here before his given name, as is customary in Japan.) In the mid-1920s—generally an extraordinarily productive period for modern Japanese letters—he joined two newly founded journals: in 1923, the journal *Literary Annals* founded by playwright Kikuchi Kan, and in 1924 *Literary Age,* whose coeditor he became together with well-known novelist Kawabata Yasunari. In the latter journal, he published a short story called "Heads and Bellies" the same year, which attracted attention for its innovative style. *Literary Age* became the rallying point for a group of young writers who were dissatisfied with the traditions of Japanese naturalism and the "I-novel," which was very popular in the early decades of the century. Instead, Yokomitsu and others called for a literature that reveals the essence of things in a sudden shock of intuition—not by merely presenting their surface appearance nor individuals' subjective perceptions of them. This group of writers came to be known as the "New Sensation School," a name that a journalist bestowed on them. In 1925, Yokomitsu published the most important theoretical manifesto of the group, a piece entitled "New Sensation Theory" in the pages of *Literary Age;* the second section of this essay, entitled "Sensation and New Sensation," spells out a literary program according to which the grasp for the essence of things goes hand in hand with the call for a new kind of literary symbolism. Even though this particular group dissolved quickly, Yokomitsu continued to publish short stories and other prose writings until his death in 1947.

Sensation and New Sensation[1]

Up to now various interpretations have been put forward concerning the role of the sensations in literature. Still, I think one is bound to admit that this interpretative effort has been on a very limited scale. Undoubtedly when criticism is but a limited apprehension of a factor of great potential, the environment conducive to the growth of works of art will be similarly limited in its scope, a fact which one need not illustrate with examples. Thus with regard to the portrayal of the sensations, or sense impressions, in the works of the "New Sensation Group," which has now so suddenly come to the fore, one comes across, at times and in various places, those

1. Translated by Dennis Keene.

people of a similarly limited apprehension who, because of their very limitations, direct the most violent hostility towards this factor in the artistic world because of this considerable sensationalistic power it possesses. This was only to be expected, and this is not indicative of any failure of understanding on their part or ours. What has happened is no more than a change in the handling of those sensations which have been described up to now, a change from handling them in an objective manner to a subjective one, describing them at that point where they burst into life. However, it would certainly be onerous to give this new point of view a precise and adequate theoretical form. For example, even if we were first able to make a categorical analysis in objective terms and then to create similar subjective categories, we would still be left with the problem of finding some system of references between the two sets of categories. However, success in such a venture would necessarily lead to the setting of our overall basic aesthetic concepts in order, and to the declaration of the birth of a fundamental revolution in the world of art. I shall limit myself to hints and suggestions only in this matter, preferring the risky business of leaping head first into the adventure of the internal workings of the new sensations.

Indeed my own fundamental idea on sensation, which is the distinctive aspect of the "New Sensation Group" in this respect, is, to put it briefly, that sensation is an intuitive explosion of subjectivity that rips off the external aspects of nature to give direct access to the thing in itself. This is a rather extravagant way of putting it, and as such does not yet enable us to grasp what is actually new in the new sensation. Here there is one essential word, which is the word "subjectivity" in the sense in which it is used here, namely as that which sets in motion those faculties by which we apprehend the various existences of things in themselves. Now, cognition is obviously a synthesis of understanding and sensibility, and yet the question is whether the understanding and the sensibilities which constitute this cognitive faculty which apprehends these various existences, whether these can be said to take on, in conjunction with the development of the subjectivity that directly enters into the thing in itself, a dynamic form which responds in an increased sensationalistic way; a question of considerable import for the elucidation of a new basic concept for the new sensation. Sensation is the representation of that process which controls the representational faculty of external objectivity, and also of pure objectivity which is never an object for subjectivity.

The concept of sensation which operates in literature is generally speaking a simplified form of sensation; that is, not the sensation itself but a sensationalist representation of that sensation. And yet we must make the most definite distinction between the sensation itself and the actual bodily faculties. If we leave this point until later, then what in fact is it that is new in this new sensation we have already talked about? The difference between sensation and new sensation is this: that the objectivity of the object which bursts into life is not purely objective, but is rather the representation of that emotional cognition which has broken away from subjective objectivity, incorporating as it does both a formal appearance and also the idea of a generalized consciousness within it. And it is thus that the new sensationalist method is able to appear in a more dynamic form to the understanding than the sensationalist method by virtue of the fact that it gives a more material representation of an emotional apprehension. Still, one must always point out that, as far as this sensationalist bursting into life is concerned, the distinction between the objective and the subjective form is a real distinction.

---·❈❈❈·---

Oswald de Andrade
1890–1954

Born in São Paulo, Brazil, to a wealthy family, Oswald de Andrade, along with Mário de Andrade (no relation), would become identified with Brazilian modernism and the watershed event in Brazilian literary history known as "The Week of Modern Art" of 1922. That historic week set the course for a self-declared national literary independence, even though many of its elements originated in the modernist movements of Europe. Oswald de Andrade, who studied law, traveled to Europe in 1912, the peak year of Futurism in Paris, where he came into contact with the new literary and artistic currents championed by that movement. He devoted himself to literary and cultural journalism upon his return, and he was instrumental in a number of national debates on the course of Brazilian literary culture. His nativist bent took a radical turn and resulted in the *Manifesto Antropofágico* of 1928—the Cannibalist Manifesto. He used the imagery of the cannibals because he viewed Brazil as devouring foreign culture and, in the process, producing a revolutionary culture of its own. After the market crash of 1929 and the advent of the Depression, during which de Andrade's family fortune endured great losses, he became a militant member of the Brazilian Communist Party. He wrote a number of novels and plays, but his greatest impact was his polemical literary essays and his poetry. He obtained a professorship in literature at the University of São Paulo in 1945 and died in his native city nine years later.

Cannibalist Manifesto[1]

Cannibalism alone unites us. Socially. Economically. Philosophically.

. . .

The world's single law. Disguised expression of all individualism, of all collectivisms. Of all religions. Of all peace treaties.

. . .

Tupi or not tupi,[2] that is the question.

. . .

Down with every catechism. And down with the Gracchi's[3] mother.

. . .

I am only concerned with what is not mine. Law of Man. Law of the cannibal.

. . .

We're tired of all the suspicious Catholic husbands who've been given starring roles. Freud put an end to the mystery of Woman and to other horrors of printed psychology.

. . .

What clashed with the truth was clothing, that raincoat placed between the inner and outer worlds. The reaction against the dressed man. American movies will inform us.

. . .

Children of the sun, mother of the living. Discovered and loved ferociously with all the hypocrisy of *saudade*,[4] by the immigrants, by slaves and by the *touristes*. In the land of the Great Snake.[5]

---

1. Translated by Leslie Bary.
2. Tupi refers to the Brazilian indigenous people and their language. The author is punning on Hamlet's famous soliloquy "To be, or not to be: that is the question" in

Shakespeare's *Hamlet* 3.1.
3. Distinguished Roman family from 2nd century B.C.E.
4. "Nostalgia."
5. The Amazon.

It was because we never had grammars, nor collections of old plants. And we never knew what urban, suburban, frontier and continental were. Lazy in the *mapamundi*[6] of Brazil.

A participatory consciousness, a religious rhythmics.

Down with all the importers of canned consciousness. The palpable existence of life. And the pre-logical mentality for Mr. Lévy-Bruhl[7] to study.

. . .

We want the Carib Revolution. Greater than the French Revolution. The unification of all productive revolts for the progress of humanity. Without us, Europe wouldn't even have its meager declaration of the rights of man.

The Golden Age heralded by America. The Golden Age. And all the *girls*.

. . .

Heritage. Contact with the Carib[8] side of Brazil. *Où Villegaignon print terre.* Montaigne.[9] Natural man. Rousseau.[1] From the French Revolution[2] to Romanticism, to the Bolshevik Revolution,[3] to the Surrealist Revolution and Keyserling's[4] technicized barbarian. We push onward.

. . .

We were never catechized. We live by a somnambulistic law. We made Christ to be born in Bahia.[5] Or in Belém do Pará.[6]

. . .

But we never permitted the birth of logic among us.

. . .

Down with Father Vieira.[7] Author of our first loan, to make a commission. The illiterate king had told him: put that on paper, but without a lot of lip. The loan was made. Brazilian sugar was signed away. Vieira left the money in Portugal and brought us the lip.

. . .

The spirit refuses to conceive a spirit without a body. Anthropomorphism. Need for the cannibalistic vaccine. To maintain our equilibrium, against meridian religions. And against outside inquisitions.

. . .

We can attend only to the oracular world.

. . .

6. World map.
7. Lucien Lévy-Bruhl (1857–1939), French philosopher and anthropologist.
8. Indigenous people of the Caribbean, whose mispronounced name gave rise to Shakespeare's character Caliban in *The Tempest,* and to "cannibal."
9. Michel Eyquem de Montaigne (1533–1592), author of essays on diverse cultures and their practices, including "Of Cannibals," where he argues that many European customs are more barbaric than ritual cannibalism. *"Où Villegaignon print terre"* in Montagine's essay refers to Antarctic France, then the French designation for Brazil.
1. Jean-Jacques Rousseau (1712–1778), French philosopher associated most often with the idea of "the noble savage."
2. Antimonarchical movement and rule by the National Assembly, 1789–1791. Considered the threshold of modern regimes and break with traditional monarchy.

3. Also known as the February Revolution of 1917, dethroned the Czar Nicholas II and installed a provisional government, which was succeeded in turn by the October Revolution of the workers known as the Red Guards, thereby initiating the Soviet era of the 20th century.
4. Count Hermann Alexander Keyserling, Estonian-Austrian philosopher, author, spiritual leader, and founder of the School of Wisdom (1920).
5. Northeastern state of Brazil.
6. City in the Amazonian region of Pará, Brazil.
7. Father Antonio Vieira, Jesuit missionary to Brazil and defender of the indigenous populations in the Amazon region. He headed the mission to the Amazon between 1653 and 1661 but was expelled by the slave-holding Portuguese settlers and imprisoned by the Inquisition. Here, however, Andrade refers to Vieira's 1649 proposal to found a company for the exploitation of the sugar produced in Maranhão.

We already had justice, the codification of vengeance. Science, the codification of Magic. Cannibalism. The permanent transformation of the Tabu into a totem.[8]

. . .

Down with the reversible world, and against objectified ideas. Cadaverized. The stop of thought that is dynamic. The individual as victim of the system. Source of classical injustices. Of romantic injustices. And the forgetting of inner conquests.

. . .

Routes. Routes. Routes. Routes. Routes. Routes. Routes.[9]

. . .

The Carib instinct.

. . .

Death and life of all hypotheses. From the equation "Self, part of the Cosmos" to the axiom "Cosmos, part of the Self." Subsistence. Experience. Cannibalism.

. . .

Down with the vegetable elites. In communication with the soil.

. . .

We were never catechized. What we really made was Carnaval. The Indian dressed as senator of the Empire. Making believe he's Pitt.[1] Or performing in Alencar's[2] operas, full of worthy Portuguese sentiments.

. . .

We already had Communism. We already had Surrealist language. The Golden Age.

. . .

Catiti Catiti
Imara Notiá
Notiá Imara
Ipejú.[3]

. . .

Magic and life. We had the description and allocation of tangible goods, moral goods, and royal goods. And we knew how to transpose mystery and death with the help of a few grammatical forms.

. . .

I asked a man what the Law was. He answered that it was the guarantee of the exercise of possibility. That man was named Galli Mathias.[4] I ate him.

. . .

Only where there is mystery is there no determinism. But what does that have to do with us?

. . .

8. In going from "taboo" to "totem" Andrade wishes to reverse the sequence explained by Freud in his treatise *Totem and Taboo* (1913) in the establishment of civilized culture; that is, Andrade advocates going back from the patriarchal authority (imperial Portugal in this case) to the liberatory rites of totemistic cannibalism.
9. The Portuguese term is *roteiros*, which does mean routes but also means ship's logbooks and navigational charts. The implication is perpetual discovery.
1. William Pitt (1759–1806), British statesman and advisor to the king. Associated with government spending, fiscal deficits, taxation, and colonial policy.

2. Jose Martiniano de Alencar (1829–1877), Brazilian jurist, conservative politician, and novelist, exemplar of Brazilian Romanticism. The opera referred to is an 1870 Italian adaptation of Alencar's Indianist novel *O Guarani* (1857).
3. In Tupi, "New moon, oh, new moon, blow memories of me [to the man I want]." The author takes the phrase from *O selvagem* (1876), a work on the Brazilian Indians by José Vieira Couto Magalhães.
4. *Galimatias*, a French term meaning nonsense, incoherent speech, or contorted reasoning, made into a name and surname here by Andrade.

Down with the histories of Man that begin at Cape Finisterre. The undated world. Unrubrified. Without Napoleon. Without Caesar.

. . .

The determination of progress by catalogues and television sets. Only machinery. And blood transfusers.

. . .

Down with the antagonistic sublimations. Brought here in caravels.

. . .

Down with the truth of missionary peoples, defined by the sagacity of a cannibal, the Viscount of Cairu:[5]—It's a lie told again and again.

. . .

But those who came here weren't crusaders. They were fugitives from a civilization we are eating, because we are strong and vindictive like the Jabuti.

. . .

If God is the consciousness of the Uncreated Universe, Guaraci[6] is the mother of the living. Jaci[7] is the mother of plants.

. . .

We never had speculation. But we had divination. We had Politics, which is the science of distribution. And a social system in harmony with the planet.

. . .

The migrations. The flight from tedious states. Against urban scleroses. Against the Conservatories and speculative tedium.

. . .

From William James[8] and Voronoff.[9] The transfiguration of the Taboo into a totem. Cannibalism.

. . .

The paterfamilias and the creation of the Morality of the Stork: Real ignorance of things + lack of imagination + sense of authority in the face of curious offspring.

. . .

One must depart from a profound atheism in order to arrive at the idea of God. But the Carib didn't need to. Because he had Guaraci.

. . .

The created object reacts like the Fallen Angels. Next, Moses day-dreams. What do we have to do with that?

. . .

Before the Portuguese discovered Brazil, Brazil had discovered happiness.

. . .

Down with the torch-bearing Indian. The Indian son of Mary, the stepson of Catherine of Medici[1] and the godson of Dom Antonio de Mariz.[2]

---

5. José da Silva Lisboa, Viscount of Cairu (1756–1835), Brazilian author, liberal politician, and economist who opened up Brazilian markets and resources to international interests.
6. Tupi sun goddess, mother of all humans.
7. Tupi moon goddess.
8. American philosopher, biologist, and psychologist. From 1865 to 1866 he formed part of a Harvard University natural science expedition to the Amazonian region of Brazil.
9. Serge Voronoff (1866–1951), Russian-born biologist and physiologist. Director of experimental surgery at the

Collège de France, he specialized in grafting animal genital glands into the human body, specifically for recovery of one's youth and vigor.
1. Political strong woman (1519–1589) of the European Renaissance, she defined power politics between Catholics and Protestants at a time when these were the contending ideologies in the life of Europe. In an apocryphal story based on Alencar's novel O Guarani, she is said to be the godmother of an Indian baptized in Saint-Malo.
2. Portuguese nobleman in O Guarani (1857), José de Alencar's novel based on Brazilian indigenous culture.

Joy is the proof of nines.

. . .

In the matriarchy of Pindorama.[3]

. . .

Down with Memory as a source of custom. The renewal of personal experience.

. . .

We are concretists. Ideas take charge, react, and burn people in public squares. Let's get rid of ideas and other paralyses. By means of routes. Believe in signs; believe in sextants and in stars.

. . .

Down with Goethe,[4] the Gracchi's mother, and the court of Dom João VI.[5]

. . .

Joy is the proof by nines.

. . .

The struggle between what we might call the Uncreated and the Creation—illustrated by the permanent contradiction between Man and his Taboo. Everyday love and the capitalist way of life. Cannibalism. Absorption of the sacred enemy. To transform him into a totem. The human adventure. The earthly goal. Even so, only the pure elites managed to realize carnal cannibalism, which carries within itself the highest meaning of life and avoids all the ills identified by Freud[6]—catechist ills. What result is not a sublimation of the sexual instinct. It is the thermometrical scale of the cannibal instinct. Carnal at first, this instinct becomes elective, and creates friendship. When it is affective, it creates love. When it is speculative, it creates science. It takes detours and moves around. At times it is degraded. Low cannibalism, agglomerated with the sins of catechism—envy, usury, calumny, murder. We are acting against this plague of a supposedly cultured and Christianized peoples. Cannibals.

Down with Anchieta[7] singing of the eleven thousand virgins of Heaven, in the land of Iracema[8]—the patriarch João Ramalho,[9] founder of São Paulo.

. . .

Our independence has not yet been proclaimed. An expression typical of Dom João VI: "My son, put this crown on your head, before some adventurer puts it on his!" We expelled the dynasty. We must still expel the Bragantine spirit, the decrees and the snuff-box of Maria da Fonte.[1]

---

3. The Tupi name of Brazil, literally meaning "country of palm trees."
4. German poet, novelist, dramatist, and essayist (1749–1832), often identified as Germany's greatest writer.
5. Dom João de Bragança. Regent of Portugal as of 1792, who fled Napoleon's invasion and moved the royal court to Rio de Janeiro, Brazil, in 1807. He succeeded to the Portuguese throne in 1816 when his mother died.
6. Sigmund Freud (1856–1939), founder of modern psychology and psychiatry, his theories on dreams and the unconscious were influential for modern literature and its manifestos. His treatise *Totem and Taboo* (1913) is invoked throughout the *Manifesto*.
7. José de Anchieta (1533–1597), Jesuit priest and missionary to Brazilian Indians. He is one of the cofounders

of São Paulo and is known as the "Apostle of Brazil."
8. Name of an Indian princess-protagonist in a novel by the same title by José Martiniano de Alencar.
9. João Ramalho (1490–1580), one of the first colonists of southern Brazil, where his ship wrecked in 1513. He married the daughter of an Indian chief. By 1532, when he was discovered, he was totally assimilated to the indigenous life of the region. A founder of the settlement of Piratininga, he led the Indians against the Jesuits who were trying to found São Paulo.
1. Legendary conservative strongwoman, symbol of the old patriarchal regime in Portugal, opposed to the liberal Dom Pedro I who counsels his son here, advice that would lead to the independence of Brazil from Portugal.

Down with the dressed and oppressive social reality registered by Freud—reality without complexes, without madness, without prostitutions and without penitentiaries, in the matriarchy of Pindorama.

OSWALD DE ANDRADE
In Piratininga, in the 374th
Year of the Swallowing of
Bishop Sardinha.[2]

→‡◆⇄├→

André Breton
1896–1966

Leon Trotsky
1879–1940

Diego Rivera
1886–1957

As they debated the merits of fascism and Marxism, André Breton and the overwhelming majority of Surrealists saw Marxist and socialist philosophy as more conducive to the liberationist program of Surrealism. Chagrined by Stalin's repressive regime in the Soviet Union and the Moscow trials of dissidents and intellectuals in 1935 and 1936, however, Breton severely criticized Soviet communism as brutal. The Marxism he felt drawn to was that espoused by its foremost intellectual, Leon Trotsky, whose real name was Lev Davidovich Bronstein. Trotsky had been second in command following the 1917 Russian Revolution, but he had been banished by Stalin five years after he came to power in 1924, the year of Lenin's death and also the year of the Surrealist Manifesto. In 1938, when the French Foreign Ministry offered Breton a choice of posts as cultural ambassador in Czechoslovakia or Mexico, Breton chose Mexico because Trotsky was taking refuge there at the time.

Breton referred to Trotsky as the immortal theorist of permanent revolution, though the Surrealist and Marxist revolutions didn't always coincide, nor did Trotsky prove to be as immortal as Breton had thought, at least not outside his philosophy. Trotsky was murdered by Stalinist operatives in Mexico City two years later. Diego Rivera, the most celebrated of Mexico's muralist painters, had been instrumental in Mexico giving refuge to Trotsky. Rivera was in Paris in 1909, the year that Marinetti's Futurist Manifesto was published. His interests, however, gravitated toward a different sort of monumentalism, that of public art in the service of revolution. His commitment blended his interests in the Russian Revolution and his devotion to Mexico's own Revolution of 1910. The results of his political commitment as an artist extend from murals in Mexico City (see the front cover of this volume) to New York City's Rockefeller Center to Detroit's Institute of Art. When Breton, Trotsky, and Rivera coincided in Mexico in 1938, they went on a long anthropological excursion through Mexico. The result of their conversation on the question of the artist's role in the new society is the coauthored manifesto included here.

---

2. Pedro Fernandes Sardinha. Installed as Bishop of Salvador da Bahia in 1552, he was killed and devoured by the Indians in 1556, the event that marks the birth of Brazilian culture, according to the *Manifesto*.

Manifesto: Towards a Free Revolutionary Art[1]

We can say without exaggeration that never has civilization been menaced so seriously as today. The Vandals, with instruments which were barbarous, and so comparatively ineffective, blotted out the culture of antiquity in one corner of Europe. But today we see world civilization, united in its historic destiny, reeling under the blows of reactionary forces armed with the entire arsenal of modern technology. We are by no means thinking only of the world war that draws near. Even in times of "peace," the position of art and science has become absolutely intolerable.

Insofar as it originates with an individual, insofar as it brings into play subjective talents to create something which brings about an objective enriching of culture, any philosophical, sociological, scientific, or artistic discovery seems to be the fruit of a precious *chance,* that is to say, the manifestation, more or less spontaneous, of necessity. Such creations cannot be slighted, whether from the standpoint of general knowledge (which interprets the existing world), or of revolutionary knowledge (which, the better to change the world, requires an exact analysis of the laws which govern its movement). Specifically, we cannot remain indifferent to the intellectual conditions under which creative activity takes place, nor should we fail to pay all respect to those particular laws which govern intellectual creation.

In the contemporary world we must recognize the ever more widespread destruction of those conditions under which intellectual creation is possible. From this follows of necessity an increasingly manifest degradation not only of the work of art but also of the specifically "artistic" personality. The regime of Hitler, now that it has rid Germany of all those artists whose work expressed the slightest sympathy for liberty, however superficial, has reduced those who still consent to take up pen or brush to the status of domestic servants of the regime, whose task it is to glorify it on order, according to the worst possible aesthetic conventions. If reports may be believed, it is the same in the Soviet Union, where Thermidorean[2] reaction is now reaching its climax.

It goes without saying that we do not identify ourselves with the currently fashionable catchword: "Neither fascism nor communism!" a shibboleth which suits the temperament of the Philistine, conservative and frightened, clinging to the tattered remnants of the "democratic" past. True art, which is not content to play variations on ready-made models but rather insists on expressing the inner needs of man and of mankind in its time—true art is unable *not* to be revolutionary, *not* to aspire to a complete and radical reconstruction of society. This it must do, were it only to deliver intellectual creation from the chains which bind it, and to allow all mankind to raise itself to those heights which only isolated geniuses have achieved in the past. We recognize that only the social revolution can sweep clear the path for a new culture. If, however, we reject all solidarity with the bureaucracy now in control of the Soviet Union, it is precisely because, in our eyes, it represents not communism but its most treacherous and dangerous enemy.

The totalitarian regime of the U.S.S.R., working through the so-called "cultural" organizations it controls in other countries, has spread over the entire world a deep twilight hostile to every sort of spiritual value. A twilight of filth and blood in which, disguised as intellectuals and artists, those men steep themselves who have made of servility a career, of lying for pay a custom, and of the palliation of crime a source of

1. Translated by Dwight MacDonald.
2. Thermidor was the eleventh month of the French Revolutionary calendar. The reference here is to the coup of 9 Thermidor (27 July, 1794) that marked a turning point in the French Revolution and the return of the bourgeoisie and the newly rich.

pleasure. The official art of Stalinism mirrors with a blatancy unexampled in history their efforts to put a good face on their mercenary profession.

The repugnance which this shameful negation of the principles of art inspires in the artistic world—a negation which even slave states have never dared carry so far—should give rise to an active, uncomprising condemnation. The *opposition* of writers and artists is one of the forces which can usefully contribute to the discrediting and overthrow of regimes which are destroying, along with the right of the proletariat to aspire to a better world, every sentiment of nobility and even of human dignity.

The communist revolution is not afraid of art. It realizes that the role of the artist in a decadent capitalist society is determined by the conflict between the individual and various social forms which are hostile to him. This fact alone, insofar as he is conscious of it, makes the artist the natural ally of revolution. The process of *sublimation,* which here comes into play, and which psychoanalysis has analyzed, tries to restore the broken equilibrium between the integral "ego" and the outside elements it rejects. This restoration works to the advantage of the "ideal of self," which marshals against the unbearable present reality all those powers of the interior world, of the "self," which are *common to all men* and which are constantly flowering and developing. The need for emancipation felt by the individual spirit has only to follow its natural course to be led to mingle its stream with this primeval necessity: the need for the emancipation of man.

The conception of the writer's function which the young Marx worked out is worth recalling. "The writer," he declared, "naturally must make money in order to live and write, but he should not under any circumstances live and write in order to make money. The writer by no means looks at his work as a means. It is *an end in itself* and so little a means in the eyes of himself and of others that if necessary he sacrifices his existence to the existence of his work. . . . *The first condition of the freedom of the press is that it is not a business activity.*" It is more than ever fitting to use this statement against those who would regiment intellectual activity in the direction of ends foreign to itself, and prescribe, in the guise of so-called "reasons of State," the themes of art. The free choice of these themes and the absence of all restrictions on the range of his explorations—these are possessions which the artist has a right to claim as inalienable. In the realm of artistic creation, the imagination must escape from all constraint and must, under no pretext, allow itself to be placed under bonds. To those who would urge us, whether for today or for tomorrow, to consent that art should submit to a discipline which we hold to be radically incompatible with its nature, we give a flat refusal, and we repeat our deliberate intention of standing by the formula: *complete freedom for art.*

We recognize, of course, that the revolutionary State has the right to defend itself against the counterattack of the bourgeoisie, even when this drapes itself in the flag of science or art. But there is an abyss between these enforced and temporary measures of revolutionary self-defense and the pretension to lay commands on intellectual creation. If, for the better development of the forces of material production, the revolution must build a *socialist* regime with centralized control, to develop intellectual creation an *anarchist* regime of individual liberty should from the first be established. No authority, no dictation, not the least trace of orders from above! Only on a base of friendly cooperation, without the constraint from outside, will it be possible for scholars and artists to carry out their tasks, which will be more far-reaching than ever before in history.

It should be clear by now that in defending freedom of thought we have no intention of justifying political indifference, and that it is far from our wish to revive a so-called "pure" art which generally serves the extremely impure ends of reaction. No, our conception of the role of art is too high to refuse it an influence on the fate of society. We believe that the supreme task of art in our epoch is to take part actively and consciously in the preparation of the revolution. But the artist cannot serve the struggle for freedom unless he subjectively assimilates its social content, unless he feels in his very nerves its meaning and drama and freely seeks to give his own inner world incarnation in his art.

In the present period of the death agony of capitalism, democratic as well as fascist, the artist sees himself threatened with the loss of his right to live and continue working. He sees all avenues of communication choked with the debris of capitalist collapse. Only naturally, he turns to the Stalinist organizations, which hold out the possibility of escaping from his isolation. But if he is to avoid complete demoralization, he cannot remain there, because of the impossibility of delivering his own message and the degrading servility which these organizations exact from him in exchange for certain material advantages. He must understand that his place is elsewhere, not among those who betray the cause of the revolution and of mankind, but among those who with unshaken fidelity bear witness to this revolution, among those who, for this reason, are alone able to bring it to fruition, and along with it the ultimate free expression of all forms of human genius.

The aim of this appeal is to find a common ground on which may be reunited all revolutionary writers and artists, the better to serve the revolution by their art and to defend the liberty of that art itself against the usurpers of the revolution. We believe that aesthetic, philosophical, and political tendencies of the most varied sort can find here a common ground. Marxists can march here hand in hand with anarchists, provided both parties uncompromisingly reject the reactionary police-patrol spirit represented by Joseph Stalin and by his henchman, García Oliver.[3]

We know very well that thousands on thousands of isolated thinkers and artists are today scattered throughout the world, their voices drowned out by the loud choruses of well-disciplined liars. Hundreds of small local magazines are trying to gather youthful forces about them, seeking new paths and not subsidies. Every progressive tendency in art is destroyed by fascism as "degenerate." Every free creation is called "fascist" by the Stalinists. Independent revolutionary art must now gather its forces for the struggle against reactionary persecution. It must proclaim aloud its right to exist. Such a union of forces is the aim of the *International Federation of Independent Revolutionary Art* which we believe it is now necessary to form.

We by no means insist on every idea put forth in this manifesto, which we ourselves consider only a first step in the new direction. We urge every friend and defender of art, who cannot but realize the necessity for this appeal, to make himself heard at once. We address the same appeal to all those publications of the left-wing which are ready to participate in the creation of the International Federation and to consider its task and its methods of action.

When a preliminary international contact has been established through the press and by correspondence, we will proceed to the organization of local and national congresses on a modest scale. The final step will be the assembling of a world congress which will officially mark the foundation of the International Federation.

---

3. Juan García Oliver (1901–1980), minister of justice to the ill-fated Republican government during the Spanish Civil War of 1936.

Our aims:

> The independence of art—for the revolution;
> The revolution—for the complete liberation of art!

Hu Shi
1891–1962

Hu Shi was a writer, scholar, and diplomat who in the early twentieth century participated in the so-called May Fourth Movement, a broad-based rebellion against traditional cultural Chinese values, and particularly against Confucian ethics, which were perceived to perpetuate rigidly authoritarian political and social structures. The origins of this movement can be traced back to the foundation of the journal *New Youth* in 1915, where a generation of young and often Western-trained scholars and intellectuals published their ideas. The movement reached its peak in 1919 in protests against the Chinese signing of the Treaty of Versailles, which would have ceded Chinese territory to the Japanese.

Reform of the classical Chinese literary language was considered a crucial part of the changes that would lead to a different culture and society. Hu Shi's essay "Some Modest Proposals for the Reform of Literature," was published in *New Youth* in 1917, the year in which Hu returned to China after completing a doctorate at Columbia University in New York, where he studied under the pragmatist philosopher John Dewey. Hu's essay vigorously advocates a dynamic, vernacular literature as an alternative to what Hu perceived as the ossified forms of expression of the literary tradition. But implicitly, what is at stake is more than a change in literary expression. Some of these implications became visible in 1922, when Hu helped to establish a modernized, simplified Chinese as the official written language. Since classical Chinese, which had been used before, was far removed from the spoken language of the day, it was very difficult to learn and contributed to the persistence of illiteracy among the population. The change in official language opened up writing to a far broader public.

from Some Modest Proposals for the Reform of Literature[1]

Those engaged in the present discourse on literary reform are myriad. How am I, unlearned and unlettered, qualified to speak on the subject? Yet I have over the past few years, with the benefit of my friends' argumentation, pondered and studied this matter a fair degree and the results achieved are perhaps not unworthy of discussion. So I summarize the opinions I hold and list them in eight points; I have divided them in this fashion for the investigation of those interested in literary reform.

It is my belief that those wishing to discuss literary reform today should begin with eight matters, which are as follows:

- I. Writing should have substance
- II. Do not imitate the ancients
- III. Emphasize the technique of writing
- IV. Do not moan without an illness
- V. Eliminate hackneyed and formal language

---

1. Translated by Kirk A. Denton.

VI. Do not use allusions
VII. Do not use parallelism
VIII. Do not avoid vulgar diction

I. WRITING SHOULD HAVE SUBSTANCE

The greatest malady of letters in our nation today is language without substance.[2] All one ever hears is "If writing is without form, it will not travel far."[3] But nothing is said about language without substance, nor what function form should serve. What I mean by substance is not the "literature conveys the *Dao*"[4] of the ancients. What I mean by substance are the two following points:

A. *Feeling.* In the "Great Preface" to the *Book of Songs* is written: "Feelings come from within and are shaped through language. If language is insufficient to express one's feelings, then one may sigh; if sighing is insufficient, then one may chant or sing; if chanting or singing is insufficient, then one may dance with one's hands and feet." This is what I mean by feeling. Feeling is the soul of literature. Literature without feeling is like a man without a soul, nothing but a wooden puppet, a walking corpse. (What people call aesthetic feeling is only one kind of feeling.)

B. *Thought.* By "thought" I mean one's views, perceptions, and ideals. Thought need not depend on literature for transmission, but literature is enriched by thought and thought is enriched by the value of literature. This is why the prose of Zhuangzi, the poetry of Tao Yuanming and Du Fu, the lyric meters of Xin Qiji, and the fictional narratives of Shi Nai'an are eternal.[5] As the brain is to man's body, so is thought to literature. If a man cannot think, though he be attractive in appearance and capable of laughter, tears, and feelings, is this really sufficient for him? Such is the case with literature.

Without these two kinds of substance, literature is like a beauty without a soul or a brain; though she have a lovely and ample exterior, she is nonetheless inferior. The greatest reason for the deterioration of literature is that the literati have become mired in poetics and are without any kind of far-reaching thought or sincere feeling. The harm of an overly formalist literature lies in this so-called language without substance. And should we wish to save it from this fault, we must save it with substance, by which I mean only feeling and thought.

II. DO NOT IMITATE THE ANCIENTS

Literature has changed from dynasty to dynasty, each dynasty having its own literature. The Zhou and Qin dynasties had their literatures, the Wei and Jin had theirs, as did the Tang, Song, Yuan, and Ming. This is not just a personal opinion held by me alone, but a truth of the progression of civilization. As for prose, there are the styles of the *Book of History,*[6] the philosophers of the pre-Qin period, the Han historians Sima

2. This expression comes from the classical *Book of Changes,* in which the gentleman is exhorted to "have substance in his words" in order to have "stability in his actions."
3. A saying attributed to Confucius.
4. The "Way," or moral path stressed by Confucian philosophers.
5. Hu Shi refers here to the 4th-century B.C.E. Daoist

philosopher Zhuangzi, the two great poets, Tao Qian (365–427) and Du Fu (712–770), the song lyricist Xin Qiji (1140–1207) and Shi Nai'an, reputed author of a popular novel centered around a group of bandits, *The Water Margin* (c. 14th century).
6. Also known as the *Book of Documents,* one of the five Confucian classics.

Qian and Ban Gu, the essayists Han Yu, Liu Zongyuan, Ouyang Xiu, and Su Shi, the dialogues of Zhu Xi, and the fictional narratives of Shi Nai'an and Cao Xueqin.[7] This is the progression of literature. To turn our attention to verse, poems such as "The Pushpin Song" and "Song of Five Sons"[8] constitute the earliest period. Then follow the poems in the *Book of Songs,* Qu Yuan's *sao,* and Xunzi's rhyme-prose.[9] From Su Wu and Li Ling of the Western Han to the Wei-Jin period, and the *paibi* parallel style of the Southern dynasties, to the flourishing of regulated verse in the Tang and Du Fu and Bai Juyi's[1] "realism" (as in Du Fu's "Recruiting Officer of Shihao" and "Jiang Village" or Bai Juyi's "New Ballads"). The regulated verse form flourished in the Tang, but was later replaced by the lyric meter and the dramatic song (*qu*). From the Tang and Five Dynasties period to the short form in the beginning of the Song marks one period of the lyric meter. The lyrics of Su Shi, Liu Yong, Xin Qiji, and Jiang Kui form another period.[2] The *zaju* and *chuanqi* dramas of the Yuan are another. All these periods have changed with the times, and each has its own characteristics. Our generation, looking back with a historical, progressive perspective, is most certainly unable to say that the literature of the ancients is superior to that of the present. The prose of the *Zuo Commentary* and *Records of the Grand Historian* is miraculous indeed, but do they cede much to that of Shi Nai'an's *Water Margin?* And the rhyme-prose of the "Three Capitals" and "Two Capitals"[3] is but dregs in comparison to the Tang regulated verse and the Song lyric meter. We see from the above that literature develops and does not stand still. Tang people should not write poems of the Shang and Zhou, and Song people should not write rhyme-prose like Sima Xiangru or Yang Xiong.[4] Were they to do so, their results would certainly not be fine. One cannot be skillful if one goes against Heaven, turns one's back on one's age, and defies the footsteps of progress.

Since we now understand the principle of literary development, I can proceed to a discussion of what I mean by "not imitating the ancients." In contemporary China, in creating a literature for today, one must not imitate the Tang, Song, Zhou, or the Qin. I once saw the "Inaugural Remarks of the National Assembly" and it read: "Most glorious National Assembly, the end of penumbrous times is nigh." This is evidence that today there is a desire to model literature after the Three Dynasties of antiquity. When we look at today's "great writers," the lesser writers model themselves after Yao Nai and

7. Sima Qian's *Records of the Grand Historian* (c. 100 B.C.E.) offered the first comprehensive history of China, from the beginnings to the Han dynasty. Ban Gu (32–92 C.E.) was a poet and author of the history of the Former Han. Han Yu (768–824), Liu Zongyuan (773–819), Ouyang Xiu (1007–1072), and Su Shi (1037–1101) were masters of ancient Chinese prose style. Zhu Xi (1130–1200) was the most influential philosopher of early modern China, whose dialogues with his students record his comments on a broad range of topics. Cao Xueqin (1715–1763) wrote the great novel, *The Story of the Stone.*
8. Anonymous folk songs that probably weren't actually earlier than the *Book of Songs,* an anthology compiled by the 6th century B.C.E. and one of the Five Classics.
9. Qu Yuan (340?-278 B.C.E.) was said to have written many poems in a southern anthology known as the *Songs of Chu,* of which the most famous, "Encountering Sorrow," is believed to lament his banishment—owing to slander—from the court of the kingdom of Chu. The 3rd century

B.C.E. philosopher Xunzi employed rhymed riddles in his essays, from which a later genre known as the rhapsody or *fu,* translated here as rhyme-prose, was said to derive.
1. Also known as Bo Juyi (772–846), he was a prolific poet whose New Ballads critiqued contemporary inequities and abuses.
2. Liu Yong (987–1053) was known for his colloquial and sensuous song lyrics employing longer forms than had previously been used. Jiang Kui (1155–1221) wrote criticism on the song lyric and composed some of the few surviving examples of Song dynasty music.
3. Two famous examples of *fu,* which was well-suited to lavish description of sites. The "Three Capitals" was composed by the poet Zuo Si (c. 253–307) and the "Two Capitals" by the historian Ban Gu.
4. Sima Xiangru (179–117 B.C.E.) was the best-known writer of rhapsodies during the Han, and Yang Xiong (53 B.C.E.–18 C.E.) was recognized for his philosophical writings and his *fu.*

Zeng Guofan of the Tongcheng School,[5] the greater writers take the Tang-Song essayists Han Yu and Ouyang Xiu as their masters, while the greatest follow the prose of the Qin-Han or Wei-Jin periods and feel that there is no literature to speak of after the Six Dynasties. But the difference between these is like the difference between one hundred steps and fifty steps; they all belittle literature. Even if it resembles the ancients in spirit, it still amounts to nothing more than adding several "realistic counterfeits" to a museum. Is this literature? Yesterday I saw a poem by Chen Boyan[6] that reads as follows:

> In the Garden of Waves I copied lines from Du Fu,
> Half a year passed, many brushes worn thin.
> All I have to show for myself are tears,
> Though friends passed by commenting on my "skillful creations."
> The myriad souls are all silent,
> The more I look up to Du Fu the higher he becomes.
> I turn these feelings over in my bosom
> And leisurely read Qu Yuan's tragic *sao*.

This amply represents the imitative psychology of today's "poets of the first rank." The root of their sickness lies in spending "half a year passed with many brushes worn thin" in being slavish scriveners to the ancients, resulting in sighs about "the more I look up to him the higher he becomes." If we free ourselves from this kind of slavery and no longer write poems of the ancients and only write our own poems, we will not end with this sort of defeatism.

Whenever I mention contemporary literature, only vernacular fiction (Wu Woyao, Li Baojia, and Liu E)[7] can be compared without shame to the world's literary "first rank." This is for no other reason than that they do not imitate the ancients (although they owe much to *The Scholars*,[8] *The Water Margin,* and *The Story of the Stone,* they are not imitative works). And it is only because they faithfully write about the contemporary situation that they can become true literature. All other poets or ancient-style essayists who study this or that style have no literary value. Those today with a determination to pursue literature should understand precisely the nature of that in which they are engaged.

III. EMPHASIZE THE TECHNIQUE OF WRITING

Many poets and essayists today neglect syntactic structure. Examples are legion and not worth raising; they are especially numerous in writings of parallel prose and regulated verse. Neglecting syntactic structure means there will be an absence of "communication." This is clear enough, and there is no need to go into further detail.

IV. DO NOT MOAN WITHOUT AN ILLNESS

This is not easy to discuss. Today's youth often affect a tragic view of the world. When they adopt a sobriquet it is most often something like "Cold Ashes," "Dead

---

5. Yao Nai (1731–1815) was the founder of the Tongcheng school (named after his hometown), known for its clear and elegant—but definitely classical—prose style, which was admired and popularized by Zeng Guofan (1811–1872).
6. Also known as Chen Sanli (1852–1937), he was a late Qing reformer who was banished from government service and then dedicated himself to classical prose and poetry.

7. Wu Woyao (1866–1910) and Li Baojia (1867–1906) were journalists and novelists based in Shanghai whose satirical and sentimental writings captured the political and social collapse of late Qing dynasty China. The novel *The Travels of Lao Can* by Liu E (1857–1909) similarly exposes the old regime's demise.
8. A novel by Wu Jingzi (1701–1754), noted for its critique of traditional Chinese society, with a focus on the civil service examination system.

Ashes," or "Lifeless." In their poems and prose they write of such things as old age before a setting sun, desolation facing the autumn winds. When spring arrives, they dread its swift departure, and when flowers bloom, they fear their premature withering. These are the tragic voices of a fallen country. The old should not act thus—how much more so the young! The long-term effect of this is to foster a sense of despondency, which leads to a lack of regard for action or service to one's country, and which only knows the voice of lamentation or the literature of despair. This kind of literature will hasten writers to their grave and sap the will of its readers. This is what I mean by moaning without an illness. I am perfectly aware of the ills facing our nation today, but what effect can sobbing and tears have on a sick nation in such a perilous state? I only wish that contemporary writers become Fichtes and Mazzinis and not the likes of Jia Yi, Wang Can, Qu Yuan, or Xie Ao.[9] That they are unable to actually be like Jia Yi, Wang Can, Qu Yuan, or Xie Ao but instead write poems and essays about women, fine wine, depression, and discouragement makes them beneath contempt.

V. ELIMINATE HACKNEYED AND FORMAL LANGUAGE

Today one is called a poet if one can summon up from memory a few literary clichés. Poetry and prose are filled with stale and hackneyed diction, like "time waits for no man," "slings and arrows," "desolation," "solitary drifting," "the common man," "poor scholar," "sinking sun," "fragrant flowers," "spring boudoir," "melancholy soul," "home is where the heart is," "cry of the cuckoo," "lonely as a solitary shadow," "words formed by migrating geese," "jade pavilion," "elixir of love," "gray-eyed morn," and the like, an endless and most despicable gush. The long-term effect of this malady on our nation will be to give birth to poetry and prose that have the appearance of literature but really are not. Now I will demonstrate this tendency with a lyric:

> Like tiny peas, the twinkling flames of an evening lamp
> Cast a flickering shadow on a solitary figure,
> Helter-skelter and adrift.
> Beneath his kingfisher-blue covers
> Under his roof of interlocking butterfly-tile,
> How can he ward off the cold of an autumn's night?
> The tiny strings of the pipa murmur
> Early at Dingzi Lian,
> Heavy frost frolicked about.
> Enchanting notes lofted above
> After lingering momentarily round the columns.[1]

Glancing quickly at this piece we sense that its words and lines do form a lyric, when in point of fact it is but a list of clichés. "Kingfisher-blue covers" and "butterfly-tile" may be appropriate for Bai Juyi's "Song of Eternal Sorrow," but there they refer to the emperor's covers and the tiles of the imperial palace. "Dingzi Lian" and "tiny

9. Jia Yi (200–168 B.C.E.), politician and poet of the Western Han, was banished for criticizing the government and wrote a well-known *fu* lamenting the death of Qu Yuan, an exile and eventual suicide for similar reasons. Wang Can (177–217) lamented the chaos of warfare in his poetry. Xie Ao (1249–1295) was known as a patriotic poet who critiqued life under the Mongol occupation of China.

1. In later versions of this essay, Hu Shi indicates that this poem was written by "his friend" Hu Xiansu, who studied in the United States at the same time as Hu Shi and later became a member of the conservative Critical Review Group. Dingzi Lian may here refer to a pleasure quarter in Ming dynasty Nanjing. [Translator's note.]

strings" are stock phrases. This lyric was written in America, so the poet's "evening lamp" could not have "twinkled" "like little peas" and his abode had no "columns" around which the notes could linger. As for "heavy frost frolicked about," this is even more absurd. Whoever saw heavy frost "frolicking about"?

What I mean by the necessity of eliminating hackneyed and formulaic language can only be achieved through the creation of new phrases to describe and portray what people see and hear with their own eyes and ears or personally live through. It is indeed a great talent in writing to be able to mesh with reality and arrive at the goal of describing your object or conveying meaning. Those who employ hackneyed and formulaic language are indolent and unwilling to create new phrases to describe their objects.

VI. DO NOT USE ALLUSIONS

Among the eight propositions that I have proffered, that which has been most singled out for attack is the one most misunderstood. My friend Jiang Kanghu[2] dispatched a letter in which he writes:

> The term "allusion" has both a broad and narrow sense. Ornateness and grandiloquence have since days of yore been raised by the ancients as something to be strictly prohibited. If idiomatic expressions and anecdotes are eliminated, this will not only be a loss in terms of style, but a disaster for the function of writing. The most wonderful mood that writing can evoke is through simple words with broad and varied connotations. I could not succeed in writing this present passage without allusions. Not only can poetry not be written without allusions, neither can letters nor even speeches. The letters I receive are replete with such allusions as "a second self," "broadness of mind," "fail to get to the root of the problem," "miss the forest for the trees," "calamity of nature," "make the deaf hear and the dumb speak," "join forces and forge ahead," "I'm pleased to humbly submit," "Parnassian world," "an honorable retreat of a hundred leagues," "fill the firmament," "sharp instruments of power," and "ironclad proof." If we try to extricate them all and replace them with vulgar language and vulgar words, how will we be able to speak? Whether one uses ornate or simple diction is ultimately a trivial matter. What I fear is that if we change these allusions into other words, though we might have five times as many words, the connotations cannot in the end be as perfect. What then?

* * *

I am proposing that allusions in the narrow definition of the word not be employed. What I mean by this use of allusion is when men of letters are incapable of creating their own words and expressions to write about what is before their eyes or in their hearts and instead borrow, in part or wholly inapposite, anecdotes and hackneyed language to do it for them, allowing them to muddle along. The allusions in the "broad" definition discussed above are, excluding the fifth category, all metaphors or similes. But they use one thing as a metaphor for another, not as a substitute for it. The narrow definition of allusion, on the other hand, sees allusion as substituting for language; because they are

2. Jiang Kanghu founded the Chinese Socialist Party in 1911. When it was banned in 1913, Jiang went into exile in the United States, where he was at the time Hu Shi wrote this essay. He later returned to China to teach at Peking University. [Translator's note.]

unable to directly express themselves, they can only let allusion speak for them. This is what I mean by the distinction between what is and what is not allusion. And yet we still must distinguish between the skilled use of allusion and its crude or clumsy use. Skilled use is occasionally acceptable. Crude use should be eliminated altogether.

* * *

The problem in using allusion is that it causes people to lose the original meaning behind the metaphor. Crude uses of allusion are when the host and guest are reversed, so to speak, and the reader becomes lost in the complexity of historical fact and allusion and ends up forgetting the object the writer set out to compare. When the ancients wrote long poems, they only used a handful of allusions (Du Fu's "Journey North" and Bai Juyi's "Temple of Truth Realized" do not make use of a single allusion). Men today cannot write long poems without using allusion. I once read a poem with eighty-four couplets which made over one hundred allusions, none of which was used skillfully.

* * *

This reflects not only an indolence beyond salvation, but a self-deception and a deception of others.

Men of letters devote much time and energy to all these various sorts of allusions. Once you are stung with their poison, there is no recovery. This is why I have advocated not employing allusions.

VII. Do Not Use Parallelism

Parallelism is a characteristic of human language. For this reason we find occasional parallel lines even in such ancient texts as those by Confucius and Laozi. For example:

> The way that can be spoken is not the constant way;
> The name that can be named is not the constant name.
> The nameless was the beginning of heaven and earth;
> The named was the mother of the myriad creatures.
> Let there forever be non-being so we may see their subtlety;
> Let there forever be being so we may see their outcome.[3]

Or the following parallel lines from the *Analects*:

> In food [the gentleman] does not seek satiety,
> Nor in his dwelling does he seek ease and comfort.

> Poverty without sycophancy
> Wealth without arrogance.

> You love his goats,
> I love his rites.[4]

Yet these are all not far from natural language, without a trace of being forced or artificially constructed, especially since rules had yet to be established as to the length of lines, tones, or diction. As for the decadent literature of subsequent generations, it was without substance and showy to such a degree that it led to the advent of parallel prose, regulated verse, and extended regulated verse. There are some excellent works written in parallel prose and in regulated verse, but these are rare in the final analysis.

3. From the *Dao de jing* attributed to Laozi, ch. 45.   4. These passages can be found in the *Analects*, 1.14, 1.15, and 3.17.

Why is this? Is it not because they constrict man's freedom to such an extent? (Not a single excellent work of long regulated verse can be mentioned.) Now, in our discussion of literary reform, we must "first stand fast on what is of greater importance"[5] and not waste our useful talents on minute detail and subtle technique. This is why I have proposed the elimination of parallel prose and regulated verse. Even if they cannot be eliminated, we should nonetheless look upon them as mere literary tricks, not something to be undertaken with any urgency.

Today people still look down upon vernacular fiction as the lesser tradition and are not aware that Shi Nai'an, Cao Xueqin, and Wu Woyao are the truly canonical and that parallel prose and regulated verse are the lesser tradition. I know that when you hear this there will certainly be some among you who simply cannot bear it.

VIII. Do Not Avoid Vulgar Diction

Since my literary canon is composed only of Shi Nai'an, Cao Xueqin, and Wu Woyao, I have the theory of "do not avoid vulgar diction." (Refer to Section II above.) And yet for a long time the spoken and literary languages in our country have been turning their backs on each other. Ever since the importation of Buddhist scriptures, translators have been aware of the fact that the classical language is deficient in conveying meaning, so they have used in their translations an ordinary and simple language, whose style verged on the vernacular. Later, Buddhist lectures and catechisms mostly made use of the vernacular, which gave rise to the dialogue form. When the Song neo-Confucians used the vernacular in the scholarly lectures of their dialogues, this form became the standard in scholarship. (Ming scholars later followed this style.) By this time, the vernacular had already long since entered rhymed prose, as can be seen in the vernacular poetry and lyrics of the Tang and Song. By the end of the Yuan dynasty, northern China had already been under the occupation of a foreign race for more than three hundred years (Liao, Jin, and Yuan dynasties). In these three hundred years, China developed an incipient popular literature, out of which emerged the novels *The Water Margin, The Journey to the West,* and *The Romance of the Three Kingdoms* and innumerable dramas (Guan Hanqing et al. each produced more than ten different dramas; no period in the history of Chinese literature exceeded this in terms of wealth of productivity). Looking back from our contemporary perspective, the Yuan should without doubt be seen as the most vigorous period of Chinese literature, producing the greatest number of immortal works. At that time, Chinese literature came closest to a union of spoken and written languages, and the vernacular itself had nearly become a literary language. If this tendency had not been arrested, then a "living literature" might have appeared in China and the great endeavor of Dante and Luther might have developed in old Cathay. (In the Middle Ages in Europe, each country had its own vulgar spoken language and Latin was the literary language. All written works used Latin, just as the classical language was used in China. Later, in Italy appeared Dante and other literary giants who first used their own vulgar language to write. Other countries followed suit, and national languages began to replace Latin. When Luther created Protestantism, he began by translating the *Old Testament* and the *New Testament* into German, which ushered in German literature. England, France, and other countries followed this pattern. Today the most widely circulated English Bible is a translation dating from 1611, only 300 years

5. From the work of Confucius's disciple, *Mencius*, 6A.15.

ago. Hence, all contemporary literature in the various European nations developed from the vulgar languages of that time. The rise of literary giants began with a "living literature" replacing a dead literature in Latin. When there is a living literature, there will be a national language based on the unity of the spoken and written languages.) Unexpectedly, this tendency was suddenly arrested during the Ming. The government had already been using the "eight-legged essay" to select its civil servants, and scholars like Li Mengyang [1472–1529] and the followers of the "former seven masters" raised "archaism" as the most lofty of literary goals. So the once-in-a-millennium opportunity to effect the unity of the spoken and written languages died a premature death, midway in the process. Yet, from today's perspective of historical evolution, we can say with complete certainty that vernacular literature is really the canonical and will be a useful tool for developing future literature. (My "certainty" is only my opinion, one shared by few of my contemporaries.) For this reason, I propose the appropriate use of vulgar diction in the writing of prose and poetry. It is preferable to use the living words of the twentieth century than the dead words of three millennia past (like "Most glorious National Assembly, the end of penumbrous times is nigh"); it is preferable to use the language of *The Water Margin* and *The Journey to the West,* which is known in every household, than the language of the Qin, Han, and Six Dynasties, which is limited and not universally understood.

CONCLUSION

The eight points related above are the result of my recent investigation and contemplation of this important question. Since I am studying in a far-off foreign land, I have little leisure for reading, so I must ask my learned elders back home for their scrutiny and circumspection, for there may well be places in need of severe rectification. These eight points are all fundamental to literature and merit investigation. So I have drafted this essay and hope that it elicits some response from those who care about this issue, both here and in China. I have called them "modest proposals" to underscore the sense of their incompleteness and to respectfully seek the redaction of my compatriots.

▨ END OF CROSSCURRENTS: THE ART OF THE MANIFESTO ▨

—◆—

Joseph Conrad
1857–1924

One of the greatest English novelists, Joseph Conrad didn't seriously begin to learn English until the age of twenty-one. He was already embarked on decades of world travel that would shape his fiction when he finally decided, in 1894, to become a full-time writer. By then, he had long lived in exile from his native Poland—a country no longer even present on the map at that time, carved up between Russia and the Austro-Hungarian empire. Born Josef Teodor Konrad Korzeniowski, he was the son of a noble-born Polish poet and patriot, Apollo, whose ardent nationalism led to his arrest by the Russian government in 1861. The four-year-old Josef and his mother Eva followed Apollo into exile in a bleak village in northern Russia. Ill with tuberculosis, Eva died there in 1865; Apollo also became ill, and was allowed to return to Cracow, where he died in 1869 when Josef was twelve. Josef was raised thereafter by his cultured, cosmopolitan uncle Tadeusz Bobrowski, but he was bored and restless in school in Cracow, and so his uncle eventually sent him to Switzerland with a private tutor. Before long, the tutor had resigned, and instead of returning to Cracow, the sixteen-year-old Josef slipped away to Marseilles and joined the French merchant navy.

He spent the following twenty years as a sailor and eventually as a merchant ship captain, working first for the French merchant marine and then for British companies. His ships took him around the world, to the eastern Mediterranean, Indonesia, China, Thailand, the Philippines, South America, the West Indies, and Africa, giving him the opportunity to see first-hand the unsettling effects of the rising tide of European imperial expansion. At one point he supplemented his observations with active involvement in political conflict: In 1878 he and several friends bought a ship to smuggle guns into Spain on behalf of a claimant to the throne. This effort collapsed, and Conrad was wounded not long after, either in a duel (as he claimed) or else (as his uncle believed) in a suicide attempt. Heavily in debt, he left France and switched into the British merchant marine, where he served for the next sixteen years.

Based in London in 1889 for several months between ships, he began to write *Almayer's Folly,* a novel closely based on some of his South Seas experiences, but in 1890 he interrupted this project to fulfill a childhood dream of sailing up the Congo River. Using an aunt's influence, he went to Brussels and gained an appointment to pilot an aging steamboat upriver—the basis for his most famous novella, *Heart of Darkness* (serialized in 1899, published in book form in 1902). The Congo at the time was controlled by a private corporation set up by King Leopold II of Belgium for personal profit. The king's company was being promoted as a perfect marriage of the noble work of civilization and the profits of free enterprise, a perspective advanced by the explorer-journalist Henry Morton Stanley in the Resonance below (page 117). There, Stanley appeals to the businessmen of Manchester to support Leopold's unfettered control over the Congo, stressing both the higher goals of civilization and also the direct profits to be made by selling wedding dresses and burial clothes to the native inhabitants.

A diary Conrad kept during his journey (excerpted in the Resonance below, page 115) shows his experience of a much grimmer reality. His work included transporting a sick agent of the Belgian Company downriver; his charge, Georges Klein, died en route. Conrad's encounter with Klein ("Little," in German) provided the germ of the plot of his novella, whose protagonist Marlow journeys upriver to encounter the mysterious, threatening, eloquent company agent Mister Kurtz. Conrad returned to England after four months in the Congo, beset with fever and with a deepening tragic sense of the imperial enterprise and of life overall. "Before the Congo," he later wrote, "I was a mere animal." He became active in the efforts led by the Irish diplomat Roger Casement to expose the cruelty of imperial practices in the Congo, and in his fiction he explored the fatal slippage of idealism into corruption, in language and practice alike.

In 1894 Conrad's life changed in decisive ways. His uncle Bobrowski died, and Conrad decided to settle permanently in England; he Anglicized his name as "Joseph Conrad," and later married an Englishwoman, Jessie George. He also took a temporary break, which proved to be permanent, from sailing, and completed *Almayer's Folly,* which soon found a publisher. Determined to make a living as a writer, he began a second novel while the first was still in press, and was soon able to establish friendships with some of England's leading writers, including such figures as Bernard Shaw and H. G. Wells. His English friends regarded him with some bemusement as a master of English prose and yet an exotic foreigner; Wells described Conrad driving a carriage rapidly along a country lane, urging his horses on with imperious commands in Polish. General readers were slow to recognize the excellence of his fiction, and such major early works as *Lord Jim, Nostromo,* and *The Secret Agent* sold

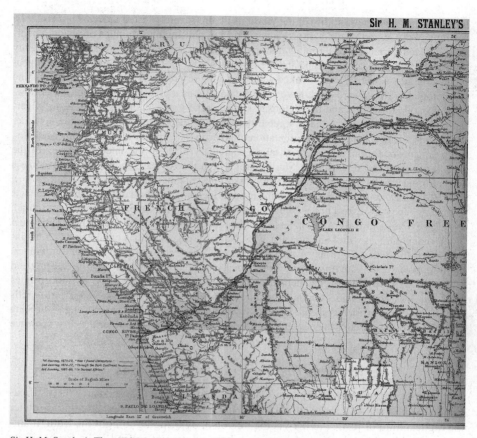

Sir H. M. Stanley's Three African Journeys, c. 1895; detail. When Conrad's Marlow dreamed of voyaging "into the yellow" of the empty spaces on African maps (pp. 64 and 66), he would have been looking at a map like this one. The Congo Free State is shown in yellow on the map, with red, green and blue lines tracing Stanley's travels in the 1870s and 1880s across east and central Africa and up and down the Congo River, as he explored the borders of King Leopold's African domain.

poorly. As late as 1910 Conrad still considered returning to sea. Gradually, though, he reached a wider public with his tales of the sea and of imperial and political intrigue, becoming a best-selling writer with his novels *Chance* (1910) and *Victory* (1915). World War I only deepened his pessimism about modern life, but he continued to pursue his artistic vocation with undiminished intensity.

In his preface to his early novella *The Nigger of the "Narcissus"* (1897), Conrad issued a personal manifesto for the critical responsibility of the artist, who must seek the truth of life by descending "within himself, and in that lonely region of stress and strife, if he be deserving and fortunate, he finds the terms of his appeal . . . to snatch in a moment of courage, from the remorseless rush of time, a passing phase of life." Conrad insists that this lonely descent into self is not a matter of aesthetic withdrawal but instead should be the basis for "the solidarity . . . which binds men to each other and all mankind to the visible world." That solidarity, however, and even the visibility of the world itself, are severely tested in *Heart of Darkness*. Like many of Conrad's works, it presents a world of shifting uncertainties of vision, understanding, and moral choice. From its multiple framing of stories inside stories to its uncanny portrayal of the African landscape and the Congolese and the displaced Europeans who people it, Conrad's narrative has provoked widely varying responses. Many critics, including the postcolonial critic Edward Said, have seen the novella as a pivotal exposure of the hollowness of imperial rhetoric and the viciousness of imperial practice; others, such as the Nigerian novelist Chinua Achebe, have argued that Conrad's heartfelt imperial critique nonetheless coexists with a stereotyped presentation of African racial primitivism. For other readers, the political dimensions of the story take a secondary place to the interior journey of the story's principal narrator, Charlie Marlow, for whom the African landscape may become a kind of projection of his own hallucinatory loss of psychic moorings.

Heart of Darkness has been one of the most influential narratives of the twentieth century. Chinua Achebe's own great novel *Things Fall Apart* (page 871) is in part a response to Conrad, as Achebe gives a directly African perspective on the European imperial presence. The Nobel Prize–winning travel writer and novelist V. S. Naipaul (page 519) has often expressed his indebtedness to Conrad's writing. A notable reuse of Conrad's novella can be found in Francis Ford Coppola's 1979 film *Apocalypse Now,* which cast Marlon Brando in the role of Kurtz and set the story in the midst of the Vietnam War. The novella's haunting blend of stark realities and multiplying uncertainties continues to unsettle and captivate readers today. As Marlow tells his tale to a group of friends aboard a pleasure yacht in the Thames River, his Congo—or King Leopold's Congo—oscillates between an image of all that is uncivilized, or the secret essence of civilization itself.

Preface to *The Nigger of the "Narcissus"*[1]

A work that aspires, however humbly, to the condition of art should carry its justification in every line. And art itself may be defined as a single-minded attempt to render the highest kind of justice to the visible universe, by bringing to light the truth, manifold and one, underlying its every aspect. It is an attempt to find in its forms, in its colours, in its light, in its shadows, in the aspects of matter, and in the facts of life what of each is fundamental, what is enduring and essential—their one illuminating and convincing quality—the very truth of their existence. The artist, then, like the thinker or the scientist, seeks the truth and makes his appeal. Impressed by the aspect of the world the thinker plunges into ideas, the scientist into facts—whence, presently, emerging they make their appeal to those qualities of our being that fit us best for the hazardous enterprise of living. They speak authoritatively to our common sense, to our intelligence, to our desire of peace, or to our desire of unrest; not seldom to our prejudices, sometimes to our fears, often to our egoism—but always to our credulity. And their words are heard with reverence, for their concern is with weighty matters: with the cultivation of our minds and the proper care of our bodies, with the attainment of our ambitions, with the perfection of the means and the glorification of our precious aims.

It is otherwise with the artist.

Confronted by the same enigmatical spectacle the artist descends within himself, and in that lonely region of stress and strife, if he be deserving and fortunate,

---

1. Conrad's novella *The Nigger of the "Narcissus"* deals with the tragic death of a black seaman aboard a merchant ship named the *Narcissus;* Conrad had served as first mate on a ship of that name in the Indian Ocean in 1883. He published the novella in *The New Review* in 1897, then added this preface when it came out in book form in 1898.

he finds the terms of his appeal. His appeal is made to our less obvious capacities: to that part of our nature which, because of the warlike conditions of existence, is necessarily kept out of sight within the more resisting and hard qualities—like the vulnerable body within a steel armour. His appeal is less loud, more profound, less distinct, more stirring—and sooner forgotten. Yet its effect endures for ever. The changing wisdom of successive generations discards ideas, questions facts, demolishes theories. But the artist appeals to that part of our being which is not dependent on wisdom; to that in us which is a gift and not an acquisition—and, therefore, more permanently enduring. He speaks to our capacity for delight and wonder, to the sense of mystery surrounding our lives; to our sense of pity, and beauty, and pain; to the latent feeling of fellowship with all creation—and to the subtle but invincible conviction of solidarity that knits together the loneliness of innumerable hearts, to the solidarity in dreams, in joy, in sorrow, in aspirations, in illusions, in hope, in fear, which binds men to each other, which binds together all humanity—the dead to the living and the living to the unborn.

It is only some such train of thought, or rather of feeling, that can in a measure explain the aim of the attempt, made in the tale which follows, to present an unrestful episode in the obscure lives of a few individuals out of all the disregarded multitude of the bewildered, the simple, and the voiceless. For, if any part of truth dwells in the belief confessed above, it becomes evident that there is not a place of splendour or a dark corner of the earth that does not deserve, if only a passing glance of wonder and pity. The motive, then, may be held to justify the matter of the work; but this preface, which is simply an avowal of endeavour, cannot end here—for the avowal is not yet complete.

Fiction—if it at all aspires to be art—appeals to temperament. And in truth it must be, like painting, like music, like all art, the appeal of one temperament to all the other innumerable temperaments whose subtle and resistless power endows passing events with their true meaning, and creates the moral, the emotional atmosphere of the place and time. Such an appeal to be effective must be an impression conveyed through the senses; and, in fact, it cannot be made in any other way, because temperament, whether individual or collective, is not amenable to persuasion. All art, therefore, appeals primarily to the senses, and the artistic aim when expressing itself in written words must also make its appeal through the senses, if its high desire is to reach the secret spring of responsive emotions. It must strenuously aspire to the plasticity of sculpture, to the colour of painting, and to the magic suggestiveness of music—which is the art of arts. And it is only through complete, unswerving devotion to the perfect blending of form and substance; it is only through an unremitting never-discouraged care for the shape and ring of sentences that an approach can be made to plasticity, to colour, and that the light of magic suggestiveness may be brought to play for an evanescent instant over the commonplace surface of words: of the old, old words, worn thin, defaced by ages of careless usage.

The sincere endeavour to accomplish that creative task, to go as far on that road as his strength will carry him, to go undeterred by faltering, weariness, or reproach, is the only valid justification for the worker in prose. And if his conscience is clear, his answer to those who, in the fullness of a wisdom which looks for immediate profit, demand specifically to be edified, consoled, amused; who demand to be promptly improved, or encouraged, or frightened, or shocked, or charmed, must run thus: My task which I am trying to achieve is, by the power of the written word to make you hear, to make you feel—it is, before all, to make you see. That—and no more, and it is every-thing. If I succeed, you shall find there according to your deserts: encouragement, consolation, fear, charm—all you demand—and, perhaps, also that glimpse of truth for which you have forgotten to ask.

To snatch in a moment of courage, from the remorseless rush of time, a passing phase of life, is only the beginning of the task. The task approached in tenderness and faith is to hold up unquestioningly, without choice and without fear, the rescued frag-ment before all eyes in the light of a sincere mood. It is to show its vibration, its colour, its form; and through its movement, its form, and its colour, reveal the sub-stance of its truth—disclose its inspiring secret: the stress and passion within the core of each convincing moment. In a single-minded attempt of that kind, if one be deserv-ing and fortunate, one may perchance attain to such clearness of sincerity that at last the presented vision of regret or pity, of terror or mirth, shall awaken in the hearts of the beholders that feeling of unavoidable solidarity; of the solidarity in mysterious origin, in toil, in joy, in hope, in uncertain fate, which binds men to each other and all mankind to the visible world.

It is evident that he who, rightly or wrongly, holds by the convictions expressed above cannot be faithful to any one of the temporary formulas of his craft. The endur-ing part of them—the truth which each only imperfectly veils—should abide with him as the most precious of his possessions, but they all: Realism, Romanticism, Natural-ism, even the unofficial sentimentalism (which, like the poor, is exceedingly difficult to get rid of), all these gods must, after a short period of fellowship, abandon him—even on the very threshold of the temple—to the stammerings of his conscience and to the outspoken consciousness of the difficulties of his work. In that uneasy solitude the supreme cry of Art for Art itself, loses the exciting ring of its apparent immorality. It sounds far off. It has ceased to be a cry, and is heard only as a whisper, often in-comprehensible, but at times and faintly encouraging.

Sometimes, stretched at ease in the shade of a roadside tree, we watch the mo-tions of a labourer in a distant field, and after a time, begin to wonder languidly as to what the fellow may be at. We watch the movements of his body, the waving of his arms, we see him bend down, stand up, hesitate, begin again. It may add to the charm of an idle hour to be told the purpose of his exertions. If we know he is trying to lift a stone, to dig a ditch, to uproot a stump, we look with a more real interest at his efforts; we are disposed to condone the jar of his agitation upon the restfulness of the land-scape; and even, if in a brotherly frame of mind, we may bring ourselves to forgive his failure. We understood his object, and, after all, the fellow has tried, and perhaps he had not the strength—and perhaps he had not the knowledge. We forgive, go on our way—and forget.

And so it is with the workman of art. Art is long and life is short, and success is very far off. And thus, doubtful of strength to travel so far, we talk a little about the aim—the aim of art, which, like life itself, is inspiring, difficult—obscured by mists. It is not in the clear logic of a triumphant conclusion; it is not in the unveiling of one of those heartless secrets which are called the Laws of Nature. It is not less great, but only more difficult.

To arrest, for the space of a breath, the hands busy about the work of the earth, and compel men entranced by the sight of distant goals to glance for a moment at the surrounding vision of form and colour, of sunshine and shadows; to make them pause for a look, for a sigh, for a smile—such is the aim, difficult and evanescent, and reserved only for a very few to achieve. But sometimes, by the deserving and the fortunate, even that task is accomplished. And when it is accomplished—behold!—all the truth of life is there: a moment of vision, a sigh, a smile—and the return to an eternal rest.

Heart of Darkness

1

The *Nellie,* a cruising yawl,[1] swung to her anchor without a flutter of the sails, and was at rest. The flood had made, the wind was nearly calm, and being bound down the river, the only thing for it was to come to and wait for the turn of the tide.

The sea-reach of the Thames stretched before us like the beginning of an interminable waterway. In the offing the sea and the sky were welded together without a joint, and in the luminous space the tanned sails of the barges drifting up with the tide seemed to stand still in red clusters of canvas sharply peaked, with gleams of varnished sprits. A haze rested on the low shores that ran out to sea in vanishing flatness. The air was dark above Gravesend, and farther back still seemed condensed into a mournful gloom, brooding motionless over the biggest, and the greatest, town on earth.[2]

The Director of Companies was our captain and our host. We four affectionately watched his back as he stood in the bows looking to seaward. On the whole river there was nothing that looked half so nautical. He resembled a pilot, which to a seaman is trustworthiness personified. It was difficult to realise his work was not out there in the luminous estuary, but behind him, within the brooding gloom.

Between us there was, as I have already said somewhere, the bond of the sea. Besides holding our hearts together through long periods of separation, it had the effect of making us tolerant of each other's yarns—and even convictions. The Lawyer—the best of old fellows—had, because of his many years and many virtues, the only cushion on deck, and was lying on the only rug. The Accountant had brought out already a box of dominoes, and was toying architecturally with the bones. Marlow sat cross-legged right aft, leaning against the mizzen-mast.[3] He had sunken cheeks, a yellow complexion, a straight back, an ascetic aspect, and, with his arms dropped, the palms of hands outwards, resembled an idol. The Director, satisfied the anchor had good hold, made his way aft and sat down amongst us. We exchanged a few words lazily. Afterwards there was silence on board the yacht. For some reason or other we did not begin that game of dominoes. We felt meditative, and fit for nothing but placid staring. The day was ending in a serenity of still and exquisite brilliance. The water shone pacifically; the sky, without a speck, was a benign immensity of unstained light; the very mist on the Essex marshes was like a gauzy and radiant fabric, hung from the wooded rises inland, and draping the low shores in diaphanous folds. Only the gloom to the west, brooding over the upper reaches, became more sombre every minute, as if angered by the approach of the sun.

And at last, in its curved and imperceptible fall, the sun sank low, and from glowing white changed to a dull red without rays and without heat, as if about to go out suddenly, stricken to death by the touch of that gloom brooding over a crowd of men.

Forthwith a change came over the waters, and the serenity became less brilliant but more profound. The old river in its broad reach rested unruffled at the decline of

---

1. A two-masted ship.
2. London. Gravesend is the last major town on the

Thames estuary, from which the river joins the North Sea.
3. A secondary mast at the stern of the ship.

day, after ages of good service done to the race that peopled its banks, spread out in the tranquil dignity of a waterway leading to the uttermost ends of the earth. We looked at the venerable stream not in the vivid flush of a short day that comes and departs for ever, but in the august light of abiding memories. And indeed nothing is easier for a man who has, as the phrase goes, "followed the sea" with reverence and affection, than to evoke the great spirit of the past upon the lower reaches of the Thames. The tidal current runs to and fro in its unceasing service, crowded with memories of men and ships it has borne to the rest of home or to the battles of the sea. It had known and served all the men of whom the nation is proud, from Sir Francis Drake to Sir John Franklin, knights all, titled and untitled—the great knights-errant of the sea.[4] It had borne all the ships whose names are like jewels flashing in the night of time, from the *Golden Hind* returning with her round flanks full of treasure, to be visited by the Queen's Highness and thus pass out of the gigantic tale, to the *Erebus* and *Terror,* bound on other conquests—and that never returned. It had known the ships and the men. They had sailed from Deptford, from Greenwich, from Erith—the adventurers and the settlers; kings' ships and the ships of men on 'Change; captains, admirals, the dark "interlopers" of the Eastern trade, and the commissioned "generals" of East India fleets.[5] Hunters for gold or pursuers of fame, they all had gone out on that stream, bearing the sword, and often the torch, messengers of the might within the land, bearers of a spark from the sacred fire. What greatness had not floated on the ebb of that river into the mystery of an unknown earth! . . . The dreams of men, the seed of commonwealths, the germs of empires.

The sun set; the dusk fell on the stream, and lights began to appear along the shore. The Chapman lighthouse, a three-legged thing erect on a mudflat, shone strongly. Lights of ships moved in the fairway—a great stir of lights going up and going down. And farther west on the upper reaches the place of the monstrous town was still marked ominously on the sky, a brooding gloom in sunshine, a lurid glare under the stars.

"And this also," said Marlow suddenly, "has been one of the dark places of the earth."

He was the only man of us who still "followed the sea." The worst that could be said of him was that he did not represent his class. He was a seaman, but he was a wanderer too, while most seamen lead, if one may so express it, a sedentary life. Their minds are of the stay-at-home order, and their home is always with them—the ship; and so is their country—the sea. One ship is very much like another, and the sea is always the same. In the immutability of their surroundings the foreign shores, the foreign faces, the changing immensity of life, glide past, veiled not by a sense of mystery but by a slightly disdainful ignorance; for there is nothing mysterious to a seaman unless it be the sea itself, which is the mistress of his existence and as inscrutable as Destiny. For the rest, after his hours of work, a casual stroll or a casual spree on shore suffices to unfold for him the secret of a whole continent, and generally he finds the secret not worth knowing. The yarns of seamen have a direct simplicity, the whole meaning of which lies within the shell of a cracked nut. But Marlow was not typical (if his propensity to spin yarns be excepted), and to him the meaning of an episode

4. Sir Francis Drake (1540–1596) was captain of the *Golden Hind* in the service of Queen Elizabeth I; his reputation came from the successful raids he mounted against Spanish ships returning laden with gold from the New World (South America). In 1845 Sir John Franklin led an expedition in the *Erebus* and *Terror* in search of the Northwest Passage (to the Pacific); all perished.
5. Deptford, Greenwich, and Erith lie on the Thames between London and Gravesend; "men on 'Change" are brokers on the Stock Exchange; the East India Company, a commercial and trading concern, became *de facto* ruler of large tracts of India in the 18th and 19th centuries.

was not inside like a kernel but outside, enveloping the tale which brought it out only as a glow brings out a haze, in the likeness of one of these misty halos that sometimes are made visible by the spectral illumination of moonshine.

His remark did not seem at all surprising. It was just like Marlow. It was accepted in silence. No one took the trouble to grunt even; and presently he said, very slow,—

"I was thinking of very old times, when the Romans first came here, nineteen hundred years ago[6]—the other day. . . . Light came out of this river since—you say Knights? Yes; but it is like a running blaze on a plain, like a flash of lightning in the clouds. We live in the flicker—may it last as long as the old earth keeps rolling! But darkness was here yesterday. Imagine the feelings of a commander of a fine—what d'ye call 'em?—trireme in the Mediterranean, ordered suddenly to the north; run over-land across the Gauls in a hurry;[7] put in charge of one of these craft the legionaries,—a wonderful lot of handy men they must have been too—used to build, apparently by the hundred, in a month or two, if we may believe what we read. Imagine him here—the very end of the world, a sea the colour of lead, a sky the colour of smoke, a kind of ship about as rigid as a concertina—and going up this river with stores, or orders, or what you like. Sandbanks, marshes, forests, savages,—precious little to eat fit for a civilised man, nothing but Thames water to drink. No Falernian wine here, no going ashore. Here and there a military camp lost in a wilderness, like a needle in a bundle of hay—cold, fog, tempests, disease, exile, and death,—death skulking in the air, in the water, in the bush. They must have been dying like flies here. Oh yes—he did it. Did it very well, too, no doubt, and without thinking much about it either, except afterwards to brag of what he had gone through in his time, perhaps. They were men enough to face the darkness. And perhaps he was cheered by keeping his eye on a chance of pro-motion to the fleet at Ravenna by-and-by, if he had good friends in Rome and survived the awful climate. Or think of a decent young citizen in a toga—perhaps too much dice, you know—coming out here in the train of some prefect, or tax-gatherer, or trader even, to mend his fortunes. Land in a swamp, march through the woods, and in some inland post feel the savagery, the utter savagery, had closed round him,—all that mysterious life of the wilderness that stirs in the forest, in the jungles, in the hearts of wild men. There's no initiation either into such mysteries. He has to live in the midst of the incomprehensible, which is also detestable. And it has a fascination, too, that goes to work upon him. The fascination of the abomination—you know. Imagine the growing regrets, the longing to escape, the powerless disgust, the surrender, the hate."

He paused.

"Mind," he began again, lifting one arm from the elbow, the palm of the hand outwards, so that, with his legs folded before him, he had the pose of a Buddha preaching in European clothes and without a lotus-flower—"Mind, none of us would feel exactly like this. What saves us is efficiency—the devotion to efficiency. But these chaps were not much account, really. They were no colonists; their administra-tion was merely a squeeze, and nothing more, I suspect. They were conquerors, and for that you want only brute force—nothing to boast of, when you have it, since your strength is just an accident arising from the weakness of others. They grabbed what they could get for the sake of what was to be got. It was just robbery with violence,

---

6. A Roman force under Julius Caesar landed in Britain in 55 B.C.E., but it was not until 43 C.E. that the Emperor Claudius decided to conquer the island.

7. A trireme is an ancient warship, propelled by oars-men; the Gauls were the pre-Roman tribes who occupied present-day France; they were subdued by Julius Caesar between 58–50 B.C.E.

aggravated murder on a great scale, and men going at it blind—as is very proper for those who tackle a darkness. The conquest of the earth, which mostly means the taking it away from those who have a different complexion or slightly flatter noses than ourselves, is not a pretty thing when you look into it too much. What redeems it is the idea only. An idea at the back of it; not a sentimental pretence but an idea; and an unselfish belief in the idea—something you can set up, and bow down before, and offer a sacrifice to. . . ."

He broke off. Flames glided in the river, small green flames, red flames, white flames, pursuing, overtaking, joining, crossing each other—then separating slowly or hastily. The traffic of the great city went on in the deepening night upon the sleepless river. We looked on, waiting patiently—there was nothing else to do till the end of the flood; but it was only after a long silence, when he said, in a hesitating voice, "I suppose you fellows remember I did once turn fresh-water sailor for a bit," that we knew we were fated, before the ebb began to run, to hear about one of Marlow's inconclusive experiences.

"I don't want to bother you much with what happened to me personally," he began, showing in this remark the weakness of many tellers of tales who seem so often unaware of what their audience would best like to hear; "yet to understand the effect of it on me you ought to know how I got out there, what I saw, how I went up that river to the place where I first met the poor chap. It was the farthest point of navigation and the culminating point of my experience. It seemed somehow to throw a kind of light on everything about me—and into my thoughts. It was sombre enough too— and pitiful—not extraordinary in any way—not very clear either. No, not very clear. And yet it seemed to throw a kind of light.

"I had then, as you remember, just returned to London after a lot of Indian Ocean, Pacific, China Seas—a regular dose of the East—six years or so, and I was loafing about, hindering you fellows in your work and invading your homes, just as though I had got a heavenly mission to civilise you. It was very fine for a time, but after a bit I did get tired of resting. Then I began to look for a ship—I should think the hardest work on earth. But the ships wouldn't even look at me. And I got tired of that game too.

"Now when I was a little chap I had a passion for maps. I would look for hours at South America, or Africa, or Australia, and lose myself in all the glories of exploration. At that time there were many blank spaces on the earth, and when I saw one that looked particularly inviting on a map (but they all look that) I would put my finger on it and say, When I grow up I will go there. The North Pole was one of these places, I remember. Well, I haven't been there yet, and shall not try now. The glamour's off. Other places were scattered about the Equator, and in every sort of latitude all over the two hemispheres. I have been in some of them, and . . . well, we won't talk about that. But there was one yet—the biggest, the most blank, so to speak—that I had a hankering after.

"True, by this time it was not a blank space any more. It had got filled since my boyhood with rivers and lakes and names. It had ceased to be a blank space of delightful mystery—a white patch for a boy to dream gloriously over. It had become a place of darkness. But there was in it one river especially, a mighty big river, that you could see on the map, resembling an immense snake uncoiled, with its head in the sea, its body at rest curving afar over a vast country, and its tail lost in the depths of the land. And as I looked at the map of it in a shop-window, it fascinated me as a snake would a bird—a silly little bird. Then I remembered there was a big concern, a Company for trade on that river. Dash it all! I thought to myself, they can't trade without using some kind of craft on that lot of fresh water—steamboats! Why shouldn't I try to get charge of one. I went on along Fleet Street, but could not shake off the idea. The snake had charmed me.

"You understand it was a Continental concern, that Trading Society; but I have a lot of relations living on the Continent, because it's cheap and not so nasty as it looks, they say.

"I am sorry to own I began to worry them. This was already a fresh departure for me. I was not used to get things that way, you know. I always went my own road and on my own legs where I had a mind to go. I wouldn't have believed it of myself; but, then—you see—I felt somehow I must get there by hook or by crook. So I worried them. The men said 'My dear fellow,' and did nothing. Then—would you believe it?—I tried the women. I, Charlie Marlow, set the women to work—to get a job. Heavens! Well, you see, the notion drove me. I had an aunt, a dear enthusiastic soul. She wrote: 'It will be delightful. I am ready to do anything, anything for you. It is a glorious idea. I know the wife of a very high personage in the Administration, and also a man who has lots of influence with,' &c., &c. She was determined to make no end of fuss to get me appointed skipper of a river steamboat, if such was my fancy.

"I got my appointment—of course; and I got it very quick. It appears the Company had received news that one of their captains had been killed in a scuffle with the natives. This was my chance, and it made me the more anxious to go. It was only months and months afterwards, when I made the attempt to recover what was left of the body, that I heard the original quarrel arose from a misunderstanding about some hens. Yes, two black hens. Fresleven—that was the fellow's name, a Dane—thought himself wronged somehow in the bargain, so he went ashore and started to hammer the chief of the village with a stick. Oh, it didn't surprise me in the least to hear this, and at the same time to be told that Fresleven was the gentlest, quietest creature that ever walked on two legs. No doubt he was; but he had been a couple of years already out there engaged in the noble cause, you know, and he probably felt the need at last of asserting his self-respect in some way. Therefore he whacked the old nigger mercilessly, while a big crowd of his people watched him, thunderstruck, till some man,—I was told the chief's son,—in desperation at hearing the old chap yell, made a tentative jab with a spear at the white man—and of course it went quite easy between the shoulder-blades. Then the whole population cleared into the forest, expecting all kinds of calamities to happen, while, on the other hand, the steamer Fresleven commanded left also in a bad panic, in charge of the engineer, I believe. Afterwards nobody seemed to trouble much about Fresleven's remains, till I got out and stepped into his shoes. I couldn't let it rest, though; but when an opportunity offered at last to meet my predecessor, the grass growing through his ribs was tall enough to hide his bones. They were all there. The supernatural being had not been touched after he fell. And the village was deserted, the huts gaped black, rotting, all askew within the fallen enclosures. A calamity had come to it, sure enough. The people had vanished. Mad terror had scattered them, men, women, and children, through the bush, and they had never returned. What became of the hens I don't know either. I should think the cause of progress got them, anyhow. However, through this glorious affair I got my appointment, before I had fairly begun to hope for it.

"I flew around like mad to get ready, and before forty-eight hours I was crossing the Channel to show myself to my employers, and sign the contract. In a very few hours I arrived in a city that always makes me think of a whited sepulchre.[8] Prejudice no doubt. I had no difficulty in finding the Company's offices. It was the biggest thing in the town, and everybody I met was full of it. They were going to run an over-sea empire, and make no end of coin by trade.

"A narrow and deserted street in deep shadow, high houses, innumerable windows with venetian blinds, a dead silence, grass sprouting between the stones, imposing carriage archways right and left, immense double doors standing ponderously ajar. I slipped through one of these cracks, went up a swept and ungarnished staircase, as arid as a desert, and opened the first door I came to. Two women, one fat and the other slim, sat on straw-bottomed chairs, knitting black wool. The slim one got up and walked straight at me—still knitting with downcast eyes—and only just as I began to think of getting out of her way, as you would for a somnambulist, stood still, and looked up. Her dress was as plain as an umbrella-cover, and she turned round without a word and preceded me into a waiting-room. I gave my name, and looked about. Deal table in the middle, plain chairs all round the walls, on one end a large shining map, marked with all the colours of a rainbow. There was a vast amount of red—good to see at any time, because one knows that some real work is done in there, a deuce of a lot of blue, a little green, smears of orange, and, on the East Coast, a purple patch, to show where the jolly pioneers of progress drink the jolly lager-beer.[9] However, I wasn't going into any of these. I was going into the yellow. Dead in the centre. And the river was there—fascinating—deadly—like a snake. Ough! A door opened, a white-haired secretarial head, but wearing a compassionate expression, appeared, and a skinny forefinger beckoned me into the sanctuary. Its light was dim, and a heavy writing-desk squatted in the middle. From behind that structure came out an impression of pale plumpness in a frock-coat. The great man himself. He was five feet six, I should judge, and had his grip on the handle-end of ever so many millions. He shook hands, I fancy, murmured vaguely, was satisfied with my French. *Bon voyage.*

"In about forty-five seconds I found myself again in the waiting-room with the compassionate secretary, who, full of desolation and sympathy, made me sign some document. I believe I undertook amongst other things not to disclose any trade secrets. Well, I am not going to.

"I began to feel slightly uneasy. You know I am not used to such ceremonies, and there was something ominous in the atmosphere. It was just as though I had been let into some conspiracy—I don't know—something not quite right; and I was glad to get out. In the outer room the two women knitted black wool feverishly. People were arriving, and the younger one was walking back and forth introducing them. The old one sat on her chair. Her flat cloth slippers were propped up on a foot-warmer, and a cat reposed on her lap. She wore a starched white affair on her head, had a wart on one cheek, and silver-rimmed spectacles hung on the tip of her nose. She glanced at me above the glasses. The swift and indifferent placidity of that look troubled me. Two youths with foolish and cheery countenances were being piloted over, and she threw at them the same quick glance of unconcerned wisdom. She seemed to know all about them and about me too. An eerie feeling came over me. She seemed uncanny and fateful. Often far away there I thought of these two, guarding the door of Dark-

8. Brussels was the headquarters of the Société Anonyme Belge pour le Commerce du Haut-Congo (Belgian Corporation for Trade in the Upper Congo), with which Conrad obtained his post through the influence of his aunt, Marguerite Poradowska.

9. British territories were traditionally marked in red on colonial maps; lager was originally a continental beer, not much drunk in England.

ness, knitting black wool as for a warm pall, one introducing, introducing continuously to the unknown, the other scrutinising the cheery and foolish faces with unconcerned old eyes. *Ave!* Old knitter of black wool. *Morituri te salutant.*[1] Not many of those she looked at ever saw her again—not half, by a long way.

"There was yet a visit to the doctor. 'A simple formality,' assured me the secretary, with an air of taking an immense part in all my sorrows. Accordingly a young chap wearing his hat over the left eyebrow, some clerk I suppose,—there must have been clerks in the business, though the house was as still as a house in a city of the dead,—came from somewhere upstairs, and led me forth. He was shabby and careless, with ink-stains on the sleeves of his jacket, and his cravat was large and billowy, under a chin shaped like the toe of an old boot. It was a little too early for the doctor, so I proposed a drink, and thereupon he developed a vein of joviality. As we sat over our vermouths he glorified the Company's business, and by-and-by I expressed casually my surprise at him not going out there. He became very cool and collected all at once. 'I am not such a fool as I look, quoth Plato to his disciples,' he said sententiously, emptied his glass with great resolution, and we rose.

"The old doctor felt my pulse, evidently thinking of something else the while. 'Good, good for there,' he mumbled, and then with a certain eagerness asked me whether I would let him measure my head. Rather surprised, I said Yes, when he produced a thing like calipers and got the dimensions back and front and every way, taking notes carefully. He was an unshaven little man in a threadbare coat like a gaberdine, with his feet in slippers, and I thought him a harmless fool. 'I always ask leave, in the interests of science, to measure the crania of those going out there,' he said. 'And when they come back too?' I asked. 'Oh, I never see them,' he remarked; 'and moreover, the changes take place inside, you know.' He smiled, as if at some quiet joke. 'So you are going out there. Famous. Interesting too.' He gave me a searching glance, and made another note. 'Ever any madness in your family?' he asked, in a matter-of-fact tone. I felt very annoyed. 'Is that question in the interests of science too?' 'It would be,' he said, without taking notice of my irritation, 'interesting for science to watch the mental changes of individuals, on the spot, but . . .' 'Are you an alienist?'[2] I interrupted. 'Every doctor should be—a little,' answered that original, imperturbably. 'I have a little theory which you Messieurs who go out there must help me to prove. This is my share in the advantages my country shall reap from the possession of such a magnificent dependency. The mere wealth I leave to others. Pardon my questions, but you are the first Englishman coming under my observation . . .' I hastened to assure him I was not in the least typical. 'If I were,' said I, 'I wouldn't be talking like this with you.' 'What you say is rather profound, and probably erroneous,' he said, with a laugh. 'Avoid irritation more than exposure to the sun. Adieu. How do you English say, eh? Good-bye. Ah! Good-bye. Adieu. In the tropics one must before everything keep calm.' . . . He lifted a warning forefinger. . . . '*Du calme, du calme. Adieu.*'

"One thing more remained to do—say good-bye to my excellent aunt. I found her triumphant. I had a cup of tea—the last decent cup of tea for many days—and in a room that most soothingly looked just as you would expect a lady's drawing-room to look, we had a long quiet chat by the fireside. In the course of these confidences it became quite plain to me I had been represented to the wife of the high

---

1. Hail! . . . Those who are about to die salute you!—traditional cry of Roman gladiators.   2. A psychologist.

dignitary, and goodness knows to how many more people besides, as an exceptional and gifted creature—a piece of good fortune for the Company—a man you don't get hold of every day. Good heavens! and I was going to take charge of a twopenny-half-penny river-steamboat with a penny whistle attached! It appeared, however, I was also one of the Workers, with a capital—you know. Something like an emissary of light, something like a lower sort of apostle. There had been a lot of such rot let loose in print and talk just about that time, and the excellent woman, living right in the rush of all that humbug, got carried off her feet. She talked about 'weaning those ignorant millions from their horrid ways,' till, upon my word, she made me quite uncomfortable. I ventured to hint that the Company was run for profit.

"'You forget, dear Charlie, that the labourer is worthy of his hire,' she said, brightly.[3] It's queer how out of touch with truth women are. They live in a world of their own, and there had never been anything like it, and never can be. It is too beautiful altogether, and if they were to set it up it would go to pieces before the first sunset. Some confounded fact we men have been living contentedly with ever since the day of creation would start up and knock the whole thing over.

"After this I got embraced, told to wear flannel, be sure to write often, and so on—and I left. In the street—I don't know why—a queer feeling came to me that I was an impostor. Odd thing that I, who used to clear out for any part of the world at twenty-four hours' notice, with less thought than most men give to the crossing of a street, had a moment—I won't say of hesitation, but of startled pause, before this commonplace affair. The best way I can explain it to you is by saying that, for a second or two, I felt as though, instead of going to the centre of a continent, I were about to set off for the centre of the earth.

"I left in a French steamer, and she called in every blamed port they have out there, for, as far as I could see, the sole purpose of landing soldiers and custom-house officers. I watched the coast. Watching a coast as it slips by the ship is like thinking about an enigma. There it is before you—smiling, frowning, inviting, grand, mean, insipid, or savage, and always mute with an air of whispering, Come and find out. This one was almost featureless, as if still in the making, with an aspect of monotonous grimness. The edge of a colossal jungle, so dark-green as to be almost black, fringed with white surf, ran straight, like a ruled line, far, far away along a blue sea whose glitter was blurred by a creeping mist. The sun was fierce, the land seemed to glisten and drip with steam. Here and there greyish-whitish specks showed up, clustered inside the white surf, with a flag flying above them perhaps—settlements some centuries old, and still no bigger than pin-heads on the untouched expanse of their background. We pounded along, stopped, landed soldiers; went on, landed custom-house clerks to levy toll in what looked like a Godforsaken wilderness, with a tin shed and a flag-pole lost in it; landed more soldiers—to take care of the custom-house clerks, presumably. Some, I heard, got drowned in the surf; but whether they did or not, nobody seemed particularly to care. They were just flung out there, and on we went. Every day the coast looked the same, as though we had not moved; but we passed various places—trading places—with names like Gran' Bassam, Little Popo,[4] names that seemed to belong to some sordid farce acted in front of a sinister backcloth. The idleness of a passenger, my isolation amongst all these men with whom I

3. 1 Timothy 5:18.

4. Grand Bassam and Grand Popo are the names of ports where Conrad's ship called on its way to the Congo.

had no point of contact, the oily and languid sea, the uniform sombreness of the coast, seemed to keep me away from the truth of things, within the toil of a mournful and senseless delusion. The voice of the surf heard now and then was a positive pleasure, like the speech of a brother. It was something natural, that had its reason, that had a meaning. Now and then a boat from the shore gave one a momentary contact with reality. It was paddled by black fellows. You could see from afar the white of their eyeballs glistening. They shouted, sang; their bodies streamed with perspiration; they had faces like grotesque masks—these chaps; but they had bone, muscle, a wild vitality, an intense energy of movement, that was as natural and true as the surf along their coast. They wanted no excuse for being there. They were a great comfort to look at. For a time I would feel I belonged still to a world of straightforward facts; but the feeling would not last long. Something would turn up to scare it away. Once, I remember, we came upon a man-of-war anchored off the coast. There wasn't even a shed there, and she was shelling the bush. It appears the French had one of their wars going on thereabouts. Her ensign dropped limp like a rag; the muzzles of the long eight-inch guns stuck out all over the low hull; the greasy, slimy swell swung her up lazily and let her down, swaying her thin masts. In the empty immensity of earth, sky, and water, there she was, incomprehensible, firing into a continent. Pop, would go one of the eight-inch guns; a small flame would dart and vanish, a little white smoke would disappear, a tiny projectile would give a feeble screech—and nothing happened. Nothing could happen. There was a touch of insanity in the proceeding, a sense of lugubrious drollery in the sight; and it was not dissipated by somebody on board assuring me earnestly there was a camp of natives—he called them enemies!—hidden out of sight somewhere.

"We gave her letters (I heard the men in that lonely ship were dying of fever at the rate of three a day) and went on. We called at some more places with farcical names, where the merry dance of death and trade goes on in a still and earthy atmosphere as of an overheated catacomb;[5] all along the formless coast bordered by dangerous surf, as if Nature herself had tried to ward off intruders; in and out of rivers, streams of death in life, whose banks were rotting into mud, whose waters, thickened into slime, invaded the contorted mangroves, that seemed to writhe at us in the extremity of an impotent despair. Nowhere did we stop long enough to get a particularised impression, but the general sense of vague and oppressive wonder grew upon me. It was like a weary pilgrimage amongst hints for nightmares.

"It was upward of thirty days before I saw the mouth of the big river. We anchored off the seat of the government. But my work would not begin till some two hundred miles farther on. So as soon as I could I made a start for a place thirty miles higher up.

"I had my passage on a little sea-going steamer. Her captain was a Swede, and knowing me for a seaman, invited me on the bridge. He was a young man, lean, fair, and morose, with lanky hair and a shuffling gait. As we left the miserable little wharf, he tossed his head contemptuously at the shore. 'Been living there?' he asked. I said, 'Yes.' 'Fine lot these government chaps—are they not?' he went on, speaking English with great precision and considerable bitterness. 'It is funny what some people will do

5. In a letter in May 1890 Conrad wrote: "What makes me rather uneasy is the information that 60 per cent. of our Company's employés return to Europe before they have completed even six months' service. Fever and dysentery! There are others who are sent home in a hurry at the end of a year, so that they shouldn't die in the Congo." According to a 1907 report, 150 out of every 2,000 native Congolese laborers died each month while in company employ; "All along the [railroad] track one would see corpses."

for a few francs a month. I wonder what becomes of that kind when it goes up country?' I said to him I expected to see that soon. 'So-o-o!' he exclaimed. He shuffled athwart, keeping one eye ahead vigilantly. 'Don't be too sure,' he continued. 'The other day I took up a man who hanged himself on the road. He was a Swede, too.' 'Hanged himself! Why, in God's name?' I cried. He kept on looking out watchfully. 'Who knows? The sun too much for him, or the country perhaps.'

"At last we opened a reach. A rocky cliff appeared, mounds of turned-up earth by the shore, houses on a hill, others, with iron roofs, amongst a waste of excavations, or hanging to the declivity. A continuous noise of the rapids above hovered over this scene of inhabited devastation. A lot of people, mostly black and naked, moved about like ants. A jetty projected into the river. A blinding sunlight drowned all this at times in a sudden recrudescence of glare. 'There's your Company's station,' said the Swede, pointing to three wooden barrack-like structures on the rocky slope. 'I will send your things up. Four boxes did you say? So. Farewell.'

"I came upon a boiler wallowing in the grass, then found a path leading up the hill. It turned aside for the boulders, and also for an undersized railway-truck lying there on its back with its wheels in the air. One was off. The thing looked as dead as the carcass of some animal. I came upon more pieces of decaying machinery, a stack of rusty rails. To the left a clump of trees made a shady spot, where dark things seemed to stir feebly. I blinked, the path was steep. A horn tooted to the right, and I saw the black people run. A heavy and dull detonation shook the ground, a puff of smoke came out of the cliff, and that was all. No change appeared on the face of the rock. They were building a railway. The cliff was not in the way or anything; but this objectless blasting was all the work going on.

"A slight clinking behind me made me turn my head. Six black men advanced in a file, toiling up the path. They walked erect and slow, balancing small baskets full of earth on their heads, and the clink kept time with their footsteps. Black rags were wound round their loins, and the short ends behind wagged to and fro like tails. I could see every rib, the joints of their limbs were like knots in a rope; each had an iron collar on his neck, and all were connected together with a chain whose bights swung between them, rhythmically clinking. Another report from the cliff made me think suddenly of that ship of war I had seen firing into a continent. It was the same kind of ominous voice; but these men could by no stretch of imagination be called enemies. They were called criminals, and the outraged law, like the bursting shells, had come to them, an insoluble mystery from over the sea. All their meagre breasts panted together, the violently dilated nostrils quivered, the eyes stared stonily up-hill. They passed me within six inches, without a glance, with that complete, deathlike indifference of unhappy savages. Behind this raw matter one of the reclaimed, the product of the new forces at work, strolled despondently, carrying a rifle by its middle. He had a uniform jacket with one button off, and seeing a white man on the path, hoisted his weapon to his shoulder with alacrity. This was simple prudence, white men being so much alike at a distance that he could not tell who I might be. He was speedily reassured, and with a large, white, rascally grin, and a glance at his charge, seemed to take me into partnership in his exalted trust. After all, I also was a part of the great cause of these high and just proceedings.

"Instead of going up, I turned and descended to the left. My idea was to let that chain-gang get out of sight before I climbed the hill. You know I am not particularly tender; I've had to strike and to fend off. I've had to resist and to attack sometimes— that's only one way of resisting—without counting the exact cost, according to the demands of such sort of life as I had blundered into. I've seen the devil of violence, and the devil of greed, and the devil of hot desire; but, by all the stars! these were strong, lusty, red-eyed devils, that swayed and drove men—men, I tell you. But as I stood on this hillside, I foresaw that in the blinding sunshine of that land I would become acquainted with a flabby, pretending, weak-eyed devil of a rapacious and pitiless folly. How insidious he could be, too, I was only to find out several months later and a thousand miles farther. For a moment I stood appalled, as though by a warning. Finally I descended the hill, obliquely, towards the trees I had seen.

"I avoided a vast artificial hole somebody had been digging on the slope, the purpose of which I found it impossible to divine. It wasn't a quarry or a sandpit, anyhow. It was just a hole. It might have been connected with the philanthropic desire of giving the criminals something to do. I don't know. Then I nearly fell into a very narrow ravine, almost no more than a scar in the hillside. I discovered that a lot of imported drainage-pipes for the settlement had been tumbled in there. There wasn't one that was not broken. It was a wanton smash-up. At last I got under the trees. My purpose was to stroll into the shade for a moment; but no sooner within than it seemed to me I had stepped into the gloomy circle of some Inferno. The rapids were near, and an uninterrupted, uniform, headlong, rushing noise filled the mournful stillness of the grove, where not a breath stirred, not a leaf moved, with a mysterious sound—as though the tearing pace of the launched earth had suddenly become audible.

"Black shapes crouched, lay, sat between the trees, leaning against the trunks, clinging to the earth, half coming out, half effaced within the dim light, in all the attitudes of pain, abandonment, and despair. Another mine on the cliff went off, followed by a slight shudder of the soil under my feet. The work was going on. The work! And this was the place where some of the helpers had withdrawn to die.

"They were dying slowly—it was very clear. They were not enemies, they were not criminals, they were nothing earthly now,—nothing but black shadows of disease and starvation, lying confusedly in the greenish gloom. Brought from all the recesses of the coast in all the legality of time contracts, lost in uncongenial surroundings, fed on unfamiliar food, they sickened, became inefficient, and were then allowed to crawl away and rest. These moribund shapes were free as air—and nearly as thin. I began to distinguish the gleam of eyes under the trees. Then, glancing down, I saw a face near my hand. The black bones reclined at full length with one shoulder against the tree, and slowly the eyelids rose and the sunken eyes looked up at me, enormous and vacant, a kind of blind, white flicker in the depths of the orbs, which died out slowly. The man seemed young—almost a boy—but you know with them it's hard to tell. I found nothing else to do but to offer him one of my good Swede's ship's biscuits I had in my pocket. The fingers closed slowly on it and held—there was no other movement and no other glance. He had tied a bit of white worsted round his neck—Why? Where did he get it? Was it a badge—an ornament—a charm—a propitiatory act? Was there any idea at all connected with it? It looked startling round his black neck, this bit of white thread from beyond the seas.

"Near the same tree two more bundles of acute angles sat with their legs drawn up. One, with his chin propped on his knees, stared at nothing, in an intolerable and appalling manner: his brother phantom rested its forehead, as if overcome with a great weariness; and all about others were scattered in every pose of contorted collapse, as in some picture of a massacre or a pestilence. While I stood horror-struck, one of these creatures rose to his hands and knees, and went off on all-fours towards the river to drink. He lapped out of his hand, then sat up in the sunlight, crossing his shins in front of him, and after a time let his woolly head fall on his breastbone.

"I didn't want any more loitering in the shade, and I made haste towards the station. When near the buildings I met a white man, in such an unexpected elegance of get-up that in the first moment I took him for a sort of vision. I saw a high starched collar, white cuffs, a light alpaca jacket, snowy trousers, a clear silk necktie, and varnished boots. No hat. Hair parted, brushed, oiled, under a green-lined parasol held in a big white hand. He was amazing, and had a penholder behind his ear.

"I shook hands with this miracle, and I learned he was the Company's chief accountant, and that all the book-keeping was done at this station. He had come out for a moment, he said, 'to get a breath of fresh air.' The expression sounded wonderfully odd, with its suggestion of sedentary desk-life. I wouldn't have mentioned the fellow to you at all, only it was from his lips that I first heard the name of the man who is so indissolubly connected with the memories of that time. Moreover, I respected the fellow. Yes; I respected his collars, his vast cuffs, his brushed hair. His appearance was certainly that of a hairdresser's dummy; but in the great demoralisation of the land he kept up his appearance. That's backbone. His starched collars and got-up shirt-fronts were achievements of character. He had been out nearly three years; and, later on, I could not help asking him how he managed to sport such linen. He had just the faintest blush, and said modestly, 'I've been teaching one of the native women about the station. It was difficult. She had a distaste for the work.' Thus this man had verily accomplished something. And he was devoted to his books, which were in apple-pie order.

"Everything else in the station was in a muddle,—heads, things, buildings. Strings of dusty niggers with splay feet arrived and departed; a stream of manufactured goods, rubbishy cottons, beads, and brass-wire set into the depths of darkness, and in return came a precious trickle of ivory.

"I had to wait in the station for ten days—an eternity. I lived in a hut in the yard, but to be out of the chaos I would sometimes get into the accountant's office. It was built of horizontal planks, and so badly put together that, as he bent over his high desk, he was barred from neck to heels with narrow strips of sunlight. There was no need to open the big shutter to see. It was hot there too; big flies buzzed fiendishly, and did not sting, but stabbed. I sat generally on the floor, while, of faultless appearance (and even slightly scented), perching on a high stool, he wrote, he wrote. Sometimes he stood up for exercise. When a truckle-bed with a sick man (some invalided agent from up-country) was put in there, he exhibited a gentle annoyance. 'The groans of this sick person,' he said, 'distract my attention. And without that it is extremely difficult to guard against clerical errors in this climate.'

"One day he remarked, without lifting his head, 'In the interior you will no doubt meet Mr Kurtz.' On my asking who Mr Kurtz was, he said he was a first-class agent; and seeing my disappointment at this information, he added slowly, laying down his pen, 'He is a very remarkable person.' Further questions elicited from him that Mr Kurtz was at present in charge of a trading-post, a very important one, in the true ivory-country, at 'the very bottom of there. Sends in as much ivory as all the others put together . . .' He began to write again. The sick man was too ill to groan. The flies buzzed in a great peace.

"Suddenly there was a growing murmur of voices and a great tramping of feet. A caravan had come in. A violent babble of uncouth sounds burst out on the other side of the planks. All the carriers were speaking together, and in the midst of the uproar the lamentable voice of the chief agent was heard 'giving it up' tearfully for the twentieth time that day. . . . He rose slowly. 'What a frightful row,' he said. He crossed the room gently to look at the sick man, and returning, said to me, 'He does not hear.'

'What! Dead?' I asked, startled. 'No, not yet,' he answered, with great composure. Then, alluding with a toss of the head to the tumult in the station-yard, 'When one has got to make correct entries, one comes to hate those savages—hate them to the death.' He remained thoughtful for a moment. 'When you see Mr Kurtz,' he went on, 'tell him from me that everything here'—he glanced at the desk—'is very satisfactory. I don't like to write to him—with those messengers of ours you never know who may get hold of your letter—at that Central Station.' He stared at me for a moment with his mild, bulging eyes. 'Oh, he will go far, very far,' he began again. 'He will be a somebody in the Administration before long. They, above—the Council in Europe, you know—mean him to be.'

"He turned to his work. The noise outside had ceased, and presently in going out I stopped at the door. In the steady buzz of flies the homeward-bound agent was lying flushed and insensible; the other, bent over his books, was making correct entries of perfectly correct transactions; and fifty feet below the doorstep I could see the still tree-tops of the grove of death.

"Next day I left that station at last, with a caravan of sixty men, for a two-hundred-mile tramp.

"No use telling you much about that. Paths, paths, everywhere; a stamped-in network of paths spreading over the empty land, through long grass, through burnt grass, through thickets, down and up chilly ravines, up and down stony hills ablaze with heat; and a solitude, a solitude, nobody, not a hut. The population had cleared out a long time ago. Well, if a lot of mysterious niggers armed with all kinds of fearful weapons suddenly took to travelling on the road between Deal[6] and Gravesend, catching the yokels right and left to carry heavy loads for them, I fancy every farm and cottage thereabouts would get empty very soon. Only here the dwellings were gone too. Still, I passed through several abandoned villages. There's something pathetically childish in the ruins of grass walls. Day after day, with the stamp and shuffle of sixty pair of bare feet behind me, each pair under a 60-lb. load. Camp, cook, sleep, strike camp, march. Now and then a carrier dead in harness, at rest in the long grass near the path, with an empty water-gourd and his long staff lying by his side. A great silence around and above. Perhaps on some quiet night the tremor of far-off drums, sinking, swelling, a tremor vast, faint; a sound weird, appealing, suggestive, and wild—and perhaps with as profound a meaning as the sound of bells in a Christian country. Once a white man in an unbuttoned uniform, camping on the path with an armed escort of lank Zanzibaris,[7] very hospitable and festive—not to say drunk. Was looking after the upkeep of the road, he declared. Can't say I saw any road or any upkeep, unless the body of a middle-aged negro, with a bullet-hole in the forehead, upon which I absolutely stumbled three miles farther on, may be considered as a permanent improvement. I had a white companion too, not a bad chap, but rather too fleshy and with the exasperating habit of fainting on the hot hillsides, miles away from the least bit of shade and water. Annoying, you know, to hold your own coat like a parasol over a man's head while he is coming-to. I couldn't help asking him once what he meant by coming there at all. 'To make money, of course. What do you think?' he said, scornfully. Then he got fever, and had to be carried in a hammock slung under a pole. As he weighed sixteen stone I had no end of rows with the carriers. They jibbed, ran away, sneaked off with their loads in the night—quite a mutiny. So, one evening, I

6. An English port.

7. Africans from Zanzibar, in East Africa; they were widely used as mercenaries.

made a speech in English with gestures, not one of which was lost to the sixty pairs of eyes before me, and the next morning I started the hammock off in front all right. An hour afterwards I came upon the whole concern wrecked in a bush—man, hammock, groans, blankets, horrors. The heavy pole had skinned his poor nose. He was very anxious for me to kill somebody, but there wasn't the shadow of a carrier near. I remembered the old doctor,—'It would be interesting for science to watch the mental changes of individuals, on the spot.' I felt I was becoming scientifically interesting. However, all that is to no purpose. On the fifteenth day I came in sight of the big river again, and hobbled into the Central Station. It was on a back water surrounded by scrub and forest, with a pretty border of smelly mud on one side, and on the three others enclosed by a crazy fence of rushes. A neglected gap was all the gate it had, and the first glance at the place was enough to let you see the flabby devil was running that show. White men with long staves in their hands appeared languidly from amongst the buildings, strolling up to take a look at me, and then retired out of sight somewhere. One of them, a stout, excitable chap with black moustaches, informed me with great volubility and many digressions, as soon as I told him who I was, that my steamer was at the bottom of the river. I was thunderstruck. What, how, why? Oh, it was 'all right.' The 'manager himself' was there. All quite correct. 'Everybody had behaved splendidly! splendidly!'—'You must,' he said in agitation, 'go and see the general manager at once. He is waiting!'

"I did not see the real significance of that wreck at once. I fancy I see it now, but I am not sure—not at all. Certainly the affair was too stupid—when I think of it—to be altogether natural. Still. . . . But at the moment it presented itself simply as a confounded nuisance. The steamer was sunk. They had started two days before in a sudden hurry up the river with the manager on board, in charge of some volunteer skipper, and before they had been out three hours they tore the bottom out of her on stones, and she sank near the south bank. I asked myself what I was to do there, now my boat was lost. As a matter of fact, I had plenty to do in fishing my command out of the river. I had to set about it the very next day. That, and the repairs when I brought the pieces to the station, took some months.

"My first interview with the manager was curious. He did not ask me to sit down after my twenty-mile walk that morning. He was commonplace in complexion, in feature, in manners, and in voice. He was of middle size and of ordinary build. His eyes, of the usual blue, were perhaps remarkably cold, and he certainly could make his glance fall on one as trenchant and heavy as an axe. But even at these times the rest of his person seemed to disclaim the intention. Otherwise there was only an indefinable, faint expression of his lips, something stealthy—a smile—not a smile—I remember it, but I can't explain. It was unconscious, this smile was, though just after he had said something it got intensified for an instant. It came at the end of his speeches like a seal applied on the words to make the meaning of the commonest phrase appear absolutely inscrutable. He was a common trader, from his youth up employed in these parts—nothing more. He was obeyed, yet he inspired neither love nor fear, nor even respect. He inspired uneasiness. That was it! Uneasiness. Not a definite mistrust—just uneasiness—nothing more. You have no idea how effective such a . . . a . . . faculty can be. He had no genius for organising, for initiative, or for order even. That was evident in such things as the deplorable state of the station. He had no learning, and no intelligence. His position had come to him—why? Perhaps because he was never ill . . . He had served three terms of three years out there . . . Because triumphant health in the general rout of constitutions is a kind of power in itself. When he went

home on leave he rioted on a large scale—pompously. Jack ashore—with a difference—in externals only. This one could gather from his casual talk. He originated
nothing, he could keep the routine going—that's all. But he was great. He was great
by this little thing that it was impossible to tell what could control such a man. He
never gave that secret away. Perhaps there was nothing within him. Such a suspicion
made one pause—for out there there were no external checks. Once when various
tropical diseases had laid low almost every 'agent' in the station, he was heard to say,
'Men who come out here should have no entrails.' He sealed the utterance with that
smile of his, as though it had been a door opening into a darkness he had in his keeping. You fancied you had seen things—but the seal was on. When annoyed at meal-
times by the constant quarrels of the white men about precedence, he ordered an immense round table to be made, for which a special house had to be built. This was the
station's mess-room. Where he sat was the first place—the rest were nowhere. One
felt this to be his unalterable conviction. He was neither civil nor uncivil. He was
quiet. He allowed his 'boy'—an overfed young negro from the coast—to treat the
white men, under his very eyes, with provoking insolence.

"He began to speak as soon as he saw me. I had been very long on the road. He
could not wait. Had to start without me. The up-river stations had to be relieved.
There had been so many delays already that he did not know who was dead and who
was alive, and how they got on—and so on, and so on. He paid no attention to my explanations, and, playing with a stick of sealing-wax, repeated several times that the
situation was 'very grave, very grave.' There were rumours that a very important station was in jeopardy, and its chief, Mr Kurtz, was ill. Hoped it was not true. Mr Kurtz
was . . . I felt weary and irritable. Hang Kurtz, I thought. I interrupted him by saying I
had heard of Mr Kurtz on the coast. 'Ah! So they talk of him down there,' he murmured to himself. Then he began again, assuring me Mr Kurtz was the best agent he
had, an exceptional man, of the greatest importance to the Company; therefore I could
understand his anxiety. He was, he said, 'very, very uneasy.' Certainly he fidgeted on
his chair a good deal, exclaimed, 'Ah, Mr Kurtz!' broke the stick of sealing-wax and
seemed dumbfounded by the accident. Next thing he wanted to know 'how long it
would take to' . . . I interrupted him again. Being hungry, you know, and kept on my
feet too, I was getting savage. 'How can I tell?' I said. 'I haven't even seen the wreck
yet—some months, no doubt.' All this talk seemed to me so futile. 'Some months,' he
said. 'Well, let us say three months before we can make a start. Yes. That ought to do
the affair.' I flung out of his hut (he lived all alone in a clay hut with a sort of verandah) muttering to myself my opinion of him. He was a chattering idiot. Afterwards I
took it back when it was borne in upon me startlingly with what extreme nicety he
had estimated the time requisite for the 'affair.'

"I went to work the next day, turning, so to speak, my back on that station. In that
way only it seemed to me I could keep my hold on the redeeming facts of life. Still,
one must look about sometimes; and then I saw this station, these men strolling aimlessly about in the sunshine of the yard. I asked myself sometimes what it all meant.
They wandered here and there with their absurd long staves in their hands, like a lot
of faithless pilgrims bewitched inside a rotten fence. The word 'ivory' rang in the air,
was whispered, was sighed. You would think they were praying to it. A taint of imbecile rapacity blew through it all, like a whiff from some corpse. By Jove! I've never
seen anything so unreal in my life. And outside, the silent wilderness surrounding this
cleared speck on the earth struck me as something great and invincible, like evil or
truth, waiting patiently for the passing away of this fantastic invasion.

"Oh, those months! Well, never mind. Various things happened. One evening a grass shed full of calico, cotton prints, beads, and I don't know what else, burst into a blaze so suddenly that you would have thought the earth had opened to let an avenging fire consume all that trash. I was smoking my pipe quietly by my dismantled steamer, and saw them all cutting capers in the light, with their arms lifted high, when the stout man with moustaches came tearing down to the river, a tin pail in his hand, assured me that everybody was 'behaving splendidly, splendidly,' dipped about a quart of water and tore back again. I noticed there was a hole in the bottom of his pail.

"I strolled up. There was no hurry. You see the thing had gone off like a box of matches. It had been hopeless from the very first. The flame had leaped high, driven everybody back, lighted up everything—and collapsed. The shed was already a heap of embers glowing fiercely. A nigger was being beaten near by. They said he had caused the fire in some way; be that as it may, he was screeching most horribly. I saw him, later on, for several days, sitting in a bit of shade looking very sick and trying to recover himself: afterwards he arose and went out—and the wilderness without a sound took him into its bosom again. As I approached the glow from the dark I found myself at the back of two men, talking. I heard the name of Kurtz pronounced, then the words, 'take advantage of this unfortunate accident.' One of the men was the manager. I wished him a good evening. 'Did you ever see anything like it—eh? it is incredible,' he said, and walked off. The other man remained. He was a first-class agent, young, gentlemanly, a bit reserved, with a forked little beard and a hooked nose. He was stand-offish with the other agents, and they on their side said he was the manager's spy upon them. As to me, I had hardly ever spoken to him before. We got into talk, and by-and-by we strolled away from the hissing ruins. Then he asked me to his room, which was in the main building of the station. He struck a match, and I perceived that this young aristocrat had not only a silver-mounted dressing-case but also a whole candle all to himself. Just at that time the manager was the only man supposed to have any right to candles. Native mats covered the clay walls; a collection of spears, assegais,[8] shields, knives was hung up in trophies. The business intrusted to this fellow was the making of bricks—so I had been informed; but there wasn't a fragment of a brick anywhere in the station, and he had been there more than a year—waiting. It seems he could not make bricks without something, I don't know what—straw maybe. Anyway, it could not be found there, and as it was not likely to be sent from Europe, it did not appear clear to me what he was waiting for. An act of special creation perhaps. However, they were all waiting—all the sixteen or twenty pilgrims of them—for something; and upon my word it did not seem an uncongenial occupation, from the way they took it, though the only thing that ever came to them was disease—as far as I could see. They beguiled the time by backbiting and intriguing against each other in a foolish kind of way. There was an air of plotting about that station, but nothing came of it, of course. It was as unreal as everything else—as the philanthropic pretence of the whole concern, as their talk, as their government, as their show of work. The only real feeling was a desire to get appointed to a trading-post where ivory was to be had, so that they could earn percentages. They intrigued and slandered and hated each other only on that account,—but as to effectually lifting a little finger—oh, no. By heavens! there is something after all in the world allowing one man to steal a horse while another must not look at a halter. Steal a horse straight

8. Spears.

out. Very well. He has done it. Perhaps he can ride. But there is a way of looking at a halter that would provoke the most charitable of saints into a kick.

"I had no idea why he wanted to be sociable, but as we chatted in there it suddenly occurred to me the fellow was trying to get at something—in fact, pumping me. He alluded constantly to Europe, to the people I was supposed to know there—putting leading questions as to my acquaintances in the sepulchral city, and so on. His little eyes glittered like mica discs—with curiosity,—though he tried to keep up a bit of superciliousness. At first I was astonished, but very soon I became awfully curious to see what he would find out from me. I couldn't possibly imagine what I had in me to make it worth his while. It was very pretty to see how he baffled himself, for in truth my body was full of chills, and my head had nothing in it but that wretched steamboat business. It was evident he took me for a perfectly shameless prevaricator. At last he got angry, and, to conceal a movement of furious annoyance, he yawned. I rose. Then I noticed a small sketch in oils, on a panel, representing a woman, draped and blind-folded, carrying a lighted torch. The background was sombre—almost black. The movement of the woman was stately, and the effect of the torchlight on the face was sinister.

"It arrested me, and he stood by civilly, holding a half-pint champagne bottle (medical comforts) with the candle stuck in it. To my question he said Mr Kurtz had painted this—in this very station more than a year ago—while waiting for means to go to his trading-post. 'Tell me, pray,' said I, 'who is this Mr Kurtz?'

"'The chief of the Inner Station,' he answered in a short tone, looking away. 'Much obliged,' I said, laughing. 'And you are the brickmaker of the Central Station. Every one knows that.' He was silent for a while. 'He is a prodigy,' he said at last. 'He is an emissary of pity, and science, and progress, and devil knows what else. We want,' he began to declaim suddenly, 'for the guidance of the cause intrusted to us by Europe, so to speak, higher intelligence, wide sympathies, a singleness of purpose.' 'Who says that?' I asked. 'Lots of them,' he replied. 'Some even write that; and so *he* comes here, a special being, as you ought to know.' 'Why ought I to know?' I interrupted, really surprised. He paid no attention. 'Yes. To-day he is chief of the best station, next year he will be assistant-manager, two years more and . . . but I daresay you know what he will be in two years' time. You are of the new gang—the gang of virtue. The same people who sent him specially also recommended you. Oh, don't say no. I've my own eyes to trust.' Light dawned upon me. My dear aunt's influential acquaintances were producing an unexpected effect upon that young man. I nearly burst into a laugh. 'Do you read the Company's confidential correspondence?' I asked. He hadn't a word to say. It was great fun. 'When Mr Kurtz,' I continued severely, 'is General Manager, you won't have the opportunity.'

"He blew the candle out suddenly, and we went outside. The moon had risen. Black figures strolled about listlessly, pouring water on the glow, whence proceeded a sound of hissing; steam ascended in the moonlight; the beaten nigger groaned somewhere. 'What a row the brute makes!' said the indefatigable man with the moustaches, appearing near us. 'Serve him right. Transgression—punishment—bang! Pitiless, pitiless. That's the only way. This will prevent all conflagrations for the future. I was just telling the manager . . .' He noticed my companion, and became crestfallen all at once. 'Not in bed yet,' he said, with a kind of servile heartiness; 'it's so natural. Ha! Danger—agitation.' He vanished. I went on to the river-side, and the other followed me. I heard a scathing murmur at my ear, 'Heap of muffs—go to.' The pilgrims could be seen in knots gesticulating, discussing. Several had still their staves in their hands. I verily believe they took these sticks to bed with them. Beyond the fence the

forest stood up spectrally in the moonlight, and through the dim stir, through the faint
sounds of that lamentable courtyard, the silence of the land went home to one's very
heart,—its mystery, its greatness, the amazing reality of its concealed life. The hurt
nigger moaned feebly somewhere near by, and then fetched a deep sigh that made me
mend my pace away from there. I felt a hand introducing itself under my arm. 'My
dear sir,' said the fellow, 'I don't want to be misunderstood, and especially by you,
who will see Mr Kurtz long before I can have that pleasure. I wouldn't like him to get
a false idea of my disposition. . . .'

    "I let him run on, this papier-mâché Mephistopheles, and it seemed to me that if I
tried I could poke my forefinger through him, and would find nothing inside but a little loose dirt, maybe. He, don't you see, had been planning to be assistant-manager
by-and-by under the present man, and I could see that the coming of that Kurtz had
upset them both not a little. He talked precipitately, and I did not try to stop him. I had
my shoulders against the wreck of my steamer, hauled up on the slope like a carcass
of some big river animal. The smell of mud, of primeval mud, by Jove! was in my
nostrils, the high stillness of primeval forest was before my eyes; there were shiny
patches on the black creek. The moon had spread over everything a thin layer of silver—over the rank grass, over the mud, upon the wall of matted vegetation standing
higher than the wall of a temple, over the great river I could see through a sombre gap
glittering, glittering, as it flowed broadly by without a murmur. All this was great, ex-
pectant, mute, while the man jabbered about himself. I wondered whether the stillness
on the face of the immensity looking at us two were meant as an appeal or as a menace. What were we who had strayed in here? Could we handle that dumb thing, or
would it handle us? I felt how big, how confoundedly big, was that thing that couldn't
talk, and perhaps was deaf as well. What was in there? I could see a little ivory coming out from there, and I had heard Mr Kurtz was in there. I had heard enough about it
too—God knows! Yet somehow it didn't bring any image with it—no more than if I
had been told an angel or a fiend was in there. I believed it in the same way one of you
might believe there are inhabitants in the planet Mars. I knew once a Scotch sailmaker
who was certain, dead sure, there were people in Mars. If you asked him for some
idea how they looked and behaved, he would get shy and mutter something about
'walking on all-fours.' If you as much as smiled, he would—though a man of sixty—
offer to fight you. I would not have gone so far as to fight for Kurtz, but I went for
him near enough to a lie. You know I hate, detest, and can't bear a lie, not because I
am straighter than the rest of us, but simply because it appals me. There is a taint of
death, a flavour of mortality in lies,—which is exactly what I hate and detest in the
world—what I want to forget. It makes me miserable and sick, like biting something
rotten would do. Temperament, I suppose. Well, I went near enough to it by letting
the young fool there believe anything he liked to imagine as to my influence in Europe. I became in an instant as much of a pretence as the rest of the bewitched pilgrims. This simply because I had a notion it somehow would be of help to that Kurtz
whom at the time I did not see—you understand. He was just a word for me. I did not
see the man in the name any more than you do. Do you see him? Do you see the
story? Do you see anything? It seems to me I am trying to tell you a dream—making
a vain attempt, because no relation of a dream can convey the dream-sensation, that
commingling of absurdity, surprise, and bewilderment in a tremor of struggling revolt, that notion of being captured by the incredible which is of the very essence of
dreams. . . ."

    He was silent for a while.

"... No, it is impossible; it is impossible to convey the life-sensation of any given epoch of one's existence,—that which makes its truth, its meaning—its subtle and penetrating essence. It is impossible. We live, as we dream—alone. . . ."

He paused again as if reflecting, then added—

"Of course in this you fellows see more than I could then. You see me, whom you know. . . ."

It had become so pitch dark that we listeners could hardly see one another. For a long time already he, sitting apart, had been no more to us than a voice. There was not a word from anybody. The others might have been asleep, but I was awake. I listened, I listened on the watch for the sentence, for the word, that would give me the clue to the faint uneasiness inspired by this narrative that seemed to shape itself without human lips in the heavy night-air of the river.

"...Yes—I let him run on," Marlow began again, "and think what he pleased about the powers that were behind me. I did! And there was nothing behind me! There was nothing but that wretched, old, mangled steamboat I was leaning against, while he talked fluently about 'the necessity for every man to get on.' 'And when one comes out here, you conceive, it is not to gaze at the moon.' Mr Kurtz was a 'universal genius,' but even a genius would find it easier to work with 'adequate tools—intelligent men.' He did not make bricks—why, there was a physical impossibility in the way—as I was well aware; and if he did secretarial work for the manager, it was because 'no sensible man rejects wantonly the confidence of his superiors.' Did I see it? I saw it. What more did I want? What I really wanted was rivets, by heaven! Rivets. To get on with the work—to stop the hole. Rivets I wanted. There were cases of them down at the coast—cases—piled up—burst—split! You kicked a loose rivet at every second step in that station yard on the hillside. Rivets had rolled into the grove of death. You could fill your pockets with rivets for the trouble of stooping down— and there wasn't one rivet to be found where it was wanted. We had plates that would do, but nothing to fasten them with. And every week the messenger, a lone negro, letter-bag on shoulder and staff in hand, left our station for the coast. And several times a week a coast caravan came in with trade goods,—ghastly glazed calico that made you shudder only to look at it, glass beads value about a penny a quart, confounded spotted cotton handkerchiefs. And no rivets. Three carriers could have brought all that was wanted to set that steamboat afloat.

"He was becoming confidential now, but I fancy my unresponsive attitude must have exasperated him at last, for he judged it necessary to inform me he feared neither God nor devil, let alone any mere man. I said I could see that very well, but what I wanted was a certain quantity of rivets—and rivets were what really Mr Kurtz wanted, if he had only known it. Now letters went to the coast every week. . . . 'My dear sir,' he cried, 'I write from dictation.' I demanded rivets. There was a way—for an intelligent man. He changed his manner; became very cold, and suddenly began to talk about a hippopotamus; wondered whether sleeping on board the steamer (I stuck to my salvage night and day) I wasn't disturbed. There was an old hippo that had the bad habit of getting out on the bank and roaming at night over the station grounds. The pilgrims used to turn out in a body and empty every rifle they could lay hands on at him. Some even had sat up o' nights for him. All this energy was wasted, though. 'That animal has a charmed life,' he said; 'but you can say this only of brutes in this country. No man—you apprehend me?—no man here bears a charmed life.' He stood there for a moment in the moonlight with his delicate hooked nose set a little askew, and his mica eyes glittering without a wink, then, with a curt Good night, he strode off. I could see he was disturbed and considerably puzzled, which made me feel more hopeful than I had been for days. It was a great comfort to turn from that chap to my influential friend, the battered, twisted, ruined, tin-pot steamboat. I clambered on board. She rang under my feet like an empty Huntley & Palmer[9] biscuit-tin kicked along a gutter; she was nothing so solid in make, and rather less pretty in shape, but I had expended enough hard work on her to make me love her. No influential friend would have served me better. She had given me a chance to come out a bit—to find out what I could do. No, I don't like work. I had rather laze about and think of all the fine things that can be done. I don't like work—no man does—but I like what is in the work,—the chance to find yourself. Your own reality—for yourself, not for others— what no other man can ever know. They can only see the mere show, and never can tell what it really means.

"I was not surprised to see somebody sitting aft, on the deck, with his legs dangling over the mud. You see I rather chummed with the few mechanics there were in that station, whom the other pilgrims naturally despised—on account of their imperfect manners, I suppose. This was the foreman—a boiler-maker by trade—a good worker. He was a lank, bony, yellow-faced man, with big intense eyes. His aspect was worried, and his head was as bald as the palm of my hand; but his hair in falling seemed to have stuck to his chin, and had prospered in the new locality, for his beard hung down to his waist. He was a widower with six young children (he had left them in charge of a sister of his to come out there), and the passion of his life was pigeon-flying. He was an enthusiast and a connoisseur. He would rave about pigeons. After work hours he used sometimes to come over from his hut for a talk about his children and his pigeons; at work, when he had to crawl in the mud under the bottom of the steamboat, he would tie up that beard of his in a kind of white serviette[1] he brought for the purpose. It had loops to go over his ears. In the evening he could be seen squatted on the bank rinsing that wrapper in the creek with great care, then spreading it solemnly on a bush to dry.

"I slapped him on the back and shouted 'We shall have rivets!' He scrambled to his feet exclaiming 'No! Rivets!' as though he couldn't believe his ears. Then in a low voice, 'You . . . eh?' I don't know why we behaved like lunatics. I put my finger to the side of my nose and nodded mysteriously. 'Good for you!' he cried, snapped his fingers above his head, lifting one foot. I tried a jig. We capered on the iron deck. A frightful clatter came out of that hulk, and the virgin forest on the other bank of the creek sent it back in a thundering roll upon the sleeping station. It must have made some of the pilgrims sit up in their hovels. A dark figure obscured the lighted doorway of the manager's hut, vanished, then, a second or so after, the doorway itself vanished too. We stopped, and the silence driven away by the stamping of our feet flowed back again from the recesses of the land. The great wall of vegetation, an exuberant and entangled mass of trunks, branches, leaves, boughs, festoons, motionless in the moonlight, was like a rioting invasion of soundless life, a rolling wave of plants, piled up, crested, ready to topple over the creek, to sweep every little man of us out of his little existence. And it moved not. A deadened burst of mighty splashes and snorts reached us from afar, as though an ichthyosaurus had been taking a bath of glitter in the great river. 'After all,' said the boiler-maker in a reasonable tone, 'why shouldn't we get the rivets?' Why not, indeed! I did not know of any reason why we shouldn't. 'They'll come in three weeks,' I said, confidently.

9. A brand of English cookies.   1. Napkin.

"But they didn't. Instead of rivets there came an invasion, an infliction, a visitation. It came in sections during the next three weeks, each section headed by a donkey carrying a white man in new clothes and tan shoes, bowing from that elevation right and left to the impressed pilgrims. A quarrelsome band of footsore sulky niggers trod on the heels of the donkey; a lot of tents, camp-stools, tin boxes, white cases, brown bales would be shot down in the courtyard, and the air of mystery would deepen a little over the muddle of the station. Five such instalments came, with their absurd air of disorderly flight with the loot of innumerable outfit shops and provision stores, that, one would think, they were lugging, after a raid, into the wilderness for equitable division. It was an inextricable mess of things decent in themselves but that human folly made look like the spoils of thieving.

"This devoted band called itself the Eldorado Exploring Expedition,[2] and I believe they were sworn to secrecy. Their talk, however, was the talk of sordid buccaneers: it was reckless without hardihood, greedy without audacity, and cruel without courage; there was not an atom of foresight or of serious intention in the whole batch of them, and they did not seem aware these things are wanted for the work of the world. To tear treasure out of the bowels of the land was their desire, with no more moral purpose at the back of it than there is in burglars breaking into a safe. Who paid the expenses of the noble enterprise I don't know; but the uncle of our manager was leader of that lot.

"In exterior he resembled a butcher in a poor neighbourhood, and his eyes had a look of sleepy cunning. He carried his fat paunch with ostentation on his short legs, and during the time his gang infested the station spoke to no one but his nephew. You could see these two roaming about all day long with their heads close together in an everlasting confab.

"I had given up worrying myself about the rivets. One's capacity for that kind of folly is more limited than you would suppose. I said Hang!—and let things slide. I had plenty of time for meditation, and now and then I would give some thought to Kurtz. I wasn't very interested in him. No. Still, I was curious to see whether this man, who had come out equipped with moral ideas of some sort, would climb to the top after all, and how he would set about his work when there."

2

"One evening as I was lying flat on the deck of my steamboat, I heard voices approaching—and there were the nephew and the uncle strolling along the bank. I laid my head on my arm again, and had nearly lost myself in a doze, when somebody said in my ear, as it were: 'I am as harmless as a little child, but I don't like to be dictated to. Am I the manager—or am I not? I was ordered to send him there. It's incredible.' . . . I became aware that the two were standing on the shore alongside the forepart of the steamboat, just below my head. I did not move; it did not occur to me to move: I was sleepy. 'It *is* unpleasant,' grunted the uncle. 'He has asked the Administration to be sent there,' said the other, 'with the idea of showing what he could do; and I was instructed accordingly. Look at the influence that man must have. Is it not frightful?' They both agreed it was frightful, then made several bizarre remarks: 'Make rain and fine weather—one man—the Council—by the nose'—bits of absurd sentences that got the better of my drowsiness, so that I had pretty near the whole of my wits about me when the uncle said, 'The climate may do away with this difficulty

2. Eldorado, legendary land of gold in South America and the object of many fruitless 16th-century Spanish expeditions.

for you. Is he alone there?' 'Yes,' answered the manager; 'he sent his assistant down the river with a note to me in these terms: "Clear this poor devil out of the country, and don't bother sending more of that sort. I had rather be alone than have the kind of men you can dispose of with me." It was more than a year ago. Can you imagine such impudence?' 'Anything since then?' asked the other, hoarsely. 'Ivory,' jerked the nephew; 'lots of it—prime sort—lots—most annoying, from him.' 'And with that?' questioned the heavy rumble. 'Invoice,' was the reply fired out, so to speak. Then silence. They had been talking about Kurtz.

"I was broad awake by this time, but, lying perfectly at ease, remained still, having no inducement to change my position. 'How did that ivory come all this way?' growled the elder man, who seemed very vexed. The other explained that it had come with a fleet of canoes in charge of an English half-caste clerk Kurtz had with him; that Kurtz had apparently intended to return himself, the station being by that time bare of goods and stores, but after coming three hundred miles, had suddenly decided to go back, which he started to do alone in a small dug-out with four paddlers, leaving the half-caste to continue down the river with the ivory. The two fellows there seemed astounded at anybody attempting such a thing. They were at a loss for an adequate motive. As to me, I seemed to see Kurtz for the first time. It was a distinct glimpse: the dug-out, four paddling savages, and the lone white man turning his back suddenly on the headquarters, on relief, on thoughts of home—perhaps; setting his face towards the depths of the wilderness, towards his empty and desolate station. I did not know the motive. Perhaps he was just simply a fine fellow who stuck to his work for its own sake. His name, you understand, had not been pronounced once. He was 'that man.' The half-caste, who, as far as I could see, had conducted a difficult trip with great prudence and pluck, was invariably alluded to as 'that scoundrel.' The 'scoundrel' had reported that the 'man' had been very ill—had recovered imperfectly. . . . The two below me moved away then a few paces, and strolled back and forth at some little distance. I heard: 'Military post—doctor—two hundred miles—quite alone now—unavoidable delays—nine months—no news—strange rumours.' They approached again, just as the manager was saying, 'No one, as far as I know, unless a species of wandering trader—a pestilential fellow, snapping ivory from the natives.' Who was it they were talking about now? I gathered in snatches that this was some man supposed to be in Kurtz's district, and of whom the manager did not approve. 'We will not be free from unfair competition till one of these fellows is hanged for an example,' he said. 'Certainly,' grunted the other; 'get him hanged! Why not? Anything—anything can be done in this country. That's what I say; nobody here, you understand, *here,* can endanger your position. And why? You stand the climate—you outlast them all. The danger is in Europe; but there before I left I took care to—' They moved off and whispered, then their voices rose again. 'The extraordinary series of delays is not my fault. I did my possible.' The fat man sighed, 'Very sad.' 'And the pestiferous absurdity of his talk,' continued the other; 'he bothered me enough when he was here. "Each station should be like a beacon on the road towards better things, a centre for trade of course, but also for humanising, improving, instructing." Conceive you—that ass! And he wants to be manager! No, it's—' Here he got choked by excessive indignation, and I lifted my head the least bit. I was surprised to see how near they were—right under me. I could have spat upon their hats. They were looking on the ground, absorbed in thought. The manager was switching his leg with a slender twig: his sagacious relative lifted his head. 'You have been well since you came out this time?' he asked. The other gave a start. 'Who? I? Oh! Like a charm—like a charm. But the rest—oh, my goodness! All sick. They die so quick, too, that I haven't the time to send them out of the country—it's incredible!' 'H'm. Just so,' grunted the uncle. 'Ah! my boy, trust to this—I say, trust to this.' I saw him extend his short flipper of an arm for a gesture that took in the forest, the creek, the mud, the river,—seemed to beckon with a dishonouring flourish before the sunlit face of the land a treacherous appeal to the lurking death, to the hidden evil, to the profound darkness of its heart. It was so startling that I leaped to my feet and looked back at the edge of the forest, as though I had expected an answer of some sort to that black display of confidence. You know the foolish notions that come to one sometimes. The high stillness confronted these two figures with its ominous patience, waiting for the passing away of a fantastic invasion.

"They swore aloud together—out of sheer fright, I believe—then, pretending not to know anything of my existence, turned back to the station. The sun was low; and leaning forward side by side, they seemed to be tugging painfully uphill their two ridiculous shadows of unequal length, that trailed behind them slowly over the tall grass without bending a single blade.

"In a few days the Eldorado Expedition went into the patient wilderness, that closed upon it as the sea closes over a diver. Long afterwards the news came that all the donkeys were dead. I know nothing as to the fate of the less valuable animals. They, no doubt, like the rest of us, found what they deserved. I did not inquire. I was then rather excited at the prospect of meeting Kurtz very soon. When I say very soon I mean it comparatively. It was just two months from the day we left the creek when we came to the bank below Kurtz's station.

"Going up that river was like travelling back to the earliest beginnings of the world, when vegetation rioted on the earth and the big trees were kings. An empty stream, a great silence, an impenetrable forest. The air was warm, thick, heavy, sluggish. There was no joy in the brilliance of sunshine. The long stretches of the waterway ran on, deserted, into the gloom of overshadowed distances. On silvery sandbanks hippos and alligators sunned themselves side by side. The broadening waters flowed through a mob of wooded islands; you lost your way on that river as you would in a desert, and butted all day long against shoals, trying to find the channel, till you thought yourself bewitched and cut off for ever from everything you had known once—somewhere—far away—in another existence perhaps. There were moments when one's past came back to one, as it will sometimes when you have not a moment to spare to yourself; but it came in the shape of an unrestful and noisy dream, remembered with wonder amongst the overwhelming realities of this strange world of plants, and water, and silence. And this stillness of life did not in the least resemble a peace. It was the stillness of an implacable force brooding over an inscrutable intention. It looked at you with a vengeful aspect. I got used to it afterwards; I did not see it any more; I had no time. I had to keep guessing at the channel; I had to discern, mostly by inspiration, the signs of hidden banks; I watched for sunken stones; I was learning to clap my teeth smartly before my heart flew out, when I shaved by a fluke some infernal sly old snag that would have ripped the life out of the tin-pot steamboat and drowned all the pilgrims; I had to keep a look-out for the signs of dead wood we could cut up in the night for next day's steaming. When you have to attend to things of that sort, to the mere incidents of the surface, the reality—the reality, I tell you—fades. The inner truth is hidden—luckily, luckily. But I felt it all the same; I felt often its mysterious stillness watching me at my monkey tricks, just as it watches you fellows performing on your respective tight-ropes for—what is it? half-a-crown a tumble—"

"Try to be civil, Marlow," growled a voice, and I knew there was at least one listener awake besides myself.

"I beg your pardon. I forgot the heartache which makes up the rest of the price. And indeed what does the price matter, if the trick be well done? You do your tricks very well. And I didn't do badly either, since I managed not to sink that steamboat on my first trip. It's a wonder to me yet. Imagine a blindfolded man set to drive a van over a bad road. I sweated and shivered over that business considerably, I can tell you. After all, for a seaman, to scrape the bottom of the thing that's supposed to float all the time under his care is the unpardonable sin. No one may know of it, but you never forget the thump—eh? A blow on the very heart. You remember it, you dream of it, you wake up at night and think of it—years after—and go hot and cold all over. I don't pretend to say that steamboat floated all the time. More than once she had to wade for a bit, with twenty cannibals splashing around and pushing. We had enlisted some of these chaps on the way for a crew. Fine fellows—cannibals—in their place. They were men one could work with, and I am grateful to them. And, after all, they did not eat each other before my face: they had brought along a provision of hippo-meat which went rotten, and made the mystery of the wilderness stink in my nostrils. Phoo! I can sniff it now. I had the manager on board and three or four pilgrims with their staves—all complete. Sometimes we came upon a station close by the bank, clinging to the skirts of the unknown, and the white men rushing out of a tumbledown hovel, with great gestures of joy and surprise and welcome, seemed very strange,—had the appearance of being held there captive by a spell. The word 'ivory' would ring in the air for a while—and on we went again into the silence, along empty reaches, round the still bends, between the high walls of our winding way, reverberating in hollow claps the ponderous beat of the stern-wheel. Trees, trees, millions of trees, massive, immense, running up high; and at their foot, hugging the bank against the stream, crept the little begrimed steamboat, like a sluggish beetle crawling on the floor of a lofty portico. It made you feel very small, very lost, and yet it was not altogether depressing that feeling. After all, if you were small, the grimy beetle crawled on—which was just what you wanted it to do. Where the pilgrims imagined it crawled to I don't know. To some place where they expected to get something, I bet! For me it crawled towards Kurtz—exclusively; but when the steam-pipes started leaking we crawled very slow. The reaches opened before us and closed behind, as if the forest had stepped leisurely across the water to bar the way for our return. We penetrated deeper and deeper into the heart of darkness. It was very quiet there. At night sometimes the roll of drums behind the curtain of trees would run up the river and remain sustained faintly, as if hovering in the air high over our heads, till the first break of day. Whether it meant war, peace, or prayer we could not tell. The dawns were heralded by the descent of a chill stillness; the woodcutters slept, their fires burned low; the snapping of a twig would make you start. We were wanderers on a prehistoric earth, on an earth that wore the aspect of an unknown planet. We could have fancied ourselves the first of men taking possession of an accursed inheritance, to be subdued at the cost of profound anguish and of excessive toil. But suddenly, as we struggled round a bend, there would be a glimpse of rush walls, of peaked grass-roofs, a burst of yells, a whirl of black limbs, a mass of hands clapping, of feet stamping, of bodies swaying, of eyes rolling, under the droop of heavy and motionless foliage. The steamer toiled along slowly on the edge of a black and incomprehensible frenzy. The prehistoric man was cursing us, praying to us, welcoming us—who could tell? We were cut off from the comprehension of our surroundings; we glided past like phantoms, wondering and secretly appalled, as sane men would be before an enthusiastic outbreak in a madhouse. We could not understand, because we were too far and could not remember, because we were travelling in the night of first ages, of those ages that are gone, leaving hardly a sign—and no memories.

"The earth seemed unearthly. We are accustomed to look upon the shackled form of a conquered monster, but there—there you could look at a thing monstrous and free. It was unearthly, and the men were—No, they were not inhuman. Well, you know, that was the worst of it—this suspicion of their not being inhuman. It would come slowly to one. They howled, and leaped, and spun, and made horrid faces; but what thrilled you was just the thought of their humanity—like yours—the thought of your remote kinship with this wild and passionate uproar. Ugly. Yes, it was ugly enough; but if you were man enough you would admit to yourself that there was in you just the faintest trace of a response to the terrible frankness of that noise, a dim suspicion of there being a meaning in it which you—you so remote from the night of first ages—could comprehend. And why not? The mind of man is capable of any-thing—because everything is in it, all the past as well as all the future. What was there after all? Joy, fear, sorrow, devotion, valour, rage—who can tell?—but truth—truth stripped of its cloak of time. Let the fool gape and shudder—the man knows, and can look on without a wink. But he must at least be as much of a man as these on the shore. He must meet that truth with his own true stuff—with his own inborn strength. Principles? Principles won't do. Acquisitions, clothes, pretty rags—rags that would fly off at the first good shake. No; you want a deliberate belief. An appeal to me in this fiendish row—is there? Very well; I hear; I admit, but I have a voice too, and for good or evil mine is the speech that cannot be silenced. Of course, a fool, what with sheer fright and fine sentiments, is always safe. Who's that grunting? You wonder I didn't go ashore for a howl and a dance? Well, no—I didn't. Fine sentiments, you say? Fine sentiments be hanged! I had no time. I had to mess about with white-lead and strips of woollen blanket helping to put bandages on those leaky steam-pipes—I tell you. I had to watch the steering, and circumvent those snags, and get the tin-pot along by hook or by crook. There was surface-truth enough in these things to save a wiser man. And between whiles I had to look after the savage who was fireman. He was an improved specimen; he could fire up a vertical boiler. He was there below me, and, upon my word, to look at him was as edifying as seeing a dog in a parody of breeches and a feather hat, walking on his hind-legs. A few months of training had done for that really fine chap. He squinted at the steam-gauge and at the water-gauge with an evident effort of intrepidity—and he had filed teeth too, the poor devil, and the wool of his pate shaved into queer patterns, and three ornamental scars on each of his cheeks. He ought to have been clapping his hands and stamping his feet on the bank, instead of which he was hard at work, a thrall to strange witchcraft, full of im-proving knowledge. He was useful because he had been instructed; and what he knew was this—that should the water in that transparent thing disappear, the evil spirit in-side the boiler would get angry through the greatness of his thirst, and take a terrible vengeance. So he sweated and fired up and watched the glass fearfully (with an im-promptu charm, made of rags, tied to his arm, and a piece of polished bone, as big as a watch, stuck flatways through his lower lip), while the wooded banks slipped past us slowly, the short noise was left behind, the interminable miles of silence—and we crept on, towards Kurtz. But the snags were thick, the water was treacherous and shal-low, the boiler seemed indeed to have a sulky devil in it, and thus neither that fireman nor I had any time to peer into our creepy thoughts.

"Some fifty miles below the Inner Station we came upon a hut of reeds, an inclined and melancholy pole, with the unrecognisable tatters of what had been a flag of some sort flying from it, and a neatly stacked wood-pile. This was unexpected. We came to the bank, and on the stack of firewood found a flat piece of board with some faded pencil-writing on it. When deciphered it said: 'Wood for you. Hurry up. Approach cautiously.' There was a signature, but it was illegible—not Kurtz—a much longer word. Hurry up. Where? Up the river? 'Approach cautiously.' We had not done so. But the warning could not have been meant for the place where it could be only found after approach. Something was wrong above. But what—and how much? That was the question. We commented adversely upon the imbecility of that telegraphic style. The bush around said nothing, and would not let us look very far, either. A torn curtain of red twill hung in the doorway of the hut, and flapped sadly in our faces. The dwelling was dismantled; but we could see a white man had lived there not very long ago. There remained a rude table—a plank on two posts; a heap of rubbish reposed in a dark corner, and by the door I picked up a book. It had lost its covers, and the pages had been thumbed into a state of extremely dirty softness; but the back had been lovingly stitched afresh with white cotton thread, which looked clean yet. It was an extraordinary find. Its title was, 'An Inquiry into some Points of Seamanship,' by a man Tower, Towson—some such name—Master in his Majesty's Navy. The matter looked dreary reading enough, with illustrative diagrams and repulsive tables of figures, and the copy was sixty years old. I handled this amazing antiquity with the greatest possible tenderness, lest it should dissolve in my hands. Within, Towson or Towser was inquiring earnestly into the breaking strain of ships' chains and tackle, and other such matters. Not a very enthralling book; but at the first glance you could see there a singleness of intention, an honest concern for the right way of going to work, which made these humble pages, thought out so many years ago, luminous with another than a professional light. The simple old sailor, with his talk of chains and purchases, made me forget the jungle and the pilgrims in a delicious sensation of having come upon something unmistakably real. Such a book being there was wonderful enough; but still more astounding were the notes pencilled in the margin, and plainly referring to the text. I couldn't believe my eyes! They were in cipher! Yes, it looked like cipher. Fancy a man lugging with him a book of that description into this nowhere and studying it—and making notes—in cipher at that! It was an extravagant mystery.

"I had been dimly aware for some time of a worrying noise, and when I lifted my eyes I saw the wood-pile was gone, and the manager, aided by all the pilgrims, was shouting at me from the river-side. I slipped the book into my pocket. I assure you to leave off reading was like tearing myself away from the shelter of an old and solid friendship.

"I started the lame engine ahead. 'It must be this miserable trader—this intruder,' exclaimed the manager, looking back malevolently at the place we had left. 'He must be English,' I said. 'It will not save him from getting into trouble if he is not careful,' muttered the manager darkly. I observed with assumed innocence that no man was safe from trouble in this world.

"The current was more rapid now, the steamer seemed at her last gasp, the stern-wheel flopped languidly, and I caught myself listening on tiptoe for the next beat of the float, for in sober truth I expected the wretched thing to give up every moment. It was like watching the last flickers of a life. But still we crawled. Sometimes I would pick out a tree a little way ahead to measure our progress towards Kurtz by, but I lost it invariably before we got abreast. To keep the eyes so long on one thing was too much for human patience. The manager displayed a beautiful resignation. I fretted and fumed and took to arguing with myself whether or no I would talk openly with Kurtz; but before I could come to any conclusion it occurred to me that my speech or my silence, indeed any action of mine, would be a mere futility. What did it matter what any one knew or ignored? What did it matter who was manager? One gets sometimes such a flash of insight. The essentials of this affair lay deep under the surface, beyond my reach, and beyond my power of meddling.

"Towards the evening of the second day we judged ourselves about eight miles from Kurtz's station. I wanted to push on; but the manager looked grave, and told me the navigation up there was so dangerous that it would be advisable, the sun being very low already, to wait where we were till next morning. Moreover, he pointed out that if the warning to approach cautiously were to be followed, we must approach in daylight—not at dusk, or in the dark. This was sensible enough. Eight miles meant nearly three hours' steaming for us, and I could also see suspicious ripples at the upper end of the reach. Nevertheless, I was annoyed beyond expression at the delay, and most unreasonably too, since one night more could not matter much after so many months. As we had plenty of wood, and caution was the word, I brought up in the middle of the stream. The reach was narrow, straight, with high sides like a railway cutting. The dusk came gliding into it long before the sun had set. The current ran smooth and swift, but a dumb immobility sat on the banks. The living trees, lashed together by the creepers and every living bush of the undergrowth, might have been changed into stone, even to the slenderest twig, to the lightest leaf. It was not sleep—it seemed unnatural, like a state of trance. Not the faintest sound of any kind could be heard. You looked on amazed, and began to suspect yourself of being deaf—then the night came suddenly, and struck you blind as well. About three in the morning some large fish leaped, and the loud splash made me jump as though a gun had been fired. When the sun rose there was a white fog, very warm and clammy, and more blinding than the night. It did not shift or drive; it was just there, standing all round you like something solid. At eight or nine, perhaps, it lifted as a shutter lifts. We had a glimpse of the towering multitude of trees, of the immense matted jungle, with the blazing little ball of the sun hanging over it—all perfectly still—and then the white shutter came down again, smoothly, as if sliding in greased grooves. I ordered the chain, which we had begun to heave in, to be paid out again. Before it stopped running with a muffled rattle, a cry, a very loud cry, as of infinite desolation, soared slowly in the opaque air. It ceased. A complaining clamour, modulated in savage discords, filled our ears. The sheer unexpectedness of it made my hair stir under my cap. I don't know how it struck the others: to me it seemed as though the mist itself had screamed, so suddenly, and apparently from all sides at once, did this tumultuous and mournful uproar arise. It culminated in a hurried outbreak of almost intolerably excessive shrieking, which stopped short, leaving us stiffened in a variety of silly attitudes, and obstinately listening to the nearly as appalling and excessive silence. 'Good God! What is the meaning—?' stammered at my elbow one of the pilgrims,—a little fat man, with sandy hair and red whiskers, who wore side-spring boots, and pink pyjamas tucked into his socks. Two others remained open-mouthed a whole minute, then dashed into the little cabin, to rush out incontinently and stand darting scared glances, with Winchesters at 'ready' in their hands. What we could see was just the steamer we were on, her outlines blurred as though she had been on the point of dissolving, and a misty strip of water, perhaps two feet broad, around her—and that was all. The rest of the world was nowhere, as far as our eyes and ears were concerned. Just nowhere. Gone, disappeared; swept off without leaving a whisper or a shadow behind.

"I went forward, and ordered the chain to be hauled in short, so as to be ready to trip the anchor and move the steamboat at once if necessary. 'Will they attack?' whispered an awed voice. 'We will all be butchered in this fog,' murmured another. The faces twitched with the strain, the hands trembled slightly, the eyes forgot to wink. It was very curious to see the contrast of expressions of the white men and of the black fellows of our crew, who were as much strangers to that part of the river as we, though their homes were only eight hundred miles away. The whites, of course greatly discomposed, had besides a curious look of being painfully shocked by such an outrageous row. The others had an alert, naturally interested expression; but their faces were essentially quiet, even those of the one or two who grinned as they hauled at the chain. Several exchanged short, grunting phrases, which seemed to settle the matter to their satisfaction. Their headman, a young, broad-chested black, severely draped in dark-blue fringed cloths, with fierce nostrils and his hair all done up artfully in oily ringlets, stood near me. 'Aha!' I said, just for good fellowship's sake. 'Catch 'im,' he snapped, with a bloodshot widening of his eyes and a flash of sharp teeth— 'catch 'im. Give 'im to us.' 'To you, eh?' I asked; 'what would you do with them?' 'Eat 'im!' he said, curtly, and, leaning his elbow on the rail, looked out into the fog in a dignified and profoundly pensive attitude. I would no doubt have been properly horrified, had it not occurred to me that he and his chaps must be very hungry: that they must have been growing increasingly hungry for at least this month past. They had been engaged for six months (I don't think a single one of them had any clear idea of time, as we at the end of countless ages have. They still belonged to the beginnings of time—had no inherited experience to teach them, as it were), and of course, as long as there was a piece of paper written over in accordance with some farcical law or other made down the river, it didn't enter anybody's head to trouble how they would live. Certainly they had brought with them some rotten hippo-meat, which couldn't have lasted very long, anyway, even if the pilgrims hadn't, in the midst of a shocking hullabaloo, thrown a considerable quantity of it overboard. It looked like a high-handed proceeding; but it was really a case of legitimate self-defence. You can't breathe dead hippo waking, sleeping, and eating, and at the same time keep your precarious grip on existence. Besides that, they had given them every week three pieces of brass wire, each about nine inches long; and the theory was they were to buy their provisions with that currency in river-side villages. You can see how *that* worked. There were either no villages, or the people were hostile, or the director, who like the rest of us fed out of tins, with an occasional old he-goat thrown in, didn't want to stop the steamer for some more or less recondite reason. So, unless they swallowed the wire itself, or made loops of it to snare the fishes with, I don't see what good their extravagant salary could be to them. I must say it was paid with a regularity worthy of a large and honourable trading company. For the rest, the only thing to eat—though it didn't look eatable in the least—I saw in their possession was a few lumps of some stuff like half-cooked dough, of a dirty lavender colour, they kept wrapped in leaves, and now and then swallowed a piece of, but so small that it seemed done more for the looks of the thing than for any serious purpose of sustenance. Why in the name of all the gnawing devils of hunger they didn't go for us—they were thirty to five—and have a good tuck-in for once, amazes me now when I think of it. They were big powerful men, with not much capacity to weigh the consequences, with courage, with strength, even yet, though their skins were no longer glossy and their muscles no longer hard. And I saw that something restraining, one of those human secrets that baffle probability, had come into play there. I looked at them with a swift quickening of interest—not because it occurred to me I might be eaten by them before very long, though I own to you that just then I perceived—in a new light, as it were—how unwholesome the pilgrims looked, and I hoped, yes, I positively hoped, that my aspect was not so—what shall I say?—so—unappetising: a touch of fantastic vanity which fitted well with the dream-sensation that pervaded all my days at that time. Perhaps I had a little fever too. One can't live with one's finger everlastingly on one's pulse. I had often 'a little fever,' or a little touch of other things—the playful paw-strokes of the wilderness, the preliminary trifling before the more serious onslaught which came in due course. Yes; I looked at them as you would on any human being, with a curiosity of their impulses, motives, capacities, weaknesses, when brought to the test of an inexorable physical necessity. Restraint! What possible restraint? Was it superstition, disgust, patience, fear—or some kind of primitive honour? No fear can stand up to hunger, no patience can wear it out, disgust simply does not exist where hunger is; and as to superstition, beliefs, and what you may call principles, they are less than chaff in a breeze. Don't you know the devilry of lingering starvation, its exasperating torment, its black thoughts, its sombre and brooding ferocity? Well, I do. It takes a man all his inborn strength to fight hunger properly. It's really easier to face bereavement, dishonour, and the perdition of one's soul—than this kind of prolonged hunger. Sad, but true. And these chaps too had no earthly reason for any kind of scruple. Restraint! I would just as soon have expected restraint from a hyena prowling amongst the corpses of a battlefield. But there was the fact facing me—the fact dazzling, to be seen, like the foam on the depths of the sea, like a ripple on an unfathomable enigma, a mystery greater—when I thought of it—than the curious, inexplicable note of desperate grief in this savage clamour that had swept by us on the river-bank, behind the blind whiteness of the fog.

"Two pilgrims were quarrelling in hurried whispers as to which bank. 'Left.' 'No, no; how can you? Right, right, of course.' 'It is very serious,' said the manager's voice behind me; 'I would be desolated if anything should happen to Mr Kurtz before we came up.' I looked at him, and had not the slightest doubt he was sincere. He was just the kind of man who would wish to preserve appearances. That was his restraint. But when he muttered something about going on at once, I did not even take the trouble to answer him. I knew, and he knew, that it was impossible. Were we to let go our hold of the bottom, we would be absolutely in the air—in space. We wouldn't be able to tell where we were going to—whether up or down stream, or across—till we fetched against one bank or the other,—and then we wouldn't know at first which it was. Of course I made no move. I had no mind for a smash-up. You couldn't imagine a more deadly place for a shipwreck. Whether drowned at once or not, we were sure to perish speedily in one way or another. 'I authorise you to take all the risks,' he said, after a short silence. 'I refuse to take any,' I said shortly; which was just the answer he expected, though its tone might have surprised him. 'Well, I must defer to your judgment. You are captain,' he said, with marked civility. I turned my shoulder to him in sign of my appreciation, and looked into the fog. How long would it last? It was the most hopeless look-out. The approach to this Kurtz grubbing for ivory in the wretched bush was beset by as many dangers as though he had been an enchanted princess sleeping in a fabulous castle. 'Will they attack, do you think?' asked the manager, in a confidential tone.

"I did not think they would attack, for several obvious reasons. The thick fog was one. If they left the bank in their canoes they would get lost in it, as we would be if we attempted to move. Still, I had also judged the jungle of both banks quite impenetrable—and yet eyes were in it, eyes that had seen us. The river-side bushes were certainly very thick; but the undergrowth behind was evidently penetrable. However, during the short lift I had seen no canoes anywhere in the reach—certainly not abreast of the steamer. But what made the idea of attack inconceivable to me was the nature of the noise—of the cries we had heard. They had not the fierce character boding of immediate hostile intention. Unexpected, wild, and violent as they had been, they had given me an irresistible impression of sorrow. The glimpse of the steamboat had for some reason filled those savages with unrestrained grief. The danger, if any, I expounded, was from our proximity to a great human passion let loose. Even extreme grief may ultimately vent itself in violence—but more generally takes the form of apathy. . . .

"You should have seen the pilgrims stare! They had no heart to grin, or even to revile me; but I believe they thought me gone mad—with fright, maybe. I delivered a regular lecture. My dear boys, it was no good bothering. Keep a look-out? Well, you may guess I watched the fog for the signs of lifting as a cat watches a mouse; but for anything else our eyes were of no more use to us than if we had been buried miles deep in a heap of cotton-wool. It felt like it too—choking, warm, stifling. Besides, all I said, though it sounded extravagant, was absolutely true to fact. What we afterwards alluded to as an attack was really an attempt at repulse. The action was very far from being aggressive—it was not even defensive, in the usual sense: it was undertaken under the stress of desperation, and in its essence was purely protective.

"It developed itself, I should say, two hours after the fog lifted, and its commencement was at a spot, roughly speaking, about a mile and a half below Kurtz's station. We had just floundered and flopped round a bend, when I saw an islet, a mere grassy hummock of bright green, in the middle of the stream. It was the only thing of the kind; but as we opened the reach more, I perceived it was the head of a long sandbank, or rather of a chain of shallow patches stretching down the middle of the river. They were discoloured, just awash, and the whole lot was seen just under the water, exactly as a man's backbone is seen running down the middle of his back under the skin. Now, as far as I did see, I could go to the right or to the left of this. I didn't know either channel, of course. The banks looked pretty well alike, the depth appeared the same; but as I had been informed the station was on the west side, I naturally headed for the western passage.

"No sooner had we fairly entered it than I became aware it was much narrower than I had supposed. To the left of us there was the long uninterrupted shoal, and to the right a high, steep bank heavily overgrown with bushes. Above the bush the trees stood in serried ranks. The twigs overhung the current thickly, and from distance to distance a large limb of some tree projected rigidly over the stream. It was then well on in the afternoon, the face of the forest was gloomy, and a broad strip of shadow had already fallen on the water. In this shadow we steamed up—very slowly, as you may imagine. I sheered her well inshore—the water being deepest near the bank, as the sounding-pole informed me.

"One of my hungry and forbearing friends was sounding in the bows just below me. This steamboat was exactly like a decked scow.[3] On the deck there were two little teak-wood houses, with doors and windows. The boiler was in the fore-end, and the

3. A flat-bottomed boat.

machinery right astern. Over the whole there was a light roof, supported on stan-
chions. The funnel projected through that roof, and in front of the funnel a small cabin
built of light planks served for a pilot-house. It contained a couch, two camp-stools, a
loaded Martini-Henry[4] leaning in one corner, a tiny table, and the steering-wheel. It
had a wide door in front and a broad shutter at each side. All these were always
thrown open, of course. I spent my days perched up there on the extreme fore-end of
that roof, before the door. At night I slept, or tried to, on the couch. An athletic black
belonging to some coast tribe, and educated by my poor predecessor, was the helmsman. He sported a pair of brass earrings, wore a blue cloth wrapper from the waist to
the ankles, and thought all the world of himself. He was the most unstable kind of
fool I had ever seen. He steered with no end of a swagger while you were by; but if he
lost sight of you, he became instantly the prey of an abject funk, and would let that
cripple of a steamboat get the upper hand of him in a minute.

"I was looking down at the sounding-pole, and feeling much annoyed to see at
each try a little more of it stick out of that river, when I saw my poleman give up the
business suddenly, and stretch himself flat on the deck, without even taking the trouble to haul his pole in. He kept hold on it though, and it trailed in the water. At the
same time the fireman, whom I could also see below me, sat down abruptly before his
furnace and ducked his head. I was amazed. Then I had to look at the river mighty
quick, because there was a snag in the fairway. Sticks, little sticks, were flying
about—thick: they were whizzing before my nose, dropping below me, striking behind me against my pilot-house. All this time the river, the shore, the woods, were
very quiet—perfectly quiet. I could only hear the heavy splashing thump of the stern-
wheel and the patter of these things. We cleared the snag clumsily. Arrows, by Jove!
We were being shot at! I stepped in quickly to close the shutter on the landside. That
fool-helmsman, his hands on the spokes, was lifting his knees high, stamping his feet,
champing his mouth, like a reined-in horse. Confound him! And we were staggering
within ten feet of the bank. I had to lean right out to swing the heavy shutter, and I
saw a face amongst the leaves on the level with my own, looking at me very fierce
and steady; and then suddenly, as though a veil had been removed from my eyes, I
made out, deep in the tangled gloom, naked breasts, arms, legs, glaring eyes,—the
bush was swarming with human limbs in movement, glistening, of bronze colour. The
twigs shook, swayed, and rustled, the arrows flew out of them, and then the shutter
came to. 'Steer her straight,' I said to the helmsman. He held his head rigid, face forward; but his eyes rolled, he kept on lifting and setting down his feet gently, his
mouth foamed a little. 'Keep quiet!' I said in a fury. I might just as well have ordered
a tree not to sway in the wind. I darted out. Below me there was a great scuffle of feet
on the iron deck; confused exclamations; a voice screamed, 'Can you turn back?' I
caught sight of a V-shaped ripple on the water ahead. What? Another snag! A fusillade burst out under my feet. The pilgrims had opened with their Winchesters, and
were simply squirting lead into that bush. A deuce of a lot of smoke came up and
drove slowly forward. I swore at it. Now I couldn't see the ripple or the snag either. I
stood in the doorway, peering, and the arrows came in swarms. They might have been
poisoned, but they looked as though they wouldn't kill a cat. The bush began to howl.
Our wood-cutters raised a warlike whoop; the report of a rifle just at my back deaf-
ened me. I glanced over my shoulder, and the pilot-house was yet full of noise and

4. A rifle.

smoke when I made a dash at the wheel. The fool-nigger had dropped everything, to throw the shutter open and let off that Martini-Henry. He stood before the wide opening, glaring, and I yelled at him to come back, while I straightened the sudden twist out of that steamboat. There was no room to turn even if I had wanted to, the snag was somewhere very near ahead in that confounded smoke, there was no time to lose, so I just crowded her into the bank—right into the bank, where I knew the water was deep.

"We tore slowly along the overhanging bushes in a whirl of broken twigs and flying leaves. The fusillade below stopped short, as I had foreseen it would when the squirts got empty. I threw my head back to a glinting whizz that traversed the pilot-house, in at one shutter-hole and out at the other. Looking past that mad helmsman, who was shaking the empty rifle and yelling at the shore, I saw vague forms of men running bent double, leaping, gliding, distinct, incomplete, evanescent. Something big appeared in the air before the shutter, the rifle went overboard, and the man stepped back swiftly, looked at me over his shoulder in an extraordinary, profound, familiar manner, and fell upon my feet. The side of his head hit the wheel twice, and the end of what appeared a long cane clattered round and knocked over a little camp-stool. It looked as though after wrenching that thing from somebody ashore he had lost his balance in the effort. The thin smoke had blown away, we were clear of the snag, and looking ahead I could see that in another hundred yards or so I would be free to sheer off, away from the bank; but my feet felt so very warm and wet that I had to look down. The man had rolled on his back and stared straight up at me; both his hands clutched that cane. It was the shaft of a spear that, either thrown or lunged through the opening, had caught him in the side just below the ribs; the blade had gone in out of sight, after making a frightful gash; my shoes were full; a pool of blood lay very still, gleaming dark-red under the wheel; his eyes shone with an amazing lustre. The fusillade burst out again. He looked at me anxiously, gripping the spear like something precious, with an air of being afraid I would try to take it away from him. I had to make an effort to free my eyes from his gaze and attend to the steering. With one hand I felt above my head for the line of the steam-whistle, and jerked out screech after screech hurriedly. The tumult of angry and warlike yells was checked instantly, and then from the depths of the woods went out such a tremulous and prolonged wail of mournful fear and utter despair as may be imagined to follow the flight of the last hope from the earth. There was a great commotion in the bush; the shower of arrows stopped, a few dropping shots rang out sharply—then silence, in which the languid beat of the stern-wheel came plainly to my ears. I put the helm hard astarboard at the moment when the pilgrim in pink pyjamas, very hot and agitated, appeared in the doorway. 'The manager sends me—' he began in an official tone, and stopped short. 'Good God!' he said, glaring at the wounded man.

"We two whites stood over him, and his lustrous and inquiring glance enveloped us both. I declare it looked as though he would presently put to us some question in an understandable language; but he died without uttering a sound, without moving a limb, without twitching a muscle. Only in the very last moment, as though in response to some sign we could not see, to some whisper we could not hear, he frowned heavily, and that frown gave to his black death-mask an inconceivably sombre, brooding, and menacing expression. The lustre of inquiring glance faded swiftly into vacant glassiness. 'Can you steer?' I asked the agent eagerly. He looked very dubious; but I made a grab at his arm, and he understood at once I meant him to steer whether or no. To tell you the truth, I was morbidly anxious to change my shoes and socks. 'He is dead,' murmured the fellow, immensely impressed. 'No doubt about it,' said I, tugging like mad at the shoelaces. 'And, by the way, I suppose Mr Kurtz is dead as well by this time.'

"For the moment that was the dominant thought. There was a sense of extreme disappointment, as though I had found out I had been striving after something altogether without a substance. I couldn't have been more disgusted if I had travelled all this way for the sole purpose of talking with Mr Kurtz. Talking with . . . I flung one shoe overboard, and became aware that that was exactly what I had been looking forward to—a talk with Kurtz. I made the strange discovery that I had never imagined him as doing, you know, but as discoursing. I didn't say to myself, 'Now I will never see him,' or 'Now I will never shake him by the hand,' but, 'Now I will never hear him.' The man presented himself as a voice. Not of course that I did not connect him with some sort of action. Hadn't I been told in all the tones of jealousy and admiration that he had collected, bartered, swindled, or stolen more ivory than all the other agents together. That was not the point. The point was in his being a gifted creature, and that of all his gifts the one that stood out pre-eminently, that carried with it a sense of real presence, was his ability to talk, his words—the gift of expression, the bewildering, the illuminating, the most exalted and the most contemptible, the pulsating stream of light, or the deceitful flow from the heart of an impenetrable darkness.

"The other shoe went flying unto the devil-god of that river. I thought, By Jove! it's all over. We are too late; he has vanished—the gift has vanished, by means of some spear, arrow, or club. I will never hear that chap speak after all,—and my sorrow had a startling extravagance of emotion, even such as I had noticed in the howling sorrow of these savages in the bush. I couldn't have felt more of lonely desolation somehow, had I been robbed of a belief or had missed my destiny in life. . . . Why do you sigh in this beastly way, somebody? Absurd? Well, absurd. Good Lord! mustn't a man ever—Here, give me some tobacco." . . .

There was a pause of profound stillness, then a match flared, and Marlow's lean face appeared, worn, hollow, with downward folds and dropped eyelids, with an aspect of concentrated attention; and as he took vigorous draws at his pipe, it seemed to retreat and advance out of the night in the regular flicker of the tiny flame. The match went out.

"Absurd!" he cried. "This is the worst of trying to tell . . . Here you all are, each moored with two good addresses, like a hulk with two anchors, a butcher round one corner, a policeman round another, excellent appetites, and temperature normal—you hear—normal from year's end to year's end. And you say, Absurd! Absurd be—exploded! Absurd! My dear boys, what can you expect from a man who out of sheer nervousness had just flung overboard a pair of new shoes? Now I think of it, it is amazing I did not shed tears. I am, upon the whole, proud of my fortitude. I was cut to the quick at the idea of having lost the inestimable privilege of listening to the gifted Kurtz. Of course I was wrong. The privilege was waiting for me. Oh yes, I heard more than enough. And I was right, too. A voice. He was very little more than a voice. And I heard—him—it—this voice—other voices—all of them were so little more than voices—and the memory of that time itself lingers around me, impalpable, like a dying vibration of one immense jabber, silly, atrocious, sordid, savage, or simply mean, without any kind of sense. Voices, voices—even the girl herself—now—"

He was silent for a long time.

"I laid the ghost of his gifts at last with a lie," he began suddenly. "Girl! What? Did I mention a girl? Oh, she is out of it—completely. They—the women I mean—are out of it—should be out of it. We must help them to stay in that beautiful world of their own, lest ours gets worse. Oh, she had to be out of it. You should have heard the disinterred body of Mr Kurtz saying, 'My Intended.' You would have perceived directly then how completely she was out of it. And the lofty frontal bone of Mr Kurtz!

They say the hair goes on growing sometimes, but this—ah—specimen was impressively bald. The wilderness had patted him on the head, and, behold, it was like a ball—an ivory ball; it had caressed him, and—lo!—he had withered; it had taken him, loved him, embraced him, got into his veins, consumed his flesh, and sealed his soul to its own by the inconceivable ceremonies of some devilish initiation. He was its spoiled and pampered favourite. Ivory? I should think so. Heaps of it, stacks of it. The old mud shanty was bursting with it. You would think there was not a single tusk left either above or below the ground in the whole country. 'Mostly fossil,' the manager had remarked disparagingly. It was no more fossil than I am; but they call it fossil when it is dug up. It appears these niggers do bury the tusks sometimes—but evidently they couldn't bury this parcel deep enough to save the gifted Mr Kurtz from his fate. We filled the steamboat with it, and had to pile a lot on the deck. Thus he could see and enjoy as long as he could see, because the appreciation of this favour had remained with him to the last. You should have heard him say, 'My ivory.' Oh yes, I heard him. 'My Intended, my ivory, my station, my river, my—' everything belonged to him. It made me hold my breath in expectation of hearing the wilderness burst into a prodigious peal of laughter that would shake the fixed stars in their places. Everything belonged to him—but that was a trifle. The thing was to know what he belonged to, how many powers of darkness claimed him for their own. That was the reflection that made you creepy all over. It was impossible—it was not good for one either— trying to imagine. He had taken a high seat amongst the devils of the land—I mean literally. You can't understand. How could you?—with solid pavement under your feet, surrounded by kind neighbours ready to cheer you or to fall on you, stepping delicately between the butcher and the policeman, in the holy terror of scandal and gallows and lunatic asylums—how can you imagine what particular region of the first ages a man's untrammelled feet may take him into by the way of solitude—utter solitude without a policeman—by the way of silence—utter silence, where no warning voice of a kind neighbour can be heard whispering of public opinion? These little things make all the great difference. When they are gone you must fall back upon your own innate strength, upon your own capacity for faithfulness. Of course you may be too much of a fool to go wrong—too dull even to know you are being assaulted by the powers of darkness. I take it, no fool ever made a bargain for his soul with the devil: the fool is too much of a fool, or the devil too much of a devil—I don't know which. Or you may be such a thunderingly exalted creature as to be altogether deaf and blind to anything but heavenly sights and sounds. Then the earth for you is only a standing place—and whether to be like this is your loss or your gain I won't pretend to say. But most of us are neither one nor the other. The earth for us is a place to live in, where we must put up with sights, with sounds, with smells too, by Jove!— breathe dead hippo, so to speak, and not be contaminated. And there, don't you see? your strength comes in, the faith in your ability for the digging of unostentatious holes to bury the stuff in—your power of devotion, not to yourself, but to an obscure, backbreaking business. And that's difficult enough. Mind, I am not trying to excuse or even explain—I am trying to account to myself for—for—Mr Kurtz—for the shade of Mr Kurtz. This initiated wraith from the back of Nowhere honoured me with its amazing confidence before it vanished altogether. This was because it could speak English to me. The original Kurtz had been educated partly in England, and—as he was good enough to say himself—his sympathies were in the right place. His mother was half-English, his father was half-French. All Europe contributed to the making of Kurtz; and by-and-by I learned that, most appropriately, the International Society for the Suppression of Savage Customs had intrusted him with the making of a report, for its future guidance. And he had written it too. I've seen it. I've read it. It was eloquent, vibrating with eloquence, but too high-strung, I think. Seventeen pages of close writing he had found time for! But this must have been before his—let us say—nerves went wrong, and caused him to preside at certain midnight dances ending with unspeakable rites, which—as far as I reluctantly gathered from what I heard at various times—were offered up to him—do you understand?—to Mr Kurtz himself. But it was a beautiful piece of writing. The opening paragraph, however, in the light of later information, strikes me now as ominous. He began with the argument that we whites, from the point of development we had arrived at, 'must necessarily appear to them [savages] in the nature of supernatural beings—we approach them with the might as of a deity,' and so on, and so on. 'By the simple exercise of our will we can exert a power for good practically unbounded,' &c., &c. From that point he soared and took me with him. The peroration was magnificent, though difficult to remember, you know. It gave me the notion of an exotic Immensity ruled by an august Benevolence. It made me tingle with enthusiasm. This was the unbounded power of eloquence—of words—of burning noble words. There were no practical hints to interrupt the magic current of phrases, unless a kind of note at the foot of the last page, scrawled evidently much later, in an unsteady hand, may be regarded as the exposition of a method. It was very simple, and at the end of that moving appeal to every altruistic sentiment it blazed at you, luminous and terrifying, like a flash of lightning in a serene sky: 'Exterminate all the brutes!' The curious part was that he had apparently forgotten all about that valuable postscriptum, because, later on, when he in a sense came to himself, he repeatedly entreated me to take good care of 'my pamphlet' (he called it), as it was sure to have in the future a good influence upon his career. I had full information about all these things, and, besides, as it turned out, I was to have the care of his memory. I've done enough for it to give me the indisputable right to lay it, if I choose, for an everlasting rest in the dust-bin of progress, amongst all the sweepings and, figuratively speaking, all the dead cats of civilisation. But then, you see, I can't choose. He won't be forgotten. Whatever he was, he was not common. He had the power to charm or frighten rudimentary souls into an aggravated witch-dance in his honour; he could also fill the small souls of the pilgrims with bitter misgivings: he had one devoted friend at least, and he had conquered one soul in the world that was neither rudimentary nor tainted with self-seeking. No; I can't forget him, though I am not prepared to affirm the fellow was exactly worth the life we lost in getting to him. I missed my late helmsman awfully,—I missed him even while his body was still lying in the pilot-house. Perhaps you will think it passing strange this regret for a savage who was no more account than a grain of sand in a black Sahara. Well, don't you see, he had done something, he had steered; for months I had him at my back—a help—an instrument. It was a kind of partnership. He steered for me—I had to look after him, I worried about his deficiencies, and thus a subtle bond had been created, of which I only became aware when it was suddenly broken. And the intimate profundity of that look he gave me when he received his hurt remains to this day in my memory—like a claim of distant kinship affirmed in a supreme moment.

"Poor fool! If he had only left that shutter alone. He had no restraint, no restraint—just like Kurtz—a tree swayed by the wind. As soon as I had put on a dry pair of slippers, I dragged him out, after first jerking the spear out of his side, which operation I confess I performed with my eyes shut tight. His heels leaped together over the little doorstep; his shoulders were pressed to my breast; I hugged him from behind desperately. Oh! he was heavy, heavy; heavier than any man on earth, I should imagine. Then without more ado I tipped him overboard. The current snatched him as though he had been a wisp of grass, and I saw the body roll over twice before I lost sight of it for ever. All the pilgrims and the manager were then congregated on the awning-deck about the pilot-house, chattering at each other like a flock of excited magpies, and there was a scandalised murmur at my heartless promptitude. What they wanted to keep that body hanging about for I can't guess. Embalm it, maybe. But I had also heard another, and a very ominous, murmur on the deck below. My friends the woodcutters were likewise scandalised, and with a better show of reason—though I admit that the reason itself was quite inadmissible. Oh, quite! I had made up my mind that if my late helmsman was to be eaten, the fishes alone should have him. He had been a very second-rate helmsman while alive, but now he was dead he might have become a first-class temptation, and possibly cause some startling trouble. Besides, I was anxious to take the wheel, the man in pink pyjamas showing himself a hopeless duffer at the business.

"This I did directly the simple funeral was over. We were going half-speed, keeping right in the middle of the stream, and I listened to the talk about me. They had given up Kurtz, they had given up the station; Kurtz was dead, and the station had been burnt—and so on—and so on. The red-haired pilgrim was beside himself with the thought that at least this poor Kurtz had been properly revenged. 'Say! We must have made a glorious slaughter of them in the bush. Eh? What do you think? Say?' He positively danced, the bloodthirsty little gingery beggar. And he had nearly fainted when he saw the wounded man! I could not help saying, 'You made a glorious lot of smoke, anyhow.' I had seen, from the way the tops of the bushes rustled and flew, that almost all the shots had gone too high. You can't hit anything unless you take aim and fire from the shoulder; but these chaps fired from the hip with their eyes shut. The retreat, I maintained—and I was right—was caused by the screeching of the steam-whistle. Upon this they forgot Kurtz, and began to howl at me with indignant protests.

"The manager stood by the wheel murmuring confidentially about the necessity of getting well away down the river before dark at all events, when I saw in the distance a clearing on the river-side and the outlines of some sort of building. 'What's this?' I asked. He clapped his hands in wonder. 'The station!' he cried. I edged in at once, still going half-speed.

"Through my glasses I saw the slope of a hill interspersed with rare trees and perfectly free from undergrowth. A long decaying building on the summit was half buried in the high grass; the large holes in the peaked roof gaped black from afar; the jungle and the woods made a background. There was no enclosure or fence of any kind; but there had been one apparently, for near the house half-a-dozen slim posts remained in a row, roughly trimmed, and with their upper ends ornamented with round carved balls. The rails, or whatever there had been between, had disappeared. Of course the forest surrounded all that. The river-bank was clear, and on the waterside I saw a white man under a hat like a cart-wheel beckoning persistently with his whole arm. Examining the edge of the forest above and below, I was almost certain I could see movements—human forms gliding here and there. I steamed past prudently, then stopped the engines and let her drift down. The man on the shore began to shout, urging us to land. 'We have been attacked,' screamed the manager. 'I know—I know. It's all right,' yelled back the other, as cheerful as you please. 'Come along. It's all right. I am glad.'

"His aspect reminded me of something I had seen—something funny I had seen somewhere. As I manoeuvred to get alongside, I was asking myself, 'What does this fellow look like?' Suddenly I got it. He looked like a harlequin. His clothes had been made of some stuff that was brown holland[5] probably, but it was covered with patches all over, with bright patches, blue, red, and yellow,—patches on the back, patches on front, patches on elbows, on knees; coloured binding round his jacket, scarlet edging at the bottom of his trousers; and the sunshine made him look extremely gay and wonderfully neat withal, because you could see how beautifully all this patching had been done. A beardless, boyish face, very fair, no features to speak of, nose peeling, little blue eyes, smiles and frowns chasing each other over that open countenance like sunshine and shadow on a wind-swept plain. 'Look out, captain!' he cried; 'there's a snag lodged in here last night.' What! Another snag? I confess I swore shamefully. I had nearly holed my cripple, to finish off that charming trip. The harlequin on the bank turned his little pug nose up to me. 'You English?' he asked, all smiles. 'Are you?' I shouted from the wheel. The smiles vanished, and he shook his head as if sorry for my disappointment. Then he brightened up. 'Never mind!' he cried encouragingly. 'Are we in time?' I asked. 'He is up there,' he replied, with a toss of the head up the hill, and becoming gloomy all of a sudden. His face was like the autumn sky, overcast one moment and bright the next.

"When the manager, escorted by the pilgrims, all of them armed to the teeth, had gone to the house, this chap came on board. 'I say, I don't like this. These natives are in the bush,' I said. He assured me earnestly it was all right. 'They are simple people,' he added; 'well, I am glad you came. It took me all my time to keep them off.' 'But you said it was all right,' I cried. 'Oh, they meant no harm,' he said; and as I stared he corrected himself, 'Not exactly.' Then vivaciously, 'My faith, your pilot-house wants a clean-up!' In the next breath he advised me to keep enough steam on the boiler to blow the whistle in case of any trouble. 'One good screech will do more for you than all your rifles. They are simple people,' he repeated. He rattled away at such a rate he quite overwhelmed me. He seemed to be trying to make up for lots of silence, and actually hinted, laughing, that such was the case. 'Don't you talk with Mr Kurtz?' I said. 'You don't talk with that man—you listen to him,' he exclaimed with severe exaltation. 'But now—' He waved his arm, and in the twinkling of an eye was in the uttermost depths of despondency. In a moment he came up again with a jump, possessed himself of both my hands, shook them continuously, while he gabbled: 'Brother sailor . . . honour . . . pleasure . . . delight . . . introduce myself . . . Russian . . . son of an arch-priest . . . Government of Tambov[6] . . . What? Tobacco! English tobacco; the excellent English tobacco! Now, that's brotherly. Smoke? Where's a sailor that does not smoke?'

"The pipe soothed him, and gradually I made out he had run away from school, had gone to sea in a Russian ship; ran away again; served some time in English ships; was now reconciled with the arch-priest. He made a point of that. 'But when one is young one must see things, gather experience, ideas; enlarge the mind.' 'Here!' I interrupted. 'You can never tell! Here I have met Mr Kurtz,' he said, youthfully solemn and reproachful. I held my tongue after that. It appears he had persuaded a Dutch trading-house on the coast to fit him out with stores and goods, and had started for the interior with a light heart, and no more idea of what would happen to him than a baby. He had been wandering about that river for nearly two years alone, cut off from everybody and everything. 'I am not so young as I look. I am twenty-five,' he said.

---

5. A smooth linen fabric.   6. A province of Western Russia.

'At first old Van Shuyten would tell me to go to the devil,' he narrated with keen enjoyment; 'but I stuck to him, and talked and talked, till at last he got afraid I would talk the hind-leg off his favorite dog, so he gave me some cheap things and a few guns, and told me he hoped he would never see my face again. Good old Dutchman, Van Shuyten. I sent him one small lot of ivory a year ago, so that he can't call me a little thief when I get back. I hope he got it. And for the rest, I don't care. I had some wood stacked for you. That was my old house. Did you see?'

"I gave him Towson's book. He made as though he would kiss me, but restrained himself. 'The only book I had left, and I thought I had lost it,' he said, looking at it ecstatically. 'So many accidents happen to a man going about alone, you know. Canoes get upset sometimes—and sometimes you've got to clear out so quick when the people get angry.' He thumbed the pages. 'You made notes in Russian?' I asked. He nodded. 'I thought they were written in cipher,' I said. He laughed, then became serious. 'I had lots of trouble to keep these people off,' he said. 'Did they want to kill you?' I asked. 'Oh no!' he cried, and checked himself. 'Why did they attack us?' I pursued. He hesitated, then said shamefacedly, 'They don't want him to go.' 'Don't they?' I said, curiously. He nodded a nod full of mystery and wisdom. 'I tell you,' he cried, 'this man has enlarged my mind.' He opened his arms wide, staring at me with his little blue eyes that were perfectly round."

3

"I looked at him, lost in astonishment. There he was before me, in motley, as though he had absconded from a troupe of mimes, enthusiastic, fabulous. His very existence was improbable, inexplicable, and altogether bewildering. He was an insoluble problem. It was inconceivable how he had existed, how he had succeeded in getting so far, how he had managed to remain—why he did not instantly disappear. 'I went a little farther,' he said, 'then still a little farther—till I had gone so far that I don't know how I'll ever get back. Never mind. Plenty time. I can manage. You take Kurtz away quick—quick—I tell you.' The glamour of youth enveloped his particoloured rags, his destitution, his loneliness, the essential desolation of his futile wanderings. For months—for years—his life hadn't been worth a day's purchase; and there he was gallantly, thoughtlessly alive, to all appearance indestructible solely by the virtue of his few years and of his unreflecting audacity. I was seduced into something like admiration—like envy. Glamour urged him on, glamour kept him unscathed. He surely wanted nothing from the wilderness but space to breathe in and to push on through. His need was to exist, and to move onwards at the greatest possible risk, and with a maximum of privation. If the absolutely pure, uncalculating, unpractical spirit of adventure had ever ruled a human being, it ruled this be-patched youth. I almost envied him the possession of this modest and clear flame. It seemed to have consumed all thought of self so completely, that, even while he was talking to you, you forgot that it was he—the man before your eyes—who had gone through these things. I did not envy him his devotion to Kurtz, though. He had not meditated over it. It came to him, and he accepted it with a sort of eager fatalism. I must say that to me it appeared about the most dangerous thing in every way he had come upon so far.

"They had come together unavoidably, like two ships becalmed near each other, and lay rubbing sides at last. I suppose Kurtz wanted an audience, because on a certain occasion, when encamped in the forest, they had talked all night, or more probably Kurtz had talked. 'We talked of everything,' he said, quite transported at the recollection. 'I forgot there was such a thing as sleep. The night did not seem to last an hour. Everything! Everything! . . . Of love too.' 'Ah, he talked to you of love!' I said, much amused. 'It isn't what you think,' he cried, almost passionately. 'It was in general. He made me see things—things.'

"He threw his arms up. We were on deck at the time, and the headman of my wood-cutters, lounging near by, turned upon him his heavy and glittering eyes. I looked around, and I don't know why, but I assure you that never, never before, did this land, this river, this jungle, the very arch of this blazing sky, appear to me so hopeless and so dark, so impenetrable to human thought, so pitiless to human weakness. 'And, ever since, you have been with him, of course?' I said.

"On the contrary. It appears their intercourse had been very much broken by various causes. He had, as he informed me proudly, managed to nurse Kurtz through two illnesses (he alluded to it as you would to some risky feat), but as a rule Kurtz wandered alone, far in the depths of the forest. 'Very often coming to this station, I had to wait days and days before he would turn up,' he said. 'Ah, it was worth waiting for!— sometimes.' 'What was he doing? exploring or what?' I asked. 'Oh yes, of course'; he had discovered lots of villages, a lake too—he did not know exactly in what direction; it was dangerous to inquire too much—but mostly his expeditions had been for ivory. 'But he had no goods to trade with by that time,' I objected. 'There's a good lot of cartridges left even yet,' he answered, looking away. 'To speak plainly, he raided the country,' I said. He nodded. 'Not alone, surely!' He muttered something about the villages round that lake. 'Kurtz got the tribe to follow him, did he?' I suggested. He fidgeted a little. 'They adored him,' he said. The tone of these words was so extraordinary that I looked at him searchingly. It was curious to see his mingled eagerness and reluctance to speak of Kurtz. The man filled his life, occupied his thoughts, swayed his emotions. 'What can you expect?' he burst out; 'he came to them with thunder and lightning, you know—and they had never seen anything like it—and very terrible. He could be very terrible. You can't judge Mr Kurtz as you would an ordinary man. No, no, no! Now—just to give you an idea—I don't mind telling you, he wanted to shoot me too one day—but I don't judge him.' 'Shoot you!' I cried. 'What for?' 'Well, I had a small lot of ivory the chief of that village near my house gave me. You see I used to shoot game for them. Well, he wanted it, and wouldn't hear reason. He declared he would shoot me unless I gave him the ivory and then cleared out of the country, because he could do so, and had a fancy for it, and there was nothing on earth to prevent him killing whom he jolly well pleased. And it was true too. I gave him the ivory. What did I care! But I didn't clear out. No, no. I couldn't leave him. I had to be careful, of course, till we got friendly again for a time. He had his second illness then. Afterwards I had to keep out of the way; but I didn't mind. He was living for the most part in those villages on the lake. When he came down to the river, sometimes he would take to me, and sometimes it was better for me to be careful. This man suffered too much. He hated all this, and somehow he couldn't get away. When I had a chance I begged him to try and leave while there was time; I offered to go back with him. And he would say yes, and then he would remain; go off on another ivory hunt; disappear for weeks; forget himself amongst these people—forget himself—you know.' 'Why! he's mad,' I said. He protested indignantly. Mr Kurtz couldn't be mad. If I had heard him talk, only two days ago, I wouldn't dare hint at such a thing. . . . I had taken up my binoculars while we talked, and was looking at the shore, sweeping the limit of the forest at each side and at the back of the house. The consciousness of there being people in that bush, so silent, so quiet—as silent and quiet as the ruined house on the hill—made me uneasy. There was no sign on the face of nature of this amazing tale that was not so much told as suggested to me in desolate exclamations, completed by shrugs, in interrupted phrases, in hints ending in deep sighs. The woods were unmoved, like a mask—heavy, like the closed door of a prison—they looked with their air of hidden knowledge, of patient expectation, of unapproachable silence. The Russian was explaining to me that it was only lately that Mr Kurtz had come down to the river, bringing along with him all the fighting men of that lake tribe. He had been absent for several months—getting himself adored, I suppose—and had come down unexpectedly, with the intention to all appearance of making a raid either across the river or down stream. Evidently the appetite for more ivory had got the better of the—what shall I say?—less material aspirations. However, he had got much worse suddenly. 'I heard he was lying helpless, and so I came up—took my chance,' said the Russian. 'Oh, he is bad, very bad.' I directed my glass to the house. There were no signs of life, but there was the ruined roof, the long mud wall peeping above the grass, with three little square window-holes, no two of the same size; all this brought within reach of my hand, as it were. And then I made a brusque movement, and one of the remaining posts of that vanished fence leaped up in the field of my glass. You remember I told you I had been struck at the distance by certain attempts at ornamentation, rather remarkable in the ruinous aspect of the place. Now I had suddenly a nearer view, and its first result was to make me throw my head back as if before a blow. Then I went carefully from post to post with my glass, and I saw my mistake. These round knobs were not ornamental but symbolic; they were expressive and puzzling, striking and disturbing—food for thought and also for the vultures if there had been any looking down from the sky; but at all events for such ants as were industrious enough to ascend the pole. They would have been even more impressive, those heads on the stakes, if their faces had not been turned to the house. Only one, the first I had made out, was facing my way. I was not so shocked as you may think. The start back I had given was really nothing but a movement of surprise. I had expected to see a knob of wood there, you know. I returned deliberately to the first I had seen—and there it was, black, dried, sunken, with closed eyelids,—a head that seemed to sleep at the top of that pole, and, with the shrunken dry lips showing a narrow white line of the teeth, was smiling too, smiling continuously at some endless and jocose dream of that eternal slumber.

"I am not disclosing any trade secrets. In fact the manager said afterwards that Mr Kurtz's methods had ruined the district. I have no opinion on that point, but I want you clearly to understand that there was nothing exactly profitable in these heads being there. They only showed that Mr Kurtz lacked restraint in the gratification of his various lusts, that there was something wanting in him—some small matter which, when the pressing need arose, could not be found under his magnificent eloquence. Whether he knew of this deficiency himself I can't say. I think the knowledge came to him at last—only at the very last. But the wilderness had found him out early, and had taken on him a terrible vengeance for the fantastic invasion. I think it had whispered to him things about himself which he did not know, things of which he had no conception till he took counsel with this great solitude—and the whisper had proved irresistibly fascinating. It echoed loudly within him because he was hollow at the core. . . . I put down the glass, and the head that had appeared near enough to be spoken to seemed at once to have leaped away from me into inaccessible distance.

"The admirer of Mr Kurtz was a bit crestfallen. In a hurried, indistinct voice he began to assure me he had not dared to take these—say, symbols—down. He was not afraid of the natives; they would not stir till Mr Kurtz gave the word. His ascendancy was extraordinary. The camps of these people surrounded the place, and the chiefs came every day to see him. They would crawl . . . 'I don't want to know anything of the ceremonies used when approaching Mr Kurtz,' I shouted. Curious, this feeling that came over me that such details would be more intolerable than those heads drying on the stakes under Mr Kurtz's windows. After all, that was only a savage sight, while I seemed at one bound to have been transported into some lightless region of subtle horrors, where pure, uncomplicated savagery was a positive relief, being something that had a right to exist—obviously—in the sunshine. The young man looked at me with surprise. I suppose it did not occur to him Mr Kurtz was no idol of mine. He forgot I hadn't heard any of these splendid monologues on, what was it? on love, justice, conduct of life—or what not. If it had come to crawling before Mr Kurtz, he crawled as much as the veriest savage of them all. I had no idea of the conditions, he said: these heads were the heads of rebels. I shocked him excessively by laughing. Rebels! What would be the next definition I was to hear? There had been enemies, criminals, workers—and these were rebels. Those rebellious heads looked very subdued to me on their sticks. 'You don't know how such a life tries a man like Kurtz,' cried Kurtz's last disciple. 'Well, and you?' I said. 'I! I! I am a simple man. I have no great thoughts. I want nothing from anybody. How can you compare me to . . .?' His feelings were too much for speech, and suddenly he broke down. 'I don't understand,' he groaned. 'I've been doing my best to keep him alive, and that's enough. I had no hand in all this. I have no abilities. There hasn't been a drop of medicine or a mouthful of invalid food for months here. He was shamefully abandoned. A man like this, with such ideas. Shamefully! Shamefully! I—I—haven't slept for the last ten nights. . . .'

"His voice lost itself in the calm of the evening. The long shadows of the forest had slipped down-hill while we talked, had gone far beyond the ruined hovel, beyond the symbolic row of stakes. All this was in the gloom, while we down there were yet in the sunshine, and the stretch of the river abreast of the clearing glittered in a still and dazzling splendour, with a murky and overshadowed bend above and below. Not a living soul was seen on the shore. The bushes did not rustle.

"Suddenly round the corner of the house a group of men appeared, as though they had come up from the ground. They waded waist-deep in the grass, in a compact body, bearing an improvised stretcher in their midst. Instantly, in the emptiness of the landscape, a cry arose whose shrillness pierced the still air like a sharp arrow flying straight to the very heart of the land; and, as if by enchantment, streams of human beings—of naked human beings—with spears in their hands, with bows, with shields, with wild glances and savage movements, were poured into the clearing by the dark-faced and pensive forest. The bushes shook, the grass swayed for a time, and then everything stood still in attentive immobility.

"'Now, if he does not say the right thing to them we are all done for,' said the Russian at my elbow. The knot of men with the stretcher had stopped too, half-way to the steamer, as if petrified. I saw the man on the stretcher sit up, lank and with an uplifted arm, above the shoulders of the bearers. 'Let us hope that the man who can talk so well of love in general will find some particular reason to spare us this time,' I said. I resented bitterly the absurd danger of our situation, as if to be at the mercy of that atrocious phantom had been a dishonouring necessity. I could not hear a sound, but through my glasses I saw the thin arm extended commandingly, the lower jaw moving, the eyes of that apparition shining darkly far in its bony head that nodded with grotesque jerks. Kurtz—Kurtz—that means 'short' in German—don't it? Well, the name was as true as everything else in his life—and death. He looked at least seven feet long. His covering had fallen off, and his body emerged from it pitiful and appalling as from a winding-sheet. I could see the cage of his ribs all astir, the bones of his arm waving. It was as though an animated image of death carved out of old ivory had been shaking its hand with menaces at a motionless crowd of men made of dark and glittering bronze. I saw him open his mouth wide—it gave him a weirdly voracious aspect, as though he had wanted to swallow all the air, all the earth, all the men before him. A deep voice reached me faintly. He must have been shouting. He fell back suddenly. The stretcher shook as the bearers staggered forward again, and almost at the same time I noticed that the crowd of savages was vanishing without any perceptible movement of retreat, as if the forest that had ejected these beings so suddenly had drawn them in again as the breath is drawn in a long aspiration.

"Some of the pilgrims behind the stretcher carried his arms—two shot-guns, a heavy rifle, and a light revolver-carbine—the thunderbolts of that pitiful Jupiter. The manager bent over him murmuring as he walked beside his head. They laid him down in one of the little cabins—just a room for a bed-place and a camp-stool or two, you know. We had brought his belated correspondence, and a lot of torn envelopes and open letters littered his bed. His hand roamed feebly amongst these papers. I was struck by the fire of his eyes and the composed languor of his expression. It was not so much the exhaustion of disease. He did not seem in pain. This shadow looked satiated and calm, as though for the moment it had had its fill of all the emotions.

"He rustled one of the letters, and looking straight in my face said, 'I am glad.' Somebody had been writing to him about me. These special recommendations were turning up again. The volume of tone he emitted without effort, almost without the trouble of moving his lips, amazed me. A voice! a voice! It was grave, profound, vibrating, while the man did not seem capable of a whisper. However, he had enough strength in him—factitious no doubt—to very nearly make an end of us, as you shall hear directly.

"The manager appeared silently in the doorway; I stepped out at once and he drew the curtain after me. The Russian, eyed curiously by the pilgrims, was staring at the shore. I followed the direction of his glance.

"Dark human shapes could be made out in the distance, flitting indistinctly against the gloomy border of the forest, and near the river two bronze figures, leaning on tall spears, stood in the sunlight under fantastic head-dresses of spotted skins, warlike and still in statuesque repose. And from right to left along the lighted shore moved a wild and gorgeous apparition of a woman.

"She walked with measured steps, draped in striped and fringed cloths, treading the earth proudly, with a slight jingle and flash of barbarous ornaments. She carried her head high; her hair was done in the shape of a helmet; she had brass leggings to the knee, brass wire gauntlets to the elbow, a crimson spot on her tawny cheek, innumerable necklaces of glass beads on her neck; bizarre things, charms, gifts of witchmen, that hung about her, glittered and trembled at every step. She must have had the value of several elephant tusks upon her. She was savage and superb, wild-eyed and magnificent; there was something ominous and stately in her deliberate progress. And in the hush that had fallen suddenly upon the whole sorrowful land, the immense wilderness, the colossal body of the fecund and mysterious life seemed to look at her, pensive, as though it had been looking at the image of its own tenebrous and passionate soul.

"She came abreast of the steamer, stood still, and faced us. Her long shadow fell to the water's edge. Her face had a tragic and fierce aspect of wild sorrow and of dumb pain mingled with the fear of some struggling, half-shaped resolve. She stood looking at us without a stir, and like the wilderness itself, with an air of brooding over an inscrutable purpose. A whole minute passed, and then she made a step forward. There was a low jingle, a glint of yellow metal, a sway of fringed draperies, and she stopped as if her heart had failed her. The young fellow by my side growled. The pilgrims murmured at my back. She looked at us all as if her life had depended upon the unswerving steadiness of her glance. Suddenly she opened her bared arms and threw them up rigid above her head, as though in an uncontrollable desire to touch the sky, and at the same time the swift shadows darted out on the earth, swept around on the river, gathering the steamer in a shadowy embrace. A formidable silence hung over the scene.

"She turned away slowly, walked on, following the bank, and passed into the bushes to the left. Once only her eyes gleamed back at us in the dusk of the thickets before she disappeared.

"'If she had offered to come aboard I really think I would have tried to shoot her,' said the man of patches, nervously. 'I had been risking my life every day for the last fortnight to keep her out of the house. She got in one day and kicked up a row about those miserable rags I picked up in the storeroom to mend my clothes with. I wasn't decent. At least it must have been that, for she talked like a fury to Kurtz for an hour, pointing at me now and then. I don't understand the dialect of this tribe. Luckily for me, I fancy Kurtz felt too ill that day to care, or there would have been mischief. I don't understand. . . . No—it's too much for me. Ah, well, it's all over now.'

"At this moment I heard Kurtz's deep voice behind the curtain, 'Save me!—save the ivory, you mean. Don't tell me. Save *me*! Why, I've had to save you. You are interrupting my plans now. Sick! Sick! Not so sick as you would like to believe. Never mind. I'll carry my ideas out yet—I will return. I'll show you what can be done. You with your little peddling notions—you are interfering with me. I will return. I . . .'

"The manager came out. He did me the honour to take me under the arm and lead me aside. 'He is very low, very low,' he said. He considered it necessary to sigh, but neglected to be consistently sorrowful. 'We have done all we could for him—haven't we? But there is no disguising the fact, Mr Kurtz has done more harm than good to the Company. He did not see the time was not ripe for vigorous action. Cautiously, cautiously—that's my principle. We must be cautious yet. The district is closed to us for a time. Deplorable! Upon the whole, the trade will suffer. I don't deny there is a remarkable quantity of ivory—mostly fossil. We must save it, at all events—but look how precarious the position is—and why? Because the method is unsound.' 'Do you,' said I, looking at the shore, 'call it "unsound method"?' 'Without doubt,' he exclaimed, hotly. 'Don't you?' . . . 'No method at all,' I murmured after a while. 'Exactly,' he exulted. 'I anticipated this. Shows a complete want of judgment. It is my duty to point it out in the proper quarter.' 'Oh,' said I, 'that fellow—what's his name?—the brickmaker, will make a readable report for you.' He appeared confounded for a moment. It seemed to me I had never breathed an atmosphere so vile, and I turned mentally to Kurtz for relief—positively for relief. 'Nevertheless, I think Mr Kurtz is a remarkable man,' I said with emphasis. He started, dropped on me a cold heavy glance, said very quietly, 'He was,' and turned his back on me. My hour of favour was over; I found myself lumped along with Kurtz as a partisan of methods for which the time was not ripe: I was unsound! Ah! but it was something to have at least a choice of nightmares.

"I had turned to the wilderness really, not to Mr Kurtz, who, I was ready to admit, was as good as buried. And for a moment it seemed to me as if I also were buried in a vast grave full of unspeakable secrets. I felt an intolerable weight oppressing my breast, the smell of the damp earth, the unseen presence of victorious corruption, the darkness of an impenetrable night. . . . The Russian tapped me on the shoulder. I heard him mumbling and stammering something about 'brother seaman—couldn't conceal—knowledge of matters that would affect Mr Kurtz's reputation.' I waited. For him evidently Mr Kurtz was not in his grave; I suspect that for him Mr Kurtz was one of the immortals. 'Well!' said I at last, 'speak out. As it happens, I am Mr Kurtz's friend—in a way.'

"He stated with a good deal of formality that had we not been 'of the same profession,' he would have kept the matter to himself without regard to consequences. He suspected 'there was an active ill-will towards him on the part of these white men that—' 'You are right,' I said, remembering a certain conversation I had overheard. 'The manager thinks you ought to be hanged.' He showed a concern at this intelligence which amused me at first. 'I had better get out of the way quietly,' he said, earnestly. 'I can do no more for Kurtz now, and they would soon find some excuse. What's to stop them? There's a military post three hundred miles from here.' 'Well, upon my word,' said I, 'perhaps you had better go if you have any friends amongst the savages near by.' 'Plenty,' he said. 'They are simple people—and I want nothing, you know.' He stood biting his lip, then: 'I don't want any harm to happen to these whites here, but of course I was thinking of Mr Kurtz's reputation—but you are a brother seaman and—' 'All right,' said I, after a time. 'Mr Kurtz's reputation is safe with me.' I did not know how truly I spoke.

"He informed me, lowering his voice, that it was Kurtz who had ordered the attack to be made on the steamer. 'He hated sometimes the idea of being taken away—and then again . . . But I don't understand these matters. I am a simple man. He thought it would scare you away—that you would give it up, thinking him dead. I could not stop him. Oh, I had an awful time of it this last month.' 'Very well,' I said. 'He is all right now.' 'Ye-e-es,' he muttered, not very convinced apparently. 'Thanks,' said I; 'I shall keep my eyes open.' 'But quiet—eh?' he urged, anxiously. 'It would be awful for his reputation if anybody here—' I promised a complete discretion with great gravity. 'I have a canoe and three black fellows waiting not very far. I am off. Could you give me a few Martini-Henry cartridges?' I could, and did, with proper secrecy. He helped himself, with a wink at me, to a handful of my tobacco. 'Between sailors—you know—good English tobacco.' At the door of the pilot-house he turned round—'I say, haven't you a pair of shoes you could spare?' He raised one leg. 'Look.' The soles were tied with knotted strings sandal-wise under his bare feet. I rooted out an old pair, at which he looked with admiration before tucking it under his left arm. One of his pockets (bright red) was bulging with cartridges, from the other (dark blue) peeped 'Towson's Inquiry,' &c., &c. He seemed to think himself excellently well equipped for a renewed encounter with the wilderness. 'Ah! I'll never, never meet such a man again. You ought to have heard him recite poetry—his own too it was, he told me. Poetry!' He rolled his eyes at the recollection of these delights. 'Oh, he enlarged my mind!' 'Good-bye,' said I. He shook hands and vanished in the night. Sometimes I ask myself whether I had ever really seen him—whether it was possible to meet such a phenomenon! . . .

"When I woke up shortly after midnight his warning came to my mind with its hint of danger that seemed, in the starred darkness, real enough to make me get up for the purpose of having a look round. On the hill a big fire burned, illuminating fitfully a crooked corner of the station-house. One of the agents with a picket of a few of our blacks, armed for the purpose, was keeping guard over the ivory; but deep within the forest, red gleams that wavered, that seemed to sink and rise from the ground amongst confused columnar shapes of intense blackness, showed the exact position of the camp where Mr Kurtz's adorers were keeping their uneasy vigil. The monotonous beating of a big drum filled the air with muffled shocks and a lingering vibration. A steady droning sound of many men chanting each to himself some weird incantation came out from the black, flat wall of the woods as the humming of bees comes out of a hive, and had a strange narcotic effect upon my half-awake senses. I believe I dozed off leaning over the rail, till an abrupt burst of yells, an overwhelming outbreak of a pent-up and mysterious frenzy, woke me up in a bewildered wonder. It was cut short all at once, and the low droning went on with an effect of audible and soothing silence. I glanced casually into the little cabin. A light was burning within, but Mr Kurtz was not there.

"I think I would have raised an outcry if I had believed my eyes. But I didn't believe them at first—the thing seemed so impossible. The fact is, I was completely unnerved by a sheer blank fright, pure abstract terror, unconnected with any distinct shape of physical danger. What made this emotion so overpowering was—how shall I define it?—the moral shock I received, as if something altogether monstrous, intolerable to thought and odious to the soul, had been thrust upon me unexpectedly. This lasted of course the merest fraction of a second, and then the usual sense of commonplace, deadly danger, the possibility of a sudden onslaught and massacre, or something of the kind, which I saw impending, was positively welcome and composing. It pacified me, in fact, so much, that I did not raise an alarm.

"There was an agent buttoned up inside an ulster[7] and sleeping on a chair on deck within three feet of me. The yells had not awakened him; he snored very slightly; I left him to his slumbers and leaped ashore. I did not betray Mr Kurtz—it was ordered I should never betray him—it was written I should be loyal to the nightmare of my choice. I was anxious to deal with this shadow by myself alone,—and to this day I don't know why I was so jealous of sharing with any one the peculiar blackness of that experience.

"As soon as I got on the bank I saw a trail—a broad trail through the grass. I remember the exultation with which I said to myself, 'He can't walk—he is crawling on all-fours—I've got him.' The grass was wet with dew. I strode rapidly with clenched fists. I fancy I had some vague notion of falling upon him and giving him a drubbing. I don't know. I had some imbecile thoughts. The knitting old woman with the cat obtruded herself upon my memory as a most improper person to be sitting at the other end of such an affair. I saw a row of pilgrims squirting lead in the air out of Winchesters held to the hip. I thought I would never get back to the steamer, and imagined myself living alone and unarmed in the woods to an advanced age. Such silly things—you know. And I remember I confounded the beat of the drum with the beating of my heart, and was pleased at its calm regularity.

"I kept to the track though—then stopped to listen. The night was very clear: a dark blue space, sparkling with dew and starlight, in which black things stood very still. I thought I could see a kind of motion ahead of me. I was strangely cocksure of everything that night. I actually left the track and ran in a wide semicircle (I verily believe chuckling to myself) so as to get in front of that stir, of that motion I had seen—if indeed I had seen anything. I was circumventing Kurtz as though it had been a boyish game.

7. Long overcoat.

"I came upon him, and, if he had not heard me coming, I would have fallen over him too, but he got up in time. He rose, unsteady, long, pale, indistinct, like a vapour exhaled by the earth, and swayed slightly, misty and silent before me; while at my back the fires loomed between the trees, and the murmur of many voices issued from the forest. I had cut him off cleverly; but when actually confronting him I seemed to come to my senses, I saw the danger in its right proportion. It was by no means over yet. Suppose he began to shout? Though he could hardly stand, there was still plenty of vigour in his voice. 'Go away—hide yourself,' he said, in that profound tone. It was very awful. I glanced back. We were within thirty yards from the nearest fire. A black figure stood up, strode on long black legs, waving long black arms, across the glow. It had horns—antelope horns, I think—on its head. Some sorcerer, some witch-man, no doubt: it looked fiend-like enough. 'Do you know what you are doing?' I whispered. 'Perfectly,' he answered, raising his voice for that single word: it sounded to me far off and yet loud, like a hail through a speaking-trumpet. If he makes a row we are lost, I thought to myself. This clearly was not a case for fisticuffs, even apart from the very natural aversion I had to beat that Shadow—this wandering and tormented thing. 'You will be lost,' I said—'utterly lost.' One gets sometimes such a flash of inspiration, you know. I did say the right thing, though indeed he could not have been more irretrievably lost than he was at this very moment, when the foundations of our intimacy were being laid—to endure—to endure—even to the end—even beyond.

"'I had immense plans,' he muttered irresolutely. 'Yes,' said I; 'but if you try to shout I'll smash your head with—' there was not a stick or a stone near. 'I will throttle you for good,' I corrected myself. 'I was on the threshold of great things,' he pleaded, in a voice of longing, with a wistfulness of tone that made my blood run cold. 'And now for this stupid scoundrel—' 'Your success in Europe is assured in any case,' I affirmed, steadily. I did not want to have the throttling of him, you understand—and indeed it would have been very little use for any practical purpose. I tried to break the spell—the heavy, mute spell of the wilderness—that seemed to draw him to its pitiless breast by the awakening of forgotten and brutal instincts, by the memory of gratified and monstrous passions. This alone, I was convinced, had driven him out to the edge of the forest, to the bush, towards the gleam of fires, the throb of drums, the drone of weird incantations; this alone had beguiled his unlawful soul beyond the bounds of permitted aspirations. And, don't you see, the terror of the position was not in being knocked on the head—though I had a very lively sense of that danger too—but in this, that I had to deal with a being to whom I could not appeal in the name of anything high or low. I had, even like the niggers, to invoke him—himself—his own exalted and incredible degradation. There was nothing either above or below him, and I knew it. He had kicked himself loose of the earth. Confound the man! he had kicked the very earth to pieces. He was alone, and I before him did not know whether I stood on the ground or floated in the air. I've been telling you what we said—repeating the phrases we pronounced,—but what's the good? They were common everyday words,—the familiar, vague sounds exchanged on every waking day of life. But what of that? They had behind them, to my mind, the terrific suggestiveness of words heard in dreams, of phrases spoken in nightmares. Soul! If anybody had ever struggled with a soul, I am the man. And I wasn't arguing with a lunatic either. Believe me or not, his intelligence was perfectly clear—concentrated, it is true, upon himself with horrible intensity, yet clear; and therein was my only chance—barring, of course, the killing him there and then, which wasn't so good, on account of unavoidable noise. But his soul was mad. Being alone in the wilderness, it had looked within itself, and, by heavens! I tell you, it had gone mad. I had—for my sins, I suppose—to go through the ordeal of looking into it myself. No eloquence could have been so withering to one's belief in mankind as his final burst of sincerity. He struggled with himself, too. I saw it,—I heard it. I saw the inconceivable mystery of a soul that knew no restraint, no faith, and no fear, yet struggling blindly with itself. I kept my head pretty well; but when I had him at last stretched on the couch, I wiped my forehead, while my legs shook under me as though I had carried half a ton on my back down that hill. And yet I had only supported him, his bony arm clasped round my neck—and he was not much heavier than a child.

   "When next day we left at noon, the crowd, of whose presence behind the curtain of trees I had been acutely conscious all the time, flowed out of the woods again, filled the clearing, covered the slope with a mass of naked, breathing, quivering, bronze bodies. I steamed up a bit, then swung down-stream, and two thousand eyes followed the evolutions of the splashing, thumping, fierce river-demon beating the water with its terrible tail and breathing black smoke into the air. In front of the first rank, along the river, three men, plastered with bright red earth from head to foot, strutted to and fro restlessly. When we came abreast again, they faced the river, stamped their feet, nodded their horned heads, swayed their scarlet bodies; they shook towards the fierce river-demon a bunch of black feathers, a mangy skin with a pendent tail—something that looked like a dried gourd; they shouted periodically together strings of amazing words that resembled no sounds of human language; and the deep murmurs of the crowd, interrupted suddenly, were like the responses of some satanic litany.

   "We had carried Kurtz into the pilot-house: there was more air there. Lying on the couch, he stared through the open shutter. There was an eddy in the mass of human bodies, and the woman with helmeted head and tawny cheeks rushed out to the very brink of the stream. She put out her hands, shouted something, and all that wild mob took up the shout in a roaring chorus of articulated, rapid, breathless utterance.

   "'Do you understand this?' I asked.

   "He kept on looking out past me with fiery, longing eyes, with a mingled expression of wistfulness and hate. He made no answer, but I saw a smile, a smile of indefinable meaning, appear on his colourless lips that a moment after twitched convulsively. 'Do I not?' he said slowly, gasping, as if the words had been torn out of him by a supernatural power.

   "I pulled the string of the whistle, and I did this because I saw the pilgrims on deck getting out their rifles with an air of anticipating a jolly lark. At the sudden screech there was a movement of abject terror through that wedged mass of bodies. 'Don't! don't! you frighten them away,' cried some one on deck disconsolately. I pulled the string time after time. They broke and ran, they leaped, they crouched, they swerved, they dodged the flying terror of the sound. The three red chaps had fallen flat, face down on the shore, as though they had been shot dead. Only the barbarous and superb woman did not so much as flinch, and stretched tragically her bare arms after us over the sombre and glittering river.

   "And then that imbecile crowd down on the deck started their little fun, and I could see nothing more for smoke.

   "The brown current ran swiftly out of the heart of darkness, bearing us down towards the sea with twice the speed of our upward progress; and Kurtz's life was running swiftly too, ebbing, ebbing out of his heart into the sea of inexorable time. The manager was very placid, he had no vital anxieties now, he took us both in with a comprehensive and satisfied glance: the 'affair' had come off as well as could be wished. I saw the time approaching when I would be left alone of the party of 'unsound method.' The pilgrims looked upon me with disfavour. I was, so to speak, numbered with the dead. It is strange how I accepted this unforeseen partnership, this choice of nightmares forced upon me in the tenebrous land invaded by these mean and greedy phantoms.

"Kurtz discoursed. A voice! a voice! It rang deep to the very last. It survived his strength to hide in the magnificent folds of eloquence the barren darkness of his heart. Oh, he struggled! he struggled! The wastes of his weary brain were haunted by shadowy images now—images of wealth and fame revolving obsequiously round his unextinguishable gift of noble and lofty expression. My Intended, my station, my career, my ideas—these were the subjects for the occasional utterances of elevated sentiments. The shade of the original Kurtz frequented the bedside of the hollow sham, whose fate it was to be buried presently in the mould of primeval earth. But both the diabolic love and the unearthly hate of the mysteries it had penetrated fought for the possession of that soul satiated with primitive emotions, avid of lying fame, of sham distinction, of all the appearances of success and power.

"Sometimes he was contemptibly childish. He desired to have kings meet him at railway-stations on his return from some ghastly Nowhere, where he intended to accomplish great things. 'You show them you have in you something that is really profitable, and then there will be no limits to the recognition of your ability,' he would say. 'Of course you must take care of the motives—right motives—always.' The long reaches that were like one and the same reach, monotonous bends that were exactly alike, slipped past the steamer with their multitude of secular[8] trees looking patiently after this grimy fragment of another world, the forerunner of change, of conquest, of trade, of massacres, of blessings. I looked ahead—piloting. 'Close the shutter,' said Kurtz suddenly one day; 'I can't bear to look at this.' I did so. There was a silence. 'Oh, but I will wring your heart yet!' he cried at the invisible wilderness.

"We broke down—as I had expected—and had to lie up for repairs at the head of an island. This delay was the first thing that shook Kurtz's confidence. One morning he gave me a packet of papers and a photograph,—the lot tied together with a shoestring. 'Keep this for me,' he said. 'This noxious fool' (meaning the manager) 'is capable of prying into my boxes when I am not looking.' In the afternoon I saw him. He was lying on his back with closed eyes, and I withdrew quietly, but I heard him mutter, 'Live rightly, die, die . . .' I listened. There was nothing more. Was he rehearsing some speech in his sleep, or was it a fragment of a phrase from some newspaper article? He had been writing for the papers and meant to do so again, 'for the furthering of my ideas. It's a duty.'

"His was an impenetrable darkness. I looked at him as you peer down at a man who is lying at the bottom of a precipice where the sun never shines. But I had not much time to give him, because I was helping the engine-driver to take to pieces the leaky cylinders, to straighten a bent connecting-rod, and in other such matters. I lived in an infernal mess of rust, filings, nuts, bolts, spanners, hammers, ratchet-drills— things I abominate, because I don't get on with them. I tended the little forge we for-

8. Ancient.

tunately had aboard; I toiled wearily in a wretched scrap-heap—unless I had the shakes too bad to stand.

"One evening coming in with a candle I was startled to hear him say a little tremulously, 'I am lying here in the dark waiting for death.' The light was within a foot of his eyes. I forced myself to murmur, 'Oh, nonsense!' and stood over him as if transfixed.

"Anything approaching the change that came over his features I have never seen before, and hope never to see again. Oh, I wasn't touched. I was fascinated. It was as though a veil had been rent. I saw on that ivory face the expression of sombre pride, of ruthless power, of craven terror—of an intense and hopeless despair. Did he live his life again in every detail of desire, temptation, and surrender during that supreme moment of complete knowledge? He cried in a whisper at some image, at some vision,—he cried out twice, a cry that was no more than a breath—

"'The horror! The horror!'

"I blew the candle out and left the cabin. The pilgrims were dining in the mess-room, and I took my place opposite the manager, who lifted his eyes to give me a questioning glance, which I successfully ignored. He leaned back, serene, with that peculiar smile of his sealing the unexpressed depths of his meanness. A continuous shower of small flies streamed upon the lamp, upon the cloth, upon our hands and faces. Suddenly the manager's boy put his insolent black head in the doorway, and said in a tone of scathing contempt—

"'Mistah Kurtz—he dead.'

"All the pilgrims rushed out to see. I remained, and went on with my dinner. I believe I was considered brutally callous. However, I did not eat much. There was a lamp in there—light, don't you know—and outside it was so beastly, beastly dark. I went no more near the remarkable man who had pronounced a judgment upon the adventures of his soul on this earth. The voice was gone. What else had been there? But I am of course aware that next day the pilgrims buried something in a muddy hole.

"And then they very nearly buried me.

"However, as you see, I did not go to join Kurtz there and then. I did not. I remained to dream the nightmare out to the end, and to show my loyalty to Kurtz once more. Destiny. My destiny! Droll thing life is—that mysterious arrangement of merciless logic for a futile purpose. The most you can hope from it is some knowledge of yourself—that comes too late—a crop of unextinguishable regrets. I have wrestled with death. It is the most unexciting contest you can imagine. It takes place in an impalpable greyness, with nothing underfoot, with nothing around, without spectators, without clamour, without glory, without the great desire of victory, without the great fear of defeat, in a sickly atmosphere of tepid scepticism, without much belief in your own right, and still less in that of your adversary. If such is the form of ultimate wisdom, then life is a greater riddle than some of us think it to be. I was within a hair's-breadth of the last opportunity for pronouncement, and I found with humiliation that probably I would have nothing to say. This is the reason why I affirm that Kurtz was a remarkable man. He had something to say. He said it. Since I had peeped over the edge myself, I understand better the meaning of his stare, that could not see the flame of the candle, but was wide enough to embrace the whole universe, piercing enough to penetrate all the hearts that beat in the darkness. He had summed up—he had judged. 'The horror!' He was a remarkable man. After all, this was the expression of some sort of belief; it had candour, it had conviction, it had a vibrating note of revolt in its whisper, it had the appalling face of a glimpsed truth—the strange commingling of desire and hate. And it is not my own extremity I remember best—a vision of greyness without form filled with physical pain, and a careless contempt for the evanescence of all things—even of this pain itself. No! It is his extremity that I seem to have lived through. True, he had made that last stride, he had stepped over the edge, while I had been permitted to draw back my hesitating foot. And perhaps in this is the whole difference; perhaps all the wisdom, and all truth, and all sincerity, are just compressed into that inappreciable moment of time in which we step over the threshold of the invisible. Perhaps! I like to think my summing-up would not have been a word of careless contempt. Better his cry—much better. It was an affirmation, a moral victory paid for by innumerable defeats, by abominable terrors, by abominable satisfactions. But it was a victory! That is why I have remained loyal to Kurtz to the last, and even beyond, when a long time after I heard once more, not his own voice, but the echo of his magnificent eloquence thrown to me from a soul as translucently pure as a cliff of crystal.

"No, they did not bury me, though there is a period of time which I remember mistily, with a shuddering wonder, like a passage through some inconceivable world that had no hope in it and no desire. I found myself back in the sepulchral city resenting the sight of people hurrying through the streets to filch a little money from each other, to devour their infamous cookery, to gulp their unwholesome beer, to dream their insignificant and silly dreams. They trespassed upon my thoughts. They were intruders whose knowledge of life was to me an irritating pretence, because I felt so sure they could not possibly know the things I knew. Their bearing, which was simply the bearing of commonplace individuals going about their business in the assurance of perfect safety, was offensive to me like the outrageous flauntings of folly in the face of a danger it is unable to comprehend. I had no particular desire to enlighten them, but I had some difficulty in restraining myself from laughing in their faces, so full of stupid importance. I daresay I was not very well at that time. I tottered about the streets—there were various affairs to settle—grinning bitterly at perfectly respectable persons. I admit my behaviour was inexcusable, but then my temperature was seldom normal in these days. My dear aunt's endeavours to 'nurse up my strength' seemed altogether beside the mark. It was not my strength that wanted nursing, it was my imagination that wanted soothing. I kept the bundle of papers given me by Kurtz, not knowing exactly what to do with it. His mother had died lately, watched over, as I was told, by his Intended. A clean-shaved man, with an official manner and wearing gold-rimmed spectacles, called on me one day and made inquiries, at first circuitous, afterwards suavely pressing, about what he was pleased to denominate certain 'documents.' I was not surprised, because I had had two rows with the manager on the subject out there. I had refused to give up the smallest scrap out of that package, and I took the same attitude with the spectacled man. He became darkly menacing at last, and with much heat argued that the Company had the right to every bit of information about its 'territories.' And, said he, 'Mr Kurtz's knowledge of unexplored regions must have been necessarily extensive and peculiar—owing to his great abilities and to the deplorable circumstances in which he had been placed: therefore—' I assured him Mr Kurtz's knowledge, however extensive, did not bear upon the problems of commerce or administration. He invoked then the name of science. 'It would be an incalculable loss if,' &c., &c. I offered him the report on the 'Suppression of Savage Customs,' with the postscriptum torn off. He took it up eagerly, but ended by sniffing at it with an air of contempt. 'This is not what we had a right to expect,' he remarked. 'Expect nothing else,' I said. 'There are only private letters.' He withdrew upon some threat of legal proceedings, and I saw him no more;

but another fellow, calling himself Kurtz's cousin, appeared two days later, and was anxious to hear all the details about his dear relative's last moments. Incidentally he gave me to understand that Kurtz had been essentially a great musician. 'There was the making of an immense success,' said the man, who was an organist, I believe, with lank grey hair flowing over a greasy coat-collar. I had no reason to doubt his statement; and to this day I am unable to say what was Kurtz's profession, whether he ever had any—which was the greatest of his talents. I had taken him for a painter who wrote for the papers, or else for a journalist who could paint—but even the cousin (who took snuff during the interview) could not tell me what he had been—exactly. He was a universal genius—on that point I agreed with the old chap, who thereupon blew his nose noisily into a large cotton handkerchief and withdrew in senile agitation, bearing off some family letters and memoranda without importance. Ultimately a journalist anxious to know something of the fate of his 'dear colleague' turned up. This visitor informed me Kurtz's proper sphere ought to have been politics 'on the popular side.' He had furry straight eyebrows, bristly hair cropped short, an eye-glass on a broad ribbon, and, becoming expansive, confessed his opinion that Kurtz really couldn't write a bit—'but heavens! how that man could talk! He electrified large meetings. He had faith—don't you see?—he had the faith. He could get himself to believe anything—anything. He would have been a splendid leader of an extreme party.' 'What party?' I asked. 'Any party,' answered the other. 'He was an—an—extremist.' Did I not think so? I assented. Did I know, he asked, with a sudden flash of curiosity, 'what it was that had induced him to go out there?' 'Yes,' said I, and forthwith handed him the famous Report for publication, if he thought fit. He glanced through it hurriedly, mumbling all the time, judged 'it would do,' and took himself off with this plunder.

"Thus I was left at last with a slim packet of letters and the girl's portrait. She struck me as beautiful—I mean she had a beautiful expression. I know that the sunlight can be made to lie too, yet one felt that no manipulation of light and pose could have conveyed the delicate shade of truthfulness upon those features. She seemed ready to listen without mental reservation, without suspicion, without a thought for herself. I concluded I would go and give her back her portrait and those letters myself. Curiosity? Yes; and also some other feeling perhaps. All that had been Kurtz's had passed out of my hands: his soul, his body, his station, his plans, his ivory, his career. There remained only his memory and his Intended—and I wanted to give that up too to the past, in a way,—to surrender personally all that remained of him with me to that oblivion which is the last word of our common fate. I don't defend myself. I had no clear perception of what it was I really wanted. Perhaps it was an impulse of unconscious loyalty, or the fulfilment of one of those ironic necessities that lurk in the facts of human existence. I don't know. I can't tell. But I went.

"I thought his memory was like the other memories of the dead that accumulate in every man's life,—a vague impress on the brain of shadows that had fallen on it in their swift and final passage; but before the high and ponderous door, between the tall houses of a street as still and decorous as a well-kept alley in a cemetery, I had a vision of him on the stretcher, opening his mouth voraciously, as if to devour all the earth with all its mankind. He lived then before me; he lived as much as he had ever lived—a shadow insatiable of splendid appearances, of frightful realities; a shadow darker than the shadow of the night, and draped nobly in the folds of a gorgeous eloquence. The vision seemed to enter the house with me—the stretcher, the phantom-bearers, the wild crowd of obedient worshippers, the gloom of the forests, the glitter of the reach between the murky bends, the beat of the drum, regular and muffled like the beating of a heart—the heart of a conquering darkness. It was a moment of triumph for the wilderness, an invading and vengeful rush which, it seemed to me, I would have to keep back alone for the salvation of another soul. And the memory of what I had heard him say afar there, with the horned shapes stirring at my back, in the glow of fires, within the patient woods, those broken phrases came back to me, were heard again in their ominous and terrifying simplicity. I remembered his abject pleading, his abject threats, the colossal scale of his vile desires, the meanness, the torment, the tempestuous anguish of his soul. And later on I seemed to see his collected languid manner, when he said one day, 'This lot of ivory now is really mine. The Company did not pay for it. I collected it myself at a very great personal risk. I am afraid they will try to claim it as theirs though. H'm. It is a difficult case. What do you think I ought to do—resist? Eh? I want no more than justice.' . . . He wanted no more than justice—no more than justice. I rang the bell before a mahogany door on the first floor, and while I waited he seemed to stare at me out of the glassy panel—stare with that wide and immense stare embracing, condemning, loathing all the universe. I seemed to hear the whispered cry, 'The horror! The horror!'

"The dusk was falling. I had to wait in a lofty drawing-room with three long windows from floor to ceiling that were like three luminous and bedraped columns. The bent gilt legs and backs of the furniture shone in indistinct curves. The tall marble fireplace had a cold and monumental whiteness. A grand piano stood massively in a corner, with dark gleams on the flat surfaces like a sombre and polished sarcophagus. A high door opened—closed. I rose.

"She came forward, all in black, with a pale head, floating towards me in the dusk. She was in mourning. It was more than a year since his death, more than a year since the news came; she seemed as though she would remember and mourn for ever. She took both my hands in hers and murmured, 'I had heard you were coming.' I noticed she was not very young—I mean not girlish. She had a mature capacity for fidelity, for belief, for suffering. The room seemed to have grown darker, as if all the sad light of the cloudy evening had taken refuge on her forehead. This fair hair, this pale visage, this pure brow, seemed surrounded by an ashy halo from which the dark eyes looked out at me. Their glance was guileless, profound, confident, and trustful. She carried her sorrowful head as though she were proud of that sorrow, as though she would say, I—I alone know how to mourn for him as he deserves. But while we were still shaking hands, such a look of awful desolation came upon her face that I perceived she was one of those creatures that are not the playthings of Time. For her he had died only yesterday. And, by Jove! the impression was so powerful that for me too he seemed to have died only yesterday—nay, this very minute. I saw her and him in the same instant of time—his death and her sorrow—I saw her sorrow in the very moment of his death. Do you understand? I saw them together—I heard them together. She had said, with a deep catch of the breath, 'I have survived'; while my strained ears seemed to hear distinctly, mingled with her tone of despairing regret, the summing-up whisper of his eternal condemnation. I asked myself what I was doing there, with a sensation of panic in my heart as though I had blundered into a place of cruel and absurd mysteries not fit for a human being to behold. She motioned me to a chair. We sat down. I laid the packet gently on the little table, and she put her hand over it. . . . 'You knew him well,' she murmured, after a moment of mourning silence.

"'Intimacy grows quickly out there,' I said. 'I knew him as well as it is possible for one man to know another.'

"'And you admired him,' she said. 'It was impossible to know him and not to admire him. Was it?'

"'He was a remarkable man,' I said, unsteadily. Then before the appealing fixity of her gaze, that seemed to watch for more words on my lips, I went on, 'It was impossible not to—'

"'Love him,' she finished eagerly, silencing me into an appalled dumbness. 'How true! how true! But when you think that no one knew him so well as I! I had all his noble confidence. I knew him best.'

"'You knew him best,' I repeated. And perhaps she did. But with every word spoken the room was growing darker, and only her forehead, smooth and white, remained illumined by the unextinguishable light of belief and love.

"'You were his friend,' she went on. 'His friend,' she repeated, a little louder. 'You must have been, if he had given you this, and sent you to me. I feel I can speak to you—and oh! I must speak. I want you—you who have heard his last words—to know I have been worthy of him. . . . It is not pride. . . . Yes! I am proud to know I understood him better than any one on earth—he told me so himself. And since his mother died I have had no one—no one—to—to—'

"I listened. The darkness deepened. I was not even sure whether he had given me the right bundle. I rather suspect he wanted me to take care of another batch of his papers which, after his death, I saw the manager examining under the lamp. And the girl talked, easing her pain in the certitude of my sympathy; she talked as thirsty men drink. I had heard that her engagement with Kurtz had been disapproved by her people. He wasn't rich enough or something. And indeed I don't know whether he had not been a pauper all his life. He had given me some reason to infer that it was his impatience of comparative poverty that drove him out there.

"'. . . Who was not his friend who had heard him speak once?' she was saying. 'He drew men towards him by what was best in them.' She looked at me with intensity. 'It is the gift of the great,' she went on, and the sound of her low voice seemed to have the accompaniment of all the other sounds, full of mystery, desolation, and sorrow, I had ever heard—the ripple of the river, the soughing of the trees swayed by the wind, the murmurs of wild crowds, the faint ring of incomprehensible words cried from afar, the whisper of a voice speaking from beyond the threshold of an eternal darkness. 'But you have heard him! You know!' she cried.

"'Yes, I know,' I said with something like despair in my heart, but bowing my head before the faith that was in her, before that great and saving illusion that shone with an unearthly glow in the darkness, in the triumphant darkness from which I could not have defended her—from which I could not even defend myself.

"'What a loss to me—to us!'—she corrected herself with beautiful generosity; then added in a murmur, 'To the world.' By the last gleams of twilight I could see the glitter of her eyes, full of tears—of tears that would not fall.

"'I have been very happy—very fortunate—very proud,' she went on. 'Too fortunate. Too happy for a little while. And now I am unhappy for—for life.'

"She stood up; her fair hair seemed to catch all the remaining light in a glimmer of gold. I rose too.

"'And of all this,' she went on, mournfully, 'of all his promise, and of all his greatness, of his generous mind, of his noble heart, nothing remains—nothing but a memory. You and I—'

"'We shall always remember him,' I said, hastily.

"'No!' she cried. 'It is impossible that all this should be lost—that such a life should be sacrificed to leave nothing—but sorrow. You know what vast plans he had. I knew of them too—I could not perhaps understand,—but others knew of them. Something must remain. His words, at least, have not died.'

"'His words will remain,' I said.

"'And his example,' she whispered to herself. 'Men looked up to him,—his goodness shone in every act. His example—'

"'True,' I said; 'his example too. Yes, his example. I forgot that.'

"'But I do not. I cannot—I cannot believe—not yet. I cannot believe that I shall never see him again, that nobody will see him again, never, never, never.'

"She put out her arms as if after a retreating figure, stretching them black and with clasped pale hands across the fading and narrow sheen of the window. Never see him! I saw him clearly enough then. I shall see this eloquent phantom as long as I live, and I shall see her too, a tragic and familiar Shade, resembling in this gesture another one, tragic also, and bedecked with powerless charms, stretching bare brown arms over the glitter of the infernal stream, the stream of darkness. She said suddenly very low, 'He died as he lived.'

"'His end,' said I, with dull anger stirring in me, 'was in every way worthy of his life.'

"'And I was not with him,' she murmured. My anger subsided before a feeling of infinite pity.

"'Everything that could be done—' I mumbled.

"'Ah, but I believed in him more than any one on earth—more than his own mother, more than—himself. He needed me! Me! I would have treasured every sigh, every word, every sign, every glance.'

"I felt like a chill grip on my chest. 'Don't,' I said, in a muffled voice.

"'Forgive me. I—I—have mourned so long in silence—in silence. . . . You were with him—to the last? I think of his loneliness. Nobody near to understand him as I would have understood. Perhaps no one to hear. . . .'

"'To the very end,' I said, shakily. 'I heard his very last words. . . .' I stopped in a fright.

"'Repeat them,' she said in a heart-broken tone. 'I want—I want—something—something—to—to live with.'

"I was on the point of crying at her, 'Don't you hear them?' The dusk was repeating them in a persistent whisper all around us, in a whisper that seemed to swell menacingly like the first whisper of a rising wind. 'The horror! the horror!'

"'His last word—to live with,' she murmured. 'Don't you understand I loved him—I loved him—I loved him!'

"I pulled myself together and spoke slowly.

"'The last word he pronounced was—your name.'

"I heard a light sigh, and then my heart stood still, stopped dead short by an exulting and terrible cry, by the cry of inconceivable triumph and of unspeakable pain. 'I knew it—I was sure!' . . . She knew. She was sure. I heard her weeping; she had hidden her face in her hands. It seemed to me that the house would collapse before I could escape, that the heavens would fall upon my head. But nothing happened. The heavens do not fall for such a trifle. Would they have fallen, I wonder, if I had rendered Kurtz that justice which was his due? Hadn't he said he wanted only justice? But I couldn't. I could not tell her. It would have been too dark—too dark altogether. . . ."

Marlow ceased, and sat apart, indistinct and silent, in the pose of a meditating Buddha. Nobody moved for a time. "We have lost the first of the ebb," said the Director, suddenly. I raised my head. The offing was barred by a black bank of clouds, and the tranquil waterway leading to the uttermost ends of the earth flowed sombre under an overcast sky—seemed to lead into the heart of an immense darkness.

❦

RESONANCES

Joseph Conrad: from Congo Diary

Arrived at Matadi[1] on the 13th of June, 1890.

Mr Gosse, chief of the station (O.K.) retaining us for some reason of his own.

Made the acquaintance of Mr Roger Casement,[2] which I should consider as a great pleasure under any circumstances and now it becomes a positive piece of luck. Thinks, speaks well, most intelligent and very sympathetic.

Feel considerably in doubt about the future. Think just now that my life amongst the people (white) around here cannot be very comfortable. Intend avoid acquaintances as much as possible. * * *

24th. Gosse and R.C. gone with a large lot of ivory down to Boma. On G.['s] return to start to up the river. Have been myself busy packing ivory in casks. Idiotic employment. Health good up to now. * * *

Prominent characteristic of the social life here: people speaking ill of each other.

* * *

Friday, 4th July.

Left camp at 6h a.m. after a very unpleasant night. Marching across a chain of hills and then in a maze of hills. At 8:15 opened out into an undulating plain. Took bearings of a break in the chain of mountains on the other side. * * *

Saw another dead body lying by the path in an attitude of meditative repose.

In the evening three women of whom one albino passed our camp. Horrid chalky white with pink blotches. Red eyes. Red hair. Features very Negroid and ugly. Mosquitos. At night when the moon rose heard shouts and drumming in distant villages. Passed a bad night.

Saturday, 5th July. go.

Left at 6:15. Morning cool, even cold and very damp. Sky densely overcast. Gentle breeze from NE. Road through a narrow plain up to R. Kwilu. Swift-flowing and deep, 50 yds. wide. Passed in canoes. After[war]ds up and down very steep hills intersected by deep ravines. Main chain of heights running mostly NW-SE or W and E at times. Stopped at Manyamba. Camp[in]g place bad—in hollow—water very indifferent. Tent set at 10:15.

Section of today's road. NNE Distance 12 m. [a drawing]

---

1. Colonial station near the mouth of the Congo River. Conrad arrived there on his way to take up his command of a steamship upriver at Kinshasa.
2. Casement (1864–1916) and Conrad were working for the same company. Casement later served as British consul in various parts of Africa, and was the author of a report on the Congo (1904) that did much to make public the terrible conditions there. He was knighted in 1912. In 1916 he was executed by the British for his part in the Easter Rebellion in Ireland.

Today fell into a muddy puddle. Beastly. The fault of the man that carried me. After camp[in]g went to a small stream, bathed and washed clothes. Getting jolly well sick of this fun.

Tomorrow expect a long march to get to Nsona, 2 days from Manyanga. No sunshine today.

* * *

Saturday, 26th.

Left very early. Road ascending all the time. Passed villages. Country seems thickly inhabited. At 11h arrived at large market place. Left at noon and camped at 1h p.m.

[section of the day's march with notes]

a camp—a white man died here—market—govt. post—mount—crocodile pond—Mafiesa. * * *

Sunday, 27th.

Left at 8h am. Sent luggage carriers straight on to Luasi and went ourselves round by the Mission of Sutili.

Hospitable reception by Mrs Comber. All the missio[naries] absent.

The looks of the whole establishment eminently civilized and very refreshing to see after the lots of tumble-down hovels in which the State and Company agents are content to live—fine buildings. Position on a hill. Rather breezy.

Left at 3h pm. At the first heavy ascent met Mr Davis, miss[ionary] returning from a preaching trip. Rev. Bentley away in the South with his wife. * * *

Tuesday, 29th.

Left camp at 7h after a good night's rest. Continuous ascent; rather easy at first. Crossed wooded ravines and the river Lunzadi by a very decent bridge.

At 9h met Mr Louette escorting a sick agent of the Comp[an]y back to Matadi. Looking very well. Bad news from up the river. All the steamers disabled. One wrecked. Country wooded. At 10:30 camped at Inkissi. * * *

Today did not set the tent but put up in Gov[ernmen]t shimbek.[3] Zanzibari in charge—very obliging. Met ripe pineapple for the first time. On the road today passed a skeleton tied up to a post. Also white man's grave—no name. Heap of stones in the form of a cross.

Health good now.

Wednesday, 30th.

Left at 6 a.m. intending to camp at Kinfumu. Two hours' sharp walk brought me to Nsona na Nsefe. Market. ½ hour after, Harou arrived very ill with billious [sic] attack and fever. Laid him down in Gov[ernmen]t shimbek. Dose of Ipeca.[4] Vomiting bile in enormous quantities. At 11h gave him 1 gramme of quinine and lots of hot tea. Hot fit ending in heavy perspiration. At 2 p.m. put him in hammock and started for Kinfumu. Row with carriers all the way. Harou suffering much through the jerks of the hammock. Camped at a small stream.

At 4h Harou better. Fever gone. * * *

Up till noon, sky clouded and strong NW wind very chilling. From 1h pm to 4h pm sky clear and very hot day. Expect lots of bother with carriers tomorrow. Had

---

3. A group of huts.   4. A medicine.

them all called and made a speech which they did not understand. They promise good behaviour. * * *

Friday, 1st of August 1890.

* * * Row between the carriers and a man stating himself in Gov[ernmen]t employ, about a mat. Blows with sticks raining hard. Stopped it. Chief came with a youth about 13 suffering from gunshot wound in the head. Bullet entered about an inch above the right eyebrow and came out a little inside. The roots of the hair, fairly in the middle of the brow in a line with the bridge of the nose. Bone not damaged apparently. Gave him a little glycerine to put on the wound made by the bullet on coming out. Harou not very well. Mosquitos. Frogs. Beastly. Glad to see the end of this stupid tramp. Feel rather seedy. Sun rose red. Very hot day. Wind S[ou]th.

Sir Henry Morton Stanley:
from *Address to the Manchester Chamber of Commerce*[1]

There is not one manufacturer here present who could not tell me if he had the opportunity how much he personally suffered through the slackness of trade; and I dare say that you have all some vague idea that if things remain as they are the future of the cotton manufacture is not very brilliant. New inventions are continually cropping up, so that your power of producing, if stimulated, is almost incalculable; but new markets for the sale of your products are not of rapid growth, and as other nations, by prohibitive tariffs, are bent upon fostering native manufacturers to the exclusion of your own, such markets as are now open to you are likely to be taken away from you in course of time. Well, then, I come to you with at least one market where there are at present, perhaps, 6,250,000 yards of cheap cottons sold every year on the Congo banks and in the Congo markets.[2]

I was interested the other day in making a curious calculation, which was, supposing that all the inhabitants of the Congo basin were simply to have one Sunday dress each, how many yards of Manchester cloth would be required; and the amazing number was 320,000,000 yards, just for one Sunday dress! (Cheers.) Proceeding still further with these figures I found that two Sunday dresses and four everyday dresses would in one year amount to 3,840,000,000 yards, which at 2d. [two pence] per yard would be of the value of £16,000,000. The more I pondered upon these things I discovered that I could not limit these stores of cotton cloth to day dresses. I would have to provide for night dresses also—(laughter)—and these would consume 160,000,000 yards. (Cheers.) Then the grave cloths came into mind, and, as a poor lunatic, who burned Bolobo Station,[3] destroyed 30,000 yards of cloth in order that he should not be cheated out of a respectable burial, I really feared for a time that the millions would

---

1. The journalist-adventurer Henry Morton Stanley wrote *Through the Dark Continent* and other best-selling accounts of his exploits in Africa, including the finding of the lost missionary Doctor Livingstone. He delivered this address to the textile manufacturers of Manchester, England, in 1886, seeking their support for the commercial exploitation of the Congo. His speech gives a striking example of the outlook—and the rhetoric—of the people who created the conditions Conrad encountered when he went to the Congo a few years later.
2. The Congo Free State (later Zaire), a vast area of central Africa around the Congo River, was formally brought under the ownership of Leopold II of Belgium and other investors in the International Association of the Congo by the Berlin West Africa Conference of 1884–1885. Stanley's expeditions there (from 1876) had been financed by Leopold, and from 1879 Stanley had set up trading stations along the river to facilitate the exploitation of the area's natural resources.
3. The London *Times* carried frequent reports of disturbances in the Congo at this time; in March 1884, for example, Congolese attacks on foreign trading establishments at Nokki in the Lower Congo had caused the Europeans to "declare war against the natives."

get beyond measurable calculation. However, putting such accidents aside, I estimate that, if my figures of population are approximately correct, 2,000,000 die every year, and to bury these decently, and according to the custom of those who possess cloth, 16,000,000 yards will be required, while the 40,000 chiefs will require an average of 100 yards each, or 4,000,000 yards. I regarded these figures with great satisfaction, and I was about to close my remarks upon the millions of yards of cloth that Manchester would perhaps be required to produce when I discovered that I had neglected to provide for the family wardrobe or currency chest, for you must know that in the Lower Congo there is scarcely a family that has not a cloth fund of about a dozen pieces of about 24 yards each. This is a very important institution, otherwise how are the family necessities to be provided for? How are the fathers and mothers of families to go to market to buy greens, bread, oil, ground nuts, chickens, fish, and goats, and how is the petty trade to be conducted? How is ivory to be purchased, the gums, rubber, dye powders, gunpowder, copper slugs, guns, trinkets, knives, and swords to be bought without a supply of cloth? Now, 8,000,000 families at 300 yards each will require 2,400,000,000. (Cheers.) You all know how perishable such currency must be; but if you sum up these several millions of yards, and value all of them at the average price of 2d. per yard, you will find that it will be possible for Manchester to create a trade—in the course of time—in cottons in the Congo basin amounting in value to about £26,000,000 annually. (Loud cheers.) I have said nothing about Rochdale savelist, or your own superior prints, your gorgeous handkerchiefs, with their variegated patterns, your checks and striped cloths, your ticking and twills.[4] I must satisfy myself with suggesting them; your own imaginations will no doubt carry you to the limbo of immeasurable and incalculable millions. (Laughter and cheers.)

Now, if your sympathy for yourselves and the fate of Manchester has been excited sufficiently, your next natural question would be as follows: We acknowledge, sir, that you have contrived by an artful array of imposing millions to excite our attention, at least, to this field; but we beg to ask you what Manchester is to do in order that we may begin realising this sale of untold millions of yards of cotton cloth? I answer that the first thing to do is for you to ask the British Government to send a cruiser to the mouth of the Congo to keep watch and ward over that river until the European nations have agreed among themselves as to what shall be done with the river, lest one of these days you will hear that it is too late. (Hear, hear.) Secondly, to study whether, seeing that it will never do to permit Portugal to assume sovereignty over that river[5]—and England publicly disclaims any wish to possess that river for herself—it would not be as well to allow the International Association to act as guardians of international right to free trade and free entrance and exit into and out of the river. (Hear, hear.) The main point, remember, always is a guarantee that the lower river shall be free, that, however the Upper Congo may be developed, no Power, inspired by cupidity, shall seize upon the mouth of the river and build custom houses. (Hear, hear.) The Lower Congo in the future will only be valuable because down its waters will have to be floated the produce of the rich basin above to the ocean steamships. It will always have a fair trade of its own, but it bears no proportion to the almost limitless trade that the Upper Congo could furnish. If the Association could be assured that the road from Europe to Vivi[6] was for ever free, the first steps to realise the sale of those countless

4. Savelist is cheap fabric; ticking is a strong cotton or linen fabric; twill is a kind of textile weave.
5. The mouth of the Congo River had been discovered by the Portuguese in 1482.

6. A town on the Upper Congo River; from 1882 Stanley had been arguing that a railway should be built between the Lower and Upper Congo to facilitate the exploitation of the interior. It was completed in 1898.

millions of yards of cotton cloth would be taken. Over six millions of yards are now used annually; but we have no means of absorbing more, owing to the difficulties of transport. Every man capable and willing to carry a load is employed. When human power was discovered to be not further available we tested animal power and discovered it to be feebler and more costly than the other; and we have come to the conclusion that steam power must now assist us or we remain *in statu quo* [as things now stand]. But before having recourse to this steam power, and building the iron road along which your bales of cotton fabrics may roll on to the absorbing markets of the Upper Congo unceasingly, the Association pauses to ask you, and the peoples of other English cities, such as London, Liverpool, Glasgow, Birmingham, Leeds, Preston, Sheffield, who profess to understand the importance of the work we have been doing, and the absorbing power of those markets we have reached, what help you will render us, for your own sakes, to make those markets accessible? (Hear, hear.) The Association will not build that railway to the Upper Congo, nor invest one piece of sterling gold in it, unless they are assured they will not be robbed of it, and the Lower Congo will be placed under some flag that shall be a guarantee to all the world that its waters and banks are absolutely free. (Cheers.)

You will agree with me, I am sure, that trade ought to expand and commerce grow, and if we can coax it into mature growth in this Congo basin that it would be a praiseworthy achievement, honoured by men and gods; for out of this trade, this intercourse caused by peaceful barter, proceed all those blessings which you and I enjoy. The more trade thrives, the more benefits to mankind are multipled, and nearer to gods do men become. (Hear, hear.) The builders of railroads through wildernesses generally require large concessions of lands; but the proposed builders of this railway to connect the Lower with the Upper Congo do not ask for any landed concessions; but they ask for a concession of authority over the Lower Congo in order that the beneficent policy which directs the civilising work on the Upper Congo may be extended to the Lower River, and that the mode of government and action may be uniform throughout. The beneficent policy referred to is explained in the treaty made and concluded with the United States Government.[7] That treaty says: "That with the object of enabling civilisation and commerce to penetrate into Equatorial Africa the Free States of the Congo have resolved to levy no customs duties whatever. The Free States also guarantee to all men who establish themselves in their territories the right of purchasing, selling, or leasing any land and buildings, of creating factories and of trade on the sole condition that they conform to the law. The International Association of the Congo is prepared to enter into engagements with other nations who desire to secure the free admission of their products on the same terms as those agreed upon with the United States."

Here you have in brief the whole policy. I might end here, satisfied with having reminded you of these facts, which probably you had forgotten. Obedience to the laws—that is, laws drawn for protection of all—is the common law of all civilised communities, without which men would soon become demoralised. Can anybody object to that condition? Probably many of you here recollect reading those interesting letters from the Congo which were written by an English clerk in charge of an English factory. They ended with the cry of "Let us alone." In few words he meant to say, "We are doing very well as we are, we do not wish to be protected, and least of all

---

7. The United States was the first country to recognize the right of the International Association to govern the Congo territories in April 1884.

taxed—therefore, let us alone. Our customers, the natives, are satisfied with us. The native chiefs are friendly and in accord with us; the disturbances, if any occur, are local; they are not general, and they right themselves quickly enough, for the trader cannot exist here if he is not just and kind in his dealings. The obstreperous and violent white is left to himself and ruin. Therefore, let us alone." Most heartily do I echo this cry; but unfortunately the European nations will not heed this cry; they think that some mode of government is necessary to curb those inclined to be refractory, and if there is at present a necessity to exhibit judicial power and to restrict evil-minded and ill-conditioned whites, as the Congo basin becomes more and more populated this necessity will be still more apparent. At the same time, if power appears on the Congo with an arbitrary and unfeeling front—with a disposition to tax and levy burdensome tariffs just as trade begins to be established—the outlook for enterprise becomes dismal and dark indeed.[8] (Hear, hear.) * * *

No part of Africa, look where I might, appeared so promising to me as this neglected tenth part of the continent. I have often fancied myself—when I had nothing to do better than dream—gazing from some lofty height, and looking down upon this square compact patch of 800,000,000 acres, with its 80,000 native towns, its population of 40,000,000 souls, its 17,000 miles of river waters, and its 30,000 square miles of lakes, all lying torpid, lifeless, inert, soaked in brutishness and bestiality, and I have never yet descended from that airy perch in the empyrean and touched earth but I have felt a purpose glow in me to strive to do something to awaken it into life and movement, and I have sometimes half fancied that the face of aged Livingstone,[9] vague and indistinct as it were, shone through the warm, hazy atmosphere, with a benignant smile encouraging me in my purpose. * * *

Yet, though examined from every point of view, a study of the Upper Congo and its capabilities produces these exciting arrays of figures and possibilities, I would not pay a two-shilling piece for it all so long as it remains as it is. It will absorb easily the revenue of the wealthiest nation in Europe without any return. I would personally one hundred times over prefer a snug little freehold in a suburb of Manchester to being the owner of the 1,300,000 English square miles of the Congo basin if it is to remain as inaccessible as it is to-day, or if it is to be blocked by that fearful tariff-loving nation, the Portuguese. (Hear, hear.) But if I were assured that the Lower Congo would remain free, and the flag of the Association guaranteed its freedom, I would if I were able build that railway myself—build it solid and strong—and connect the Lower Congo with the Upper Congo, perfectly satisfied that I should be followed by the traders and colonists of all nations. * * * The Portuguese have had nearly 400 years given them to demonstrate to the world what they could do with the river whose mouth they discovered, and they have been proved to be incapable to do any good with it, and now civilisation is inclined to say to them, "Stand off from this broad highway into the regions beyond—(cheers); let others who are not paralytic strive to do what they can with it to bring it within the number of accessible markets. There are 40,000,000 of naked people beyond that gateway, and the cotton spinners of Manchester are waiting to clothe them. Rochdale and Preston women are waiting for the

8. The right of the International Association to govern the Congo was eventually ended in 1908, following widespread protests against the regime's brutality.

9. David Livingstone (1813–1873), Scottish explorer and missionary. His expeditions into central Africa, in search of the source of the Nile River, were heavily publicized;

when Livingstone "disappeared" in the course of what proved to be his last expedition, Stanley, then a correspondent for the *New York Herald,* was sent to find him. The two men met on the banks of Lake Tanganyika in East Africa in 1871; Stanley published an account of their meeting in *How I Found Livingstone* (1872).

word to weave them warm blue and crimson savelist. Birmingham foundries are glowing with the red metal that shall presently be made into ironwork in every fashion and shape for them, and the trinkets that shall adorn those dusky bosoms; and the ministers of Christ are zealous to bring them, the poor benighted heathen, into the Christian fold." (Cheers.)

MR JACOB BRIGHT, M.P., who was received with loud cheers, said: I have listened with extreme interest to one of the ablest, one of the most eloquent addresses which have ever been delivered in this city—(cheers); and I have heard with uncommon pleasure the views of a man whose ability, whose splendid force of character, whose remarkable heroism, have given him a world-wide reputation. (Cheers.) * * *
MR GRAFTON, M.P., moved:—

That the best thanks of this meeting be and are hereby given to Mr H. M. Stanley for his address to the members of the Chamber, and for the interesting information conveyed by him respecting the Congo and prospects of international trade on the West Coast and interior of Africa.

He remarked that Mr Stanley's name was already enrolled in the pages of history, and would be handed down to posterity with the names of the greatest benefactors of our species, such as Columbus, who had opened out the pathways of the world. Long might Mr Stanley be spared to witness the benefit of his arduous and beneficent labours. (Cheers.)

Premchand
1880–1936

Born in a village in northern India, Premchand grew up in difficult circumstances, the son of an underpaid postal clerk and a mother who died when he was eight. Fluent from birth in Hindi, the young Dhanpat Rai (his actual name) attended an Islamic *madras,* a religious school where he learned Urdu and Persian. A grandmother took charge of his upbringing, but she herself died soon thereafter. Married at age fifteen, he managed to finish high school, by which time his father had died as well; he had to suspend his schooling and took a job as an elementary school teacher, not completing a college degree until twenty years later. He then began to work for the government in a series of positions, eventually becoming Deputy Inspector of Schools, but resigned his post in the 1920s, in response to Mahatma Gandhi's call for noncooperation with the British imperial regime then still ruling India. Thereafter, he devoted himself to his writing, most importantly a total of more than 250 stories of village and city life, while also editing journals and translating Tolstoy, Chekhov, and George Eliot among others. He secured his position as one of the founders of the modern short story in two different languages, Urdu and Hindi. In 1936, at the end of his life, he chaired the first national conference of the Indian Progressive Writers' Association—a major source of activism for independence and social reform.

Soon after the turn of the century he had begun publishing short stories in magazines, under the pen name of Premchand. Indian fiction in Premchand's youth had largely consisted of romantic tales of love and adventure, but from the start Premchand brought a new realism and social concern to his fiction, giving searching portrayals of such subjects as child widowhood, prostitution, and landlords' mistreatment of peasants. Implicitly or explicitly, his stories often implicated British rule in the problems he treated, and the British government banned his first collection of stories when it appeared in Urdu in 1907. In 1914 Premchand began writing instead in Hindi, so as to reach as wide as possible an audience, but throughout his life and writings he emphasized the interdependence of the Urdu-speaking Muslim and Hindi-speaking Hindu communities in northern India. Like his Irish contemporary James Joyce, Premchand focuses on revelatory moments in ordinary life, conveyed in an apparently simple style that reveals the characters' conflicts with an irony that is by turns sympathetic and unsparing. In "My Big Brother," homegrown sibling rivalries and imported British curricula interact in comic but then surprisingly moving ways.

PRONUNCIATIONS:
    Lakshmi: LOCK-shmee
    Ravan: rah-VAN
    Premchand: PREM-chawnd

My Big Brother[1]

My big brother was five years older than me but only three grades ahead. He'd begun his studies at the same age I had but he didn't like the idea of moving hastily in an important matter like education. He wanted to lay a firm foundation for that great edifice, so he took two years to do one year's work; sometimes he even took three. If the foundation weren't well-made, how could the edifice endure?

I was the younger, he the elder—I was nine, he was fourteen. He had full right by seniority to supervise and instruct me. And I was expected to accept every order of his as law.

By nature he was very studious. He was always sitting with a book open. And perhaps to rest his brain he would sometimes draw pictures of birds, dogs and cats in the margin of his notebook. Occasionally he would write a name, a word or a sentence ten or twenty times. He might copy a couplet out several times in beautiful letters or create new words which made no rhyme or reason. Once, for example, I saw the following: Special Amina brothers and brothers, in reality brother-brother, Radheshyam, Mr Radheshyam, for one hour. Following this was the sketch of a man's face. I tried very hard to make some sense out of this rigmarole but I didn't succeed and I didn't dare ask him. He was in the ninth grade, I was in the sixth. To understand his creation was beyond my powers.

I wasn't really very keen about studying. To pick up a book and sit with it for an hour was a tremendous effort. As soon as I found a chance I'd leave the hostel[2] and go to the field and play marbles or fly paper kites or sometimes just meet a chum—what could be more fun? Sometimes we'd climb on to the courtyard walls and jump down or straddle the gate and ride it back and forth enjoying it as though it were an automobile. But as soon as I came back into the room and saw my brother's scowling face I was petrified. His first question would be, "Where were you?" Always this question, always asked in the same tone and the only answer I had was silence. I don't know why I couldn't manage to say that I'd just been outside playing. My silence was an

---

1. Translated by David Rubin, who notes that in Hindi the title means "my respected big brother." The narrator always addresses his older brother formally, while the brother addresses him informally.

2. The brothers are staying at a youth hostel in town, studying away from home.

acknowledgement of guilt and my brother's only remedy for this was to greet me with indignant words.

"If you study English this way you'll be studying your whole life and you won't get one word right! Studying English is no laughing matter that anyone who wants to can learn. Otherwise everybody and his cousin would be regular experts in English. You've got to wear out your eyes morning and night and use every ounce of energy, then maybe you'll master the subject. And even then it's just to say you have a smattering of it. Even great scholars can't write proper English, to say nothing of being able to speak it. And I ask you, how much of a blockhead are you that you can't learn a lesson from looking at me? You've seen with your own eyes how much I grind, and if you haven't seen it, there's something wrong with your eyes and with your wits as well. No matter how many shows and carnivals there may be have you ever seen me going to watch them? Every day there are cricket and hockey matches but I don't go near them. I keep on studying all the time, and even so it takes me two years or even three for one grade. So how do you expect to pass when you waste your time playing like this? If it takes me two or even three years, you'll fritter your whole life away studying in one grade. If you waste your time like this, it would be better if you just went home and played stick-ball to your heart's content. Why waste our dad's hard-earned money?"

Hearing a dressing-down like this I'd start to cry. What could I answer? I was guilty but who could endure a scolding like that? My brother was an expert in the art of giving advice. He'd say such sarcastic words, overwhelm me with such good counsel that my spirits would collapse, my courage disappear. I couldn't find in myself the power to toil so desperately, and in despair for a little while I'd think, "Why *don't* I run away from school and go back home? Why should I spoil my life fiddling with work that's beyond my capacity?" I was willing to remain a fool, but I just got dizzy from so much work. But after an hour or two the cloud of despair would dissipate and I'd resolve to study with all my might. I'd draw up a schedule on the spot. How could I start work without first making an outline, working out a plan? In my timetable the heading of play was entirely absent. Get up at the crack of dawn, wash hands and face at six, eat a snack, sit down and study. From six to eight English, eight to nine arithmetic, nine to nine-thirty history, then mealtime and afterwards off to school. A half hour's rest at 3.30 when I got back from school, geography from four to five, grammar from five to six, then a half hour's walk in front of the hostel, 6.30 to seven English composition, then supper, translation from eight to nine, Hindi from nine to ten, from ten to eleven miscellaneous, then to bed.

But it's one thing to draw up a schedule, another to follow it. It began to be neglected from the very first day. The inviting green expanse of the playground, the balmy winds, the commotion on the football field, the exciting stratagems of prisoner's-base, the speed and flurries of volley ball would all draw me mysteriously and irresistibly. As soon as I was there I forgot everything: the life-destroying schedule, the books that strained your eyes—I couldn't remember them at all. And then my big brother would have an occasion for sermons and scoldings. I would stay well out of his way, try to keep out of his sight, come into the room on tip-toe so he wouldn't know. But if he spotted me I'd just about die. It seemed that a naked sword was always swinging over my head. But just as in the midst of death and catastrophe a man may remain caught in the snares of illusion, so I, though I suffered reproaches and threats, could not renounce fun and games.

2

The yearly exams came round: my brother failed, I passed and was first in my class. Only two years difference were left between him and me. It occurred to me to taunt him. "What was the good of all your horrible self-punishment? Look at me, I went on playing and having a good time and I'm at the head of my class." But he was so sad and depressed that I felt genuinely sorry for him and it seemed shameful to me to pour salt on his wounds. But now I could be a little proud of myself and indeed my ego expanded. My brother's sway over me was over. I began to take part freely in the games, my spirits were running high. If he gave me another sermon, then I'd say straight out, "With all your grinding what kind of marks did you get? Playing and having fun I ended up first in my class." Although I didn't have the courage to say anything so outrageous it was plain from my behaviour that my brother's power over me was gone. He guessed it—his intuition was sharp and one day when I'd spent the whole morning playing stick-ball and came back exactly at meal time, he said, with all the air of pulling out a sword to rush at me:

"I see you've passed this year and you're first in your class, and you've got stuck up about it. But my dear brother, even great men live to regret their pride, and who are you compared to them? You must have read about what happened to Ravan.[3] Didn't you learn anything from his story or did you just read it without paying any attention? Just to pass an exam isn't anything, the real thing is to develop your mind. Understand the significance of what you read. Ravan was master of the earth. Such kings are called "Rulers of the World." These days the extent of the British Empire is vast, but their kings can't be called "Rulers of the World"—many countries in the world don't accept British rule, they're completely independent. But Ravan was a Ruler of the World, all the kings of the earth paid taxes to him. Great divinities were his slaves, even the gods of fire and water. But what happened to him in the end? Pride completely finished him off, destroying even his name. There wasn't anybody left to perform all his funeral rites properly. A man can commit any sin he wants but he'd better not be proud, nor give himself airs. When he turns proud he loses both this world and the next. You must have read about what happened to Satan too. He was so proud that he thought there was no truer devotee of God than himself. Finally it came about that he got shoved out of heaven into hell. Once the king of Turkey became very stuck-up too; he died begging for alms. You've just been promoted one grade and your head's turned by it—you've gone way up in the world! Understand this, you didn't pass through your own efforts but just stumbled on it by luck, like a blind man who catches hold of a quail. But you can catch a quail only once like that, no more. Sometimes in stick-ball too a lucky shot in the dark hits the goal, but nobody gets to be a good player from it, the kind who never misses a shot.

"Don't assume that because I failed I'm stupid and you're smart. When you reach my class you'll sweat right through your teeth when you have to bite into algebra and geometry and study English history—it's not easy to memorize these kings' names. There were eight Henrys—do you think it's easy to remember all the things that happened in each Henry's time? If you write Henry the Eighth instead of Henry the Seventh you get a zero. A complete flunk! You won't get a zero, not even zero. What kind of idea do you have about it anyway? There were dozens of Jameses,

---

3. In Hindu mythology, Ravan or Ravana was a demon king in south India; he was eventually defeated by the god Rama after he overreached his power and abducted Rama's wife Sita.

dozens of Williams and scores of Charleses! You get dizzy with them, your mind's in a whirl. Those poor fellows didn't have names enough to go around. After every name they have to put second, third, fourth and fifth. If anybody'd asked me I could have reeled off thousands of names. And as for geometry, well, God help you! If you write *a c b* instead of *a b c* your whole answer is marked wrong. Nobody ever asks those hard-hearted examiners what *is* the difference, after all, between *a b c* and *a c b* or why they waste their time torturing the students with it. Does it make any difference if you eat lentils, boiled rice and bread or boiled rice, lentils and bread? But what do those examiners care? They see only what they've written in their books. They expect us to learn it word for word. And this kind of parroting they call teaching! And in the long run what's the point of learning all this nonsense? If you bring this perpendicular line down on that line it will be twice the base line. I ask you, what's the point of that? If it isn't twice as long it's four times as long or half as long, what the devil do I care? But you've got to pass so you've got to memorize all this garbage.

"They say, 'Write an essay on punctuality no less than four pages long.' So now you open up your notebook in front of you, take your pen and curse the whole business. Who doesn't know that punctuality's a very good thing? Man's life is organized according to it, others love him for it and his business prospers from it. How can you write four pages on something so trifling? Do I need four pages for what I can describe in one sentence? So I consider it stupidity. It's not economizing time, it's wasting it to cram it with such nonsense. We want a man to say what he has to say quickly and then get moving. But no, you've got to drag it out to four pages, whatever you write, and they're foolscap[4] pages too. If this isn't an outrage on the students, what is it? It's a contradiction for them to ask us to write concisely. Write a concise essay on punctuality in no less than four pages. All right! If four pages is concise then maybe otherwise they'd ask us to write one or two hundred pages. Run fast and walk slow at the same time. Is that all mixed up or isn't it? We students can understand that much but those teachers don't have the sense—and despite that they claim they're teachers. When you get into my class, old man, then you'll really take a beating, and then you'll find out what's what. Just because you got a first division this time you're all puffed up—so pay attention to what I say. What if I failed, I'm still older than you, I have more experience of the world. Take what I say to heart or you'll be sorry."

It was almost time for school, otherwise I don't know when this medley of sermons would have ended. I didn't have much appetite that day. If I got a scolding like this when I passed, maybe if I'd failed I would have had to pay with my life. My brother's terrible description of studying in the ninth grade really scared me. I'm surprised I didn't run away from school and go home. But even a scolding like this didn't change my distaste for books one bit. I didn't miss one chance to play. I also studied, but much less. Well, anyway, just enough to complete each day's assignment and not be disgraced in class. But the confidence I'd gained in myself disappeared and then I began to lead a life like a thief's.

Then it was the yearly exams again and it so happened that once more I passed and my brother failed again. I hadn't done much work; but somehow or other I was in the first division. I myself was astonished. My brother had just about killed himself with work, memorizing every word in the course, studying till ten at night and

4. Legal size.

starting again at four in the morning, and from six until 9.30 before going to school. He'd grown pale. But the poor fellow failed again and I felt sorry for him. When he heard the results he broke down and cried, and so did I. My pleasure in passing was cut by half. If I'd failed my brother couldn't have felt so bad. But who can escape his fate?

There was only one grade left between my brother and me. The insidious thought crossed my mind that if he failed just once more then I'd be at the same level as him and then what grounds would he have for lecturing me? But I violently rejected this unworthy idea. After all, he'd scolded me only with the intention of helping me. At the time it was really obnoxious, but maybe it was only as a result of his advice that I'd passed so easily and with such good marks.

Now my brother had become much gentler toward me. Several times when he found occasion to scold me he did it without losing his temper. Perhaps he himself was beginning to understand that he no longer had the right to tell me off or at least not so much as before. My independence grew. I began to take unfair advantage of his toleration, I half started to imagine that I'd pass next time whether I studied or not, my luck was high. As a result, the little I'd studied before because of my brother, even that ceased. I found a new pleasure in flying kites and now I spent all my time at the sport. Still, I minded my manners with my brother and concealed my kite-flying from him. In preparation for the kite tournament I was secretly busy solving such problems as how best to secure the string and how to apply the paste mixed with ground glass in it to cut the other fellows' kites off their strings. I didn't want to let my brother suspect that my respect for him had in any way diminished.

One day, far from the hostel, I was running along like mad trying to grab hold of a kite. My eyes were on the heavens and that high-flying traveller in the skies that glided smoothly down like some soul emerging from paradise free of worldly attachments to be incarnated in a new life. A whole army of boys came racing out to welcome it with long, thick bamboo rods. Nobody was aware who was in front or in back of him. It was as though every one of them was flying along with that kite in the sky where everything is level, without cars or trams or trains.

Suddenly I collided with my brother, who was probably coming back from the market. He grabbed my hand and said angrily, "Aren't you ashamed to be running with these ragamuffins after a one-penny kite? Have you forgotten that you're not in a low grade any more? You're in the eighth now, one behind me. A man's got to have some regard for his position, after all. There was a time when by passing the eighth grade people became assistant revenue collectors. I know a whole lot of men who finished only the middle grades and today are first degree deputy magistrates or superintendents. How many eighth-grade graduates today are our leaders and newspaper editors? Great scholars work under their supervision but when you get into this same eighth grade you run around with hoodlums!

"I'm sorry to see you have so little sense. You're smart, there's no doubt of that, but what use is it if it destroys your self-respect? You must have assumed, 'I'm just one grade behind my brother so now he doesn't have any right to say anything to me.' But you're mistaken. I'm five years older than you and even if you come into my grade today—and the examiners being what they are there's no doubt that next year you'll be on an equal footing with me and maybe a year later you'll even get ahead of me—but that difference of five years between us not even God—to say nothing of you—can remove. I'm five years older than you and I always will be. The experience

I have of life and the world you can never catch up with even if you get an M.A. and a D. Litt. and even a Ph.D. Understanding doesn't come from reading books. Our mother never passed any grade and Dad probably never went beyond the fifth, but even if we studied the wisdom of the whole world mother and father would always have the right to explain to us and to correct us. Not just because they're our parents but because they'll always have more experience of the world. Maybe they don't know what kind of government they've got in America or how many wives Henry the Eighth had or how many constellations there are in the sky, but there are a thousand things they know more about than you or me. God forbid, but if I should fall sick to-day then you'd be in a pickle. You wouldn't be able to think of anything except sending a telegram to Dad. But in your place *he* wouldn't send anybody a telegram or get upset or be all flustered. First of all he'd diagnose the disease himself and try the remedy; then if it didn't work he'd call some doctor. And sickness is a serious matter. But you and I don't even know how to make our allowance last through the month. We spend what father sends us and then we're penniless again. We cut our breakfast, we have to hide from the barber and washerman. But as much as you and I spend today, Dad's maintained himself honourably and in good reputation the greater part of his life and brought up a family with seven children on half of it. Just look at our headmaster. Does he have an M.A. or doesn't he? And not from here either, but from Oxford. He gets a thousand rupees, but who runs his house? His old mother. There his degrees are useless. He used to manage the house himself, but he couldn't make both ends meet, he had to borrow. But since his mother has taken over it's as though Lakshmi[5] had come into his house. So brother, don't be so proud of having almost caught up with me and being independent now. I'll see that you don't go off the track. If you don't mind,[6] then" (showing me his fist) "I can use this too. I know you don't like hearing all this."

I was thoroughly shamed by this new approach of his. I had truly come to know my own insignificance and a new respect for my brother was born in my heart. With tears in my eyes, I said, "No, no, what you say is completely true and you have the right to say it."

My brother embraced me and said, "I don't forbid you to fly kites. I'd like to too. But what can I do? If I go off the track myself then how can I watch out for you? That's my responsibility."

Just then by chance a kite that had been cut loose passed over us with its string dangling down. A crowd of boys were chasing after it. My brother is very tall and leaping up he caught hold of the string and ran at top speed towards the hostel and I ran close behind him.

Lu Xun
1881–1936

Widely considered the finest Chinese writer of his generation, Lu Xun (the pen name of Zhou Shuren) was born in 1881 to a family of scholar-officials on China's southeast coast. He received the classical education expected of someone with his pedigree, but a scandal during his

---

5. Hindu goddess of wealth and good fortune.   6. Pay attention.

youth sent his grandfather to prison and the family fortunes went into decline. Lu Xun studied in a school whose focus on science and technology was designed to "strengthen" a new generation of Chinese for the new century. He then received a government scholarship to continue his studies in Japan, where modern Western influences had already taken root. Blaming the death of his father some years before on the failed methods of traditional Chinese quacks, he entered medical school, choosing to study Western medicine. But he was shocked by photographs revealing the abject helplessness of even healthy Chinese before foreign armies fighting on their territory during the Russo-Japanese War of 1904–1905, and he decided that China's real diseases were of the spirit rather than the body. That realization, perhaps coupled with a rather undistinguished record in medical school, led him to embark on a literary career in hopes of effecting a spiritual transformation of the nation.

Lu Xun's publishing projects in Japan didn't elicit the hoped-for response, however, and in 1909 he returned disheartened to China, where he spent the next sixteen years teaching and working in the Ministry of Education. A friend introduced him to the New Culture Movement, which aimed to reform both literature and society by revolutionizing the language of writing itself (see Hu Shi's manifesto, page 47), and urged Lu Xun to contribute something to the effort in 1917. His initial reaction, recorded in his preface to *A Call to Arms,* was one of apparent futility. But the following year his first short story, "A Madman's Diary," launched one of the movement's most trenchant critiques.

Over the next eight years Lu Xun wrote some two dozen stories, which were published in two volumes, *A Call to Arms* (1923) and *Wandering* (1926). In these works he wrestles with a number of recurring themes centering on the dilemmas and contradictions facing intellectuals committed to a thoroughgoing transformation of the culture. Recognizing the failings and abuses of traditional Chinese thought and practices, he was both unwilling to abandon them wholesale and skeptical of the ability of sweeping utopian reforms to effect real positive change. He was haunted as well by doubts about whether writing could in fact grasp and convey real knowledge, and about whether intellectuals in general could truly communicate with the common people, in whose interests they were presumably working. By 1926 these questions finally led him to abandon fiction writing altogether. Forced to flee Peking following a purge by the Nationalist government of Communists and Communist sympathizers, he turned to the more pointed essay form and to Marxist activism as a means of gaining a less ambiguous leverage over reality. His relations with leftist colleagues remained fraught, however, and he never joined the party, yet he continued writing and left behind a substantial body of work—from essays, poetry, short stories, translations, and works on premodern literature to collections of woodcuts.

PRONUNCIATIONS:
   Li Shizhen: LEE SHEE-jen
   Lu Xun: LOU SHOON
   Zhao: ja'o

Preface to *A Call to Arms*[1]

When I was young I, too, had many dreams. Most of them I later forgot, but I see nothing in this to regret. For although recalling the past may bring happiness, at times it cannot but bring loneliness, and what is the point of clinging in spirit to lonely bygone days? However, my trouble is that I cannot forget completely, and these stories stem from those things which I have been unable to forget.

---

1. Translated by Yang Xianyi and Gladys Yang, from whom the following footnotes are adapted.

For more than four years I frequented, almost daily, a pawnshop and pharmacy. I cannot remember how old I was at the time, but the pharmacy counter was exactly my height and that in the pawnshop twice my height. I used to hand clothes and trinkets up to the counter twice my height, then take the money given me with contempt to the counter my own height to buy medicine for my father, a chronic invalid. On my return home I had other things to keep me busy, for our physician was so eminent that he prescribed unusual drugs and adjuvants: aloe roots dug up in winter, sugar-cane that had been three years exposed to frost, original pairs of crickets, and ardisia that had seeded . . . most of which were difficult to come by. But my father's illness went from bad to worse until finally he died.

It is my belief that those who come down in the world will probably learn in the process what society is really like. My eagerness to go to N— and study in the K— Academy[2] seems to have shown a desire to strike out for myself, escape, and find people of a different kind. My mother had no choice but to raise eight dollars for my travelling expenses and say I might do as I pleased. That she cried was only natural, for at that time the proper thing was to study the classics and take the official examinations. Anyone who studied "foreign subjects" was a social outcast regarded as someone who could find no way out and was forced to sell his soul to foreign devils. Besides, she was sorry to part with me. But in spite of all this, I went to N— and entered the K— Academy; and it was there that I learned of the existence of physics, arithmetic, geography, history, drawing and physical training. They had no physiology course, but we saw woodblock editions of such works as *A New Course on the Human Body* and *Essays on Chemistry and Hygiene*.[3] Recalling the talk and prescriptions of physicians I had known and comparing them with what I now knew, I came to the conclusion that those physicians must be either unwitting or deliberate charlatans; and I began to feel great sympathy for the invalids and families who suffered at their hands. From translated histories I also learned that the Japanese Reformation owed its rise, to a great extent, to the introduction of Western medical science to Japan.

These inklings took me to a medical college in the Japanese countryside.[4] It was my fine dream that on my return to China I would cure patients like my father who had suffered from the wrong treatment, while if war broke out I would serve as an army doctor, at the same time promoting my countrymen's faith in reform.

I have no idea what improved methods are now used to teach microbiology, but in those days we were shown lantern slides of microbes; and if the lecture ended early, the instructor might show slides of natural scenery or news to fill up the time. Since this was during the Russo-Japanese War, there were many war slides, and I had to join in the clapping and cheering in the lecture hall along with the other students. It was a long time since I had seen any compatriots, but one day I saw a newsreel slide of a number of Chinese, one of them bound and the rest standing around him. They were all sturdy fellows but appeared completely apathetic. According to the commentary, the one with his hands bound was a spy working for the Russians who was to be beheaded by the Japanese military as a warning to others, while the Chinese beside him had come to enjoy the spectacle.

2. N— refers to Nanjing, and K— to the Kiangnan (Jiang-nan) Naval Academy where the author studied in 1898.
3. Two English books about physiology and nutrition, translated into Chinese in the mid-19th century.
4. The Sendai Medical College, where Lu Xun studied from 1904 to 1906.

Before the term was over I had left for Tokyo, because this slide convinced me that medical science was not so important after all. The people of a weak and backward country, however strong and healthy they might be, could only serve to be made examples of or as witnesses of such futile spectacles; and it was not necessarily deplorable if many of them died of illness. The most important thing, therefore, was to change their spirit; and since at that time I felt that literature was the best means to this end, I decided to promote a literary movement. There were many Chinese students in Tokyo studying law, political science, physics and chemistry, even police work and engineering, but not one studying literature and art. However, even in this uncongenial atmosphere I was fortunate enough to find some kindred spirits. We gathered the few others we needed and after discussion our first step, of course, was to publish a magazine, the title of which denoted that this was a new birth. As we were then rather classically inclined, we called it *Vita Nova* (*New Life*).

When the time for publication drew near, some of our contributors dropped out and then our funds ran out, until there were only three of us left and we were penniless. Since we had started our venture at an unlucky hour, there was naturally no one to whom we could complain when we failed; but later even we three were destined to part, and our discussions of a future dream world had to cease. So ended this abortive *Vita Nova*.

Only later did I feel the futility of it all. At that time I had not a clue. Later it seemed to me that if a man's proposals met with approval, that should encourage him to advance; if they met with opposition, that should make him fight back; but the real tragedy was for him to lift up his voice among the living and meet with no response, neither approval nor opposition, just as if he were stranded in a boundless desert completely at a loss. That was when I became conscious of loneliness.

And this sense of loneliness grew from day to day, entwining itself about my soul like some huge poisonous snake.

But in spite of my groundless sadness, I felt no indignation; for this experience had made me reflect and see that I was definitely not the type of hero who could rally multitudes at his call.

However, my loneliness had to be dispelled because it was causing me agony. So I used various means to dull my senses, to immerse myself among my fellow nationals and to turn to the past. Later I experienced or witnessed even greater loneliness and sadness which I am unwilling to recall, preferring that it should perish with my mind in the dust. Still my attempt to deaden my senses was not unsuccessful—I lost the enthusiasm and fervour of my youth.

In S— Hostel[5] was a three-roomed house with a courtyard in which grew a locust tree, and it was said that a woman had hanged herself there. Although the tree had grown so tall that its branches were now out of reach, the rooms remained deserted. For some years I stayed here, copying ancient inscriptions. I had few visitors, the inscriptions raised no political problems or issues, and so the days slipped quietly away, which was all that I desired. On summer nights, when mosquitoes swarmed, I would sit under the locust tree waving my fan and looking at specks of blue sky through chinks in the thick foliage, while belated caterpillars would fall, icy-cold, on to my neck.

The only visitor to drop in occasionally for a talk was my old friend Jin Xinyi. Having put his big portfolio on the rickety table he would take off his long gown and sit down opposite me, looking as if his heart was still beating fast because he was afraid of dogs.

5. The Shaoxing Hostel, where Lu Xun stayed in Beijing from 1912 to 1919.

"What's the use of copying these?" One night, while leafing through the inscriptions I had copied, he asked me for enlightenment on this point.

"There isn't any use."

"What's the point, then, of copying them?"

"There isn't any point."

"Why don't you write something? . . ."

I understood. They were bringing out *New Youth*,[6] but since there did not seem to have been any reaction, favourable or otherwise, no doubt they felt lonely. However I said:

"Imagine an iron house having not a single window and virtually indestructible, with all its inmates sound asleep and about to die of suffocation. Dying in their sleep, they won't feel the pain of death. Now if you raise a shout to wake a few of the lighter sleepers, making these unfortunate few suffer the agony of irrevocable death, do you really think you are doing them a good turn?"

"But if a few wake up, you can't say there is no hope of destroying the iron house."

True, in spite of my own conviction, I could not blot out hope, for hope belongs to the future. I had no negative evidence able to refute his affirmation of faith. So I finally agreed to write, and the result was my first story "A Madman's Diary." And once started I could not give up but would write some sort of short story from time to time to humour my friends, until I had written more than a dozen of them.

As far as I am concerned, I no longer feel any great urge to express myself; yet, perhaps because I have not forgotten the grief of my past loneliness, I sometimes call out to encourage those fighters who are galloping on in loneliness, so that they do not lose heart. Whether my cry is brave or sad, repellent or ridiculous, I do not care. However, since this is a call to arms I must naturally obey my general's orders. This is why I often resort to innuendoes, as when I made a wreath appear from nowhere at the son's grave in "Medicine," while in "Tomorrow" I did not say that Fourth Shan's Wife never dreamed of her little boy. For our chiefs in those days were against pessimism. And I, for my part, did not want to infect with the loneliness which I had found so bitter those young people who were still dreaming pleasant dreams, just as I had done when young.

It is clear, then, that my stories fall far short of being works of art; hence I must at least count myself fortunate that they are still known as stories and are even being brought out in one volume. Although such good fortune makes me uneasy, it still pleases me to think that they have readers in the world of men, for the time being at any rate.

So now that these stories of mine are being reprinted in one collection, for the reasons given above I have chosen to entitle it *Call to Arms.*

Beijing
3 December 1922

A Madman's Diary[1]

Two brothers, whose names I need not mention here, were both good friends of mine in high school; but after a separation of many years we gradually lost touch. Some time ago I happened to hear that one of them was seriously ill, and since I was going

---

6. This magazine played an important part in the May 4th Movement of 1919 by attacking feudalism, advocating the New Culture Movement, and spreading Marxist ideas. Jin Xinyi is an alias for Qian Xuantong, one of the editors of *New Youth.* Lu Xun was an important contributor to the magazine.

1. Translated by Yang Xianyi and Gladys Yang.

back to my old home I broke my journey to call on them. I saw only one, however, who told me that the invalid was his younger brother.

"I appreciate your coming such a long way to see us," he said, "but my brother recovered some time ago and has gone elsewhere to take up an official post." Then, laughing, he produced two volumes of his brother's diary, saying that from these the nature of his past illness could be seen and there was no harm in showing them to an old friend. I took the diary away, read it through, and found that he had suffered from a form of persecution complex. The writing was most confused and incoherent, and he had made many wild statements; moreover he had omitted to give any dates, so that only by the colour of the ink and the differences in the writing could one tell that it was not all written at one time. Certain sections, however, were not altogether disconnected, and I have copied out a part to serve as a subject for medical research. I have not altered a single illogicality in the diary and have changed only the names, even though the people referred to are all country folk, unknown to the world and of no consequence. As for the title, it was chosen by the diarist himself after his recovery, and I did not change it.

I

Tonight the moon is very bright.

I have not seen it for over thirty years, so today when I saw it I felt in unusually high spirits. I begin to realize that during the past thirty-odd years I have been in the dark; but now I must be extremely careful. Otherwise why should the Zhaos' dog have looked at me twice?

I have reason for my fear.

II

Tonight there is no moon at all, I know that this is a bad omen. This morning when I went out cautiously, Mr. Zhao had a strange look in his eyes, as if he were afraid of me, as if he wanted to murder me. There were seven or eight others who discussed me in a whisper. And they were afraid of my seeing them. So, indeed, were all the people I passed. The fiercest among them grinned at me; whereupon I shivered from head to foot, knowing that their preparations were complete.

I was not afraid, however, but continued on my way. A group of children in front were also discussing me, and the look in their eyes was just like that in Mr. Zhao's while their faces too were ghastly pale. I wondered what grudge these children could have against me to make them behave like this. I could not help calling out, "Tell me!" But then they ran away.

I wonder what grudge Mr. Zhao has against me, what grudge the people on the road have against me. I can think of nothing except that twenty years ago I trod on Mr. Gu Jiu's[2] old ledgers, and Mr. Gu was most displeased. Although Mr. Zhao does not know him, he must have heard talk of this and decided to avenge him, thus he is conspiring against me with the people on the road. But then what of the children? At that time they were not yet born, so why should they eye me so strangely today, as if they were afraid of me, as if they wanted to murder me? This really frightens me, it is so bewildering and upsetting.

I know. They must have learned this from their parents!

2. Literally, Mr. "Ancient Old."

III

I can't sleep at night. Everything requires careful consideration if one is to understand it.

Those people, some of whom have been pilloried by the magistrate, slapped in the face by the local gentry, had their wives taken away by bailiffs or their parents driven to suicide by creditors, never looked as frightened and as fierce then as they did yesterday.

The most extraordinary thing was that woman on the street yesterday who was spanking her son. "Little devil!" she cried. "I'm so angry I could eat you!" Yet all the time it was me she was looking at. I gave a start, unable to hide my alarm. Then all those long-toothed people with livid faces began to hoot with laughter. Old Chen hurried forward and dragged me home.

He dragged me home. The folk at home all pretended not to know me; they had the same look in their eyes as all the others. When I went into the study, they locked me in as if cooping up a chicken or a duck. This incident left me even more bewildered.

A few days ago a tenant of ours from Wolf Cub Village came to report the failure of the crops and told my elder brother that a notorious character in their village had been beaten to death; then some people had taken out his heart and liver, fried them in oil, and eaten them as a means of increasing their courage. When I interrupted, the tenant and my brother both stared at me. Only today have I realized that they had exactly the same look in their eyes as those people outside.

Just to think of it sets me shivering from the crown of my head to the soles of my feet.

They eat human beings, so they may eat me.

I see that the woman's "eat you," the laughter of those long-toothed people with livid faces, and the tenant's story the other day are obviously secret signs. I realize all the poison in their speech, all the daggers in their laughter. Their teeth are white and glistening: they use these teeth to eat men.

Evidently, although I am not a bad man, ever since I trod on Mr. Gu's ledgers it has been touch-and-go with me. They seem to have secrets which I cannot guess, and once they are angry they will call anyone a bad character. I remember when my elder brother taught me to write compositions, no matter how good a man was, if I produced arguments to the contrary he would mark that passage to show his approval; while if I excused evildoers he would say, "Good for you, that shows originality." How can I possibly guess their secret thoughts—especially when they are ready to eat people?

Everything requires careful consideration if one is to understand it. In ancient times, as I recollect, people often ate human beings, but I am rather hazy about it. I tried to look this up, but my history has no chronology and scrawled all over each page are the words: "Confucian Virtue and Morality." Since I could not sleep anyway, I read intently half the night until I began to see words between the lines. The whole book was filled with the two words—"Eat people."

All these words written in the book, all the words spoken by our tenant, eye me quizzically with an enigmatic smile.

I too am a man, and they want to eat me!

IV

In the morning I sat quietly for some time. Old Chen brought in lunch: one bowl of vegetables, one bowl of steamed fish. The eyes of the fish were white and hard, and its mouth was open just like those people who want to eat human beings. After a few mouthfuls I could not tell whether the slippery morsels were fish or human flesh, so I brought it all up.

I said, "Old Chen, tell my brother that I feel quite suffocated and want to have a stroll in the garden." Old Chen said nothing but went out, and presently he came back and opened the gate.

I did not move, but watched to see how they would treat me, feeling certain that they would not let me go. Sure enough! My elder brother came slowly out, leading an old man. There was a murderous gleam in his eyes, and fearing that I would see it he lowered his head, stealing side-glances at me from behind his glasses.

"You seem very well today," said my brother.

"Yes," said I.

"I have invited Mr. Ho here today to examine you."

"All right," I replied. Actually I knew quite well that this old man was the executioner in disguise! Feeling my pulse was simply a pretext for him to see how fat I was; for this would entitle him to a share of my flesh. Still I was not afraid. Although I do not eat men my courage is greater than theirs. I held out my two fists to see what he would do. The old man sat down, closed his eyes, fumbled for some time, remained motionless for a while; then opened his shifty eyes and said, "Don't let your imagination run away with you. Rest quietly for a few days, and you will be better."

Don't let your imagination run away with you! Rest quietly for a few days! By fattening me of course they'll have more to eat. But what good will it do me? How can it be "better"? The whole lot of them wanting to eat people yet stealthily trying to keep up appearances, not daring to do it outright, was really enough to make me die of laughter. I couldn't help it, I nearly split my sides, I was so amused. I knew that this laughter voiced courage and integrity. Both the old man and my brother turned pale, awed by my courage and integrity.

But my courage just makes them all the more eager to eat me, to acquire some of my courage for themselves. The old man went out of the gate, but before he had gone far he said to my brother in a low voice, "To be eaten at once!" My brother nodded. So you are in it too! This stupendous discovery, though it came as a shock, is no more than I might expect: the accomplice in eating me is my elder brother!

The eater of human flesh is my elder brother!

I am the younger brother of an eater of human flesh!

I, who will be eaten by others, am the younger brother of an eater of human flesh!

V

These few days I have been thinking again: suppose that old man were not an executioner in disguise, but a real doctor; he would be nonetheless an eater of human flesh. That book on herbs by his predecessor Li Shizhen[3] states explicitly that men's flesh can be boiled and eaten; how then can he still deny that he eats men?

As for my elder brother, I have also good reason to suspect him. When he was teaching me, he told me himself, "People exchange their sons to eat."[4] And once in discussing a bad man he said that not only did the fellow deserve to be killed, he should "have his flesh eaten and his hide slept on." I was still young at the time, and for quite a while my

3. Famous pharmacologist (1518–93). His *Compendium of Materia Medica* doesn't say that human flesh could be used as a medicine.

4. From a commentary on the canonical chronicle *Spring and Autumn Annals,* which describes the desperate conditions of a besieged population in 488 B.C.E.

heart beat faster. That story our tenant from Wolf Cub Village told the other day about eating a man's heart and liver didn't surprise him at all—he kept nodding his head. He is evidently just as cruel as before. Since it is possible to "exchange sons to eat," then anything can be exchanged, anyone can be eaten. In the past I simply listened to his explanations and let it go at that; now I know that when he gave me these explanations, not only was there human fat at the corner of his lips, but his whole heart was set on eating men.

VI

Pitch dark. I don't know whether it is day or night. The Zhaos' dog has started barking again.

The fierceness of a lion, the timidity of a rabbit, the craftiness of a fox. . . .

VII

I know their way: they are not prepared to kill outright, nor would they dare, for fear of the consequences. Instead they have banded together and set traps everywhere, to force me to kill myself. The behaviour of the men and women in the street a few days ago and my elder brother's attitude these last few days make it quite obvious. What they like best is for a man to take off his belt and hang himself from a beam; for then they can enjoy their hearts' desire without being blamed for murder. Naturally that delights them and sets them roaring with laughter. On the other hand, if a man is frightened or worried to death, though that makes him rather thin, they still nod in approval.

They only eat dead flesh! I remember reading somewhere of a hideous beast with an ugly look in its eye called "hyena," which often eats dead flesh. Even the largest bones it crunches into fragments and swallows; the mere thought of this makes your hair stand on end. Hyenas are related to wolves, wolves belong to the canine species. The other day the Zhaos' dog eyed me several times: it is obviously in the plot too as their accomplice. The old man's eyes were cast down, but that did not deceive me.

The most deplorable is my elder brother. He's a man too, so why isn't he afraid, why is he plotting with others to eat me? Does force of habit blind a man to what's wrong? Or is he so heartless that he will knowingly commit a crime?

In cursing man-eaters, I shall start with my brother. In dissuading man-eaters, I shall start with him too.

VIII

Actually such arguments should have convinced them long ago. . . .

Suddenly someone came in. He was only about twenty years old and I did not see his features very clearly. His face was wreathed in smiles, but when he nodded to me his smile didn't seem genuine. I asked him, "Is it right to eat human beings?"

Still smiling, he replied, "When there is no famine how can one eat human beings?"

I realized at once he was one of them; but still I summoned up courage to repeat my question:

"Is it right?"

"What makes you ask such a thing? You really are . . . fond of a joke. . . . It is very fine today."

"It is fine, and the moon is very bright. But I want to ask you: Is it right?"

He looked disconcerted and muttered, "No. . . ."

"No? Then why do they still do it?"

"What are you talking about?"

"What am I talking about? They are eating men now in Wolf Cub Village, and you can see it written all over the books, in fresh red ink."

His expression changed. He grew ghastly pale. "It may be so," he said staring at me. "That's the way it's always been. . . ."

"Does that make it right?"

"I refuse to discuss it with you. Anyway, you shouldn't talk about it. It's wrong for anyone to talk about it."

I leaped up and opened my eyes wide, but the man had vanished. I was soaked with sweat. He was much younger than my elder brother, but even so he was in it. He must have been taught by his parents. And I am afraid he has already taught his son; that is why even the children look at me so fiercely.

IX

Wanting to eat men, at the same time afraid of being eaten themselves, they all eye each other with the deepest suspicion.

How comfortable life would be for them if they could rid themselves of such obsessions and go to work, walk, eat and sleep at ease. They have only this one step to take. Yet fathers and sons, husbands and wives, brothers, friends, teachers and students, sworn enemies and even strangers, have all joined in this conspiracy, discouraging and preventing each other from taking this step.

X

Early this morning I went to find my elder brother. He was standing outside the hall door looking at the sky when I walked up behind him, standing between him and the door, and addressed him with exceptional poise and politeness:

"Brother, I have something to say to you."

"Go ahead then." He turned quickly towards me, nodding.

"It's nothing much, but I find it hard to say. Brother, probably all primitive people ate a little human flesh to begin with. Later, because their views altered some of them stopped and tried so hard to do what was right that they changed into men, into real men. But some are still eating people—just like reptiles. Some have changed into fish, birds, monkeys, and finally men; but those who make no effort to do what's right are still reptiles. When those who eat men compare themselves with those who don't, how ashamed they must be. Probably much more ashamed than the reptiles are before monkeys.

"In ancient times Yi Ya boiled his son for Jie and Zhou to eat; that is the old story.[5] But actually since the creation of heaven and earth by Pan Gu[6] men have been eating each other, from the time of Yi Ya's son to the time of Xu Xilin,[7] and from the time of Xu Xilin down to the man caught in Wolf Cub Village. Last year they executed a criminal in the city, and a consumptive soaked a piece of bread in his blood and sucked it.

"They want to eat me, and of course you can do nothing about it single-handed; but why must you join them? As man-eaters they are capable of anything. If they eat

5. Yi Ya, a favorite of Duke Huan of Qi in the seventh century B.C.E., was a good cook and sycophant. When the duke remarked that he had never tasted the flesh of children, Yi Ya cooked his own son for him to eat. Jie and Zhou were kings of earlier periods.

6. A mythological figure from whom, according to one legend, the entire universe derives.

7. A revolutionary executed in 1907 for assassinating a Qing official. His heart and liver were eaten.

me, they can eat you as well; members of the same group can still eat each other. But if you will just change your ways, change right away, then everyone will have peace. Although this has been going on since time immemorial, today we could make a special effort to do what is right, and say this can't be done! I'm sure you can say that, Brother. The other day when the tenant wanted the rent reduced, you said it couldn't be done."

At first he only smiled cynically, then a murderous gleam came into his eyes, and when I spoke of their secret he turned pale. Outside the gate quite a crowd had gathered, among them Mr. Zhao and his dog, all craning their necks to peer in. I could not see all their faces, some of them seemed to be masked; others were the old lot, long-toothed with livid faces, concealing their laughter. I knew they were one gang, all eaters of human flesh. But I also knew that they did not all think alike by any means. Some of them thought that since it had always been so, men should be eaten. Others knew they shouldn't eat men but still wanted to, and were afraid people might discover their secret; so although what I said made them angry they still smiled their cynical, tight-lipped smiles.

Suddenly my brother's face darkened.

"Clear off, the whole lot of you!" he roared. "What's the point of looking at a madman?"

Then I realized part of their cunning. They would never be willing to change their stand, and their plans were all laid: they had labelled me a madman. In future when I was eaten, not only would there be no trouble but people would probably be grateful to them. When our tenant spoke of the villagers eating a bad character, it was exactly the same device. This is their old trick.

Old Chen came in too in a towering temper. But they could not stop my mouth, I had to warn those people:

"You should change, change from the bottom of your hearts. You must realize that there will be no place for man-eaters in the world in future.

"If you don't change, you may all be eaten by each other. However many of you there are, you will be wiped out by the real men, just as wolves are killed by hunters—just like reptiles!"

Old Chen drove everybody away. My brother had disappeared. Old Chen advised me to go back to my room. It was pitch dark in there. The beams and rafters shook above my head. After shaking for a while they grew bigger and bigger. They piled on top of me.

The weight was so great, I couldn't move. They meant that I should die. However, knowing that the weight was false I struggled out, dripping with sweat. But I had to warn them:

"You must change at once, change from the bottom of your hearts! You must know that there'll be no place for man-eaters in future. . . ."

XI

The sun has stopped shining, the door is never opened. Just two meals day after day.

Picking up my chopsticks, I thought of my elder brother. I know now how my little sister died: it was all through him. My sister was only five at the time. I can still remember how sweet she looked, poor thing. Mother wept as if she would never stop, but he begged her not to cry, probably because he had eaten our sister himself and so this weeping made him rather ashamed. If he had any sense of shame. . . .

My sister was eaten by my brother, but I don't know whether Mother realized it or not.

I think Mother must have known, but when she wept she didn't say so outright, probably because she also thought it proper. I remember when I was four or five, sitting in the cool of the hall, my brother told me that if a man's parents were ill he should cut off a piece of his flesh and boil it for them, if he wanted to be considered a good son;[8] and Mother didn't contradict him. If one piece could be eaten, obviously so could the whole. And yet just to think of the weeping then still makes my heart bleed; that is the extraordinary thing about it!

XII

I can't bear to think of it.

It has only just dawned on me that all these years I have been living in a place where for four thousand years human flesh has been eaten. My brother had just taken over the charge of the house when our sister died, and he may well have used her flesh in our food, making us eat it unwittingly.

I may have eaten several pieces of my sister's flesh unwittingly, and now it is my turn. . . .

How can a man like myself, after four thousand years of man-eating history—even though I knew nothing about it at first—ever hope to face real men?

XIII

Perhaps there are still children who haven't eaten men?

Save the children. . . .

A Small Incident

Six years have slipped by since I came from the country to the capital. During that time the number of so-called affairs of state I have witnessed or heard about is far from small, but none of them made much impression. If asked to define their influence on me, I can only say they made my bad temper worse. Frankly speaking, they taught me to take a poorer view of people every day.

One small incident, however, which struck me as significant and jolted me out of my irritability, remains fixed even now in my memory.

It was the winter of 1917, a strong north wind was blustering, but the exigencies of earning my living forced me to be up and out early. I met scarcely a soul on the road, but eventually managed to hire a rickshaw to take me to S— Gate. Presently the wind dropped a little, having blown away the drifts of dust on the road to leave a clean broad highway, and the rickshaw man quickened his pace. We were just approaching S— Gate when we knocked into someone who slowly toppled over.

It was a grey-haired woman in ragged clothes. She had stepped out abruptly from the roadside in front of us, and although the rickshaw man had swerved, her tattered padded waistcoat, unbuttoned and billowing in the wind, had caught on the shaft. Luckily the rickshaw man had slowed down, otherwise she would certainly have had a bad fall and it might have been a serious accident.

---

8. Traditional doctrines instructed children to cut off their flesh to feed their parents, if necessary.

She huddled there on the ground, and the rickshaw man stopped. As I did not believe the old woman was hurt and as no one else had seen us, I thought this halt of his uncalled for, liable to land him in trouble and hold me up.

"It's all right," I said. "Go on."

He paid no attention—he may not have heard—but set down the shafts, took the old woman's arm and gently helped her up.

"Are you all right?" he asked.

"I hurt myself falling."

I thought: I saw how slowly you fell, how could you be hurt? Putting on an act like this is simply disgusting. The rickshaw man asked for trouble, and now he's got it. He'll have to find his own way out.

But the rickshaw man did not hesitate for a minute after hearing the old woman's answer. Still holding her arm, he helped her slowly forward. Rather puzzled by this I looked ahead and saw a police-station. Because of the high wind, there was no one outside. It was there that the rickshaw man was taking the old woman.

Suddenly I had the strange sensation that his dusty retreating figure had in that instant grown larger. Indeed, the further he walked the larger he loomed, until I had to look up to him. At the same time he seemed gradually to be exerting a pressure on me which threatened to overpower the small self hidden under my fur-lined gown.

Almost paralysed at that juncture I sat there motionless, my mind a blank, until a policeman came out. Then I got down from the rickshaw.

The policeman came up to me and said, "Get another rickshaw. He can't take you any further."

On the spur of the moment I pulled a handful of coppers from my coat pocket and handed them to the policeman. "Please give him this," I said.

The wind had dropped completely, but the road was still quiet. As I walked along thinking, I hardly dared to think about myself. Quite apart from what had happened earlier, what had I meant by that handful of coppers? Was it a reward? Who was I to judge the rickshaw man? I could give myself no answer.

Even now, this incident keeps coming back to me. It keeps distressing me and makes me try to think about myself. The politics and the fighting of those years have slipped my mind as completely as the classics I read as a child. Yet this small incident keeps coming back to me, often more vivid than in actual life, teaching me shame, spurring me on to reform, and imbuing me with fresh courage and fresh hope.

—◄═◊═►—

James Joyce
1882–1941

One of the greatest figures in European modernism, James Joyce emigrated from his native Ireland at the age of twenty-two, and spent his adult life in Italy, Switzerland, and France; yet this most cosmopolitan of writers continued to ground his fiction in the experiences of his early years in provincial Dublin. He had been born in a Dublin suburb, the eldest of "sixteen or seventeen children," as his father later hazily recalled, only ten of whom survived infancy. His father,

John, worked for the Irish nationalist movement headed by Charles Stewart Parnell in the 1880s, until Parnell's influence collapsed after he was named as an adulterer in a divorce suit in 1889. The Irish Catholic hierarchy turned against him, as did many political supporters, and a broken Parnell died in 1891, an event that prompted the nine-year-old Joyce to compose his first published poem, "Et Tu, Healy?" John Joyce lost his political appointment as a tax collector (problems with alcohol and borrowings from his own tax receipts compounded his political difficulties), and the family moved frequently in the ensuing years, to a series of increasingly rundown lodgings.

Joyce spent his adolescence in the 1890s hoping to get away from what he saw as Dublin's spiritual, political, and intellectual paralysis. A prize-winning student at a Catholic boys' school—where for a time he considered entering the priesthood—Joyce won a scholarship to study at the Jesuit-run University College, Dublin, where he pursued his wide, eclectic reading in ancient and modern authors. By the age of eighteen, he had taught himself Dano-Norwegian in order to read the works of Henrik Ibsen in the original. That year, he published an article on Ibsen in the *Fortnightly Review,* an important London journal. A few months later, he learned that Ibsen had admired the article, and Joyce wrote his hero a glowing letter in Norwegian— never answered—congratulating the aging author on his work and indicating his intention to carry on Ibsen's struggle against social and artistic conventions.

Joyce always had an ambiguous relation to his Irish literary contemporaries. In 1901 he published "The Day of the Rabblement," an essay criticizing as provincial the Irish Literary Theatre recently started by W. B. Yeats and others to promote a revival of Irish culture. Yet in the following years, he sought out Yeats and the other leading literary figures of Dublin, hoping to establish himself as a writer and reviewer. Funds were a constant concern, and an attempt to study medicine in Paris was cut short both by lack of money and by the slow death by cancer of his mother in 1903. Joyce returned home for her final illness, and abandoned his projected medical career; after a desultory year of teaching and writing, he left permanently for the Continent, where he taught for several years in a Berlitz school in Trieste. He was accompanied by Nora Barnacle, whom he had met on 16 June 1904—a day he would immortalize as "Bloomsday," the day on which his great novel *Ulysses* is set. While in Trieste, he completed *Dubliners,* a series of short stories he had begun at the suggestion of a friend who had offered him £1 each for some simple stories for a newspaper called the *Irish Homestead.* He also began an autobiographical novel, first entitled *Stephen Hero* and then rewritten as *A Portrait of the Artist as a Young Man.*

Joyce had great difficulty getting both works published. He insisted on recording the actual language Dubliners used, including vulgarities and even occasional obscenities, and he included real people—often unflatteringly portrayed—along with his fictional characters. Dublin publishers hesitated to take his work, fearing both libel and obscenity charges, and though Joyce had impressed the Irish literary establishment with his talent (as well as his arrogance), he had no obvious group of supporters. At once anti-British and antinationalist, fiercely independent yet expecting others to support him, Joyce was hard to place. This difficulty only increased as time went on, as he continually reinvented himself throughout his career. As soon as one phase of his work finally found a publisher and a small group of fervent admirers, Joyce would abandon the kind of writing they had come to admire and would make new demands on his readers' creativity, intelligence, and sheer patience.

Dubliners was published in 1914, while *Portrait* was being serialized in a magazine of experimental writing run by Harriet Weaver, who became a longtime supporter of Joyce and his work. *Portrait* was published in book form in 1916—in the United States, no Irish or English publisher having been willing to take it. By that point, Joyce was deeply engaged in what was to become one of the most influential novels of the twentieth century—*Ulysses,* the story of several intertwined lives in Dublin on 16 June 1904, centering on the adventures of Leopold Bloom, advertising salesman, and his unfaithful wife Molly. *Ulysses* has direct links with Joyce's previous fiction, including the presence of its third lead character,

Stephen Dedalus, the autobiographical hero of *Portrait.* Yet as he worked on his big new novel Joyce rapidly began to move beyond the symbolically charged realism that had characterized his earlier fiction. Like its predecessors, *Ulysses* is filled with realistic detail about Dublin life, but over the course of the book these details are increasingly caught up in an exploding universe of literary styles and cultural references—from an extended parallel with Homer's *Odyssey* to parodies of the entire history of English prose style, experiments in musical writing, and even a chapter in drama form. Arcane references to medieval scholastic philosophy intertwine with parodies of contemporary advertising language, and whole chains of reference to Dante, Shakespeare, and Mozart are developed amid visits to outhouses and brothels. Reading *Ulysses* after it was eventually published in 1922 in Paris—once again, no English or Irish publisher having been found willing to take it—a bemused Virginia Woolf was impressed by its virtuosity and ambition, but couldn't help feeling she was watching "an undergraduate scratching his pimples." T. S. Eliot, on the other hand, wrote an essay called "*Ulysses,* Order, and Myth," in which he praised the novel as one of the great achievements of modern literature, asserting that Joyce had succeeded in "giving a shape and a significance to the immense panorama of futility and anarchy which is contemporary history."

Joyce by this time was living in Paris, together with Nora—they would only formally marry late in life—and their two children. His great novel gradually came to find readers, including in the United States, where it was initially banned as obscene, until a landmark decision by a judge determined in 1928 that the book's obscenities served compelling artistic purposes. By then, Joyce was working on a yet more baffling work, *Finnegans Wake,* which would occupy him for seventeen years, until shortly before his death in 1941. An extraordinary kaleidoscope of styles and languages, the book is a riot of stories, rumors, and hearsay surrounding a series of comically embarrassing moments in the life of a hero of many names but constant initials, H.C.E.; his wife, Anna Livia Plurabelle; and their quarreling sons and daughter. At the same time, it is a compendium of Irish and world history, politics, and culture, a veritable "chaosmos of Alle," as it calls itself. Even this phantasmagoric book, though, remains set in Dublin, and it displays Joyce's abiding interest in intersections of sexual, textual, and political misfortunes, as H.C.E. loses a local election after seducing some girls, or being seduced by them, or exposing himself in Dublin's Phoenix Park, whereupon Anna Livia writes a long letter, her "mamafesta," in his defense.

When he received the commission to write some "simple stories" for the *Irish Homestead* in 1904, Joyce was already engaged in composing a series of short prose experiments that he called "epiphanies"—sketches of seemingly ordinary scenes in which the hidden truth about a person or situation is suddenly brought to the surface, often for the lead character to contemplate, sometimes only for the reader to perceive. Each of the three stories from *Dubliners* included here moves to such an epiphany; at the same time, the stories show the young Joyce trying out a range of options as a writer: the first-person narration of "Araby," the coolly distanced observation of "Clay," and the broad canvas of the dinner party of "The Dead"—appropriately, set on January 6, the Feast of the Epiphany. Written in 1907, two years after he had completed the rest of the book, this last and longest of the stories in *Dubliners* shows how its hero's world turns upside down over the course of a single evening, as Gabriel Conroy has a series of unsettling encounters with a servant, a nationalist friend, and his own wife. She reveals a past (based on actual experiences of Nora Barnacle) previously unknown to Gabriel, and dramatically different from the ordinary pleasures of food, drink, and hospitality that the story luminously evokes. As often happens in the stories and novels of Virginia Woolf, memory invades the present, breeding uncertainties that can be compared to those explored in Akutagawa Ryunosuke's modernist mystery stories as well. Like the tales that Premchand was beginning to write during the same period, the stories of *Dubliners* use close, understated observation of everyday objects and events to unfold abiding mysteries of loyalty and betrayal, rivalry and love.

from DUBLINERS

Araby

North Richmond Street, being blind,[1] was a quiet street except at the hour when the Christian Brothers' School set the boys free. An uninhabited house of two storeys stood at the blind end, detached from its neighbours in a square ground. The other houses of the street, conscious of decent lives within them, gazed at one another with brown imperturbable faces.

The former tenant of our house, a priest, had died in the back drawing-room. Air, musty from having been long enclosed, hung in all the rooms, and the waste room behind the kitchen was littered with old useless papers. Among these I found a few paper-covered books, the pages of which were curled and damp: *The Abbot,* by Walter Scott,[2] *The Devout Communicant*[3] and *The Memoirs of Vidocq.*[4] I liked the last best because its leaves were yellow. The wild garden behind the house contained a central apple-tree and a few straggling bushes under one of which I found the late tenant's rusty bicycle-pump. He had been a very charitable priest; in his will he had left all his money to institutions and the furniture of his house to his sister.

When the short days of winter came dusk fell before we had well eaten our dinners. When we met in the street the houses had grown sombre. The space of sky above us was the colour of ever-changing violet and towards it the lamps of the street lifted their feeble lanterns. The cold air stung us and we played till our bodies glowed. Our shouts echoed in the silent street. The career of our play brought us through the dark muddy lanes behind the houses where we ran the gantlet[5] of the rough tribes from the cottages, to the back doors of the dark dripping gardens where odours arose from the ashpits, to the dark odorous stables where a coachman smoothed and combed the horse or shook music from the buckled harness. When we returned to the street light from the kitchen windows had filled the areas. If my uncle was seen turning the corner we hid in the shadow until we had seen him safely housed. Or if Mangan's sister came out on the doorstep to call her brother in to his tea we watched her from our shadow peer up and down the street. We waited to see whether she would remain or go in and, if she remained, we left our shadow and walked up to Mangan's steps resignedly. She was waiting for us, her figure defined by the light from the half-opened door. Her brother always teased her before he obeyed and I stood by the railings looking at her. Her dress swung as she moved her body and the soft rope of her hair tossed from side to side.

Every morning I lay on the floor in the front parlour watching her door. The blind was pulled down to within an inch of the sash so that I could not be seen. When she came out on the doorstep my heart leaped. I ran to the hall, seized my books and followed her. I kept her brown figure always in my eye and, when we came near the point at which our ways diverged, I quickened my pace and passed her. This happened morning after morning. I had never spoken to her, except for a few casual words, and yet her name was like a summons to all my foolish blood.

1. A dead end.
2. A romantic novel concerning Mary Queen of Scots, published in 1820.
3. A religious tract written by a Franciscan friar.
4. François Vidocq was chief of detectives with the Paris

police in the early 19th century, before being dismissed from the force for falsifying records. He probably didn't write the *Memoirs*.
5. Risk, challenge (variation of "gauntlet").

Her image accompanied me even in places the most hostile to romance. On Saturday evenings when my aunt went marketing I had to go to carry some of the parcels. We walked through the flaring streets, jostled by drunken men and bargaining women, amid the curses of labourers, the shrill litanies of shop-boys who stood on guard by the barrels of pigs' cheeks, the nasal chanting of street-singers, who sang a *come-all-you* about O'Donovan Rossa,[6] or a ballad about the troubles in our native land. These noises converged in a single sensation of life for me: I imagined that I bore my chalice safely through a throng of foes. Her name sprang to my lips at moments in strange prayers and praises which I myself did not understand. My eyes were often full of tears (I could not tell why) and at times a flood from my heart seemed to pour itself out into my bosom. I thought little of the future. I did not know whether I would ever speak to her or not or, if I spoke to her, how I could tell her of my confused adoration. But my body was like a harp and her words and gestures were like fingers running upon the wires.

One evening I went into the back drawing-room in which the priest had died. It was a dark rainy evening and there was no sound in the house. Through one of the broken panes I heard the rain impinge upon the earth, the fine incessant needles of water playing in the sodden beds. Some distant lamp or lighted window gleamed below me. I was thankful that I could see so little. All my senses seemed to desire to veil themselves and, feeling that I was about to slip from them, I pressed the palms of my hands together until they trembled, murmuring: *O love! O love!* many times.

At last she spoke to me. When she addressed the first words to me I was so confused that I did not know what to answer. She asked me was I going to *Araby*. I forget whether I answered yes or no. It would be a splendid bazaar, she said; she would love to go.

—And why can't you? I asked.

While she spoke she turned a silver bracelet round and round her wrist. She could not go, she said, because there would be a retreat[7] that week in her convent. Her brother and two other boys were fighting for their caps and I was alone at the railings. She held one of the spikes, bowing her head towards me. The light from the lamp opposite our door caught the white curve of her neck, lit up her hair that rested there and, falling, lit up the hand upon the railing. It fell over one side of her dress and caught the white border of a petticoat, just visible as she stood at ease.

—It's well for you, she said.

—If I go, I said, I will bring you something.

What innumerable follies laid waste my waking and sleeping thoughts after that evening! I wished to annihilate the tedious intervening days. I chafed against the work of school. At night in my bedroom and by day in the classroom her image came between me and the page I strove to read. The syllables of the word *Araby* were called to me through the silence in which my soul luxuriated and cast an Eastern enchantment over me. I asked for leave to go to the bazaar on Saturday night. My aunt was surprised and hoped it was not some Freemason affair.[8] I answered few questions in class. I watched my master's face pass from amiability to sternness; he hoped I was not beginning to idle. I could not call my wandering thoughts together. I had hardly

6. Jeremiah O'Donovan, an Irish nationalist exiled to the United States. A *come-all-you* is a ballad beginning with the formula, "Come all you Irishmen. . . ."
7. A period of withdrawal for prayer, meditation, and religious study.
8. The Masonic Order was a guild thought to be an enemy of the Catholic Church.

any patience with the serious work of life which, now that it stood between me and my desire, seemed to me child's play, ugly monotonous child's play.

On Saturday morning I reminded my uncle that I wished to go to the bazaar in the evening. He was fussing at the hallstand, looking for the hat-brush, and answered me curtly:

—Yes, boy, I know.

As he was in the hall I could not go into the front parlour and lie at the window. I left the house in bad humour and walked slowly towards the school. The air was pitilessly raw and already my heart misgave me.

When I came home to dinner my uncle had not yet been home. Still it was early. I sat staring at the clock for some time and, when its ticking began to irritate me, I left the room. I mounted the staircase and gained the upper part of the house. The high cold empty gloomy rooms liberated me and I went from room to room singing. From the front window I saw my companions playing below in the street. Their cries reached me weakened and indistinct and, leaning my forehead against the cool glass, I looked over at the dark house where she lived. I may have stood there for an hour, seeing nothing but the brown-clad figure cast by my imagination, touched discreetly by the lamplight at the curved neck, at the hand upon the railings and at the border below the dress.

When I came downstairs again I found Mrs Mercer sitting at the fire. She was an old garrulous woman, a pawnbroker's widow, who collected used stamps for some pious purpose. I had to endure the gossip of the tea-table. The meal was prolonged beyond an hour and still my uncle did not come. Mrs Mercer stood up to go: she was sorry she couldn't wait any longer, but it was after eight o'clock and she did not like to be out late, as the night air was bad for her. When she had gone I began to walk up and down the room, clenching my fists. My aunt said:

—I'm afraid you may put off your bazaar for this night of Our Lord.

At nine o'clock I heard my uncle's latchkey in the halldoor. I heard him talking to himself and heard the hallstand rocking when it had received the weight of his overcoat. I could interpret these signs. When he was midway through his dinner I asked him to give me the money to go to the bazaar. He had forgotten.

—The people are in bed and after their first sleep now, he said.

I did not smile. My aunt said to him energetically:

—Can't you give him the money and let him go? You've kept him late enough as it is.

My uncle said he was very sorry he had forgotten. He said he believed in the old saying: *All work and no play makes Jack a dull boy.* He asked me where I was going and, when I had told him a second time he asked me did I know *The Arab's Farewell to his Steed.*[9] When I left the kitchen he was about to recite the opening lines of the piece to my aunt.

I held a florin[1] tightly in my hand as I strode down Buckingham Street towards the station. The sight of the streets thronged with buyers and glaring with gas recalled to me the purpose of my journey. I took my seat in a third-class carriage of a deserted train. After an intolerable delay the train moved out of the station slowly. It crept onward among ruinous houses and over the twinkling river. At Westland Row Station a crowd of people pressed to the carriage doors; but the porters moved

9. A sentimental poem by Caroline Norton, in which the speaker imagines his despair upon selling his favorite horse.

1. A coin worth two shillings.

them back, saying that it was a special train for the bazaar. I remained alone in the bare carriage. In a few minutes the train drew up beside an improvised wooden platform. I passed out on to the road and saw by the lighted dial of a clock that it was ten minutes to ten. In front of me was a large building which displayed the magical name.

I could not find any sixpenny entrance and, fearing that the bazaar would be closed, I passed in quickly through a turnstile, handing a shilling to a weary-looking man. I found myself in a big hall girdled at half its height by a gallery. Nearly all the stalls were closed and the greater part of the hall was in darkness. I recognised a silence like that which pervades a church after a service. I walked into the centre of the bazaar timidly. A few people were gathered about the stalls which were still open. Before a curtain, over which the words *Café Chantant*[2] were written in coloured lamps, two men were counting money on a salver.[3] I listened to the fall of the coins.

Remembering with difficulty why I had come I went over to one of the stalls and examined porcelain vases and flowered tea-sets. At the door of the stall a young lady was talking and laughing with two young gentlemen. I remarked their English accents and listened vaguely to their conversation.

—O, I never said such a thing!
—O, but you did!
—O, but I didn't!
—Didn't she say that?
—Yes. I heard her.
—O, there's a . . . fib!

Observing me the young lady came over and asked me did I wish to buy anything. The tone of her voice was not encouraging; she seemed to have spoken to me out of a sense of duty. I looked humbly at the great jars that stood like eastern guards at either side of the dark entrance to the stall and murmured:

—No, thank you.

The young lady changed the position of one of the vases and went back to the two young men. They began to talk of the same subject. Once or twice the young lady glanced at me over her shoulder.

I lingered before her stall, though I knew my stay was useless, to make my interest in her wares seem the more real. Then I turned away slowly and walked down the middle of the bazaar. I allowed the two pennies to fall against the sixpence in my pocket. I heard a voice call from one end of the gallery that the light was out. The upper part of the hall was now completely dark.

Gazing up into the darkness I saw myself as a creature driven and derided by vanity; and my eyes burned with anguish and anger.

Clay

The matron had given her leave to go out as soon as the women's tea was over and Maria looked forward to her evening out. The kitchen was spick and span: the cook said you could see yourself in the big copper boilers. The fire was nice and bright and on one of the side-tables were four very big barmbracks.[1] These barmbracks seemed

---

2. A café with musical entertainment.   1. Speckled cakes or currant buns.
3. A tray for food and drinks.

uncut; but if you went closer you would see that they had been cut into long thick even slices and were ready to be handed round at tea. Maria had cut them herself.

Maria was a very, very small person indeed but she had a very long nose and a very long chin. She talked a little through her nose, always soothingly: *Yes, my dear,* and *No, my dear.* She was always sent for when the women quarrelled over their tubs and always succeeded in making peace. One day the matron had said to her:

—Maria, you are a veritable peace-maker!

And the sub-matron and two of the Board ladies[2] had heard the compliment. And Ginger Mooney was always saying what she wouldn't do to the dummy[3] who had charge of the irons if it wasn't for Maria. Everyone was so fond of Maria.

The women would have their tea at six o'clock and she would be able to get away before seven. From Ballsbridge to the Pillar, twenty minutes; from the Pillar to Drumcondra, twenty minutes; and twenty minutes to buy the things. She would be there before eight. She took out her purse with the silver clasps and read again the words *A Present from Belfast.* She was very fond of that purse because Joe had brought it to her five years before when he and Alphy had gone to Belfast on a Whit-Monday[4] trip. In the purse were two half-crowns and some coppers. She would have five shillings clear after paying tram fare. What a nice evening they would have, all the children singing! Only she hoped that Joe wouldn't come in drunk. He was so different when he took any drink.

Often he had wanted her to go and live with them; but she would have felt herself in the way (though Joe's wife was ever so nice with her) and she had become accustomed to the life of the laundry. Joe was a good fellow. She had nursed him and Alphy too; and Joe used often say:

—Mamma is mamma but Maria is my proper mother.

After the break-up at home the boys had got her that position in the *Dublin by Lamplight* laundry,[5] and she liked it. She used to have such a bad opinion of Protestants but now she thought they were very nice people, a little quiet and serious, but still very nice people to live with. Then she had her plants in the conservatory and she liked looking after them. She had lovely ferns and wax-plants and, whenever anyone came to visit her, she always gave the visitor one or two slips from her conservatory. There was one thing she didn't like and that was the tracts[6] on the walls; but the matron was such a nice person to deal with, so genteel.

When the cook told her everything was ready she went into the women's room and began to pull the big bell. In a few minutes the women began to come in by twos and threes, wiping their steaming hands in their petticoats and pulling down the sleeves of their blouses over their red steaming arms. They settled down before their huge mugs which the cook and the dummy filled up with hot tea, already mixed with milk and sugar in huge tin cans. Maria superintended the distribution of the barmbrack and saw that every woman got her four slices. There was a great deal of laughing and joking during the meal. Lizzie Fleming said Maria was sure to get the ring and, though Fleming had said that for so many Hallow Eves, Maria had to laugh and say she didn't want any ring or man either; and when she laughed her grey-green eyes sparkled with disappointed shyness and the tip of her nose nearly met the tip of her

---

2. Members of the governing board of the Dublin by Lamplight Laundry.
3. Slang for a mute person.
4. Holiday following Whitsunday, the seventh Sunday after Easter.
5. Joyce's invented benevolent society, run by Protestant women, "saves" Dublin's prostitutes from a life on the streets by giving them honest work in a laundry. Maria works for the laundry but appears not to be a reformed prostitute herself.
6. Evangelical religious texts.

chin. Then Ginger Mooney lifted up her mug of tea and proposed Maria's health while all the other women clattered with their mugs on the table, and said she was sorry she hadn't a sup of porter[7] to drink it in. And Maria laughed again till the tip of her nose nearly met the tip of her chin and till her minute body nearly shook itself asunder because she knew that Mooney meant well though, of course, she had the notions of a common woman.

But wasn't Maria glad when the women had finished their tea and the cook and the dummy had begun to clear away the tea-things! She went into her little bedroom and, remembering that the next morning was a mass morning, changed the hand of the alarm from seven to six. Then she took off her working skirt and her house-boots and laid her best skirt out on the bed and her tiny dress-boots beside the foot of the bed. She changed her blouse too and, as she stood before the mirror, she thought of how she used to dress for mass on Sunday morning when she was a young girl; and she looked with quaint affection at the diminutive body which she had so often adorned. In spite of its years she found it a nice tidy little body.

When she got outside the streets were shining with rain and she was glad of her old brown raincloak. The tram was full and she had to sit on the little stool at the end of the car, facing all the people, with her toes barely touching the floor. She arranged in her mind all she was going to do and thought how much better it was to be independent and to have your own money in your pocket. She hoped they would have a nice evening. She was sure they would but she could not help thinking what a pity it was Alphy and Joe were not speaking. They were always falling out now but when they were boys together they used to be the best of friends: but such was life.

She got out of her tram at the Pillar and ferreted her way quickly among the crowds. She went into Downes's cakeshop but the shop was so full of people that it was a long time before she could get herself attended to. She bought a dozen of mixed penny cakes, and at last came out of the shop laden with a big bag. Then she thought what else would she buy: she wanted to buy something really nice. They would be sure to have plenty of apples and nuts. It was hard to know what to buy and all she could think of was cake. She decided to buy some plumcake but Downes's plumcake had not enough almond icing on top of it so she went over to a shop in Henry Street. Here she was a long time in suiting herself and the stylish young lady behind the counter, who was evidently a little annoyed by her, asked her was it wedding-cake she wanted to buy. That made Maria blush and smile at the young lady; but the young lady took it all very seriously and finally cut a thick slice of plumcake, parcelled it up and said:

—Two-and-four, please.

She thought she would have to stand in the Drumcondra tram because none of the young men seemed to notice her but an elderly gentleman made room for her. He was a stout gentleman and he wore a brown hard hat; he had a square red face and a greyish moustache. Maria thought he was a colonel-looking gentleman and she reflected how much more polite he was than the young men who simply stared straight before them. The gentleman began to chat with her about Hallow Eve and the rainy weather. He supposed the bag was full of good things for the little ones and said it was only right that the youngsters should enjoy themselves while they were young. Maria agreed with him and favoured him with demure nods and hems. He

---

7. A heavy, dark brown ale.

was very nice with her, and when she was getting out at the Canal Bridge she thanked him and bowed, and he bowed to her and raised his hat and smiled agreeably; and while she was going up along the terrace, bending her tiny head under the rain, she thought how easy it was to know a gentleman even when he has a drop taken.

Everybody said: *O, here's Maria!* when she came to Joe's house. Joe was there, having come home from business, and all the children had their Sunday dresses on. There were two big girls in from next door and games were going on. Maria gave the bag of cakes to the eldest boy, Alphy, to divide and Mrs Donnelly said it was too good of her to bring such a big bag of cakes and made all the children say:

—Thanks, Maria.

But Maria said she had brought something special for papa and mamma, something they would be sure to like, and she began to look for her plumcake. She tried in Downes's bag and then in the pockets of her raincloak and then on the hallstand but nowhere could she find it. Then she asked all the children had any of them eaten it—by mistake, of course—but the children all said no and looked as if they did not like to eat cakes if they were to be accused of stealing. Everybody had a solution for the mystery and Mrs Donnelly said it was plain that Maria had left it behind her in the tram. Maria, remembering how confused the gentleman with the greyish moustache had made her, coloured with shame and vexation and disappointment. At the thought of the failure of her little surprise and of the two and fourpence she had thrown away for nothing she nearly cried outright.

But Joe said it didn't matter and made her sit down by the fire. He was very nice with her. He told her all that went on in his office, repeating for her a smart answer which he had made to the manager. Maria did not understand why Joe laughed so much over the answer he had made but she said that the manager must have been a very overbearing person to deal with. Joe said he wasn't so bad when you knew how to take him, that he was a decent sort so long as you didn't rub him the wrong way. Mrs Donnelly played the piano for the children and they danced and sang. Then the two next-door girls handed round the nuts. Nobody could find the nutcrackers and Joe was nearly getting cross over it and asked how did they expect Maria to crack nuts without a nutcracker. But Maria said she didn't like nuts and that they weren't to bother about her. Then Joe asked would she take a bottle of stout[8] and Mrs Donnelly said there was port wine too in the house if she would prefer that. Maria said she would rather they didn't ask her to take anything: but Joe insisted.

So Maria let him have his way and they sat by the fire talking over old times and Maria thought she would put in a good word for Alphy. But Joe cried that God might strike him stone dead if ever he spoke a word to his brother again and Maria said she was sorry she had mentioned the matter. Mrs Donnelly told her husband it was a great shame for him to speak that way of his own flesh and blood but Joe said that Alphy was no brother of his and there was nearly being a row[9] on the head of it. But Joe said he would not lose his temper on account of the night it was and asked his wife to open some more stout. The two next-door girls had arranged some Hallow

---

8. An extra-strength ale.   9. Argument.

Eve games[1] and soon everything was merry again. Maria was delighted to see the children so merry and Joe and his wife in such good spirits. The next-door girls put some saucers on the table and then led the children up to the table, blindfold. One got the prayer-book and the other three got the water; and when one of the next-door girls got the ring Mrs Donnelly shook her finger at the blushing girl as much as to say: *O, I know all about it!* They insisted then on blindfolding Maria and leading her up to the table to see what she would get; and, while they were putting on the bandage, Maria laughed and laughed again till the tip of her nose nearly met the tip of her chin.

They led her up to the table amid laughing and joking and she put her hand out in the air as she was told to do. She moved her hand about here and there in the air and descended on one of the saucers. She felt a soft wet substance with her fingers and was surprised that nobody spoke or took off her bandage. There was a pause for a few seconds; and then a great deal of scuffling and whispering. Somebody said something about the garden, and at last Mrs Donnelly said something very cross to one of the next-door girls and told her to throw it out at once: that was no play. Maria understood that it was wrong that time and so she had to do it over again: and this time she got the prayer-book.

After that Mrs Donnelly played Miss McCloud's Reel for the children and Joe made Maria take a glass of wine. Soon they were all quite merry again and Mrs Donnelly said Maria would enter a convent before the year was out because she had got the prayer-book. Maria had never seen Joe so nice to her as he was that night, so full of pleasant talk and reminiscences. She said they were all very good to her.

At last the children grew tired and sleepy and Joe asked Maria would she not sing some little song before she went, one of the old songs. Mrs Donnelly said *Do, please, Maria!* and so Maria had to get up and stand beside the piano. Mrs Donnelly bade the children be quiet and listen to Maria's song. Then she played the prelude and said *Now, Maria!* and Maria, blushing very much, began to sing in a tiny quavering voice. She sang *I Dreamt that I Dwelt,*[2] and when she came to the second verse she sang again:

> *I dreamt that I dwelt in marble halls*
> *With vassals and serfs at my side*
> *And of all who assembled within those walls*
> *That I was the hope and the pride.*
>
> *I had riches too great to count, could boast*
> *Of a high ancestral name,*
> *But I also dreamt, which pleased me most,*
> *That you loved me still the same.*

But no one tried to show her her mistake;[3] and when she had ended her song Joe was very much moved. He said that there was no time like the long ago and no music for him like poor old Balfe, whatever other people might say; and his eyes filled up so

---

1. The primary game that Maria and the girls play is a traditional Irish Halloween game. In its original version, a blindfolded girl would be led to three plates and would choose one. Choosing the plate with a ring meant that she would soon marry; water meant she would emigrate (probably to America); and soil, or clay, meant she would soon die. In modern times, a prayer book was substituted for this unsavory third option, suggesting that the girl would enter a convent.
2. Aria from Act 2 of *The Bohemian Girl.*
3. Maria repeats the first verse rather than singing the second.

much with tears that he could not find what he was looking for and in the end he had
to ask his wife to tell him where the corkscrew was.

The Dead

Lily, the caretaker's daughter, was literally run off her feet. Hardly had she brought one
gentleman into the little pantry behind the office on the ground floor and helped him off
with his overcoat than the wheezy hall-door bell clanged again and she had to scamper
along the bare hallway to let in another guest. It was well for her she had not to attend to
the ladies also. But Miss Kate and Miss Julia had thought of that and had converted the
bathroom upstairs into a ladies' dressing-room. Miss Kate and Miss Julia were there,
gossiping and laughing and fussing, walking after each other to the head of the stairs,
peering down over the banisters and calling down to Lily to ask her who had come.

It was always a great affair, the Misses Morkan's annual dance. Everybody who
knew them came to it, members of the family, old friends of the family, the members of
Julia's choir, any of Kate's pupils that were grown up enough and even some of Mary
Jane's pupils too. Never once had it fallen flat. For years and years it had gone off in
splendid style as long as anyone could remember; ever since Kate and Julia, after the
death of their brother Pat, had left the house in Stoney Batter[1] and taken Mary Jane, their
only niece, to live with them in the dark gaunt house on Usher's Island,[2] the upper part
of which they had rented from Mr Fulham, the cornfactor on the ground floor. That was
a good thirty years ago if it was a day. Mary Jane, who was then a little girl in short
clothes, was now the main prop of the household for she had the organ in Haddington
Road.[3] She had been through the Academy[4] and gave a pupils' concert every year in the
upper room of the Antient Concert Rooms. Many of her pupils belonged to better-class
families on the Kingstown and Dalkey line.[5] Old as they were, her aunts also did their
share. Julia, though she was quite grey, was still the leading soprano in Adam and
Eve's,[6] and Kate, being too feeble to go about much, gave music lessons to beginners on
the old square piano in the back room. Lily, the caretaker's daughter, did housemaid's
work for them. Though their life was modest they believed in eating well; the best of
everything: diamond-bone sirloins, three-shilling tea and the best bottled stout.[7] But Lily
seldom made a mistake in the orders so that she got on well with her three mistresses.
They were fussy, that was all. But the only thing they would not stand was back answers.

Of course they had good reason to be fussy on such a night. And then it was long
after ten o'clock and yet there was no sign of Gabriel and his wife. Besides they were
dreadfully afraid that Freddy Malins might turn up screwed.[8] They would not wish for
worlds that any of Mary Jane's pupils should see him under the influence; and when he
was like that it was sometimes very hard to manage him. Freddy Malins always came
late but they wondered what could be keeping Gabriel: and that was what brought
them every two minutes to the banisters to ask Lily had Gabriel or Freddy come.

—O, Mr Conroy, said Lily to Gabriel when she opened the door for him, Miss
Kate and Miss Julia thought you were never coming. Good-night, Mrs Conroy.

—I'll engage[9] they did, said Gabriel, but they forget that my wife here takes three
mortal hours to dress herself.

1. A district in northwest Dublin.
2. Two adjoining quays on the south side of the River
Liffey.
3. Played the organ in a church on the Haddington Road.
4. Royal Academy of Music.
5. The train line connecting Dublin to the affluent suburbs
south of the city.
6. A Dublin church.
7. An extra-strength ale.
8. Drunk.
9. Wager.

He stood on the mat, scraping the snow from his goloshes, while Lily led his wife to the foot of the stairs and called out:

—Miss Kate, here's Mrs Conroy.

Kate and Julia came toddling down the dark stairs at once. Both of them kissed Gabriel's wife, said she must be perished alive and asked was Gabriel with her.

—Here I am as right as the mail, Aunt Kate! Go on up. I'll follow, called out Gabriel from the dark.

He continued scraping his feet vigorously while the three women went upstairs, laughing, to the ladies' dressing-room. A light fringe of snow lay like a cape on the shoulders of his overcoat and like toecaps on the toes of his goloshes; and, as the buttons of his overcoat slipped with a squeaking noise through the snow-stiffened frieze, a cold fragrant air from out-of-doors escaped from crevices and folds.

—Is it snowing again, Mr Conroy? asked Lily.

She had preceded him into the pantry to help him off with his overcoat. Gabriel smiled at the three syllables she had given his surname and glanced at her. She was a slim, growing girl, pale in complexion and with hay-coloured hair. The gas in the pantry made her look still paler. Gabriel had known her when she was a child and used to sit on the lowest step nursing a rag doll.

—Yes, Lily, he answered, and I think we're in for a night of it.

He looked up at the pantry ceiling, which was shaking with the stamping and shuffling of feet on the floor above, listened for a moment to the piano and then glanced at the girl, who was folding his overcoat carefully at the end of a shelf.

—Tell me, Lily, he said in a friendly tone, do you still go to school?

—O no, sir, she answered. I'm done schooling this year and more.

—O, then, said Gabriel gaily, I suppose we'll be going to your wedding one of these fine days with your young man, eh?

The girl glanced back at him over her shoulder and said with great bitterness:

—The men that is now is only all palaver[1] and what they can get out of you.

Gabriel coloured as if he felt he had made a mistake and, without looking at her, kicked off his goloshes and flicked actively with his muffler at his patent-leather shoes.

He was a stout tallish young man. The high colour of his cheeks pushed upwards even to his forehead where it scattered itself in a few formless patches of pale red; and on his hairless face there scintillated restlessly the polished lenses and the bright gilt rims of the glasses which screened his delicate and restless eyes. His glossy black hair was parted in the middle and brushed in a long curve behind his ears where it curled slightly beneath the groove left by his hat.

When he had flicked lustre into his shoes he stood up and pulled his waistcoat down more tightly on his plump body. Then he took a coin rapidly from his pocket.

—O Lily, he said, thrusting it into her hands, it's Christmas-time, isn't it? Just . . . here's a little. . . .

He walked rapidly towards the door.

—O no, sir! cried the girl, following him. Really, sir, I wouldn't take it.

—Christmas-time! Christmas-time! said Gabriel, almost trotting to the stairs and waving his hand to her in deprecation.

The girl, seeing that he had gained the stairs, called out after him:

—Well, thank you, sir.

1. Empty talk.

He waited outside the drawing-room door until the waltz should finish, listening to the skirts that swept against it and to the shuffling of feet. He was still discomposed by the girl's bitter and sudden retort. It had cast a gloom over him which he tried to dispel by arranging his cuffs and the bows of his tie. Then he took from his waistcoat pocket a little paper and glanced at the headings he had made for his speech. He was undecided about the lines from Robert Browning for he feared they would be above the heads of his hearers. Some quotation that they could recognise from Shakespeare or from the Melodies[2] would be better. The indelicate clacking of the men's heels and the shuffling of their soles reminded him that their grade of culture differed from his. He would only make himself ridiculous by quoting poetry to them which they could not understand. They would think that he was airing his superior education. He would fail with them just as he had failed with the girl in the pantry. He had taken up a wrong tone. His whole speech was a mistake from first to last, an utter failure.

Just then his aunts and his wife came out of the ladies' dressing-room. His aunts were two small plainly dressed old women. Aunt Julia was an inch or so taller. Her hair, drawn low over the tops of her ears, was grey; and grey also, with darker shadows, was her large flaccid face. Though she was stout in build and stood erect her slow eyes and parted lips gave her the appearance of a woman who did not know where she was or where she was going. Aunt Kate was more vivacious. Her face, healthier than her sister's, was all puckers and creases, like a shrivelled red apple, and her hair, braided in the same old-fashioned way, had not lost its ripe nut colour.

They both kissed Gabriel frankly. He was their favourite nephew, the son of their dead elder sister, Ellen, who had married T.J. Conroy of the Port and Docks.

—Gretta tells me you're not going to take a cab back to Monkstown[3] to-night, Gabriel, said Aunt Kate.

—No, said Gabriel, turning to his wife, we had quite enough of that last year, hadn't we. Don't you remember, Aunt Kate, what a cold Gretta got out of it? Cab windows rattling all the way, and the east wind blowing in after we passed Merrion. Very jolly it was. Gretta caught a dreadful cold.

Aunt Kate frowned severely and nodded her head at every word.

—Quite right, Gabriel, quite right, she said. You can't be too careful.

—But as for Gretta there, said Gabriel, she'd walk home in the snow if she were let.

Mrs Conroy laughed.

—Don't mind him, Aunt Kate, she said. He's really an awful bother, what with green shades for Tom's eyes at night and making him do the dumb-bells, and forcing Eva to eat the stirabout.[4] The poor child! And she simply hates the sight of it! . . . O, but you'll never guess what he makes me wear now!

She broke out into a peal of laughter and glanced at her husband, whose admiring and happy eyes had been wandering from her dress to her face and hair. The two aunts laughed heartily too, for Gabriel's solicitude was a standing joke with them.

—Goloshes! said Mrs Conroy. That's the latest. Whenever it's wet underfoot I must put on my goloshes. Tonight even he wanted me to put them on, but I wouldn't. The next thing he'll buy me will be a diving suit.

Gabriel laughed nervously and patted his tie reassuringly while Aunt Kate nearly doubled herself, so heartily did she enjoy the joke. The smile soon faded from Aunt

2. Thomas Moore's *Irish Melodies,* a perennial favorite volume of poetry.

3. An elegant suburb south of Dublin.
4. Porridge.

Julia's face and her mirthless eyes were directed towards her nephew's face. After a pause she asked:

—And what are goloshes, Gabriel?

—Goloshes, Julia! exclaimed her sister. Goodness me, don't you know what goloshes are? You wear them over your . . . over your boots, Gretta, isn't it?

—Yes, said Mrs Conroy. Guttapercha[5] things. We both have a pair now. Gabriel says everyone wears them on the continent.

—O, on the continent, murmured Aunt Julia, nodding her head slowly.

Gabriel knitted his brows and said, as if he were slightly angered:

—It's nothing very wonderful but Gretta thinks it very funny because she says the word reminds her of Christy Minstrels.[6]

—But tell me, Gabriel, said Aunt Kate, with brisk tact. Of course, you've seen about the room. Gretta was saying . . .

—O, the room is all right, replied Gabriel. I've taken one in the Gresham.[7]

—To be sure, said Aunt Kate, by far the best thing to do. And the children, Gretta, you're not anxious about them?

—O, for one night, said Mrs Conroy. Besides, Bessie will look after them.

—To be sure, said Aunt Kate again. What a comfort it is to have a girl like that, one you can depend on! There's that Lily, I'm sure I don't know what has come over her lately. She's not the girl she was at all.

Gabriel was about to ask his aunt some questions on this point but she broke off suddenly to gaze after her sister who had wandered down the stairs and was craning her neck over the banisters.

—Now, I ask you, she said, almost testily, where is Julia going? Julia! Julia! Where are you going?

Julia, who had gone halfway down one flight, came back and announced blandly:

—Here's Freddy.

At the same moment a clapping of hands and a final flourish of the pianist told that the waltz had ended. The drawing-room door was opened from within and some couples came out. Aunt Kate drew Gabriel aside hurriedly and whispered into his ear:

—Slip down, Gabriel, like a good fellow and see if he's all right, and don't let him up if he's screwed. I'm sure he's screwed. I'm sure he is.

Gabriel went to the stairs and listened over the banisters. He could hear two persons talking in the pantry. Then he recognised Freddy Malins' laugh. He went down the stairs noisily.

—It's such a relief, said Aunt Kate to Mrs Conroy, that Gabriel is here. I always feel easier in my mind when he's here. . . . Julia, there's Miss Daly and Miss Power will take some refreshment. Thanks for your beautiful waltz, Miss Daly. It made lovely time.

A tall wizen-faced man, with a stiff grizzled moustache and swarthy skin, who was passing out with his partner said:

—And may we have some refreshment, too, Miss Morkan?

—Julia, said Aunt Kate summarily, and here's Mr Browne and Miss Furlong. Take them in, Julia, with Miss Daly and Miss Power.

—I'm the man for the ladies, said Mr Browne, pursing his lips until his moustache bristled and smiling in all his wrinkles. You know, Miss Morkan, the reason they are so fond of me is—

5. Rubberized fabric.
6. A 19th-century blackface minstrel show.

7. The most elegant hotel in Dublin.

He did not finish his sentence, but, seeing that Aunt Kate was out of earshot, at once led the three young ladies into the back room. The middle of the room was occupied by two square tables placed end to end, and on these Aunt Julia and the caretaker were straightening and smoothing a large cloth. On the sideboard were arrayed dishes and plates, and glasses and bundles of knives and forks and spoons. The top of the closed square piano served also as a sideboard for viands[8] and sweets. At a smaller sideboard in one corner two young men were standing, drinking hop-bitters.[9]

Mr Browne led his charges thither and invited them all, in jest, to some ladies' punch, hot, strong and sweet. As they said they never took anything strong he opened three bottles of lemonade for them. Then he asked one of the young men to move aside, and, taking hold of the decanter, filled out for himself a goodly measure of whisky. The young men eyed him respectfully while he took a trial sip.

—God help me, he said, smiling, it's the doctor's orders.

His wizened face broke into a broader smile, and the three young ladies laughed in musical echo to his pleasantry, swaying their bodies to and fro, with nervous jerks of their shoulders. The boldest said:

—O, now, Mr Browne, I'm sure the doctor never ordered anything of the kind.

Mr Browne took another sip of his whisky and said, with sidling mimicry:

—Well, you see, I'm like the famous Mrs Cassidy, who is reported to have said: *Now, Mary Grimes, if I don't take it, make me take it, for I feel I want it.*

His hot face had leaned forward a little too confidentially and he had assumed a very low Dublin accent so that the young ladies, with one instinct, received his speech in silence. Miss Furlong, who was one of Mary Jane's pupils, asked Miss Daly what was the name of the pretty waltz she had played; and Mr Browne, seeing that he was ignored, turned promptly to the two young men who were more appreciative.

A red-faced young woman, dressed in pansy, came into the room, excitedly clapping her hands and crying:

—Quadrilles![1] Quadrilles!

Close on her heels came Aunt Kate, crying:

—Two gentlemen and three ladies, Mary Jane!

—O, here's Mr Bergin and Mr Kerrigan, said Mary Jane. Mr Kerrigan, will you take Miss Power? Miss Furlong, may I get you a partner, Mr Bergin. O, that'll just do now.

—Three ladies, Mary Jane, said Aunt Kate.

The two young gentlemen asked the ladies if they might have the pleasure, and Mary Jane turned to Miss Daly.

—O, Miss Daly, you're really awfully good, after playing for the last two dances, but really we're so short of ladies to-night.

—I don't mind in the least, Miss Morkan.

—But I've a nice partner for you, Mr Bartell D'Arcy, the tenor. I'll get him to sing later on. All Dublin is raving about him.

—Lovely voice, lovely voice! said Aunt Kate.

As the piano had twice begun the prelude to the first figure Mary Jane led her recruits quickly from the room. They had hardly gone when Aunt Julia wandered slowly into the room, looking behind her at something.

8. Meats.
9. Dry ale.

1. A French square dance.

—What is the matter, Julia? asked Aunt Kate anxiously. Who is it?

Julia, who was carrying in a column of table-napkins, turned to her sister and said, simply, as if the question had surprised her:

—It's only Freddy, Kate, and Gabriel with him.

In fact right behind her Gabriel could be seen piloting Freddy Malins across the landing. The latter, a young man of about forty, was of Gabriel's size and build, with very round shoulders. His face was fleshy and pallid, touched with colour only at the thick hanging lobes of his ears and at the wide wings of his nose. He had coarse features, a blunt nose, a convex and receding brow, tumid and protruded lips. His heavy-lidded eyes and the disorder of his scanty hair made him look sleepy. He was laughing heartily in a high key at a story which he had been telling Gabriel on the stairs and at the same time rubbing the knuckles of his left fist backwards and forwards into his left eye.

—Good-evening, Freddy, said Aunt Julia.

Freddy Malins bade the Misses Morkan good-evening in what seemed an off-hand fashion by reason of the habitual catch in his voice and then, seeing that Mr Browne was grinning at him from the sideboard, crossed the room on rather shaky legs and began to repeat in an undertone the story he had just told to Gabriel.

—He's not so bad, is he? said Aunt Kate to Gabriel.

Gabriel's brows were dark but he raised them quickly and answered:

—O no, hardly noticeable.

—Now, isn't he a terrible fellow! she said. And his poor mother made him take the pledge on New Year's Eve. But come on, Gabriel, into the drawing-room.

Before leaving the room with Gabriel she signalled to Mr Browne by frowning and shaking her forefinger in warning to and fro. Mr Browne nodded in answer and, when she had gone, said to Freddy Malins:

—Now, then, Teddy, I'm going to fill you out a good glass of lemonade just to buck you up.

Freddy Malins, who was nearing the climax of his story, waved the offer aside impatiently but Mr Browne, having first called Freddy Malins' attention to a disarray in his dress, filled out and handed him a full glass of lemonade. Freddy Malins' left hand accepted the glass mechanically, his right hand being engaged in the mechanical readjustment of his dress. Mr Browne, whose face was once more wrinkling with mirth, poured out for himself a glass of whisky while Freddy Malins exploded, before he had well reached the climax of his story, in a kink of high-pitched bronchitic laughter and, setting down his untasted and overflowing glass, began to rub the knuckles of his left fist backwards and forwards into his left eye, repeating words of his last phrase as well as his fit of laughter would allow him.

Gabriel could not listen while Mary Jane was playing her Academy piece, full of runs and difficult passages, to the hushed drawing-room. He liked music but the piece she was playing had no melody for him and he doubted whether it had any melody for the other listeners, though they had begged Mary Jane to play something. Four young men, who had come from the refreshment-room to stand in the door-way at the sound of the piano, had gone away quietly in couples after a few minutes. The only persons who seemed to follow the music were Mary Jane herself, her hands racing along the key-board or lifted from it at the pauses like those of a priest-ess in momentary imprecation, and Aunt Kate standing at her elbow to turn the page.

Gabriel's eyes, irritated by the floor, which glittered with beeswax under the heavy chandelier, wandered to the wall above the piano. A picture of the balcony scene in *Romeo and Juliet* hung there and beside it was a picture of the two murdered princes[2] in the Tower which Aunt Julia had worked in red, blue and brown wools when she was a girl. Probably in the school they had gone to as girls that kind of work had been taught, for one year his mother had worked for him as a birthday present a waistcoat of purple tabinet,[3] with little foxes' heads upon it, lined with brown satin and having round mulberry buttons. It was strange that his mother had had no musical talent though Aunt Kate used to call her the brains carrier of the Morkan family. Both she and Julia had always seemed a little proud of their serious and matronly sister. Her photograph stood before the pierglass.[4] She held an open book on her knees and was pointing out something in it to Constantine who, dressed in a man-o'-war suit, lay at her feet. It was she who had chosen the names for her sons for she was very sensible of the dignity of family life. Thanks to her, Constantine was now senior curate in Balbriggan[5] and, thanks to her, Gabriel himself had taken his degree in the Royal University.[6] A shadow passed over his face as he remembered her sullen opposition to his marriage. Some slighting phrases she had used still rankled in his memory; she had once spoken of Gretta as being country cute and that was not true of Gretta at all. It was Gretta who had nursed her during all her last long illness in their house at Monkstown.

He knew that Mary Jane must be near the end of her piece for she was playing again the opening melody with runs of scales after every bar and while he waited for the end the resentment died down in his heart. The piece ended with a trill of octaves in the treble and a final deep octave in the bass. Great applause greeted Mary Jane as, blushing and rolling up her music nervously, she escaped from the room. The most vigorous clapping came from the four young men in the doorway who had gone away to the refreshment-room at the beginning of the piece but had come back when the piano had stopped.

Lancers[7] were arranged. Gabriel found himself partnered with Miss Ivors. She was a frank-mannered talkative young lady, with a freckled face and prominent brown eyes. She did not wear a low-cut bodice and the large brooch which was fixed in the front of her collar bore on it an Irish device.

When they had taken their places she said abruptly:

—I have a crow to pluck with you.

—With me? said Gabriel.

She nodded her head gravely.

—What is it? asked Gabriel, smiling at her solemn manner.

—Who is G. C.? answered Miss Ivors, turning her eyes upon him.

Gabriel coloured and was about to knit his brows, as if he did not understand, when she said bluntly:

—O, innocent Amy! I have found out that you write for *The Daily Express*.[8] Now, aren't you ashamed of yourself?

—Why should I be ashamed of myself? asked Gabriel, blinking his eyes and trying to smile.

—Well, I'm ashamed of you, said Miss Ivors frankly. To say you'd write for a rag like that. I didn't think you were a West Briton.[9]

---

2. The young sons of Edward IV, murdered in the Tower of London by order of their uncle, Edward III.
3. Silk and wool fabric.
4. A large high mirror.
5. A seaport southeast of Dublin.
6. The Royal University of Ireland, established in 1882.

7. A type of quadrille for 8 or 16 people.
8. A conservative paper opposed to the struggle for Irish independence.
9. Disparaging term for people wishing to identify Ireland as British.

A look of perplexity appeared on Gabriel's face. It was true that he wrote a literary column every Wednesday in *The Daily Express,* for which he was paid fifteen shillings. But that did not make him a West Briton surely. The books he received for review were almost more welcome than the paltry cheque. He loved to feel the covers and turn over the pages of newly printed books. Nearly every day when his teaching in the college was ended he used to wander down the quays to the second-hand booksellers, to Hickey's on Bachelor's Walk, to Webb's or Massey's on Aston's Quay, or to O'Clohissey's in the by-street. He did not know how to meet her charge. He wanted to say that literature was above politics. But they were friends of many years' standing and their careers had been parallel, first at the University and then as teachers: he could not risk a grandiose phrase with her. He continued blinking his eyes and trying to smile and murmured lamely that he saw nothing political in writing reviews of books.

When their turn to cross had come he was still perplexed and inattentive. Miss Ivors promptly took his hand in a warm grasp and said in a soft friendly tone:

—Of course, I was only joking. Come, we cross now.

When they were together again she spoke of the University question[1] and Gabriel felt more at ease. A friend of hers had shown her his review of Browning's poems. That was how she had found out the secret: but she liked the review immensely. Then she said suddenly:

—O, Mr Conroy, will you come for an excursion to the Aran Isles[2] this summer? We're going to stay there a whole month. It will be splendid out in the Atlantic. You ought to come. Mr Clancy is coming, and Mr Kilkelly and Kathleen Kearney. It would be splendid for Gretta too if she'd come. She's from Connacht,[3] isn't she?

—Her people are, said Gabriel shortly.

—But you will come, won't you? said Miss Ivors, laying her warm hand eagerly on his arm.

—The fact is, said Gabriel, I have already arranged to go—

—Go where? asked Miss Ivors.

—Well, you know, every year I go for a cycling tour with some fellows and so—

—But where? asked Miss Ivors.

—Well, we usually go to France or Belgium or perhaps Germany, said Gabriel awkwardly.

—And why do you go to France and Belgium, said Miss Ivors, instead of visiting your own land?

—Well, said Gabriel, it's partly to keep in touch with the languages and partly for a change.

—And haven't you your own language to keep in touch with—Irish? asked Miss Ivors.

—Well, said Gabriel, if it comes to that, you know, Irish is not my language.

Their neighbours had turned to listen to the cross-examination. Gabriel glanced right and left nervously and tried to keep his good humour under the ordeal which was making a blush invade his forehead.

---

1. Ireland's oldest most and prestigious university, Trinity College, was open only to Protestants; the "University question" involved, in part, the provision of quality university education to Catholics.

2. Islands off the west coast of Ireland where the people still retained their traditional culture and spoke Irish.
3. A province on the west coast of Ireland.

—And haven't you your own land to visit, continued Miss Ivors, that you know nothing of, your own people, and your own country?

—O, to tell you the truth, retorted Gabriel suddenly, I'm sick of my own country, sick of it!

—Why? asked Miss Ivors.

Gabriel did not answer for his retort had heated him.

—Why? repeated Miss Ivors.

They had to go visiting together and, as he had not answered her, Miss Ivors said warmly:

—Of course, you've no answer.

Gabriel tried to cover his agitation by taking part in the dance with great energy. He avoided her eyes for he had seen a sour expression on her face. But when they met in the long chain he was surprised to feel his hand firmly pressed. She looked at him from under her brows for a moment quizzically until he smiled. Then, just as the chain was about to start again, she stood on tiptoe and whispered into his ear:

—West Briton!

When the lancers were over Gabriel went away to a remote corner of the room where Freddy Malins' mother was sitting. She was a stout feeble old woman with white hair. Her voice had a catch in it like her son's and she stuttered slightly. She had been told that Freddy had come and that he was nearly all right. Gabriel asked her whether she had had a good crossing. She lived with her married daughter in Glasgow and came to Dublin on a visit once a year. She answered placidly that she had had a beautiful crossing and that the captain had been most attentive to her. She spoke also of the beautiful house her daughter kept in Glasgow, and of all the nice friends they had there. While her tongue rambled on Gabriel tried to banish from his mind all memory of the unpleasant incident with Miss Ivors. Of course the girl or woman, or whatever she was, was an enthusiast but there was a time for all things. Perhaps he ought not to have answered her like that. But she had no right to call him a West Briton before people, even in joke. She had tried to make him ridiculous before people, heckling him and staring at him with her rabbit's eyes.

He saw his wife making her way towards him through the waltzing couples. When she reached him she said into his ear:

—Gabriel, Aunt Kate wants to know won't you carve the goose as usual. Miss Daly will carve the ham and I'll do the pudding.

—All right, said Gabriel.

—She's sending in the younger ones first as soon as this waltz is over so that we'll have the table to ourselves.

—Were you dancing? asked Gabriel.

—Of course I was. Didn't you see me? What words had you with Molly Ivors?

—No words. Why? Did she say so?

—Something like that. I'm trying to get that Mr D'Arcy to sing. He's full of conceit, I think.

—There were no words, said Gabriel moodily, only she wanted me to go for a trip to the west of Ireland and I said I wouldn't.

His wife clasped her hands excitedly and gave a little jump.

—O, do go, Gabriel, she cried. I'd love to see Galway again.

—You can go if you like, said Gabriel coldly.

She looked at him for a moment, then turned to Mrs Malins and said:

—There's a nice husband for you, Mrs Malins.

While she was threading her way back across the room Mrs Malins, without adverting to the interruption, went on to tell Gabriel what beautiful places there were in Scotland and beautiful scenery. Her son-in-law brought them every year to the lakes and they used to go fishing. Her son-in-law was a splendid fisher. One day he caught a fish, a beautiful big big fish, and the man in the hotel boiled it for their dinner.

Gabriel hardly heard what she said. Now that supper was coming near he began to think again about his speech and about the quotation. When he saw Freddy Malins coming across the room to visit his mother Gabriel left the chair free for him and retired into the embrasure of the window. The room had already cleared and from the back room came the clatter of plates and knives. Those who still remained in the drawing-room seemed tired of dancing and were conversing quietly in little groups. Gabriel's warm trembling fingers tapped the cold pane of the window. How cool it must be outside! How pleasant it would be to walk out alone, first along by the river and then through the park! The snow would be lying on the branches of the trees and forming a bright cap on the top of the Wellington Monument.[4] How much more pleasant it would be there than at the supper-table!

He ran over the headings of his speech: Irish hospitality, sad memories, the Three Graces, Paris, the quotation from Browning. He repeated to himself a phrase he had written in his review: *One feels that one is listening to a thought-tormented music.* Miss Ivors had praised the review. Was she sincere? Had she really any life of her own behind all her propagandism? There had never been any ill-feeling between them until that night. It unnerved him to think that she would be at the supper-table, looking up at him while he spoke with her critical quizzing eyes. Perhaps she would not be sorry to see him fail in his speech. An idea came into his mind and gave him courage. He would say, alluding to Aunt Kate and Aunt Julia: *Ladies and Gentlemen, the generation which is now on the wane among us may have had its faults but for my part I think it had certain qualities of hospitality, of humour, of humanity, which the new and very serious and hypereducated generation that is growing up around us seems to me to lack.* Very good: that was one for Miss Ivors. What did he care that his aunts were only two ignorant old women?

A murmur in the room attracted his attention. Mr Browne was advancing from the door, gallantly escorting Aunt Julia, who leaned upon his arm, smiling and hanging her head. An irregular musketry of applause escorted her also as far as the piano and then, as Mary Jane seated herself on the stool, and Aunt Julia, no longer smiling, half turned so as to pitch her voice fairly into the room, gradually ceased. Gabriel recognised the prelude. It was that of an old song of Aunt Julia's—*Arrayed for the Bridal.*[5] Her voice, strong and clear in tone, attacked with great spirit the runs which embellish the air and though she sang very rapidly she did not miss even the smallest of the grace notes. To follow the voice, without looking at the singer's face, was to feel and share the excitement of swift and secure flight. Gabriel applauded loudly with all the others at the close of the song and loud applause was borne in from the invisible supper-table. It sounded so genuine that a little colour struggled into Aunt Julia's face as she bent to replace in the music-stand the old leather-bound song-book that had her initials on the cover. Freddy Malins, who had listened with his head perched sideways to hear her better, was still applauding when everyone else had

---

4. A monument to the Duke of Wellington, an Irish-born English military hero, located in Phoenix Park, Dublin's major public park.

5. A popular but challenging song set to music from Bellini's opera *I Puritani* (1835).

ceased and talking animatedly to his mother who nodded her head gravely and slowly in acquiescence. At last, when he could clap no more, he stood up suddenly and hurried across the room to Aunt Julia whose hand he seized and held in both his hands, shaking it when words failed him or the catch in his voice proved too much for him.

—I was just telling my mother, he said, I never heard you sing so well, never. No, I never heard your voice so good as it is to-night. Now! Would you believe that now? That's the truth. Upon my word and honour that's the truth. I never heard your voice sound so fresh and so . . . so clear and fresh, never.

Aunt Julia smiled broadly and murmured something about compliments as she released her hand from his grasp. Mr Browne extended his open hand towards her and said to those who were near him in the manner of a showman introducing a prodigy to an audience:

—Miss Julia Morkan, my latest discovery!

He was laughing very heartily at this himself when Freddy Malins turned to him and said:

—Well, Browne, if you're serious you might make a worse discovery. All I can say is I never heard her sing half so well as long as I am coming here. And that's the honest truth.

—Neither did I, said Mr. Browne. I think her voice has greatly improved.

Aunt Julia shrugged her shoulders and said with meek pride:

—Thirty years ago I hadn't a bad voice as voices go.

—I often told Julia, said Aunt Kate emphatically, that she was simply thrown away in that choir. But she never would be said by me.

She turned as if to appeal to the good sense of the others against a refractory child while Aunt Julia gazed in front of her, a vague smile of reminiscence playing on her face.

—No, continued Aunt Kate, she wouldn't be said or led by anyone, slaving there in that choir night and day, night and day. Six o'clock on Christmas morning! And all for what?

—Well, isn't it for the honour of God, Aunt Kate? asked Mary Jane, twisting round on the piano-stool and smiling.

Aunt Kate turned fiercely on her niece and said:

—I know all about the honour of God, Mary Jane, but I think it's not at all honourable for the pope to turn out the women out of the choirs that have slaved there all their lives and put little whipper-snappers of boys over their heads.[6] I suppose it is for the good of the Church if the pope does it. But it's not just, Mary Jane, and it's not right.

She had worked herself into a passion and would have continued in defence of her sister for it was a sore subject with her but Mary Jane, seeing that all the dancers had come back, intervened pacifically:

—Now, Aunt Kate, you're giving scandal to Mr Browne who is of the other persuasion.

Aunt Kate turned to Mr Browne, who was grinning at this allusion to his religion, and said hastily:

—O, I don't question the pope's being right. I'm only a stupid old woman and I wouldn't presume to do such a thing. But there's such a thing as common everyday politeness and gratitude. And if I were in Julia's place I'd tell that Father Healy straight up to his face . . .

6. In 1903 the Pope had ordered all Catholic churches to start using all-male choirs.

—And besides, Aunt Kate, said Mary Jane, we really are all hungry and when we are hungry we are all very quarrelsome.

—And when we are thirsty we are also quarrelsome, added Mr Browne.

—So that we had better go to supper, said Mary Jane, and finish the discussion afterwards.

On the landing outside the drawing-room Gabriel found his wife and Mary Jane trying to persuade Miss Ivors to stay for supper. But Miss Ivors, who had put on her hat and was buttoning her cloak, would not stay. She did not feel in the least hungry and she had already overstayed her time.

—But only for ten minutes, Molly, said Mrs Conroy. That won't delay you.

—To take a pick itself, said Mary Jane, after all your dancing.

—I really couldn't, said Miss Ivors.

—I am afraid you didn't enjoy yourself at all, said Mary Jane hopelessly.

—Ever so much, I assure you, said Miss Ivors, but you really must let me run off now.

—But how can you get home? asked Mrs Conroy.

—O, it's only two steps up the quay.

Gabriel hesitated a moment and said:

—If you will allow me, Miss Ivors, I'll see you home if you really are obliged to go.

But Miss Ivors broke away from them.

—I won't hear of it, she cried. For goodness sake go in to your suppers and don't mind me. I'm quite well able to take care of myself.

—Well, you're the comical girl, Molly, said Mrs Conroy frankly.

—*Beannacht libh,*[7] cried Miss Ivors, with a laugh, as she ran down the staircase.

Mary Jane gazed after her, a moody puzzled expression on her face, while Mrs Conroy leaned over the banisters to listen for the hall-door. Gabriel asked himself was he the cause of her abrupt departure. But she did not seem to be in ill humour: she had gone away laughing. He stared blankly down the staircase.

At that moment Aunt Kate came toddling out of the supper-room, almost wringing her hands in despair.

—Where is Gabriel? she cried. Where on earth is Gabriel? There's everyone waiting in there, stage to let, and nobody to carve the goose!

—Here I am, Aunt Kate! cried Gabriel, with sudden animation, ready to carve a flock of geese, if necessary.

A fat brown goose lay at one end of the table and at the other end, on a bed of creased paper strewn with sprigs of parsley, lay a great ham, stripped of its outer skin and peppered over with crust crumbs, a neat paper frill round its shin and beside this was a round of spiced beef. Between these rival ends ran parallel lines of side-dishes: two little minsters of jelly, red and yellow; a shallow dish full of blocks of blancmange and red jam, a large green leaf-shaped dish with a stalk-shaped handle, on which lay bunches of purple raisins and peeled almonds, a companion dish on which lay a solid rectangle of Smyrna figs, a dish of custard topped with grated nut-meg, a small bowl full of chocolates and sweets wrapped in gold and silver papers and a glass vase in which stood some tall celery stalks. In the centre of the table there stood, as sentries to a fruit-stand which upheld a pyramid of oranges and American apples, two squat old-fashioned decanters of cut glass, one containing port and the other dark sherry. On the closed square piano a pudding in a huge yellow

7. Farewell (Irish).

dish lay in waiting and behind it were three squads of bottles of stout and ale and minerals, drawn up according to the colours of their uniforms, the first two black, with brown and red labels, the third and smallest squad white, with transverse green sashes.

Gabriel took his seat boldly at the head of the table and, having looked to the edge of the carver, plunged his fork firmly into the goose. He felt quite at ease now for he was an expert carver and liked nothing better than to find himself at the head of a well-laden table.

—Miss Furlong, what shall I send you? he asked. A wing or a slice of the breast?

—Just a small slice of the breast.

—Miss Higgins, what for you?

—O, anything at all, Mr Conroy.

While Gabriel and Miss Daly exchanged plates of goose and plates of ham and spiced beef Lily went from guest to guest with a dish of hot floury potatoes wrapped in a white napkin. This was Mary Jane's idea and she had also suggested apple sauce for the goose but Aunt Kate had said that plain roast goose without apple sauce had always been good enough for her and she hoped she might never eat worse. Mary Jane waited on her pupils and saw that they got the best slices and Aunt Kate and Aunt Julia opened and carried across from the piano bottles of stout and ale for the gentlemen and bottles of minerals for the ladies. There was a great deal of confusion and laughter and noise, the noise of orders and counter-orders, of knives and forks, of corks and glass-stoppers. Gabriel began to carve second helpings as soon as he had finished the first round without serving himself. Everyone protested loudly so that he compromised by taking a long draught of stout for he had found the carving hot work. Mary Jane settled down quietly to her supper but Aunt Kate and Aunt Julia were still toddling round the table, walking on each other's heels, getting in each other's way and giving each other unheeded orders. Mr Browne begged of them to sit down and eat their suppers and so did Gabriel but they said there was time enough so that, at last, Freddy Malins stood up and, capturing Aunt Kate, plumped her down on her chair amid general laughter.

When everyone had been well served Gabriel said, smiling:

—Now, if anyone wants a little more of what vulgar people call stuffing let him or her speak.

A chorus of voices invited him to begin his own supper and Lily came forward with three potatoes which she had reserved for him.

—Very well, said Gabriel amiably, as he took another preparatory draught, kindly forget my existence, ladies and gentlemen, for a few minutes.

He set to his supper and took no part in the conversation with which the table covered Lily's removal of the plates. The subject of talk was the opera company which was then at the Theatre Royal. Mr Bartell D'Arcy, the tenor, a dark-complexioned young man with a smart moustache, praised very highly the leading contralto of the company but Miss Furlong thought she had a rather vulgar style of production. Freddy Malins said there was a negro chieftain singing in the second part of the Gaiety pantomime who had one of the finest tenor voices he had ever heard.

—Have you heard him? he asked Mr Bartell D'Arcy across the table.

—No, answered Mr Bartell D'Arcy carelessly.

—Because, Freddy Malins explained, now I'd be curious to hear your opinion of him. I think he has a grand voice.

—It takes Teddy to find out the really good things, said Mr Browne familiarly to the table.

—And why couldn't he have a voice too? asked Freddy Malins sharply. Is it because he's only a black?

Nobody answered this question and Mary Jane led the table back to the legitimate opera. One of her pupils had given her a pass for *Mignon.* Of course it was very fine, she said, but it made her think of poor Georgina Burns. Mr Browne could go back farther still, to the old Italian companies that used to come to Dublin—Tietjens, Ilma de Murzka, Campanini, the great Trebelli, Giuglini, Ravelli, Aramburo.[8] Those were the days, he said, when there was something like singing to be heard in Dublin. He told too of how the top gallery of the old Royal used to be packed night after night, of how one night an Italian tenor had sung five encores to *Let Me Like a Soldier Fall,* introducing a high C every time, and of how the gallery boys would sometimes in their enthusiasm unyoke the horses from the carriage of some great *prima donna* and pull her themselves through the streets to her hotel. Why did they never play the grand old operas now, he asked, *Dinorah, Lucrezia Borgia?* Because they could not get the voices to sing them: that was why.

—O, well, said Mr Bartell D'Arcy, I presume there are as good singers to-day as there were then.

—Where are they? asked Mr Browne defiantly.

—In London, Paris, Milan, said Mr Bartell D'Arcy warmly. I suppose Caruso,[9] for example, is quite as good, if not better than any of the men you have mentioned.

—Maybe so, said Mr Browne. But I may tell you I doubt it strongly.

—O, I'd give anything to hear Caruso sing, said Mary Jane.

—For me, said Aunt Kate, who had been picking a bone, there was only one tenor. To please me, I mean. But I suppose none of you ever heard of him.

—Who was he, Miss Morkan? asked Mr Bartell D'Arcy politely.

—His name, said Aunt Kate, was Parkinson. I heard him when he was in his prime and I think he had then the purest tenor voice that was ever put into a man's throat.

—Strange, said Mr Bartell D'Arcy. I never even heard of him.

—Yes, yes, Miss Morkan is right, said Mr Browne. I remember hearing of old Parkinson but he's too far back for me.

—A beautiful pure sweet mellow English tenor, said Aunt Kate with enthusiasm.

Gabriel having finished, the huge pudding was transferred to the table. The clatter of forks and spoons began again. Gabriel's wife served out spoonfuls of the pudding and passed the plates down the table. Midway down they were held up by Mary Jane, who replenished them with raspberry or orange jelly or with blancmange and jam. The pudding was of Aunt Julia's making and she received praises for it from all quarters. She herself said that it was not quite brown enough.

—Well, I hope, Miss Morkan, said Mr Browne, that I'm brown enough for you because, you know, I'm all brown.

All the gentlemen, except Gabriel, ate some of the pudding out of compliment to Aunt Julia. As Gabriel never ate sweets the celery had been left for him. Freddy Malins also took a stalk of celery and ate it with his pudding. He had been told that celery was a capital thing for the blood and he was just then under doctor's care. Mrs Malins, who had been silent all through the supper, said that her son was going down to

---

8. Famous 19th-century opera singers.   9. Enrico Caruso (1874–1921), a famous tenor.

Mount Melleray[1] in a week or so. The table then spoke to Mount Melleray, how bracing the air was down there, how hospitable the monks were and how they never asked for a penny-piece from their guests.

—And do you mean to say, asked Mr Browne incredulously, that a chap can go down there and put up there as if it were a hotel and live on the fat of the land and then come away without paying a farthing?

—O, most people give some donation to the monastery when they leave, said Mary Jane.

—I wish we had an institution like that in our Church, said Mr Browne candidly.

He was astonished to hear that the monks never spoke, got up at two in the morning and slept in their coffins. He asked what they did it for.

—That's the rule of the order, said Aunt Kate firmly.

—Yes, but why? asked Mr Browne.

Aunt Kate repeated that it was the rule, that was all. Mr Browne still seemed not to understand. Freddy Malins explained to him, as best he could, that the monks were trying to make up for the sins committed by all the sinners in the outside world. The explanation was not very clear for Mr Browne grinned and said:

—I like that idea very much but wouldn't a comfortable spring bed do them as well as a coffin?

—The coffin, said Mary Jane, is to remind them of their last end.

As the subject had grown lugubrious it was buried in a silence of the table during which Mrs Malins could be heard saying to her neighbour in an indistinct undertone:

—They are very good men, the monks, very pious men.

The raisins and almonds and figs and apples and oranges and chocolates and sweets were now passed about the table and Aunt Julia invited all the guests to have either port or sherry. At first Mr Bartell D'Arcy refused to take either but one of his neighbours nudged him and whispered something to him upon which he allowed his glass to be filled. Gradually as the last glasses were being filled the conversation ceased. A pause followed, broken only by the noise of the wine and by unsettlings of chairs. The Misses Morkan, all three, looked down at the tablecloth. Someone coughed once or twice and then a few gentlemen patted the table gently as a signal for silence. The silence came and Gabriel pushed back his chair and stood up.

The patting at once grew louder in encouragement and then ceased altogether. Gabriel leaned his ten trembling fingers on the tablecloth and smiled nervously at the company. Meeting a row of upturned faces he raised his eyes to the chandelier. The piano was playing a waltz tune and he could hear the skirts sweeping against the drawing-room door. People, perhaps, were standing in the snow on the quay outside, gazing up at the lighted windows and listening to the waltz music. The air was pure there. In the distance lay the park where the trees were weighted with snow. The Wellington Monument wore a gleaming cap of snow that flashed westward over the white field of Fifteen Acres.[2]

He began:

—Ladies and Gentlemen.

—It has fallen to my lot this evening, as in years past, to perform a very pleasing task but a task for which I am afraid my poor powers as a speaker are all too inadequate.

---

1. A monastery in southern Ireland, specializing in the treatment of alcoholics.   2. A section of Phoenix Park.

—No, no! said Mr Browne.

—But, however that may be, I can only ask you tonight to take the will for the deed and to lend me your attention for a few moments while I endeavour to express to you in words what my feelings are on this occasion.

—Ladies and Gentlemen. It is not the first time that we have gathered together under this hospitable roof, around this hospitable board. It is not the first time that we have been the recipients—or perhaps, I had better say, the victims—of the hospitality of certain good ladies.

He made a circle in the air with his arm and paused. Everyone laughed or smiled at Aunt Kate and Aunt Julia and Mary Jane who all turned crimson with pleasure. Gabriel went on more boldly:

—I feel more strongly with every recurring year that our country has no tradition which does it so much honour and which it should guard so jealously as that of its hospitality. It is a tradition that is unique as far as my experience goes (and I have visited not a few places abroad) among the modern nations. Some would say, perhaps, that with us it is rather a failing than anything to be boasted of. But granted even that, it is, to my mind, a princely failing, and one that I trust will long be cultivated among us. Of one thing, at least, I am sure. As long as this one roof shelters the good ladies aforesaid—and I wish from my heart it may do so for many and many a long year to come—the tradition of genuine warm-hearted courteous Irish hospitality, which our forefathers have handed down to us and which we in turn must hand down to our descendants, is still alive among us.

A hearty murmur of assent ran round the table. It shot through Gabriel's mind that Miss Ivors was not there and that she had gone away discourteously: and he said with confidence in himself:

—Ladies and Gentlemen.

—A new generation is growing up in our midst, a generation actuated by new ideas and new principles. It is serious and enthusiastic for these new ideas and its enthusiasm, even when it is misdirected, is, I believe, in the main sincere. But we are living in a sceptical and, if I may use the phrase, a thought-tormented age: and sometimes I fear that this new generation, educated or hypereducated as it is, will lack those qualities of humanity, of hospitality, of kindly humour which belonged to an older day. Listening to-night to the names of all those great singers of the past it seemed to me, I must confess, that we were living in a less spacious age. Those days might, without exaggeration, be called spacious days: and if they are gone beyond recall let us hope, at least, that in gatherings such as this we shall still speak of them with pride and affection, still cherish in our hearts the memory of those dead and gone great ones whose fame the world will not willingly let die.

—Hear, hear! said Mr Browne loudly.

—But yet, continued Gabriel, his voice falling into a softer inflection, there are always in gatherings such as this sadder thoughts that will recur to our minds: thoughts of the past, of youth, of changes, of absent faces that we miss here to-night. Our path through life is strewn with many such sad memories: and were we to brood upon them always we could not find the heart to go on bravely with our work among the living. We have all of us living duties and living affections which claim, and rightly claim, our strenuous endeavours.

—Therefore, I will not linger on the past. I will not let any gloomy moralising intrude upon us here to-night. Here we are gathered together for a brief moment from the bustle and rush of our everyday routine. We are met here as friends, in the spirit of good-fellowship, as colleagues, also to a certain extent, in the true spirit of *camaraderie,* and as the guests of—what shall I call them?—the Three Graces[3] of the Dublin musical world.

The table burst into applause and laughter at this sally. Aunt Julia vainly asked each of her neighbors in turn to tell her what Gabriel had said.

—He says we are the Three Graces, Aunt Julia, said Mary Jane.

Aunt Julia did not understand but she looked up, smiling, at Gabriel, who continued in the same vein:

—Ladies and Gentlemen.

—I will not attempt to play to-night the part that Paris[4] played on another occasion. I will not attempt to choose between them. The task would be an invidious one and one beyond my poor powers. For when I view them in turn, whether it be our chief hostess herself, whose good heart, whose too good heart, has become a byword with all who know her, or her sister, who seems to be gifted with perennial youth and whose singing must have been a surprise and a revelation to us all to-night, or, last but not least, when I consider our youngest hostess, talented, cheerful, hard-working and the best of nieces, I confess, Ladies and Gentlemen, that I do not know to which of them I should award the prize.

Gabriel glanced down at his aunts and, seeing the large smile on Aunt Julia's face and the tears which had risen to Aunt Kate's eyes, hastened to his close. He raised his glass of port gallantly, while every member of the company fingered a glass expectantly, and said loudly:

—Let us toast them all three together. Let us drink to their health, wealth, long life, happiness and prosperity and may they long continue to hold the proud and self-won position which they hold in their profession and the position of honour and affection which they hold in our hearts.

All the guests stood up, glass in hand, and, turning towards the three seated ladies, sang in unison, with Mr Browne as leader:

> *For they are jolly gay fellows,*
> *For they are jolly gay fellows,*
> *For they are jolly gay fellows,*
> *Which nobody can deny.*

Aunt Kate was making frank use of her handkerchief and even Aunt Julia seemed moved. Freddy Malins beat time with his pudding-fork and the singers turned towards one another, as if in melodious conference, while they sang, with emphasis:

> *Unless he tells a lie,*
> *Unless he tells a lie.*

Then, turning once more towards their hostesses, they sang:

> *For they are jolly gay fellows,*
> *For they are jolly gay fellows,*
> *For they are jolly gay fellows,*
> *Which nobody can deny.*

3. Companions to the Muses in Greek mythology.
4. Paris was the judge of a divine beauty contest in which Hera, Athena, and Aphrodite competed; his selection of Aphrodite was, indirectly, the cause of the Trojan War.

The acclamation which followed was taken up beyond the door of the supper-room by many of the other guests and renewed time after time, Freddy Malins acting as officer with his fork on high.

The piercing morning air came into the hall where they were standing so that Aunt Kate said:

—Close the door, somebody. Mrs Malins will get her death of cold.

—Browne is out there, Aunt Kate, said Mary Jane.

—Browne is everywhere, said Aunt Kate, lowering her voice.

Mary Jane laughed at her tone.

—Really, she said archly, he is very attentive.

—He has been laid on here like the gas, said Aunt Kate in the same tone, all during the Christmas.

She laughed herself this time good-humouredly and then added quickly:

—But tell him to come in, Mary Jane, and close the door. I hope to goodness he didn't hear me.

At that moment the hall-door was opened and Mr Browne came in from the doorstep, laughing as if his heart would break. He was dressed in a long green overcoat with mock astrakhan cuffs and collar and wore on his head an oval fur cap. He pointed down the snow-covered quay from where the sound of shrill prolonged whistling was borne in.

—Teddy will have all the cabs in Dublin out, he said.

Gabriel advanced from the little pantry behind the office, struggling into his overcoat and looking round the hall, said:

—Gretta not down yet?

—She's getting on her things, Gabriel, said Aunt Kate.

—Who's playing up there? asked Gabriel.

—Nobody. They're all gone.

—O no, Aunt Kate, said Mary Jane. Bartell D'Arcy and Miss O'Callaghan aren't gone yet.

—Someone is strumming at the piano, anyhow, said Gabriel.

Mary Jane glanced at Gabriel and Mr Browne and said with a shiver:

—It makes me feel cold to look at you two gentlemen muffled up like that. I wouldn't like to face your journey home at this hour.

—I'd like nothing better this minute, said Mr Browne stoutly, than a rattling fine walk in the country or a fast drive with a good spanking goer between the shafts.

—We used to have a very good horse and trap at home, said Aunt Julia sadly.

—The never-to-be-forgotten Johnny, said Mary Jane, laughing.

Aunt Kate and Gabriel laughed too.

—Why, what was wonderful about Johnny? asked Mr Browne.

—The late lamented Patrick Morkan, our grandfather, that is, explained Gabriel, commonly known in his later years as the old gentleman, was a glue-boiler.

—O, now, Gabriel, said Aunt Kate, laughing, he had a starch mill.

—Well, glue or starch, said Gabriel, the old gentleman had a horse by the name of Johnny. And Johnny used to work in the old gentleman's mill, walking round and round in order to drive the mill. That was all very well; but now comes the tragic part about Johnny. One fine day the old gentleman thought he'd like to drive out with the quality to a military review in the park.

—The Lord have mercy on his soul, said Aunt Kate compassionately.

—Amen, said Gabriel. So the old gentleman, as I said, harnessed Johnny and put on his very best tall hat and his very best stock collar and drove out in grand style from his ancestral mansion somewhere near Back Lane, I think.

Everyone laughed, even Mrs Malins, at Gabriel's manner and Aunt Kate said:

—O now, Gabriel, he didn't live in Back Lane, really. Only the mill was there.

—Out from the mansion of his forefathers, continued Gabriel, he drove with Johnny. And everything went on beautifully until Johnny came in sight of King Billy's statue:[5] and whether he fell in love with the horse King Billy sits on or whether he thought he was back again in the mill, anyhow he began to walk round the statue.

Gabriel paced in a circle round the hall in his goloshes amid the laughter of the others.

—Round and round he went, said Gabriel, and the old gentleman, who was a very pompous old gentleman, was highly indignant. *Go on, sir! What do you mean, sir? Johnny! Johnny! Most extraordinary conduct! Can't understand the horse!*

The peals of laughter which followed Gabriel's imitation of the incident were interrupted by a resounding knock at the hall-door. Mary Jane ran to open it and let in Freddy Malins. Freddy Malins, with his hat well back on his head and his shoulders humped with cold, was puffing and steaming after his exertions.

—I could only get one cab, he said.

—O, we'll find another along the quay, said Gabriel.

—Yes, said Aunt Kate. Better not keep Mrs Malins standing in the draught.

Mrs Malins was helped down the front steps by her son and Mr Browne and, after many manoeuvres, hoisted into the cab. Freddy Malins clambered in after her and spent a long time settling her on the seat, Mr Browne helping him with advice. At last she was settled comfortably and Freddy Malins invited Mr Browne into the cab. There was a good deal of confused talk, and then Mr Browne got into the cab. The cabman settled his rug over his knees, and bent down for the address. The confusion grew greater and the cabman was directed differently by Freddy Malins and Mr Browne, each of whom had his head out through a window of the cab. The difficulty was to know where to drop Mr Browne along the route and Aunt Kate, Aunt Julia and Mary Jane helped the discussion from the doorstep with cross-directions and contradictions and abundance of laughter. As for Freddy Malins he was speechless with laughter. He popped his head in and out of the window every moment, to the great danger of his hat, and told his mother how the discussion was progressing till at last Mr Browne shouted to the bewildered cabman above the din of everybody's laughter:

—Do you know Trinity College?

—Yes, sir, said the cabman.

—Well, drive bang up against Trinity College gates, said Mr Browne, and then we'll tell you where to go. You understand now?

—Yes, sir, said the cabman.

—Make like a bird for Trinity College.

—Right, sir, cried the cabman.

The horse was whipped up and the cab rattled off along the quay amid a chorus of laughter and adieus.

5. A statue of William of Orange, who defeated the Irish Catholic forces in the Battle of the Boyne in 1690, which stood in College Green in front of Trinity College in the heart of Dublin. It was seen as a symbol of British imperial oppression.

Gabriel had not gone to the door with the others. He was in a dark part of the hall gazing up the staircase. A woman was standing near the top of the first flight, in the shadow also. He could not see her face but he could see the terracotta and salmonpink panels of her skirt which the shadow made appear black and white. It was his wife. She was leaning on the banisters, listening to something. Gabriel was surprised at her stillness and strained his ear to listen also. But he could hear little save the noise of laughter and dispute on the front steps, a few chords struck on the piano and a few notes of a man's voice singing.

He stood still in the gloom of the hall, trying to catch the air that the voice was singing and gazing up at his wife. There was grace and mystery in her attitude as if she were a symbol of something. He asked himself what is a woman standing on the stairs in the shadow, listening to distant music, a symbol of. If he were a painter he would paint her in that attitude. Her blue felt hat would show off the bronze of her hair against the darkness and the dark panels of her skirt would show off the light ones. *Distant Music* he would call the picture if he were a painter.

The hall-door was closed; and Aunt Kate, Aunt Julia and Mary Jane came down the hall, still laughing.

—Well, isn't Freddy terrible? said Mary Jane. He's really terrible.

Gabriel said nothing but pointed up the stairs towards where his wife was standing. Now that the hall-door was closed the voice and the piano could be heard more clearly. Gabriel held up his hand for them to be silent. The song seemed to be in the old Irish tonality and the singer seemed uncertain both of his words and of his voice. The voice, made plaintive by distance and by the singer's hoarseness, faintly illuminated the cadence of the air with words expressing grief:

> *O, the rain falls on my heavy locks*
> *And the dew wets my skin,*
> *My babe lies cold . . .*[6]

–O, exclaimed Mary Jane. It's Bartell D'Arcy singing and he wouldn't sing all the night. O, I'll get him to sing a song before he goes.

—O do, Mary Jane, said Aunt Kate.

Mary Jane brushed past the others and ran to the staircase but before she reached it the singing stopped and the piano was closed abruptly.

—O, what a pity! she cried. Is he coming down, Gretta?

Gabriel heard his wife answer yes and saw her come down towards them. A few steps behind her were Mr Bartell D'Arcy and Miss O'Callaghan.

—O, Mr D'Arcy, cried Mary Jane, it's downright mean of you to break off like that when we were all in raptures listening to you.

—I have been at him all the evening, said Miss O'Callaghan, and Mrs Conroy too and he told us he had a dreadful cold and couldn't sing.

—O, Mr D'Arcy, said Aunt Kate, now that was a great fib to tell.

—Can't you see that I'm as hoarse as a crow? said Mr D'Arcy roughly.

He went into the pantry hastily and put on his overcoat. The others, taken aback by his rude speech, could find nothing to say. Aunt Kate wrinkled her brows and made signs to the others to drop the subject. Mr D'Arcy stood swathing his neck carefully and frowning.

6. From a traditional ballad, *The Lass of Aughrim,* about a peasant girl seduced by a nobleman. She brings their baby to the castle door, only to be turned away; she and her child then die by drowning.

—It's the weather, said Aunt Julia, after a pause.

—Yes, everybody has colds, said Aunt Kate readily, everybody.

—They say, said Mary Jane, we haven't had snow like it for thirty years; and I read this morning in the newspapers that the snow is general all over Ireland.

—I love the look of snow, said Aunt Julia sadly.

—So do I, said Miss O'Callaghan. I think Christmas is never really Christmas unless we have the snow on the ground.

—But poor Mr D'Arcy doesn't like the snow, said Aunt Kate, smiling.

Mr D'Arcy came from the pantry, full swathed and buttoned, and in a repentant tone told them the history of his cold. Everyone gave him advice and said it was a great pity and urged him to be very careful of his throat in the night air. Gabriel watched his wife who did not join in the conversation. She was standing right under the dusty fanlight and the flame of the gas lit up the rich bronze of her hair which he had seen her drying at the fire a few days before. She was in the same attitude and seemed unaware of the talk about her. At last she turned towards them and Gabriel saw that there was colour on her cheeks and that her eyes were shining. A sudden tide of joy went leaping out of his heart.

—Mr D'Arcy, she said, what is the name of that song you were singing?

—It's called *The Lass of Aughrim,* said Mr D'Arcy, but I couldn't remember it properly. Why? Do you know it?

—*The Lass of Aughrim,* she repeated. I couldn't think of the name.

—It's a very nice air, said Mary Jane. I'm sorry you were not in voice to-night.

—Now, Mary Jane, said Aunt Kate, don't annoy Mr D'Arcy. I won't have him annoyed.

Seeing that all were ready to start she shepherded them to the door where good-night was said:

—Well, good-night, Aunt Kate, and thanks for the pleasant evening.

—Good-night, Gabriel. Good-night, Gretta!

—Good-night, Aunt Kate, and thanks ever so much. Good-night, Aunt Julia.

—O, good-night, Gretta, I didn't see you.

—Good-night, Mr D'Arcy. Good-night, Miss O'Callaghan.

—Good-night, Miss Morkan.

—Good-night, again.

—Good-night, all. Safe home.

—Good-night. Good-night.

The morning was still dark. A dull yellow light brooded over the houses and the river; and the sky seemed to be descending. It was slushy underfoot; and only streaks and patches of snow lay on the roofs, on the parapets of the quay and on the area railings. The lamps were still burning redly in the murky air and, across the river, the palace of the Four Courts[7] stood out menacingly against the heavy sky.

She was walking on before him with Mr Bartell D'Arcy, her shoes in a brown parcel tucked under one arm and her hands holding her skirt up from the slush. She had no longer any grace of attitude but Gabriel's eyes were still bright with happiness. The blood went bounding along his veins; and the thoughts went rioting through his brain, proud, joyful, tender, valorous.

She was walking on before him so lightly and so erect that he longed to run after her noiselessly, catch her by the shoulders and say something foolish and affectionate

7. The Irish law courts.

into her ear. She seemed to him so frail that he longed to defend her against something and then to be alone with her. Moments of their secret life together burst like stars upon his memory. A heliotrope envelope was lying beside his breakfast-cup and he was caressing it with his hand. Birds were twittering in the ivy and the sunny web of the curtain was shimmering along the floor: he could not eat for happiness. They were standing on the crowded platform and he was placing a ticket inside the warm palm of her glove. He was standing with her in the cold, looking in through a grated window at a man making bottles in a roaring furnace. It was very cold. Her face, fragrant in the cold air, was quite close to his; and suddenly she called out to the man at the furnace:

—Is the fire hot, sir?

But the man could not hear her with the noise of the furnace. It was just as well. He might have answered rudely.

A wave of yet more tender joy escaped from his heart and went coursing in warm flood along his arteries. Like the tender fires of stars moments of their life together, that no one knew of or would ever know of, broke upon and illumined his memory. He longed to recall to her those moments, to make her forget the years of their dull existence together and remember only their moments of ecstasy. For the years, he felt, had not quenched his soul or hers. Their children, his writing, her household cares had not quenched all their souls' tender fire. In one letter that he had written to her then he had said: *Why is it that words like these seem to me so dull and cold? Is it because there is no word tender enough to be your name?*

Like distant music these words that he had written years before were borne towards him from the past. He longed to be alone with her. When the others had gone away, when he and she were in their room in the hotel, then they would be alone together. He would call her softly:

—Gretta!

Perhaps she would not hear at once: she would be undressing. Then something in his voice would strike her. She would turn and look at him. . . .

At the corner of Winetavern Street they met a cab. He was glad of its rattling noise as it saved him from conversation. She was looking out of the window and seemed tired. The others spoke only a few words, pointing out some building or street. The horse galloped along wearily under the murky morning sky, dragging his old rattling box after his heels, and Gabriel was again in a cab with her, galloping to catch the boat, galloping to their honeymoon.

As the cab drove across O'Connell Bridge Miss O'Callaghan said:

—They say you never cross O'Connell Bridge without seeing a white horse.

—I see a white man this time, said Gabriel.

—Where? asked Mr Bartell D'Arcy.

Gabriel pointed to the statue, on which lay patches of snow.[8] Then he nodded familiarly to it and waved his hand.

—Good-night, Dan, he said gaily.

When the cab drew up before the hotel Gabriel jumped out and, in spite of Mr Bartell D'Arcy's protest, paid the driver. He gave the man a shilling over his fare. The man saluted and said:

—A prosperous New Year to you, sir.

—The same to you, said Gabriel cordially.

8. A statue of Daniel O'Connell, 19th-century nationalist leader.

She leaned for a moment on his arm in getting out of the cab and while standing at the curbstone, bidding the others good-night. She leaned lightly on his arm, as lightly as when she had danced with him a few hours before. He had felt proud and happy then, happy that she was his, proud of her grace and wifely carriage. But now, after the kindling again of so many memories, the first touch of her body, musical and strange and perfumed, sent through him a keen pang of lust. Under cover of her silence he pressed her arm closely to his side; and, as they stood at the hotel door, he felt that they had escaped from their lives and duties, escaped from home and friends and run away together with wild and radiant hearts to a new adventure.

An old man was dozing in a great hooded chair in the hall. He lit a candle in the office and went before them to the stairs. They followed him in silence, their feet falling in soft thuds on the thickly carpeted stairs. She mounted the stairs behind the porter, her head bowed in the ascent, her frail shoulders curved as with a burden, her skirt girt tightly about her. He could have flung his arms about her hips and held her still for his arms were trembling with desire to seize her and only the stress of his nails against the palms of his hands held the wild impulse of his body in check. The porter halted on the stairs to settle his guttering candle. They halted too on the steps below him. In the silence Gabriel could hear the falling of the molten wax into the tray and the thumping of his own heart against his ribs.

The porter led them along a corridor and opened a door. Then he set his unstable candle down on a toilet-table and asked at what hour they were to be called in the morning.

—Eight, said Gabriel.

The porter pointed to the tap of the electric-light and began a muttered apology but Gabriel cut him short.

—We don't want any light. We have light enough from the street. And I say, he added, pointing to the candle, you might remove that handsome article, like a good man.

The porter took up his candle again, but slowly for he was surprised by such a novel idea. Then he mumbled good-night and went out. Gabriel shot the lock to.

A ghostly light from the street lamp lay in a long shaft from one window to the door. Gabriel threw his overcoat and hat on a couch and crossed the room towards the window. He looked down into the street in order that his emotion might calm a little. Then he turned and leaned against a chest of drawers with his back to the light. She had taken off her hat and cloak and was standing before a large swinging mirror, unhooking her waist. Gabriel paused for a few moments, watching her, and then said:

—Gretta!

She turned away from the mirror slowly and walked along the shaft of light towards him. Her face looked so serious and weary that the words would not pass Gabriel's lips. No, it was not the moment yet.

—You looked tired, he said.

—I am a little, she answered.

—You don't feel ill or weak?

—No, tired: that's all.

She went on to the window and stood there, looking out. Gabriel waited again and then, fearing that diffidence was about to conquer him, he said abruptly:

—By the way, Gretta!

—What is it?

—You know that poor fellow Malins? he said quickly.

—Yes. What about him?

—Well, poor fellow, he's a decent sort of chap after all, continued Gabriel in a false voice. He gave me back that sovereign I lent him and I didn't expect it really. It's a pity he wouldn't keep away from that Browne, because he's not a bad fellow at heart.

He was trembling now with annoyance. Why did she seem so abstracted? He did not know how he could begin. Was she annoyed, too, about something? If she would only turn to him or come to him of her own accord! To take her as she was would be brutal. No, he must see some ardour in her eyes first. He longed to be master of her strange mood.

—When did you lend him the pound? she asked, after a pause.

Gabriel strove to restrain himself from breaking out into brutal language about the sottish Malins and his pound. He longed to cry to her from his soul, to crush her body against his, to overmaster her. But he said:

—O, at Christmas, when he opened that little Christmas-card shop in Henry Street.

He was in such a fever of rage and desire that he did not hear her come from the window. She stood before him for an instant, looking at him strangely. Then, suddenly raising herself on tiptoe and resting her hands lightly on his shoulders, she kissed him.

—You are a very generous person, Gabriel, she said.

Gabriel, trembling with delight at her sudden kiss and at the quaintness of her phrase, put his hands on her hair and began smoothing it back, scarcely touching it with his fingers. The washing had made it fine and brilliant. His heart was brimming over with happiness. Just when he was wishing for it she had come to him of her own accord. Perhaps her thoughts had been running with his. Perhaps she had felt the impetuous desire that was in him and then the yielding mood had come upon her. Now that she had fallen to him so easily he wondered why he had been so diffident.

He stood, holding her head between his hands. Then, slipping one arm swiftly about her body and drawing her towards him, he said softly:

—Gretta dear, what are you thinking about?

She did not answer nor yield wholly to his arm. He said again, softly:

—Tell me what it is, Gretta. I think I know what is the matter. Do I know?

She did not answer at once. Then she said in an outburst of tears:

—O, I am thinking about that song, *The Lass of Aughrim.*

She broke loose from him and ran to the bed and, throwing her arms across the bed-rail, hid her face. Gabriel stood stock-still for a moment in astonishment and then followed her. As he passed in the way of the cheval-glass he caught sight of himself in full length, his broad, well-filled shirt-front, the face whose expression always puzzled him when he saw it in a mirror and his glimmering gilt-rimmed eyeglasses. He halted a few paces from her and said:

—What about the song? Why does that make you cry?

She raised her head from her arms and dried her eyes with the back of her hand like a child. A kinder note than he had intended went into his voice.

—Why, Gretta? he asked.

—I am thinking about a person long ago who used to sing that song.

—And who was the person long ago? asked Gabriel, smiling.

—It was a person I used to know in Galway when I was living with my grandmother, she said.

The smile passed away from Gabriel's face. A dull anger began to gather again at the back of his mind and the dull fires of his lust began to glow angrily in his veins.

—Someone you were in love with? he asked ironically.

—It was a young boy I used to know, she answered, named Michael Furey. He used to sing that song, *The Lass of Aughrim.* He was very delicate.

Gabriel was silent. He did not wish her to think that he was interested in this delicate boy.

—I can see him so plainly, she said after a moment. Such eyes as he had: big dark eyes! And such an expression in them—an expression!

—O then, you were in love with him? said Gabriel.

—I used to go out walking with him, she said, when I was in Galway.

A thought flew across Gabriel's mind.

—Perhaps that was why you wanted to go to Galway with that Ivors girl? he said coldly.

She looked at him and asked in surprise:

—What for?

Her eyes made Gabriel feel awkward. He shrugged his shoulders and said:

—How do I know? To see him perhaps.

She looked away from him along the shaft of light towards the window in silence.

—He is dead, she said at length. He died when he was only seventeen. Isn't it a terrible thing to die so young as that?

—What was he? asked Gabriel, still ironically.

—He was in the gasworks, she said.

Gabriel felt humiliated by the failure of his irony and by the evocation of this figure from the dead, a boy in the gasworks. While he had been full of memories of their secret life together, full of tenderness and joy and desire, she had been comparing him in her mind with another. A shameful consciousness of his own person assailed him. He saw himself as a ludicrous figure, acting as a pennyboy[9] for his aunts, a nervous well-meaning sentimentalist, orating to vulgarians and idealising his own clownish lusts, the pitiable fatuous fellow he had caught a glimpse of in the mirror. Instinctively he turned his back more to the light lest she might see the shame that burned upon his forehead.

He tried to keep up his tone of cold interrogation but his voice when he spoke was humble and indifferent.

—I suppose you were in love with this Michael Furey, Gretta, he said.

—I was great with him at that time, she said.

Her voice was veiled and sad. Gabriel, feeling now how vain it would be to try to lead her whither he had purposed, caressed one of her hands and said, also sadly:

—And what did he die of so young, Gretta? Consumption, was it?

—I think he died for me, she answered.[1]

A vague terror seized Gabriel at this answer as if, at that hour when he had hoped to triumph, some impalpable and vindictive being was coming against him, gathering forces against him in its vague world. But he shook himself free of it with an effort of reason and continued to caress her hand. He did not question her again for he felt that she would tell him of herself. Her hand was warm and moist: it did not respond to his touch but he continued to caress it just as he had caressed her first letter to him that spring morning.

—It was in the winter, she said, about the beginning of the winter when I was going to leave my grandmother's and come up here to the convent. And he was ill at the time

9. Errand boy.

1. Gretta here echoes the words of Yeats's Cathleen ní Houlihan: "Singing I am about a man I knew one time, yellow-haired Donough that was hanged in Galway. . . . He died for love of me: many a man has died for love of me." The play was first performed in Dublin on 2 April 1902.

in his lodgings in Galway and wouldn't be let out and his people in Oughterard[2] were written to. He was in decline, they said, or something like that. I never knew rightly.

She paused for a moment and sighed.

—Poor fellow, she said. He was very fond of me and he was such a gentle boy. We used to go out together, walking, you know, Gabriel, like the way they do in the country. He was going to study singing only for his health. He had a very good voice, poor Michael Furey.

—Well; and then? asked Gabriel.

—And then when it came to the time for me to leave Galway and come up to the convent he was much worse and I wouldn't be let see him so I wrote a letter saying I was going up to Dublin and would be back in the summer and hoping he would be better then.

She paused for a moment to get her voice under control and then went on:

—Then the night before I left I was in my grandmother's house in Nuns' Island, packing up, and I heard gravel thrown up against the window. The window was so wet I couldn't see so I ran downstairs as I was and slipped out the back into the garden and there was the poor fellow at the end of the garden, shivering.

—And did you not tell him to go back? asked Gabriel.

—I implored him to go home at once and told him he would get his death in the rain. But he said he did not want to live. I can see his eyes as well as well! He was standing at the end of the wall where there was a tree.

—And did he go home? asked Gabriel.

—Yes, he went home. And when I was only a week in the convent he died and he was buried in Oughterard where his people came from. O, the day I heard that, that he was dead!

She stopped, choking with sobs, and, overcome by emotion, flung herself face downward on the bed, sobbing in the quilt. Gabriel held her hand for a moment longer, irresolutely, and then, shy of intruding on her grief, let it fall gently and walked quietly to the window.

She was fast asleep.

Gabriel, leaning on his elbow, looked for a few moments unresentfully on her tangled hair and half-open mouth, listening to her deep-drawn breath. So she had had that romance in her life: a man had died for her sake. It hardly pained him now to think how poor a part he, her husband, had played in her life. He watched her while she slept as though he and she had never lived together as man and wife. His curious eyes rested long upon her face and on her hair: and, as he thought of what she must have been then, in that time of her first girlish beauty, a strange friendly pity for her entered his soul. He did not like to say even to himself that her face was no longer beautiful but he knew that it was no longer the face for which Michael Furey had braved death.

Perhaps she had not told him all the story. His eyes moved to the chair over which she had thrown some of her clothes. A petticoat string dangled to the floor. One boot stood upright, its limp upper fallen down: the fellow of it lay upon its side. He wondered at his riot of emotions of an hour before. From what had it proceeded? From his aunt's supper, from his own foolish speech, from the wine and dancing, the merry-making when saying good-night in the hall, the pleasure of the walk along the river in the snow. Poor Aunt Julia! She, too, would soon be a shade with the shade of Patrick Morkan and

2. A small village in western Ireland.

his horse. He had caught that haggard look upon her face for a moment when she was singing *Arrayed for the Bridal*. Soon, perhaps, he would be sitting in that same drawing-room, dressed in black, his silk hat on his knees. The blinds would be drawn down and Aunt Kate would be sitting beside him, crying and blowing her nose and telling him how Julia had died. He would cast about in his mind for some words that might console her, and would find only lame and useless ones. Yes, yes: that would happen very soon.

The air of the room chilled his shoulders. He stretched himself cautiously along under the sheets and lay down beside his wife. One by one they were all becoming shades. Better pass boldly into that other world, in the full glory of some passion, than fade and wither dismally with age. He thought of how she who lay beside him had locked in her heart for so many years that image of her lover's eyes when he had told her that he did not wish to live.

Generous tears filled Gabriel's eyes. He had never felt like that himself towards any woman but he knew that such a feeling must be love. The tears gathered more thickly in his eyes and in the partial darkness he imagined he saw the form of a young man standing under a dripping tree. Other forms were near. His soul had approached that region where dwell the vast hosts of the dead. He was conscious of, but could not apprehend, their wayward and flickering existence. His own identity was fading out into a grey impalpable world: the solid world itself which these dead had one time reared and lived in was dissolving and dwindling.

A few light taps upon the pane made him turn to the window. It had begun to snow again. He watched sleepily the flakes, silver and dark, falling obliquely against the lamplight. The time had come for him to set out on his journey westward. Yes, the newspapers were right: snow was general all over Ireland. It was falling on every part of the dark central plain, on the treeless hills, falling softly upon the Bog of Allen and, farther westward, softly falling into the dark mutinous Shannon waves.[3] It was falling, too, upon every part of the lonely churchyard on the hill where Michael Furey lay buried. It lay thickly drifted on the crooked crosses and headstones, on the spears of the little gate, on the barren thorns. His soul swooned slowly as he heard the snow falling faintly through the universe and faintly falling, like the descent of their last end, upon all the living and the dead.

— ⊨◆⊨ →

Virginia Woolf
1882–1941

"On or about December, 1910," Virginia Woolf once wrote in an essay on fiction, "human character changed." That month saw the opening of a major exhibit of post-Impressionist art in London, and it is characteristic of Woolf to consider that art has the power to change human nature itself. A proper Victorian by upbringing and an avant-garde artist by vocation, Virginia Woolf was deeply interested in the ways human nature was changing in her times, both through artistic revolutions and through the social upheavals that culminated in World War I and its aftermath. By 1910 her own life had changed in many ways from the life she had experienced in her childhood as the young Adeline Virginia Stephen, daughter of the prosperous editor and as-

---

3. Where Ireland's longest river, the Shannon, empties into the sea.

piring philosopher Sir Leslie Stephen, editor of the massive *Dictionary of National Biography*. Her mother, Julia—artistic in temperament, and a famous beauty often sketched by Pre-Raphaelite artist friends—died in 1895, when Virginia was thirteen. A mental breakdown, the first of what became Woolf's recurrent bouts of mental instability, quickly followed. Two years later, her half-sister Stella died in childbirth, and within another two years her brother Thoby died of typhoid.

Having grown up an intensely literary child in a pervasively literary and artistic household, the young Virginia Stephen was nevertheless kept away from the public routes to education offered to her brothers, who attended prestigious private schools and went on to Oxford. Like most upper-class British women of her generation, Woolf and her sisters were educated at home, and never went to college. Woolf read voraciously, and her independence of mind and habits fostered her later freedom to experiment, yet she remained keenly aware of her exclusion from the wealth of resources offered by Oxford and Cambridge. Her path-breaking essay *A Room of One's Own* (1928), on the intellectual and material conditions needed for women to write fiction, opens with a scene in which an angelic beadle prohibits her from entering an Edenlike university library. All her life, Woolf was to be a full member of upper-class British society and yet also in important ways an outsider to it: as a pacifist as World War II approached; as an entirely committed writer when women were supposed to devote most of their attention to husband and children; as someone romantically drawn to women as well as to men, notably to her intimate friend Vita Sackville-West, to whom she dedicated her 1928 novel *Orlando,* whose hero changes sex and becomes a heroine part way into the book.

Following her father's death in 1904, Virginia began to publish her work. Together with her surviving brother Adrian and her artist sister Vanessa, she set up house in Bloomsbury Square in London, forming the center for a loose group of free-thinking artists, writers, and other intellectuals. In 1912 she married Leonard Woolf, himself an outsider as a socialist, an anti-imperialist, and a Jew in the often genially anti-Semitic culture of Edwardian England. The Woolfs founded the Hogarth Press, which published their own books and those of many others, including work by their friends T. S. Eliot, E. M. Forster, and Katherine Mansfield, together with the first English translations of the works of Sigmund Freud.

Once she began publishing, Woolf was extraordinarily productive, creating a wide variety of work. She explored the finest nuances of consciousness and perception in her major novels, starting with *The Voyage Out* (1915). Her work became increasingly experimental as time went on; along with James Joyce she became a pioneering practitioner of the technique of "interior monologue," following the twists and turns of an individual's consciousness from within, most notably in her great novels *Mrs Dalloway* (1925) and *To the Lighthouse* (1927)—a loving, ironic recreation of her parents in the form of the charming, self-centered philosopher Mr. Ramsay and his magnetic, manipulative wife Mrs. Ramsay, who humors her husband and shelters her brood of eight children until her sudden, untimely death. Later Woolf experimented with a shifting, polyphonic multiplicity of voices in *The Waves* (1931) and used a fragmented, drama-based style for her last novel, *Between the Acts* (1941). The pressures for war were building as she was completing this novel, and Woolf grew increasingly depressed. She and Leonard anticipated that the Nazis would soon invade England; they expected that certainly Leonard—and probably Woolf herself, as well as many of their friends—would be killed if the invasion were to succeed. Fearing the onset of a new mental breakdown, Woolf drowned herself in a river near her country home in March of 1941.

By then she had produced not only a major body of fiction but also several volumes of sparkling essays and reviews for "the common reader," whom she hoped to reach even in her most experimental work. She also wrote voluminous diaries and masses of letters (several volumes have been published both of the diaries and of the letters). Together, these works show a life in which conversation, reflection, and writing were constant means of self-understanding and of engagement with the wider world.

The blending of social framing and psychological insight is fully evident in the two stories given here, two of her most compelling short fictions. Like the "epiphanies" of James Joyce, these stories center on an ordinary yet suddenly revelatory moment. "The Lady in the Looking-Glass: A Reflection" (1929) takes vision itself as its theme. The lady of the title is absent for most of the story; an invisible narrator builds a world around her absence by examining what can be seen, or inferred, in the mirror above her mantelpiece. Literature has long been described as "holding a mirror up to nature," though by Woolf's time writers were often revising this image to express less direct sorts of mirroring. In the 1890s, Oscar Wilde had described his art as a *cracked* looking-glass, while in *Ulysses,* Joyce went Wilde one better by having Stephen Dedalus describe Irish art as the cracked mirror "of a servant." Woolf's mirror in turn conceals as well as reveals, and the final appearance of the lady in the looking-glass yields a very different epiphany than we have been led to expect.

For Woolf, as for contemporaries of hers from Joseph Conrad in England to Akutagawa Ryunosuke in Japan, truth can't be reflected directly but must be perceived in fragments, by indirection. Seen rightly, even the smallest image or incident can reveal multiple facets and possibilities, as in "Mrs Dalloway in Bond Street" (1923), in which a woman simply goes out to buy a pair of gloves. This story was the germ of what was to become the novel *Mrs Dalloway.* As she was expanding this story, Woolf clearly had it in mind when writing an essay in 1925 on "Modern Fiction." "Examine for a moment an ordinary mind on an ordinary day," she says:

> The mind receives a myriad impressions—trivial, fantastic, evanescent, or engraved with the sharpness of steel. From all sides they come, an incessant shower of innumerable atom; and, as they fall, as they shape themselves into the life of Monday or Tuesday, the accent falls differently from of old; the moment of importance came not here but there; so that, if a writer were a free man and not a slave, if he could write what he chose, not what he must, if he could base his work upon his own feeling and not upon convention, there would be no plot, no comedy, no tragedy, no love interest or catastrophe in the accepted style, and perhaps not a single button sewn on as the Bond Street tailors would have it.

Mrs Dalloway in Bond Street

Mrs Dalloway said she would buy the gloves herself. Big Ben was striking as she stepped out into the street. It was eleven o'clock and the unused hour was fresh as if issued to children on a beach. But there was something solemn in the deliberate swing of the repeated strokes; something stirring in the murmur of wheels and the shuffle of footsteps.

No doubt they were not all bound on errands of happiness. There is much more to be said about us than that we walk the streets of Westminster.[1] Big Ben too is nothing but steel rods consumed by rust were it not for the care of H.M's Office of Works. Only for Mrs Dalloway the moment was complete; for Mrs Dalloway June was fresh. A happy childhood—and it was not to his daughters only that Justin Parry had seemed a fine fellow (weak of course on the Bench); flowers at evening, smoke rising; the caw of rooks falling from ever so high, down down through the October air—there is nothing to take the place of childhood. A leaf of mint brings it back: or a cup with a blue ring.

Poor little wretches, she sighed, and pressed forward. Oh, right under the horses' noses, you little demon! and there she was left on the kerb stretching her hand out, while Jimmy Dawes grinned on the further side.

---

1. District of central London, including the Houses of Parliament (with their famous clock tower "Big Ben"); it is also a fashionable residential area.

A charming woman, posed, eager, strangely white-haired for her pink cheeks, so Scope Purvis, C.B., saw her as he hurried to his office. She stiffened a little, waiting for Durtnall's van to pass. Big Ben struck the tenth; struck the eleventh stroke. The leaden circles dissolved in the air. Pride held her erect, inheriting, handing on, acquainted with discipline and with suffering. How people suffered, how they suffered, she thought, thinking of Mrs Foxcroft at the Embassy last night decked with jewels, eating her heart out, because that nice boy was dead, and now the old Manor House (Durtnall's van passed) must go to a cousin.

"Good morning to you," said Hugh Whitbread raising his hat rather extravagantly by the china shop, for they had known each other as children. "Where are you off to?"

"I love walking in London," said Mrs Dalloway. "Really it's better than walking in the country!"

"We've just come up," said Hugh Whitbread. "Unfortunately to see doctors."

"Milly?" said Mrs Dalloway, instantly compassionate.

"Out of sorts," said Hugh Whitbread. "That sort of thing. Dick all right?"

"First rate!" said Clarissa.

Of course, she thought, walking on, Milly is about my age—fifty—fifty-two. So it is probably *that*. Hugh's manner had said so, said it perfectly—dear old Hugh, thought Mrs Dalloway, remembering with amusement, with gratitude, with emotion, how shy, like a brother—one would rather die than speak to one's brother—Hugh had always been, when he was at Oxford, and came over, and perhaps one of them (drat the thing!) couldn't ride. How then could women sit in Parliament? How could they do things with men? For there is this extraordinarily deep instinct, something inside one; you can't get over it; it's no use trying; and men like Hugh respect it without our saying it, which is what one loves, thought Clarissa, in dear old Hugh.

She had passed through the Admiralty Arch and saw at the end of the empty road with its thin trees Victoria's white mound, Victoria's billowing motherliness, amplitude and homeliness, always ridiculous, yet how sublime thought Mrs Dalloway, remembering Kensington Gardens and the old lady in horn spectacles and being told by Nanny to stop dead still and bow to the Queen. The flag flew above the Palace. The King and Queen were back then. Dick had met her at lunch the other day—a thoroughly nice woman. It matters so much to the poor, thought Clarissa, and to the soldiers. A man in bronze stood heroically on a pedestal with a gun on her left hand side—the South African war. It matters, thought Mrs Dalloway walking towards Buckingham Palace. There it stood four-square, in the broad sunshine, uncompromising, plain. But it was character she thought; something inborn in the race; what Indians respected. The Queen went to hospitals, opened bazaars—the Queen of England, thought Clarissa, looking at the Palace. Already at this hour a motor car passed out at the gates; soldiers saluted; the gates were shut. And Clarissa, crossing the road, entered the Park, holding herself upright.

June had drawn out every leaf on the trees. The mothers of Westminster with mottled breasts gave suck to their young. Quite respectable girls lay stretched on the grass. An elderly man, stooping very stiffly, picked up a crumpled paper, spread it out flat and flung it away. How horrible! Last night at the Embassy Sir Dighton had said, "If I want a fellow to hold my horse, I have only to put up my hand." But the religious question is far more serious than the economic, Sir Dighton had said, which she thought extraordinarily interesting, from a man like Sir Dighton. "Oh, the country will never know what it has lost," he had said, talking, of his own accord, about dear Jack Stewart.

She mounted the little hill lightly. The air stirred with energy. Messages were passing from the Fleet to the Admiralty. Piccadilly and Arlington Street and the

Mall seemed to chafe the very air in the Park and lift its leaves hotly, brilliantly, upon waves of that divine vitality which Clarissa loved. To ride; to dance; she had adored all that. Or going on long walks in the country, talking, about books, what to do with one's life, for young people were amazingly priggish—oh, the things one had said! But one had conviction. Middle age is the devil. People like Jack'll never know that, she thought; for he never once thought of death, never, they said, knew he was dying. And now can never mourn—how did it go?—a head grown grey.... From the contagion of the world's slow stain.... Have drunk their cup a round or two before.... From the contagion of the world's slow stain![2] She held herself upright.

But how Jack would have shouted! Quoting Shelley, in Piccadilly! "You want a pin," he would have said. He hated frumps. "My God Clarissa! My God Clarissa!"—she could hear him now at the Devonshire House party, about poor Sylvia Hunt in her amber necklace and that dowdy old silk. Clarissa held herself upright for she had spoken aloud and now she was in Piccadilly, passing the house with the slender green columns, and the balconies; passing club windows full of newspapers; passing old Lady Burdett Coutt's house where the glazed white parrot used to hang; and Devonshire House, without its gilt leopards; and Claridge's, where she must remember Dick wanted her to leave a card on Mrs Jepson or she would be gone. Rich Americans can be very charming. There was St James's Palace; like a child's game with bricks; and now—she had passed Bond Street—she was by Hatchard's book shop. The stream was endless—endless—endless. Lords, Ascot, Hurlingham[3]—what was it? What a duck, she thought, looking at the frontispiece of some book of memoirs spread wide in the bow window, Sir Joshua perhaps or Romney; arch, bright, demure; the sort of girl—like her own Elizabeth—the only *real* sort of girl. And there was that absurd book, *Soapy Sponge,* which Jum used to quote by the yard; and Shakespeare's Sonnets. She knew them by heart. Phil and she had argued all day about the Dark Lady, and Dick had said straight out at dinner that night that he had never heard of her. Really, she had married him for that! He had never read Shakespeare! There must be some little cheap book she could buy for Milly—*Cranford*[4] of course! Was there ever anything so enchanting as the cow in petticoats? If only people had that sort of humour, that sort of self-respect now, thought Clarissa, for she remembered the broad pages; the sentences ending; the characters—how one talked about them as if they were real. For all the great things one must go to the past, she thought. From the contagion of the world's slow stain.... Fear no more the heat o' the sun.... And now can never mourn, can never mourn, she repeated, her eyes straying over the window; for it ran in her head; the test of great poetry; the moderns had never written anything one wanted to read about death, she thought; and turned.

Omnibuses joined motor cars; motor cars vans; vans taxicabs; taxicabs motor cars—here was an open motor car with a girl, alone. Up till four, her feet tingling, I know, thought Clarissa, for the girl looked washed out, half asleep, in the corner of the car after the dance. And another car came; and another. No! No! No! Clarissa smiled good-naturedly. The fat lady had taken every sort of trouble, but diamonds! orchids! at this hour of the morning! No! No! No! The excellent policeman would, when the time came, hold up his hand. Another motor car passed. How utterly unattractive! Why should a girl of that age paint black round her eyes? And a young man

2. From *Adonais* (stanza 40), Percy Shelley's elegy on the early death of Keats.
3. Locations of fashionable sporting events (cricket, horse racing, and polo).
4. Popular novel by Elizabeth Gaskell (1810–1865).

with a girl, at this hour, when the country—The admirable policeman raised his hand and Clarissa acknowledging his sway, taking her time, crossed, walked towards Bond Street; saw the narrow crooked street, the yellow banners; the thick notched telegraph wires stretched across the sky.

A hundred years ago her great-great-grandfather, Seymour Parry, who ran away with Conway's daughter, had walked down Bond Street. Down Bond Street the Parrys had walked for a hundred years, and might have met the Dalloways (Leighs on the mother's side) going up. Her father got his clothes from Hill's. There was a roll of cloth in the window, and here just one jar on a black table, incredibly expensive; like the thick pink salmon on the ice block at the fishmonger's. The jewels were exquisite—pink and orange stars, paste, Spanish, she thought, and chains of old gold; starry buckles, little brooches which had been worn on sea-green satin by ladies with high head-dresses. But no looking! One must economise. She must go on past the picture dealer's where one of the odd French pictures hung, as if people had thrown confetti—pink and blue—for a joke. If you had lived with pictures (and it's the same with books and music) thought Clarissa, passing the Aeolian Hall, you can't be taken in by a joke.

The river of Bond Street was clogged. There, like a queen at a tournament, raised, regal, was Lady Bexborough. She sat in her carriage, upright, alone, looking through her glasses. The white glove was loose at her wrist. She was in black, quite shabby, yet, thought Clarissa, how extraordinarily it tells, breeding, self-respect, never saying a word too much or letting people gossip; an astonishing friend; no one can pick a hole in her after all these years, and now, there she is, thought Clarissa, passing the Countess who waited powdered, perfectly still, and Clarissa would have given anything to be like that, the mistress of Clarefield, talking politics, like a man. But she never goes anywhere, thought Clarissa, and it's quite useless to ask her, and the carriage went on and Lady Bexborough was borne past like a queen at a tournament, though she had nothing to live for and the old man is failing and they say she is sick of it all, thought Clarissa and the tears actually rose to her eyes as she entered the shop.

"Good morning," said Clarissa in her charming voice. "Gloves," she said with her exquisite friendliness and putting her bag on the counter began, very slowly, to undo the buttons. "White gloves," she said. "Above the elbow," and she looked straight into the shopwoman's face—but this was not the girl she remembered? She looked quite old. "These really don't fit," said Clarissa. The shop-girl looked at them. "Madame wears bracelets?" Clarissa spread out her fingers. "Perhaps it's my rings," And the girl took the grey gloves with her to the end of the counter.

Yes, thought Clarissa, it's the girl I remember, she's twenty years older. . . . There was only one other customer, sitting sideways at the counter, her elbow poised, her bare hand drooping vacant; like a figure on a Japanese fan, thought Clarissa, too vacant perhaps, yet some men would adore her. The lady shook her head sadly. Again the gloves were too large. She turned round the glass. "Above the wrist," she reproached the grey-headed woman, who looked and agreed.

They waited; a clock ticked; Bond Street hummed, dulled, distant; the woman went away holding gloves. "Above the wrist," said the lady, mournfully, raising her voice. And she would have to order chairs, ices, flowers, and cloak-room tickets, thought Clarissa. The people she didn't want would come; the others wouldn't. She would stand by the door. They sold stockings—silk stockings. A lady is known by her gloves and her shoes, old Uncle William used to say. And through the hanging silk stockings, quivering silver she looked at the lady, sloping shouldered, her

hand drooping, her bag slipping, her eyes vacantly on the floor. It would be intolerable if dowdy women came to her party! Would one have liked Keats if he had
worn red socks? Oh, at last—she drew into the counter and it flashed into her
mind:

"Do you remember before the war you had gloves with pearl buttons?"

"French gloves, Madame?"

"Yes, they were French," said Clarissa. The other lady rose very sadly and took
her bag, and looked at the gloves on the counter. But they were all too large—always
too large at the wrist.

"With pearl buttons," said the shop-girl, who looked ever so much older. She
split the lengths of tissue paper apart on the counter. With pearl buttons, thought
Clarissa, perfectly simple—how French!

"Madame's hands are so slender," said the shop-girl, drawing the glove firmly,
smoothly, down over her rings. And Clarissa looked at her arm in the looking-glass.
The glove hardly came to the elbow. Were there others half an inch longer? Still it
seemed tiresome to bother her—perhaps the one day in the month, thought Clarissa,
when it's an agony to stand. "Oh, don't bother," she said. But the gloves were brought.

"Don't you get fearfully tired," she said in her charming voice, "standing? When
d'you get your holiday?"

"In September, Madame, when we're not so busy."

When we're in the country thought Clarissa. Or shooting. She has a fortnight at
Brighton. In some stuffy lodging. The landlady takes the sugar. Nothing would be
easier than to send her to Mrs Lumley's right in the country (and it was on the tip of
her tongue). But then she remembered how on their honeymoon Dick had shown her
the folly of giving impulsively. It was much more important, he said, to get trade with
China. Of course he was right. And she could feel the girl wouldn't like to be given
things. There she was in her place. So was Dick. Selling gloves was her job. She had
her own sorrows quite separate, "and now can never mourn, can never mourn," the
words ran in her head, "From the contagion of the world's slow stain," thought
Clarissa holding her arm stiff, for there are moments when it seems utterly futile (the
glove was drawn off leaving her arm flecked with powder)—simply one doesn't believe, thought Clarissa, any more in God.

The traffic suddenly roared; the silk stockings brightened. A customer came in.

"White gloves," she said, with some ring in her voice that Clarissa remembered.

It used, thought Clarissa, to be so simple. Down, down through the air came the
caw of the rooks. When Sylvia died, hundreds of years ago, the yew hedges looked so
lovely with the diamond webs in the mist before early church. But if Dick were to die
to-morrow? As for believing in God—no, she would let the children choose, but for
herself, like Lady Bexborough, who opened the bazaar, they say, with the telegram in
her hand—Roden, her favourite, killed—she would go on. But why, if one doesn't believe? For the sake of others, she thought taking the glove in her hand. The girl would
be much more unhappy if she didn't believe.

"Thirty shillings," said the shop-woman. "No, pardon me Madame, thirty-five.
The French gloves are more."

For one doesn't live for oneself, thought Clarissa.

And then the other customer took a glove, tugged it, and it split.

"There!" she exclaimed.

"A fault of the skin," said the grey-headed woman hurriedly. "Sometimes a drop
of acid in tanning. Try this pair, Madame."

"But it's an awful swindle to ask two pound ten!"

Clarissa looked at the lady; the lady looked at Clarissa.

"Gloves have never been quite so reliable since the war," said the shop-girl, apologising, to Clarissa.

But where had she seen the other lady?—elderly, with a frill under her chin; wearing a black ribbon for gold eyeglasses; sensual, clever, like a Sargent drawing. How one can tell from a voice when people are in the habit, thought Clarissa, of making other people—"It's a shade too tight," she said—obey. The shop-woman went off again. Clarissa was left waiting. Fear no more she repeated, playing her finger on the counter. Fear no more the heat o' the sun. Fear no more she repeated. There were little brown spots on her arm. And the girl crawled like a snail. Thou thy wordly task hast done. Thousands of young men had died that things might go on. At last! Half an inch above the elbow; pearl buttons; five and a quarter. My dear slowcoach, thought Clarissa, do you think I can sit here the whole morning? Now you'll take twenty-five minutes to bring me my change!

There was a violent explosion in the street outside. The shop-women cowered behind the counters. But Clarissa, sitting very upright, smiled at the other lady. "Miss Anstruther!" she exclaimed.

The Lady in the Looking-Glass: A Reflection

People should not leave looking-glasses hanging in their rooms any more than they should leave open cheque books or letters confessing some hideous crime. One could not help looking, that summer afternoon, in the long glass that hung outside in the hall. Chance had so arranged it. From the depths of the sofa in the drawing-room one could see reflected in the Italian glass not only the marble-topped table opposite, but a stretch of the garden beyond. One could see a long grass path leading between banks of tall flowers until, slicing off an angle, the gold rim cut it off.

The house was empty, and one felt, since one was the only person in the drawing-room, like one of those naturalists who, covered with grass and leaves, lie watching the shyest animals—badgers, otters, kingfishers—moving about freely, themselves unseen. The room that afternoon was full of such shy creatures, lights and shadows, curtains blowing, petals falling—things that never happen, so it seems, if someone is looking. The quiet old country room with its rugs and stone chimney pieces, its sunken bookcases and red and gold lacquer cabinets, was full of such nocturnal creatures. They came pirouetting across the floor, stepping delicately with high-lifted feet and spread tails and pecking allusive beaks as if they had been cranes or flocks of elegant flamingoes whose pink was faded, or peacocks whose trains were veined with silver. And there were obscure flushes and darkenings too, as if a cuttlefish had suddenly suffused the air with purple; and the room had its passions and rages and envies and sorrows coming over it and clouding it, like a human being. Nothing stayed the same for two seconds together.

But, outside, the looking-glass reflected the hall table, the sunflowers, the garden path so accurately and so fixedly that they seemed held there in their reality unescapably. It was a strange contrast—all changing here, all stillness there. One could not help looking from one to the other. Meanwhile, since all the doors and windows were open in the heat, there was a perpetual sighing and ceasing sound, the voice of the transient and the perishing, it seemed, coming and going like human breath, while in the looking-glass things had ceased to breathe and lay still in the trance of immortality.

Half an hour ago the mistress of the house, Isabella Tyson, had gone down the grass path in her thin summer dress, carrying a basket, and had vanished, sliced off by the gilt rim of the looking-glass. She had gone presumably into the lower garden to pick flowers; or as it seemed more natural to suppose, to pick something light and fantastic and leafy and trailing, traveller's joy, or one of those elegant sprays of convolvulus that twine round ugly walls and burst here and there into white and violet blossoms. She suggested the fantastic and the tremulous convolvulus rather than the upright aster, the starched zinnia, or her own burning roses alight like lamps on the straight posts of their rose trees. The comparison showed how very little, after all these years, one knew about her; for it is impossible that any woman of flesh and blood of fifty-five or sixty should be really a wreath or a tendril. Such comparisons are worse than idle and superficial—they are cruel even, for they come like the convolvulus itself trembling between one's eyes and the truth. There must be truth; there must be a wall. Yet it was strange that after knowing her all these years one could not say what the truth about Isabella was; one still made up phrases like this about convolvulus and traveller's joy. As for facts, it was a fact that she was a spinster; that she was rich; that she had bought this house and collected with her own hands—often in the most obscure corners of the world and at great risk from poisonous stings and Oriental diseases—the rugs, the chairs, the cabinets which now lived their nocturnal life before one's eyes. Sometimes it seemed as if they knew more about her than we, who sat on them, wrote at them, and trod on them so carefully, were allowed to know. In each of these cabinets were many little drawers, and each almost certainly held letters, tied with bows of ribbon, sprinkled with sticks of lavender or rose leaves. For it was another fact—if facts were what one wanted—that Isabella had known many people, had had many friends; and thus if one had the audacity to open a drawer and read her letters, one would find the traces of many agitations, of appointments to meet, of upbraidings for not having met, long letters of intimacy and affection, violent letters of jealousy and reproach, terrible final words of parting—for all those interviews and assignations had led to nothing—that is, she had never married, and yet, judging from the mask-like indifference of her face, she had gone through twenty times more of passion and experience than those whose loves are trumpeted forth for all the world to hear. Under the stress of thinking about Isabella, her room became more shadowy and symbolic; the corners seemed darker, the legs of chairs and tables more spindly and hieroglyphic.

Suddenly these reflections were ended violently and yet without a sound. A large black form loomed into the looking-glass; blotted out everything, strewed the table with a packet of marble tablets veined with pink and grey, and was gone. But the picture was entirely altered. For the moment it was unrecognisable and irrational and entirely out of focus. One could not relate these tablets to any human purpose. And then by degrees some logical process set to work on them and began ordering and arranging them and bringing them into the fold of common experience. One realised at last that they were merely letters. The man had brought the post.

There they lay on the marble-topped table, all dripping with light and colour at first and crude and unabsorbed. And then it was strange to see how they were drawn in and arranged and composed and made part of the picture and granted that stillness and immortality which the looking-glass conferred. They lay there invested with a new reality and significance and with a greater heaviness, too, as if it would have needed a chisel to dislodge them from the table. And, whether it was fancy or not, they seemed to have become not merely a handful of casual letters but to be tablets graven with eternal truth—if one could read them, one would know everything there was to be known about Isabella, yes, and about life, too. The pages inside those marble-looking envelopes must be cut deep and scored thick with meaning. Isabella would come in, and take them, one by one, very slowly, and open them, and read them carefully word by word, and then with a profound sigh of comprehension, as if she had seen to the bottom of everything, she would tear the envelopes to little bits and tie the letters together and lock the cabinet drawer in her determination to conceal what she did not wish to be known.

The thought served as a challenge. Isabella did not wish to be known—but she should no longer escape. It was absurd, it was monstrous. If she concealed so much and knew so much one must prize her open with the first tool that came to hand—the imagination. One must fix one's mind upon her at that very moment. One must fasten her down there. One must refuse to be put off any longer with sayings and doings such as the moment brought forth—with dinners and visits and polite conversations. One must put oneself in her shoes. If one took the phrase literally, it was easy to see the shoes in which she stood, down in the lower garden, at this moment. They were very narrow and long and fashionable—they were made of the softest and most flexible leather. Like everything she wore, they were exquisite. And she would be standing under the high hedge in the lower part of the garden, raising the scissors that were tied to her waist to cut some dead flower, some overgrown branch. The sun would beat down on her face, into her eyes; but no, at the critical moment a veil of cloud covered the sun, making the expression of her eyes doubtful—was it mocking or tender, brilliant or dull? One could only see the indeterminate outline of her rather faded, fine face looking at the sky. She was thinking, perhaps, that she must order a new net for the strawberries; that she must send flowers to Johnson's widow; that it was time she drove over to see the Hippesleys in their new house. Those were the things she talked about at dinner certainly. But one was tired of the things that she talked about at dinner. It was her profounder state of being that one wanted to catch and turn to words, the state that is to the mind what breathing is to the body, what one calls happiness or unhappiness. At the mention of those words it became obvious, surely, that she must be happy. She was rich; she was distinguished; she had many friends; she travelled—she bought rugs in Turkey and blue pots in Persia. Avenues of pleasure radiated this way and that from where she stood with her scissors raised to cut the trembling branches while the lacy clouds veiled her face.

Here with a quick movement of her scissors she snipped the spray of traveller's joy and it fell to the ground. As it fell, surely some light came in too, surely one could penetrate a little farther into her being. Her mind then was filled with tenderness and regret. . . . To cut an overgrown branch saddened her because it had once lived, and life was dear to her. Yes, and at the same time the fall of the branch would suggest to her how she must die herself and all the futility and evanescence of things. And then again quickly catching this thought up, with her instant good sense, she thought life had treated her well; even if fall she must, it was to lie on the earth and moulder sweetly into the roots of violets. So she stood thinking. Without making any thought precise—for she was one of those reticent people whose minds hold their thoughts enmeshed in clouds of silence—she was filled with thoughts. Her mind was like her room, in which lights advanced and retreated, came pirouetting and stepping delicately, spread their tails, pecked their way; and then her whole being was suffused, like the room again, with a cloud of some profound knowledge, some unspoken regret, and then she was full of locked drawers, stuffed with letters, like her cabinets. To talk of "prizing her open" as if she were an oyster, to use any but the finest and subtlest and most pliable tools upon her was impious and absurd. One must imagine—here was she in the looking-glass. It made one start.

She was so far off at first that one could not see her clearly. She came lingering and pausing, here straightening a rose, there lifting a pink to smell it, but she never stopped; and all the time she became larger and larger in the looking-glass, more and more completely the person into whose mind one had been trying to penetrate. One verified her by degrees—fitted the qualities one had discovered into this visible body. There were her grey-green dress, and her long shoes, her basket, and something sparkling at her throat. She came so gradually that she did not seem to derange the pattern in the glass, but only to bring in some new element which gently moved and altered the other objects as if asking them, courteously, to make room for her. And the letters and the table and the grass walk and the sunflowers which had been waiting in the looking-glass separated and opened out so that she might be received among them. At last there she was, in the hall. She stopped dead. She stood by the table. She stood perfectly still. At once the looking-glass began to pour over her a light that seemed to fix her; that seemed like some acid to bite off the unessential and superficial and to leave only the truth. It was an enthralling spectacle. Everything dropped from her—clouds, dress, basket, diamond—all that one had called the creeper and convolvulus. Here was the hard wall beneath. Here was the woman herself. She stood naked in that pitiless light. And, there was nothing. Isabella was perfectly empty. She had no thoughts. She had no friends. She cared for nobody. As for her letters, they were all bills. Look, as she stood there, old and angular, veined and lined, with her high nose and her wrinkled neck, she did not even trouble to open them.

People should not leave looking-glasses hanging in their rooms.

A ROOM OF ONE'S OWN   In the fall of 1928 Virginia Woolf delivered lectures at two women's colleges at Cambridge University, where women were still not being admitted to the older, far better funded men's colleges, despite strong agitation for reform. Revised for publication, Woolf's talks became *A Room of One's Own* (1929), one of the most influential works in modern feminist writing. Woolf makes a double argument in her essay, both material and psychological. On the material level, Woolf insists that women writers have the need for the same degree of privacy and material support that the major male writers traditionally had. On the psychological level, she asserts that the great goal of literary work isn't a "separate but equal" status for women's writing but instead an inspired, transcendent "androgyny," in which the literary work can fuse the perspectives of both sexes, bound to neither alone.

Woolf's work has inspired many later feminist thinkers, while provoking controversy as well. Not all of Woolf's young audience at Newnham and Girton Colleges agreed with her claim that they would need an independent income to fuel their creative flame; and later feminists have questioned whether her advocacy of androgyny works against her claim that women's sentences are different from men's. Woolf's essayistic method has sparked debate as well: some readers have wanted her to come to her points more directly and clarify her terms more fully; many others, however, have responded to the essay's subtle weaving of images and ironies into deeply resonant patterns. Far from shunning controversy, Woolf herself welcomed it. As the book was about to appear, she wrote in her diary that what she really feared was "that I shall get no criticism, except the evasive jocular kind . . . that the press will be kind & talk of its charm, and sprightliness & also I shall be attacked for a feminist & hinted at for a sapphist. . . . I am afraid it will not be taken seriously." Her book did indeed receive such responses when it first appeared ("Mrs. Woolf speaks for her sex with as much fancy as logic," the *New York Times* brightly observed, while the *Yale Review* praised "its quiet, demure laughter"), but in the decades since then, *A Room of One's Own* has come to be seen as a foundational text for modern feminist thought and a masterpiece of creative nonfiction by a great novelist in her prime.

from A Room of One's Own
Chapter 1

But, you may say, we asked you to speak about women and fiction—what has that got to do with a room of one's own?[1] I will try to explain. When you asked me to speak about women and fiction I sat down on the banks of a river and began to wonder what the words meant. They might mean simply a few remarks about Fanny Burney; a few more about Jane Austen; a tribute to the Brontës and a sketch of Haworth Parsonage under snow; some witticisms if possible about Miss Mitford; a respectful allusion to George Eliot; a reference to Mrs Gaskell and one would have done.[2] But at second sight the words seemed not so simple. The title women and fiction might mean, and you may have meant it to mean, women and what they are like; or it might mean women and the fiction that they write; or it might mean women and the fiction that is written about them; or it might mean that somehow all three are inextricably mixed together and you want me to consider them in that light. But when I began to consider the subject in this last way, which seemed the most interesting, I soon saw that it had one fatal drawback. I should never be able to come to a conclusion. I should never be able to fulfil what is, I understand, the first duty of a lecturer—to hand you after an hour's discourse a nugget of pure truth to wrap up between the pages of your notebooks and keep on the mantelpiece for ever. All I could do was to offer you an opinion upon one minor point—a woman must have money and a room of her own if she is to write fiction; and that, as you will see, leaves the great problem of the true nature of woman and the true nature of fiction unsolved. I have shirked the duty of coming to a conclusion upon these two questions—women and fiction remain, so far as I am concerned, unsolved problems. But in order to make some amends I am going to do what I can to show you how I arrived at this opinion about the room and the money. I am going to develop in your presence as fully and freely as I can the train of thought which led me to think this. Perhaps if I lay bare the ideas, the prejudices, that lie behind this statement you will find that they have some bearing upon women and some upon fiction. At any rate, when a subject is highly controversial—and any question about sex is that—one cannot hope to tell the truth. One can only show how one came to hold whatever opinion one does hold. One can only give one's audience the chance of drawing their own conclusions as they observe the limitations, the prejudices, the idiosyncrasies of the speaker. Fiction here is likely to contain more truth than fact. Therefore I propose, making use of all the liberties and licences of a novelist, to tell you the story of the two days that preceded my coming here—how, bowed down by the weight of the subject which you have laid upon my shoulders, I pondered it, and made it work in and out of my daily life. I need not say that what I am about to describe has no existence; Oxbridge is an invention; so is Fernham;[3] "I" is only a convenient term for somebody who has no real being. Lies will flow from my lips, but there may perhaps be some truth mixed up with them; it is for you to seek out this truth and to decide whether any part of it is worth keeping. If not, you will of course throw the whole of it into the wastepaper basket and forget all about it.

---

1. Woolf delivered her essay in a shorter version to meetings first at two women's colleges, Newnham and Girton, Cambridge University, in October 1928.
2. Important 19th-century novelists.

3. "Oxbridge" was in fact the common slang term for Oxford and Cambridge universities. "Fernham" suggests Newnham College.

Here then was I (call me Mary Beton, Mary Seton, Mary Carmichael[4] or by any name you please—it is not a matter of any importance) sitting on the banks of a river a week or two ago in fine October weather, lost in thought. That collar I have spoken of, women and fiction, the need of coming to some conclusion on a subject that raises all sorts of prejudices and passions, bowed my head to the ground. To the right and left bushes of some sort, golden and crimson, glowed with the colour, even it seemed burnt with the heat, of fire. On the further bank the willows wept in perpetual lamentation, their hair about their shoulders. The river reflected whatever it chose of sky and bridge and burning tree, and when the undergraduate had oared his boat through the reflections they closed again, completely, as if he had never been. There one might have sat the clock round lost in thought. Thought—to call it by a prouder name than it deserved—had let its line down into the stream. It swayed, minute after minute, hither and thither among the reflections and the weeds, letting the water lift it and sink it, until—you know the little tug—the sudden conglomeration of an idea at the end of one's line: and then the cautious hauling of it in, and the careful laying of it out? Alas, laid on the grass how small, how insignificant this thought of mine looked; the sort of fish that a good fisherman puts back into the water so that it may grow fatter and be one day worth cooking and eating. I will not trouble you with that thought now, though if you look carefully you may find it for yourselves in the course of what I am going to say.

But however small it was, it had, nevertheless, the mysterious property of its kind—put back into the mind, it became at once very exciting, and important; and as it darted and sank, and flashed hither and thither, set up such a wash and tumult of ideas that it was impossible to sit still. It was thus that I found myself walking with extreme rapidity across a grass plot. Instantly a man's figure rose to intercept me. Nor did I at first understand that the gesticulations of a curious-looking object, in a cut-away coat and evening shirt, were aimed at me. His face expressed horror and indignation. Instinct rather than reason came to my help; he was a Beadle; I was a woman. This was the turf; there was the path. Only the Fellows and Scholars are allowed here; the gravel is the place for me.[5] Such thoughts were the work of a moment. As I re-gained the path the arms of the Beadle sank, his face assumed its usual repose, and though turf is better walking than gravel, no very great harm was done. The only charge I could bring against the Fellows and Scholars of whatever the college might happen to be was that in protection of their turf, which has been rolled for 300 years in succession, they had sent my little fish into hiding.

What idea it had been that had sent me so audaciously trespassing I could not now remember. The spirit of peace descended like a cloud from heaven, for if the spirit of peace dwells anywhere, it is in the courts and quadrangles of Oxbridge on a fine October morning. Strolling through those colleges past those ancient halls the roughness of the present seemed smoothed away; the body seemed contained in a miraculous glass cabinet through which no sound could penetrate, and the mind, freed from any contact with facts (unless one trespassed on the turf again), was at liberty to settle down upon whatever meditation was in harmony with the moment. As chance would have it, some stray memory of some old essay about revisiting Oxbridge in the

---

4. Three of the four Marys who by tradition were attendants to Mary Queen of Scots (executed in 1567), and who figure in many Scottish ballads; the fourth was Mary Hamilton.

5. A beadle is a disciplinary officer. The fellows of Oxbridge colleges typically tutor the undergraduates, who are divided into scholars and commoners. The commoners form the majority of the student body.

long vacation brought Charles Lamb to mind—Saint Charles, said Thackeray,[6] putting a letter of Lamb's to his forehead. Indeed, among all the dead (I give you my thoughts as they came to me), Lamb is one of the most congenial; one to whom one would have liked to say, Tell me then how you wrote your essays? For his essays are superior even to Max Beerbohm's, I thought, with all their perfection, because of that wild flash of imagination, that lightning crack of genius in the middle of them which leaves them flawed and imperfect, but starred with poetry. Lamb then came to Oxbridge perhaps a hundred years ago. Certainly he wrote an essay—the name escapes me—about the manuscript of one of Milton's poems which he saw here.[7] It was *Lycidas* perhaps, and Lamb wrote how it shocked him to think it possible that any word in *Lycidas* could have been different from what it is. To think of Milton changing the words in that poem seemed to him a sort of sacrilege. This led me to remember what I could of *Lycidas* and to amuse myself with guessing which word it could have been that Milton had altered, and why. It then occurred to me that the very manuscript itself which Lamb had looked at was only a few hundred yards away, so that one could follow Lamb's footsteps across the quadrangle to that famous library where the treasure is kept. Moreover, I recollected, as I put this plan into execution, it is in this famous library that the manuscript of Thackeray's *Esmond* is also preserved. The critics often say that *Esmond* is Thackeray's most perfect novel. But the affectation of the style, with its imitation of the eighteenth century, hampers one, so far as I remember; unless indeed the eighteenth-century style was natural to Thackeray—a fact that one might prove by looking at the manuscript and seeing whether the alterations were for the benefit of the style or of the sense. But then one would have to decide what is style and what is meaning, a question which—but here I was actually at the door which leads into the library itself. I must have opened it, for instantly there issued, like a guardian angel barring the way with a flutter of black gown instead of white wings, a deprecating, silvery, kindly gentleman, who regretted in a low voice as he waved me back that ladies are only admitted to the library if accompanied by a Fellow of the College or furnished with a letter of introduction.

That a famous library has been cursed by a woman is a matter of complete indifference to a famous library. Venerable and calm, with all its treasures safe locked within its breast, it sleeps complacently and will, so far as I am concerned, so sleep for ever. Never will I wake those echoes, never will I ask for that hospitality again, I vowed as I descended the steps in anger. Still an hour remained before luncheon, and what was one to do? Stroll on the meadows? sit by the river? Certainly it was a lovely autumn morning; the leaves were fluttering red to the ground; there was no great hardship in doing either. But the sound of music reached my ear. Some service or celebration was going forward. The organ complained magnificently as I passed the chapel door. Even the sorrow of Christianity sounded in that serene air more like the recollection of sorrow than sorrow itself; even the groanings of the ancient organ seemed lapped in peace. I had no wish to enter had I the right, and this time the verger might have stopped me, demanding perhaps my baptismal certificate, or a letter of introduction from the Dean. But the outside of these magnificent buildings is often as beautiful as the inside. Moreover, it was amusing enough to watch the congregation

---

6. William Makepeace Thackeray (1811–1863), novelist and journalist, Woolf's father's first father-in-law.
7. Lamb's *Oxford in the Vacation*—describing the locales Lamb himself was too poor to attend in term time. The manuscript of Milton's elegy *Lycidas* (1638) is in the Wren Library of Trinity College, Cambridge, together with that of Thackeray's novel *The History of Henry Esmond* (1852).

assembling, coming in and going out again, busying themselves at the door of the chapel like bees at the mouth of a hive. Many were in cap and gown; some had tufts of fur on their shoulders; others were wheeled in bath-chairs; others, though not past middle age, seemed creased and crushed into shapes so singular that one was reminded of those giant crabs and crayfish who heave with difficulty across the sand of an aquarium. As I leant against the wall the University indeed seemed a sanctuary in which are preserved rare types which would soon be obsolete if left to fight for existence on the pavement of the Strand.[8] Old stories of old deans and old dons came back to mind, but before I had summoned up courage to whistle—it used to be said that at the sound of a whistle old Professor —— instantly broke into a gallop—the venerable congregation had gone inside. The outside of the chapel remained. As you know, its high domes and pinnacles can be seen, like a sailing-ship always voyaging never arriving, lit up at night and visible for miles, far away across the hills. Once, presumably, this quadrangle with its smooth lawns, its massive buildings, and the chapel itself was marsh too, where the grasses waved and the swine rootled. Teams of horses and oxen, I thought, must have hauled the stone in wagons from far countries, and then with infinite labour the grey blocks in whose shade I was now standing were poised in order one on top of another, and then the painters brought their glass for the windows, and the masons were busy for centuries up on that roof with putty and cement, spade and trowel. Every Saturday somebody must have poured gold and silver out of a leathern purse into their ancient fists, for they had their beer and skittles presumably of an evening. An unending stream of gold and silver, I thought, must have flowed into this court perpetually to keep the stones coming and the masons working; to level, to ditch, to dig and to drain. But it was then the age of faith, and money was poured liberally to set these stones on a deep foundation, and when the stones were raised, still more money was poured in from the coffers of kings and queens and great nobles to ensure that hymns should be sung here and scholars taught. Lands were granted; tithes were paid. And when the age of faith was over and the age of reason had come, still the same flow of gold and silver went on; fellowships were founded; lectureships endowed; only the gold and silver flowed now, not from the coffers of the king, but from the chests of merchants and manufacturers, from the purses of men who had made, say, a fortune from industry, and returned, in their wills, a bounteous share of it to endow more chairs, more lectureships, more fellowships in the university where they had learnt their craft. Hence the libraries and laboratories; the observatories; the splendid equipment of costly and delicate instruments which now stands on glass shelves, where centuries ago the grasses waved and the swine rootled. Certainly, as I strolled round the court, the foundation of gold and silver seemed deep enough; the pavement laid solidly over the wild grasses. Men with trays on their heads went busily from staircase to staircase. Gaudy blossoms flowered in window-boxes. The strains of the gramophone blared out from the rooms within. It was impossible not to reflect—the reflection whatever it may have been was cut short. The clock struck. It was time to find one's way to luncheon.

It is a curious fact that novelists have a way of making us believe that luncheon parties are invariably memorable for something very witty that was said, or for something very wise that was done. But they seldom spare a word for what was eaten. It is part of the novelist's convention not to mention soup and salmon and ducklings, as if

8. A thoroughfare in central London.

soup and salmon and ducklings were of no importance whatsoever, as if nobody ever smoked a cigar or drank a glass of wine. Here, however, I shall take the liberty to defy that convention and to tell you that the lunch on this occasion began with soles, sunk in a deep dish, over which the college cook had spread a counterpane of the whitest cream, save that it was branded here and there with brown spots like the spots on the flanks of a doe. After that came the partridges, but if this suggests a couple of bald, brown birds on a plate you are mistaken. The partridges, many and various, came with all their retinue of sauces and salads, the sharp and the sweet, each in its order; their potatoes, thin as coins but not so hard; their sprouts, foliated as rosebuds but more succulent. And no sooner had the roast and its retinue been done with than the silent serving-man, the Beadle himself perhaps in a milder manifestation, set before us, wreathed in napkins, a confection which rose all sugar from the waves. To call it pudding and so relate it to rice and tapioca would be an insult. Meanwhile the wine-glasses had flushed yellow and flushed crimson; had been emptied; had been filled. And thus by degrees was lit, halfway down the spine, which is the seat of the soul, not that hard little electric light which we call brilliance, as it pops in and out upon our lips, but the more profound, subtle and subterranean glow, which is the rich yellow flame of rational intercourse. No need to hurry. No need to sparkle. No need to be anybody but oneself. We are all going to heaven and Vandyck[9] is of the company—in other words, how good life seemed, how sweet its rewards, how trivial this grudge or that grievance, how admirable friendship and the society of one's kind, as, lighting a good cigarette, one sunk among the cushions in the window-seat.

If by good luck there had been an ash-tray handy, if one had not knocked the ash out of the window in default, if things had been a little different from what they were, one would not have seen, presumably, a cat without a tail. The sight of that abrupt and truncated animal padding softly across the quadrangle changed by some fluke of the subconscious intelligence the emotional light for me. It was as if some one had let fall a shade. Perhaps the excellent hock was relinquishing its hold. Certainly, as I watched the Manx cat pause in the middle of the lawn as if it too questioned the universe, something seemed lacking, something seemed different. But what was lacking, what was different, I asked myself, listening to the talk. And to answer that question I had to think myself out of the room, back into the past, before the war indeed,[1] and to set before my eyes the model of another luncheon party held in rooms not very far distant from these; but different. Everything was different. Meanwhile the talk went on among the guests, who were many and young, some of this sex, some of that; it went on swimmingly, it went on agreeably, freely, amusingly. And as it went on I set it against the background of that other talk, and as I matched the two together I had no doubt that one was the descendant, the legitimate heir of the other. Nothing was changed; nothing was different save only—here I listened with all my ears not entirely to what was being said, but to the murmur or current behind it. Yes, that was it—the change was there. Before the war at a luncheon party like this people would have said precisely the same things but they would have sounded different, because in those days they were accompanied by a sort of humming noise, not articulate, but musical, exciting, which changed the value of the words themselves. Could one set that humming noise to words? Perhaps with the help of the poets one could. A book lay

9. Sir Anthony Van Dyck, prominent 17th-century society   1. World War I.
painter.

beside me and, opening it, I turned casually enough to Tennyson. And here I found
Tennyson was singing:

> There has fallen a splendid tear
>   From the passion-flower at the gate.
> She is coming, my dove, my dear;
>   She is coming, my life, my fate;
> The red rose cries, "She is near, she is near";
>   And the white rose weeps, "She is late";
> The larkspur listens, "I hear, I hear";
>   And the lily whispers, "I wait."[2]

Was that what men hummed at luncheon parties before the war? And the
women?

> My heart is like a singing bird
>   Whose nest is in a water'd shoot;
> My heart is like an apple tree
>   Whose boughs are bent with thick-set fruit;
> My heart is like a rainbow shell
>   That paddles in a halcyon sea;
> My heart is gladder than all these
>   Because my love is come to me.[3]

Was that what women hummed at luncheon parties before the war?
There was something so ludicrous in thinking of people humming such things
even under their breath at luncheon parties before the war that I burst out laughing,
and had to explain my laughter by pointing at the Manx cat, who did look a little absurd, poor beast, without a tail, in the middle of the lawn. Was he really born so, or
had he lost his tail in an accident? The tailless cat, though some are said to exist in the
Isle of Man, is rarer than one thinks. It is a queer animal, quaint rather than beautiful.
It is strange what a difference a tail makes—you know the sort of things one says as a
lunch party breaks up and people are finding their coats and hats.

This one, thanks to the hospitality of the host, had lasted far into the afternoon.
The beautiful October day was fading and the leaves were falling from the trees in the
avenue as I walked through it. Gate after gate seemed to close with gentle finality behind me. Innumerable beadles were fitting innumerable keys into well-oiled locks;
the treasure-house was being made secure for another night. After the avenue one
comes out upon a road—I forget its name—which leads you, if you take the right
turning, along to Fernham.[4] But there was plenty of time. Dinner was not till half-past
seven. One could almost do without dinner after such a luncheon. It is strange how a
scrap of poetry works in the mind and makes the legs move in time to it along the
road. Those words—

> There has fallen a splendid tear
>   From the passion-flower at the gate.
> She is coming, my dove, my dear—

2. From Lord Alfred Tennyson's *Maud* (1855), lines
908–915.
3. The first stanza of Christina Rossetti's poem *A Birth-day* (1857).

4. Both Girton and Newnham colleges, established only
in the late 19th century, are outside the old university area
of Cambridge.

sang in my blood as I stepped quickly along towards Headingley. And then, switching off into the other measure, I sang, where the waters are churned up by the weir:

> My heart is like a singing bird
>   Whose nest is in a water'd shoot;
> My heart is like an apple tree—

What poets, I cried aloud, as one does in the dusk, what poets they were!

In a sort of jealousy, I suppose, for our own age, silly and absurd though these comparisons are, I went on to wonder if honestly one could name two living poets now as great as Tennyson and Christina Rossetti were then. Obviously it is impossible, I thought, looking into those foaming waters, to compare them. The very reason why the poetry excites one to such abandonment, such rapture, is that it celebrates some feeling that one used to have (at luncheon parties before the war perhaps), so that one responds easily, familiarly, without troubling to check the feeling, or to compare it with any that one has now. But the living poets express a feeling that is actually being made and torn out of us at the moment. One does not recognize it in the first place; often for some reason one fears it; one watches it with keenness and compares it jealously and suspiciously with the old feeling that one knew. Hence the difficulty of modern poetry; and it is because of this difficulty that one cannot remember more than two consecutive lines of any good modern poet. For this reason—that my memory failed me—the argument flagged for want of material. But why, I continued, moving on towards Headingley, have we stopped humming under our breath at luncheon parties? Why has Alfred ceased to sing

> She is coming, my dove, my dear?

Why has Christina ceased to respond

> My heart is gladder than all these
> Because my love is come to me?

Shall we lay the blame on the war? When the guns fired in August 1914, did the faces of men and women show so plain in each other's eyes that romance was killed? Certainly it was a shock (to women in particular with their illusions about education, and so on) to see the faces of our rulers in the light of the shell-fire. So ugly they looked—German, English, French—so stupid. But lay the blame where one will, on whom one will, the illusion which inspired Tennyson and Christina Rossetti to sing so passionately about the coming of their loves is far rarer now than then. One has only to read, to look, to listen, to remember. But why say "blame"? Why, if it was an illusion, not praise the catastrophe, whatever it was, that destroyed illusion and put truth in its place? For truth . . . those dots mark the spot where, in search of truth, I missed the turning up to Fernham. Yes indeed, which was truth and which was illusion, I asked myself. What was the truth about these houses, for example, dim and festive now with their red windows in the dusk, but raw and red and squalid, with their sweets and their boot-laces, at nine o'clock in the morning? And the willows and the river and the gardens that run down to the river, vague now with the mist stealing over them, but gold and red in the sunlight—which was the truth, which was the illusion about them? I spare you the twists and turns of my cogitations, for no conclusion was found on the road to Headingley, and I ask you to suppose that I soon found out my mistake about the turning and retraced my steps to Fernham.

As I have said already that it was an October day, I dare not forfeit your respect and imperil the fair name of fiction by changing the season and describing lilacs hanging over garden walls, crocuses, tulips and other flowers of spring. Fiction must stick to facts, and the truer the facts the better the fiction—so we are told. Therefore it was still autumn and the leaves were still yellow and falling, if anything, a little faster than before, because it was now evening (seven twenty-three to be precise) and a breeze (from the south-west to be exact) had risen. But for all that there was something odd at work:

> My heart is like a singing bird
> Whose nest is in a water'd shoot;
> My heart is like an apple tree
> Whose boughs are bent with thick-set fruit—

perhaps the words of Christina Rossetti were partly responsible for the folly of the fancy—it was nothing of course but a fancy—that the lilac was shaking its flowers over the garden walls, and the brimstone butterflies were scudding hither and thither, and the dust of the pollen was in the air. A wind blew, from what quarter I know not, but it lifted the half-grown leaves so that there was a flash of silver grey in the air. It was the time between the lights when colours undergo their intensification and purples and golds burn in window-panes like the beat of an excitable heart; when for some reason the beauty of the world revealed and yet soon to perish (here I pushed into the garden, for, unwisely, the door was left open and no beadles seemed about), the beauty of the world which is so soon to perish, has two edges, one of laughter, one of anguish, cutting the heart asunder. The gardens of Fernham lay before me in the spring twilight, wild and open, and in the long grass, sprinkled and carelessly flung, were daffodils and bluebells, not orderly perhaps at the best of times, and now wind-blown and waving as they tugged at their roots. The windows of the building, curved like ships' windows among generous waves of red brick, changed from lemon to silver under the flight of the quick spring clouds. Somebody was in a hammock, somebody, but in this light they were phantoms only, half guessed, half seen, raced across the grass—would no one stop her?—and then on the terrace, as if popping out to breathe the air, to glance at the garden, came a bent figure, formidable yet humble, with her great forehead and her shabby dress—could it be the famous scholar, could it be J——H—— herself?[5] All was dim, yet intense too, as if the scarf which the dusk had flung over the garden were torn asunder by star or sword—the flash of some terrible reality leaping, as its way is, out of the heart of the spring. For youth——

Here was my soup. Dinner was being served in the great dining-hall. Far from being spring it was in fact an evening in October. Everybody was assembled in the big dining-room. Dinner was ready. Here was the soup. It was a plain gravy soup. There was nothing to stir the fancy in that. One could have seen through the transparent liquid any pattern that there might have been on the plate itself. But there was no pattern. The plate was plain. Next came beef with its attendant greens and potatoes—a homely trinity, suggesting the rumps of cattle in a muddy market, and sprouts curled and yellowed at the edge, and bargaining and cheapening, and women with string bags on Monday morning. There was no reason to complain of human nature's daily food, seeing that the supply was sufficient and coal-miners doubtless were sitting down to less. Prunes and custard followed. And if any one complains that prunes, even when mitigated by custard, are an uncharitable vegetable (fruit they are not),

5. Jane Harrison, a famous classical scholar.

stringy as a miser's heart and exuding a fluid such as might run in misers' veins who have denied themselves wine and warmth for eighty years and yet not given to the poor, he should reflect that there are people whose charity embraces even the prune. Biscuits and cheese came next, and here the water-jug was liberally passed round, for it is the nature of biscuits to be dry, and these were biscuits to the core. That was all. The meal was over. Everybody scraped their chairs back; the swing-doors swung violently to and fro; soon the hall was emptied of every sign of food and made ready no doubt for breakfast next morning. Down corridors and up staircases the youth of England went banging and singing. And was it for a guest, a stranger (for I had no more right here in Fernham than in Trinity or Somerville or Girton or Newnham or Christchurch),[6] to say, "The dinner was not good," or to say (we were now, Mary Seton and I, in her sitting-room), "Could we not have dined up here alone?" for if I had said anything of the kind I should have been prying and searching into the secret economies of a house which to the stranger wears so fine a front of gaiety and courage. No, one could say nothing of the sort. Indeed, conversation for a moment flagged. The human frame being what it is, heart, body and brain all mixed together, and not contained in separate compartments as they will be no doubt in another million years, a good dinner is of great importance to good talk. One cannot think well, love well, sleep well, if one has not dined well. The lamp in the spine does not light on beef and prunes. We are all *probably* going to heaven, and Vandyck is, we *hope*, to meet us round the next corner—that is the dubious and qualifying state of mind that beef and prunes at the end of the day's work breed between them. Happily my friend, who taught science, had a cupboard where there was a squat bottle and little glasses— (but there should have been sole and partridge to begin with)—so that we were able to draw up to the fire and repair some of the damages of the day's living. In a minute or so we were slipping freely in and out among all those objects of curiosity and interest which form in the mind in the absence of a particular person, and are naturally to be discussed on coming together again—how somebody has married, another has not; one thinks this, another that; one has improved out of all knowledge, the other most amazingly gone to the bad—with all those speculations upon human nature and the character of the amazing world we live in which spring naturally from such beginnings. While these things were being said, however, I became shamefacedly aware of a current setting in of its own accord and carrying everything forward to an end of its own. One might be talking of Spain or Portugal, of book or racehorse, but the real interest of whatever was said was none of those things, but a scene of masons on a high roof some five centuries ago. Kings and nobles brought treasure in huge sacks and poured it under the earth. This scene was for ever coming alive in my mind and placing itself by another of lean cows and a muddy market and withered greens and the stringy hearts of old men—these two pictures, disjointed and disconnected and nonsensical as they were, were for ever coming together and combating each other and had me entirely at their mercy. The best course, unless the whole talk was to be distorted, was to expose what was in my mind to the air, when with good luck it would fade and crumble like the head of the dead king when they opened the coffin at Windsor. Briefly, then, I told Miss Seton about the masons who had been all those years on the roof of the chapel, and about the kings and queens and nobles bearing sacks of gold and silver on their shoulders, which they shovelled into the earth; and then how

6. Trinity, Girton, and Newnham are colleges of Cambridge University; Somerville and Christchurch are at Oxford.

the great financial magnates of our own time came and laid cheques and bonds, I suppose, where the others had laid ingots and rough lumps of gold. All that lies beneath the colleges down there, I said; but this college, where we are now sitting, what lies beneath its gallant red brick and the wild unkempt grasses of the garden? What force is behind the plain china off which we dined, and (here it popped out of my mouth before I could stop it) the beef, the custard and the prunes?

Well, said Mary Seton, about the year 1860—Oh, but you know the story, she said, bored, I suppose, by the recital. And she told me—rooms were hired. Committees met. Envelopes were addressed. Circulars were drawn up. Meetings were held; letters were read out; so-and-so has promised so much; on the contrary, Mr——won't give a penny. The *Saturday Review* has been very rude. How can we raise a fund to pay for offices? Shall we hold a bazaar? Can't we find a pretty girl to sit in the front row? Let us look up what John Stuart Mill said on the subject.[7] Can any one persuade the editor of the——to print a letter? Can we get Lady——to sign it? Lady——is out of town. That was the way it was done, presumably, sixty years ago, and it was a prodigious effort, and a great deal of time was spent on it. And it was only after a long struggle and with the utmost difficulty that they got thirty thousand pounds together.[8] So obviously we cannot have wine and partridges and servants carrying tin dishes on their heads, she said. We cannot have sofas and separate rooms. "The amenities," she said, quoting from some book or other, "will have to wait."[9]

At the thought of all those women working year after year and finding it hard to get two thousand pounds together, and as much as they could do to get thirty thousand pounds, we burst out in scorn at the reprehensible poverty of our sex. What had our mothers been doing then that they had no wealth to leave us? Powdering their noses? Looking in at shop windows? Flaunting in the sun at Monte Carlo? There were some photographs on the mantel-piece. Mary's mother—if that was her picture—may have been a wastrel in her spare time (she had thirteen children by a minister of the church), but if so her gay and dissipated life had left too few traces of its pleasures on her face. She was a homely body; an old lady in a plaid shawl which was fastened by a large cameo; and she sat in a basket-chair, encouraging a spaniel to look at the camera, with the amused, yet strained expression of one who is sure that the dog will move directly the bulb is pressed. Now if she had gone into business; had become a manufacturer of artificial silk or a magnate on the Stock Exchange; if she had left two or three hundred thousand pounds to Fernham, we could have been sitting at our ease tonight and the subject of our talk might have been archaeology, botany, anthropology, physics, the nature of the atom, mathematics, astronomy, relativity, geography. If only Mrs Seton and her mother and her mother before her had learnt the great art of making money and had left their money, like their fathers and their grandfathers before them, to found fellowships and lectureships and prizes and scholarships appropriated to the use of their own sex, we might have dined very tolerably up here alone off a bird and a bottle of wine; we might have looked forward without undue confidence to a pleasant and honourable lifetime spent in the shelter of one of the liberally

---

7. In 1869 Mill published his essay *The Subjection of Women*, which argued forcefully for women's suffrage and their right to equality with men.

8. "We are told that we ought to ask for £30,000 at least. . . . It is not a large sum, considering that there is to be but one college of this sort for Great Britain, Ireland and the Colonies, and considering how easy it is to raise immense sums for boys' schools. But considering how few people really wish women to be educated, it is a good deal."–Lady Stephen, *Life of Miss Emily Davies* [Woolf's note].

9. Every penny which could be scraped together was set aside for building, and the amenities had to be postponed.–R. Strachey, *The Cause* [Woolf's note].

endowed professions. We might have been exploring or writing; mooning about the venerable places of the earth; sitting contemplative on the steps of the Parthenon, or going at ten to an office and coming home comfortably at half-past four to write a little poetry. Only, if Mrs Seton and her like had gone into business at the age of fifteen, there would have been—that was the snag in the argument—no Mary. What, I asked, did Mary think of that? There between the curtains was the October night, calm and lovely, with a star or two caught in the yellowing trees. Was she ready to resign her share of it and her memories (for they had been a happy family, though a large one) of games and quarrels up in Scotland, which she is never tired of praising for the fineness of its air and the quality of its cakes, in order that Fernham might have been endowed with fifty thousand pounds or so by a stroke of the pen? For, to endow a college would necessitate the suppression of families altogether. Making a fortune and bearing thirteen children—no human being could stand it. Consider the facts, we said. First there are nine months before the baby is born. Then the baby is born. Then there are three or four months spent in feeding the baby. After the baby is fed there are certainly five years spent in playing with the baby. You cannot, it seems, let children run about the streets. People who have seen them running wild in Russia say that the sight is not a pleasant one. People say, too, that human nature takes its shape in the years between one and five. If Mrs Seton, I said, had been making money, what sort of memories would you have had of games and quarrels? What would you have known of Scotland, and its fine air and cakes and all the rest of it? But it is useless to ask these questions, because you would never have come into existence at all. Moreover, it is equally useless to ask what might have happened if Mrs Seton and her mother and her mother before her had amassed great wealth and laid it under the foundations of college and library, because, in the first place, to earn money was impossible for them, and in the second, had it been possible, the law denied them the right to possess what money they earned. It is only for the last forty-eight years that Mrs Seton has had a penny of her own. For all the centuries before that it would have been her husband's property—a thought which, perhaps, may have had its share in keeping Mrs Seton and her mothers off the Stock Exchange.[1] Every penny I earn, they may have said, will be taken from me and disposed of according to my husband's wisdom—perhaps to found a scholarship or to endow a fellowship in Balliol or Kings,[2] so that to earn money, even if I could earn money, is not a matter that interests me very greatly. I had better leave it to my husband.

At any rate, whether or not the blame rested on the old lady who was looking at the spaniel, there could be no doubt that for some reason or other our mothers had mismanaged their affairs very gravely. Not a penny could be spared for "amenities"; for partridges and wine, beadles and turf, books and cigars, libraries and leisure. To raise bare walls out of the bare earth was the utmost they could do.

So we talked standing at the window and looking, as so many thousands look every night, down on the domes and towers of the famous city beneath us. It was very beautiful, very mysterious in the autumn moonlight. The old stone looked very white and venerable. One thought of all the books that were assembled down there; of the pictures of old prelates and worthies hanging in the panelled rooms; of the painted

1. The late 19th century saw the passage of legislation designed to improve the legal status of women. In 1870 the Married Women's Property Act allowed women to retain £200 of their own earnings (which previously had automatically become the property of her husband); in 1884 a further act gave married women the same rights over property as unmarried women, and allowed them to carry on trades or businesses using their property.

2. Balliol is a college of Oxford University; King's is at Cambridge.

windows that would be throwing strange globes and crescents on the pavement; of the tablets and memorials and inscriptions; of the fountains and the grass; of the quiet rooms looking across the quiet quadrangles. And (pardon me the thought) I thought, too, of the admirable smoke and drink and the deep armchairs and the pleasant carpets: of the urbanity, the geniality, the dignity which are the offspring of luxury and privacy and space. Certainly our mothers had not provided us with anything comparable to all this—our mothers who found it difficult to scrape together thirty thousand pounds, our mothers who bore thirteen children to ministers of religion at St Andrews.

So I went back to my inn, and as I walked through the dark streets I pondered this and that, as one does at the end of the day's work. I pondered why it was that Mrs Seton had no money to leave us; and what effect poverty has on the mind; and what effect wealth has on the mind; and I thought of the queer old gentlemen I had seen that morning with tufts of fur upon their shoulders; and I remembered how if one whistled one of them ran; and I thought of the organ booming in the chapel and of the shut doors of the library; and I thought how unpleasant it is to be locked out; and I thought how it is worse perhaps to be locked in; and, thinking of the safety and prosperity of the one sex and of the poverty and insecurity of the other and of the effect of tradition and of the lack of tradition upon the mind of a writer, I thought at last that it was time to roll up the crumpled skin of the day, with its arguments and its impressions and its anger and its laughter, and cast it into the hedge. A thousand stars were flashing across the blue wastes of the sky. One seemed alone with an inscrutable society. All human beings were laid asleep—prone, horizontal, dumb. Nobody seemed stirring in the streets of Oxbridge. Even the door of the hotel sprang open at the touch of an invisible hand—not a boots was sitting up to light me to bed, it was so late.

from *Chapter 3*

It would have been impossible, completely and entirely, for any woman to have written the plays of Shakespeare in the age of Shakespeare. Let me imagine, since facts are so hard to come by, what would have happened had Shakespeare had a wonderfully gifted sister, called Judith, let us say. Shakespeare himself went, very probably—his mother was an heiress—to the grammar school, where he may have learnt Latin—Ovid, Virgil, and Horace—and the elements of grammar and logic. He was, it is well known, a wild boy who poached rabbits, perhaps shot a deer, and had, rather sooner than he should have done, to marry a woman in the neighbourhood, who bore him a child rather quicker than was right. That escapade sent him to seek his fortune in London. He had, it seemed, a taste for the theatre; he began by holding horses at the stage door. Very soon he got work in the theatre, became a successful actor, and lived at the hub of the universe, meeting everybody, knowing everybody, practising his art on the boards, exercising his wits in the streets, and even getting access to the palace of the queen. Meanwhile his extraordinarily gifted sister, let us suppose, remained at home. She was as adventurous, as imaginative, as agog to see the world as he was. But she was not sent to school. She had no chance of learning grammar and logic, let alone of reading Horace and Virgil. She picked up a book now and then, one of her brother's perhaps, and read a few pages. But then her parents came in and told her to mend the stockings or mind the stew and not moon about with books and papers. They would have spoken sharply but kindly, for they were substantial people who knew the conditions of life for a woman and loved their daughter—indeed, more likely than not she was the apple of her father's eye. Perhaps she scribbled some pages up in an apple loft on the sly, but was careful to hide them or set fire to them. Soon, however, before she was out of her teens, she was to be betrothed to the son of a neighbouring wool-stapler. She cried out that marriage was hateful to her, and for that she was severely beaten by her father. Then he ceased to scold her. He begged her instead not to hurt him, not to shame him in this matter of her marriage. He would give her a chain of beads or a fine petticoat, he said; and there were tears in his eyes. How could she disobey him? How could she break his heart? The force of her own gift alone drove her to it. She made up a small parcel of her belongings, let herself down by a rope one summer's night and took the road to London. She was not seventeen. The birds that sang in the hedge were not more musical than she was. She had the quickest fancy, a gift like her brother's, for the tune of words. Like him, she had a taste for the theatre. She stood at the stage door; she wanted to act, she said. Men laughed in her face. The manager—a fat, loose-lipped man—guffawed. He bellowed something about poodles dancing and women acting—no woman, he said, could possibly be an actress. He hinted—you can imagine what. She could get no training in her craft. Could she even seek her dinner in a tavern or roam the streets at midnight? Yet her genius was for fiction and lusted to feed abundantly upon the lives of men and women and the study of their ways. At last—for she was very young, oddly like Shakespeare the poet in her face, with the same grey eyes and rounded brows—at last Nick Greene the actor-manager took pity on her; she found herself with child by that gentleman and so—who shall measure the heat and violence of the poet's heart when caught and tangled in a woman's body?—killed herself one winter's night and lies buried at some cross-roads where the omnibuses now stop outside the Elephant and Castle.[3]

That, more or less, is how the story would run, I think, if a woman in Shakespeare's day had had Shakespeare's genius. But for my part, I agree with the deceased bishop, if such he was—it is unthinkable that any woman in Shakespeare's day should have had Shakespeare's genius. For genius like Shakespeare's is not born among labouring, un-educated, servile people. It was not born in England among the Saxons and the Britons. It is not born today among the working classes. How, then, could it have been born among women whose work began, according to Professor Trevelyan,[4] almost before they were out of the nursery, who were forced to it by their parents and held to it by all the power of law and custom? Yet genius of a sort must have existed among women as it must have existed among the working classes. Now and again an Emily Brontë or a Robert Burns blazes out and proves its presence. But certainly it never got itself on to paper. When, however, one reads of a witch being ducked, of a woman possessed by devils, of a wise woman selling herbs, or even of a very remarkable man who had a mother, then I think we are on the track of a lost novelist, a suppressed poet, of some mute and inglorious Jane Austen, some Emily Brontë who dashed her brains out on the moor or mopped and mowed about the highways crazed with the torture that her gift had put her to. Indeed, I would venture to guess that Anon, who wrote so many poems without signing them, was often a woman. It was a woman Edward Fitzgerald,[5] I think, suggested who made the ballads and the folk-songs, crooning them to her children, be-guiling her spinning with them, or the length of the winter's night.

This may be true or it may be false—who can say?—but what is true in it, so it seemed to me, reviewing the story of Shakespeare's sister as I had made it, is that any

---

3. A tavern on the outskirts of South London.
4. George Trevelyan (1876–1962), historian.

5. Poet and translator (1809–1883).

woman born with a great gift in the sixteenth century would certainly have gone crazed, shot herself, or ended her days in some lonely cottage outside the village, half witch, half wizard, feared and mocked at. For it needs little skill in psychology to be sure that a highly gifted girl who had tried to use her gift for poetry would have been so thwarted and hindered by other people, so tortured and pulled asunder by her own contrary instincts, that she must have lost her health and sanity to a certainty. No girl could have walked to London and stood at a stage door and forced her way into the presence of actor-managers without doing herself a violence and suffering an anguish which may have been irrational—for chastity may be a fetish invented by certain societies for unknown reasons—but were none the less inevitable. Chastity had then, it has even now, a religious importance in a woman's life, and has so wrapped itself round with nerves and instincts that to cut it free and bring it to the light of day demands courage of the rarest. To have lived a free life in London in the sixteenth century would have meant for a woman who was poet and playwright a nervous stress and dilemma which might well have killed her. Had she survived, whatever she had written would have been twisted and deformed, issuing from a strained and morbid imagination. And undoubtedly, I thought, looking at the shelf where there are no plays by women, her work would have gone unsigned. That refuge she would have sought certainly. It was the relic of the sense of chastity that dictated anonymity to women even so late as the nineteenth century. Currer Bell, George Eliot, George Sand,[6] all the victims of inner strife as their writings prove, sought ineffectively to veil themselves by using the name of a man. Thus they did homage to the convention, which if not implanted by the other sex was liberally encouraged by them (the chief glory of a woman is not to be talked of, said Pericles, himself a much-talked-of man), that publicity in women is detestable.[7] Anonymity runs in their blood. The desire to be veiled still possesses them. They are not even now as concerned about the health of their fame as men are, and, speaking generally, will pass a tombstone or a signpost without feeling an irresistible desire to cut their names on it, as Alf, Bert or Chas. must do in obedience to their instinct, which murmurs if it sees a fine woman go by, or even a dog, Ce chien est à moi [that dog is mine]. And, of course, it may not be a dog, I thought, remembering Parliament Square, the Sieges Allee[8] and other avenues; it may be a piece of land or a man with curly black hair. It is one of the great advantages of being a woman that one can pass even a very fine negress without wishing to make an Englishwoman of her.

That woman, then, who was born with a gift of poetry in the sixteenth century, was an unhappy woman, a woman at strife against herself. All the conditions of her life, all her own instincts, were hostile to the state of mind which is needed to set free whatever is in the brain. * * * There would always have been that assertion—you cannot do this, you are incapable of doing that—to protest against, to overcome. Probably for a novelist this germ is no longer of much effect; for there have been women novelists of merit. But for painters it must still have some sting in it; and for musicians, I imagine, is even now active and poisonous in the extreme. The woman composer stands where the actress stood in the time of Shakespeare. Nick Greene, I thought, remembering the story I had made about Shakespeare's sister, said that a

6. Currer Bell, pen name of Charlotte Brontë; George Eliot, pen name of Mary Ann Evans; George Sand, pen name of Amandine Aurore Lucille Dupin (1804–1876).
7. The Athenian statesman Pericles was reported by the historian Thucydides to have said, "That woman is most praiseworthy whose name is least bandied about on men's lips, whether for praise or dispraise."
8. Victory Road, a thoroughfare in Berlin.

woman acting put him in mind of a dog dancing. Johnson repeated the phrase two hundred years later of women preaching.[9] And here, I said, opening a book about music, we have the very words used again in this year of grace, 1928, of women who try to write music. "Of Mlle. Germaine Tailleferre one can only repeat Dr. Johnson's dictum concerning a woman preacher, transposed into terms of music. 'Sir, a woman's composing is like a dog's walking on his hind legs. It is not done well, but you are surprised to find it done at all.'"[1] So accurately does history repeat itself.

Thus, I concluded, shutting Mr Oscar Browning's life and pushing away the rest, it is fairly evident that even in the nineteenth century a woman was not encouraged to be an artist. On the contrary, she was snubbed, slapped, lectured and exhorted. Her mind must have been strained and her vitality lowered by the need of opposing this, of disproving that. For here again we come within range of that very interesting and obscure masculine complex which has had so much influence upon the woman's movement; that deep-seated desire, not so much that she shall be inferior as that he shall be superior, which plants him wherever one looks, not only in front of the arts, but barring the way to politics too, even when the risk to himself seems infinitesimal and the suppliant humble and devoted. Even Lady Bessborough, I remembered, with all her passion for politics, must humbly bow herself and write to Lord Granville Leveson-Gower:[2] ". . . notwithstanding all my violence in politics and talking so much on that subject, I perfectly agree with you that no woman has any business to meddle with that or any other serious business, farther than giving her opinion (if she is ask'd)." And so she goes on to spend her enthusiasm where it meets with no obstacle whatsoever upon that immensely important subject, Lord Granville's maiden speech in the House of Commons. The spectacle is certainly a strange one, I thought. The history of men's opposition to women's emancipation is more interesting perhaps than the story of that emancipation itself. An amusing book might be made of it if some young student at Girton or Newnham would collect examples and deduce a theory—but she would need thick gloves on her hands, and bars to protect her of solid gold.

But what is amusing now, I recollected, shutting Lady Bessborough, had to be taken in desperate earnest once. Opinions that one now pastes in a book labelled cock-a-doodle-dum and keeps for reading to select audiences on summer nights once drew tears, I can assure you. Among your grandmothers and great-grandmothers there were many that wept their eyes out. Florence Nightingale shrieked aloud in her agony.[3] Moreover, it is all very well for you, who have got yourselves to college and enjoy sitting-rooms—or is it only bed-sitting-rooms?—of your own to say that genius should disregard such opinions; that genius should be above caring what is said of it. Unfortunately, it is precisely the men or women of genius who mind most what is said of them. Remember Keats. Remember the words he had cut on his tombstone. Think of Tennyson; think—but I need hardly multiply instances of the undeniable, if very unfortunate, fact that it is the nature of the artist to mind excessively what is said about him. Literature is strewn with the wreckage of men who have minded beyond reason the opinions of others.

And this susceptibility of theirs is doubly unfortunate, I thought, returning again to my original enquiry into what state of mind is most propitious for creative work,

9. Samuel Johnson (1709–1784), poet and man of letters.
1. *A Survey of Contemporary Music,* Cecil Gray, page 246 [Woolf's note].
2. Lady Bessborough (1761–1821), correspondent of the British statesman Lord Granville.
3. See *Cassandra,* by Florence Nightingale, printed in *The Cause,* by R. Strachey [Woolf's note].

because the mind of an artist, in order to achieve the prodigious effort of freeing whole and entire the work that is in him, must be incandescent, like Shakespeare's mind, I conjectured, looking at the book which lay open at *Antony and Cleopatra.* There must be no obstacle in it, no foreign matter unconsumed.

For though we say that we know nothing about Shakespeare's state of mind, even as we say that, we are saying something about Shakespeare's state of mind. The reason perhaps why we know so little of Shakespeare—compared with Donne or Ben Jonson or Milton—is that his grudges and spites and antipathies are hidden from us. We are not held up by some "revelation" which reminds us of the writer. All desire to protest, to preach, to proclaim an injury, to pay off a score, to make the world the witness of some hardship or grievance was fired out of him and consumed. Therefore his poetry flows from him free and unimpeded. If ever a human being got his work expressed completely, it was Shakespeare. If ever a mind was incandescent, unimpeded, I thought, turning again to the bookcase, it was Shakespeare's mind.

from *Chapter 4*

The extreme activity of mind which showed itself in the later eighteenth century among women—the talking, and the meeting, the writing of essays on Shakespeare, the translating of the classics—was founded on the solid fact that women could make money by writing. Money dignifies what is frivolous if unpaid for. It might still be well to sneer at "blue stockings with an itch for scribbling," but it could not be denied that they could put money in their purses. Thus, towards the end of the eighteenth century a change came about which, if I were rewriting history, I should describe more fully and think of greater importance than the Crusades or the Wars of the Roses. The middle-class woman began to write. For if *Pride and Prejudice* matters, and *Middlemarch* and *Villette* and *Wuthering Heights* matter,[4] then it matters far more than I can prove in an hour's discourse that women generally, and not merely the lonely aristocrat shut up in her country house among her folios and her flatterers, took to writing. Without those forerunners, Jane Austen and the Brontës and George Eliot could no more have written than Shakespeare could have written without Marlowe, or Marlowe without Chaucer, or Chaucer without those forgotten poets who paved the ways and tamed the natural savagery of the tongue. For masterpieces are not single and solitary births; they are the outcome of many years of thinking in common, of thinking by the body of the people, so that the experience of the mass is behind the single voice. Jane Austen should have laid a wreath upon the grave of Fanny Burney, and George Eliot done homage to the robust shade of Eliza Carter—the valiant old woman who tied a bell to her bedstead in order that she might wake early and learn Greek. All women together ought to let flowers fall upon the tomb of Aphra Behn[5] which is, most scandalously but rather appropriately, in Westminster Abbey, for it was she who earned them the right to speak their minds. It is she—shady and amorous as she was—who makes it not quite fantastic for me to say to you tonight: Earn five hundred a year by your wits.

---

4. *Pride and Prejudice* (1813), a novel by Jane Austen; *Middlemarch* (1871–1872) by George Eliot; *Villette* (1853) by Charlotte Brontë; *Wuthering Heights* (1847) by Emily Brontë.

5. A dramatist and the first English woman to earn a living by writing (1640–1689). Westminster Abbey, in central London, is the burial place of many of the English kings and queens, as well as of famous poets and statesmen.

Here, then, one had reached the early nineteenth century. And here, for the first time, I found several shelves given up entirely to the works of women. But why, I could not help asking, as I ran my eyes over them, were they, with very few exceptions, all novels? The original impulse was to poetry. The "supreme head of song" was a poetess. Both in France and in England the women poets precede the women novelists. Moreover, I thought, looking at the four famous names, what had George Eliot in common with Emily Brontë? Did not Charlotte Brontë fail entirely to understand Jane Austen? Save for the possibly relevant fact that not one of them had a child, four more incongruous characters could not have met together in a room—so much so that it is tempting to invent a meeting and a dialogue between them. Yet by some strange force they were all compelled, when they wrote, to write novels. Had it something to do with being born of the middle class, I asked; and with the fact, which Miss Emily Davies a little later was so strikingly to demonstrate,[6] that the middle-class family in the early nineteenth century was possessed only of a single sitting-room between them? If a woman wrote, she would have to write in the common sitting-room. And, as Miss Nightingale was so vehemently to complain,—"women never have an half hour . . . that they can call their own"—she was always interrupted. Still it would be easier to write prose and fiction there than to write poetry or a play. Less concentration is required. Jane Austen wrote like that to the end of her days. "How she was able to effect all this," her nephew writes in his Memoir, "is surprising, for she had no separate study to repair to, and most of the work must have been done in the general sitting-room, subject to all kinds of casual interruptions. She was careful that her occupation should not be suspected by servants or visitors or any persons beyond her own family party."[7] Jane Austen hid her manuscripts or covered them with a piece of blotting-paper. Then, again, all the literary training that a woman had in the early nineteenth century was training in the observation of character, in the analysis of emotion. Her sensibility had been educated for centuries by the influences of the common sitting-room. People's feelings were impressed on her; personal relations were always before her eyes. Therefore, when the middle-class woman took to writing, she naturally wrote novels, even though, as seems evident enough, two of the four famous women here named were not by nature novelists. Emily Brontë should have written poetic plays; the overflow of George Eliot's capacious mind should have spread itself when the creative impulse was spent upon history or biography. They wrote novels, however; one may even go further, I said, taking *Pride and Prejudice* from the shelf, and say that they wrote good novels. Without boasting or giving pain to the opposite sex, one may say that *Pride and Prejudice* is a good book. At any rate, one would not have been ashamed to have been caught in the act of writing *Pride and Prejudice*. Yet Jane Austen was glad that a hinge creaked, so that she might hide her manuscript before any one came in. To Jane Austen there was something discreditable in writing *Pride and Prejudice*. And, I wondered, would *Pride and Prejudice* have been a better novel if Jane Austen had not thought it necessary to hide her manuscript from visitors? I read a page or two to see; but I could not find any signs that her circumstances had harmed her work in the slightest. That, perhaps, was the chief miracle about it. Here was a woman about the year 1800 writing without hate, without

6. (Sarah) Emily Davies was prominent in the movement to secure university education for women in the 19th century and was chief founder of Girton College, Cambridge (1873).

7. *Memoir of Jane Austen,* by her nephew, James Edward Austen-Leigh [Woolf's note].

bitterness, without fear, without protest, without preaching. That was how Shakespeare wrote, I thought, looking at *Antony and Cleopatra;* and when people compare Shakespeare and Jane Austen, they may mean that the minds of both had consumed all impediments; and for that reason we do not know Jane Austen and we do not know Shakespeare, and for that reason Jane Austen pervades every word that she wrote, and so does Shakespeare. If Jane Austen suffered in any way from her circumstances it was in the narrowness of life that was imposed upon her. It was impossible for a woman to go about alone. She never travelled; she never drove through London in an omnibus or had luncheon in a shop by herself. But perhaps it was the nature of Jane Austen not to want what she had not. Her gift and her circumstances matched each other completely. But I doubt whether that was true of Charlotte Brontë, I said, opening *Jane Eyre* and laying it beside *Pride and Prejudice.*[8]

I opened it at chapter twelve and my eye was caught by the phrase, "Anybody may blame me who likes." What were they blaming Charlotte Brontë for, I wondered? And I read how Jane Eyre used to go up on to the roof when Mrs Fairfax was making jellies and looked over the fields at the distant view. And then she longed— and it was for this that they blamed her—that "then I longed for a power of vision which might overpass that limit; which might reach the busy world, towns, regions full of life I had heard of but never seen: that then I desired more of practical experience than I possessed; more of intercourse with my kind, of acquaintance with variety of character than was here within my reach. I valued what was good in Mrs Fairfax, and what was good in Adèle; but I believed in the existence of other and more vivid kinds of goodness, and what I believed in I wished to behold.

"Who blames me? Many, no doubt, and I shall be called discontented. I could not help it: the restlessness was in my nature; it agitated me to pain sometimes. . . .

"It is vain to say human beings ought to be satisfied with tranquillity: they must have action; and they will make it if they cannot find it. Millions are condemned to a stiller doom than mine, and millions are in silent revolt against their lot. Nobody knows how many rebellions ferment in the masses of life which people earth. Women are supposed to be very calm generally: but women feel just as men feel; they need exercise for their faculties and a field for their efforts as much as their brothers do; they suffer from too rigid a restraint, too absolute a stagnation, precisely as men would suffer; and it is narrow-minded in their more privileged fellow-creatures to say that they ought to confine themselves to making puddings and knitting stockings, to playing on the piano and embroidering bags. It is thoughtless to condemn them, or laugh at them, if they seek to do more or learn more than custom has pronounced necessary for their sex.

"When thus alone I not unfrequently heard Grace Poole's laugh . . ."

That is an awkward break, I thought. It is upsetting to come upon Grace Poole all of a sudden. The continuity is disturbed. One might say, I continued, laying the book down beside *Pride and Prejudice,* that the woman who wrote those pages had more genius in her than Jane Austen; but if one reads them over and marks that jerk in them, that indignation, one sees that she will never get her genius expressed whole

---

8. Woolf now goes on to describe parts of the plot of *Jane Eyre;* Jane Eyre, a penniless orphan, having suffered greatly during her schooling, takes up the post of governess to Adèle, the daughter of Mr. Rochester, a man of strange moods. Rochester falls in love with Jane, who agrees to marry him; however this is prevented by Rochester's mad wife—whom Rochester has locked in the attic, concealing her existence from Jane—who tears Jane's wedding veil on the eve of the marriage. Rochester at first tells Jane that Grace Poole, a servant, had been responsible for this and other strange events, including the uncanny laughter occasionally heard in the house.

and entire. Her books will be deformed and twisted. She will write in a rage where she should write calmly. She will write foolishly where she should write wisely. She will write of herself where she should write of her characters. She is at war with her lot. How could she help but die young, cramped and thwarted?

One could not but play for a moment with the thought of what might have happened if Charlotte Brontë had possessed say three hundred a year—but the foolish woman sold the copyright of her novels outright for fifteen hundred pounds; had somehow possessed more knowledge of the busy world, and towns and regions full of life; more practical experience, and intercourse with her kind and acquaintance with a variety of character. In those words she puts her finger exactly not only upon her own defects as a novelist but upon those of her sex at that time. She knew, no one better, how enormously her genius would have profited if it had not spent itself in solitary visions over distant fields; if experience and intercourse and travel had been granted her. But they were not granted; they were withheld; and we must accept the fact that all those good novels, *Villette, Emma, Wuthering Heights, Middlemarch,* were written by women without more experience of life than could enter the house of a respectable clergyman; written too in the common sitting-room of that respectable house and by women so poor that they could not afford to buy more than a few quires of paper at a time upon which to write *Wuthering Heights* or *Jane Eyre.* One of them, it is true, George Eliot, escaped after much tribulation, but only to a secluded villa in St John's Wood. And there she settled down in the shadow of the world's disapproval.[9] "I wish it to be understood," she wrote, "that I should never invite any one to come and see me who did not ask for the invitation"; for was she not living in sin with a married man and might not the sight of her damage the chastity of Mrs Smith or whoever it might be that chanced to call? One must submit to the social convention, and be "cut off from what is called the world." At the same time, on the other side of Europe, there was a young man living freely with this gipsy or with that great lady; going to the wars; picking up unhindered and uncensored all that varied experience of human life which served him so splendidly later when he came to write his books. Had Tolstoi lived at the Priory in seclusion with a married lady "cut off from what is called the world," however edifying the moral lesson, he could scarcely, I thought, have written *War and Peace.* ***

I do not want, and I am sure that you do not want me, to broach that very dismal subject, the future of fiction, so that I will only pause here one moment to draw your attention to the great part which must be played in that future so far as women are concerned by physical conditions. The book has somehow to be adapted to the body, and at a venture one would say that women's books should be shorter, more concentrated, than those of men, and framed so that they do not need long hours of steady and uninterrupted work. For interruptions there will always be. Again, the nerves that feed the brain would seem to differ in men and women, and if you are going to make them work their best and hardest, you must find out what treatment suits them—whether these hours of lectures, for instance, which the monks devised, presumably, hundreds of years ago, suit them—what alternations of work and rest they need, interpreting rest not as doing nothing but as doing something but something that is different; and what should that difference be? All this should be discussed and discovered; all this is part of the question of women and fiction. And yet, I continued, approaching the bookcase again, where shall I find that elaborate study of the psychology of

---

9. Following a strictly religious childhood, the novelist George Eliot lost her faith and eloped with G. H. Lewes, a married man, with whom she lived for the rest of his life; her family never forgave her.

women by a woman? If through their incapacity to play football women are not going
to be allowed to practise medicine——

Happily my thoughts were now given another turn.

from *Chapter 6*

Next day the light of the October morning was falling in dusty shafts through the un-
curtained windows, and the hum of traffic rose from the street. London then was
winding itself up again; the factory was astir; the machines were beginning. It was
tempting, after all this reading, to look out of the window and see what London was
doing on the morning of the twenty-sixth of October 1928. And what was London doing? Nobody, it seemed, was reading *Antony and Cleopatra*. London was wholly indifferent, it appeared, to Shakespeare's plays. Nobody cared a straw—and I do not
blame them—for the future of fiction, the death of poetry or the development by the
average woman of a prose style completely expressive of her mind. If opinions upon
any of these matters had been chalked on the pavement, nobody would have stooped
to read them. The nonchalance of the hurrying feet would have rubbed them out in
half an hour. Here came an errand-boy; here a woman with a dog on a lead. The fascination of the London street is that no two people are ever alike; each seems bound on
some private affair of his own. There were the business-like, with their little bags;
there were the drifters rattling sticks upon area railings; there were affable characters
to whom the streets serve for clubroom, hailing men in carts and giving information
without being asked for it. Also there were funerals to which men, thus suddenly reminded of the passing of their own bodies, lifted their hats. And then a very distinguished gentleman came slowly down a doorstep and paused to avoid collision with a
bustling lady who had, by some means or other, acquired a splendid fur coat and a
bunch of Parma violets. They all seemed separate, self-absorbed, on business of their
own.

At this moment, as so often happens in London, there was a complete lull and
suspension of traffic. Nothing came down the street; nobody passed. A single leaf detached itself from the plane tree at the end of the street, and in that pause and suspension fell. Somehow it was like a signal falling, a signal pointing to a force in things
which one had overlooked. It seemed to point to a river, which flowed past, invisibly,
round the corner, down the street, and took people and eddied them along, as the
stream at Oxbridge had taken the undergraduate in his boat and the dead leaves. Now
it was bringing from one side of the street to the other diagonally a girl in patent
leather boots, and then a young man in a maroon overcoat; it was also bringing a taxi-
cab; and it brought all three together at a point directly beneath my window; where
the taxi stopped; and the girl and the young man stopped; and they got into the taxi;
and then the cab glided off as if it were swept on by the current elsewhere.

The sight was ordinary enough; what was strange was the rhythmical order with
which my imagination had invested it; and the fact that the ordinary sight of two people getting into a cab had the power to communicate something of their own seeming
satisfaction. The sight of two people coming down the street and meeting at the corner seems to ease the mind of some strain, I thought, watching the taxi turn and make
off. Perhaps to think, as I had been thinking these two days, of one sex as distinct
from the other is an effort. It interferes with the unity of the mind. Now that effort had
ceased and that unity had been restored by seeing two people come together and get
into a taxi-cab. The mind is certainly a very mysterious organ, I reflected, drawing my

head in from the window, about which nothing whatever is known, though we depend upon it so completely. Why do I feel that there are severances and oppositions in the mind, as there are strains from obvious causes on the body? What does one mean by "the unity of the mind," I pondered, for clearly the mind has so great a power of concentrating at any point at any moment that it seems to have no single state of being. It can separate itself from the people in the street, for example, and think of itself as apart from them, at an upper window looking down on them. Or it can think with other people spontaneously, as, for instance, in a crowd waiting to hear some piece of news read out. It can think back through its fathers or through its mothers, as I have said that a woman writing thinks back through her mothers. Again if one is a woman one is often surprised by a sudden splitting off of consciousness, say in walking down Whitehall,[1] when from being the natural inheritor of that civilisation, she becomes, on the contrary, outside of it, alien and critical. Clearly the mind is always altering its focus, and bringing the world into different perspectives. But some of these states of mind seem, even if adopted spontaneously, to be less comfortable than others. In order to keep oneself continuing in them one is unconsciously holding something back, and gradually the repression becomes an effort. But there may be some state of mind in which one could continue without effort because nothing is required to be held back. And this perhaps, I thought, coming in from the window, is one of them. For certainly when I saw the couple get into the taxi-cab the mind felt as if, after being divided, it had come together again in a natural fusion. The obvious reason would be that it is natural for the sexes to co-operate. One has a profound, if irrational, instinct in favour of the theory that the union of man and woman makes for the greatest satisfaction, the most complete happiness. But the sight of the two people getting into the taxi and the satisfaction it gave me made me also ask whether there are two sexes in the mind corresponding to the two sexes in the body, and whether they also require to be united in order to get complete satisfaction and happiness. And I went on amateurishly to sketch a plan of the soul so that in each of us two powers preside, one male, one female; and in the man's brain, the man predominates over the woman, and in the woman's brain, the woman predominates over the man. The normal and comfortable state of being is that when the two live in harmony together, spiritually co-operating. If one is a man, still the woman part of the brain must have effect; and a woman also must have intercourse with the man in her. Coleridge perhaps meant this when he said that a great mind is androgynous.[2] It is when this fusion takes place that the mind is fully fertilised and uses all its faculties. Perhaps a mind that is purely masculine cannot create, any more than a mind that is purely feminine, I thought. ＊ ＊ ＊

One must turn back to Shakespeare then, for Shakespeare was androgynous; and so was Keats and Sterne and Cowper and Lamb and Coleridge. Shelley perhaps was sexless. Milton and Ben Jonson had a dash too much of the male in them. So had Wordsworth and Tolstoi. In our time Proust was wholly androgynous, if not perhaps a little too much of a woman. But that failing is too rare for one to complain of it, since without some mixture of the kind the intellect seems to predominate and the other faculties of the mind harden and become barren. However, I consoled myself with the reflection that this is perhaps a passing phase; much of what I have said in obedience to

---

1. A main thoroughfare in central London and site of government offices.

2. The poet Samuel Taylor Coleridge made the remark in September 1832—"a great mind must be androgynous"—and it was duly recorded in his *Table Talk*.

my promise to give you the course of my thoughts will seem out of date; much of what flames in my eyes will seem dubious to you who have not yet come of age.

Even so, the very first sentence that I would write here, I said, crossing over to the writing-table and taking up the page headed Women and Fiction, is that it is fatal for any one who writes to think of their sex. It is fatal to be a man or woman pure and simple; one must be woman-manly or man-womanly. It is fatal for a woman to lay the least stress on any grievance; to plead even with justice any cause; in any way to speak consciously as a woman. And fatal is no figure of speech; for anything written with that conscious bias is doomed to death. It ceases to be fertilised. Brilliant and effective, powerful and masterly, as it may appear for a day or two, it must wither at nightfall; it cannot grow in the minds of others. Some collaboration has to take place in the mind between the woman and the man before the act of creation can be accomplished. Some marriage of opposites has to be consummated. The whole of the mind must lie wide open if we are to get the sense that the writer is communicating his experience with perfect fullness. There must be freedom and there must be peace. Not a wheel must grate, not a light glimmer. The curtains must be close drawn. The writer, I thought, once his experience is over, must lie back and let his mind celebrate its nuptials in darkness. He must not look or question what is being done. Rather, he must pluck the petals from a rose or watch the swans float calmly down the river. And I saw again the current which took the boat and the undergraduate and the dead leaves; and the taxi took the man and the woman, I thought, seeing them come together across the street, and the current swept them away, I thought, hearing far off the roar of London's traffic, into that tremendous stream.

Here, then, Mary Beton ceases to speak. She has told you how she reached the conclusion—the prosaic conclusion—that it is necessary to have five hundred a year and a room with a lock on the door if you are to write fiction or poetry. She has tried to lay bare the thoughts and impressions that led her to think this. She has asked you to follow her flying into the arms of a Beadle, lunching here, dining there, drawing pictures in the British Museum, taking books from the shelf, looking out of the window. While she has been doing all these things, you no doubt have been observing her failings and foibles and deciding what effect they have had on her opinions. You have been contradicting her and making whatever additions and deductions seem good to you. That is all as it should be, for in a question like this truth is only to be had by laying together many varieties of error. And I will end now in my own person by anticipating two criticisms, so obvious that you can hardly fail to make them.

No opinion has been expressed, you may say, upon the comparative merits of the sexes even as writers. That was done purposely, because, even if the time had come for such a valuation—and it is far more important at the moment to know how much money women had and how many rooms than to theorise about their capacities— even if the time had come I do not believe that gifts, whether of mind or character, can be weighed like sugar and butter, not even in Cambridge, where they are so adept at putting people into classes and fixing caps on their heads and letters after their names. I do not believe that even the Table of Precedency which you will find in Whitaker's *Almanac*[3] represents a final order of values, or that there is any sound reason to suppose that a Commander of the Bath will ultimately walk in to dinner behind a Master in Lunacy. All this pitting of sex against sex, of quality against quality; all this claim-

3. A compendium of general information first published in 1868.

ing of superiority and imputing of inferiority, belong to the private-school stage of human existence where there are "sides," and it is necessary for one side to beat another side, and of the utmost importance to walk up to a platform and receive from the hands of the Headmaster himself a highly ornamental pot. As people mature they cease to believe in sides or in Headmasters or in highly ornamental pots. At any rate, where books are concerned, it is notoriously difficult to fix labels of merit in such a way that they do not come off. Are not reviews of current literature a perpetual illustration of the difficulty of judgment? "This great book," "this worthless book," the same book is called by both names. Praise and blame alike mean nothing. No, delightful as the pastime of measuring may be, it is the most futile of all occupations, and to submit to the decrees of the measurers the most servile of attitudes. So long as you write what you wish to write, that is all that matters; and whether it matters for ages or only for hours, nobody can say. But to sacrifice a hair of the head of your vision, a shade of its colour, in deference to some Headmaster with a silver pot in his hand or to some professor with a measuring-rod up his sleeve, is the most abject treachery, and the sacrifice of wealth and chastity which used to be said to be the greatest of human disasters, a mere flea-bite in comparison.

Next I think that you may object that in all this I have made too much of the importance of material things. * * * Intellectual freedom depends upon material things. Poetry depends upon intellectual freedom. And women have always been poor, not for two hundred years merely, but from the beginning of time. Women have had less intellectual freedom than the sons of Athenian slaves. Women, then, have not had a dog's chance of writing poetry. That is why I have laid so much stress on money and a room of one's own. However, thanks to the toils of those obscure women in the past, of whom I wish we knew more, thanks, curiously enough, to two wars, the Crimean which let Florence Nightingale out of her drawing-room, and the European War which opened the doors to the average woman some sixty years later, these evils are in the way to be bettered. Otherwise you would not be here tonight, and your chance of earning five hundred pounds a year, precarious as I am afraid that it still is, would be minute in the extreme. * * *

Here I would stop, but the pressure of convention decrees that every speech must end with a peroration. And a peroration addressed to women should have something, you will agree, particularly exalting and ennobling about it. I should implore you to remember your responsibilities, to be higher, more spiritual; I should remind you how much depends upon you, and what an influence you can exert upon the future. But those exhortations can safely, I think, be left to the other sex, who will put them, and indeed have put them, with far greater eloquence than I can compass. When I rummage in my own mind I find no noble sentiments about being companions and equals and influencing the world to higher ends. I find myself saying briefly and prosaically that it is much more important to be oneself than anything else. Do not dream of influencing other people, I would say, if I knew how to make it sound exalted. Think of things in themselves.

And again I am reminded by dipping into newspapers and novels and biographies that when a woman speaks to women she should have something very unpleasant up her sleeve. Women are hard on women. Women dislike women. Women . . . but are you not sick to death of the word? I can assure you that I am. Let us agree, then, that a paper read by a woman to women should end with something particularly disagreeable.

But how does it go? What can I think of? The truth is, I often like women. I like their unconventionality. I like their subtlety. I like their anonymity. I like—but I must not run on in this way. That cupboard there,—you say it holds clean table-napkins only; but what if Sir Archibald Bodkin were concealed among them?[4] Let me then adopt a sterner tone. Have I, in the preceding words, conveyed to you sufficiently the warnings and reprobation of mankind? I have told you the very low opinion in which you were held by Mr Oscar Browning. I have indicated what Napoleon once thought of you and what Mussolini thinks now. Then, in case any of you aspire to fiction, I have copied out for your benefit the advice of the critic about courageously acknowledging the limitations of your sex. I have referred to Professor X and given prominence to his statement that women are intellectually, morally and physically inferior to men. I have handed on all that has come my way without going in search of it, and here is a final warning—from Mr John Langdon Davies.[5] Mr John Langdon Davies warns women "that when children cease to be altogether desirable, women cease to be altogether necessary." I hope you will make a note of it.

How can I further encourage you to go about the business of life? Young women, I would say, and please attend, for the peroration is beginning, you are, in my opinion, disgracefully ignorant. You have never made a discovery of any sort of importance. You have never shaken an empire or led an army into battle. The plays of Shakespeare are not by you, and you have never introduced a barbarous race to the blessings of civilisation. What is your excuse? It is all very well for you to say, pointing to the streets and squares and forests of the globe swarming with black and white and coffee-coloured inhabitants, all busily engaged in traffic and enterprise and love-_making, we have had other work on our hands. Without our doing, those seas would be unsailed and those fertile lands a desert. We have borne and bred and washed and taught, perhaps to the age of six or seven years, the one thousand six hundred and twenty-three million human beings who are, according to statistics, at present in existence, and that, allowing that some had help, takes time.

There is truth in what you say—I will not deny it. But at the same time may I remind you that there have been at least two colleges for women in existence in England since the year 1866; that after the year 1880 a married woman was allowed by law to possess her own property; and that in 1919—which is a whole nine years ago—she was given a vote? May I also remind you that the most of the professions have been open to you for close on ten years now? When you reflect upon these immense privileges and the length of time time during which they have been enjoyed, and the fact that there must be at this moment some two thousand women capable of earning over five hundred a year in one way or another, you will agree that the excuse of lack of opportunity, training, encouragement, leisure and money no longer holds good. Moreover, the economists are telling us that Mrs Seton has had too many children. You must, of course, go on bearing children, but, so they say, in twos and threes, not in tens and twelves.

Thus, with some time on your hands and with some book learning in your brains—you have had enough of the other kind, and are sent to college partly, I suspect, to be uneducated—surely you should embark upon another stage of your very long, very laborious and highly obscure career. A thousand pens are ready to suggest

4. Sir Archibald Bodkin was then Director of Public Prosecutions; his office had been responsible for the 1928 prosecution of Radclyffe Hall's novel *The Well of Loneliness* on a charge of obscenity. It was subsequently banned. Woolf had wanted to give evidence in the book's defense at the trial, but expert witnesses were not allowed by the presiding magistrate.
5. *A Short History of Women,* by John Langford Davies [Woolf's note].

what you should do and what effect you will have. My own suggestion is a little fantastic, I admit; I prefer, therefore, to put it in the form of fiction.

I told you in the course of this paper that Shakespeare had a sister; but do not look for her in Sir Sidney Lee's life of the poet. She died young—alas, she never wrote a word. She lies buried where the omnibuses now stop, opposite the Elephant and Castle. Now my belief is that this poet who never wrote a word and was buried at the crossroads still lives. She lives in you and in me, and in many other women who are not here tonight, for they are washing up the dishes and putting the children to bed. But she lives; for great poets do not die; they are continuing presences; they need only the opportunity to walk among us in the flesh. This opportunity, as I think, it is now coming within your power to give her. For my belief is that if we live another century or so—I am talking of the common life which is the real life and not of the little separate lives which we live as individuals—and have five hundred a year each of us and rooms of our own; if we have the habit of freedom and the courage to write exactly what we think; if we escape a little from the common sitting-room and see human beings not always in their relation to each other but in relation to reality; and the sky, too, and the trees or whatever it may be in themselves; if we look past Milton's bogey, for no human being should shut out the view; if we face the fact, for it is a fact, that there is no arm to cling to, but that we go alone and that our relation is to the world of reality and not only to the world of men and women, then the opportunity will come and the dead poet who was Shakespeare's sister will put on the body which she has so often laid down. Drawing her life from the lives of the unknown who were her forerunners, as her brother did before her, she will be born. As for her coming without that preparation, without that effort on our part, without that determination that when she is born again she shall find it possible to live and write her poetry, that we cannot expect, for that would be impossible. But I maintain that she would come if we worked for her, and that so to work, even in poverty and obscurity, is worth while.

—•—≡◆≡—•—

Akutagawa Ryunosuke
1892–1927

In a life framed by melancholy and early death, Akutagawa Ryunosuke became a prolific and pathbreaking short-story writer and essayist. Nine months after his birth in Tokyo, his mother went insane and died; his father, a struggling tradesman, couldn't hold his family together, and sent his son to be raised by an uncle, whose surname—Akutagawa—the boy later adopted as a substitute family name. A brilliant student, Akutagawa founded a literary magazine with two friends while still a student at Tokyo Imperial University, where he studied English, writing a senior thesis on the Victorian poet, painter, and socialist William Morris. At the same time, increasingly unhappy with the rhetoric of progress and the cultural compromises of modern Japan, Akutagawa pursued studies in classical Japanese and Chinese literature.

His early interests are seen in his influential story "Rashōmon" ("The Rashō Gate"), which he published in a university magazine in 1915. Set at a major gateway into the medieval capitol of Kyoto, this stark, uncanny tale depicts a period of social collapse at the close of the brilliant cultural flowering of the Heian period (794–1184) when such foundational works of Japanese prose as *The Tale of Genji* and *Tales of the Heike* had been written. In Akutagawa's story, questions of right and wrong, survival and sacrilege develop in a strange confrontation between two desperate commoners. Akutagawa relates this tale without comment, setting up dizzying shifts in perspective on the events as they unfold.

After graduation from college, Akutagawa married, began a family, and wrote incessantly, producing more than 150 stories in a decade. He carried his interest in multiple perspectives still further in "In a Grove" (1922), a short story that takes the form of testimonies given to a magistrate in a murder case, culminating in the confessions of three characters—one of them a ghost, speaking through a medium—all of whom claim to have been the murderer. "Rashōmon" and "In a Grove" achieved international fame after the film director Kurosawa Akira combined them to create *Rashomon* (1950), a brilliant exploration of ambiguities of perception, evidence, and character. Kurosawa's *Rashomon* was the first Japanese film to win major prizes abroad, and brought international attention to the thriving postwar Japanese film industry.

Akutagawa didn't live to see his stories receive this new level of attention. Depressed and in deteriorating health, he committed suicide by taking an overdose of sleeping pills in 1927, at the age of thirty-five. He explained this decision with a chill calm in his suicide note, "A Note Forwarded to a Certain Old Friend"—the friend's anonymity increasing the sense of Akutagawa's isolation. Yet his readers recognized Akutagawa as a brilliant innovator, someone who could combine close naturalistic observation with uncanny hints of mystery and psychological complexity. Akutagawa's use of multiple, conflicting perspectives preceded comparable experiments in modernist narratives—from Virginia Woolf's *The Waves* (1931) to William Faulkner's *Absalom, Absalom!* (1936). In his highly individual synthesis of Japanese and Western literary modes, Akutagawa is a major product of the turn-of-the-century, post-Meiji Japanese culture from which he felt so deeply estranged.

PRONUNCIATIONS:
Akutagawa Ryonosuke: ah-koo-tah-GAW-wah rie-YOU-noh-SUE-kay
Kurosawa Akira: koo-row-SAH-wah ah-KEY-rah
Kanazawa no Takehiro: kah-nah-ZAH-wah noh tah-ka-HE-row
Tajomaru: tah-joe-MAH-rue

Rashōmon[1]

It was a chilly evening. A servant of a samurai stood under the Rashōmon, waiting for a break in the rain.

No one else was under the wide gate. On the thick column, its crimson lacquer rubbed off here and there, perched a cricket. Since the Rashōmon stands on Sujaku Avenue, a few other people at least, in sedge hat or nobleman's headgear, might have been expected to be waiting there for a break in the rain storm. But no one was near except this man.

For the past few years the city of Kyōto had been visited by a series of calamities, earthquakes, whirlwinds, and fires, and Kyōto had been greatly devastated. Old chronicles say that broken pieces of Buddhist images and other Buddhist objects, with their lacquer, gold, or silver leaf worn off, were heaped up on roadsides to be sold as firewood. Such being the state of affairs in Kyōto, the repair of the Rashōmon was out of the question. Taking advantage of the devastation, foxes and other wild animals made their dens in the ruins of the gate, and thieves and robbers found a home there

---

1. Translated by T. Kojima.

too. Eventually it became customary to bring unclaimed corpses to this gate and abandon them. After dark it was so ghostly that no one dared approach.

Flocks of crows flew in from somewhere. During the daytime these cawing birds
circled round the ridgepole of the gate. When the sky overhead turned red in the after-
light of the departed sun, they looked like so many grains of sesame flung across the
gate. But on that day not a crow was to be seen, perhaps because of the lateness of the
hour. Here and there the stone steps, beginning to crumble, and with rank grass growing in their crevices, were dotted with the white droppings of crows. The servant, in a
worn blue kimono, sat on the seventh and highest step, vacantly watching the rain.
His attention was drawn to a large pimple irritating his right cheek.

As has been said, the servant was waiting for a break in the rain. But he had no particular idea of what to do after the rain stopped. Ordinarily, of course, he would have returned to his master's house, but he had been discharged just before. The prosperity of
the city of Kyōto had been rapidly declining, and he had been dismissed by his master,
whom he had served many years, because of the effects of this decline. Thus, confined
by the rain, he was at a loss to know where to go. And the weather had not a little to do
with his depressed mood. The rain seemed unlikely to stop. He was lost in thoughts of
how to make his living tomorrow, helpless incoherent thoughts protesting an inexorable
fate. Aimlessly he had been listening to the pattering of the rain on the Sujaku Avenue.

The rain, enveloping the Rashōmon, gathered strength and came down with a
pelting sound that could be heard far away. Looking up, he saw a fat black cloud impale itself on the tips of the tiles jutting out from the roof of the gate.

He had little choice of means, whether fair or foul, because of his helpless circumstances. If he chose honest means, he would undoubtedly starve to death beside
the wall or in the Sujaku gutter. He would be brought to this gate and thrown away
like a stray dog. If he decided to steal . . . His mind, after making the same detour time
and again, came finally to the conclusion that he would be a thief.

But doubts returned many times. Though determined that he had no choice, he
was still unable to muster enough courage to justify the conclusion that he must become a thief.

After a loud fit of sneezing he got up slowly. The evening chill of Kyōto made
him long for the warmth of a brazier. The wind in the evening dusk howled through
the columns of the gate. The cricket which had been perched on the crimson-
lacquered column was already gone.

Ducking his neck, he looked around the gate, and drew up the shoulders of the
blue kimono which he wore over his thin underwear. He decided to spend the night
there, if he could find a secluded corner sheltered from wind and rain. He found a
broad lacquered stairway leading to the tower over the gate. No one would be there,
except the dead, if there were any. So, taking care that the sword at his side did not
slip out of the scabbard, he set foot on the lowest step of the stairs.

A few seconds later, halfway up the stairs, he saw a movement above. Holding
his breath and huddling cat-like in the middle of the broad stairs leading to the tower,
he watched and waited. A light coming from the upper part of the tower shone
faintly upon his right cheek. It was the cheek with the red, festering pimple visible
under his stubbly whiskers. He had expected only dead people inside the tower, but
he had only gone up a few steps before he noticed a fire above, about which someone was moving. He saw a dull, yellow, flickering light which made the cobwebs
hanging from the ceiling glow in a ghostly way. What sort of person would be making a light in the Rashōmon . . . and in a storm? The unknown, the evil terrified him.

As quietly as a lizard, the servant crept up to the top of the steep stairs. Crouching on all fours, and stretching his neck as far as possible, he timidly peeped into the tower.

As rumor had said, he found several corpses strewn carelessly about the floor. Since the glow of the light was feeble, he could not count the number. He could only see that some were naked and others clothed. Some of them were women, and all were lolling on the floor with their mouths open or their arms outstretched showing no more signs of life than so many clay dolls. One would doubt that they had ever been alive, so eternally silent they were. Their shoulders, breasts, and torsos stood out in the dim light; other parts vanished in shadow. The offensive smell of these decomposed corpses brought his hand to his nose.

The next moment his hand dropped and he stared. He caught sight of a ghoulish form bent over a corpse. It seemed to be an old woman, gaunt, gray-haired, and nunnish in appearance. With a pine torch in her right hand, she was peeping into the face of a corpse which had long black hair.

Seized more with horror than curiosity, he even forgot to breathe for a time. He felt the hair of his head and body stand on end. As he watched, terrified, she wedged the torch between two floor boards and, laying hands on the head of the corpse, began to pull out the long hairs one by one, as a monkey kills the lice of her young. The hair came out smoothly with the movement of her hands.

As the hair came out, fear faded from his heart, and his hatred toward the old woman mounted. It grew beyond hatred, becoming a consuming antipathy against all evil. At this instant if anyone had brought up the question of whether he would starve to death or become a thief—the question which had occurred to him a little while ago—he would not have hesitated to choose death. His hatred toward evil flared up like the piece of pine wood which the old woman had stuck in the floor.

He did not know why she pulled out the hair of the dead. Accordingly, he did not know whether her case was to be put down as good or bad. But in his eyes, pulling out the hair of the dead in the Rashōmon on this stormy night was an unpardonable crime. Of course it never entered his mind that a little while ago he had thought of becoming a thief.

Then, summoning strength into his legs, he rose from the stairs and strode, hand on sword, right in front of the old creature. The hag turned, terror in her eyes, and sprang up from the floor, trembling. For a small moment she paused, poised there, then lunged for the stairs with a shriek.

"Wretch! Where are you going?" he shouted, barring the way of the trembling hag who tried to scurry past him. Still she attempted to claw her way by. He pushed her back to prevent her . . . they struggled, fell among the corpses, and grappled there. The issue was never in doubt. In a moment he had her by the arm, twisted it, and forced her down to the floor. Her arms were all skin and bones, and there was no more flesh on them than on the shanks of a chicken. No sooner was she on the floor than he drew his sword and thrust the silver-white blade before her very nose. She was silent. She trembled as if in a fit, and her eyes were open so wide that they were almost out of their sockets, and her breath come in hoarse gasps. The life of this wretch was his now. This thought cooled his boiling anger and brought a calm pride and satisfaction. He looked down at her, and said in a somewhat calmer voice:

"Look here, I'm not an officer of the High Police Commissioner. I'm a stranger who happened to pass by this gate. I won't bind you or do anything against you, but you must tell me what you're doing up here."

Then the old woman opened her eyes still wider, and gazed at his face intently with the sharp red eyes of a bird of prey. She moved her lips, which were wrinkled into her nose, as though she were chewing something. Her pointed Adam's apple moved in her thin throat. Then a panting sound like the cawing of a crow came from her throat:

"I pull the hair . . . I pull out the hair . . . to make a wig."

Her answer banished all unknown from their encounter and brought disappointment. Suddenly she was only a trembling old woman there at his feet. A ghoul no longer: only a hag who makes wigs from the hair of the dead—to sell, for scraps of food. A cold contempt seized him. Fear left his heart, and his former hatred entered. These feelings must have been sensed by the other. The old creature, still clutching the hair she had pulled off the corpse, mumbled out these words in her harsh broken voice:

"Indeed, making wigs out of the hair of the dead may seem a great evil to you, but these that are here deserve no better. This woman, whose beautiful black hair I was pulling, used to sell cut and dried snake flesh at the guard barracks, saying that it was dried fish. If she hadn't died of the plague, she'd be selling it now. The guards liked to buy from her, and used to say her fish was tasty. What she did couldn't be wrong, because if she hadn't, she would have starved to death. There was no other choice. If she knew I had to do this in order to live, she probably wouldn't care."

He sheathed his sword, and, with his left hand on its hilt, he listened to her meditatively. His right hand touched the big pimple on his cheek. As he listened, a certain courage was born in his heart—the courage which he had not had when he sat under the gate a little while ago. A strange power was driving him in the opposite direction of the courage which he had had when he seized the old woman. No longer did he wonder whether he should starve to death or become a thief. Starvation was so far from his mind that it was the last thing that would have entered it.

"Are you sure?" he asked in a mocking tone, when she finished talking. He took his right hand from his pimple, and, bending forward, seized her by the neck and said sharply:

"Then it's right if I rob you. I'd starve if I didn't."

He tore her clothes from her body and kicked her roughly down on the corpses as she struggled and tried to clutch his leg. Five steps, and he was at the top of the stairs. The yellow clothes he had wrested off were under his arm, and in a twinkling he had rushed down the steep stairs into the abyss of night. The thunder of his descending steps pounded in the hollow tower, and then it was quiet.

Shortly after that the hag raised up her body from the corpses. Grumbling and groaning, she crawled to the top stair by the still flickering torchlight, and through the gray hair which hung over her face, she peered down to the last stair in the torch light.

Beyond this was only darkness . . . unknowing and unknown.

In a Grove[1]

THE STORY OF A WOODCUTTER QUESTIONED BY THE GRAND MAGISTRATE

Yes, it's just as you say. I was the one who found the body. Like always, I went deep into the mountains this morning to cut cedars. I found the body in a grove hidden in the shadows of the mountain. Where was it? Four or five hundred yards off the Yamashina station road.[2] It's a deserted grove where small cedars grow among the bamboo.

---

1. Translated by Seiji M. Lippit.   2. A road leading out of Kyoto through deserted countryside.

The body lay face up and was clothed in a light-blue hunting robe with a courtier's hat from the capital. The wound was caused by just a single sword stroke—but it was to his chest, and so the bamboo leaves around him were stained with dark blood. No, he was no longer bleeding. The wound seemed to be dry already. What's more, a huge horsefly was clinging to the wound as if it didn't even hear my footsteps.

Did I see a long sword? No, there was nothing. There was only a piece of rope at the foot of a nearby cedar. And then—yes, there was also a comb in addition to the rope. These were the only two items near the corpse. But the grass and bamboo leaves were completely trampled, so the man must have struggled painfully before being killed. Was there no horse? There's no chance a horse could enter there. A thicket separates it from the road where horses pass.

The Story of a Travelling Priest Questioned by the Grand Magistrate

I believe I met the deceased man yesterday. It was—let me see—about noon yesterday. The location was on the road from Sekiyama to Yamashina. He was leading a woman on a horse toward the barrier. She was wearing a cloth covering over her head, so I never saw her face. The only thing that I saw was the color of the cloth—I believe it was a dark red and blue pattern. The horse was reddish dapple-gray, with its mane cropped close. Its height? I think it must have been more than four feet. But of course as a priest I know little of these matters. The man carried a bow along with the sword he had at his side. I still remember the twenty or so arrows stuck in his black-lacquered quiver.

I never dreamed he would end up like this. Truly, human life is as ephemeral as dew and as brief as lightning. Ah, what a terrible, sad fate!

The Story of a Police Official Questioned by the Grand Magistrate

The man I captured? He is most certainly Tajomaru, the notorious bandit. Of course, when I caught him he'd fallen from his horse and was moaning in pain on the stone bridge at Awataguchi. The time? It was last night, soon after the first watch of the evening. When I nearly captured him the time before, he was also carrying this long sword and wearing this dark blue hunting robe. Yet this time, as you see, he also had a bow. Is that so? The dead man was also carrying one—well then, the murderer must be none other than Tajomaru. The leather-covered bow with black-lacquer quiver, the seventeen arrows with hawk-feather quills—these must have belonged to the man. Yes. Just as you say, the horse is a reddish dapple-gray with a short-cropped mane. It must have been an act of providence he was thrown by that animal. It was standing just beyond the bridge dragging its long halter and eating grass by the roadside.

Of all the bandits lurking about the capital, this Tajomaru is especially known to target women. It's rumored he was behind the murder of a woman and a young girl in the mountains behind the Pindola at the Toribe temple last autumn. If he did kill the man, there's no telling what he may have done with the woman on the gray horse. It's not my place to say so, but won't you investigate this matter as well?

The Story of an Old Woman Questioned by the Grand Magistrate

Yes, this dead man is my daughter's husband. But he's not from the capital. He's a samurai from the province of Wakasa. His name was Kanazawa no Takehiro, and he was twenty-six years of age. No, he had a gentle nature, so he wouldn't have had any enemies.

My daughter? Her name is Masago and she's nineteen years old. She's strong-willed like a man, so she's never known any man other than Takehiro. Her face is small and oval-shaped, slightly dark with a birthmark under her left eye.

Takehiro left for Wakasa yesterday with my daughter. What a terrible fate to end up like this! But what has happened to my daughter? I'm resigned to my son-in-law's fate, but I'm still worried about her. Please—my only request is that you find my daughter, even if you have to bend every blade of grass. How I hate that thief Tajomaru! If he killed not only my son-in-law but my daughter too. . . . (Her voice trails off into sobbing.)

TAJOMARU'S CONFESSION

Yes, I killed the man—but not the woman. Then where is she? That I don't know. Wait a moment! No matter how much you torture me, I can't tell you what I don't know. And now that you've caught me I have no intention of hiding anything like a coward.

It was yesterday, just past noon, when I saw the man and woman. A slight breeze happened to lift the woman's veil, and I caught a glimpse of her face. One brief look—and the next moment it was hidden again. Maybe it was because I only caught a glimpse, but the woman's face seemed to me like a Boddhisatva's.[3] In that one instant, I decided to make her mine, even if it meant killing the man.

Killing a man is not as difficult as you may think. If I wanted to have the woman, I had to kill him. Of course, when I kill a man I use the sword at my side, but you—you don't use swords, you kill with power and money. Sometimes, you even kill with words that sound like they're full of kindness. There may be no blood, and the man may still breathe, but you've killed him all the same. When you think about it, it's not so easy to tell who is guiltier, you or I. (An ironic smile.)

Still, I would've been happy to have her without killing the man. In fact, I decided to take the woman without killing him, if I could. But that was impossible in the middle of the Yamashina station road. So I hatched a plan to lure them into the mountains.

It was a simple plan. I fell in with them and told them a story—that I'd discovered an old tomb up in the mountains filled with swords and mirrors and that I'd buried them in a grove in the shadow of the mountains unknown to anyone. If I could only find someone to take them, I'd be willing to sell them off cheaply. As I spoke the man grew more and more interested in my story. And then—well, greed is a terrifying thing. In half an instant the two of them were following me with their horse up the mountain path.

When we came to the grove, I said the treasure was buried inside and told them to come have a look. The man was consumed with desire, so of course he agreed. But the woman stayed on her horse and said she would wait. It was only natural after seeing that thick grove. In fact, this fell into my plan perfectly, so I left her alone and entered the grove with the man.

For a while the grove is just bamboo. But some fifty meters in, there's a stand of cedars that opens up a bit. There was no better place to carry out my scheme. Pushing my way through the trees, I uttered a believable enough lie, that the treasure was buried by the cedars. When the man heard these words he rushed forward towards the trees. As the bamboo thinned out we came to the place where the cedars grow. But as

---

3. A Buddhist saint or enlightened being, especially one who remains in the world to help those who suffer.

soon as we had reached this place I pinned him to the ground. He had a long sword by his side and seemed strong enough, but caught by surprise like that there was nothing he could do. Soon enough he was bound to the trunk of a nearby cedar. The rope? A rope is indispensable for a thief like me, since you never know when you might have to scale a wall. I had it by my side. I stuffed bamboo leaves into his mouth so he wouldn't cry out, and it was all over.

After dealing with the man I returned to the woman and told her he'd suddenly fallen ill, that she'd better come have a look. There's no need to tell you I was on the mark once more! The woman took off her sedge hat and I led her by the hand into the grove. When we came to the clearing, she saw the man tied to the base of a tree. One look and she quickly drew a dagger from her sleeve. I've never seen such a strong-willed woman. If I'd let my guard down for an instant, she would've stabbed me in the side. Even dodging her blade as she swung wildly at me I could've been injured. But I'm Tajomaru, after all, so I took the dagger from her without even drawing my own sword. Strong as she was, she was helpless without a weapon. At last, just as I had planned, I was able to take her without killing the man.

Yes—without killing him. I had no desire to take his life on top of it all. I left the woman sobbing on the ground behind me and was about to run from the grove when she grabbed onto my arm as if she'd gone mad. And when I listened to her words through her sobbing, I found she was saying: one of you must die, either you or my husband. It's worse than death, she said, to be shamed like this before two men. She even said through her tears that she would follow whomever was left alive. Then I was seized with a brutal urge to kill the man. (A dark excitement.)

When you hear this, you must think I'm more cruel than you are. But that's because you didn't see her face just then. Because you didn't see her eyes at that moment, lit up like fire. When I looked into her eyes I felt a desire to make her my wife, even if it meant being struck down by lightning. To make her my wife—this was the only thought in my mind. It was not just a question of mere lust, as you may think. If it were only lust, I would've kicked her down and run away. Then the man would've been spared from staining my blade with his blood. Yet as I stared into the woman's face in that shadowy grove, I knew I couldn't leave there without killing him.

But even though I'd decided to take his life, I refused to kill him like a coward. I cut his bonds and told him to take up his sword. (The rope you found at the root of the tree was the one I threw down just then.) The man was pale as he drew his sword. Without a word he jumped at me savagely. There's no need to tell you the outcome of the duel. My blade found his chest on the twenty-third stroke. On the twenty-third stroke—make sure you take note of it! I'm still impressed by the fact. No one else has ever crossed swords with me twenty times. (Energetic laughter.)

As soon as he fell, I threw down my bloody sword and turned back to the woman. But then—yes, she was nowhere to be found. I searched the stand of cedars, but there was no trace of her left among the fallen bamboo leaves. I tried to listen for her, but all I could hear was the death-rattle in the man's throat.

Maybe she ran from the grove to call for help when our sword-fight began. When that thought crossed my mind. I knew my own life was in danger, so I grabbed the man's sword and his bow and arrows, and ran back to the mountain path. I found the woman's horse there grazing quietly on the grass. It's a waste of time to describe what happened next. But before I entered the capital I got rid of the man's sword. That's the end of my confession. All along I knew I would hang from the gallows one day, so go ahead and do your worst. (A defiant attitude.)

THE CONFESSION OF THE WOMAN WHO CAME TO KIYOMIZU TEMPLE[4]

After the man wearing the dark blue robe raped me, he looked at my husband bound to the tree and laughed mockingly. How mortified my husband must have felt! No matter how hard he struggled, the cord binding him only bit deeper into his body. Without even thinking, I stumbled over to his side. No, I tried to run over to him when the man kicked me down to the ground. It was just then. In my husband's eyes, I saw an indescribable light. Even now when I recall his eyes I can't help but tremble. Even though he could not speak, he said everything in his heart with that one look. It was not a look of anger or even sadness, but one of icy contempt. It was that look, rather than the man's kick, that made me cry out and finally lose consciousness.

When I awoke the man in the dark blue robe had left. Only my husband remained, still tied to the base of the cedar. Finally I raised myself from the bamboo leaves and looked into his eyes once again. Yet the expression in his eyes had not changed. They still had the same cold look of contempt tinged with hatred. Shame, despair, anger—I don't know how to describe my feelings at that moment. I stood up trembling and approached his side.

"Now that things have come to this, I cannot stay with you any longer. I am resigned to die. Yet—yet I ask you to die as well. You have witnessed my shame. I cannot leave you alive by yourself this way."

It took all of my strength to say this. Yet still my husband looked at me with disdain. I clutched my breast, which felt as if it were torn asunder, and looked for his long sword. But the thief must have taken it, for the sword and even the bow and arrows were nowhere to be seen in the grove. Yet fortunately my dagger at least was on the ground by my feet. I raised the dagger and then spoke once again to my husband.

"Then I ask you to give your life to me. I will follow soon after."

When he heard these words he finally moved his lips. Of course his mouth was filled with bamboo leaves, so no sound emerged. But when I saw his face, I understood what he was trying to say. Still eyeing me with contempt he had said simply, "Kill me." Then, as if in a dream, I stabbed my husband's chest through his silk robe.

I must have fainted once more. When I was able to look about at last, my husband, still bound, was long dead. The western sun cast a single beam of light on his pale face through the bamboo and cedar trees. Stifling my tears, I unbound his body and cast the rope aside. And then—and then what happened to me? I have no strength left to speak of it. In any case I didn't have the strength to take my own life. I pressed the dagger to my neck, threw myself into the lake at the foot of the mountains, and tried every other way. Living on like this without even the strength to die brings me only shame. (A sad smile.) Even the merciful Kannon[5] must have forsaken such an unfortunate woman as I. After killing my husband, being raped by the thief, what is left for me? What am I to do . . . ? (Suddenly, fierce sobbing.)

THE STORY OF THE GHOST TOLD BY A MEDIUM

After raping my wife, the thief sat by her side on the ground, consoling her in various ways. Of course I couldn't speak. My body was bound to the base of the tree. Yet the whole time I tried to make eye contact with my wife. Don't believe anything this man says, no matter what he says don't trust him—I tried to communicate such

---

4. A large temple complex in the wooded hills outside of Kyoto.

5. Bodhisattva of compassion and mercy, often prayed to in Japan for aid in childbirth.

thoughts to her. But my wife sat there vacantly among the fallen leaves and stared quietly into her lap. Did it not appear to me as if she were listening to the thief? I struggled with feelings of jealousy. Yet the thief moved skillfully from one argument to another. Now that your body has been violated, things will not go well between you and your husband. Why not leave him and be my wife instead? It was only because of your beauty that I did such a thing. These were the brazen things he said in the end.

After listening to him my wife raised her head as though spellbound. I have never seen her as beautiful as she was at that moment. Yet what did this beautiful wife of mine say to the thief as I sat bound in front of her? Even as I wander in the darkness, every time I recall my wife's words I burn with anger. In a clear voice she said, "Then take me with you anywhere." (A long silence.)

That was not the extent of my wife's sin. If it were, I would not suffer as I do in the abyss. She grasped the thief's hand as though in a dream and was about to leave the grove, when suddenly the color drained from her face and she pointed to me as I sat bound to the cedar. "Kill that man! As long as he is alive I cannot be with you." As though she had gone mad, my wife screamed these words over and over again. "Kill that man!" Even now, like some tempest these words threaten to blast me into the faraway darkness. Have such hateful words ever been uttered by human mouth? Have human ears ever heard such cursed words? Have ever . . . (Suddenly, scattered mocking laughter.) Even the thief paled when he heard those words. "Kill that man!" my wife screamed as she clung to his arm. He stared at her and did not say whether he would kill me. Suddenly, he kicked her down onto the fallen bamboo leaves. (Once more, scattered mocking laughter.) The thief quietly folded his arms and looked at me. "What do you want me to do with this woman? Kill her or spare her? Just nod in response. Shall I kill her?" For these words, I can almost forgive the thief his crimes. (Again, a long silence.)

While I hesitated my wife screamed and ran off into the thicket. The thief sprang after her, but he was unable to grasp even her sleeve. I stared at the scene before me as if it were some kind of phantasm.

After my wife had run off the thief picked up the long sword and my bow and arrows, and he cut the rope binding me in a single spot. "Now my own life's in danger." I remember him muttering these words as he left the grove. Afterwards all was still. No, there still lingered the sound of someone crying. I listened carefully as I undid my bonds. Then I realized the sobbing voice was my own. (For the third time, a long silence.)

At last I raised my spent body from the base of the cedar. My wife's fallen dagger glinted on the ground before me. I took it in my hand and stabbed myself once in the chest. I could feel something raw coming up into my mouth. Yet there was no pain. Only, as my chest grew colder the surrounding world grew ever more still. Ah, what stillness! Not even a bird in the sky above this grove in the shadows of the mountains. Only a lonely shaft of sunlight behind the cedars and bamboo. The shaft of sunlight—even that gradually dimmed. Then even the cedars and bamboo were no longer visible. As I lay there, I was enveloped in deep stillness.

Then, someone approached me with stealthy footsteps. I tried to look over. But by then the darkness had pressed in all around me. The hand of someone—someone I couldn't see—quietly drew the dagger from my chest. At the same time blood surged into my mouth once more. And I sank forever into the blackness of the abyss. . . .

A Note Forwarded to a Certain Old Friend[1]

There is as yet no one who has written about the mentality of the suicide as such. This may be due to the pride of the suicide or to the lack of psychological interest in the suicide. I am thinking of explaining clearly this mentality in the last letter that I am sending to you. Of course, there is no particular reason for telling you of the motives of my committing suicide. Lenau[2] describes a suicide in his short story. The protagonist of this short story does not himself know why he commits suicide. On the third page of the newspaper, for instance, you will discover various kinds of motives of suicide, such as difficulties of living, pains from sickness, mental sufferings, and others. However, according to my experience, these are not *the whole of the motives*. Moreover, in most cases, these merely exhibit the processes that lead to the motives. Generally, the suicide as described by Lenau would not know why he commits suicide. The act of suicide like any other act involves complex motives. But, at least in my case, the motive is merely a vague anxiety, an anxiety with respect to my future. Probably you do not trust my words. However, 2 years of experience teaches me that, so long as one does not resemble me and does not live in a situation like mine, my words disappear like a song in the wind. Accordingly, I do not blame you.

For these 2 years I have been thinking unceasingly about my dying. It was also during these years that I had read Mainländer[3] seriously. Mainländer describes skillfully, in abstract words, the process leading to death. But I am thinking of describing the same thing more concretely. Before such desire, the compassion etc. toward my family amount to nothing. Probably, this comment will necessarily seem to you *inhuman*. Nevertheless, if I am inhuman, I am inhuman only in part.

My duty is to write everything honestly. (I have already analyzed the vague anxiety with respect to my future. I believe that in general this is fully described in my *Life of a Certain Fool*. Even in this work, however, I did not write specifically about the social conditions that had faced me,—the feudalistic factors that had cast their shadows upon me. The reason why I did not write about them specifically is that even now we human beings are more or less under the shadow of the feudalistic age. In addition to presenting the stage, I attempted to write about the actions—mostly mine— of characters, backgrounds, and lightings. Moreover, one can certainly doubt whether I could have understood clearly the social conditions in which I myself was involved.)—What I pondered first of all was how I could die without torment. No doubt, hanging was the most suitable means for this purpose. But, when I imagined myself hanging, luxuriously enough, I felt an aesthetic abhorrence. (I remember that once when I was in love with a woman, I lost my love suddenly because of her poor handwriting.) Nor could drowning serve the purpose at all, since I was able to swim. Moreover, even if drowning were successful, it would come to be more tormenting than hanging. Death by a train gave me more immediate aesthetic abhorrence than any other methods. Death by way of a pistol or a knife has a possibility of failure because of trembling hands. Likewise jumping from a building would be ignominious. On the basis of these considerations, I decided to die by taking drugs. Dying by taking drugs would be more tormenting than hanging. However, besides giving no aesthetic abhorrence, this had the advantage of the insurance against revival. But, undoubtedly,

1. Translated by A. Inoue.
2. Nikolaus Lenau (1802–1850), a pessimistic Austrian poet.

3. Philip Mainländer, author of *The Philosophy of Redemption* (1876), on the philosophies of Kant and Schopenhauer.

it would not be easy to find the drug. As I had made up my mind to commit suicide, I took every opportunity to try to secure the drug. At the same time, I tried to acquire knowledge about toxicology.

Then what I considered was the place to commit suicide. My family must rely on my inheritance after my death. In my inheritance there was nothing but about 0.08 acres of land, my house, my copyright, and my savings of two thousand yen. I suffered from thinking that my house would be difficult to sell because of my suicide. Accordingly I felt an envy toward the bourgeois who can easily afford a villa. You will find a certain ridiculousness in my words. I now, too, feel a certain ridiculousness in them. But, when I thought about this, I felt quite literally an inconvenience. This inconvenience, however, could not be avoided. I am only thinking of committing suicide in such a way that my corpse could not be seen by anyone except my family.

However, I was at least half attached to life, even after I decided upon the method. Accordingly, I needed a "spring-board" to jump into death. (I do not think committing suicide is a sin as foreigners believe. Actually, Gotama[4] accepts the suicide of his disciple in the Agama sûtra. In spite of this acceptance the literary sycophants would say that suicide is sin except in the "unavoidable" situation. However, from a more objective point of view, the "unavoidable" situation is not found merely in the crisis in which a suicide must die helplessly and therefore more tragically. Whoever commits suicide does so only when it is "unavoidable" to him. Before this unavoidable situation, the one who commits suicide must first have resolute courage.) The instrument that serves for the "spring-board" is after all a woman. Kleist, before he committed suicide, often induced his friends (his male ones) to bear his company. Also, Racine was about to drown himself in the Seine with Molière and Boileau.[5] But, unfortunately, I had no such friends. However, a woman whom I had known agreed to die with me, although this ended as an impossible proposal for us. In the meantime, I gained confidence in dying without a "spring-board." It happened this way, not because I despaired of the fact that there was nobody who would die with me. Rather, it was because I gradually became sentimental and wished to be kind to my wife, even when we were separated by death. At the same time, it was because I had found that committing suicide by myself was easier than doing so with another. Here there was also the advantage of being able to choose freely the time of my suicide.

Finally, what I planned was to commit suicide so craftily that my family would not be suspicious. With respect to this, I somehow reached a certain degree of confidence after several months of preparation. (I cannot write in detail about these matters because of the people who had felt close to me. Even if I had written about these details it is sure that this would not constitute from the legal point of view an abetting the crime of suicide. [There is no more comic charge than this. If this law were applied, it would increase greatly the number of criminals. Pharmacists, gunshop keepers and razor sellers, however much they may say "We don't know," so far as one's will appears in one's words and expressions, they must be suspected at least a little. Moreover, society and the law itself encourage crimes. Finally, what a kind heart most of these criminals have!]) Calmly finishing these preparations, I was now merely playing with death. My feelings hereafter would be close to the words of Mainländer.

4. Gautama Buddha, founder of Buddhism.
5. Heinrich von Kleist, major German dramatist and short-story writer, committed suicide with a woman friend in 1811 at age 34. The 17th-century French playwright Jean Racine was said to have been saved from a suicide attempt by his writer friends Molière and Boileau.

We human beings fear death instinctively because of our being "the man-animal." What is called human vitality is actually nothing but a synonym for animality. I am also but one instance of "the man-animal." However, seeing that I tire of lust and the appetites, I may be losing this animality. The world in which I am now living is a morbid and nervous world that is as perfectly serene as ice. Last night I talked with a prostitute about her wages (!), and felt sad for us human beings who "live for the sake of living." If, by our own choice, we could enter the eternal sleep with resignations, we would certainly have peace, though we might not have happiness. However, it is not certain when I could commit suicide resolutely. But, to me, nature is more beautiful than ever before. You will laugh at my contradiction of both loving the beauty of nature and wishing to commit suicide. But the beauty of nature exists for me in its reflections upon my eyes at the last moment. I saw, loved and also understood more than others. Of that much I feel more or less content amidst my incessant sufferings. Please do not publish this letter for at least several years after my death. For it is not necessarily improbable that my suicide is like a death from sickness.

Additional Note: Having read the biography of Empedocles,[6] I recognized the real antiquity of the desire to become one with God. However, as long as I remained conscious, this note is from one who does not attempt to become God himself. No, this note is from one who attempts to be a great man of stupidity. You probably remember that twenty years ago we argued about "Empedocles at Etna"[7] under the bo-tree. At that age, I was one of those who wished to become one with God.

---

6. Greek philosopher and poet (5th century B.C.E.) who declared himself divine and flung himself into a volcano to prove his immortality.

7. Poem by the Victorian poet Matthew Arnold portraying Empedocles' reflections before his suicide. Gautama Buddha achieved union with God while meditating under a bo tree.

⇒⊹ PERSPECTIVES ⊹⇐
Modernist Memory

One of the defining ironies of twentieth-century literary modernism resides in its paradoxical relationship to memory. While modernists labored mightily to eradicate or at least transcend the past, they had an obsession with memory and remembering. The writers featured here offer an array of literary engagements with memory and the pursuit of remembrance, beginning with T. S. Eliot, whose work is an ambivalent engagement with the past and its rearticulation to the present through poetic language. Eliot's abandonment of his native St. Louis, Missouri, for England was a pursuit of his own ancestral and poetic beginnings and an engagement with a past he sought to leave behind, only to encounter an even more distant past foreshadowing the future. Hence, in his *Four Quartets* Eliot adopts Mary Queen of Scots's enigmatic motto before her execution, "In my end is my beginning." For his part, the poet Constantine Cavafy was a native son of Alexandria, Egypt, a city that hinges the ancient civilizations of the East and the West and the cultures of antiquity and modernity. Cavafy accordingly reaches for a cultural memory that extends to classical Greek literature and its epic tradition. Federico García Lorca, Carlos Drummond de Andrade, Octavio Paz, and Emile Habiby each trip over historical memory in its ironic, lyrical, surprising, but also painful, assaults on the poetic imagination.

⊹⊷⇒⊹⇐⊷⊹

T. S. Eliot
1888–1965

Thomas Stearns Eliot, an American-born poet and playwright who became a British citizen, is one of the towering presences in modern literature. After its publication in 1922, his poem *The Waste Land* achieved international fame as one of the most poignant expressions of the alienation and despair of the modern age. Also revolutionary in the fragmentation of its lyrical form, *The Waste Land* is stitched together from textual fragments that echo a wide range of literary traditions from Sanskrit to Dante and that connect to each other by means of underlying mythological themes. Along with Eliot's poetic and dramatic work, his criticism equally accounts for his extraordinary stature in modernist literature. In hundreds of essays and reviews, Eliot revisited and partly redefined the British literary canon, setting out principles of literary criticism that were to become foundational for the New Criticism that dominated British and American universities from the early 1930s to the late 1950s. Forty years of work as an editor with the publisher Faber and Faber equally contributed to shaping the literary scene. While he was considered a revolutionary poet in the 1910s and 1920s, the combined weight of Eliot's poetry and criticism turned him into a prime representative of the literary establishment by the 1940s, a figure against whose influence a younger generation of poets rose up to rebel: His winning the Nobel Prize in literature in 1948 sealed the conversion of one of the foremost innovators of modern poetry into the figurehead of a new literary standard.

But it wasn't only Eliot's steadily growing reputation as a poet and critic that changed his status as a writer. His own worldview underwent a radical change only five years after the publication of *The Waste Land:* In 1927, Eliot converted to the Anglican church and only a few months later was naturalized as a British citizen. His literary mode of expression changed in similarly fundamental ways, moving away from the fragmentation, meaninglessness, and isolation portrayed in his earlier works to a much more centered and religious outlook. His greatest achievement in this later mode is a set of four poems called *Four Quartets* (1943); there is considerable debate among critics as to whether this work or the earlier *Waste Land* qualifies as his best poetry, and which one expresses the essence of modernist lyric more successfully.

"The Love Song of J. Alfred Prufrock" belongs to Eliot's earliest work, and it is in fact the poem that first made him visible on London's literary scene. Written between 1910 and 1911 and first published in the magazines *Poetry* and *Catholic Anthology* in 1915 with the help of fellow poet Ezra Pound, "Prufrock" addresses a middle-aged man's anxiety over the passing of time and his own aging; but this specific unease is associated in the poem with more diffuse fears over what the meaning of human existence might be and how it could be found or expressed in a society that exhausts itself in empty social rituals and linguistic clichés. Far from offering an alternative to these oppressive social conventions, however, Prufrock's own voice sounds hollow and uncertain. In counterpoint to nineteenth-century poet Robert Browning's dramatic monologues, on whose model Eliot draws in the poem, Prufrock is as fragmented and empty as the society that surrounds him; his condition prefigures the broader panorama of stagnation and estrangement Eliot was to portray in *The Waste Land*.

The Love Song of J. Alfred Prufrock

> *S'io credessi che mia risposta fosse*
> *a persona che mai tornasse al mondo,*
> *questa fiamma staria senza più scosse.*
> *Ma per ciò che giammai di questo fondo*
> *non tornò vivo alcun, s'i'odo il vero,*
> *senza tema d'infamia ti rispondo.*[1]

Let us go then, you and I,
When the evening is spread out against the sky
Like a patient etherised upon a table;
Let us go, through certain half-deserted streets,
5   The muttering retreats
Of restless nights in one-night cheap hotels
And sawdust restaurants with oyster-shells:
Streets that follow like a tedious argument
Of insidious intent
10 To lead you to an overwhelming question . . .
Oh, do not ask, "What is it?"
Let us go and make our visit.

In the room the women come and go
Talking of Michelangelo.

15 The yellow fog that rubs its back upon the window-panes,
The yellow smoke that rubs its muzzle on the window-panes,
Licked its tongue into the corners of the evening,
Lingered upon the pools that stand in drains,
Let fall upon its back the soot that falls from chimneys,
20 Slipped by the terrace, made a sudden leap,
And seeing that it was a soft October night,
Curled once about the house, and fell asleep.

---

1. From Dante's *Inferno* (27.61–66). Dante asks one of the damned souls for its name, and it replies: "If I thought my answer were for one who could return to the world, I would not reply, but as none ever did return alive from this depth, without fear of infamy I answer thee."

And indeed there will be time
For the yellow smoke that slides along the street
25   Rubbing its back upon the window-panes;
There will be time, there will be time
To prepare a face to meet the faces that you meet;
There will be time to murder and create,
And time for all the works and days of hands
30   That lift and drop a question on your plate;
Time for you and time for me,
And time yet for a hundred indecisions,
And for a hundred visions and revisions,
Before the taking of a toast and tea.

35   In the room the women come and go
Talking of Michelangelo.

And indeed there will be time
To wonder, "Do I dare?" and, "Do I dare?"
Time to turn back and descend the stair,
40   With a bald spot in the middle of my hair—
(They will say: "How his hair is growing thin!")
My morning coat, my collar mounting firmly to the chin,
My necktie rich and modest, but asserted by a simple pin—
(They will say: "But how his arms and legs are thin!")
45   Do I dare
Disturb the universe?
In a minute there is time
For decisions and revisions which a minute will reverse.

For I have known them all already, known them all—
50   Have known the evenings, mornings, afternoons,
I have measured out my life with coffee spoons;
I know the voices dying with a dying fall
Beneath the music from a farther room.
        So how should I presume?

55   And I have known the eyes already, known them all—
The eyes that fix you in a formulated phrase,
And when I am formulated, sprawling on a pin,
When I am pinned and wriggling on the wall,
Then how should I begin
60   To spit out all the butt-ends of my days and ways?
        And how should I presume?

And I have known the arms already, known them all—
Arms that are braceleted and white and bare
(But in the lamplight, downed with light brown hair!)
65   Is it perfume from a dress
That makes me so digress?
Arms that lie along a table, or wrap about a shawl.
        And should I then presume?

And how should I begin?

70   Shall I say, I have gone at dusk through narrow streets
And watched the smoke that rises from the pipes
Of lonely men in shirt-sleeves, leaning out of windows? . . .

I should have been a pair of ragged claws
Scuttling across the floors of silent seas.

      . . .

75   And the afternoon, the evening, sleeps so peacefully!
Smoothed by long fingers,
Asleep . . . tired . . . or it malingers,
Stretched on the floor, here beside you and me.
Should I, after tea and cakes and ices,
80   Have the strength to force the moment to its crisis?
But though I have wept and fasted, wept and prayed,
Though I have seen my head (grown slightly bald) brought in upon a platter,[2]
I am no prophet—and here's no great matter;
I have seen the moment of my greatness flicker,
85   And I have seen the eternal Footman hold my coat, and snicker,
And in short, I was afraid.

And would it have been worth it, after all,
After the cups, the marmalade, the tea,
Among the porcelain, among some talk of you and me,
90   Would it have been worth while,
To have bitten off the matter with a smile,
To have squeezed the universe into a ball
To roll it towards some overwhelming question,
To say: "I am Lazarus, come from the dead,
95   Come back to tell you all, I shall tell you all"[3]—
If one, settling a pillow by her head,
    Should say: "That is not what I meant at all.
    That is not it, at all."

And would it have been worth it, after all,
100   Would it have been worth while,
After the sunsets and the dooryards and the sprinkled streets,
After the novels, after the teacups, after the skirts that trail along the floor—
And this, and so much more?—
It is impossible to say just what I mean!
105   But as if a magic lantern[4] threw the nerves in patterns on a screen:
Would it have been worth while
If one, settling a pillow or throwing off a shawl,
And turning toward the window, should say:

2. Cf. Matthew 14. John the Baptist was beheaded by Herod and his head was brought to his wife, Herodias, on a platter.
3. Cf. John 11. Jesus raised Lazarus from the grave after he had been dead four days.
4. A device that employs a candle to project images, rather like a slide projector.

"That is not it at all,

110   That is not what I meant, at all."

                     . . .

No! I am not Prince Hamlet, nor was meant to be;

Am an attendant lord, one that will do

To swell a progress, start a scene or two,

Advise the prince; no doubt, an easy tool,

115 Deferential, glad to be of use,

Politic, cautious, and meticulous;

Full of high sentence, but a bit obtuse;

At times, indeed, almost ridiculous—

Almost, at times, the Fool.

120 I grow old . . . I grow old . . .

I shall wear the bottoms of my trousers rolled.

Shall I part my hair behind? Do I dare to eat a peach?

I shall wear white flannel trousers, and walk upon the beach.

I have heard the mermaids singing, each to each.

125 I do not think that they will sing to me.

I have seen them riding seaward on the waves

Combing the white hair of the waves blown back

When the wind blows the water white and black.

We have lingered in the chambers of the sea

130 By sea-girls wreathed with seaweed red and brown

Till human voices wake us, and we drown.

The Waste Land[1]

"Nam Sibyllam quidem Cumis ego ipse oculis meis vidi in ampulla

pendere, et cum illi pueri dicerent: Σίβυλλα τί θέλεις;

respondebat illa: ἀποθανεῖν θέλω."[2]

For Ezra Pound
il miglior fabbro.[3]

I. THE BURIAL OF THE DEAD

April is the cruellest month, breeding

Lilacs out of the dead land, mixing

---

1. Not only the title, but the plan and a good deal of the incidental symbolism of the poem were suggested by Miss Jessie L. Weston's book on the Grail legend: *From Ritual to Romance* (Cambridge). Indeed, so deeply am I indebted, Miss Weston's book will elucidate the difficulties of the poem much better than my notes can do; and I recommend it (apart from the great interest of the book itself) to any who think such elucidation of the poem worth the trouble. To another work of anthropology I am indebted in general, one which has influenced our generation profoundly; I mean *The Golden Bough;* I have used especially the two volumes *Adonis, Attis, Osiris.* Anyone who is acquainted with these works will immediately recognize in the poem certain references to vegetation cere- monies [Eliot's note]. Sir James Frazer (1854–1941) brought out the 12 volumes of *The Golden Bough,* a vast work of anthropology, comparative mythology and religion, between 1890 and 1915, with a supplement published in 1936.

2. From the *Satyricon* of Petronius (1st century C.E.). "For once I myself saw with my own eyes the Sybil at Cumae hanging in a cage, and when the boys said to her, 'Sybil, what do you want?' she replied, 'I want to die.'" The Sybil was granted anything she wished by Apollo, if only she would be his; she made the mistake of asking for everlasting life, without asking for eternal youth.

3. "The better craftsman." Pound played a crucial role in editing *The Waste Land* before its publication.

Memory and desire, stirring
Dull roots with spring rain.
5   Winter kept us warm, covering
Earth in forgetful snow, feeding
A little life with dried tubers.
Summer surprised us, coming over the Starnbergersee[4]
With a shower of rain; we stopped in the colonnade,
10   And went on in sunlight, into the Hofgarten,[5]
And drank coffee, and talked for an hour.
Bin gar keine Russin, stamm' aus Litauen, echt deutsch.[6]
And when we were children, staying at the arch-duke's,
My cousin's, he took me out on a sled,
15   And I was frightened. He said, Marie,
Marie, hold on tight. And down we went.
In the mountains, there you feel free.
I read, much of the night, and go south in the winter.

What are the roots that clutch, what branches grow
20   Out of this stony rubbish? Son of man,[7]
You cannot say, or guess, for you know only
A heap of broken images, where the sun beats,
And the dead tree gives no shelter, the cricket no relief,[8]
And the dry stone no sound of water. Only
25   There is shadow under this red rock,
(Come in under the shadow of this red rock),
And I will show you something different from either
Your shadow at morning striding behind you
Or your shadow at evening rising to meet you;
30   I will show you fear in a handful of dust.

> *Frisch weht der Wind*
> *Der Heimat zu*
> *Mein Irisch Kind,*
> *Wo weilest du?*[9]

35   "You gave me hyacinths first a year ago;
They called me the hyacinth girl."
—Yet when we came back, late, from the hyacinth garden,
Your arms full, and your hair wet, I could not
Speak, and my eyes failed, I was neither
40   Living nor dead, and I knew nothing,

---

4. A lake near Munich.
5. A public park in Munich, with a zoo and cafés.
6. "I'm not a Russian at all; I come from Lithuania, a true German."
7. Cf. Ezekiel 2.7 [Eliot's note]. Ezekiel 2.8 reads: "But thou, son of man, hear what I say unto thee; Be not thou rebellious like that rebellious house: open thy mouth, and eat that I give thee."
8. Cf. Ecclesiastes 12.5 [Eliot's note]. "They shall be afraid of that which is high, and fears shall be in the way, and the almond tree shall flourish, and the grasshopper shall be a burden, and desire shall fail."
9. V. *Tristan and Isolde*, i, verses 5–8 [Eliot's note]. In Wagner's opera, Tristan sings this about Isolde, the woman he is leaving behind as he sails for home: "Fresh blows the wind to the homeland; my Irish child, where are you staying?"

Looking into the heart of light, the silence.
Oed' und leer das Meer.[1]

Madame Sosostris, famous clairvoyante,
Had a bad cold, nevertheless
45   Is known to be the wisest woman in Europe,
With a wicked pack of cards.[2] Here, said she,
Is your card, the drowned Phoenician Sailor,
(Those are pearls that were his eyes.[3] Look!)
Here is Belladonna, the Lady of the Rocks,
50   The lady of situations.
Here is the man with three staves, and here the Wheel,
And here is the one-eyed merchant, and this card,
Which is blank, is something he carries on his back,
Which I am forbidden to see. I do not find
55   The Hanged Man.[4] Fear death by water.
I see crowds of people, walking round in a ring.
Thank you. If you see dear Mrs. Equitone,
Tell her I bring the horoscope myself:
One must be so careful these days.

60   Unreal City,[5]
Under the brown fog of a winter dawn,
A crowd flowed over London Bridge, so many,
I had not thought death had undone so many.[6]
Sighs, short and infrequent, were exhaled,[7]
65   And each man fixed his eyes before his feet.
Flowed up the hill and down King William Street,
To where Saint Mary Woolnoth kept the hours
With a dead sound on the final stroke of nine.[8]
There I saw one I knew, and stopped him, crying: "Stetson!
70   You who were with me in the ships at Mylae![9]

1. Id. iii, verse 24 [Eliot's note]. Tristan is dying and wait-ing for Isolde to come to him, but a shepherd, whom Tris-tan has hired to keep watch for her ship, reports only "Desolate and empty the sea."
2. I am not familiar with the exact constitution of the Tarot pack of cards, from which I have obviously de-parted to suit my own convenience. The Hanged Man, a member of the traditional pack, fits my purpose in two ways: because he is associated in my mind with the Hanged God of Frazer, and because I associated him with the hooded figure in the passage of the disciples to Em-maus in Part V. The Phoenician Sailor and the Merchant appear later; also the "crowds of people," and Death by Water is executed in Part IV. The Man with Three Staves (an authentic member of the Tarot pack) I associate, quite arbitrarily, with the Fisher King Himself [Eliot's note].
3. From Ariel's song, in Shakespeare's *The Tempest*: "Full fathom five thy father lies; / Of his bones are coral made; / Those are pearls that were his eyes: / Nothing of him that doth fade, / But doth suffer a sea-change" (1.2.399–403).

4. The tarot card that depicts a man hanging by one foot from a cross.
5. Cf. Baudelaire: "Fourmillante cité, cité pleine de rêves, / Où le spectre en plein jour raccroche le passant" [Eliot's note]. From *The Flowers of Evil*. "Swarming city, city full of dreams, / where in plain daylight the spectre accosts the passer-by."
6. Cf. *Inferno*, iii.55–7: "si lunga tratta / di gente, ch'io non avrei mai creduto / che morte tanta n'avesse disfatta" [Eliot's note]. "Such an endless train, / Of people, it never would have entered in my head / There were so many men whom death had slain."
7. Cf. *Inferno*, iv. 25–7: "Ouivi, secondo che per as-coltare, / non avea pianto, ma' che di sospiri, / che l'aura eterna facevan tremare" [Eliot's note]. "We heard no loud complaint, no crying there, / No sound of grief except the sound of sighing / Quivering forever through the eternal air."
8. A phenomenon which I have often noticed [Eliot's note].
9. The Battle of Mylae (260 B.C.E.) in the First Punic War.

That corpse you planted last year in your garden,
Has it begun to sprout? Will it bloom this year?
Or has the sudden frost disturbed its bed?
O keep the Dog far hence, that's friend to men,[1]
75 Or with his nails he'll dig it up again!
You! hypocrite lecteur!—mon semblable,—mon frère!"[2]

II. A GAME OF CHESS[3]

The Chair she sat in, like a burnished throne,[4]
Glowed on the marble, where the glass
Held up by standards wrought with fruited vines
80 From which a golden Cupidon peeped out
(Another hid his eyes behind his wing)
Doubled the flames of sevenbranched candelabra
Reflecting light upon the table as
The glitter of her jewels rose to meet it,
85 From satin cases poured in rich profusion.
In vials of ivory and coloured glass
Unstoppered, lurked her strange synthetic perfumes,
Unguent, powdered, or liquid—troubled, confused
And drowned the sense in odours; stirred by the air
90 That freshened from the window, these ascended
In fattening the prolonged candle-flames,
Flung their smoke into the laquearia,[5]
Stirring the pattern on the coffered ceiling.
Huge sea-wood fed with copper
95 Burned green and orange, framed by the coloured stone,
In which sad light a carvèd dolphin swam.
Above the antique mantel was displayed
As though a window gave upon the sylvan scene[6]
The change of Philomel, by the barbarous king[7]
100 So rudely forced; yet there the nightingale[8]
Filled all the desert with inviolable voice
And still she cried, and still the world pursues,
"Jug Jug" to dirty ears.
And other withered stumps of time

1. Cf. the Dirge in Webster's *White Devil* [Eliot's note].
2. *V.* Baudelaire, Preface to *Fleurs du Mal* [Eliot's note]. "Hypocrite reader—my double—my brother!"
3. Cf. Thomas Middleton's drama *A Game at Chess* (1625), a political satire.
4. Cf. *Antony and Cleopatra*, II. ii. 190 [Eliot's note].
5. "Laquearia. *V. Aeneid*, I.726: "dependent lychni laque-aribus aureis / incensi, et noctem flammis funalia vin-cunt." [Eliot's note]. "Burning lamps hang from the gold-panelled ceiling / And torches dispel the night with their flames"; a *laquearia* is a panelled ceiling. The passage from Virgil's *Aeneid* describes the banquet given by Dido for her lover Aeneas.
6. "Sylvan scene. *V.* Milton, *Paradise Lost*, iv. 140 [Eliot's note]. "And over head up grew / Insuperable height of loftiest shade, / Cedar, and Pine, and Fir, and branching Palm, / A Silvan Scene, and as the ranks ascend / Shade above shade, a woody Theatre / Of stateliest view." The passage describes the Garden of Eden, as seen through Satan's eyes. A sylvan scene is one taking place in a forest.
7. *V.* Ovid, *Metamorphoses*, vi, Philomela [Eliot's note]. Philomela was raped by King Tereus, her sister's husband, and was then changed into a nightingale.
8. Cf. Part III, l. 204 [Eliot's note].

105   Were told upon the walls; staring forms
Leaned out, leaning, hushing the room enclosed.
Footsteps shuffled on the stair.
Under the firelight, under the brush, her hair
Spread out in fiery points

110   Glowed into words, then would be savagely still.

    "My nerves are bad to-night. Yes, bad. Stay with me.
Speak to me. Why do you never speak. Speak.
    What are you thinking of? What thinking? What?
I never know what you are thinking. Think."

115   I think we are in rats' alley[9]
Where the dead men lost their bones.

"What is that noise?"
                The wind under the door.[1]
    "What is that noise now? What is the wind doing?"

120   Nothing again nothing.
                          "Do
"You know nothing? Do you see nothing? Do you remember
Nothing?"
    I remember

125   Those are pearls that were his eyes.
"Are you alive, or not? Is there nothing in your head?"[2]
                                  But

O O O O that Shakespeherian Rag—[3]
It's so elegant

130   So intelligent
"What shall I do now? What shall I do?"
"I shall rush out as I am, and walk the street
With my hair down, so. What shall we do tomorrow?
What shall we ever do?"

135   The hot water at ten.
And if it rains, a closed car at four.
And we shall play a game of chess,
Pressing lidless eyes and waiting for a knock upon the door.[4]

When Lil's husband got demobbed,° I said—   *demobilized*

140   I didn't mince my words, I said to her myself,
HURRY UP PLEASE ITS TIME[5]
Now Albert's coming back, make yourself a bit smart.
He'll want to know what you done with that money he gave you
To get yourself some teeth. He did, I was there.

9. Cf. Part III, 1. 195 [Eliot's note].
1. Cf. Webster: "Is the wind in that door still?" [Eliot's note]. From John Webster's *The Devil's Law Case*, 3.2.162. The doctor asks this question when he discovers that a "murder victim" is still breathing.
2. Cf. Part I, l. 37, 48 [Eliot's note].

3. Quoting an American ragtime song featured in Ziegfield's Follies of 1912.
4. Cf. the game of chess in Middleton's *Women beware Women* [Eliot's note].
5. A British pub-keeper's call for a last round before closing.

145 You have them all out, Lil, and get a nice set,
He said, I swear, I can't bear to look at you.
And no more can't I, I said, and think of poor Albert,
He's been in the army four years, he wants a good time,
And if you don't give it him, there's others will, I said.
150 Oh is there, she said. Something o' that, I said.
Then I'll know who to thank, she said, and give me a straight look.
HURRY UP PLEASE ITS TIME
If you don't like it you can get on with it, I said.
Others can pick and choose if you can't.
155 But if Albert makes off, it won't be for lack of telling.
You ought to be ashamed, I said, to look so antique.
(And her only thirty-one.)
I can't help it, she said, pulling a long face,
It's them pills I took, to bring it off, she said.
160 (She's had five already, and nearly died of young George.)
The chemist[6] said it would be all right, but I've never been the same.
You *are* a proper fool, I said.
Well, if Albert won't leave you alone, there it is, I said,
What you get married for if you don't want children?
165 HURRY UP PLEASE ITS TIME
Well, that Sunday Albert was home, they had a hot gammon,°   *ham*
And they asked me in to dinner, to get the beauty of it hot—
HURRY UP PLEASE ITS TIME
HURRY UP PLEASE ITS TIME
170 Goonight Bill. Goonight Lou. Goonight May. Goonight.
Ta ta. Goonight. Goonight.
Good night, ladies, good night, sweet ladies, good night, good night.[7]

III. THE FIRE SERMON

The river's tent is broken; the last fingers of leaf
Clutch and sink into the wet bank. The wind
175 Crosses the brown land, unheard. The nymphs are departed.
Sweet Thames, run softly, till I end my song.[8]
The river bears no empty bottles, sandwich papers,
Silk handkerchiefs, cardboard boxes, cigarette ends
Or other testimony of summer nights. The nymphs are departed.
180 And their friends, the loitering heirs of City directors;
Departed, have left no addresses.
By the waters of Leman[9] I sat down and wept . . .
Sweet Thames, run softly till I end my song,

6. Pharmacist.
7. Ophelia speaks these words in Shakespeare's *Hamlet,* and they are understood by the King as certain evidence of her insanity: "Good night ladies, good night. Sweet ladies, good night, good night" (4.5.72–73).
8. V. Spenser, *Prothalamion* [Eliot's note]; Spenser's poem (1596) celebrates the double marriage of Lady Elizabeth and Lady Katherine Somerset.
9. Lake Geneva. The line echoes Psalm 137, in which, exiled in Babylon, the Hebrew poets are too full of grief to sing.

Sweet Thames, run softly, for I speak not loud or long.
185 But at my back in a cold blast I hear
The rattle of the bones, and chuckle spread from ear to ear.

A rat crept softly through the vegetation
Dragging its slimy belly on the bank
While I was fishing in the dull canal
190 On a winter evening round behind the gashouse
Musing upon the king my brother's wreck
And on the king my father's death before him.[1]
White bodies naked on the low damp ground
And bones cast in a little low dry garret,
195 Rattled by the rat's foot only, year to year.
But at my back from time to time I hear[2]
The sound of horns and motors, which shall bring[3]
Sweeney to Mrs. Porter in the spring.
O the moon shone bright on Mrs. Porter[4]
200 And on her daughter
They wash their feet in soda water
Et O ces voix d'enfants, chantant dans la coupole![5]

Twit twit twit
Jug jug jug jug jug jug
205 So rudely forc'd.
Tereu

Unreal City
Under the brown fog of a winter noon
Mr. Eugenides, the Smyrna[6] merchant
210 Unshaven, with a pocket full of currants
C.i.f.[7] London: documents at sight,
Asked me in demotic° French   *vulgar*
To luncheon at the Cannon Street Hotel[8]
Followed by a weekend at the Metropole.[9]

215 At the violet hour, when the eyes and back
Turn upward from the desk, when the human engine waits
Like a taxi throbbing waiting,

---

1. Cf. *The Tempest*, I. ii [Eliot's note].
2. Cf. Marvell, *To His Coy Mistress* [Eliot's note]. "But at my back I always hear / Time's wingèd chariot hurrying near."
3. Cf. Day, *Parliament of Bees:* "When of the sudden, listening, you shall hear, / A noise of horns and hunting, which shall bring / Actaeon to Diana in the spring, / Where all shall see her naked skin . . ." [Eliot's note].
4. I do not know the origin of the ballad from which these are taken: it was reported to me from Sydney, Australia [Eliot's note]. Sung by Australian soldiers in World War I: "O the moon shone bright on Mrs. Porter / And on the daughter / Of Mrs. Porter / They wash their feet in soda water / And so they oughter / To keep them clean."

5. V. Verlaine, *Parsifal* [Eliot's note]. "And O those children's voices singing in the dome." Paul Verlaine's sonnet describes Parsifal, who keeps himself pure in hopes of seeing the holy grail, and has his feet washed before entering the castle.
6. Seaport in western Turkey.
7. The currants were quoted at a price "carriage and insurance free to London"; and the Bill of Lading, etc., were to be handed to the buyer upon payment of the sight draft [Eliot's note].
8. A Hotel in London near the train station used for travel to and from continental Europe.
9. An upscale seaside resort hotel in Brighton.

I Tiresias,[1] though blind, throbbing between two lives,
Old man with wrinkled female breasts, can see
220 At the violet hour, the evening hour that strives
Homeward, and brings the sailor home from sea,[2]
The typist home at teatime, clears her breakfast, lights
Her stove, and lays out food in tins.
Out of the window perilously spread
225 Her drying combinations touched by the sun's last rays,
On the divan are piled (at night her bed)
Stockings, slippers, camisoles, and stays.
I Tiresias, old man with wrinkled dugs
Perceived the scene, and foretold the rest—
230 I too awaited the expected guest.
He, the young man carbuncular,° arrives,   *pimply*
A small house agent's clerk, with one bold stare,
One of the low on whom assurance sits
As a silk hat on a Bradford[3] millionaire.
235 The time is now propitious, as he guesses,
The meal is ended, she is bored and tired,
Endeavours to engage her in caresses
Which still are unreproved, if undesired.
Flushed and decided, he assaults at once;
240 Exploring hands encounter no defence;
His vanity requires no response,
And makes a welcome of indifference.
(And I Tiresias have foresuffered all
Enacted on this same divan or bed;
245 I who have sat by Thebes below the wall
And walked among the lowest of the dead.)

1. Tiresias, although a mere spectator and not indeed a "character," is yet the most important personage in the poem, uniting all the rest. Just as the one-eyed merchant, seller of currants, melts into the Phoenician Sailor, and the latter is not wholly distinct from Ferdinand Prince of Naples, so all the women are one woman, and the two sexes meet in Tiresias. What Tiresias *sees*, in fact, is the substance of the poem. The whole passage from Ovid is of great anthropological interest: ". . .Cum Iunone iocos et 'maior vestra profecto est / Quam, quae contingit maribus,' dixisse, 'voluptas.' / Illa negat; placuit quae sit sententia docti / Quaerere Tiresiae: venus huic erat utraque nota. / Nam duo magnorum viridi coeuntia silva / Corpora serpentum baculi violaverat ictu / Deque viro factus, mirabile, femina septem / Egerat autumnos; octavo rursus eosdem / Vidit et 'est vestrae si tanta potentia plagae,' / Dixit 'ut auctoris sortem in contraria mutet, / Nunc quoque vos feriam!' percussis anguibus isdem / Forma prior rediit genetivaque venit imago. / Arbiter hic igitur sumptus de lite iocosa / Dicta Iovis firmat; gravius Saturnia iusto / Nec pro materia fertur doluisse suique / Iudicis aeterna damnavit lumina nocte, / At pater omnipotens (neque enim licet inrita cuiquam / Facta dei fecisse deo) pro lumine adempto / Scire futura dedit poenamque levavit honore" [Eliot's note]. This passage from Ovid's *Metamorphoses* describes Tiresias's sex change: "[The story goes that once Jove, having drunk a great deal,] jested with Juno. He said, 'Your pleasure in love is really greater than that enjoyed by men.' She denied it; so they decided to seek the opinion of the wise Tiresias, for he knew both aspects of love. For once, with a blow of his staff, he had committed violence on two huge snakes as they copulated in the green forest; and—wonderful to tell—was turned from a man into a woman and thus spent seven years. In the eighth year he saw the same snakes again and said: 'If a blow struck at you is so powerful that it changes the sex of the giver, I will now strike at you again.' With these words he struck the snakes, and his former shape was restored to him and he became as he had been born. So he was appointed arbitrator in the playful quarrel, and supported Jove's statement. It is said that Saturnia [i.e., Juno] was quite disproportionately upset, and condemned the arbitrator to perpetual blindness. But the almighty father (for no god may undo what has been done by another god), in return for the sight that was taken away, gave him the power to know the future and so lightened the penalty paid by the honor."

2. This may not appear as exact as Sappho's lines but I had in mind the "longshore" or "dory" fisherman, who returns at nightfall [Eliot's note]. "Hesperus, thou bringst home all things bright morning scattered: thou bringest the sheep, the goat, the child to the mother."

3. An industrial town in Yorkshire; many of its residents became wealthy during World War I.

Bestows one final patronising kiss,
And gropes his way, finding the stairs unlit . . .

She turns and looks a moment in the glass,
250   Hardly aware of her departed lover;
Her brain allows one half-formed thought to pass:
"Well now that's done: and I'm glad it's over."
When lovely woman stoops to folly and[4]
Paces about her room again, alone,
255   She smoothes her hair with automatic hand,
And puts a record on the gramophone.

"This music crept by me upon the waters"[5]
And along the Strand, up Queen Victoria Street.
O City city, I can sometimes hear
260   Beside a public bar in Lower Thames Street,
The pleasant whining of a mandoline
And a clatter and a chatter from within
Where fishmen lounge at noon: where the walls
Of Magnus Martyr[6] hold
265   Inexplicable splendour of Ionian white and gold.

> The river sweats[7]
> Oil and tar
> The barges drift
> With the turning tide
> 270   Red sails
> Wide
> To leeward, swing on the heavy spar.
> The barges wash
> Drifting logs
> 275   Down Greenwich reach
> Past the Isle of Dogs.[8]
>   Weialala leia
>   Wallala leialala

> Elizabeth and Leicester[9]
> 280   Beating oars

---

4. V. Goldsmith, the song in *The Vicar of Wakefield* [Eliot's note]. Oliver Goldsmith's character Olivia, on returning to the place where she was seduced, sings, "When lovely woman stoops to folly / And finds too late that men betray / What charm can soothe her melancholy, / What art can wash her guilt away? / The only art her guilt to cover, / To hide her shame from every eye, / To give repentance to her lover / And wring his bosom—is to die."
5. V. *The Tempest,* as above [Eliot's note].
6. The interior of St. Magnus Martyr is to my mind one of the finest among Wren's interiors. See *The Proposed Demolition of Nineteen City Churches* (P.S. King & Son, Ltd.) [Eliot's note].
7. The Song of the (three) Thames-daughters begins here. From line 292 to 306 inclusive they speak in turn. V. *Götterdämmerung,* III.I: the Rhine-daughters [Eliot's note].

In Richard Wagner's opera *Twilight of the Gods,* the Rhine maidens, when their gold is stolen, lament that the beauty of the river is gone.
8. Greenwich is a borough on the south bank of the River Thames; the Isle of Dogs is a peninsula in East London formed by a sharp bend in the Thames called Greenwich Reach.
9. V. Froude, *Elizabeth,* vol. I, Ch. iv, letter of De Quadra to Philip of Spain: "In the afternoon we were in a barge, watching the games on the river. (The Queen) was alone with Lord Robert and myself on the poop, when they began to talk nonsense, and went so far that Lord Robert at last said, as I was on the spot there was no reason why they should not be married if the queen pleased" [Eliot's note].

The stern was formed
A gilded shell
Red and gold
The brisk swell
285 Rippled both shores
Southwest wind
Carried down stream
The peal of bells
White towers
290   Weialala leia
            Wallala leialala

"Trams and dusty trees.
Highbury bore me. Richmond and Kew[1]
Undid me. By Richmond I raised my knees
295 Supine on the floor of a narrow canoe."

"My feet are at Moorgate,[2] and my heart
Under my feet. After the event
He wept. He promised 'a new start.'
I made no comment. What should I resent?"

300 "On Margate Sands.[3]
I can connect
Nothing with nothing.
The broken fingernails of dirty hands.
My people humble people who expect
305 Nothing."
            la la

To Carthage then I came[4]

Burning burning burning burning[5]
O Lord Thou pluckest me out[6]
310 O Lord Thou pluckest

burning

IV. DEATH BY WATER

Phlebas the Phoenician, a fortnight dead,
Forgot the cry of gulls, and the deep sea swell

1. "Cf. *Purgatorio*, V. 133: "Ricorditi di me, che son la Pia; / Siena mi fe', disfecemi Maremma." [Eliot's note]. "Remember me, that I am called Piety; / Sienna made me and Maremma undid me." Highbury, Richmond, and Kew are suburbs of London near the Thames.
2. A slum in East London.
3. A seaside resort in the Thames estuary.
4. *V.* St. Augustine's *Confessions*: "to Carthage then I came, where a cauldron of unholy loves sang all about mine ears" [Eliot's note].
5. The complete text of the Buddha's Fire Sermon (which corresponds in importance to the Sermon on the Mount) from which these words are taken, will be found translated in the late Henry Clarke Warren's *Buddhism in Translation* (Harvard Oriental Series). Mr. Warren was one of the great pioneers of Buddhist studies in the Occident [Eliot's note].
6. From St. Augustine's *Confessions* again. The collocation of these two representatives of eastern and western asceticism, as the culmination of this part of the poem, is not an accident [Eliot's note]. Augustine writes: "I entangle my steps with these outward beauties, but thou pluckest me out, O Lord, Thou pluckest me out."

And the profit and loss.
                          A current under sea
315   Picked his bones in whispers. As he rose and fell
He passed the stages of his age and youth
Entering the whirlpool.
                          Gentile or Jew
320   O you who turn the wheel and look to windward,
Consider Phlebas, who was once handsome and tall as you.

V. WHAT THE THUNDER SAID[7]

After the torchlight red on sweaty faces
After the frosty silence in the gardens
After the agony in stony places
325   The shouting and the crying
Prison and palace and reverberation
Of thunder of spring over distant mountains
He who was living is now dead
We who were living are now dying
330   With a little patience

Here is no water but only rock
Rock and no water and the sandy road
The road winding above among the mountains
Which are mountains of rock without water
335   If there were water we should stop and drink
Amongst the rock one cannot stop or think
Sweat is dry and feet are in the sand
If there were only water amongst the rock
Dead mountain mouth of carious° teeth that cannot spit   *rotting*
340   Here one can neither stand nor lie nor sit
There is not even silence in the mountains
But dry sterile thunder without rain
There is not even solitude in the mountains
But red sullen faces sneer and snarl
345   From doors of mudcracked houses
                              If there were water

And no rock
If there were rock
And also water
350   And water
A spring
A pool among the rock
If there were the sound of water only
Not the cicada
355   And dry grass singing

---

7. In the first part of Part V three themes are employed: the journey to Emmaus, the approach to the Chapel Perilous (see Miss Weston's book), and the present decay of eastern Europe [Eliot's note].

But sound of water over a rock
Where the hermit-thrush sings in the pine trees
Drip drop drip drop drop drop drop[8]
But there is no water

360 Who is the third who walks always beside you?
When I count, there are only you and I together[9]
But when I look ahead up the white road
There is always another one walking beside you
Gliding wrapt in a brown mantle, hooded
365 I do not know whether a man or a woman
—But who is that on the other side of you?

What is that sound high in the air[1]
Murmur of maternal lamentation
Who are those hooded hordes swarming
370 Over endless plains, stumbling in cracked earth
Ringed by the flat horizon only
What is the city over the mountains
Cracks and reforms and bursts in the violet air
Falling towers
375 Jerusalem Athens Alexandria
Vienna London
Unreal

A woman drew her long black hair out tight
And fiddled whisper music on those strings
380 And bats with baby faces in the violet light
Whistled, and beat their wings
And crawled head downward down a blackened wall
And upside down in air were towers
Tolling reminiscent bells, that kept the hours
385 And voices singing out of empty cisterns and exhausted wells

In this decayed hole among the mountains
In the faint moonlight, the grass is singing
Over the tumbled graves, about the chapel
There is the empty chapel, only the wind's home.

---

8. This is *Turdus aonalaschkae pallasii*, the hermit-thrush which I have heard in Quebec County. Chapman says (*Handbook of Birds of Eastern North America*) "it is most at home in secluded woodland and thickety retreats. . . . Its notes are not remarkable for variety or volume, but in purity and sweetness of tone and exquisite modulation they are unequalled." Its "water-dripping song" is justly celebrated [Eliot's note].
9. The following lines were stimulated by the account of one of the Antarctic expeditions (I forget which, but I think one of Shackleton's): it was related that the party of explorers, at the extremity of their strength, had the constant delusion that there was one more member than could actually be counted [Eliot's note]. There seems also to be an echo of the account of Jesus meeting his disciples on the road to Emmaus: "Jesus himself drew near, and went with them. But their eyes were holden that they should not know him" (Luke 24.13–16).
1. Cf. Hermann Hesse, *Blick ins Chaos:* "Schon ist halb Europa, schon ist zumindest der halbe Osten Europas auf dem Wege zum Chaos, fährt betrunken im heiligen Wahn am Abgrund entlang und singt dazu, singt betrunken und hymnisch wie Dmitri Karamasoff sang. Ueber diese Lieder lacht der Bürger beleidigt, der Heilige und Seher hört sie mit Tränen" [Eliot's note]. "Already half of Europe, already at least half of Eastern Europe, on the way to chaos, drives drunk in sacred infatuation along the edge of the precipice, singing drunkenly, as though singing hymns, as Dmitri Karamazov sang. The offended bourgeois laughs at the songs; the saint and the seer hear them with tears."

380 It has no windows, and the door swings,
     Dry bones can harm no one.
     Only a cock stood on the rooftree
     Co co rico co co rico
     In a flash of lightning. Then a damp gust
395 Bringing rain

     Ganga[2] was sunken, and the limp leaves
     Waited for rain, while the black clouds
     Gathered far distant, over Himavant.[3]
     The jungle crouched, humped in silence.
400 Then spoke the thunder
     DA
     Datta: what have we given?[4]
     My friend, blood shaking my heart
     The awful daring of a moment's surrender
405 Which an age of prudence can never retract
     By this, and this only, we have existed
     Which is not to be found in our obituaries
     Or in memories draped by the beneficent spider[5]
     Or under seals broken by the lean solicitor
410 In our empty rooms
     DA
     Dayadhvam: I have heard the key[6]
     Turn in the door once and turn once only
     We think of the key, each in his prison
415 Thinking of the key, each confirms a prison
     Only at nightfall, aethereal rumours
     Revive for a moment a broken Coriolanus[7]
     DA
     Damyata: The boat responded
420 Gaily, to the hand expert with sail and oar
     The sea was calm, your heart would have responded
     Gaily, when invited, beating obedient
     To controlling hands

---

2. The river Ganges.

3. The Himalayas.

4. "Datta, dayadhvam, damyata" (Give, sympathize, control). The fable of the meaning of the Thunder is found in the *Brihadaranyaka—Upanishad*, 5, I. A translation is found in Deussen's *Sechzig Upanishads des Veda*, p. 489 [Eliot's note]. "That very thing is repented even today by the heavenly voice, in the form of thunder, in the form of thunder as 'Da,' 'Da,' 'Da'. . . . Therefore one should practice these three things: self-control, alms-giving, and compassion."

5. Cf. Webster, *The White Devil*, v. vi: ". . . they'll remarry / Ere the worm pierce your winding-sheet, ere the spider / make a thin curtain for your epitaphs" [Eliot's note].

6. Cf. *Inferno*, xxxiii. 46: "ed io sentii chiavar l'uscio di sotto / all'orrible torre." Also F. H. *Bradley, Appearance and Reality*, p. 346: "My external sensations are no less private to myself than are my thoughts or my feelings. In either case my experience falls within my own circle, a circle closed on the outside; and, with all its elements alike, every sphere is opaque to the others which surround it. . . . In brief, regarded as an existence which appears in a soul, the whole world for each is peculiar and private to that soul." [Eliot's note]. In the passage from the *Inferno*, Ugolino tells Dante of his imprisonment and starvation until he became so desperate that he ate his children: "And I heard below me the door of the horrible tower being locked."

7. In Shakespeare's play of the same name, Coriolanus is a Roman general who is exiled and later leads the enemy in an attack against the Romans.

I sat upon the shore
425 Fishing, with the arid plain behind me[8]
Shall I at least set my lands in order?
London Bridge is falling down falling down falling down
Poi s'ascose nel foco che gli affina[9]
Quando fiam uti chelidon—O swallow swallow[1]
430 *Le Prince d'Aquitaine à la tour abolie*[2]
These fragments I have shored against my ruins
Why then Ile fit you. Hieronymo's mad againe.[3]
Datta. Dayadhvam. Damyata.
Shantih   shantih   shantih[4]

Constantine Cavafy
1863–1933

Born Konstantinos Petrou Kavafis in Alexandria, Egypt, to a Greek family from Istanbul, Turkey, Constantine Cavafy has enjoyed a posthumous reputation much greater than his fame during his lifetime. He spent a number of his formative years in England, lived for a couple of years in Istanbul as an adolescent, and then lived for a time in France. He was fluent in Turkish, English, French, and Italian, but he wrote in Greek, his mother tongue. He was employed as a clerk at a government office in the Ministry of Public Works of Egypt in his native Alexandria. Though he became one of the most prominent poets of the Greek language in the twentieth century, he visited Greece only occasionally and for very brief periods. His first publications were chapbooks of verse privately printed in 1904 and 1910. While his reputation as a poet grew in Alexandria, the English-reading public was not familiar with Cavafy's work until the British novelist E. M. Forster helped distribute his poetry after the two met in Alexandria in 1917, a meeting from which a long friendship and correspondence would ensue. There is an unadorned directness to Cavafy's poetry. As the English poet W. H. Auden has noted, imagery, simile, and metaphor are largely absent from Cavafy's poems, which are given to plain, factual statement. The themes of Cavafy's poetry are often historical, focused principally on Alexandrian Greek and Roman history. In their unadorned simplicity, however, Cavafy's poems express a skepticism and nonconformist critique of traditional morality, religious values, and nationalistic enthusiasms. His sense of history is keen, as is his insight into the illusions of historical grandeur. He was among the first to write openly of homosexuality, yet the self-centeredness of passion does not escape his scrutiny or his skepticism.

8. *V.* Weston, *From Ritual to Romance;* chapter on the Fisher King [Eliot's note].

9. *V. Purgatorio*, xxvi.148: "Ara vos prec per aquella valor / que vos condus al som de l'escalina, / sovegna vos a temps de ma dolor." / "Poi s'ascose nel foco che gli affina" [Eliot's note]. In this passage, the poet Arnaut Daniel speaks to Dante: "Now I pray you, by the goodness that guides you to the top of this staircase, be mindful in time of my suffering."

1. *V. Pervigilium Veneris.* Cf. Philomela in Parts II and III [Eliot's note]. Philomel asks, "When shall I be a swallow?"

2. *V.* Gerard de Nerval, Sonnet *El Desdichado* [Eliot's note]. "The Prince of Aquitaine in the ruined tower."

3. *V.* Kyd's *Spanish Tragedy* [Eliot's note]. The subtitle of Kyd's play is, "Hieronymo's Mad Againe." His son having been murdered, Hieronymo is asked to compose a court play, to which he responds "Why then Ile fit you"; his son's murder is avenged in the course of the play.

4. Shantih. Repeated as here, a formal ending to an Upanishad. "The Peace which passeth understanding" is a feeble translation of the content of this word [Eliot's note]. The Upanishads are poetic commentaries on the Hindu Scriptures.

PRONUNCIATIONS:
Cavafy: cah-VAH-fee
Laistrygonians: LAY-strih-GO-nee-ans
Poseidon: poh-SIGH-dun

Days of 1908[1]

He was out of work that year,
so he lived off card games,
backgammon, and borrowed money.

He was offered a job at three pounds a month
5   in a small stationery store,
but he turned it down without the slightest hesitation.
It wasn't suitable. It wasn't the right pay for him,
a reasonably educated young man, twenty-five years old.

He won two, maybe three dollars a day—sometimes.
10   How much could he expect to make out of cards and backgammon
in the cafés of his social level, working-class places,
however cleverly he played, however stupid the opponents he chose?
His borrowing—that was even worse.
He rarely picked up a dollar, usually no more than half that,
15   and sometimes he had to come down to even less.

For a week or so, sometimes longer,
when he managed to escape those horrible late nights,
he'd cool himself at the baths, and with a morning swim.

His clothes were a terrible mess.
20   He always wore the same suit,
a very faded cinnamon-brown suit.

O summer days of nineteen hundred and eight,
from your perspective
the cinnamon-brown suit was tastefully excluded.

25   Your perspective has preserved him
as he was when he took off, threw off,
those unworthy clothes, that mended underwear,
and stood stark naked, impeccably handsome, a miracle—
his hair uncombed, swept back,
30   his limbs a little tanned
from his morning nakedness at the baths and on the beach.

Ithaka[1]

As you set out for Ithaka
hope the voyage is a long one,
full of adventure, full of discovery.

---

1. Translated by Edmund Keeley and Philip Sherrard.

1. Home and ultimate destination of Homer's epic hero in the *Odyssey.*

Laistrygonians[2] and Cyclops,[3]
5   angry Poseidon[4]—don't be afraid of them:
        you'll never find things like that on your way
        as long as you keep your thoughts raised high,
        as long as a rare excitement
        stirs your spirit and your body.
10   Laistrygonians and Cyclops,
        wild Poseidon—you won't encounter them
        unless you bring them along inside your soul,
        unless your soul sets them up in front of you.

        Hope the voyage is a long one.
15   May there be many a summer morning when,
        with what pleasure, what joy,
        you come into harbors seen for the first time;
        may you stop at Phoenician trading stations
        to buy fine things,
20   mother of pearl and coral, amber and ebony,
        sensual perfume of every kind—
        as many sensual perfumes as you can;
        and may you visit many Egyptian cities
        to gather stores of knowledge from their scholars.

25   Keep Ithaka always in your mind.
        Arriving there is what you are destined for.
        But do not hurry the journey at all.
        Better if it lasts for years,
        so you are old by the time you reach the island,
30   wealthy with all you have gained on the way,
        not expecting Ithaka to make you rich.

        Ithaka gave you the marvelous journey.
        Without her you would not have set it out.
        She has nothing left to give you now.

35   And if you find her poor, Ithaka won't have fooled you.
        Wise as you will have become, so full of experience,
        you will have understood by then what these Ithakas mean.

━━●━ ≡◆≡ ━●━━

Claude McKay
1890–1948

Born and raised in Jamaica in what was then the colonial British West Indies, Claude McKay published two books of poetry in Jamaican dialect while still in his early twenties. He came to

---

2. In Homer's *Odyssey* 10.80 and 12.1, they are man-eating giants encountered by Odysseus at the northernmost shores of the earth.
3. Greek, "Round Eye." A mythical monster of huge proportions with a single eye in the middle of the forehead.

The best-known Cyclops is Polyphemus, blinded by Odysseus in Homer's *Odyssey* 9.110–130.
4. Greek god of the sea and father of the Cyclops Polyphemus.

the United States in 1912 on a scholarship and studied first at the Tuskegee Institute in Alabama and then at Kansas State Teachers College. He moved to New York in 1914, where he wrote for the *Liberator,* a journal of avant-garde art and politics, of which he became a co-editor. Rejecting the accommodationist mode of the Tuskegee Institute's founder Booker T. Washington, McKay began to write militant verse, emerging as a major voice of the Harlem Renaissance with his volumes *Spring in New Hampshire* (1920) and *Harlem Shadows* (1922), in which the following poems appeared. He wrote mostly prose thereafter, including the first bestseller by a black writer, *Home to Harlem* (1928), a novel about a black soldier returning from World War I.

McKay had a peripatetic life, living between 1922 and 1934 in the Soviet Union, France, Spain, and Morocco, before returning to the United States. His autobiography, *A Long Way from Home* (1937), signals the theme of displacement that figures in many of his poems as well. In the poems given here, McKay overlays New York and Jamaica as sites of memory and desire, seeing both locales as transitional spaces between a lost African past and a not yet realized future of full freedom. McKay's work is fully modernist in such themes, though unlike modernists such as T. S. Eliot he favored formal stanza patterns and rhyme schemes. Yet his embrace of traditional forms and diction marked a deliberate, modern break from the dialect writing that McKay himself and other Caribbean and African-American writers had often used in the past, in a radical traditionalism that allowed him to give his shifting memory-scapes a directly political force.

The Tropics in New York

Bananas ripe and green, and gingerroot,
    Cocoa in pods and alligator pears,
And tangerines and mangoes and grapefruit,
    Fit for the highest prize at parish fairs,

5   Set in the window, bringing memories
    Of fruit trees laden by low-singing rills,°   *streams*
And dewy dawns, and mystical blue skies
    In benediction over nunlike hills.

My eyes grew dim, and I could no more gaze;
10   A wave of longing through my body swept,
And, hungry for the old, familiar ways,
    I turned aside and bowed my head and wept.

Flame-Heart

So much have I forgotten in ten years,
    So much in ten brief years! I have forgot
What time the purple apples come to juice,
    And what month brings the shy forget-me-not.
5   I have forgot the special, startling season
    Of the pimento's flowering and fruiting;
What time of year the ground doves brown the fields
    And fill the noonday with their curious fluting.
I have forgotten much, but still remember
10   The poinsettia's red, blood-red warm in December.

I still recall the honey-fever grass,
    But cannot recollect the high days when
We rooted them out of the ping-wing path
    To stop the mad bees in the rabbit pen.

15   I often try to think in what sweet month
            The languid painted ladies used to dapple
        The yellow byroad mazing from the main,
            Sweet with the golden threads of the rose apple.
        I have forgotten—strange—but quite remember
20   The poinsettia's red, blood-red in warm December.

        What weeks, what months, what time of the mild year
            We cheated school to have our fling at tops?
        What days our wine-thrilled bodies pulsed with joy
            Feasting upon blackberries in the copse?°   *thicket*
25   Oh, some I know! I have embalmed the days,
            Even the sacred moments when we played,
        All innocent of passion, uncorrupt,
            At noon and evening in the flame-heart's shade.
        We were so happy, happy, I remember,
30   Beneath the poinsettia's red in warm December.

Outcast

        For the dim regions whence my fathers came
        My spirit, bondaged by the body, longs.
        Word felt, but never heard, my lips would frame;
        My soul would sing forgotten jungle songs.
5   I would go back to darkness and to peace,
        But the great western world holds me in fee,
        And I may never hope for full release
        While to its alien gods I bend my knee.
        Something in me is lost, forever lost,
10   Some vital thing has gone out of my heart,
        And I must walk the way of life a ghost
        Among the sons of earth, a thing apart.

        For I was born, far from my native clime,
        Under the white man's menace, out of time.

—◄━━═◆═━━►—

Federico García Lorca
1898–1936

Poet, playwright, painter, and pianist, Federico García Lorca was born in the province of Granada, Spain, and was educated in the provincial capital and in Madrid. He is best known for his gypsy ballads (*Romancero Gitano*, 1928) and his intensely lyrical poetic tragedies, evocative of the harshness, honor, and passion of Spanish peasant life. He traveled to New York in 1929, an experience that yielded a volume of surreal poems published posthumously in 1940 with the title *Poeta en Nueva York*. García Lorca was murdered by General Franco's Nationalist partisans shortly after the Spanish Civil War broke out in 1936, and his body was never found. His literary corpus, however, has come to symbolize the republican cause and resistance to the fascist agenda in mid-twentieth-century Europe, for which the Spanish Civil War served as dress rehearsal for launching World War II.

In the poem from *Poet in New York* printed here, "Unsleeping City," García Lorca counters the "nocturn," traditionally a meditative poem, with the insomnia of Surrealism and the jar-
ring images that disrupt any meditation or peaceful reflection. García Lorca's nocturnal Surrealism consists of an inescapable assault by the illogical and haunting dreamscape of the modern
city epitomized by New York. More a waking nightmare than a dream, the sleepwalking
through these psychological states of lunacy and dread is typical of the irrational free associations that define the surreal. The strained juxtaposition and blending of natural elements, colors, faculties, and symbols that one would associate with the poetic undermine the expectations
of the reader and subvert customary poetic logic.

Unsleeping City[1]
(Brooklyn Bridge Nocturne)

No sleep in the sky; nobody, nobody.
No one lies sleeping.
The spawn of the moon sniff the cabins, and circle.
The living iguanas arrive and set tooth on the sleepless.
5   The heartstricken one who takes flight will meet on the corners
the incredible mute crocodile under the timid reproach of the stars.

No sleep upon earth; nobody, nobody.
No one lies sleeping.
The corpse in the furthermost graveyard
10   that was three years berating
the landscape of drought that he held on his knees,
and the boy that they buried this morning—he whimpered so much
they called out the mastiffs to quiet him.

Life is no dream! Beware and beware and beware!
15   We tumble downstairs to eat of the damp of the earth
or we climb to the snowy divide with the choir of dead dahlias.
But neither dream nor forgetfulness, is:
brute flesh is. Kisses that tether our mouths
in a mesh of raw veins.
20   Whomsoever his woe brings to grief, it will grieve without quarter.
Whom death brings to dread will carry that death on his shoulders.

On a day,
the horses will thrive in the taverns,
the ravening ant
25   will assail yellow heavens withheld in the eyes of a cow.

On a time
we shall see, rearisen, the anatomized butterflies,
and walking the ways of gray sponge and a stillness of boats,
behold our rings glisten and the roses gush forth from our tongues.
30   Beware and beware and beware!
Those still keeping watch on the print of the paw and the cloudburst,
the boy in his tears, who cannot interpret the bridge's invention,

1. Translated by Ben Belitt.

the dead with no more than a head and a shoe now—
drive them all to the wall where snake and iguana are waiting,
35   where the bear's fang lies ready
and the mummified hand of the child
and the pelt of the camel in a raging blue ague, stands on end.

No sleep under heaven; nobody, nobody.
No one lies sleeping.
40   And should one shut an eye,
lay on the whip, my boys, lay on the whip!
Let eye's panorama be open, I say,
let bitter sores rankle!
No sleep upon earth; nobody, nobody,
45   no one, I tell you.
No one lies sleeping.
But if any should find in the night the mosses' excess on his temples—
down with the trapdoors and let there be seen in the moon
the perfidious goblets, the theater's skull, and the bane.

⊷ ⚎⚏⚎ ⊶

Carlos Drummond de Andrade
1902–1987

Journalist, pharmacologist, newspaper editor, and civil servant, Carlos Drummond de Andrade was born to a landowning family of Portuguese and Scottish extraction in the little town of Itibara, state of Minas Gerais, Brazil. In 1934, he moved to Rio de Janeiro as a civil servant in the Ministry of Education, from which he would retire in 1966. His first book of poetry dates from 1930. Two years earlier, his poem "In the Middle of the Road" appeared in the modernist journal *Antropofagia* ("Cannibalism") of São Paulo. This unorthodox poem, matter-of-fact, unadorned, pared down to a minimal and seemingly unimportant incident, would cause a scandal among the poetry establishment of the day. A perennial candidate for the Nobel Prize for his poetry, Drummond de Andrade was also an award-winning translator of French novels into Portuguese.

In the Middle of the Road[1]

In the middle of the road there was a stone
there was a stone in the middle of the road
there was a stone
in the middle of the road there was a stone.
5   Never should I forget this event
in the life of my fatigued retinas.
Never should I forget that in the middle of the road
there was a stone
there was a stone in the middle of the road
10   in the middle of the road there was a stone.

---

1. Translated by Elizabeth Bishop.

Emile Habiby
1922–1998

Emile Habiby is perhaps the most important Arab novelist to emerge from Palestine. He is the only Palestinian Arab to win the highest literary honors both from the Palestine Liberation Organization and from Israel. In 1990, PLO Chairman Yassir Arafat bestowed on him the illustrious Al-Quds Prize for his role in furthering the cause of Palestinian literature. In 1992, the Israeli Prime Minister Yitzak Shamir awarded him the Israel Prize for Literature for his role in promoting tolerance and mutual understanding through his writing. Habiby deserved both, but the award of the Israeli prize raised wide controversy both in the Arab world and in Israel.

Habiby was born in Haifa in 1922 to a Christian Orthodox middle-class family. In 1942 he began working as a news announcer for the Palestinian broadcasting station in Jerusalem; in 1949 Habiby was a lone voice calling for the acceptance of the UN plan for the division of Palestine into an Arab and a Jewish state. Soon after the creation of Israel, he became a political activist for the cause of Palestinians and founded the League of Liberation of Palestine, which eventually became the Israeli Communist Party. Habiby was elected in 1952 to the Israeli parliament, a seat he held for twenty years. In the 1950s, he became the chief editor of his party's newspaper, *al-Ittihad* (The Union), which called for the unity of Arabs and Jews in a secular, democratic, and multi-ethnic state in Palestine. Under Habiby, *al-Ittihad* published the new Palestinian poetry of resistance that emerged in the late 1950s and early 1960s, articulating a strong sense of hope and the quest for an Arab identity among Palestinians in Israel. He continued to play this cultural and literary role until his death in 1998.

Emile Habiby started writing late in life. Unlike the majority of contemporary Palestinian writers, who emerged from the refugee camps established after 1947, Habiby lived his childhood in the Palestine of the British mandate, and remained in his native city after the creation of Israel. He could thus represent the continuity of the Palestinian experience in modern Arabic literature. The devastating shock of the 1967 war turned Habiby's left-wing optimism into bitter sarcasm and biting humor, which he channeled into his literary work. Structural irony is at the core of his second and most famous novel, *The Secret Life of Saeed, the Pessoptimist* (1974), which highlights the theme of Palestinians' survival in the face of Zionist attempts to eradicate their identity. This novel has been translated into sixteen languages. *The Pessoptimist* uses a fine mixture of the ironic and reflexive narrative pioneered by the eighteenth-century British novelist Laurence Sterne in *Tristram Shandy*, infusing this Shandean style with humorous Arabic anecdotal narrative. It consists of three parts, each devoted to a major phase in the recent history of Palestine and entitled with the name of a woman who is both the beloved of the hero and a symbol of Palestine.

In this work and in Habiby's other novels and plays, literature becomes an arena for recording what one may call the infrastructure of Palestinian identity: its history, geography, oral tradition, folk culture, popular lore, proverbs, and even fragments of its written literature. The collective culture is shown as much in the realistic account of daily events as in flights into fantasy and imagination. Beneath the deformed narrative space of present-day Israel, the author uses a powerful nostalgia to invoke the sacrosanct Palestine around every corner and behind every street name.

PRONUNCIATIONS:
Habiby: hah-BEE-bee
Saeed: sah-EED
Safsharsheck: SAFF-shar-shek

from The Secret Life of Saeed, the Ill-Fated Pessoptimist[1]

Saeed Reports How His Life in Israel Was All Due to the Munificence of an Ass

Let's start at the beginning. My whole life has been strange, and a strange life can only end strangely. When I asked my extraterrestrial friend why he took me in, he merely replied, "What alternative did you have?"

So when did it all begin?

When I was born again, thanks to an ass.

During the fighting in 1948 they waylaid us and opened fire, shooting my father, may he rest in peace. I escaped because a stray donkey came into the line of fire and they shot it, so it died in place of me. My subsequent life in Israel, then, was really a gift from that unfortunate beast. What value then, honored sir, should we assign to this life of mine?

I consider myself quite remarkable. You've no doubt read of dogs lapping up poisoned water and dying to warn their masters and save their lives. And of horses, too, racing the wind bearing their wounded riders to safety, only to die of exhaustion themselves.[2] But I'm the first man, to my knowledge, to be saved by a mulish donkey, an animal unable either to race the wind or to bark. I truly am remarkable. That must be why the men from outer space chose me.

Tell me, please do, what makes one truly remarkable? Must one be different from all the rest or, indeed, be very much one of them?

You said you never noticed me before. That's because you lack sensitivity, my good friend. How very often you have seen my name in the leading newspapers. Didn't you read of the hundreds imprisoned by Haifa police when that melon exploded in Hanatir Square, now Paris Square? Afterwards every Arab they found in Lower Haifa, pedestrian or on wheels, they put in jail. The papers published the names of everyone notable who was caught, but merely gave general reference to the rest.

The rest—yes, that's me! The papers haven't ignored me. How can you claim not to have heard of me? I truly am remarkable. For no paper with wide coverage, having sources, resources, advertisements, celebrity writers, and a reputation, can ignore me. Those like me are everywhere—towns, villages, bars, everywhere. I am "the rest." I am remarkable indeed! * * *

Three: Saeed Gives His Ancestry

Saeed, the ill-fated Pessoptimist—my name fits my appearance precisely. The Pessoptimist family is truly noble and long established in our land. It traces its origins to a Cypriot girl from Aleppo. Tamerlane, unable to find room for her head in his pyramid of skulls, for all its reported dimensions of 20,000 arms length by 10 high, sent her with one of his lieutenants to Baghdad, where she was to clean herself up and await his return. But she made a fool of the man. They say, and this is a family secret, that this was the cause of the infamous massacre. Anyway, she ran off with a Bedouin of the Tuwaisat tribe named Abjar, of whom a poet has said:

> *Abjar, Abjar, son of Abjar,*
> *Divorced his wife when he couldn't feed her.*

---

1. Translated by Salmal Jayyusi and Trevor LeGassick.   2. These are well-known popular stories.

He divorced her when he found she had deceived him with Loaf, son of Hunger, from the Jaftlick lowlands, who in turn divorced her in Beersheba. Our forefathers went on divorcing our grandmothers until our journey brought us to a flat and fragrant land at the shore of the sea called Acre, then on to Haifa at the other side of the bay. We continued this practice of divorcing our wives right up until the state was founded.

After the first misfortunes, those of 1948,[3] the members of our great family became scattered, living in all of the Arab countries not yet occupied.[4] And so I have relatives working in the very Arabian Aal Rabi court, with posts in the Bureau of Translation—both from and into Persian, I might add. And I have one who has specialized in lighting the cigarettes of different kings. We also had a captain in Syria, a major in Iraq and a lieutenant-colonel in Lebanon. The last mentioned, however, died of a heart attack when the Intra Bank[5] there, the country's biggest, went bankrupt. The first Arab to be appointed by the government of Israel as head of the Committee for Distribution of Dandelion and Watercress in Upper Galilee is from our family, even though his mother, so they say, was a divorced Circassian girl. And he still claims, so far unsuccessfully, distribution rights for Lower Galilee too. My father, may he rest in peace, did many favors for the state before it was founded. These services of his are known in detail by his good friend Adon (Mr., that is) Safsarsheck, the retired police officer.

After my father fell a martyr on the open road and I was redeemed by the ass, my family took the boat to Acre. When we found that we were in no danger, and that everyone was busy saving their skins, we fled to Lebanon to save ours. And there we sold them to live.

When we had nothing left to sell, I recalled my father's behest to me as he breathed his last, there on the open road. "Go," he had said, "to Mr. Safsarsheck and say to him: 'My father, before his martyrdom, sent you his compliments and asked you to fix me up.'"

And fix me he did.

Four: Saeed Enters Israel for the First Time

I crossed the border into Israel in the car of a doctor affiliated with the Arab Salvation Army. He used to flirt with my sister in his clinic in Haifa. When we emigrated to Tyre, in Lebanon, we found him awaiting us. And when I came to suspect what was going on between him and my sister, he began treating me as his dearest friend. Then his wife began to fancy me.

One day, the doctor asked me, "Can you keep a secret?"

I replied, "Like a star over two lovers."

"Then hold your tongue, for my wife won't hold hers."

And so, for my sister's sake, I held mine.

When I revealed to him my desire to sneak into Israel, he promptly volunteered to take me in his car. "It will be better for you to go," he said.

"And for you too," I responded.

"God bless you then," he said.

And my mother did bless us farewell.

---

3. The loss of Palestine and the establishment of the state of Israel. It is referred to as the first misfortune since the occupation of the rest of Palestine, Gaza, and the West Bank in 1967 is the second misfortune.
4. In addition to the rest of Palestine, lands of three more Arab countries, Egypt, Syria, and Lebanon, were occupied in 1967.
5. A well-known Lebanese bank that went bankrupt in the 1960s.

We reached Tarshiha just as the sun and the villagers were abandoning it. The Arab guards stopped us. When the doctor showed them his papers, they greeted us warmly. I still felt scared though. But the doctor joked and swore with them, and they laughed and swore back.

In Maaliya we slept. But before dawn I awoke to hear whispering coming from the doctor's bed nearby. I held my breath and made out a woman's voice whispering that her husband would not be awake that early. I told myself that this could not be my sister since she as yet had no husband. So I went contentedly back to sleep.

We lunched at the home of that woman's father in Abu Snan, which was at that time in no-man's-land; that is, it was territory frequented only by spies, cattle merchants, and stray donkeys.

They hired an ass for me and I rode it down to Kufr Yasif. This was in the summer of 1948. And it was riding this donkey as I descended from Abu Snan to Kufr Yasif that I celebrated my twenty-fourth birthday.

They directed me to the headquarters of the military governor. I entered it still riding the donkey. It proudly mounted the three steps at the building's entrance. Soldiers rushed towards me amazed. I shouted, "Safsarsheck, Safsarsheck!"

A fat soldier ran toward me shouting, "I am the military governor, dismount!"

"I am so-and-so, the son of so-and-so," I replied, "and I shall only alight at the door of Mr. Safsarsheck." He swore at me violently but I shouted, "I claim sanctuary with Adon Safsarsheck."

But he merely cursed Mr. Safsarsheck.

So I dismounted from the donkey.

Five: Research on the Origins of the Pessoptimists

When I alighted from the donkey, I found that I was taller than the military governor. I felt much relieved at being bigger than him without the help of the donkey's legs. So I settled comfortably into a chair in the school they had converted into the governor's headquarters. The blackboards were being used as Ping-Pong tables.

There I sat, at ease, thanking God for making me taller than the military governor without the help of the donkey's legs.

That's the way our family is and why we bear the name Pessoptimist. For this word combines two qualities, pessimism and optimism, that have been blended perfectly in the character of all members of our family since our first divorced mother, the Cypriot. It is said that the first to so name us was Tamerlane, following the second massacre of Baghdad. This was when it was reported to him that my first ancestor, Abjar son of Abjar, mounted on his horse outside the city walls, had stared back at the tongues of flame and shouted, "After me, the deluge!"

Take me, for example, I don't differentiate between optimism and pessimism and am quite at a loss as to which of the two characterizes me. When I awake each morning I thank the Lord he did not take my soul during the night. If harm befalls me during the day, I thank Him that it was no worse. So which am I, a pessimist or an optimist?

My mother is also a Pessoptimist. My older brother used to work at the port of Haifa. One day a storm blew up and overturned the crane he was operating, throwing them both onto the rocks and down into the sea. They collected his remains and brought them to us. Neither his head nor his insides could be found. He had been married less than a month and his bride sat weeping and bewailing her hard luck. My mother sat there too, crying silently.

Suddenly my mother became agitated and started beating her hands together. She said hoarsely: "It's best it happened like this and not some other way!"

None of us was surprised at her conclusion except the bride, who was not from our family and therefore did not understand our kind of wisdom. She almost lost her mind and began screaming in my mother's face, "What do you mean, 'some other way'? You ill-fated [this, of course, was the name of my father, may he rest in peace] hag! What worse way could there have been?"

My mother did not appreciate this childish outburst and answered with all the calm assurance of a fortuneteller: "For you to have run off during his life, my girl, to have run away with some other man." One should remember, of course, that my mother knew our family history all too well.

My brother's widow did indeed run off with another man two years later and he turned out to be sterile. When my mother heard that he was so, she repeated her favorite saying, "And why should we not praise God?"

So what are we then? Optimists or pessimists?

Six: How Saeed First Participated in the War of Independence

Now let's return, my dear sir, to the headquarters of the military governor and how, as soon as he cursed Adon Safsarsheck I alighted from the donkey. It became clear to me very soon indeed that in cursing a person one is sometimes really expressing jealousy rather than contempt.

As soon as I seated myself in the chair, cheered by the thought that I was taller than the military governor even without the donkey's legs, he hurried to the telephone and gabbled some words of which I could only distinguish two, namely, *ill-fated* and *Safsarsheck,* both names to be associated with me for a long time. When finished, he threw down the receiver and screamed in my face to get up. I did so.

"I am Abu Isaac. Follow me," he ordered. So I followed him to a jeep parked near the entrance. My donkey was standing beside it, sniffing.

"Let's go," said Abu Isaac. He climbed into his jeep and I mounted my donkey. But he shrieked in fury, and my donkey and I so shook with fear that I fell from its back and found myself in the car next to the military governor. It proceeded westward along a dirt road flanked by stalks of sesame.

"Where to?" I asked.

"Acre. And shut up!" he replied.

So shut up I did. After continuing for a few minutes he brought the jeep to a sudden halt and jumped from it like a shot, his gun in his hand. He raced into the sesame stalks, parting them with his paunch. I saw a peasant woman crouching down there, in her lap a child, its eyes wide in terror.

"From which village?" demanded the governor.

The mother remained crouching, staring at him askance, although he stood right over her, huge as a mountain.

"From Berwah?" he yelled.

She made no response but continued to stare at him.

He then pointed his gun straight at the child's head and screamed, "Reply, or I'll empty this into him!"

At this I tensed, ready to spring at him come what may. After all, the blood of youth surged hot within me, at my age then of twenty-four. And not even a stone could have been unmoved at this sight. However, I recalled my father's final counsel and my mother's blessing and then said to myself, "I certainly shall attack him if he fires his gun. But so far he is merely threatening her." I remained at the ready.

The woman did reply, "Yes, from Berwah."

"Are you returning there?" he demanded.

"Yes, returning."

"Didn't we warn you," he yelled, "that anyone returning there will be killed? Don't you all understand the meaning of discipline? Do you think it's the same as chaos? Get up and run ahead of me. Go back anywhere you like to the east. And if I ever see you again on this road I'll show you no mercy."

The woman stood up and, gripping her child by the hand, set off toward the east, not once looking back. Her child walked beside her, and he too never looked back.

At this point I observed the first example of that amazing phenomenon that was to occur again and again until I finally met my friends from outer space. For the further the woman and child went from where we were, the governor standing and I in the jeep, the taller they grew. By the time they merged with their own shadows in the sinking sun they had become bigger than the plain of Acre itself. The governor still stood there awaiting their final disappearance, while I remained huddled in the jeep. Finally he asked in amazement, "Will they never disappear?"

This question, however, was not directed at me.

Berwah is the village of the poet Mahmoud Darwish,[6] who said fifteen years later:

> I laud the executioner, victor over a dark-eyed maiden;
> Hurrah for the vanquisher of villages, hurrah for the butcher of infants.

Was he this very child? Had he gone on walking eastward after releasing himself from his mother's hand, leaving her in the shadows?

Now why am I, my good sir, relating this trivial incident to you? For many reasons. And among them is this phenomenon of bodies growing ever larger the farther they move from our sight.

Another reason is that this incident provides further proof that the name of our ancient family inspires respect in the hearts of the authorities of the state of Israel. For were it not for this respect, the governor would most certainly have emptied his gun into my head when he saw me tense up, in readiness to attack him.

Yet another reason is that I felt for the first time that I was fulfilling the mission of my father, may he rest in peace, and serving the state, even if only after its establishment. So I thought to myself, Why should I not be on familiar terms with the military governor?

I therefore took the liberty to blurt out: "Er, this vehicle of yours, what make is it?"

"Shut up!" he replied. And I did.

It was that same poet of Berwah mentioned above who later said:

> We know best about those devils
> Who of children prophets make.

He realized only quite recently that those same devils could also render a whole nation utterly and completely forgotten.

---

6. The most famous Palestinian poet (see p. 1035) whose family returned to the village despite the military orders to the contrary.

Octavio Paz
1914–1998

Perhaps Mexico's most distinguished man of letters in the twentieth century, Octavio Paz was the epitome of a public intellectual—a writer who assumes a principled role in the political arena and emerges as the social conscience of his time. Poet, essayist, and editor, Paz was also a member of Mexico's diplomatic corps starting in 1945. In this capacity, he served in France, Japan, and Switzerland before being posted to India in 1962. He resigned as Ambassador to India in 1968 following the Mexican government's bloody putdown of a major student uprising in Mexico City during the Olympic Games. A consistent champion of human rights, he was equally critical of authoritarian regimes of the right and of the left during a time when, in theory, one could only be on the left or on the right as an intellectual. Paz came by his political commitment through his family legacy, his father having been a supporter of the peasant leader and revolutionary Emiliano Zapata during the Mexican Revolution (1910). One of the foremost spokesmen and practitioners of modern poetry, Paz had a keen sense of other genres of art and of modernist aesthetics. He wrote profusely as a poet and as a critic and essayist, his most famous book being *The Labyrinth of Solitude* (1950), a diagnosis of Mexican culture and its violent history. Paz held a number of distinguished academic positions including at Cambridge and Harvard and was the recipient of a number of international literary prizes on his way to receiving the Nobel Prize in literature in 1990.

The selections that follow exemplify the diversity of what critics and historians consider "high modernism." While this designation has tended to focus on the aesthetic and experimental qualities of these writings, as a constellation they demonstrate the full range of the modernist era that extends from recollection and the psychology of self-consciousness to the highly political and ironic acts of linguistic experimentation and social commitment.

A Wind Called Bob Rauschenberg[1]

Landscape fallen from Saturn,
abandoned landscape,
plains of nuts and wheels and bars,
asthmatic turbines, broken propellers,
5   electrical scars,
desolate landscape:
the objects sleep side by side,
great flocks of things and things and things,
the objects sleep with eyes open
10   and slowly fall within themselves,
they fall without moving,
their fall is the stillness of a plain under the moon,
their sleep is a falling with no return,
a descent toward a space with no beginning,
15   the objects fall,
        objects are falling,
they fall from my mind that thinks them,
they fall from my eyes that don't see them,

---

1. Translated by Eliot Weinberger. Robert Rauschenberg (1925–), American painter and designer, influential in the history of Pop Art.

they fall from my thoughts that speak them,
they fall like letters, letters, letters,
20   a rain of letters on a derelict landscape.

Fallen landscape,
strewn over itself, a great ox,
an ox crepuscular as this century that ends,
things sleep side by side—
25   iron and cotton, silk and coal,
synthetic fibers and grains of wheat,
screws and the wing-bones of a sparrow,
the crane, the woolen quilt, the family portrait,
the headlight, the crank and the hummingbird feather—
30   things sleep and talk in their sleep,
the wind blows over the things,
and what the things say in their sleep
the lunar wind says brushing past them,
it says it with reflections and colors that burn and sparkle,
35   the wind speaks forms that breathe and whirl,
the things hear them talking, and take fright at the sound,
they were born mute, and now they sing and laugh,
they were paralytic, and now they dance,
the wind joins them and separates and joins them,
40   plays with them, unmakes and remakes them,
invents other things, never seen nor heard,
their unions and disjunctions
are clusters of tangible enigmas,
strange and changing forms of passion,
45   constellations of desire, rage, love,
figures of encounters and goodbyes.

The landscape opens its eyes and sits up,
sets out walking followed by its shadow,
it is a stela of dark murmurs
50   that are the languages of fallen matter,
the wind stops and hears the clamor of the elements,
sand and water talking in low voices,
the howl of pilings as they battle the salt,
the rash confidence of fire,
55   the soliloquy of ashes,
the interminable conversation of the universe.
Talking with the things and with ourselves
the universe talks to itself:
we are its tongue and ears, its words and silences.
60   The wind hears what the universe says
and we hear what the wind says,
rustling the submarine foliage of language,
the secret vegetation of the underworld and the undersky:
man dreams the dream of things,
65   time thinks the dreams of men.

Central Park

Green and black thickets, bare spots,
leafy river knotting into itself:
it runs motionless through the leaden buildings
and there, where light turns to doubt
and stone wants to be shadow, it vanishes.
Don't cross Central Park at night.

Day falls, night flares up,
Alechinsky draws a magnetic rectangle,
a trap of lines, a corral of ink:
inside there is a fallen beast,
two eyes and a twisting rage.
Don't cross Central Park at night.

There are no exits or entrances,
enclosed in a ring of light
the grass beast sleeps with eyes open,
the moon exhumes razors,
the water in the shadows has become green fire.
Don't cross Central Park at night.

There are no entrances but everyone,
in the middle of a phrase dangling from the telephone,
from the top of the fountain of silence or laughter,
from the glass cage of the eye that watches us,
everyone, all of us are falling in the mirror.
Don't cross Central Park at night.

The mirror is made of stone and the stone now is shadow,
there are two eyes the color of anger,
a ring of cold, a belt of blood,
there is a wind that scatters the reflections
of Alice, dismembered in the pond.
Don't cross Central Park at night.

Open your eyes: now you are inside yourself,
you sail in a boat of monosyllables
across the mirror-pond, you disembark
at the Cobra dock: it is a yellow taxi
that carries you to the land of flames
across Central Park at night.

➥ END OF PERSPECTIVES: MODERNIST MEMORY ➦

5

10

15

20

25

30

35

Franz Kafka
1883–1924

Compared to many other modern novelists, Franz Kafka wrote little, and three of his major novels remained incomplete at his death. Yet in spite of its small bulk, his fiction has become one of the most towering achievements of European modernism: Throughout the twentieth century, Kafka's stories deeply influenced writers across different continents and languages, from the Argentinean short-story writer Jorge Luis Borges to the Japanese novelist Abe Kobo and the American cartoon artist Art Spiegelman. Profoundly enigmatic, Kafka's novels and stories resist attempts at defining their meaning conclusively, but it is precisely their indeterminacy that allows readers from very different backgrounds to understand his works as reflecting a part of their own condition. Indeed, in several languages the adjective "kafkaesque" has become part of the common modern vocabulary as a description of situations that are difficult, intricate, alienating, or absurd.

This usage loosely reflects the kind of predicament Kafka's protagonists typically find themselves confronted with. An event occurs that can't really be explained in terms of ordinary experience and commonsense rationality; as they investigate what the meaning of this event might be, Kafka's characters move gradually away from normal life and become more and more deeply entangled with incomprehensible processes and authorities. In the encounter with immensely powerful but impenetrable structures of authority—whether they are familial, civic, legal, or religious—Kafka's characters come to question their own identities and beliefs about the world, but they are unable to formulate more adequate ones. Sometimes the protagonists die without ever having understood what it was that threw their lives off their normal course in the first place. As they find themselves in an environment that is unintelligible at best and hostile at worst, Kafka's characters experience what is often considered one of the quintessentially modern conditions: *alienation*, the estrangement of the individual from normal social bonds and activities.

The reasons for this alienation in Kafka's fictional world have been hotly debated over the decades. Some readers (among them Max Brod, Kafka's friend and literary executor) have claimed that Kafka's characters exemplify the predicament of a humankind that needs and seeks out religious redemption but is forever cut off from divine mercy or access to salvation. Others emphasize that Kafka's descriptions of impersonal, inefficient, and incomprehensible institutions reflect some aspects of German sociologist Max Weber's famous characterization of modern bureaucracies. In this view, Kafka's characters would illustrate the condition of the typical modern citizen, whose life, in large part, is determined by abstract bureaucratic networks. Yet others have argued that Kafka's stories refer more specifically to the experience of a particular social group, the bourgeois middle class in an advanced capitalist society, and even more specifically to the double alienation implicit in Kafka's own status as a Jew of mixed German and Czech heritage living in Prague in the waning years of the Austro-Hungarian Empire. And finally, it has been suggested that the best way to approach Kafka's stories is through a psychoanalytical perspective that would foreground Kafka's own extremely troubled relation to his father as one of the basic sources of his characters' conflicted encounters with authority.

The reason that it is often difficult to decide which of these and other interpretations might be the most appropriate lies in the fact that many of Kafka's stories have the structure of a *parable*, a story that describes concrete and everyday events in order to illustrate an abstract concept or condition; unlike allegories, parables are usually not self-explanatory but require interpretive comment. Kafka's parables, however, stand on their own, and his brief reflection "On Parables" shows just how ambiguous the relation to the real can remain in this genre. An understanding of Kafka's texts is further complicated by the fact that even at the most literal level of the plot, they don't remain in the realm of ordinary experience in the way biblical parables do.

Rather, many of them start out with what appears at first sight to be an everyday situation, which then mutates into nightmarish circumstances that clearly fall outside the realm of commonsense reality. In *The Trial,* Kafka's protagonist is informed by two officials on what seems like an ordinary morning that a lawsuit has been initiated against him, but he is not told what crime he is accused of, and still doesn't know months later when he is sentenced to death. In *The Metamorphosis,* Gregor Samsa wakes up in the morning with every intention of going to work, only to find himself transformed into a beetle lying on its back. Kafka's literary mastery is most obvious in his ability to make such fantastic occurrences appear perfectly real to the reader.

The apparent simplicity of Kafka's style subtly heightens the enigma of his works. Especially compared to other Prague authors writing in German at the same time, his style is strikingly concrete and literal, without any obvious display of metaphor, symbol, or ornate syntax. But precisely in stripping his fiction of the ordinary trappings of "literary" diction, Kafka often pushes language to an extreme where even very simple words become problematic: What, really, is a "trial" or a "judgment"? How are we to imagine the "singing" of the mouse performer in "Josephine the Singer," who hardly seems to make audible sounds at all? Since words like these don't seem to function in Kafka's texts in quite the way they do in ordinary language, readers have always been tempted to give a variety of symbolic meanings to them. But Kafka's own language stubbornly refuses to yield firm evidence of what these meanings might be. This has led some of his successors, such as the French novelist Alain Robbe-Grillet, to claim that, in fact, Kafka's fiction belongs to an entirely different kind of literature that does away with metaphor as the basis of narrative meaning.

Kafka's work consists not only of narrative fiction but also of extensive diaries and letters that he wrote during most of his life; indeed all of his life was accompanied by constant acts of writing. The diaries and letters reveal an intensely introspective mind that steadily scrutinizes itself and others: "Every person is lost in himself beyond hope of rescue, and one's sole consolation in this is to observe other people and the laws governing them and everything," he noted in a 1914 diary entry. Kafka felt and thought deeply about each of his family and friendship relations and often agonized over what he perceived as his own shortfalls in fulfilling others' expectations. But his letters and diaries are not only fascinating psychological documents; they are also quite often accomplished literary texts. The "Letter to His Father," beyond what it might reveal about Kafka's family experience, is a striking example of character construction, and some of the diary entries contain narrative fragments whose quality rivals that of Kafka's fiction. Though they were never meant for literary publication, they convey the sense of a man who lived almost every aspect of his life through writing. "My happiness, my abilities and every possibility of being useful in any way have always been in the literary field," he wrote in his diary in 1911.

The world that is reflected in Kafka's fiction as well as in his letters and diaries is that of Prague at the turn of the twentieth century, where Kafka was born in 1883 as the first child of Hermann Kafka, who came from a Czech-Jewish family, and his mother, Julie, who was German-Jewish. At the time, Prague formed part of the Empire of Austria-Hungary and was home to three different groups: the Czech majority and significant minorities of Jews and Germans. Jews occupied a somewhat ambiguous position between the Czech majority and the ruling German elite; Prague Jews had for a long time deeply identified with German culture, and it was not unusual for Jewish children to be sent to German-language schools. Kafka attended such a school in Prague from 1893 to 1901. In November 1901 he entered Prague's German University and studied law, graduating in June 1906. After the mandatory first year of unpaid practical experience in law, he started working for a private insurance company, Assicurazioni Generali, but he disliked the working atmosphere and long hours so much that less than a year later, he moved to the Workers' Accident Insurance Institute, for which he continued to work until shortly before his death in 1924.

Kafka's youth was overshadowed by personal, professional, and medical troubles. Some of the most important and intimate relationships in his life were also the most complex and conflicted. He had an intensely ambivalent relationship with his father, who first ran a small business selling women's clothing and later ran an asbestos factory in which his son sometimes helped out. Kafka's ambivalence emerges clearly in the "Letter to His Father," written in 1919 but never actually sent. According to this letter, the father's professional success, self-assurance, and willingness to ignore others' desires stood in stark contrast with the son's self-doubt and uncertainty regarding his success as a writer as well as in his relationships with women. This conflict led Kafka to a mixture of admiration and repulsion and to simultaneous desires to please his father and rebel against him, which precluded any effective communication or deep understanding. Kafka's relationship with his fiancée, Felice Bauer, was similarly troubled: in their five-year relationship between 1912 and 1917, the couple were twice engaged, but both times Kafka broke the engagement in intense self-doubt over his own inability to sustain a marriage and to reconcile it with his devotion to literature.

Kafka's professional life proved no less conflicted. He often agonized over the obligation to earn a living through legal work that he experienced as tedious and burdensome instead of devoting himself to the work that he considered to be his real vocation, writing. His attempt to carve out time to write outside of a long workday frequently led to sleepless nights and ill health during his time at Assicurazioni Generali, and he moved to the Workers' Accident Insurance Institute partly for the more moderate hours required there. Nevertheless, his life remained divided between tedious work that was financially necessary and the work he passionately cared about but was unable to live from. Illness was a constant presence in Kafka's life, starting in his childhood, but it gradually became a more and more serious threat to both his work and his life. From about 1912 on, he complained of insomnia and severe headaches, and symptoms of tuberculosis manifested themselves in 1917. In 1920 and 1921 he was forced to spend several months at a sanatorium. Only a few months before his death in March 1924, he wrote his haunting story "Josephine the Singer," which celebrates the profound significance of artistic creation, only to deny its social relevance. Perhaps not coincidentally, Kafka instructed his friend Max Brod shortly before his death to destroy all his literary works; Brod ignored this instruction and preserved Kafka's unpublished texts for posterity. Kafka died on 3 June 1924, from laryngeal tuberculosis, just a month short of his forty-first birthday.

The Metamorphosis[1]

1

When Gregor Samsa woke up one morning from unsettling dreams, he found himself changed in his bed into a monstrous vermin. He was lying on his back as hard as armor plate, and when he lifted his head a little, he saw his vaulted brown belly, sectioned by arch-shaped ribs, to whose dome the cover, about to slide off completely, could barely cling. His many legs, pitifully thin compared with the size of the rest of him, were waving helplessly before his eyes.

"What's happened to me?" he thought. It was no dream. His room, a regular human room, only a little on the small side, lay quiet between the four familiar walls. Over the table, on which an unpacked line of fabric samples was all spread out—Samsa was a traveling salesman—hung the picture which he had recently cut out of a glossy magazine and lodged in a pretty gilt frame. It showed a lady done up in a fur hat and a fur boa,[2] sitting upright and raising up against the viewer a heavy fur muff in which her whole forearm had disappeared.

Gregor's eyes then turned to the window, and the overcast weather—he could hear raindrops hitting against the metal window ledge—completely depressed him. "How about going back to sleep for a few minutes and forgetting all this nonsense,"

---

1. Translated by Stanley Corngold.   2. A long, thin scarf made of feathers or fur that women wear around their necks or shoulders.

he thought, but that was completely impracticable, since he was used to sleeping on his right side and in his present state could not get into that position. No matter how hard he threw himself onto his right side, he always rocked onto his back again. He must have tried it a hundred times, closing his eyes so as not to have to see his squirming legs, and stopped only when he began to feel a slight, dull pain in his side, which he had never felt before.

"Oh God," he thought, "what a grueling job I've picked! Day in, day out—on the road. The upset of doing business is much worse than the actual business in the home office, and, besides, I've got the torture of traveling, worrying about changing trains, eating miserable food at all hours, constantly seeing new faces, no relationships that last or get more intimate. To the devil with it all!" He feld a slight itching up on top of his belly; shoved himself slowly on his back closer to the bedpost, so as to be able to lift his head better; found the itchy spot, studded with small white dots which he had no idea what to make of; and wanted to touch the spot with one of his legs but immediately pulled it back, for the contact sent a cold shiver through him.

He slid back again into his original position. "This getting up so early," he thought, "makes anyone a complete idiot. Human beings have to have their sleep. Other traveling salesmen live like harem women. For instance, when I go back to the hotel before lunch to write up the business I've done, these gentlemen are just having breakfast. That's all I'd have to try with my boss; I'd be fired on the spot. Anyway, who knows if that wouldn't be a very good thing for me. If I didn't hold back for my parents' sake, I would have quit long ago, I would have marched up to the boss and spoken my piece from the bottom of my heart. He would have fallen off the desk! It is funny, too, the way he sits on the desk and talks down from the heights to the employees, especially when they have to come right up close on account of the boss's being hard of hearing. Well, I haven't given up hope completely; once I've gotten the money together to pay off my parents' debt to him—that will probably take another five or six years—I'm going to do it without fail. Then I'm going to make the big break. But for the time being I'd better get up, since my train leaves at five."

And he looked over at the alarm clock, which was ticking on the chest of drawers. "God Almighty!" he thought. It was six-thirty, the hands were quietly moving forward, it was actually past the half-hour, it was already nearly a quarter to. Could it be that the alarm hadn't gone off? You could see from the bed that it was set correctly for four o'clock; it certainly had gone off, too. Yes, but was it possible to sleep quietly through a ringing that made the furniture shake? Well, he certainly hadn't slept quietly, but probably all the more soundly for that. But what should he do now? The next train left at seven o'clock; to make it he would have to hurry like a madman, and the line of samples wasn't packed yet, and he himself didn't feel especially fresh and ready to march around. And even if he did make the train, he could not avoid getting it from the boss, because the messenger boy had been waiting at the five-o'clock train and would have long ago reported his not showing up. He was a tool of the boss, without brains or backbone. What if he were to say he was sick? But that would be extremely embarrassing and suspicious because during his five years with the firm Gregor had not been sick even once. The boss would be sure to come with the health-insurance doctor, blame his parents for their lazy son, and cut off all excuses by quoting the health-insurance doctor, for whom the world consisted of people who were completely healthy but afraid to work. And, besides, in this case would he be so very wrong? In fact, Gregor felt fine, with the exception of his drowsiness, which was really unnecessary after sleeping so late, and he even had a ravenous appetite.

Just as he was thinking all this over at top speed, without being able to decide to get out of bed—the alarm clock had just struck a quarter to seven—he heard a cautious knocking at the door next to the head of his bed. "Gregor," someone called—it was his mother—"it's a quarter to seven. Didn't you want to catch the train?" What a soft voice! Gregor was shocked to hear his own voice answering, unmistakably his own voice, true, but in which, as if from below, an insistent distressed chirping intruded, which left the clarity of his words intact only for a moment really, before so badly garbling them as they carried that no one could be sure if he had heard right. Gregor had wanted to answer in detail and to explain everything, but given the circumstances, confined himself to saying, "Yes, yes, thanks, Mother, I'm just getting up." The wooden door must have prevented the change in Gregor's voice from being noticed outside, because his mother was satisfied with this explanation and shuffled off. But their little exchange had made the rest of the family aware that, contrary to expectations, Gregor was still in the house, and already his father was knocking on one of the side doors, feebly but with his fist. "Gregor, Gregor," he called, "what's going on?" And after a little while he called again in a deeper, warning voice, "Gregor! Gregor!" At the other side door, however, his sister moaned gently, "Gregor? Is something the matter with you? Do you want anything?" Toward both sides Gregor answered: "I'm all ready," and made an effort, by meticulous pronunciation and by inserting long pauses between individual words, to eliminate everything from his voice that might betray him. His father went back to his breakfast, but his sister whispered, "Gregor, open up, I'm pleading with you." But Gregor had absolutely no intention of opening the door and complimented himself instead on the precaution he had adopted from his business trips, of locking all the doors during the night even at home.

First of all he wanted to get up quietly, without any excitement; get dressed; and, the main thing, have breakfast, and only then think about what to do next, for he saw clearly that in bed he would never think things through to a rational conclusion. He remembered how even in the past he had often felt some kind of slight pain, possibly caused by lying in an uncomfortable position, which, when he got up, turned out to be purely imaginary, and he was eager to see how today's fantasy would gradually fade away. That the change in his voice was nothing more than the first sign of a bad cold, an occupational ailment of the traveling salesman, he had no doubt in the least.

It was very easy to throw off the cover; all he had to do was puff himself up a little, and it fell off by itself. But after this, things got difficult, especially since he was so unusually broad. He would have needed hands and arms to lift himself up, but instead of that he had only his numerous little legs, which were in every different kind of perpetual motion and which, besides, he could not control. If he wanted to bend one, the first thing that happened was that it stretched itself out; and if he finally succeeded in getting this leg to do what he wanted, all the others in the meantime, as if set free, began to work in the most intensely painful agitation. "Just don't stay in bed being useless," Gregor said to himself.

First he tried to get out of bed with the lower part of his body, but this lower part—which by the way he had not seen yet and which he could not form a clear picture of—proved too difficult to budge; it was taking so long; and when finally, almost out of his mind, he lunged forward with all his force, without caring, he had picked the wrong direction and slammed himself violently against the lower bedpost, and the searing pain he felt taught him that exactly the lower part of his body was, for the moment anyway, the most sensitive.

He therefore tried to get the upper part of his body out of bed first and warily turned his head toward the edge of the bed. This worked easily, and in spite of its width and weight, the mass of his body finally followed, slowly, the movement of his head. But when at last he stuck his head over the edge of the bed into the air, he got too scared to continue any further, since if he finally let himself fall in this position, it would be a miracle if he didn't injure his head. And just now he had better not for the life of him lose consciousness; he would rather stay in bed.

But when, once again, after the same exertion, he lay in his original position, sighing, and again watched his little legs struggling, if possible more fiercely, with each other and saw no way of bringing peace and order into this mindless motion, he again told himself that it was impossible for him to stay in bed and that the most rational thing was to make any sacrifice for even the smallest hope of freeing himself from the bed. But at the same time he did not forget to remind himself occasionally that thinking things over calmly—indeed, as calmly as possible—was much better than jumping to desperate decisions. At such moments he fixed his eyes as sharply as possible on the window, but unfortunately there was little confidence and cheer to be gotten from the view of the morning fog, which shrouded even the other side of the narrow street. "Seven o'clock already," he said to himself as the alarm clock struck again, "seven o'clock already and still such a fog." And for a little while he lay quietly, breathing shallowly, as if expecting, perhaps, from the complete silence the return of things to the way they really and naturally were.

But then he said to himself, "Before it strikes a quarter past seven, I must be completely out of bed without fail. Anyway, by that time someone from the firm will be here to find out where I am, since the office opens before seven." And now he started rocking the complete length of his body out of the bed with a smooth rhythm. If he let himself topple out of bed in this way, his head, which on falling he planned to lift up sharply, would presumably remain unharmed. His back seemed to be hard; nothing was likely to happen to it when it fell onto the carpet. His biggest misgiving came from his concern about the loud crash that was bound to occur and would probably create, if not terror, at least anxiety behind all the doors. But that would have to be risked.

When Gregor's body already projected halfway out of bed—the new method was more of a game than a struggle, he only had to keep on rocking and jerking himself along—he thought how simple everything would be if he could get some help. Two strong persons—he thought of his father and the maid—would have been completely sufficient; they would only have had to shove their arms under his arched back, in this way scoop him off the bed, bend down with their burden, and then just be careful and patient while he managed to swing himself down onto the floor, where his little legs would hopefully acquire some purpose. Well, leaving out the fact that the doors were locked, should he really call for help? In spite of all his miseries, he could not repress a smile at this thought.

He was already so far along that when he rocked more strongly he could hardly keep his balance, and very soon he would have to commit himself, because in five minutes it would be a quarter past seven—when the doorbell rang. "It's someone from the firm," he said to himself and almost froze, while his little legs only danced more quickly. For a moment everything remained quiet. "They're not going to answer," Gregor said to himself, captivated by some senseless hope. But then, of course, the maid went to the door as usual with her firm stride and opened up. Gregor only had to hear the visitor's first word of greeting to know who it was—the office manager himself. Why was only Gregor condemned to work for a firm where at the slightest omission they immediately suspected the worst? Were all employees louts without exception, wasn't there a single loyal, dedicated worker among them who, when he had not fully utilized a few hours of the morning for the firm, was driven half-mad by pangs of conscience and was actually unable to get out of bed? Really, wouldn't it have been enough to send one of the apprentices to find out—if this prying were absolutely necessary—did the manager himself have to come, and did the whole innocent family have to be shown in this way that the investigation of this suspicious affair could be entrusted only to the intellect of the manager? And more as a result of the excitement produced in Gregor by these thoughts than as a result of any real decision, he swung himself out of bed with all his might. There was a loud thump, but it was not a real crash. The fall was broken a little by the carpet, and Gregor's back was more elastic than he had thought, which explained the not very noticeable muffled sound. Only he had not held his head carefully enough and hit it; he turned it and rubbed it on the carpet in anger and pain.

"Something fell in there," said the manager in the room on the left. Gregor tried to imagine whether something like what had happened to him today could one day happen even to the manager; you really had to grant the possibility. But as if in rude reply to this question, the manager took a few decisive steps in the next room and made his patent leather boots creak. From the room on the right his sister whispered, to inform Gregor, "Gregor, the manager is here." "I know," Gregor said to himself; but he did not dare raise his voice enough for his sister to hear.

"Gregor," his father now said from the room on the left, "the manager has come and wants to be informed why you didn't catch the early train. We don't know what we should say to him. Besides, he wants to speak to you personally. So please open the door. He will certainly be so kind as to excuse the disorder of the room." "Good morning, Mr. Samsa," the manager called in a friendly voice. "There's something the matter with him," his mother said to the manager while his father was still at the door, talking. "Believe me, sir, there's something the matter with him. Otherwise how would Gregor have missed a train? That boy has nothing on his mind but the business. It's almost begun to rile me that he never goes out nights. He's been back in the city for eight days now, but every night he's been home. He sits there with us at the table, quietly reading the paper or studying timetables. It's already a distraction for him when he's busy working with his fretsaw.[3] For instance, in the span of two or three evenings he carved a little frame. You'll be amazed how pretty it is; it's hanging inside his room. You'll see it right away when Gregor opens the door. You know, I'm glad that you've come, sir. We would never have gotten Gregor to open the door by ourselves; he's so stubborn. And there's certainly something wrong with him, even though he said this morning there wasn't." "I'm coming right away," said Gregor slowly and deliberately, not moving in order not to miss a word of the conversation. "I haven't any other explanation myself," said the manager. "I hope it's nothing serious. On the other hand, I must say that we businessmen—fortunately or unfortunately, whichever you prefer—very often simply have to overcome a slight indisposition for business reasons." "So can the manager come in now?" asked his father, impatient, and knocked on the door again. "No," said Gregor. In the room on the left there was an embarrassing silence; in the room on the right his sister began to sob.

3. A small fine-toothed saw that is used to cut creative, decorative patterns in wood.

Why didn't his sister go in to the others? She had probably just got out of bed and not even started to get dressed. Then what was she crying about? Because he didn't get up and didn't let the manager in, because he was in danger of losing his job, and because then the boss would start hounding his parents about the old debts? For the time being, certainly, her worries were unnecessary. Gregor was still here and hadn't the slightest intention of letting the family down. True, at the moment he was lying on the carpet, and no one knowing his condition could seriously have expected him to let the manager in. But just because of this slight discourtesy, for which an appropriate excuse would easily be found later on, Gregor could not simply be dismissed. And to Gregor it seemed much more sensible to leave him alone now than to bother him with crying and persuasion. But it was just the uncertainty that was tormenting the others and excused their behavior.

"Mr. Samsa," the manager now called, raising his voice, "what's the matter? You barricade yourself in your room, answer only 'yes' and 'no,' cause your parents serious, unnecessary worry, and you neglect—I mention this only in passing—your duties to the firm in a really shocking manner. I am speaking here in the name of your parents and of your employer and ask you in all seriousness for an immediate, clear explanation. I'm amazed, amazed. I thought I knew you to be a quiet, reasonable person, and now you suddenly seem to want to start strutting about, flaunting strange whims. The head of the firm did suggest to me this morning a possible explanation for your tardiness—it concerned the cash payments recently entrusted to you—but really, I practically gave my word of honor that this explanation could not be right. But now, seeing your incomprehensible obstinacy, I am about to lose even the slightest desire to stick up for you in any way at all. And your job is not the most secure. Originally I intended to tell you all this in private, but since you make me waste my time here for nothing, I don't see why your parents shouldn't hear too. Your performance of late has been very unsatisfactory; I know it is not the best season for doing business, we all recognize that; but a season for not doing any business, there is no such thing, Mr. Samsa, such a thing cannot be tolerated."

"But, sir," cried Gregor, beside himself, in his excitement forgetting everything else, "I'm just opening up, in a minute. A slight indisposition, a dizzy spell, prevented me from getting up. I'm still in bed. But I already feel fine again. I'm just getting out of bed. Just be patient for a minute! I'm not as well as I thought yet. But really I'm fine. How something like this could just take a person by surprise! Only last night I was fine, my parents can tell you, or wait, last night I already had a slight premonition. They must have been able to tell by looking at me. Why didn't I report it to the office! But you always think that you'll get over a sickness without staying home. Sir! Spare my parents! There's no basis for any of the accusations that you're making against me now; no one has ever said a word to me about them. Perhaps you haven't seen the last orders I sent in. Anyway, I'm still going on the road with the eight o'clock train; these few hours of rest have done me good. Don't let me keep you, sir. I'll be at the office myself right away, and be so kind as to tell them this, and give my respects to the head of the firm."

And while Gregor hastily blurted all this out, hardly knowing what he was saying, he had easily approached the chest of drawers, probably as a result of the practice he had already gotten in bed, and now he tried to raise himself up against it. He actually intended to open the door, actually present himself and speak to the manager; he was eager to find out what the others, who were now so anxious to see him, would say at the sight of him. If they were shocked, then Gregor had no further responsibility and could be calm. But if they took everything calmly, then he, too, had no reason to get excited and could, if he hurried, actually be at the station by eight o'clock. At first he slid off the polished chest of drawers a few times, but at last, giving himself a final push, he stood upright; he no longer paid any attention to the pains in his abdomen, no matter how much they were burning. Now he let himself fall against the back of a nearby chair, clinging to its slats with his little legs. But by doing this he had gotten control of himself and fell silent, since he could now listen to what the manager was saying.

"Did you understand a word?" the manager was asking his parents. "He isn't trying to make fools of us, is he?" "My God," cried his mother, already in tears, "maybe he's seriously ill, and here we are, torturing him. Grete! Grete!" she then cried. "Mother?" called his sister from the other side. They communicated by way of Gregor's room. "Go to the doctor's immediately. Gregor is sick. Hurry, get the doctor. Did you just hear Gregor talking?" "That was the voice of an animal," said the manager, in a tone conspicuously soft compared with the mother's yelling. "Anna! Anna!" the father called through the foyer into the kitchen, clapping his hands, "get a locksmith right away!" And already the two girls were running with rustling skirts through the foyer—how could his sister have gotten dressed so quickly?—and tearing open the door to the apartment. The door could not be heard slamming; they had probably left it open, as is the custom in homes where a great misfortune has occurred.[4]

But Gregor had become much calmer. It was true that they no longer understood his words, though they had seemed clear enough to him, clearer than before, probably because his ear had grown accustomed to them. But still, the others now believed that there was something the matter with him and were ready to help him. The assurance and confidence with which the first measures had been taken did him good. He felt integrated into human society once again and hoped for marvelous, amazing feats from both the doctor and the locksmith, without really distinguishing sharply between them. In order to make his voice as clear as possible for the crucial discussions that were approaching, he cleared his throat a little—taking pains, of course, to do so in a very muffled manner, since this noise, too, might sound different from human coughing, a thing he no longer trusted himself to decide. In the next room, meanwhile, everything had become completely still. Perhaps his parents were sitting at the table with the manager, whispering; perhaps they were all leaning against the door and listening.

Gregor slowly lugged himself toward the door, pushing the chair in front of him, then let go of it, threw himself against the door, held himself upright against it—the pads on the bottom of his little legs exuded a little sticky substance—and for a moment rested there from the exertion. But then he got started turning the key in the lock with his mouth. Unfortunately it seemed that he had no real teeth—what was he supposed to grip the key with?—but in compensation his jaws, of course, were very strong; with their help he actually got the key moving and paid no attention to the fact that he was undoubtedly hurting himself in some way, for a brown liquid came out of his mouth, flowed over the key, and dripped onto the floor. "Listen," said the manager in the next room, "he's turning the key." This was great encouragement to Gregor; but everyone should have cheered him on, his father and mother too. "Go, Gregor," they should have called, "keep going, at that lock, harder, harder!" And in the delusion that

4. Kafka is referring to a common popular belief that opening a house's doors and windows after a stroke of ill fortune, especially a death, will help to clear bad influences and spirits from the residence.

they were all following his efforts with suspense, he clamped his jaws madly on the key with all the strength he could muster. Depending on the progress of the key, he danced around the lock; holding himself upright only by his mouth, he clung to the key, as the situation demanded, or pressed it down again with the whole weight of his body. The clearer click of the lock as it finally snapped back literally woke Gregor up. With a sigh of relief he said to himself, "So I didn't need the locksmith after all," and laid his head down on the handle in order to open wide one wing of the double doors.

Since he had to use this method of opening the door, it was really opened very wide while he himself was still invisible. He first had to edge slowly around the one wing of the door, and do so very carefully if he was not to fall flat on his back just before entering. He was still busy with this difficult maneuver and had no time to pay attention to anything else when he heard the manager burst out with a loud "Oh!"—it sounded like a rush of wind—and now he could see him, standing closest to the door, his hand pressed over his open mouth, slowly backing away, as if repulsed by an invisible, unrelenting force. His mother—in spite of the manager's presence she stood with her hair still unbraided from the night, sticking out in all directions—first looked at his father with her hands clasped, then took two steps toward Gregor, and sank down in the midst of her skirts spreading out around her, her face completely hidden on her breast. With a hostile expression his father clenched his fist, as if to drive Gregor back into his room, then looked uncertainly around the living room, shielded his eyes with his hands, and sobbed with heaves of his powerful chest.

Now Gregor did not enter the room after all but leaned against the inside of the firmly bolted wing of the door, so that only half his body was visible and his head above it, cocked to one side and peeping out at the others. In the meantime it had grown much lighter; across the street one could see clearly a section of the endless, grayish-black building opposite—it was a hospital—with its regular windows starkly piercing the façade; the rain was still coming down, but only in large, separately visible drops that were also pelting the ground literally one at a time. The breakfast dishes were laid out lavishly on the table, since for his father breakfast was the most important meal of the day, which he would prolong for hours while reading various newspapers. On the wall directly opposite hung a photograph of Gregor from his army days, in a lieutenant's uniform, his hand on his sword, a carefree smile on his lips, demanding respect for his bearing and his rank. The door to the foyer was open, and since the front door was open too, it was possible to see out onto the landing and the top of the stairs going down.

"Well," said Gregor—and he was thoroughly aware of being the only one who had kept calm—"I'll get dressed right away, pack up my samples, and go. Will you, will you please let me go? Now, sir, you see, I'm not stubborn and I'm willing to work; traveling is a hardship, but without it I couldn't live. Where are you going, sir? To the office? Yes? Will you give an honest report of everything? A man might find for a moment that he was unable to work, but that's exactly the right time to remember his past accomplishments and to consider that later on, when the obstacle has been removed, he's bound to work all the harder and more efficiently. I'm under so many obligations to the head of the firm, as you know very well. Besides, I also have my parents and my sister to worry about. I'm in a tight spot, but I'll also work my way out again. Don't make things harder for me than they already are. Stick up for me in the office, please. Traveling salesmen aren't well liked there, I know. People think they make a fortune leading the gay life. No one has any particular reason to rectify this prejudice. But you, sir, you have a better perspective on things than the rest of the

office, an even better perspective, just between the two of us, than the head of the firm
himself, who in his capacity as owner easily lets his judgment be swayed against an
employee. And you also know very well that the traveling salesman, who is out of the
office practically the whole year round, can so easily become the victim of gossip, co-
incidences, and unfounded accusations, against which he's completely unable to defend himself, since in most cases he knows nothing at all about them except when he
returns exhausted from a trip, and back home gets to suffer on his own person the
grim consequences, which can no longer be traced back to their causes. Sir, don't go
away without a word to tell me you think I'm at least partly right!"

But at Gregor's first words the manager had already turned away and with curled
lips looked back at Gregor only over his twitching shoulder. And during Gregor's
speech he did not stand still for a minute but, without letting Gregor out of his sight,
backed toward the door, yet very gradually, as if there were some secret prohibition
against leaving the room. He was already in the foyer, and from the sudden movement
with which he took his last step from the living room, one might have thought he had
just burned the sole of his foot. In the foyer, however, he stretched his right hand far
out toward the staircase, as if nothing less than an unearthly deliverance were awaiting him there.

Gregor realized that he must on no account let the manager go away in this mood
if his position in the firm were not to be jeopardized in the extreme. His parents did
not understand this too well; in the course of the years they had formed the conviction
that Gregor was set for life in this firm; and furthermore, they were so preoccupied
with their immediate troubles that they had lost all consideration for the future. But
Gregor had this forethought. The manager must be detained, calmed down, convinced, and finally won over; Gregor's and the family's future depended on it! If only
his sister had been there! She was perceptive; she had already begun to cry when Gregor was still lying calmly on his back. And certainly the manager, this ladies' man,
would have listened to her; she would have shut the front door and in the foyer talked
him out of his scare. But his sister was not there; Gregor had to handle the situation
himself. And without stopping to realize that he had no idea what his new faculties of
movement were, and without stopping to realize either that his speech had possibly—
indeed, probably—not been understood again, he let go of the wing of the door; he
shoved himself through the opening, intending to go to the manager, who was already
on the landing, ridiculously holding onto the banisters with both hands; but groping
for support, Gregor immediately fell down with a little cry onto his numerous little
legs. This had hardly happened when for the first time that morning he had a feeling of
physical well-being; his little legs were on firm ground; they obeyed him completely,
as he noted to his joy; they even strained to carry him away wherever he wanted to go;
and he already believed that final recovery from all his sufferings was imminent. But
at that very moment, as he lay on the floor rocking with repressed motion, not far from
his mother and just opposite her, she, who had seemed so completely self-absorbed,
all at once jumped up, her arms stretched wide, her fingers spread, and cried, "Help,
for God's sake, help!" held her head bent as if to see Gregor better, but inconsistently
darted madly backward instead; had forgotten that the table laden with the breakfast
dishes stood behind her; sat down on it hastily, as if her thoughts were elsewhere,
when she reached it; and did not seem to notice at all that near her the big coffeepot
had been knocked over and coffee was pouring in a steady stream onto the rug.

"Mother, Mother," said Gregor softly and looked up at her. For a minute the
manager had completely slipped his mind; on the other hand at the sight of the

spilling coffee he could not resist snapping his jaws several times in the air. At this his mother screamed once more, fled from the table, and fell into the arms of his father, who came rushing up to her. But Gregor had no time now for his parents; the manager was already on the stairs; with his chin on the banister, he was taking a last look back. Gregor was off to a running start, to be as sure as possible of catching up with him; the manager must have suspected something like this, for he leaped down several steps and disappeared; but still he shouted "Agh," and the sound carried through the whole staircase. Unfortunately the manager's flight now seemed to confuse his father completely, who had been relatively calm until now, for instead of running after the manager himself, or at least not hindering Gregor in his pursuit, he seized in his right hand the manager's cane, which had been left behind on a chair with his hat and over-coat, picked up in his left hand a heavy newspaper from the table, and stamping his feet, started brandishing the cane and the newspaper to drive Gregor back into his room. No plea of Gregor's helped, no plea was even understood; however humbly he might turn his head, his father merely stamped his feet more forcefully. Across the room his mother had thrown open a window in spite of the cool weather, and leaning out, she buried her face, far outside the window, in her hands. Between the alley and the staircase a strong draft was created, the window curtains blew in, the newspapers on the table rustled, single sheets fluttered across the floor. Pitilessly his father came on, hissing like a wild man. Now Gregor had not had any practice at all walking in re-verse, it was really very slow going. If Gregor had only been allowed to turn around, he could have gotten into his room right away, but he was afraid to make his father impatient by this time-consuming gyration, and at any minute the cane in his father's hand threatened to come down on his back or his head with a deadly blow. Finally, however, Gregor had no choice, for he noticed with horror that in reverse he could not even keep going in one direction; and so, incessantly throwing uneasy side-glances at his father, he began to turn around as quickly as possible, in reality turning only very slowly. Perhaps his father realized his good intentions, for he did not interfere with him; instead, he even now and then directed the maneuver from afar with the tip of his cane. If only his father did not keep making this intolerable hissing sound! It made Gregor lose his head completely. He had almost finished the turn when—his mind continually on this hissing—he made a mistake and even started turning back around to his original position. But when he had at last successfully managed to get his head in front of the opened door, it turned out that his body was too broad to get through as it was. Of course in his father's present state of mind it did not even remotely occur to him to open the other wing of the door in order to give Gregor enough room to pass through. He had only the fixed idea that Gregor must return to his room as quickly as possible. He would never have allowed the complicated preliminaries Gregor needed to go through in order to stand up on one end and perhaps in this way fit through the door. Instead he drove Gregor on, as if there were no obstacle, with exceptional loud-ness; the voice behind Gregor did not sound like that of only a single father; now this was really no joke anymore, and Gregor forced himself—come what may—into the doorway. One side of his body rose up, he lay lop-sided in the opening, one of his flanks was scraped raw, ugly blotches marred the white door, soon he got stuck and could not have budged any more by himself, his little legs on one side dangled trem-blingly in midair, those on the other were painfully crushed against the floor—when from behind his father gave him a hard shove, which was truly his salvation, and bleeding profusely, he flew far into his room. The door was slammed shut with the cane, then at last everything was quiet.

2

It was already dusk when Gregor awoke from his deep, comalike sleep. Even if he had not been disturbed, he would certainly not have woken up much later, for he felt that he had rested and slept long enough, but it seemed to him that a hurried step and a cautious shutting of the door leading to the foyer had awakened him. The light of the electric street-lamps lay in pallid streaks on the ceiling and on the upper parts of the furniture, but underneath, where Gregor was, it was dark. Groping clumsily with his antennae, which he was only now beginning to appreciate, he slowly dragged himself toward the door to see what had been happening there. His left side felt like one single long, unpleasantly tautening scar, and he actually had to limp on his two rows of legs. Besides, one little leg had been seriously injured in the course of the morning's events—it was almost a miracle that only one had been injured—and dragged along lifelessly.

Only after he got to the door did he notice what had really attracted him—the smell of something to eat. For there stood a bowl filled with fresh milk, in which small slices of white bread were floating. He could almost have laughed for joy, since he was even hungrier than he had been in the morning, and he immediately dipped his head into the milk, almost to over his eyes. But he soon drew it back again in disappointment; not only because he had difficulty eating on account of the soreness in his left side—and he could eat only if his whole panting body cooperated—but because he didn't like the milk at all, although it used to be his favorite drink, and that was certainly why his sister had put it in the room; in fact, he turned away from the bowl almost with repulsion and crawled back to the middle of the room.

In the living room, as Gregor saw through the crack in the door, the gas had been lit, but while at this hour of the day his father was in the habit of reading the afternoon newspaper in a loud voice to his mother and sometimes to his sister too, now there wasn't a sound. Well, perhaps this custom of reading aloud, which his sister was always telling him and writing him about, had recently been discontinued altogether. But in all the other rooms too it was just as still, although the apartment certainly was not empty. "What a quiet life the family has been leading," Gregor said to himself, and while he stared rigidly in front of him into the darkness, he felt very proud that he had been able to provide such a life in so nice an apartment for his parents and his sister. But what now if all the peace, the comfort, the contentment were to come to a horrible end? In order not to get involved in such thoughts, Gregor decided to keep moving, and he crawled up and down the room.

During the long evening, first one of the side doors and then the other was opened a small crack and quickly shut again; someone had probably had the urge to come in and then had had second thoughts. Gregor now settled into position right by the living-room door, determined somehow to get the hesitating visitor to come in, or at least to find out who it might be; but the door was not opened again, and Gregor waited in vain. In the morning, when the doors had been locked, everyone had wanted to come in; now that he had opened one of the doors and the others had evidently been opened during the day, no one came in, and now the keys were even inserted on the outside.

It was late at night when the light finally went out in the living room, and now it was easy for Gregor to tell that his parents and his sister had stayed up so long, since, as he could distinctly hear, all three were now retiring on tiptoe. Certainly no one would come in to Gregor until the morning; and so he had ample time to consider undisturbed how best to rearrange his life. But the empty high-ceilinged room in which he was forced to lie flat on the floor made him nervous, without his being able to tell why—since it was, after all, the room in which be had lived for the past five years—and turning half unconsciously and not without a slight feeling of shame, he scuttled under the couch where, although his back was a little crushed and he could not raise his head any more, he immediately felt very comfortable and was only sorry that his body was too wide to go completely under the couch.

There he stayed the whole night, which he spent partly in a sleepy trance, from which hunger pangs kept waking him with a start, partly in worries and vague hopes, all of which, however, led to the conclusion that for the time being he would have to lie low and, by being patient and showing his family every possible consideration, help them bear the inconvenience which he simply had to cause them in his present condition.

Early in the morning—it was still almost night—Gregor had the opportunity of testing the strength of the resolutions he had just made, for his sister, almost fully dressed, opened the door from the foyer and looked in eagerly. She did not see him right away, but when she caught sight of him under the couch—God, he had to be somewhere, he couldn't just fly away—she became so frightened that she lost control of herself and slammed the door shut again. But, as if she felt sorry for her behavior, she immediately opened the door again and came in on tiptoe, as if she were visiting someone seriously ill or perhaps even a stranger. Gregor had pushed his head forward just to the edge of the couch and was watching her. Would she notice that he had left the milk standing, and not because he hadn't been hungry, and would she bring in a dish of something he'd like better? If she were not going to do it of her own free will, he would rather starve than call it to her attention, although, really, he felt an enormous urge to shoot out from under the couch, throw himself at his sister's feet, and beg her for something good to eat. But his sister noticed at once, to her astonishment, that the bowl was still full, only a little milk was spilled around it; she picked it up immediately—not with her bare hands, of course, but with a rag—and carried it out. Gregor was extremely curious to know what she would bring him instead, and he racked his brains on the subject. But he would never have been able to guess what his sister, in the goodness of her heart, actually did. To find out his likes and dislikes, she brought him a wide assortment of things, all spread out on an old newspapers: old, half-rotten vegetables; bones left over from the evening meal, caked with congealed white sauce; some raisins and almonds; a piece of cheese, which two days before Gregor had declared inedible; a plain slice of bread, a slice of bread and butter, and one with butter and salt. In addition to all this she put down some water in the bowl apparently permanently earmarked for Gregor's use. And out of a sense of delicacy, since she knew that Gregor would not eat in front of her, she left hurriedly and even turned the key, just so that Gregor should know that he might make himself as comfortable as he wanted. Gregor's legs began whirring now that he was going to eat. Besides, his bruises must have completely healed, since he no longer felt any handicap, and marveling at this he thought how, over a month ago, he had cut his finger very slightly with a knife and how this wound was still hurting him only the day before yesterday. "Have I become less sensitive?" he thought, already sucking greedily at the cheese, which had immediately and forcibly attracted him ahead of all the other dishes. One right after the other, and with eyes streaming with tears of contentment, he devoured the cheese, the vegetables, and the sauce; the fresh foods, on the other hand, he did not care for; he couldn't even stand their smell and even dragged the things he wanted to eat a bit farther away. He had finished with everything long since and was just lying lazily at the same spot when his sister slowly turned the key as a sign for him to withdraw. That immediately startled him, although he was almost asleep, and he scuttled under the couch again. But it took great self-control for him to stay under the couch even for the short time his sister was in the room, since his body had become a little bloated from the heavy meal, and in his cramped position he could hardly breathe. In between slight attacks of suffocation he watched with bulging eyes as his unsuspecting sister took a broom and swept up, not only his leavings, but even the foods which Gregor had left completely untouched—as if they too were no longer usable—and dumping everything hastily into a pail, which she covered with a wooden lid, she carried everything out. She had hardly turned her back when Gregor came out from under the couch, stretching and puffing himself up.

This, then, was the way Gregor was fed each day, once in the morning, when his parents and the maid were still asleep, and a second time in the afternoon after everyone had had dinner, for then his parents took a short nap again, and the maid could be sent out by his sister on some errand. Certainly they did not want him to starve either, but perhaps they would not have been able to stand knowing any more about his meals than from hearsay, or perhaps his sister wanted to spare them even what was possibly only a minor torment, for really, they were suffering enough as it was.

Gregor could not find out what excuses had been made to get rid of the doctor and the locksmith on that first morning, for since the others could not understand what he said, it did not occur to any of them, not even to his sister, that he could understand what they said, and so he had to be satisfied, when his sister was in the room, with only occasionally hearing her sighs and appeals to the saints. It was only later, when she had begun to get used to everything—there could never, of course, be any question of a complete adjustment—that Gregor sometimes caught a remark which was meant to be friendly or could be interpreted as such. "Oh, he liked what he had today," she would say when Gregor had tucked away a good helping, and in the opposite case, which gradually occurred more and more frequently, she used to say, almost sadly, "He's left everything again."

But if Gregor could not get any news directly, he overheard a great deal from the neighboring rooms, and as soon as he heard voices, he would immediately run to the door concerned and press his whole body against it. Especially in the early days, there was no conversation that was not somehow about him, if only implicitly. For two whole days there were family consultations at every mealtime about how they should cope; this was also the topic of discussion between meals, for at least two members of the family were always at home, since no one probably wanted to stay home alone and it was impossible to leave the apartment completely empty. Besides, on the very first day the maid—it was not completely clear what and how much she knew of what had happened—had begged his mother on bended knees to dismiss her immediately; and when she said goodbye a quarter of an hour later, she thanked them in tears for the dismissal, as if for the greatest favor that had ever been done to her in this house, and made a solemn vow, without anyone asking her for it, not to give anything away to anyone.

Now his sister, working with her mother, had to do the cooking too; of course that did not cause her much trouble, since they hardly ate anything. Gregor was always hearing one of them pleading in vain with one of the others to eat and getting no answer except, "Thanks, I've had enough," or something similar. They did not seem to drink anything either. His sister often asked her father if he wanted any beer and gladly offered to go out for it herself; and when he did not answer, she said, in order to remove any hesitation on his part, that she could also send the janitor's wife to get it, but then his father finally answered with a definite "No," and that was the end of that.

In the course of the very first day his father explained the family's financial situation and prospects to both the mother and the sister. From time to time he got up from the table to get some kind of receipt or notebook out of the little strongbox he had rescued from the collapse of his business five years before. Gregor heard him open the complicated lock and secure it again after taking out what he had been looking for. These explanations by his father were to some extent the first pleasant news Gregor had heard since his imprisonment. He had always believed that his father had not been able to save a penny from the business, at least his father had never told him anything to the contrary, and Gregor, for his part, had never asked him any questions. In those days Gregor's sole concern had been to do everything in his power to make the family forget as quickly as possible the business disaster which had plunged everyone into a state of total despair. And so he had begun to work with special ardor and had risen almost overnight from stock clerk to traveling salesman, which of course had opened up very different moneymaking possibilities, and in no time his successes on the job were transformed, by means of commissions, into hard cash that could be plunked down on the table at home in front of his astonished and delighted family. Those had been wonderful times, and they had never returned, at least not with the same glory, although later on Gregor earned enough money to meet the expenses of the entire family and actually did so. They had just gotten used to it, the family as well as Gregor, the money was received with thanks and given with pleasure, but no special feeling of warmth went with it anymore. Only his sister had remained close to Gregor, and it was his secret plan that she, who, unlike him, loved music and could play the violin movingly, should be sent next year to the Conservatory, regardless of the great expense involved, which could surely be made up for in some other way. Often during Gregor's short stays in the city, the Conservatory would come up in his conversations with his sister, but always merely as a beautiful dream which was not supposed to come true, and his parents were not happy to hear even these innocent allusions; but Gregor had very concrete ideas on the subject and he intended solemnly to announce his plan on Christmas Eve.

Thoughts like these, completely useless in his present state, went through his head as he stood glued to the door, listening. Sometimes out of general exhaustion he could not listen anymore and let his head bump carelessly against the door, but immediately pulled it back again, for even the slight noise he made by doing this had been heard in the next room and made them all lapse into silence. "What's he carrying on about in there now?" said his father after a while, obviously turning toward the door, and only then would the interrupted conversation gradually be resumed.

Gregor now learned in a thorough way—for his father was in the habit of often repeating himself in his explanations, partly because he himself had not dealt with these matters for a long time, partly, too, because his mother did not understand everything the first time around—that in spite of all their misfortunes a bit of capital, a very little bit, certainly, was still intact from the old days, which in the meantime had increased a little through the untouched interest. But besides that, the money Gregor had brought home every month—he had kept only a few dollars for himself—had never been completely used up and had accumulated into a tidy principal. Behind his door Gregor nodded emphatically, delighted at this unexpected foresight and thrift. Of course he actually could have paid off more of his father's debt to the boss with this extra money, and the day on which he could have gotten rid of his job would have been much closer, but now things were undoubtedly better the way his father had arranged them.

Now this money was by no means enough to let the family live off the interest; the principal was perhaps enough to support the family for one year, or at the most two, but that was all there was. So it was just a sum that really should not be touched and that had to be put away for a rainy day; but the money to live on would have to be earned. Now his father was still healthy, certainly, but he was an old man who had not worked for the past five years and who in any case could not be expected to undertake too much; during these five years, which were the first vacation of his hard-working yet unsuccessful life, he had gained a lot of weight and as a result had become fairly sluggish. And was his old mother now supposed to go out and earn money, when she suffered from asthma, when a walk through the apartment was already an ordeal for her, and when she spent every other day lying on the sofa under the open window, gasping for breath? And was his sister now supposed to work—who for all her seventeen years was still a child and whom it would be such a pity to deprive of the life she had led until now, which had consisted of wearing pretty clothes, sleeping late, helping in the house, enjoying a few modest amusements, and above all playing the violin? At first, whenever the conversation turned to the necessity of earning money, Gregor would let go of the door and throw himself down on the cool leather sofa which stood beside it, for he felt hot with shame and grief.

Often he lay there the whole long night through, not sleeping a wink and only scrabbling on the leather for hours on end. Or, not balking at the huge effort of pushing an armchair to the window, he would crawl up to the window sill and, propped up in the chair, lean against the window, evidently in some sort of remembrance of the feeling of freedom he used to have from looking out the window. For, in fact, from day to day he saw things even a short distance away less and less distinctly; the hospital opposite, which he used to curse because he saw so much of it, was now completely beyond his range of vision, and if he had not been positive that he was living in Charlotte Street—a quiet but still very much a city street—he might have believed that he was looking out of his window into a desert where the gray sky and the gray earth were indistinguishably fused. It took his observant sister only twice to notice that his armchair was standing by the window for her to push the chair back to the same place by the window each time she had finished cleaning the room, and from then on she even left the inside casement of the window open.

If Gregor had only been able to speak to his sister and thank her for everything she had to do for him, he could have accepted her services more easily; as it was, they caused him pain. Of course his sister tried to ease the embarrassment of the whole situation as much as possible, and as time went on, she naturally managed it better and better, but in time Gregor, too, saw things much more clearly. Even the way she came in was terrible for him. Hardly had she entered the room than she would run straight to the window without taking time to close the door—though she was usually so careful to spare everyone the sight of Gregor's room—then tear open the casements with eager hands, almost as if she were suffocating, and remain for a little while at the window even in the coldest weather, breathing deeply. With this racing and crashing she frightened Gregor twice a day; the whole time he cowered under the couch, and yet he knew very well that she would certainly have spared him this if only she had found it possible to stand being in a room with him with the window closed.

One time—it must have been a month since Gregor's metamorphosis, and there was certainly no particular reason any more for his sister to be astonished at Gregor's appearance—she came a little earlier than usual and caught Gregor still looking out the window, immobile and so in an excellent position to be terrifying. It would not have surprised Gregor if she had not come in, because his position prevented her from immediately opening the window, but not only did she not come in, she even sprang back and locked the door; a stranger might easily have thought that Gregor had been lying in wait for her, wanting to bite her. Of course Gregor immediately hid under the couch, but he had to wait until noon before his sister came again, and she seemed much more uneasy than usual. He realized from this that the sight of him was still repulsive to her and was bound to remain repulsive to her in the future, and that she probably had to overcome a lot of resistance not to run away at the sight of even the small part of his body that jutted out from under the couch. So, to spare her even this sight, one day he carried the sheet on his back to the couch—the job took four hours—and arranged it in such a way that he was now completely covered up and his sister could not see him even when she stooped. If she had considered this sheet unnecessary, then of course she could have removed it, for it was clear enough that it could not be for his own pleasure that Gregor shut himself off altogether, but she left the sheet the way it was, and Gregor thought that he had even caught a grateful look when one time he cautiously lifted the sheet a little with his head in order to see how his sister was taking the new arrangement.

During the first two weeks, his parents could not bring themselves to come in to him, and often he heard them say how much they appreciated his sister's work, whereas until now they had frequently been annoyed with her because she had struck them as being a little useless. But now both of them, his father and his mother, often waited outside Gregor's room while his sister straightened it up, and as soon as she came out she had to tell them in great detail how the room looked, what Gregor had eaten, how he had behaved this time, and whether he had perhaps shown a little improvement. His mother, incidentally, began relatively soon to want to visit Gregor, but his father and his sister at first held her back with reasonable arguments to which Gregor listened very attentively and of which he whole-heartedly approved. But later she had to be restrained by force, and then when she cried out, "Let me go to Gregor, he is my unfortunate boy! Don't you understand that I have to go to him?" Gregor thought that it might be a good idea after all if his mother did come in, not every day of course, but perhaps once a week; she could still do everything much better than his sister, who, for all her courage, was still only a child and in the final analysis had perhaps taken on such a difficult assignment only out of childish flightiness.

Gregor's desire to see his mother was soon fulfilled. During the day Gregor did not want to show himself at the window, if only out of consideration for his parents, but he couldn't crawl very far on his few square yards of floor space, either; he could hardly put up with just lying still even at night; eating soon stopped giving him the slightest pleasure, so, as a distraction, he adopted the habit of crawling crisscross over the walls and the ceiling. He especially liked hanging from the ceiling; it was completely different from lying on the floor; one could breathe more freely; a faint swinging sensation went through the body; and in the almost happy absent-mindedness which Gregor felt up there, it could happen to his own surprise that he let go and plopped onto the floor. But now, of course, he had much better control of his body than before and did not hurt himself even from such a big drop. His sister immediately noticed the new entertainment Gregor had discovered for himself—after all, he left behind traces of his sticky substance wherever he crawled—and so she got it into her head to make it possible for Gregor to crawl on an altogether wider scale by taking out the furniture which stood in his way—mainly the chest of drawers and the desk. But she was not able to do this by herself; she did not dare ask her father for help; the maid would certainly not have helped her, for although this girl, who was about sixteen, was bravely sticking it out after the previous cook had left, she had asked for the favor of locking herself in the kitchen at all times and of only opening the door on special request. So there was nothing left for his sister to do except to get her mother one day when her father was out. And his mother did come, with exclamations of excited joy, but she grew silent at the door of Gregor's room. First his sister looked to see, of course, that everything in the room was in order; only then did she let her mother come in. Hurrying as fast as he could, Gregor had pulled the sheet down lower still and pleated it more tightly—it really looked just like a sheet accidentally thrown over the couch. This time Gregor also refrained from spying from under the sheet; he renounced seeing his mother for the time being and was simply happy that she had come after all. "Come on, you can't see him," his sister said, evidently leading her mother in by the hand. Now Gregor could hear the two frail women moving the old chest of drawers—heavy for anyone—from its place and his sister insisting on doing the harder part of the job herself, ignoring the warnings of her mother, who was afraid that she would overexert herself. It went on for a long time. After struggling for a good quarter of an hour, his mother said that they had better leave the chest where it was, because, in the first place, it was too heavy, they would not finish before his father came, and with the chest in the middle of the room, Gregor would be completely barricaded; and, in the second place, it was not at all certain that they were doing Gregor a favor by removing his furniture. To her the opposite seemed to be the case; the sight of the bare wall was heart-breaking; and why shouldn't Gregor also have the same feeling, since he had been used to his furniture for so long and would feel abandoned in the empty room. "And doesn't it look," his mother concluded very softly—in fact she had been almost whispering the whole time, as if she wanted to avoid letting Gregor, whose exact whereabouts she did not know, hear even the sound of her voice, for she was convinced that he did not understand the words—"and doesn't it look as if by removing his furniture we were showing him that we have given up all hope of his getting better and are leaving him to his own devices without any consideration? I think the best thing would be to try to keep the room exactly the way it was before, so that when Gregor comes back to us again, he'll find everything unchanged and can forget all the more easily what's happened in the meantime."

When he heard his mother's words, Gregor realized that the monotony of family life, combined with the fact that not a soul had addressed a word directly to him, must have addled his brain in the course of the past two months, for he could not explain to himself in any other way how in all seriousness he could have been anxious to have his room cleared out. Had he really wanted to have his warm room, comfortably fitted with furniture that had always been in the family, changed into a cave, in which, of course, he would be able to crawl around unhampered in all directions but at the cost of simultaneously, rapidly, and totally forgetting his human past? Even now he had been on the verge of forgetting, and only his mother's voice, which he had not heard for so long, had shaken him up. Nothing should be removed; everything had to stay; he could not do without the beneficial influence of the furniture on his state of mind; and if the furniture prevented him from carrying on this senseless crawling around, then that was no loss but rather a great advantage.

But his sister unfortunately had a different opinion; she had become accustomed, certainly not entirely without justification, to adopt with her parents the role of the particularly well-qualified expert whenever Gregor's affairs were being discussed;

and so her mother's advice was now sufficient reason for her to insist, not only on the removal of the chest of drawers and the desk, which was all she had been planning at first, but also on the removal of all the furniture with the exception of the indispensable couch. Of course it was not only childish defiance and the self-confidence she had recently acquired so unexpectedly and at such a cost that led her to make this demand; she had in fact noticed that Gregor needed plenty of room to crawl around in; and on the other hand, as best she could tell, he never used the furniture at all. Perhaps, however, the romantic enthusiasm of girls her age, which seeks to indulge itself at every opportunity, played a part, by tempting her to make Gregor's situation even more terrifying in order that she might do even more for him. Into a room in which Gregor ruled the bare walls all alone, no human being beside Grete was ever likely to set foot.

And so she did not let herself be swerved from her decision by her mother, who, besides, from the sheer anxiety of being in Gregor's room, seemed unsure of herself, soon grew silent, and helped her daughter as best she could to get the chest of drawers out of the room. Well, in a pinch Gregor could do without the chest, but the desk had to stay. And hardly had the women left the room with the chest, squeezing against it and groaning, than Gregor stuck his head out from under the couch to see how he could feel his way into the situation as considerately as possible. But unfortunately it had to be his mother who came back first, while in the next room Grete was clasping the chest and rocking it back and forth by herself, without of course budging it from the spot. His mother, however, was not used to the sight of Gregor, he could have made her ill, and so Gregor, frightened, scuttled in reverse to the far end of the couch but could not stop the sheet from shifting a little at the front. That was enough to put his mother on the alert. She stopped, stood still for a moment, and then went back to Grete.

Although Gregor told himself over and over again that nothing special was happening, only a few pieces of furniture were being moved, he soon had to admit that this coming and going of the women, their little calls to each other, the scraping of the furniture along the floor had the effect on him of a great turmoil swelling on all sides, and as much as he tucked in his head and his legs and shrank until his belly touched the floor, he was forced to admit that he would not be able to stand it much longer. They were clearing out his room; depriving him of everything that he loved; they had already carried away the chest of drawers, in which he kept the fretsaw and other tools; were now budging the desk firmly embedded in the floor, the desk he had done his homework on when he was a student at business college, in high school, yes, even in public school—now he really had no more time to examine the good intentions of the two women, whose existence, besides, he had almost forgotten, for they were so exhausted that they were working in silence, and one could hear only the heavy shuffling of their feet.

And so he broke out—the women were just leaning against the desk in the next room to catch their breath for a minute—changed his course four times, he really didn't know what to salvage first, then he saw hanging conspicuously on the wall, which was otherwise bare already, the picture of the lady all dressed in furs, hurriedly crawled up on it and pressed himself against the glass, which gave a good surface to stick to and soothed his hot belly. At least no one would take away this picture, while Gregor completely covered it up. He turned his head toward the living-room door to watch the women when they returned.

They had not given themselves much of a rest and were already coming back; Grete had put her arm around her mother and was practically carrying her. "So what should we take now?" said Grete and looked around. At that her eyes met Gregor's as he clung to the wall. Probably only because of her mother's presence she kept her self-control, bent her head down to her mother to keep her from looking around, and said, though in a quavering and thoughtless voice: "Come, we'd better go back into the living room for a minute." Grete's intent was clear to Gregor, she wanted to bring his mother into safety and then chase him down from the wall. Well, just let her try! He squatted on his picture and would not give it up. He would rather fly in Grete's face.

But Grete's words had now made her mother really anxious; she stepped to one side, caught sight of the gigantic brown blotch on the flowered wallpaper, and before it really dawned on her that what she saw was Gregor, cried in a hoarse, bawling voice: "Oh, God, Oh, God!"; and as if giving up completely, she fell with outstretched arms across the couch and did not stir. "You, Gregor!" cried his sister with raised fist and piercing eyes. These were the first words she had addressed directly to him since his metamorphosis. She ran into the next room to get some kind of spirits to revive her mother; Gregor wanted to help too—there was time to rescue the picture—but he was stuck to the glass and had to tear himself loose by force; then he too ran into the next room, as if he could give his sister some sort of advice, as in the old days; but then had to stand behind her doing nothing while she rummaged among various little bottles; moreover, when she turned around she was startled, a bottle fell on the floor and broke, a splinter of glass wounded Gregor in the face, some kind of corrosive medicine flowed around him; now without waiting any longer, Grete grabbed as many little bottles as she could carry and ran with them inside to her mother; she slammed the door behind her with her foot. Now Gregor was cut off from his mother, who was perhaps near death through his fault; he could not dare open the door if he did not want to chase away his sister, who had to stay with his mother; now there was nothing for him to do except wait; and tormented by self-reproaches and worry, he began to crawl, crawled over everything, walls, furniture and ceiling, and finally in desperation, as the whole room was beginning to spin, fell down onto the middle of the big table.

A short time passed; Gregor lay there prostrate; all around, things were quiet, perhaps that was a good sign. Then the doorbell rang. The maid, of course, was locked up in her kitchen and so Grete had to answer the door. His father had come home. "What's happened?" were his first words; Grete's appearance must have told him everything. Grete answered in a muffled voice, her face was obviously pressed against her father's chest: "Mother fainted, but she's better now. Gregor's broken out." "I knew it," his father said. "I kept telling you, but you women don't want to listen." It was clear to Gregor that his father had put the worst interpretation on Grete's all-too-brief announcement and assumed that Gregor was guilty of some outrage. Therefore Gregor now had to try to calm his father down, since he had neither the time nor the ability to enlighten him. And so he fled to the door of his room and pressed himself against it for his father to see, as soon as he came into the foyer, that Gregor had the best intentions of returning to his room immediately and that it was not necessary to drive him back; if only the door were opened for him, he would disappear at once.

But his father was in no mood to notice such subtleties; "Ah!" he cried as he entered, in a tone that sounded as if he were at once furious and glad. Gregor turned his head away from the door and lifted it toward his father. He had not really imagined his father looking like this, as he stood in front of him now; admittedly Gregor had been too absorbed recently in his newfangled crawling to bother as much as before about events in the rest of the house and should really have been prepared to find some changes. And yet, and yet—was this still his father? Was this the same man who in the old days used to lie wearily buried in bed when Gregor left on a business trip; who greeted him on his return in the evening, sitting in his bathrobe in the armchair, who actually had difficulty getting to his feet but as a sign of joy only lifted up his arms; and who, on the rare occasions when the whole family went out for a walk, on a few Sundays in June and on the major holidays, used to shuffle along with great effort between Gregor and his mother, who were slow walkers themselves, always a little more slowly than they, wrapped in his old overcoat, always carefully planting down his crutch-handled cane, and, when he wanted to say something, nearly always stood still and assembled his escort around him? Now, however, he was holding himself very erect, dressed in a tight-fitting blue uniform with gold buttons, the kind worn by messengers at banking concerns; above the high stiff collar of the jacket his heavy chin protruded; under his bushy eyebrows his black eyes darted bright, piercing glances; his usually rumpled white hair was combed flat, with a scrupulously exact, gleaming part. He threw his cap—which was adorned with a gold monogram, proba-bly that of a bank—in an arc across the entire room onto the couch, and with the tails of his long uniform jacket slapped back, his hands in his pants pockets, went for Gre-gor with a sullen look on his face. He probably did not know himself what he had in mind; still he lifted his feet unusually high off the floor, and Gregor staggered at the gigantic size of the soles of his boots. But he did not linger over this, he had known right from the first day of his new life that his father considered only the strictest treat-ment called for in dealing with him. And so he ran ahead of his father, stopped when his father stood still, and scooted ahead again when his father made even the slightest movement. In this way they made more than one tour of the room, without anything decisive happening; in fact the whole movement did not even have the appearance of a chase because of its slow tempo. So Gregor kept to the floor for the time being, es-pecially since he was afraid that his father might interpret a flight onto the walls or the ceiling as a piece of particular nastiness. Of course Gregor had to admit that he would not be able to keep up even this running for long, for whenever his father took one step, Gregor had to execute countless movements. He was already beginning to feel winded, just as in the old days he had not had very reliable lungs. As he now stag-gered around, hardly keeping his eyes open in order to gather all his strength for the running; in his obtuseness not thinking of any escape other than by running; and hav-ing almost forgotten that the walls were at his disposal, though here of course they were blocked up with elaborately carved furniture full of notches and points—at that moment a lightly flung object hit the floor right near him and rolled in front of him. It was an apple; a second one came flying right after it; Gregor stopped dead with fear; further running was useless, for his father was determined to bombard him. He had filled his pockets from the fruit bowl on the buffet and was now pitching one apple af-ter another, for the time being without taking good aim. These little red apples rolled around on the floor as if electrified, clicking into each another. One apple, thrown weakly, grazed Gregor's back and slid off harmlessly. But the very next one that came flying after it literally forced its way into Gregor's back; Gregor tried to drag himself away, as if the startling, unbelievable pain might disappear with a change of place; but he felt nailed to the spot and stretched out his body in a complete confusion of all his senses. With his last glance he saw the door of his room burst open as his mother rushed out ahead of his screaming sister, in her chemise, for his sister had partly un-dressed her while she was unconscious in order to let her breathe more freely; saw his mother run up to his father and on the way her unfastened petticoats slide to the floor one by one; and saw as, stumbling over the skirts, she forced herself onto his father, and embracing him, in complete union with him—but now Gregor's sight went dim—her hands clasping his father's neck, begged for Gregor's life.

3

Gregor's serious wound, from which he suffered for over a month—the apple remained imbedded in his flesh as a visible souvenir since no one dared to remove it—seemed to have reminded even his father that Gregor was a member of the family, in spite of his present pathetic and repulsive shape, who could not be treated as an enemy; that, on the contrary, it was the commandment of family duty to swallow their disgust and endure him, endure him and nothing more.

And now, although Gregor had lost some of his mobility probably for good because of his wound, and although for the time being he needed long, long minutes to get across his room, like an old war veteran—crawling above ground was out of the question—for this deterioration of his situation he was granted compensation which in his view was entirely satisfactory: every day around dusk the living-room door—which he was in the habit of watching closely for an hour or two beforehand—was opened, so that, lying in the darkness of his room, invisible from the living room, he could see the whole family sitting at the table under the lamp and could listen to their conversation, as it were with general permission; and so it was completely different from before.

Of course these were no longer the animated conversations of the old days, which Gregor used to remember with a certain nostalgia in small hotel rooms when he'd had to throw himself wearily into the damp bedding. Now things were mostly very quiet. Soon after supper his father would fall asleep in his armchair; his mother and sister would caution each other to be quiet; his mother, bent low under the light, sewed delicate lingerie for a clothing store; his sister, who had taken a job as a salesgirl, was learning shorthand and French in the evenings in order to attain a better position some time in the future. Sometimes his father woke up, and as if he had absolutely no idea that he had been asleep, said to his mother, "Look how long you're sewing again today!" and went right back to sleep, while mother and sister smiled wearily at each other.

With a kind of perverse obstinacy his father refused to take off his official uniform even in the house; and while his robe hung uselessly on the clothes hook, his father dozed, completely dressed, in his chair, as if he were always ready for duty and were waiting even here for the voice of his superior. As a result his uniform, which had not been new to start with, began to get dirty in spite of all the mother's and sister's care, and Gregor would often stare all evening long at this garment, covered with stains and gleaming with its constantly polished gold buttons, in which the old man slept most uncomfortably and yet peacefully.

As soon as the clock struck ten, his mother tried to awaken his father with soft encouraging words and then persuade him to go to bed, for this was no place to sleep properly, and his father badly needed his sleep, since he had to be at work at six o'clock. But with the obstinacy that had possessed him ever since he had become a messenger, he always insisted on staying at the table a little longer, although he invariably fell asleep and then could be persuaded only with the greatest effort to exchange his armchair for bed. However much mother and sister might pounce on him with little admonitions, he would slowly shake his head for a quarter of an hour at a time, keeping his eyes closed, and would not get up. Gregor's mother plucked him by the sleeves, whispered blandishments into his ear, his sister dropped her homework in order to help her mother, but all this was of no use. He only sank deeper into his armchair. Not until the women lifted him up under his arms did he open his eyes, look alternately at mother and sister, and usually say, "What a life. So this is the peace of my old age." And leaning on the two women, he would get up laboriously, as if he were the greatest weight on himself, and let the women lead him to the door, where, shrugging them off, he would proceed independently, while Gregor's mother threw down her sewing, and his sister her pen, as quickly as possible so as to run after his father and be of further assistance.

Who in this overworked and exhausted family had time to worry about Gregor any more than was absolutely necessary? The household was stinted more and more; now the maid was let go after all; a gigantic bony cleaning woman with white hair fluttering about her head came mornings and evenings to do the heaviest work; his mother took care of everything else, along with all her sewing. It even happened that various pieces of family jewelry, which in the old days his mother and sister had been overjoyed to wear at parties and celebrations, were sold, as Gregor found out one evening from the general discussion of the prices they had fetched. But the biggest complaint was always that they could not give up the apartment, which was much too big for their present needs, since no one could figure out how Gregor was supposed to be moved. But Gregor understood easily that it was not only consideration for him which prevented their moving, for he could easily have been transported in a suitable crate with a few air holes; what mainly prevented the family from moving was their complete hopelessness and the thought that they had been struck by a misfortune as none of their relatives and acquaintances had ever been hit. What the world demands of poor people they did to the utmost of their ability; his father brought breakfast for the minor officials at the bank, his mother sacrificed herself to the underwear of strangers, his sister ran back and forth behind the counter at the request of the customers; but for anything more than this they did not have the strength. And the wound in Gregor's back began to hurt anew when mother and sister, after getting his father to bed, now came back, dropped their work, pulled their chairs close to each other and sat cheek to cheek; when his mother, pointing to Gregor's room, said, "Close that door, Grete"; and when Gregor was back in darkness, while in the other room the women mingled their tears or stared dry-eyed at the table.

Gregor spent the days and nights almost entirely without sleep. Sometimes he thought that the next time the door opened he would take charge of the family's affairs again, just as he had done in the old days; after this long while there again appeared in his thoughts the boss and the manager, the salesmen and the trainees, the handyman who was so dense, two or three friends from other firms, a chambermaid in a provincial hotel—a happy fleeting memory—a cashier in a millinery store, whom he had courted earnestly but too slowly—they all appeared, intermingled with strangers or people he had already forgotten; but instead of helping him and his family, they were all inaccessible, and he was glad when they faded away. At other times he was in no mood to worry about his family, he was completely filled with rage at his miserable treatment, and although he could not imagine anything that would pique his appetite, he still made plans for getting into the pantry to take what was coming to him, even if he wasn't hungry. No longer considering what she could do to give Gregor a special treat, his sister, before running to business every morning and afternoon, hurriedly shoved any old food into Gregor's room with her foot; and in the evening, regardless of whether the food had only been toyed with or—the most usual case— had been left completely untouched, she swept it out with a swish of the broom. The cleaning up of Gregor's room, which she now always did in the evenings, could not be done more hastily. Streaks of dirt ran along the walls, fluffs of dust and filth lay here and there on the floor. At first, whenever his sister came in, Gregor would place himself in those corners which were particularly offending, meaning by his position in a sense to reproach her. But he could probably have stayed there for weeks without his sister's showing any improvement; she must have seen the dirt as clearly as he did, but she had just decided to leave it. At the same time she made sure—with an irritableness that was completely new to her and which had in fact infected the whole family—that the cleaning of Gregor's room remain her province. One time his mother had submitted Gregor's room to a major housecleaning, which she managed only after employing a couple of pails of water—all this dampness, of course, irritated Gregor too and he lay prostrate, sour and immobile, on the couch—but his mother's punishment was not long in coming. For hardly had his sister noticed the difference in Gregor's room that evening than, deeply insulted, she ran into the living room and, in spite of her mother's imploringly uplifted hands, burst out in a fit of crying, which his parents—his father had naturally been startled out of his armchair—at first watched in helpless amazement; until they too got going; turning to the right, his father blamed his mother for not letting his sister clean Gregor's room; but turning to the left, he screamed at his sister that she would never again be allowed to clean Gregor's room; while his mother tried to drag his father, who was out of his mind with excitement, into the bedroom; his sister, shaken with sobs, hammered the table with her small fists; and Gregor hissed loudly with rage because it did not occur to any of them to close the door and spare him such a scene and a row.

But even if his sister, exhausted from her work at the store, had gotten fed up with taking care of Gregor as she used to, it was not necessary at all for his mother to take her place and still Gregor did not have to be neglected. For now the cleaning woman was there. This old widow, who thanks to her strong bony frame had probably survived the worst in a long life, was not really repelled by Gregor. Without being in the least inquisitive, she had once accidentally opened the door of Gregor's room, and at the sight of Gregor—who, completely taken by surprise, began to race back and forth although no one was chasing him—she had remained standing, with her hands folded on her stomach, marveling. From that time on she never failed to open the door a crack every morning and every evening and peek in hurriedly at Gregor. In the beginning she also used to call him over to her with words she probably considered friendly, like, "Come over here for a minute, you old dung beetle!" or "Look at that old dung beetle!" To forms of address like these Gregor would not respond but remained immobile where he was, as if the door had not been opened. If only they had given this cleaning woman orders to clean up his room every day, instead of letting her disturb him uselessly whenever the mood took her. Once, early in the morning— heavy rain, perhaps already a sign of approaching spring, was beating on the window panes—Gregor was so exasperated when the cleaning woman started in again with her phrases that he turned on her, of course slowly and decrepitly, as if to attack. But the cleaning woman, instead of getting frightened, simply lifted up high a chair near the door, and as she stood there with her mouth wide open, her intention was clearly to shut her mouth only when the chair in her hand came crashing down on Gregor's back. "So, is that all there is?" she asked when Gregor turned around again, and she quietly put the chair back in the corner.

Gregor now hardly ate anything anymore. Only when he accidentally passed the food laid out for him would he take a bite into his mouth just for fun, hold it in for hours, and then mostly spit it out again. At first he thought that his grief at the state of his room kept him off food, but it was the very changes in his room to which he quickly became adjusted. His family had gotten into the habit of putting in this room things for which they could not find any other place, and now there were plenty of these, since one of the rooms in the apartment had been rented to three boarders. These serious gentlemen—all three had long beards, as Gregor was able to register once through a crack in the door—were obsessed with neatness, not only in their room, but since they had, after all, moved in here, throughout the entire household and especially in the kitchen. They could not stand useless, let alone dirty junk. Besides, they had brought along most of their own household goods. For this reason many things had become superfluous, and though they certainly weren't salable, on the other hand they could not just be thrown out. All these things migrated into Gregor's room. Likewise the ash can and the garbage can from the kitchen. Whatever was not being used at the moment was just flung into Gregor's room by the cleaning woman, who was always in a big hurry; fortunately Gregor generally saw only the object involved and the hand that held it. Maybe the cleaning woman intended to reclaim the things as soon as she had a chance or else to throw out everything together in one fell swoop, but in fact they would have remained lying wherever they had been thrown in the first place if Gregor had not squeezed through the junk and set it in motion, at first from necessity, because otherwise there would have been no room to crawl in, but later with growing pleasure, although after such excursions, tired to death and sad, he did not budge again for hours.

Since the roomers sometimes also had their supper at home in the common living room, the living-room door remained closed on certain evenings, but Gregor found it very easy to give up the open door, for on many evenings when it was opened he had not taken advantage of it, but instead, without the family's noticing, had lain in the darkest corner of his room. But once the cleaning woman had left the living-room door slightly open, and it also remained opened a little when the roomers came in in the evening and the lamp was lit. They sat down at the head of the table where in the old days his father, his mother, and Gregor had eaten, unfolded their napkins, and picked up their knives and forks. At once his mother appeared in the doorway with a platter of meat, and just behind her came his sister with a platter piled high with potatoes. A thick vapor steamed up from the food. The roomers bent over the platters set in front of them as if to examine them before eating, and in fact the one who sat in the middle, and who seemed to be regarded by the other two as an authority, cut into a piece of meat while it was still on the platter, evidently to find out whether it was tender enough or whether it should perhaps be sent back to the kitchen. He was satisfied, and mother and sister, who had been watching anxiously, sighed with relief and began to smile.

The family itself ate in the kitchen. Nevertheless, before going into the kitchen, his father came into this room and, bowing once, cap in hand, made a turn around the table. The roomers rose as one man and mumbled something into their beards. When they were alone again, they ate in almost complete silence. It seemed strange to Gregor that among all the different noises of eating he kept picking up the sound of their chewing teeth, as if this were a sign to Gregor that you needed teeth to eat with and that even with the best make of toothless jaws you couldn't do a thing. "I'm hungry enough," Gregor said to himself, full of grief, "but not for these things. Look how these roomers are gorging themselves, and I'm dying!"

On this same evening—Gregor could not remember having heard the violin during the whole time—the sound of violin playing came from the kitchen. The roomers had already finished their evening meal, the one in the middle had taken out a newspaper, given each of the two others a page, and now, leaning back, they read and smoked. When the violin began to play, they became attentive, got up, and went on tiptoe to the door leading to the foyer, where they stood in a huddle. They must have been heard in the kitchen, for his father called, "Perhaps the playing bothers you, gentlemen? It can be stopped right away." "On the contrary," said the middle roomer. "Wouldn't the young lady like to come in to us and play in here where it's much roomier and more comfortable?" "Oh, certainly," called Gregor's father, as if he were the violinist. The boarders went back into the room and waited. Soon Gregor's father came in with the music stand, his mother with the sheet music, and his sister with the violin. Calmly his sister got everything ready for playing; his parents—who had never rented out rooms before and therefore behaved toward the roomers with excessive politeness—did not even dare sit down on their own chairs; his father leaned against the door, his right hand inserted between two buttons of his uniform coat, which he kept closed; but his mother was offered a chair by one of the roomers, and since she left the chair where the roomer just happened to put it, she sat in a corner to one side.

His sister began to play. Father and mother, from either side, attentively followed the movements of her hands. Attracted by the playing, Gregor had dared to come out a little further and already had his head in the living room. It hardly surprised him that lately he was showing so little consideration for the others; once such consideration had been his greatest pride. And yet he would never have had better reason to keep hidden; for now, because of the dust which lay all over his room and blew around at the slightest movement, he too was completely covered with dust; he dragged around with him on his back and along his sides fluff and hairs and scraps of food; his indifference to everything was much too deep for him to have gotten on his back and scrubbed himself clean against the carpet, as once he had done several times a day. And in spite of his state, he was not ashamed to inch out a little farther on the immaculate living-room floor.

Admittedly no one paid any attention to him. The family was completely absorbed by the violin-playing; the roomers, on the other hand, who at first had stationed themselves, hands in pockets, much too close behind his sister's music stand, so that they could all have followed the score, which certainly must have upset his sister, soon withdrew to the window, talking to each other in an undertone, their heads lowered, where they remained, anxiously watched by his father. It now seemed only too obvious that they were disappointed in their expectation of hearing beautiful or entertaining violin-playing, had had enough of the whole performance, and continued to let their peace be disturbed only out of politeness. Especially the way they all blew the cigar smoke out of their nose and mouth toward the ceiling suggested great nervousness. And yet his sister was playing so beautifully. Her face was inclined to one side, sadly and probingly her eyes followed the lines of music. Gregor crawled forward a little farther, holding his head close to the floor, so that it might be possible to catch her eye. Was he an animal, that music could move him so? He felt as if the way to the unknown nourishment he longed for were coming to light. He was determined to force himself on until he reached his sister, to pluck at her skirt, and to let her know in this way that she should bring her violin into his room, for no one here appreciated her playing the way he would appreciate it. He would never again let her out of his room—at least not for as long as he lived; for once, his nightmarish looks would be of use to him; he would be at all the doors of his room at the same time and hiss and spit at the aggressors; his sister, however, should not be forced to stay with him, but would do so of her own free will; she should sit next to him on the couch, bending her ear down to him, and then he would confide to her that he had had the firm intention of sending her to the Conservatory, and that, if the catastrophe had not intervened, he would have announced this to everyone last Christmas—certainly Christmas had come and gone?—without taking notice of any objections. After this declaration his sister would burst into tears of emotion, and Gregor would raise himself up to her shoulder and kiss her on the neck which, ever since she started going out to work, she kept bare, without a ribbon or collar.

"Mr. Samsa!" the middle roomer called to Gregor's father and without wasting another word pointed his index finger at Gregor, who was slowly moving forward. The violin stopped, the middle roomer smiled first at his friends, shaking his head, and then looked at Gregor again. Rather than driving Gregor out, his father seemed to consider it more urgent to start by soothing the roomers although they were not at all upset, and Gregor seemed to be entertaining them more than the violin-playing. He rushed over to them and tried with outstretched arms to drive them into their room and at the same time with his body to block their view of Gregor. Now they actually did get a little angry—it was not clear whether because of his father's behavior or because of their dawning realization of having had without knowing it such a next door neighbor as Gregor. They demanded explanations from his father; in their turn they raised their arms, plucked excitedly at their beards, and, dragging their feet, backed off toward their room. In the meantime his sister had overcome the abstracted mood into which she had fallen after her playing had been so suddenly interrupted; and all at once, after holding violin and bow for a while in her slackly hanging hands and continuing to follow the score as if she were still playing, she pulled herself together, laid the instrument on the lap of her mother—who was still sitting in her chair, fighting for breath, her lungs violently heaving—and ran into the next room, which the roomers, under pressure from her father, were nearing more quickly than before. One could see the covers and bolsters on the beds, obeying his sister's practiced hands, fly up and arrange themselves. Before the boarders had reached the room, she had finished turning down the beds and had slipped out. Her father seemed once again to be gripped by his perverse obstinacy to such a degree that he completely forgot any respect still due his tenants. He drove them on and kept on driving until, already at the bedroom door, the middle boarder stamped his foot thunderingly and thus brought him to a standstill. "I herewith declare," he said, raising his hand and casting his eyes around for Gregor's mother and sister too, "that in view of the disgusting conditions prevailing in this apartment and family"—here he spat curtly and decisively on the floor—"I give notice as of now. Of course I won't pay a cent for the days I have been living here, either; on the contrary, I shall consider taking some sort of action against you with claims that—believe me—will be easy to substantiate." He stopped and looked straight in front of him, as if he were expecting something. And in fact his two friends at once chimed in with the words, "We too give notice as of now." Thereupon he grabbed the door knob and slammed the door with a bang.

Gregor's father, his hands groping, staggered to his armchair and collapsed into it; it looked as if he were stretching himself out for his usual evening nap, but the heavy drooping of his head, as if it had lost all support, showed that he was certainly not asleep. All this time Gregor had lain quietly at the spot where the roomers had surprised him. His disappointment at the failure of his plan—but perhaps also the weakness caused by so much fasting—made it impossible for him to move. He was afraid with some certainty that in the very next moment a general debacle would burst over him, and he waited. He was not even startled by the violin as it slipped from under his mother's trembling fingers and fell off her lap with a reverberating clang.

"My dear parents," said his sister and by way of an introduction pounded her hand on the table, "things can't go on like this. Maybe you don't realize it, but I do. I won't pronounce the name of my brother in front of this monster, and so all I say is: we have to try to get rid of it. We've done everything humanly possible to take care of it and to put up with it; I don't think anyone can blame us in the least."

"She's absolutely right," said his father to himself. His mother, who still could not catch her breath, began to cough dully behind her hand, a wild look in her eyes.

His sister rushed over to his mother and held her forehead. His father seemed to have been led by Grete's words to more definite thoughts, had sat up, was playing with the cap of his uniform among the plates which were still lying on the table from the roomers' supper, and from time to time looked at Gregor's motionless form.

"We must try to get rid of it," his sister now said exclusively to her father, since her mother was coughing too hard to hear anything. "It will be the death of you two, I can see it coming. People who already have to work as hard as we do can't put up with this constant torture at home, too. I can't stand it anymore either." And she broke out crying so bitterly that her tears poured down onto her mother's face, which she wiped off with mechanical movements of her hand.

"Child," said her father kindly and with unusual understanding, "but what can we do?"

Gregor's sister only shrugged her shoulders as a sign of the bewildered mood that had now gripped her as she cried, in contrast with her earlier confidence.

"If he could understand us," said her father, half questioning; in the midst of her crying Gregor's sister waved her hand violently as a sign that that was out of the question.

"If he could understand us," his father repeated and by closing his eyes, absorbed his daughter's conviction of the impossibility of the idea, "then maybe we could come to an agreement with him. But the way things are——"

"It has to go," cried his sister. "That's the only answer, Father. You just have to try to get rid of the idea that it's Gregor. Believing it for so long, that is our real misfortune. But how can it be Gregor? If it were Gregor, he would have realized long ago that it isn't possible for human beings to live with such a creature, and he would have gone away of his own free will. Then we wouldn't have a brother, but we'd be able to go on living and honor his memory. But as things are, this animal persecutes us, drives the roomers away, obviously wants to occupy the whole apartment and for us to sleep in the gutter. Look, Father," she suddenly shrieked, "he's starting in again!" And in a fit of terror that was completely incomprehensible to Gregor, his sister abandoned even her mother, literally shoved herself off from her chair, as if she would rather sacrifice her mother than stay near Gregor, and rushed behind her father, who, upset only by her behavior, also stood up and half-lifted his arms in front of her as if to protect her.

But Gregor had absolutely no intention of frightening anyone, let alone his sister. He had only begun to turn around in order to trek back to his room; certainly his movements did look peculiar, since his ailing condition made him help the complicated turning maneuver along with his head, which he lifted up many times and knocked against the floor. He stopped and looked around. His good intention seemed to have been recognized; it had only been a momentary scare. Now they all watched him, silent and sad. His mother lay in her armchair, her legs stretched out and pressed together, her eyes almost closing from exhaustion; his father and his sister sat side by side, his sister had put her arm around her father's neck.

Now maybe they'll let me turn around, Gregor thought and began his labors again. He could not repress his panting from the exertion, and from time to time he had to rest. Otherwise no one harassed him; he was left completely on his own. When he had completed the turn, he immediately began to crawl back in a straight line. He was astonished at the great distance separating him from his room and could not understand at all how, given his weakness, he had covered the same distance a little while ago almost without realizing it. Constantly intent only on rapid crawling, he hardly noticed that not a word, not an exclamation from his family interrupted him. Only when he was already in the doorway did he turn his head—not completely, for he felt his neck stiffening; nevertheless he still saw that behind him nothing had changed except that his sister had gotten up. His last glance ranged over his mother, who was now fast asleep.

He was hardly inside his room when the door was hurriedly slammed shut, firmly bolted, and locked. Gregor was so frightened at the sudden noise behind him that his little legs gave way under him. It was his sister who had been in such a hurry. She had been standing up straight, ready and waiting, then she had leaped forward nimbly, Gregor had not even heard her coming, and she cried "Finally!" to her parents as she turned the key in the lock.

"And now?" Gregor asked himself, looking around in the darkness. He soon made the discovery that he could no longer move at all. It did not surprise him; rather, it seemed unnatural that until now he had actually been able to propel himself on these thin little legs. Otherwise he felt relatively comfortable. He had pains, of course, throughout his whole body, but it seemed to him that they were gradually getting fainter and fainter and would finally go away altogether. The rotten apple in his back and the inflamed area around it, which were completely covered with fluffy dust, already hardly bothered him. He thought back on his family with deep emotion and love. His conviction that he would have to disappear was, if possible, even firmer than his sister's. He remained in this state of empty and peaceful reflection until the tower clock struck three in the morning. He still saw that outside the window everything was beginning to grow light. Then, without his consent, his head sank down to the floor, and from his nostrils streamed his last weak breath.

When early in the morning the cleaning woman came—in sheer energy and impatience she would slam all the doors so hard although she had often been asked not to, that once she arrived, quiet sleep was no longer possible anywhere in the apartment—she did not at first find anything out of the ordinary on paying Gregor her usual short visit. She thought that he was deliberately lying motionless, pretending that his feelings were hurt; she credited him with unlimited intelligence. Because she happened to be holding the long broom, she tried from the doorway to tickle Gregor with it. When this too produced no results, she became annoyed and jabbed Gregor a little, and only when she had shoved him without any resistance to another spot did she begin to take notice. When she quickly became aware of the true state of things, she opened her eyes wide, whistled softly, but did not dawdle; instead, she tore open the door of the bedroom and shouted at the top of her voice into the darkness: "Come and have a look, it's croaked; it's lying there, dead as a doornail!"

The couple Mr. and Mrs. Samsa sat up in their marriage bed and had a struggle overcoming their shock at the cleaning woman before they could finally grasp her message. But then Mr. and Mrs. Samsa hastily scrambled out of bed, each on his side, Mr. Samsa threw the blanket around his shoulders, Mrs. Samsa came out in nothing but her nightgown; dressed this way, they entered Gregor's room. In the meantime the door of the living room had also opened, where Grete had been sleeping since the roomers had moved in; she was fully dressed, as if she had not been asleep at all; and her pale face seemed to confirm this. "Dead?" said Mrs. Samsa and look inquiringly at the cleaning woman, although she could scrutinize everything for herself and could recognize the truth even without scrunity. "I'll say," said the cleaning woman, and to prove it she pushed Gregor's corpse with her broom a good distance sideways. Mrs. Samsa made a movement as if to hold the broom back but did not do it. "Well," said Mr. Samsa, "now we can thank God!" He crossed himself, and the three women followed his example. Grete, who never took her eyes off the corpse, said, "Just look how thin he was. Of course he didn't eat anything for such a long time. The food came out again just the way it went in." As a matter of fact, Gregor's body was completely flat and dry; this was obvious now for the first time, really, since the body was no longer raised up by his little legs and nothing else distracted the eye.

"Come in with us for a little while, Grete," said Mrs. Samsa with a melancholy smile, and Grete, not without looking back at the corpse, followed her parents into their bedroom. The cleaning woman shut the door and opened the window wide. Although it was early in the morning, there was already some mildness mixed in with the fresh air. After all, it was already the end of March.

The three boarders came out of their room and looked around in astonishment for their breakfast; they had been forgotten. "Where's breakfast?" the middle roomer grumpily asked the cleaning woman. But she put her finger to her lips and then hastily and silently beckoned the boarders to follow her into Gregor's room. They came willingly and then stood, their hands in the pockets of their somewhat shabby jackets, in the now already very bright room, surrounding Gregor's corpse.

At that point the bedroom door opened, and Mr. Samsa appeared in his uniform, his wife on one arm, his daughter on the other. They all looked as if they had been crying; from time to time Grete pressed her face against her father's sleeve.

"Leave my house immediately," said Mr. Samsa and pointed to the door, without letting go of the women. "What do you mean by that?" said the middle roomer, somewhat nonplussed, and smiled with a sugary smile. The two others held their hands behind their back and incessantly rubbed them together, as if in joyful anticipation of a big argument, which could only turn out in their favor. "I mean just what I say," answered Mr. Samsa and with his two companions marched in a straight line toward the roomer. At first the roomer stood still and looked at the floor, as if the thoughts inside his head were fitting themselves together in a new order. "So, we'll go, then," he said and looked up at Mr. Samsa as if, suddenly overcome by a fit of humility, he were asking for further permission even for this decision. Mr. Samsa merely nodded briefly several times, his eyes wide open. Thereupon the roomer actually went immediately into the foyer, taking long strides; his two friends had already been listening for a while, their hands completely still, and now they went hopping right after him, as if afraid that Mr. Samsa might get into the foyer ahead of them and interrupt the contact with their leader. In the foyer all three took their hats from the coatrack, pulled their canes from the umbrella stand, bowed silently, and left the apartment. In a suspicious mood which proved completely unfounded, Mr. Samsa led the two women out onto the landing; leaning over the banister, they watched the three roomers slowly but steadily going down the long flight of stairs, disappearing on each landing at a particular turn of the stairway and a few moments later emerging again; the farther down they got, the more the Samsa family's interest in them wore off, and when a butcher's boy with a carrier on his head came climbing up the stairs with a proud bearing, toward them and then up on past them, Mr. Samsa and the women quickly left the banister and all went back, as if relieved, into their apartment.

They decided to spend this day resting and going for a walk; they not only deserved a break in their work, they absolutely needed one. And so they sat down at the table and wrote three letters of excuse, Mr. Samsa to the management of the bank, Mrs. Samsa to her employer, and Grete to the store owner. While they were writing, the cleaning woman came in to say that she was going, since her morning's work was done. The three letter writers at first simply nodded without looking up, but as the cleaning woman still kept lingering, they looked up, annoyed. "Well?" asked Mr. Samsa. The cleaning woman stood smiling in the doorway, as if she had some great good news to announce to the family but would do so only if she were thoroughly questioned. The little ostrich feather which stood almost upright on her hat and which had irritated Mr. Samsa the whole time she had been with them swayed lightly in all directions. "What do you want?" asked Mrs. Samsa, who inspired the most respect in the cleaning woman. "Well," the cleaning woman answered, and for good-natured laughter could not immediately go on, "look, you don't have to worry about getting rid of the stuff next door. It's already been taken care of." Mrs. Samsa and Grete bent down over their letters, as if to continue writing; Mr. Samsa, who noticed that the cleaning woman was now about to start describing everything in detail, stopped her with a firmly outstretched hand. But since she was not going to be permitted to tell her story, she remembered that she was in a great hurry, cried, obviously insulted, "So long, everyone," whirled around wildly, and left the apartment with a terrible slamming of doors.

"We'll fire her tonight," said Mr. Samsa, but did not get an answer from either his wife or his daughter, for the cleaning woman seemed to have ruined their barely regained peace of mind. They got up, went to the window, and stayed there, holding each other tight. Mr. Samsa turned around in his chair toward them and watched them quietly for a while. Then he called, "Come on now, come over here. Stop brooding over the past. And have a little consideration for me, too." The women obeyed him at once, hurried over to him, fondled him, and quickly finished their letters.

Then all three of them left the apartment together, something they had not done in months, and took the trolley into the open country on the outskirts of the city. The car, in which they were the only passengers, was completely filled with warm sunshine. Leaning back comfortably in their seats, they discussed their prospects for the time to come, and it seemed on closer examination that these weren't bad at all, for all three positions—about which they had never really asked one another in any detail—were exceedingly advantageous and especially promising for the future. The greatest immediate improvement in their situation would come easily, of course, from a change in apartments; they would now take a smaller and cheaper apartment, but one better situated and in every way simpler to manage than the old one, which Gregor had picked for them. While they were talking in this vein, it occurred almost simultaneously to Mr. and Mrs. Samsa, as they watched their daughter getting livelier and livelier, that lately, in spite of all the troubles which had turned her cheeks pale, she had blossomed into a good-looking, shapely girl. Growing quieter and communicating almost unconsciously through glances, they thought that it would soon be time, too, to find her a good husband. And it was like a confirmation of their new dreams and good intentions when at the end of the ride their daughter got up first and stretched her young body.

Parables
The Trees[1]

For we are as treetrunks in the snow. They appear to lie flat on the surface, and with a little push one should be able to shift them. No, one cannot, for they are fixed firmly to the ground. But look, even that is mere appearance.

The Next Village[2]

MY grandfather used to say: "Life is astoundingly short. To me, looking back over it, life seems so foreshortened that I scarcely understand, for instance, how a young man can decide to ride over to the next village without being afraid that—not to mention accidents—even the span of a normal happy life may fall far short of the time needed for such a journey."

The Cares of a Family Man[3]

Some say the word Odradek is of Slavonic origin, and try to account for it on that basis. Others again believe it to be of German origin, only influenced by Slavonic. The uncertainty of both interpretations allows one to assume with justice that neither is accurate, especially as neither of them provides an intelligent meaning of the word.

No one, of course, would occupy himself with such studies if there were not a creature called Odradek. At first glance it looks like a flat star-shaped spool for thread, and indeed it does seem to have thread wound upon it; to be sure, they are only old, broken-off bits of thread, knotted and tangled together, of the most varied sorts and colors. But it is not only a spool, for a small wooden crossbar sticks out of the middle of the star, and another small rod is joined to that at a right angle. By means of this latter rod on one side and one of the points of the star on the other, the whole thing can stand upright as if on two legs.

One is tempted to believe that the creature once had some sort of intelligible shape and is now only a broken-down remnant. Yet this does not seem to be the case; at least there is no sign of it; nowhere is there an unfinished or unbroken surface to suggest anything of the kind; the whole thing looks senseless enough, but in its own way perfectly finished. In any case, closer scrutiny is impossible, since Odradek is extraordinarily nimble and can never be laid hold of.

He lurks by turns in the garret, the stairway, the lobbies, the entrance hall. Often for months on end he is not to be seen; then he has presumably moved into other houses; but he always comes faithfully back to our house again. Many a time when you go out of the door and he happens just to be leaning directly beneath you against the banisters you feel inclined to speak to him. Of course, you put no difficult questions to him, you treat him—he is so diminutive that you cannot help it—rather like a child. "Well, what's your name?" you ask him. "Odradek," he says. "And where do you live?" "No fixed abode," he says and laughs; but it is only the kind of laughter that has no lungs behind it. It sounds rather like the rustling of fallen leaves. And that is usually the end of the conversation. Even these answers are not always forthcoming; often he stays mute for a long time, as wooden as his appearance.

---

1. Translated by J. A. Underwood.
2. Translated by Willa and Edwin Muir.

3. Translated by Willa and Edwin Muir.

I ask myself, to no purpose, what is likely to happen to him? Can he possibly die? Anything that dies has had some kind of aim in life, some kind of activity, which has worn out; but that does not apply to Odradek. Am I to suppose, then, that he will always be rolling down the stairs, with ends of thread trailing after him, right before the feet of my children, and my children's children? He does no harm to anyone that one can see; but the idea that he is likely to survive me I find almost painful.

Give It Up![4]

It was very early in the morning, the streets clean and deserted, I was on my way to the station. As I compared the tower clock with my watch I realized it was much later than I had thought and that I had to hurry; the shock of this discovery made me feel uncertain of the way, I wasn't very well acquainted with the town as yet; fortunately, there was a policeman at hand, I ran to him and breathlessly asked him the way. He smiled and said: "You asking me the way?" "Yes," I said, "since I can't find it myself." "Give it up! Give it up!" said he, and turned with a sudden jerk, like someone who wants to be alone with his laughter.

On Parables[5]

Many complain that the words of the wise are always merely parables and of no use in daily life, which is the only life we have. When the sage says: "Go over," he does not mean that we should cross to some actual place, which we could do anyhow if the labor were worth it; he means some fabulous yonder, something unknown to us, something that he cannot designate more precisely either, and therefore cannot help us here in the very least. All these parables really set out to say merely that the incomprehensible is incomprehensible, and we know that already. But the cares we have to struggle with every day: that is a different matter.

Concerning this a man once said: Why such reluctance? If you only followed the parables you yourselves would become parables and with that rid of all your daily cares.

Another said: I bet that is also a parable.

The first said: You have won.

The second said: But unfortunately only in parable.

The first said: No, in reality: in parable you have lost.

Anna Akhmatova
1889–1966

Anna Andreyevna Gorenko ("Akhmatova" was an assumed name) was born near Odessa, Ukraine, the daughter of a naval officer. She lived most of her life in Saint Petersburg (Leningrad) and died in Domodedovo, near Moscow. The ups and downs of her life and poetic career are a telling reflection of the tumultuous history of her time. She started writing poetry at age eleven and published her first books of poems in her early twenties shortly after she joined the Poets' Guild, a group that was to found Russian Acmeism. This was the avant-garde of Russ-

---

4. Translated by Tania and James Stern.   5. Translated by Willa and Edwin Muir.

ian modernism that sought to turn Russian literature away from the belated romanticism being expressed by the poets who referred to themselves as Symbolists. In 1910, Akhmatova married a fellow Acmeist poet, Nikolai Stepanovich Gumilyov, with whom she traveled to Paris and Western Europe in the course of 1910 and 1911. There she met a number of modernist poets and artists, among them the Italian painter Amadeo Modigliani, who drew several portraits of the fetching Akhmatova. She had a son, Lev, by Gumilyov, whom she divorced in 1918. Gumilyov was arrested and shot as a counterrevolutionary in August 1921. Their son would be arrested, in turn, for the first time in 1934 and in 1949 for the third time. He was finally released from prison in 1956.

Akhmatova's third volume of poetry, *The White Flock,* appeared in 1917 just before the Bolshevik Revolution. She went on to publish two more collections of poems, *Plantain* (1921) and *Anno Domini MCMXXI* (1922), after which her career as published poet was interrupted by political vicissitudes until 1940, when she was permitted to resume publication of her poems. During the siege of Leningrad in World War II, Akhmatova was evacuated from the city. She spent the war years in Tashkent, Uzbekistan. Following the war and her return to Leningrad, she was targeted in August 1946 by the cultural freeze under the Stalinist regime, with a Communist Party henchman referring to her as "half-nun, half-whore." Her cycle of poems on the Stalinist terror, *Requiem,* was begun in 1934 with the first arrest of her son but was only published in Munich in 1963. Akhmatova's succinct poetic rendering of her struggles as a poet began with "Muse," a poem she wrote in 1924 but that wasn't published until 1940. Here, she identifies the source of her strength and reveals as well her identification with another poet, Dante, whose infernal times would find their afterlife in the posterity of poetic expression dictated by the redemptive voice of the muse. After the fall of Stalin, Akhmatova was rehabilitated, and her status became that of a national poet. In 1962 she met with Robert Frost in Leningrad, and in 1965 she traveled to Oxford University, where she was awarded an honorary doctorate in letters. Akhmatova is considered one of Russia's most important poets, and her work is viewed as a monument to the indomitable spirit of Russia's people in the darkest days of the twentieth century.

PRONUNCIATION:
   Akhmatova: akh-MAH-toh-vah

The Muse[1]

When at night I await her coming,
It seems that life hangs by a strand.
What are honors, what is youth, what is freedom,
Compared to that dear guest with rustic pipe in hand.
And she entered. Drawing aside her shawl
She gazed attentively at me.
I said to her: "Was it you who dictated to Dante[2]
The pages of *The Inferno?*" She replied: "It was I."

I am not with those[1]

I am not with those who abandoned their land
To the lacerations of the enemy.
I am deaf to their coarse flattery,
I won't give them my songs.

1. Translated by Judith Hemschemeyer.
2. Dante Alighieri (1265–1321), Florentine poet and au-

thor of the *Divine Comedy.*
1. Translated by Judith Hemschemeyer.

5 But to me the exile is forever pitiful,
Like a prisoner, like someone ill.
Dark is your road, wanderer,
Like wormwood smells the bread of strangers.

But here, in the blinding smoke of the conflagration
10 Destroying what's left of youth,
We have not deflected from ourselves
One single stroke.

And we know that in the final accounting,
Each hour will be justified . . .
15 But there is no people on earth more tearless
More simple and more full of pride.

July 1922
Petersburg

Boris Pasternak[1]

He who compared himself to a horse's eye,
squints, looks, sees, recognises,
and already the puddles shine
like a fused diamond, the ice pines away.

5 The backwoods rest in a lilac haze,
platforms, logs, leaves, clouds,
the engine whistles, the crunch of melon peel,
a timid hand in a fragrant kid glove.

There is a ringing, a thundering, a gnashing, the crash of surf,
10 and then suddenly quiet: this means
he is treading the pine needles, fearful lest
he should scare awake the light dream-sleep of space.

This means he is counting the grains
in the empty ears; this means
15 he has come again from some funeral
to the cursed, black, Daryal Gorge.[2]

Moscow languor burns again,
death's little bells ring in the distance—
Who has got lost two steps from home,
20 where the snow is waist deep and an end to everything?

For comparing smoke with Laocoön,[3]
for singing of the graveyard thistle,

1. Translated by Richard McKane. Boris Pasternak (1890–1960) was a Russian poet and translator who was most influential in Russian poetry of the 20th century (see p. 306). Akhmatova wrote this poem in 1936, after Pasternak had run afoul of Stalin's repression of experimental poetry and was not allowed to publish.
2. Located in the central Caucasus Mountains of what was then Soviet Georgia. A historic passage and invasion route between east and west, it appears in Mikhail Lermontov's narrative poem *The Demon* (1829–1841).
3. Ancient sculptural grouping found in Rome in 1506, it depicts the Trojan priest Laocoön, who was strangled with his sons by sea snakes sent by the gods who favored the Greeks in the Trojan War because he tried to warn the Trojans against bringing the wooden horse into the city (Virgil, *Aeneid*, bk. 2).

for filling the earth with a new sound
in a new space of mirrored stanzas,

25 he is rewarded with a form of eternal childhood,
with the bounty and vigilance of the stars,
the whole world was his inheritance
and he shared it with everyone.

Why is this century worse[1]

Why is this century worse than those that have gone before?
In a stupor of sorrow and grief
it located the blackest wound
but somehow couldn't heal it.
5 The earth's sun is still shining in the West
and the roofs of towns sparkle in its rays,
while here death marks houses with crosses
and calls in the crows and the crows fly over.

Requiem[1]
1935–1940

No, not under the vault of alien skies,[2]
And not under the shelter of alien wings—
I was with my people then,
There, where my people, unfortunately, were.

1961

INSTEAD OF A PREFACE

In the terrible years of the Yezhov terror,[3] I spent seventeen months in the prison lines of Leningrad. Once, someone "recognized" me. Then a woman with bluish lips standing behind me, who of course had never heard me called by name before, woke up from the stupor to which everyone had succumbed and whispered in my ear (everyone spoke in whispers there):

"Can you describe this?"

And I answered: "Yes, I can."

Then something that looked like a smile passed over what had once been her face.

April 1, 1957
Leningrad

DEDICATION

Mountains bow down to this grief,
Mighty rivers cease to flow,

1. Translated by Richard McKane.
1. Translated by Judith Hemschemeyer. The poem's verses were written at various times during and after the imprisonment of her son, Lev Gumilov, in 1935 and the arrest of her lover Nikolai Punin later that year. Her son was arrested again in 1939 and condemned to a labor camp in Siberia, where he remained until 1941; he was imprisoned again from 1949–1956.
2. Quoting "Message to Siberia," by Alexander Pushkin (1799–1837).
3. A major purge in 1937–1938, led by Nikolai Yezhov, head of Stalin's secret police.

But the prison gates hold firm,
And behind them are the "prisoners' burrows"
5   And mortal woe,
For someone a fresh breeze blows,
For someone the sunset luxuriates—
We wouldn't know, we are those who everywhere
Hear only the rasp of the hateful key
10   And the soldiers' heavy tread.
We rose as if for an early service,
Trudged through the savaged capital
And met there, more lifeless than the dead;
The sun is lower and the Neva[4] mistier,
15   But hope keeps singing from afar.
The verdict . . . And her tears gush forth,
Already she is cut off from the rest,
As if they painfully wrenched life from her heart,
As if they brutally knocked her flat,
20   But she goes on . . . Staggering . . . Alone . . .
Where now are my chance friends
Of those two diabolical years?
What do they imagine is in Siberia's storms,[5]
What appears to them dimly in the circle of the moon?
25   I am sending my farewell greeting to them.

March 1940

PROLOGUE

That was when the ones who smiled
Were the dead, glad to be at rest.
And like a useless appendage, Leningrad
Swung from its prisons.
30   And when, senseless from torment,
Regiments of convicts marched,
And the short songs of farewell
Were sung by locomotive whistles.
The stars of death stood above us
35   And innocent Russia writhed
Under bloody boots
And under the tires of the Black Marias.[6]

I

They led you away at dawn,
I followed you, like a mourner,

4. The famous river around which St. Petersburg (Leningrad) was built.
5. Wives of male prisoners spared execution were allowed to move to Siberia, to be near their husbands' prison camps.
6. Police vans.

40 In the dark front room the children were crying,
By the icon shelf the candle was dying.
On your lips was the icon's chill.[7]
The deathly sweat on your brow . . . Unforgettable!—
I will be like the wives of the Streltsy,[8]
45 Howling under the Kremlin towers.

1935

II

Quietly flows the quiet Don,[9]
Yellow moon slips into a home.

He slips in with cap askew,
He sees a shadow, yellow moon.

50 This woman is ill,
This woman is alone,

Husband in the grave,[1] son in prison,
Say a prayer for me.

III

No, it is not I, it is somebody else who is suffering.
55 I would not have been able to bear what happened,
Let them shroud it in black,
And let them carry off the lanterns . . .
                                                    Night.

1940

IV

You should have been shown, you mocker,
Minion of all your friends,
60 Gay little sinner of Tsarskoye Selo[2]
What would happen in your life—
How three-hundredth in line, with a parcel,
You would stand by the Kresty prison,
Your fiery tears
65 Burning through the New Year's ice.
Over there the prison poplar bends,
And there's no sound—and over there how many
Innocent lives are ending now . . .

7. When he was arrested at their apartment in 1935, Akhmatova's husband had kissed an icon (religious painting) in farewell.
8. Rebellious troops executed by Peter the Great in 1698 as their wives watched.

9. A river flowing into the Black Sea.
1. Akhmatova's first husband, the poet Nikolai Gumilov, executed in 1921.
2. Town outside Leningrad where Akhmatova grew up, site of the tsars' summer palace and elaborate gardens.

V

For seventeen months I've been crying out,
Calling you home.
I flung myself at the hangman's feet,
You are my son and my horror.
Everything is confused forever,
And it's not clear to me
Who is a beast now, who is a man,
And how long before the execution.
And there are only dusty flowers,
And the chinking of the censer, and tracks
From somewhere to nowhere.
And staring me straight in the eyes,
And threatening impending death,
Is an enormous star.

1939

VI

The light weeks will take flight,
I won't comprehend what happened.
Just as the white nights[3]
Stared at you, dear son, in prison
So they are staring again,
With the burning eyes of a hawk,
Talking about your lofty cross,
And about death.

1939

VII: THE SENTENCE

And the stone word fell
On my still-living breast.
Never mind, I was ready,
I will manage somehow.

Today I have so much to do:
I must kill memory once and for all,
I must turn my soul to stone,
I must learn to live again—

Unless . . . Summer's ardent rustling
Is like a festival outside my window.

---

3. Midsummer nights in which the sun barely sets.

For a long time I've foreseen this
Brilliant day, deserted house.

June 22, 1939[4]
Fountain House

VIII: To Death

You will come in any case—so why not now?
I am waiting for you—I can't stand much more.
105 I've put out the light and opened the door
For you, so simple and miraculous.
So come in any form you please,
Burst in as a gas shell
Or, like a gangster, steal in with a length of pipe,
110 Or poison me with your typhus fumes.
Or be that fairy tale you've dreamed up,
So sickeningly familiar to everyone—
In which I glimpse the top of a pale blue cap[5]
And the house attendant white with fear.
115 Now it doesn't matter anymore. The Yenisey[6] swirls,
The North Star shines.
And the final horror dims
The blue luster of beloved eyes.

August 19, 1939
Fountain House

IX

Now madness half shadows
120 My soul with its wing,
And makes it drunk with fiery wine
And beckons toward the black ravine.

And I've finally realized
That I must give in,
125 Overhearing myself
Raving as if it were somebody else.

And it does not allow me to take
Anything of mine with me.
(No matter how much I plead with it,
130 No matter how much I supplicate):

Not the terrible eyes of my son—
Suffering turned to stone,

---

4. The date her son was sentenced to labor camp in
Siberia.
5. Often worn by the secret police.

6. Several prison camps were built along this Siberian
river.

Not the day of the terror,
Not the hour I met with him in prison,

135 Not the sweet coolness of his hands,
Not the trembling shadow of the lindens,
Not the far-off, fragile sound—
Of the final words of consolation.

May 4, 1940
Fountain House

X: CRUCIFIXION

"Do not weep for Me, Mother,
I am in the grave."[7]

1

A choir of angels sang the praises of that momentous hour,
140 And the heavens dissolved in fire.
To his Father He said: "Why hast Thou forsaken me!"[8]
And to his Mother: "Oh, do not weep for Me . . ."

1940
Fountain House

2

Mary Magdalene beat her breast and sobbed,
The beloved disciple turned to stone,
145 But where the silent Mother stood, there
No one glanced and no one would have dared.

1943
Tashkent

EPILOGUE I

I learned how faces fall,
How terror darts from under eyelids,
How suffering traces lines
150 Of stiff cuneiform on cheeks,
How locks of ashen-blonde or black
Turn silver suddenly,
Smiles fade on submissive lips
And fear trembles in a dry laugh.
155 And I pray not for myself alone,
But for all those who stood there with me
In cruel cold, and in July's heat,
At that blind, red wall.

7. From a Russian Orthodox prayer sung at Easter, in which Jesus comforts his mother, Mary.

8. Jesus's last words on the cross, according to Matthew's gospel (27:46).

EPILOGUE II

Once more the day of remembrance draws near.[9]
160   I see, I hear, I feel you:

The one they almost had to drag at the end,
And the one who tramps her native land no more,

And the one who, tossing her beautiful head,
Said, "Coming here's like coming home."

165   I'd like to name them all by name,
But the list has been confiscated and is nowhere to be found.

I have woven a wide mantle for them
From their meager, overheard words.

I will remember them always and everywhere,
170   I will never forget them no matter what comes.

And if they gag my exhausted mouth
Through which a hundred million scream,

Then may the people remember me
On the eve of my remembrance day.

175   And if ever in this country
They decide to erect a monument to me,

I consent to that honor
Under these conditions—that it stand

Neither by the sea, where I was born:
180   My last tie with the sea is broken,

Nor in the tsar's garden near the cherished pine stump,
Where an inconsolable shade looks for me,

But here, where I stood for three hundred hours,
And where they never unbolted the doors for me.

185   This, lest in blissful death
I forget the rumbling of the Black Marias,

Forget how that detested door slammed shut
And an old woman howled like a wounded animal.

And may the melting snow stream like tears
190   From my motionless lids of bronze,

And a prison dove coo in the distance,
And the ships of the Neva sail calmly on.

March 1940

---

9. "Remembrance Day" is a Russian Orthodox church service held a year after someone's death.

≈+ PERSPECTIVES +≈

Modernism and Revolution in Russia

Rupture, radical break, and drastic discontinuity are marks of modernism. When the artistic split with the past was coupled with political revolution, the intensity of the rift between past and present was compounded, in some instances to such extremes that it would prove fatal for the writers themselves. Of the five writers featured in this section, two (Mayakovski and Tsvetaeva) died violent deaths at their own hand (Mandelstam's suicide attempt proved unsuccessful), and three endured imprisonment and exile, internal or external (Pasternak, Tsvetaeva, and Mandelstam). One would also be awarded the Nobel Prize in Literature (Pasternak). Russia's Bolshevik Revolution of 1917 coincided, not altogether incidentally, with Russian literature's passage from a neo-Romantic aesthetic called Symbolism, in poetry especially, to various modernist movements that went by a number of "-isms." The most shrill of these revolutionary ruptures was expressed by Mayakovski, who was also a graphic designer and painter of broadsides and billboards for the Russian Revolution; one of his most characteristic poems is entitled "At the Top of My Voice."

A revolutionary new age meant a new language, and the Russian language was to be subjected to drastic forms of typographic and verbal experimentation by these authors. In all revolutionary moments, once the rupture crystallizes into regime, the force and energy of change usually passes into harsh forms of repression and curtailment, lest the breakage spin out of control, and the attained transformations themselves become the next targets of the revolutionary dynamic. And so it was with Lenin's death and Stalin's succession in 1924. Russian modernism under Stalinism found itself on precarious ground, and its innovative experiments came up against official suspicion and repressive containment. Stalinism's thirty-year repression would channel literary and artistic modernism into ideologically controlled social-materialist "modernization." As with its effects on the literary legacy of the Russian Revolution, the political, environmental, and technological ravages of that modernizing program are still being assessed today in post-Soviet Russia and in the other republics of the former Soviet Union.

+— ≈◆≈ —+

Vladimir Mayakovski
1893–1930

Vladimir Mayakovski was born in the country of Georgia, at that time part of the Russian empire, and moved to Moscow with his family after his father, a forest ranger, died in 1906. Two years later he joined the Bolshevik faction of the Russian Social Democratic Party; he was imprisoned for six months shortly afterward for subversive activities. In 1912 Mayakovski moved to Saint Petersburg and was one of the principal actors in Russia's own Futurist revolution in the arts and literature. He was co-author of "A Slap in the Face of Public Taste" (1912), a manifesto that sought to reform Russian culture by attacking such canonical figures as Pushkin, Dostoevsky, and Tolstoi. A talented painter and draftsman who was trained at the Stroganov School of Industrial Arts and also at the Moscow Institute of Painting, Sculpture, and Architecture, he would put his talents in the service of the Russian Revolution by painting posters and billboards for the Russian Telegraph Agency between 1919 and 1921. He was also a playwright and scriptwriter and starred in a number of his own films.

Mayakovski's artistic inclinations and revolutionary spirit, however, would prove problematic for the Revolution itself. His most consistent production was political verse of epic proportions in praise of the Bolshevik Revolution, though his long poem "150,000,000" (1921–1922) was a political allegory and satire against capitalism. The poem joined Futurist poetics to revolutionary enthusiasm, but it only managed to elicit the perplexity and irritation of Lenin, who called the poem preposterous and stupid. Mayakovski attained his greatest renown as a result of his 3,000-line poem "Vladimir Ilyich Lenin" upon the death of the Bolshevik leader in 1924. With Stalin's rise to power, however, Mayakovski's poetic resources would be devoted mostly to defending himself in the face of what he saw as growing Soviet philistinism. Ironically, his fame as Russia's foremost revolutionary poet would not be assured until he was posthumously, and by fiat, proclaimed as such by Stalin. Mayakovski shot himself in 1930, leaving an unfinished poem entitled "At the Top of My Voice" as his suicide testament.

PRONUNCIATION:
   Mayakovski: MY-ah-COFF-skee

Listen![1]

Now, listen!
Surely, if the stars are lit
there's somebody who longs for them,
somebody who wants them to shine a bit,
5   somebody who calls it, that wee speck
                              of spittle, a gem?

And overridden
by blizzards of midday dust,
tears in to God,
10   afraid that it's too late,
and sobbing,
kisses the sinewy hand outthrust,
swears
that he can't, simply can't bear a starless
15   fate:

There must be a star, there must!
. . . Then goes about anxious,
though tranquil seeming,
whispering to somebody,
20   "You're better?
Not afraid?

All right?"
Now listen,
it must be for somebody stars are set gleaming,
25   somebody who longs
for one star at least
over the rooftops to come alight?

Fed Up

Couldn't sit home.
Annensky, Tyutchev, Fet . . .[1]

---

1. Translated by Dorian Rottenberg, as are the next two poems.

1. Russian Symbolist poets against whom Mayakovski is rebelling.

Driven by boredom
again among people to roam
5 I go
to cinema, pub, café.

At table.
An aura of hope seems to shine.
One beat my silly heart misses.
10 What if
the past week has so altered this silly countryman of mine,
that I'll scorch off his cheeks with kisses?

Cautious, I lift up my eyes, peer about,
digging into the jacketed populace.
15 "Back out!
Back out!
BACK OUT!"
yells tear from my heart,
overrunning my face, moody and hopeless.

20 Unheeding,
here's what my eyes abut on:
a little to the right, unheard-of, unseen,
thoroughly absorbed in a leg of mutton,
the most puzzling creature there's ever been.

25 You look and marvel—is it eating or not?
You watch and wonder—does it breathe or not?
Five feet of pinkish, featureless dough,
not so much as a tag in a convenient spot.

Only, lolling on the shoulders, sleek silk bladders,
30 glistening cheeks all space annex.
Raging and tearing, my heart yells madder,
"Back out, now!
What next?"

I swing to the left: mouth-agape;
35 then again to the right, in opinion flinching.
To the observer of the second wry shape,
the first
seems the double of Leonardo da Vinci.[2]

No humans! Can you comprehend
40 the outcry of a thousand days' pain?
The soul doesn't want to go dumb till the end,
yet to whom complain?

I'll fling myself down,
rub my face raw

2. Italian Renaissance painter, architect, engineer, mathematician, and philosopher (1452–1519).

45   on the curbstone, washing it from my hot tears' font,
with love-thirsty lips plant a thousand kisses and more
on the tram's intelligent front.

Home I'll go,
to the wallpaper cling.
50   Where else are roses more worth my wooing?
Dear, blotchy thing,
shall I read you *Plain as Mooing?*

FOR HISTORY

When all are accommodated in heaven and hell,
55   accounts drawn up for both saint and retrograde,
in the year 1916—
remember well—
handsome people vanished from Petrograd.[3]

Ode to the Revolution[1]

To you,
whistled at,
jeered at by artillery,
to you,
5   slashed by vicious-tongued bayonets' blows,
I exultantly raise
over all the vile hollering
this ode's
ceremonial
10   "O's."
O bestial!
O childish!
O penniworth!
O great!
15   What epithets haven't been piled on your doings?
Double-faced, how will you turn out yet?
As a splendid edifice
or a heap of ruins?
To the engine-driver
20   in soot-clouds dense,
to the miner, boring through ore-bed layers,
reverently
you burn your incense,
glorifying man's labour.
25   And tomorrow
St. Basil
Cathedral's rafters

---

3. Capital of Russia until 1918. Formerly Saint Petersburg, it was renamed Petrograd in 1914, changed to Leningrad in 1924, and restored to its original name in 1991.
1. The title refers to the Soviet Revolution of 1917.

rear in vain, imploring your mercy,
while your boar-faced six-inchers
30   roar with devilish laughter,
into the Kremlin's millennia bursting.
The *Slava,*
its sirens half-choked, screaming,
wheezes on its life's last cruise.
35   To the sinking cruiser
you send your seamen,
where a kitten,
forgotten,
mews.
40   And after,
a mob with drunken shouts,
mustachios twisted in bravado coarse,
you drove grey-haired admirals with rifle butts
head-down from the bridge in Helsingfors.
45   Yesterday's wounds are still licked and nursed,
yet again blood from fresh-cut arteries shines.
From the philistine comes
"O, be thrice accursed!"
and from me,
50   a poet,
"Thrice blessed be, sublime!"

On Trash[1]

Glory, glory, glory to the heroes!!!

Incidentally,
for them
enough tribute's been stashed.
5   Now
let's thrash out
about trash.

In revolutionary laps the storm is hardly heard.
It's surfaced with a Soviet mish-mash of slime.
10   And emerging
from behind the back of the USSR[2]
purred
the Philistines.

(Don't take me literally,
15   It's not against the petty-bourgeoisie I'm rising.
It's the Philistines,
whatever their class or estate,
I'm eulogising.)

---

1. Translated by Herbert Marshall.   2. Union of Soviet Socialist Republics, 1922–1991.

Still image from Sergei Mikhailovich Eisenstein's *Battleship Potemkin,* 1925. Eisenstein's avant-garde film, set in the Ukranian city of Odessa, celebrates the 1905 uprising against tsarism in Russia. In one of the central scenes, tsarist militia violently subdue the insurgent crowd; the regime's brutality is vividly foregrounded by close-up shots of the soldiers' boots marching down the famous Odessa steps, trampling objects and people that stand in the way of their relentless advance.

        From all the boundlessness of Russia they gathered,
20   from the very first day of our Soviet Constitution,
        they poured in,
        quick-changing their feathers,
        and ensconced themselves in every institution.

        Callousing their behinds from five-year sittings,
25   shiny-hard as washbasin toilets,
        they live till now—
        quiet as water flitting.
        In cosy parlours and comfy bedrooms coiling.
        And in the evening
30   mean and nasty,
        they watch the wife,—
        piano-learning's the fashion—
        and say to her,
        by the samovar basking:
35   "Comrade Natasha!
        Got an anniversary rise—
        24 thousand.
        The Official Tariff.

Hey,
40   I'll order a pair of breeches,
Pacific-ocean wide,
out of them
I'll rear
like a coral reef!"
45   Then Natasha:
"And for me a dress with emblems displayed.
Without hammers and sickles one can't appear at all!
For how else
today
50   could I figure
at the RevMilSoviet Ball?"
On the wall Marx,
in a red, red frame.
On *Izvestia*[3] a cat preens, staring.
55   And hanging from the ceiling
chirrups inane
a moulting canary.

Marx from the wall looked on appalled . . .
Then suddenly
60   opened his mouth
and bawled:
"The Revolution by Philistine meshes' entangled.
A Philistine-existence's more terrible than
                               Wrangel!

65   Hurry!
Wring that damned canary's neck—
so that Communism
by canaries won't be wrecked!"

◄┤═◊═├►

Boris Pasternak
1890–1960

Boris Pasternak was born in Moscow, where his father was a successful painter, his mother a concert pianist. He studied composition for six years and then philosophy at Marburg University in Germany, but abandoned music and philosophy for poetry upon his return to Moscow in 1913, where he became involved with the Centrifuge group of Futurists. His first two books of poetry were in the Futurist vein, though it was with his third and fourth volumes of poems, *My Sister Life* (written in 1917 and published in 1922) and *Themes and Variations* (1923), that he became recognized as one of Russia's leading new poets. A poet with an individualist and idiosyncratic vision, he never warmed up to utilitarian Soviet poetry. He ran into great difficulties

3. "News," one of two largest circulation newspapers under the Soviet Union. Now an independent paper.

during the decade of the 1930s, which he considered the years of his silent war with Stalin. Unable to publish his own poetry during those years, he translated Shakespeare, Goethe, Schiller, Shelley, Byron, Keats, as well as Verlaine and Rilke, whom he had met early in his career as an aspiring poet.

During World War II, with censorship authorities distracted by the war, Pasternak was able to resume publishing—*On Early Trains* (1943) and *Expanses of Land* (1945), translated as *The Breadth of the Earth*. In the last decade of his life, faced with declining health, he concentrated on what he considered his testament as witness to the events before, during, and after the Russian Revolution of 1917, his novel *Doctor Zhivago*, which he finished but wasn't allowed to publish in the Soviet Union. It appeared in Italy in 1957, and the following year Pasternak was awarded the Nobel Prize. This led to what has become known as the "Pasternak Affair," the result of which was that he was obliged by the Soviet authorities to decline the prize and was ostracized by the Soviet establishment. His poetry would not appear again until after his death. Reflecting his intense work with the English and German Romantic poets as their translator into Russian, Pasternak's poetry has a decidedly Romantic flavor, and his most autobiographical volume of poems, *Safe Conduct* (1931), is the most revealing of the poet's relationship to poetry and of his vocation as a writer.

O Had I Known . . .[1]

O had I known that thus it happens,
When first I started, that at will
Your lines with blood in them destroy you,
Roll up into your throat and kill,

5   My answer to this kind of joking
Had been a most decisive "no",
So distant was the start, so timid
The first approach—what could one know?

But older age is Rome, demanding
10 From actors not a gaudy blend
Of props and reading, but in earnest
A tragedy, with tragic end.

A slave is sent to the arena
When feeling has produced a line,
15 Then breathing soil and fate take over
And art has done and must resign.

On Early Trains[1]

Near Moscow living, I, this winter,
In blizzard, chill and snow,
On business when it was essential
Always caught the train to town.

5   When I went out on some occasions
The street was black as pitch.

1. Translated by Lydia Pasternak Slater.   1. Translated by George Reavey.

And through the forests dark I scattered
My tread that creaked at every step.

Confronting me at the highway crossing
10   White willows straggled in the waste.
Above, the constellations towered
In January's frozen ditch.

At the backyards, normally
The mail train or Number Forty
15   Tried hard to overhaul me, but I
Was aiming at the Six O'Clock.

Then the cunning wrinkles of the light
In feelers gathered round.
A searchlight sped full speed upon
20   The staggered viaduct.

In the compartment's stifling heat,
I gave myself up wholly
To a surge of inborn weakness
I'd sucked in from the breast.

25   Through all the trials of the past,
The years of war and hardship,
I silently identified
Russia's inimitable features.

Mastering my adoration,
30   And deifying, I observed:
Here were locksmiths, workers,
Students, and peasant women.

In them I found no servile traits
Such as great need imposes,
35   And, like any gentlemen, they bore
Discomfort and bad news.

Closely packed as in a carriage,
In every kind of pose,
Adults and children were engrossed
40   In reading as though they'd been wound up.

Then Moscow met us in the gloom
Which sometimes shone like silver,
And leaving the ambiguous light,
We walked out of the subway.

45   Posterity shoved me to the wall,
And splashed me on the way,
With fresh birdcherry soap
And sweetly smelling honeycake.

Peredelkino, early 1941

Hamlet[1]

The murmurs ebb; onto the stage I enter.
I am trying, standing in the door,
To discover in the distant echoes
What the coming years may hold in store.

5   The nocturnal darkness with a thousand
Binoculars is focused onto me.
Take away this cup, O Abba, Father,
Everything is possible to thee.

I am fond of this thy stubborn project,
10   And to play my part I am content.
But another drama is in progress,
And, this once, O let me be exempt.

But the plan of action is determined,
And the end irrevocably sealed.
15   I am alone; all round me drowns in falsehood:
Life is not a walk across a field.

—◄═◆═►—

Andrei Bely
1880–1934

Andrei Bely is the pen name of Boris Nikolaevich Bugaev, who was born in Moscow as the son of a mathematics professor. He is significant as a transitional figure between Russian Symbolism and modernism. He is an important figure for his essays on the philosophy of art and poetry, collected in such early books as *Symbolism* and *A Green Meadow,* both of which appeared in 1910, and in *On the Border of Two Centuries* (1931) and *Between Two Revolutions* (1934). Bely sought an overall philosophy that would explain the aesthetics of art and literature. In the process, he recapitulated a good deal of Romantic theory and philosophy, but he also anticipated the methods of Russian Formalism as well as the technologies of abstract art and experimental poetry that defined the avant-garde movements in the first two decades of the twentieth century. His own poetry and prose fiction are equally marked by this vacillation between the romantic conventions of Symbolism and the technical experiments of modernism and avant-garde writing. Writer/critics such as Nabokov consider his novel *Saint Petersburg* to be as important and as defining of twentieth-century literature as the greatest works of Kafka, Joyce, and Proust.

PRONUNCIATION:
    Andrei Bely: ahn-DRAY BYEL-lee

---

1. Translated by Lydia Pasternak Slater.

from The Magic of Words[1]

I

Language is the most powerful instrument of creation. In naming an object with a word I assert its existence. All knowledge results from the naming. Knowledge is not possible without the word. The process of knowing something is the forging of relationships between words which are subsequently transferred to objects which correspond to the words. Grammatical forms, which make sentence construction possible, are possible only when words exist; the logical articulation of speech occurs only later. In asserting that creation precedes knowledge I assert the primacy of creation, not only in its epistemological priority but also in its genetic sequence.

Figurative speech is made up of words which express logically my inexpressible impression of the things that surround me. Living speech is always the music of the inexpressible. "A thought that is spoken is a lie", says Tyutchev,[2] and he is right if, by a thought, he understands something that is expressed in a series of terminological concepts. But the living, spoken word is not a lie. It is the expression of the secret essence of my nature, and, inasmuch as my nature is nature in general, the word is an expression of the innermost secrets of nature. Every word is a sound. I can understand the spatial and causal relationships outside me by means of the word. If words did not exist, the world would not exist either. Isolated from its surroundings, my "I" does not exist at all; nor does the world exist, isolated from me; "I" and "world" come into being only in the process of their joining through sound. Consciousness and nature which lie outside the individual become contiguous and are joined only in the process of naming. Thus consciousness, nature and world come into being for the knower only when he is able to create names; there is no nature, world or knower outside language. Primal creation is inherent in the word; the word links the wordless, invisible world, which swarms in the subconscious depths of my personal consciousness, with the wordless, meaningless world which swarms outside my person. The word creates a new, third world, a world of sound symbols through which the secrets of the worlds, confined both outside and inside me, are illuminated. Then the outside world pours into my soul just as the inside world spills over into the dawn, into the rustle of trees; I re-create for myself all that surrounds me, on the outside and the inside, through words and only through words, for I am a *word* and only a *word.* * * *

All that is felt in me by my senses decays when I die; my body becomes a rotting corpse which stinks; but when the process of decay ends I appear before the gaze of those who have loved me in a row of beautiful crystals. The ideal term is an eternal crystal obtained only by way of its final decay. The word-image is like a living human being; it creates, affects and changes its content. An ordinary, prosaic word, one having lost its sound and descriptive imagery and not having as yet become an ideal term, is a stinking, rotting corpse.

There are few ideal terms because there have been so few living words; all our life is filled with rotting words which give off an unbearable stink; the use of these words infects us with the poison of a corpse, because the word is the direct expression of life.

---

1. Translated by T. G. West.

2. Feodor Ivanovich Tyutchev (1903–1973), Russian diplomat, lyrical poet, and essayist.

And thus the only thing to which our vitality commits us is the creation of words. We must harness our power in the combining of words; in so doing we forge a weapon with which to combat the living corpses which impinge upon our activities; we must become barbarians, executioners of the popular word, if we cannot first breathe life into it. * * *

Armed with the defence of words, man re-creates everything he sees, invades the limits of the unknown like a warrior and, if he triumphs, his words thunder, flare up with the sparks of constellations, shroud his listeners with the darkness of interplanetary space, send them off to an unknown planet where rainbows gleam, rivers murmur and huge cities tower up, in which his listeners, as though dreaming, find themselves exhausted in a four-cornered enclosure called a room, where they dream that someone is speaking to them; they think the *word* of the speaker comes from the speaker; and that it is authentic. If this is how it seems to them, then the magic of words has been realized and the illusion of knowledge begins to have an effect; it then begins to seem that there is some hidden meaning behind the words, that knowledge is separable from the word; but meanwhile the whole dream of knowledge has been created by the word; the knower always speaks aloud or mentally; all knowledge is an illusion which follows the word. * * *

All knowledge is the fireworks of words with which I fill the emptiness surrounding me; if my words sparkle with colours, they create the illusion of light; and this illusion of light is knowledge. No one convinces anyone. No one proves anything to anyone; every argument is a battle of words, is magic; I speak only in order to cast a spell; a battle with words which has the appearance of a dispute is the filling up of emptiness with one thing or the other: at this point it is normal to silence an opponent with rotten words; but this is not persuasion—the opponent, upon returning home after the argument, is sickened by the rotten words. In early times emptiness was filled with light by the fires of images; this was the process of mythic creation. The word gave rise to the descriptive symbol—the metaphor; the metaphor seemed to be something that really existed; the word gave rise to myth, and myth gave rise to religion, religion to philosophy, and philosophy to the term.

It is better to shoot off word-rockets purposelessly into emptiness than to allow dust to gather in the same place. The former is the effect of living language, the latter, that of dead language. We often prefer the latter. We are half alive, half dead.

* * *

Poetic speech is directly bound to mythical creation; the striving for a figurative combination of words is a basic characteristic of poetry.

The real power of creation cannot be measured by consciousness; consciousness always comes after creation; the striving for a combination of words and consequently for the creation of images which emerge out of a new word formation is indicative of the fact that the basis of a creative assertion of life is alive, independent of whether consciousness justifies this striving or not. Such an assertion of the power of creation in words is religious; it exists in spite of consciousness.

And thus the new word of life is nurtured by poetry in a period of general decay. We revel in words because we are conscious of the significance of new, magical words with which, again and again, we are able to cast a spell on the darkness of night which looms above us. We are still alive, but we are alive because we are supported by words.

Play with words is a characteristic of youth; beneath the dust of the fragments of decayed culture we invoke and conjure with the sounds of words. We know that this is the only legacy which will be of use to our children.

Our children will forge the new symbol of belief out of luminous words; the crisis of knowledge will appear to them to be just the death of old words. Mankind is alive as long as the poetry of language exists; the poetry of language is alive.

We are alive.

・━━ ≡◆≡ ━━・

Marina Tsvetaeva
1892–1941

Daughter of the founder of Moscow's Museum of Fine Arts and of a concert pianist, Marina Tsvetaeva has emerged as one of the most important Russian poets of the twentieth century. Though her work was neglected during her lifetime, her tumultuous life and violent death at her own hand have become symptomatic of the historical period she lived in. The lyrical intensity of her poetry likewise reflects the turmoil of her personal and political life. She spent most of her childhood in Western Europe, attending schools in Switzerland, Germany, and France, and was fluent in French and German. She married Sergei Yakovlevich Efron in 1912. He would become a Tsarist army officer, and they would have a son and two daughters, one of whom died of starvation in 1920 during the famine following the 1917 Russian Revolution. In 1922 Tsvetaeva went into exile with her family, first to Berlin, then Prague, and then to Paris, where she lived until 1938. Her husband became progressively pro-Soviet, and he assassinated a Soviet defector in Paris on the orders of the Soviet secret police, after which he fled to the Soviet Union.

Shunned by the Russian émigré community and destitute, Tsvetaeva returned in 1938 to Russia, where her children and husband already lived. A year later, her husband was shot, and her remaining daughter was sent to a labor camp. Ostracized by publishers and fellow writers, she found it impossible to publish her work. When the German army invaded the Soviet Union in 1941, Tsvetaeva and her son were evacuated to the village of Elabuga in the Tatar Autonomous Republic. There, in despair, she hanged herself. Tsvetaeva's poetry is thematically diverse and ranges from childhood recollection (*Evening Album*, 1918) to female sexuality ("Girlfriend"), political allegory ("The Ratcatcher: A Lyrical Satire," 1925), and death—her own ("The Day Will Come," 1916) and the death of many around her ("Poem of the End," 1924). Tsvetaeva was intensely engaged with the most important poets of her time. She corresponded with and wrote poems to and/or about such key figures as Bely, Pasternak, Rilke, and Akhmatova.

PRONUNCIATION:
   Tsvetaeva: TSFETT-eye-AY-vah

The Poet[1]
1

A poet's speech begins   a great way off.
A poet is   carried far away by speech

by way of planets, signs, and the ruts
of roundabout parables, between *yes* and *no,*
5   in his hands even sweeping gestures from a bell-tower
become hook-like. For the way of comets

1. Translated by Elaine Feinstein.

is the poet's way. And the blown-apart
links of causality   are his links. Look up
after him without hope. The eclipses of
10   poets are not foretold in the calendar.

He is the one that mixes up the cards
and confuses arithmetic and weight.
He is   the *questioner* from the desk
the one who beats Kant[2] on the head,

15   the one in the stone graves of the Bastille[3]
who remains like a tree in its loveliness.
And yet the one whose traces have always vanished,
the train everyone always arrives
too late to catch

              for the path of comets
20   is the path of poets: they burn without warming,
pick without cultivating. They are: an explosion, a breaking in—
and the mane of their path makes the   curve of a
graph   cannot be foretold by the calendar.

2

There are superfluous people about in
25   this world, out of sight, who
aren't listed in any directory: and
home for them is   a rubbish heap.

They are hollow, jostled creatures:
who keep silent, dumb as dung, they are
30   nails   catching in your silken hem
dirt   imagined under your wheels.

Here they are, ghostly and invisible, the
sign is on them, like the speck of the leper.
People like Job in this world who
35   might even have envied him. If.

We are poets, which has the sound of outcast.
Nevertheless, we step out from our shores.
We dare contend for godhead, with goddesses,
and for the Virgin   with the gods themselves.

3

40   Now what shall I do here, blind and fatherless?
Everyone else can see and has a father.
Passion in this world has to leap anathema

---

2. Immanuel Kant (1724–1804). German philosopher and one of the greatest figures in Western philosophy, he was born in Konigsberg, Prussia (now Kaliningrad, Russia).

3. Fortress and state prison in Paris, stormed by the people on 14 July 1789. Symbol of the French Revolution and of popular uprisings ever since.

as it might be over the walls of a trench
and weeping   is called a cold in the head.

45   What shall I do, by nature and trade
a singing creature (like a wire—sunburn! Siberia!)
as I go over the bridge of my enchanted
visions, that cannot be weighed, in a
world that deals only in weights and measures?

50   What shall I do, singer and first-born, in a
world where the deepest black is grey,
and inspiration is kept in   a thermos?
with all this immensity
in a measured world?

Readers of Newspapers

It crawls, the underground snake,
crawls, with its load of people.
And each one   has his
newspaper, his skin
5   disease; a twitch of chewing;
newspaper *caries*.
Masticators of gum,
readers of newspapers.

And who are the readers? old men? athletes?
10   soldiers? No face, no features,
no age. Skeletons—there's no
face, only the newspaper page.

All Paris   is dressed
this way from forehead to navel.
15   Give it up, girl, or
you'll give birth to
a reader of newspapers.

Sway/he lived with his sister,
Swaying/he killed his father,
20   They blow themselves up with pettiness
as if they were swaying with drink.

For such gentlemen   what
is the sunset or the sunrise?
They swallow emptiness,
25   these readers of newspapers.

For news   read: calumnies,
For news   read: embezzling,
in every column   slander
every paragraph some   disgusting thing.

30   With what, at the Last Judgement
      will you come before the light?
      Grabbers of small moments,
      readers of newspapers.

      Gone! lost! vanished! so,
35   the old maternal terror.
      But mother, the Gutenberg Press
      is more terrible than Schwarz' powder.

      It's better to go to a graveyard
      than into the   prurient
40   sickbay of scab-scratchers,
      these readers of newspapers.

      And who is it rots our sons
      now in the prime of their life?
      Those corrupters of blood
45   the *writers* of newspapers.

      Look, friends   much
      stronger than in these lines, do
      I think this, when with
      a manuscript in my hand

50   I stand before the face
      there is no   emptier place
      than before the absent
      face of an editor of news
                      papers' evil filth.

❯—≡◈≡—❮

Osip Mandelstam
1891–1938

Osip Mandelstam was born in Warsaw, Poland, but lived most of his life in Saint Petersburg, with Russian as his "native" language. His father was a successful leather goods merchant and his mother a piano teacher. He visited Paris in 1907 and spent two semesters studying old French literature in Heidelberg, Germany, in 1910. He registered as a student of Romance and Germanic philology at the University of Saint Petersburg between 1911 and 1917 but never completed his degree. He published his first poems in 1909 in the Acmeist journal *Apollon* and befriended the Acmeist poets Anna Akhmatova and her husband Nikolai Gumilyov, whom he joined as a member of the Poets' Guild in 1911. Mandelstam had strong ambivalences toward the 1917 Bolshevik Revolution and an unhappy history with the Soviet regime. His first book of poems, *Stone* (1913, expanded in 1916), gained wide acceptance, and his second collection, *Tristia* (1922), consolidated his reputation as a poet. In the 1920s he came under attack as being out of step with the Soviet age and supported himself by writing children's books and translating a number of writers into Russian, including Upton Sinclair. Between 1920 and 1925 his work consisted mostly of prose, though in 1928 his third book of poetry, *Poems,* would appear along with his collected essays on literature and criticism. In 1930 he made a long voyage which resulted in his book *Journey to Armenia* (1933). He was not published in the Soviet Union again for over thirty years. He was arrested for the first time in 1934 when Stalin took a personal interest in his poetry. His imprisonment and attempted suicide were followed by internal exile until 1937. Relentless in his anti-Stalinist writing, he was re-arrested for "counter-revolutionary" activities in 1938 and sentenced to five years of hard labor. He succumbed to a heart attack on the way to a labor camp on 27 December 1938. His work was published in the West to international acclaim starting in the 1970s, when his widow, Nadezhda Mandelstam, published her memoirs, *Hope Against Hope* (1971) and *Hope Abandoned* (1974), which depict life under Soviet rule during the Stalin era.

To A. A. A. (Akhmatova)[1]

Save my language forever for its smell of disaster and smoke,
For its resin of mutual endurance, its shameless drudgery's tar,
The way Novgorod well water, sickly sweet and pitch-black,
At Christmas should reflect a seven-finned star.

5   And for its sake, my father, my friend, my rough-tongued accomplice,
I, your outcaste brother, my people's black sheep,
I'm ready to dig crude timber-roofed wells
Where princes can be sunk in tubs by the Horde.

If these old headsman's blocks would just show me affection—
10   Like aiming at death, you play at knocking down sticks in a park—
For its sake I'd wear an iron shirt all life long
And for Tsar Peter's beheadings fetch a great axe from the woods.

                              3 May 1931, Khmel'nitskaya

We live, not feeling . . .[1]

We live, not feeling the country beneath us,
Our speech inaudible ten steps away,
But where they're up to half a conversation—
They'll speak of the Kremlin mountain man.

5   His thick fingers are fat like worms,
And his words certain as pound weights.
His cockroach whiskers laugh,
And the tops of his boots glisten.

And all around his rabble of thick-skinned leaders,
10   He plays through services of half-people.
Some whistle, some meow, some snivel,
He alone merely caterwauls and prods.

Like horseshoes he forges decree after decree—
Some get it in the forehead, some in the brow,
15   some in the groin, and some in the eye.

1. Translated by Bernard Meares.   1. Translated by Albert C. Todd.

By denying me the seas . . .[1]

By denying me the seas, the right to run and fly,
By holding my foot firm on the constraining earth,
What have you achieved? A splendid calculation,
But you couldn't seize my muttering lips thereby.

1935, Voronezh

END OF PERSPECTIVES: MODERNISM AND REVOLUTION IN RUSSIA

William Butler Yeats
1865–1939

Heir to a lingering British Romanticism and yet also a major modernist innovator; a Protestant in largely Catholic Ireland and a mystic in largely rationalist London; deeply introspective yet a highly public figure, at once fascinated and horrified by the politics of a violent age— William Butler Yeats was a pivotal figure both in international modernism and in the revival of Irish culture in his time. He was born to a Protestant family in Dublin; his father, John Butler Yeats, was a struggling painter and amateur philosopher, while his mother, Susan Pollexfen, had come from an old family in County Sligo in the rural northwest. Throughout his career, Yeats would explore manifold ways to combine the techniques and concerns of the English literary tradition with the historical and mythic resources of Catholic and pre-Christian Ireland.

Yeats's double perspective was fostered early. When he was three, his family moved to London, where his father pursued studies as a painter; the family's life in London was culturally rich but financially precarious. Yeats hated London, which he found cold and foreign, and treasured summer stays with his mother's family in County Sligo, warmly evoked in his early poem "The Lake Isle of Innisfree." Yeats's parents had three more children while in London, one of whom died in childhood; his surviving brother, Jack, became an important painter, while his sisters, Lil and Lolly, went on to found a press devoted to Irish culture. The family returned to Ireland in 1880, when Yeats was fifteen, settling in the village of Howth outside Dublin. Yeats found Dublin far more congenial than London, and attempted (with little success) to follow his father's footsteps as a painter, while also writing poetry with growing success. Though he never went to college, his first poems were published in a Dublin University literary magazine when he was twenty.

By this time Yeats was developing lifelong interests in two quite different directions: political and mystical. The 1880s were a time of widespread agitation for the freeing of Ireland from British colonial rule, and Yeats began attending meetings of various political and debating societies. At the same time, breaking with his father's rationalist humanism, he and several friends formed a "Hermetic Society" to explore mystical teachings of spiritual guides from India. After he moved with his family once again back to London in 1887, Yeats furthered these interests by studying with the charismatic Madame Blavatsky, whose 1877 book *Isis Unveiled* had become a bible for Theosophy, an Indian-derived mystical movement that stressed

1. Translated by Bernard Meares.

universal brotherhood, reincarnation, occult knowledge derived from communication with departed spirits, and a higher wisdom underlying all religions.

Yeats published his first book of poems, *The Wanderings of Oisin and Other Poems*, in 1889; among its readers was the revolutionary patriot and statuesque beauty Maud Gonne, who appeared at his lodgings with an introduction from a mutual friend and declared that Yeats's poetry had brought her to tears. For the next five decades Yeats would write poetry to and about Gonne, who came to symbolize for him the endless idealism—and, he felt, the dangerous fanaticism—of revolutionary political engagement. Maud Gonne is widely understood to stand behind figures such as Helen of Troy in poems such as "No Second Troy." Yeats proposed many times to Gonne, who always refused him, eventually marrying a fellow revolutionary, Major John MacBride, who was executed for his role in the Irish Rebellion against British rule in 1916, the subject of Yeats's haunting poem "Easter 1916." Yeats later said of his hopeless pursuit of Gonne that he might as well have proposed "to a statue in a museum." In 1917, he went so far as to propose to Gonne's adopted daughter, Iseult; like her mother, she turned him down. Shortly thereafter, he married an old friend, Georgiana Hyde-Lees, herself both an intellectual and someone interested in mysticism.

Both Yeats's mystical research and his contemplation of the endless ebb and flow of Irish politics fed into the elaborate personal mythology he gradually developed, which centered on a universal storehouse of experience and knowledge to which he gave the name *Spiritus Mundi*, or the World Spirit. Brought to fullest form in his 1928 book *A Vision*, Yeats's theory involved two great, antithetical historical "gyres" or spirals, which reverse position every two thousand years, in an apocalyptic explosion that leads to a new birth of a revived archaic culture. This vision underlies poems such as "The Second Coming." Yeats was inspired not only by his work in theosophy and comparative mythology but also by his close study of the works of the Romantic poet-painter William Blake, who similarly sought to fuse radically opposite elements into what Blake called "fearful symmetries."

Such concerns might have led to a purely private, esoteric poetry, but Yeats remained closely involved with Irish culture and politics. Settled permanently back in Dublin in the 1890s, he became a moving force in the revival of Irish drama at the Abbey Theatre, and he began to write plays based on traditional Irish stories, such as those from the medieval prose epic *The Táin*. His plays often had directly contemporary implications: In his play *The Countess Cathleen*, his heroine sells her soul to protect her peasants from starvation. Politics came to a critical juncture with the Easter Rising of 1916, whose dramatic initial proclamation—read from the steps of the central post office in Dublin—is given below as a Resonance for "Easter 1916." The British quickly crushed this rebellion and executed its leaders, many of them Yeats's friends. Several conflict-filled years followed, culminating in the establishment of the Irish Free State in 1922 and the partition of the country, with the largely Protestant northern counties remaining a colony of England. Yeats was made a senator of the new Irish state in 1922. He wasn't temperamentally suited to full-time political involvement, though, and soon returned to his writing, increasingly suspicious of the violence of popular politics and mourning the loss of an older aristocratic culture; in the 1930s he even flirted briefly with fascism.

Yeats remained a highly individualistic figure, and he continued to write innovative poetry to the end of his life; in 1923 he became the first Irish writer to be awarded the Nobel Prize. Many of his most powerful poems, such as "Byzantium," date from the 1930s, including his extraordinary poetic last testament, "Under Ben Bulben," which concludes with the epitaph he asked to have carved on his tombstone after his death, not long after he wrote it. Yeats's poems together form one of the century's most remarkable confrontations of an individual sensibility with the broadest social and political forces of history. His verses subtly dissect and adapt the traditional verse forms they use, and like his friend Ezra Pound and his contemporary Rainer Maria Rilke, he is one of the greatest masters of intense observation, rotating objects and images within poems and from one poem to another so that they display their many facets—historical, cultural, and individual—to our view.

The Lake Isle of Innisfree[1]

I will arise and go now, and go to Innisfree,
And a small cabin build there, of clay and wattles° made: *woven twigs*
Nine bean-rows will I have there, a hive for the honey-bee,
And live alone in the bee-loud glade.

5   And I shall have some peace there, for peace comes dropping slow,
Dropping from the veils of the morning to where the cricket sings;
There midnight's all a glimmer, and noon a purple glow,
And evening full of the linnet's° wings.   *song bird*

I will arise and go now, for always night and day
10   I hear lake water lapping with low sounds by the shore;
While I stand on the roadway, or on the pavements grey,
I hear it in the deep heart's core.

Who Goes with Fergus?[1]

Who will go drive with Fergus now,
And pierce the deep wood's woven shade,
And dance upon the level shore?
Young man, lift up your russet brow,
5   And lift your tender eyelids, maid,
And brood on hopes and fear no more.

And no more turn aside and brood
Upon love's bitter mystery;
For Fergus rules the brazen° cars,   *brass*
10   And rules the shadows of the wood,
And the white breast of the dim sea
And all dishevelled wandering stars.

No Second Troy[1]

Why should I blame her that she filled my days
With misery, or that she would of late
Have taught to ignorant men most violent ways,
Or hurled the little streets upon the great,
5   Had they but courage equal to desire?
What could have made her peaceful with a mind
That nobleness made simple as a fire,
With beauty like a tightened bow, a kind
That is not natural in an age like this,
10   Being high and solitary and most stern?

1. A small island in Lough Gill outside the city of Sligo, near the border with Northern Ireland.
1. The poem is a lyric from the second scene of Yeats's play *The Countess Cathleen*. Fergus was an ancient Irish king who gave up his throne to feast, fight, and hunt.
1. Yeats here compares Maud Gonne to Helen of Troy; the Trojan War began from two kings' rivalry over Helen.

Why, what could she have done, being what she is?
Was there another Troy for her to burn?

The Wild Swans at Coole[1]

The trees are in their autumn beauty,
The woodland paths are dry,
Under the October twilight the water
Mirrors a still sky;
5   Upon the brimming water among the stones
Are nine-and-fifty swans.

The nineteenth autumn has come upon me
Since I first made my count;
I saw, before I had well finished,
10   All suddenly mount
And scatter wheeling in great broken rings
Upon their clamorous wings.

I have looked upon those brilliant creatures,
And now my heart is sore.
15   All's changed since I, hearing at twilight,
The first time on this shore,
The bell-beat of their wings above my head,
Trod with a lighter tread.

Unwearied still, lover by lover,
20   They paddle in the cold
Companionable streams or climb the air;
Their hearts have not grown old;
Passion or conquest, wander where they will,
Attend upon them still.

But now they drift on the still water,
25   Mysterious, beautiful;
Among what rushes will they build,
By what lake's edge or pool
Delight men's eyes when I awake some day
30   To find they have flown away?

Easter 1916[1]

I have met them at close of day
Coming with vivid faces
From counter or desk among grey
Eighteenth-century houses.
5   I have passed with a nod of the head
Or polite meaningless words,
Or have lingered awhile and said

1. Coole Park was the name of the estate of Yeats's patron
Lady Gregory in Galway.

1. The Irish Republic was declared on Easter Monday
1916.

Polite meaningless words,
And thought before I had done
10   Of a mocking tale or a gibe°   *taunt*
To please a companion
Around the fire at the club,
Being certain that they and I
But lived where motley° is worn: *jester's outfit*
15   All changed, changed utterly:
A terrible beauty is born.

That woman's days were spent
In ignorant good-will,
Her nights in argument
20   Until her voice grew shrill.[2]
What voice more sweet than hers
When, young and beautiful,
She rode to harriers?°   *hunting dogs*
This man[3] had kept a school
25   And rode our wingèd horse;
This other his helper and friend[4]
Was coming into his force;
He might have won fame in the end,
So sensitive his nature seemed,
30   So daring and sweet his thought.
This other man[5] I had dreamed
A drunken, vainglorious lout.
He had done most bitter wrong
To some who are near my heart,
35   Yet I number him in the song;
He, too, has resigned his part
In the casual comedy;
He, too, has been changed in his turn,
Transformed utterly:
40   A terrible beauty is born.

Hearts with one purpose alone
Through summer and winter seem
Enchanted to a stone
To trouble the living stream.
45   The horse that comes from the road,
The rider, the birds that range
From cloud to tumbling cloud,
Minute by minute they change;
A shadow of cloud on the stream
50   Changes minute by minute;

2. Countess Markiewicz, née Constance Gore-Booth, played a prominent part in the Easter Rising and was sentenced to be executed; her sentence was later reduced to imprisonment.
3. Padraic Pearse.
4. Thomas MacDonagh, poet executed for his role in the rebellion.
5. Major John MacBride, briefly married to Maud Gonne, was also executed.

A horse-hoof slides on the brim,
And a horse plashes within it;
The long-legged moor-hens dive,
And hens to moor-cocks call;
55   Minute by minute they live:
The stone's in the midst of all.

Too long a sacrifice
Can make a stone of the heart.
O when may it suffice?
60   That is Heaven's part, our part
To murmur name upon name,
As a mother names her child
When sleep at last has come
On limbs that had run wild.
65   What is it but nightfall?
No, no, not night but death;
Was it needless death after all?
For England may keep faith
For all that is done and said.
70   We know their dream; enough
To know they dreamed and are dead;
And what if excess of love
Bewildered them till they died?
I write it out in a verse—
75   MacDonagh and MacBride
And Connolly[6] and Pearse
Now and in time to be,
Wherever green is worn,
Are changed, changed utterly:
80   A terrible beauty is born.

RESONANCE

Proclamation of the Irish Republic

Poblacht na h Eireann[1]

THE PROVISIONAL GOVERNMENT OF THE IRISH REPUBLIC
TO THE PEOPLE OF IRELAND

Irishmen and Irishwomen:

In the name of God and of the dead generations from which she receives her old tradition of nationhood, Ireland, through us, summons her children to her flag and strikes for her freedom.

Having organised and trained her manhood through her secret revolutionary organisation, the Irish Republican Brotherhood, and through her open military organisa-

---

6. James Connolly, Marxist commander-in-chief of the Easter rebels; also executed.

1. *Irish Republic,* in the Irish language.

tions, the Irish Volunteers and the Irish Citizen Army, having patiently perfected her discipline, having resolutely waited for the right moment to reveal itself, she now seizes that moment, and, supported by her exiled children in America and by gallant allies in Europe, but relying in the first on her own strength, she strikes in full confidence of victory.

We declare the right of the people of Ireland to the ownership of Ireland, and to the unfettered control of Irish destinies, to be sovereign and indefeasible. The long usurpation of that right by a foreign people and government has not extinguished the right, nor can it ever be extinguished except by the destruction of the Irish people. In every generation the Irish have asserted their right to National freedom and sovereignty; six times during the past three hundred years they have asserted it in arms. Standing on that fundamental right and again asserting it in arms in the face of the world, we hereby proclaim the Irish Republic as a Sovereign Independent State, and we pledge our lives and the lives of our comrades-in-arms to the cause of its freedom, of its welfare, and of its exaltation among the nations.

The Irish Republic is entitled to, and hereby claims, the allegiance of every Irishman and Irishwoman. The Republic guarantees religious and civil liberty, equal rights and equal opportunities to all its citizens, and declares its resolve to pursue the happiness and prosperity of the whole nation and of all its parts, cherishing all the children of the nation equally, and oblivious of the differences carefully fostered by an alien government, which have divided a minority from the majority in the past.

Until our arms have brought the opportune moment for the establishment of a permanent National Government, representative of the whole people of Ireland and elected by the suffrages of all her men and women,[2] the Provisional Government, hereby constituted, will administer the civil and military affairs of the Republic in trust for the people.

We place the cause of the Irish Republic under the protection of the Most High God, Whose blessing we invoke upon our arms, and we pray that no one who serves that cause will dishonor it by cowardice, inhumanity, or rapine. In this supreme hour the Irish nation must, by its valour and discipline and by the readiness of its children to sacrifice themselves for the common good, prove itself worthy of the august destiny to which it is called.

Signed on Behalf of the Provisional Government,

THOMAS J. CLARKE,
SEAN MACDIARMADA,
THOMAS MACDONAGH,
P. H. PEARSE,
EAMONN CEANNT,
JAMES CONNOLLY,
JOSEPH PLUNKETT.

Easter 1916

2. This call for women's suffrage in the Irish Republic predates full British women's suffrage by 12 years, and American women's suffrage by four years.

The Second Coming[1]

Turning and turning in the widening gyre°   *circle or spiral*
The falcon cannot hear the falconer;
Things fall apart; the centre cannot hold;
Mere anarchy is loosed upon the world,

5 The blood-dimmed tide is loosed, and everywhere
The ceremony of innocence is drowned;
The best lack all conviction, while the worst
Are full of passionate intensity.

Surely some revelation is at hand;

10 Surely the Second Coming is at hand.
The Second Coming! Hardly are those words out
When a vast image out of *Spiritus Mundi*[2]
Troubles my sight: somewhere in sands of the desert
A shape with lion body and the head of a man,

15 A gaze blank and pitiless as the sun,
Is moving its slow thighs, while all about it
Reel shadows of the indignant desert birds.
The darkness drops again; but now I know
That twenty centuries of stony sleep

20 Were vexed to nightmare by a rocking cradle,
And what rough beast, its hour come round at last,
Slouches towards Bethlehem to be born?

Sailing to Byzantium[1]

1

That is no country for old men. The young
In one another's arms, birds in the trees,
—Those dying generations—at their song,
The salmon-falls, the mackerel-crowded seas,

5 Fish, flesh, or fowl, commend all summer long
Whatever is begotten, born, and dies.
Caught in that sensual music all neglect
Monuments of unageing intellect.

2

An aged man is but a paltry thing,

10 A tattered coat upon a stick, unless
Soul clap its hands and sing, and louder sing
For every tatter in its mortal dress,
Nor is there singing school but studying
Monuments of its own magnificence;

15 And therefore I have sailed the seas and come
To the holy city of Byzantium.

---

1. Traditionally, the return of Christ to earth on Judgment Day. In Yeats's private mythology, the signal of the end of a 2,000-year cycle, at which point history reverses and a new age is born.
2. A storehouse of images and symbols common to all humankind; similar to Carl Jung's notion of the collective unconscious.
1. Constantinople, now called Istanbul, capital of the Byzantine Empire and the holy city of Eastern Christianity.

3

O sages standing in God's holy fire
As in the gold mosaic of a wall,
Come from the holy fire, perne° in a gyre,   *spin*
20   And be the singing-masters of my soul.
Consume my heart away; sick with desire
And fastened to a dying animal
It knows not what it is; and gather me
Into the artifice of eternity.

4

25   Once out of nature I shall never take
My bodily form from any natural thing,
But such a form as Grecian goldsmiths make
Of hammered gold and gold enamelling
To keep a drowsy Emperor awake;—
30   Or set upon a golden bough to sing
To lords and ladies of Byzantium
Of what is past, or passing, or to come.

Byzantium

The unpurged images of day recede;
The Emperor's drunken soldiery are abed;
Night resonance recedes, night-walkers' song
After great cathedral gong;
5   A starlit or a moonlit dome disdains
All that man is,
All mere complexities,
The fury and the mire of human veins.

Before me floats an image, man or shade,
10   Shade more than man, more image than a shade;
For Hades' bobbin° bound in mummy-cloth   *spool*
May unwind the winding path;
A mouth that has no moisture and no breath
Breathless mouths may summon;
15   I hail the superhuman;
I call it death-in-life and life-in-death.

Miracle, bird or golden handiwork,
More miracle than bird or handiwork,
Planted on the starlit golden bough,
20   Can like the cocks of Hades crow,
Or, by the moon embittered, scorn aloud
In glory of changeless metal
Common bird or petal
And all complexities of mire or blood.

25   At midnight on the Emperor's pavement flit
Flames that no faggot° feeds, nor steel has lit,   *bundle of sticks*
Nor storm disturbs, flames begotten of flame,
Where blood-begotten spirits come

And all complexities of fury leave,
30   Dying into a dance,
An agony of trance,
An agony of flame that cannot singe a sleeve.

Astraddle on the dolphin's mire and blood,
Spirit after spirit! The smithies break the flood,
35   The golden smithies of the Emperor!
Marbles of the dancing floor
Break bitter furies of complexity,
Those images that yet
Fresh images beget,
40   That dolphin-torn, that gong-tormented sea.

Under Ben Bulben[1]

1

Swear by what the Sages spoke
Round the Mareotic Lake[2]
That the Witch of Atlas[3] knew,
Spoke and set the cocks a-crow.

5   Swear by those horsemen, by those women
Complexion and form prove superhuman,
That pale, long-visaged company
That airs an immortality
Completeness of their passions won;
10   Now they ride the wintry dawn
Where Ben Bulben sets the scene.

Here's the gist of what they mean.

2

Many times man lives and dies
Between his two eternities,
15   That of race and that of soul,
And ancient Ireland knew it all.
Whether man dies in his bed
Or the rifle knocks him dead,
A brief parting from those dear
20   Is the worst man has to fear.
Though grave-diggers' toil is long,
Sharp their spades, their muscle strong,
They but thrust their buried men
Back in the human mind again.

3

25   You that Mitchel's prayer have heard,
"Send war in our time, O Lord!"[4]

1. A mountain in County Sligo.
2. An ancient region south of Alexandria, Egypt, known as a center of Neoplatonism.
3. *The Witch of Atlas* is the title of a poem by Percy Shelley.
4. John Mitchel, revolutionary patriot, wrote "Give us war in our time, O Lord!" while in prison.

Know that when all words are said
And a man is fighting mad,
Something drops from eyes long blind,
30   He completes his partial mind,
For an instant stands at ease,
Laughs aloud, his heart at peace.
Even the wisest man grows tense
With some sort of violence
35   Before he can accomplish fate,
Know his work or choose his mate.

4

Poet and sculptor do the work,
Nor let the modish painter shirk
What his great forefathers did,
40   Bring the soul of man to God,
Make him fill the cradles right.

Measurement began our might:
Forms a stark Egyptian[5] thought,
Forms that gentler Phidias wrought.
45   Michael Angelo left a proof
On the Sistine Chapel roof,
Where but half-awakened Adam
Can disturb globe-trotting Madam
Till her bowels are in heat,
50   Proof that there's a purpose set
Before the secret working mind:
Profane perfection of mankind.

Quattrocento[6] put in paint
On backgrounds for a God or Saint
55   Gardens where a soul's at ease;
Where everything that meets the eye,
Flowers and grass and cloudless sky
Resemble forms that are, or seem
When sleepers wake and yet still dream,
60   And when it's vanished still declare,
With only bed and bedstead there,
That Heavens had opened.
                                Gyres run on;
When that greater dream had gone
Calvert and Wilson, Blake and Claude,[7]
65   Prepared a rest for the people of God,
Palmer's phrase,[8] but after that
Confusion fell upon our thought.

---

5. Plotinus, 3rd-century C.E. Egyptian-born philosopher, founder of Neoplatonism.
6. Fifteenth-century artists of Italy's Renaissance.
7. Edward Calvert (1799–1883), English painter and engraver, disciple of Blake; Richard Wilson (1714–1782), British landscape painter; Claude Lorrain (1600–1682), French landscape painter.
8. Samuel Palmer (1805–1881), English painter of visionary landscapes and admirer of Blake.

5

Irish poets learn your trade,
Sing whatever is well made,
70   Scorn the sort now growing up
All out of shape from toe to top,
Their unremembering hearts and heads
Base-born products of base beds.
Sing the peasantry, and then
75   Hard-riding country gentlemen,
The holiness of monks, and after
Porter-drinkers' randy° laughter;   *lusty*
Sing the lords and ladies gay
That were beaten into the clay
80   Through seven heroic centuries;⁹
Cast your mind on other days
That we in coming days may be
Still the indomitable Irishry.

6

Under bare Ben Bulben's head
85   In Drumcliff¹ churchyard Yeats is laid.
An ancestor was rector there
Long years ago; a church stands near,
By the road an ancient cross.
No marble, no conventional phrase,
90   On limestone quarried near the spot
By his command these words are cut:

> *Cast a cold eye*
> *On life, on death.*
> *Horseman, pass by!*

—✦—

Rainer Maria Rilke
1875–1926

Rainer Maria Rilke's poetic talents evolved gradually. He was born in Prague in 1875, and his life was turned upside down by his parents' separation when he was just eight years old. He stayed with his mother and was then sent to a military school, an experience that he recalled with horror throughout his later life. After concluding his high school education, he studied literature, art history, and law for several semesters at the universities of Prague, Munich, and Berlin but never completed a degree. In Munich, he had a love affair of several years' duration with Lou Andreas-Salomé, a writer and psychoanalyst who introduced him to many outstanding writers, artists, and intellectuals of the period; they remained lifelong friends after the end of their affair.

9. I.e., the seven centuries since the conquest of Ireland by Henry II.

1. A village lying on the slopes of Ben Bulben, where Yeats was buried.

He began by writing rather conventional verse in his youth. Although some of his early work achieved commercial success, it was with the publication of *New Poems* between 1907 and 1908 that Rilke began to create genuinely modernist works. With poems like "The Panther," Rilke introduced the "Ding-Gedicht," or "object poem," which attempts to capture the invisible essence of an artifact or landscape through a description of its physical features. He went on to write a novel, *The Notebooks of Malte Laurids Brigge* (1910), which ranks among the best-known texts about the experience of the modern city. But Rilke's most important achievements continued to be in poetry. In the winter of 1911–1912, he wrote the first two of ten *Duino Elegies*, named after a castle near Trieste (Italy), where he resided when he composed them, thanks to the generosity of a friend. The Fourth Elegy, much darker in tone, was written during World War I in Munich. It took Rilke a full decade to complete the volume: Only in 1922, with great effort and struggle, was he able to compose the final elegies. Once the entire sequence was completed, however, Rilke immediately felt that they were the major achievement of his poetic career, and critics have generally agreed with him. The *Sonnets to Orpheus*, which he wrote immediately afterward, came to him, according to his own account, quickly and like an unexpected gift, quite different in kind from the decade-long efforts that led to the *Duino Elegies*.

Already in the *New Poems*, but especially in the *Duino Elegies* and the *Sonnets to Orpheus,* Rilke's poetic language can be difficult in its extreme abstractness, as in the following burst of imagery from the Second Elegy:

> pollen of blossoming godhead,
> hinges of light, corridors, stairways, thrones,
> spaces of being, shields of felicity, tumults
> of stormily-rapturous feeling, and suddenly, separate,
> mirrors.

It is difficult to say what these images might refer to. But this language does arise from Rilke's underlying concern with the transcendental dimensions of human existence: he sees spiritual essences as imbuing even the most material and concrete aspects of nature, culture, and the human body. The task of the individual (and the poet in particular) is to understand and give form to these essences. As a consequence, the boundaries between the visible and the invisible, life and death, and the material and the transcendental are constantly blurred in Rilke's thought and poetic expression: the ideal forms of existence he calls "angels," beings who do not even distinguish between life and death, as he indicates in the First Elegy. Humans are not able to reach this level of transcendence, but the *Duino Elegies* explore certain types of individuals who might come closer than ordinary humans to the angels' state of being: lovers, heroes, saints, and sometimes children. Yet even limited experiences of genuine transcendence are terrifying and ultimately prove that it isn't accessible to humans as such. The paradoxes and abstractions that result from Rilke's attempt to capture in poetry the longing for such transcendence are often of extraordinary verbal beauty, even when they aren't completely intelligible. His aspiration toward a "pure" poetry that would not be entangled in the corruption of the world, and that might in some sense take the place that religion once held, links his work to Symbolist poetry and to such poets as Stéphane Mallarmé and William Butler Yeats.

During most of his writing life, Rilke was perpetually in motion, spending only a few months or at most a few years in one place at a time and living and traveling at different times in Germany, Austria, France, Italy, Russia, Spain, and Switzerland, where he died in 1926. Not even marriage and the birth of a daughter tied him more permanently to one place. Quite often, affluent friends would make their residences available to him for a time to work on a writing project. But he remained extremely individualistic and viewed solitude as a basic condition of human life.

PRONUNCIATION:
Rilke: REAL-cuh

The Panther[1]

JARDIN DES PLANTES, PARIS

His gaze has been so worn by the procession
Of bars that it no longer makes a bond.
Around, a thousand bars seem to be flashing,
And in their flashing show no world beyond.

5   The lissom steps which round out and re-enter
That tightest circuit of their turning drill
Are like a dance of strength about a center
Wherein there stands benumbed a mighty will.

Only from time to time the pupil's shutter
10 Will draw apart: an image enters then,
To travel through the tautened body's utter
Stillness—and in the heart to end.

from Duino Elegies[1]

The First Elegy

Who, if I cried, would hear me among the angelic
orders? And even if one of them suddenly
pressed me against his heart, I should fade in the strength of his
stronger existence. For Beauty's nothing
5   but beginning of Terror we're still just able to bear,
and why we adore it so is because it serenely
disdains to destroy us. Each single angel is terrible.
And so I keep down my heart, and swallow the call-note
of depth-dark sobbing. Alas, who is there
10 we can make use of? Not angels, not men;
and already the knowing brutes are aware
that we don't feel very securely at home
within our interpreted world. There remains, perhaps,
some tree on a slope, to be looked at day after day,
15 there remains for us yesterday's walk and the cupboard-love loyalty
of a habit that liked us and stayed and never gave notice.
Oh, and there's Night, there's Night, when wind full of cosmic space
feeds on our faces: for whom would she not remain,
longed for, mild disenchantress, painfully there
20 for the lonely heart to achieve? Is she lighter for lovers?
Alas, with each other they only conceal their lot!
Don't you know yet?—Fling the emptiness out of your arms
into the spaces we breathe—maybe that the birds
will feel the extended air in more intimate flight.

25 Yes, the Springs had need of you. Many a star
was waiting for you to espy it. Many a wave

---

1. Translated by Walter Arndt.   1. Translated by J. B. Leishman and Stephen Spender.

would rise on the past towards you; or, else, perhaps,
as you went by an open window, a violin
would be giving itself to someone. All this was a trust.

30   But were you equal to it? Were you not always
distracted by expectation, as though all this
were announcing someone to love? (As if you could hope
to conceal her, with all those great strange thoughts
going in and out and often staying overnight!)

35   No, when longing comes over you, sing the great lovers: the fame
of all they can feel is far from immortal enough.
Those whom you almost envied, those forsaken, you found
so far beyond the requited in loving. Begin
ever anew their never attainable praise.

40   Consider: the Hero continues, even his fall
was a pretext for further existence, an ultimate birth.
But lovers are taken back by exhausted Nature
into herself, as though such creative force
could never be re-exerted. Have you so fully remembranced

45   Gaspara Stampa,[2] that any girl, whose beloved's
eluded her, may feel, from that far intenser
example of loving: "if I could become like her!"?
Ought not these oldest sufferings of ours to be yielding
more fruit by now? Is it not time that, in loving,

50   we freed ourselves from the loved one, and, quivering, endured:
as the arrow endures the string, to become, in the gathering out-leap,
something more than itself? For staying is nowhere.

Voices, voices. Hear, O my heart, as only
saints have heard: heard till the giant-call

55   lifted them off the ground; yet they went impossibly
on with their kneeling, in undistracted attention:
so inherently hearers. Not that you could endure
the voice of God—far from it. But hark to the suspiration,
the uninterrupted news that grows out of silence.

60   Rustling towards you now from those youthfully-dead.
Whenever you entered a church in Rome or in Naples
were you not always being quietly addressed by their fate?
Or else an inscription sublimely imposed itself on you,
as, lately, the tablet in Santa Maria Formosa.[3]

65   What they require of me? I must gently remove the appearance
of suffered injustice, that hinders
a little, at times, their purely-proceeding spirits.

True, it is strange to inhabit the earth no longer,
to use no longer customs scarcely acquired,

70   not to interpret roses, and other things
that promise so much, in terms of a human future;

---

2. A 16th-century Italian poet who composed two hundred sonnets about the man whom she loved and who left her. She died at age thirty-one.

3. A famous church in Venice, Italy.

to be no longer all that one used to be
in endlessly anxious hands, and to lay aside
even one's proper name like a broken toy.
75   Strange, not to go on wishing one's wishes. Strange,
to see all that was once relation so loosely fluttering
hither and thither in space. And it's hard, being dead,
and full of retrieving before one begins to espy
a trace of eternity.—Yes, but all of the living
80   make the mistake of drawing too sharp distinctions.
Angels, (they say) are often unable to tell
whether they move among living or dead. The eternal
torrent whirls all the ages through either realm
for ever, and sounds above their voices in both.

85   They've finally no more need of us, the early-departed,
one's gently weaned from terrestrial things as one mildly
outgrows the breasts of a mother. But we, that have need of
such mighty secrets, we, for whom sorrow's so often
source of blessedest progress, could we exist without them?
90   Is the story in vain, how once, in the mourning for Linos,[4]
venturing earliest music pierced barren numbness, and how,
in the horrified space an almost deified youth
suddenly quitted for ever, emptiness first
felt the vibration that now charms us and comforts and helps?

The Second Elegy

Every Angel is terrible. Still, though, alas!
I invoke you, almost deadly birds of the soul,
knowing what you are. Oh, where are the days of Tobias,[1]
when one of the shining-most stood on the simple threshold,
5   a little disguised for the journey, no longer appalling,
(a youth to the youth as he curiously peered outside).
Let the archangel perilous now, from behind the stars,
step but a step down hitherwards: high up-beating,
our heart would out-beat us. Who are you?

10   Early successes, Creation's pampered darlings,
ranges, summits, dawn-red ridges
of all beginning,—pollen of blossoming godhead,
hinges of light, corridors, stairways, thrones,
spaces of being, shields of felicity, tumults
15   of stormily-rapturous feeling, and suddenly, separate,
mirrors, drawing up their own
outstreamed beauty into their faces again.

---

4. In Greek mythology, a figure who personifies lamentation.
1. Allusion to the story of Tobias in the Book of Tobit, one of the books that wasn't included in the Bible. As his death approaches, Tobit sends his son Tobias to recover money he has left with another man; Tobias encounters the angel Raphael, who guides him to the right place.

For we, when we feel, evaporate; oh, we
breathe ourselves out and away; from ember to ember
yielding a fainter scent. True, someone may tell us:
"You've got in my blood, the room, the Spring's
growing full of you" . . . What's the use? He cannot retain us.
We vanish within and around him. And those that have beauty,
oh, who shall hold them back? Incessant appearance
comes and goes in their faces. Like dew from the morning grass
exhales from us that which is ours, like heat
from a smoking dish. O smile, whither? O upturned glance:
new, warm, vanishing wave of the heart—alas,
but we *are* all that. Does the cosmic space
we dissolve into taste of us, then? Do the angels really
only catch up what is theirs, what has streamed from them, or at times,
as though through an oversight, is a little of our
existence in it as well? Is there just so much of us
mixed with their features as that vague look in the faces
of pregnant women? Unmarked by them in their whirling
return to themselves. (How should they remark it?)

Lovers, if Angels could understand them, might utter
strange things in the midnight air. For it seems that everything's
trying to hide us. Look, the trees exist; the houses
we live in still stand where they were. We only
pass everything by like a transposition of air.
And all combines to suppress us, partly as shame,
perhaps, and partly as inexpressible hope.

Lovers, to you, each satisfied in the other,
I turn with my question about us. You grasp yourselves. Have you proofs?
Look, with me it may happen at times that my hands
grow aware of each other, or else that my hard-worn face
seeks refuge within them. That gives me a little
sensation. But who, just for that, could presume to exist?
You, though, that go on growing
in the other's rapture till, overwhelmed, he implores
"No more"; you that under each other's hands
grow more abundant like vintage grapes;
sinking at times, but only because the other
has so completely emerged; I ask you about us. I know
why you so blissfully touch: because the caress persists,
because it does not vanish, the place that you
so tenderly cover; because you perceive thereunder
pure duration. Until your embraces almost
promise eternity. Yet, when you've once withstood
the startled first encounter, the window-longing,
and that first walk, just once, through the garden together:
Lovers, are you the same? When you lift yourselves
up to each other's lips—drink unto drink:
oh, how strangely the drinker eludes his part!

20
25
30
35
40
45
50
55
60
65

On Attic stelês,[2] did not the circumspection
of human gesture amaze you? Were not love and farewell
so lightly laid upon shoulders, they seemed to be made
of other stuff than with us? Remember the hands,
70   how they rest without pressure, though power is there in the torsos.
The wisdom of those self-masters was this: we have got so far;
ours is to touch one another like this; the gods
may press more strongly upon us. But that is the gods' affair.
If only we could discover some pure, contained,
75   narrow, human, own little strip of orchard
in between river and rock! For our heart transcends us
just as it did those others. And we can no longer
gaze after it into figures that soothe it, or godlike
bodies, wherein it achieves a grander restraint.

The Fourth Elegy

O trees of life, when will your winter come?
We're never single-minded, unperplexed,
like migratory birds. Outstript and late,
we suddenly thrust into the wind, and fall
5   into unfeeling ponds. We comprehend
flowering and fading simultaneously.
And somewhere lions still roam, all unaware,
in being magnificent, of any weakness.

We, though, while we're intent upon one thing,
10   can feel the cost and conquest of another.
Hostility's our first response. Aren't lovers
for ever reaching verges in each other,—
lovers, that looked for spaces, hunting, home?
Then, for the sudden sketchwork of a moment,
15   a ground of contrast's painfully prepared,
to make us see it. For they're very clear
with us, we that don't know our feeling's shape,
but only that which forms it from outside.
Who's not sat tense before his own heart's curtain?
20   Up it would go: the scenery was parting.
Easy to understand. The well-known garden,
swaying a little. Then appeared the dancer.
Not *the!* Enough! However light he foots it,
he's just disguised, and turns into a bourgeois,
25   and passes through the kitchen to his dwelling.
I will not have those half-filled masks! No, no,
rather the doll. That's full. I'll force myself

2. Greek columns or upright slabs of stone that are inscribed or decorated with images, often commemorating the dead.

to bear the husk, the wire, and even the face
that's all outside. Here! I'm already waiting.
30   Even if the lights go out, even if I'm told
"There's nothing more,"—even if greyish draughts
of emptiness come drifting from the stage,—
even if of all my silent forebears none
sits by me any longer, not a woman,
35   not even the boy with the brown squinting eyes:
I'll still remain. For one can always watch.

Am I not right? You, to whom life would taste
so bitter, Father, when you tasted mine,
that turbid first infusion of my Must,
40   you kept on tasting as I kept on growing,
and, fascinated by the after-taste
of such queer future, tried my clouded gaze,—
you, who so often since you died, my Father,
have been afraid within my inmost hope,
45   surrendering realms of that serenity
the dead are lords of for my bit of fate,—
am I not right? And you, am I not right,—
you that would love me for that small beginning
of love for you I always turned away from,
50   because the space within your faces changed,
even while I loved it, into cosmic space
where you no longer were . . . , when I feel like it,
to wait before the puppet stage,—no, rather
gaze so intensely on it that at last,
55   to upweigh my gaze, an angel has to come
and play a part there, snatching up the husks?
Angel and doll! Then there's at last a play.
Then there unites what we continually
part by our being there. Then at last
60   can spring from our own turning years the cycle
of the whole going-on. Over and above us
there's then the angel playing. Look, the dying,—
surely they must suspect how full of pretext
is all that we accomplish here, where nothing
65   is what it really is. O hours of childhood,
hours when behind the figures there was more
than the mere past, and when what lay before us
was not the future! We were growing, and sometimes
impatient to grow up, half for the sake
70   of those who'd nothing left but their grown-upness.
Yet, when alone, we entertained ourselves
with everlastingness: there we would stand,
within the gap left between world and toy,
upon a spot which, from the first beginning,
75   had been established for a pure event.

Who'll show a child just as it is? Who'll place it
within its constellation, with the measure
of distance in its hand? Who'll make its death
from grey bread, that grows hard,—or leave it there,
80   within the round mouth, like the choking core
of a sweet apple? . . . . . . Minds of murderers
are easily divined. But this, though: death,
the whole of death,—even before life's begun,
to hold it all so gently, and be good:
85   this is beyond description!

Sonnets to Orpheus[1]
1.1

A tree ascending there. O pure transcension!
O Orpheus[2] sings! O tall tree in the ear!
All noise suspended, yet in that suspension
what new beginning, beckoning, change, appear!

5   Creatures of silence pressing through the clear
disintricated wood from lair and nest;
and neither cunning, it grew manifest,
had made them breathe so quietly, nor fear,

but only hearing. Roar, cry, bell they found
10   within their hearts too small. And where before
less than a hut had harboured what came thronging,

a refuge tunnelled out of dimmest longing
with lowly entrance through a quivering door,
you built them temples in their sense of sound.

1.2

And almost maiden-like was what drew near
from that twin-happiness of song and lyre,
and shone so clearly through her spring attire,
and made herself a bed within my ear.

5   And slept in me sleep that was everything:
the trees I'd always loved, the unrevealed,
treadable distances, the trodden field,
and all my strangest self-discovering.

She slept the world. O singing god, and stayed,
10   while you were shaping her, with no desire
to wake, and only rose to fall asleep?

---

1. Translated by J.B. Leishman.
2. In Greek mythology, Orpheus was a poet, singer, and lyre player who could move even the natural world with his art. He followed his deceased wife, Eurydice, into the underworld to release her from death and won the ap-proval of the gods but lost her when he turned around and looked at her before the appointed moment during the journey back. He was killed by a band of female follow-ers of the god Bacchus.

Where is her death? Oh, shall you find this deep
unsounded theme before your song expire?
Sinking to where from me? . . . Almost a maid . . .

1.3

A god can do it. But can a man expect
to penetrate the narrow lyre and follow?
His sense is discord. Temples for Apollo³
are not found where two heart-ways intersect.

5   For song, as taught by you, is not desire,
not wooing of something finally attained;
song is existence. For the god unstrained.
But when shall we *exist?* And he require

the earth and heavens to exist for us?
10   It's more than being in love, boy, though your ringing
voice may have flung your dumb mouth open thus:

learn to forget those fleeting ecstasies.
Far other is the breath of real singing.
An aimless breath. A stirring in the god. A breeze.

1.5

Raise no commemorating stone. The roses
shall blossom every summer for his sake.
For this is Orpheus. His metamorphosis
in this one and in that. We should not take

5   thought about other names. Once and for all,
it's Orpheus when there's song. He comes and goes.
Is it not much if sometimes, by some small
number of days, he shall outlive the rose?

Could you but feel his passing's needfulness!
10   Though he himself may dread the hour drawing nigher.
Already, when his words pass earthliness,

he passes with them far beyond your gaze.
His hands unhindered by the trellised lyre,
in all his over-steppings he obeys.

3. In Greek mythology, the god of sun, light, and poetry, but also a god habitually distant from humans, communicating with them from far away.

PERSPECTIVES

Poetry About Poetry

Many literary cultures feature poems and prose pieces in which poets inquire into the sources and meanings of their craft. As the selections on definitions of literature and the poet in ancient India, medieval China, and early modern Europe show in the first three volumes of this anthology, writers across ages and cultures have wrestled with questions about what their own authority and vocation might be, what sources of imagination they should draw on, and how they should relate to their finished work and their readers. Sometimes such concerns are voiced in essays and manifestos that stand apart from the literary text proper, but often they also emerge as integral parts of the work itself. The poems in this section are both poetry and poetics, both works of art and reflections on what that art really is, and as such they shed light on how twentieth-century poets approach the central problems of their craft.

One of these basic questions is what source of imagination the poet relies on, in an age in which appeals to the intervention of the Muse or divine inspiration have lost credibility as legitimations of poetic works. Portuguese poet Fernando Pessoa directly takes on this issue in "The ancients used to invoke," humorously showing how the modern poet has only his or her own self to fall back on. But modern poets are also unsure whether a poem can be simply the authentic expression of the poet's own deeply felt sentiments, since even what the poet genuinely experiences becomes an artifice once it is translated into lyrical language. Chilean poet Pablo Neruda evokes a very different image in his "Ars Poetica," which draws upon an older concept of the poet as seer or prophet. Yet this poet seems to be a victim rather than a master of his vocation as words and images visit him. Torn between the idea that poetry might be a privileged vehicle of transcendent truths in an increasingly secular world, and the alternative view that the pleasures of poetry derive mainly from the artifices and elegance of its linguistic surfaces, Pessoa, Neruda, and others strive to understand the modern poet's role, sometimes seriously and sometimes playfully.

The question of what can be considered authentic in lyrical poetry connects directly to the ways in which the poet can or should create new poetic language. Drawing on achievements of the past, Neruda plays with the conventional idiom of love poetry and its invocations of nature in "Tonight I can write," and American poet Ezra Pound turns to the poetry of predecessor Walt Whitman as a source of innovation. Pessoa and Turkish poet Nazim Hikmet, by contrast, take a more aggressive stance toward the literary past by inveighing against what they view as hackneyed lyrical languages: stereotypical equations between a poet's mood and natural landscapes, and stale metaphors involving roses and nightingales. Instead, Hikmet celebrates the modern age with its skyscrapers and railroads, its speed and technological inventiveness as the poet's new "muse" and source of original language. This rhetoric of energetic rupture with the outmoded forms of past art often appears in self-definitions of twentieth-century avant-garde groups in literature and the arts, as is evident from the sample of manifestos that opens this volume. But the new faith in steel and speed as engines of creation carries a particular charge in a genre such as poetry, which has traditionally often been associated with nature, quiet reflection, and intimate feelings.

Not all the poets selected here present themselves as masters of language who can choose their themes and styles at will. Some of them portray themselves not as finding words but being found by them, and describe lyrical language as a kind of independent being with its own desires and intentions that it imposes upon the poet. Neruda offers a glimpse of the poet as being urged on by words, but Italian poet Eugenio Montale even more forcefully portrays his verses as dynamic and sometimes even irritating forces with a mind of their own. Implicitly at least, such descriptions harken back to the notion of the poet inspired by the Muse, in that they cast the writer as a recipient rather than a creator of language; but what is distinctly modern is that the words don't seem to originate in some privileged source of truth but simply lead a life all their own.

Native Canadian poet Daniel David Moses explores the issue of poetic control in a different dimension: that of the poet's and the poem's relation to the reader. He reflects on this relationship even as he establishes it when we read his lines. This is only one version of the often amusing, sometimes puzzling, and occasionally disturbing questions that arise when we read poems about poetry, or any literary texts that explore their own conditions of existence: Can a poet show that he is inspired by claiming he is not? How can one find a justification for poetic language even as one writes it? Should a poem about how to be lyrically innovative demonstrate such innovation in its own language? Doesn't a well-crafted poem about how lyrical verses lead a life of their own prove the opposite of what it claims? Can an author get a reader interested in a piece about how to get readers interested? If these questions and paradoxes sometimes make one laugh and sometimes leave one's head spinning, that is just the point of such self-referentiality.

Ezra Pound
1885–1972

T. S. Eliot, whom Ezra Pound had helped substantially in shaping his major poem *The Waste Land*, once wrote that "Mr. Pound is more responsible for the XXth Century revolution in poetry than is any other individual." Few would deny Pound's fundamental role in the shaping of modern poetry. During the twelve years he lived in London (1908–1920), Pound published multiple volumes of his own poetry and started to work on what was to become his masterpiece, the *Cantos*. This epic sequence of poems took him five decades to complete (1915–1969); integrating ancient Greek, Chinese, medieval French, as well as British and American poetic traditions, the *Cantos* have become one of the cornerstone achievements of modern poetry. In the mid-1910s, Pound also helped to found the avant-garde movements of Imagism and Vorticism, which sought to translate modernist forms of perception into innovative forms of poetry and visual art. He also worked tirelessly as an editor and critic to support, publish, and comment on poetry that he considered valuable. Many of those whose efforts he promoted went on to become noted modernist writers of their own. T. S. Eliot, James Joyce, William Carlos Williams, H. D., and Marianne Moore are only a few of the writers whose talents he recognized and supported.

In 1920, Pound moved to Paris and four years later settled in Rapallo, Italy, where he became more and more interested in Mussolini's fascist politics. His engagement with fascism culminated in a series of anti-American and anti-Semitic radio speeches that were broadcast between 1941 and 1943. These broadcasts led to his being indicted for treason in 1943 and arrested by the U.S. Army in 1945; during several weeks of imprisonment at the U.S. Army Disciplinary Training Center, he wrote *The Pisan Cantos,* which won the Bollingen Prize for Poetry in 1949 amidst public uproar. Late in 1945, Pound had been taken back to the United States and reindicted, but he was found mentally insane and interned at Saint Elizabeth's Hospital for the Criminally Insane in Washington, D.C., where he was confined for twelve and a half years. When he was released in 1958, at age seventy-two, he took up residence in Italy again and remained there, except for occasional travel, for the rest of his life.

Pound's poetry is a continuous engagement with poetic tradition. In the poem "A Pact," which first appeared in the magazine *Poetry* in 1913, Pound explicitly acknowledges the importance of his great American predecessor, the nineteenth-century poet Walt Whitman. But while he admired Whitman's poetry for its "impulse" and energy, he also criticized it severely for its lack of "technique" and what appeared to him as a random, sporadic use of various poetic patterns of the day. His view of Whitman, as a consequence, remained conflicted. "From an examination of Walt made twelve years ago the present writer carried away the impression that there are thirty well-written pages of Whitman; he is now unable to find them," he remarked acerbically in his *ABC of Reading*. Yet traces of Whitman's influence can be found

throughout Pound's poetry all the way to some of the later *Cantos;* it is this persistent if sometimes reluctantly accepted influence that Pound acknowledges in "A Pact."

A Pact

I make a pact with you, Walt Whitman[1]—
I have detested you long enough.
I come to you as a grown child
Who has had a pig-headed father;
5   I am old enough now to make friends.
It was you that broke the new wood,
Now is a time for carving.
We have one sap and one root—
Let there be commerce between us.

Eugenio Montale
1896–1981

Eugenio Montale was born in Genoa, Italy. After receiving a degree in accounting in 1915, he
studied voice with the famous baritone Ernesto Sivori. Sivori's death and then World War I
(1915–1918), in which Montale served as an infantry officer, interrupted his singing career, and
he turned to literature. His first poetic works appeared after the war, in 1925, and dealt with his
native region. He moved to Florence in 1928 to serve as director of a cultural center and library,
a position from which he was dismissed ten years later because of his unwillingness to join the
Fascist regime that governed Italy at the time. His second book of poems, *The Occasions*
(1939), dealt with the philosophical questions of the time and confirmed Montale as the poetic
and philosophical voice of his generation, particularly those who were opposed to the Fascist
ideology that dominated a number of European countries at the time. By the mid-twentieth century, Montale's reputation as poet and essayist was unquestionable. Starting in 1961, he was
honored with doctorates from a number of universities around Europe, and in 1967 the president of Italy named him "senator for life" in recognition of his literary and cultural contributions. This made it possible for him to leave the position he had occupied since 1948 as music
critic and general editor of *Il Corriere della Sera,* one of Italy's most important dailies, and focus on his poetry. He also published a number of books of essays that deal with the metaphysical and existential questions that often mark his poetry, reflecting on the predicament of his
generation, which experienced two world wars and all their attendant cruelty. Montale is also
recognized for his translations into Italian of William Shakespeare, Gerard Manley Hopkins,
William Butler Yeats, and T. S. Eliot. He was awarded the Nobel Prize in literature in 1975.

Rhymes[1]

Rhymes are pests, worse
than the nuns of St. Vincent, knocking at your door
nonstop. You can't just turn them away

---

1. Walt Whitman (1819–1992) was the most important
American poet of the nineteenth century. His work
Leaves of Grass in particular was enormously influential

among subsequent generations of poets.
1. Translated by William Arrowsmith.

5 and they're tolerable so long as they're outside.
    The polite poet stays aloof, disguising
    or outwitting them (the rhymes), or trying to sneak
    them by. But they're fanatical, blazing
    with zeal and sooner or later they're back (rhymes
    and biddies), pounding at your door and poems,
10 same as always.

Poetry

I

The agonizing question
whether inspiration is hot or cold
is not a matter of thermodynamics.
Raptus[1] doesn't produce, the void doesn't conduce,
5 there's no poetry á la sorbet or barbecued.
It's more a matter of very
importunate words
rushing
from oven or deep freeze.
10 The source doesn't matter. No sooner are they out
than they look around and seem to be saying:
What am I doing here?

II

Poetry
rejects with horror
15 the glosses of commentators.
But it's unclear that the excessively mute
is sufficient unto itself
or to the property man who's stumbled onto it,
unaware that he's
20 the author.

Fernando Pessoa
1888–1935

Orphaned by the death of his father when he was very young, Fernando Pessoa would spend his life in a lively conversation with the seventy-two alter egos, or alternative personas, whom he created as "heteronyms" and to whom he attributed many of his writings—poetic and critical. His first three books (he only published four during his lifetime) were in English, in which he was fluent. Though born in Lisbon, he spent his teenage years in Durban, South Africa, where his widowed mother moved after marrying the Portuguese consul to South Africa. He published his first book in Portuguese in 1933, *Message,* a message that went unnoticed. Nonetheless, Pessoa is considered one of the most innovative poets of European modernism, a reputation based on a voluminous trunk of writings he left behind, an archive of some 25,426 documents, now in the National

---

1. "Being caught" (Latin), the root of both "rapture" and "rape."

Library of Portugal. His writings began to appear in the 1940s, among them his most extensive work, *The Book of Disquietude,* attributed to one of his heteronyms, a certain "Bernardo
Soares, Assistant Bookkeeper in the City of Lisbon." This is Pessoa's most autobiographical
work, characterized by its author as a "factless autobiography." In his adult life, Pessoa
worked as a commercial translator and business correspondent for international companies
based in Lisbon. He was also a regular contributor of poetry and critical reviews to avant-
garde journals of Portuguese modernism, principally *Orpheu* and his own short-lived literary
magazine, *Athena.* He was a confirmed bachelor whose sociability was limited to literary discussions in the Café Brasileiro de Chiado, Lisbon, in front of which his statue still greets poets
and presides over literary conversations.

Autopsychography[1]

The poet is a faker. He
Fakes it so completely,
He even fakes he's suffering
The pain he's really feeling.

5   And those of us who read his writing
Fully feel while reading
Not that pain of his that's double,
But one completely fictional.

So on its tracks goes round and round,
10   To entertain the reason,
That wound-up little train
We call the heart of man.

This

They say I fake or lie
In everything I write.
No, it's simply that
With me imagination
5   Feels—I don't use
The heart.

All I dream or go through,
All I fail or lose out
On, is like a terrace
10   Facing something else
Again. And that's the lovely
Thing.

It's why I write
Steeped in things not readily
15   At hand—free of emotions,
Serious about what isn't.
Feelings? That's the reader's
Lot.

---

1. Translated by Edwin Honig, as are the next two poems. An "autopsychography" is a written self-analysis.

Today I read nearly two pages

Today I read nearly two pages
In a book by a mystic poet
And I laughed like someone who'd been sobbing.

Mystic poets are sick philosophers,
5 And philosophers are mad men.

Because mystic poets say that flowers feel
And say that stones have souls
And rivers have ecstasies in moonlight.

But flowers wouldn't be flowers if they felt anything—
10 They'd be people;
And if stones had souls they'd be living things, not stones;
And if rivers had ecstasies in moonlight,
They'd be sick people.

Only if you don't know what flowers, stones, and rivers are
15 Can you talk about their feelings.
To talk about the souls of flowers, stones, and rivers
Is to talk about yourself, about your delusions.
Thank God stones are just stones,
20 And rivers, just rivers,
And flowers, just flowers.

As for myself, I write out the prose of my poems,
And I am satisfied,
Because I know that all I know is Nature from the outside;
I don't understand it from the inside,
25 Because Nature hasn't any inside;
Otherwise, it wouldn't be Nature.

The ancients used to invoke[1]

The ancients used to invoke the Muses.
We invoke ourselves.
I don't know if the Muses appeared—
Invoked and invocation must have had some conformity—
5 But I know we don't appear.
How often I have leaned
Over the well I suppose I am
And bleated "Ah!" to hear an echo,
And have not heard more than what I saw—
10 The vague dim dawn-grey of the water answering the light
Down there in the uselessness at the bottom . . .
No echo for me . . .
Only, vaguely, a face,
Which must be mine since it can't be someone else's.

1. Translated by Jonathan Griffin.

15 It is a thing almost invisible,
  Except as and when luminously I see
  There at the bottom . . .
  In the silence and the false light at the bottom . . .

  What a Muse! . . .

Pablo Neruda
1904–1973

Born Neftalí Ricardo Reyes, Pablo Neruda assumed a pen name at age sixteen to avoid embarrassing his father, who was set against his son's literary inclinations. His mother had died when he was an infant. He legalized the name "Pablo Neruda" in 1946, after publishing half a dozen books of poetry under his assumed name. Neruda's poetic trajectory developed from the intimate lyricism of an introspective young poet to the bardic voice of a socially committed writer that resonates throughout the American continent. Neruda came into the public arena early in his career, having been named Chile's consul to Burma (now Myanmar) at the age of twenty-three. He would hold a number of diplomatic posts in East Asian and European capitals in the course of his life. It was the Spanish Civil War (1936–1939) that politicized Neruda and his poetry most intensely. The poetry he wrote between 1925 and 1931 for the first edition of his visionary book *Residence on Earth* already expressed a strong commitment in the face of rising fascism. He supported the Republican cause in Spain's Civil War and embraced communism. In 1945 he was elected to the Chilean senate as a member of the Communist Party, a position he was obliged to relinquish when right-wing extremists took over the government. Shortly after another right-wing takeover, he died of cancer on 23 September 1973, within days of the military coup that toppled the leftist government of Salvador Allende.

 Neruda's poetic voice ranges from love poetry to "elemental odes" devoted to material things of daily life. He considered Walt Whitman his most significant poetic predecessor, and, like Whitman, he sang all things American, grand and ordinary. His *Canto General* (1950) was a paean to American history, its glories and its shame, its ideals of freedom, and its political squalor. Neruda was awarded the Nobel Prize in literature in 1971 and is considered by many to be the greatest Latin American poet of the twentieth century.

Tonight I can write the saddest lines[1]

 Tonight I can write the saddest lines,

 Write, for example, "The night is shattered
 and the blue stars shiver in the distance."

 The night wind revolves in the sky and sings.

5 Tonight I can write the saddest lines.
 I loved her, and sometimes she loved me too.

 Through nights like this one I held her in my arms.
 I kissed her again and again under the endless sky.

 She loved me, sometimes I loved her too.
10 How could one not have loved her great still eyes.

---

1. Translated by W. S. Merwin.

Tonight I can write the saddest lines.
To think that I do not have her. To feel that I have lost her.

To hear the immense night, still more immense without her.
And the verse falls to the soul like dew to the pasture.

15 What does it matter that my love could not keep her.
The night is shattered and she is not with me.

This is all. In the distance someone is singing. In the distance.
My soul is not satisfied that it has lost her.

My sight searches for her as though to go to her.
20 My heart looks for her, and she is not with me.

The same night whitening the same trees.
We, of that time, are no longer the same.

I no longer love her, that's certain, but how I loved her.
My voice tried to find the wind to touch her hearing.

25 Another's. She will be another's. Like my kisses before.
Her voice. Her bright body. Her infinite eyes.

I no longer love her, that's certain, but maybe I love her.
Love is so short, forgetting is so long.

Because through nights like this one I held her in my arms
30 my soul is not satisfied that it has lost her.

Though this be the last pain that she makes me suffer
and these the last verses that I write for her.

Ars Poetica[1]

Between shadow and space, young girls and garrisons,
saddled with a strange heart, with funereal dreams,
taken suddenly pale, my forehead withered
by the rage of a widower's grief for each day of lost life—
5 oh for each invisible drop I drink in a stupor
and for each sound I harbour, trembling,
I nurse the same far thirst, the same cold fever,
a noise in labour, a devious anguish—
as if thieves or emanations were coming—
10 in the enveloping shell, rooted, profound,
like a humiliated scullion, a bell cracked a little,
a mirror tarnished, the fug of a deserted house
whose guests come in at night sloshed to perdition,
with a stench of clothes scattered on the floor
15 and a yearning for flowers—
another way to put it perhaps, a touch less sadly:
but the hard truth is if you want it so,
this wind that whacks at my breast,

---

1. Translated by Nathaniel Tarm. "Ars poetica" means "the art of poetry" (Latin).

the unbounded expanse of night collapsing in my bedroom,
20   the morning's rumours afire with sacrifice
now beg of me this prophecy I have, with mournfulness
and a lurch of objects calling without answers,
with a truceless movement, a name I can't make out.

⊷ ⇌◆⇌ ⊷

Wallace Stevens
1879–1955

Born and raised in Reading, Pennsylvania, Wallace Stevens attended Harvard for three years, but
his family couldn't pay for a fourth year. At Harvard, he studied English, German, and French literature. When he left the university in 1897, he went to New York City to pursue a career in literature and journalism. He worked as a reporter for the New York *Tribune* for a year, after which he
succumbed to family pressure and to the shock of his experiences as a reporter and entered the
New York Law School. In 1904 he was admitted to the New York State Bar and practiced law in
New York until 1916, when he moved to Hartford, Connecticut, to work for the Hartford Accident and Indemnity Company. He worked for the same insurance firm, rising to vice president,
until his death in 1955, continuing to write poetry all the while, publishing in literary journals and
magazines. He published his first book of poetry, *Harmonium,* in 1923 with Knopf, a publishing
house that brought out all of his books, including his *Collected Poems* in 1954, a volume that was
awarded the Pulitzer Prize the following year, shortly before Stevens's death from cancer. A volume of lectures and essays on poetry, *The Necessary Angel,* appeared in 1951. His uncollected
writings appeared in 1957 as *Opus Posthumous,* and his daughter, Holly Stevens, selected and
published his *Letters* in 1966.

The scholars of Stevens's work see America and Americanness as the constant preoccupations in his poetry. His earliest and most enduring influence in this regard dates from his
days at Harvard, where he studied with the Spanish-American poet and philosopher George
Santayana. It was through this long-lasting relationship that Stevens never ceased examining
the connections between the European literary tradition and America's literary culture. In
Latin poets such as Virgil, Stevens found many of his themes and developed his fascination
with words and etymologies. From the Italian Dante he took the form of the three-verse stro-
phe, the tercet, which one finds throughout Stevens's poetry. French Modernist poets such as
Baudelaire, Mallarmé, Valéry, and Laforgue resonate in Stevens, as do Shakespeare, the
British Romantics, and modern Irish poets such as Yeats. Stevens's poetic career enacts an
extended dialogue between America and Europe, often adapting the European tradition to an
American culture that Stevens and some of his contemporaries anxiously considered a literary canon still in the making. The thematic breadth of Stevens's poetry is as wide as his technical experimentation and philosophical exploration. He ranges from the religious to the humorous and from the ironic to the idealistic. The objects of his poems extend from the
common and everyday to the sublime. For most of his contemporaries, he was not, and, for
many, still is not, an easy poet; but he certainly will continue to be an enduring one.

Anecdote of the Jar

I placed a jar in Tennessee,
And round it was, upon a hill.
It made the slovenly wilderness
Surround that hill.

5   The wilderness rose up to it,
    And sprawled around, no longer wild.
    The jar was round upon the ground
    And tall and of a port in air.

    It took dominion everywhere.
10 The jar was gray and bare.
    It did not give of bird or bush,
    Like nothing else in Tennessee.

Of Modern Poetry

    The poem of the mind in the act of finding
    What will suffice. It has not always had
    To find: the scene was set; it repeated what
    Was in the script.
                        Then the theatre was changed
5   To something else. Its past was a souvenir.
    It has to be living, to learn the speech of the place.
    It has to face the men of the time and to meet
    The women of the time. It has to think about war
    And it has to find what will suffice. It has
10 To construct a new stage. It has to be on that stage
    And, like an insatiable actor, slowly and
    With meditation, speak words that in the ear,
    In the delicatest ear of the mind, repeat,
    Exactly, that which it wants to hear, at the sound
15 Of which, an invisible audience listens,
    Not to the play, but to itself, expressed
    In an emotion as of two people, as of two
    Emotions becoming one. The actor is
    A metaphysician in the dark, twanging
20 An instrument, twanging a wiry string that gives
    Sounds passing through sudden rightnesses, wholly
    Containing the mind, below which it cannot descend,
    Beyond which it has no will to rise.
                                        It must
    Be the finding of a satisfaction, and may
25 Be of a man skating, a woman dancing, a woman
    Combing. The poem of the act of the mind.

Of Mere Being

    The palm at the end of the mind,
    Beyond the last thought, rises
    In the bronze decor,

    A gold-feathered bird
5   Sings in the palm, without human meaning,
    Without human feeling, a foreign song.

You know then that it is not the reason
That makes us happy or unhappy.
The bird sings. Its feathers shine.

10   The palm stands on the edge of space.
The wind moves slowly in the branches.
The bird's fire-fangled feathers dangle down.

+— ⚎◆⚎ —+

Nazim Hikmet
1902–1963

The greatest poet of modern Turkey, Nazim Hikmet spent eighteen years as a political prisoner in his home country and lived the last thirteen years of his life in exile. He was born in Salonica (Thessaloniki, Greece) when it was still part of the Ottoman Empire. He was educated in Istanbul and worked as a teacher in eastern Turkey. In 1922, attracted by the Russian Revolution and its promise for social justice, he made his way to Moscow and studied sociology and economics at the University of Moscow. He returned home in 1924 following Turkey's war of independence, only to be arrested for his leftist writings and publications. He managed to escape and returned to Moscow in 1926, where he met Vladimir Mayakovski and worked in the theater until a general amnesty allowed him to return to Turkey in 1928. As a member of the outlawed Turkish Communist Party, he was arrested repeatedly on a number of trumped-up charges and spent five of the next ten years in prison.

Between 1929 and 1936 he published nine books that revolutionized Turkish poetry. An experimental poet in form and subject matter, he wrote in free verse about ordinary people's daily struggles, inflecting poetry with his lifelong social commitment. He also published several plays and novels while working at a number of jobs as bookbinder, editor, journalist, translator, and screenwriter. In 1938 he was sentenced to a twenty-eight-year prison term for sedition, ostensibly for inciting the Turkish naval forces to revolt. In fact, the government was angry because the naval cadets were reading his long 1936 poem *The Epic of Sheik Bedreddin,* based on a peasant rebellion in the fifteenth century against Ottoman rule. This was the last of his books to appear in Turkey during his lifetime. In 1949 an international committee that included Pablo Picasso, Paul Robeson, and Jean-Paul Sartre campaigned for his release, which came about in 1950 in a general amnesty. Attempts on his life followed, and in 1951 he managed to escape and made his way to Moscow. In 1959, stripped of his Turkish citizenship, he became a Polish citizen. He died of a heart attack in Moscow in 1963.

Hikmet's "Regarding Art" is a proclamation of poetry as the domain of the ordinary, the man-made, the daily, and the concrete and a rejection of poetry as the lyrical flight of the sentimental and the pursuit of the otherworldly.

PRONUNCIATION:
   Nazim Hikmet: nah-ZEEM HEEK-met

Regarding Art[1]

Sometimes I, too, tell the ah's
of my heart one by one

1. Translated by Randy Blasing and Mutlu Konuk.

like the blood-red beads
of a ruby rosary strung
5   on strands of golden hair!

But my
poetry's muse
takes to the air
on wings made of steel
10   like the I-beams
      of my suspension bridges!

I don't pretend
    the nightingale's lament
to the rose isn't easy on the ears . . .
15   But the language
      that really speaks to me
are Beethoven[2] sonatas played
on copper, iron, wood, bone, and catgut . . .

You can *have*
20   galloping off
in a cloud of dust!
Me, I wouldn't trade
for the purest-bred
    Arabian steed
25   the sixty mph
      of my iron horse
        running on iron tracks!

Sometimes my eye is caught like a big dumb fly
by the masterly spider webs in the corners of my room.
30   But I really look up
to the seventy-seven-story, reinforced-concrete mountains
      my blue-shirted builders create!

Were I to meet
the male beauty
35   "young Adonis, god of Byblos,"[3]
on a bridge, I'd probably never notice;
but I can't help staring into my philosopher's glassy eyes
or my fireman's square face
      red as a sweating sun!

40   Though I can smoke
third-class cigarettes filled
on my electric workbenches,
I can't roll tobacco—even the finest—
in paper by hand and smoke it!
45   I didn't—

2. Ludvig van Beethoven (1770–1827), German composer.

3. The Babylonian god Tammuz, associated with natural regeneration and the cycles of death and birth.

wouldn't—trade
my wife dressed in her leather cap and jacket
for Eve's nakedness!
Maybe I don't have a "poetic soul"?
50   What can I do
            when I love my own children
                    more
                than Mother Nature's!

━━ ✦ ━━

Bei Dao
b. 1949

Bei Dao (meaning "Northern Island") is the pen name of Zhao Zhenkai. He was born in Beijing to parents originally from Shanghai; his father was a government bureaucrat, his mother a medical doctor. He took part in the Cultural Revolution promulgated by Mao Zedong in the 1960s, but became disillusioned with Maoist authoritarianism. The authorities responded to his criticism by sending him into internal exile in the countryside. There he worked in construction and lived in isolation for over a decade. His experience turned him to spiritual contemplation and to new forms of poetry. He experimented with free verse and, starting in the early 1970s, was identified with the "misty poets," so named because of the elusive nature of their language and poetic subjects—a challenge to the simplicity and broad appeal that Mao expected of art. Bei Dao's poetry would be adopted by the April Fifth Democracy Movement of 1976, whose members demonstrated peacefully in Beijing's Tiananmen Square. In 1978 Bei Dao cofounded the first unofficial, non-government-sponsored literary journal, *Jintian* ("Today"), which would be closed down by the government two years later. By 1989, Bei Dao was forced into exile. He was in Berlin during the Tiananmen Square massacre of that year and wasn't allowed to return to China. Though he attempted returning in 1994, he was detained at the Beijing airport and deported. Since his exile, he has lived in a half dozen European countries, principally in Stockholm, Sweden, where in 1990 he resumed publication of the journal he founded, and then in the United States. He has been inducted into the American Academy of Arts and Letters as an honorary member, but his poems continue to reflect his displacement across continents and literary traditions.

PRONUNCIATION:
    Bei Dao: BAY DOW

He Opens Wide a Third Eye . . .[1]

He opens wide a third eye
the star above his head
warm currents from both east and west
have formed an archway
5   the expressway passes through the setting sun
two mountain peaks have ridden the camel to collapse

---

1. Translated by Bonnie S. McDougall and Chen Maiping.

its skeleton has been pressed deep down
into a layer of coal

He sits in the narrow cabin under water
10   calm as ballast
schools of fish around him flash and gleam
freedom, that golden coffin lid
hangs high above the prison
the people queueing behind the giant rock
15   are waiting to enter the emperor's
memory

The exile of words has begun

Old Snow

When heavy snow revives an ancient language
maps of national territories change shape
on this continent
snow shows deep concern
5   for a foreigner's small room

Before my door
lies a three metre long steel rail

Factories go bankrupt, governments fall
outdated newspapers converge
10   into a decomposed ocean
old snow comes constantly, new snow comes not at all
the art of creation is lost
windows retreat
. . . five magpies fly past

15   Unexpected sunlight is an event

Green frogs start their hibernation
the postmen's strike drags on
no news of any kind

Daniel David Moses
b. 1952

"The Line," a poem from Daniel David Moses's collection *The White Line* (1990), plays on
the double meaning of the title word that is established at the beginning: "this line / I'm feeding you" refers both to the poet who writes poems for a reader and to a fisherman baiting his
prey. Moses again and again delays giving an answer to the question, "What is a poem?" but
skillfully reels us in by making us go on from one line to the next. One reason it is as difficult
to stop reading this poem as it is for a fish to get off a hook is Moses's use of enjambment; by
letting his sentences run over one end of the line into the next (and thereby, of course, raising
the question of what a "line" in a poem really is and does), he makes it hard for the reader to

stop at the end of any one of them. Only in the final question does the end of the sentence coincide with the end of the line—and of the poem.

Daniel David Moses, a Native Canadian playwright and poet of the Delaware tribe, grew up on the Six Nations Reservation in southern Ontario. He completed college at York University and a Master of Fine Arts degree at the University of British Columbia. After working part time in Toronto in the early 1980s, he started supporting himself exclusively by writing from 1986 on. Besides *White Line,* he has published another volume of poetry, *Delicate Bodies* (1980), and a series of plays, among them *Coyote City* (produced in 1988), *Almighty Voice and His Wife* (produced in 1991), and *The Indian Medicine Shows* (produced in 1996).

The Line

This is not the poem, this line
I'm feeding you. And the thought
that this line is not the poem
is not it either. Instead

5   the thought of what this line is
not is the weight that sinks it
in. And though this image of
that thought as a weight is quite
a neat figure of speech, you

10   know what it's not—though it did
this time let the line smoothly
arc to this spot, and now lets
it reach down to one other,
one further rhyme—the music

15   of which almost does measure
up, the way it keeps the line
stirring through the dampening
air. Oh, you know you can hear
the lure in that. As you know

20   you've known from the start the self
referring this line's doing
was a hook—a sharp, twisted
bit of wit that made you look
and see how clear it is no

25   part of this line or its gear
could be the poem. Still it cast
and kept the line reeling out
till now at last the hook's on
to itself and about to

30   tie this line I'm feeding you
up with a knot. Referring
to itself has got the line
and us nowhere. So clever's
not what the poem is about

35   either. We're left hanging there
while something like a snout starts
nudging at your ear, nibbling
near my mouth—and it's likely

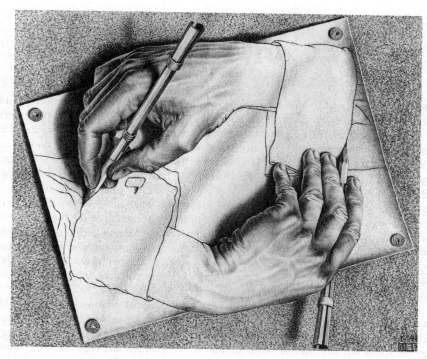

M. C. Escher, *Drawing Hands,* lithograph, 1948. Dutch artist M. C. Escher's drawings frequently foreground the ways in which we usually convert a two-dimensional canvas into an illusion of three-dimensional space. By reminding us that this three-dimensionality is only make-believe, Escher forces us to reflect on the strategies and materials by means of which we represent the world to ourselves, and reminds us that we cannot perceive the world without such procedures.

```
          it's the poem about to take
40        the bait. From the inside ought
          to be a great way to learn
          what the poem is. And we'll use
          this line when the poem's drawn it
          taut and fine as breath to tell
45        what we know, where we are and
          where we'll go—unless the line
          breaks. How would it feel, knowing,
          at last, what the poem really
          is, to lack the line to speak?
```

END OF PERSPECTIVES: POETRY ABOUT POETRY

Bertolt Brecht
1898–1956

Bertolt Brecht is one of a handful of modernist playwrights who transformed twentieth-century theater. Born in Augsburg, Germany, to a middle-class family, Brecht started writing poems and plays while he was still in high school. During World War I, a heart problem prevented him from being drafted into the army as early as his friends, but in 1918, after he'd already concluded high school and taken courses in medicine at the university in Munich, he served in an army hospital for about three months. He continued to take university courses intermittently until 1921, among them courses in drama, but never came close to completing a degree. Instead, he focused his energies on finding ways to stage his plays and publish poetry at a time when Germany was undergoing a profound political and economic crisis after having lost World War I. Setting his hopes on the German capital, Brecht went to Berlin for the first time in the fall of 1921, but success was slow in coming. Going back and forth between Berlin and Bavaria for the next few years, Brecht suffered considerable hardship; he even had to be admitted to the Charité Hospital in Berlin at one point for undernourishment. But some of his plays did begin to be performed, among them his first play *Baal* (performed in 1923), and *Edward II*.

Several of Brecht's friends were very alarmed at the fascist uprising in Munich in 1923 and resettled in Berlin in early 1924; Brecht followed them later the same year. In Berlin, he gradually became better and better known and began to develop an interest in representing on stage the social mechanisms that shape an individual's thoughts and behavior. Conventional drama, with its main focus on the individual, didn't seem well suited to this purpose. As an alternative, Brecht developed what he would eventually call "epic theater," a kind of play that doesn't invite the spectators' identification with the characters on stage but again and again reminds them that what they see is a particular representation of reality that they need to confront critically. "When I get my hands on a theatre," he said during this period, "I'll hire two clowns. They'll come on stage during the intermission and act the role of the public. They'll exchange views on the play and the audience. And make bets on how it ends." His interest in a theater that inspires critical reflection on society was reinforced through his encounter with Marxism. The sociologist Fritz Sternberg and the communist theoretician Karl Korsch introduced Brecht to Karl Marx's thought and writings, which won him over for life: From the late 1920s on, Brecht's life and work were deeply shaped by his commitment to Marxism.

In the meantime, his career reached its first peak with the performance of *The Threepenny Opera* in 1928. Based on John Gay's eighteenth-century satire *The Beggar's Opera* and written in collaboration with the well-known composer Kurt Weill, *The Threepenny Opera* suffered a series of mishaps and conflictive rehearsals as it was being put on, but it became an instant success and remained on stage for over a year. It was the most successful German play of the 1920s and illustrates many of the characteristic features of Brecht's work: extensive collaboration with other writers and artists, the creative use of already existing literary or historical material, the foregrounding of social issues rather than individual conflicts, the fusion of music and performance, the blending of popular culture and high art, and a persistent sense of humor. Initially more popular among the public than among critics, *The Threepenny Opera* has become one of Brecht's best-known masterpieces.

His enormous success with this opera put Brecht's career on a firmer foundation, but political developments immediately began to unsettle it again. The Nazi rise to power put outspoken Marxists such as Brecht at great risk, and he left Germany in 1933, spending the next decade and a half in exile. While he was living in Denmark from 1933 to 1939, his German citizenship was withdrawn and his books were burned. Fleeing from Nazi invasions, he moved to Sweden in 1939 and then to Finland; finally, he emigrated to the United States with his family in 1941. Life in Los Angeles, where he would spend most of his time while in American exile, came as a shock to him. The complacent materialism of his surroundings proved hard to reconcile with the consciousness of ongoing slaughter all across Europe, and he was disgusted by what he perceived as American superficiality and crass money-mindedness. A large community of German emigré artists and intellectuals had already settled in Los Angeles and provided some support. But there were also frequent conflicts within this community between Jews and non-Jews, those who were successful in the United States and those who were not, and sometimes simply between opposed personalities with different social and political backgrounds (such as an ongoing hostility between Brecht and the novelist Thomas Mann). In spite of many efforts, Brecht was never able to gain an entry into the Hollywood motion picture world; his scripts were considered too political and uncompromising to please an American public. Very few of his plays were performed, and the ones that were met with little success. On the whole, his experience in the United States was far from a happy one. The gathering hostility against communism throughout the 1940s further contributed to unsettling him, culminating in 1947, when he was called to testify in front of the House Un-American Activities Committee, a committee established to root out communist influences in American political and cultural life.

Despite the many difficulties Brecht had to confront during his years in exile, he produced some of his best work, especially during his stay in Scandinavia: not only plays, but also poems and important theoretical essays. This work includes major plays such as *Mutter Courage und ihre Kinder* (*Mother Courage and Her Children*, 1941), *The Life of Galilei* (1943), *The Good Woman of Sezuan* (1943), *The Resistible Rise of Arturo Ui* (1947), and *The Caucasian Chalk Circle* (1948). In these plays, Brecht uses a variety of devices to achieve what he called the "alienation effect" (*Verfremdungseffekt*), a crucial cornerstone of his theory of "epic theater." The alienation effect is designed to ensure that the audience doesn't experience events on the stage as an illusion of reality but as a representation of events that is to be viewed and evaluated with critical detachment. In Brecht's intent, this critical stance would ideally carry over to the audience's attitude toward real social structures. In one of his theoretical essays ("The Courage Model"), he argues:

> Too much heightening of the illusion in the setting, together with a "magnetic" way of acting that gives the spectator the illusion of being present at a fleeting, accidental, "real" event, create such an impression of naturalness that one can no longer interpose one's judgment, imagination or reactions, and must simply conform by sharing in the experience and becoming one of "nature's" objects. The illusion created by the theatre must be a partial one, in order that it may always be recognized as an illusion. Reality, however complete, has to be altered by being turned into art, so that it can be seen to be alterable and be treated as such.

In other words, the political project of Brecht's plays is based on a rejection of the blending of "world" and "stage" that had been a commonplace of the theater for centuries and that had been exploited by the Nazis in their highly theatrical mass rallies. Precisely by disrupting the theatrical illusion of reality with narrative or "epic" devices that are absent from conventional drama, Brecht hoped to create a basis for the critical understanding that he considered a prerequisite for social change.

Brecht returned to Europe in 1947, settling at first in Zurich, Switzerland, where he began to reestablish connections with the theater world, hoping that a base outside German territory would make it easier to make contact with all the different occupied zones in the former Germany. In 1949 he went to Berlin to stage *Mother Courage* at a theater in the Soviet sector, with his wife, the actress Helene Weigel, in the main role. This project initiated his return to Berlin and the formation of his own theater company, the Berliner Ensemble. After the separation of Germany into two states in 1949, Brecht became one of the most prominent intellectual and artistic figures in East Germany. Yet his status remained contested: He was continuously

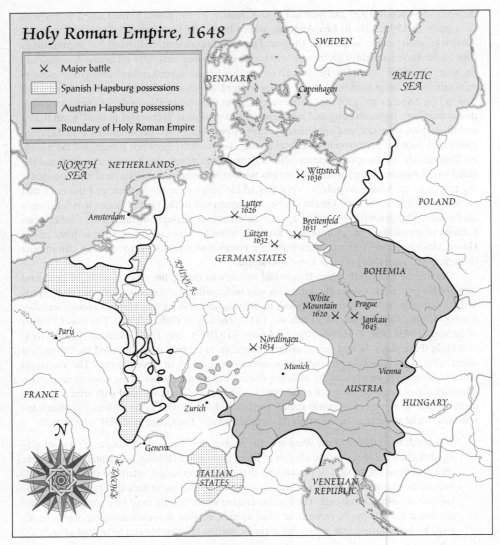

Holy Roman Empire, 1648

✕ Major battle

▒ Spanish Hapsburg possessions

▒ Austrian Hapsburg possessions

── Boundary of Holy Roman Empire

SWEDEN

BALTIC SEA

DENMARK

Copenhagen

NORTH SEA

NETHERLANDS

Amsterdam

POLAND

✕ Wittstock 1636

✕ Lutter 1626

✕ Breitenfeld 1631

✕ Lützen 1632

GERMAN STATES

BOHEMIA

White Mountain 1620 ✕

Prague ✕

✕ Jankau 1645

RHINE R.

✕ Nördlingen 1634

Munich

Vienna

Paris

FRANCE

AUSTRIA

HUNGARY

Zurich

N

Geneva

RHONE R.

ITALIAN STATES

VENETIAN REPUBLIC

The Holy Roman Empire after the Treaty of Westphalia, 1648. The Treaty ended the Thirty Year's War, which reduced the population within the Empire's German states by more than one-third. Millions died. It would be the most destructive war in Europe until the twentieth century.

exasperated with East German political authorities and the "socialist realist" standards they expected him to conform to, as well as with the increasingly stifled and restricted intellectual climate. But he defended the objectives of the East German state when he traveled abroad, which often led public opinion in the West to write him off as a mere lackey of the Eastern bloc.

Controversies over Brecht's life and work have persisted since his death in 1956: his relationships with his numerous mistresses and with his collaborators, as well as the question of whether politics drowns out aesthetic value or enhances his plays, have remained contentious issues. *Mother Courage* is one of the examples that is often cited in such debates. Brecht wanted to show in this play how war affects the life of ordinary citizens so deeply that they themselves perpetuate it. He commented at one point, speaking of himself in the third person, that "the play . . . shows that Courage has learnt nothing from the disasters that befall her. The play was written in 1938, when the writer foresaw a great war; he was not convinced that humanity was necessarily going to learn anything from the tragedy which he expected to strike it. . . . But even if Courage learns nothing else at least the audience can, in my view, learn something by observing her." Many critics, however, have argued that what makes this play compelling is not its political perspective but its main character. Mother Courage's relentless will to survive, her ingenuity, and her wit make the spectator sympathize with her to some degree, and the effect of the play may depend on factors that are quite different from those Brecht postulated in his theory. These complex questions regarding the content of his plays and the way in which they engage the audience have made Brecht one of the most enduring presences in twentieth-century theater.

PRONUNCIATIONS:
   Eilif: EYE-liff
   Kattrin: CAH-treen

Mother Courage and Her Children[1]
A Chronicle of the Thirty Years' War

Characters

MOTHER COURAGE	A CLERK
KATTRIN, *her mute daughter*	YOUNG SOLDIER
EILIF, *her elder son*	AN OLDER SOLDIER
SWISS CHEESE, *her younger son*	A PEASANT
THE RECRUITER	THE PEASANT'S WIFE
THE SERGEANT	THE YOUNG MAN
THE COOK	THE OLD WOMAN
THE GENERAL	ANOTHER PEASANT
THE CHAPLAIN	THE PEASANT WOMAN
THE ORDNANCE OFFICER	A YOUNG PEASANT
YVETTE POTTIER	THE LIEUTENANT
THE MAN WITH THE PATCH OVER HIS EYE	SOLDIERS
THE OTHER SERGEANT	A VOICE
THE OLD COLONEL	

1

Spring, 1624. General Oxenstjerna recruits troops in Dalarna for the Polish campaign.[2] The canteen woman, Anna Fierling, known as Mother Courage, loses a son.

   Highway near a city.

   A sergeant and a recruiter stand shivering.

---

1. Translated by Ralph Manheim.
2. The Thirty Years' War, which lasted from 1618 to 1648, was one of the most protracted confrontations between Catholic and Protestant forces in Europe. It took place for the most part on German soil. Originally a conflict between Protestant Bohemians and their Catholic King Ferdinand, it soon included Ferdinand's allies Poland, Bavaria, and Spain. Sweden entered the war on the Protestant side under King Gustav II Adolf in 1630. The first scene shows recruitment efforts on behalf of the Swedish Chancellor, Oxenstjerna, in preparation for Sweden's intervention into the war.

THE RECRUITER: How can anybody get a company together in a place like this? Sergeant, sometimes I feel like committing suicide. The general wants me to recruit four platoons by the twelfth, and the people around here are so depraved I can't sleep at night. I finally get hold of a man, I close my eyes and pretend not to see that he's chicken-breasted and he's got varicose veins, I get him good and drunk and he signs up. While I'm paying for the drinks, he steps out, I follow him to the door because I smell a rat: Sure enough, he's gone, like a fart out of a goose. A man's word doesn't mean a thing, there's no honor, no loyalty. This place has undermined my faith in humanity, sergeant.

THE SERGEANT: It's easy to see these people have gone too long without a war. How can you have morality without a war, I ask you? Peace is a mess, it takes a war to put things in order. In peacetime the human race goes to the dogs. Man and beast are treated like so much dirt. Everybody eats what they like, a big piece of cheese on white bread, with a slice of meat on top of the cheese. Nobody knows how many young men or good horses there are in that town up ahead, they've never been counted. I've been in places where they hadn't had a war in as much as seventy years, the people had no names, they didn't even know who they were. It takes a war before you get decent lists and records; then your boots are done up in bales and your grain in sacks, man and beast are properly counted and marched away, because people realize that without order they can't have a war.

THE RECRUITER: How right you are!

THE SERGEANT: Like all good things, a war is hard to get started. But once it takes root, it's vigorous; then people are as scared of peace as dice players are of laying off, because they'll have to reckon up their losses. But at first they're scared of war. It's the novelty.

THE RECRUITER: Say, there comes a wagon. Two women and two young fellows. Keep the old woman busy, sergeant. If this is another flop, you won't catch me standing out in this April wind any more.

[*A Jew's harp[3] is heard. Drawn by two young men, a covered wagon approaches. In the wagon sit Mother Courage and her mute daughter Kattrin.*]

MOTHER COURAGE: Good morning, sergeant.

SERGEANT [*barring the way*]: Good morning, friends. Who are you?

MOTHER COURAGE : Business people. [*Sings.*]

> Hey, Captains, make the drum stop drumming
> And let your soldiers take a seat.
> Here's Mother Courage, with boots she's coming
> To help along their aching feet.
> How can they march off to the slaughter
> With baggage, cannon, lice and fleas
> Across the rocks and through the water
> Unless their boots are in one piece?
>> The spring is come. Christian, revive!
>> The snowdrifts melt. The dead lie dead.
>> And if by chance you're still alive
>> It's time to rise and shake a leg.

3. Or "mouth organ," a horseshoe-shaped instrument held between the teeth while the metal strip that connects the two ends is made to vibrate with a finger.

O Captains, don't expect to send them
To death with nothing in their crops.
First you must let Mother Courage mend them
In mind and body with her schnapps.
On empty bellies it's distressing
To stand up under shot and shell.
But once they're full, you have my blessing
To lead them to the jaws of hell.
      The spring is come. Christian, revive!
      The snowdrifts melt, the dead lie dead.
      And if by chance you're still alive
      It's time to rise and shake a leg.

THE SERGEANT: Halt, you scum. Where do you belong?

THE ELDER SON: Second Finnish Regiment.

THE SERGEANT: Where are your papers?

MOTHER COURAGE: Papers?

THE YOUNGER SON: But she's Mother Courage!

THE SERGEANT: Never heard of her. Why Courage?

MOTHER COURAGE: They call me Courage, sergeant, because when I saw ruin staring me in the face I drove out of Riga[4] through cannon fire with fifty loaves of bread in my wagon. They were getting moldy, it was high time, I had no choice.

THE SERGEANT: No wisecracks. Where are your papers?

MOTHER COURAGE [*fishing a pile of papers out of a tin box and climbing down*]: Here are my papers, sergeant. There's a whole missal, picked it up in Alt-Ötting to wrap cucumbers in, and a map of Moravia, God knows if I'll ever get there, if I don't it's a total loss. And this here certifies that my horse hasn't got foot-and-mouth disease, too bad, he croaked on us, he cost fifteen guilders, but not out of my pocket, glory be. Is that enough paper?

THE SERGEANT: Are you trying to pull my leg? I'll teach you to get smart. You know you need a license.

MOTHER COURAGE: You mind your manners and don't go telling my innocent children that I'd go anywhere near your leg, it's indecent. I want no truck with you. My license in the Second Regiment is my honest face, and if you can't read it, that's not my fault. I'm not letting anybody put his seal on it.

THE RECRUITER: Sergeant, I detect a spirit of insubordination in this woman. In our camp we need respect for authority.

MOTHER COURAGE: Wouldn't sausage be better?

THE SERGEANT: Name.

MOTHER COURAGE: Anna Fierling.[5]

THE SERGEANT: Then you're all Fierlings?

MOTHER COURAGE: What do you mean? Fierling is my name. Not theirs.

THE SERGEANT: Aren't they all your children?

MOTHER COURAGE: That they are, but why should they all have the same name? [*Pointing at the elder son.*] This one, for instance. His name is Eilif Nojocki. How come? Because his father always claimed to be called Kojocki or Mojocki. The boy remembers him well, except the one he remembers was somebody else, a

4. Located on the Baltic Sea, Riga is the capital of what is now Latvia.   5. Pronounced "FEAR-ling."

Frenchman with a goatee. But aside from that, he inherited his father's intelligence; that man could strip the pants off a peasant's ass without his knowing it. So, you see, we've each got our own name.

THE SERGEANT: Each different, you mean?

MOTHER COURAGE: Don't act so innocent.

THE SERGEANT: I suppose that one's a Chinaman? [*Indicating the younger son.*]

MOTHER COURAGE: Wrong. He's Swiss.

THE SERGEANT: After the Frenchman?

MOTHER COURAGE: What Frenchman? I never heard of any Frenchman. Don't get everything balled up or we'll be here all day. He's Swiss, but his name is Fejos, the name has nothing to do with his father. He had an entirely different name, he was an engineer, built fortifications, but he drank. [*Swiss Cheese nods, beaming; the mute Kattrin is also tickled.*]

THE SERGEANT: Then how can his name be Fejos?

MOTHER COURAGE: I wouldn't want to offend you, but you haven't got much imagination. Naturally his name is Fejos because when he came I was with a Hungarian, it was all the same to him, he was dying of kidney trouble though he never touched a drop, a very decent man. The boy takes after him.

THE SERGEANT: But you said he wasn't his father?

MOTHER COURAGE: He takes after him all the same. I call him Swiss Cheese, how come, because he's good at pulling the wagon. [*Pointing at her daughter.*] Her name is Kattrin Haupt, she's half German.

THE SERGEANT: A fine family, I must say.

MOTHER COURAGE: Yes, I've been all over the world with my wagon.

THE SERGEANT: It's all being taken down. [*He takes it down.*] You're from Bamberg, Bavaria. What brings you here?

MOTHER COURAGE: I couldn't wait for the war to kindly come to Bamberg.

THE RECRUITER: You wagon pullers ought to be called Jacob Ox and Esau Ox.[6] Do you ever get out of harness?

EILIF: Mother, can I clout him one on the kisser? I'd like to.

MOTHER COURAGE: And I forbid you. You stay put. And now, gentlemen, wouldn't you need a nice pistol, or a belt buckle, yours is all worn out, sergeant.

THE SERGEANT: I need something else. I'm not blind. Those young fellows are built like tree trunks, big broad chests, sturdy legs. Why aren't they in the army? That's what I'd like to know.

MOTHER COURAGE [*quickly*]: Nothing doing, sergeant. My children aren't cut out for soldiers.

THE RECRUITER: Why not? There's profit in it, and glory. Peddling shoes is woman's work. [*To Eilif.*] Step up; let's feel if you've got muscles or if you're a sissy.

MOTHER COURAGE: He's a sissy. Give him a mean look and he'll fall flat on his face.

THE RECRUITER: And kill a calf if it happens to be standing in the way. [*Tries to lead him away.*]

MOTHER COURAGE: Leave him alone. He's not for you.

THE RECRUITER: He insulted me. He referred to my face as a kisser. Him and me will now step out in the field and discuss this thing as man to man.

EILIF: Don't worry, mother. I'll take care of him.

---

6. An allusion to Jacob and Esau, Isaac's rival sons (Genesis 25–36).

MOTHER COURAGE: You stay put. You no-good! I know you, always fighting. He's got a knife in his boot, he's a knifer.

THE RECRUITER: I'll pull it out of him like a milk tooth. Come on, boy.

MOTHER COURAGE: Sergeant, I'll report you to the colonel. He'll throw you in the lock-up. The lieutenant is courting my daughter.

THE SERGEANT: No rough stuff, brother. [*To Mother Courage.*] What have you got against the army? Wasn't his father a soldier? Didn't he die fair and square? You said so yourself.

MOTHER COURAGE: He's only a child. You want to lead him off to slaughter, I know you. You'll get five guilders for him.

THE RECRUITER: He'll get a beautiful cap and top boots.

EILIF: Not from you.

MOTHER COURAGE: Oh, won't you come fishing with me? said the fisherman to the worm. [*To Swiss Cheese.*] Run and yell that they're trying to steal your brother. [*She pulls a knife.*] Just try and steal him. I'll cut you down, you dogs. I'll teach you to put him in your war! We do an honest business in ham and shirts, we're peaceful folk.

THE SERGEANT: I can see by the knife how peaceful you are. You ought to be ashamed of yourself, put that knife away, you bitch. A minute ago you admitted you lived off war, how else would you live, on what? How can you have a war without soldiers?

MOTHER COURAGE: It doesn't have to be my children.

THE SERGEANT: I see. You'd like the war to eat the core and spit out the apple. You want your brood to batten on war, tax-free. The war can look out for itself, is that it? You call yourself Courage, eh? And you're afraid of the war that feeds you. Your sons aren't afraid of it, I can see that.

EILIF: I'm not afraid of any war.

THE SERGEANT: Why should you be? Look at me: Has the soldier's life disagreed with me? I was seventeen when I joined up.

MOTHER COURAGE: You're not seventy yet.

THE SERGEANT: I can wait.

MOTHER COURAGE: Sure. Under ground.

THE SERGEANT: Are you trying to insult me? Telling me I'm going to die?

MOTHER COURAGE: But suppose it's the truth? I can see the mark on you. You look like a corpse on leave.

SWISS CHEESE: She's got second sight. Everybody says so. She can tell the future.

THE RECRUITER: Then tell the sergeant his future. It might amuse him.

THE SERGEANT: I don't believe in that stuff.

MOTHER COURAGE: Give me your helmet. [*He gives it to her.*]

THE SERGEANT: It doesn't mean any more than taking a shit in the grass. But go ahead for the laugh.

MOTHER COURAGE [*takes a sheet of parchment and tears it in two*]: Eilif, Swiss Cheese, Kattrin: That's how we'd all be torn apart if we got mixed up too deep in the war. [*To the sergeant.*] Seeing it's you, I'll do it for nothing. I make a black cross on this piece. Black is death.

SWISS CHEESE: She leaves the other one blank. Get it?

MOTHER COURAGE: Now I fold them, and now I shake them up together. Same as we're all mixed up together from the cradle to the grave. And now you draw, and you'll know the answer. [*The sergeant hesitates.*]

THE RECRUITER [*to Eilif*]: I don't take everybody, I'm known to be picky and choosy, but you've got spirit, I like that.

THE SERGEANT [*fishing in the helmet*]: Damn foolishness! Hocus-pocus!

SWISS CHEESE: He's pulled a black cross. He's through.

THE RECRUITER: Don't let them scare you, there's not enough bullets for everybody.

THE SERGEANT [*hoarsely*]: You've fouled me up.

MOTHER COURAGE: You fouled yourself up the day you joined the army. And now we'll be going, there isn't a war every day, I've got to take advantage.

THE SERGEANT: Hell and damnation! Don't try to hornswoggle me. We're taking your bastard to be a soldier.

EILIF: I'd like to be a soldier, mother.

MOTHER COURAGE: You shut your trap, you Finnish devil.

EILIF: Swiss Cheese wants to be a soldier too.

MOTHER COURAGE: That's news to me. I'd better let you draw too, all three of you. [*She goes to the rear to mark crosses on slips of parchment.*]

THE RECRUITER [*to Eilif*]: It's been said to our discredit that a lot of religion goes on in the Swedish camp, but that's slander to blacken our reputation. Hymn singing only on Sunday, one verse! And only if you've got a voice.

MOTHER COURAGE [*comes back with the slips in the sergeant's helmet*]: Want to sneak away from their mother, the devils, and run off to war like calves to a salt lick. But we'll draw lots on it, then they'll see that the world is no vale of smiles with a "Come along, son, we're short on generals." Sergeant, I'm very much afraid they won't come through the war. They've got terrible characters, all three of them. [*She holds out the helmet to Eilif.*] There. Pick a slip. [*He picks one and unfolds it. She snatches it away from him.*] There you have it. A cross! Oh, unhappy mother that I am, oh, mother of sorrows. Has he got to die? Doomed to perish in the springtime of his life? If he joins the army, he'll bite the dust, that's sure. He's too brave, just like his father. If he's not smart, he'll go the way of all flesh, the slip proves it. [*She roars at him.*] Are you going to be smart?

EILIF: Why not?

MOTHER COURAGE: The smart thing to do is to stay with your mother, and if they make fun of you and call you a sissy, just laugh.

THE RECRUITER: If you're shitting in your pants, we'll take your brother.

MOTHER COURAGE: I told you to laugh. Laugh! And now you pick, Swiss Cheese. I'm not so worried about you, you're honest. [*He picks a slip.*] Oh! Why, have you got that strange look? It's got to be blank. There can't be a cross on it. No, I can't lose you. [*She takes the slip.*] A cross? Him too? Maybe it's because he's so stupid. Oh, Swiss Cheese, you'll die too, unless you're very honest the whole time, the way I've taught you since you were a baby, always bringing back the change when I sent you to buy bread. That's the only way you can save yourself. Look, sergeant, isn't that a black cross?

THE SERGEANT: It's a cross all right. I don't see how I could have pulled one. I always stay in the rear. [*To the recruiter.*] It's on the up and up. Her own get it too.

SWISS CHEESE: I get it too. But I can take a hint.

MOTHER COURAGE [*to Kattrin*]: Now you're the only one I'm sure of, you're a cross yourself because you've got a good heart. [*She holds up the helmet to Kattrin in the wagon, but she herself takes out the slip.*] It's driving me to despair. It can't be right, maybe I mixed them wrong. Don't be too good-natured, Kattrin, don't, there's a cross on your path too. Always keep very quiet, that ought to be easy seeing you're dumb. Well, now you know. Be careful, all of you, you'll need to be. And now we'll climb up and drive on. [*She returns the sergeant's helmet and climbs up into the wagon.*]

THE RECRUITER [*to the sergeant*]: Do something!

THE OTHER SERGEANT: I'm not feeling so good.

THE RECRUITER: Maybe you caught cold when you took your helmet off in the wind. Tell her you want to buy something. Keep her busy. [*Aloud.*] You could at least take a look at that buckle, sergeant. After all, selling things is these good people's living. Hey, you, the sergeant wants to buy that belt buckle.

MOTHER COURAGE: Half a guilder. A buckle like that is worth two guilders. [*She climbs down.*]

THE SERGEANT: It's not new. This wind! I can't examine it here. Let's go where it's quiet. [*He goes behind the wagon with the buckle.*]

MOTHER COURAGE: I haven't noticed any wind.

THE SERGEANT: Maybe it is worth half a guilder. It's silver.

MOTHER COURAGE [*joins him behind the wagon*]: Six solid ounces.

THE RECRUITER [*to Eilif*]: And then we'll have a drink, just you and me. I've got your enlistment bonus right here. Come on. [*Eilif stands undecided.*]

MOTHER COURAGE: All right. Half a guilder.

THE SERGEANT: I don't get it. I always stay in the rear. There's no safer place for a sergeant. You can send the men up forward to win glory. You've spoiled my dinner. It won't go down, I know it, not a bite.

MOTHER COURAGE: Don't take it to heart. Don't let it spoil your appetite. Just keep behind the lines. Here, take a drink of schnapps, man. [*She hands him the bottle.*]

THE RECRUITER [*has taken Eilif's arm and is pulling him away toward the rear*]: A bonus of ten guilders, and you'll be a brave man and you'll fight for the king, and the women will tear each other's hair out over you. And you can clout me one on the kisser for insulting you. [*Both go out.*]

[*Mute Kattrin jumps down from the wagon and emits raucous sounds.*]

MOTHER COURAGE: Just a minute, Kattrin, just a minute. The sergeant's paying up. [*Bites the half guilder.*] I'm always suspicious of money. I'm a burnt child, sergeant. But your coin is good. And now we'll be going. Where's Eilif?

SWISS CHEESE: He's gone with the recruiter.

MOTHER COURAGE [*stands motionless, then*]: You simple soul. [*To Kattrin.*] I know. You can't talk, you couldn't help it.

THE SERGEANT: You could do with a drink yourself, mother. That's the way it goes. Soldiering isn't the worst thing in the world. You want to live off the war, but you want to keep you and yours out of it. Is that it?

MOTHER COURAGE: Now you'll have to pull with your brother, Kattrin.

[*Brother and sister harness themselves to the wagon and start pulling. Mother Courage walks beside them. The wagon rolls off.*]

THE SERGEANT [*looking after them*]:

> If you want the war to work for you
> You've got to give the war its due.

2

In 1625 and 1626 Mother Courage crosses Poland in the train of the Swedish armies. Outside the fortress of Wallhof she meets her son again.—A capon[1] is successfully sold, the brave son's fortunes are at their zenith.

> *The general's tent.*

> *Beside it the kitchen. The thunder of cannon. The cook is arguing with Mother Courage, who is trying to sell him a capon.*

THE COOK: Sixty hellers for that pathetic bird?

MOTHER COURAGE: Pathetic bird? You mean this plump beauty? Are you trying to tell me that a general who's the biggest eater for miles around—God help you if you haven't got anything for his dinner—can't afford a measly sixty hellers?

THE COOK: I can get a dozen like it for ten hellers right around the corner.

MOTHER COURAGE: What, you'll find a capon like this right around the corner? With a siege on and everybody so starved you can see right through them. Maybe you'll scare up a rat, maybe, I say, 'cause they've all been eaten, I've seen five men chasing a starved rat for hours. Fifty hellers for a giant capon in the middle of a siege.

THE COOK: We're not besieged; they are. We're the besiegers, can't you get that through your head?

MOTHER COURAGE: But we haven't got anything to eat either, in fact we've got less than the people in the city. They've hauled it all inside. I hear their life is one big orgy. And look at us. I've been around to the peasants, they haven't got a thing.

THE COOK: They've got plenty. They hide it.

MOTHER COURAGE [*triumphantly*]: Oh, no! They're ruined, that's what they are. They're starving. I've seen them. They're so hungry they're digging up roots. They lick their fingers when they've eaten a boiled strap. That's the situation. And here I've got a capon and I'm supposed to let it go for forty hellers.

THE COOK: Thirty, not forty. Thirty, I said.

MOTHER COURAGE: It's no common capon. They tell me this bird was so talented that he wouldn't eat unless they played music, he had his own favorite march. He could add and subtract, that's how intelligent he was. And you're trying to tell me forty hellers is too much. The general will bite your head off if there's nothing to eat.

THE COOK: You know what I'm going to do? [*He takes a piece of beef and sets his knife to it.*] Here I've got a piece of beef. I'll roast it. Think it over. This is your last chance.

MOTHER COURAGE: Roast and be damned. It's a year old.

THE COOK: A day old. That ox was running around only yesterday afternoon, I saw him with my own eyes.

MOTHER COURAGE: Then he must have stunk on the hoof.

THE COOK: I'll cook it five hours if I have to. We'll see if it's still tough. [*He cuts into it.*]

MOTHER COURAGE: Use plenty of pepper, maybe the general won't notice the stink.

> [*The general, a chaplain and Eilif enter the tent.*]

THE GENERAL [*slapping Eilif on the back*]: All right, son, into your general's tent you go, you'll sit at my right hand. You've done a heroic deed and you're a pious trooper, because this is a war of religion and what you did was done for God, that's

1. A castrated rooster.

what counts with me. I'll reward you with a gold bracelet when I take the city. We come here to save their souls and what do those filthy, shameless peasants do? They drive their cattle away. And they stuff their priests with meat, front and back. But you taught them a lesson. Here's a tankard of red wine for you. [*He pours.*] We'll down it in one gulp. [*They do so.*] None for the chaplain, he's got his religion. What would you like for dinner, sweetheart?

EILIF: A scrap of meat. Why not?

THE GENERAL: Cook! Meat!

THE COOK: And now he brings company when there's nothing to eat.

[*Wanting to listen, Mother Courage makes him stop talking.*]

EILIF: Cutting down peasants whets the appetite.

MOTHER COURAGE: God, it's my Eilif.

THE COOK: Who?

MOTHER COURAGE: My eldest. I haven't seen hide nor hair of him in two years, he was stolen from me on the highway. He must be in good if the general invites him to dinner, and what have you got to offer? Nothing. Did you hear what the general's guest wants for dinner? Meat! Take my advice, snap up this capon. The price is one guilder.

THE GENERAL [*has sat down with Eilif. Bellows*]: Food, Lamb, you lousy, no-good cook, or I'll kill you.

THE COOK: All right, hand it over. This is extortion.

MOTHER COURAGE: I thought it was a pathetic bird.

THE COOK: Pathetic is the word. Hand it over. Fifty hellers! It's highway robbery.

MOTHER COURAGE: One guilder, I say. For my eldest son, the general's honored guest, I spare no expense.

THE COOK [*gives her the money*]: Then pluck it at least while I make the fire.

MOTHER COURAGE [*sits down to pluck the capon*]: Won't he be glad to see me! He's my brave, intelligent son. I've got a stupid one too, but he's honest. The girl's a total loss. But at least she doesn't talk, that's something.

THE GENERAL: Take another drink, son, it's my best Falerno,[2] I've only got another barrel or two at the most, but it's worth it to see that there's still some true faith in my army. The good shepherd here just looks on, all he knows how to do is preach. Can he do anything? No. And now, Eilif my son, tell us all about it, how cleverly you hoodwinked those peasants and captured those twenty head of cattle. I hope they'll be here soon.

EILIF: Tomorrow. Maybe the day after.

MOTHER COURAGE: Isn't my Eilif considerate, not bringing those oxen in until tomorrow, or you wouldn't have even said hello to my capon.

EILIF: Well, it was like this: I heard the peasants were secretly—mostly at night—rounding up the oxen they'd hidden in a certain forest. The city people had arranged to come and get them. I let them round the oxen up, I figured they'd find them easier than I would. I made my men ravenous for meat, put them on short rations for two days until their mouths watered if they even heard a word beginning with *me* . . . like measles.

THE GENERAL: That was clever of you.

EILIF: Maybe. The rest was a pushover. Except the peasants had clubs and there were three times more of them and they fell on us like bloody murder. Four of them

2. An Italian wine.

drove me into a clump of bushes, they knocked my sword out of my hand and yelled: Surrender! Now what'll I do, I says to myself, they'll make hash out of me.

THE GENERAL: What did you do?

EILIF: I laughed.

THE GENERAL: You laughed?

EILIF: I laughed. Which led to a conversation. The first thing you know, I'm bargaining. Twenty guilders is too much for that ox, I say, how about fifteen? Like I'm meaning to pay. They're flummoxed, they scratch their heads. Quick, I reach for my sword and mow them down. Necessity knows no law. See what I mean?

THE GENERAL: What do you say to that, shepherd?

CHAPLAIN: Strictly speaking, that maxim is not in the Bible. But our Lord was able to turn five loaves into five hundred.[3] So there was no question of poverty; he could tell people to love their neighbors because their bellies were full. Nowadays it's different.

THE GENERAL [laughs]: Very different. All right, you Pharisee,[4] take a swig. [To Eilif.] You mowed them down, splendid, so my fine troops could have a decent bite to eat. Doesn't the Good Book say: "Whatsoever thou doest for the least of my brethren, thou doest for me"?[5] And what have you done for them? You've got them a good chunk of beef for their dinner. They're not used to moldy crusts; in the old days they had a helmetful of white bread and wine before they went out to fight for God.

EILIF: Yes, I reached for my sword and I mowed them down.

THE GENERAL: You're a young Caesar. You deserve to see the king.

EILIF: I have, in the distance. He shines like a light. He's my ideal.

THE GENERAL: You're something like him already, Eilif. I know the worth of a brave soldier like you. When I find one, I treat him like my own son. [He leads him to the map.] Take a look at the situation, Eilif; we've still got a long way to go.

MOTHER COURAGE [who has been listening starts plucking her capon furiously]: He must be a rotten general.

THE COOK: Eats like a pig, but why rotten?

MOTHER COURAGE: Because he needs brave soldiers, that's why. If he planned his campaigns right, what would he need brave soldiers for? The run-of-the-mill would do. Take it from me, whenever you find a lot of virtues, it shows that something's wrong.

THE COOK: I'd say it proves that something is all right.

MOTHER COURAGE: No, that something's wrong. See, when a general or a king is real stupid and leads his men up shit creek, his troops need courage, that's a virtue. If he's stingy and doesn't hire enough soldiers, they've all got to be Herculeses.[6] And if he's a slob and lets everything go to pot, they've got to be as sly as serpents or they're done for. And if he's always expecting too much of them, they need an extra dose of loyalty. A country that's run right, or a good king or a good general, doesn't need any of these virtues. You don't need virtues in a decent country, the people can all be perfectly ordinary, medium-bright, and cowards too for my money.

THE GENERAL: I bet your father was a soldier.

EILIF: A great soldier, I'm told. My mother warned me about it. Makes me think of a song.

THE GENERAL: Sing it! [Bellowing.] Where's that food!

3. The story of Christ feeding a large crowd with five loaves of bread and two fish is told in all the gospels (Matthew 14:13–21, etc.). None of them mentions 500 loaves of bread.
4. The Pharisees were an important, learned Jewish sect,

often characterized in the New Testament as hypocrites.
5. Matthew 25:40.
6. Hercules was a hero of Greek mythology, endowed with unusual strength and courage, who successfully solved extremely difficult and demanding tasks.

EILIF: It's called: The Song of the Old Wife and the Soldier.

[*He sings, doing a war dance with his saber.*]

> *A gun or a pike, they can kill who they like*
> *And the torrent will swallow a wader*
> *You had better think twice before battling with ice*
> *Said the old wife to the soldier.*
> *Cocking his rifle he leapt to his feet*
> *Laughing for joy as he heard the drum beat*
> *The wars cannot hurt me, he told her.*
> *He shouldered his gun and he picked up his knife*
> *To see the wide world. That's the soldier's life.*
> *Those were the words of the soldier.*
>
> *Ah, deep will they lie who wise counsel defy*
> *Learn wisdom from those that are older*
> *Oh, don't venture too high or you'll fall from the sky*
> *Said the old wife to the soldier.*
> *But the young soldier with knife and with gun*
> *Only laughed a cold laugh and stepped into the run.*
> *The water can't hurt me, he told her.*
> *And when the moon on the rooftop shines white*
> *We'll be coming back. You can pray for that night.*
> *Those were the words of the soldier.*

MOTHER COURAGE [*in the kitchen, continues the song, beating a pot with a spoon*]:

> *Like the smoke you'll be gone and no warmth linger on*
> *And your deeds only leave me the colder!*
> *Oh, see the smoke race. Oh, dear God keep him safe!*
> *That's what she said of the soldier.*

EILIF: What's that?

MOTHER COURAGE [*goes on singing*]:

> *And the young soldier with knife and with gun*
> *Was swept from his feet till he sank in the run*
> *And the torrent swallowed the waders.*
> *Cold shone the moon on the rooftop white*
> *But the soldier was carried away with the ice*
> *And what was it she heard from the soldiers?*
>
> *Like the smoke he was gone and no warmth lingered on*
> *And his deeds only left her the colder.*
> *Ah, deep will they lie who wise counsel defy!*
> *That's what she said to the soldiers.*

THE GENERAL: What do they think they're doing in my kitchen?

EILIF [*has gone into the kitchen. He embraces his mother*]: Mother! It's you! Where are the others?

MOTHER COURAGE [*in his arms*]: Snug as a bug in a rug. Swiss Cheese is paymaster of the Second Regiment; at least he won't be fighting, I couldn't keep him out altogether.

EILIF: And how about your feet?

MOTHER COURAGE: Well, it's hard getting my shoes on in the morning.

THE GENERAL [*has joined them*]: Ah, so you're his mother. I hope you've got more sons for me like this fellow here.

EILIF: Am I lucky! There you're sitting in the kitchen hearing your son being praised.

MOTHER COURAGE: I heard it all right! [*She gives him a slap in the face.*]

EILIF [*holding his cheek*]: For capturing the oxen?

MOTHER COURAGE: No. For not surrendering when the four of them were threatening to make hash out of you! Didn't I teach you to take care of yourself? You Finnish devil! [*The general and the chaplain laugh.*]

3

Three years later Mother Courage and parts of a Finnish regiment are taken prisoner. She is able to save her daughter and her wagon, but her honest son dies.

  Army camp.

  Afternoon. On a pole the regimental flag. Mother Courage has stretched a clothesline between her wagon, on which all sorts of merchandise is hung in display, and a large cannon. She and Kattrin are folding washing and piling it on the cannon. At the same time she is negotiating with an ordnance officer over a sack of bullets. Swiss Cheese, now in the uniform of a paymaster, is looking on. A pretty woman, Yvette Pottier, is sitting with a glass of brandy in front of her, sewing a gaudy-colored bat. She is in her stocking feet, her red high-heeled shoes are on the ground beside her.

THE ORDNANCE OFFICER: I'll let you have these bullets for two guilders. It's cheap, I need the money, because the colonel's been drinking with the officers for two days and we're out of liquor.

MOTHER COURAGE: That's ammunition for the troops. If it's found here, I'll be court-martialed. You punks sell their bullets and the men have nothing to shoot at the enemy.

THE ORDNANCE OFFICER: Don't be hard-hearted, you scratch my back, I'll scratch yours.

MOTHER COURAGE: I'm not taking any army property. Not at that price.

THE ORDNANCE OFFICER: You can sell it for five guilders, maybe eight, to the ordnance officer of the Fourth before the day is out, if you're quiet about it and give him a receipt for twelve. He hasn't an ounce of ammunition left.

MOTHER COURAGE: Why don't you do it yourself?

THE ORDNANCE OFFICER: Because I don't trust him, he's a friend of mine.

MOTHER COURAGE [*takes the sack*]: Hand it over. [*To Kattrin.*] Take it back there and pay him one and a half guilders. [*In response to the ordnance officer's protest.*] One and a half guilders, I say. [*Kattrin drags the sack behind the wagon, the ordnance officer follows her. Mother Courage to Swiss Cheese.*] Here's your underdrawers, take good care of them, this is October, might be coming on fall, I don't say it will be, because I've learned that nothing is sure to happen the way we think, not even the seasons. But whatever happens, your regimental funds have to be in order. Are your funds in order?

SWISS CHEESE: Yes, mother.

MOTHER COURAGE: Never forget that they made you paymaster because you're honest and not brave like your brother, and especially because you're too simple-minded to get the idea of making off with the money. That's a comfort to me. And don't go mislaying your drawers.

SWISS CHEESE: No, mother. I'll put them under my mattress. [*Starts to go.*]

ORDNANCE OFFICER: I'll go with you, paymaster.

MOTHER COURAGE: Just don't teach him any of your tricks. [*Without saying good-bye the ordnance officer goes out with Swiss Cheese.*]

YVETTE [*waves her hand after the ordnance officer*]: You might say good-bye, officer.

MOTHER COURAGE [*to Yvette*]: I don't like to see those two together. He's not the right kind of company for my Swiss Cheese. But the war's getting along pretty well. More countries are joining in all the time, it can go on for another four, five years, easy. With a little planning ahead, I can do good business if I'm careful. Don't you know you shouldn't drink in the morning with your sickness?

YVETTE: Who says I'm sick, it's slander.

MOTHER COURAGE: Everybody says so.

YVETTE: Because they're all liars. Mother Courage, I'm desperate. They all keep out of my way like I'm a rotten fish on account of those lies. What's the good of fixing my hat? [*She throws it down.*] That's why I drink in the morning, I never used to, I'm getting crow's-feet, but it doesn't matter now. In the Second Finnish Regiment they all know me. I should have stayed home when my first love walked out on me. Pride isn't for the likes of us. If we can't put up with shit, we're through.

MOTHER COURAGE: Just don't start in on your Pieter and how it all happened in front of my innocent daughter.

YVETTE: She's just the one to hear it, it'll harden her against love.

MOTHER COURAGE: Nothing can harden them.

YVETTE: Then I'll talk about it because it makes me feel better. It begins with my growing up in fair Flanders, because if I hadn't I'd never have laid eyes on him and I wouldn't be here in Poland now, because he was an army cook, blond, a Dutchman, but skinny. Kattrin, watch out for the skinny ones, but I didn't know that then, and another thing I didn't know is that he had another girl even then, and they all called him Pete the Pipe, because he didn't even take his pipe out of his mouth when he was doing it, that's all it meant to him. [*She sings the Song of Fraternization.*]

> *When I was only sixteen*
> *The foe came into our land.*
> *He laid aside his sabre*
> *And with a smile he took my hand.*
> > *After the May parade*
> > *The May light starts to fade.*
> > *The regiment dressed by the right*
> > *Then drums were beaten, that's the drill.*
> > *The foe took us behind the hill*
> > *And fraternized all night.*
>
> *There were so many foes came*
> *And mine worked in the mess.*
> *I loathed him in the daytime.*
> *At night I loved him none the less.*
> > *After the May parade*
> > *The May light starts to fade.*
> > *The regiment dressed by the right*
> > *Then drums were beaten, that's the drill.*
> > *The foe took us behind the hill*
> > *And fraternized all night.*

> *The love which came upon me*
> *Was wished on me by fate.*
> *My friends could never grasp why*
> *I found it hard to share their hate.*
> *The fields were wet with dew*
> *When sorrow first I knew,*
> *The regiment dressed by the right*
> *Then drums were beaten, that's the drill*
> *And then the foe, my lover still*
> *Went marching from our sight.*

Well, I followed him, but I never found him. That was five years ago. [*She goes behind the wagon with an unsteady gait.*]

MOTHER COURAGE: You've left your hat.

YVETTE: Anybody that wants it can have it.

MOTHER COURAGE: Let that be a lesson to you, Kattrin. Have no truck with soldiers. It's love that makes the world go round, so you'd better watch out. Even with a civilian it's no picnic. He says he'd kiss the ground you put your little feet on, talking of feet, did you wash yours yesterday, and then you're his slave. Be glad you're dumb, that way you'll never contradict yourself or want to bite your tongue off because you've told the truth, it's a gift of God to be dumb. Here comes the general's cook, I wonder what he wants. [*The cook and the chaplain enter.*]

THE CHAPLAIN: I've got a message for you from your son Eilif. The cook here thought he'd come along, he's taken a shine to you.

THE COOK: I only came to get a breath of air.

MOTHER COURAGE: You can always do that here if you behave, and if you don't, I can handle you. Well, what does he want? I've got no money to spare.

THE CHAPLAIN: Actually he wanted me to see his brother, the paymaster.

MOTHER COURAGE: He's not here any more, or anywhere else either. He's not his brother's paymaster. I don't want him leading him into temptation and being smart at his expense. [*Gives him money from the bag slung around her waist.*] Give him this, it's a sin, he's speculating on mother love and he ought to be ashamed.

THE COOK: He won't do it much longer, then he'll be marching off with his regiment, maybe to his death, you never can tell. Better make it a little more, you'll be sorry later. You women are hard-hearted, but afterwards you're sorry. A drop of brandy wouldn't have cost much when it was wanted, but it wasn't given, and later, for all you know, he'll be lying in the cold ground and you can't dig him up again.

THE CHAPLAIN: Don't be sentimental, cook. There's nothing wrong with dying in battle, it's a blessing, and I'll tell you why. This is a war of religion. Not a common war, but a war for the faith, and therefore pleasing to God.

THE COOK: That's a fact. In a way you could call it a war, because of the extortion and killing and looting, not to mention a bit of rape, but it's a war of religion, which makes it different from all other wars, that's obvious. But it makes a man thirsty all the same, you've got to admit that.

THE CHAPLAIN [*to Mother Courage, pointing at the cook*]: I tried to discourage him, but he says you've turned his head, he sees you in his dreams.

THE COOK [*lights a short-stemmed pipe*]: All I want is a glass of brandy from your fair hand, nothing more sinful. I'm already so shocked by the jokes the chaplain's been telling me, I bet I'm still red in the face.

MOTHER COURAGE: And him a clergyman! I'd better give you fellows something to drink or you'll be making me immoral propositions just to pass the time.

THE CHAPLAIN: This is temptation, said the deacon, and succumbed to it. [*Turning toward Kattrin as he leaves.*] And who is this delightful young lady?

MOTHER COURAGE: She's not delightful, she's a respectable young lady.

[*The chaplain and the cook go behind the wagon with Mother Courage. Kattrin looks after them, then she walks away from the washing and approaches the hat. She picks it up, sits down and puts on the red shoes. From the rear Mother Courage is heard talking politics with the chaplain and the cook.*]

MOTHER COURAGE: The Poles here in Poland shouldn't have butted in. All right, our king marched his army into their country. But instead of keeping the peace, the Poles start butting into their own affairs and attack the king while he's marching quietly through the landscape. That was a breach of the peace and the blood is on their head.

THE CHAPLAIN: Our king had only one thing in mind: freedom. The emperor had everybody under his yoke, the Poles as much as the Germans; the king[1] had to set them free.

THE COOK: I see it this way, your brandy's first-rate, I can see why I liked your face, but we were talking about the king. This freedom he was trying to introduce into Germany cost him a fortune, he had to levy a salt tax in Sweden, which, as I said, cost the poor people a fortune. Then he had to put the Germans in jail and break them on the rack because they liked being the emperor's slaves. Oh yes, the king made short shrift of anybody that didn't want to be free. In the beginning he only wanted to protect Poland against wicked people, especially the emperor, but the more he ate the more he wanted, and pretty soon he was protecting all of Germany. But the Germans didn't take it lying down and the king got nothing but trouble for all his kindness and expense, which he naturally had to defray from taxes, which made for bad blood, but that didn't discourage him. He had one thing in his favor, the word of God, which was lucky, because otherwise people would have said he was doing it all for himself and what he hoped to get out of it. As it was, he always had a clear conscience and that was all he really cared about.

MOTHER COURAGE: It's easy to see you're not a Swede, or you wouldn't talk like that about the Hero-King.

THE CHAPLAIN: You're eating his bread, aren't you?

THE COOK: I don't eat his bread, I bake it.

MOTHER COURAGE: He can't be defeated because his men believe in him. [*Earnestly.*] When you listen to the big wheels talk, they're making war for reasons of piety, in the name of everything that's fine and noble. But when you take another look, you see that they're not so dumb; they're making war for profit. If they weren't, the small fry like me wouldn't have anything to do with it.

THE COOK: That's a fact.

THE CHAPLAIN: And it wouldn't hurt you as a Dutchman to take a look at that flag up there before you express opinions in Poland.

MOTHER COURAGE: We're all good Protestants here! Prosit!

[*Kattrin has started strutting about with Yvette's hat on, imitating Yvette's gait.*]

1. Gustav II Adolf of Sweden, who marched into Poland against the Holy Roman Emperor Ferdinand II of Habsburg.

[*Suddenly cannon fire and shots are heard. Drums. Mother Courage, the cook and the chaplain run out from behind the wagon, the two men still with glasses in hand. The ordnance officer and a soldier rush up to the cannon and try to push it away.*]

MOTHER COURAGE: What's going on? Let me get my washing first, you lugs. [*She tries to rescue her washing.*]

THE ORDNANCE OFFICER: The Catholics. They're attacking. I don't know as we'll get away. [*To the soldier.*] Get rid of the gun! [*Runs off.*]

THE COOK: Christ, I've got to find the general. Courage, I'll be back for a little chat in a day or two. [*Rushes out.*]

MOTHER COURAGE: Stop, you've forgotten your pipe.

THE COOK [*from the distance*]: Keep it for me! I'll need it.

MOTHER COURAGE: Just when we were making a little money!

THE CHAPLAIN: Well, I guess I'll be going too. It might be dangerous though, with the enemy so close. Blessed are the peaceful is the best motto in wartime. If only I had a cloak to cover up with.

MOTHER COURAGE: I'm not lending any cloaks, not on your life. I've had bitter experience in that line.

THE CHAPLAIN: But my religion puts me in special danger.

MOTHER COURAGE [*bringing him a cloak*]: It's against my better conscience. And now run along.

THE CHAPLAIN: Thank you kindly, you've got a good heart. But maybe I'd better sit here a while. The enemy might get suspicious if they see me running.

MOTHER COURAGE [*to the soldier*]: Leave it lay, you fool, you won't get paid extra. I'll take care of it for you, you'd only get killed.

THE SOLDIER [*running away*]: I tried. You're my witness.

MOTHER COURAGE: I'll swear it on the Bible. [*Sees her daughter with the hat.*] What are you doing with that floozy hat? Take it off, have you gone out of your mind? Now of all times, with the enemy on top of us? [*She tears the hat off Kattrin's head.*] You want them to find you and make a whore out of you? And those shoes! Take them off, you woman of Babylon! [*She tries to pull them off.*] Jesus Christ, chaplain, make her take those shoes off! I'll be right back. [*She runs to the wagon.*]

YVETTE [*enters, powdering her face*]: What's this I hear? The Catholics are coming? Where's my hat? Who's been stamping on it? I can't be seen like this if the Catholics are coming. What'll they think of me? I haven't even got a mirror. [*To the chaplain.*] How do I look? Too much powder?

THE CHAPLAIN: Just right.

YVETTE: And where are my red shoes? [*She doesn't see them because Kattrin hides her feet under her skirt.*] I left them here. I've got to get back to my tent. In my bare feet. It's disgraceful! [*Goes out.*]

[*Swiss Cheese runs in carrying a small box.*]

MOTHER COURAGE [*comes out with her hands full of ashes. To Kattrin*]: Ashes. [*To Swiss Cheese.*] What you got there?

SWISS CHEESE: The regimental funds.

MOTHER COURAGE: Throw it away! No more paymastering for you.

SWISS CHEESE: I'm responsible for it. [*He goes rear.*]

MOTHER COURAGE [*to the chaplain*]: Take your clergyman's coat off, chaplain, or they'll recognize you, cloak or no cloak. [*She rubs Kattrin's face with ashes.*] Hold still! There. With a little dirt you'll be safe. What a mess! The sentries were drunk. Hide your light under a bushel, as the Good Book says. When a soldier, especially a Catholic, sees a clean face, she's a whore before she knows it. Nobody feeds them for weeks. When they finally loot some provisions, the next thing they want is women. That'll do it. Let me look at you. Not bad. Like you'd been wallowing in a pigsty. Stop shaking. You're safe now. [*To Swiss Cheese.*] What did you do with the cashbox?

SWISS CHEESE: I thought I'd put it in the wagon.

MOTHER COURAGE [*horrified*]: What! In my wagon? Of all the sinful stupidity! If my back is turned for half a second! They'll hang us all!

SWISS CHEESE: Then I'll put it somewhere else, or I'll run away with it.

MOTHER COURAGE: You'll stay right here. It's too late.

THE CHAPLAIN [*still changing, comes forward*]: Heavens, the flag!

MOTHER COURAGE [*takes down the regimental flag*]: Bozhe moi![2] I'm so used to it I don't see it. Twenty-five years I've had it.

[*The cannon fire grows louder.*]

[*Morning, three days later. The cannon is gone. Mother Courage, Kattrin, the chaplain and Swiss Cheese are sitting dejectedly over a meal.*]

SWISS CHEESE: This is the third day I've been sitting here doing nothing; the sergeant has always been easy on me, but now he must be starting to wonder: where can Swiss Cheese be with the cashbox?

MOTHER COURAGE: Be glad they haven't tracked you down.

THE CHAPLAIN: What about me? I can't hold a service here either. The Good Book says: "Whosoever hath a full heart, his tongue runneth over."[3] Heaven help me if mine runneth over.

MOTHER COURAGE: That's the way it is. Look what I've got on my hands: one with a religion and one with a cashbox. I don't know which is worse.

THE CHAPLAIN: Tell yourself that we're in the hands of God.

MOTHER COURAGE: I don't think we're that bad off, but all the same I can't sleep at night. If it weren't for you, Swiss Cheese, it'd be easier. I think I've put myself in the clear. I told them I was against the antichrist; he's a Swede with horns, I told them, and I'd noticed the left horn was kind of worn down. I interrupted the questioning to ask where I could buy holy candles cheap. I knew what to say because Swiss Cheese's father was a Catholic and he used to make jokes about it. They didn't really believe me, but their regiment had no provisioner, so they looked the other way. Maybe we stand to gain. We're prisoners, but so are lice on a dog.

THE CHAPLAIN: This milk is good. Though there's not very much of it or of anything else. Maybe we'll have to cut down on our Swedish appetites. But such is the lot of the vanquished.

MOTHER COURAGE: Who's vanquished? Victory and defeat don't always mean the same thing to the big wheels up top and the small fry underneath. Not by a long shot. In some cases defeat is a blessing to the small fry. Honor's lost, but nothing

2. My God! (Russian).

3. "For out of the abundance of the heart the mouth speaks" (Matthew 12:34, Luke 6:45).

else. One time in Livonia[4] our general got such a shellacking from the enemy that in the confusion I laid hands on a beautiful white horse from the baggage train. That horse pulled my wagon for seven months, until we had a victory and they checked up. On the whole, you can say that victory and defeat cost us plain people plenty. The best thing for us is when politics gets bogged down. [*To Swiss Cheese.*] Eat!

SWISS CHEESE: I've lost my appetite. How's the sergeant going to pay the men?

MOTHER COURAGE: Troops never get paid when they're running away.

SWISS CHEESE: But they've got it coming to them. If they're not paid, they don't need to run. Not a step.

MOTHER COURAGE: Swiss Cheese, you're too conscientious, it almost frightens me. I brought you up to be honest, because you're not bright, but somewhere it's got to stop. And now me and the chaplain are going to buy a Catholic flag and some meat. Nobody can buy meat like the chaplain, he goes into a trance and heads straight for the best piece, I guess it makes his mouth water and that shows him the way. At least they let me carry on my business. Nobody cares about a shopkeeper's religion, all they want to know is the price. Protestant pants are as warm as any other kind.

THE CHAPLAIN: Like the friar said when somebody told him the Lutherans were going to stand the whole country on its head. They'll always need beggars, he says. [*Mother Courage disappears into the wagon.*] But she's worried about that cashbox. They've taken no notice of us so far, they think we're all part of the wagon, but how long can that go on?

SWISS CHEESE: I can take it away.

THE CHAPLAIN: That would be almost more dangerous. What if somebody sees you? They've got spies. Yesterday morning, just as I'm relieving myself, one of them jumps out of the ditch. I was so scared I almost let out a prayer. That would have given me away. I suppose they think they can tell a Protestant by the smell of his shit. He was a little runt with a patch over one eye.

MOTHER COURAGE [*climbing down from the wagon with a basket*]: Look what I've found. You shameless slut! [*She holds up the red shoes triumphantly.*] Yvette's red shoes! She's swiped them in cold blood. It's your fault. Who told her she was a delightful young lady? [*She puts them into the basket.*] I'm giving them back. Stealing Yvette's shoes! She ruins herself for money, that I can understand. But you'd like to do it free of charge, for pleasure. I've told you, you'll have to wait for peace. No soldiers! Just wait for peace with your worldly ways.

THE CHAPLAIN: She doesn't seem very worldly to me.

MOTHER COURAGE: Too worldly for me. In Dalarna she was like a stone, which is all they've got around there. The people used to say: We don't see the cripple. That's the way I like it. That way she's safe. [*To Swiss Cheese.*] You leave that box where it is, hear? And keep an eye on your sister, she needs it. The two of you will be the death of me. I'd sooner take care of a bag of fleas. [*She goes off with the chaplain. Kattrin starts clearing away the dishes.*]

SWISS CHEESE: Won't be many more days when I can sit in the sun in my shirtsleeves. [*Kattrin points to a tree.*] Yes, the leaves are all yellow. [*Kattrin asks him, by means of gestures, whether he wants a drink.*] Not now. I'm thinking. [*Pause.*] She

---

4. A region that included present-day northern Latvia and southern Estonia.

says she can't sleep. I'd better get the cashbox out of here, I've found a hiding place. All right, get me a drink. [*Kattrin goes behind the wagon.*] I'll hide it in the rabbit hole down by the river until I can take it away. Maybe late tonight. I'll go get it and take it to the regiment. I wonder how far they've run in three days? Won't the sergeant be surprised! Well, Swiss Cheese, this is a pleasant disappointment, that's what he'll say. I trust you with the regimental cashbox and you bring it back.

[*As Kattrin comes out from behind the wagon with a glass of brandy, she comes face to face with two men. One is a sergeant. The other removes his hat and swings it through the air in a ceremonious greeting. He has a patch over one eye.*]

THE MAN WITH THE PATCH: Good morning, my dear. Have you by any chance seen a man from the headquarters of the Second Finnish Regiment?

[*Scared out of her wits, Kattrin runs front, spilling the brandy. The two exchange looks and withdraw after seeing Swiss Cheese sitting there.*]

SWISS CHEESE [*starting up from his thoughts*]: You've spilled half of it. What's the fuss about? Poke yourself in the eye? I don't understand you. I'm getting out of here. I've made up my mind, it's best. [*He stands up. She does everything she can think of to call his attention to the danger. He only evades her.*] I wish I could understand you. Poor thing, I know you're trying to tell me something, you just can't say it. Don't worry about spilling the brandy, I'll be drinking plenty more. What's one glass? [*He takes the cashbox out of the wagon and bides it under his jacket.*] I'll be right back. Let me go, you're making me angry. I know you mean well. If only you could talk.

[*When she tries to hold him back, he kisses her and tears himself away. He goes out. She is desperate, she races back and forth, uttering short inarticulate sounds. The chaplain and Mother Courage come back. Kattrin gesticulates wildly at her mother.*]

MOTHER COURAGE: What's the matter? You're all upset. Has somebody hurt you? Where's Swiss Cheese? Tell it to me in order, Kattrin. Your mother understands you. What, the no-good's taken the cashbox? I'll hit him over the head with it, the sneak. Take your time, don't talk nonsense, use your hands, I don't like it when you howl like a dog, what will the chaplain think? It gives him the creeps. A one-eyed man?

THE CHAPLAIN: The one-eyed man is a spy. Did they arrest Swiss Cheese? [*Kattrin shakes her head and shrugs her shoulders.*] We're done for.

MOTHER COURAGE [*takes a Catholic flag out of her basket. The chaplain fastens it to the flagpole*]: Hoist the new flag!

THE CHAPLAIN [*bitterly*]: All good Catholics here.

[*Voices are heard from the rear. The two men bring in Swiss Cheese.*]

SWISS CHEESE: Let me go, I haven't got anything. Stop twisting my shoulder, I'm innocent.

THE SERGEANT: He belongs here. You know each other.

MOTHER COURAGE: What makes you think that?

SWISS CHEESE: I don't know them. I don't even know who they are. I had a meal here, it cost me ten hellers. Maybe you saw me sitting here, it was too salty.

THE SERGEANT: Who are you anyway?

MOTHER COURAGE: We're respectable people. And it's true. He had a meal here. He said it was too salty.

THE SERGEANT: Are you trying to tell me you don't know each other?

MOTHER COURAGE: Why should I know him? I don't know everybody. I don't ask people what their name is or if they're heathens; if they pay, they're not heathens. Are you a heathen?

SWISS CHEESE: Of course not.

THE CHAPLAIN: He ate his meal and he behaved himself. He didn't open his mouth except when he was eating. Then you have to.

THE SERGEANT: And who are you?

MOTHER COURAGE: He's only my bartender. You gentlemen must be thirsty, I'll get you a drink of brandy, you must be hot and tired.

THE SERGEANT: We don't drink on duty. [*To Swiss Cheese.*] You were carrying something. You must have hidden it by the river. You had something under your jacket when you left here.

MOTHER COURAGE: Was it really him?

SWISS CHEESE: I think you must have seen somebody else. I saw a man running with something under his jacket. You've got the wrong man.

MOTHER COURAGE: That's what I think too, it's a misunderstanding. These things happen. I'm a good judge of people, I'm Mother Courage, you've heard of me, everybody knows me. Take it from me, this man has an honest face.

THE SERGEANT: We're looking for the cashbox of the Second Finnish Regiment. We know what the man in charge of it looks like. We've been after him for two days. You're him.

SWISS CHEESE: I'm not.

THE SERGEANT: Hand it over. If you don't you're a goner, you know that. Where is it?

MOTHER COURAGE [*with urgency*]: He'd hand it over, wouldn't he, knowing he was a goner if he didn't? I've got it, he'd say, take it, you're stronger. He's not that stupid. Speak up, you stupid idiot, the sergeant's giving you a chance.

SWISS CHEESE: But I haven't got it.

THE SERGEANT: In that case come along. We'll get it out of you. [*They lead him away.*]

MOTHER COURAGE [*shouts after them*]: He'd tell you. He's not that stupid. And don't twist his shoulder off! [*Runs after them.*]

[*The same evening. The chaplain and mute Kattrin are washing dishes and scouring knives.*]

THE CHAPLAIN: That boy's in trouble. There are cases like that in the Bible. Take the Passion of our Lord and Saviour.
There's an old song about it. [*He sings the Song of the Hours.*]

> In the first hour Jesus mild
> Who had prayed since even
> Was betrayed and led before
> Pontius the heathen.
>
> Pilate found him innocent
> Free from fault and error.
> Therefore, having washed his hands
> Sent him to King Herod.
>
> In the third hour he was scourged
> Stripped and clad in scarlet
> And a plaited crown of thorns
> Set upon his forehead.

On the Son of Man they spat
Mocked him and made merry.
Then the cross of death was brought
Given him to carry.

At the sixth hour with two thieves
To the cross they nailed him
And the people and the thieves
Mocked him and reviled him.

This is Jesus King of Jews
Cried they in derision
Till the sun withdrew its light
From that awful vision.

At the ninth hour Jesus wailed
Why hast thou me forsaken?
Soldiers brought him vinegar
Which he left untaken.

Then he yielded up the ghost
And the earth was shaken.
Rended was the temple's veil
And the saints were wakened.

Soldiers broke the two thieves' legs
As the night descended
Thrust a spear in Jesus' side
When his life had ended.

Still they mocked, as from his wound
Flowed the blood and water
Thus blasphemed the Son of Man
With their cruel laughter.

MOTHER COURAGE [*enters in a state of agitation*]: His life's at stake. But they say the sergeant will listen to reason. Only it mustn't come out that he's our Swiss Cheese, or they'll say we've been giving him aid and comfort. All they want is money. But where will we get the money? Hasn't Yvette been here? I met her just now, she's latched onto a colonel, he's thinking of buying her a provisioner's business.

THE CHAPLAIN: Are you really thinking of selling?

MOTHER COURAGE: How else can I get the money for the sergeant?

THE CHAPLAIN: But what will you live on?

MOTHER COURAGE: That's the hitch.

[*Yvette Pottier comes in with a doddering colonel.*]

YVETTE [*embracing Mother Courage*]: My dear Mother Courage. Here we are again! [*Whispering.*] He's willing. [*Aloud.*] This is my dear friend who advises me on business matters. I just chanced to hear that you wish to sell your wagon, due to circumstances. I might be interested.

MOTHER COURAGE: Mortgage it, not sell it, let's not be hasty. It's not so easy to buy a wagon like this in wartime.

YVETTE [*disappointed*]: Only mortgage it? I thought you wanted to sell it. In that case, I don't know if I'm interested. [*To the colonel.*] What do you think?

THE COLONEL: Just as you say, my dear.

MOTHER COURAGE: It's only being mortgaged.

YVETTE: I thought you needed money.

MOTHER COURAGE [*firmly*]: I need the money, but I'd rather run myself ragged looking for an offer than sell now. The wagon is our livelihood. It's an opportunity for you, Yvette, God knows when you'll find another like it and have such a good friend to advise you. See what I mean?

YVETTE: My friend thinks I should snap it up, but I don't know. If it's only being mortgaged . . . Don't you agree that we ought to buy?

THE COLONEL: Yes, my dear.

MOTHER COURAGE: Then you'll have to look for something that's for sale, maybe you'll find something if you take your time and your friend goes around with you. Maybe in a week or two you'll find the right thing.

YVETTE: Then we'll go looking, I love to go looking for things, and I love to go around with you, Poldi, it's a real pleasure. Even if it takes two weeks. When would you pay the money back if you get it?

MOTHER COURAGE: I can pay it back in two weeks, maybe one.

YVETTE: I can't make up my mind, Poldi, chéri, tell me what to do. [*She takes the colonel aside.*] I know she's got to sell, that's definite. The lieutenant, you know who I mean, the blond one, he'd be glad to lend me the money. He's mad about me, he says I remind him of somebody. What do you think?

THE COLONEL: Keep away from that lieutenant. He's no good. He'll take advantage. Haven't I told you I'd buy you something, pussykins?

YVETTE: I can't accept it from you. But then if you think the lieutenant might take advantage . . . Poldi, I'll accept it from you.

THE COLONEL: I hope so.

YVETTE: Your advice is to take it?

THE COLONEL: That's my advice.

YVETTE [*goes back to Mother Courage*]: My friend advises me to do it. Write me out a receipt, say the wagon belongs to me complete with stock and furnishings when the two weeks are up. We'll take inventory right now, then I'll bring you the two hundred guilders. [*To the colonel.*] You go back to camp, I'll join you in a little while, I've got to take inventory, I don't want anything missing from my wagon. [*She kisses him. He leaves. She climbs up in the wagon.*] I don't see very many boots.

MOTHER COURAGE: Yvette. This is no time to inspect your wagon if it is yours. You promised to see the sergeant about my Swiss Cheese, you've got to hurry. They say he's to be court-martialed in an hour.

YVETTE: Just let me count the shirts.

MOTHER COURAGE [*pulls her down by the skirt*]: You hyena, it's Swiss Cheese, his life's at stake. And don't tell anybody where the offer comes from, in heaven's name say it's your gentleman friend, or we'll all get it, they'll say we helped him.

YVETTE: I've arranged to meet One-Eye in the woods, he must be there already.

THE CHAPLAIN: And there's no need to start out with the whole two hundred, offer a hundred and fifty, that's plenty.

MOTHER COURAGE: Is it your money? You just keep out of this. Don't worry, you'll get your bread and soup. Go on now and don't haggle. It's his life. [*She gives Yvette a push to start her on her way.*]

THE CHAPLAIN: I didn't mean to butt in, but what are we going to live on? You've got an unemployable daughter on your hands.

MOTHER COURAGE: You muddlehead, I'm counting on the regimental cashbox. They'll allow for his expenses, won't they?

THE CHAPLAIN: But will she handle it right?

MOTHER COURAGE: It's in her own interest. If I spend her two hundred, she gets the wagon. She's mighty keen on it, how long can she expect to hold on to her colonel? Kattrin, you scour the knives, use pumice. And you, don't stand around like Jesus on the Mount of Olives, bestir yourself, wash those glasses, we're expecting at least fifty for dinner, and then it'll be the same old story: "Oh my feet, I'm not used to running around, I don't run around in the pulpit." I think they'll set him free. Thank God they're open to bribery. They're not wolves, they're human and out for money. Bribe-taking in humans is the same as mercy in God. It's our only hope. As long as people take bribes, you'll have mild sentences and even the innocent will get off once in a while.

YVETTE [comes in panting]: They want two hundred. And we've got to be quick. Or it'll be out of their hands. I'd better take One-Eye to see my colonel right away. He confessed that he'd had the cashbox, they put the thumb screws on him. But he threw it in the river when he saw they were after him. The box is gone. Should I run and get the money from my colonel?

MOTHER COURAGE: The box is gone? How will I get my two hundred back?

YVETTE: Ah, so you thought you could take it out of the cashbox? You thought you'd put one over on me. Forget it. If you want to save Swiss Cheese, you'll just have to pay, or maybe you'd like me to drop the whole thing and let you keep your wagon?

MOTHER COURAGE: This is something I hadn't reckoned with. But don't rush me, you'll get the wagon, I know it's down the drain, I've had it for seventeen years. Just let me think a second, it's all so sudden. What'll I do, I can't give them two hundred, I guess you should have bargained. If I haven't got a few guilders to fall back on, I'll be at the mercy of the first Tom, Dick, or Harry. Say I'll give them a hundred and twenty, I'll lose my wagon anyway.

YVETTE: They won't go along. One-Eye's in a hurry, he's so keyed-up he keeps looking behind him. Hadn't I better give them the whole two hundred?

MOTHER COURAGE [in despair]: I can't do it. Thirty years I've worked. She's twenty-five and no husband. I've got her to keep too. Don't needle me, I know what I'm doing. Say a hundred and twenty or nothing doing.

YVETTE: It's up to you. [Goes out quickly.]

[Mother Courage looks neither at the chaplain nor at her daughter. She sits down to help Kattrin scour the knives.]

MOTHER COURAGE: Don't break the glasses. They're not ours any more. Watch what you're doing, you'll cut yourself. Swiss Cheese will be back, I'll pay two hundred if I have to. You'll have your brother. With eighty guilders we can buy a peddler's pack and start all over. Worse things have happened.

THE CHAPLAIN: The Lord will provide.

MOTHER COURAGE: Rub them dry. [They scour the knives in silence. Suddenly Kattrin runs sobbing behind the wagon.]

YVETTE [comes running]: They won't go along. I warned you. One-Eye wanted to run out on me, he said it was no use. He said we'd hear the drums any minute, meaning he'd been sentenced. I offered a hundred and fifty. He didn't even bother to shrug his shoulders. When I begged and pleaded, he promised to wait till I'd spoken to you again.

MOTHER COURAGE: Say I'll give him the two hundred. Run.

[*Yvette runs off. They sit in silence. The chaplain has stopped washing the glasses.*]

Maybe I bargained too long.

[*Drums are heard in the distance. The chaplain stands up and goes to the rear. Mother Courage remains seated. It grows dark. The drums stop. It grows light again. Mother Courage has not moved.*]

YVETTE [*enters, very pale*]: Now you've done it with your haggling and wanting to keep your wagon. Eleven bullets he got, that's all. I don't know why I bother with you any more, you don't deserve it. But I've picked up a little information. They don't believe the cashbox is really in the river. They suspect it's here and they think you were connected with him. They're going to bring him here, they think maybe you'll give yourself away when you see him. I'm warning you: You don't know him, or you're all dead ducks. I may as well tell you, they're right behind me. Should I keep Kattrin out of the way? [*Mother Courage shakes her head.*] Does she know? Maybe she didn't hear the drums or maybe she didn't understand.

MOTHER COURAGE: She knows. Get her.

[*Yvette brings Kattrin, who goes to her mother and stands beside her. Mother Courage takes her by the hand. Two soldiers come in with a stretcher on which something is lying under a sheet. The sergeant walks beside them. They set the stretcher down.*]

THE SERGEANT: We've got a man here and we don't know his name. We need it for the records. He had a meal with you. Take a look, see if you know him. [*He removes the sheet.*] Do you know him? [*Mother Courage shakes her head.*] What? You'd never seen him before he came here for a meal? [*Mother Courage shakes her head.*] Pick him up. Throw him on the dump. Nobody knows him. [*They carry him away.*]

4

Mother Courage sings the Song of the Great Capitulation.

    Outside an officer's tent.

    Mother Courage is waiting. A clerk looks out of the tent.

THE CLERK: I know you. You had a Protestant paymaster at your place, he was hiding. I wouldn't put in any complaints if I were you.

MOTHER COURAGE: I'm putting in a complaint. I'm innocent. If I take this lying down, it'll look as if I had a guilty conscience. First they ripped up my whole wagon with their sabers, then they wanted me to pay a fine of five talers for no reason at all.

THE CLERK: I'm advising you for your own good: Keep your trap shut. We haven't got many provisioners and we'll let you keep on with your business, especially if you've got a guilty conscience and pay a fine now and then.

MOTHER COURAGE: I'm putting in a complaint.

THE CLERK: Have it your way. But you'll have to wait till the captain can see you. [*Disappears into the tent.*]

A YOUNG SOLDIER [*enters in a rage*]: Bouque la Madonne! Where's that stinking captain? He embezzled my reward and now he's drinking it up with his whores. I'm going to get him!

AN OLDER SOLDIER [*comes running after him*]: Shut up. They'll put you in the stocks!

THE YOUNG SOLDIER: Come on out, you crook! I'll make chops out of you. Embezzling my reward! Who jumps in the river? Not another man in the whole squad, only me. And I can't even buy myself a beer. I won't stand for it. Come on out and let me cut you to pieces!

THE OLDER SOLDIER: Holy Mary! He'll ruin himself.

MOTHER COURAGE: They didn't give him a reward?

THE YOUNG SOLDIER: Let me go. I'll run you through too, the more the merrier.

THE OLDER SOLDIER: He saved the colonel's horse and they didn't give him a reward. He's young, he hasn't been around long.

MOTHER COURAGE: Let him go, he's not a dog, you don't have to tie him up. Wanting a reward is perfectly reasonable. Why else would he distinguish himself?

THE YOUNG SOLDIER: And him drinking in there! You're all a lot of yellowbellies. I distinguished myself and I want my reward.

MOTHER COURAGE: Young man, don't shout at me. I've got my own worries and besides, go easy on your voice, you may need it. You'll be hoarse when the captain comes out, you won't be able to say boo and he won't be able to put you in the stocks till you're blue in the face. People that yell like that don't last long, maybe half an hour, then they're so exhausted you have to sing them to sleep.

THE YOUNG SOLDIER: I'm not exhausted and who wants to sleep? I'm hungry. They make our bread out of acorns and hemp seed, and they skimp on that. He's whoring away my reward and I'm hungry. I'll murder him.

MOTHER COURAGE: I see. You're hungry. Last year your general made you cut across the fields to trample down the grain. I could have sold a pair of boots for ten guilders if anybody'd had ten guilders and if I'd had any boots. He thought he'd be someplace else this year, but now he's still here and everybody's starving. I can see that you might be good and mad.

THE YOUNG SOLDIER: He can't do this to me, save your breath, I won't put up with injustice.

MOTHER COURAGE: You're right, but for how long? How long won't you put up with injustice? An hour? Two hours? You see, you never thought of that, though it's very important, because it's miserable in the stocks when it suddenly dawns on you that you *can* put up with injustice.

THE YOUNG SOLDIER: I don't know why I listen to you. Bouque la Madonne! Where's the captain?

MOTHER COURAGE: You listen to me because I'm not telling you anything new. You know your temper has gone up in smoke, it was a short temper and you need a long one, but that's a hard thing to come by.

THE YOUNG SOLDIER: Are you trying to say I've no right to claim my reward?

MOTHER COURAGE: Not at all. I'm only saying your temper isn't long enough, it won't get you anywhere. Too bad. If you had a long temper, I'd even egg you on. Chop the bastard up, that's what I'd say, but suppose you don't chop him up, because your tail's drooping and you know it. I'm left standing there like a fool and the captain takes it out on me.

THE OLDER SOLDIER: You're right. He's only blowing off steam.

THE YOUNG SOLDIER: We'll see about that. I'll cut him to pieces. [*He draws his sword.*] When he comes out, I'll cut him to pieces.

THE CLERK [*looks out*]: The captain will be here in a moment. Sit down.

[*The young soldier sits down.*]

MOTHER COURAGE: There he sits. What did I tell you? Sitting, aren't you? Oh, they know us like a book, they know how to handle us. Sit down! And down we sit. You can't start a riot sitting down. Better not stand up again, you won't be able to stand the way you were standing before. Don't be embarrassed on my account, I'm no better, not a bit of it. We were full of piss and vinegar, but they've bought it off. Look at me. No back talk, it's bad for business. Let me tell you about the great ca-pitulation. [*She sings the Song of the Great Capitulation.*]

> *When I was young, no more than a spring chicken*
> *I too thought that I was really quite the cheese*

(No common peddler's daughter, not I with my looks and my talent and striving for higher things!)

> *One little hair in the soup would make me sicken*
> *And at me no man would dare to sneeze.*

(It's all or nothing, no second best for me. I've got what it takes, the rules are for somebody else!)

> *But a chickadee*
> *Sang wait and see!*
> *And you go marching with the show*
> *In step, however fast or slow*
> *And rattle off your little song:*
> *It won't be long.*
> *And then the whole thing slides.*
> *You think God provides—*
> *But you've got it wrong.*

> *And before one single year had wasted*
> *I had learned to swallow down the bitter brew*

(Two kids on my hands and the price of bread and who do they take me for anyway!)

> *Man, the double-edged shellacking that I tasted*
> *On my ass and knees I was when they were through.*

(You've got to get along with people, one good turn deserves another, no use try-ing to ram your head through the wall!)

> *And the chickadee*
> *Sang wait and see!*
> *And she goes marching with the show*
> *In step, however fast or slow*
> *And rattles off her little song:*
> *It won't be long.*
> *And then the whole thing slides*
> *You think God provides—*
> *But you've got it wrong.*

> *I've seen many fired by high ambition*
> *No star's big or high enough to reach out for.*

(It's ability that counts, where there's a will there's a way, one way or another we'll swing it!)

Then while moving mountains they get a suspicion
That to wear a straw hat is too big a chore.

(No use being too big for your britches!)

And the chickadee
Sings wait and see!
And they go marching with the show
In step, however fast or slow
And rattle off their little song:
It won't be long.
And then the whole thing slides!
You think God provides—
But you've got it wrong!

MOTHER COURAGE [*to the young soldier*]: So here's what I think: Stay here with your sword if your anger's big enough, I know you have good reason, but if it's a short quick anger, better make tracks!

THE YOUNG SOLDIER: Kiss my ass! [*He staggers off, the older soldier after him.*]

THE CLERK [*sticking his head out*]: The captain is here. You can put in your complaint now.

MOTHER COURAGE: I've changed my mind. No complaint. [*She goes out.*]

5

Two years have passed. The war has spread far and wide. With scarcely a pause Mother Courage's little wagon rolls through Poland, Moravia, Bavaria, Italy, and back again to Bavaria. 1631. Tilly's victory at Magdeburg costs Mother Courage four officers' shirts.[1]

Mother Courage's wagon has stopped in a devastated village.

Thin military music is heard from the distance. Two soldiers at the bar are being waited on by Kattrin and Mother Courage. One of them is wearing a lady's fur coat over his shoulders.

MOTHER COURAGE: What's that? You can't pay? No money, no schnapps. Plenty of victory marches for the Lord but no pay for the men.

THE SOLDIER: I want my schnapps. I came too late for the looting. The general skunked us: permission to loot the city for exactly one hour. Says he's not a monster; the mayor must have paid him.

THE CHAPLAIN [*staggers in*]: There's still some wounded in the house. The peasant and his family. Help me, somebody, I need linen.

[*The second soldier goes out with him. Kattrin gets very excited and tries to persuade her mother to hand out linen.*]

MOTHER COURAGE: I haven't got any. The regiment's bought up all my bandages. You think I'm going to rip up my officers' shirts for the likes of them?

THE CHAPLAIN [*calling back*]: I need linen, I tell you.

---

1. Johann Tserclaes, Graf von Tilly (1559–1632), was field marshal of Maximilian, Duke of Bavaria, who sided with Ferdinand II on the Catholic side. He was eventually defeated by Gustav II Adolf of Sweden in 1631. Magdeburg is located about 80 miles southwest of Berlin.

MOTHER COURAGE [*sitting down on the wagon steps to keep Kattrin out*]: Nothing doing. They don't pay, they got nothing to pay with.

THE CHAPLAIN [*bending over a woman whom he has carried out*]: Why did you stay
here in all that gunfire?

THE PEASANT WOMAN [*feebly*]: Farm.

MOTHER COURAGE: You won't catch them leaving their property. And I'm expected to
foot the bill. I won't do it.

THE FIRST SOLDIER: They're Protestants. Why do they have to be Protestants?

MOTHER COURAGE: Religion is the least of their worries. They've lost their farm.

THE SECOND SOLDIER: They're no Protestants. They're Catholics like us.

THE FIRST SOLDIER: How do we know who we're shooting at?

A PEASANT [*whom the Chaplain brings in*]: They got my arm.

THE CHAPLAIN: Where's the linen?

[*All look at Mother Courage, who does not move.*]

MOTHER COURAGE: I can't give you a thing. What with all my taxes, duties, fees and
bribes! [*Making guttural sounds, Kattrin picks up a board and threatens her
mother with it.*] Are you crazy? Put that board down, you slut, or I'll smack you.
I'm not giving anything, you can't make me, I've got to think of myself. [*The
chaplain picks her up from the step and puts her down on the ground. Then he
fishes out some shirts and tears them into strips.*] My shirts! Half a guilder apiece!
I'm ruined!

[*The anguished cry of a baby is heard from the house.*]

THE PEASANT: The baby's still in there!

[*Kattrin runs in.*]

THE CHAPLAIN [*to the woman*]: Don't move. They're bringing him out.

MOTHER COURAGE: Get her out of there. The roof'll cave in.

THE CHAPLAIN: I'm not going in there again.

MOTHER COURAGE [*torn*]: Don't run hog-wild with my expensive linen.

[*Kattrin emerges from the ruins carrying an infant.*]

MOTHER COURAGE: Oh, so you've found another baby to carry around with you? Give
that baby back to its mother this minute, or it'll take me all day to get it away from
you. Do you hear me? [*To the second soldier.*] Don't stand there gaping, go back
and tell them to stop that music, I can see right here that they've won a victory.
Your victory's costing me a pretty penny.

[*Kattrin rocks the baby in her arms, humming a lullaby.*]

MOTHER COURAGE: There she sits, happy in all this misery; give it back this minute,
the mother's coming to. [*She pounces on the first soldier who has been helping
himself to the drinks and is now making off with the bottle.*] Pshagreff! Beast!
Haven't you had enough victories for today? Pay up.

FIRST SOLDIER: I'm broke.

MOTHER COURAGE [*tears the fur coat off him*]: Then leave the coat here, it's stolen
anyway.

THE CHAPLAIN: There's still somebody in there.

6

Outside Ingolstadt in Bavaria Mother Courage attends the funeral of Tilly, the imperial field marshal. Conversations about heroes and the longevity of the war. The chaplain deplores the waste of his talents. Mute Kattrin gets the red shoes. 1632.

Inside Mother Courage's tent.

A bar open to the rear. Rain. In the distance drum rolls and funeral music. The chaplain and the regimental clerk are playing a board game. Mother Courage and her daughter are taking inventory.

THE CHAPLAIN: The procession's starting.

MOTHER COURAGE: It's a shame about the general—socks: twenty-two pairs—I hear he was killed by accident. On account of the fog in the fields. He's up front encouraging the troops. "Fight to the death, boys," he sings out. Then he rides back, but he gets lost in the fog and rides back forward. Before you know it he's in the middle of the battle and stops a bullet—lanterns: we're down to four. [*A whistle from the rear. She goes to the bar.*] You men ought to be ashamed, running out on your late general's funeral! [*She pours drinks.*]

THE CLERK: They shouldn't have been paid before the funeral. Now they're getting drunk instead.

THE CHAPLAIN [*to the clerk*]: Shouldn't you be at the funeral?

THE CLERK: In this rain?

MOTHER COURAGE: With you it's different, the rain might spoil your uniform. It seems they wanted to ring the bells, naturally, but it turned out the churches had all been shot to pieces by his orders, so the poor general won't hear any bells when they lower him into his grave. They're going to fire a three-gun salute instead, so it won't be too dull—seventeen sword belts.

CRIES [*from the bar*]: Hey! Brandy!

MOTHER COURAGE: Money first! No, you can't come into my tent with your muddy boots! You can drink outside, rain or no rain. [*To the clerk.*] I'm only letting officers in. It seems the general had been having his troubles. Mutiny in the Second Regiment because he hadn't paid them. It's a war of religion, he says, should they profit by their faith?

[*Funeral march. All look to the rear.*]

THE CHAPLAIN: Now they're marching past the body.

MOTHER COURAGE: I feel sorry when a general or an emperor passes away like this, maybe he thought he'd do something big, that posterity would still be talking about and maybe put up a statue in his honor, conquer the world, for instance, that's a nice ambition for a general, he doesn't know any better. So he knocks himself out, and then the common people come and spoil it all, because what do they care about greatness, all they care about is a mug of beer and maybe a little company. The most beautiful plans have been wrecked by the smallness of the people that are supposed to carry them out. Even an emperor can't do anything by himself, he needs the support of his soldiers and his people. Am I right?

THE CHAPLAIN [*laughing*]: Courage, you're right, except about the soldiers. They do their best. With those fellows out there, for instance, drinking their brandy in the rain, I'll undertake to carry on one war after another for a hundred years, two at once if I have to, and I'm not a general by trade.

MOTHER COURAGE: Then you don't think the war might stop?

THE CHAPLAIN: Because the general's dead? Don't be childish. They grow by the dozen, there'll always be plenty of heroes.

MOTHER COURAGE: Look here, I'm not asking you for the hell of it. I've been wondering whether to lay in supplies while they're cheap, but if the war stops, I can throw them out the window.

THE CHAPLAIN: I understand. You want a serious answer. There have always been people who say: "The war will be over some day." I say there's no guarantee the war will ever be over. Naturally a brief intermission is conceivable. Maybe the war needs a breather, a war can even break its neck, so to speak. There's always a chance of that, nothing is perfect here below. Maybe there never will be a perfect war, one that lives up to all our expectations. Suddenly, for some unforeseen reason, a war can bog down, you can't think of everything. Some little oversight and your war's in trouble. And then you've got to pull it out of the mud. But the kings and emperors, not to mention the pope, will always come to its help in adversity. On the whole, I'd say this war has very little to worry about, it'll live to a ripe old age.

A SOLDIER [*sings at the bar*]:

> *A drink, and don't be slow!*
> *A soldier's got to go*
> *And fight for his religion.*

Make it double, this is a holiday.

MOTHER COURAGE: If I could only be sure . . .

THE CHAPLAIN: Figure it out for yourself. What's to stop the war?

THE SOLDIER [*sings*]:

> *Your breasts, girl, don't be slow!*
> *A soldier's got to go*
> *And ride away to Pilsen.*[1]

THE CLERK [*suddenly*]: But why can't we have peace? I'm from Bohemia, I'd like to go home when the time comes.

THE CHAPLAIN: Oh, you'd like to go home? Ah, peace! What becomes of the hole when the cheese has been eaten?

THE SOLDIER [*sings*]:

> *Play cards, friends, don't be slow!*
> *A soldier's got to go*
> *No matter if it's Sunday.*
>
> *A prayer, priest, don't be slow!*
> *A soldier's got to go*
> *And die for king and country.*

THE CLERK: In the long run nobody can live without peace.

THE CHAPLAIN: The way I see it, war gives you plenty of peace. It has its peaceful moments. War meets every need, including the peaceful ones, everything's taken care of, or your war couldn't hold its own. In a war you can shit the same as in the dead of peace, you can stop for a beer between battles, and even on the march you can

---

1. A town near Prague in West Bohemia, in what is now the Czech Republic.

always lie down on your elbows and take a little nap by the roadside. You can't play cards when you're fighting; but then you can't when you're plowing in the dead of peace either, but after a victory the sky's the limit. Maybe you've had a leg shot off, at first you raise a howl, you make a big thing of it. But then you calm down or they give you schnapps, and in the end you're hopping around again and the war's no worse off than before. And what's to prevent you from multiplying in the thick of the slaughter, behind a barn or someplace, in the long run how can they stop you, and then the war has your progeny to help it along. Take it from me, the war will always find an answer. Why would it have to stop?

[Kattrin has stopped working and is staring at the chaplain.]

MOTHER COURAGE: Then I'll buy the merchandise. You've convinced me. *[Kattrin suddenly throws down a basket full of bottles and runs out.]* Kattrin! *[Laughs.]* My goodness, the poor thing's been hoping for peace. I promised her she'd get a husband when peace comes. *[She runs after her.]*

THE CLERK *[getting up]*: I win, you've been too busy talking. Pay up.

MOTHER COURAGE *[comes back with Kattrin]*: Be reasonable, the war'll go on a little longer and we'll make a little more money, then peace will be even better. Run along to town now, it won't take you ten minutes, and get the stuff from the Golden Lion, only the expensive things, we'll pick up the rest in the wagon later, it's all arranged, the regimental clerk here will go with you. They've almost all gone to the general's funeral, nothing can happen to you. Look sharp, don't let them take anything away from you, think of your dowry.

[Kattrin puts a kerchief over her head and goes with the clerk.]

THE CHAPLAIN: Is it all right letting her go with the clerk?

MOTHER COURAGE: Who'd want to ruin her? She's not pretty enough.

THE CHAPLAIN: I've come to admire the way you handle your business and pull through every time. I can see why they call you Mother Courage.

MOTHER COURAGE: Poor people need courage. Why? Because they're sunk. In their situation it takes gumption just to get up in the morning. Or to plow a field in the middle of a war. They even show courage by bringing children into the world, because look at the prospects. The way they butcher and execute each other, think of the courage they need to look each other in the face. And putting up with an emperor and a pope takes a whale of a lot of courage, because those two are the death of the poor. *[She sits down, takes a small pipe from her pocket and smokes.].* You could be making some kindling.

THE CHAPLAIN *[reluctantly takes his jacket off and prepares to chop]*: Chopping wood isn't really my trade, you know, I'm a shepherd of souls.

MOTHER COURAGE: Sure. But I have no soul and I need firewood.

THE CHAPLAIN: What's that pipe?

MOTHER COURAGE: Just a pipe.

THE CHAPLAIN: No, it's not "just a pipe," it's a very particular pipe.

MOTHER COURAGE: Really?

THE CHAPLAIN: It's the cook's pipe from the Oxenstjerna regiment.

MOTHER COURAGE: If you know it all, why the mealy-mouthed questions?

THE CHAPLAIN: I didn't know if *you* knew. You could have been rummaging through your belongings and laid hands on some pipe and picked it up without thinking.

MOTHER COURAGE: Yes. Maybe that's how it was.

THE CHAPLAIN: Except it wasn't. You knew who that pipe belongs to.

MOTHER COURAGE: What of it?

THE CHAPLAIN: Courage, I'm warning you. It's my duty. I doubt if you ever lay eyes on the man again, but that's no calamity, in fact you're lucky. If you ask me, he wasn't steady. Not at all.

MOTHER COURAGE: What makes you say that? He was a nice man.

THE CHAPLAIN: Oh, you think he was nice? I differ. Far be it from me to wish him any harm, but I can't say he was nice. I'd say he was a scheming Don Juan. If you don't believe me, take a look at his pipe. You'll have to admit that it shows up his character.

MOTHER COURAGE: I don't see anything. It's beat up.

THE CHAPLAIN: It's half bitten through. A violent man. That is the pipe of a ruthless, violent man, you must see that if you've still got an ounce of good sense.

MOTHER COURAGE: Don't wreck my chopping block.

THE CHAPLAIN: I've told you I wasn't trained to chop wood. I studied theology. My gifts and abilities are being wasted on muscular effort. The talents that God gave me are lying fallow. That's a sin. You've never heard me preach. With one sermon I can whip a regiment into such a state that they take the enemy for a flock of sheep. Then men care no more about their lives than they would about a smelly old sock that they're ready to throw away in hopes of final victory. God has made me eloquent. You'll swoon when you hear me preach.

MOTHER COURAGE: I don't want to swoon. What good would that do me?

THE CHAPLAIN: Courage, I've often wondered if maybe you didn't conceal a warm heart under that hard-bitten talk of yours. You too are human, you need warmth.

MOTHER COURAGE: The best way to keep this tent warm is with plenty of firewood.

THE CHAPLAIN: Don't try to put me off. Seriously, Courage, I sometimes wonder if we couldn't make our relationship a little closer. I mean, seeing that the whirlwind of war has whirled us so strangely together.

MOTHER COURAGE: Seems to me it's close enough. I cook your meals and you do chores, such as chopping wood, for instance.

THE CHAPLAIN [*goes toward her*]: You know what I mean by "closer"; it has nothing to do with meals and chopping wood and such mundane needs. Don't harden your heart, let it speak.

MOTHER COURAGE: Don't come at me with that ax. That's too close a relationship.

THE CHAPLAIN: Don't turn it to ridicule. I'm serious, I've given it careful thought.

MOTHER COURAGE: Chaplain, don't be silly. I like you, I don't want to have to scold you. My aim in life is to get through, me and my children and my wagon. I don't think of it as mine and besides I'm not in the mood for private affairs. Right now I'm taking a big risk, buying up merchandise with the general dead and everybody talking peace. What'll you do if I'm ruined? See? You don't know. Chop that wood, then we'll be warm in the evening, which is a good thing in times like these. Now what? [*She stands up.*]

[*Enter Kattrin out of breath, with a wound across her forehead and over one eye. She is carrying all sorts of things, packages, leather goods, a drum, etc.*]

MOTHER COURAGE: What's that? Assaulted? On the way back? She was assaulted on the way back. Must have been that soldier that got drunk here! I shouldn't have let you go! Throw the stuff down! It's not bad, only a flesh wound. I'll bandage it, it'll heal in a week. They're worse than wild beasts. [*She bandages the wound.*]

THE CHAPLAIN: I can't find fault with them. At home they never raped anybody. I blame the people that start wars, they're the ones that dredge up man's lowest instincts.

MOTHER COURAGE: Didn't the clerk bring you back? That's because you're respectable, they don't give a damn. It's not a deep wound, it won't leave a mark. There, all bandaged. Don't fret, I've got something for you. I've been keeping it for you on the sly, it'll be a surprise. [*She fishes Yvette's red shoes out of a sack.*] See? You've always wanted them. Now you've got them. Put them on quick before I regret it. It won't leave a mark, though I wouldn't mind if it did. The girls that attract them get the worst of it. They drag them around till there's nothing left of them. If you don't appeal to them, they won't harm you. I've seen girls with pretty faces, a few years later they'd have given a wolf the creeps. They can't step behind a bush without fearing the worst. It's like trees. The straight tall ones get chopped down for ridgepoles, the crooked ones enjoy life. In other words, it's a lucky break. The shoes are still in good condition, I've kept them nicely polished.

[*Kattrin leaves the shoes where they are and crawls into the wagon.*]

THE CHAPLAIN: I hope she won't be disfigured.

MOTHER COURAGE: There'll be a scar. She can stop waiting for peace.

THE CHAPLAIN: She didn't let them take anything.

MOTHER COURAGE: Maybe I shouldn't have drummed it into her. If I only knew what went on in her head. One night she stayed out, the only time in all these years. Afterwards she traipsed around as usual, except she worked harder. I never could find out what happened. I racked my brains for quite some time. [*She picks up the articles brought by Kattrin and sorts them angrily.*] That's war for you! A fine way to make a living!

[*Cannon salutes are heard.*]

THE CHAPLAIN: Now they're burying the general. This is a historic moment.

MOTHER COURAGE: To me it's a historic moment when they hit my daughter over the eye. She's a wreck, she'll never get a husband now, and she's so crazy about children. It's the war that made her dumb too, a soldier stuffed something in her mouth when she was little. I'll never see Swiss Cheese again and where Eilif is, God knows. God damn the war.

7

Mother Courage at the height of her business career.

Highway.

The chaplain, Mother Courage and her daughter Kattrin are pulling the wagon. New wares are hanging on it. Mother Courage is wearing a necklace of silver talers.

MOTHER COURAGE: Stop running down the war. I won't have it. I know it destroys the weak, but the weak haven't a chance in peacetime either. And war is a better provider. [*Sings.*]

> *If you're not strong enough to take it*
> *The victory will find you dead.*
> *A war is only what you make it.*
> *It's business, not with cheese but lead.*

And what good is it staying in one place? The stay-at-homes are the first to get it. [*Sings.*]

> *Some people think they'd like to ride out*
> *The war, leave danger to the brave*
> *And dig themselves a cozy hideout—*
> *They'll dig themselves an early grave.*
> *I've seen them running from the thunder*
> *To find a refuge from the war*
> *But once they're resting six feet under*
> *They wonder what they hurried for.*

[*They plod on.*]

8

In the same year Gustavus Adolphus, King of Sweden, is killed at the battle of Lützen. Peace threatens to ruin Mother Courage's business. Her brave son performs one heroic deed too many and dies an ignominious death.

A camp.

A summer morning. An old woman and her son are standing by the wagon. The son is carrying a large sack of bedding.

MOTHER COURAGE's voice [*from the wagon*]: Does it have to be at this unearthly hour?

THE YOUNG MAN: We've walked all night, twenty miles, and we've got to go back today.

MOTHER COURAGE's voice: What can I do with bedding? The people haven't any houses.

THE YOUNG MAN: Wait till you've seen it.

THE OLD WOMAN: She won't take it either. Come on.

THE YOUNG MAN: They'll sell the roof from over our heads for taxes. Maybe she'll give us three guilders if you throw in the cross. [*Bells start ringing.*] Listen, mother!

VOICES [*from the rear*]: Peace! The king of Sweden is dead!

MOTHER COURAGE [*sticks her head out of the wagon. She has not yet done her hair*]: Why are the bells ringing in the middle of the week?

THE CHAPLAIN [*crawls out from under the wagon*]: What are they shouting?

MOTHER COURAGE: Don't tell me peace has broken out when I've just taken in more supplies.

THE CHAPLAIN [*shouting toward the rear*]: Is it true? Peace?

VOICE: Three weeks ago, they say. But we just found out.

THE CHAPLAIN [*to Mother Courage*]: What else would they ring the bells for?

VOICE: There's a whole crowd of Lutherans, they've driven their carts into town. They brought the news.

THE YOUNG MAN: Mother, it's peace. What's the matter?

[*The old woman has collapsed.*]

MOTHER COURAGE [*going back into the wagon*]: Heavenly saints! Kattrin, peace! Put your black dress on! We're going to church. We owe it to Swiss Cheese. Can it be true?

THE YOUNG MAN: The people here say the same thing. They've made peace. Can you get up? [*The old woman stands up, still stunned.*] I'll get the saddle shop started again. I promise. Everything will be all right. Father will get his bed back. Can you walk? [*To the chaplain.*] She fainted. It was the news. She thought peace would never come again. Father said it would. We'll go straight home. [*Both go out.*]

MOTHER COURAGE's voice: Give her some brandy.

THE CHAPLAIN: They're gone.

MOTHER COURAGE's voice: What's going on in camp?

THE CHAPLAIN: A big crowd. I'll go see. Shouldn't I put on my clericals?

MOTHER COURAGE's voice: Better make sure before you step out in your antichrist costume. I'm glad to see peace, even if I'm ruined. At least I've brought two of my children through the war. Now I'll see my Eilif again.

THE CHAPLAIN: Look who's coming down the road. If it isn't the general's cook!

THE COOK [*rather bedraggled, carrying a bundle*]: Can I believe my eyes? The chaplain!

THE CHAPLAIN: Courage! A visitor!

[*Mother Courage climbs down.*]

THE COOK: Didn't I promise to come over for a little chat as soon as I had time? I've never forgotten your brandy, Mrs. Fierling.

MOTHER COURAGE: Mercy, the general's cook! After all these years! Where's Eilif, my eldest?

THE COOK: Isn't he here yet? He left ahead of me, he was coming to see you too.

THE CHAPLAIN: I'll put on my clericals, wait for me. [*Goes out behind the wagon.*]

MOTHER COURAGE: Then he'll be here any minute. [*Calls into the wagon.*] Kattrin, Eilif's coming! Bring the cook a glass of brandy! [*Kattrin does not appear.*] Put a lock of hair over it, and forget it! Mr. Lamb is no stranger. [*Gets the brandy herself.*] She won't come out. Peace doesn't mean a thing to her, it's come too late. They hit her over the eye, there's hardly any mark, but she thinks people are staring at her.

THE COOK: Ech, war! [*He and Mother Courage sit down.*]

MOTHER COURAGE: Cook, you find me in trouble. I'm ruined.

THE COOK: What? Say, that's a shame.

MOTHER COURAGE: Peace has done me in. Only the other day I stocked up. The chaplain's advice. And now they'll all demobilize and leave me sitting on my merchandise.

THE COOK: How could you listen to the chaplain? If I'd had time, I'd have warned you against him, but the Catholics came too soon. He's a fly-by-night. So now he's the boss here?

MOTHER COURAGE: He washed my dishes and helped me pull the wagon.

THE COOK: Him? Pulling? I guess he's told you a few of his jokes too, I wouldn't put it past him, he has an unsavory attitude toward women, I tried to reform him, it was hopeless. He's not steady.

MOTHER COURAGE: Are you steady?

THE COOK: If nothing else, I'm steady. Prosit!

MOTHER COURAGE: Steady is no good. I've only lived with one steady man, thank the Lord. I never had to work so hard, he sold the children's blankets when spring came, and he thought my harmonica was unchristian. In my opinion you're not doing yourself any good by admitting you're steady.

THE COOK: You've still got your old bite, but I respect you for it.

MOTHER COURAGE: Don't tell me you've been dreaming about my old bite.

THE COOK: Well, here we sit, with the bells of peace and your world-famous brandy, that hasn't its equal.

MOTHER COURAGE: The bells of peace don't strike my fancy right now. I don't see them paying the men, they're behind-hand already. Where does that leave me with my famous brandy? Have you been paid?

THE COOK [*hesitantly*]: Not really. That's why we demobilized ourselves. Under the circumstances, I says to myself, why should I stay on? I'll go see my friends in the meantime. So here we are.

MOTHER COURAGE: You mean you're out of funds?

THE COOK: If only they'd stop those damn bells! I'd be glad to go into some kind of business. I'm sick of being a cook. They give me roots and shoe leather to work with, and then they throw the hot soup in my face. A cook's got a dog's life these days. I'd rather be in combat, but now we've got peace. [*The chaplain appears in his original dress.*] We'll discuss it later.

THE CHAPLAIN: It's still in good condition. There were only a few moths in it.

THE COOK: I don't see why you bother. They won't take you back. Who are you going to inspire now to be an honest soldier and earn his pay at the risk of his life? Besides, I've got a bone to pick with you. Advising this lady to buy useless merchandise on the ground that the war would last forever.

THE CHAPLAIN [*heatedly*]: And why, I'd like to know, is it any of your business?

THE COOK: Because it's unscrupulous. How can you meddle in other people's business and give unsolicited advice?

THE CHAPLAIN: Who's meddling? [*To Mother Courage.*] I didn't know you were accountable to this gentleman, I didn't know you were so intimate with him.

MOTHER COURAGE: Don't get excited, the cook is only giving his private opinion. And you can't deny that your war was a dud.

THE CHAPLAIN: Courage, don't blaspheme against peace. You're a battlefield hyena.

MOTHER COURAGE: What am I?

THE COOK: If you insult this lady, you'll hear from me.

THE CHAPLAIN: I'm not talking to you. Your intentions are too obvious. [*To Mother Courage.*] But when I see you picking up peace with thumb and forefinger like a snotty handkerchief, it revolts my humanity; you don't want peace, you want war, because you profit by it, but don't forget the old saying: "He hath need of a long spoon that eateth with the devil."

MOTHER COURAGE: I've no use for war and war hasn't much use for me. Anyway, I'm not letting anybody call me a hyena, you and me are through.

THE CHAPLAIN: How can you complain about peace when it's such a relief to everybody else? On account of the old rags in your wagon?

MOTHER COURAGE: My merchandise isn't old rags, it's what I live off, and so did you.

THE CHAPLAIN: Off war, you mean. Aha!

THE COOK [*to the chaplain*]: You're a grown man, you ought to know there's no sense in giving advice. [*To Mother Courage.*] The best thing you can do now is to sell off certain articles quick, before the prices hit the floor. Dress yourself and get started, there's no time to lose.

MOTHER COURAGE: That's very sensible advice. I think I'll do it.

THE CHAPLAIN: Because the cook says so!

MOTHER COURAGE: Why didn't *you* say so? He's right, I'd better run over to the market. [*She goes into the wagon.*]

THE COOK: My round, chaplain. No presence of mind. Here's what you should have said: me give you advice? All I ever did was talk politics! Don't try to take me on. Cockfighting is undignified in a clergyman.

THE CHAPLAIN: If you don't shut up, I'll murder you, undignified or not.

THE COOK [*taking off his shoes and unwinding the wrappings from his feet*]: If the war hadn't made a godless bum out of you, you could easily come by a parsonage now that peace is here. They won't need cooks, there's nothing to cook, but people still do a lot of believing, that hasn't changed.

THE CHAPLAIN: See here, Mr. Lamb. Don't try to squeeze me out. Being a bum has made me a better man. I couldn't preach to them any more.

[*Yvette Pottier enters, elaborately dressed in black, with a cane. She is much older and fatter and heavily powdered. Behind her a servant.*]

YVETTE: Hello there! Is this the residence of Mother Courage?

CHAPLAIN: Right you are. With whom have we the pleasure?

YVETTE: The Countess Starhemberg, my good people. Where is Mother Courage?

THE CHAPLAIN [*calls into the wagon*]: Countess Starhemberg wishes to speak to you!

MOTHER COURAGE: I'm coming.

YVETTE: It's Yvette!

MOTHER COURAGE's voice: My goodness! It's Yvette!

YVETTE: Just dropped in to see how you're doing. [*The cook has turned around in horror.*] Pieter!

THE COOK: Yvette!

YVETTE: Blow me down! How did you get here?

THE COOK: In a cart.

THE CHAPLAIN: Oh, you know each other? Intimately?

YVETTE: I should think so. [*She looks the cook over.*] Fat!

THE COOK: You're not exactly willowy yourself.

YVETTE: All the same I'm glad I ran into you, you bum. Now I can tell you what I think of you.

THE CHAPLAIN: Go right ahead, spare no details, but wait until Courage comes out.

MOTHER COURAGE [*comes out with all sorts of merchandise*]: Yvette! [*They embrace.*] But what are you in mourning for?

YVETTE: Isn't it becoming? My husband the colonel died a few years ago.

MOTHER COURAGE: The old geezer that almost bought my wagon?

YVETTE: His elder brother.

MOTHER COURAGE: You must be pretty well fixed. It's nice to find somebody that's made a good thing out of the war.

YVETTE: Oh well, it's been up and down and back up again.

MOTHER COURAGE: Let's not say anything bad about colonels. They make money by the bushel.

THE CHAPLAIN: If I were you, I'd put my shoes back on again. [*To Yvette.*] Countess Starhemberg, you promised to tell us what you think of this gentleman.

THE COOK: Don't make a scene here.

MOTHER COURAGE: He's a friend of mine, Yvette.

YVETTE: He's Pete the Pipe, that's who he is.

THE COOK: Forget the nicknames, my name is Lamb.

MOTHER COURAGE [*laughs*]: Pete the Pipe! That drove the women crazy! Say, I've saved your pipe.

THE CHAPLAIN: And smoked it.

YVETTE: It's lucky I'm here to warn you. He's the worst rotter that ever infested the coast of Flanders. He ruined more girls than he's got fingers.

THE COOK: That was a long time ago. I've changed.

YVETTE: Stand up when a lady draws you into a conversation! How I loved this man! And all the while he was seeing a little bandylegged brunette, ruined her too, naturally.

THE COOK: Seems to me I started you off on a prosperous career.

YVETTE: Shut up, you depressing wreck! Watch your step with him, his kind are dangerous even when they've gone to seed.

MOTHER COURAGE [*to Yvette*]: Come along, I've got to sell my stuff before the prices drop. Maybe you can help me, with your army connections. [*Calls into the wagon.*] Kattrin, forget about church, I'm running over to the market. When Eilif comes, give him a drink. [*Goes out with Yvette.*]

YVETTE [*in leaving*]: To think that such a man could lead me astray! I can thank my lucky stars that I was able to rise in the world after that. I've put a spoke in your wheel, Pete the Pipe, and they'll give me credit for it in heaven when my time comes.

THE CHAPLAIN: Our conversation seems to illustrate the old adage: The mills of God grind slowly. What do you think of my jokes now?

THE COOK: I'm just unlucky. I'll come clean: I was hoping for a hot meal. I'm starving. And now they're talking about me, and she'll get the wrong idea. I think I'll beat it before she comes back.

THE CHAPLAIN: I think so too.

THE COOK: Chaplain, I'm fed up on peace already. Men are sinners from the cradle, fire and sword are their natural lot. I wish I were cooking for the general again, God knows where he is, I'd roast a fine fat capon, with mustard sauce and a few carrots.

THE CHAPLAIN: Red cabbage. Red cabbage with capon.

THE COOK: That's right, but he wanted carrots.

THE CHAPLAIN: He was ignorant.

THE COOK: That didn't prevent you from gorging yourself.

THE CHAPLAIN: With repugnance.

THE COOK: Anyway you'll have to admit those were good times.

THE CHAPLAIN: I might admit that.

THE COOK: Now you've called her a hyena, your good times here are over. What are you staring at?

THE CHAPLAIN: Eilif! [*Eilif enters, followed by soldiers with pikes. His hands are fettered. He is deathly pale.*] What's wrong?

EILIF: Where's mother?

THE CHAPLAIN: Gone to town.

EILIF: I heard she was here. They let me come and see her.

THE COOK [*to the soldiers*]: Where are you taking him?

A SOLDIER: No good place.

THE CHAPLAIN: What has he done?

THE SOLDIER: Broke into a farm. The peasant's wife is dead.

THE CHAPLAIN: How could you do such a thing?

EILIF: It's what I've been doing all along.

THE COOK: But in peacetime!

EILIF: Shut your trap. Can I sit down till she comes?

THE SOLDIER: We haven't time.

THE CHAPLAIN: During the war they honored him for it, he sat at the general's right hand. Then it was bravery. Couldn't we speak to the officer?

THE SOLDIER: No use. What's brave about taking a peasant's cattle?

THE COOK: It was stupid.

EILIF: If I'd been stupid, I'd have starved, wise guy.

THE COOK: And for being smart your head comes off.

THE CHAPLAIN: Let's get Kattrin at least.

EILIF: Leave her be. Get me a drink of schnapps.

THE SOLDIER: No time. Let's go!

THE CHAPLAIN: And what should we tell your mother?

EILIF: Tell her it wasn't any different, tell her it was the same. Or don't tell her anything. [*The soldiers drive him away.*]

THE CHAPLAIN: I'll go with you on your hard journey.

EILIF: I don't need any sky pilot.

THE CHAPLAIN: You don't know yet. [*He follows him.*]

THE COOK [*calls after them*]: I'll have to tell her, she'll want to see him.

THE CHAPLAIN: Better not tell her anything. Or say he was here and he'll come again, maybe tomorrow. I'll break it to her when I get back. [*Hurries out.*]

[*The cook looks after them, shaking his head, then he walks anxiously about. Finally he approaches the wagon.*]

THE COOK: Hey! Come on out! I can see why you'd hide from peace. I wish I could do it myself. I'm the general's cook, remember? Wouldn't you have a bite to eat, to do me till your mother gets back? A slice of ham or just a piece of bread while I'm waiting. [*He looks in.*] She's buried her head in a blanket.

[*The sound of gunfire in the rear.*]

MOTHER COURAGE [*runs in. She is out of breath and still has her merchandise*]: Cook, the peace is over, the war started up again three days ago. I hadn't sold my stuff yet when I found out. Heaven be praised! They're shooting each other up in town, the Catholics and Lutherans. We've got to get out of here. Kattrin, start packing. What have *you* got such a long face about? What's wrong?

THE COOK: Nothing.

MOTHER COURAGE: Something's wrong, I can tell by your expression.

THE COOK: Maybe it's the war starting up again. Now I probably won't get anything hot to eat before tomorrow night.

MOTHER COURAGE: That's a lie, cook.

THE COOK: Eilif was here. He couldn't stay.

MOTHER COURAGE: He was here? Then we'll see him on the march. I'm going with our troops this time. How does he look?

THE COOK: The same.

MOTHER COURAGE: He'll never change. The war couldn't take him away from me. He's smart. Could you help me pack? [*She starts packing.*] Did he tell you anything? Is he in good with the general? Did he say anything about his heroic deeds?

THE COOK [*gloomily*]: They say he's been at one of them again.

MOTHER COURAGE: Tell me later, we've got to be going. [*Kattrin emerges.*] Kattrin, peace is over. We're moving. [*To the cook.*] What's the matter with you?

THE COOK: I'm going to enlist.

MOTHER COURAGE: I've got a suggestion. Why don't . . . ? Where's the chaplain?

THE COOK: Gone to town with Eilif.

MOTHER COURAGE: Then come a little way with me, Lamb. I need help.

THE COOK: That incident with Yvette . . .

MOTHER COURAGE: It hasn't lowered you in my estimation. Far from it. Where there's smoke there's fire. Coming?

THE COOK: I won't say no.

MOTHER COURAGE: The Twelfth Regiment has shoved off. Take the shaft. Here's a chunk of bread. We'll have to circle around to meet the Lutherans. Maybe I'll see Eilif tonight. He's my favorite. It's been a short peace. And we're on the move again.

[*She sings, while the cook and Kattrin harness themselves to the wagon.*]

> *From Ulm to Metz, from Metz to Pilsen*
> *Courage is right there in the van.*
> *The war both in and out of season*
> *With shot and shell will feed its man.*
> *But lead alone is not sufficient*
> *The war needs soldiers to subsist!*
> *Its diet elseways is deficient.*
> *The war is hungry! So enlist!*

9

The great war of religion has been going on for sixteen years. Germany has lost more than half its population. Those whom the slaughter has spared have been laid low by epidemics. Once-flourishing countrysides are ravaged by famine. Wolves prowl through the charred ruins of the cities. In the fall of 1634 we find Mother Courage in Germany, in the Fichtelgebirge, at some distance from the road followed by the Swedish armies. Winter comes early and is exceptionally severe. Business is bad, begging is the only resort. The cook receives a letter from Utrecht[1] and is dismissed.

Outside a half-demolished presbytery.

Gray morning in early winter. Gusts of wind. Mother Courage and the cook in shabby sheepskins by the wagon.

THE COOK: No light. Nobody's up yet.

MOTHER COURAGE: But it's a priest. He'll have to crawl out of bed to ring the bells. Then he'll get himself a nice bowl of hot soup.

THE COOK: Go on, you saw the village, everything's been burned to a crisp.

MOTHER COURAGE: But somebody's here, I heard a dog bark.

THE COOK: If the priest's got anything, he won't give it away.

MOTHER COURAGE: Maybe if we sing . . .

THE COOK: I've had it up to here. [*Suddenly.*] I got a letter from Utrecht. My mother's died of cholera and the tavern belongs to me. Here's the letter if you don't believe me. It's no business of yours what my aunt says about my evil ways, but never mind, read it.

MOTHER COURAGE [*reads the letter*]: Lamb, I'm sick of roaming around, myself. I feel like a butcher's dog that pulls the meat cart but doesn't get any for himself. I've nothing left to sell and the people have no money to pay for it. In Saxony a man in rags tried to foist a cord of books on me for two eggs, and in Württemberg they'd have let their plow go for a little bag of salt. What's the good of plowing? Nothing

---

1. A city near Amsterdam in the Netherlands.

grows but brambles. In Pomerania they say the villagers have eaten up all the babies, and that nuns have been caught at highway robbery.

THE COOK: It's the end of the world.

MOTHER COURAGE: Sometimes I have visions of myself driving through hell, selling sulphur and brimstone, or through heaven peddling refreshments to the roaming souls. If me and the children I've got left could find a place where there's no shooting, I wouldn't mind a few years of peace and quiet.

THE COOK: We could open up the tavern again. Think it over, Anna. I made up my mind last night; with or without you, I'm going back to Utrecht. In fact I'm leaving today.

MOTHER COURAGE: I'll have to talk to Kattrin. It's kind of sudden, and I don't like to make decisions in the cold with nothing in my stomach. Kattrin! [*Kattrin climbs out of the wagon.*] Kattrin, I've got something to tell you. The cook and me are thinking of going to Utrecht. They've left him a tavern there. You'd be living in one place, you'd meet people. A lot of men would be glad to get a nice, well-behaved girl, looks aren't everything. I'm all for it. I get along fine with the cook. I've got to hand it to him: He's got a head for business. We'd eat regular meals, wouldn't that be nice? And you'd have your own bed, wouldn't you like that? It's no life on the road, year in year out. You'll go to rack and ruin. You're crawling with lice already. We've got to decide, you see, we could go north with the Swedes, they must be over there. [*She points to the left.*] I think we'll do it, Kattrin.

THE COOK: Anna, could I have a word with you alone?

MOTHER COURAGE: Get back in the wagon, Kattrin.

[*Kattrin climbs back in.*]

THE COOK: I interrupted you because I see there's been a misunderstanding. I thought it was too obvious to need saying. But if it isn't, I'll just have to say it. You can't take her, it's out of the question. Is that plain enough for you?

[*Kattrin sticks her head out of the wagon and listens.*]

MOTHER COURAGE: You want me to leave Kattrin?

THE COOK: Look at it this way. There's no room in the tavern. It's not one of those places with three taprooms. If the two of us put our shoulder to the wheel, we can make a living, but not three, it can't be done. Kattrin can keep the wagon.

MOTHER COURAGE: I'd been thinking she could find a husband in Utrecht.

THE COOK: Don't make me laugh! How's she going to find a husband? At her age? And dumb! And with that scar!

MOTHER COURAGE: Not so loud.

THE COOK: Shout or whisper, the truth's the truth. And that's another reason why I can't have her in the tavern. The customers won't want a sight like that staring them in the face. Can you blame them?

MOTHER COURAGE: Shut up. Not so loud, I say.

THE COOK: There's a light in the presbytery. Let's sing.

MOTHER COURAGE: How could she pull the wagon by herself? She's afraid of the war. She couldn't stand it. The dreams she must have! I hear her groaning at night. Especially after battles. What she sees in her dreams, God knows. It's pity that makes her suffer so. The other day the wagon hit a hedgehog, I found it hidden in her blanket.

THE COOK: The tavern's too small. [*He calls.*] Worthy gentleman and members of the household! We shall now sing the Song of Solomon, Julius Caesar, and other great men, whose greatness didn't help them any. Just to show you that we're

God-fearing people ourselves, which makes it hard for us, especially in the winter.
[*They sing.*]

> *You saw the wise King Solomon*
> *You know what came of him.*
> *To him all hidden things were plain.*
> *He cursed the hour gave birth to him*
> *And saw that everything was vain.*
> *How great and wise was Solomon!*
> *Now think about his case. Alas*
> *A useful lesson can be won.*
> *It's wisdom that had brought him to that pass!*
> *How happy is the man with none!*

Our beautiful song proves that virtues are dangerous things, better steer clear of them, enjoy life, eat a good breakfast, a bowl of hot soup, for instance. Take me, I haven't got any soup and wish I had, I'm a soldier, but what has my bravery in all those battles got me, nothing, I'm starving, I'd be better off if I'd stayed home like a yellowbelly. And I'll tell you why.

> *You saw the daring Caesar next*
> *You know what he became.*
> *They deified him in his life*
> *But then they killed him just the same.*
> *And as they raised the fatal knife*
> *How loud he cried: "You too, my son!"*
> *Now think about his case. Alas*
> *A useful lesson can be won.*
> *It's daring that had brought him to that pass!*
> *How happy is the man with none!*

[*In an undertone.*] They're not even looking out. Worthy gentleman and members of the household! Maybe you'll say, all right, if bravery won't keep body and soul together, try honesty. That may fill your belly or at least get you a drop to drink. Let's look into it.

> *You've heard of honest Socrates*
> *Who never told a lie.*
> *They weren't so grateful as you'd think*
> *Instead they sentenced him to die*
> *And handed him the poisoned drink.*
> *How honest was the people's noble son!*
> *Now think about his case. Alas*
> *A useful lesson can be won.*
> *His honesty had brought him to that pass.*
> *How happy is the man with none!*

Yes, they tell us to be charitable and to share what we have, but what if we haven't got anything? Maybe philanthropists have a rough time of it too, it stands to reason, they need a little something for themselves. Yes, charity is a rare virtue, because it doesn't pay.

> *St. Martin couldn't bear to see*
> *His fellows in distress.*

He saw a poor man in the snow.
"Take half my cloak!" He did, and lo!
They both of them froze none the less.
He thought his heavenly reward was won.
Now think about his case. Alas
A useful lesson can be won.
Unselfishness had brought him to that pass.
How happy is the man with none!

That's our situation. We're God-fearing folk, we stick together, we don't steal, we don't murder, we don't set fire to anything! You could say that we set an example which bears out the song, we sink lower and lower, we seldom see any soup, but if we were different, if we were thieves and murderers, maybe our bellies would be full. Because virtue isn't rewarded, only wickedness, the world needn't be like this, but it is.

And here you see God-fearing folk
Observing God's ten laws.
So far He hasn't taken heed.
You people sitting warm indoors
Help to relieve our bitter need!
Our virtue can be counted on.
Now think about our case. Alas
A useful lesson can be won.
The fear of God has brought us to this pass.
How happy is the man with none!

VOICE [*from above*]: Hey, down there! Come on up! We've got some good thick soup.

MOTHER COURAGE: Lamb, I couldn't get anything down. I know what you say makes sense, but is it your last word? We've always been good friends.

THE COOK: My last word. Think it over.

MOTHER COURAGE: I don't need to think it over. I won't leave her.

THE COOK: It wouldn't be wise, but there's nothing I can do. I'm not inhuman, but it's a small tavern. We'd better go in now, or there won't be anything left, we'll have been singing in the cold for nothing.

MOTHER COURAGE: I'll get Kattrin.

THE COOK: Better bring it down for her. They'll get a fright if the three of us barge in.

[*They go out.*]

[*Kattrin climbs out of the wagon. She is carrying a bundle. She looks around to make sure the others are gone. Then she spreads out an old pair of the cook's trousers and a skirt belonging to her mother side by side on a wheel of the wagon so they can easily be seen. She is about to leave with her bundle when Mother Courage comes out of the house.*]

MOTHER COURAGE [*with a dish of soup*]: Kattrin! Stop! Kattrin! Where do you think you're going with that bundle? Have you taken leave of your wits? [*She examines the bundle.*] She's packed her things. Were you listening? I've told him it's no go with Utrecht and his lousy tavern, what would we do there? A tavern's no place for you and me. The war still has a thing or two up its sleeve for us. [*She sees the trousers and skirt.*] You're stupid. Suppose I'd seen that and you'd been gone? [*Kattrin tries to leave, Mother Courage holds her back.*] And don't go thinking I've given him the gate on your account. It's the wagon. I won't part with the wagon, I'm used to it, it's not you, it's the wagon. We'll go in the other direction, we'll put the cook's stuff out here where he'll find it, the fool. [*She climbs up and throws down a few odds and ends to join the trousers.*] There. Now we're shut of him, you won't see me taking anyone else into the business. From now on it's you and me. This winter will go by like all the rest. Harness up, it looks like snow.

[*They harness themselves to the wagon, turn it around and pull it away. When the cook comes out he sees his things and stands dumbfounded.*]

10

Throughout 1635 Mother Courage and her daughter Kattrin pull the wagon over the roads of central Germany in the wake of the increasingly bedraggled armies.

Highway.

Mother Courage and Kattrin are pulling the wagon. They come to a peasant's house. A voice is heard singing from within.

THE VOICE:

> The rose bush in our garden
> Rejoiced our hearts in spring
> It bore such lovely flowers.
> We planted it last season
> Before the April showers.
> A garden is a blessèd thing
> It bore such lovely flowers.
>
> When winter comes a-stalking
> And gales great snow storms bring
> They trouble us but little.
> We've lately finished caulking
> The roof with moss and wattle.
> A sheltering roof's a blessèd thing
> When winter comes a-stalking.

[*Mother Courage and Kattrin have stopped to listen. Then they move on.*]

11

January 1636. The imperial troops threaten the Protestant city of Halle. The stone speaks. Mother Courage loses her daughter and goes on alone. The end of the war is not in sight.

The wagon, much the worse for wear, is standing beside a peasant house with an enormous thatch roof. The house is built against the side of a stony hill. Night.

A lieutenant and three soldiers in heavy armor step out of the woods.

THE LIEUTENANT: I don't want any noise. If anybody yells, run him through with your pikes.

FIRST SOLDIER: But we need a guide. We'll have to knock if we want them to come out.

THE LIEUTENANT: Knocking sounds natural. It could be a cow bumping against the barn wall.

[*The soldiers knock on the door. A peasant woman opens. They hold their hands over her mouth. Two soldiers go in.*]

A MAN'S VOICE [*inside*]: Who's there?

[*The soldiers bring out a peasant and his son.*]

THE LIEUTENANT [*points to the wagon, in which Kattrin has appeared*]: There's another one. [*A soldier pulls her out.*] Anybody else live here?

THE PEASANT COUPLE: This is our son.—That's a dumb girl.—Her mother's gone into the town on business.—Buying up people's belongings, they're selling cheap because they're getting out.—They're provisioners.

THE LIEUTENANT: I'm warning you to keep quiet, one squawk and you'll get a pike over the head. All right. I need somebody who can show us the path into the city. [*Points to the young peasant.*] You. Come here!

THE YOUNG PEASANT: I don't know no path.

THE SECOND SOLDIER [*grinning*]: He don't know no path.

THE YOUNG PEASANT: I'm not helping the Catholics.

THE LIEUTENANT [*to the second soldier*]: Give him a feel of your pike!

THE YOUNG PEASANT [*forced down on his knees and threatened with the pike*]: You can kill me. I won't do it.

THE FIRST SOLDIER: I know what'll make him think twice. [*He goes over to the barn.*] Two cows and an ox. Get this: If you don't help us, I'll cut them down.

THE YOUNG PEASANT: Not the animals!

THE PEASANT WOMAN [*in tears*]: Captain, spare our animals or we'll starve.

THE LIEUTENANT: If he insists on being stubborn, they're done for.

THE FIRST SOLDIER: I'll start with the ox.

THE YOUNG PEASANT [*to the old man*]: Do I have to? [*The old woman nods.*] I'll do it.

THE PEASANT WOMAN: And thank you kindly for your forbearance, Captain, for ever and ever, amen.

[*The peasant stops her from giving further thanks.*]

THE FIRST SOLDIER: Didn't I tell you? With them it's the animals that come first.

[*Led by the young peasant, the lieutenant and the soldiers continue on their way.*]

THE PEASANT: I wish I knew what they're up to. Nothing good.

THE PEASANT WOMAN: Maybe they're only scouts.—What are you doing?

THE PEASANT [*putting a ladder against the roof and climbing up*]: See if they're alone. [*On the roof.*] Men moving in the woods. All the way to the quarry. Armor in the clearing. And a cannon. It's more than a regiment. God have mercy on the city and everybody in it.

THE PEASANT WOMAN: See any light in the city?

THE PEASANT: No. They're all asleep. [*He climbs down.*] If they get in, they'll kill everybody.

THE PEASANT WOMAN: The sentry will see them in time.

THE PEASANT: They must have killed the sentry in the tower on the hill, or he'd have blown his horn.

THE PEASANT WOMAN: If there were more of us . . .

THE PEASANT: All by ourselves up here with a cripple . . .

THE PEASANT WOMAN: We can't do a thing. Do you think . . .

THE PEASANT: Not a thing.

THE PEASANT WOMAN: We couldn't get down there in the dark.

THE PEASANT: The whole hillside is full of them. We can't even give a signal.

THE PEASANT WOMAN: They'd kill us.

THE PEASANT: No, we can't do a thing.

THE PEASANT WOMAN [*to Kattrin*]: Pray, poor thing, pray! We can't stop the bloodshed. If you can't talk, at least you can pray. He'll hear you if nobody else does. I'll help you. [*All kneel, Kattrin behind the peasants.*] Our Father which art in heaven, hear our prayer. Don't let the town perish with everybody in it, all asleep and unsuspecting. Wake them, make them get up and climb the walls and see the enemy coming through the night with cannon and pikes, through the fields and down the hillside. [*Back to Kattrin.*] Protect our mother and don't let the watchman sleep, wake him before it's too late. And succor our brother-in-law, he's in there with his four children, let them not perish, they're innocent and don't know a thing. [*To Kattrin, who groans.*] The littlest is less than two, the oldest is seven. [*Horrified, Kattrin stands up.*] Our Father, hear us, for Thou alone canst help, we'll all be killed, we're weak, we haven't any pikes or anything, we are powerless and in Thine hands, we and our animals and the whole farm, and the city too, it's in Thine hands, and the enemy is under the walls with great might.

[*Kattrin has crept unnoticed to the wagon, taken something out of it, put it under her apron and climbed up the ladder to the roof of the barn.*]

THE PEASANT WOMAN: Think upon the children in peril, especially the babes in arms and the old people that can't help themselves and all God's creatures.

THE PEASANT: And forgive us our trespasses as we forgive them that trespass against us. Amen.

[*Kattrin, sitting on the roof, starts beating the drum that she has taken out from under her apron.*]

THE PEASANT WOMAN: Jesus! What's she doing?

THE PEASANT: She's gone crazy.

THE PEASANT WOMAN: Get her down, quick!

[*The peasant runs toward the ladder, but Kattrin pulls it up on the roof.*]

THE PEASANT WOMAN: She'll be the death of us all.

THE PEASANT: Stop that, you cripple!

THE PEASANT WOMAN: She'll have the Catholics down on us.

THE PEASANT [*looking around for stones*]: I'll throw rocks at you.

THE PEASANT WOMAN: Have you no pity? Have you no heart? We're dead if they find out it's us! They'll run us through!

[*Kattrin stares in the direction of the city, and goes on drumming.*]

THE PEASANT WOMAN [*to the peasant*]: I told you not to let those tramps stop here. What do they care if the soldiers drive our last animals away?

THE LIEUTENANT [*rushes in with his soldiers and the young peasant*]: I'll cut you to pieces!

THE PEASANT WOMAN: We're innocent, captain. We couldn't help it. She sneaked up there. We don't know her.

THE LIEUTENANT: Where's the ladder?

THE PEASANT: Up top.

THE LIEUTENANT [*to Kattrin*]: Throw down that drum. It's an order!

[*Kattrin goes on drumming.*]

THE LIEUTENANT: You're all in this together! This'll be the end of you!

THE PEASANT: They've felled some pine trees in the woods over there. We could get one and knock her down . . .

THE FIRST SOLDIER [*to the lieutenant*]: Request permission to make a suggestion. [*He whispers something in the lieutenant's ear. He nods.*] Listen. We've got a friendly proposition. Come down, we'll take you into town with us. Show us your mother and we won't touch a hair of her head.

[*Kattrin goes on drumming.*]

THE LIEUTENANT [*pushes him roughly aside*]: She doesn't trust you. No wonder with your mug. [*He calls up.*] If I give you my word? I'm an officer, you can trust my word of honor. [*She drums still louder.*]

THE LIEUTENANT: Nothing is sacred to her.

THE YOUNG PEASANT: It's not just her mother, lieutenant!

THE FIRST SOLDIER: We can't let this go on. They'll hear it in the city.

THE LIEUTENANT: We'll have to make some kind of noise that's louder than the drums. What could we make noise with?

THE FIRST SOLDIER: But we're not supposed to make noise.

THE LIEUTENANT: An innocent noise, stupid. A peaceable noise.

THE PEASANT: I could chop wood.

THE LIEUTENANT: That's it, chop! [*The peasant gets an ax and chops at a log.*] Harder! Harder! You're chopping for your life.

[*Listening, Kattrin has been drumming more softly. Now she looks anxiously around and goes on drumming as before.*]

THE LIEUTENANT [*to the peasant*]: Not loud enough. [*To the first soldier.*] You chop too.

THE PEASANT: There's only one ax. [*Stops chopping.*]

THE LIEUTENANT: We'll have to set the house on fire. Smoke her out.

THE PEASANT: That won't do any good, captain. If the city people see fire up here, they'll know what's afoot.

[*Still drumming, Kattrin has been listening again. Now she laughs.*]

THE LIEUTENANT: Look, she's laughing at us. I'll shoot her down, regardless. Get the musket!

[*Two soldiers run out. Kattrin goes on drumming.*]

THE PEASANT WOMAN: I've got it, captain. That's their wagon over there. If we start smashing it up, she'll stop. The wagon's all they've got.

THE LIEUTENANT [*to the young peasant*]: Smash away. [*To Kattrin.*] We'll smash your wagon if you don't stop.

[*The young peasant strikes a few feeble blows at the wagon.*]

THE PEASANT WOMAN: Stop it, you beast!

[*Kattrin stares despairingly at the wagon and emits pitiful sounds. But she goes on drumming.*]

THE LIEUTENANT: Where are those stinkers with the musket?

THE FIRST SOLDIER: They haven't heard anything in the city yet, or we'd hear their guns.

THE LIEUTENANT [*to Kattrin*]: They don't hear you. And now we're going to shoot you down. For the last time: Drop that drum!

THE YOUNG PEASANT [*suddenly throws the plank away*]: Keep on drumming! Or they'll all be killed! Keep on drumming, keep on drumming . . .

[*The soldier throws him down and hits him with his pike. Kattrin starts crying, but goes on drumming.*]

THE PEASANT WOMAN: Don't hit him in the back! My God, you're killing him.

[*The soldiers run in with the musket.*]

THE SECOND SOLDIER: The colonel's foaming at the mouth. We'll be court-martialed.

THE LIEUTENANT: Set it up! Set it up! [*To Kattrin, while the musket is being set up on its stand.*] For the last time: Stop that drumming! [*Kattrin in tears drums as loud as she can.*] Fire!

[*The soldiers fire. Kattrin is hit. She beats the drum a few times more and then slowly collapses.*]

THE LIEUTENANT: Now we'll have some quiet.

[*But Kattrin's last drumbeats are answered by the city's cannon. A confused hubbub of alarm bells and cannon is heard in the distance.*]

FIRST SOLDIER: She's done it.

1 2

Night, toward morning. The fifes and drums of troops marching away.

Outside the wagon Mother Courage sits huddled over her daughter. The peasant couple are standing beside them.

THE PEASANT [*hostile*]: You'll have to be going, woman. There's only one more regiment to come. You can't go alone.

MOTHER COURAGE: Maybe I can get her to sleep. [*She sings.*]

> Lullaby baby
> What stirs in the hay?
> The neighbor brats whimper
> Mine are happy and gay.
> They go in tatters
> And you in silk down
> Cut from an angel's
> Best party gown.
>
> They've nothing to munch on
> And you will have pie
> Just tell your mother
> In case it's too dry.
> Lullaby baby
> What stirs in the hay?
> The one lies in Poland
> The other—who can say?

Now she's asleep. You shouldn't have told her about your brother-in-law's children.

THE PEASANT: Maybe it wouldn't have happened if you hadn't gone to town to swindle people.

MOTHER COURAGE: I'm glad she's sleeping now.

THE PEASANT WOMAN: She's not sleeping, you'll have to face it, she's dead.

THE PEASANT: And it's time you got started. There are wolves around here, and what's worse, marauders.

MOTHER COURAGE: Yes.

[*She goes to the wagon and takes out a sheet of canvas to cover the body with.*]

THE PEASANT WOMAN: Haven't you anybody else? Somebody you can go to?

MOTHER COURAGE: Yes, there's one of them left. Eilif.

THE PEASANT [*while Mother Courage covers the body*]: Go find him. We'll attend to this one, give her a decent burial. Set your mind at rest.

MOTHER COURAGE: Here's money for your expenses. [*She gives the peasant money.*]

[*The peasant and his son shake hands with her and carry Kattrin away.*]

THE PEASANT WOMAN [*on the way out*]: Hurry up!

MOTHER COURAGE [*harnesses herself to the wagon*]: I hope I can pull the wagon alone. I'll manage, there isn't much in it. I've got to get back in business.

[*Another regiment marches by with fifes and drums in the rear.*]

MOTHER COURAGE: Hey, take me with you! [*She starts to pull.*]

[*Singing is heard in the rear.*]

> *With all the killing and recruiting*
> *The war will worry on a while.*
> *In ninety years they'll still be shooting.*
> *It's hardest on the rank-and-file.*
> *Our food is swill, our pants all patches*
> *The higher-ups steal half our pay*
> *And still we dream of God-sent riches.*
> *Tomorrow is another day!*
> > *The spring is come! Christian, revive!*
> > *The snowdrifts melt, the dead lie dead!*
> > *And if by chance you're still alive*
> > *It's time to rise and shake a leg.*

Primo Levi
1919–1987

Primo Levi was born to a middle-class Jewish family in Turin, Italy. His family had long assimilated into Italian life, and Levy only discovered his Jewishness when he came up against the racial laws enacted in 1938 by Mussolini's Fascist regime. Levi graduated first in his class as a chemist from the University of Turin in 1941, the year in which Italy joined World War II as a German ally. Active in the resistance against the Fascist cause, Levi was captured in northern Italy in 1943 and imprisoned in an Italian transit camp, from which he was transferred to Auschwitz. He was one of fifteen men and nine women from the railroad convoy of 650 who survived. Levi's training as a chemist made him a valuable asset to the Germans, who spared him from the gas chamber and forced him to work in a laboratory. He was liberated by the Soviets in 1945 and returned to Turin, where he worked as a chemist, becoming general manager of a paint factory in 1961. In 1977 he retired to devote himself to writing full time. He committed suicide in 1987.

Primo Levi's life and writing are marked by his wartime experience and by the guilt of having survived when so many others perished in the German concentration camps. In matter-of-fact scientist's language, Levi recorded his prison recollections in a memoir in 1947 entitled *Se questo e un uomo (If This Is a Man*, translated into English as *Survival in Auschwitz)*. There he details the dehumanizing conditions in the concentration camps. The book sold more than half a million copies in Italy and has been translated into many languages as a classic document of human cruelty and suffering at mid-twentieth century. In 1963, Levi published a sequel, *La tregua (The Truce / The Reawakening),* which documents his wanderings in Eastern Europe and the Soviet Union. The nightmares of Auschwitz never cease to haunt Levi in this picaresque itinerary. In *The Periodic Table* (1975), he organizes his haunting recollections into the Russian chemist Mendeleyev's periodic table, distilling his autobiography to correspond to each of the twenty-one chemical elements. In Levi's last completed work, *The Drowned and the Saved,* published the year before his death, he wonders how much of the concentration camp still forms part of modern life and how enduring it might be in human history. He explores the paradoxical similarities between those who perpetrate cruelty and those who must endure it, showing how violence and oppression dehumanize both victim and oppressor.

The Two Flags[1]

Bertrando was born and grew up in a country called Lantania that had a very beautiful flag: or at least that was how it seemed to Bertrando, to all of his friends and fellow students, and to the greater part of his compatriots. It was different from all the others: against a bright purple ground stood out an orange oval, and in this rose a volcano, green at the bottom and white with snow at its top, surmounted by a plume of smoke.

In Bertrando's country there were no volcanoes; but there was one in the bordering country, Gunduwia, with which Lantania had been for centuries at war, or at any rate in a hostile relationship. Indeed, the Lantanic national poem, in a passage of debatable interpretation, mentioned the volcano as the "Lantanic altar of fire."

In all of Lantania's schools it was taught that the annexation of the volcano by the Gunduwians had been an act of banditry, and that the first duty of every Lantanian was to train militarily, hate Gunduwia with all his might, and prepare for the inevitable and desirable war, which was going to bend Gunduwian arrogance and reconquer the volcano. That this volcano every three or four years devastated thousands of villages and every year caused disastrous earthquakes was of no importance: Lantanic it was and Lantanic it must be again.

In any case, how not hate a country like Gunduwia? That very name, so grim, so sepulchral, inspired aversion. The Lantanians were a contentious and litigious people, they brawled or knifed each other for the slightest divergence of opinion, but they all agreed on the fact that Gunduwia was a country of scoundrels and bullies.

1. Translated by Raymond Rosenthal.

As for their flag, it represented them perfectly: it could not have been uglier, it was flat and silly, clumsy both in colors and design. Nothing more than a brown disk in a yellow field: not an image, not a symbol. A coarse, vulgar, and excremental flag. The Gunduwians must really be imbeciles, must have been since time immemorial for having chosen it and drenched it with their blood when they died in battle, something that happened three or four times a century. Furthermore, they were notoriously avaricious and wasteful, lewd and prudish, reckless and cowardly.

Bertrando was a proper young man, respectful of laws and traditions, and the very sight of his country's flag caused a wave of pride and self-assurance to course through his veins. The combination of those three noble colors, green, orange, and purple, when he sometimes recognized them joined in a spring meadow, made him strong and happy, glad to be a Lantanian, glad to be in this world, but also ready to die for his flag, best if wrapped in it.

Conversely, since his earliest childhood, since his memory began, the Gunduwian yellow and brown had been odious to him: disagreeable if taken separately, hateful to the point of nausea when placed side by side. Bertrando was a sensitive and emotional youth, and the sight of the enemy flag reproduced for derision on wall posters or in satirical vignettes put him in a bad mood and gave him an itch at the nape of the neck and elbows, intense salivation, and a certain dizziness.

Once, during a concert, he had found himself next to a pretty girl who inadvertently, of course, was wearing a yellow blouse and a brown skirt; Bertrando had been compelled to get up and move away and, since there were no other seats, to listen to the concert standing up; if he hadn't been rather shy, he would have told that girl exactly what she deserved. Bertrando liked apricots and medlars, but he ate them with his eyes shut so as to avoid the disgusting sight of the brown pit that stood out against the yellowish pulp.

Also, the sound of the Gunduwian language, which was harsh, guttural, almost inarticulate, had similar effects on Bertrando. It seemed to him scandalous that in certain Lantanian schools the enemy tongue should be taught, and that there even should be academicians who studied its history and origins, its grammar and syntax, and translated its literature. What sort of literature could that be? What good could come from that yellow-brown land of perverts and degenerates?

And yet there had been a professor who claimed he could prove that Lantanian and Gunduwian descended from one and the same language, extinct now for three thousand years, documented by a number of inscriptions on tombstones. Absurd, or rather insufferable. There are things that *cannot* be true, that must be ignored, not mentioned, buried. If it had been up to Bertrando, all Gunduwophiles would be buried three meters deep under the ground, along with all those (unfortunately, almost all of them young!) who, out of snobbism, surreptitiously listened to Gunduwian radio and repeated its obscene lies.

Not that the border between the two countries was hermetic. It was well patrolled on both sides by guards who shot readily, but there was a pass, and every so often trade delegations passed through it in both directions because the two economies were complementary. To everyone's surprise, there also passed through smugglers, with considerable loads that the border guards did not seem to notice.

Once Bertrando had watched a Gunduwian delegation pass through the main street of the capital. Those bastards were not really so different from the Lantanians: aside from their ridiculous way of dressing, they would have been difficult to pick out if not for their shifty eyes and their typically sly expressions. Bertrando had come closer, to sniff and find out whether it was true that they stank, but the police had prevented him. Of course, they had to stink. In the Lantanian subconscious there had been established for centuries an etymological nexus between Gunduwia and stench (*kumt* in Lantanian). Conversely, it was known to everyone that in Gunduwian *latnen* are boils, and to Lantanians this seemed a vicious buffoonery that must be washed in blood.

Now it so happened that, after long secret negotiations, the presidents of the two countries made it known that in the spring they would meet. After an embarrassed silence, the Lantanian daily newspaper began to leak unaccustomed material: photographs of the Gunduwian capital with its imposing cathedral and its beautiful parks; images of Gunduwian children, well groomed and with laughing eyes. A book was published in which it was shown how, in remote times, a Lantano-Gunduwian fleet had routed a ragtag fleet of pirate junks ten times stronger in number. And finally it became known that in the stadium of the Lantanian capital a soccer match would take place between each country's best teams.

Bertrando was one of the first to rush out and buy his ticket of admission, but it was already too late: he had to resign himself to spending five times as much buying from the scalpers. It was a splendid day, and the stadium was packed; there was not a breath of wind, and the two flags hung slack from the gigantic masts. At the appointed hour the umpire blew the starting whistle, and at the same instant there rose a sustained breeze. The two flags, side by side for the first time, fluttered gloriously: the Lantanian purple-orange-green next to the Gunduwian's yellow-brown.

Bertrando felt a gelid, searing shiver run down his spine, like a rapier threading his vertebrae. His eyes must be lying, they could not be transmitting to him that double message, that impossible, lacerating yes-no. He experienced revulsion and love to a degree that poisoned him. All around him he saw a crowd, as divided as he, explode. He felt all his muscles contract painfully, adductors and abductors, enemies to each other, the smooth and the striated, and the tireless muscles of the heart; all his glands secreted tumultuously, inundating him with warring hormones. His jaws locked as though from tetanus and he fell to the ground like a block of wood.

from Survival in Auschwitz[1]
The Journey

I was captured by the Fascist Militia on December 13, 1943. I was twenty-four, with little wisdom, no experience, and a decided tendency—encouraged by the life of segregation forced on me for the previous four years by the racial laws—to live in an unrealistic world of my own, a world inhabited by civilized Cartesian phantoms,[2] by sincere male and bloodless female friendships. I cultivated a moderate and abstract sense of rebellion.

It had been by no means easy to flee into the mountains and to help set up what, both in my opinion and in that of friends little more experienced than myself, should have become a partisan band affiliated with the Resistance movement *Justice and Liberty*. Contacts, arms, money and the experience needed to acquire them were all missing. We lacked capable men, and instead we were swamped by a deluge of outcasts, in good or bad faith, who came from the plain in search of a non-existent mili-

1. Translated by Stuart Woolf.
2. The French philosopher René Descartes (1596–1650) gave precedence to abstract reasoning as antidote to doubt.

tary or political organization, of arms, or merely of protection, a hiding place, a fire, a pair of shoes.

At that time I had not yet been taught the doctrine I was later to learn so hurriedly in the Lager:[3] that man is bound to pursue his own ends by all possible means, while he who errs but once pays dearly. So that I can only consider the following sequence of events justified. Three Fascist Militia companies, which had set out in the night to surprise a much more powerful and dangerous band than ours, broke into our refuge one spectral snowy dawn and took me down to the valley as a suspect person.

During the interrogations that followed, I preferred to admit my status of "Italian citizen of Jewish race." I felt that otherwise I would be unable to justify my presence in places too secluded even for an evacuee; while I believed (wrongly as was subsequently seen) that the admission of my political activity would have meant torture and certain death. As a Jew, I was sent to Fossoli, near Modena,[4] where a vast detention camp, originally meant for English and American prisoners-of-war, collected all the numerous categories of people not approved of by the new-born Fascist Republic.[5]

At the moment of my arrival, that is, at the end of January, 1944, there were about one hundred and fifty Italian Jews in the camp, but within a few weeks their number rose to over six hundred. For the most part they consisted of entire families captured by the Fascists or Nazis through their imprudence or following secret accusations. A few had given themselves up spontaneously, reduced to desperation by the vagabond life, or because they lacked the means to survive, or to avoid separation from a captured relation, or even—absurdly—"to be in conformity with the law." There were also about a hundred Jugoslavian military internees and a few other foreigners who were politically suspect.

The arrival of a squad of German SS men[6] should have made even the optimists doubtful; but we still managed to interpret the novelty in various ways without drawing the most obvious conclusions. Thus, despite everything, the announcement of the deportation caught us all unawares.

On February 20, the Germans had inspected the camp with care and had publicly and loudly upbraided the Italian commissar for the defective organization of the kitchen service and for the scarce amount of wood distributed for heating; they even said that an infirmary would soon be opened. But on the morning of the 21st we learned that on the following day the Jews would be leaving. All the Jews, without exception. Even the children, even the old, even the ill. Our destination? Nobody knew. We should be prepared for a fortnight of travel. For every person missing at the roll-call, ten would be shot.

Only a minority of ingenuous and deluded souls continued to hope; we others had often spoken with the Polish and Croat refugees and we knew what departure meant.

For people condemned to death, tradition prescribes an austere ceremony, calculated to emphasize that all passions and anger have died down, and that the act of justice represents only a sad duty towards society which moves even the executioner to pity for the victim. Thus the condemned man is shielded from all external cares, he is granted solitude and, should he want it, spiritual comfort; in short, care is taken that he should feel around him neither hatred nor arbitrariness, only necessity and justice, and by means of punishment, pardon.

3. Literally, "storage place." The "holding tank" for German prisoners destined for concentration camps.
4. Provincial capital in north-central Italy.
5. Fascist regime of Italy (1922–1943) under the dictator-

ship of Benito Mussolini.
6. The German SS, or "Storm Toopers," were the elite cadre of Hitler's military forces.

But to us this was not granted, for we were many and time was short. And in any case, what had we to repent, for what crime did we need pardon? The Italian commissar accordingly decreed that all services should continue to function until the final notice: the kitchens remained open, the corvées[7] for cleaning worked as usual, and even the teachers of the little school gave lessons until the evening, as on other days. But that evening the children were given no homework.

And night came, and it was such a night that one knew that human eyes would not witness it and survive. Everyone felt this: not one of the guards, neither Italian nor German, had the courage to come and see what men do when they know they have to die.

All took leave from life in the manner which most suited them. Some praying, some deliberately drunk, others lustfully intoxicated for the last time. But the mothers stayed up to prepare the food for the journey with tender care, and washed their children and packed the luggage; and at dawn the barbed wire was full of children's washing hung out in the wind to dry. Nor did they forget the diapers, the toys, the cushions and the hundred other small things which mothers remember and which children always need. Would you not do the same? If you and your child were going to be killed tomorrow, would you not give him to eat today?

In hut 6A old Gattegno lived with his wife and numerous children and grandchildren and his sons and daughters-in-law. All the men were carpenters; they had come from Tripoli after many long journeys, and had always carried with them the tools of their trade, their kitchen utensils, and their accordions and violins to play and dance to after the day's work. They were happy and pious folk. Their women were the first to silently and rapidly finish the preparations for the journey in order to have time for mourning. When all was ready, the food cooked, the bundles tied together, they unloosened their hair, took off their shoes, placed the Yahrzeit[8] candles on the ground and lit them according to the customs of their fathers, and sat on the bare soil in a circle for the lamentations, praying and weeping all the night. We collected in a group in front of their door, and we experienced within ourselves a grief that was new for us, the ancient grief of the people that has no land, the grief without hope of the exodus which is renewed every century.

Dawn came on us like a betrayer; it seemed as though the new sun rose as an ally of our enemies to assist in our destruction. The different emotions that overcame us, of resignation, of futile rebellion, of religious abandon, of fear, of despair, now joined together after a sleepless night in a collective, uncontrolled panic. The time for meditation, the time for decision was over, and all reason dissolved into a tumult, across which flashed the happy memories of our homes, still so near in time and space, as painful as the thrusts of a sword.

Many things were then said and done among us; but of these it is better that there remain no memory.

With the absurd precision to which we later had to accustom ourselves, the Germans held the roll-call. At the end the officer asked *"Wieviel Stück?"*[9] The corporal saluted smartly and replied that there were six hundred and fifty "pieces" and that all was in order. They then loaded us on to the buses and took us to the station of Carpi. Here the train was waiting for us, with our escort for the journey. Here we received the first blows: and it was so new and senseless that we felt no pain, neither in body nor in spirit. Only a profound amazement: how can one hit a man without anger?

---

7. Unpaid workers.
8. In Judaism, the anniversary of the death of a relative,   observed with mourning candles and religious recitations.
9. "How many pieces?"

There were twelve goods wagons for six hundred and fifty men; in mine we were only forty-five, but it was a small wagon. Here then, before our very eyes, under our very feet, was one of those notorious transport trains, those which never return, and of which, shuddering and always a little incredulous, we had so often heard speak. Exactly like this, detail for detail: goods wagons closed from the outside, with men, women and children pressed together without pity, like cheap merchandise, for a journey towards nothingness, a journey down there, towards the bottom. This time it is us who are inside.

Sooner or later in life everyone discovers that perfect happiness is unrealizable, but there are few who pause to consider the antithesis: that perfect unhappiness is equally unattainable. The obstacles preventing the realization of both these extreme states are of the same nature: they derive from our human condition which is opposed to everything infinite. Our ever-insufficient knowledge of the future opposes it: and this is called, in the one instance, hope, and in the other, uncertainty of the following day. The certainty of death opposes it: for it places a limit on every joy, but also on every grief. The inevitable material cares oppose it: for as they poison every lasting happiness, they equally assiduously distract us from our misfortunes, and make our consciousness of them intermittent and hence supportable.

It was the very discomfort, the blows, the cold, the thirst that kept us aloft in the void of bottomless despair, both during the journey and after. It was not the will to live, nor a conscious resignation; for few are the men capable of such resolution, and we were but a common sample of humanity.

The doors had been closed at once, but the train did not move until evening. We had learnt of our destination with relief. Auschwitz:[1] a name without significance for us at that time, but it at least implied some place on this earth.

The train travelled slowly, with long, unnerving halts. Through the slit we saw the tall pale cliffs of the Adige Valley and the names of the last Italian cities disappear behind us. We passed the Brenner[2] at midday of the second day and everyone stood up, but no one said a word. The thought of the return journey stuck in my heart, and I cruelly pictured to myself the inhuman joy of that other journey, with doors open, no one wanting to flee, and the first Italian names . . . and I looked around and wondered how many, among that poor human dust, would be struck by fate. Among the forty-five people in my wagon only four saw their homes again; and it was by far the most fortunate wagon.

We suffered from thirst and cold; at every stop we clamoured for water, or even a handful of snow, but we were rarely heard; the soldiers of the escort drove off anybody who tried to approach the convoy. Two young mothers, nursing their children, groaned night and day, begging for water. Our state of nervous tension made the hunger, exhaustion and lack of sleep seem less of a torment. But the hours of darkness were nightmares without end.

There are few men who know how to go to their deaths with dignity, and often they are not those whom one would expect. Few know how to remain silent and respect the silence of others. Our restless sleep was often interrupted by noisy and futile disputes, by curses, by kicks and blows blindly delivered to ward off some encroaching and inevitable contact. Then someone would light a candle, and its mournful flicker would reveal an obscure agitation, a human mass, extended across the floor, confused and continuous, sluggish and aching, rising here and there in sudden convulsions and immediately collapsing again in exhaustion.

1. City in southeast Poland, where the Nazis established   2. Alpine pass between Austria and Italy.
concentration camps and forced labor camps.

Through the slit, known and unknown names of Austrian cities, Salzburg, Vienna, then Czech, finally Polish names. On the evening of the fourth day the cold became intense; the train ran through interminable black pine forests, climbing perceptibly. The snow was high. It must have been a branch line as the stations were small and almost deserted. During the halts, no one tried anymore to communicate with the outside world: we felt ourselves by now "on the other side." There was a long halt in open country. The train started up with extreme slowness, and the convoy stopped for the last time, in the dead of night, in the middle of a dark silent plain.

On both sides of the track rows of red and white lights appeared as far as the eye could see; but there was none of that confusion of sounds which betrays inhabited places even from a distance. By the wretched light of the last candle, with the rhythm of the wheels, with every human sound now silenced, we awaited what was to happen.

Next to me, crushed against me for the whole journey, there had been a woman. We had known each other for many years, and the misfortune had struck us together, but we knew little of each other. Now, in the hour of decision, we said to each other things that are never said among the living. We said farewell and it was short; everybody said farewell to life through his neighbour. We had no more fear.

The climax came suddenly. The door opened with a crash, and the dark echoed with outlandish orders in that curt, barbaric barking of Germans in command which seems to give vent to a millennial anger. A vast platform appeared before us, lit up by reflectors. A little beyond it, a row of lorries. Then everything was silent again. Someone translated: we had to climb down with our luggage and deposit it alongside the train. In a moment the platform was swarming with shadows. But we were afraid to break that silence: everyone busied himself with his luggage, searched for someone else, called to somebody, but timidly, in a whisper.

A dozen SS men stood around, legs akimbo, with an indifferent air. At a certain moment they moved among us, and in a subdued tone of voice, with faces of stone, began to interrogate us rapidly, one by one, in bad Italian. They did not interrogate everybody, only a few: "How old? Healthy or ill?" And on the basis of the reply they pointed in two different directions.

Everything was as silent as an aquarium, or as in certain dream sequences. We had expected something more apocalyptic: they seemed simple police agents. It was disconcerting and disarming. Someone dared to ask for his luggage: they replied, "luggage afterwards." Someone else did not want to leave his wife: they said, "together again afterwards." Many mothers did not want to be separated from their children: they said "good, good, stay with child." They behaved with the calm assurance of people doing their normal duty of every day. But Renzo stayed an instant too long to say goodbye to Francesca, his fiancée, and with a single blow they knocked him to the ground. It was their everyday duty.

In less than ten minutes all the fit men had been collected together in a group. What happened to the others, to the women, to the children, to the old men, we could establish neither then nor later: the night swallowed them up, purely and simply. Today, however, we know that in that rapid and summary choice each one of us had been judged capable or not of working usefully for the Reich; we know that of our convoy no more than ninety-six men and twenty-nine women entered the respective camps of Monowitz-Buna and Birkenau, and that of all the others, more than five hundred in number, not one was living two days later. We also know that not even this tenuous principle of discrimination between fit and unfit was always followed, and that later the simpler method was often adopted of merely opening both doors of the wagon without warning or instructions to the new arrivals. Those who by chance climbed down on one side of the convoy entered the camp; the others went to the gas chamber.

This is the reason why three-year-old Emilia died: the historical necessity of killing the children of Jews was self-demonstrative to the Germans. Emilia, daughter of Aldo Levi of Milan, was a curious, ambitious, cheerful, intelligent child; her parents had succeeded in washing her during the journey in the packed car in a tub with tepid water which the degenerate German engineer had allowed them to draw from the engine that was dragging us all to death.

Thus, in an instant, our women, our parents, our children disappeared. We saw them for a short while as an obscure mass at the other end of the platform; then we saw nothing more.

Instead, two groups of strange individuals emerged into the light of the lamp. They walked in squads, in rows of three, with an odd, embarrassed step, head dangling in front, arms rigid. On their heads they wore comic berets and were all dressed in long striped overcoats, which even by night and from a distance looked filthy and in rags. They walked in a large circle around us, never drawing near, and in silence began to busy themselves with our luggage and to climb in and out of the empty wagons.

We looked at each other without a word. It was all incomprehensible and mad, but one thing we had understood. This was the metamorphosis that awaited us. Tomorrow we would be like them.

Without knowing how I found myself loaded on to a lorry[3] with thirty others; the lorry sped into the night at full speed. It was covered and we could not see outside, but by the shaking we could tell that the road had many curves and bumps. Are we unguarded? Throw ourselves down? It is too late, too late, we are all "down." In any case we are soon aware that we are not without guard. He is a strange guard, a German soldier bristling with arms. We do not see him because of the thick darkness, but we feel the hard contact every time that a lurch of the lorry throws us all in a heap. At a certain point he switches on a pocket torch[4] and instead of shouting threats of damnation at us, he asks us courteously, one by one, in German and in pidgin language, if we have any money or watches to give him, seeing that they will not be useful to us anymore. This is no order, no regulation: it is obvious that it is a small private initiative of our Charon.[5] The matter stirs us to anger and laughter and brings relief. * * *

THE CANTO OF ULYSSES

There were six of us, scraping and cleaning the inside of an underground petrol tank; the daylight only reached us through a small manhole. It was a luxury job because no one supervised us; but it was cold and damp. The powder of the rust burnt under our eyelids and coated our throats and mouths with a taste almost like blood.

The rope-ladder hanging from the manhole began to sway: someone was coming. Deutsch extinguished his cigarette, Goldner woke Sivadjan; we all began to vigorously scrape the resonant steelplate wall.

It was not the *Vorarbeiter*,[6] it was only Jean, the Pikolo of our Kommando. Jean was an Alsatian student; although he was already twenty-four, he was the youngest Häftling[7]

3. Truck.
4. Flashlight.
5. In Greek mythology, Charon is the ferryman who conveys the dead across the River Styx to the underworld.
6. Foreman.
7. Underling.

of the Chemical Kommando. So that he was given the post of Pikolo, which meant the messenger-clerk, responsible for the cleaning of the hut, for the distribution of tools, for the washing of bowls, and for keeping record of the working hours of the Kommando.

Jean spoke French and German fluently: as soon as we recognized his shoes on the top step of the ladder we all stopped scraping.

"*Also, Pikolo, was gibt es Neues?*"[8]

"*Qu'est ce qu'il-y-a comme soupe aujourd'hui?*"[9]

. . . in what mood was the Kapo?[1] And the affair of the twenty-five lashes given to Stern? What was the weather like outside? Had he read the newspaper? What smell was coming from the civilian kitchen? What was the time?

Jean was liked a great deal by the Kommando. One must realize that the post of Pikolo represented a quite high rank in the hierarchy of the Prominents: the Pikolo (who is usually no more than seventeen years old) does no manual work, has an absolute right to the remainder of the daily ration to be found on the bottom of the vat, and can stay all day near the stove. He "therefore" has the right to a supplementary half-ration and has a good chance of becoming the friend and confidant of the Kapo, from whom he officially receives discarded clothes and shoes. Now Jean was an exceptional Pikolo. He was shrewd and physically robust, and at the same time gentle and friendly: although he continued his secret individual struggle against the camp and against death, he did not neglect his human relationships with less privileged comrades; at the same time he had been so able and persevering that he had managed to establish himself in the confidence of Alex, the Kapo.

Alex had kept all his promises. He had shown himself a violent and unreliable rogue, with an armour of solid and compact ignorance and stupidity, always excepting his intuition and consummate technique as convict-keeper. He never let slip an opportunity of proclaiming his pride in his pure blood and his green triangle, and displayed a lofty contempt for his ragged and starving chemists: "*Ihr Doktoren! Ihr Intelligenten!*"[2] he sneered every day, watching them crowd around with their bowls held out for the distribution of the ration. He was extremely compliant and servile before the civilian *Meister* and with the SS he kept up ties of cordial friendship.

He was clearly intimidated by the register of the Kommando and by the daily report of work, and this had been the path that Pikolo had chosen to make himself indispensable. It had been a long, cautious and subtle task which the entire Kommando had followed for a month with bated breath; but at the end the porcupine's defence was penetrated, and Pikolo confirmed in his office to the satisfaction of all concerned.

Although Jean had never abused his position, we had already been able to verify that a single word of his, said in the right tone of voice and at the right moment, had great power; many times already it had saved one of us from a whipping or from being denounced to the SS. We had been friends for a week: we discovered each other during the unusual occasion of an air-raid alarm, but then, swept by the fierce rhythm of the Lager, we had only been able to greet each other fleetingly, at the latrines, in the washroom.

Hanging with one hand on the swaying ladder, he pointed to me: "*Aujourd'hui c'est Primo qui viendra avec moi chercher la soupe.*"[3]

---

8. "What's new?'
9. "What's today's soup?"
1. Chief.

2. "You doctors! You intellectuals!"
3. "Today Primo's the one who's getting the soup with me."

Until yesterday it had been Stern, the squinting Transylvanian; now he had fallen into disgrace for some story of brooms stolen from the store, and Pikolo had managed to support my candidature as assistant to the *"Essenholen,"*[4] the daily corvée of the ration.

He climbed out and I followed him, blinking in the brightness of the day. It was warmish outside, the sun drew a faint smell of paint and tar from the greasy earth, which made me think of a holiday beach of my infancy. Pikolo gave me one of the two wooden poles, and we walked along under a clear June sky.

I began to thank him, but he stopped me: it was not necessary. One could see the Carpathians covered in snow. I breathed in the fresh air, I felt unusually light-hearted.

"Tu es fou de marcher si vite. On a le temps, tu sais,"[5] The ration was collected half a mile away; one had to return with the pot weighing over a hundred pounds supported on the two poles. It was quite a tiring task, but it meant a pleasant walk there without a load, and the ever-welcome chance of going near the kitchens.

We slowed down. Pikolo was expert. He had chosen the path cleverly so that we would have to make a long detour, walking at least for an hour, without arousing suspicion. We spoke of our houses, of Strasbourg and Turin, of the books we had read; of what we had studied, of our mothers: how all mothers resemble each other! His mother too had scolded him for never knowing how much money he had in his pocket; his mother too would have been amazed if she had known that he had found his feet, that day by day he was finding his feet.

An SS man passed on a bicycle. It is Rudi, the *Blockführer.*[6] Halt! Attention! Take off your beret! *"Sale brute, celui-là. Ein ganz gemeiner Hund."*[7] Can he speak French and German with equal facility? Yes, he thinks indifferently in both languages. He spent a month in Liguria,[8] he likes Italy, he would like to learn Italian: I would be pleased to teach him Italian: why not try? We can do it. Why not immediately, one thing is as good as another, the important thing is not to lose time, not to waste this hour.

Limentani from Rome walks by, dragging his feet, with a bowl hidden under his jacket. Pikolo listens carefully, picks up a few words of our conversation and repeats them smiling: *"Zup-pa, cam-po, acqua."*[9]

Frenkl the spy passes. Quicken our pace, one never knows, he does evil for evil's sake.

. . . The canto of Ulysses.[1] Who knows how or why it comes into my mind. But we have no time to change, this hour is already less than an hour. If Jean is intelligent he will understand. He *will* understand—today I feel capable of so much.

. . . Who is Dante? What is the Comedy? That curious sensation of novelty which one feels if one tries to explain briefly what is the Divine Comedy. How the Inferno is divided up, what are its punishments. Virgil is Reason, Beatrice is Theology.

Jean pays great attention, and I begin slowly and accurately:

> *Then of that age-old fire the loftier horn*
> *Began to mutter and move, as a wavering flame*

4. Mess hall.
5. "You're crazy to be walking so fast. There is time, you know."
6. Cell commander.
7. "A filthy brute, that one. Just a common mutt."
8. A region in northwest Italy that borders France.
9. "Soup, field, water."

1. The canto of Ulysses is the 26th Canto of Dante's *Inferno*, one of the three books of the *Divine Comedy*. The Homeric hero is condemned to one of the "malbolge" for having dared to go beyond the frontiers of the known world. In the pages that follow, Levi often cites from this canto.

> *Wrestles against the wind and is over-worn;*
> *And, like a speaking tongue vibrant to frame*
> *Language, the tip of it flickering to and fro*
> *Threw out a voice and answered: "When I came . . ."*

Here I stop and try to translate. Disastrous—poor Dante and poor French! All the same, the experience seems to promise well: Jean admires the bizarre simile of the tongue and suggests the appropriate word to translate "age-old."

And after "When I came?" Nothing. A hole in my memory. "Before Aeneas ever named it so." Another hole. A fragment floats into my mind, not relevant: ". . . nor piety To my old father, nor the wedded love That should have comforted Penelope . . . ," is it correct?

". . . So on the open sea I set forth."

Of this I am certain, I am sure, I can explain it to Pikolo, I can point out why "I set forth" is not *"je me mis,"* it is much stronger and more audacious, it is a chain which has been broken, it is throwing oneself on the other side of a barrier, we know the impulse well. The open sea: Pikolo has travelled by sea, and knows what it means: it is when the horizon closes in on itself, free, straight ahead and simple, and there is nothing but the smell of the sea; sweet things, ferociously far away.

We have arrived at Kraftwerk, where the cable-laying Kommando works. Engineer Levi must be here. Here he is, one can only see his head above the trench. He waves to me, he is a brave man, I have never seen his morale low, he never speaks of eating.

"Open sea, open sea." I know it rhymes with "left me": ". . . and that small band of comrades that had never left me," but I cannot remember if it comes before or after. And the journey as well, the foolhardy journey beyond the Pillars of Hercules, how sad, I have to tell it in prose—a sacrelege. I have only rescued two lines, but they are worth stopping for:

> *". . . that none should prove so hardy*
> *To venture the uncharted distances . . ."*

"to venture": I had to come to the Lager to realize that it is the same expression as before "I set forth." But I say nothing to Jean, I am not sure that it is an important observation. How many things there are to say, and the sun is already high, midday is near. I am in a hurry, a terrible hurry.

Here, listen Pikolo, open your ears and your mind, you have to understand, for my sake:

> *"Think of your breed; for brutish ignorance*
> *Your mettle was not made; you were made men,*
> *To follow after knowledge and excellence."*

As if I also was hearing it for the first time: like the blast of a trumpet, like the voice of God. For a moment I forget who I am and where I am.

Pikolo begs me to repeat it. How good Pikolo is, he is aware that it is doing me good. Or perhaps it is something more: perhaps, despite the wan translation and the pedestrian, rushed commentary, he has received the message, he has felt that it has to do with him, that it has to do with all men who toil, and with us in particular; and that it has to do with us two, who dare to reason of these things with the poles for the soup on our shoulders.

> *"My little speech made every one so keen . . ."*

. . . and I try, but in vain, to explain how many things this "keen" means. There is another lacuna here, this time irreparable. ". . . the light kindles and grows Beneath the moon" or something like it; but before it? . . . Not an idea, *"keine Ahnung"*[2] as they say here. Forgive me, Pikolo, I have forgotten at least four triplets.

"Ça ne fait rien, vas-y tout de même."[3]

> *". . . When at last hove up a mountain, grey*
> *With distance, and so lofty and so steep,*
> *I never had seen the like on any day."*

Yes, yes, "so lofty and so steep," not "very steep," a consecutive proposition. And the mountains when one sees them in the distance . . . the mountains . . . oh, Pikolo, Pikolo, say something, speak, do not let me think of my mountains which used to show up against the dusk of evening as I returned by train from Milan to Turin!

Enough, one must go on, these are things that one thinks but does not say. Pikolo waits and looks at me.

I would give today's soup to know how to connect "the like on any day" to the last lines. I try to reconstruct it through the rhymes, I close my eyes, I bite my fingers—but it is no use, the rest is silence. Other verses dance in my head: " . . . The sodden ground belched wind . . . ," no, it is something else. It is late, it is late, we have reached the kitchen, I must finish;

> *"And three times round she went in roaring smother*
> *With all the waters; at the fourth the poop*
> *Rose, and the prow went down, as pleased Another."*

I keep Pikolo back, it is vitally necessary and urgent that he listen, that he understand this "as pleased Another" before it is too late; tomorrow he or I might be dead, or we might never see each other again, I must tell him, I must explain to him about the Middle Ages, about the so human and so necessary and yet unexpected anachronism, but still more, something gigantic that I myself have only just seen, in a flash of intuition, perhaps the reason for our fate, for our being here today. . . .

We are now in the soup queue, among the sordid, ragged crowd of soup-carriers from other Kommandos. Those just arrived press against our backs. *"Kraut und Rüben? Kraut und Rüben."* The official announcement is made that the soup today is of cabbages and turnips: *"Choux et navets. Kaposzta és répak."*

> *"And over our heads the hollow seas closed up."*

---

2. No idea.   3. "No matter. Go on anyway."

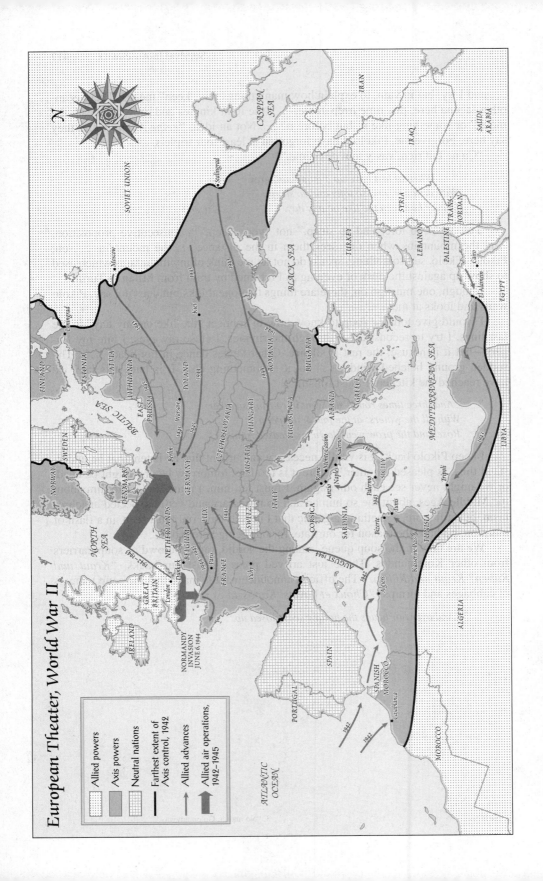

European Theater, World War II

Allied powers

Axis powers

Neutral nations

Farthest extent of Axis control, 1942

Allied advances

Allied air operations, 1942–1945

ATLANTIC OCEAN

IRELAND

GREAT BRITAIN
London

NORTH SEA

NORMANDY INVASION JUNE 6, 1944

Dunkirk

NETHERLANDS

BELGIUM

LUX.

FRANCE

Paris

1944–1945

1943–1945

1944

Vichy

SWITZ.

GERMANY

Berlin

1945

EAST PRUSSIA

1943

Warsaw

POLAND

1945

LITHUANIA

LATVIA

ESTONIA

1941

Leningrad

FINLAND

NORWAY

SWEDEN

DENMARK

BALTIC SEA

Moscow

1943

Kiev

1941

1944

SOVIET UNION

Stalingrad

1942

CASPIAN SEA

IRAN

IRAQ

SAUDI ARABIA

SYRIA

LEBANON

JORDAN

TRANS-JORDAN

PALESTINE

Cairo

EGYPT

El Alamein

1942

LIBYA

MEDITERRANEAN SEA

Tripoli

TUNISIA

Tunis

Bizerte

Kasserine Pass

1942

1943

Algiers

AUGUST 1944

SPANISH MOROCCO

Casablanca

1942

1942

MOROCCO

ALGERIA

PORTUGAL

SPAIN

CORSICA

SARDINIA

SICILY

Palermo

ITALY

1945

Rome

Anzio

Monte Cassino

Naples

Salerno

1943

CZECHOSLOVAKIA

AUSTRIA

HUNGARY

1944

YUGOSLAVIA

ROMANIA

BULGARIA

ALBANIA

GREECE

1945

BLACK SEA

TURKEY

⇌ PERSPECTIVES ⇌
Echoes of War

Growing up in the twentieth century, it is easy to assume that one's own era is more humane and civilized than that of earlier periods, and one might be tempted to look at history as a steady if uneven evolution away from violence and brutality. Yet the twentieth century's history of military conflict is staggering, and its number of war dead easily dwarfs that of any earlier century, from two World Wars to wars of independence from colonial power, from "proxy wars" in Africa and Asia during the long Cold War to violent ethnic conflict in Eastern Europe, Africa, and Central America. Few areas of the globe have been spared involvement in bloody conflict over the last hundred years, and the attempt to cope with war, violence, destruction, loss, and mourning looms large in twentieth-century literature across cultures and generations. Novelists as well as playwrights and poets have struggled with the difficult issues that arise when one's community becomes involved in violent conflict and have suggested ways of thinking through the particular circumstances as well as the more general historical, political, social, moral, and cultural dilemmas that accompany such violence.

Loyalty is one of the most complex of the issues that arise in the context of war. What importance does a country's call to arms carry in relation to other values? Under what circumstances should it be obeyed or resisted? Unflinching loyalty such as that described by Japanese writer Mishima Yukio and Polish poet Zbigniew Herbert is not weakened by defeat or even death. Such a view contrasts sharply with Yosano Akiko's call to her brother to preserve his life: In a movement that was very unusual for her time, Yosano used loyalty to family ties as a means of putting in question the necessity of unconditional loyalty to the highest political power. In Herbert, by contrast, loyalty means not so much obedience to state institutions as the coherence of one's personal identity, which persists even beyond the realities of military defeat. A larger question arises through the comparative study of these texts and also emerges in other sections such as "Postcolonial Conditions": To what extent is our sense of identity dependent upon the needs of the communities we are part of? How can conflicting loyalties to family, ethnic group, religious community, city, region, and nation be negotiated in situations of danger, violence, and confrontation?

A somewhat different set of questions is brought to the fore by poets who focus on those who die in wars and those who remember them. These questions figure prominently in the poems of Rupert Brooke and Wilfred Owen, both of whom fought in the trenches during World War I. What real or symbolic meanings do the living attach to the dying? Are these meanings in keeping with those proclaimed by official justifications for war, or in subtle ways opposed to them? Israeli poet Yehuda Amichai raises this question in regard both to victims of the Nazi Holocaust and those who died fighting for the establishment of a Jewish homeland. In this context, the process of remembering—which is sometimes an effort, sometimes an involuntary onslaught—becomes a central focus of attention that in some respects harkens back to the investigation of memory in classic modernist texts (see Perspectives: Modernist Memory, page 224). How does one's memory of the dead balance love and celebration with mourning and loss? What manifestations of grief, loss, and memory are appropriate for those who didn't die merely "private" deaths but lost their lives in the name of a larger communal cause? How should such communal causes be reconsidered in view of the lives lost on their behalf? Lyrical poetry, with its long historical tradition of the *elegy*, the poem written on the occasion of someone's death to memorialize the deceased person's life and passing, is a particularly apt vehicle for such reflections.

Some of the texts presented here, however, focus on life rather than death during times of war and explore how the war experience transforms the perspective and identity of those who survive. Austrian poet and novelist Ingeborg Bachmann investigates this question in a short

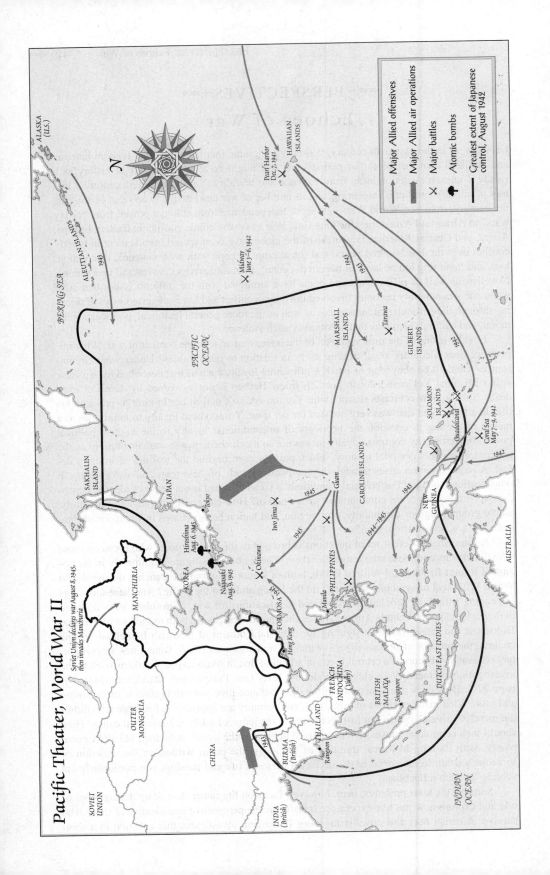

Pacific Theater, World War II

Soviet Union declares war August 8, 1945, then invades Manchuria

SOVIET UNION

ALASKA (U.S.)

OUTER MONGOLIA

MANCHURIA

BEERING SEA

ALEUTIAN ISLANDS
1943

PACIFIC OCEAN

KOREA

CHINA

SAKHALIN ISLAND

JAPAN

Tokyo
1945

Hiroshima
Aug. 6, 1945

Nagasaki
Aug. 9, 1945

Iwo Jima
1945

Okinawa
1945

Midway
June 3–6, 1942

HAWAIIAN ISLANDS

Pearl Harbor
Dec. 7, 1941

Guam
1944–1945

MARSHALL ISLANDS
1943

GILBERT ISLANDS

Tarawa

CAROLINE ISLANDS

FORMOSA

Hong Kong

BURMA (British)
1943

Rangoon

THAILAND

FRENCH INDOCHINA (Vichy)

BRITISH MALAYA

Singapore

DUTCH EAST INDIES

PHILIPPINES
1945

Manila

SOLOMON ISLANDS

Guadalcanal

Coral Sea
May 7–9, 1942

NEW GUINEA
1942
1943

AUSTRALIA

INDIA (British)

INDIAN OCEAN

N

Legend

→ Major Allied offensives

⇨ Major Allied air operations

✕ Major battles

☢ Atomic bombs

— Greatest extent of Japanese control, August 1942

story that forces the reader to confront war from the perspective of children who have only the most rudimentary understanding of the Second World War unfolding right around them. Yehuda Amichai and Paul Celan examine this topic more indirectly, while Cuban writer Alejo Carpentier makes it very explicit in a short story that subtly fuses the moments at the beginnings of military conflicts that span three millennia from the Trojan War to the wars of the twentieth century. How do combatants make the transition from the routines of daily life to the extremes of combat? What hopes, fears, and aspirations accompany this transition? While the relationship between normal, daily life and the realities of armed combat is discussed in Bachmann's short story in the specific context of World War II, Alejo Carpentier's story is consciously designed to make the reader feel the universality of war as a human experience across the most varied historical stages, geographical locations, and technological manifestations. Even more explicitly than in Zbigniew Herbert's "Report from the Besieged City," which fuses what seem to be several hundred years of combat into the description of one siege, all historical wars become one continuously repeated event in Carpentier's "Like the Night."

Beyond their explicit content, all of the texts in this section can be understood as investigations of what language might be appropriate to capture the experience of war and death. How can horror be turned into literature? Do the beauty and pleasures of the literary text run the risk of betraying the suffering and violence implicit in the subject matter? Perhaps no other text in the twentieth century has exemplified this dilemma better than Paul Celan's Holocaust poem "Death Fugue." Its startling lyrical beauty is as easy to perceive as its horrifying theme, the experience of death camps. Do the two go together? Does accomplished literary style effectively convey or dangerously detract from the deadly seriousness of the portrayed situation? This is perhaps the most difficult question the "Echoes of War" texts ask their readers.

Yosano Akiko
1878–1942

Yosano Akiko was born in 1878 near Osaka to a family of prosperous confectioners (her name is listed here in the order common in Japanese, with the family name preceding the given name). In early twentieth-century Tokyo, she became well-known as a poet, critic, and activist on behalf of women's right to education and suffrage. She contributed to the magazine *Myoojoo,* edited by Yosano Tekkan (whom she was later to marry), and joined his New Poetry Society in 1900. In her first volume of poetry, *Tangled Hair* (1901), she used *tanka,* a traditional Japanese verse form, to celebrate passion and sexuality in an unusually outspoken manner. After accompanying her husband to France in 1912, she began to translate Murasaki Shikibu's eleventh-century *Tale of Genji* into modern Japanese. Back in Japan in 1921, she founded the Bunka Gakuin School for girls, and subsequently worked there as a teacher while also writing literary criticism.

Her 1904 poem "I Beg You, Brother: Do Not Die" has become the most famous Japanese antiwar poem of the twentieth century. It is addressed to Yosano's brother Chuuzaburoo, who was fighting with General Nogi Maresuke's Third Army in China in the Russo-Japanese War. Japan's successful effort to drive the Russians out of northern China and increase its own influence in the region enjoyed wide support among the Japanese population. Explicitly critical of the war effort and the Emperor, the poem invokes the family as a value more central than the military objectives of the state. Revealing the rift between state interest and family interest in this way was a daring move in Yosano's day and provoked a storm of anger and outrage when the poem was published.

I Beg You, Brother: Do Not Die[1]

Oh my little brother, I weep for you
And beg you: do not die—
You, last-born and most beloved.
Did our parents
5   Put a blade into your hand
And teach you to kill men?
"Kill men and die in battle," did they say
And raise you so 'til twenty-four?

It is you who are to carry on the name
10   You who are to be master of
This proud, old merchant house.
I beg you: do not die.
What concern is it of yours
If the Russian fortress[2] falls or stands?
15   Of this, the merchant household code
Says nothing.

I beg you: do not die.
His Imperial Majesty—he himself—
Enters not the field of battle.
20   So vast and deep his sacred heart:
He cannot wish for you to spill
Your own blood and another's,
To die the death of beasts,
To think such death is glory!

25   Oh my little brother
I beg you: do not die in battle.
To add to mother's grief
When she lost father this autumn past,
They took her son
30   And left her to protect the house.
I hear of "peace" in this great Emperor's reign,
And yet our mother's hair grows ever whiter.

Your pliant, young bride crouches weeping
In the shadows of the shop curtains.
35   Do you think of her, or have you forgotten?
Imagine the heart of this sweet girl—
Not ten months were you together!
Who else has she in all the world
To care for her but you?
40   I beg you, brother: do not die.

---

1. Translated by Jay Rubin.   2. Port Arthur.

Rupert Brooke
1887–1915

The first of the young British poets who rose to prominence during World War I, Rupert Brooke found his vocation as a poet in the "Great War" that killed him just as it was beginning. He died of blood poisoning while still en route to his first real battle station in the eastern Mediterranean—an oddly appropriate end for an always precocious poet. Son of a teacher at England's prestigious Rugby School, Brooke had begun publishing poems in national journals while still attending college at Cambridge, and he brought out a well-received first volume of poems in 1912 when he was twenty-five. Already at Cambridge he had became locally famous as a personality as much as a poet: urbane, skeptical, a brilliant talker, a socialist and sometime vegetarian, and a heartbreakingly handsome youth. Friends described him as "a young golden Apollo," "almost ludicrously beautiful," and someone "whose moods seemed to be merely a disguise for the radiance of an early summer's morning." Brooke's early poems ranged widely in theme and form, treating such disparate subjects as lost loves, the mental world of fish, and the beauties of the South Seas, where he spent several months in 1913 after suffering a nervous breakdown.

Brooke's ultimate direction as a poet was uncertain and might never have become clear but for the advent of the war, which brought a sharp focus to his work. He enlisted immediately after war was declared in August 1914: "Well, if Armageddon's *on*," he remarked, "I suppose one should be there." During his months of training and an initial, inconclusive posting to Antwerp, he began to write poems that combined premonitions of death with a newfound patriotism. Especially notable was a series of sonnets written in 1914 as he prepared to sail to the Mediterranean. Published in book form under the title *Nineteen Fourteen,* Brooke's war poems gave him a new prominence that was heightened by his death soon thereafter. Writing in the London *Times* on the day his death was announced, future Prime Minister Winston Churchill wrote that "A voice had become audible, a note had been struck, more true, more thrilling, more able to do justice to the nobility of our youth in arms engaged in this present war, than any other."

Peace

Now, God be thanked Who has matched us with His hour,
    And caught our youth, and wakened us from sleeping,
With hand made sure, clear eye, and sharpened power,
    To turn, as swimmers into cleanness leaping,
5   Glad from a world grown old and cold and weary,
    Leave the sick hearts that honour could not move,
And half-men, and their dirty songs and dreary,
    And all the little emptiness of love!

Oh! we, who have known shame, we have found release there,
10   Where there's no ill, no grief, but sleep has mending,
        Naught broken save this body, lost but breath;
Nothing to shake the laughing heart's long peace there
    But only agony, and that has ending;
        And the worst friend and enemy is but Death.

The Soldier

If I should die, think only this of me:
    That there's some corner of a foreign field
That is for ever England. There shall be
    In that rich earth a richer dust concealed;
5   A dust whom England bore, shaped, made aware,
    Gave, once, her flowers to love, her ways to roam,
A body of England's, breathing English air,
    Washed by the rivers, blest by suns of home.

And think, this heart, all evil shed away,
10   A pulse in the eternal mind, no less
    Gives somewhere back the thoughts by England given;
Her sights and sounds; dreams happy as her day;
    And laughter, learnt of friends; and gentleness,
    In hearts at peace, under an English heaven.

Wilfred Owen
1893–1918

Born on the Welsh border in the region of Shropshire, Wilfred Owen never found a settled place in English society during his life. He was trained in a technical school and then spent two years in an informal apprenticeship to an evangelical vicar of the Church of England. Increasingly unhappy with the established church's response to poverty and social injustice, Owen decided not to seek ordination and instead enlisted in the army in 1915. He was posted to France in 1916 as a lieutenant with the Lancashire Fusiliers, a unit that saw heavy losses in trench warfare. Owen himself was blown out of a foxhole, and though he survived, he suffered a mental breakdown, diagnosed as "shell shock," a new term born of the brutal conditions of bombardment during months in the trenches. He was sent to a military hospital in Edinburgh to recover. There, he began to edit the hospital's magazine, in which he included anonymous poems of his own about his battlefield experiences. He wrote almost all of his poetry during the fourteen months of his convalescence, before he was posted back to France in September 1918. He was killed two months later, one week before the war's end.

One of his fellow convalescents in Edinburgh was the poet Siegfried Sassoon, seven years his senior, who became a close friend and confidant as Owen developed his highly individual poetic vision, at once realistic and surreal, of battlefield landscapes in which earth and hell mingle together. Owen's verse often employs shifting, ambiguous patterns of rhyme and off-rhyme and uneven stanza lengths that disorient classical forms even as they play on a rich poetic heritage from ancient Romans such as Horace to British Romantics such as Keats and Shelley. Sassoon published his friend's poetry in 1920; by then a famous war poet himself, Sassoon credited Owen as the greater artist: "My trench-sketches were like rockets, sent up to illuminate the darkness. . . . It was Owen who revealed how, out of realistic horror and scorn, poetry might be made."

Anthem for Doomed Youth

What passing-bells for these who die as cattle?
    Only the monstrous anger of the guns.

Only the stuttering rifles' rapid rattle
Can patter out their hasty orisons.°   *prayers*
5   No mockeries now for them; no prayers nor bells,
      Nor any voice of mourning save the choirs,—
The shrill, demented choirs of wailing shells;
      And bugles calling for them from sad shires.

What candles may be held to speed them all?
10   Not in the hands of boys, but in their eyes
Shall shine the holy glimmers of good-byes.
      The pallor of girls' brows shall be their pall;°   *coffin covering*
Their flowers the tenderness of patient minds,
And each slow dusk a drawing-down of blinds.

Strange Meeting

It seemed that out of battle I escaped
Down some profound dull tunnel, long since scooped
Through granites which titanic wars had groined.°   *joined together*
Yet also there encumbered sleepers groaned,
5   Too fast in thought or death to be bestirred.
Then, as I probed them, one sprang up, and stared
With piteous recognition in fixed eyes,
Lifting distressful hands, as if to bless.
And by his smile, I knew that sullen hall,—
10 By his dead smile I knew we stood in Hell.
With a thousand pains that vision's face was grained;
Yet no blood reached there from the upper ground,
And no guns thumped, or down the flues made moan.
"Strange friend," I said, "here is no cause to mourn."
15 "None," said that other, "save the undone years,
The hopelessness. Whatever hope is yours,
Was my life also; I went hunting wild
After the wildest beauty in the world,
Which lies not calm in eyes, or braided hair,
20 But mocks the steady running of the hour,
And if it grieves, grieves richlier than here.
For by my glee might many men have laughed,
And of my weeping something had been left,
Which must die now. I mean the truth untold,
25 The pity of war, the pity war distilled.
Now men will go content with what we spoiled,
Or, discontent, boil bloody, and be spilled.
They will be swift with swiftness of the tigress.
None will break ranks, though nations trek from progress.
30 Courage was mine, and I had mystery,
Wisdom was mine, and I had mastery:
To miss the march of this retreating world
Into vain citadels that are not walled.
Then, when much blood had clogged their chariot-wheels,

35   I would go up and wash them from sweet wells,
    Even with truths that lie too deep for taint.
    I would have poured my spirit without stint
    But not through wounds; not on the cess of war.
    Foreheads of men have bled where no wounds were.
40   I am the enemy you killed, my friend.
    I knew you in this dark: for so you frowned
    Yesterday through me as you jabbed and killed.
    I parried; but my hands were loath and cold.
    Let us sleep now . . ."

Dulce et Decorum Est[1]

    Bent double, like old beggars under sacks,
    Knock-kneed, coughing like hags, we cursed through sludge,
    Till on the haunting flares we turned our backs,
    And towards our distant rest began to trudge.
5   Men marched asleep. Many had lost their boots,
    But limped on, blood-shod. All went lame, all blind;
    Drunk with fatigue; deaf even to the hoots
    Of tired, outstripped Five-Nines[2] that dropped behind.

    Gas! Gas! Quick, boys!—An ecstasy of fumbling
10   Fitting the clumsy helmets just in time,
    But someone still was yelling out and stumbling
    And flound'ring like a man in fire or lime[3] . . . .
    Dim through the misty panes and thick green light,
    As under a green sea, I saw him drowning.

15   In all my dreams before my helpless sight
    He plunges at me, guttering, choking, drowning.

    If in some smothering dreams, you too could pace
    Behind the wagon that we flung him in,
    And watch the white eyes writhing in his face,
20   His hanging face, like a devil's sick of sin;
    If you could hear, at every jolt, the blood
    Come gargling from the froth-corrupted lungs
    Obscene as cancer, bitter as the cud
    Of vile, incurable sores on innocent tongues,—
25   My friend, you would not tell with such high zest
    To children ardent for some desperate glory,
    The old Lie: Dulce et decorum est
    Pro patria mori.

1. From the *Odes* of the Roman satirist Horace (65–8 B.C.E.): Dulce et decorum est pro patria mori (sweet and fitting it is to die for your fatherland).
2. Artillery shells used by the Germans.

3. Calcium oxide, a powerfully caustic alkali used, among other purposes, for cleaning the flesh off the bones of corpses.

Yukio Mishima
1925–1970

One of the greatest—and most disturbing—writers of the twentieth century, Yukio Mishima wrote hundreds of novels, plays, and stories before ending his life by committing ritual suicide at the age of forty-five. Born in Tokyo as Kimitake Hiraoka, he was the son of a government official and grandson of a former provincial governor. He was educated at Peers School, created for the children of the new, Western-style aristocracy established in the Meiji Restoration of 1868. There he began writing, publishing his first work at age sixteen, using the pen name "Mishima" so that people would not identify it as the work of a high school student. From his student days onward, Mishima had an ambivalent fascination for Western culture, admiring especially "decadent" writers such as Oscar Wilde while also decrying the vulgar materialism and moral corruption that he saw as part and parcel of Meiji-era Japan's tilting toward the West. He devoted intense study to classical Japanese literature, and he remains best known in Japan as a great modern practitioner of the traditional drama form of Noh.

His stories and novels, however, brought him his greatest fame abroad, and he was several times nominated for the Nobel Prize. His most ambitious novelistic project was a series of four volumes collectively called *The Sea of Fertility,* which span six decades from 1910 to 1970. Over the course of these volumes, a student (then a lawyer and judge) named Honda observes what appear to be successive reincarnations of his closest childhood friend, Kiyoaki—a personal embodiment of the dualities of a culture caught between a decayed classical tradition and an artificial imported culture. In the second selection below, set in wartime Tokyo, Honda observes the drastic yet strangely beautiful destruction the city has undergone as a result of Allied firebombing.

Mishima wrote constantly even as he maintained a complex personal life, with a wife and two children and also extensive forays into Tokyo's gay subculture. He became devoted to the movement known as Bushido, which stressed traditional values, loyalty to the Emperor, military strength, and self-sacrifice. Like others in the movement, and like the hero of his story "Patriotism," Mishima felt that the Western-style parliamentary government introduced in 1868 lacked courage and principles and allowed the Western powers free rein in Asia even as Western influence was subtly corrupting Japanese culture at home. In 1968 he created the Shield Society, a virtual private army. On 25 November 1970, the day he completed *The Sea of Fertility,* he led a small group of followers in storming the headquarters of Japan's Self-Defense Force, the much-reduced military establishment allowed Japan after its defeat in World War II. Taking the commander hostage, he addressed the local garrison from the commander's balcony, urging them to join him in restoring imperial power and samurai values. Greeted with catcalls from the troops—as he had expected—he went into the commander's office and committed ritual suicide, slashing his stomach open with a sword.

Mishima's story "Patriotism" eerily anticipates this highly theatrical closing chapter of his life, though in a much more secluded, domestic setting. The story is set in the turbulent days of February 1936, a time of economic crisis and growing conflict as Japan jockeyed with Western powers for control of China. Feeling hampered by an indecisive civilian government, a growing number of ultranationalist military officers were agitating for the government's overthrow and the return of full authority to the Emperor. On the night of February 26, a group of young officers shot several leading statesmen; the Prime Minister himself was a target, but the rebels killed his brother-in-law by mistake. The rebels held much of downtown Tokyo for three days before the leaders were captured and executed on February 29. In his opening paragraph, Mishima recounts the true story of the ritual suicide, or *seppuku,* of one of the rebels' comrades; he then imagines in detail what might have been the man's last hours together with his wife. Written in Mishima's characteristically deadpan style, the story suggests an intense identification—as much with the young lieutenant's wife as with the officer himself—tinged with a hint of mockery. In its oddly calm presentation of horrific events occurring in the stillness of a quiet household, "Patriotism" powerfully conveys the echoes of the conflict beyond the newly-wed couple's sliding doors.

PRONUNCIATIONS:
   Yukio Mishima: YOU-key-oh ME-shee-mah
   Shinji Takeyama: SHIN-jee tah-key-YAH-mah
   Reiko: RAY-koh

Patriotism[1]

1

On the twenty-eighth of February, 1936 (on the third day, that is, of the February 26 Incident), Lieutenant Shinji Takeyama of the Konoe Transport Battalion—profoundly disturbed by the knowledge that his closest colleagues had been with the mutineers from the beginning, and indignant at the imminent prospect of Imperial troops attacking Imperial troops—took his officer's sword and ceremonially disemboweled himself in the eight-mat room of his private residence in the sixth block of Aoba-chō, in Yotsuya Ward. His wife, Reiko, followed him, stabbing herself to death. The lieutenant's farewell note consisted of one sentence: "Long live the Imperial Forces." His wife's, after apologies for her unfilial conduct in thus preceding her parents to the grave, concluded: "The day which, for a soldier's wife, had to come, has come. . . ." The last moments of this heroic and dedicated couple were such as to make the gods themselves weep. The lieutenant's age, it should be noted, was thirty-one, his wife's twenty-three; and it was not half a year since the celebration of their marriage.

2

Those who saw the bride and bridegroom in the commemorative photograph—perhaps no less than those actually present at the lieutenant's wedding—had exclaimed in wonder at the bearing of this handsome couple. The lieutenant, majestic in military uniform, stood protectively beside his bride, his right hand resting upon his sword, his officer's cap held at his left side. His expression was severe, and his dark brows and wide-gazing eyes well conveyed the clear integrity of youth. For the beauty of the bride in her white over-robe no comparisons were adequate. In the eyes, round beneath soft brows, in the slender, finely shaped nose, and in the full lips, there was both sensuousness and refinement. One hand, emerging shyly from a sleeve of the over-robe, held a fan, and the tips of the fingers, clustering delicately, were like the bud of a moonflower.

   After the suicide, people would take out this photograph and examine it, and sadly reflect that too often there was a curse on these seemingly flawless unions. Perhaps it was no more than imagination, but looking at the picture after the tragedy it al-

---

1. Translated by Geoffrey Sargeant.

most seemed as if the two young people before the gold-lacquered screen were gazing, each with equal clarity, at the deaths which lay before them.

Thanks to the good offices of their go-between, Lieutenant General Ozeki, they had
been able to set themselves up in a new home at Aoba-chō in Yotsuya. "New home" is
perhaps misleading. It was an old three-room rented house backing onto a small garden.
As neither the six- nor the four-and-a-half-mat room downstairs was favored by the sun,
they used the upstairs eight-mat room as both bedroom and guest room. There was no
maid, so Reiko was left alone to guard the house in her husband's absence.

The honeymoon trip was dispensed with on the grounds that these were times of
national emergency. The two of them had spent the first night of their marriage at this
house. Before going to bed, Shinji, sitting erect on the floor with his sword laid before
him, had bestowed upon his wife a soldierly lecture. A woman who had become the
wife of a soldier should know and resolutely accept that her husband's death might
come at any moment. It could be tomorrow. It could be the day after. But, no matter
when it came—he asked—was she steadfast in her resolve to accept it? Reiko rose to
her feet, pulled open a drawer of the cabinet, and took out what was the most prized of
her new possessions, the dagger her mother had given her. Returning to her place, she
laid the dagger without a word on the mat before her, just as her husband had laid his
sword. A silent understanding was achieved at once, and the lieutenant never again
sought to test his wife's resolve.

In the first few months of her marriage Reiko's beauty grew daily more radiant,
shining serene like the moon after rain.

As both were possessed of young, vigorous bodies, their relationship was passionate. Nor was this merely a matter of the night. On more than one occasion, returning home straight from maneuvers, and begrudging even the time it took to remove
his mud-splashed uniform, the lieutenant had pushed his wife to the floor almost as
soon as he had entered the house. Reiko was equally ardent in her response. For a little more or a little less than a month, from the first night of their marriage Reiko knew
happiness, and the lieutenant, seeing this, was happy too.

Reiko's body was white and pure, and her swelling breasts conveyed a firm and
chaste refusal; but, upon consent, those breasts were lavish with their intimate, welcoming warmth. Even in bed these two were frighteningly and awesomely serious. In
the very midst of wild, intoxicating passions, their hearts were sober and serious.

By day the lieutenant would think of his wife in the brief rest periods between
training; and all day long, at home, Reiko would recall the image of her husband.
Even when apart, however, they had only to look at the wedding photograph for their
happiness to be once more confirmed. Reiko felt not the slightest surprise that a man
who had been a complete stranger until a few months ago should now have become
the sun about which her whole world revolved.

All these things had a moral basis, and were in accordance with the Education
Rescript's injunction that "husband and wife should be harmonious." Not once did
Reiko contradict her husband, nor did the lieutenant ever find reason to scold his wife.
On the god shelf below the stairway, alongside the tablet from the Great Ise Shrine,
were set photographs of their Imperial Majesties, and regularly every morning, before
leaving for duty, the lieutenant would stand with his wife at this hallowed place and
together they would bow their heads low. The offering water was renewed each
morning, and the sacred sprig of *sasaki* was always green and fresh. Their lives were
lived beneath the solemn protection of the gods and were filled with an intense happiness which set every fiber in their bodies trembling.

3

Although Lord Privy Seal Saitō's house was in their neighborhood, neither of them heard any noise of gunfire on the morning of February 26. It was a bugle, sounding muster in the dim, snowy dawn, when the ten-minute tragedy had already ended, which first disrupted the lieutenant's slumbers. Leaping at once from his bed, and without speaking a word, the lieutenant donned his uniform, buckled on the sword held ready for him by his wife, and hurried swiftly out into the snow-covered streets of the still darkened morning. He did not return until the evening of the twenty-eighth.

Later, from the radio news, Reiko learned the full extent of this sudden eruption of violence. Her life throughout the subsequent two days was lived alone, in complete tranquillity, and behind locked doors.

In the lieutenant's face, as he hurried silently out into the snowy morning, Reiko had read the determination to die. If her husband did not return, her own decision was made: she too would die. Quietly she attended to the disposition of her personal possessions. She chose her sets of visiting kimonos as keepsakes for friends of her schooldays, and she wrote a name and address on the stiff paper wrapping in which each was folded. Constantly admonished by her husband never to think of the morrow, Reiko had not even kept a diary and was now denied the pleasure of assiduously rereading her record of the happiness of the past few months and consigning each page to the fire as she did so. Ranged across the top of the radio were a small china dog, a rabbit, a squirrel, a bear, and a fox. There were also a small vase and a water pitcher. These comprised Reiko's one and only collection. But it would hardly do, she imagined, to give such things as keepsakes. Nor again would it be quite proper to ask specifically for them to be included in the coffin. It seemed to Reiko, as these thoughts passed through her mind, that the expressions on the small animals' faces grew even more lost and forlorn.

Reiko took the squirrel in her hand and looked at it. And then, her thoughts turning to a realm far beyond these child-like affections, she gazed up into the distance at the great sunlike principle which her husband embodied. She was ready, and happy, to be hurtled along to her destruction in that gleaming sun chariot—but now, for these few moments of solitude, she allowed herself to luxuriate in this innocent attachment to trifles. The time when she had genuinely loved these things, however, was long past. Now she merely loved the memory of having once loved them, and their place in her heart had been filled by more intense passions, by a more frenzied happiness. . . . For Reiko had never, even to herself, thought of those soaring joys of the flesh as a mere pleasure. The February cold, and the icy touch of the china squirrel, had numbed Reiko's slender fingers; yet, even so, in her lower limbs, beneath the ordered repetition of the pattern which crossed the skirt of her trim *meisen* kimono, she could feel now, as she thought of the lieutenant's powerful arms reaching out toward her, a hot moistness of the flesh which defied the snows.

She was not in the least afraid of the death hovering in her mind. Waiting alone at home, Reiko firmly believed that everything her husband was feeling or thinking now, his anguish and distress, was leading her—just as surely as the power in his flesh—to a welcome death. She felt as if her body could melt away with ease and be transformed to the merest fraction of her husband's thought.

Listening to the frequent announcements on the radio, she heard the names of several of her husband's colleagues mentioned among those of the insurgents. This was news of death. She followed the developments closely, wondering anxiously, as the situation became daily more irrevocable, why no Imperial ordinance was sent down, and watching what had at first been taken as a movement to restore the nation's honor come gradually to be branded with the infamous name of mutiny. There was no communication from the regiment. At any moment, it seemed, fighting might commence in the city streets, where the remains of the snow still lay.

Toward sundown on the twenty-eighth Reiko was startled by a furious pounding on the front door. She hurried downstairs. As she pulled with fumbling fingers at the bolt, the shape dimly outlined beyond the frosted-glass panel made no sound, but she knew it was her husband. Reiko had never known the bolt on the sliding door to be so stiff. Still it resisted. The door just would not open.

In a moment, almost before she knew she had succeeded, the lieutenant was standing before her on the cement floor inside the porch, muffled in a khaki greatcoat, his top boots heavy with slush from the street. Closing the door behind him, he returned the bolt once more to its socket. With what significance, Reiko did not understand.

"Welcome home."

Reiko bowed deeply, but her husband made no response. As he had already unfastened his sword and was about to remove his greatcoat, Reiko moved around behind to assist. The coat, which was cold and damp and had lost the odor of horse dung it normally exuded when exposed to the sun, weighed heavily upon her arm. Draping it across a hanger, and cradling the sword and leather belt in her sleeves, she waited while her husband removed his top boots and then followed behind him into the "living room." This was the six-mat room downstairs.

Seen in the clear light from the lamp, her husband's face, covered with a heavy growth of bristle, was almost unrecognizably wasted and thin. The cheeks were hollow, their luster and resilience gone. In his normal good spirits he would have changed into old clothes as soon as he was home and have pressed her to get supper at once, but now he sat before the table still in his uniform, his head drooping dejectedly. Reiko refrained from asking whether she should prepare the supper.

After an interval the lieutenant spoke.

"I knew nothing. They hadn't asked me to join. Perhaps out of consideration, because I was newly married. Kanō, and Homma too, and Yamaguchi."

Reiko recalled momentarily the faces of high-spirited young officers, friends of her husband, who had come to the house occasionally as guests.

"There may be an Imperial ordinance sent down tomorrow. They'll be posted as rebels, I imagine. I shall be in command of a unit with orders to attack them. . . . I can't do it. It's impossible to do a thing like that."

He spoke again.

"They've taken me off guard duty, and I have permission to return home for one night. Tomorrow morning, without question, I must leave to join the attack. I can't do it, Reiko."

Reiko sat erect with lowered eyes. She understood clearly that her husband had spoken of his death. The lieutenant was resolved. Each word, being rooted in death, emerged sharply and with powerful significance against this dark, unmovable background. Although the lieutenant was speaking of his dilemma, already there was no room in his mind for vacillation.

However, there was a clarity, like the clarity of a stream fed from melting snows, in the silence which rested between them. Sitting in his own home after the long two-day ordeal, and looking across at the face of his beautiful wife, the lieutenant was for the first time experiencing true peace of mind. For he had at once known, though she said nothing, that his wife divined the resolve which lay beneath his words.

"Well, then . . ." The lieutenant's eyes opened wide. Despite his exhaustion they were strong and clear, and now for the first time they looked straight into the eyes of his wife. "Tonight I shall cut my stomach."

Reiko did not flinch.

Her round eyes showed tension, as taut as the clang of a bell.

"I am ready," she said. "I ask permission to accompany you."

The lieutenant felt almost mesmerized by the strength in those eyes. His words flowed swiftly and easily, like the utterances of a man in delirium, and it was beyond his understanding how permission in a matter of such weight could be expressed so casually.

"Good. We'll go together. But I want you as a witness, first, for my own suicide. Agreed?"

When this was said a sudden release of abundant happiness welled up in both their hearts. Reiko was deeply affected by the greatness of her husband's trust in her. It was vital for the lieutenant, whatever else might happen, that there should be no irregularity in his death. For that reason there had to be a witness. The fact that he had chosen his wife for this was the first mark of his trust. The second, and even greater mark, was that though he had pledged that they should die together he did not intend to kill his wife first—he had deferred her death to a time when he would no longer be there to verify it. If the lieutenant had been a suspicious husband, he would doubtless, as in the usual suicide pact, have chosen to kill his wife first.

When Reiko said, "I ask permission to accompany you," the lieutenant felt these words to be the final fruit of the education which he had himself given his wife, starting on the first night of their marriage, and which had schooled her, when the moment came, to say what had to be said without a shadow of hesitation. This flattered the lieutenant's opinion of himself as a self-reliant man. He was not so romantic or conceited as to imagine that the words were spoken spontaneously, out of love for her husband.

With happiness welling almost too abundantly in their hearts, they could not help smiling at each other. Reiko felt as if she had returned to her wedding night.

Before her eyes was neither pain nor death. She seemed to see only a free and limitless expanse opening out into vast distances.

"The water is hot. Will you take your bath now?"

"Ah yes, of course."

"And supper . . .?"

The words were delivered in such level, domestic tones that the lieutenant came near to thinking, for the fraction of a second, that everything had been a hallucination.

"I don't think we'll need supper. But perhaps you could warm some sake?"

"As you wish."

As Reiko rose and took a *tanzen* gown from the cabinet for after the bath, she purposely directed her husband's attention to the opened drawer. The lieutenant rose, crossed to the cabinet, and looked inside. From the ordered array of paper wrappings he read, one by one, the addresses of the keepsakes. There was no grief in the lieutenant's response to this demonstration of heroic resolve. His heart was filled with tenderness. Like a husband who is proudly shown the childish purchases of a young wife, the lieutenant, overwhelmed by affection, lovingly embraced his wife from behind and implanted a kiss upon her neck.

Reiko felt the roughness of the lieutenant's unshaven skin against her neck. This sensation, more than being just a thing of this world, was for Reiko almost the world itself, but now—with the feeling that it was soon to be lost forever—it had freshness beyond all her experience. Each moment had its own vital strength, and the senses in every corner of her body were reawakened. Accepting her husband's caresses from behind, Reiko raised herself on the tips of her toes, letting the vitality seep through her entire body.

"First the bath, and then, after some sake . . . lay out the bedding upstairs, will you?"

The lieutenant whispered the words into his wife's ear. Reiko silently nodded.

Flinging off his uniform, the lieutenant went to the bath. To faint background noises of slopping water Reiko tended the charcoal brazier in the living room and began the preparations for warming the sake.

Taking the *tanzen,* a sash, and some underclothes, she went to the bathroom to ask how the water was. In the midst of a coiling cloud of steam the lieutenant was sitting cross-legged on the floor, shaving, and she could dimly discern the rippling movements of the muscles on his damp, powerful back as they responded to the movement of his arms.

There was nothing to suggest a time of any special significance. Reiko, going busily about her tasks, was preparing side dishes from odds and ends in stock. Her hands did not tremble. If anything, she managed even more efficiently and smoothly than usual. From time to time, it is true, there was a strange throbbing deep within her breast. Like distant lightning, it had a moment of sharp intensity and then vanished without a trace. Apart from that, nothing was in any way out of the ordinary.

The lieutenant, shaving in the bathroom, felt his warmed body miraculously healed at last of the desperate tiredness of the days of indecision and filled—in spite of the death which lay ahead—with pleasurable anticipation. The sound of his wife going about her work came to him faintly. A healthy physical craving, submerged for two days, reasserted itself.

The lieutenant was confident there had been no impurity in that joy they had experienced when resolving upon death. They had both sensed at that moment—though not, of course, in any clear and conscious way—that those permissible pleasures which they shared in private were once more beneath the protection of Righteousness and Divine Power, and of a complete and unassailable morality. On looking into each other's eyes and discovering there an honorable death, they had felt themselves safe once more behind steel walls which none could destroy, encased in an impenetrable armor of Beauty and Truth. Thus, so far from seeing any inconsistency or conflict between the urges of his flesh and the sincerity of his patriotism, the lieutenant was even able to regard the two as parts of the same thing.

Thrusting his face close to the dark, cracked, misted wall mirror, the lieutenant shaved himself with great care. This would be his death face. There must be no unsightly blemishes. The clean-shaven face gleamed once more with a youthful luster, seeming to brighten the darkness of the mirror. There was a certain elegance, he even felt, in the association of death with this radiantly healthy face.

Just as it looked now, this would become his death face! Already, in fact, it had half departed from the lieutenant's personal possession and had become the bust above a dead soldier's memorial. As an experiment he closed his eyes tight. Everything was wrapped in blackness, and he was no longer a living, seeing creature.

Returning from the bath, the traces of the shave glowing faintly blue beneath his smooth cheeks, he seated himself beside the now well-kindled charcoal brazier. Busy though Reiko was, he noticed, she had found time lightly to touch up her face. Her cheeks were gay and her lips moist. There was no shadow of sadness to be seen. Truly, the lieutenant felt, as he saw this mark of his young wife's passionate nature, he had chosen the wife he ought to have chosen.

As soon as the lieutenant had drained his sake cup he offered it to Reiko. Reiko had never before tasted sake, but she accepted without hesitation and sipped timidly.

"Come here," the lieutenant said.

Reiko moved to her husband's side and was embraced as she leaned backward across his lap. Her breast was in violent commotion, as if sadness, joy, and the potent sake were mingling and reacting within her. The lieutenant looked down into his wife's face. It was the last face he would see in this world, the last face he would see of his wife. The lieutenant scrutinized the face minutely, with the eyes of a traveler bidding farewell to splendid vistas which he will never revisit. It was a face he could not tire of looking at—the features regular yet not cold, the lips lightly closed with a soft strength. The lieutenant kissed those lips, unthinkingly. And suddenly, though there was not the slightest distortion of the face into the unsightliness of sobbing, he noticed that tears were welling slowly from beneath the long lashes of the closed eyes and brimming over into a glistening stream.

When, a little later, the lieutenant urged that they should move to the upstairs bedroom, his wife replied that she would follow after taking a bath. Climbing the stairs alone to the bedroom, where the air was already warmed by the gas heater, the lieutenant lay down on the bedding with arms outstretched and legs apart. Even the time at which he lay waiting for his wife to join him was no later and no earlier than usual.

He folded his hands beneath his head and gazed at the dark boards of the ceiling in the dimness beyond the range of the standard lamp. Was it death he was now waiting for? Or a wild ecstasy of the senses? The two seemed to overlap, almost as if the object of this bodily desire was death itself. But, however that might be, it was certain that never before had the lieutenant tasted such total freedom.

There was the sound of a car outside the window. He could hear the screech of its tires skidding in the snow piled at the side of the street. The sound of its horn re-echoed from nearby walls. . . . Listening to these noises he had the feeling that this house rose like a solitary island in the ocean of a society going as restlessly about its business as ever. All around, vastly and untidily, stretched the country for which he grieved. He was to give his life for it. But would that great country, with which he was prepared to remonstrate to the extent of destroying himself, take the slightest heed of his death? He did not know; and it did not matter. His was a battlefield without glory, a battlefield where none could display deeds of valor: it was the front line of the spirit.

Reiko's footsteps sounded on the stairway. The steep stairs in this old house creaked badly. There were fond memories in that creaking, and many a time, while waiting in bed, the lieutenant had listened to its welcome sound. At the thought that he would hear it no more he listened with intense concentration, striving for every corner of every moment of this precious time to be filled with the sound of those soft footfalls on the creaking stairway. The moments seemed transformed to jewels, sparkling with inner light.

Reiko wore a Nagoya sash about the waist of her *yukata*,[2] but as the lieutenant reached toward it, its redness sobered by the dimness of the light, Reiko's hand moved to his assistance and the sash fell away, slithering swiftly to the floor. As she

2. A light cotton robe with wide sleeves.

stood before him, still in her *yukata,* the lieutenant inserted his hands through the side slits beneath each sleeve, intending to embrace her as she was; but at the touch of his finger tips upon the warm naked flesh, and as the armpits closed gently about his hands, his whole body was suddenly aflame.

In a few moments the two lay naked before the glowing gas heater.

Neither spoke the thought, but their hearts, their bodies, and their pounding breasts blazed with the knowledge that this was the very last time. It was as if the words "The Last Time" were spelled out, in invisible brushstrokes, across every inch of their bodies.

The lieutenant drew his wife close and kissed her vehemently. As their tongues explored each other's mouths, reaching out into the smooth, moist interior, they felt as if the still-unknown agonies of death had tempered their senses to the keenness of red-hot steel. The agonies they could not yet feel, the distant pains of death, had refined their awareness of pleasure.

"This is the last time I shall see your body," said the lieutenant. "Let me look at it closely." And, tilting the shade on the lampstand to one side, he directed the rays along the full length of Reiko's outstretched form.

Reiko lay still with her eyes closed. The light from the low lamp clearly revealed the majestic sweep of her white flesh. The lieutenant, not without a touch of egocentricity, rejoiced that he would never see this beauty crumble in death.

At his leisure, the lieutenant allowed the unforgettable spectacle to engrave itself upon his mind. With one hand he fondled the hair, with the other he softly stroked the magnificent face, implanting kisses here and there where his eyes lingered. The quiet coldness of the high, tapering forehead, the closed eyes with their long lashes beneath faintly etched brows, the set of the finely shaped nose, the gleam of teeth glimpsed between full, regular lips, the soft cheeks and the small, wise chin . . . these things conjured up in the lieutenant's mind the vision of a truly radiant death face, and again and again he pressed his lips tight against the white throat—where Reiko's own hand was soon to strike—and the throat reddened faintly beneath his kisses. Returning to the mouth he laid his lips against it with the gentlest of pressures, and moved them rhythmically over Reiko's with the light rolling motion of a small boat. If he closed his eyes, the world became a rocking cradle.

Wherever the lieutenant's eyes moved his lips faithfully followed. The high, swelling breasts, surmounted by nipples like the buds of a wild cherry, hardened as the lieutenant's lips closed about them. The arms flowed smoothly downward from each side of the breast, tapering toward the wrists, yet losing nothing of their roundness or symmetry, and at their tips were those delicate fingers which had held the fan at the wedding ceremony. One by one, as the lieutenant kissed them, the fingers withdrew behind their neighbor as if in shame. . . . The natural hollow curving between the bosom and the stomach carried in its lines a suggestion not only of softness but of resilient strength, and while it gave forewarning of the rich curves spreading outward from there to the hips it had, in itself, an appearance only of restraint and proper discipline. The whiteness and richness of the stomach and hips was like milk brimming in a great bowl, and the sharply shadowed dip of the navel could have been the fresh impress of a raindrop, fallen there that very moment. Where the shadows gathered more thickly, hair clustered, gentle and sensitive, and as the agitation mounted in the now no longer passive body there hung over this region a scent like the smoldering of fragrant blossoms, growing steadily more pervasive.

At length, in a tremulous voice, Reiko spoke.

"Show me. . . . Let me look too, for the last time."

Never before had he heard from his wife's lips so strong and unequivocal a request. It was as if something which her modesty had wished to keep hidden to the end had suddenly burst its bonds of constraint. The lieutenant obediently lay back and surrendered himself to his wife. Lithely she raised her white, trembling body, and—burning with an innocent desire to return to her husband what he had done for her—placed two white fingers on the lieutenant's eyes, which gazed fixedly up at her, and gently stroked them shut.

Suddenly overwhelmed by tenderness, her cheeks flushed by a dizzying uprush of emotion, Reiko threw her arms about the lieutenant's close-cropped head. The bristly hairs rubbed painfully against her breast, the prominent nose was cold as it dug into her flesh, and his breath was hot. Relaxing her embrace, she gazed down at her husband's masculine face. The severe brows, the closed eyes, the splendid bridge of the nose, the shapely lips drawn firmly together . . . the blue, clean-shaven cheeks reflecting the light and gleaming smoothly. Reiko kissed each of these. She kissed the broad nape of the neck, the strong, erect shoulders, the powerful chest with its twin circles like shields and its russet nipples. In the armpits, deeply shadowed by the ample flesh of the shoulders and chest, a sweet and melancholy odor emanated from the growth of hair, and in the sweetness of this odor was contained, somehow, the essence of young death. The lieutenant's naked skin glowed like a field of barley, and everywhere the muscles showed in sharp relief, converging on the lower abdomen about the small, unassuming navel. Gazing at the youthful, firm stomach, modestly covered by a vigorous growth of hair, Reiko thought of it as it was soon to be, cruelly cut by the sword, and she laid her head upon it, sobbing in pity, and bathed it with kisses.

At the touch of his wife's tears upon his stomach the lieutenant felt ready to endure with courage the cruelest agonies of his suicide.

What ecstasies they experienced after these tender exchanges may well be imagined. The lieutenant raised himself and enfolded his wife in a powerful embrace, her body now limp with exhaustion after her grief and tears. Passionately they held their faces close, rubbing cheek against cheek. Reiko's body was trembling. Their breasts, moist with sweat, were tightly joined, and every inch of the young and beautiful bodies had become so much one with the other that it seemed impossible there should ever again be a separation. Reiko cried out. From the heights they plunged into the abyss, and from the abyss they took wing and soared once more to dizzying heights. The lieutenant panted like the regimental standard-bearer on a route march. . . . As one cycle ended, almost immediately a new wave of passion would be generated, and together—with no trace of fatigue—they would climb again in a single breathless movement to the very summit.

4

When the lieutenant at last turned away, it was not from weariness. For one thing, he was anxious not to undermine the considerable strength he would need in carrying out his suicide. For another, he would have been sorry to mar the sweetness of these last memories by overindulgence.

Since the lieutenant had clearly desisted, Reiko too, with her usual compliance, followed his example. The two lay naked on their backs, with fingers interlaced, staring fixedly at the dark ceiling. The room was warm from the heater, and even when the sweat had ceased to pour from their bodies they felt no cold. Outside, in the hushed night, the sounds of passing traffic had ceased. Even the noises of the trains and streetcars around Yotsuya station did not penetrate this far. After echoing through the region bounded by the moat, they were lost in the heavily wooded park fronting the broad driveway before Akasaka Palace. It was hard to believe in the tension gripping this whole quarter, where the two factions of the bitterly divided Imperial Army now confronted each other, poised for battle.

Savoring the warmth glowing within themselves, they lay still and recalled the ecstasies they had just known. Each moment of the experience was relived. They remembered the taste of kisses which had never wearied, the touch of naked flesh, episode after episode of dizzying bliss. But already, from the dark boards of the ceiling, the face of death was peering down. These joys had been final, and their bodies would never know them again. Not that joy of this intensity—and the same thought had occurred to them both—was ever likely to be re-experienced, even if they should live on to old age.

The feel of their fingers intertwined—this too would soon be lost. Even the wood-grain patterns they now gazed at on the dark ceiling boards would be taken from them. They could feel death edging in, nearer and nearer. There could be no hesitation now. They must have the courage to reach out to death themselves, and to seize it.

"Well, let's make our preparations," said the lieutenant. The note of determination in the words was unmistakable, but at the same time Reiko had never heard her husband's voice so warm and tender.

After they had risen, a variety of tasks awaited them.

The lieutenant, who had never once before helped with the bedding, now cheerfully slid back the door of the closet, lifted the mattress across the room by himself, and stowed it away inside.

Reiko turned off the gas heater and put away the lamp standard. During the lieutenant's absence she had arranged this room carefully, sweeping and dusting it to a fresh cleanness, and now—if one overlooked the rosewood table drawn into one corner—the eight-mat room gave all the appearance of a reception room ready to welcome an important guest.

"We've seen some drinking here, haven't we? With Kanō and Homma and Noguchi . . ."

"Yes, they were great drinkers, all of them."

"We'll be meeting them before long, in the other world. They'll tease us, I imagine, when they find I've brought you with me."

Descending the stairs, the lieutenant turned to look back into this calm, clean room, now brightly illuminated by the ceiling lamp. There floated across his mind the faces of the young officers who had drunk there, and laughed, and innocently bragged. He had never dreamed then that he would one day cut open his stomach in this room.

In the two rooms downstairs husband and wife busied themselves smoothly and serenely with their respective preparations. The lieutenant went to the toilet, and then to the bathroom to wash. Meanwhile Reiko folded away her husband's padded robe, placed his uniform tunic, his trousers, and a newly cut bleached loincloth in the bathroom, and set out sheets of paper on the living-room table for the farewell notes. Then she removed the lid from the writing box and began rubbing ink from the ink tablet. She had already decided upon the wording of her own note.

Reiko's fingers pressed hard upon the cold gilt letters of the ink tablet, and the water in the shallow well at once darkened, as if a black cloud had spread across it.[3] She stopped thinking that this repeated action, this pressure from her fingers, this rise and fall of faint sound, was all and solely for death. It was a routine domestic task, a

---

3. The couple uses the traditional means of writing, with a brush, first preparing the ink by mixing powdered ink with water.

simple paring away of time until death should finally stand before her. But somehow, in the increasingly smooth motion of the tablet rubbing on the stone, and in the scent from the thickening ink, there was unspeakable darkness.

Neat in his uniform, which he now wore next to his skin, the lieutenant emerged from the bathroom. Without a word he seated himself at the table, bolt upright, took a brush in his hand, and stared undecidedly at the paper before him.

Reiko took a white silk kimono with her and entered the bathroom. When she reappeared in the living room, clad in the white kimono and with her face lightly made up, the farewell note lay completed on the table beneath the lamp. The thick black brushstrokes said simply:

"Long Live the Imperial Forces—Army Lieutenant Takeyama Shinji."

While Reiko sat opposite him writing her own note, the lieutenant gazed in silence, intensely serious, at the controlled movement of his wife's pale fingers as they manipulated the brush.

With their respective notes in their hands—the lieutenant's sword strapped to his side, Reiko's small dagger thrust into the sash of her white kimono—the two of them stood before the god shelf and silently prayed. Then they put out all the downstairs lights. As he mounted the stairs the lieutenant turned his head and gazed back at the striking, white-clad figure of his wife, climbing behind him, with lowered eyes, from the darkness beneath.

The farewell notes were laid side by side in the alcove of the upstairs room. They wondered whether they ought not to remove the hanging scroll, but since it had been written by their go-between, Lieutenant General Ozeki, and consisted, moreover, of two Chinese characters signifying "Sincerity," they left it where it was. Even if it were to become stained with splashes of blood, they felt that the lieutenant general would understand.

The lieutenant, sitting erect with his back to the alcove, laid his sword on the floor before him.

Reiko sat facing him, a mat's width away. With the rest of her so severely white the touch of rouge on her lips seemed remarkably seductive.

Across the dividing mat they gazed intently into each other's eyes. The lieutenant's sword lay before his knees. Seeing it, Reiko recalled their first night and was overwhelmed with sadness. The lieutenant spoke, in a hoarse voice:

"As I have no second to help me I shall cut deep. It may look unpleasant, but please do not panic. Death of any sort is a fearful thing to watch. You must not be discouraged by what you see. Is that all right?"

"Yes."

Reiko nodded deeply.

Looking at the slender white figure of his wife the lieutenant experienced a bizarre excitement. What he was about to perform was an act in his public capacity as a soldier, something he had never previously shown his wife. It called for a resolution equal to the courage to enter battle; it was a death of no less degree and quality than death in the front line. It was his conduct on the battlefield that he was now to display.

Momentarily the thought led the lieutenant to a strange fantasy. A lonely death on the battlefield, a death beneath the eyes of his beautiful wife . . . in the sensation that he was now to die in these two dimensions, realizing an impossible union of them both, there was sweetness beyond words. This must be the very pinnacle of good fortune, he thought. To have every moment of his death observed by those beautiful eyes—it was like being borne to death on a gentle, fragrant breeze. There was some special favor here. He did not understand precisely what it was, but it was a domain unknown to others: a dispensation granted to no one else had been permitted to himself. In the radiant, bridelike figure of his white-robed wife the lieutenant seemed to see a vision of all those things he had loved and for which he was to lay down his life—the Imperial Household, the Nation, the Army Flag. All these, no less than the wife who sat before him, were presences observing him closely with clear and never-faltering eyes.

Reiko too was gazing intently at her husband, so soon to die, and she thought that never in this world had she seen anything so beautiful. The lieutenant always looked well in uniform, but now, as he contemplated death with severe brows and firmly closed lips, he revealed what was perhaps masculine beauty at its most superb.

"It's time to go," the lieutenant said at last.

Reiko bent her body low to the mat in a deep bow. She could not raise her face. She did not wish to spoil her make-up with tears, but the tears could not be held back.

When at length she looked up she saw hazily through the tears that her husband had wound a white bandage around the blade of his now unsheathed sword, leaving five or six inches of naked steel showing at the point.

Resting the sword in its cloth wrapping on the mat before him, the lieutenant rose from his knees, resettled himself cross-legged, and unfastened the hooks of his uniform collar. His eyes no longer saw his wife. Slowly, one by one, he undid the flat brass buttons. The dusky brown chest was revealed, and then the stomach. He unclasped his belt and undid the buttons of his trousers. The pure whiteness of the thickly coiled loincloth showed itself. The lieutenant pushed the cloth down with both hands, further to ease his stomach, and then reached for the white-bandaged blade of his sword. With his left hand he massaged his abdomen, glancing downward as he did so.

To reassure himself on the sharpness of his sword's cutting edge the lieutenant folded back the left trouser flap, exposing a little of his thigh, and lightly drew the blade across the skin. Blood welled up in the wound at once, and several streaks of red trickled downward, glistening in the strong light.

It was the first time Reiko had ever seen her husband's blood, and she felt a violent throbbing in her chest. She looked at her husband's face. The lieutenant was looking at the blood with calm appraisal. For a moment—though thinking at the same time that it was hollow comfort—Reiko experienced a sense of relief.

The lieutenant's eyes fixed his wife with an intense, hawk-like stare. Moving the sword around to his front, he raised himself slightly on his hips and let the upper half of his body lean over the sword point. That he was mustering his whole strength was apparent from the angry tension of the uniform at his shoulders. The lieutenant aimed to strike deep into the left of his stomach. His sharp cry pierced the silence of the room.

Despite the effort he had himself put into the blow, the lieutenant had the impression that someone else had struck the side of his stomach agonizingly with a thick rod of iron. For a second or so his head reeled and he had no idea what had happened. The five or six inches of naked point had vanished completely into his flesh, and the white bandage, gripped in his clenched fist, pressed directly against his stomach.

He returned to consciousness. The blade had certainly pierced the wall of the stomach, he thought. His breathing was difficult, his chest thumped violently, and in some far deep region, which he could hardly believe was a part of himself, a fearful and excruciating pain came welling up as if the ground had split open to disgorge a boiling stream of molten rock. The pain came suddenly nearer, with terrifying speed. The lieutenant bit his lower lip and stifled an instinctive moan.

Was this *seppuku*?[4]—he was thinking. It was a sensation of utter chaos, as if the sky had fallen on his head and the world was reeling drunkenly. His will power and courage, which had seemed so robust before he made the incision, had now dwindled to something like a single hairlike thread of steel, and he was assailed by the uneasy feeling that he must advance along this thread, clinging to it with desperation. His clenched fist had grown moist. Looking down, he saw that both his hand and the cloth about the blade were drenched in blood. His loincloth too was dyed a deep red. It struck him as incredible that, amidst this terrible agony, things which could be seen could still be seen, and existing things existed still.

The moment the lieutenant thrust the sword into his left side and she saw the deathly pallor fall across his face, like an abruptly lowered curtain, Reiko had to struggle to prevent herself from rushing to his side. Whatever happened, she must watch. She must be a witness. That was the duty her husband had laid upon her. Opposite her, a mat's space away, she could clearly see her husband biting his lip to stifle the pain. The pain was there, with absolute certainty, before her eyes. And Reiko had no means of rescuing him from it.

The sweat glistened on her husband's forehead. The lieutenant closed his eyes, and then opened them again, as if experimenting. The eyes had lost their luster, and seemed innocent and empty like the eyes of a small animal.

The agony before Reiko's eyes burned as strong as the summer sun, utterly remote from the grief which seemed to be tearing herself apart within. The pain grew steadily in stature, stretching upward. Reiko felt that her husband had already become a man in a separate world, a man whose whole being had been resolved into pain, a prisoner in a cage of pain where no hand could reach out to him. But Reiko felt no pain at all. Her grief was not pain. As she thought about this, Reiko began to feel as if someone had raised a cruel wall of glass high between herself and her husband.

Ever since her marriage her husband's existence had been her own existence, and every breath of his had been a breath drawn by herself. But now, while her husband's existence in pain was a vivid reality, Reiko could find in this grief of hers no certain proof at all of her own existence.

With only his right hand on the sword the lieutenant began to cut sideways across his stomach. But as the blade became entangled with the entrails it was pushed constantly outward by their soft resilience; and the lieutenant realized that it would be necessary, as he cut, to use both hands to keep the point pressed deep into his stomach. He pulled the blade across. It did not cut as easily as he had expected. He directed the strength of his whole body into his right hand and pulled again. There was a cut of three or four inches.

The pain spread slowly outward from the inner depths until the whole stomach reverberated. It was like the wild clanging of a bell. Or like a thousand bells which jangled simultaneously at every breath he breathed and every throb of his pulse, rocking his whole being. The lieutenant could no longer stop himself from moaning. But by now the blade had cut its way through to below the navel, and when he noticed this he felt a sense of satisfaction, and a renewal of courage.

The volume of blood had steadily increased, and now it spurted from the wound as if propelled by the beat of the pulse. The mat before the lieutenant was drenched red with splattered blood, and more blood overflowed onto it from pools which gath-

4. Ritual suicide.

ered in the folds of the lieutenant's khaki trousers. A spot, like a bird, came flying across to Reiko and settled on the lap of her white silk kimono.

By the time the lieutenant had at last drawn the sword across to the right side of his stomach, the blade was already cutting shallow and had revealed its naked tip, slippery with blood and grease. But, suddenly stricken by a fit of vomiting, the lieutenant cried out hoarsely. The vomiting made the fierce pain fiercer still, and the stomach, which had thus far remained firm and compact, now abruptly heaved, opening wide its wound, and the entrails burst through, as if the wound too were vomiting. Seemingly ignorant of their master's suffering, the entrails gave an impression of robust health and almost disagreeable vitality as they slipped smoothly out and spilled over into the crotch. The lieutenant's head drooped, his shoulders heaved, his eyes opened to narrow slits, and a thin trickle of saliva dribbled from his mouth. The gold markings on his epaulettes caught the light and glinted.

Blood was scattered everywhere. The lieutenant was soaked in it to his knees, and he sat now in a crumpled and listless posture, one hand on the floor. A raw smell filled the room. The lieutenant, his head drooping, retched repeatedly, and the movement showed vividly in his shoulders. The blade of the sword, now pushed back by the entrails and exposed to its tip, was still in the lieutenant's right hand.

It would be difficult to imagine a more heroic sight than that of the lieutenant at this moment, as he mustered his strength and flung back his head. The movement was performed with sudden violence, and the back of his head struck with a sharp crack against the alcove pillar. Reiko had been sitting until now with her face lowered, gazing in fascination at the tide of blood advancing toward her knees, but the sound took her by surprise and she looked up.

The lieutenant's face was not the face of a living man. The eyes were hollow, the skin parched, the once so lustrous cheeks and lips the color of dried mud. The right hand alone was moving. Laboriously gripping the sword, it hovered shakily in the air like the hand of a marionette and strove to direct the point at the base of the lieutenant's throat. Reiko watched her husband make this last, most heart-rending, futile exertion. Glistening with blood and grease, the point was thrust at the throat again and again. And each time it missed its aim. The strength to guide it was no longer there. The straying point struck the collar and the collar badges. Although its hooks had been unfastened, the stiff military collar had closed together again and was protecting the throat.

Reiko could bear the sight no longer. She tried to go to her husband's help, but she could not stand. She moved through the blood on her knees, and her white skirts grew deep red. Moving to the rear of her husband, she helped no more than by loosening the collar. The quivering blade at last contacted the naked flesh of the throat. At that moment Reiko's impression was that she herself had propelled her husband forward; but that was not the case. It was a movement planned by the lieutenant himself, his last exertion of strength. Abruptly he threw his body at the blade, and the blade pierced his neck, emerging at the nape. There was a tremendous spurt of blood and the lieutenant lay still, cold blue-tinged steel protruding from his neck at the back.

5

Slowly, her socks slippery with blood, Reiko descended the stairway. The upstairs room was now completely still.

Switching on the ground-floor lights, she checked the gas jet and the main gas plug and poured water over the smoldering, half-buried charcoal in the brazier. She stood before the upright mirror in the four-and-a-half-mat room and held up her skirts. The bloodstains made it seem as if a bold, vivid pattern was printed across the lower half of her white kimono. When she sat down before the mirror, she was conscious of the dampness and coldness of her husband's blood in the region of her thighs, and she shivered. Then, for a long while, she lingered over her toilet preparations. She applied the rouge generously to her cheeks, and her lips too she painted heavily. This was no longer make-up to please her husband. It was make-up for the world which she would leave behind, and there was a touch of the magnificent and the spectacular in her brushwork. When she rose, the mat before the mirror was wet with blood. Reiko was not concerned about this.

Returning from the toilet, Reiko stood finally on the cement floor of the porchway. When her husband had bolted the door here last night it had been in preparation for death. For a while she stood immersed in the consideration of a simple problem. Should she now leave the bolt drawn? If she were to lock the door, it could be that the neighbors might not notice their suicide for several days. Reiko did not relish the thought of their two corpses putrifying before discovery. After all, it seemed, it would be best to leave it open. . . . She released the bolt, and also drew open the frosted-glass door a fraction. . . . At once a chill wind blew in. There was no sign of anyone in the midnight streets, and stars glittered ice-cold through the trees in the large house opposite.

Leaving the door as it was, Reiko mounted the stairs. She had walked here and there for some time and her socks were no longer slippery. About halfway up, her nostrils were already assailed by a peculiar smell.

The lieutenant was lying on his face in a sea of blood. The point protruding from his neck seemed to have grown even more prominent than before. Reiko walked heedlessly across the blood. Sitting beside the lieutenant's corpse, she stared intently at the face, which lay on one cheek on the mat. The eyes were opened wide, as if the lieutenant's attention had been attracted by something. She raised the head, folding it in her sleeve, wiped the blood from the lips, and bestowed a last kiss.

Then she rose and took from the closet a new white blanket and a waist cord. To prevent any derangement of her skirts, she wrapped the blanket about her waist and bound it there firmly with the cord.

Reiko sat herself on a spot about one foot distant from the lieutenant's body. Drawing the dagger from her sash, she examined its dully gleaming blade intently, and held it to her tongue. The taste of the polished steel was slightly sweet.

Reiko did not linger. When she thought how the pain which had previously opened such a gulf between herself and her dying husband was now to become a part of her own experience, she saw before her only the joy of herself entering a realm her husband had already made his own. In her husband's agonized face there had been something inexplicable which she was seeing for the first time. Now she would solve that riddle. Reiko sensed that at last she too would be able to taste the true bitterness and sweetness of that great moral principle in which her husband believed. What had until now been tasted only faintly through her husband's example she was about to savor directly with her own tongue.

Reiko rested the point of the blade against the base of her throat. She thrust hard. The wound was only shallow. Her head blazed, and her hands shook uncontrollably. She gave the blade a strong pull sideways. A warm substance flooded into her mouth, and everything before her eyes reddened, in a vision of spouting blood. She gathered her strength and plunged the point of the blade deep into her throat.

from The Temple of Dawn[1]

[TOKYO IN WARTIME]

When Honda's thinking had evolved this far, everything around him took on an unanticipated appearance.

This particular day, he happened to have been invited to a villa in Shoto in the Shibuya district concerning a prolonged lawsuit and was waiting in the second-floor reception room. No lodgings were available, and when the plaintiff came up to Tokyo on matters of litigation, he stayed at the house of some wealthy man from his home region. The owner had long since left Tokyo for Karuizawa to avoid the bombings.

The administrative suit was being conducted with a leisureliness that stood above time. It had, in fact, been initiated by a law promulgated in 1899, and the origin of the dispute itself went back to post-Restoration days several decades earlier. The accused in this case was the government, and even the defendant's title had changed from Minister of Agriculture and Commerce to that of Agriculture and Forestry with the reorganization of the cabinet. Lawyers representing the plaintiff covered several generations, and now, if Honda, who had been entrusted with the case, won, according to the original agreement one third of the entire land accruing to the plaintiff would be his remuneration. However, he did not expect that the litigation would be over in his lifetime.

Thus he came to the Shibuya villa only to pass the time, using the work as a pretext. In reality he came in anticipation of the polished rice and chicken that his client usually brought as a gift from the country.

The client, who should have long since arrived, was not there yet. He was no doubt having difficulty with the trains.

The June afternoon was too warm for his civilian uniform and gaiters, so Honda opened the tall, oblong English window and stood by it to catch some air. Having had no military experience, he could not to this day manage his gaiters properly, and they tended to slip off his legs and to bunch around his calves, giving him the sensation of dragging a pilgrim's bag around his legs when he walked. His wife Rié always feared that the loose gaiters might get caught in the crowded streetcars and trip him.

Perspiration seeped through the lumpy areas of the gaiters today. The vulgarly shiny summer uniform, made of some staple fiber, retained every crease, and Honda knew that the back of his jacket must be puckered into ugly wrinkles from sitting. But it was no use straightening it.

From the window, he could see all the way to the Shibuya Station area bathed in June light. The residential parts of the immediate vicinity had survived relatively intact, but the area from the foot of the plateau up to the station was freshly bombed ruins spotted with half-destroyed concrete buildings. The air raids that had razed the area had occurred, only the week before, on the nights of May twenty-fourth and twenty-fifth, 1945, during which a total of five hundred B-29s had fire-bombed various residential parts of Tokyo. The odor of the conflagration still remained, and the memory of the hellish scene still lingered in the light of day.

The odor, like that of a crematorium, was mixed with more ordinary smells such as those from kitchens or bonfires, commingling with the pungent tang of chemicals as in a pharmaceutical factory or machinery. The smell of burnt-out ruins was already familiar to Honda. Fortunately his house in Hongo had not yet been touched.

---

1. Translated by E. D. Saunders and C. S. Seigle.

In the continuous metallic whine of bombs drilling through the night sky above, followed by a series of explosions and the release of fire bombs, he could always hear something inhuman, something like the voices of women cheering somewhere in the sky. Honda realized later that these were the cries of the damned.

In the burnt-out ruins, the debris had turned rusty, and the crushed roofs had remained untouched. Pillars of various heights stood everywhere like blackened pickets, and ashes crumbled from them to dance in the faint breeze.

Here and there something glittered brightly—for the most part, the remains of shattered panes of glass, glass surfaces burned and warped, pieces of broken bottles that reflected the sun. These little fragments harvested all the June light they could gather to them. Honda beheld for the first time the brilliance of the rubble.

The concrete foundations of houses were clearly limned under the crumbled walls. High and low, each was lit by the afternoon sun. For this reason, the entire ruin had the appearance of a type mold for a sheet of newsprint. But the predominant shade was the light reddish brown of a flowerpot, not the gloomy gray unevenness of a newspaper mold.

There was little greenery, for the area had been mostly commercial. Some half-burned trees were still standing along the streets.

Many shattered office buildings had paneless windows on this side, through which one could see the light reflecting in the glass on the far side, and the window frames were blackened, probably by the soot that had been deposited by the shooting flames.

It was a sloping area with a complex mesh of back streets on different levels. The concrete stairs and steps that remained led expectantly to nothing. Nothing remained either above or below them. In the field of rubble too there was no starting point, no destination; only the stairways adhered to direction.

All was quiet, but there were faint stirrings and things would rise softly. When he looked, it seemed like some hallucination, in which blackened corpses ravaged by countless vermin began to stir. They were ashes caught in the breeze, rising everywhere. There were white ashes and black ashes. Some floating ash adhered to a crumbling wall and rested there. Ashes of straw, ashes of books, ashes from a secondhand bookstall, ashes from a quilt maker's shop, floating about individually, commingling indiscriminately, moving, shifting over the face of the devastation.

An area of asphalt road gleamed blackly with water spurting from a ruptured main.

The sky was strangely spacious and the summer clouds immaculately white.

This was the world presented to Honda's five senses at this very moment. His plentiful savings had enabled him to accept only those legal cases that suited him during the war, and the study of samsara and reincarnation which entirely filled his leisure time seemed designed for the purpose of making this devastation manifest.[2] The destroyer was Honda himself.

The vast panorama of devastation before his eyes, resembling the end of the world, was not the end itself, nor was it the beginning. It was a world that imperturbably regenerated itself from instant to instant. *Alaya* consciousness,[3] perturbed by nothing, accepted this expanse of reddish ruin as one world, relinquishing it the next moment, accepting in the same way other worlds in which the color of destruction deepened with every day, with every month.

---

2. Honda has been studying Indian philosophy, seeking to integrate it with his work in Western-based law. Samsara is the Hindu doctrine of the repeated cycle of birth and death that souls undergo before they achieve enlightenment and are freed from the world.

3. In one school of Buddhist thought, the world is essentially a mental construct, continually being destroyed and then reborn in the observer's consciousness (*yuishiki*, in Japanese) from a general storehouse (*alaya*) of past materials and experiences.

Honda felt no emotion as he compared this sight with the city as it had been. Only when his eyes caught the bright reflections of the fragments of broken glass in the ruins and he was momentarily blinded did he understand with the sureness of his senses that the glass, the whole ruin would disappear the next instant to make way for another. He would resist catastrophe with catastrophe, and he would deal with the infinite disintegration and desolation with ever more gigantic and all-inclusive instantaneously repeated devastation. Yes, he must grasp with his mind the instant-by-instant, inevitable total destruction and prepare for the carnage of an uncertain future. He was elated to the point of trembling with these refreshing ideas that he had gleaned from Yuishiki doctrine.

Paul Celan
1920–1970

Is it possible to write poetry and novels about the Holocaust? What kind of language would be appropriate to describe so horrendous an event? Who would be entitled to write it? These questions gave rise to protracted and controversial debates in the German-speaking world after World War II. Paul Celan's poem "Death Fugue," first written in 1944 or 1945 but not published in Germany until 1952, had a crucial impact on this debate and has remained one of the most lasting translations of the Holocaust experience into poetry. Originally entitled "Death Tango," it captures the experience of concentration camp inmates who were forced to dig graves but also play music for the Nazi overseers who ended up murdering most of them. With a broad range of allusions to the Bible, German fairy tales, the music of Johann Sebastian Bach, and literary texts by Johann Wolfgang von Goethe and Heinrich Heine, the rhythmic repetitions of "Death Fugue" convey a sense of the tedium and despair of life in the death camps and yet also of the high ideals and cultural traditions that are buried along with the victims. Harking back to Romantic and Symbolist forms of poetic expression, "Death Fugue" also incorporates some of the stark metaphoric contrasts—e.g., "black milk"—that were typical of Surrealism.

The use of the pronoun "we" might lead one to believe that the poem was in fact written in a concentration camp. It was not, although Paul Celan—a pseudonym based on his real name, Paul Ancel/Antschel, which he adopted after World War II—did have firsthand experience of Nazi camps. Born in 1920 to a German-Jewish family in Czernowitz (which was then part of Romania), he witnessed the German occupation during the war; his parents were deported and died, and he himself was interned in a forced-labor camp from 1942 to 1944. After his release, he lived in Bucharest under Soviet occupation and in 1948 emigrated to Paris, where he spent the rest of his life. After *Poppy and Memory,* in which "Death Fugue" appeared in 1952, nine more volumes of his poetry were published, two posthumously. As his career advanced, Celan's poetry grew more and more elliptic and hermetic and gave rise to vigorous debates over its meaning. Besides his treatment of the Holocaust, Celan's complex relationship to his own Jewishness, to Judaism in general, and to the German language and literary tradition became subjects of often heated controversy. In spite of great public recognition of his work, Celan was plagued by psychological breakdowns that eventually led to his suicide in 1970. His poetry, both difficult and gripping, remains one of the most forceful engagements with the question of how war, violence, and the enjoyment of lyrical beauty might be brought together.

Death Fugue[1]

Black milk of dawn we drink it at dusk
we drink it at noon and at daybreak we drink it at night

1. Translated by Joachim Neugroschel.

Pablo Picasso, *Guernica*, 1937. At the height of the Spanish Civil War, the fascist forces of General Francisco Franco terror-bombed the northern Spanish city of Guernica, an ancient center of Basque culture. The Spanish-born Picasso had made his career in France from an early age and had been fairly removed from Spanish affairs, but the civil war galvanized him into active support for the Republican forces. He painted this huge mural (almost 12 feet high and over 25 feet wide) in just a month, using muted tones of grey and black and formal gestures found on ancient Greek vases to convey the horror of modern, mechanized war, as animals, people, and an entire culture feel the force of the unseen bombs.

>   we drink and we drink
>   we are digging a grave in the air there's room for us all
> 5   A man lives in the house he plays with the serpents he writes
>   he writes when it darkens to Germany your golden hair Margarete
>   he writes it and steps outside and the stars all aglisten he whistles for his
>   hounds
>   he whistles for his Jews he has them dig a grave in the earth
>   he commands us to play for the dance
>
> 10 Black milk of dawn we drink you at night
>   we drink you at daybreak and noon we drink you at dusk
>   we drink and we drink
>   A man lives in the house he plays with the serpents he writes
>   he writes when it darkens to Germany your golden hair Margarete
> 15 Your ashen hair Shulamite[2] we are digging a grave in the air there's room
>   for us all
>
>   He shouts cut deeper in the earth to some the rest of you sing and play
>   he reaches for the iron in his belt he heaves it his eyes are blue
>   make your spades cut deeper the rest of you play for the dance
>
>   Black milk of dawn we drink you at night
> 20 we drink you at noon and at daybreak we drink you at dusk
>   we drink and we drink
>   a man lives in the house your golden hair Margarete
>   your ashen hair Shulamite he plays with the serpents

2. Allusions to Gretchen, the tragic heroine of Goethe's *Faust*, and to the biblical *Song of Songs*.

He shouts play death more sweetly death is a master from Germany
25   he shouts play the violins darker you'll rise as smoke in the air
then you'll have a grave in the clouds there's room for you all

Black milk of dawn we drink you at night
we drink you at noon death is a master from Germany
we drink you at dusk and at daybreak we drink and we drink you
30   death is a master from Germany his eye is blue
he shoots you with bullets of lead his aim is true
a man lives in the house your golden hair Margarete
he sets his hounds on us he gives us a grave in the air
he plays with the serpents and dreams death is a master from Germany

35   your golden hair Margarete
your ashen hair Shulamite

Zbigniew Herbert
1924–1998

Zbigniew Herbert was born in Lvov, at that time in eastern Poland and now part of Ukraine. He studied literature, painting, economics, law, and philosophy at a number of institutions in Poland and then worked at a number of low-paying jobs. He refused to write within officially mandated communist guidelines and was forced to circulate his writing in the literary underground, where he developed a wide reputation for his poetry and essays as well as his translations. He moved to Warsaw in 1950, and his first book of poetry, *String of Light,* was published in 1956. He later lived for several years in France, but returned to Warsaw, where he lived until his death. He eventually won a number of international literary prizes. A subtle and complex sense of irony underlies Herbert's poetry. He is best known for *Mr. Cogito,* a cycle of poems that began to appear in 1974. He saw irony as an instrument of liberation from authoritarian structures, a theme exemplified best by his *Report from the Besieged City and Other Poems* (1983). His essays, of which *The Barbarian in the Garden* (1962) may be the best known, chronicle his journeys through classical European sites and the history of European culture including painting, architecture, and sculpture.

Herbert considers the poet to be chronicler of his people. In "Report from the Besieged City," he dramatizes this role, basing the survival of the city on its last chronicler, though his chronicle, the poem, is nothing more than the record of war's perennial depredations.

PRONUNCIATION:
Zbigniew: ZBIG-nee-you

Report from the Besieged City[1]
Too old to carry arms and fight like the others—

they graciously gave me the inferior role of chronicler
I record—I don't know for whom—the history of the siege

1. Translated by John and Bogdana Carpenter.

I am supposed to be exact but I don't know when the invasion began
two hundred years ago in December in September perhaps yesterday at dawn
everyone here suffers from a loss of the sense of time

all we have left is the place the attachment to the place
we still rule over the ruins of temples specters of gardens and houses
if we lose the ruins nothing will be left

I write as I can in the rhythm of interminable weeks
monday: empty storehouses a rat became the unit of currency
tuesday: the mayor murdered by unknown assailants
wednesday: negotiations for a cease-fire the enemy has imprisoned our
        messengers
we don't know where they are held that is the place of torture
thursday: after a stormy meeting a majority of voices rejected
the motion of the spice merchants for unconditional surrender
friday: the beginning of the plague saturday: our invincible defender
N. N. committed suicide sunday: no more water we drove back
an attack at the eastern gate called the Gate of the Alliance

all of this is monotonous I know it can't move anyone

I avoid any commentary I keep a tight hold on my emotions I write about
        the facts
only they it seems are appreciated in foreign markets
yet with a certain pride I would like to inform the world
that thanks to the war we have raised a new species of children
our children don't like fairy tales they play at killing
awake and asleep they dream of soup of bread and bones
just like dogs and cats

in the evening I like to wander near the outposts of the City
along the frontier of our uncertain freedom
I look at the swarms of soldiers below their lights
I listen to the noise of drums barbarian shrieks
truly it is inconceivable the City is still defending itself
the siege has lasted a long time the enemies must take turns
nothing unites them except the desire for our extermination
Goths the Tartars Swedes troops of the Emperor regiments of the
        Transfiguration
who can count them
the colors of their banners change like the forest on the horizon
from delicate bird's yellow in spring through green through red to winter's
        black

and so in the evening released from facts I can think
about distant ancient matters for example our
friends beyond the sea I know they sincerely sympathize
they send us flour lard sacks of comfort and good advice
they don't even know their fathers betrayed us
our former allies at the time of the second Apocalypse

45   their sons are blameless they deserve our gratitude therefore we are grateful
     they have not experienced a siege as long as eternity
     those struck by misfortune are always alone
     the defenders of the Dalai Lama[2] the Kurds the Afghan mountaineers

     now as I write these words the advocates of conciliation
50   have won the upper hand over the party of inflexibles
     a normal hesitation of moods fate still hangs in the balance

     cemeteries grow larger the number of defenders is smaller
     yet the defense continues it will continue to the end
     and if the City falls but a single man escapes
55   he will carry the City within himself on the roads of exile
     he will be the City
     we look in the face of hunger the face of fire face of death
     worst of all—the face of betrayal

     and only our dreams have not been humiliated

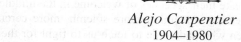

Alejo Carpentier
1904–1980

Born in Havana to a Cuban mother and a French architect father, Alejo Carpentier lived and studied in Paris for a number of years after his family moved there when he was twelve. He studied music in Paris and architecture upon the family's return to Cuba. He abandoned his studies for journalism, which he practiced until his arrest for leftist political activities. He was subsequently exiled to France. Upon his return from exile, he delved into the musical traditions of Cuba and the Caribbean, as well as into the slave trade of the colonial period. These ethnographic studies have figured prominently in his writings as musicologist, cultural historian, and novelist. In 1945 he felt obliged to abandon his native island once more, moving to Caracas, Venezuela, where he lived until the Cuban Revolution of 1956. He returned to Cuba then and served in a number of official capacities for the revolutionary government; a long career in governmental service culminated in his posting as ambassador to France, a position he held at the time of his death in Paris in 1980.

A bridge between the cultural history of the Caribbean and the avant-garde modernist movements of Europe, Carpentier had a profound understanding of the European Baroque period, the aesthetic traditions of Afro-Caribbean cultures, and a direct involvement in such movements as Surrealism, a cross-cultural familiarity he was able to translate into his literary work and into his critical and historical writings. This syncretism would result in what has come to be known as "magical realism." Time, history, and the migration of cultures are the most common themes of his literary works.

PRONUNCIATION:
     Alejo Carpentier: all-EH-ho car-pen-TIER

---

2. Spiritual leader of Tibet, forced into exile by the Chinese Communist government.

Like the Night[1]

And he traveled like the night.

—ILIAD, BOOK I.

I

Although the headlands still lay in shadow, the sea between them was beginning to turn green when the lookout blew his conch to announce that the fifty black ships sent us by King Agamemnon had arrived. Hearing the signal, those who had been waiting for so many days on the dung-covered threshing floors began carrying the wheat toward the shore, where rollers were already being made ready so that the vessels could be brought right up to the walls of the fortress. When the keels touched the sand, there was a certain amount of wrangling with the steersmen, because the Mycenaeans had so often been told about our complete ignorance of nautical matters that they tried to keep us at a distance with their poles. Moreover, the beach was now crowded with children, who got between the soldiers' legs, hindered their movements, and scrambled up the sides of the ships to steal nuts from under the oarsmen's benches. The transparent waves of dawn were breaking amid cries, insults, tussles, and blows, and our leading citizens could not make their speeches of welcome in the middle of such pandemonium. I had been expecting something more solemn, more ceremonious, from our meeting with these men who had come to fetch us to fight for them, and I walked off, feeling somewhat disillusioned, toward the fig tree on whose thickest branch I often sat astride, gripping the wood with my knees, because it reminded me somewhat of a woman's body.

As the ships were drawn out of the water and the tops of the mountains behind began to catch the sun, my first bad impression gradually faded; it had clearly been the result of a sleepless night of waiting, and also of my having drunk too heavily the day before with the young men recently arrived on the coast from inland, who were to embark with us soon after dawn. As I watched the procession of men carrying jars, black wineskins, and baskets moving toward the ships, a warm pride swelled within me, and a sense of my superiority as a soldier. That oil, that resinated wine, and above all that wheat from which biscuits would be cooked under the cinders at night while we slept in the shelter of the wet prows in some mysterious and unknown bay on the way to the Great City of Ships—the grain that I had helped to winnow with my shovel—all these things were being put on board for me; nor need I tire my long, muscular limbs, and arms designed for handling an ashwood pike, with tasks fit only for men who knew nothing but the smell of the soil, men who looked at the earth over the sweating backs of their animals or spent their lives crouched over it, weeding, uprooting, and raking, in almost the same attitudes as their own browsing cattle. These men would never pass under the clouds that at this time of day darken the distant green islands, whence the acrid-scented silphium was brought. They would never know the wide streets of the Trojans' city, the city we were now going to surround, attack, and destroy.

For days and days, the messengers sent us by the Mycenaean king had been telling us about Priam's insolence and the sufferings that threatened our people because of the arrogant behavior of his subjects. They had been jeering at our manly

---

1. Translated by F. Partridge.

way of life; and, trembling with rage, we had heard of the challenges hurled at us long-haired Achaeans by the men of Ilium[2] although our courage is unmatched by any other race. Cries of rage were heard, fists clenched and shaken, oaths sworn with the hands palms upward, and shields thrown against the walls, when we heard of the abduction of Helen of Sparta. While wine flowed from skins into helmets, in loud voices the emissaries told us of her marvelous beauty, her noble bearing and adorable way of walking, and described the cruelties she had endured in her miserable captivity. That same evening, when the whole town was seething with indignation, we were told that the fifty black ships were being sent. Fires were lighted in the bronze foundries while old women brought wood from the mountains.

And now, several days later, here I was gazing at the vessels drawn up at my feet, with their powerful keels and their masts at rest between the bulwarks like a man's virility between his thighs; I felt as if in some sense I was the owner of those timbers, transformed by some portentous carpentry unknown to our people into racehorses of the ocean, ready to carry us where the greatest adventure of all time was now unfolding like an epic. And I, son of a harness maker and grandson of a castrator of bulls, was to have the good fortune to go where those deeds were being done whose luster reached us in sailors' stories; I was to have the honor of seeing the walls of Troy, of following noble leaders and contributing my energy and strength to the cause of rescuing Helen of Sparta—a manly undertaking and the supreme triumph of a war that would give us prosperity, happiness, and pride in ourselves forever. I took a deep breath of the breeze blowing from the olive-covered hillside and thought how splendid it would be to die in such a just conflict, for the cause of Reason itself. But the idea of being pierced by an enemy lance made me think of my mother's grief and also of another, perhaps even profounder grief, though in this case the news would have to be heard with dry eyes because the hearer was head of the family. I walked slowly down to the town by the shepherds' path. Three kids were gamboling in the thyme-scented air. Down on the beach the loading of wheat was still going on.

II

The impending departure of the ships was being celebrated on all sides with thrumming of guitars and clashing of cymbals. The sailors from *La Gallarda* were dancing the zarambeque with enfranchised Negresses, and singing familiar coplas[3]—like the song of the *Moza del Retoño,* wherein groping hands supplied the blanks left in the words. Meanwhile the loading of wine, oil, and grain was still going on, with the help of the overseer's Indian servants, who were impatient to return to their native land. Our future chaplain was on his way to the harbor, driving before him two mules loaded with the bellows and pipes of a wooden organ. Whenever I met any of the men from the ships, there were noisy embraces, exaggerated gestures, and enough laughter and boasting to bring the women to their windows. We seemed to be men of a different race, expressly created to carry out exploits beyond the ken of the baker, the wool carder, and the merchant who hawked holland shirts embroidered by parties of nuns in their patios. In the middle of the square, their brass instruments flashing in the sun, the Captain's six trumpeters were playing popular airs while the Burgundian drummers thundered on their instruments, and a sackbut with a mouthpiece like a dragon was bellowing as if it wanted to bite.

2. Troy.   3. Couplets.

In his shop, smelling of calfskin and Cordovan leather, my father was driving his awl into a stirrup strap with the halfheartedness of someone whose mind is elsewhere. When he saw me, he took me in his arms with serene sadness, perhaps remembering the horrible death of Cristobalillo, the companion of my youthful escapades, whom the Indians of the Dragon's Mouth[4] had pierced with their arrows. But he knew that everyone was wild to embark for the Indies then—although most men in possession of their senses were already realizing that it was the "madness of many for the gain of a few." He spoke in praise of good craftsmanship and told me that a man could gain as much respect by carrying the harness maker's standard in the Corpus Christi procession as from dangerous exploits. He pointed out the advantages of a well-provided table, a full coffer, and a peaceful old age. But, probably having realized that the excitement in the town was steadily increasing and that my mood was not attuned to such sensible reasoning, he gently led me to the door of my mother's room.

This was the moment I had most dreaded, and I could hardly restrain my own tears when I saw hers, for we had put off telling her of my departure until everyone knew that my name had been entered in the books of the Casa de la Contratación.[5] I thanked her for the vows she had made to the Virgin of Navigators in exchange for my speedy return, and promised her everything she asked of me, such as to have no sinful dealings with the women of those far-off countries, whom the Devil kept in a state of paradisal nakedness in order to confuse and mislead unwary Christians, even if they were not actually corrupted by the sight of such a careless display of flesh. Then, realizing that it was useless to make demands of someone who was already dreaming of what lay beyond the horizon, my mother began asking me anxiously about the safety of the ships and the skill of their pilots. I exaggerated the solidity and seaworthiness of *La Gallarda,* declaring that her pilot was a veteran of the Indies and a comrade of Nuño García. And to distract her from her fears, I told her about the wonders of the New World, where all diseases could be cured by the Claw of the Great Beast and by bezoar stones; I told her, too, that in the country of the Omeguas there was a city built entirely of gold, so large that it would take a good walker a night and two days to cross it, and that we should surely go there unless we found our fortune in some not-yet-discovered regions inhabited by rich tribes for us to conquer. Gently shaking her head, my mother then said that travelers returned from the Indies told lying, boastful stories, and spoke of Amazons and anthropophagi,[6] of terrible Bermudan tempests and poisoned spears that transformed into a statue anyone they pierced.

Seeing that she confronted all my hopeful remarks with unpleasant facts, I talked to her of our high-minded aims and tried to make her see the plight of all the poor idol worshippers who did not even know the sign of the Cross. We should win thousands of souls to our holy religion and carry out Christ's commandments to the Apostles. We were soldiers of God as well as soldiers of the King, and by baptizing the Indians and freeing them from their barbarous superstitions our nation would win imperishable glory and greater happiness, prosperity, and power than all the Kingdoms of Europe. Soothed by my remarks, my mother hung a scapulary around my neck and gave me various ointments against the bites of poisonous creatures, at the same time making me promise that I would never go to sleep without wearing some woolen socks

4. The mouth of the Orinoco River in northeast South America.

5. Customs House in Seville, Spain, which coordinated

colonial trade during Spain's empire in the Americas.

6. Cannibals.

she had made for me herself. And as the cathedral bells began to peal, she went to look for an embroidered shawl that she wore only on very important occasions. On the way to church I noticed that in spite of everything my parents had, as it were, grown in stature because of their pride in having a son in the Captain's fleet, and that they greeted people more often and more demonstratively than usual. It is always gratifying to have a brave son on his way to fight for a splendid and just cause. I looked toward the harbor. Grain was still being carried onto the ships.

III

I used to call her my sweetheart, although no one yet knew that we were in love. When I saw her father near the ships, I realized that she would be alone, so I followed the dreary jetty battered by the winds, splashed with green water, and edged with chains and rings green with slime until I reached the last house, the one with green shutters that were always closed. Hardly had I sounded the tarnished knocker when the door opened, and I entered the house along with a gust of wind full of sea spray. The lamps had already been lighted because of the mist. My sweetheart sat down beside me in a deep armchair covered in old brocade and rested her head on my shoulder with such a sad air of resignation that I did not dare question those beloved eyes, which seemed to be gazing at nothing, but with an air of amazement. The strange objects that filled the room now took on a new significance for me. Some link bound me to the astrolabe, the compass, and the wind rose, as well as to the sawfish hanging from the beams of the ceiling and the charts by Mercator and Ortelius[7] spread out on either side of the fireplace among maps of the heavens populated by Bears, Dogs, and Archers.

Above the whistling of the wind as it crept under the doors, I heard the voice of my sweetheart asking how our preparations were going. Reassured to find that it was possible to talk of something other than ourselves, I told her about the Sulpicians and Recollects who were to embark with us, and praised the piety of the gentlemen and farmers chosen by the man who would take possession of these far-off countries in the name of the King of France. I told her what I knew of the great River Colbert,[8] bordered with ancient trees draped in silvery moss, its red waters flowing majestically beneath a sky white with herons. We were taking provisions for six months. The lowest decks of the *Belle* and the *Aimable* were full of corn. We were undertaking the important task of civilizing the vast areas of forest lying between the burning Gulf of Mexico and Chicagua, and we would teach new skills to the inhabitants.

Just when I thought my sweetheart was listening most attentively to what I was saying, she suddenly sat up, and said with unexpected vehemence that there was nothing glorious about the enterprise that had set all the town bells ringing since dawn. Last night, with her eyes inflamed with weeping, her anxiety to know something about the world across the sea to which I was going had driven her to pick up Montaigne's *Essais*[9] and read everything to do with America in the chapter on Coaches. There she had learned about the treachery of the Spaniards, and how they had succeeded in passing themselves off as gods, with their horses and bombards. Aflame

---

7. Gerardus Marcator (1512–1594) invented the "Mercator projection" used for many maps ever since. German geographer Abraham Ortelius's *Theatrum orbis terrarum* (1570) was the first modern atlas of the world.

8. The name the French gave to the Mississippi River in the 17th century.

9. Michel Eyquem de Montaigne (1533–1592) wrote on diverse cultures and their practices, including his essay "Of Cannibals," which refers to the New World, the destination of this expedition.

with virginal indignation, my sweetheart showed me the passage in which the skeptical Bordelais[1] says of the Indians that "we have made use of their ignorance and inexperience to draw them more easily into fraud, luxury, avarice, and all manner of inhumanity and cruelty by the example of our life and pattern of our customs." Blinded by
her distress at such perfidy, this devout young woman who always wore a gold cross
on her bosom actually approved of a writer who could impiously declare that the savages of the New World had no reason to exchange their religion for ours, their own
having served them very well for a long time.

I realized that these errors came only from the resentment of a girl in love—and a
very charming girl—against the man who was forcing her to wait for him for so long
merely because he wanted to make his fortune quickly in a much-proclaimed undertaking. But although I understood this, I felt deeply wounded by her scorn for my
courage and her lack of interest in an adventure that would make my name famous;
for the news of some exploit of mine, or of some region I had pacified, might well
lead to the King's conferring a title on me, even though it might involve a few Indians
dying by my hand. No great deed is achieved without a struggle, and as for our holy
faith, the Word must be imposed with blood. But it was jealousy that made my sweetheart paint such an ugly picture of the island of Santo Domingo, where we were to
make a landing, describing it in adorably unsuitable words as "a paradise of wicked
women." It was obvious that in spite of her chastity, she knew what sort of women
they were who often embarked for Cap Français from a jetty nearby under the supervision of the police and amid shouts of laughter and coarse jokes from the sailors.
Someone, perhaps one of the servants, may have told her that a certain sort of abstinence is not healthy for a man, and she was imagining me beset by greater perils than
the floods, storms, and water dragons that abound in American rivers, in some Eden
of nudity and demoralizing heat.

In the end I began to be annoyed that we should be having this wrangle instead of
the tender farewells I had expected at such a moment. I started abusing the cowardice
of women, their incapacity for heroism, the way their philosophy was bounded by
baby linen and workboxes, when a loud knocking announced the untimely return of
her father. I jumped out of a back window, unnoticed by anyone in the marketplace,
for passersby, fishermen, and drunkards—already numerous even so early in the
evening—had gathered around a table on which a man stood shouting. I took him at
first for a hawker trying to sell Orvieto elixir, but he turned out to be a hermit demanding the liberation of the holy places. I shrugged my shoulders and went on my
way. Some time ago I had been on the point of enlisting in Foulques de Neuilly's[2]
crusade. A malignant fever—cured thanks to God and my sainted mother's ointments—most opportunely kept me shivering in bed on the day of departure: that adventure ended, as everyone knows, in a war between Christians and Christians. The
crusades had fallen into disrepute. Besides, I had other things to think about.

IV

The wind had died down. Still annoyed by my stupid quarrel with my betrothed, I
went off to the harbor to look at the ships. They were all moored to the jetty, side by
side, with hatches open, receiving thousands of sacks of wheat flour between their

1. Montaigne, native of Bordeaux.
2. Fr. Foulques de Neuilly, French preacher, whom Pope
Innocent III appointed in 1199 to preach the Fourth
Crusade.

brightly camouflaged sides. The infantry regiments were slowly going up the gang-ways amid the shouts of stevedores, blasts from the boatswain's whistle, and signals tearing through the mist to set the cranes in motion. On the decks, shapeless objects and menacing machines were being heaped together under tarpaulins. From time to time an aluminum wing revolved slowly above the bulwarks before disappearing into the darkness of the hold. The generals' horses, suspended from webbing bands, trav-eled over the roofs of the shops like the horses of the Valkyries.[3] I was standing on a high iron gangway watching the final preparations, when suddenly I became agoniz-ingly aware that there were only a few hours left—scarcely thirteen—before I too should have to board one of those ships now being loaded with weapons for my use. Then I thought of women; of the days of abstinence lying ahead; of the sadness of dy-ing without having once more taken my pleasure from another warm body.

Full of impatience, and still angry because I had not got even a kiss from my sweetheart, I strode off toward the house where the dancers lived. Christopher, very drunk, was already shut into his girl's room. My girl embraced me, laughing and crying, saying that she was proud of me, that I looked very handsome in my uniform, and that a fortune-teller had read the cards and told her that no harm would come to me during the Great Landing. She more than once called me a "hero," as if she knew how cruelly her flattery contrasted with my sweetheart's unjust remarks. I went out onto the roof. The lights were coming on in the town, outlining the gigantic geometry of the buildings in luminous points. Below, in the streets, was a confused swarm of heads and hats.

At this distance, it was impossible to tell women from men in the evening mist. Yet it was in order that this crowd of unknown human beings should go on existing that I was due to make my way to the ships soon after dawn. I should plow the stormy ocean during the winter months and land on a remote shore under attack from steel and fire, in defense of my countrymen's principles. It was the last time a sword would be brandished over the maps of the West. This time we should finish off the new Teu-tonic Order[4] for good and all, and advance as victors into that longed-for future when man would be reconciled with man. My mistress laid her trembling hand on my head, perhaps guessing at the nobility of my thoughts. She was naked under the half-open flaps of her dressing gown.

V

I returned home a few hours before dawn, walking unsteadily from the wine with which I had tried to cheat the fatigue of a body surfeited with enjoyment of another body. I was hungry and sleepy, and at the same time deeply disturbed by the thought of my approaching departure. I laid my weapons and belt on a stool and threw myself on my bed. Then I realized, with a start of surprise, that someone was lying under the thick woolen blanket; and I was just stretching out my hand for my knife when I found myself embraced by two burning-hot arms, which clasped me around the neck like the arms of a drowning man while two inexpressibly smooth legs twined themselves between mine. I was struck dumb with astonishment when I saw that the person who had slipped into my bed was my sweetheart. Between her sobs, she told me how she had escaped in the darkness, had run away in terror from

3. In Germanic mythology, warrior maidens of the god Odin. They decided who would die and who would live in battle.

4. Germany.

barking dogs and crept furtively through my father's garden to the window of my room. Here she had waited for me in terror and impatience. After our stupid quarrel that afternoon, she had thought of the dangers and sufferings lying in wait for me, with that sense of impotent longing to lighten a soldier's hazardous lot which women so often express by offering their own bodies, as if the sacrifice of their jealously guarded virginity at the moment of departure and without hope of enjoyment, this reckless abandonment to another's pleasure, could have the propitiatory power of ritual ablation.

There is a unique and special freshness in an encounter with a chaste body never touched by a lover's hands, a felicitous clumsiness of response, an intuitive candor that, responding to some obscure promptings, divines and adopts the attitudes that favor the closest possible physical union. As I lay in my sweetheart's arms and felt the little fleece that timidly brushed against one of my thighs, I grew more and more angry at having exhausted my strength in all-too-familiar coupling, in the absurd belief that I was ensuring my future serenity by means of present excesses. And now that I was being offered this so desirable compliance, I lay almost insensible beneath my sweetheart's tremulous and impatient body. I would not say that my youth was incapable of catching fire once again that night under the stimulus of this new pleasure. But the idea that it was a virgin who was offering herself to me, and that her closed and intact flesh would require a slow and sustained effort on my part, filled me with an obsessive fear of failure.

I pushed my sweetheart to one side, kissing her gently on the shoulders, and began telling her with assumed sincerity what a mistake it would be for our nuptial joys to be marred by the hurry of departure; how ashamed she would be if she became pregnant, and how sad it was for children to grow up with no father to teach them how to get green honey out of hollow tree trunks and look for cuttlefish under stones. She listened, her large bright eyes burning in the darkness, and I was aware that she was in the grip of a resentment drawn from the underworld of the instincts and felt nothing but scorn for a man who, when offered such an opportunity, invoked reason and prudence instead of taking her by force, leaving her bleeding on the bed like a trophy of the chase, defiled, with breasts bitten, but having become a woman in her hour of defeat.

Just then we heard the lowing of cattle going to be sacrificed on the shore and the watchmen blowing their conchs. With scorn showing clearly in her face, my sweetheart got quickly out of bed without letting me touch her, and with a gesture not so much of modesty as of someone taking back what he had been on the point of selling too cheap, she covered those charms which had suddenly begun to enflame my desire. Before I could stop her, she had jumped out of the window. I saw her running away as fast as she could among the olives, and I realized in that instant that it would be easier for me to enter the city of Troy without a scratch than to regain what I had lost.

When I went down to the ships with my parents, my soldier's pride had been replaced by an intolerable sense of disgust, of inner emptiness and self-depreciation. And when the steersmen pushed the ships away from the shore with their strong poles, and the masts stood erect between the rows of oarsmen, I realized that the display, excesses, and feasting that precede the departure of soldiers to the battlefield were now over. There was no time now for garlands, laurel wreaths, wine drinking in every house, envious glances from weaklings, and favors from women. Instead, our lot would consist of bugle calls, mud, rain-soaked bread, the arrogance of our leaders, blood spilled in error, the sickly, tainted smell of gangrene. I already felt less confident that my courage would contribute to the power and happiness of the long-haired

Achaeans.[5] A veteran soldier, going to war because it was his profession and with no more enthusiasm than a sheep shearer on his way to the pen, was telling anyone prepared to listen that Helen of Sparta was very happy to be in Troy, and that when she disported herself in Paris' bed, her hoarse cries of enjoyment brought blushes to the cheeks of the virgins who lived in Priam's palace. It was said that the whole story of the unhappy captivity of Leda's daughter, and of the insults and humiliations the Trojans had subjected her to, was simply war propaganda, inspired by Agamemnon with the consent of Menelaus. In fact, behind this enterprise and the noble ideals it had set up as a screen, a great many aims were concealed which would not benefit the combatants in the very least: above all, so the old soldier said, to sell more pottery, more cloth, more vases decorated with scenes from chariot races, and to open new ways of access to Asia, whose peoples had a passion for barter, and so put an end once and for all to Trojan competition.

Too heavily loaded with flour and men, the ship responded slowly to the oars. I gazed for a long time at the sunlit houses of my native town. I was nearly in tears. I took off my helmet and hid my eyes behind its crest; I had taken great trouble to make it round and smooth, like the magnificent crests of the men who could order their accoutrements of war from the most highly skilled craftsmen and who were voyaging on the swiftest and longest ship.

—◆—

Nazim Hikmet
1902–1963

The great experimental Turkish poet Nazim Hikmet spent eighteen years as a political prisoner in Turkey and the last thirteen years in exile.

His poem "Gioconda and SI-YA-U" weaves war and art into the fabric of history, and history, in turn, becomes the poet's redemption and instrument of human solidarity. Hsiao San, the Chinese poet in the title of the poem, and Hikmet were fellow travelers in the cause of social justice, each having endured official government persecution throughout their lives for their commitment and political campaigns.

For more on Nazim Hikmet, see his prior listing, page 348.

Gioconda and SI-YA-U[1]

to the memory of my friend SI-YA-U,
whose head was cut off in Shanghai

A CLAIM

Renowned Leonardo's
world-famous
"La Gioconda"

---

5. All references to peoples, places, and characters in this section are to the primal war epic in the Western tradition—Homer's *Iliad.*

1. Translated by Randy Blasing and Mutlu Konuk. *La Gioconda* is a painting by Leonardo da Vinci from 1506, commonly known as the Mona Lisa. SI-YA-U, Hsiao San (born 1896), was a friend of the poet, whom he thought was executed in Shanghai, China, in 1927. It turned out not to have been the case. But the Chinese translation of Hikmet's poem, along with the works of Hsiao San, were burned during the Cultural Revolution of the 1960s.

has disappeared.[2]

5   And in the space
vacated by the fugitive
a copy has been placed.

The poet inscribing
the present treatise
10   knows more than a little
about the fate
of the real Gioconda.
She fell in love
with a seductive
15   graceful youth:
a honey-tongued
almond-eyed Chinese
named SI-YA-U.
Gioconda ran off
20   after her lover;
Gioconda was burned
in a Chinese city.

I, Nazim Hikmet,
authority
25   on this matter,
thumbing my nose at friend and foe
five times a day,
undaunted,
claim
30   I can prove it;
if I can't,
I'll be ruined and banished
forever from the realm of poesy.

Ingeborg Bachmann
1926–1973

The experience of World War II is a recurring theme in Ingeborg Bachmann's poetry and fiction. She was born in Klagenfurt, Austria, in 1926 and came of age during the war years. She completed a doctorate in philosophy and became one of the best-known German-language poets during the 1950s, the focus of a genuine celebrity cult. In the early 1960s, however, she turned away from poetry and from then on wrote only fiction, in which the experience of fascism and war is often intertwined with reflections on women's oppression by men. After the breakup of a five-year love affair with the Swiss novelist and playwright Max Frisch in 1963, however, her physical and psychological health declined. The deeply distraught female protagonist of her novel *Malina*

---

2. In 1924, when Hikmet and Hsiao San met in Paris, Leonardo's masterpiece did indeed go missing from the Louvre Museum for a while.

(1971) is as much a reflection of her own condition as a description of patriarchal structures that lead to both fascism and sexism. Bachmann died during a fire in her home in Rome in 1973.

The short story "Youth in an Austrian Town" is the first in Ingeborg Bachmann's volume of stories *The Thirtieth Year* (1961). It is a story about what war looks like from the perspective of growing children, and at the same time offers a meditation on memory. The juxtaposition and occasional intermingling of children's and adult perspectives allows the narrator to reveal the horrors of war through seemingly trivial changes in daily routine whose meaning the children do not yet grasp, while we as adult readers understand their implications clearly.

Youth in an Austrian Town[1]

On fine October days, as you come out of the Radetzkystrasse, you can see by the Municipal Theatre a group of trees in the sunshine. The first tree, which stands in front of those dark-red cherry trees that bear no fruit, is so ablaze with autumn, such an immense patch of gold, that it looks like a torch dropped by an angel. And now it is burning, and the autumn wind and frost cannot put it out.

Who, faced with this tree, is going to talk to me about falling leaves and the white death? Who will prevent me from holding it with my eyes and believing that it will always glow before me as it does at this moment and that it is not subject to the laws of the world?

In its light the town too is recognizable again, with pale convalescent houses under the dark hair of their tiles, and the canal that every now and then brings in a boat from the sea which ties up in its heart. The docks are undoubtedly dead now that freight is brought to the town quicker by train and lorry; but flowers and fruit still fall from the high quay onto the pondlike water, the snow drops off the boughs, the melted snow comes rushing noisily down, then washes back and raises a wave and with the wave a ship whose bright-coloured sail was set on our arrival.

People rarely moved to this town from another town, because its attractions were too few; they came from the villages, because the farms had grown too small, and they looked for accommodation on the outskirts where it was cheapest. Here there were still fields and gravel pits, big market gardens and allotments on which year after year the owners grew turnips, cabbages and beans, the bread of the poorest settlers. These settlers dug their own cellars, standing in the seepage. They nailed up their own rafters during the brief evenings between spring and autumn, and heaven knows whether they ever in their lives saw the ceremony that takes place when the roof is put on.

This didn't worry their children, for they had already grown familiar with the ever-changing smells that came from far away, when the bonfires were burning and the gypsies speaking strange languages settled fleetingly in the no-man's-land between cemetery and airfield.

In the tenement in the Durchlasstrasse the children have to take off their shoes and play in stockinged feet, because they live above the landlord. They are only allowed to whisper and for the rest of their lives they will never lose the habit of whispering. At school the teachers say to them: "You should be beaten till you open your mouths. Beaten. . . ." Between the reproach for talking too loud and the reproach for talking too softly, they settle down in silence.

The Durchlasstrasse, Tunnel Street, did not get its name from the game in which the robbers march through a tunnel, but for a long time the children thought it

1. Translated by Michael Bullock.

did. It wasn't until later, when their legs carried them farther, that they saw the tunnel, the little underpass, over which the train passed on its way to Vienna. Inquisitive people who wanted to go to the airfield had to walk through this tunnel, across the fields and right through all the embroideries of autumn. Someone had the idea of putting the airfield next to the cemetery, and the people in K always said it was convenient for burying the pilots who for a time made training flights here. The pilots never did anyone the favour of crashing. The children always yelled: "An airman! An airman!" They raised their arms towards them as though to catch them, and stared into the cloud zoo in which the airmen moved among animals' heads and masks.

The children take the silver paper off the bars of chocolate and whistle the *Maria Saaler Geläut* on it. At school the children's heads are examined for lice by a woman doctor. The children don't know what the time is, because the clock on the parish church has stopped. They always come home late from school. The children! They know their names when put to it, but they prick up their ears only when someone calls out "Children".

Homework: down strokes and up strokes in neat writing, exercises in profit and loss, the profit of new horizons against the loss of dreams, learning things off by heart with the help of memory aids. Their task: to learn an alphabet and the multiplication tables, an orthography and the ten commandments, among the fumes of oiled floors, of a few hundred children's lives, dwarfs' overcoats, burnt India-rubbers, among tears and scoldings, standing in the corner, kneeling and unsilenceable chatter.

The children take off old words and put on new ones. They hear about Mount Sinai and they see the Ulrichsberg with its turnip fields, larches and firs, mixed up with cedars and thorn bushes, and they eat sorrel and gnaw the corn cobs before they grow hard and ripe, or bring them home and roast them on the glowing embers. The stripped cobs disappear into the wooden box and are used as tinder, and cedar and olive wood is laid on top, smoulders, warms from far away and casts shadows on the wall.

The time of trophies, the time of Christmases, without looking forward, without looking back, the time of the pumpkin nights, of ghosts and terrors without end. In good, in evil—without hope.

The children have no future. They are afraid of the whole world. They don't picture the world; they picture only the geography of a hopscotch square, because its frontiers can be drawn in chalk. On one or two legs they hop the frontiers from one region to another.

One day the children move into the Henselstrasse. Into a house without a landlord, into an estate that has crawled out tame and hidebound from under mortgages. They live two streets away from the Beethovenstrasse, in which all the houses are spacious and centrally heated, and one street away from the Radetzkystrasse, through which the trams run, electric-red and with huge muzzles. They have become the possessors of a garden, in which roses are planted in the front and little apple trees and blackcurrant bushes at the back. The trees are no taller than the children, and they grow up together. On the left they have neighbours with a boxer dog, and on the right children who eat bananas and spend the day swinging on a horizontal bar and rings which they have put up in the garden. They make friends with the dog Ali and compete with the children next door, who always know better and can do things better.

They prefer to be by themselves; they make themselves a den in the attic and often shout out loud in their hiding place, trying out their crippled voices. They utter little low cries of rebellion in front of spiders' webs.

The cellar is spoiled for them by mice and the smell of apples. They go down every day, pick out the rotten fruit, cut out the bad bits and eat what is left. Because the day never comes on which all the rotten apples have been eaten, because more apples are always turning rotten and nothing must be thrown away, they hunger after an alien, forbidden fruit. They don't like the apples, their relations or the Sundays on which they have to go for walks on the Kreuzberg above the house, naming the flowers, naming the birds.

In the summer the children blink through the green shutters into the sunshine; in winter they make a snowman and stick pieces of coal in its head for eyes. They learn French. *Madeleine est une petite fille. Elle regarde la rue.*[2] They play the piano. "The Champagne Song". "The Last Rose of Summer". "The Rustle of Spring".

They no longer spell. They read newspapers, from which the sex murderer jumps out at them. He becomes the shadow thrown by the trees in the dusk as they come home from Bible lessons, and he causes the rustling of the swaying lilac along the front gardens; the snowball bushes and the phloxes part for a moment and reveal his figure. They feel the strangler's grip, the mystery contained in the word sex that is more to be feared than the murderer.

The children read their eyes sore. They wake up tired because they spent too long in the evening in wild Kurdistan or with the gold-diggers in Alaska.[3] They eavesdrop on a conversation between lovers and wish they had a dictionary in which to look up all the words they don't understand. They rack their brains about their bodies and a quarrel that takes place at night in their parents' bedroom. They laugh at every opportunity; they can scarcely contain themselves and fall off the bench for laughing, get up and go on laughing, till they get cramps.

But the sex murderer is soon found in a village, in the Rosental, in a barn, with tufts of hay and the grey photographic mist in his face that makes him forever unrecognizable, not only in the morning paper.

There is no money in the house. No more coins drop into the piggy bank. In front of children adults speak only in veiled hints. They cannot guess that the country is in the process of selling itself and the sky along with it, the sky at which everyone tugs until it tears and a black hole appears.

At table the children sit in silence, chewing for a long time on a mouthful, while a storm crackles on the radio and the announcer's voice flashes round the kitchen like ball-lightning and ends up where the saucepan lid rises in alarm above the potatoes in their burst jackets. The electric cables are cut. Columns of marching men pass through the streets. The flags strike together over their heads. "We shall march on and on till everything crashes in ruins," they sing outside. The time signal sounds, and the children start giving each other silent news with practised fingers.

The children are in love but do not know with what. They talk in gibberish, muse themselves into an indefinable pallor, and when they are completely at a loss they invent a language that maddens them. My fish. My hook. My fox. My snare. My fire. You my water. You my current. My earth. You my if. And you my but. Either. Or. My everything . . . my everything. . . . They push one another, go for each other with their fists and scuffle over a counter-word that doesn't exist.

It's nothing. Those children!

2. "Madeleine is a little girl. She looks at the street."
3. An allusion to the 19th-century novelist Karl May, whose adventure books were extremely popular among German-speaking youth throughout much of the 20th century. One of his novels is called *In Wild Kurdistan.*

They develop temperatures, they vomit, get the shivers, sore throats, whooping cough, measles, scarlet fever; they reach the crisis, are given up, are suspended between life and death; and one day they lie there numb and shaky, with new thoughts about everything. They are told that war has broken out.

For a few more winters, until the bombs fling up its ice, there is skating on the pond under the Kreuzberg. The fine glassy surface in the centre is reserved for the girls in flared skirts who perform inside edges, outside edges and figure-eights; the circle round this belongs to the speed skaters. In the warming-room the bigger boys pull on the bigger girls' skates and their ear-flaps touch the leather that is like swan's necks as it is stretched over thin legs. You have to have skates that screw on in order to count as a real skater, and those who, like the children, have only wooden skates attached with straps retire into remote corners of the pond or look on.

In the evening, when the skaters of both sexes have slipped off their boots, slung them over their shoulders and stepped up onto the wooden stands to say goodbye, when all the faces, like fresh young moons, are shining in the dusk, the lights go on under the snow canopies. The loudspeakers are switched on, and the sixteen-year-old twins, who are known throughout the town, come down the wooden steps, he in blue trousers and a white sweater and she in a gauzy blue nothing over her flesh-pink tights. They wait nonchalantly for the music to strike up before leaping down onto the ice from the last step but one—she with a beating of wings, he plunging like a magnificent swimmer—and reach the centre with a few deep, powerful thrusts. There she launches out into the first figure, and he holds out to her a hoop of light through which she springs, encircled by a haze, as the gramophone needle begins to scratch and the music grates to an end. The old gentlemen's eyes widen under their frosty brows, and the man with the snow shovel clearing the long-distance skating track round the outside of the pond, his feet wrapped in rags, rests his chin on the handle of his shovel and follows the girl's steps as though they led into eternity.

The children get one more surprise: the next lot of Christmas trees really do fall from heaven. On fire. And the unexpected present which the children receive is more free time.

During air raid alarms they are allowed to leave their exercise books lying on their desks and go down into the shelter. Later they are allowed to save up sweets for the wounded, to knit socks and weave raffia baskets for the men who are fighting on land, on sea and in the air. And to write a composition commemorating those under the earth and on the ground. And later still they are allowed to dig trenches between the cemetery and the airfield, which is already paying tribute to the cemetery. They are allowed to forget their Latin and learn to distinguish between the sounds of the engines in the sky. They don't have to wash so often any more; no one bothers about their finger nails now. The children mend their skipping ropes, because there are no longer any new ones, and they talk about time fuses and landmines. The children play "Let the robbers march through" among the ruins, but often they merely sit there staring into space, and they no longer hear when people call out "Children" to them. There are enough bits of rubble for hopscotch, but the children shiver because they are soaking wet and cold.

Children die, and the children learn the dates of the Seven Years War and the Thirty Years War,[4] and they wouldn't care if they mixed up all the hostilities, the pretext and the cause, for the exact differentiation of which they could get good marks in history.

---

4. The Seven Years' War (1756–1763) was the last major European war before the French Revolution, and the Thirty Years' War (1618–1648) was the last great war over religious issues in Europe.

They bury the dog Ali and then his owners. The time of veiled hints is past. People speak in their presence of shooting in the back of the neck, of hanging, liquidating, blowing up, and what they don't hear and see they smell, as they smell the dead of St Ruprecht, who cannot be dug out because they have been buried under the movie theatre into which they slipped surreptitiously to see *Romance in a Minor Key*.[5] Juveniles were not admitted, but then they were admitted to the great dying and murdering which took place a few days later and every day after that.

There is no more light in the house. No glass in the windows. No door on the hinges. Nobody stirs and nobody rises.

The Glan does not flow upstream and downstream. The little river stands still, and Zigulln Castle[6] stands still and does not rise.

St George stands in the New Square, stands with his club and does not strike the dragon. Next to him stands the Empress and she does not rise either.

O town. Town. Privet town with all its roots dangling. There is no light and no bread in the house. The children are told: "Keep quiet, keep quiet whatever you do."

Among these walls, between the ring roads, how many walls are still standing? Is the bird Wonderful still alive? He has been silent for seven years. Seven years are over. You my place, you no place, above clouds, beneath karst, under night, over day, my town and my river. I your current, you my earth.

Town with the Viktringer Ring and the St Veiter Ring. . . . All the ring roads ought to be named by their names like the great starry ways that looked no larger to children, and all the alleys, Citadel Alley and Corn Alley, yes, that's what they were called, Paradise Alley, not to forget the squares, Hay Square and Holy Ghost Square, so that everything here shall be named, once and for all, so that all the squares shall be named. Current and earth.

And one day nobody gives the children report cards any more, and they can go. They are called upon to step into life. Spring descends with clear, raging waters and gives birth to a blade of grass. There is no need to tell the children it is peace. They go away, with their hands in their ragged pockets and a whistle that is meant as a warning to themselves.

Because at that time, at that place, I was among children and we had created fresh space, I gave up the Henselstrasse, as well as the view of the Kreuzberg, and took as my witnesses all the fir trees, the jays and the eloquent foliage. And because I have become aware that the innkeeper no longer gives a groschen[7] for an empty soda siphon and no longer pours out lemonade for me, I leave to others the path through the Durchlasstrasse and pull the collar of my coat up higher when I cross it without a glance on my way to the graves outside, a passer-through whose origins are evident to no one. Where the town comes to an end, where the gravel pits are, where the sieves stand full of pebbles and the sand has stopped singing, you can sit down for a moment and take your head in your hands. Then you know that everything was as it was, that everything is as it is, and you abandon the attempt to find a reason for everything. For there is no wand that touches you, no transformation. The lime trees and the elder bush . . .? Nothing touches your heart. No slopes from former times,

5. A popular German film from 1942–1943 that presents a melodramatic love story.
6. Located in Klagenfurt, Bachmann's home town in southern Austria.
7. A small coin.

no risen house. Nor the tower of Zigulln, the two captive bears, the ponds, the roses, the gardens full of laburnum. In the motionless recollection before departure, before all departures, what can be revealed to us? Very little is left to reveal things to us, and youth has no part in what is left, nor has the town in which it was passed.

Only when the tree outside the theatre works the miracle, when the torch burns, do I manage to see everything mingled, like the waters in the sea: the early confinement in darkness while the aeroplanes flew above incandescent clouds; the New Square and its absurd monuments looking out upon Utopia; the sirens that wailed in those days with a sound like the lift in a skyscraper; the slices of dry bread and jam containing a stone on which I bit by the shores of the Atlantic.

→ ⇒◈⇒ →

Yehuda Amichai
1924–2000

Yehuda Amichai was born in Germany and emigrated to Palestine in 1935. After the establishment of Israel in 1948, he attended Hebrew University in Jerusalem, where he studied Hebrew literature and the Bible and then taught in secondary schools. His first book of poetry, *Now and in Other Days,* was published in 1955. He coined new idioms and interjected prose passages and colloquial slang into his Hebrew poetry, and in 1982 he won the Israel Prize for his experimental poetry and innovations in the language of poetry in Hebrew. He also wrote two novels, a number of short stories, radio sketches, and children's literature. He has been widely translated into a number of languages, principally into English. His innovative style engages the ordinary in daily life even in the extraordinary circumstances of war—tanks, airplanes, implements, and governmental contracts.

Seven Laments for the War-Dead[1]
1

    Mr. Beringer, whose son
    fell at the Canal that strangers dug
    so ships could cross the desert,
    crosses my path at Jaffa Gate.

5   He has grown very thin, has lost
    the weight of his son.
    That's why he floats so lightly in the alleys
    and gets caught in my heart like little twigs
    that drift away.

2

10   As a child he would mash his potatoes
    to a golden mush.
    And then you die.
    A living child must be cleaned
    when he comes home from playing.

---

1. Translated by Chana Bloch and Stephen Mitchell.

15   But for a dead man
      earth and sand are clear water, in which
      his body goes on being bathed and purified
      forever.

                           3

      The Tomb of the Unknown Soldier
20   across there. On the enemy's side. A good landmark
      for gunners of the future.

      Or the war monument in London
      at Hyde Park Corner, decorated
      like a magnificent cake: yet another soldier
25   lifting head and rifle,
      another cannon, another eagle, another
      stone angel.

      And the whipped cream of a huge marble flag
      poured over it all
30   with an expert hand.

      But the candied, much-too-red cherries
      were already gobbled up
      by the glutton of hearts. Amen.

                           4

      I came upon an old zoology textbook,
35   Brehm, Volume II, *Birds:*
      in sweet phrases, an account of the life of the starling,
      swallow, and thrush. Full of mistakes in an antiquated
      Gothic typeface, but full of love, too. "Our feathered
      friends." "Migrate from us to the warmer climes."
40   Nest, speckled egg, soft plumage, nightingale,
      stork. "The harbingers of spring." The robin,
      red-breasted.

      Year of publication: 1913, Germany,
      on the eve of the war that was to be
45   the eve of all my wars.
      My good friend who died in my arms, in
      his blood,
      on the sands of Ashdod. 1948, June.

      Oh my friend,
50   red-breasted.

                           5

      Dicky was hit.
      Like the water tower at Yad Mordechai.

Hit. A hole in the belly. Everything
came flooding out.

55   But he has remained standing like that
in the landscape of my memory
like the water tower at Yad Mordechai.

He fell not far from there,
a little to the north, near Huleikat.

6

60   Is all of this
sorrow? I don't know.
I stood in the cemetery dressed in
the camouflage clothes of a living man: brown pants
and a shirt yellow as the sun.

65   Cemeteries are cheap; they don't ask for much.
Even the wastebaskets are small, made for holding
tissue paper
that wrapped flowers from the store.
Cemeteries are a polite and disciplined thing.
70   "I shall never forget you," in French
on a little ceramic plaque.
I don't know who it is that won't ever forget:
he's more anonymous than the one who died.

Is all of this sorrow? I guess so.
75   "May ye find consolation in the building
of the homeland." But how long
can you go on building the homeland
and not fall behind in the terrible
three-sided race
80   between consolation and building and death?

Yes, all of this is sorrow. But leave
a little love burning always
like the small bulb in the room of a sleeping baby
that gives him a bit of security and quiet love
85   though he doesn't know what the light is
or where it comes from.

7

Memorial Day for the war-dead: go tack on
the grief of all your losses—
including a woman who left you—
90   to the grief of losing them; go mix
one sorrow with another, like history,
that in its economical way
heaps pain and feast and sacrifice
onto a single day for easy reference.

95   Oh sweet world, soaked like bread
in sweet milk for the terrible
toothless God. "Behind all this,
some great happiness is hiding." No use
crying inside and screaming outside.

100   Behind all this, some great happiness may
be hiding.

Memorial day. Bitter salt, dressed up as
a little girl with flowers.
Ropes are strung out the whole length of the route

105   for a joint parade: the living and the dead together.
Children move with the footsteps of someone else's grief
as if picking their way through broken glass.

The flautist's mouth will stay pursed for many days.
A dead soldier swims among the small heads

110   with the swimming motions of the dead,
with the ancient error the dead have
about the place of the living water.
A flag loses contact with reality and flies away.
A store window decked out with beautiful dresses for women

115   in blue and white. And everything
in three languages: Hebrew, Arabic, and Death.

A great royal beast has been dying all night long
under the jasmine,
with a fixed stare at the world.

120   A man whose son died in the war
walks up the street
like a woman with a dead fetus in her womb.
"Behind all this, some great happiness is hiding."

Little Ruth[1]

Sometimes I remember you, little Ruth,
we were separated in our distant childhood and they burned you in the camps.
If you were alive now, you would be a woman of sixty-five,
a woman on the verge of old age. At twenty you were burned

5   and I don't know what happened to you in your short life
since we separated. What did you achieve, what insignia
did they put on your shoulders, your sleeves, your
brave soul, what shining stars
did they pin on you, what decorations for valor, what

10   medals for love hung around your neck,
what peace upon you, *peace unto you.*
And what happened to the unused years of your life?
Are they still packed away in pretty bundles,
were they added to my life? Did you turn me

1. Translated by Barbara and Benjamin Harshav.

15   into your bank of love like the banks in Switzerland
where assets are preserved even after their owners are dead?
Will I leave all this to my children
whom you never saw?
You gave your life to me, like a wine dealer
20   who remains sober himself.
You sober in death, lucid in the dark
for me, drunk on life, wallowing in my forgetfulness.

Now and then, I remember you in times
unbelievable. And in places not made for memory
25   but for the transient, the passing that does not remain.
Like in an airport, when the arriving travelers
stand tired at the revolving conveyor belt
that brings their suitcases and packages,
and they identify theirs with cries of joy
30   as at a resurrection and go out into their lives;
and there is one suitcase that returns and disappears again
and returns again, ever so slowly, in the empty hall,
again and again it passes.
This is how your quiet figure passes by me,
35   this is how I remember you until
the conveyor belt stands still. *And they stood still. Amen.*

⇥ END OF PERSPECTIVES: ECHOES OF WAR ⇤

Samuel Beckett
1906–1989

In Samuel Beckett's play *Endgame,* one of the characters asks anxiously, "We're not beginning to . . . to . . . mean something?" Whereupon another character responds, "Mean something! You and I, mean something! [Brief laugh.] Ah that's a good one!" This refusal of conventionally understood meaning—whether biographical, psychological, symbolic, or philosophical—characterizes Beckett's groundbreaking work in drama as well as his significant achievements in fiction. In both genres, Beckett persistently attempts to capture the human condition reduced to its barest essentials: through denuded landscapes or tightly enclosed spaces, sparse objects, handicapped or immobilized bodies, repeated gestures, and characters who have no way of escaping from their constrained existential situations. Sometimes they don't even have a voice of their own, functioning instead as an echo of other, perhaps imaginary voices. Yet their fatigue and boredom with their own suicidal despair are always counteracted by their irrepressible urge to keep on talking, adding yet another sentence to the dialogue, telling yet another story. Typically, such characters go back and forth between the assertion that all is over and that nothing will ever stop: "I can't go on, I'll go on," says the narrator in the very last line of Beckett's novel *The Unnamable* (1953), and the only character in his late play *Not I* (1973) is a disembodied mouth speaking incessantly.

The endeavor to get down to essentials and to subtract, reduce, and condense words is quite visible in the steadily diminishing bulk of Beckett's writing; while his works were never voluminous, in the 1940s he did write several full-length novels. By the 1960s and 1970s, he was publishing pieces whose very titles evoked brevity and inconsequence (such as *Ends and Odds* [1974–1976] or *Fizzles* [1976]), and they did indeed tend to become ever shorter: *Come and Go* (1967) and *Lessness* (1970) reduced their linguistic inventory to just a few dozen words or sentences, and some of his late plays such as *Quad* (1984) or *Acts Without Words I* and *Acts Without Words II* dispensed with language altogether, reducing theater to movement and gesture. Yet over a writing career that spanned four decades, Beckett never did stop writing. Instead, he invented ever-new ways to express the absence of meaning that lies at the core of his aesthetics: he once summarized his project as "the expression that there is nothing to express, nothing with which to express, nothing from which to express, no power to express, no desire to express, together with the obligation to express."

Yet this statement by no means implies that Beckett's works are tedious, bleak, and cheerless to read. On the contrary, many of them are uproariously funny, and some of his plays can be performed either as deadly serious drama or as vaudeville slapstick. A good example of this ambivalence is Beckett's most famous work, *Waiting for Godot,* which was an immediate success at its first performance in Paris in 1953 and established his reputation as a major playwright. Its four characters, Vladimir, Estragon, Lucky, and Pozzo, can be played either as existentialist heroes confronted with the absurdity of human life or as clowns who experience life's lack of meaning as a kind of cosmic comedy. The comedian Bert Lahr, in fact—best known as the Cowardly Lion in *The Wizard of Oz*—performed one of the roles in the play's Broadway debut. Beckett's fiction similarly oscillates between slapstick and bitter irony. A reader may be deeply disturbed at the spectacle of the character Molloy dragging himself through the mud with his crutches or laugh out loud at Molloy's insistence that even in this unlikely position, he never fails to doff his hat to passing ladies. While it isn't inappropriate to refer to Beckett as a pessimist, nihilist, or existentialist, he is also one of the twentieth century's great humorists, and his flair for comedy is what sets him apart from such writers as Franz Kafka, Jean-Paul Sartre, or Albert Camus, who also foreground the absurdity of an existence into which humans find themselves thrown without their consent.

Nor does Beckett's rejection of expression and meaning imply that his texts can't or shouldn't be interpreted. In fact, they challenge us to explore precisely the reasons and strategies through which they elude common procedures of sense making. Quite often, Beckett's texts take up problems of philosophy and language that have a long tradition in Western thought and pursue them to a logical impasse from which there is no conceptual escape. Many readers have noted the influence of French philosopher René Descartes on Beckett's work: Descartes's statement "I think, therefore I am" splits the thinking mind into the one who thinks and the one who observes the thinking, a self-referentiality that is often reflected in the relationship between similar or symbiotic characters in Beckett's fiction and plays. How the workings of human consciousness can be represented in literary language at all is a question that takes on a good deal of urgency in this context, one that was also explored by the Irish novelist James Joyce, whom Beckett met and worked with in Paris. In an early essay on the French novelist Marcel Proust, Beckett discussed the problematic connection between past and present self as they are established in the human mind by memory. His own works foreground this theme through characters who seem able to call up only fragments of their former lives. From Dante Alighieri, who is frequently alluded to, Beckett takes an interest in the various kinds of hell that people's lives can become and that they can create for each other—but without the sense of theological justice that informed Dante's *Inferno*. Frequently, then, what makes it difficult to attribute meaning to Beckett's texts is the fact that they question precisely the tools—rationality, logic, chronology, and transparent language—that we normally use to establish such meaning.

The multiple echoes of earlier writings in Beckett's texts point to a writer with a broad knowledge of varied languages and traditions. Born in a suburb of Dublin in 1906, he grew up in a middle-class, Anglo-Irish, Protestant family. From 1923 to 1927 he attended Trinity College in Dublin, where he studied French and Italian. In 1928 he went to Paris on a fellowship to teach English at the École Normale Supérieure and met his countryman James Joyce during his stay. Two years later, in 1930, he returned to Ireland to become a lecturer of French at Trinity College; he completed his master's degree in December 1931 and shortly afterward resigned from teaching, which he disliked intensely. In the following years, he lived and traveled in England, France, Italy, and Germany and finally settled in Paris in 1937. A year later he met Suzanne Deschevaux-Dumesnil, who became his life companion and, in 1961, his wife; she was an indispensable help in getting his first novel, *Murphy,* published in 1938 after it had been rejected by dozens of publishers.

Since Ireland was a neutral power in World War II, Beckett was able to remain in Paris during the Nazi occupation. But he joined an underground resistance group in 1941 and was forced to flee to Roussillon in the unoccupied south of France when some members of his group were arrested by the Germans in 1942. In Roussillon, he worked as a farm laborer until the end of the war and composed his novel *Watt.* In 1945 he worked for some time as an interpreter for the Irish Red Cross in Normandy. He returned to Paris in the winter of 1945, and was awarded the *Croix de guerre* and the *Médaille de la Résistance* for his participation in the French Resistance. Beckett lived and wrote in Paris for the rest of his life; while his main achievements continued to be in drama and narrative, he also ventured into radio plays, a television play, and a film script. He was awarded the Nobel Prize in literature in 1969, and at his eightieth birthday he was celebrated as one of the most important writers of the twentieth century. He died in Paris at the age of eighty-three.

The period following World War II was one of the most productive in Beckett's life: In the late 1940s, he switched from English to French as his principal literary medium and wrote his most important narrative work, a trilogy of novels entitled *Molloy, Malone Dies,* and *The Unnamable,* which were published between 1951 and 1953. He also completed *Waiting for Godot,* followed in 1957 by *Endgame,* which portrays a bunkerlike setting where human existences that have run far beyond meaning nevertheless stubbornly refuse to end. With its hints at a cultural landscape devastated perhaps by war, perhaps by holocaust, or maybe just by the sheer absurdity of life, *Endgame* is an even starker, more stripped-down play than *Godot.* Yet as in *Godot,* the moments of bleakest despair give rise to the most sweeping comedy.

Endgame[1]
A Play in One Act

Characters

NAGG	HAMM
NELL	CLOV

Bare interior.

Grey light.

Left and right back, high up, two small windows, curtains drawn. Front right, a door. Hanging near door, its face to wall, a picture. Front left, touching each other, covered with an old sheet, two ashbins. Center, in an armchair on castors, covered with an old sheet, Hamm. Motionless by the door, his eyes fixed on Hamm, Clov. Very red face. Brief tableau.

---

1. Written in French, then translated into English by Beckett himself. Beckett dedicated the play to its first director, Roger Blin.

Clov goes and stands under window left. Stiff, staggering walk. He looks up at window left. He turns and looks at window right. He goes and stands under window right. He looks up at window right. He turns and looks at window left. He goes out, comes back immediately with a small step-ladder, carries it over and sets it down under window left, gets up on it, draws back curtain. He gets down, takes six steps (for example) towards window right, goes back for ladder, carries it over and sets it down under window right, gets up on it, draws back curtain. He gets down, takes three steps towards window left, goes back for ladder, carries it over and sets it down under window left, gets up on it, looks out of window. Brief laugh. He gets down, takes one step towards window right, goes back for ladder, carries it over and sets it down under window right, gets up on it, looks out of window. Brief laugh. He gets down, goes with ladder towards ashbins, halts, turns, carries back ladder and sets it down under window right, goes to ashbins, removes sheet covering them, folds it over his arm. He raises one lid, stoops and looks into bin. Brief laugh. He closes lid. Same with other bin. He goes to Hamm, removes sheet covering him, folds it over his arm. In a dressing-gown, a stiff toque[2] on his head, a large blood-stained handkerchief over his face, a whistle hanging from his neck, a rug over his knees, thick socks on his feet, Hamm seems to be asleep. Clov looks him over. Brief laugh. He goes to door, halts, turns towards auditorium.

CLOV [*fixed gaze, tonelessly*]: Finished, it's finished, nearly finished, it must be nearly finished. [*Pause.*] Grain upon grain, one by one, and one day, suddenly, there's a heap, a little heap, the impossible heap. [*Pause.*] I can't be punished any more. [*Pause.*] I'll go now to my kitchen, ten feet by ten feet by ten feet, and wait for him to whistle me. [*Pause.*] Nice dimensions, nice proportions, I'll lean on the table, and look at the wall, and wait for him to whistle me.

[*He remains a moment motionless, then goes out. He comes back immediately, goes to window right, takes up the ladder and carries it out. Pause. Hamm stirs. He yawns under the handkerchief. He removes the handkerchief from his face. Very red face. Black glasses.*]

HAMM: Me—[*he yawns*]—to play. [*He holds the handkerchief spread out before him.*]

Old stancher! [*He takes off his glasses, wipes his eyes, his face, the glasses, puts them on again, folds the handkerchief and puts it back neatly in the breast-pocket of his dressing-gown. He clears his throat, joins the tips of his fingers.*]

Can there be misery—[*he yawns*]—loftier than mine? No doubt. Formerly. But now? [*Pause.*] My father? [*Pause.*] My mother? [*Pause.*] My . . . dog? [*Pause.*] Oh I am willing to believe they suffer as much as such creatures can suffer. But does that mean their sufferings equal mine? No doubt. [*Pause.*] No, all is a—[*he yawns*]—bsolute, [*proudly*] the bigger a man is the fuller he is. [*Pause. Gloomily.*] And the emptier. [*He sniffs.*] Clov! [*Pause.*] No, alone. [*Pause.*] What dreams! Those forests! [*Pause.*] Enough, it's time it ended, in the shelter too. [*Pause.*] And yet I hesitate, I hesitate to . . . to end. Yes, there it is, it's time it ended and yet I hesitate to—[*he yawns*]—to end. [*Yawns.*] God, I'm tired, I'd be better off in bed.

---

2. A round brimless hat.

[*He whistles. Enter Clov immediately. He halts beside the chair.*]

You pollute the air! [*Pause.*] Get me ready, I'm going to bed.

CLOV: I've just got you up.

HAMM: And what of it?

CLOV: I can't be getting you up and putting you to bed every five minutes, I have things to do. [*Pause.*]

HAMM: Did you ever see my eyes?

CLOV: No.

HAMM: Did you never have the curiosity, while I was sleeping, to take off my glasses and look at my eyes?

CLOV: Pulling back the lids? [*Pause.*] No.

HAMM: One of these days I'll show them to you. [*Pause.*] It seems they've gone all white. [*Pause.*] What time is it?

CLOV: The same as usual.

HAMM [*gesture towards window right*]: Have you looked?

CLOV: Yes.

HAMM: Well?

CLOV: Zero.

HAMM: It'd need to rain.

CLOV: It won't rain. [*Pause.*]

HAMM: Apart from that, how do you feel?

CLOV: I don't complain.

HAMM: You feel normal?

CLOV [*irritably*]: I tell you I don't complain.

HAMM: I feel a little queer. [*Pause.*] Clov!

CLOV: Yes.

HAMM: Have you not had enough?

CLOV: Yes! [*Pause.*] Of what?

HAMM: Of this . . . this . . . thing.

CLOV: I always had. [*Pause.*] Not you?

HAMM [*gloomily*]: Then there's no reason for it to change.

CLOV: It may end. [*Pause.*] All life long the same questions, the same answers.

HAMM: Get me ready.

[*Clov does not move.*]

Go and get the sheet.

[*Clov does not move.*]

Clov!

CLOV: Yes.

HAMM: I'll give you nothing more to eat.

CLOV: Then we'll die.

HAMM: I'll give you just enough to keep you from dying. You'll be hungry all the time.

CLOV: Then we won't die. [*Pause.*] I'll go and get the sheet.

[*He goes towards the door.*]

HAMM: No!

[*Clov halts.*]

I'll give you one biscuit per day. [*Pause.*] One and a half. [*Pause.*] Why do you
stay with me?

CLOV: Why do you keep me?

HAMM: There's no one else.

CLOV: There's nowhere else. [*Pause.*]

HAMM: You're leaving me all the same.

CLOV: I'm trying.

HAMM: You don't love me.

CLOV: No.

HAMM: You loved me once.

CLOV: Once!

HAMM: I've made you suffer too much. [*Pause.*] Haven't I?

CLOV: It's not that.

HAMM [*shocked*]: I haven't made you suffer too much?

CLOV: Yes!

HAMM [*relieved*]: Ah you gave me a fright! [*Pause. Coldly.*] Forgive me. [*Pause.
Louder.*] I said, Forgive me.

CLOV: I heard you. [*Pause.*] Have you bled?

HAMM: Less. [*Pause.*] Is it not time for my pain-killer?

CLOV: No. [*Pause.*]

HAMM: How are your eyes?

CLOV: Bad.

HAMM: How are your legs?

CLOV: Bad.

HAMM: But you can move.

CLOV: Yes.

HAMM [*violently*]: Then move!

[*Clov goes to back wall, leans against it with his forehead and hands.*]

Where are you?

CLOV: Here.

HAMM: Come back!

[*Clov returns to his place beside the chair.*]

Where are you?

CLOV: Here.

HAMM: Why don't you kill me?

CLOV: I don't know the combination of the cupboard. [*Pause.*]

HAMM: Go and get two bicycle-wheels.

CLOV: There are no more bicycle-wheels.

HAMM: What have you done with your bicycle?

CLOV: I never had a bicycle.

HAMM: The thing is impossible.

CLOV: When there were still bicycles I wept to have one. I crawled at your feet. You
told me to go to hell. Now there are none.

HAMM: And your rounds? When you inspected my paupers. Always on foot?

CLOV: Sometimes on horse.

[*The lid of one of the bins lifts and the hands of Nagg appear, gripping the rim. Then his head emerges. Nightcap. Very white face. Nagg yawns, then listens.*]

I'll leave you, I have things to do.

HAMM: In your kitchen?

CLOV: Yes.

HAMM: Outside of here it's death. [*Pause.*] All right, be off.

[*Exit Clov. Pause.*]

We're getting on.

NAGG: Me pap!

HAMM: Accursed progenitor!

NAGG: Me pap!

HAMM: The old folks at home! No decency left! Guzzle, guzzle, that's all they think of.

[*He whistles. Enter Clov. He halts beside the chair.*]

Well! I thought you were leaving me.

CLOV: Oh not just yet, not just yet.

NAGG: Me pap!

HAMM: Give him his pap.

CLOV: There's no more pap.

HAMM [*to Nagg*]: Do you hear that? There's no more pap. You'll never get any more pap.

NAGG: I want me pap!

HAMM: Give him a biscuit.

[*Exit Clov.*]

Accursed fornicator! How are your stumps?

NAGG: Never mind me stumps.

[*Enter Clov with biscuit.*]

CLOV: I'm back again, with the biscuit.

[*He gives biscuit to Nagg who fingers it, sniffs it.*]

NAGG [*plaintively*]: What is it?

CLOV: Spratt's medium.

NAGG [*as before*]: It's hard! I can't!

HAMM: Bottle him!

[*Clov pushes Nagg back into the bin, closes the lid.*]

CLOV [*returning to his place beside the chair*]: If age but knew!

HAMM: Sit on him!

CLOV: I can't sit.

HAMM: True. And I can't stand.

CLOV: So it is.

HAMM: Every man his speciality. [*Pause.*] No phone calls? [*Pause.*] Don't we laugh?

CLOV [*after reflection*]: I don't feel like it.

HAMM [*after reflection*]: Nor I. [*Pause.*] Clov!

CLOV: Yes.

HAMM: Nature has forgotten us.

CLOV: There's no more nature.

HAMM: No more nature! You exaggerate.

CLOV: In the vicinity.

HAMM: But we breathe, we change! We lose our hair, our teeth! Our bloom! Our ideals!

CLOV: Then she hasn't forgotten us.

HAMM: But you say there is none.

CLOV [*sadly*]: No one that ever lived ever thought so crooked as we.

HAMM: We do what we can.

CLOV: We shouldn't. [*Pause.*]

HAMM: You're a bit of all right, aren't you?

CLOV: A smithereen. [*Pause.*]

HAMM: This is slow work. [*Pause.*] Is it not time for my pain-killer?

CLOV: No. [*Pause.*] I'll leave you, I have things to do.

HAMM: In your kitchen?

CLOV: Yes.

HAMM: What, I'd like to know.

CLOV: I look at the wall.

HAMM: The wall! And what do you see on your wall? Mene, mene?[3] Naked bodies?

CLOV: I see my light dying.

HAMM: Your light dying! Listen to that! Well, it can die just as well here, *your* light. Take a look at me and then come back and tell me what you think of *your* light. [*Pause.*]

CLOV: You shouldn't speak to me like that. [*Pause.*]

HAMM [*coldly*]: Forgive me. [*Pause. Louder.*] I said, Forgive me.

CLOV: I heard you.

[*The lid of Nagg's bin lifts. His hands appear, gripping the rim. Then his head emerges. In his mouth the biscuit. He listens.*]

HAMM: Did your seeds come up?

CLOV: No.

HAMM: Did you scratch round them to see if they had sprouted?

CLOV: They haven't sprouted.

HAMM: Perhaps it's still too early.

CLOV: If they were going to sprout they would have sprouted. [*Violently.*] They'll never sprout!

[*Pause. Nagg takes biscuit in his hand.*]

HAMM: This is not much fun. [*Pause.*] But that's always the way at the end of the day, isn't it, Clov?

CLOV: Always.

HAMM: It's the end of the day like any other day, isn't it, Clov?

CLOV: Looks like it. [*Pause.*]

HAMM [*anguished*]: What's happening, what's happening?

3. A phrase that appears written by a supernatural hand on a wall of the Babylonian king Belshazzar's palace in the book of Daniel. The inscription, "mene, mene, tekel, upharsin," is translated by the prophet Daniel as "God has numbered the days of your kingdom and brought it to an end" (Daniel 5:26); Belshazzar is killed the same night.

CLOV: Something is taking its course. [*Pause.*]
HAMM: All right, be off.

[*He leans back in his chair, remains motionless. Clov does not move, heaves a great groaning sigh. Hamm sits up.*]

I thought I told you to be off.
CLOV: I'm trying.

[*He goes to door, halts.*]

Ever since I was whelped.

[*Exit Clov.*]

HAMM: We're getting on.

[*He leans back in his chair, remains motionless. Nagg knocks on the lid of the other bin. Pause. He knocks harder. The lid lifts and the hands of Nell appear, gripping the rim. Then her head emerges. Lace cap. Very white face.*]

NELL: What is it, my pet? [*Pause.*] Time for love?
NAGG: Were you asleep?
NELL: Oh no!
NAGG: Kiss me.
NELL: We can't.
NAGG: Try.

[*Their heads strain towards each other, fail to meet, fall apart again.*]

NELL: Why this farce, day after day? [*Pause.*]
NAGG: I've lost me tooth.
NELL: When?
NAGG: I had it yesterday.
NELL [*elegiac*]: Ah yesterday!

[*They turn painfully towards each other.*]

NAGG: Can you see me?
NELL: Hardly. And you?
NAGG: What?
NELL: Can you see me?
NAGG: Hardly.
NELL: So much the better, so much the better.
NAGG: Don't say that. [*Pause.*] Our sight has failed.
NELL: Yes.

[*Pause. They turn away from each other.*]

NAGG: Can you hear me?
NELL: Yes. And you?
NAGG: Yes. [*Pause.*] Our hearing hasn't failed.
NELL: Our what?
NAGG: Our hearing.
NELL: No. [*Pause.*] Have you anything else to say to me?
NAGG: Do you remember—

NELL: No.

NAGG: When we crashed on our tandem and lost our shanks.

[*They laugh heartily.*]

NELL: It was in the Ardennes.

[*They laugh less heartily.*]

NAGG: On the road to Sedan.[4]

[*They laugh still less heartily.*]

Are you cold?

NELL: Yes, perished. And you?

NAGG: [*Pause.*] I'm freezing. [*Pause.*] Do you want to go in?

NELL: Yes.

NAGG: Then go in.

[*Nell does not move.*]

Why don't you go in?

NELL: I don't know. [*Pause.*]

NAGG: Has he changed your sawdust?

NELL: It isn't sawdust. [*Pause. Wearily.*] Can you not be a little accurate, Nagg?

NAGG: Your sand then. It's not important.

NELL: It is important. [*Pause.*]

NAGG: It was sawdust once.

NELL: Once!

NAGG: And now it's sand. [*Pause.*] From the shore. [*Pause. Impatiently.*] Now it's sand he fetches from the shore.

NELL: Now it's sand.

NAGG: Has he changed yours?

NELL: No.

NAGG: Nor mine. [*Pause.*] I won't have it! [*Pause. Holding up the biscuit.*] Do you want a bit?

NELL: No. [*Pause.*] Of what?

NAGG: Biscuit. I've kept you half. [*He looks at the biscuit. Proudly.*] Three quarters. For you. Here. [*He proffers the biscuit.*] No? [*Pause.*] Do you not feel well?

HAMM [*wearily*]: Quiet, quiet, you're keeping me awake. [*Pause.*] Talk softer. [*Pause.*] If I could sleep I might make love. I'd go into the woods. My eyes would see . . . the sky, the earth. I'd run, run, they wouldn't catch me. [*Pause.*] Nature! [*Pause.*] There's something dripping in my head. [*Pause.*] A heart, a heart in my head. [*Pause.*]

NAGG [*soft*]: Do you hear him? A heart in his head! [*He chuckles cautiously.*]

NELL: One mustn't laugh at those things, Nagg. Why must you always laugh at them?

NAGG: Not so loud!

NELL [*without lowering her voice*]: Nothing is funnier than unhappiness, I grant you that. But—

NAGG [*shocked*]: Oh!

---

4. A town in the Ardennes, a wooded region in northern France.

NELL: Yes, yes, it's the most comical thing in the world. And we laugh, we laugh, with a will, in the beginning. But it's always the same thing. Yes, it's like the funny story we have heard too often, we still find it funny, but we don't laugh any more. [*Pause.*] Have you anything else to say to me?

NAGG: No.

NELL: Are you quite sure? [*Pause.*] Then I'll leave you.

NAGG: Do you not want your biscuit? [*Pause.*] I'll keep it for you. [*Pause.*] I thought you were going to leave me.

NELL: I am going to leave you.

NAGG: Could you give me a scratch before you go?

NELL: No. [*Pause.*] Where?

NAGG: In the back.

NELL: No. [*Pause.*] Rub yourself against the rim.

NAGG: It's lower down. In the hollow.

NELL: What hollow?

NAGG: The hollow! [*Pause.*] Could you not? [*Pause.*] Yesterday you scratched me there.

NELL [*elegiac*]: Ah yesterday!

NAGG: Could you not? [*Pause.*] Would you like me to scratch you? [*Pause.*] Are you crying again?

NELL: I was trying. [*Pause.*]

HAMM: Perhaps it's a little vein. [*Pause.*]

NAGG: What was that he said?

NELL: Perhaps it's a little vein.

NAGG: What does that mean? [*Pause.*] That means nothing. [*Pause.*] Will I tell you the story of the tailor?

NELL: No. [*Pause.*] What for?

NAGG: To cheer you up.

NELL: It's not funny.

NAGG: It always made you laugh. [*Pause.*] The first time I thought you'd die.

NELL: It was on Lake Como.[5] [*Pause.*] One April afternoon. [*Pause.*] Can you believe it?

NAGG: What?

NELL: That we once went out rowing on Lake Como. [*Pause.*] One April afternoon.

NAGG: We had got engaged the day before.

NELL: Engaged!

NAGG: You were in such fits that we capsized. By rights we should have been drowned.

NELL: It was because I felt happy.

NAGG [*indignant*]: It was not, it was not, it was my story and nothing else. Happy! Don't you laugh at it still? Every time I tell it. Happy!

NELL: It was deep, deep. And you could see down to the bottom. So white. So clean.

NAGG: Let me tell it again. [*Raconteur's*[6] *voice.*] An Englishman, needing a pair of striped trousers in a hurry for the New Year festivities, goes to his tailor who takes his measurements.

　　[*Tailor's voice.*]

"That's the lot, come back in four days, I'll have it ready."
Good. Four days later.

---

5. A scenic lake in northern Italy.　　　　　6. A talented storyteller.

[*Tailor's voice.*]

"So sorry, come back in a week, I've made a mess of the seat." Good, that's all right, a neat seat can be very ticklish. A week later.

[*Tailor's voice.*]

"Frightfully sorry, come back in ten days, I've made a hash of the crotch." Good, can't be helped, a snug crotch is always a teaser. Ten days later.

[*Tailor's voice.*]

"Dreadfully sorry, come back in a fortnight, I've made a balls of the fly." Good, at a pinch, a smart fly is a stiff proposition. [*Pause. Normal voice.*] I never told it worse. [*Pause. Gloomy.*] I tell this story worse and worse.

[*Pause. Raconteur's voice.*]

Well, to make it short, the bluebells are blowing and he ballockses the buttonholes.

[*Customer's voice.*]

"God damn you to hell, Sir, no, it's indecent, there are limits! In six days, do you hear me, six days, God made the world. Yes Sir, no less Sir, the WORLD! And you are not bloody well capable of making me a pair of trousers in three months!"

[*Tailor's voice, scandalized.*]

"But my dear Sir, my dear Sir, look—[*disdainful gesture, disgustedly*]—at the world—[*pause*] and look—[*loving gesture, proudly*]—at my TROUSERS!"

[*Pause. He looks at Nell who has remained impassive, her eyes unseeing, breaks into a high forced laugh, cuts it short, pokes his head towards Nell, launches his laugh again.*]

HAMM: Silence!

[*Nagg starts, cuts short his laugh.*]

NELL: You could see down to the bottom.

HAMM [*exasperated*]: Have you not finished? Will you never finish? [*With sudden fury.*] Will this never finish?

[*Nagg disappears into his bin, closes the lid behind him. Nell does not move. Frenziedly.*]

My kingdom for a nightman![7]

[*He whistles. Enter Clov.*]

Clear away this muck! Chuck it in the sea!

[*Clov goes to bins, halts.*]

NELL: So white.
HAMM: What? What's she blathering about?

---

7. Someone who empties outhouses. Hamm's phrasing alludes to Richard III's call, "My kingdom for a horse!" in Shakespeare's tragedy *Richard III* 5.4.

[*Clov stoops, takes Nell's hand, feels her pulse.*]

NELL [*to Clov*]: Desert!

[*Clov lets go her hand, pushes her back in the bin, closes the lid.*]

CLOV [*returning to his place beside the chair*]: She has no pulse.
HAMM: What was she drivelling about?
CLOV: She told me to go away, into the desert.
HAMM: Damn busybody! Is that all?
CLOV: No.
HAMM: What else?
CLOV: I didn't understand.
HAMM: Have you bottled her?
CLOV: Yes.
HAMM: Are they both bottled?
CLOV: Yes.
HAMM: Screw down the lids.

[*Clov goes towards door.*]

Time enough.

[*Clov halts.*]

My anger subsides, I'd like to pee.
CLOV [*with alacrity*]: I'll go and get the catheter.

[*He goes towards door.*]

HAMM: Time enough.

[*Clov halts.*]

Give me my pain-killer.
CLOV: It's too soon. [*Pause.*] It's too soon on top of your tonic, it wouldn't act.
HAMM: In the morning they brace you up and in the evening they calm you down. Unless it's the other way round. [*Pause.*] That old doctor, he's dead naturally?
CLOV: He wasn't old.
HAMM: But he's dead?
CLOV: Naturally. [*Pause.*] *You* ask *me* that? [*Pause.*]
HAMM: Take me for a little turn.

[*Clov goes behind the chair and pushes it forward.*]

Not too fast!

[*Clov pushes chair.*]

Right round the world!

[*Clov pushes chair.*]

Hug the walls, then back to the center again.

[*Clov pushes chair.*]

I was right in the center, wasn't I?

CLOV [*pushing*]: Yes.

HAMM: We'd need a proper wheel-chair. With big wheels. Bicycle wheels! [*Pause.*]
Are you hugging?

CLOV [*pushing*]: Yes.

HAMM [*groping for wall*]: It's a lie! Why do you lie to me?

CLOV [*bearing closer to wall*]: There! There!

HAMM: Stop!

[*Clov stops chair close to back wall. Hamm lays his hand against wall.*]

Old wall! [*Pause.*] Beyond is the . . . other hell. [*Pause. Violently.*] Closer! Closer!
Up against!

CLOV: Take away your hand.

[*Hamm withdraws his hand. Clov rams chair against wall.*]

There!

[*Hamm leans towards wall, applies his ear to it.*]

HAMM: Do you hear?

[*He strikes the wall with his knuckles.*]

Do you hear? Hollow bricks!

[*He strikes again.*]

All that's hollow! [*Pause. He straightens up. Violently.*] That's enough. Back!

CLOV: We haven't done the round.

HAMM: Back to my place!

[*Clov pushes chair back to center.*]

Is that my place?

CLOV: Yes, that's your place.

HAMM: Am I right in the center?

CLOV: I'll measure it.

HAMM: More or less! More or less!

CLOV [*moving chair slightly*]: There!

HAMM: I'm more or less in the center?

CLOV: I'd say so.

HAMM: You'd say so! Put me right in the center!

CLOV: I'll go and get the tape.

HAMM: Roughly! Roughly!

[*Clov moves chair slightly.*]

Bang in the center!

CLOV: There! [*Pause.*]

HAMM: I feel a little too far to the left.

[*Clov moves chair slightly.*]

Now I feel a little too far to the right.

[*Clov moves chair slightly.*]

I feel a little too far forward.

[*Clov moves chair slightly.*]

Now I feel a little too far back.

[*Clov moves chair slightly.*]

Don't stay there [*i.e. behind the chair*], you give me the shivers.

[*Clov returns to his place beside the chair.*]

CLOV: If I could kill him I'd die happy. [*Pause.*]
HAMM: What's the weather like?
CLOV: As usual.
HAMM: Look at the earth.
CLOV: I've looked.
HAMM: With the glass?
CLOV: No need of the glass.
HAMM: Look at it with the glass.
CLOV: I'll go and get the glass

[*Exit Clov.*]

HAMM: No need for the glass!

[*Enter Clov with telescope.*]

CLOV: I'm back again, with the glass.

[*He goes to window right, looks up at it.*]

I need the steps.
HAMM: Why? Have you shrunk?

[*Exit Clov with telescope.*]

I don't like that, I don't like that.

[*Enter Clov with ladder, but without telescope.*]

CLOV: I'm back again, with the steps.

[*He sets down ladder under window right, gets up on it, realizes he has not the telescope, gets down.*]

I need the glass.

[*He goes towards door.*]

HAMM [*violently*]: But you have the glass!
CLOV [*halting, violently*]: No, I haven't the glass!

[*Exit Clov.*]

HAMM: This is deadly.

[*Enter Clov with telescope. He goes towards ladder.*]

CLOV: Things are livening up.

[*He gets up on the ladder, raises the telescope, lets it fall.*]

I did it on purpose.

[*He gets down, picks up the telescope, turns it on auditorium.*]

I see . . . a multitude . . . in transports . . . of joy. [*Pause.*] That's what I call a magnifier.

[*He lowers the telescope, turns towards Hamm.*]

Well? Don't we laugh?

HAMM [*after reflection*]: I don't.

CLOV [*after reflection*]: Nor I.

[*He gets up on ladder, turns the telescope on the without.*]

Let's see.

[*He looks, moving the telescope.*]

Zero . . . [*he looks*] . . . zero . . . [*he looks*] . . . and zero.

HAMM: Nothing stirs. All is—

CLOV: Zer—

HAMM [*violently*]: Wait till you're spoken to! [*Normal voice.*] All is . . . all is . . . all is what? [*Violently.*] All is what?

CLOV: What all is? In a word? Is that what you want to know? Just a moment.

[*He turns the telescope on the without, looks, lowers the telescope, turns towards Hamm.*]

Corpsed. [*Pause.*] Well? Content?

HAMM: Look at the sea.

CLOV: It's the same.

HAMM: Look at the ocean!

[*Clov gets down, takes a few steps towards window left, goes back for ladder, carries it over and sets it down under window left, gets up on it, turns the telescope on the without, looks at length. He starts, lowers the telescope, examines it, turns it again on the without.*]

CLOV: Never seen anything like that!

HAMM [*anxious*]: What? A sail? A fin? Smoke?

CLOV [*looking*]: The light is sunk.

HAMM [*relieved*]: Pah! We all knew that.

CLOV [*looking*]: There was a bit left.

HAMM: The base.

CLOV [*looking*]: Yes.

HAMM: And now?

CLOV [*looking*]: All gone.

HAMM: No gulls?

CLOV [*looking*]: Gulls!

HAMM: And the horizon? Nothing on the horizon?

CLOV [*lowering the telescope, turning towards Hamm, exasperated*]: What in God's name could there be on the horizon? [*Pause.*]

HAMM: The waves, how are the waves?

CLOV: The waves?

[*He turns the telescope on the waves.*]

Lead.

HAMM: And the sun?

CLOV [*looking*]: Zero.

HAMM: But it should be sinking. Look again.

CLOV [*looking*]: Damn the sun.

HAMM: Is it night already then?

CLOV [*looking*]: No.

HAMM: Then what is it?

CLOV [*looking*]: Gray.

[*Lowering the telescope, turning towards Hamm, louder.*]

Gray! [*Pause. Still louder.*] GRRAY! [*Pause. He gets down, approaches Hamm from behind, whispers in his ear.*]

HAMM [*starting*]: Gray! Did I hear you say gray?

CLOV: Light black. From pole to pole.

HAMM: You exaggerate. [*Pause.*] Don't stay there, you give me the shivers.

[*Clov returns to his place beside the chair.*]

CLOV: Why this farce, day after day?

HAMM: Routine. One never knows. [*Pause.*] Last night I saw inside my breast. There was a big sore.

CLOV: Pah! You saw your heart.

HAMM: No, it was living. [*Pause. Anguished.*] Clov!

CLOV: Yes.

HAMM: What's happening?

CLOV: Something is taking its course. [*Pause.*]

HAMM: Clov!

CLOV [*impatiently*]: What is it?

HAMM: We're not beginning to . . . to . . . mean something?

CLOV: Mean something! You and I, mean something! [*Brief laugh.*] Ah that's a good one!

HAMM: I wonder. [*Pause.*] Imagine if a rational being came back to earth, wouldn't he be liable to get ideas into his head if he observed us long enough. [*Voice of rational being.*] Ah, good, now I see what it is, yes, now I understand what they're at!

[*Clov starts, drops the telescope and begins to scratch his belly with both hands. Normal voice.*]

And without going so far as that, we ourselves . . . [*with emotion*] . . . we ourselves . . . at certain moments . . . [*Vehemently.*] To think perhaps it won't all have been for nothing!

CLOV [*anguished, scratching himself*]: I have a flea!

HAMM: A flea! Are there still fleas?

CLOV: On me there's one. [*Scratching.*] Unless it's a crablouse.

HAMM [*very perturbed*]: But humanity might start from there all over again! Catch him, for the love of God!

CLOV: I'll go and get the powder.

[*Exit Clov.*]

HAMM: A flea! This is awful! What a day!

[*Enter Clov with a sprinkling-tin.*]

CLOV: I'm back again, with the insecticide.

HAMM: Let him have it!

[*Clov loosens the top of his trousers, pulls it forward and shakes powder into the aperture. He stoops, looks, waits, starts, frenziedly shakes more powder, stoops, looks, waits.*]

CLOV: The bastard!

HAMM: Did you get him?

CLOV: Looks like it.

[*He drops the tin and adjusts his trousers.*]

Unless he's laying doggo.

HAMM: Laying! Lying you mean. Unless he's *lying* doggo.

CLOV: Ah? One says lying? One doesn't say laying?

HAMM: Use your head, can't you. If he was laying we'd be bitched.

CLOV: Ah. [*Pause.*] What about that pee?

HAMM: I'm having it.

CLOV: Ah that's the spirit, that's the spirit! [*Pause.*]

HAMM [*with ardour*]: Let's go from here, the two of us! South! You can make a raft and the currents will carry us away, far away, to other . . . mammals!

CLOV: God forbid!

HAMM: Alone, I'll embark alone! Get working on that raft immediately. Tomorrow I'll be gone for ever.

CLOV [*hastening towards door*]: I'll start straight away.

HAMM: Wait!

[*Clov halts.*]

Will there be sharks, do you think?

CLOV: Sharks? I don't know. If there are there will be.

[*He goes towards door.*]

HAMM: Wait!

[*Clov halts.*]

Is it not yet time for my pain-killer?

CLOV [*violently*]: No!

[*He goes towards door.*]

HAMM: Wait!

[*Clov halts.*]

How are your eyes?

CLOV: Bad.

HAMM: But you can see.

CLOV: All I want.

HAMM: How are your legs?

CLOV: Bad.

HAMM: But you can walk.

CLOV: I come . . . and go.

HAMM: In my house. [*Pause. With prophetic relish.*] One day you'll be blind, like me. You'll be sitting there, a speck in the void, in the dark, for ever, like me. [*Pause.*] One day you'll say to yourself, I'm tired, I'll sit down, and you'll go and sit down. Then you'll say, I'm hungry, I'll get up and get something to eat. But you won't get up. You'll say, I shouldn't have sat down, but since I have I'll sit on a little longer, then I'll get up and get something to eat. But you won't get up and you won't get anything to eat. [*Pause.*] You'll look at the wall a while, then you'll say, I'll close my eyes, perhaps have a little sleep, after that I'll feel better, and you'll close them. And when you open them again there'll be no wall any more. [*Pause.*] Infinite emptiness will be all around you, all the resurrected dead of all the ages wouldn't fill it, and there you'll be like a little bit of grit in the middle of the steppe. [*Pause.*] Yes, one day you'll know what it is, you'll be like me, except that you won't have anyone with you, because you won't have had pity on anyone and because there won't be anyone left to have pity on. [*Pause.*]

CLOV: It's not certain. [*Pause.*] And there's one thing you forget.

HAMM: Ah?

CLOV: I can't sit down.

HAMM [*impatiently*]: Well you'll lie down then, what the hell! Or you'll come to a standstill, simply stop and stand still, the way you are now. One day you'll say, I'm tired, I'll stop. What does the attitude matter? [*Pause.*]

CLOV: So you all want me to leave you.

HAMM: Naturally.

CLOV: Then I'll leave you.

HAMM: You can't leave us.

CLOV: Then I won't leave you. [*Pause.*]

HAMM: Why don't you finish us? [*Pause.*] I'll tell you the combination of the cupboard if you promise to finish me.

CLOV: I couldn't finish you.

HAMM: Then you won't finish me. [*Pause.*]

CLOV: I'll leave you, I have things to do.

HAMM: Do you remember when you came here?

CLOV: No. Too small, you told me.

HAMM: Do you remember your father.

CLOV [*wearily*]: Same answer. [*Pause.*] You've asked me these questions millions of times.

HAMM: I love the old questions. [*With fervour.*] Ah the old questions, the old answers, there's nothing like them! [*Pause.*] It was I was a father to you.

CLOV: Yes. [*He looks at Hamm fixedly.*] You were that to me.

HAMM: My house a home for you.

CLOV: Yes. [*He looks about him.*] This was that for me.

HAMM [*proudly*]: But for me, [*gesture towards himself*] no father. But for Hamm, [*gesture towards surroundings*] no home. [*Pause.*]

CLOV: I'll leave you.

HAMM: Did you ever think of one thing?

CLOV: Never.

HAMM: That here we're down in a hole. [*Pause.*] But beyond the hills? Eh? Perhaps it's still green. Eh? [*Pause.*] Flora! Pomona! [*Ecstatically.*] Ceres![8] [*Pause.*] Perhaps you won't need to go very far.

CLOV: I can't go very far. [*Pause.*] I'll leave you.

HAMM: Is my dog ready?

CLOV: He lacks a leg.

HAMM: Is he silky?

CLOV: He's a kind of Pomeranian.

HAMM: Go and get him.

CLOV: He lacks a leg.

HAMM: Go and get him!

[*Exit Clov.*]

We're getting on.

[*Enter Clov holding by one of its three legs a black toy dog.*]

CLOV: Your dogs are here.

[*He hands the dog to Hamm who feels it, fondles it.*]

HAMM: He's white, isn't he?

CLOV: Nearly.

HAMM: What do you mean, nearly? Is he white or isn't he?

CLOV: He isn't. [*Pause.*]

HAMM: You've forgotten the sex.

CLOV [*vexed*]: But he isn't finished. The sex goes on at the end. [*Pause.*]

HAMM: You haven't put on his ribbon.

CLOV [*angrily*]: But he isn't finished, I tell you! First you finish your dog and then you put on his ribbon! [*Pause.*]

HAMM: Can he stand?

CLOV: I don't know.

HAMM: Try.

[*He hands the dog to Clov who places it on the ground.*]

Well?

CLOV: Wait!

[*He squats down and tries to get the dog to stand on its three legs, fails, lets it go. The dog falls on its side.*]

HAMM [*impatiently*]: Well?

CLOV: He's standing.

---

8. Flora, Pomona, and Ceres: the Roman goddesses of flowering plants, fruits, and grains.

HAMM [*groping for the dog*]: Where? Where is he?

[*Clov holds up the dog in a standing position.*]

CLOV: There.

[*He takes Hamm's hand and guides it towards the dog's head.*]

HAMM [*his hand on the dog's head*]: Is he gazing at me?
CLOV: Yes.
HAMM [*proudly*]: As if he were asking me to take him for a walk?
CLOV: If you like.
HAMM [*as before*]: Or as if he were begging me for a bone.

[*He withdraws his hand.*]

Leave him like that, standing there imploring me.

[*Clov straightens up. The dog falls on its side.*]

CLOV: I'll leave you.
HAMM: Have you had your visions?
CLOV: Less.
HAMM: Is Mother Pegg's light on?
CLOV: Light! How could anyone's light be on?
HAMM: Extinguished!
CLOV: Naturally it's extinguished. If it's not on it's extinguished.
HAMM: No, I mean Mother Pegg.
CLOV: But naturally she's extinguished! [*Pause.*] What's the matter with you today?
HAMM: I'm taking my course. [*Pause.*] Is she buried?
CLOV: Buried! Who would have buried her?
HAMM: You.
CLOV: Me! Haven't I enough to do without burying people?
HAMM: But you'll bury me.
CLOV: No I won't bury you. [*Pause.*]
HAMM: She was bonny once, like a flower of the field. [*With reminiscent leer.*] And a great one for the men!
CLOV: We too were bonny—once. It's a rare thing not to have been bonny—once. [*Pause.*]
HAMM: Go and get the gaff.[9]

[*Clov goes to door, halts.*]

CLOV: Do this, do that, and I do it. I never refuse. Why?
HAMM: You're not able to.
CLOV: Soon I won't do it any more.
HAMM: You won't be able to any more.

[*Exit Clov.*]

Ah the creatures, the creatures, everything has to be explained to them.

[*Enter Clov with gaff.*]

---

9. A fishing pole designed for catching large fish.

CLOV: Here's your gaff. Stick it up.

[*He gives the gaff to Hamm who, wielding it like a puntpole, tries to move his chair.*]

HAMM: Did I move?

CLOV: No.

[*Hamm throws down the gaff.*]

HAMM: Go and get the oilcan.

CLOV: What for?

HAMM: To oil the castors.

CLOV: I oiled them yesterday.

HAMM: Yesterday! What does that mean? Yesterday!

CLOV [*violently*]: That means that bloody awful day, long ago, before this bloody awful day. I use the words you taught me. If they don't mean anything any more, teach me others. Or let me be silent. [*Pause.*]

HAMM: I once knew a madman who thought the end of the world had come. He was a painter—and engraver. I had a great fondness for him. I used to go and see him, in the asylum. I'd take him by the hand and drag him to the window. Look! There! All that rising corn! And there! Look! The sails of the herring fleet! All that loveliness! [*Pause.*] He'd snatch away his hand and go back into his corner. Appalled. All he had seen was ashes. [*Pause.*] He alone had been spared. [*Pause.*] Forgotten. [*Pause.*] It appears the case is . . . was not so . . . so unusual.

CLOV: A madman? When was that?

HAMM: Oh way back, way back, you weren't in the land of the living.

CLOV: God be with the days!

[*Pause. Hamm raises his toque.*]

HAMM: I had a great fondness for him.

[*Pause. He puts on his toque again.*]

He was a painter—and engraver.

CLOV: There are so many terrible things.

HAMM: No, no, there are not so many now. [*Pause.*] Clov!

CLOV: Yes.

HAMM: Do you not think this has gone on long enough?

CLOV: Yes! [*Pause.*] What?

HAMM: This . . . this . . . thing.

CLOV: I've always thought so. [*Pause.*] You not?

HAMM [*gloomily*]: Then it's a day like any other day.

CLOV: As long as it lasts. [*Pause.*] All life long the same inanities.

HAMM: I can't leave you.

CLOV: I know. And you can't follow me. [*Pause.*]

HAMM: If you leave me how shall I know?

CLOV [*briskly*]: Well you simply whistle me and if I don't come running it means I've left you. [*Pause.*]

HAMM: You won't come and kiss me goodbye?

CLOV: Oh I shouldn't think so. [*Pause.*]

HAMM: But you might be merely dead in your kitchen.

CLOV: The result would be the same.

HAMM: Yes, but how would I know, if you were merely dead in your kitchen?

CLOV: Well . . . sooner or later I'd start to stink.

HAMM: You stink already. The whole place stinks of corpses.

CLOV: The whole universe.

HAMM [angrily]: To hell with the universe. [Pause.] Think of something.

CLOV: What?

HAMM: An idea, have an idea. [Angrily.] A bright idea!

CLOV: Ah good.

[He starts pacing to and fro, his eyes fixed on the ground, his hands behind his back. He halts.]

The pains in my legs! It's unbelievable! Soon I won't be able to think any more.

HAMM: You won't be able to leave me.

[Clov resumes his pacing.]

What are you doing?

CLOV: Having an idea.

[He paces.]

Ah!

[He halts.]

HAMM: What a brain! [Pause.] Well?

CLOV: Wait! [He meditates. Not very convinced.] Yes . . . [Pause. More convinced.] Yes! [He raises his head.] I have it! I set the alarm. [Pause.]

HAMM: This is perhaps not one of my bright days, but frankly—

CLOV: You whistle me. I don't come. The alarm rings. I'm gone. It doesn't ring. I'm dead. [Pause.]

HAMM: Is it working? [Pause. Impatiently.] The alarm, is it working?

CLOV: Why wouldn't it be working?

HAMM: Because it's worked too much.

CLOV: But it's hardly worked at all.

HAMM [angrily]: Then because it's worked too little!

CLOV: I'll go and see.

[Exit Clov. Brief ring of alarm off. Enter Clov with alarm-clock. He holds it against Hamm's ear and releases alarm. They listen to it ringing to the end. Pause.]

Fit to wake the dead! Did you hear it?

HAMM: Vaguely.

CLOV: The end is terrific!

HAMM: I prefer the middle. [Pause.] Is it not time for my pain-killer?

CLOV: No! [He goes to door, turns.] I'll leave you.

HAMM: It's time for my story. Do you want to listen to my story?

CLOV: No.

HAMM: Ask my father if he wants to listen to my story.

[Clov goes to bins, raises the lid of Nagg's, stoops, looks into it. Pause. He straightens up.]

CLOV: He's asleep.
HAMM: Wake him.

[*Clov stoops, wakes Nagg with the alarm. Unintelligible words. Clov straightens up.*]

CLOV: He doesn't want to listen to your story.
HAMM: I'll give him a bon-bon.

[*Clov stoops. As before.*]

CLOV: He wants a sugar-plum.
HAMM: He'll get a sugar-plum.

[*Clov stoops. As before.*]

CLOV: It's a deal.

[*He goes towards door. Nagg's hands appear, gripping the rim. Then the head emerges. Clov reaches door, turns.*]

Do you believe in the life to come?
HAMM: Mine was always that.

[*Exit Clov.*]

Got him that time!
NAGG: I'm listening.
HAMM: Scoundrel! Why did you engender me?
NAGG: I didn't know.
HAMM: What? What didn't you know?
NAGG: That it'd be you. [*Pause.*] You'll give me a sugar-plum?
HAMM: After the audition.
NAGG: You swear?
HAMM: Yes.
NAGG: On what?
HAMM: My honor. [*Pause. They laugh heartily.*]
NAGG: Two.
HAMM: One.
NAGG: One for me and one for—
HAMM: One! Silence! [*Pause.*] Where was I? [*Pause. Gloomily.*] It's finished, we're finished. [*Pause.*] Nearly finished. [*Pause.*] There'll be no more speech. [*Pause.*] Something dripping in my head, ever since the fontanelles.[1] [*Stifled hilarity of Nagg.*] Splash, splash, always on the same spot. [*Pause.*] Perhaps it's a little vein. [*Pause.*] A little artery. [*Pause. More animated.*] Enough of that, it's story time, where was I? [*Pause. Narrative tone.*] The man came crawling towards me, on his belly. Pale, wonderfully pale and thin, he seemed on the point of—[*Pause. Normal tone.*] No, I've done that bit. [*Pause. Narrative tone.*] I calmly filled my pipe—the meerschaum, lit it with . . . let us say a vesta,[2] drew a few puffs. Aah! [*Pause.*] Well, what is it *you* want? [*Pause.*] It was an extra-ordinarily bitter day, I remember, zero by the thermometer. But considering it was Christmas Eve there was nothing . . . extra-ordinary about that. Seasonable weather, for once in

1. Soft gaps between an infant's skull bones.   2. A match.

a way. [*Pause.*] Well, what ill wind blows you my way? He raised his face to me, black with mingled dirt and tears. [*Pause. Normal tone.*] That should do it.

[*Narrative tone.*]

No no, don't look at me, don't look at me. He dropped his eyes and mumbled something, apologies I presume. [*Pause.*] I'm a busy man, you know, the final touches, before the festivities, you know what it is. [*Pause. Forcibly.*] Come on now, what is the object of this invasion? [*Pause.*] It was a glorious bright day, I remember, fifty by the heliometer, but already the sun was sinking down into the . . . down among the dead.

[*Normal tone.*]

Nicely put, that.

[*Narrative tone.*]

Come on now, come on, present your petition and let me resume my labors.

[*Pause. Normal tone.*]

There's English for you. Ah well . . .

[*Narrative tone.*]

It was then he took the plunge. It's my little one, he said. Tsstss, a little one, that's bad. My little boy, he said, as if the sex mattered. Where did he come from? He named the hole. A good half-day, on horse. What are you insinuating? That the place is still inhabited? No no, not a soul, except himself and the child—assuming he existed. Good. I enquired about the situation at Kov, beyond the gulf. Not a sinner. Good. And you expect me to believe you have left your little one back there, all alone, and alive into the bargain? Come now! [*Pause.*] It was a howling wild day, I remember, a hundred by the anenometer.[3] The wind was tearing up the dead pines and sweeping them . . . away.

[*Pause. Normal tone.*]

A bit feeble, that.

[*Narrative tone.*]

Come on, man, speak up, what is it you want from me, I have to put up my holly. [*Pause.*]

Well to make it short it finally transpired that what he wanted from me was . . . bread for his brat? Bread? But I have no bread, it doesn't agree with me. Good. Then perhaps a little corn?

[*Pause. Normal tone.*]

That should do it.

[*Narrative tone.*]

Corn, yes, I have corn, it's true, in my granaries. But use your head. I give you some corn, a pound, a pound and a half, you bring it back to your child and you

3. An instrument used to measure wind speed.

make him—if he's still alive—a nice pot of porridge, [*Nagg reacts*] a nice pot and a half of porridge, full of nourishment. Good. The colors come back into his little cheeks—perhaps. And then? [*Pause.*] I lost patience. [*Violently.*] Use your head, can't you, use your head, you're on earth, there's no cure for that! [*Pause.*] It was an exceedingly dry day, I remember, zero by the hygrometer. Ideal weather, for my lumbago. [*Pause. Violently.*] But what in God's name do you imagine? That the earth will awake in spring? That the rivers and seas will run with fish again? That there's manna in heaven still for imbeciles like you? [*Pause.*] Gradually I cooled down, sufficiently at least to ask him how long he had taken on the way. Three whole days. Good. In what condition he had left the child. Deep in sleep. [*Forcibly.*] But deep in what sleep, deep in what sleep already? [*Pause.*] Well to make it short I finally offered to take him into my service. He had touched a chord. And then I imagined already that I wasn't much longer for this world. [*He laughs. Pause.*] Well? [*Pause.*] Well? Here if you were careful you might die a nice natural death, in peace and comfort. [*Pause.*] Well? [*Pause.*] In the end he asked me would I consent to take in the child as well—if he were still alive. [*Pause.*] It was the moment I was waiting for. [*Pause.*] Would I consent to take in the child . . . [*Pause.*] I can see him still, down on his knees, his hands flat on the ground, glaring at me with his mad eyes, in defiance of my wishes. [*Pause. Normal tone.*] I'll soon have finished with this story. [*Pause.*] Unless I bring in other characters. [*Pause.*] But where would I find them? [*Pause.*] Where would I look for them? [*Pause. He whistles. Enter Clov.*] Let us pray to God.

NAGG: Me sugar-plum!

CLOV: There's a rat in the kitchen!

HAMM: A rat! Are there still rats?

CLOV: In the kitchen there's one.

HAMM: And you haven't exterminated him?

CLOV: Half. You disturbed us.

HAMM: He can't get away?

CLOV: No.

HAMM: You'll finish him later. Let us pray to God.

CLOV: Again!

NAGG: Me sugar-plum!

HAMM: God first! [*Pause.*] Are you right?

CLOV [*resigned*]: Off we go.

HAMM [*to Nagg*]: And you?

NAGG [*clasping his hands, closing his eyes, in a gabble*]: Our Father which art—

HAMM: Silence! In silence! Where are your manners? [*Pause.*] Off we go. [*Attitudes of prayer. Silence. Abandoning his attitude, discouraged.*] Well?

CLOV [*abandoning his attitude*]: What a hope! And you?

HAMM: Sweet damn all! [*To Nagg.*] And you?

NAGG: Wait! [*Pause. Abandoning his attitude.*] Nothing doing!

HAMM: The bastard! He doesn't exist!

CLOV: Not yet.

NAGG: Me sugar-plum!

HAMM: There are no more sugar-plums! [*Pause.*]

NAGG: It's natural. After all I'm your father. It's true if it hadn't been me it would have been someone else. But that's no excuse. [*Pause.*] Turkish Delight, for example, which no longer exists, we all know that, there is nothing in the world I love more. And one day I'll ask you for some, in return for a kindness, and you'll promise it to me. One must live with the times. [*Pause.*] Whom did you call when you were a tiny boy, and were frightened, in the dark? Your mother? No. Me. We let you cry. Then we moved you out of earshot, so that we might sleep in peace. [*Pause.*] I was asleep, as happy as a king, and you woke me up to have me listen to you. It wasn't indispensable, you didn't really need to have me listen to you. Besides I didn't listen to you. [*Pause.*] I hope the day will come when you'll really need to have me listen to you, and need to hear my voice, any voice. [*Pause.*] Yes, I hope I'll live till then, to hear you calling me like when you were a tiny boy, and were frightened, in the dark, and I was your only hope. [*Pause. Nagg knocks on lid of Nell's bin. Pause.*] Nell! [*Pause. He knocks louder. Pause. Louder.*] Nell! [*Pause. Nagg sinks back into his bin, closes the lid behind him. Pause.*]

HAMM: Our revels now are ended.[4]

[*He gropes for the dog.*]

The dog's gone.

CLOV: He's not a real dog, he can't go.

HAMM [*groping*]: He's not there.

CLOV: He's lain down.

HAMM: Give him up to me.

[*Clov picks up the dog and gives it to Hamm. Hamm holds it in his arms. Pause. Hamm throws away the dog.*]

Dirty brute!

[*Clov begins to pick up the objects lying on the ground.*]

What are you doing?

CLOV: Putting things in order. [*He straightens up. Fervently.*] I'm going to clear everything away! [*He starts picking up again.*]

HAMM: Order!

CLOV [*straightening up*]: I love order. It's my dream. A world where all would be silent and still and each thing in its last place, under the last dust. [*He starts picking up again.*]

HAMM [*exasperated*]: What in God's name do you think you are doing?

CLOV [*straightening up*]: I'm doing my best to create a little order.

HAMM: Drop it!

[*Clov drops the objects he has picked up.*]

CLOV: After all, there or elsewhere. [*He goes towards door.*]

HAMM [*irritably*]: What's wrong with your feet?

CLOV: My feet?

HAMM: Tramp! Tramp!

CLOV: I must have put on my boots.

HAMM: Your slippers were hurting you? [*Pause.*]

CLOV: I'll leave you.

HAMM: No!

4. Quoting the exiled magician Prospero in Shakespeare's *The Tempest* (4.1): "Our revels are now ended. These our actors / As I foretold you, were all spirits, and / Are melted into air, into thin air."

CLOV: What is there to keep me here?

HAMM: The dialogue. [*Pause.*] I've got on with my story. [*Pause.*] I've got on with it well. [*Pause. Irritably.*] Ask me where I've got to.

CLOV: Oh, by the way, your story?

HAMM [*surprised*]: What story?

CLOV: The one you've been telling yourself all your days.

HAMM: Ah you mean my chronicle?

CLOV: That's the one. [*Pause.*]

HAMM [*angrily*]: Keep going, can't you, keep going!

CLOV: You've got on with it, I hope.

HAMM [*modestly*]: Oh not very far, not very far. [*He sighs.*] There are days like that, one isn't inspired. [*Pause.*] Nothing you can do about it, just wait for it to come. [*Pause.*] No forcing, no forcing, it's fatal. [*Pause.*] I've got on with it a little all the same. [*Pause.*] Technique, you know. [*Pause. Irritably.*] I say I've got on with it a little all the same.

CLOV [*admiringly*]: Well I never! In spite of everything you were able to get on with it!

HAMM [*modestly*]: Oh not very far, you know, not very far, but nevertheless, better than nothing.

CLOV: Better than nothing! Is it possible?

HAMM: I'll tell you how it goes. He comes crawling on his belly—

CLOV: Who?

HAMM: What?

CLOV: Who do you mean, he?

HAMM: Who do I mean! Yet another.

CLOV: Ah him! I wasn't sure.

HAMM: Crawling on his belly, whining for bread for his brat. He's offered a job as gardener. Before—

[*Clov bursts out laughing.*]

What is there so funny about that?

CLOV: A job as gardener!

HAMM: Is that what tickles you?

CLOV: It must be that.

HAMM: It wouldn't be the bread?

CLOV: Or the brat. [*Pause.*]

HAMM: The whole thing is comical, I grant you that. What about having a good guffaw the two of us together?

CLOV [*after reflection*]: I couldn't guffaw again today.

HAMM [*after reflection*]: Nor I. [*Pause.*] I continue then. Before accepting with gratitude he asks if he may have his little boy with him.

CLOV: What age?

HAMM: Oh tiny.

CLOV: He would have climbed the trees.

HAMM: All the little odd jobs.

CLOV: And then he would have grown up.

HAMM: Very likely. [*Pause.*]

CLOV: Keep going, can't you, keep going!

HAMM: That's all. I stopped there. [*Pause.*]

CLOV: Do you see how it goes on.

HAMM: More or less.

CLOV: Will it not soon be the end?

HAMM: I'm afraid it will.

CLOV: Pah! You'll make up another.

HAMM: I don't know. [*Pause.*] I feel rather drained. [*Pause.*] The prolonged creative effort. [*Pause.*] If I could drag myself down to the sea! I'd make a pillow of sand for my head and the tide would come.

CLOV: There's no more tide. [*Pause.*]

HAMM: Go and see is she dead.

[*Clov goes to bins, raises the lid of Nell's, stoops, looks into it. Pause.*]

CLOV: Looks like it.

[*He closes the lid, straightens up. Hamm raises his toque. Pause. He puts it on again.*]

HAMM [*with his hand to his toque*]: And Nagg?

[*Clov raises lid of Nagg's bin, stoops, looks into it. Pause.*]

CLOV: Doesn't look like it. [*He closes the lid, straightens up.*]

HAMM [*letting go his toque*]: What's he doing?

[*Clov raises lid of Nagg's bin, stoops, looks into it. Pause.*]

CLOV: He's crying. [*He closes lid, straightens up.*]

HAMM: Then he's living. [*Pause.*] Did you ever have an instant of happiness?

CLOV: Not to my knowledge. [*Pause.*]

HAMM: Bring me under the window.

[*Clov goes towards chair.*]

I want to feel the light on my face.

[*Clov pushes chair.*]

Do you remember, in the beginning, when you took me for a turn? You used to hold the chair too high. At every step you nearly tipped me out. [*With senile quaver.*] Ah great fun, we had, the two of us, great fun. [*Gloomily.*] And then we got into the way of it.

[*Clov stops the chair under window right.*]

There already? [*Pause. He tilts back his head.*] Is it light?

CLOV: It isn't dark.

HAMM [*angrily*]: I'm asking you is it light.

CLOV: Yes. [*Pause.*]

HAMM: The curtain isn't closed?

CLOV: No.

HAMM: What window is it?

CLOV: The earth.

HAMM: I knew it! [*Angrily.*] But there's no light there! The other!

[*Clov pushes chair towards window left.*]

The earth!

Clov stops the chair under window left. Hamm tilts back his head.]

That's what I call light! [*Pause.*] Feels like a ray of sunshine. [*Pause.*] No?

CLOV: No.

HAMM: It isn't a ray of sunshine I feel on my face?

CLOV: No. [*Pause.*]

HAMM: Am I very white? [*Pause. Angrily.*] I'm asking you am I very white!

CLOV: Not more so than usual. [*Pause.*]

HAMM: Open the window.

CLOV: What for?

HAMM: I want to hear the sea.

CLOV: You wouldn't hear it.

HAMM: Even if you opened the window?

CLOV: No.

HAMM: Then it's not worth while opening it?

CLOV: No.

HAMM [*violently*]: Then open it!

[*Clov gets up on the ladder, opens the window. Pause.*]

Have you opened it?

CLOV: Yes. [*Pause.*]

HAMM: You swear you've opened it?

CLOV: Yes. [*Pause.*]

HAMM: Well . . .! [*Pause.*] It must be very calm. [*Pause. Violently.*] I'm asking you is it very calm!

CLOV: Yes.

HAMM: It's because there are no more navigators. [*Pause.*] You haven't much conversation all of a sudden. Do you not feel well?

CLOV: I'm cold.

HAMM: What month are we? [*Pause.*] Close the window, we're going back.

[*Clov closes the window, gets down, pushes the chair back to its place, remains standing behind it, head bowed.*]

Don't stay there, you give me the shivers!

[*Clov returns to his place beside the chair.*]

Father! [*Pause. Louder.*] Father! [*Pause.*] Go and see did he hear me.

[*Clov goes to Nagg's bin, raises the lid, stoops. Unintelligible words. Clov straightens up.*]

CLOV: Yes.

HAMM: Both times?

[*Clov stoops. As before.*]

CLOV: Once only.

HAMM: The first time or the second?

[*Clov stoops. As before.*]

CLOV: He doesn't know.

HAMM: It must have been the second.
CLOV: We'll never know.

[*He closes lid.*]

HAMM: Is he still crying?
CLOV: No.
HAMM: The dead go fast. [*Pause.*] What's he doing?
CLOV: Sucking his biscuit.
HAMM: Life goes on.

[*Clov returns to his place beside the chair.*]

Give me a rug, I'm freezing.
CLOV: There are no more rugs. [*Pause.*]
HAMM: Kiss me. [*Pause.*] Will you not kiss me?
CLOV: No.
HAMM: On the forehead.
CLOV: I won't kiss you anywhere. [*Pause.*]
HAMM [*holding out his hand*]: Give me your hand at least. [*Pause.*] Will you not give
   me your hand?
CLOV: I won't touch you. [*Pause.*]
HAMM: Give me the dog.

[*Clov looks round for the dog.*]

No!
CLOV: Do you not want your dog?
HAMM: No.
CLOV: Then I'll leave you.
HAMM [*head bowed, absently*]: That's right.

[*Clov goes to door, turns.*]

CLOV: If I don't kill that rat he'll die.
HAMM [*as before*]: That's right.

[*Exit Clov. Pause.*]

Me to play.

[*He takes out his handkerchief, unfolds it, holds it spread out before him.*]

We're getting on. [*Pause.*] You weep, and weep, for nothing, so as not to laugh,
and little by little . . . you begin to grieve.

[*He folds the handkerchief, puts it back in his pocket, raises his head.*]

All those I might have helped. [*Pause.*] Helped! [*Pause.*] Saved. [*Pause.*] Saved!
[*Pause.*] The place was crawling with them! [*Pause. Violently.*] Use your head,
can't you, use your head, you're on earth, there's no cure for that! [*Pause.*] Get out
of here and love one another! Lick your neighbor as yourself! [*Pause. Calmer.*]
When it wasn't bread they wanted it was crumpets. [*Pause. Violently.*] Out of my
sight and back to your petting parties! [*Pause.*] All that, all that! [*Pause.*] Not even

a real dog! [*Calmer.*] The end is in the beginning and yet you go on. [*Pause.*] Perhaps I could go on with my story, end it and begin another. [*Pause.*] Perhaps I could throw myself out on the floor.

[*He pushes himself painfully off his seat, falls back again.*]

Dig my nails into the cracks and drag myself forward with my fingers. [*Pause.*] It will be the end and there I'll be, wondering what can have brought it on and wondering what can have . . . [*he hesitates*] . . . why it was so long coming. [*Pause.*] There I'll be, in the old shelter, alone against the silence and . . . [*he hesitates*] . . . the stillness. If I can hold my peace, and sit quiet, it will be all over with sound, and motion, all over and done with. [*Pause.*] I'll have called my father and I'll have called my . . . [*he hesitates*] . . . my son. And even twice, or three times, in case they shouldn't have heard me, the first time, or the second. [*Pause.*] I'll say to myself, He'll come back. [*Pause.*] And then? [*Pause.*] And then? [*Pause.*] He couldn't, he has gone too far. [*Pause.*] And then? [*Pause. Very agitated.*] All kinds of fantasies! That I'm being watched! A rat! Steps! Breath held and then . . . [*He breathes out.*] Then babble, babble, words, like the solitary child who turns himself into children, two, three, so as to be together, and whisper together, in the dark. [*Pause.*] Moment upon moment, pattering down, like the millet grains of . . . [*he hesitates*] . . . that old Greek, and all life long you wait for that to mount up to a life.[5] [*Pause. He opens his mouth to continue, renounces.*] Ah let's get it over!

[*He whistles. Enter Clov with alarm-clock. He halts beside the chair.*]

What? Neither gone nor dead?
CLOV: In spirit only.
HAMM: Which?
CLOV: Both.
HAMM: Gone from me you'd be dead.
CLOV: And vice versa.
HAMM: Outside of here it's death! [*Pause.*] And the rat?
CLOV: He's got away.
HAMM: He can't go far. [*Pause. Anxious.*] Eh?
CLOV: He doesn't need to go far. [*Pause.*]
HAMM: Is it not time for my pain-killer?
CLOV: Yes.
HAMM: Ah! At last! Give it to me! Quick! [*Pause.*]
CLOV: There's no more pain-killer. [*Pause.*]
HAMM [*appalled*]: Good . . .! [*Pause.*] No more pain-killer!
CLOV: No more pain-killer. You'll never get any more pain-killer. [*Pause.*]
HAMM: But the little round box. It was full!
CLOV: Yes. But now it's empty.

[*Pause. Clov starts to move about the room. He is looking for a place to put down the alarm-clock.*]

5. Hamm is referring to Zeno of Elea (5th century B.C.E.), who is known for his philosophical paradoxes. One of them is based on the sound a bushel of millet makes when it falls on the floor: since this sound is caused by the grains, each grain must make a sound when striking the ground. This sound, however, can't be heard, so the apparent sound is really an accumulation of silences.

HAMM [*soft*]: What'll I do? [*Pause. In a scream.*] What'll I do?

[*Clov sees the picture, takes it down, stands it on the floor with its face to the wall, hangs up the alarm-clock in its place.*]

What are you doing?

CLOV: Winding up.

HAMM: Look at the earth.

CLOV: Again!

HAMM: Since it's calling to you.

CLOV: Is your throat sore? [*Pause.*] Would you like a lozenge? [*Pause.*] No. [*Pause.*]
    Pity.

[*Clov goes, humming, towards window right, halts before it, looks up at it.*]

HAMM: Don't sing.

CLOV [*turning towards Hamm*]: One hasn't the right to sing any more?

HAMM: No.

CLOV: Then how can it end?

HAMM: You want it to end?

CLOV: I want to sing.

HAMM: I can't prevent you.

[*Pause. Clov turns towards window right.*]

CLOV: What did I do with that steps? [*He looks around for ladder.*] You didn't see that
    steps? [*He sees it.*] Ah, about time. [*He goes towards window left.*] Sometimes I won-
    der if I'm in my right mind. Then it passes over and I'm as lucid as before. [*He gets up
    on ladder, looks out of window.*] Christ, she's under water! [*He looks.*] How can that
    be? [*He pokes forward his head, his hand above his eyes.*] It hasn't rained. [*He wipes
    the pane, looks. Pause.*] Ah what a fool I am! I'm on the wrong side! [*He gets down,
    takes a few steps towards window right.*] Under water! [*He goes back for ladder.*]
    What a fool I am! [*He carries ladder towards window right.*] Sometimes I wonder if
    I'm in my right senses. Then it passes off and I'm as intelligent as ever.

[*He sets down ladder under window right, gets up on it, looks out of window. He turns towards Hamm.*]

Any particular sector you fancy? Or merely the whole thing?

HAMM: Whole thing.

CLOV: The general effect? Just a moment. [*He looks out of window. Pause.*]

HAMM: Clov.

CLOV [*absorbed*]: Mmm.

HAMM: Do you know what it is?

CLOV [*as before*]: Mmm.

HAMM: I was never there. [*Pause.*] Clov!

CLOV [*turning towards Hamm, exasperated*]: What is it?

HAMM: I was never there.

CLOV: Lucky for you. [*He looks out of window.*]

HAMM: Absent, always. It all happened without me. I don't know what's happened.
    [*Pause.*] Do you know what's happened? [*Pause.*] Clov!

CLOV [*turning towards Hamm, exasperated*]: Do you want me to look at this muck-
    heap, yes or no?

HAMM: Answer me first.

CLOV: What?

HAMM: Do you know what's happened?

CLOV: When? Where?

HAMM [*violently*]: When! What's happened? Use your head, can't you! What has happened?

CLOV: What for Christ's sake does it matter? [*He looks out of window.*]

HAMM: I don't know. [*Pause. Clov turns towards Hamm.*]

CLOV [*harshly*]: When old Mother Pegg asked you for oil for her lamp and you told her to get out to hell, you knew what was happening then, no? [*Pause.*] You know what she died of, Mother Pegg? Of darkness.

HAMM [*feebly*]: I hadn't any.

CLOV [*as before*]: Yes, you had. [*Pause.*]

HAMM: Have you the glass?

CLOV: No, it's clear enough as it is.

HAMM: Go and get it.

> [*Pause. Clov casts up his eyes, brandishes his fists. He loses balance, clutches on to the ladder. He starts to get down, halts.*]

CLOV: There's one thing I'll never understand. [*He gets down.*] Why I always obey you. Can you explain that to me?

HAMM: No. . . . Perhaps it's compassion. [*Pause.*] A kind of great compassion. [*Pause.*] Oh you won't find it easy, you won't find it easy.

> [*Pause. Clov begins to move about the room in search of the telescope.*]

CLOV: I'm tired of our goings on, very tired. [*He searches.*] You're not sitting on it?

> [*He moves the chair, looks at the place where it stood, resumes his search.*]

HAMM [*anguished*]: Don't leave me there! [*Angrily Clov restores the chair to its place.*] Am I right in the center?

CLOV: You'd need a microscope to find this—[*He sees the telescope.*] Ah, about time.

> [*He picks up the telescope, gets up on the ladder, turns the telescope on the without.*]

HAMM: Give me the dog.

CLOV [*looking*]: Quiet!

HAMM [*angrily*]: Give me the dog!

> [*Clov drops the telescope, clasps his hands to his head. Pause. He gets down precipitately, looks for the dog, sees it, picks it up, hastens towards Hamm and strikes him violently on the head with the dog.*]

CLOV: There's your dog for you!

> [*The dog falls to the ground. Pause.*]

HAMM: He hit me!

CLOV: You drive me mad, I'm mad!

HAMM: If you must hit me, hit me with the axe. [*Pause.*] Or with the gaff, hit me with the gaff. Not with the dog. With the gaff. Or with the axe.

> [*Clov picks up the dog and gives it to Hamm who takes it in his arms.*]

CLOV [*imploringly*]: Let's stop playing!
HAMM: Never! [*Pause.*] Put me in my coffin.
CLOV: There are no more coffins.
HAMM: Then let it end!

[*Clov goes towards ladder.*]

With a bang!

[*Clov gets up on ladder, gets down again, looks for telescope, sees it, picks it up, gets up ladder, raises telescope.*]

Of darkness! And me? Did anyone ever have pity on me?
CLOV [*lowering the telescope, turning towards Hamm*]: What? [*Pause.*] Is it me you're referring to?
HAMM [*angrily*]: An aside, ape! Did you never hear an aside before? [*Pause.*] I'm warming up for my last soliloquy.
CLOV: I warn you. I'm going to look at this filth since it's an order. But it's the last time. [*He turns the telescope on the without.*] Let's see. [*He moves the telescope.*] Nothing ... nothing ... good ... good ... nothing ... goo—[*He starts, lowers the telescope, examines it, turns it again on the without. Pause.*] Bad luck to it!
HAMM: More complications!

[*Clov gets down.*]

Not an underplot, I trust.

[*Clov moves ladder nearer window, gets up on it, turns telescope on the without.*]

CLOV [*dismayed*]: Looks like a small boy!
HAMM [*sarcastic*]: A small ... boy!
CLOV: I'll go and see.

[*He gets down, drops the telescope, goes towards door, turns.*]

I'll take the gaff.

[*He looks for the gaff, sees it, picks it up, hastens towards door.*]

HAMM: No!

[*Clov halts.*]

CLOV: No? A potential procreator?
HAMM: If he exists he'll die there or he'll come here. And if he doesn't ... [*Pause.*]
CLOV: You don't believe me? You think I'm inventing? [*Pause.*]
HAMM: It's the end, Clov, we've come to the end. I don't need you any more. [*Pause.*]
CLOV: Lucky for you. [*He goes towards door.*]
HAMM: Leave me the gaff.

[*Clov gives him the gaff, goes towards door, halts, looks at alarm-clock, takes it down, looks round for a better place to put it, goes to bins, puts it on lid of Nagg's bin. Pause.*]

CLOV: I'll leave you. [*He goes towards door.*]
HAMM: Before you go ...

[*Clov halts near door.*]

. . . say something.

CLOV: There is nothing to say.

HAMM: A few words . . . to ponder . . . in my heart.

CLOV: Your heart!

HAMM: Yes. [*Pause. Forcibly.*] Yes! [*Pause.*] With the rest, in the end, the shadows, the murmurs, all the trouble, to end up with. [*Pause.*] Clov. . . . He never spoke to me. Then, in the end, before he went, without my having asked him, he spoke to me. He said . . .

CLOV [*despairingly*]: Ah . . .!

HAMM: Something . . . from your heart.

CLOV: My heart!

HAMM: A few words . . . from your heart. [*Pause.*]

CLOV [*fixed gaze, tonelessly, towards auditorium*]: They said to me, That's love, yes, yes, not a doubt, now you see how—

HAMM: Articulate!

CLOV [*as before*]: How easy it is. They said to me, That's friendship, yes, yes, no question, you've found it. They said to me, Here's the place, stop, raise your head and look at all that beauty. That order! They said to me, Come now, you're not a brute beast, think upon these things and you'll see how all becomes clear. And simple! They said to me, What skilled attention they get, all these dying of their wounds.

HAMM: Enough!

CLOV [*as before*]: I say to myself—sometimes, Clov, you must learn to suffer better than that if you want them to weary of punishing you—one day. I say to my-self—sometimes, Clov, you must be there better than that if you want them to let you go—one day. But I feel too old, and too far, to form new habits. Good, it'll never end, I'll never go. [*Pause.*] Then one day, suddenly, it ends, it changes, I don't understand, it dies, or it's me, I don't understand, that either. I ask the words that remain—sleeping, waking, morning, evening. They have nothing to say. [*Pause.*] I open the door of the cell and go. I am so bowed I only see my feet, if I open my eyes, and between my legs a little trail of black dust. I say to myself that the earth is extinguished, though I never saw it lit. [*Pause.*] It's easy going. [*Pause.*] When I fall I'll weep for happiness. [*Pause. He goes towards door.*]

HAMM: Clov!

[*Clov halts, without turning.*]

Nothing.

[*Clov moves on.*]

Clov!

[*Clov halts, without turning.*]

CLOV: This is what we call making an exit.

HAMM: I'm obliged to you, Clov. For your services.

CLOV [*turning, sharply*]: Ah pardon, it's I am obliged to you.

HAMM: It's we are obliged to each other.

[*Pause. Clov goes towards door.*]

One thing more.

[*Clov halts.*]

A last favor.

[*Exit Clov.*]

Cover me with the sheet. [*Long pause.*] No? Good. [*Pause.*] Me to play. [*Pause. Wearily.*] Old endgame lost of old, play and lose and have done with losing. [*Pause. More animated.*] Let me see. [*Pause.*] Ah yes!

[*He tries to move the chair, using the gaff as before. Enter Clov, dressed for the road. Panama hat, tweed coat, raincoat over his arm, umbrella, bag. He halts by the door and stands there, impassive and motionless, his eyes fixed on Hamm, till the end. Hamm gives up.*]

Good. [*Pause.*] Discard. [*He throws away the gaff, makes to throw away the dog, thinks better of it.*] Take it easy. [*Pause.*] And now? [*Pause.*] Raise hat. [*He raises his toque.*] Peace to our . . . arses. [*Pause.*] And put on again. [*He puts on his toque.*] Deuce. [*Pause. He takes off his glasses.*] Wipe. [*He takes out his handkerchief and, without unfolding it, wipes his glasses.*] And put on again. [*He puts on his glasses, puts back the handkerchief in his pocket.*] We're coming. A few more squirms like that and I'll call. [*Pause.*] A little poetry. [*Pause.*] You prayed—[*Pause. He corrects himself.*] You CRIED for night; it comes—[*Pause. He corrects himself.*] It FALLS: now cry in darkness. [*He repeats, chanting.*] You cried for night; it falls: now cry in darkness. [*Pause.*] Nicely put, that. [*Pause.*] And now? [*Pause.*] Moments for nothing, now as always, time was never and time is over, reckoning closed and story ended. [*Pause. Narrative tone.*] If he could have his child with him. . . . [*Pause.*] It was the moment I was waiting for. [*Pause.*] You don't want to abandon him? You want him to bloom while you are withering? Be there to solace your last million last moments? [*Pause.*] He doesn't realize, all he knows is hunger, and cold, and death to crown it all. But you! You ought to know what the earth is like, nowadays. Oh I put him before his responsibilities! [*Pause. Normal tone.*] Well, there we are, there I am, that's enough. [*He raises the whistle to his lips, hesitates, drops it. Pause.*] Yes, truly! [*He whistles. Pause. Louder. Pause.*] Good. [*Pause.*] Father! [*Pause. Louder.*] Father! [*Pause.*] Good. [*Pause.*] We're coming. [*Pause.*] And to end up with? [*Pause.*] Discard. [*He throws away the dog. He tears the whistle from his neck.*] With my compliments.

[*He throws whistle towards auditorium. Pause. He sniffs. Soft.*]

Clov!

[*Long pause.*]

No? Good.

[*He takes out the handkerchief.*]

Since that's the way we're playing it . . .

[*He unfolds handkerchief*]

. . . let's play it that way . . .

[*He unfolds*]

. . . and speak no more about it . . .

[*he finishes unfolding*]

. . . speak no more.

[*He holds handkerchief spread out before him.*]

Old stancher!

[*Pause.*]

You . . . remain.

[*Pause. He covers his face with handkerchief, lowers his arms to armrests, remains motionless.*]

[*Brief tableau.*]

Curtain

➤ PERSPECTIVES ➤
Cosmopolitan Exiles

Unprecedented mobility is one of the twentieth century's characteristic attributes. Automobiles, propeller planes, and then jet planes brought distant regions ever closer together; and redefined frontiers, revised border crossing protocols, and repeatedly reconfigured national states made people's mobility inevitable to a degree never possible in previous human history. Unfortunately, such displacements were not always voluntary or happy. Cosmopolitan centers of culture became sites of literary and cultural production in ways that human history had rarely witnessed before. But those artists and writers who found themselves in such centers of culture frequently were there only by virtue of expulsion or in search of refuge. Their flight, in either case, often meant long or even lifetime exile.

Cosmopolitan locales existed as early as antiquity, notably in Alexandria in northern Egypt, and ancient exiles first experienced the ambiguities of belonging nowhere and everywhere. As early as the first century C.E., the Greek biographer Plutarch wrote to his young friend Menemachus, himself in exile from his native Sardis in modern Turkey, that "the exclusion from one city is the freedom to choose from all. . . . On this account, you will find that few men of the greatest good sense and wisdom have been buried in their own country." It is hard to believe that in the twentieth century, wise men were more numerous than in any previous time. Yet the fate described in Plutarch's comforting letter to his young friend proved to be the fate of more writers in the twentieth century than of any other. These writers often dramatized this experience of displacement, and it invariably forms the setting for their literary production. The twentieth century's literature has been defined by the cross-fertilization within the cosmopolitan centers where these writers interacted, personally or through their works. Amid the pain and hardship of dislocation, these writers found recompense in the enrichment of their writings, and literature has been the greatest beneficiary of their displacements.

César Vallejo
1892–1938

Born in Santiago de Chuco, Peru, César Vallejo was the youngest of eleven children. His parents wanted him to become a Catholic priest, as were his two grandfathers, notwithstanding strictures of the Catholic Church on celibacy. In a family genealogy that reflects the history of the conquest and colonization of the New World, Vallejo's father and mother were the children of Spanish priests from Galicia and Chimú Indian women from northern Peru. His poetic vocation won out over any religious calling, however, and he began writing poetry in 1913, publishing his first book, *The Black Messengers,* in 1918. In 1920 he was imprisoned for political reasons, and two years later he published his second book, *Trilce,* his most enigmatic and one of the most difficult in the Spanish language. He abandoned his native country for exile in Europe in 1923, never to return; he lived in poverty in Paris, earning a meager living as a journalist. In 1931 he joined the Congress of Antifascist Writers (Madrid) and published a novel, *Tungsteno.* A Marxist with a strong commitment to social justice, he aligned himself with the republican cause during the Spanish Civil War (1936–1939). He died in Paris, leaving two volumes of poetry that were published posthumously as *Poemas humanos/Human Poems* and *España, aparta de mi este cáliz* (1940, translated as *Spain, Take this Cup from Me*).

Brooding and hermetic are two terms most often used to describe Vallejo's poetry. His first book, *The Black Messengers,* has the keening quality, the inconsolable plaint associated with the Inca heritage of his maternal genealogy. *Trilce,* his second book, is impenetrably complex and inflected with the poetic experiments of the early twentieth century. He reaches a level of greater comprehensibility with his later poetry, especially the poetry written during the Spanish Civil War, because of the political solidarity he sought to express in his social commitment and in his broader identification with the human condition and its vicissitudes. His poems would never lose their Andean plaintive quality, even after his self-imposed and definitive exile from his Peruvian homeland.

PRONUNCIATION:
    César Vallejo: CHAY-zar va-YEH-ho

Agape[1]

Today no one's come to call;
nor have they asked me for anything this afternoon.

I haven't seen even one cemetery flower
in such a happy procession of lights.
5   Forgive me, Lord: how little I have died!

This afternoon everybody, everybody passes by
without calling on me or asking me for anything.

And I don't know what it is they forgot and that's here
feeling bad in my hands, like something strange.

10   I've gone to the door,
and I want to shout out to everybody:
If you're missing something, here it is!

Because every afternoon of this life,
I don't know what doors they slam in my face,
15   and my soul is seized by something strange.
Today no one's come;
and today how little I have died this afternoon!

Our Daily Bread

FOR ALEJANDRO GAMBOA

You drink your breakfast . . . The damp earth
of a cemetery smells of beloved blood.
The city in winter . . . The bitter crossing
of a cart that seems to drag along
5   a feeling of abstinence in chains!

You want to knock on all the doors,
and ask for who knows who; and then
see the poor, and, crying quietly,
give little pieces of fresh bread to everyone.
10   And to strip the rich of their vineyards
with the two blessed hands

---

1. Translated by Richard Schaaf and Kathleen Ross. "Agape" (pronounced "ah-GAH-pay") is the New Testament term for divine love.

    that with a blow of light
    flew off unnailed from the Cross!

    Morning eyelashes, don't wake up!
15 Give us our daily bread,
    Lord . . .!

    All my bones belong to others;
    perhaps I stole them!
    I took for my own what was
20 meant, perhaps, for another;
    and I think that, had I not been born,
    another poor man would be drinking this coffee!
    I am an awful thief . . . Where will I go!

    And at this cold hour when the earth
25 smells of human dust and is so sad,
    I want to knock on all the doors
    and beg who knows who to forgive me,
    and bake him little pieces of fresh bread
    here, in the oven of my heart . . .!

Good Sense[1]

—There is, mother, a place in the world called Paris. A very big place and far off and once again big.

My mother turns up the collar of my overcoat, not because it is beginning to snow, but so it can begin to snow.

My father's wife is in love with me, coming and advancing backward toward my birth and chestward toward my death. For I am hers twice: by the farewell and by the return. I close her, on coming back. That is why her eyes had given so much to me, brimming with me, caught red-handed with me, making herself happen through finished works, through consummated pacts.

Is my mother confessed by me, named by me. Why doesn't she give as much to my other brothers? To Victor, for example, the eldest, who is so old now, that people say: He looks like his mother's younger brother! Perhaps because I have traveled so much! Perhaps because I have lived more!

My mother grants a charter of colorful beginning to my stories of return. Before my returning life, remembering that I traveled during two hearts through her womb, she blushes and remains mortally livid, when I say, in the treatise of the soul: That night I was happy. But more often she becomes sad; more often she could become sad.

—My son, you look so old!

And files along the yellow color to cry, for she finds me aged, in the swordblade, in the rivermouth of my face. She cries from me, becomes sad from me. What need will there be for my youth, if I am always to be her son? Why do mothers ache finding their sons old, if the age of the sons never reaches that of their mothers? And why, if the sons, the more they approach death, the more they approach their parents? My mother cries because I am old from my time and because never will I grow old from hers!

---

1. Translated by Clayton Eshleman and José Rubia Barcia.

My farewell set off from a point in her being, more external than the point in her being to which I return. I am, because of the excessive time-limit of my return, more the man before my mother than the son before my mother. There resides the candor which today makes us glow with three flames. I say to her then until I hush:

    —There is, mother, in the world, a place called Paris. A very big place and very far off and once again big.

    My father's wife, on hearing me, eats her lunch and her mortal eyes descend softly down my arms.

Black Stone on a White Stone[1]

I will die in Paris with a sudden shower,
a day I can already remember.
I will die in Paris—and I don't budge—
maybe a Thursday, like today is, in autumn.

5   Thursday it will be, because today, Thursday, when I prose
these poems, the humeri[2] that I have put on
by force and, never like today, have I turned,
with all my road, to see myself alone.

César Vallejo has died, they beat him,
10   everyone, without him doing anything to them;
they gave it to him hard with a stick and hard

also with a rope; witnesses are
the Thursday days and the humerus bones,
the loneliness, the rain, the roads . . .

Vladimir Nabokov
1899–1977

The experience of exile is as crucial to Vladimir Nabokov's own experience as it is to that of many of the characters in his novels. Born in 1899 in Saint Petersburg, Russia, into a family of wealthy aristocrats, Nabokov found his prospects rising even higher when an uncle left him a large fortune in land and money in 1916. But the leisurely artistic career that he might have anticipated came to nothing in the aftermath of the Bolshevik Revolution in 1917. The Nabokov family had to flee in 1919, first to the Crimea, then to London, and finally to Berlin. Nabokov himself, however, stayed in England and completed a degree in Slavic and Romance languages at Cambridge University in 1922. He then rejoined his family in Berlin and started to write poems, plays, short stories, and novels under the pseudonym "V. Sirin" for the Russian émigré community. In 1937 he fled from the Nazis to Paris and then emigrated to the United States with his wife and son when the Germans invaded France. He had already written his first English-language novel in the late 1930s, *The Real Life of Sebastian Knight,* and while he earned a living teaching literature at Stanford, Wellesley, and Cornell, he went on to become one of the best-known American novelists of the twentieth century. His most famous novel, *Lolita* (1955), revolves around the illicit love of a middle-aged man for a young teenage girl. The book's

1. Translated by Clayton Eshleman and José Rubia Barcia.   2. Upper-arm bones.

shocking subject and the author's ironic sympathy with his hero, Humbert Humbert, made American publishers wary, and it was first published in Paris. Finally released in the United States, it became a best-seller, and it was twice turned into a movie (in 1962 and 1997). Nabokov continued to treat controversial issues in his fiction—homosexuality in *Pale Fire* (1962) and incest in *Ada, or Ardor* (1969). In 1959, Nabokov returned to Europe and settled in Montreux, Switzerland.

The protagonists of Nabokov's novels are often homeless or exiled, though sometimes from places of their own imagination rather than from actual geographic locations. In some cases, their nostalgia is for a lost time of their lives rather than for a place they had to abandon, but in each case, they develop odd obsessions to deal with their loss. Their stories are told in a highly self-referential, narrative idiom that often parodies a well-known genre (such as the mystery or the psychoanalytic case study), frequently highlighting and commenting on its own procedures. This self-conscious attitude is also obvious in "An Evening of Russian Poetry," a poem that comments humorously on Nabokov's experience as a foreign writer on the American academic lecture circuit. While it plays with clichés about Russia and Russian literature, it is also a poem about poetry: The experience of exile, in this framework, becomes the occasion for literary play built upon a foundation of loss. Many of Nabokov's most successful works similarly combine reflections on serious moral and social issues with a playful use of language that reminds the reader that literature, even at its most realistic, always operates in an order of reality all its own.

An Evening of Russian Poetry

" . . . seems to be the best train. Miss Ethel Winter of the
Department of English will meet you at the station and . . ."
FROM A LETTER ADDRESSED TO THE VISITING SPEAKER.

The subject chosen for tonight's discussion
is everywhere, though often incomplete:
when their basaltic° banks become too steep,   *volcanic rock*
most rivers use a kind of rapid Russian,
5   and so do children talking in their sleep.
My little helper at the magic lantern,
insert that slide and let the colored beam
project my name or any such like phantom
in Slavic characters upon the screen.
10   The other way, the other way. I thank you.

On mellow hills the Greek, as you remember,
fashioned his alphabet from cranes in flight;
his arrows crossed the sunset, then the night.
Our simple skyline and a taste for timber,
15   the influence of hives and conifers,
reshaped the arrows and the borrowed birds.
Yes, Sylvia?

          "Why do you speak of words
when all we want is knowledge nicely browned?"

Because all hangs together—shape and sound,
20   heather and honey, vessel and content.
Not only rainbows—every line is bent,
and skulls and seeds and all good worlds are round,
like Russian verse, like our colossal vowels:

those painted eggs, those glossy pitcher flowers
25   that swallow whole a golden bumblebee,
those shells that hold a thimble and the sea.
Next question.

"Is your prosody[1] like ours?"

Well, Emmy, our pentameter may seem
to foreign ears as if it could not rouse
30   the limp iambus from its pyrrhic dream.[2]
But close your eyes and listen to the line.
The melody unwinds; the middle word
is marvelously long and serpentine:
you hear one beat, but you have also heard
35   the shadow of another, then the third
touches the gong, and then the fourth one sighs.

It makes a very fascinating noise;
it opens slowly, like a grayish rose
in pedagogic films of long ago.

40   The rhyme is the line's birthday, as you know,
and there are certain customary twins
in Russian as in other tongues. For instance,
love automatically rhymes with blood,
nature with liberty, sadness with distance,
45   humane with everlasting, prince with mud,
moon with a multitude of words, but sun
and song and wind and life and death with none.

Beyond the seas where I have lost a scepter,
I hear the neighing of my dappled nouns,
50   soft participles coming down the steps,
treading on leaves, trailing their rustling gowns,
and liquid verbs in *ahla* and in *ili,*
Aonian grottoes, nights in the Altai,[3]
black pools of sound with "l"s for water lilies.
55   The empty glass I touched is tinkling still,
but now 'tis covered by a hand and dies.

"Trees? Animals? Your favorite precious stone?"

The birch tree, Cynthia, the fir tree, Joan.
Like a small caterpillar on its thread,
60   my heart keeps dangling from a leaf long dead
but hanging still, and still I see the slender
white birch that stands on tiptoe in the wind,

---

1. Use of meter, pitch and rhythm.
2. A pentameter line has five rhythmic "feet"; the iambus is an unstressed syllable followed by a stressed one, and a pyrrhic foot has two unstressed syllables. Nabokov is punning on the phrase "pyrrhic victory," named for the

Greek king Pyrrhus who won a battle with such heavy losses that he later lost the war.
3. Aonia was a region in ancient Greece. The Altai is a mountain range in Central Asia in the former Soviet Union.

and firs beginning where the garden ends,
the evening ember glowing through their cinders.

65   Among the animals that haunt our verse,
that bird of bards, regale of night, comes first:
scores of locutions mimicking its throat
render its every whistling, bubbling, bursting,
flutelike or cuckoolike or ghostlike note.

70   But lapidary epithets[4] are few;
we do not deal in universal rubies.
The angle and the glitter are subdued;
our riches lie concealed. We never liked
the jeweler's window in the rainy night.

75   My back is Argus-eyed.[5] I live in danger.
False shadows turn to track me as I pass
and, wearing beards, disguised as secret agents,
creep in to blot the freshly written page
and read the blotter in the looking glass.

80   And in the dark, under my bedroom window,
until, with a chill whir and shiver, day
presses its starter, warily they linger
or silently approach the door and ring
the bell of memory and run away.

85   Let me allude, before the spell is broken,
to Pushkin,[6] rocking in his coach on long
and lonely roads: he dozed, then he awoke,
undid the collar of his traveling cloak,
and yawned, and listened to the driver's song.

90   Amorphous sallow bushes called *rakeety,*
enormous clouds above an endless plain,
songline and skyline endlessly repeated,
the smell of grass and leather in the rain.
And then the sob, the syncope (Nekrasov!),[7]

95   the panting syllables that climb and climb,
obsessively repetitive and rasping,
dearer to some than any other rhyme.
And lovers meeting in a tangled garden,
dreaming of mankind, of untrammeled life,

100   mingling their longings in the moonlit garden,
where trees and hearts are larger than in life.
This passion for expansion you may follow
throughout our poetry. We want the mole
to be a lynx or turn into a swallow

105   by some sublime mutation of the soul.

---

4. Beautifully crafted, gemlike expressions.
5. Argus was a hundred-eyed monster in Greek mythology.
6. Aleksandr Pushkin (1799–1837), one of the greatest Russian poets.
7. Syncope (derived from the word for a skipping of

heartbeat) means an interruption of the normal rhythmic pattern in a musical work or in verse. Nikolai Alekseyevich Nekrasov (1821–1877) was a highly political Russian poet and editor.

But to unneeded symbols consecrated,
escorted by a vaguely infantile
path for bare feet, our roads were always fated
to lead into the silence of exile.

110 Had I more time tonight I would unfold
the whole amazing story—*neighuklúzhe,*
nevynossímo[8]—but I have to go.

What did I say under my breath? I spoke
to a blind songbird hidden in a hat,
115 safe from my thumbs and from the eggs I broke
into the gibus[9] brimming with their yolk.
And now I must remind you in conclusion,
that I am followed everywhere and that
space is collapsible, although the bounty
120 of memory is often incomplete:
once in a dusty place in Mora County
(half town, half desert, dump mound and mesquite)
and once in West Virginia (a muddy
red road between an orchard and a veil
125 of tepid rain) it came, that sudden shudder,
a Russian something that I could inhale
but could not see. Some rapid words were uttered—
and then the child slept on, the door was shut.

The conjurer collects his poor belongings—
130 the colored handkerchief, the magic rope,
the double-bottomed rhymes, the cage, the song.
You tell him of the passes you detected.
The mystery remains intact. The check
comes forward in its smiling envelope.

135 *"How would you say 'delightful talk' in Russian?"*
"How would you say 'good night'?"

Oh, that would be:
Bezónnitza, tvoy vzor oonýl i stráshen;
lubóv moyá, otstóopnika prostée.
(Insomnia, your stare is dull and ashen,
140 my love, forgive me this apostasy.)

Czeslaw Milosz
b. 1911

Czeslaw Milosz was born in Szetejnie, a Lithuanian town under the Russian czarist government at the time. Following World War I, his family moved to Vilna, Lithuania, where he had a strict Roman Catholic education. His first collection of poetry appeared in 1933, and he received a

---

8. Russian for "clumsily, unbearably."   9. A collapsible hat worn to the opera.

law degree in 1934, after which he spent a year in Paris. He worked for a radio station in Vilna in 1936, a position from which he was dismissed because of his leftist politics, whereupon he moved to Warsaw. There he became a leading figure in what was called the Zagary group, which believed in impending catastrophe. By 1939 the group's prophecies became reality with the German invasion of Poland and the start of World War II. Milosz was always wary of aesthetic formalism, nationalism, anti-Semitism, and ideological dogma. He was part of the Resistance movement during World War II, and he witnessed the Holocaust firsthand. After the war, already an established poet, he was appointed to a post in the diplomatic service by the new Communist government of Poland. Between 1946 and 1951, he served in Washington and in Paris, but he was becoming increasingly unhappy with Communist authoritarianism, and in 1951 he defected and sought asylum in France. His 1953 book *The Captive Mind* exposed the conditions of life under Stalinism. He lived in Paris between 1951 and 1960, a most prolific period in his poetic career. In 1960 he moved to the United States, where he served as professor of Slavic languages at the University of California, Berkeley. He became a U.S. citizen in 1970 and in 1980 was awarded the Nobel Prize in literature. His writing ranges across many genres in addition to poetry—essays, autobiography, literary history, and criticism. He has also translated a wide range of authors into Polish, including Shakespeare, Milton, T. S. Eliot, Walt Whitman, and Charles Baudelaire.

One of Milosz's earliest poems, "Fear-Dream," concludes by speaking of "A refugee from fictitious States, who will want me here?" Milosz never ceased rephrasing this question. His poetic corpus is the simultaneous embodiment of exile and cosmopolitanism, with cosmopolitanism serving as a precarious position from which he reflects on and interrogates— now ironically, now wistfully—the condition of exile he lived in for a greater part of the twentieth century. The four poems printed here constitute a microcosm of that itinerary and its poetic record.

PRONUNCIATION:
   Czeslaw Milosz: CHESS-law mill-OHSH

Child of Europe[1]

1

We, whose lungs fill with the sweetness of day,
Who in May admire trees flowering,
Are better than those who perished.

We, who taste of exotic dishes,
5   And enjoy fully the delights of love,
Are better than those who were buried.

We, from the fiery furnaces, from behind barbed wires
On which the winds of endless autumns howled,
We, who remember battles where the wounded air roared in paroxysms
        of pain,
10   We, saved by our own cunning and knowledge.

By sending others to the more exposed positions,
Urging them loudly to fight on,
Ourselves withdrawing in certainty of the cause lost.

---

1. Translated by Jan Darowski.

Having the choice of our own death and that of a friend,
15 We chose his, coldly thinking: let it be done quickly.

We sealed gas chamber doors, stole bread,
Knowing the next day would be harder to bear than the day before.

As befits human beings, we explored good and evil.
Our malignant wisdom has no like on this planet.

20 Accept it as proven that we are better than they,
The gullible, hot-blooded weaklings, careless with their lives.

2

Treasure your legacy of skills, child of Europe,
Inheritor of Gothic cathedrals, of baroque churches,
Of synagogues filled with the wailing of a wronged people.
25 Successor of Descartes, Spinoza,[2] inheritor of the word "honor,"
Posthumous child of Leonidas,[3]
Treasure the skills acquired in the hour of terror.

You have a clever mind which sees instantly
The good and bad of any situation.
30 You have an elegant, skeptical mind which enjoys pleasures
Quite unknown to primitive races.

Guided by this mind you cannot fail to see
The soundness of the advice we give you:
Let the sweetness of day fill your lungs.
35 For this we have strict but wise rules.

3

There can be no question of force triumphant.
We live in the age of victorious justice.

Do not mention force, or you will be accused
Of upholding fallen doctrines in secret.

40 He who has power, has it by historical logic.
Respectfully bow to that logic.

Let your lips, proposing a hypothesis,
Not know about the hand faking the experiment.

Let your hand, faking the experiment,
45 Not know about the lips proposing a hypothesis.

Learn to predict a fire with unerring precision.
Then burn the house down to fulfill the prediction.

2. René Descartes (1596–1650), French mathematician
and philosopher. Baruch Spinoza (1632–1677), Dutch
philosopher, translator, and lens grinder.
3. King of Sparta, d. 480 B.C.E.

4

Grow your tree of falsehood from a small grain of truth.
Do not follow those who lie in contempt of reality.

50   Let your lie be even more logical than the truth itself,
So the weary travelers may find repose in the lie.

After the Day of the Lie gather in select circles,
Shaking with laughter when our real deeds are mentioned.

Dispensing flattery called: perspicacious thinking.
55   Dispensing flattery called: a great talent.

We, the last who can still draw joy from cynicism.
We, whose cunning is not unlike despair.

A new, humorless generation is now arising,
It takes in deadly earnest all we received with laughter.

5

60   Let your words speak not through their meanings,
But through them against whom they are used.

Fashion your weapon from ambiguous words.
Consign clear words to lexical limbo.

Judge no words before the clerks have checked
65   In their card index by whom they were spoken.

The voice of passion is better than the voice of reason.
The passionless cannot change history.

6

Love no country: countries soon disappear.
Love no city: cities are soon rubble.

70   Throw away keepsakes, or from your desk
A choking, poisonous fume will exude.

Do not love people: people soon perish.
Or they are wronged and call for your help.

Do not gaze into the pools of the past.
75   Their corroded surface will mirror
A face different from the one you expected.

7

He who invokes history is always secure.
The dead will not rise to witness against him.

You can accuse them of any deeds you like.
80   Their reply will always be silence.

Their empty faces swim out of the deep dark.
You can fill them with any features desired.

Proud of dominion over people long vanished,
Change the past into your own, better likeness.

8

85   The laughter born of the love of truth
Is now the laughter of the enemies of the people.

Gone is the age of satire. We no longer need mock
The senile monarch with false courtly phrases.

Stern as befits the servants of a cause,
90   We will permit ourselves only sycophantic humor.

Tight-lipped, guided by reasons only,
Cautiously let us step into the era of the unchained fire.

Encounter[1]

We were riding through frozen fields in a wagon at dawn.
A red wing rose in the darkness.

And suddenly a hare ran across the road.
One of us pointed to it with his hand.

5   That was long ago. Today neither of them is alive,
Not the hare, nor the man who made the gesture.

O my love, where are they, where are they going
The flash of a hand, streak of movement, rustle of pebbles.
I ask not out of sorrow, but in wonder.

Dedication[1]

You whom I could not save
Listen to me.
Try to understand this simple speech as I would be ashamed of another.
I swear, there is in me no wizardry of words.
5   I speak to you with silence like a cloud or a tree.

What strengthened me, for you was lethal.
You mixed up farewell to an epoch with the beginning of a new one,
Inspiration of hatred with lyrical beauty,
Blind force with accomplished shape.

10   Here is the valley of shallow Polish rivers. And an immense bridge
Going into white fog. Here is a broken city,
And the wind throws the screams of gulls on your grave
When I am talking with you.

---

1. Translated by Czeslaw Milosz and Lillian Vallu.   1. Translated by Czeslaw Milosz.

15   What is poetry which does not save
     Nations or people?
     A connivance with official lies,
     A song of drunkards whose throats will be cut in a moment,
     Readings for sophomore girls.
     That I wanted good poetry without knowing it,
20   That I discovered, late, its salutary aim,
     In this and only this I find salvation.

     They used to pour millet on graves or poppy seeds
     To feed the dead who would come disguised as birds.
     I put this book here for you, who once lived
25   So that you should visit us no more.

Fear-Dream[1]

     Orsha[2] is a bad station. In Orsha a train risks stopping for days.
     Thus perhaps in Orsha I, six years old, got lost
     And the repatriation train was starting, about to leave me behind,
     Forever. As if I grasped that I would have been somebody else,
5   A poet of another language, of a different fate.
     As if I guessed my end at the shores of Kolyma[3]
     Where the bottom of the sea is white with human skulls.
     And a great dread visited me then,
     The one destined to be the mother of all my fears.

10   A trembling of the small before the great. Before the Empire.
     Which constantly marches westward, armed with bows, lariats, rifles,
     Riding in a troika, pummeling the driver's back,
     Or in a jeep, wearing fur hats, with a file full of conquered countries.
     And I just flee, for a hundred, three hundred years,
15   On the ice, swimming across, by day, by night, on and on.
     Abandoning by my river a punctured cuirass and a coffer with king's
         grants.
     Beyond the Dnieper, then the Niemen, then the Bug and the Vistula.[4]

     Finally I arrive in a city of high houses and long streets
     And am oppressed by fear, for I am just a villager
20   Who only pretends to follow what they discuss so shrewdly
     And tries to hide from them his shame, his defeat.

     Who will feed me here, as I walk in the cloudy dawn
     With small change in my pocket, for one coffee, no more?
     A refugee from fictitious States, who will want me here?

---

1. Translated by Czeslaw Milosz and Robert Hass.
2. City in northeast Belarus near the western Russian
border.
3. Gold mining range in northeast Russia, mined with
slave labor during the Stalinist era. Also, a river that flows
north to the Arctic Ocean.
4. Major rivers running through eastern Europe. The Vis-
tula is Poland's principal waterway.

V. S. Naipaul
b. 1932

Vidiadhar Surajprasad Naipaul was born on the Caribbean island of Trinidad to an East Indian family. His Hindu grandfather came to the West Indies from India as an indentured servant. Naipaul attended Queen's Royal College in Port of Spain and received a government scholarship, which enabled him to study at Oxford University starting in 1950. After his 1953 graduation, he settled permanently in England, working as a journalist and freelance writer, hosting the program *Caribbean Voices* for the BBC and serving as literary critic for *The New Statesman* between 1957 and 1961. He was knighted by Queen Elizabeth II in 1989, and in 2001 he was awarded the Nobel Prize in literature, having written many novels including what is often considered his masterpiece, *A House for Mr. Biswas* (1961). Naipaul has traveled extensively, especially in the 1960s and 1970s, with his travels resulting in such important works as *The Middle Passage* (1962), which deals with the painful history of the West Indies; *India: A Wounded Civilization* (1977); and a controversial treatise on the corruption of Islam, *Among the Believers: An Islamic Journey* (1981). His novels tend to be autobiographical, often exploring the deplorable consequences of colonialism and imperialism, with *A Bend in the River* (1979) and *The Enigma of Arrival* (1987) most prominent among such works. The selection from *Prologue to an Autobiography* printed here is exemplary of this fictionalized documentation as self-narration.

Inextricably meshed into colonial history and the history of the British empire in particular, Naipaul is a controversial figure. Among critics and scholars of colonial cultural history and postcolonial studies, there has been a debate as to Naipaul's possible complicity with colonial discourse. At the heart of the controversy is the question of whether or not Naipaul has indeed succeeded in "writing back" to the empire, countering its effects from its very metropolitan center that has all but assimilated him into its ceremonial rites (including his being knighted by the queen) and its institutional power structures as canonized author. Entire courses are now taught on the phenomenon of the former colonial subject who comes into the heart of the imperial metropolis as a cosmopolitan author. Unlike many postcolonial cosmopolitans, however, Naipaul has responded to critical controversy surrounding his social role as a writer by focusing uncompromisingly on the writing itself. This has further provoked controversy and defines yet another dimension of displacement for the writer at the heart of the metropolis.

from Prologue to an Autobiography

It is now nearly thirty years since, in a BBC room in London, on an old BBC typewriter, and on smooth, "non-rustle" BBC script paper, I wrote the first sentence of my first publishable book. I was some three months short of my twenty-third birthday. I had left Oxford ten months before, and was living in London, trying to keep afloat and, in between, hoping to alleviate my anxiety but always only adding to it, trying to get started as a writer.

At Oxford I had been supported by a Trinidad government scholarship. In London I was on my own. The only money I got—eight guineas a week, less "deductions"—came from the BBC Caribbean Service. My only piece of luck in the past year, and even in the past two years, had been to get a part-time job editing and presenting a weekly literary programme for the Caribbean.

The Caribbean Service was on the second floor of what had been the Langham Hotel, opposite Broadcasting House. On this floor the BBC had set aside a room for people like me, "freelances"—to me then not a word suggesting freedom and valour, but suggesting only people on the fringe of a mighty enterprise, a depressed and suppliant class: I would have given a lot to be "staff."

The freelances' room didn't encourage thoughts of radio glory; it was strictly for the production of little scripts. Something of the hotel atmosphere remained: in the great Victorian-Edwardian days of the Langham Hotel (it was mentioned in at least one Sherlock Holmes story), the freelances' room might have been a pantry. It was at the back of the heavy brick building, and gloomy when the ceiling lights were turned off. It wasn't cheerful when the lights were on: ochre walls with a pea-green dado, the gloss paint tarnished; a radiator below the window, with grit on the sill; two or three chairs, a telephone, two tables and two old standard typewriters.

It was in that Victorian-Edwardian gloom, and at one of those typewriters, that late one afternoon, without having any idea where I was going, and not perhaps intending to type to the end of the page, I wrote: *Every morning when he got up Hat would sit on the banister of his back verandah and shout across, "What happening there, Bogart?"*

That was a Port of Spain memory. It seemed to come from far back, but it was only eleven or twelve years old. It came from the time when we—various branches of my mother's family—were living in Port of Spain, in a house that belonged to my mother's mother. We were country people, Indians, culturally still Hindus; and this move to Port of Spain was in the nature of a migration; from the Hindu and Indian countryside to the white-negro-mulatto town.

Hat was our neighbour on the street. He wasn't negro or mulatto. But we thought of him as half-way there. He was a Port of Spain Indian. The Port of Spain Indians—there were pockets of them—had no country roots, were individuals, hardly a community, and were separate from us for an additional reason: many of them were Madrassis, descendants of South Indians, not Hindi-speaking, and not people of caste. We didn't see in them any of our own formalities or restrictions; and though we lived raggedly ourselves (and were far too numerous for the house), we thought of the other Indians in the street only as street people.

That shout of "Bogart!" was in more than one way a shout from the street. And, to add to the incongruity, it was addressed to someone in our yard: a young man, very quiet, yet another person connected in some way with my mother's family. He had come not long before from the country and was living in the separate one-room building at the back of our yard.

We called this room the "servant room." Port of Spain houses, up to the 1930s, were built with these separate servant rooms—verandah-less little boxes, probably descended in style from the ancillary "negro-houses" of slave times. I suppose that in one or two houses in our street servants of the house actually lived in the servant room. But generally it wasn't so. Servant rooms, because of the privacy they offered, were in demand, and not by servants.

It was wartime. The migration of my own family into the town had become part of a more general movement. People of all conditions were coming into Port of Spain to work at the two American bases. One of those bases had been built on recently reclaimed land just at the end of our street—eight houses down. Twice a day we heard the bugles; Americans, formal in their uniforms, with their khaki ties tucked into their shirts, were another part of the life of our street. The street was busy; the yards were crowded. Our yard was more crowded than most. No servant ever lodged in our servant room. Instead, the room sheltered a succession of favoured transients, on their way to better things. Before the big family rush, some of these transients had been outsiders; but now they were mostly relations or people close to the family, like Bogart.

The connection of Bogart with my mother's family was unusual. At the turn of the century Bogart's father and my mother's father had travelled out together from India as indentured immigrants. At some time during the long and frightening journey they had sworn a bond of brotherhood; that was the bond that was being honoured by their descendants.

Bogart's people were from the Punjab, and handsome. The two brothers we had got to know were ambitious men, rising in white-collar jobs. One was a teacher; the other (who had passed through the servant room) was a weekend sportsman who, in the cricket season, regularly got his name in the paper. Bogart didn't have the education or the ambition of his brothers; it wasn't clear what he did for a living. He was placid, without any pronounced character, detached, and in that crowded yard oddly solitary.

Once he went away. When he came back, some weeks or months later, it was said that he had been "working on a ship". Port of Spain was a colonial port, and we thought of sailors as very rough, the dregs. So this business of working on a ship—though it suggested money as well as luck, for the jobs were not easy to come by—also held suggestions of danger. It was something for the reckless and the bohemian. But it must have suited Bogart, because after a time he went away—disappeared—again.

There was a story this time that he had gone to Venezuela. He came back; but I had no memory of his return. His adventures—if he had had any—remained unknown to me. I believe I was told that the first time he had gone away, to work on the ship, he had worked as a cook. But that might have been a story I made up myself. All that I knew of Bogart while he lived in the servant room was what, as a child, I saw from a distance. He and his comings and goings were part of the confusion and haphazardness and crowd of that time.

I saw a little more of him four or five years later. The war was over. The American base at the end of the street was closed. The buildings were pulled down, and the local contractor, who knew someone in our family, gave us the run of the place for a few days, to pick up what timber we wanted. My mother's extended family was breaking up into its component parts; we were all leaving my grandmother's house. My father had bought a house of his own; I used timber from the old American base to make a new front gate. Soon I had got the Trinidad government scholarship that was to take me to Oxford.

Bogart was still reportedly a traveller. And in Trinidad now he was able to do what perhaps he had always wanted to do: to put as much distance as possible between himself and people close to him. He was living in Carenage, a seaside village five miles or so west of Port of Spain. Carenage was a negro-mulatto place, with a Spanish flavour ('pagnol, in the local French patois). There were few Indians in Carenage; that would have suited Bogart.

With nothing to do, waiting to go away, I was restless, and I sometimes cycled out to Carenage. It was pleasant after the hot ride to splash about in the rocky sea, and pleasant after that to go and have a Coca-Cola at Bogart's. He lived in a side street, a wandering lane, with yards that were half bush, half built-up. He was a tailor now, apparently with customers; and he sat at his machine in his open shop, welcoming but undemonstrative, as placid, as without conversation, and as solitary as ever. But he was willing to play with me. He was happy to let me paint a sign-board for his shop. The idea was mine, and he took it seriously. He had a carpenter build a board of new wood; and on this, over some days, after priming and painting, I did the sign. He put it up over his shop door, and I thought it looked genuine, a real sign. I was amazed; it was the first sign-board I had ever done.

The time then came for me to go to England. I left Bogart in Carenage. And that was where he had continued to live in my memory, faintly, never a figure in the foreground: the man who had worked on a ship, then gone to Venezuela, sitting placidly ever after at his sewing machine, below my sign, in his little concrete house-and-shop.

That was Bogart's story, as I knew it. And—after all our migrations within Trinidad, after my own trip to England and my time at Oxford—that was all the story I had in mind when—after two failed attempts at novels—I sat at the typewriter in the freelances' room in the Langham Hotel, to try once more to be a writer. And luck was with me that afternoon. *Every morning when he got up Hat would sit on the banister of his back verandah and shout across, "What happening there, Bogart?"* Luck was with me, because that first sentence was so direct, so uncluttered, so without complications, that it provoked the sentence that was to follow. *Bogart would turn in his bed and mumble softly, so that no one heard, "What happening there, Hat?"*

The first sentence was true. The second was invention. But together—to me, the writer—they had done something extraordinary. Though they had left out everything—the setting, the historical time, the racial and social complexities of the people concerned—they had suggested it all; they had created the world of the street. And together, as sentences, words, they had set up a rhythm, a speed, which dictated all that was to follow.

The story developed a first-person narrator. And for the sake of speed, to avoid complications, to match the rhythm of what had gone before, this narrator could not be myself. My narrator lived alone with his mother in a house on the street. He had no father; he had no other family. So, very simply, all the crowd of my mother's extended family, as cumbersome in real life as it would have been to a writer, was abolished; and, again out of my wish to simplify, I had a narrator more in tune with the life of the street than I had been.

Bogart's tailoring business, with the sign-board I had done for him, I transferred from the Carenage side street to the Port of Spain servant room, and with it there came some hint of the silent companionableness I had found in Bogart at that later period. The servant room and the street—the houses, the pavements, the open yards, the American base at the end of the street—became like a stage set. Anyone might walk down the street; anyone might turn up in the servant room. It was enough—given the rhythm of the narrative and its accumulating suggestions of street life—for the narrator to say so. So Bogart could come and go, without fuss. When, in the story, he left the servant room for the first time, it took little—just the dropping of a few names—to establish the idea of the street as a kind of club.

So that afternoon in the Langham Hotel Port of Spain memories, disregarded until then, were simplified and transformed. The speed of the narrative—that was the speed of the writer. And everything that was later to look like considered literary devices came only from the anxiety of the writer. I wanted above all to take the story to the end. I feared that if I stopped too long anywhere I might lose faith in what I was doing, give up once more, and be left with nothing.

Speed dictated the solution of the mystery of Bogart. He wished to be free (of Hindu family conventions, but this wasn't stated in the story). He was without ambition, and had no skill; in spite of the sign-board, he was hardly a tailor. He was an unremarkable man, a man from the country, to whom mystery and the name of Bogart had been given by the street, which had its own city sense of drama. If Bogart spent whole afternoons in his servant room playing Patience, it was because he had no other way of passing the time. If, until he fell into the character of the film Bogart, he had no conversation, it was because he had little to say. The street saw him as sensual, lazy, cool. He was in fact passive. The emotional entanglements that called him away from the street were less than heroic. With women, Bogart—unlike most men of the street—had taken the easy way out. He was that flabby, emasculated thing, a bigamist. So, looking only for freedom, the Bogart of my story had ended up as a man on the run. It was only in the solitude of his servant room that he could be himself, at peace. It was only with the men and boys of the street that he could be a man.

The story was short, three thousand words, two foolscap sheets and a bit. I had— a conscious piece of magic that afternoon—set the typewriter at single space, to get as much as possible on the first sheet and also to create the effect of the printed page.

People were in and out of the freelances' room while I typed. Some would have dropped by at the BBC that afternoon for the company and the chat, and the off-chance of a commission by a producer for some little script. Some would have had work to do.

I suppose Ernest Eytle would have come in, to sit at the other typewriter and to peck, with many pauses, at the "links" or even a "piece" for the magazine pro-gramme. And Ernest's beautifully spoken words, crackling over the short wave that evening, would suggest a busy, alert man, deep in the metropolitan excitements of London, sparing a few minutes for his radio talk. He was a mulatto from British Guiana. He was dark-suited, fat and slow; when, some years later, I heard he had died, I was able mentally to transfer him, without any change, and without any feeling of shock, to a coffin. As much as broadcasting, Ernest liked the pub life around Broadcasting House. This sitting at the typewriter in the gloomy freelances' room was like an imposition; and Ernest, whenever he paused to think, would rub a heavy hand down his forehead to his eyebrows, which he pushed back the wrong way; and then, like a man brushing away cobwebs, he would appear to dust his cheek, his nose, his lips, and chin.

Having done that with Ernest, I should say that my own typing posture in those days was unusual. My shoulders were thrown back as far as they could go; my spine was arched. My knees were drawn right up; my shoes rested on the topmost struts of the chair, left side and right side. So, with my legs wide apart, I sat at the typewriter with something like a monkey crouch.

The freelances' room was like a club: chat, movement, the separate anxieties of young or youngish men below the passing fellowship of the room. That was the atmosphere I was writing in. That was the atmosphere I gave to Bogart's Port of Spain street. Partly for the sake of speed, and partly because my memory or imagination couldn't rise to it, I had given his servant room hardly any furniture: the Langham room itself was barely furnished. And I benefited from the fellowship of the room that afternoon. Without that fellowship, without the response of the three men who read the story, I might not have wanted to go on with what I had begun.

I passed the three typed sheets around.

John Stockbridge was English. He worked for many BBC programmes, domestic and overseas. Unlike the rest of us, he carried a briefcase; and that briefcase suggested method, steadiness, many commissions. At our first meeting in the freelances' room three or four months before, he hadn't been too friendly—he no doubt saw me as an Oxford man, untrained, stepping just like that into regular radio work, taking the bread out of the mouths of more experienced men. But then his attitude towards me had become one of school-masterly concern. He wanted to rescue me from what, with his English eyes, he saw as my self-neglect. He wanted me to make a better job of myself, to present myself well, to wear better clothes, and especially to get rid of my dingy working-class overcoat. (I knew nothing about clothes, but I had always thought the overcoat was wrong: it had been chosen for me, before I went up to Oxford, by the Maltese manageress of an Earl's Court boarding house.) Now, after he had read the story, John made a serious face and spoke a prodigious prophecy about my future as a writer. On such little evidence! But it was his way of finally accepting my ambition and my London life, and giving me a little blessing.

Andrew Salkey was a Jamaican. He worked in a nightclub, was also trying to get started as a writer, and had just begun to do broadcasts, talks and readings. He compared learning to write with trying to wrap a whip around a rail; he thought I had begun to make the whip "stick." He detected, and made me take out, one or two early sentences where I had begun to lose faith in the material and had begun to ridicule, not the characters, but the idea that what I was doing was a real story.

The most wholehearted acceptance came from Gordon Woolford. He was from British Guiana. He came from a distinguished colonial family. He said he had some African ancestry, but it didn't show. Some deep trouble with his father had kept Gordon away from his family and committed him, after a privileged pre-war upbringing in Belgium and England, to a hard bohemian life in London. He was an unusually handsome man, in his mid-thirties. He had married a French girl, whom he had met when she was an assistant in one of the big London stores. That marriage had just broken up. Gordon was writing a novel about it, *On the Rocks;* it wasn't something he was going to finish. He changed jobs often; he loved writing; his favourite book—at least it was always with him during his drinking bouts—was *Scoop.*

Something in the Bogart story touched Gordon. When he finished reading the story he folded the sheets carefully; with a gesture as of acceptance he put the sheets in his inner jacket pocket; and then he led me out to the BBC club—he was not on the wagon that day. He read the story over again, and he made me read it with him, line by line, assessing the words and the tone: we might have been rehearsing a broadcast. The manuscript still has his foldmarks and his wine stains.

During the writing of the Bogart story some memory—very vague, as if from a forgotten film—had come to me of the man who in 1938 or 1939, five years before Bogart, had lived in his servant room. He was a negro carpenter; the small sheltered space between the servant room and the back fence was at once his kitchen and workshop. I asked him one day what he was making. He said—wonderfully to the six-year-old child who had asked the question—that he was making "the thing without a name."

It was the carpenter's story that I settled down to write the next day in the freelances' room. I had little to go on. But I had a street, already peopled; I had an atmosphere; and I had a narrator. I stuck to the magic of the previous day: the non-rustle BBC paper, the typewriter set at single space. And I was conscious, with Gordon Woolford's help, of certain things I had stumbled on the previous day: never to let the words get too much in the way, to be fast, to add one concrete detail to another, and above all to keep the tone right.

I mentally set the servant room in another yard. *The only thing that Popo, who called himself a carpenter, ever built was the little galvanized-iron workshop under the mango tree at the back of his yard.* And then scattered memories, my narrator, the life of the street, and my own childhood sense (as a six-year-old coming suddenly to Port of Spain from the Hindu rigours of my grandmother's house in the country) of the intensity of the pleasures of people on the street, gave the carpenter a story. He was an idler, a happy man, a relisher of life; but then his wife left him.

Over the next few days the street grew. Its complexities didn't need to be pointed; they simply became apparent. People who had only been names in one story got dialogue in the next, then became personalities; and old personalities became more familiar. Memory provided the material; city folklore as well, and city songs. An item from a London evening paper (about a postman throwing away his letters) was used. My narrator consumed material, and he seemed to be able to process every kind of material.

Even Gordon was written into the street. We were on the top of a bus one evening, going back from the BBC to Kilburn, the Irish working-class area where I lived in two rooms in the house of a BBC commissionaire. Gordon was talking of some early period of his life, some period of luxury and promise. Then he broke off, said, "But that was a long time ago," and looked down through the reflections of glass into the street. That went to my heart. Within a few days I was to run it into the memory of a negro ballad-maker, disturbed but very gentle, who had called at my grandmother's house in Port of Spain one day to sell copies of his poems, single printed sheets, and had told me a little of his life.

The stories became longer. They could no longer be written in a day. They were not always written in the freelances' room. The technique became more conscious; it was not always possible to write fast. Beginnings, and the rhythms they established, didn't always come naturally; they had to be worked for. And then the material, which at one time had seemed inexhaustible, dried up. I had come to the end of what I could do with the street, in that particular way. *My mother said, "You getting too wild in this place. I think is high time you leave."* My narrator left the street, as I had left Trinidad five years before. And the excitement I had lived with for five or six weeks was over.

I had written a book, and I felt it to be real. That had been my ambition for years, and an urgent ambition for the past year. And I suppose that if the book had had some response outside the freelances' room I might have been a little more secure in my talent, and my later approach to writing would have been calmer; it is just possible.

But I knew only anxiety. The publisher that Andrew Salkey took the book to sent no reply for three months (the book remained unpublished for four years). And—by now one long year out of Oxford—I was trying to write another, and discovering that to have written a book was not to be a writer. Looking for a new book, a new narrative, episodes, I found myself as uncertain, and as pretending to be a writer, as I had been before I had written the story of Bogart.

To be a writer, I thought, was to have the conviction that one could go on. I didn't have that conviction. And even when the new book had been written I didn't think of myself as a writer. I thought I should wait until I had written three. And when, a year after writing the second, I had written the third, I thought I should wait until I had written six. On official forms I described myself as a "broadcaster", thinking the word nondescript, suitable to someone from the freelances' room; until a BBC man, "staff," told me it was boastful.

So I became "writer." Though to myself an unassuageable anxiety still attached to the word, and I was still, for its sake, practising magic. I never bought paper to write on. I preferred to use "borrowed", non-rustle BBC paper; it seemed more casual, less likely to attract failure. I never numbered my pages, for fear of not getting to the end. (This drew the only comment Ernest Eytle made about my writing. Sitting idly at his typewriter one day in the freelances' room, he read some of my pages, apparently with goodwill. Then, weightily, he said, "I'll tell you what you should do with this." I waited. He said, "You should number the pages. In case they get mixed up.") And on the finished manuscripts of my first four books—half a million words—I never with my own hand typed or wrote my name. I always asked someone else to do that for me. Such anxiety; such ambition.

The ways of my fantasy, the process of creation, remained mysterious to me. For everything that was false or didn't work and had to be discarded, I felt that I alone was responsible. For everything that seemed right I felt I had only been a vessel. There was the recurring element of luck, or so it seemed to me. True, and saving, knowledge of my subject—beginning with Bogart's street—always seemed to come during the writing.

This element of luck isn't so mysterious to me now. As diarists and letter-writers repeatedly prove, any attempt at narrative can give value to an experience which might otherwise evaporate away. When I began to write about Bogart's street I began to sink into a tract of experience I hadn't before contemplated as a writer. This blindness might seem extraordinary in someone who wanted so much to be a writer. Half a writer's work, though, is the discovery of his subject. And a problem for me was that my life had been varied, full of upheavals and moves: from my grandmother's Hindu house in the country, still close to the rituals and social ways of village India; to Port of Spain, the negro and G.I. life of its streets, the other, ordered life of my colonial English school, which was called Queen's Royal College; and then Oxford, London and the freelances' room at the BBC. Trying to make a beginning as a writer, I didn't know where to focus.

In England I was also a colonial. Out of the stresses of that, and out of my worship of the name of writer, I had without knowing it fallen into the error of thinking of writing as a kind of display. My very particularity—which was the subject sitting on my shoulder—had been encumbering me.

The English or French writer of my age had grown up in a world that was more or less explained. He wrote against a background of knowledge. I couldn't be a writer in the same way, because to be a colonial, as I was, was to be spared knowledge. It was to live in an intellectually restricted world; it was to accept those restrictions. And the restrictions could become attractive.

Every morning when he got up Hat would sit on the banister of his back veran-dah and shout across, "What happening there, Bogart?" That was a good place to begin. But I couldn't stay there. My anxiety constantly to prove myself as a writer, the need to write another book and then another, led me away.

There was much in that call of "Bogart!" that had to be examined. It was spoken by a Port of Spain Indian, a descendant of nineteenth-century indentured immigrants from South India; and Bogart was linked in a special Hindu way with my mother's family. So there was a migration from India to be considered, a migration within the British Empire. There was my Hindu family, with its fading memories of India; there was India itself. And there was Trinidad, with its past of slavery, its mixed population, its racial antagonisms and its changing political life; once part of Venezuela and the Spanish Empire, now English-speaking, with the American base and an open-air cinema at the end of Bogart's street. And just across the Gulf of Paria was Venezuela, the sixteenth-century land of El Dorado, now a country of dictators, but drawing Bogart out of his servant room with its promise of Spanish sexual adventure and the promise of a job in its oilfields.

And there was my own presence in England, writing: the career wasn't possible in Trinidad, a small, mainly agricultural colony: my vision of the world couldn't exclude that important fact.

So step by step, book by book, though seeking each time only to write another book, I eased myself into knowledge. To write was to learn. Beginning a book, I always felt I was in possession of all the facts about myself; at the end I was always surprised. The book before always turned out to have been written by a man with incomplete knowledge. And the very first, the one begun in the freelances' room, seemed to have been written by an innocent, a man at the beginning of knowledge both about himself and the writing career that had been his ambition from childhood.

Adonis (Ali Ahmad Sa'id)
b. 1930

Adonis is the pen name of the Syrian-born poet, journalist, and literary critic Ali Ahmad Sa'id. Born in 1930 to a poor peasant family in a village near the port city of Latakia, he was encouraged by his father to learn hundreds of lines of poetry by heart. After attending his village school, due to his early poetic talent in praising Syria's leaders, he was given a scholarship to complete his secondary education in Latakia and then to study philosophy at Damascus University. While he was studying at Latakia, he joined the Syrian National Socialist Party (SNSP), one of several parties with fascist tendencies that sprang up in the Arab world in the early 1940s. His work in the SNSP led to his imprisonment in 1955. After his release, he left Syria and settled in Lebanon in 1956.

Adonis published his early poems in newspapers and literary journals while still a student, then after graduation worked as a journalist. In 1954 he published his first collection, *The Earth Said,* followed by *Early Poems,* 1957. In the same year, Yusuf al-Khal, a leading Lebanese poet and intellectual of the SNSP, established the literary journal *Shi'r* (Poetry) and attracted a number of young Arab poets to work with him. *Shi'r* was devoted to the promotion of modernist poetry and the translation of French and English modernist poetry. Al-Khal had a tremendous influence on Adonis, who became his most talented disciple: The link between the two is often compared to that of Ezra Pound and T. S. Eliot. Under the influence of French modernist poets, he published the book that established his fame as a significant Arab poet, *Songs of Mihyar the Damascene* (1961). Adonis continued to consolidate his stature as a major Arab poet of modernism with the collections *The Book of Transformations* (1965) and *The Theatre and the Mirrors* (1968).

Since the closure of *Shi'r* in 1968, Adonis has had a checkered career poetically, culturally, and politically. He continued to publish poetry prolifically, but none of his recent work, some of which is contrived or marred by overwriting, reaches the acme he achieved in *Songs of Mihyar* with its blend of subtle insights, innovative imagery, and sensitive lyricism. Culturally he established the journal *Mawaqif* (Situations, 1968–1995), in which he continued to promote modernist and visionary poetry inspired by the tradition of the Sufis. At the same time he obtained a doctorate at St. Joseph University in Beirut in 1973. In his journal and doctoral thesis, he calls for changing the stagnating Arab society and culture and for the transformation of language and patterns of thought. But the irony is that in Adonis's tenacious call for change, some old doctrines of the SNSP persist in different guises, appearing in his ardent support for the Ayatollah Khomeini's revolution in Iran and for Islamic Orthodoxy in Saudi Arabia. However, Adonis remains one of the most controversial figures of contemporary Arabic poetry, a poet whose work perpetuates a fascinating blend of revolution and anarchy.

PRONUNCIATION:
  Adonis: ah-DOH-nees

A Mirror for Khalida[1]

1. THE WAVE

Khalida,
you are a branch in leaf—
a voyage that drowns each day
in the fountains of your eyes—
5   a wave that helps me see
how starlight,
clouds
and sands beneath a wind
are one.

2. UNDERWATER

10   We sleep beneath a cloth
woven from the harvests
of the night.
O night of dust . . .
Cymbals and alleluias
15   chorus
in our blood.
Underwater suns
glitter
the dark to dawn.

3. LOST

20   . . . once,
encircled by your arms,
I lost my way.
My lips were fortresses
succumbing to a conquest
25   they desired.
Nearer,
nearer you breathed,
your waist—a sultan,
your hands—the messengers
30   of armies in reserve,
your eyes—lovers
in hiding.
Joined,
lost together,
35   we dared a forest of fire,
me—risking the first step
toward it
you—pointing the way.

---

1. Translated by Samuel Hazo. Khalida is the poet's wife, a well-known literary critic who has written extensively on her husband's poetry.

4. FATIGUE

Darling, an old fatigue
40   invades our house.
It looms in every drawer
and balcony.
It waits until you sleep
before it vanishes.
45   How anxious I become
about its going and coming.
I scout the house,
interrogate the plants,
pray for a glimpse of it
50   and wonder how, why, where.
The winds,
the branches
come and go.
But you—never.

5. DEATH

55   After our seconds together
time turns back to time.
I hear footsteps
repeated
down a road.
60   The house is nothing
but a house.
The bed forgets the fire
of its past and dies.
Pillows are only pillows
65   now.

⇥ END OF PERSPECTIVES: COSMOPOLITAN EXILES ⇤

Jorge Luis Borges
1899–1986

One of the most cosmopolitan of modern writers, Jorge Luis Borges was born in Buenos Aires, Argentina, and spent his formative years in Geneva, Switzerland, after his family was trapped there during World War I while traveling in Europe. He learned German and French in addition to his native Spanish and English (his maternal ancestry was part English) and graduated from the Collège de Geneve. The family moved back to Buenos Aires following the war, after living for some time in Spain, where Borges came in contact with a number of avant-garde poets and where he published his first poem, "Hymn to the Sea," in the avant-garde journal *Grecia*. Borges's first published work was a translation into Spanish of Oscar Wilde's short story "The

Happy Prince" when Borges was barely ten years old. Son of a psychology teacher with an extensive family library, Borges would spend most of his life in libraries, starting with his first job in 1939 as librarian in a municipal library in Buenos Aires. He held that position until the populist coup of the military strongman Juan Domingo Perón in 1946, at which time Borges was "promoted" to inspector of rabbits and poultry in the municipal market. Borges, whose rancor ran deep and proved implacable, never forgave Perón, and his politics, often anachronistic and deliberately provocative, were formed by this experience. Upon the fall of the Peronist regime in 1955, Borges was named Director of the National Library of Argentina, a post he held until his retirement in 1973, when Perón returned from exile to the presidency of Argentina. Genetically prone to blindness, Borges became the third director of his country's National Library to have this disability. As with most ironies, the irony of this was not lost on Borges, and several of his writings deal with this turn of fate.

While Borges began his career as a poet and wrote (or later dictated) poetry all his life, he is better known as a literary critic, essayist, and author of enigmatic short stories. His influence as a prose writer extends worldwide, with his works having been translated into many languages. As a critic, he introduced most of the Anglo-American and European modernists to the reading public of his country through his weekly column that appeared between 1936 and 1939 in a ladies' journal called *El Hogar* (The Home). During this period he was also writing some of his classic tales, which were gathered into a collection in 1941 under the title of *The Garden of the Forking Paths,* whose title story became one of his best known works.

Always fascinated by limit states of reason and rationality, Borges explores the thresholds between fantasy and reality, between the imagination and the materiality of the world. Deeply influenced by Idealist philosophers such as Arthur Schopenhauer and Bishop George Berkeley, whom he often cites, Borges speculates in his poetry and in his prose about the possibility that the world as we imagine it could well be a figment of someone else's imagination that imagines us imagining. In this sense, the authorship of the world is as compelling a problem for Borges as his and other writers' authorship of literary worlds. A self-proclaimed unbeliever, Borges doesn't view this as a religious problem but as a problem of the imagination. He is fascinated by creation, but he is not a creationist. The question of the creator, always with a lowercase "c," is of the same order as the question of a Creator with a capital "C." Very much in the metaphysical tradition of the Idealists and mathematicians, Borges sees creation as the product of an imaginative calculus. And he sees the world as a text—really, as a hypertext—whose myriad links could lead to an infinite number of other texts and other links. "The Garden of Forking Paths" and "The Library of Babel" printed here dramatize this open-ended nature of the world and its analog, writing, in Borges's characteristic fashion.

In this regard, Borges anticipated the possibilities of a "world wide web" much before this phenomenon became a commonplace part of our life. And in poems like "The Web" printed here, he had already speculated on what he refers to as "the fatal web of cause and effect / that no man can foresee, nor any god." There is much irony here, and ironic subterfuge, often self-directed, is everywhere in Borges. Even in his death, which he speculates about in this poem, he trumped fate ironically when he chose to go to Geneva upon realizing that he was dying.

Borges's essays on philosophy and literature are likewise speculative and hypertextual. He considers philosophy and metaphysics as branches of literature—that is, of imaginative creation. As a result, he always finds it more interesting to imagine the question rather than find the solution. And in this respect, he never ceases to be fascinated with the masters of the detective genre, Edgar Allan Poe, G. K. Chesterton, and the friend and mentor Borges inherited from his father in Buenos Aires, Macedonio Fernández, a writer who could never finish a novel because no single solution interested him as much as the problem the work explored. His only finished novel has fifty-nine different possible endings.

In addition to his own tales, Borges coauthored a number of stories with his lifetime friend and collaborator, Bioy Casares, publishing their joint productions in the detective genre under the pseudonym of "Bustos Domecq." Borges's translations include works by such authors as Virginia Woolf, Franz Kafka, and William Faulkner. A perennial candidate for the Nobel Prize, which eluded him, he shared the Prix Formentor with Samuel Beckett in 1961, a turning point in Borges's international recognition and world acclaim as one of the key literary figures of the twentieth century.

PRONUNCIATION:
Jorge Luis Borges: HOAR-hay lou-EES BOHR-hays

The Garden of Forking Paths[1]
FOR VICTORIA OCAMPO

On page 242 of *The History of the World War,* Liddell Hart tells us that an Allied offensive against the Serre-Montauban line (to be mounted by thirteen British divisions backed by one thousand four hundred artillery pieces) had been planned for July 24, 1916, but had to be put off until the morning of the twenty-ninth. Torrential rains (notes Capt. Liddell Hart) were the cause of that delay—a delay that entailed no great consequences, as it turns out. The statement which follows—dictated, reread, and signed by Dr. Yu Tsun, former professor of English in the *Hochschule*[2] at Tsingtao—throws unexpected light on the case. The two first pages of the statement are missing.

. . . and I hung up the receiver. Immediately afterward, I recognised the voice that had answered in German. It was that of Capt. Richard Madden. Madden's presence in Viktor Runeberg's flat meant the end of our efforts and (though this seemed to me quite secondary, or *should have seemed*) our lives as well. It meant that Runeberg had been arrested, or murdered.[3] Before the sun set on that day, I would face the same fate. Madden was implacable—or rather, he was obliged to be implacable. An Irishman at the orders of the English, a man accused of a certain lack of zealousness, perhaps even treason, how could he fail to embrace and give thanks for this miraculous favour—the discovery, capture, perhaps death, of two agents of the German Empire? I went upstairs to my room; absurdly, I locked the door, and then I threw myself, on my back, onto my narrow iron bed. Outside the window were the usual rooftops and the overcast six o'clock sun. I found it incredible that this day, lacking all omens and premonitions, should be the day of my implacable death. Despite my deceased father, despite my having been a child in a symmetrical garden in Hai Feng—was I, now, about to die? Then I reflected that all things happen to *oneself,* and happen precisely, precisely *now.* Century follows century, yet events occur only *in the present;* countless men in the air, on the land and sea, yet everything that truly happens, happens *to me.* . . . The almost unbearable memory of Madden's horsey face demolished those mental ramblings. In the midst of my hatred and my terror (now I don't mind talking about terror—now that I have foiled Richard Madden, now that my neck hungers for the rope), it occurred to me that that brawling and undoubtedly happy warrior did not suspect that I possessed the Secret—the name of the exact location of the new British artillery park on the Ancre.[4] A bird furrowed the grey sky, and I blindly translated it

---

1. Translated by Andrew Hurley.
2. "College" in German.
3. Here an "Editor's" footnote—by Borges— reads as follows: "A bizarre and despicable supposition. The Prussian spy Hans Rabener, alias Viktor Runeberg, had turned

an automatic pistol on his arresting officer, Capt. Richard Madden. Madden, in self-defense, inflicted the wound on Rabener that caused his subsequent death."
4. The River Ancre, France. Borges is also punning on "encre," "ink" in French.

into an aeroplane, and that aeroplane into many (in the French sky), annihilating the artillery park with vertical bombs. If only my throat, before a bullet crushed it, could cry out that name so that it might be heard in Germany. . . . But my human voice was so terribly inadequate. How was I to make it reach the Leader's ear—the ear of that sick and hateful man who knew nothing of Runeberg and me save that we were in Staffordshire, and who was vainly awaiting word from us in his arid office in Berlin, poring infinitely through the newspapers? . . . *I must flee,* I said aloud. I sat up noiselessly, in needless but perfect silence, as though Madden were already just outside my door. Something—perhaps the mere show of proving that my resources were nonexistent—made me go through my pockets. I found what I knew I would find: the American watch, the nickel-plated chain and quadrangular coin, the key ring with the compromising and useless keys to Runeberg's flat, the notebook, a letter I resolved to destroy at once (and never did), the false passport, one crown, two shillings, and a few odd pence, the red-and-blue pencil, the handkerchief, the revolver with its single bullet. Absurdly, I picked it up and hefted it, to give myself courage. I vaguely reflected that a pistol shot can be heard at a considerable distance. In ten minutes, my plan was ripe. The telephone book gave me the name of the only person able to communicate the information: he lived in a suburb of Fenton, less than a half hour away by train.

I am a coward. I can say that, now that I have carried out a plan whose dangerousness and daring no man will deny. I know that it was a terrible thing to do. I did not do it for Germany. What do I care for a barbaric country that has forced me to the ignominy of spying? Furthermore, I know of a man of England—a modest man—who in my view is no less a genius than Goethe.[5] I spoke with him for no more than an hour, but for one hour he was Goethe. . . . No—I did it because I sensed that the Leader looked down on the people of my race—the countless ancestors whose blood flows through my veins. I wanted to prove to him that a yellow man could save his armies. And I had to escape from Madden. His hands, his voice, could beat upon my door at any moment. I silently dressed, said good-bye to myself in the mirror, made my way downstairs, looked up and down the quiet street, and set off. The train station was not far from my flat, but I thought it better to take a cab. I argued that I ran less chance of being recognised that way; the fact is, I felt I was visible and vulnerable—infinitely vulnerable—in the deserted street. I recall that I told the driver to stop a little ways from the main entrance to the station. I got down from the cab with willed and almost painful slowness. I would be going to the village of Ashgrove, but I bought a ticket for a station farther down the line. The train was to leave at eight-fifty, scant minutes away. I had to hurry; the next train would not be until nine-thirty. There was almost no one on the platform. I walked through the cars; I recall a few workmen, a woman dressed in mourning weeds, a young man fervently reading Tacitus' *Annals,*[6] and a cheerful-looking wounded soldier. The train pulled out at last. A man I recognised ran, vainly, out to the end of the platform; it was Capt. Richard Madden. Shattered, trembling, I huddled on the other end of the seat, far from the feared window.

From that shattered state I passed into a state of almost abject cheerfulness. I told myself that my duel had begun, and that in dodging my adversary's thrust—even by forty minutes, even thanks to the slightest smile from fate—the first round had gone

5. Johann Wolfgang Goethe (1749–1832), German poet, novelist, dramatist, and essayist, often identified as Germany's greatest writer.

6. Cornelius Tacitus (c. 56–120 C.E.), historian of the Roman Empire. His *Annals* narrate the intrigue, corruption, and terror during the reigns of Tiberius, Claudius, and Nero.

to me. I argued that this small win prefigured total victory. I argued that the win was not really even so small, since without the precious hour that the trains had given me, I'd be in gaol, or dead. I argued (no less sophistically) that my cowardly cheerfulness proved that I was a man capable of following this adventure through to its successful end. From that weakness I drew strength that was never to abandon me. I foresee that mankind will resign itself more and more fully every day to more and more horrendous undertakings; soon there will be nothing but warriors and brigands. I give them this piece of advice: *He who is to perform a horrendous act should imagine to himself that it is already done, should impose upon himself a future as irrevocable as the past.* That is what I did, while my eyes—the eyes of a man already dead—registered the flow of that day perhaps to be my last, and the spreading of the night. The train ran sweetly, gently, through woods of ash trees. It stopped virtually in the middle of the countryside. No one called out the name of the station. "Ashgrove?" I asked some boys on the platform. "Ashgrove," they said, nodding. I got off the train.

A lamp illuminated the platform, but the boys' faces remained within the area of shadow. "Are you going to Dr. Stephen Albert's house?" one queried. Without waiting for an answer, another of them said: "The house is a far way, but you'll not get lost if you follow that road there to the left, and turn left at every crossing." I tossed them a coin (my last), went down some stone steps, and started down the solitary road. It ran ever so slightly downhill and was of elemental dirt. Branches tangled overhead, and the low round moon seemed to walk along beside me.

For one instant, I feared that Richard Madden had somehow seen through my desperate plan, but I soon realized that that was impossible. The boy's advice to turn always to the left reminded me that that was the common way of discovering the central lawn of a certain type of maze. I am something of a *connoisseur* of mazes: not for nothing am I the great-grandson of that Ts'ui Pen who was governor of Yunan province and who renounced all temporal power in order to write a novel containing more characters than the *Hung Lu Meng*[7] and construct a labyrinth in which all men would lose their way. Ts'ui Pen devoted thirteen years to those disparate labours, but the hand of a foreigner murdered him and his novel made no sense and no one ever found the labyrinth. It was under English trees that I meditated on that lost labyrinth: I pictured it perfect and inviolate on the secret summit of a mountain; I pictured its outlines blurred by rice paddies, or underwater; I pictured it as infinite—a labyrinth not of octagonal pavillions and paths that turn back upon themselves, but of rivers and provinces and kingdoms. . . . I imagined a labyrinth of labyrinths, a maze of mazes, a twisting, turning, ever-widening labyrinth that contained both past and future and somehow implied the stars. Absorbed in those illusory imaginings, I forgot that I was a pursued man; I felt myself, for an indefinite while, the abstract perceiver of the world. The vague, living countryside, the moon, the remains of the day did their work in me; so did the gently downward road, which forestalled all possibility of weariness. The evening was near, yet infinite.

The road dropped and forked as it cut through the now-formless meadows. A keen and vaguely syllabic song, blurred by leaves and distance, came and went on the gentle gusts of breeze. I was struck by the thought that a man may be the enemy of other men, the enemy of other men's other moments, yet not be the enemy of a country—of fireflies, words, gardens, watercourses, zephyrs. It was amidst such thoughts

---

7. Cao Xueqin's novel *Dream of the Red Chamber* (1791), China's elaborate family saga with more than 400 characters.

that I came to a high rusty gate. Through the iron bars I made out a drive lined with poplars, and a gazebo of some kind. Suddenly, I realised two things—the first trivial, the second almost incredible: the music I had heard was coming from that gazebo, or pavillion, and the music was Chinese. That was why unconsciously I had fully given myself over to it. I do not recall whether there was a bell or whether I had to clap my hands to make my arrival known.

The sputtering of the music continued, but from the rear of the intimate house, a lantern was making its way toward me—a lantern cross-hatched and sometimes blotted out altogether by the trees, a paper lantern the shape of a drum and the colour of the moon. It was carried by a tall man. I could not see his face because the light blinded me. He opened the gate and slowly spoke to me in my own language.

"I see that the compassionate Hsi P'eng has undertaken to remedy my solitude. You will no doubt wish to see the garden?"

I recognised the name of one of our consuls, but I could only disconcertedly repeat, "The garden?"

"The garden of forking paths."

Something stirred in my memory, and I spoke with incomprehensible assurance. "The garden of my ancestor Ts'ui Pen."

"Your ancestor? Your illustrious ancestor? Please—come in."

The dew-drenched path meandered like the paths of my childhood. We came to a library of Western and Oriental books. I recognised, bound in yellow silk, several handwritten volumes of the Lost Encyclopedia compiled by the third emperor of the Luminous Dynasty but never printed.[8] The disk on the gramophone revolved near a bronze phoenix. I also recall a vase of *famille rose*[9] and another, earlier by several hundred years, of that blue colour our artificers copied from the potters of ancient Persia. . . .

Stephen Albert, with a smile, regarded me. He was, as I have said, quite tall, with sharp features, grey eyes, and a grey beard. There was something priestlike about him, somehow, but something sailorlike as well; later he told me he had been a missionary in Tientsin "before aspiring to be a Sinologist."

We sat down, I on a long low divan, he with his back to the window and a tall circular clock. I figured that my pursuer, Richard Madden, could not possibly arrive for at least an hour. My irrevocable decision could wait.

"An amazing life, Ts'ui Pen's," Stephen Albert said. "Governor of the province in which he had been born, a man learned in astronomy, astrology, and the unwearying interpretation of canonical books, a chess player, a renowned poet and calligrapher—he abandoned it all in order to compose a book and a labyrinth. He renounced the pleasures of oppression, justice, the populous marriage bed, banquets, and even erudition in order to sequester himself for thirteen years in the Pavillion of Limpid Solitude. Upon his death, his heirs found nothing but chaotic manuscripts. The family, as you perhaps are aware, were about to deliver them to the fire, but his counsellor—a Taoist or Buddhist monk—insisted upon publishing them."

"To this day," I replied, "we who are descended from Ts'ui Pen execrate that monk. It was senseless to publish those manuscripts. The book is a contradictory jum-

---

8. The third emperor of the Ming, or "Luminous," Dynasty was Yung-lo, and the Encyclopedia is one he commissioned between 1403 and 1408. Originally 11,000 volumes, only 370 volumes now survive.

9. Eighteenth-century pink enamel pottery.

ble of irresolute drafts. I once examined it myself; in the third chapter the hero dies, yet in the fourth he is alive again. As for Ts'ui Pen's other labor, his Labyrinth . . ."

"Here is the Labyrinth," Albert said, gesturing towards a tall lacquered writing cabinet.

"An ivory labyrinth!" I exclaimed. "A very small sort of labyrinth . . ."

"A labyrinth of symbols," he corrected me. "An invisible labyrinth of time. I, an English barbarian, have somehow been chosen to unveil the diaphanous mystery. Now, more than a hundred years after the fact, the precise details are irrecoverable, but it is not difficult to surmise what happened, Ts'ui Pen must at one point have remarked, 'I shall retire to write a book,' and at another point, 'I shall retire to construct a labyrinth.' Everyone pictured two projects; it occurred to no one that book and labyrinth were one and the same. The Pavillion of Limpid Solitude was erected in the centre of a garden that was, perhaps, most intricately laid out; that fact might well have suggested a physical labyrinth. Ts'ui Pen died; no one in all the wide lands that had been his could find the labyrinth. The novel's confusion—confusedness, I mean, of course—suggested to me that it was that labyrinth. Two circumstances lent me the final solution of the problem—one, the curious legend that Ts'ui Pen had intended to construct a labyrinth which was truly infinite, and two, a fragment of a letter I discovered."

Albert stood. His back was turned to me for several moments; he opened a drawer in the black-and-gold writing cabinet. He turned back with a paper that had once been crimson but was now pink and delicate and rectangular. It was written in Ts'ui Pen's renowned calligraphy. Eagerly yet uncomprehendingly I read the words that a man of my own lineage had written with painstaking brushstrokes: *I leave to several futures (not to all) my garden of forking paths.* I wordlessly handed the paper back to Albert. He continued:

"Before unearthing this letter, I had wondered how a book could be infinite. The only way I could surmise was that it be a cyclical, or circular, volume, a volume whose last page would be identical to the first, so that one might go on indefinitely. I also recalled that night at the centre of the *1001 Nights,* when the queen Scheherazade (through some magical distractedness on the part of the copyist) begins to retell, verbatim, the story of the 1001 Nights, with the risk of returning once again to the night on which she is telling it—and so on, *ad infinitum.* I also pictured to myself a platonic, hereditary sort of work, passed down from father to son, in which each new individual would add a chapter or with reverent care correct his elders' pages. These imaginings amused and distracted me, but none of them seemed to correspond even remotely to Ts'ui Pen's contradictory chapters. As I was floundering about in the mire of these perplexities, I was sent from Oxford the document you have just examined. I paused, as you may well imagine, at the sentence 'I leave to several futures (not to all) my garden of forking paths.' Almost instantly, I saw it—the garden of forking paths was the chaotic novel; the phrase 'several futures (not all)' suggested to me the image of a forking in *time,* rather than in space. A full rereading of the book confirmed my theory. In all fictions, each time a man meets diverse alternatives, he chooses one and eliminates the others; in the work of the virtually impossible-to-disentangle Ts'ui Pen, the character chooses—simultaneously—all of them. *He creates,* thereby, 'several futures,' several *times,* which themselves proliferate and fork. That is the explanation for the novel's contradictions. Fang, let us say, has a secret; a stranger knocks at his door; Fang decides to kill him. Naturally, there are various possible outcomes—Fang can kill the intruder, the intruder can kill Fang, they can both live, they can both be killed, and so on. In Ts'ui Pen's novel, *all* the outcomes in fact occur; each is the starting point for further bifurcations. Once in a while, the paths of that labyrinth converge: for example, you come to this house, but in one of the possible pasts you are my enemy, in another my friend. If you can bear my incorrigible pronunciation, we shall read a few pages."

His face, in the vivid circle of the lamp, was undoubtedly that of an old man, though with something indomitable and even immortal about it. He read with slow precision two versions of a single epic chapter. In the first, an army marches off to battle through a mountain wilderness; the horror of the rocks and darkness inspires in them a disdain for life, and they go on to an easy victory. In the second, the same army passes through a palace in which a ball is being held; the brilliant battle seems to them a continuation of the *fête,* and they win it easily.

I listened with honourable veneration to those ancient fictions, which were themselves perhaps not as remarkable as the fact that a man of my blood had invented them and a man of a distant empire was restoring them to me on an island in the West in the course of a desperate mission. I recall the final words, repeated in each version like some secret commandment: "Thus the heroes fought, their admirable hearts calm, their swords violent, they themselves resigned to killing and to dying."

From that moment on, I felt all about me and within my obscure body an invisible, intangible pullulation—not that of the divergent, parallel, and finally coalescing armies, but an agitation more inaccessible, more inward than that, yet one those armies somehow prefigured. Albert went on:

"I do not believe that your venerable ancestor played at idle variations. I cannot think it probable that he would sacrifice thirteen years to the infinite performance of a rhetorical exercise. In your country, the novel is a subordinate genre; at that time it was a genre beneath contempt. Ts'ui Pen was a novelist of genius, but he was also a man of letters, and surely would not have considered himself a mere novelist. The testimony of his contemporaries proclaims his metaphysical, mystical leanings—and his life is their fullest confirmation. Philosophical debate consumes a good part of his novel. I know that of all problems, none disturbed him, none gnawed at him like the unfathomable problem of time. How strange, then, that that problem should be the *only* one that does not figure in the pages of his *Garden.* He never even uses the word. How do you explain that wilful omission?"

I proposed several solutions—all unsatisfactory. We discussed them; finally, Stephen Albert said:

"In a riddle whose answer is chess, what is the only word that must not be used?"

I thought for a moment.

"The word 'chess,'" I replied.

"Exactly," Albert said. "*The Garden of Forking Paths* is a huge riddle, or parable, whose subject is time; that secret purpose forbids Ts'ui Pen the merest mention of its name. To *always* omit one word, to employ awkward metaphors and obvious circumlocutions, is perhaps the most emphatic way of calling attention to that word. It is, at any rate, the tortuous path chosen by the devious Ts'ui Pen at each and every one of the turnings of his inexhaustible novel. I have compared hundreds of manuscripts, I have corrected the errors introduced through the negligence of copyists, I have reached a hypothesis for the plan of that chaos, I have reestablished, or believe I've reestablished, its fundamental order—I have translated the entire work; and I know that not once does the word 'time' appear. The explanation is obvious: *The Garden of Forking Paths* is an incomplete, but not false, image of the universe as conceived by Ts'ui Pen. Unlike Newton and Schopenhauer,[1] your ancestor did not believe in a uniform and absolute time; he believed in an infinite series of times, a growing, dizzying web of divergent, convergent, and parallel times. That fabric of times that approach one another, fork, are snipped off, or are simply unknown for centuries, contains *all* possibilities. In most of those times, we do not exist; in some, you exist but I do not; in others, I do and you do not; in others still, we both do. In this one, which the favouring hand of chance has dealt me, you have come to my home; in another, when you come through my garden you find me dead; in another, I say these same words, but I am an error, a ghost."

"In all," I said, not without a tremble, "I am grateful for, and I venerate, your re-creation of the garden of Ts'ui Pen."

"Not in all," he whispered with a smile. "Time forks, perpetually, into countless futures. In one of them, I am your enemy."

I felt again that pullulation I have mentioned. I sensed that the dew-drenched garden that surrounded the house was saturated, infinitely, with invisible persons. Those persons were Albert and myself—secret, busily at work, multiform—in other dimensions of time. I raised my eyes and the gossamer nightmare faded. In the yellow-and-black garden there was but a single man—but that man was as mighty as a statue, and that man was coming down the path, and he was Capt. Richard Madden.

"The future is with us," I replied, "but I am your friend. May I look at the letter again?"

Albert rose once again. He stood tall as he opened the drawer of the tall writing cabinet; he turned his back to me for a moment. I had cocked the revolver. With utmost care, I fired. Albert fell without a groan, without a sound, on the instant. I swear that he died instantly—one clap of thunder.

The rest is unreal, insignificant. Madden burst into the room and arrested me. I have been sentenced to hang. I have most abhorrently triumphed: I have communicated to Berlin the secret name of the city to be attacked. Yesterday it was bombed—I read about it in the same newspapers that posed to all of England the enigma of the murder of the eminent Sinologist Stephen Albert by a stranger, Yu Tsun. The Leader solved the riddle. He knew that my problem was how to report (over the deafening noise of the war) the name of the city named Albert, and that the only way I could find was murdering a person of that name. He does not know (no one can know) my endless contrition, and my weariness.

The Library of Babel[1]

By this art you may contemplate the variation of the 23 letters. . . .
Anatomy of Melancholy,[2] pt. 2, sec. 2, mem. 4

The universe (which others call the Library) is composed of an indefinite, perhaps infinite number of hexagonal galleries. In the center of each gallery is a ventilation shaft, bounded by a low railing. From any hexagon one can see the floors above and below—one after another, endlessly. The arrangement of the galleries is always the

---

1. Isaac Newton (1642–1727), English physicist and mathematician who formulated laws of gravity and motion. Arthur Schopenhauer (1788–1860), German philosopher whose Idealist notions of the world as the individual's will and ideas are often cited by Borges.
1. Translated by Andrew Hurley.

2. An ironic treatise published in 1621 by the bibliophile Robert Burton. Burton's private library contained more than 2,000 volumes. The epigraph refers to the alphabet, whose 23 letters and their possible combinations constitute any library.

same: Twenty bookshelves, five to each side, line four of the hexagon's six sides; the height of the bookshelves, floor to ceiling, is hardly greater than the height of a normal librarian. One of the hexagon's free sides opens onto a narrow sort of vestibule, which in turn opens onto another gallery, identical to the first—identical in fact to all. To the left and right of the vestibule are two tiny compartments. One is for sleeping, upright; the other, for satisfying one's physical necessities. Through this space, too, there passes a spiral staircase, which winds upward and downward into the remotest distance. In the vestibule there is a mirror, which faithfully duplicates appearances. Men often infer from this mirror that the Library is not infinite—if it were, what need would there be for that illusory replication? I prefer to dream that burnished surfaces are a figuration and promise of the infinite. . . . Light is provided by certain spherical fruits that bear the name "bulbs." There are two of these bulbs in each hexagon, set crosswise. The light they give is insufficient, and unceasing.

Like all the men of the Library, in my younger days I traveled; I have journeyed in quest of a book, perhaps the catalog of catalogs. Now that my eyes can hardly make out what I myself have written, I am preparing to die, a few leagues from the hexagon where I was born. When I am dead, compassionate hands will throw me over the railing; my tomb will be the unfathomable air, my body will sink for ages, and will decay and dissolve in the wind engendered by my fall, which shall be infinite. I declare that the Library is endless. Idealists argue that the hexagonal rooms are the necessary shape of absolute space, or at least of our *perception* of space. They argue that a triangular or pentagonal chamber is inconceivable. (Mystics claim that their ecstasies reveal to them a circular chamber containing an enormous circular book with a continuous spine that goes completely around the walls. But their testimony is suspect, their words obscure. That cyclical book is God.) Let it suffice for the moment that I repeat the classic dictum: *The Library is a sphere whose exact center is any hexagon and whose circumference is unattainable.*

Each wall of each hexagon is furnished with five bookshelves; each bookshelf holds thirty-two books identical in format; each book contains four hundred ten pages; each page, forty lines; each line, approximately eighty black letters. There are also letters on the front cover of each book; those letters neither indicate nor prefigure what the pages inside will say. I am aware that that lack of correspondence once struck men as mysterious. Before summarizing the solution of the mystery (whose discovery, in spite of its tragic consequences, is perhaps the most important event in all history), I wish to recall a few axioms.

First: *The Library has existed ab aeternitate.* That truth, whose immediate corollary is the future eternity of the world, no rational mind can doubt. Man, the imperfect librarian, may be the work of chance or of malevolent demiurges; the universe, with its elegant appointments—its bookshelves, its enigmatic books, its indefatigable staircases for the traveler, and its water closets for the seated librarian—can only be the handiwork of a god. In order to grasp the distance that separates the human and the divine, one has only to compare these crude trembling symbols which my fallible hand scrawls on the cover of a book with the organic letters inside—neat, delicate, deep black, and inimitably symmetrical.

Second: *There are twenty-five orthographic symbols.* That discovery enabled mankind, three hundred years ago, to formulate a general theory of the Library and thereby satisfactorily solve the riddle that no conjecture had been able to divine—the formless and chaotic nature of virtually all books. One book, which my father once saw in a hexagon in circuit 15–94, consisted of the letters M C V perversely repeated from the first line to the last. Another (much consulted in this zone) is a mere labyrinth of letters whose penultimate page contains the phrase *O Time thy pyramids*. This much is known: For every rational line or forthright statement there are leagues of senseless cacophony, verbal nonsense, and incoherency. (I know of one semi-barbarous zone whose librarians repudiate the "vain and superstitious habit" of trying to find sense in books, equating such a quest with attempting to find meaning in dreams or in the chaotic lines of the palm of one's hand. . . . They will acknowledge that the inventors of writing imitated the twenty-five natural symbols, but contend that that adoption was fortuitous, coincidental, and that books in themselves have no meaning. That argument, as we shall see, is not entirely fallacious.)

For many years it was believed that those impenetrable books were in ancient or far-distant languages. It is true that the most ancient peoples, the first librarians, employed a language quite different from the one we speak today; it is true that a few miles to the right, our language devolves into dialect and that ninety floors above, it becomes incomprehensible. All of that, I repeat, is true—but four hundred ten pages of unvarying M C V's cannot belong to any language, however dialectal or primitive it may be. Some have suggested that each letter influences the next, and that the value of M C V on page 71, line 3, is not the value of the same series on another line of another page, but that vague thesis has not met with any great acceptance. Others have mentioned the possibility of codes; that conjecture has been universally accepted, though not in the sense in which its originators formulated it.

Some five hundred years ago, the chief of one of the upper hexagons came across a book as jumbled as all the others, but containing almost two pages of homogeneous lines. He showed his find to a traveling decipherer, who told him that the lines were written in Portuguese; others said it was Yiddish. Within the century experts had determined what the language actually was: a Samoyed-Lithuanian dialect of Guaraní, with inflections from classical Arabic. The content was also determined: the rudiments of combinatory analysis, illustrated with examples of endlessly repeating variations. Those examples allowed a librarian of genius to discover the fundamental law of the Library. This philosopher observed that all books, however different from one another they might be, consist of identical elements: the space, the period, the comma, and the twenty-two letters of the alphabet. He also posited a fact which all travelers have since confirmed: *In all the Library, there are no two identical books*. From those incontrovertible premises, the librarian deduced that the Library is "total"—perfect, complete, and whole—and that its bookshelves contain all possible combinations of the twenty-two orthographic symbols (a number which, though unimaginably vast, is not infinite)—that is, all that is able to be expressed, in every language. *All*—the detailed history of the future, the autobiographies of the archangels, the faithful catalog of the Library, thousands and thousands of false catalogs, the proof of the falsity of those false catalogs, a proof of the falsity of the *true* catalog, the gnostic gospel of Basilides,[3] the commentary upon that gospel, the commentary on the commentary on that gospel, the true story of your death, the translation of every book into every language, the interpolations of every book into all books, the treatise Bede could have written (but did not) on the mythology of the Saxon people, the lost books of Tacitus.[4]

---

3. Scholar and teacher in 2nd-century C.E. Alexandria, Egypt. His *Exegetica*, a major commentary on the Bible, consisted of 24 books.

4. The Venerable Bede (c. 673–735) was an English historian and Benedictine monk. Cornelius Tacitus (c. 56–120 C.E.), historian of the Roman Empire.

When it was announced that the Library contained all books, the first reaction was unbounded joy. All men felt themselves the possessors of an intact and secret treasure. There was no personal problem, no world problem, whose eloquent solution did not exist—somewhere in some hexagon. The universe was justified; the universe suddenly became congruent with the unlimited width and breadth of humankind's hope. At that period there was much talk of The Vindications—books of *apologiae* and prophecies that would vindicate for all time the actions of every person in the universe and that held wondrous arcana for men's futures. Thousands of greedy individuals abandoned their sweet native hexagons and rushed downstairs, upstairs, spurred by the vain desire to find their Vindication. These pilgrims squabbled in the narrow corridors, muttered dark imprecations, strangled one another on the divine staircases, threw deceiving volumes down ventilation shafts, were themselves hurled to their deaths by men of distant regions. Others went insane. . . . The Vindications do exist (I have seen two of them, which refer to persons in the future, persons perhaps not imaginary), but those who went in quest of them failed to recall that the chance of a man's finding his own Vindication, or some perfidious version of his own, can be calculated to be zero.

At that same period there was also hope that the fundamental mysteries of mankind—the origin of the Library and of time—might be revealed. In all likelihood those profound mysteries can indeed be explained in words; if the language of the philosophers is not sufficient, then the multiform Library must surely have produced the extraordinary language that is required, together with the words and grammar of that language. For four centuries, men have been scouring the hexagons. . . . There are official searchers, the "inquisitors." I have seen them about their tasks: they arrive exhausted at some hexagon, they talk about a staircase that nearly killed them—rungs were missing—they speak with the librarian about galleries and staircases, and, once in a while, they take up the nearest book and leaf through it, searching for disgraceful or dishonorable words. Clearly, no one expects to discover anything.

That unbridled hopefulness was succeeded, naturally enough, by a similarly disproportionate depression. The certainty that some bookshelf in some hexagon contained precious books, yet that those precious books were forever out of reach, was almost unbearable. One blasphemous sect proposed that the searches be discontinued and that all men shuffle letters and symbols until those canonical books, through some improbable stroke of chance, had been constructed. The authorities were forced to issue strict orders. The sect disappeared, but in my childhood I have seen old men who for long periods would hide in the latrines with metal disks and a forbidden dice cup, feebly mimicking the divine disorder.

Others, going about it in the opposite way, thought the first thing to do was eliminate all worthless books. They would invade the hexagons, show credentials that were not always false, leaf disgustedly through a volume, and condemn entire walls of books. It is to their hygienic, ascetic rage that we lay the senseless loss of millions of volumes. Their name is execrated today, but those who grieve over the "treasures" destroyed in that frenzy overlook two widely acknowledged facts: One, that the Library is so huge that any reduction by human hands must be infinitesimal. And two, that each book is unique and irreplaceable, but (since the Library is total) there are always several hundred thousand imperfect facsimiles—books that differ by no more than a single letter, or a comma. Despite general opinion, I daresay that the consequences of the depredations committed by the Purifiers have been exaggerated by the horror those same fanatics inspired. They were spurred on by the holy zeal to reach—someday, through unrelenting effort—the books of the Crimson Hexagon—books smaller than natural books, books omnipotent, illustrated, and magical.

We also have knowledge of another superstition from that period: belief in what was termed the Book-Man. On some shelf in some hexagon, it was argued, there must exist a book that is the cipher and perfect compendium *of all other books,* and some librarian must have examined that book; this librarian is analogous to a god. In the language of this zone there are still vestiges of the sect that worshiped that distant librarian. Many have gone in search of Him. For a hundred years, men beat every possible path—and every path in vain. How was one to locate the idolized secret hexagon that sheltered Him? Someone proposed searching by regression: To locate book A, first consult book B, which tells where book A can be found; to locate book B, first consult book C, and so on, to infinity. . . . It is in ventures such as these that I have squandered and spent my years. I cannot think it unlikely that there is such a total book on some shelf in the universe. I pray to the unknown gods that some man—even a single man, tens of centuries ago—has perused and read that book. If the honor and wisdom and joy of such a reading are not to be my own, then let them be for others. Let heaven exist, though my own place be in hell. Let me be tortured and battered and annihilated, but let there be one instant, one creature, wherein thy enormous Library may find its justification.

Infidels claim that the rule in the Library is not "sense," but "non-sense," and that "rationality" (even humble, pure coherence) is an almost miraculous exception. They speak, I know, of "the feverish Library, whose random volumes constantly threaten to transmogrify into others, so that they affirm all things, deny all things, and confound and confuse all things, like some mad and hallucinating deity." Those words, which not only proclaim disorder but exemplify it as well, prove, as all can see, the infidels' deplorable taste and desperate ignorance. For while the Library contains all verbal structures, all the variations allowed by the twenty-five orthographic symbols, it includes not a single absolute piece of nonsense. It would be pointless to observe that the finest volume of all the many hexagons that I myself administer is titled *Combed Thunder,* while another is titled *The Plaster Cramp,* and another, *Axaxaxas mlö.* Those phrases, at first apparently incoherent, are undoubtedly susceptible to cryptographic or allegorical "reading"; that reading, that justification of the words' order and existence, is itself verbal and, *ex hypothesi,* already contained somewhere in the Library. There is no combination of characters one can make—*dhcmrlchtdj,* for example—that the divine Library has not foreseen and that in one or more of its secret tongues does not hide a terrible significance. There is no syllable one can speak that is not filled with tenderness and terror, that is not, in one of those languages, the mighty name of a god. To speak is to commit tautologies. This pointless, verbose epistle already exists in one of the thirty volumes of the five bookshelves in one of the countless hexagons—as does its refutation. (A number *n* of the possible languages employ the same vocabulary; in some of them, the *symbol* "library" possesses the correct definition "everlasting, ubiquitous system of hexagonal galleries," while a library—the thing—is a loaf of bread or a pyramid or something else, and the six words that define it themselves have other definitions. You who read me—are you certain you understand my language?)

Methodical composition distracts me from the present condition of humanity. The certainty that everything has already been written annuls us, or renders us phantasmal. I know districts in which the young people prostrate themselves before books and like savages kiss their pages, though they cannot read a letter. Epidemics, heretical discords, pilgrimages that inevitably degenerate into brigandage have decimated the population. I believe I mentioned the suicides, which are more and more frequent every year. I am perhaps misled by old age and fear, but I suspect that the human species—the *only* species—teeters at the verge of extinction, yet that the Library—enlightened, solitary, infinite, perfectly unmoving, armed with precious volumes, pointless, incorruptible, and secret—will endure.

I have just written the word "infinite." I have not included that adjective out of mere rhetorical habit; I hereby state that it is not illogical to think that the world is infinite. Those who believe it to have limits hypothesize that in some remote place or places the corridors and staircases and hexagons may, inconceivably, end—which is absurd. And yet those who picture the world as unlimited forget that the number of possible books is *not*. I will be bold enough to suggest this solution to the ancient problem: *The Library is unlimited but periodic.* If an eternal traveler should journey in any direction, he would find after untold centuries that the same volumes are repeated in the same disorder—which, repeated, becomes order: the Order. My solitude is cheered by that elegant hope.

Borges and I[1]

It's Borges, the other one, that things happen to. I walk through Buenos Aires and I pause—mechanically now, perhaps—to gaze at the arch of an entryway and its inner door; news of Borges reaches me by mail, or I see his name on a list of academics or in some biographical dictionary. My taste runs to hourglasses, maps, seventeenth-century typefaces, etymologies, the taste of coffee, and the prose of Robert Louis Stevenson;[2] Borges shares those preferences, but in a vain sort of way that turns them into the accoutrements of an actor. It would be an exaggeration to say that our relationship is hostile—I live, I allow myself to live, so that Borges can spin out his literature, and that literature is my justification. I willingly admit that he has written a number of sound pages, but those pages will not save *me*, perhaps because the good in them no longer belongs to any individual, not even to that other man, but rather to language itself, or to tradition. Beyond that, I am doomed—utterly and inevitably—to oblivion, and fleeting moments will be all of me that survives in that other man. Little by little, I have been turning everything over to him, though I know the perverse way he has of distorting and magnifying everything. Spinoza[3] believed that all things wish to go on being what they are—stone wishes eternally to be stone, and tiger, to be tiger. I shall endure in Borges, not in myself (if, indeed, I am anybody at all), but I recognize myself less in his books than in many others', or in the tedious strumming of a guitar. Years ago I tried to free myself from him, and I moved on from the mythologies of the slums and outskirts of the city to games with time and infinity, but those games belong to Borges now, and I shall have to think up other things. So my life is a point-counterpoint, a kind of fugue, and a falling away—and everything

1. Translated by Andrew Hurley.
2. Scottish author (1850–1894) of adventure tales and stories that explore embodiments of good and evil, often cited by Borges.
3. Dutch philosopher Baruch Spinoza (1632–1677).

winds up being lost to me, and everything falls into oblivion, or into the hands of the other man.

I am not sure which of us it is that's writing this page.

The Cult of the Phoenix[1]

Those who write that the cult of the Phoenix had its origin in Heliopolis,[2] and claim that it derives from the religious restoration that followed the death of the reformer Amenhotep IV,[3] cite the writings of Herodotus and Tacitus and the inscriptions on Egyptian monuments, but they are unaware, perhaps willfully unaware, that the cult's designation as "the cult of the Phoenix" can be traced back no farther than to Hrabanus Maurus[4] and that the earliest sources (the *Saturnalia*, say, or Flavius Josephus)[5] speak only of "the People of the Practice" or "the People of the Secret." In the conventicles of Ferrara, Gregorovius[6] observed that mention of the Phoenix was very rare in the spoken language; in Geneva, I have had conversations with artisans who did not understand me when I asked whether they were men of the Phoenix but immediately admitted to being men of the Secret. Unless I am mistaken, much the same might be said about Buddhists: The name by which the world knows them is not the name that they themselves pronounce.

On one altogether too famous page, Moklosich has equated the members of the cult of the Phoenix with the gypsies. In Chile and in Hungary, there are both gypsies and members of the sect; apart from their ubiquity, the two groups have very little in common. Gypsies are horse traders, pot-makers, blacksmiths, and fortune-tellers; the members of the cult of the Phoenix are generally contented practitioners of the "liberal professions." Gypsies are of a certain physical type, and speak, or used to speak, a secret language; the members of the cult are indistinguishable from other men, and the proof of this is that they have never been persecuted. Gypsies are picturesque, and often inspire bad poets; ballads, photographs, and boleros fail to mention the members of the cult. . . . Martin Buber[7] says that Jews are essentially sufferers; not all the members of the cult are, and some actively abhor pathos. That public and well-known truth suffices to refute the vulgar error (absurdly defended by Urmann) which sees the roots of the Phoenix as lying in Israel. People's reasoning goes more or less this way: Urmann was a sensitive man; Urmann was a Jew; Urmann made a habit of visiting the members of the cult in the Jewish ghettos of Prague; the affinity that Urmann sensed proves a real relationship. In all honesty, I cannot concur with that conclusion. That the members of the cult should, in a Jewish milieu, resemble Jews proves nothing; what cannot be denied is that they, like Hazlitt's infinite Shakespeare,[8] resemble every man in the world. They are all things to all men, like the Apostle; a few days ago, Dr. Juan Francisco Amaro, of Paysandú, pondered the ease with which they assimilate, the ease with which they "naturalize" themselves.

---

1. Translated by Andrew Hurley.
2. Ancient city in northern Egypt, a center of sun-worship.
3. Egyptian pharaoh, 15th-century B.C.E., discussed by the ancient Greek and Roman historians Herodotus and Tacitus.
4. German scholar and theologian (c. 780–856).
5. The Roman philosopher Macrobius's *Saturnalia* consists of dialogue in seven books, mainly an assessment of

Virgil. Flavius Josephus (c. 37–100 C.E.), scholar and historian from Jerusalem, was author of *Antiquities of the Jews*.
6. Ferdiannd Gregorovius (1821–1891), German historian.
7. Viennese Jewish philosopher (1878–1965).
8. The scholar William Hazlitt defined the modern reading of Shakespeare through his *Characters of Shakespeare's Plays* (1817).

I have said that the history of the cult records no persecutions. That is true, but since there is no group of human beings that does not include adherents of the sect of the Phoenix, it is also true that there has been no persecution or severity that the members of the cult have not suffered *and carried out*. In the wars of the Western world and in the distant wars of Asia, their blood has been spilled for centuries, under enemy flags; it is hardly worth their while to identify themselves with every nation on the globe.

Lacking a sacred book to unite them as the Scriptures unite Israel, lacking a common memory, lacking that other memory that is a common language, scattered across the face of the earth, diverse in color and in feature, there is but one thing—the Secret—that unites them, and that *will* unite them until the end of time. Once, in addition to the Secret there was a legend (and perhaps a cosmogonic myth), but the superficial men of the Phoenix have forgotten it, and today all that is left to them is the dim and obscure story of a punishment. A punishment, or a pact, or a privilege—versions differ; but what one may dimly see in all of them is the judgment of a God who promises eternity to a race of beings if its men, generation upon generation, perform a certain ritual. I have compared travelers' reports, I have spoken with patriarchs and theologians; I can attest that the performance of that ritual is the only religious practice observed by the members of the cult. The ritual is, in fact, the Secret. The Secret, as I have said, is transmitted from generation to generation, but tradition forbids a mother from teaching it to her children, as it forbids priests from doing so; initiation into the mystery is the task of the lowest individuals of the group. A slave, a leper, or a beggar plays the role of mystagogue. A child, too, may catechize another child. The act itself is trivial, the matter of a moment's time, and it needs no description. The materials used are cork, wax, or gum arabic. (In the liturgy there is mention of "slime"; pond slime is often used as well.) There are no temples dedicated expressly to the cult's worship, but ruins, cellars, or entryways are considered appropriate sites. The Secret is sacred, but that does not prevent its being a bit ridiculous; the performance of it is furtive, even clandestine, and its adepts do not speak of it. There are no decent words by which to call it, but it is understood that all words somehow name it, or rather, that they inevitably allude to it—and so I have said some insignificant thing in conversation and have seen adepts smile or grow uncomfortable because they sensed I had touched upon the Secret. In Germanic literatures there are poems written by members of the cult whose nominal subject is the sea or twilight; more than once I have heard people say that these poems are, somehow, symbols of the Secret. *Orbis terrarum est speculum Ludi*,[9] goes an apocryphal saying reported by du Cange in his Glossary. A kind of sacred horror keeps some of the faithful from performing that simplest of rituals; they are despised by the other members of the sect, but they despise themselves even more. Those, on the other hand, who deliberately renounce the Practice and achieve direct commerce with the Deity command great respect; such men speak of that commerce using figures from the liturgy, and so we find that John of the Rood[1] wrote as follows:

> Let the Nine Firmaments be told
> That God is delightful as the Cork and Mire.

9. "The Earth is the mirror of the Game." Borges is punning on an old adage, "The earth is the mirror of God," attributing his version to an obscure French historian and linguist, Charles du Fresne du Cange (1610–1688).
1. Also known as "John of the Cross"; medieval mystical theologian, author of *The Dark Night of the Soul*.

On three continents I have merited the friendship of many worshipers of the Phoenix; I know that the Secret at first struck them as banal, shameful, vulgar, and (stranger still) unbelievable. They could not bring themselves to admit that their parents had ever stooped to such acts. It is odd that the Secret did not die out long ago; but in spite of the world's vicissitudes, in spite of wars and exoduses, it does, in its full awesomeness, come to all the faithful. Someone has even dared to claim that by now it is instinctive.

The Web[1]

Which of my cities will I die in?
Geneva, where revelation came to me
through Virgil and Tacitus, certainly not from Calvin?[2]
Montevideo, where Luis Melian Lafinur,[3]
blind and heavy with years, died among the archives
of that impartial history of Uruguay
he never wrote?
Nara, where in a Japanese inn
I slept on the floor and dreamed the terrible
image of Buddha I had touched sightlessly
but saw in my dream?
Buenos Aires, where I'm almost a foreigner,
given my many years, or else a habitual target
for autograph hunters?
Austin, Texas, where my mother and I
in the autumn of '61 discovered America?
Others will know it too and will forget it.
What language am I doomed to die in?
The Spanish my ancestors used
to call for the charge or bid at truco?° *a card game*
The English of that Bible
my grandmother read from at the desert's edge?
Others will know it too and will forget it.
What time will it be?
In the dove-colored twilight when color fades away
or in the twilight of the crow
when night abstracts and simplifies
all visible things, or at an odd moment—
two in the afternoon?
Others will know it too and will forget it.
These questions are digressions, not from fear
but from impatient hope,
part of the fatal web of cause and effect
that no man can foresee, nor any god.

1. Translated by Alistair Reid.
2. Virgil and Tacitus, classical Rome's greatest poet and historian; John Calvin (1509–1564), French Protestant theologian whose sect emphasized strict morality in a sinful world.
3. One of Borges's ancestors.

~∞~

RESONANCE

Gabriel García Márquez: I Sell My Dreams[1]

One morning at nine o'clock, while we were having breakfast on the terrace of the Havana Riviera Hotel under a bright sun, a huge wave picked up several cars that were driving down the avenue along the seawall or parked on the pavement, and embedded one of them in the side of the hotel. It was like an explosion of dynamite that sowed panic on all twenty floors of the building and turned the great entrance window to dust. The many tourists in the lobby were thrown into the air along with the furniture, and some were cut by the hailstorm of glass. The wave must have been immense, because it leaped over the wide two-way street between the seawall and the hotel and still had enough force to shatter the window.

The cheerful Cuban volunteers, with the help of the fire department, picked up the debris in less than six hours, and sealed off the gate to the sea and installed another, and everything returned to normal. During the morning nobody worried about the car encrusted in the wall, for people assumed it was one of those that had been parked on the pavement. But when the crane lifted it out of its setting, the body of a woman was found secured behind the steering wheel by a seat belt. The blow had been so brutal that not a single one of her bones was left whole. Her face was destroyed, her boots had been ripped apart, and her clothes were in shreds. She wore a gold ring shaped like a serpent, with emerald eyes. The police established that she was the housekeeper for the new Portuguese ambassador and his wife. She had come to Havana with them two weeks before and had left that morning for the market, driving a new car. Her name meant nothing to me when I read it in the newspaper, but I was intrigued by the snake ring and its emerald eyes. I could not find out, however, on which finger she wore it.

This was a crucial piece of information, because I feared she was an unforgettable woman whose real name I never knew, and who wore a similar ring on her right forefinger, which in those days was even more unusual than it is now. I had met her thirty-four years earlier in Vienna, eating sausage with boiled potatoes and drinking draft beer in a tavern frequented by Latin American students. I had come from Rome that morning, and I still remember my immediate response to her splendid soprano's bosom, the languid foxtails on her coat collar, and that Egyptian ring in the shape of a serpent. She spoke an elementary Spanish in a metallic accent without pausing for breath, and I thought she was the only Austrian at the long wooden table. But no, she had been born in Colombia and had come to Austria between the wars, when she was little more than a child, to study music and voice. She was about thirty, and did not carry her years well, for she had never been pretty and had begun to age before her time. But she was a charming human being. And one of the most awe-inspiring.

---

1. Translated by Edith Grossman. Colombia's Nobel Prize-winning novelist Gabriel García Márquez (b. 1928) is one of the foremost practitioners of "magic realism," creating naturalistic worlds in which fantastic events occur. Borges has been an important inspiration for García Márquez, and "I Sell My Dreams" evokes him through the Chilean poet Pablo Neruda, who figures in this story and who speaks of him. Behind both writers is Lewis Carroll, author of the famous dream-tale *Alice's Adventures in Wonderland.* Borges used a line from Carroll's *Through the Looking Glass,* "And if he left off dreaming about you . . . ," as epigraph for a short story, "The Circular Ruins." Consumed by the creative process that engenders their literary worlds, many authors, including Borges and García Márquez, begin to wonder whether they themselves might not be figments of someone else's dreams.

Vienna was still an old imperial city, whose geographical position between the two irreconcilable worlds left behind by the Second World War had turned it into a paradise of black marketeering and international espionage. I could not have imagined a more suitable spot for my fugitive compatriot, who still ate in the students' tavern on the corner only out of loyalty to her origins, since she had more than enough money to buy meals for all her table companions. She never told her real name, and we always knew her by the Germanic tongue twister that we Latin American students in Vienna invented for her: Frau Frieda. I had just been introduced to her when I committed the happy impertinence of asking how she had come to be in a world so distant and different from the windy cliffs of Quindío, and she answered with a devastating:

"I sell my dreams."

In reality, that was her only trade. She had been the third of eleven children born to a prosperous shopkeeper in old Caldas, and as soon as she learned to speak she instituted the fine custom in her family of telling dreams before breakfast, the time when their oracular qualities are preserved in their purest form. When she was seven she dreamed that one of her brothers was carried off by a flood. Her mother, out of sheer religious superstition, forbade the boy to swim in the ravine, which was his favorite pastime. But Frau Frieda already had her own system of prophecy.

"What that dream means," she said, "isn't that he's going to drown, but that he shouldn't eat sweets."

Her interpretation seemed an infamy to a five-year-old boy who could not live without his Sunday treats. Their mother, convinced of her daughter's oracular talents, enforced the warning with an iron hand. But in her first careless moment the boy choked on a piece of caramel that he was eating in secret, and there was no way to save him.

Frau Frieda did not think she could earn a living with her talent until life caught her by the throat during the cruel Viennese winters. Then she looked for work at the first house where she would have liked to live, and when she was asked what she could do, she told only the truth: "I dream." A brief explanation to the lady of the house was all she needed, and she was hired at a salary that just covered her minor expenses, but she had a nice room and three meals a day—breakfast in particular, when the family sat down to learn the immediate future of each of its members: the father, a refined financier; the mother, a joyful woman passionate about Romantic chamber music; and two children, eleven and nine years old. They were all religious and therefore inclined to archaic superstitions, and they were delighted to take in Frau Frieda, whose only obligation was to decipher the family's daily fate through her dreams.

She did her job well, and for a long time, above all during the war years, when reality was more sinister than nightmares. Only she could decide at breakfast what each should do that day, and how it should be done, until her predictions became the sole authority in the house. Her control over the family was absolute: Even the faintest sigh was breathed by her order. The master of the house died at about the time I was in Vienna, and had the elegance to leave her a part of his estate on the condition that she continue dreaming for the family until her dreams came to an end.

I stayed in Vienna for more than a month, sharing the straitened circumstances of the other students while I waited for money that never arrived. Frau Frieda's unexpected and generous visits to the tavern were like fiestas in our poverty-stricken regime. One night, in a beery euphoria, she whispered in my ear with a conviction that permitted no delay.

"I only came to tell you that I dreamed about you last night," she said. "You must leave right away and not come back to Vienna for five years."

Her conviction was so real that I boarded the last train to Rome that same night. As for me, I was so influenced by what she said that from then on I considered myself a survivor of some catastrophe I never experienced. I still have not returned to Vienna.

Before the disaster in Havana, I had seen Frau Frieda in Barcelona in so unexpected and fortuitous a way that it seemed a mystery to me. It happened on the day Pablo Neruda[2] stepped on Spanish soil for the first time since the Civil War, on a stopover during a long sea voyage to Valparaíso. He spent a morning with us hunting big game in the secondhand bookstores, and at Porter he bought an old, dried-out volume with a torn binding for which he paid what would have been his salary for two months at the consulate in Rangoon. He moved through the crowd like an invalid elephant, with a child's curiosity in the inner workings of each thing he saw, for the world appeared to him as an immense wind-up toy with which life invented itself.

I have never known anyone closer to the idea one has of a Renaissance pope: He was gluttonous and refined. Even against his will, he always presided at the table. Matilde, his wife, would put a bib around his neck that belonged in a barbershop rather than a dining room, but it was the only way to keep him from taking a bath in sauce. That day at Carvalleiras was typical. He ate three whole lobsters, dissecting them with a surgeon's skill, and at the same time devoured everyone else's plate with his eyes and tasted a little from each with a delight that made the desire to eat contagious: clams from Galicia, mussels from Cantabria, prawns from Alicante, sea cucumbers from the Costa Brava. In the meantime, like the French, he spoke of nothing but other culinary delicacies, in particular the prehistoric shellfish of Chile, which he carried in his heart. All at once he stopped eating, tuned his lobster's antennae, and said to me in a very quiet voice:

"There's someone behind me who won't stop looking at me."

I glanced over his shoulder, and it was true. Three tables away sat an intrepid woman in an old-fashioned felt hat and a purple scarf, eating without haste and staring at him. I recognized her right away. She had grown old and fat, but it was Frau Frieda, with the snake ring on her index finger.

She was traveling from Naples on the same ship as Neruda and his wife, but they had not seen each other on board. We invited her to have coffee at our table, and I encouraged her to talk about her dreams in order to astound the poet. He paid no attention, for from the very beginning he had announced that he did not believe in prophetic dreams.

"Only poetry is clairvoyant," he said.

After lunch, during the inevitable stroll along the Ramblas, I lagged behind with Frau Frieda so that we could renew our memories with no other ears listening. She told me she had sold her properties in Austria and retired to Oporto, in Portugal, where she lived in a house that she described as a fake castle on a hill, from which one could see all the way across the ocean to the Americas. Although she did not say so, her conversation made it clear that, dream by dream, she had taken over the entire fortune of her ineffable patrons in Vienna. That did not surprise me, however, because I had always thought her dreams were no more than a stratagem for surviving. And I told her so.

She laughed her irresistible laugh. "You're as impudent as ever," she said. And said no more, because the rest of the group had stopped to wait for Neruda to finish talking in Chilean slang to the parrots along the Rambla de los Pájaros. When we resumed our conversation, Frau Frieda changed the subject.

"By the way," she said, "you can go back to Vienna now."

2. Chilean poet, diplomat, and winner of the 1971 Nobel Prize in literature.

Only then did I realize that thirteen years had gone by since our first meeting.

"Even if your dreams are false, I'll never go back," I told her. "Just in case."

At three o'clock we left her to accompany Neruda to his sacred siesta, which he took in our house after solemn preparations that in some way recalled the Japanese tea ceremony. Some windows had to be opened and others closed to achieve the perfect degree of warmth, and there had to be a certain kind of light from a certain direction, and absolute silence. Neruda fell asleep right away, and woke ten minutes later, as children do, when we least expected it. He appeared in the living room refreshed, and with the monogram of the pillowcase imprinted on his cheek.

"I dreamed about that woman who dreams," he said.

Matilde wanted him to tell her his dream.

"I dreamed she was dreaming about me," he said.

"That's right out of Borges," I said.

He looked at me in disappointment.

"Has he written it already?"

"If he hasn't he'll write it sometime," I said. "It will be one of his labyrinths."[3]

As soon as he boarded the ship at six that evening, Neruda took his leave of us, sat down at an isolated table, and began to write fluid verses in the green ink he used for drawing flowers and fish and birds when he dedicated his books. At the first "All ashore" we looked for Frau Frieda, and found her at last on the tourist deck, just as we were about to leave without saying good-bye. She too had taken a siesta.

"I dreamed about the poet," she said.

In astonishment I asked her to tell me her dream.

"I dreamed he was dreaming about me," she said, and my look of amazement disconcerted her. "What did you expect? Sometimes, with all my dreams, one slips in that has nothing to do with real life."

I never saw her again or even wondered about her until I heard about the snake ring on the woman who died in the Havana Riviera disaster. And I could not resist the temptation of questioning the Portuguese ambassador when we happened to meet some months later at a diplomatic reception. The ambassador spoke about her with great enthusiasm and enormous admiration. "You cannot imagine how extraordinary she was," he said. "You would have been obliged to write a story about her." And he went on in the same tone, with surprising details, but without the clue that would have allowed me to come to a final conclusion.

"In concrete terms," I asked at last, "what did she do?"

"Nothing," he said, with a certain disenchantment. "She dreamed."

Naguib Mahfouz
b. 1911

Naguib Mahfouz, the first Arab writer to win the Nobel Prize in literature (1988), was born in the popular quarter of al-Jammaliyyah in the heart of old Cairo in 1911. His urban upbringing

3. Borges had indeed already written it, in a short story called "The Circular Ruins."

prepared him for the role of the scribe of this teeming metropolis, to which he devoted his life and prodigal work. He inscribes its life, space, and modern history into the hearts of Arab readers and familiarizes them with its ways and norms. His vivid recollections of old Cairo were an everlasting source of inspiration for his work, from his early short stories up to his last novel, *Echoes of an Autobiography,* 1994.

Mahfouz's father was a middle-class civil servant who provided his family with a comfortable life. After a few years in the *kuttab,* the traditional Qur'anic school, Mahfouz completed his primary and secondary education in Cairo and then went to Cairo University, where he studied philosophy. Upon his graduation in 1934, he worked for the university, contemplated postgraduate study, and registered for a doctorate in philosophy, but he soon abandoned this academic endeavor and embarked on a career of literary creativity.

He started publishing articles and short stories soon after his graduation and in 1938 published his first book, *Whispers of Madness,* a collection of short stories. In 1939 he published his first novel, *Absurd Fates.* The two ensuing novels were historical works written as part of a grand plan to relate the history of Egypt from the time of the pharaohs to the present. But his historical setting was merely a textual strategy to root the work in Egypt's glorious history, thus participating in the process of shaping its national identity.

But after writing three novels without making a dent in the vast history of Egypt—he was still in the early Pharaonic period—he turned his attention to the reality of his time. This coincided with World War II, which proved to be an important period in Mahfouz's career because during the turbulent years of the war, he became increasingly aware of the need to avoid historical metaphor and deal directly with the burning social issues of the time. The title of his first realistic novel, *New Cairo,* written in the first year of the war but not appearing until 1943, sums up the project of his realistic novels. They are concerned with the transformation of Cairo both as a city and as a distinct urban culture, juxtaposing the urban space of old and new Cairo as the symbol of the clash of cultural values that affect many of the inhabitants of this teeming Third-World metropolis. The novels of this phase reflect various facets of the trauma of change and its social, human, and political ramifications.

This culminated in the *Cairo Trilogy—Palace Walk* (1955), *Palace of Desire* (1956), and *Sugar Street* (1957)—the masterpiece of his Cairene urban chronicles. The *Trilogy* spans half a century of Egypt's quest for national identity and modernization over three different generations. It is the greatest family saga of modern Arabic literature and the work that enshrined middle-class morality and culture. Inspired by John Galsworthy's *Forsyte Saga,* it reflects the cultural and political development of a society in turmoil under the pressures of British occupation and draws a highly detailed map of Egypt's social and political orientations in the first half of the twentieth century. The *Trilogy* ends with the death of the patriarch and the birth of a new child, heralding the end of one era and the beginning of a new one. The prophecy came true, for the completion of the trilogy coincided with Gamal Abdel Nasser's revolution of 1952, which ended the *ancien régime.*

The radical change brought by this revolution led Mahfouz to a long period of contemplation in which he stopped writing for five years. In 1959 he published a major novel, *The Children of Gebalawy,* which was serialized in the newspaper *Al-Ahram.* As soon as its serialization was completed, the Azhar, the major religious authority in Egypt, banned its publication in book form. But in 1966 the book was published in Beirut and was allowed calmly into Cairo until it was banned again when Salman Rushdie's *Satanic Verses* was condemned as blasphemous. Mahfouz's novel didn't satirize Islam as Rushdie's had, but it gave a narrative account of creation and humanity's spiritual and intellectual development through three religions—Judaism, Christianity, and Islam—with humanity reaching the peak of intellectual and spiritual maturity with the age of reason. The final section of the novel posits scientific and rational knowledge as the new creed for humanity, and this enraged the religious establishment. Yet the novel can be read as Mahfouz's contribution to the search for a new direction after Egypt achieved its independence. It was his implicit advice to the new officers to adopt a more liberal and rational attitude toward the complex sociopolitical reality of Egypt, advice that was not heeded.

This provoked Mahfouz to start a series of six novels constituting his output in the 1960s and forming what critics call the period of critical-realism in his development. Since these are highly critical political novels emphasizing the importance of freedom and the dire consequences of its absence from society as a whole, they can be seen as documents of the disappointment of Mahfouz's generation in Nasser's regime or as documents of defiance and glorification of the spirit of rebellion. Mahfouz's repartee and sharp sense of humor endows many of these novels, particularly *Chatter on the Nile* (1966), with a fine criticism that turns the novel into one of the most powerful commentaries on corruption and tyranny.

The realization of the prophecy of doom enshrined in *Miramar* (1967), the last novel of this period, came as a shock nonetheless and led to another period of silence in Mahfouz's career. But instead of turning his attention to writing motion pictures, as he did in the years of silence in the 1950s, he poured his energy into short stories and one-act plays. These works are marked by symbolic, even surrealistic, structures used to portray the complexity and absurdity of the unexpected events that followed the 1967 defeat of Arab forces by Israel and Israel's occupation of the Sinai Peninsula, long part of Egypt. His first novel after four years, *Love in the Rain* (1973), was solely concerned with the impact of this tragic event on the Egyptian psyche. The following novel, *Karnak* (1974), written immediately after the death of Nasser, was a harsh and strongly critical re-evaluation of the police state and its responsibility for the destruction of the spirit of opposition, the younger generation, and the will to fight for the country.

The 1970s and 1980s witnessed a marked increase in Mahfouz's productivity. In these two decades he wrote as many novels as he had written in the preceding forty years of his career, with more than twenty novels and eight collections of short stories. Although many of the novels were quickly written and loosely structured and some of them are closer to movie treatments than fully developed novels, Mahfouz had a strong urge to record a rapidly shifting reality. Among these numerous works, however, three novels stand out as some of the best examples of the modern Arabic novel with their subtle intertextuality and original narrative structure. *The Epic of Harafish* (1977) from which there is a selection included here, is a remarkable achievement that rivals the *Trilogy* in its richness, texture, and complexity. It distills the rich tradition of popular story telling and subjects its textual strategies to the demands of modernistic narrative. *The Arabian Nights and Days* (1982) is an ambitious attempt to inscribe the modern preoccupations of the Arab world into the fantastic world of *The Arabian Nights*. Mahfouz posits the modern novel as a rival to the great classic of Arabic narrative and succeeds in reproducing the magic world of the old classic but with a completely modern slant. The dialogue with classical narrative forms, in these two and other novels of this period, enhances Mahfouz's recent work and provides it with potent appeal to the wider reading public without detracting from its complexity and subtlety.

Mahfouz's major novel of the 1980s, *The Talk of Morning and Evening,* is the most significant Arabic novel of the 1980s, subverting narrative structure in order to portray the fragmentation of Egyptian society under the successive failures of the process of modernization.

The world of Naguib Mahfouz is a vast and extremely rich one that extends from Pharaonic times down to the present day. Although the space of his world is mainly Cairo and predominantly the old quarter in which he spent his childhood, he weaves the urban scene into an elaborate and highly significant metaphor for the whole national condition. On the literary plain, his career spans the whole process of the development of the Arabic novel from the historical to the modernistic and lyrical. He earned the Arabic novel respect and popularity and lived to see it flourish in the work of numerous writers throughout the Arab world.

Zaabalawi[1]

Finally I became convinced that I had to find Sheikh Zaabalawi.

The first time I had heard his name had been in a song:

> *Oh what's become of the world, Zaabalawi?*
> *They've turned it upside down and taken away its taste.*

It had been a popular song in my childhood, and one day it had occurred to me to demand of my father, in the way children have of asking endless questions:

"Who is Zaabalawi?"

He had looked at me hesitantly as though doubting my ability to understand the answer. However, he had replied, "May his blessing descend upon you, he's a true-saint of God, a remover of worries and troubles. Were it not for him I would have died miserably—"

In the years that followed, I heard my father many a time sing the praises of this good saint and speak of the miracles he performed. The days passed and brought with them many illnesses, for each one of which I was able, without too much trouble and at a cost I could afford, to find a cure, until I became afflicted with that illness for which no one possesses a remedy. When I had tried everything in vain and was overcome by despair, I remembered by chance what I had heard in my childhood: Why, I asked myself, should I not seek out Sheikh Zaabalawi? I recollected my father saying that he had made his acquaintance in Khan Gaafar at the house of Sheikh Qamar, one of those sheikhs who practiced law in the religious courts, and so I took myself off to his house. Wishing to make sure that he was still living there, I made inquiries of a vendor of beans whom I found in the lower part of the house.

"Sheikh Qamar!" he said, looking at me in amazement. "He left the quarter ages ago. They say he's now living in Garden City and has his office in al-Azhar Square."

I looked up the office address in the telephone book and immediately set off to the Chamber of Commerce Building, where it was located. On asking to see Sheikh Qamar, I was ushered into a room just as a beautiful woman with a most intoxicating perfume was leaving it. The man received me with a smile and motioned me toward a fine leather-upholstered chair. Despite the thick soles of my shoes, my feet were conscious of the lushness of the costly carpet. The man wore a lounge suit and was smoking a cigar; his manner of sitting was that of someone well satisfied both with himself and with his worldly possessions. The look of warm welcome he gave me left no doubt in my mind that he thought me a prospective client, and I felt acutely embarrassed at encroaching upon his valuable time.

"Welcome!" he said, prompting me to speak.

---

1. Translated by Denys Johnson-Davies. Zaabalawi is a name of a popular Sufi saint.

"I am the son of your old friend Sheikh Ali al-Tatawi," I answered so as to put an end to my equivocal position.

A certain languor was apparent in the glance he cast at me; the languor was not total in that he had not as yet lost all hope in me.

"God rest his soul," he said. "He was a fine man."

The very pain that had driven me to go there now prevailed upon me to stay.

"He told me," I continued, "of a devout saint named Zaabalawi whom he met at Your Honor's. I am in need of him, sir, if he be still in the land of the living."

The languor became firmly entrenched in his eyes, and it would have come as no surprise if he had shown the door to both me and my father's memory.

"That," he said in the tone of one who has made up his mind to terminate the conversation, "was a very long time ago and I scarcely recall him now."

Rising to my feet so as to put his mind at rest regarding my intention of going, I asked, "Was he really a saint?"

"We used to regard him as a man of miracles."

"And where could I find him today?" I asked, making another move toward the door.

"To the best of my knowledge he was living in the Birgawi Residence in al-Azhar," and he applied himself to some papers on his desk with a resolute movement that indicated he would not open his mouth again. I bowed my head in thanks, apologized several times for disturbing him, and left the office, my head so buzzing with embarrassment that I was oblivious to all sounds around me.

I went to the Birgawi Residence, which was situated in a thickly populated quarter. I found that time had so eaten away at the building that nothing was left of it save an antiquated façade and a courtyard that, despite being supposedly in the charge of a caretaker, was being used as a rubbish dump. A small, insignificant fellow, a mere prologue to a man, was using the covered entrance as a place for the sale of old books on theology and mysticism.

When I asked him about Zaabalawi, he peered at me through narrow, inflamed eyes and said in amazement, "Zaabalawi! Good heavens, what a time ago that was! Certainly he used to live in this house when it was habitable. Many were the times he would sit with me talking of bygone days, and I would be blessed by his holy presence. Where, though, is Zaabalawi today?"

He shrugged his shoulders sorrowfully and soon left me, to attend to an approaching customer. I proceeded to make inquiries of many shopkeepers in the district. While I found that a large number of them had never even heard of Zaabalawi, some, though recalling nostalgically the pleasant times they had spent with him, were ignorant of his present whereabouts, while others openly made fun of him, labeled him a charlatan, and advised me to put myself in the hands of a doctor—as though I had not already done so. I therefore had no alternative but to return disconsolately home.

With the passing of days like motes in the air, my pains grew so severe that I was sure I would not be able to hold out much longer. Once again I fell to wondering about Zaabalawi and clutching at the hope his venerable name stirred within me. Then it occurred to me to seek the help of the local sheikh of the district; in fact, I was surprised I had not thought of this to begin with. His office was in the nature of a small shop, except that it contained a desk and a telephone, and I found him sitting at his desk, wearing a jacket over his striped galabeya. As he did not interrupt his conversation with a man sitting beside him, I stood waiting till the man had gone. The sheikh then looked up at me coldly. I told myself that I should win him over by the usual methods, and it was not long before I had him cheerfully inviting me to sit down.

"I'm in need of Sheikh Zaabalawi," I answered his inquiry as to the purpose of my visit.

He gazed at me with the same astonishment as that shown by those I had previously encountered.

"At least," he said, giving me a smile that revealed his gold teeth, "he is still alive. The devil of it is, though, he has no fixed abode. You might well bump into him as you go out of here, on the other hand you might spend days and months in fruitless searching."

"Even you can't find him!"

"Even I! He's a baffling man, but I thank the Lord that he's still alive!"

He gazed at me intently, and murmured, "It seems your condition is serious."

"Very."

"May God come to your aid! But why don't you go about it systematically?" He spread out a sheet of paper on the desk and drew on it with unexpected speed and skill until he had made a full plan of the district, showing all the various quarters, lanes, alleyways, and squares. He looked at it admiringly and said, "These are dwelling-houses, here is the Quarter of the Perfumers, here the Quarter of the Coppersmiths, the Mouski, the police and fire stations. The drawing is your best guide. Look carefully in the cafés, the places where the dervishes perform their rites,[2] the mosques and prayerrooms, and the Green Gate,[3] for he may well be concealed among the beggars and be indistinguishable from them. Actually, I myself haven't seen him for years, having been somewhat preoccupied with the cares of the world, and was only brought back by your inquiry to those most exquisite times of my youth."

I gazed at the map in bewilderment. The telephone rang, and he took up the receiver.

"Take it," he told me, generously. "We're at your service."

Folding up the map, I left and wandered off through the quarter, from square to street to alleyway, making inquiries of everyone I felt was familiar with the place. At last the owner of a small establishment for ironing clothes told me, "Go to the calligrapher Hassanein in Umm al-Ghulam—they were friends."

I went to Umm al-Ghulam, where I found old Hassanein working in a deep, narrow shop full of signboards and jars of color. A strange smell, a mixture of glue and perfume, permeated its every corner. Old Hassanein was squatting on a sheepskin rug in front of a board propped against the wall; in the middle of it he had inscribed the world "Allah" in silver lettering. He was engrossed in embellishing the letters with prodigious care. I stood behind him, fearful of disturbing him or breaking the inspiration that flowed to his masterly hand. When my concern at not interrupting him had lasted some time, he suddenly inquired with unaffected gentleness, "Yes?"

Realizing that he was aware of my presence, I introduced myself. "I've been told that Sheikh Zaabalawi is your friend; I'm looking for him," I said.

His hand came to a stop. He scrutinized me in astonishment. "Zaabalawi! God be praised!" he said with a sigh.

"He *is* a friend of yours, isn't he?" I asked eagerly.

2. Dervishes are a pious group of people interested primarily in worship. Their rite is a weekly evening concert that is open to the faithful.

3. One of the gates of the Mosque of al-Husain in old Cairo.

"He was, once upon a time. A real man of mystery: he'd visit you so often that people would imagine he was your nearest and dearest, then would disappear as though he'd never existed. Yet saints are not to be blamed."

The spark of hope went out with the suddenness of a lamp snuffed by a power-cut.

"He was so constantly with me," said the man, "that I felt him to be a part of everything I drew. But where is he today?"

"Perhaps he is still alive?"

"He's alive, without a doubt. . . . He had impeccable taste, and it was due to him that I made my most beautiful drawings."

"God knows," I said, in a voice almost stifled by the dead ashes of hope, "how dire my need for him is, and no one knows better than you of the ailments in respect to which he is sought."

"Yes, yes. May God restore you to health. He is in truth, as is said of him, a man, and more. . . ."

Smiling broadly, he added, "And his face possesses an unforgettable beauty. But where is he?"

Reluctantly I rose to my feet, shook hands, and left. I continued wandering eastward and westward through the quarter, inquiring about Zaabalawi from everyone who, by reason of age or experience, I felt might be likely to help me. Eventually I was informed by a vendor of lupine that he had met him a short while ago at the house of Sheikh Gad, the well-known composer. I went to the musician's house in Tabakshiyya, where I found him in a room tastefully furnished in the old style, its walls redolent with history. He was seated on a divan, his famous lute beside him, concealing within itself the most beautiful melodies of our age, while somewhere from within the house came the sound of pestle and mortar and the clamor of children. I immediately greeted him and introduced myself, and was put at my ease by the unaffected way in which he received me. He did not ask, either in words or gesture, what had brought me, and I did not feel that he even harbored any such curiosity. Amazed at his understanding and kindness, which boded well, I said, "O Sheikh Gad, I am an admirer of yours, having long been enchanted by the renderings of your songs."

"Thank you," he said with a smile.

"Please excuse my disturbing you," I continued timidly, "but I was told that Zaabalawi was your friend, and I am in urgent need of him."

"Zaabalawi!" he said, frowning in concentration. "You need him? God be with you, for who knows, O Zaabalawi, where you are."

"Doesn't he visit you?" I asked eagerly.

"He visited me some time ago. He might well come right now; on the other hand I mightn't see him till death!"

I gave an audible sigh and asked, "What made him like that?"

The musician took up his lute. "Such are saints or they would not be saints," he said, laughing.

"Do those who need him suffer as I do?"

"Such suffering is part of the cure!"

He took up the plectrum and began plucking soft strains from the strings. Lost in thought, I followed his movements. Then, as though addressing myself, I said, "So my visit has been in vain."

He smiled, laying his cheek against the side of the lute. "God forgive you," he said, "for saying such a thing of a visit that has caused me to know you and you me!"

I was much embarrassed and said apologetically, "Please forgive me; my feelings of defeat made me forget my manners."

"Do not give in to defeat. This extraordinary man brings fatigue to all who seek him. It was easy enough with him in the old days, when his place of abode was known. To-day, though, the world has changed, and after having enjoyed a position attained only by potentates, he is now pursued by the police on a charge of false pretenses. It is therefore no longer an easy matter to reach him, but have patience and be sure that you will do so."

He raised his head from the lute and skillfully fingered the opening bars of a melody. Then he sang:

> *"I make lavish mention, even though I blame myself, of those I love,*
> *For the stories of the beloved are my wine."*

With a heart that was weary and listless, I followed the beauty of the melody and the singing.

"I composed the music to this poem in a single night," he told me when he had finished. "I remember that it was the eve of the Lesser Bairam. Zaabalawi was my guest for the whole of that night, and the poem was of his choosing. He would sit for a while just where you are, then would get up and play with my children as though he were one of them. Whenever I was overcome by weariness or my inspiration failed me, he would punch me playfully in the chest and joke with me, and I would bubble over with melodies, and thus I continued working till I finished the most beautiful piece I have ever composed."

"Does he know anything about music?"

"He is the epitome of things musical. He has an extremely beautiful speaking voice, and you have only to hear him to want to burst into song and to be inspired to creativity. . . ."

"How was it that he cured those diseases before which men are powerless?"

"That is his secret. Maybe you will learn it when you meet him."

But when would that meeting occur? We relapsed into silence, and the hubbub of children once more filled the room.

Again the sheikh began to sing. He went on repeating the words "and I have a memory of her" in different and beautiful variations until the very walls danced in ec-stasy. I expressed my wholehearted admiration, and he gave me a smile of thanks. I then got up and asked permission to leave, and he accompanied me to the front door. As I shook him by the hand, he said, "I hear that nowadays he frequents the house of Hagg Wanas al-Damanhouri. Do you know him?"

I shook my head, though a modicum of renewed hope crept into my heart.

"He is a man of private means," the sheikh told me, "who from time to time vis-its Cairo, putting up at some hotel or other. Every evening, though, he spends at the Negma Bar[4] in Alfi Street."

I waited for nightfall and went to the Negma Bar. I asked a waiter about Hagg Wanas, and he pointed to a corner that was semisecluded because of its position be-hind a large pillar with mirrors on all four sides. There I saw a man seated alone at a table with two bottles in front of him, one empty, the other two-thirds empty. There were no snacks or food to be seen,[5] and I was sure that I was in the presence of a hard-

---

4. Mahfouz often links drinking in bars (something that is transgressive in the Muslim culture) to spirituality, and to Sufis.

5. In Arabic culture, it is customary to have snacks with alcoholic drinks.

ened drinker. He was wearing a loosely flowing silk galabeya and a carefully wound turban; his legs were stretched out toward the base of the pillar, and as he gazed into the mirror in rapt contentment, the sides of his face, rounded and handsome despite the fact that he was approaching old age, were flushed with wine. I approached quietly till I stood but a few feet away from him. He did not turn toward me or give any indication that he was aware of my presence.

"Good evening, Mr. Wanas," I greeted him cordially.

He turned toward me abruptly, as though my voice had roused him from slumber, and glared at me in disapproval. I was about to explain what had brought me when he interrupted in an almost imperative tone of voice that was nonetheless not devoid of an extraordinary gentleness, "First, please sit down, and second, please get drunk!"

I opened my mouth to make my excuses, but, stopping up his ears with his fingers, he said, "Not a word till you do what I say."

I realized I was in the presence of a capricious drunkard and told myself that I should at least humor him a bit. "Would you permit me to ask one question?" I said with a smile, sitting down.

Without removing his hands from his ears he indicated the bottle. "When engaged in a drinking bout like this, I do not allow any conversation between myself and another unless, like me, he is drunk, otherwise all propriety is lost and mutual comprehension is rendered impossible."

I made a sign indicating that I did not drink.

"That's your lookout," he said offhandedly. "And that's my condition!"

He filled me a glass, which I meekly took and drank. No sooner had the wine settled in my stomach than it seemed to ignite. I waited patiently till I had grown used to its ferocity, and said, "It's very strong, and I think the time has come for me to ask you about—"

Once again, however, he put his fingers in his ears. "I shan't listen to you until you're drunk!"

He filled up my glass for the second time. I glanced at it in trepidation; then, overcoming my inherent objection, I drank it down at a gulp. No sooner had the wine come to rest inside me than I lost all willpower. With the third glass, I lost my memory, and with the fourth the future vanished. The world turned round about me, and I forgot why I had gone there. The man leaned toward me attentively, but I saw him—saw everything—as a mere meaningless series of colored planes. I don't know how long it was before my head sank down onto the arm of the chair and I plunged into deep sleep. During it, I had a beautiful dream the like of which I had never experienced. I dreamed that I was in an immense garden surrounded on all sides by luxuriant trees, and the sky was nothing but stars seen between the entwined branches, all enfolded in an atmosphere like that of sunset or a sky overcast with cloud. I was lying on a small hummock of jasmine petals, more of which fell upon me like rain, while the lucent spray of a fountain unceasingly sprinkled the crown of my head and my temples. I was in a state of deep contentedness, of ecstatic serenity. An orchestra of warbling and cooing played in my ear. There was an extraordinary sense of harmony between me and my inner self, and between the two of us and the world, everything being in its rightful place, without discord or distortion. In the whole world there was no single reason for speech or movement, for the universe moved in a rapture of ecstasy. This lasted but a short while. When I opened my eyes, consciousness struck at me like a policeman's fist, and I saw Wanas al-Damanhouri peering at me with concern. Only a few drowsy customers were left in the bar.

"You have slept deeply," said my companion. "You were obviously hungry for sleep."

I rested my heavy head in the palms of my hands. When I took them away in astonishment and looked down at them, I found that they glistened with drops of water.

"My head's wet," I protested.

"Yes, my friend tried to rouse you," he answered quietly.

"Somebody saw me in this state?"

"Don't worry, he is a good man. Have you not heard of Sheikh Zaabalawi?"

"Zaabalawi!" I exclaimed, jumping to my feet.

"Yes," he answered in surprise. "What's wrong?"

"Where is he?"

"I don't know where he is now. He was here and then he left."

I was about to run off in pursuit but found I was more exhausted than I had imagined. Collapsed over the table, I cried out in despair, "My sole reason for coming to you was to meet him! Help me to catch up with him or send someone after him."

The man called a vendor of prawns and asked him to seek out the sheikh and bring him back. Then he turned to me. "I didn't realize you were afflicted. I'm very sorry. . . ."

"You wouldn't let me speak," I said irritably.

"What a pity! He was sitting on this chair beside you the whole time. He was playing with a string of jasmine petals he had around his neck,[6] a gift from one of his admirers, then, taking pity on you, he began to sprinkle some water on your head to bring you around."

"Does he meet you here every night?" I asked, my eyes not leaving the doorway through which the vendor of prawns had left.

"He was with me tonight, last night, and the night before that, but before that I hadn't seen him for a month."

"Perhaps he will come tomorrow," I answered with a sigh.

"Perhaps."

"I am willing to give him any money he wants."

Wanas answered sympathetically, "The strange thing is that he is not open to such temptations, yet he will cure you if you meet him."

"Without charge?"

"Merely on sensing that you love him."

The vendor of prawns returned, having failed in his mission.

I recovered some of my energy and left the bar, albeit unsteadily. At every street corner I called out "Zaabalawi!" in the vague hope that I would be rewarded with an answering shout. The street boys turned contemptuous eyes on me till I sought refuge in the first available taxi.

The following evening I stayed up with Wanas al-Damanhouri till dawn, but the sheikh did not put in an appearance. Wanas informed me that he would be going away to the country and would not be returning to Cairo until he had sold the cotton crop.

I must wait, I told myself; I must train myself to be patient. Let me content myself with having made certain of the existence of Zaabalawi, and even of his affection for me, which encourages me to think that he will be prepared to cure me if a meeting takes place between us.

6. In Arabic culture, jasmine is a symbol of purity and innocence.

Sometimes, however, the long delay wearied me. I would become beset by despair and would try to persuade myself to dismiss him from my mind completely. How many weary people in this life know him not or regard him as a mere myth! Why, then, should I torture myself about him in this way?

No sooner, however, did my pains force themselves upon me than I would again begin to think about him, asking myself when I would be fortunate enough to meet him. The fact that I ceased to have any news of Wanas and was told he had gone to live abroad did not deflect me from my purpose; the truth of the matter was that I had become fully convinced that I had to find Zaabalawi.

Yes, I have to find Zaabalawi.

Hanzal and the Policeman[1]

The sound of heavy footsteps reverberated ominously within his breast, and the "humph" that accompanied it was a forewarning of pain and trouble. It was the police-constable approaching in the dark. He longed to run away, but could not. With great difficulty he managed to lift himself up and to throw his weight against the wall at the corner of the lane. He staggered. At any moment now he might collapse. With difficulty he opened his eyes and focused them in the direction of his oncoming doom. Several times, he tried to move in the dark but could not, and his thoughts and recollections were all scattered. His face, colourless, dusty and rugged, looked numb by the light of the street-lamp. He wore nothing but the remains of a torn *gallabeyya*[2] and his frenzied entrails burnt with a craving for the forbidden shot.

"Hanzal, come here . . ."

That fateful call, that was followed by blows and kicks. In a desperate, sickly voice he pleaded.

"Constable, have mercy on me, for God's sake."

He stood facing him, blocking the light of the street lamp, with his gun hanging from his shoulder. Hanzal pressed himself harder against the wall of Shanafiry Lane. In his fear, he tried to resist the faintness that threatened to overcome him; he whined miserably. But what was the matter? Why did the policeman not shout and scold and strike?

"Have you had the shot?"

"No, I swear I haven't."

"But you're in a stupor, or you seem to be."

"That's because I haven't taken it."

"Come with me, the officer wants you."

There came a sigh from his maddened, famished breast.

"I beg you . . ." he cried.

But the hand that was laid on his shoulder was not an iron grip, nor was it a policeman's clutch; it was a human hand. Surprised, Hanzal could not utter a word, so the policeman said:

"Come on, don't be afraid."

"I've done nothing wrong!"

He led him along gently and whispered soothingly:

"You'll find that everything's all right. Don't be afraid."

---

1. Translated by Azza Kararah, rev. David Kirkhaus. Hanzal is a name derived from the word meaning "extremely bitter." It conjures up misery and a harsh life.
2. Long outer garment.

He stood in the superintendant's room, about a yard away from the door, which was closed behind him. He could neither step forward nor raise his eyes and meet the glance that would be directed towards him from a stern face. The bright light shone on his mud-bespattered and almost naked body. Here, between the smooth white walls and the imposing furniture, he appeared like something that time had forgotten. A thunderbolt was what Hanzal expected, but to his surprise the commissioner's tone was a human one. Everything was surprising that night.

"Good evening, Hanzal. Sit down."

God in heaven! What on earth was happening?

"Heaven forbid, sir. I am your unworthy servant."

But the officer cast a reproving look at him and pointed a peremptory finger at a leather armchair. He hesitated for a long while, but seeing that there was nothing for it he gave in and perched himself on the edge of the chair with eyes fixed on his dusty feet. They looked so huge, like the feet of a statue, under their layers of grime. Hanzal could still not really believe these signs of courtesy and in an obsequious voice he said:

"Captain, sir, I'm a poor man with a lot that can be held against me, but my misery is far greater than my wrongdoings . . . and in God's eyes mercy is a higher thing than justice."

The officer retorted in a voice that was both gentle and earnest:

"Don't worry, Hanzal. I know your ill doings are very many, but your sufferings are greater. You know your wrongdoings best . . . The constable is not to be blamed for his cruelty to you, for the law is the law. But new conditions call for a change of treatment . . . a change in everything. As for us, it is true we are policemen, but we are also human."

Full of bewilderment he kept on gazing in wonder at the office while trying very hard to overcome his feeling of faintness. The man cast a pitying glance at him. "Trust in me, Hanzal," he said. "You must believe everything you hear and everything you see. You cannot concentrate because you have not had your shot. All your money is gone, and you have not had your shot. The poison-peddlar has no mercy and wants his price in advance. But you will be cured of all this . . ."

"I'm a wretch," Hanzal replied, whimpering. "All my life has been sheer bad luck. I used to be strong and now I'm weak. I was a trader and now I'm bankrupt, I've loved and suffered, I've become an addict and a beggar."

"You'll leave the sanatorium a better man and then we shall meet again."

In the yard of the police station he was surrounded by a group of policemen. Instinctively, from habit, he cowered as though to avoid a blow. Their thick lips broke into smiles under wayward moustaches!

"You!"

"Yes, Hanzal. Everything has changed."

"Get well soon, Hanzal."

"Let bygones be bygones."

He was carried away half-asleep and soon gave in altogether, in the carriage that lulled him to infinity. He opened his eyes in a strange room; it was dazzling white and brilliantly lit. He saw a strange face bending over him and he felt weak and sick, afraid and utterly lonely.

"The shot, the shot, Uncle Matbouli!" he humbly begged.

A soft laugh tickled his ear and a pungent smell penetrated his nose. He suffered a devastating hunger in his head and senses; the sides of his head were splitting, then he lost consciousness.

Hanzal left the sanatorium a new man, just as the police officer had promised. His features glowed for the first time and he swaggered along in a voluminous white *gallabeyya*. He had shaved his beard and his moustache looked healthy and strong once more. He wore bright yellow slippers, while the lion tattooed on his wrist was visible again, as well as the bird on his temple under the ornate turban. A policeman walked along with him, like a friend. Everything was friendly. His clear, dark skin gleamed in the sun. He had to laugh; surely, he said to himself, he must have lost weight with all this cleaning. He was wide awake, he could see, he could hear; he loved the police constable and he no longer felt that gnawing pain inside him. He was so full of self-confidence that he felt he could fly. He had faith in everything around him and was not surprised when police constables came towards him and congratulated him. There, in the yard of the police station, they all crowded round him and cordially shook him by the hand. He was not over-surprised either when he saw the police officer standing up to greet him. He was deeply moved and humbly he stooped forward in order to kiss the officer's hand. But he was received with open arms and embraced with kindness. He broke down with bashfulness and gratitude and his eyes overflowed with tears. The man seated him in the armchair and then went back to his own seat behind the desk. He gave a gentle, clear laugh:

"Congratulations on your recovery," he said.

Hanzal's eyes swam with unshed tears.

"Now you can start afresh," the officer went on.

His tears flowed freely:

"Thanks be to God and to you," he answered.

"Do not exaggerate. Thanks are due to God alone."

The officer then opened a book in front of him and with a pen he wrote something at the top of the white sheet; quietly, with a look in his eyes, as deep as moonlight, he said, "State your wishes, Hanzal." Hanzal was confused and could not reply. His lips moved and with them his uncouth moustache, but he remained tongue-tied. The officer urged him on, "State your wishes, Hanzal. That is an order," he was saying.

"But . . ."

"No buts—state your wishes."

He hesitated a while, then said, "All I want is God's protection."

"Make yourself clear. State your wishes. That is an order."

Hanzal remembered a mother's prayer, tales at night, tunes on the fiddle; then he chuckled, "I used to go around the streets with a fruit cart," he said.

"A fruit shop in the Hussainia," said the officer, writing in his book, "double shelves, electric light for better display . . ."

In a daze, Hanzal enquired, "And the money?"

"Do not trouble yourself, that is our responsibility and a matter for the public concern. Speak up and state your wishes. That is an order."

Hanzal found new courage which he drew from his new personality and from the fruit shop.

"Saneyya[3] Bayoumi, who sells liver," he said in a shaking voice. "The truth . . ."

The officer interrupted while his hand continued to write:

---

3. In Arabic the name means a "the one radiating with light and joy." It is often used to allude to Egypt itself.

"No need to explain, everything is known, known to the policeman at the station and by all the other police. Known also to the watchman in the market place. Saneyya is a bold and a pretty girl, and she is not yet married in spite of all that has taken place. There was a time when she was more harm to you than the heroin you were taking. And the crueller she became, the worse your condition grew. She has deserted you, but she will come back to you. Let it be a fruit and liver shop. There will be nothing else like it in the Hussainia. Just like a very exclusive grocer's. Anything else?"

Greatly moved, he bent his head and, as in a dream, he saw green pastures in which red, purple-fringed flowers grew; and in his ears a tune sounded, repeating the refrain *Tell me my heart's desire*. But then, he saw a dark blur, like a cloud of flies, and his whole body winced.

"I fear, sir," he said, pitifully, "this friendliness of the police may not last; because not the least of my miseries, in the past, was the way the police behaved. They were always after me and my cart, with reason or without; they'd confiscate my stock and beat me up. As for that business over Saneyya, it was Constable Hassouna who first began to turn her head."

The pleasant, clear laugh rose again.

"You will not find one enemy among the police," the officer retorted, in a tone that left no room for doubt. "From now on, and for good, they will be your faithful friends. State your wishes, Hanzal. That is an order."

Hanzal felt an intoxicating courage that had never been his, even in the days of his youthful exploits. A courage that was backed by a fruit and liver shop, by the love of Saneyya and the friendship of the police.

"There's many poor like me," he said, "and you, sir, you probably don't know them."

"I know everything," the officer broke in, though his hand never stopped writing, "Tell us who they are and every one of them will have his shop, his woman and the friendship of the police. All this will come true, and so state your wishes. That is an order."

Hanzal laughed very loud and pressed his hands hard together.

"This is too much like a dream," he said.

"Reality is a kind of dream; dreams are a kind of reality. State your wishes. That is an order."

He took a deep, full, confident breath.

"How many prisoners really deserve to be in prison?" he said, musingly.

The officer answered while his hand still continued to run over the paper:

"Everyone who does not really deserve prison will be let out, even if it leaves the prisons empty."

Full of exaltation Hanzal cried out:

"Long live justice! Long live the Superintendent!"

The courtyard of Hanzal's house in Shanafiry Lane then witnessed a party of a unique kind, at which the Superintendent and the constables, the poor and the one-time jail-birds, were there. Saneyya wore an orange dress with a green shawl round her shoulders so that no part of her plump body was visible, except a wrist adorned with a golden bracelet and an ankle encircled by a silver bangle with dangling crescents.[4] She herself served the drinks, tamarind and *karkadeh*[5] while, in a corner, a

---

4. Her outfit suggests the old flag of Egypt, which was green with a crescent and stars.

5. A common popular drink made of hibiscus flowers, often served on joyous occasions.

band with a touch of Mohammed Ali Street[6] blared out its welcome. They all enjoyed their freedom; even the policemen danced and sang under the eyes of their superior officer. Then a Koran-reciter rose amidst his followers and started a chant in praise of the Prophet:

With his advent came the light of truth.

The poor, the ex-convicts and the policemen all sighed with satisfaction and Saneyya's joyous trilling-cry sounded like the descant of a reed pipe. Then finally, at the close of the festivities, the police officer stood up and addressed them all, and said, "It never rains but it pours . . . and these are only the first drops. Goodnight to you all."

Once more, Saneyya uttered her trilling-cry and the guests began to leave. The day was just breaking, the roosters glorified God and the silence glorified Him too.

Hanzal stretched himself on a couch to rest, and Saneyya sat down by his head and toyed with the forelock of his hair. He was happy, peaceful and contented, and wished that things would remain as they were for ever.

"You're the source of all things good," he said gently.

Her fingers went down to his temple as though she wished to feed the bird that was tattooed there. He went on to say:

"I don't think of all that's happened as miraculous. The real miracle is that your heart should have softened after being . . ."

Her hand slipped down to his cheek, then to his chin and finally rested at his throat. He surrendered himself to her caresses and in the depths of his heart he longed for this moment never to end. But, suddenly, he became aware of a strange feeling, a kind of pressure on his throat, a pressure too great for any kind of fondling. He wanted to ask her not to press so hard, but his voice would not come out and still the pressure increased. He stretched out his hand to remove hers from his neck but he felt as though a nightmare or incubus were pressing him down; he felt as though a heavy weight, a sandbag or part of a wall, had fallen on his head. He wanted to cry out, to stand up, to move, but could not. He turned his head brusquely to get rid of this torture and scraped it against the couch, or rather against something that felt like the ground—dust and mud. A strange feeling overwhelmed him, new in its nature, its flavour, the depth of its sadness. He heard a well-known, mocking, voice shouting at him.

"And so now you go to sleep in the middle of the road!"

How very like the police constable's voice this sounded. The old police constable with his rough voice that was always a forewarning of trouble. He felt suffocated. Saneyya's hand knew no mercy. Suddenly the wall was lifted from his chest and he sat up moaning in the dark. He seemed to make out the shadow of a giant blocking the light of the street lamp and towering up towards the stars. The cocks of dawn were crowing and a rifle appeared behind the shoulder of this spectre. The pain upon his chest gave way when the heavy boot was lifted from it.

"Constable," he called out, "what of the police superintendent's promises?"

The policeman kicked Hanzal savagely.

"The Superintendent's promise!" he cried. "You crazy dope-fiend . . . Come along to the station."

Hanzal looked around in terror and bewilderment; and all he found was a slumbering street, an enveloping darkness, a silence . . . no party, no trace of a party . . . no Saneyya . . . nothing.

---

6. The street of popular Arabic music and musicians.

from The Harafish[1]
The Thief Who Stole the Melody

THE NINTH TALE IN THE EPIC OF THE HARAFISH

1

Fate decreed that Samaha should live. Gradually he recovered his health and strength. The last battle had scarred and disfigured him, and he looked ugly and intimidating. He took over as chief of the clan without a struggle and enjoyed unlimited power. Nur rejoiced at her good fortune and her decisive victory over Sanbala, who was obliged to return to her aged father's house to give birth to a son. She named him Fath al-Bab, after her maternal grandfather. Shams al-Din's legacy was divided between his two sons, Samaha and Fath al-Bab, and his widow Sanbala. Samaha appointed himself his stepbrother's guardian. Since no one dared oppose him, most of his father's wealth fell into his steely grasp.

"You abandoned my father," he said to Sanbala, "you left him alone when he was dying. It would be unfair for you to inherit any of his money. Don't expect a penny of Fath al-Bab's share to come your way either. Think of some of it as protection money and the rest as punishment for your sins!"

2

Samaha created a legend around himself. He declared that he had only entered the battle against al-Kalabshi to defend his father, in spite of the animosity between them, and that the men who had gone over to his side had done so spontaneously, driven by a noble impulse. Nobody believed a word of this. It was widely known that he had been plotting against the chief, had incited some of his men to rebel, and had merely profited from the occasion to seize power. His detractors accused him of not defending his father as he ought to have done, and of being glad when he died. But he knew nothing of this and continued to bathe in his manufactured glory.

His reign hung over the alley like the shadow of a huge mountain, but to his credit he brought the neighboring chiefs to heel, and restored the alley to its former position of power. He built a sumptuous house where he installed his mother, and divided his own time between the bar, the smoking den, and the neighborhood brothels.

3

Suma al-Kalabshi died and his daughter Sanbala inherited a small fortune which she shared with her ten sisters. Soon afterward she married a moneylender's clerk, who was reluctant to welcome his wife's son by her first marriage. Things grew worse when he and Sanbala had children of their own, and Fath al-Bab grew up in a miserable atmosphere, clinging to his mother and avoiding the master of the house. He felt a growing sense of pain and isolation which was not eased by his excellent performance at Quran school or his gentle nature and good behavior. When he was nine years old his mother took him to the chief.

"Here's your brother," she said. "It's time you took him under your wing."

---

1. Translated by Catherine Cobham. The historical meaning of *harafish* is the "rabble or riffraff." In the novel it means the common people in a positive sense.

Samaha examined him. He looked handsome, frail, sad, but his heart didn't warm to him. "What's wrong with him? He looks half-starved!"

"He's not. But he's a delicate boy."

"To see him, you wouldn't think he was descended from clan chiefs on both sides! It's more appropriate for you to take care of him," he said, trying to shrug off the unwanted burden.

Her eyes filled with tears. "He's not happy with me, there's nothing more I can do."

Samaha, feeling obliged to take him, presented the child to his mother. She protested vigorously. "I don't have the energy to look after children anymore."

The truth was that she was horrified at the idea of raising her co-wife's son. Samaha was at a loss, and the boy had to bear his humiliation and distress without a murmur. Seeing his plight, an old woman, a friend of Nur's, volunteered to look after him. Sahar the midwife was a widow without children of her own, and a descendant of the Nagis.[2] She lived in a two-room basement in a building which had belonged to Galal, the minaret man. She was good-hearted, proud of her lineage, and with her for the first time Fath al-Bab had a cozy, untroubled life, which helped him bear the separation from his mother.

4

One day a pretty young girl caught Samaha's eye. She wasn't his for the taking like his other women. He saw her passing in a carriage and found out where she lived. In her beautiful face he detected a familiarity which made him think some hidden affinity existed between them. He soon discovered why. It turned out that she was Firdus, Radi's granddaughter. His attraction was based on lust for her and a desire to possess her, but it was so powerful that it made him think seriously about marriage for the first time in his dissolute life. Added to that, he was tempted by the fact that she owned the cereal business and was a Nagi like him. His mother was amazed when he asked her to arrange the engagement, but overjoyed at the same time.

"What makes us a good match," chuckled Samaha, "is that we're both descended from beautiful, crazy Zahira, the mankiller!"

He was so ugly, so bad that he deserved to be turned down, but who would refuse the clan chief?

5

Firdus married Samaha. Beauty united with the Beast. He had been beautiful once until the clubs rearranged his face. But he was endlessly proud of his origins and his unrivaled strength. Contrary to expectations, the marriage succeeded and they were happy. Samaha became manager of the cereal business and its virtual owner. From his office he unleashed his iron will, and ran the business and directed the gang's military operations with equal zeal. Marriage brought pleasant days and youth and beauty into his life, palatial ease, the habits of refined living against a background of fine artifacts and furnishings, and all the splendors and diversions of wealth and luxury. He did not give up his riotous excesses, but confined them to his marriage nest, installing gilded water pipes and calabashes[3] to enhance his pleasure. Managing the cereal business

---

2. In Arabic "Nagi" means "the saved one." He is the founder of the area and the source of its people.

3. In the popular part of Cairo, a water pipe is the most-used instrument for smoking and calabashes are used for drinking a primitive kind of beer.

taught him a love of money, and as he began to amass a fortune he decided to follow in the footsteps of the eccentric Galal and impose his authority not only on people but on objects of value.

6

Firdus demonstrated that she was intelligent as well as lucky. She loved her husband, gave him children with warmth and tenderness, was tireless in her efforts to make him more cultured and genteel and to possess him completely, but she did this gently, stealthily, without a hint of aggression or arrogance. She did not set great store by the office of clan chief, but was happy to enjoy all its privileges. As a Nagi herself, she extolled the virtues of the legendary chiefs of old with their justice and integrity; at the same time, as a member of the bourgeoisie, she had an aversion to such purity which favored heroic poverty and muzzled the powerful and rich. She was happy for the memory to be a blessing and a source of pride, as long as the clan system of the present was there to achieve power and wealth. There was no harm in Samaha doing what he wanted provided that it was in her house, protected by a gilded veil of wealth and respectability.

The days passed; she was happy. The rich grew richer and the poor grew poorer.

7

Fath al-Bab continued his education in the Quran school, and learned the Holy Book by heart. He was happy in the affectionate atmosphere of his new home. The shadow of fear had lifted from his soul, revealing a wealth of feelings and a prodigious imagination. He was a boy with a clear, light brown skin, jet-black eyes, a dimple in his chin, a graceful physique, and a pleasant, intelligent air. He forgot his mother, just as she forgot him, and centered all his affection on the midwife Sahar. He loved and revered her, and she explained things to him that he'd never thought about before.

As they sat together in the evenings she would say to him, "We're both descended from the blessed Ashur al-Nagi."

Then she would go on to talk with conviction of the distant past as if to her it was a living, breathing reality. "He came from very noble origins, but his father wanted to protect him from the wrath of a tyrannical clan chief. In a dream he was ordered to leave the boy on the path in the sacred shadow of the monastery."

Fath al-Bab cursed those who called his ancestor a foundling.

Sahar recited, "He came from very noble origins. He was raised by a good man and grew up to be a strong and powerful youth. One night an angel came to him and told him to leave the alley to escape from the plague. He called on the people in the alley to flee with him but they laughed at him, and he departed sadly with his wife and child. When he returned, he saved the alley from suffering and shame, just as God had saved him from death."

She would go on to tell the tale of Ashur's life—his return, his sojourn in the Bannan house, his reign as chief, his covenant—until the boy's eyes were filled with tears.

"Then one day he disappeared. He never came back, so people thought he was dead, but the truth is that he never died."

"Is he still alive today?" asked Fath al-Bab expectantly.

"He'll be alive forever!"

"Why doesn't he come back here?"

"Only God knows the answer to that."

"Might he turn up unexpectedly?"

"Quite possibly."

"Does he know what my brother did?"

"Of course, son."

"Why did he keep quiet about it?"

"Who knows?"

"Doesn't he care about injustice?"

"Of course he does."

"So why doesn't he do anything about it?"

"Who knows? Perhaps because he's angry that people seem indifferent to the tyrant that rules them."

Fath al-Bab was silent. "Is all that really true?" he demanded finally.

"Have I ever lied to you?"

8

As Fath al-Bab went back and forth to school, he saw Ashur everywhere. He made his heart pound, quickened his imagination, set his hopes and passions alight. He saw him in the mosque, the fountain, the animals' trough. He saw him on the path by the old wall that enclosed the monastery garden and in the little square in front of the monastery. Hour after hour Ashur had contemplated those walls, that closed door, the tall mulberry trees, just as he was doing now. The air was still moist with his breath, with the murmurings of his voice. With his desires and dreams. The secret of his whereabouts was hidden in the folds of the unknown, out of reach of the sun's streaming rays. One day he would definitely return. That's what Sahar had said, and she always told the truth. He would wave his rough stick and Samaha with his ugly face would vanish. That would be the end of his black reign of tyranny, his bloody avarice, his hoarded wealth. The harafish would rejoice at the day of salvation and swim in a sea of light. The madman's minaret[4] would come tumbling down and treachery and foolishness would be buried under its rubble for all time.

Or is it really true that he's ignoring us because we let the tyrant get away with it?

He loved his ancestor. He wanted to please him. But where would he get the strength from, when he had been built skinny as a shadow?

9

When Fath al-Bab reached adolescence Sahar began thinking about his future. She consulted Sheikh Mugahid Ibrahim.

"Find him an apprenticeship," he advised.

"He's one of the best pupils at Quran school," she declared proudly.

"Aren't you Madame Firdus' midwife?"

"Yes."

"Talk to her about him. And I'll prepare the ground with Samaha."

10

"Fath al-Bab is a remarkable boy," said Sahar to Firdus. "He's your flesh and blood; and the obvious candidate for a job in his brother's business."

Firdus was quite agreeable and promised to talk to her husband.

---

4. The minaret whose building takes place in the seventh part of this ten-part novel.

11

Samaha examined his stepbrother carefully. "He's made like a girl," he muttered with scorn.

"That's just the way he is. He has a lot of skills."

"Such as?"

"He knows the Quran by heart. He can write and do sums."

He turned to the boy and asked sarcastically, "Are you trustworthy or light-fingered like the rest of our famous family?"

"I fear God and respect my ancestor," declared Fath al-Bab vehemently.

"The one who built the minaret?"

"Ashur al-Nagi!"

Samaha glowered. His face changed.

"He's an innocent child," Sahar said quickly.

"It's your ancestor Ashur who taught us to steal," said Samaha viciously.

Fath al-Bab was surprised and hurt. Scared he would say something detrimental to his chances, Sahar said, "I can guarantee that he's reliable and serious, as God's my witness."

So Fath al-Bab joined the business as assistant storekeeper.

12

Fath al-Bab threw himself into his work. The warehouse occupied a vast basement with as much floor space as the shop itself. Sacks of cereal were piled up on shelves and on the ground, but they were constantly being shifted, the scales were never idle, and he was kept busy registering the movement of goods all day long. He met with his brother at least once every morning to report to him on the purchases and sales. The chief was pleased with his energy and keenness, and saw that he had engaged someone who would unconsciously keep an eye on the storekeeper.

"I encourage hard workers and stamp on idleness," he said in his normal fashion.

13

Following Sahar's advice Fath al-Bab called on Nur, mother of his boss, to pay his respects. Nothing remained of her former beauty, and she gave him a chilly reception, making it plain that she could not forget an affront.

"How's your mother?" she asked him.

"I stopped living with her because her new husband didn't like me, and I haven't seen her since."

"Heartless. That's her only excuse."

He left, privately vowing not to see her again if he could avoid it.

14

Again on Sahar's insistence he visited Firdus. She welcomed him affectionately and he was entranced by her beauty and elegance.

"I've heard nice things about how hard you work," she told him.

But he noticed that she didn't call her children. Perhaps she was reluctant to introduce a simple worker like him as their uncle. This hurt him, but he decided to do his best to forget it. He left, his senses charmed by her. He vowed not to visit her again either.

15

Through hard work he gained confidence and pride. He began to imitate grown men, grew a mustache, and wore a fine headcloth around his skullcap. He became an habitué of the mosque and developed a close bond with Sheikh Sayyid Osman. He spent an hour in the café each evening, drinking cinnamon tea and smoking a water pipe, and never went home without taking a stroll around the monastery square, for he had developed a passion for the dervishes' anthems.

16

A mysterious pain consumed his entrails. His breast overflowed with longing, and burned with a secret fire. The sight of women entranced him, the sound of their voices made his heart tremble. His companions tried to tempt him to become acquainted with the bar, the hashish den, the whorehouses, but the past screamed a warning in his ears. The past burdened with memories of the minaret and the lusts and perversions which had destroyed his family's prestige. As if Sahar could read his thoughts, she said to him one day, "It's time you were married."

He was delighted at the idea; it seemed like the way out he had been searching for.

But before long the horizon grew dark, threatening storms that nobody could have foretold.

17

Strange rumors came from outside the alley. The Nile was not going to flood that year. People wondered what to make of this. Some said one catastrophe would follow another until nothing was left. Was it true? Food would become scarce. Perhaps there would be a famine. It would be prudent to lay in provisions for the future. Those with money followed this advice. The harafish looked on and laughed, refusing to believe that they would be deprived of the morsel of bread which they snatched by the sweat of their brows, or were given in alms.

The air filled with a humming sound and was tinged a repulsive yellow. Specters of anxiety were on the march day and night.

18

The wheel of misfortune raced ahead at full speed. Prices rose by the hour. Black clouds darkened the sky. Food shops only stayed open half the day for lack of supplies. Complaints and lamentations jostled together in the air. There were demonstrations in front of the flour and bean shops. People could no longer talk of anything but food. It was the sole topic of conversation in the bar, the hashish den, the café. Sparks flew and a fire was kindled. Even the notables complained openly but no one believed them, and their plump, pink faces let them down.

"It's an epidemic!" said Anba the bar owner.

Prices went on rising, especially the prices of cereals.

"There's not enough left to feed the birds!" cried Samaha.

However one night Fath al-Bab said to Sahar, "What a liar he is! The warehouse is full. The prices he's asking are just protection money in another form."

"Hold your tongue, son," she implored anxiously.

"He's barbaric. He doesn't know what compassion means."

19

The atmosphere became gloomier, uglier. Prices went crazy. Beans, lentils, tea, and coffee were scarce. Rice and sugar vanished altogether. Bread was hard to find. As nerves grew more frayed, there were signs that people began to stop caring. Thefts mounted. Chickens and rabbits disappeared. At night people were held up and robbed on their doorsteps. The clan went about issuing warnings and threats, calling for good behavior and solidarity, their voices loud and their stomachs full.

Life bared its cruel fangs as the days passed. The specter of starvation loomed large, like the madman's minaret. It was said that people were eating horses, donkeys, dogs and cats, and would soon be eating one another.

20

In that cold, sickly time a strange day blazed briefly like a glimpse of another world. Ihsan, Samaha's daughter, married the timber merchant's son. It was an extravagant and flamboyant celebration such as the alley had never witnessed before, flying in the face of the hard times and the famine. Firdus announced that she would feed the harafish. The hungry flocked to the wedding, and as soon as the trays appeared, balanced on the servants' heads, they attacked like wild beasts. Massed together like so many grains of dust on a windy day, they grabbed at the food, pulling, pushing, snatching from one another, then arguing and fighting until blood flowed mingling with the meat broth. The people were drunk on the chaos and commotion; a wave of them surged to the door of the bar and rolled through it, devouring all the food in their path, drinking greedily straight from the barrels. Then they rushed back into the alley whooping with delight and threw bricks at the ghosts that inhabited their slums and squats.

The whole alley gave itself over to frantic carousing till day-break.

21

The following day the alley was subjected to a revenge attack. Samaha's men were deployed at strategic points, and the chief walked the length of the alley from the archway to the main square. Not one of the harafish escaped without being beaten up and humiliated. Panic spread, people ran for cover, the shops closed, the café, the smoking dens were deserted. That day nobody even went to the mosque to pray.

22

Fath al-Bab sat with Sahar, dejected and sad. "Ashur will never return," he began.

The old woman gave him a sorrowful glance.

"He's still angry with us," he went on.

"This is worse than the plague in Ashur's time," muttered Sahar.

"And they're still singing hymns to joy in the monastery!"

"Perhaps they're prayers, my son."

"Wouldn't it be proper for them to give some of what they've got to ordinary people?"

"You shouldn't criticize them," she said with feeling.

"They've got the mulberries and the kitchen garden stuffed with vegetables."

She held her hand up in a gesture of warning.

He sighed. "It's Samaha who's the devil incarnate," he finished lamely.

23

A pinprick of light pierced the darkness. A murmur of compassion broke the silence. The secret did not go beyond the slums and derelict buildings where the harafish lived. They were intent on preserving it, sensing that their life depended on it. Someone had received a sack of food. "From Ashur al-Nagi," a voice had whispered, then a dim shape had melted away in the darkness. The first time it had been under the archway, then on the path by the monastery wall, then several times in the slums themselves. The harafish talked about it in low voices. They knew instinctively that they were being sought out by a secret benefactor, that the food was intended for them. Bread from heaven. A miracle taking place in the darkness of night. A window opening onto mercy. Ashur al-Nagi or his spirit moving among them. The blank, solid walls of existence bursting apart to reveal the unknown.

The blood coursed through their veins and their hearts beat with new life.

A sack of mercy, accompanied by Ashur al-Nagi's whisper.

24

The joy of newfound happiness loosed their tongues, which danced to the melodies of their wishes and prayers. They repeated Ashur's name until he seemed to acquire a physical presence. They said nothing of the sacks of food, but it was widely rumored that Ashur returned to life under cover of night. Samaha's men ridiculed this fairy story: they were on guard at night and hadn't seen anybody. Samaha summoned Sayyid Osman, the imam of the mosque. "The people have gone mad with hunger," he began.

The sheikh inclined his head.

"Have you heard what they're saying about Ashur's return?" continued Samaha.

The sheikh gave another nod of his head.

"What do you think about it?" demanded Samaha.

"It's not true."

"It's also blasphemy."

"It is indeed," said the sheikh sorrowfully.

"Do your duty then."

So the sheikh addressed the people, warning them against superstition and blasphemy. "If Ashur had really risen from the dead, he would have brought you food," he declared confidently.

25

The darkness was transformed into a magic arena crisscrossed by a network of channels linking souls to one another. The air was drunk with enchanted whisperings. Unknown to the watchmen secret conversations burst into life, intense and passionate.

"Are you Ashur al-Nagi?"

But the whisperings melted back into the night like a lost soul. These whisperings roused the sleeper, confirmed that the warehouses were full, cursed greed—greed, not drought, was mankind's enemy. These whisperings suggested that it was better to take a risk than die of hunger. Pointed out that there was a time when the clan slept and were vulnerable. Asked what could stand in their way, if they all broke out together. Challenged them, demanded how they could hesitate when Ashur al-Nagi was on their side.

The darkness was transformed into a magic arena. The air was drunk with enchanted whisperings. The invisible was full of mysterious powers.

26

There was another force working relentlessly to uncover the secret of the manna from heaven. Samaha came upon a scandal at the heart of his business. Damir al-Husni, the chief's warehouse supervisor, cried out in fear. "I'm innocent, as God's my witness."

"Half the stuff's gone from the warehouse," said Samaha savagely.

"I'm innocent, chief."

"You're guilty until proved innocent."

"Don't destroy a man who's given his life to serve you."

"You're the one who has the keys."

"I hand them into you every evening."

"And I find them in their place every morning and give them back to you!"

"Perhaps someone takes them and puts them back in the meantime."

"Without me knowing?"

"It could be someone who's free to come and go," said Damir desperately.

A cruel light blazed in Samaha's eyes, enough to call the demons from their lairs. His face ugly with malice, he declared, "If you're lying, you're dead. Whoever it is, he'd better start saying his prayers."

27

Fath al-Bab sneaked out from behind the fountain in the pitch-dark and made for the door of the warehouse. Cautiously he turned the key and pushed the door gently open. He closed it behind him and advanced a few paces, guided by the light of memory.

Suddenly the place was flooded with light. Fath al-Bab stopped dead in his tracks. Terrifying, cruel faces emerged in the lamp's glow. Samaha, Damir al-Husni, some of the fiercest of Samaha's men. His eyes collided violently with theirs. The silence impaled them all, whistled in their ears like the hissing of snakes. The air crackled with the heat released as their wild, primitive instincts asserted themselves. His brother's look engulfed him, transfixed him, dismembered him. He felt the poison coursing through his veins, and a sense of absolute defeat and loss. His hopes vanished and he plunged into despair, waiting for his sentence to be pronounced as if it related to someone else.

The words came cold, scornful, bitter. "What brings you here at this time of night?"

There was nothing for it but to confess, be brave, hope for the best. He spoke with unexpected calm. "You already know."

"What are you doing here at this time of night?" repeated Samaha as if he hadn't heard.

"I've come to save people from death," he declared boldly.

"Is this how you repay my kindness?"

"I had to do this."

"So you're Ashur al-Nagi?"

He said nothing.

"You will be hung by your feet from the ceiling, Ashur," declared Samaha spitefully, "and left to die slowly."

28

The whispered words took root in the minds of the harafish and were changed into a destructive force. A flood swept through the alley, such as had never been seen before. The harafish divided into groups and broke into the houses of Samaha's men. It was a little before dawn, the time when everyone was sound asleep. Taken by surprise in their beds, they were overwhelmed and defeated by the sheer numbers of their assailants. Their houses were looted. Their aura of magic was stripped away, leaving behind permanent scars and infirmities. The dawn call to prayers was inaudible through their screaming. The harafish streamed out into the alley, stormed the warehouses, sacking and destroying. Samaha's was their prime target. They left nothing standing, and plundered the contents down to the last grain of cereal. They saw Fath al-Bab hanging from a beam, arms dangling, unconscious or dead. They cut him down and laid him on the ground barely alive. When day broke they had control of the alley. People crowded in the windows and behind the wooden lattices and shouted in fear. At the sound of the commotion the chief's door opened and he appeared in the doorway like a wild bear, gripping his club.

29

All eyes turned toward him. The harafish stood stock-still, resolute, and full of hate, yet keeping silent and waiting expectantly. Here was the terrible beast! But they were drunk with victory and unafraid. However, they hesitated. Perhaps he was waiting for his men to join him, not yet aware of what had happened to them. He'd soon guess, if he hadn't already. He was facing the harafish alone, with only his strength, his club, and his fabled powers to protect him.

"What's the meaning of this?" he shouted, unabashed.

No one answered him. Cries for help floated down from the windows, and tales of looting and pillage.

"What have you done, you sons of whores?" he roared again.

Nobody said a word. They were neither discouraged nor emboldened.

"What've you done, you sons of whores?" he repeated savagely.

Like a stone being thrown into the midst of the silence, a voice cried, "Your grandfather was a whore's son."

There was a roar of laughter and Samaha leapt forward, brandishing his stick.

"Let's see if there's a man among you sniveling lot," he shouted.

Silence descended on them like a lead weight, but nobody retreated. Samaha prepared to attack. At that moment Fath al-Bab appeared, pale and unsteady on his feet. "Throw stones at him," he ordered, leaning on the wall for support.

At once the harafish exploded into life, pelting Samaha with bricks and rubble. The attack halted when the rain began to fall. Blood poured from his wounds, staining his face and clothes. He reeled back, moaning. The stick fell from his hand and he collapsed on his doorstep.

They swooped on his house. Its inhabitants fled over the roofs, while the harafish looted and wrecked until only a heap of ruins remained.

30

Fath al-Bab's role in the battle quickly became well known. A legend was born and he was invited to be clan chief. The young man was ill at ease. He was not deluded by the victory into having a false view of himself. He had never held a club in his life, and his fragile body could not withstand a beating from bare fists. "We'll choose a clan chief," he said to his supporters, "and oblige him to rule like Ashur."

But they were prisoners of their emotions and roared, "You are our chief. Nobody else will do!"

Fath al-Bab found himself chief of the clan without a struggle.

31

Thanks to two men in the clan—Danqal and Hamida—the clan preserved its standing in the alley and in the surrounding neighborhood. Danqal and Hamida, like most of the other members of the clan, were survivors of the previous regime, but Fath al-Bab maintained absolute authority through his personal charm and the power of the harafish who came out in force to support him, intoxicated by the triumph of their rebellion.

During this time Nur died and Firdus and her children took refuge with her family—Radi's branch—having lost most of their riches and gone down the social scale.

32

The people were eager for justice. The harafish were filled with hope and the notables with misgivings. Fath al-Bab was convinced that justice should not have to wait a single day. "We must revive Ashur al-Nagi's ideals," he said to his two aides.

Danqal and Hamida distributed charity, promises, hopes, and the wounds began to heal. Fath al-Bab noticed that they collected protection money and redistributed it in his name, and that the men of the clan still enjoyed their privileges, kept a good part of the money, and lived as heroes and thugs. He was plagued with apprehension. Fearing a gradual return to the old ways, he summoned his men. "What are you doing about justice? What's happened to Ashur al-Nagi's covenant?"

"The situation's changed," said Danqal. "We have to proceed one step at a time."

"Justice can't be postponed," said Fath al-Bab angrily.

"Your men won't be satisfied with living like ordinary people," replied Danqal with a new boldness.

"If we don't begin with ourselves we won't achieve anything," cried Fath al-Bab passionately.

"If we do, the whole clan system will be shaken to its foundations."

"Didn't Ashur live by the sweat of his brow?"

"It's impossible to bring back those days," said Hamida.

"Impossible?"

"One step at a time," said Danqal unenthusiastically.

If he had been a proper clan chief, one word from him would have settled the matter. "What's the point?" he asked himself sadly. "Seeing that I'll never have Ashur's strength."

Had the harafish already forgotten their destructive power?

33

In a moment of angry despair, Fath al-Bab announced to Danqal and Hamida that he was resigning as clan chief. The two men were anxious and asked him to give them some time, promising to fulfill his demands. They went to their friend, Sheikh Mugahid Ibrahim. "Our chief's angry. We don't share the same ideas. What do you think?"

"He wants to revive Ashur al-Nagi's covenant, doesn't he?" said the old man wrathfully.

"That's right."

"Give power to the harafish, oppress the notables, make us the laughingstock of the neighborhood!"

"But he's threatened to give up being chief," said Danqal gloomily.

"Not now!" exclaimed Mugahid Ibrahim. "Let the image of their hopes remain in place until we can be quite sure that they have reverted to their normal state, and completely forgotten their crazy outburst. Give him half of what he's asking for."

"He wants all or nothing," said Hamida crossly.

Mugahid Ibrahim pondered for a moment with a scowl on his face, then declared firmly, "He must remain chief for a while. Use force if necessary."

34

Danqal and Hamida went to find Fath al-Bab in his modest dwelling.

"We've done all we can but we've come up against insurmountable obstacles. The men don't like it. They're threatening to get nasty," Danqal told him.

"But you two are the most powerful members of the clan," muttered Fath al-Bab in amazement.

"There are a lot of them and they're the ones who are against you."

"I'll give up being chief," he said decisively.

"If you do that we can't be answerable for your safety," said Hamida.

"Don't leave the house from now on," continued Danqal. "One step outside will cost you your life."

35

Fath al-Bab realized all too plainly the predicament he was in.

"I'm a prisoner. They've got me surrounded," he complained to Sahar.

"There's nothing you can do. Just keep hoping," sighed the old woman.

"I can't stop fighting for Ashur's beliefs. I'd despise myself forever," he cried in anguish.

"What can you do against their power?"

He paused for a moment, his thoughts confused. "The harafish," he muttered finally.

"They'll kill you if you try and make contact with them."

36

Fath al-Bab remained under house arrest. Nobody knew the reason outside the clan, and people surmised that he must be ill or have decided to withdraw from the world. He was under surveillance day and night. Even Sahar was not allowed out. He knew for certain that his life depended on the enthusiasm of the harafish, and that he would be of no consequence the day their legend died and they lapsed back into ignominy. The clan grew more vigilant: they kept the harafish under constant watch and committed acts of terror and violence.

One day Hamida jumped on Danqal, thrashed him, and reigned supreme as the most powerful member of the clan. When he felt sure that the harafish were docile he proclaimed himself chief.

Fath al-Bab thought his detention would end, since there was no longer any justification for it.

"What's past is past," he said to the new chief. "Let me lead a normal life and earn my living like the rest of the human race."

But Hamida refused. "I don't trust you. Stay where you are, and you can live without having to work for it!"

37

So ended the story of Fath al-Bab and his crusade. A brief burst of sunshine in a long, cloudy day. One morning his shattered body was found at the foot of the minaret. Many wept for him, some rejoiced. People said he was demented with sorrow at having the leadership snatched away from him, and had climbed to the top of his mad ancestor's minaret in the night and, in an act of profanity, thrown himself into the void.

So ended the story of Fath al-Bab and his holy war.

The Arabian Nights and Days[1]
Shahriyar

Following the dawn prayer, with clouds of darkness defying the vigorous thrust of light, the vizier Dandan[2] was called to a meeting with the sultan Shahriyar. Dandan's composure vanished. The heart of a father quaked within him as, putting on his clothes, he mumbled, "Now the outcome will be resolved—your fate, Shahrzad."

He went by the road that led up to the mountain on an old jade, followed by a troop of guards; preceding them was a man bearing a torch, in weather that radiated dew and a gentle chilliness. Three years[3] he had spent between fear and hope, between death and expectation; three years spent in the telling of stories; and, thanks to those stories, Shahrzad's life span had been extended. Yet, like everything, the stories had come to an end, had ended yesterday. So what fate was lying in wait for you, O beloved daughter of mine?

He entered the palace that perched on top of the mountain. The chamberlain led him to a rear balcony that overlooked a vast garden. Shahriyar was sitting in the light shed by a single lamp, bare-headed,[4] his hair luxuriantly black, his eyes gleaming in his long face, his large beard spreading across the top of his chest. Dandan kissed the ground before him, feeling, despite their long association, an inner fear for a man whose history had been filled with harshness, cruelty, and the spilling of innocent blood.

The sultan signaled for the sole lamp to be extinguished. Darkness took over and the specters of the trees giving out a fragrant aroma were cast into semi-obscurity.

"Let there be darkness so that I may observe the effusion of the light," Shahriyar muttered.

Dandan felt a certain optimism.

"May God grant Your Majesty enjoyment of everything that is best in the night and the day."

Silence. Dandan could discern behind his expression neither contentment nor displeasure, until the sultan quietly said, "It is our wish that Shahrzad remain our wife."

Dandan jumped to his feet and bent over the sultan's head, kissing it with a sense of gratitude that brought tears from deep inside him.

"May God support you in your rule forever and ever."

---

1. Translated by Denys Johnson-Davies.
2. In Mahfouz's rendering of *The Arabian Nights,* Dandan is the vizier and the father of Shahrzad in the frame story.
3. "Three years" is the period that Mahfouz assigns to the 1,001 nights of the tales of Shahrzad, during which she manages to abate the brutality of Shahriyar.
4. The Sultan is not wearing his turban, the symbol of power and authority.

"Justice," said the sultan, as though remembering his victims, "possesses disparate methods, among them the sword and among them forgiveness. God has His own wisdom."

"May God direct your steps to His wisdom, Your Majesty."

"Her stories are white magic," he said delightedly. "They open up worlds that invite reflection."

The vizier was suddenly intoxicated with joy.

"She bore me a son and my troubled spirits were put at peace."

"May Your Majesty enjoy happiness both here and in the here-after."

"Happiness!" muttered the sultan sharply.

Dandan felt anxious for some reason. The crowing of the roosters rang out. As though talking to himself, the sultan said, "Existence itself is the most inscrutable thing in existence."

But his tone of perplexity vanished when he exclaimed, "Look. Over there!"

Dandan looked toward the horizon and saw it aglow with hallowed joy.

Shahrzad

Dandan asked permission to see his daughter Shahrzad. A handmaid led him to the rose room with its rose-colored carpet and curtains, and the divans and cushions in shades of red. There he was met by Shahrzad and her sister Dunyazad.

"I am overwhelmed with happiness, thanks be to God, Lord of the Worlds."

Shahrzad sat him down beside her while Dunyazad withdrew to her closet.

"I was saved from a bloody fate by our Lord's mercy," said Shahrzad.

But the man was barely mumbling his thanks as she added bitterly, "May God have mercy on those innocent virgins."

"How wise you are and how courageous!"

"But you know, father," she said in a whisper, "that I am unhappy."

"Be careful, daughter, for thoughts assume concrete forms in palaces and give voice."

"I sacrificed myself," she said sorrowfully, "in order to stem the torrent of blood."

"God has His wisdom," he muttered.

"And the Devil his supporters," she said in a fury.

"He loves you, Shahrzad," he pleaded.

"Arrogance and love do not come together in one heart. He loves himself first and last."

"Love also has its miracles."

"Whenever he approaches me I breathe the smell of blood."

"The sultan is not like the rest of humankind."

"But a crime is a crime. How many virgins has he killed![5] How many pious and God-fearing people has he wiped out! Only hypocrites are left in the kingdom."

"My trust in God has never been shaken," he said sadly.

"As for me, I know that my spiritual station lies in patience, as the great sheikh taught me."

To this Dandan said with a smile, "What an excellent teacher and what an excellent pupil!"

---

5. Before his marriage to Shahrzad, every night the Sultan would marry a new virgin, deflower her, and kill her the following morning.

The Sheikh[6]

Sheikh Abdullah al-Balkhi lived in a simple dwelling in the old quarter. His dreamy gaze was reflected in the hearts of many of his old and more recent students and was deeply engraved in the hearts of his disciples. With him, complete devotion was no more than a prologue, for he was a Sheikh of the Way, having attained a high plane in the spiritual station of love and contentment.

When he had left his place of seclusion for the reception room, Zubeida, his young and only daughter, came to him and said happily, "The city is rejoicing, father."

"Hasn't the doctor Abdul Qadir al-Maheeni arrived yet?" he inquired, not heeding her words.

"Maybe he's on his way, father, but the city is rejoicing because the sultan has consented that Shahrzad should be his wife and he has renounced the shedding of blood."

Nothing dislodges him from his calm, however: the contentment in his heart neither diminishes nor increases. Zubeida is a daughter and a disciple, but she is still at the beginning of the Way. Hearing a knock at the door, she left, saying, "Your friend has come on his usual visit."

The doctor Abdul Qadir al-Maheeni entered. The two of them embraced, then he seated himself on a mattress alongside his friend. As usual the conversation was conducted in the light from a lamp in a small recess.

"You have no doubt heard the good news?" said Abdul Qadir.

"I know what it is my business to know," he said with a smile.

"Voices are lifted in prayer for Shahrzad, showing that it is you who primarily deserve the credit," said the doctor.

"Credit is for the Beloved alone," he said in reproof.

"I too am a believer, yet I follow promises and deductions. Had she not been a pupil of yours as a young girl, Shahrzad would not, despite what you may say, have found stories to divert the sultan from shedding blood."

"My friend, the only trouble with you is that you overdo your submission to the intellect."

"It is the ornament of man."

"It is through intellect that we come to know the limits of the intellect."

"There are believers," said Abdul Qadir, "who are of the opinion that it has no limits."

"I have failed in drawing many to the Way—you at the head of them."

"People are poor creatures, master, and are in need of someone to enlighten them about their lives."

"Many a righteous soul will save a whole people," said the sheikh with confidence.

"Ali al-Salouli is the governor of our quarter—how can the quarter be saved from his corruption?" inquired the doctor, suddenly showing resentment.

"But those who strive are of different ranks," the sheikh said sadly.

"I am a doctor and what is right for the world is what concerns me."

The sheikh patted his hand gently and the doctor smiled and said, "But you are goodness itself and good luck."

"I give thanks to God, for no joy carries me away, no sadness touches me."

---

6. This section is an addition to the original frame story by Mahfouz. In this change he is attributing the success of the woman, Shahrzad, in taming her bloodthirsty husband to a man, her teacher, Abdullah al-Balkhi, a wise sheikh "of the Way"—Sufi mystic philosophy.

"As for me, dear friend, I am sad. Whenever I remember the God-fearing who have been martyred for saying the truth in protest against the shedding of blood and the plundering of property, my sadness increases."

"How strongly are we bound to material things!"

"Noble and God-fearing people have been martyred," bewailed Abdul Qadir. "How sorry I am for you, O my city, which today is controlled solely by hypocrites! Why, master, are only the worst cattle left in the stalls?"[7]

"How numerous are the lovers of vile things!"

Sounds of piping and drumming reached them from the fringes of the quarter and they realized that the people were celebrating the happy news. At this the doctor decided to make his way to the Café of the Emirs.

The Café of the Emirs[8]

The café was centered on the right-hand side of the large commercial street. Square in shape, it had a spacious courtyard, with its entrance opening onto the public way and its windows overlooking neighboring sections of the city. Along its sides were couches for the higher-class customers, while in a circle in the middle were ranged mattresses for the common folk to sit on. A variety of things to drink were served, both hot and cold according to the season; also available were the finest sorts of hashish and electuaries. At night many were the high-class customers to be found there, the likes of Sanaan al-Gamali and his son Fadil, Hamdan Tuneisha and Karam al-Aseel, Sahloul and Ibrahim al-Attar the druggist and his son Hasan, Galil al-Bazzaz the draper, Nur al-Din, and Shamloul the hunchback.

There were also ordinary folk like Ragab the porter and his crony Sindbad, Ugr the barber and his son Aladdin, Ibrahim the water-carrier and Ma'rouf the cobbler. There was general merriment on this happy night, and soon the doctor Abdul Qadir al-Maheeni had joined the group that included Ibrahim al-Attar, Karam al-Aseel the millionaire, and Sahloul the bric-a-brac merchant and furnisher. That night they had recovered from a fear that had held sway over them; every father of a beautiful virgin daughter felt reassured and was promised a sleep free from frightening specters.

"Let us recite the Fatiha over the souls of the victims," several voices rang out.

"Of virgins and God-fearing men."[9]

"Farewell to tears."

"Praise and thanks be to God, Lord of the Worlds."

"And long life to Shahrzad, the pearl of women."

"Thanks to those beautiful stories."

"It is nothing but God's mercy that has descended."

The merriment and conversation continued until the voice of Ragab the porter was heard saying with astonishment, "Are you mad, Sindbad?"

And Ugr, who was keen to put his nose into everything, asked, "What's got into him on this happy night?"

"It seems he's come to hate his work and is tired of the city. He no longer wants to be a porter."

"Does he have ambitions to be in charge of the quarter?"

---

7. A common Egyptian proverb.
8. Mahfouz uses the café as the public space in which much of the democratic interaction between people takes place in many of his works.
9. In Mahfouz's tale, good men as well as virgins are suffering the effects of corruption and tyranny.

"He went to a ship's captain and kept insisting till he agreed to take him on as a servant."

Ibrahim the water-carrier said, "Whoever gives up an assured livelihood on dry land to run away after some vague one on water must be really crazy."

"Water that from earliest times has derived its sustenance from corpses," said Ma'rouf the cobbler.

To which Sindbad said defiantly, "I am fed up with lanes and alleys. I am also fed up with carrying furniture around, with no hope of seeing anything new. Over there is another life: the river joins up with the sea and the sea penetrates deeply into the unknown, and the unknown brings forth islands and mountains, living creatures and angels and devils. It is a magical call that cannot be resisted. I said to myself, 'Try your luck, Sindbad, and throw yourself into the arms of the invisible.'"

Nur al-Din the perfume-seller said, "In movement is a blessing."[1]

"A beautiful salutation from a childhood comrade," said Sindbad.

Ugr the barber demanded sarcastically, "Are you making out that you're upper-class, porter?"

"We sat side by side in the prayer room receiving lessons from our master, Abdullah al-Balkhi," said Nur al-Din.

"And, like many others, I contented myself with learning the rudiments of reading and religion," said Sindbad.

"The dry land will not be lessened by your leaving, nor the sea increased," said Ugr.

At this the doctor Abdul Qadir al-Maheeni said to him, "Go in God's protection, but keep your wits about you—it would be good if you were able to record the wonderful sights you come across, for God has ordered us to do so. When are you departing?"

"Tomorrow morning," he muttered. "I leave you in the care of God the Living, the Eternal."

"How sad it is to part from you, Sindbad," said his comrade Ragab the porter.

Sanaan al-Gamali
I

Time gives a special knock inside and wakes him. He directs his gaze toward a window close to the bed and through it sees the city wrapped around in darkness. Sleep has stripped it of all movement and sound as it nestles in a silence replete with cosmic calm.

Separating himself from Umm Saad's[2] warm body, he stepped onto the floor, where his feet sank into the downy texture of the Persian carpet. He stretched out his arm as he groped for where the candlestick stood and bumped into something solid and hard. Startled, he muttered, "What's this?"

A strange voice issued forth, a voice the like of which he had never heard: the voice of neither a human nor an animal. It robbed him of all sensation—it was as though it were sweeping throughout the whole city. The voice spoke angrily, "You trod on my head, you blind creature!"

He fell to the ground in fear. He was a man without the tiniest atom of valor: he excelled at nothing but buying and selling and bargaining.

"You trod on my head, you ignorant fellow," said the voice.

"Who are you?" he said in a quaking voice.

1. An Egyptian proverb.   2. His wife, literally the mother of their son, Saad.

"I am Qumqam."

"Qumqam?"

"A genie from among the city's dwellers."[3]

Almost vanishing in terror, he was struck speechless.

"You hurt me and you must be punished."

His tongue was incapable of putting up any defense.

"I heard you yesterday, you hypocrite," Qumqam continued, "and you were saying that death is a debt we have to pay, so what are you doing pissing yourself with fear?"

"Have mercy on me!" he finally pleaded. "I am a family man."

"My punishment will descend only on you."

"Not for a single moment did I think of disturbing you."

"What troublesome creatures you are! You don't stop yearning to enslave us in order to achieve your vile objectives. Have you not satisfied your greed by enslaving the weak among you?"

"I swear to you . . ."

"I have no faith in a merchant's oath," he interrupted him.

"I ask mercy and plead pardon from you," he said.

"You would make me do that?"

"Your big heart . . ." he said anxiously.

"Don't try to cheat me as you do your customers."

"Do it for nothing, for the love of God."

"There is no mercy without a price and no pardon without a price."

He glimpsed a sudden ray of hope.

"I'll do as you want," he said fervently.

"Really?"

"With all the strength I possess," he said eagerly.

"Kill Ali al-Salouli," he said with frightening calm.

The joy drowned in an unexpected defeat, like something brought at great risk from across the seas whose worthlessness has become apparent on inspection.

"Ali al-Salouli, the governor of our quarter?" he asked in horror.

"None other."

"But he is a governor and lives in the guarded House of Happiness, while I am nothing but a merchant."

"Then there is no mercy, no pardon," he exclaimed.

"Sir, why don't you kill him yourself?"

"He has brought me under his power with black magic," he said with exasperation, "and he makes use of me in accomplishing purposes that my conscience does not approve of."

"But you are a force surpassing black magic."

"We are nevertheless subject to specific laws. Stop arguing—you must either accept or refuse."

"Have you no other wishes?" said Sanaan urgently. "I have plenty of money, also goods from India and China."

"Don't waste time uselessly, you fool."

---

3. The genies are mentioned in the Qur'an, and therefore the Muslims believe in their existence, and they constitute a significant part of the popular culture. There are, however, bad genies and good ones, and they dwell among the people and are often controlled, through magic, by some of them.

In utter despair, he said, "I'm at your disposal."

"Take care not to attempt to trick me."

"I have resigned myself to my fate."[4]

"You will be in my grasp even if you were to take refuge in the mountains of Qaf at the ends of the world."

At that, Sanaan felt a sharp pain in his arm. He let out a scream that tore at his depths.

II

Sanaan opened his eyes to the voice of Umm Saad saying, "What's made you sleep so late?" She lit the candle and he began to look about him in a daze. If it were a dream, why did it fill him more than wakefulness itself? He was so alive that he was terrified. Nevertheless he entertained thoughts of escape, and feelings of grateful calm took control of him. The world was brought back to its proper perspective after total ruin. How wonderful was the sweetness of life after the torture of hellfire!

"I take refuge in God from the accursed Devil," he sighed.

Umm Saad looked at him as she tucked scattered locks of hair inside the kerchief round her head, sleep having affected the beauty of her face with a sallow hue. Intoxicated with the sensation of having made his escape, he said, "Praise be to God, Who has rescued me from grievous trouble."

"May God protect us, O father of Fadil."

"A terrible dream, Umm Saad."

"God willing, all will be well."

She led the way to the bathroom and lit a small lamp in the recess. Following her, he said, "I spent part of my night with a genie."

"How is that, you being the God-fearing man you are?"

"I shall recount it to Sheikh Abdullah al-Balkhi. Go now in peace that I may make my ablutions."

As he was doing so and washing his left forearm, he stopped, trembling all over.

"O my Lord!"

He began looking aghast at the wound, which was like a bite. It was no illusion that he was seeing, for blood had broken through where the fangs had penetrated the flesh.

"It is not possible."

In terror he hurried off toward the kitchen. As she was lighting the oven, Umm Saad asked, "Have you made your ablutions?"

"Look," he said, stretching out his arm.

"What has bitten you?" the woman gasped.

"I don't know."

Overcome by anxiety, she said, "But you slept so well."

"I don't know what happened."

"Had it happened during the day . . . ."

"It didn't happen during the day," he interrupted her.

They exchanged an uneasy look fraught with suppressed thoughts.

"Tell me about the dream," she said with dread.

"I told you it was a genie," he said dejectedly. "It was a dream, though."

Once again they exchanged glances and the pain of anxiety.

---

4. Fate is a basic concept in Islamic belief. It is normally preordained, and there is no escape from its dictates.

"Let it be a secret," said Umm Saad warily.

He understood the secret of her fears that corresponded to his own, for if mention were made of the genie, he did not know what would happen to his reputation as a merchant on the morrow, nor to what the reputation of his daughter Husniya and his son Fadil would be exposed. The dream could bring about total ruin. Also, he was sure of nothing.

"A dream's a dream," said Umm Saad, "and the secret of the wound is known to God alone."

"This is what one must remind oneself," he said in despair.

"The important thing now is for you to have it treated without delay, so go now to your friend Ibrahim the druggist."

How could he arrive at the truth? He was so burdened with anxiety that he was enraged and boiled with anger. He felt his position going from bad to worse. All his feelings were charged with anger and resentment, while his nature deteriorated as though he were being created anew in a form that was at variance with his old deep-rooted gentleness. No longer could he put up with the woman's glances; he began to hate them, to loathe her very thoughts. He felt a desire to destroy everything that existed. Unable to control himself, he pierced her with a glance filled with hatred and resentment, as though it were she who was responsible for his plight. Turning his back on her, he went off.

"This is not the Sanaan of old," she muttered.

He found Fadil and Husniya in the living room in a dim light that spilled out through the holes of the wooden latticework. Their faces were distraught at the way his excited voice had been raised. His anger increased and, very unlike himself, he shouted, "Get out of my sight!"

He closed the door of his room behind him and began examining his arm. Fadil boldly joined him.

"I trust you are all right, father," he said anxiously.

"Leave me alone," he said gruffly.

"Did a dog bite you?"

"Who said so?"

"My mother."

He appreciated her wisdom in saying this and he agreed, but his mood did not improve.

"It's nothing. I'm fine, but leave me on my own."

"You should go to the druggist."

"I don't need anybody to tell me that," he said with annoyance.

Outside, Fadil said to Husniya, "How changed father is!"

III

For the first time in his life, Sanaan al-Gamali left his house without performing his prayers. He went at once to the shop of Ibrahim the druggist, an old friend and neighbor in the commercial street. When the druggist saw his arm, he said in astonishment, "What sort of dog was this! But then there are so many stray dogs . . ."

He set about making a selection of herbs, saying, "I have a prescription that never fails."

He boiled up the herbs until they deposited a sticky sediment. Having washed the wound with rose water, he covered it with the mixture, spreading it over with a wooden spatula, then bound up the arm with Damascene muslin, muttering, "May it be healed, God willing."

At which, despite himself, Sanaan said, "Or let the Devil do what he may."

Ibrahim the druggist looked quizzically into his friend's flushed face, amazed at how much he had changed.

"Don't allow a trifling wound to affect your gentle nature."

With a melancholy face, Sanaan made off, saying, "Ibrahim, don't trust this world."

How apprehensive he was! It was as though he had been washed in a potion of fiery peppers. The sun was harsh and hot, people's faces were glum.

Fadil had arrived at the shop before him and met him with a beaming smile which only increased his ill humor. He cursed the heat, despite his well-known acceptance of all kinds of weather. He greeted no one and scarcely returned a greeting. He was cheered by neither face nor word. He laughed at no joke and took no warning note at a funeral passing. No comely face brought him pleasure. What had happened? Fadil worked harder in order to intervene as far as possible between his father and the customers. More than one inquired of Fadil in a whisper, "What's up with your father today?"

The young man could only reply, "He's indisposed—may God show you no ill."

IV

It was not long before his condition was made known to the habitués of the Café of the Emirs. He made his way to them with a gloomy countenance and either sat in silence or engaged only in distracted conversation. He no longer made his amusing comments; quickly dispirited, he soon left the café.

"A wild dog bit him," Ibrahim the druggist said.

And Galil the draper commented, "He's utterly lost to us."

While Karam al-Aseel, the man with millions and the face of a monkey, said, "But his business is flourishing."

And the doctor Abdul Qadir al-Maheeni said, "The value of money evaporates when you're ill."

And Ugr the barber, the only one among those sitting on the floor who would sometimes thrust himself into the conversation of the upper-class customers, said philosophically, "What is a man? A bite from a dog or a fly's sting . . ."

But Fadil shouted at him, "My father's fine. It's only that he's indisposed—he'll be all right by daybreak."

But he went deeper and deeper into a state that became difficult to control. Finally, one night he swallowed a crazy amount of dope and left the café full of energy and ready to brave the unknown. Disliking the idea of going home, he went stumbling around in the dark, driven on by crazed fantasies. He hoped for some action that might dispel his rebellious state of tension and relieve it of its torment. He brought to mind women from his family who were long dead and they appeared before him naked and in poses that were sexually suggestive and seductive, and he regretted not having had his way with a single one of them. He passed by the cul-de-sac of Sheikh Abdullah al-Balkhi and for an instant thought of visiting him and confiding to him what had occurred, but he hurried on. In the light of a lamp hanging down from the top of the door of one of the houses he saw a young girl of ten going her way carrying a large metal bowl. He rushed toward her, blocking her way and inquiring, "Where are you going, little girl?"

"I'm going back to my mother," she replied innocently.

He plunged into the darkness till he could see her no more.

"Come here," he said, "and I'll show you something nice."

He picked her up in his arms and the water from the pickles spilt over his silken garment. He took her under the stairway of the elementary school. The girl was puzzled by his strange tenderness and didn't feel at ease with him.

"My mother's waiting," she said nervously.

But he had stirred her curiosity as much as her fears. His age, which reminded her of her father, induced in her a sort of trust, a trust in which an unknown disquiet was mixed with the anticipation of some extraordinary dream. She let out a wailing scream which tore apart his compassionate excitement and sent terrifying phantoms into his murky imagination. He quickly stifled her mouth with the trembling palm of his hand. A sudden return to his senses was like a slap in the face, as he came back to earth.

"Don't cry. Don't be frightened," he whispered entreatingly.

Despair washed over him until it demolished the pillars on which the earth was supported. Out of total devastation he heard the tread of approaching footsteps. Quickly he grasped the thin neck in hands that were alien to him. Like a rapacious beast whose foot has slipped, he tumbled down into an abyss. He realized that he was finished and noticed that a voice was calling, "Baseema . . . Baseema, my girl."

In utter despair he said to himself, "It is inevitable."

It became clear that the footsteps were approaching his hiding-place. The light from a lamp showed up dimly. He was driven by a desire to go out carrying the body with him. Then the presence of something heavy overtook his own collapsing presence, the memory of the dream took him by storm. He heard the voice of two days ago inquiring, "Is this what we pledged ourselves to?"

"You are a fact, then, and not a dire dream," he said in surrender.

"You are without doubt mad."

"I agree, but you are the cause."

"I never asked you to do something evil," the voice said angrily.

"There's no time for arguing. Save me, so that I can carry out for you what was agreed."

"This is what I came for, but you don't understand."

He felt himself traveling in a vacuum in an intensely silent world. Then he again heard the voice. "No one will find a trace of you. Open your eyes and you will find that you are standing in front of the door of your house. Enter in peace. I shall be waiting."

V

With a superhuman effort Sanaan took control of himself. Umm Saad did not feel that his condition had deteriorated. Taking refuge behind his eyelids in the darkness, he set about calling to mind what he had done. He was another person, the killer-violator was another person. His soul had begotten wild beings of which he had no experience. Now, divested of his past and having buried all his hopes, he was presenting himself to the unknown. Though he hadn't slept, no movement escaped him to indicate that he had been without sleep. Early in the morning there came the sound of wailing. Umm Saad disappeared for a while, then returned and said, "O mother of Baseema, may God be with you."

"What's happened?" he asked, lowering his gaze.

"What's got into people, father of Fadil? The girl's been raped and murdered under the elementary school stairway. A mere child, O Lord. Under the skin of certain humans lie savage beasts."

He bowed his head until his beard lay disheveled against his chest.

"I take my refuge in God from the accursed Devil," he muttered.

"These beasts know neither God nor Prophet."

The woman burst into tears.

He began to ask himself: Was it the genie? Was it the dope he had swallowed? Or was it Sanaan al-Gamali?

VI

The thoughts of everyone in the quarter were in turmoil. The crime was the sole subject of conversation. Ibrahim the druggist, as he prepared him more medicine, said, "The wound has not healed, but there is no longer any danger from it." Then, as he bound his arm with muslin, "Have you heard of the crime?"

"I take refuge in God," he said in disgust.

"The criminal's not human. Our sons marry directly they reach puberty."

"He's a madman, there's no doubt of that."

"Or he's one of those vagabonds who haven't got the means to marry. They are milling around the streets like stray dogs."

"Many are saying that."

"What is Ali al-Salouli doing in the seat of government?"

At mention of the name he quaked, remembering the pact he had made, a pact that hung over his head like a sword. "Busy with his own interests," he concurred, "and counting the presents and the bribes."

"The favors he rendered us merchants cannot be denied," said the druggist, "but he should remember that his primary duty is to maintain things as they are for us."

Sanaan went off with the words, "Don't put your trust in the world, Ibrahim."

VII

The governor of the quarter, Ali al-Salouli, knew from his private secretary Buteisha Murgan what was being said about security. He was frightened that the reports would reach the vizier Dandan and that he would pass them on to the sultan, so he called the chief of police, Gamasa al-Bulti, and said to him, "Have you heard what is being said about security during my time in office?"

The chief of police's inner calm had not changed when he had learned about his superior's secrets—and acts of corruption.

"Excuse me, governor," he said, "but I have not been negligent or remiss in sending out spies. However, the villain has left no trace and we haven't found a single witness. I myself have interrogated dozens of vagabonds and beggars, but it's an unfathomable crime, unlike anything that has previously happened."

"What a fool you are! Arrest all the vagabonds and beggars—you're an expert on the effective means of interrogation."[5]

"We haven't the prisons to take them," said Gamasa warily.

"What prisons, fellow? Do you want to impose upon the public treasury the expense of providing them with food?" said the governor in a rage. "Drive them into the open and seek the help of the troops—and bring me the criminal before nightfall."

---

5. A clear euphemism for torture.

VIII

The police swooped down on the plots of wasteland and arrested the beggars and vagabonds, then drove them in groups into the open. No complaint and no oath availed, no exception was made of old men. Force was used against them until they prayed fervently for help to God and to His Prophet and the members of his family.

Sanaan al-Gamali followed the news with anxious alarm: he was the guilty one, of this there was no doubt, and yet he was going about free and at large, being treated with esteem. How was it that he had become the very pivot of all this suffering? And someone unknown was lying in wait for him, someone indifferent to all that had occurred, while he was utterly lost, succumbing without condition. As for the old Sanaan, he had died and been obliterated, nothing being left of him but a confused mind that chewed over memories as though they were delusions.

He became conscious of a clamor sweeping down the commercial street. It was Ali al-Salouli, governor of the quarter, making his way at the head of a squadron of cavalry, reminding people of the governor's power and vigilance, a challenge to any disorder. As he proceeded he replied to the greetings of the merchants to right and left. This was the man he had undertaken to kill. His heart overflowed with fear and loathing. This was the secret of his torment. It was he who had chosen to liberate the genie from his black magic. It was the genie alone who had done this. His escape was conditional on his doing away with al-Salouli. His eyes became fixed on the dark, well-filled face, pointed beard and stocky body. When he passed in front of the shop of Ibrahim the druggist, the owner hurried up to him and they shook hands warmly. Then, passing before Sanaan's shop, he happened to glance toward it and smiled so that Sanaan had no choice but to cross over and shake him by the hand, at which al-Salouli said to him, "We'll be seeing you soon, God willing."

Sanaan al-Gamali returned to the shop, asking himself what he had meant. Why was he inviting him to a meeting? Why? Was he finding the path made easy for him in a way he had not expected? A shudder passed through him from top to toe. In a daze he repeated his words, "I'll be seeing you soon, God willing."

IX

When he lay down to sleep that night the other presence took control and the voice said mockingly, "You eat, drink, and sleep, and it is for me to exercise patience!"

"It's an onerous assignment. Those with such power as yourself do not realize how onerous," he said miserably.

"But it's easier than killing the little girl."

"What a waste! I had long been thought of as among the best of the good."

"External appearances do not deceive me."

"They were not simply external appearances."

"You have forgotten things that would bring sweat to one's brow with shame."

"Perfection is God's alone,"[6] he said in confusion.

"I also don't deny your good points, and it was for this that I nominated you to be saved."[7]

"If you hadn't forced your way into my life, I wouldn't have got myself involved in this crime."

---

6. A well-known Islamic formula.
7. Referring on the one hand to the immediate escape from the situation and on the other to the Sufi concept of salvation through performing good deeds, in this case saving the quarter from the tyranny of its corrupt ruler.

"Don't lie," he said sharply. "You alone are responsible for your crime."

"I don't understand you."

"I really judged you too favorably."

"If only you'd just left me alone!"

"I'm a believing genie and I told myself, 'This man's goodness exceeds his wickedness. Certainly he has suspicious relations with the chief of police and doesn't hesitate to exploit times of inflation, but he is the most honest of merchants, also he is charitable and undertakes his religious devotions and is merciful to the poor.' Thus I chose you to be saved, to be the saving of the quarter from the head of corruption, and the saving of your sinful self. Yet instead of attaining the visible target, your whole structure collapsed and you committed this repugnant crime."

Sanaan moaned and kept silent, while the voice continued, "The chance is still there."

"And the crime?" he asked helplessly.

"Life gives opportunities for both reflection and repentance."

"But the man is an impregnable fortress," he said in a voice clinging to a vestige of hope.

"He will invite you to meet him."

"That seems unlikely."

"He will invite you—be sure and be prepared."

Sanaan thought for a while, then inquired, "Will you promise me deliverance?"

"I chose you only for deliverance."

So exhausted was Sanaan that he fell into a deep sleep.

X

He was getting ready to go to the café when Umm Saad said, "There's a messenger from the governor waiting for you in the reception room."

He found the private secretary, Buteisha Murgan, waiting for him with his sparkling eyes and short beard.

"The governor wants to see you."

His heart beat fast. He realized that he was going off to commit the gravest crime in the history of the quarter. Perhaps it worried him that Buteisha Murgan should be acquainted with the circumstances surrounding his visit, but he took reassurance in Qumqam's promise.

"Wait for me," he said, "till I put on my clothes."

"I shall go ahead of you so as not to attract attention."

So the man was bent on keeping the secret nature of the meeting, thus facilitating his task: He began anointing himself with musk, while Umm Saad watched, nursing a sense of unease that had not left her since the night of the dream. She was held by a feeling that she was living with another man and that the old Sanaan had vanished into darkness. Without her noticing, he slipped into his pocket a dagger with a handle of pure silver that he had received as a gift from India.[8]

---

8. India is associated in the popular imagination with magic and powerful potions, linking the dagger to the genie. This is a clear indication of the scale of torture that took place in the investigation. The reader knows the real perpetrator of the crime, while the narrative tells us of this large number of those innocent who confess under police brutality to a crime they did not commit.

XI

Ali al-Salouli received him in his summer mansion at the governorate's garden, appearing in a flowing white robe and with his head bare, which lessened the awe his position bestowed. A table stood in front of him on which were assembled long-necked bottles, glasses, and various nuts, dried fruits, and sweets, which gave evidence of conviviality. He seated him on a cushion alongside him and asked Buteisha Murgan to stay on.

"Welcome to you, Master Sanaan, true merchant and noble man."

Sanaan mumbled something, hiding his confusion with a smile.

"It is thanks to you, O deputy of the sultan."

Murgan filled three glasses. Sanaan wondered whether Murgan would stay until the end of the meeting. Maybe it was an opportunity that would not be repeated, so what should he do?

"It's a pleasant summer night," said al-Salouli. "Do you like the summer?"

"I love all seasons."

"You are one of those with whom God is content, and it is by His complete contentment that we start a new and productive life."

Impelled by curiosity, Sanaan said, "I ask God to complete His favor to us."

They drank, and became elated and invigorated from the wine.

"We have cleansed our quarter of riffraff for you," al-Salouli continued.

"What firmness and determination!" he said with secret sadness.

"We scarcely hear now of a theft or other crime," said Buteisha Murgan.

"Have you discovered who the culprit is?" asked Sanaan cautiously.

"Those confessing to the crime number over fifty," said al-Salouli, laughing.

Murgan laughed too, but said, "The true culprit is doubtless among them."

"It's Gamasa al-Bulti's problem," said al-Salouli.

"We must also increase the exhortations at the mosques and at religious festivals," said Murgan.

Sanaan was beginning to despair, but then al-Salouli gave a special sign to Murgan, who left the place. Even so, the guards were dispersed throughout the garden and there was no way of escape. But not for an instant was he unmindful of Qumqam's promise.

"Let's close the discussion of crimes and criminals," said al-Salouli, changing his tone of voice.

"May your night be a pleasant one, sir," said Sanaan, smiling.

"The fact is that I invited you for more than one reason."

"I'm at your disposal."

"I would like to marry your daughter," he said confidently.

Sanaan was amazed. He was saddened too about an opportunity that was fated to miscarry before it was born. He nevertheless said, "This is a big honor, the greatest of happiness."

"And I also have a daughter as a gift for your son Fadil."

Chasing away his bewilderment, Sanaan said, "He's a lucky young man."

For a while the other was silent and then continued, "As for the final request, it relates to the public welfare."

There gleamed in Sanaan's eyes an inquiring look, at which the governor said, "The contractor Hamdan Tuneisha is your relative, is he not?"

"Yes, sir."

"The point is that I have made up my mind to construct a road alongside the desert the whole length of the quarter."

"A truly excellent project."

"When will you bring him to me here?" he asked in a meaningful tone.

Feeling how ironic the situation was, he said, "Our appointment will be for to-morrow evening, sir."

Al-Salouli gave him a piercing glance and inquired with a smile, "I wonder whether he will come duly prepared?"

"Just as you envisage," said Sanaan with shrewd subtlety.[9]

Al-Salouli laughed and said jovially, "You're intelligent, Sanaan—and don't for-get that we are related!"

Sanaan suddenly feared he would summon Buteisha Murgan, and he said to him-self, "It's now or the chance will vanish forever."

The man had facilitated things for him without knowing it by relaxing and stretching out his legs and turning over on his back, his eyes closed. Sanaan was im-mersed in thoughts about the crime and hurling himself into what destiny still re-mained to him. Unsheathing the dagger, and aiming it at the heart, he stabbed with a strength drawn from determination, despair, and a final desire to escape. The gover-nor gave a violent shuddering, as though wrestling with some unknown force. His face was convulsed and became crazily glazed. He started to bring his arms together as though to clutch at the dagger, but he was unable to. His terrified eyes uttered un-heard words, then he was forever motionless.

XII

Trembling, Sanaan stared at the dagger, whose blade had disappeared from sight, and at the gushing blood. With difficulty he wrested his eyes away and looked fearfully toward the closed door. The silence was rent by the throbbing in his temples, and for the first time he caught sight of the lamps hanging in the corners. He also noted a wooden lectern decorated with mother-of-pearl on which rested a large copy of the Quran. In all his agonies he pleaded to Qumqam, his genie and his fate. The invisible presence enveloped him and he heard the voice saying with satisfaction, "Well done!" Then, joyfully, "Now Qumqam is freed from the black magic."

"Save me," said Sanaan. "I abhor this place and this scene."

The voice said with sympathetic calm, "My faith prevents me from interfering now that I have taken possession of my free will."

"I don't understand what you're saying," he said in terror.

"Your fault, Sanaan, is that you don't think like a human being."

"O Lord, there is no time for discussion. Do you intend to abandon me to my fate?"

"That is exactly what my duty requires of me."

"How despicable! You have deceived me."

"No, rather I have granted you an opportunity of salvation seldom given to a liv-ing soul."

"Did you not interfere in my life and cause me to kill this man?"

"I was eager to free myself from the evil of black magic, so I chose you because of your faith, despite the way you fluctuated between good and evil. I reckoned you were more worthy than anyone else to save your quarter and yourself."

"But you did not make clear your thoughts to me," he said desperately.

"I made them sufficiently clear for one who thinks."

9. Sanaan is playing along with al-Salouli's expectation of receiving a generous bribe.

"Underhand double-dealing. Who said I was responsible for the quarter?"

"It is a general trust from which no person is free, but it is especially incumbent upon the likes of you, who are not devoid of good intentions."

"Did you not save me from my plight under the stairway of the elementary school?"

"Indeed it was difficult for me to accept that you should, by reason of my intervention, suffer the worst of endings without hope of atonement or repentance, so I decided to give you a new chance."

"And now I have undertaken what I pledged myself to you to do, so it is your duty to save me."

"Then it is a plot and your role in it is that of the instrument, and worthiness, atonement, repentance, and salvation are put an end to."

He went down on his knees and pleaded, "Have mercy on me. Save me."

"Don't waste your sacrifice on the air."

"It's a black outcome."

"He who does good is not troubled by the consequences."

"I don't want to be a hero!" he cried out in terror.

"Be a hero, Sanaan. That is your destiny," said Qumqam sorrowfully.

The voice began to fade as it said, "May God be with you and I ask Him to forgive both you and me."

Sanaan let out a scream that reached the ears of Buteisha Murgan and the men of the guard outside.

⇒ PERSPECTIVES ⇐
The 1001 Nights in the Twentieth Century

For some five hundred years now, the *Tales of the Thousand and One Nights,* known also as *The Arabian Nights,* has served as a storehouse of tales and narrative frames for writers from many literary traditions around the world. An anonymous collection, with many tales about its own origins, the *Thousand and One Nights* has been amended, augmented, appropriated, accommodated, and intertextualized in many traditions of writing. These tales have been retold orally even more often, with the number and nature of the stories constantly shifting, even as the fictional teller's own name takes differing forms: Sheherazade, or Scheherazade, or Shahrazad. The twentieth century was consistent with this legacy of rewriting and retelling, and the authors featured in this section operate very much in the tradition of invoking and/or imbedding tales from the *Thousand and One Nights* into their works. As narratives that deliberately engage previous narratives, these works are more properly metanarratives that trace the genealogy of their own textual histories, as is the case with the Turkish novelist and translator Güneli Gün. Her novel *The Road to Baghdad* grows out of her participation in the writing seminars of the American novelist John Barth and his fiction, which antedates Gün's own. Barth, in fact, figures as a character in Gün's narrative alongside the characters from the *Thousand and One Nights*—while Barth's own story "Dunyazadiad," from his collection *Chimera,* includes Scheherazade and Barth himself as characters. The magical quality of tale-telling that transports teller and listener alike to faraway places had already found its way into such texts as Italo Calvino's *Invisible Cities,* whose distant and exotic cities turn out to be none other than the narrator's home city of Venice. The stories offered here share a special focus on dialogue—the tale as conversation as in Calvino, or tale-telling as collaboration or sisterly complicity as in Barth and Djebar.

The frame tale of the *Thousand and One Nights* has always been especially influential, with its accounts of unbridled passion, deceit, and royal violence and with the infinite narrative resourcefulness of the heroine Scheherazade aided by her sister and accomplice Dunyazad. Sisterhood and female solidarity are binding threads that run through the diverse tales of the *Thousand and One Nights,* and the pervasive concern of twentieth-century literature with issues of gender and sexuality converges in Algerian novelist Assia Djebar's *A Sister to Sheherazade* featured here. Metanarrativity, intertextuality, and framed embeddedness are signature strategies of twentieth-century literature especially. It is inevitable that the *Thousand and One Nights,* whose technical procedures and agglomerated stories have initiated many of these narrative strategies, should take its place so prominently in the century's international literary corpus.

Güneli Gün
b. 1944

Born in Urfa, Turkey, near the headwaters of the Euphrates River, Güneli Gün was educated in the United States at Hollins College in Virginia, the University of Iowa Writers' Workshop, and the Johns Hopkins University Writing Seminars. She lives in Oberlin, Ohio, and has taught creative writing, feminist studies, and translation at the Middle East Technical University in Ankara, Turkey, and at Oberlin College. Her first novel, *Book of Trances,* was published in 1979. Her picaresque, feminist novel *On the Road to Baghdad* (1991) has been translated into Turkish and a number of other languages. It was adapted for the stage and performed at the Sadler's Wells Theatre in London. She has translated a number of Turkish works into English and won the American Literary Translators Association's Outstanding Translation Award for the translation of the Orhan Pamuk's novel *The New Life.*

Gün's narrative is characterized by a vernacular swiftness and a colloquial theatricality. A deliberately mannered, self-conscious simulation of her tale's prototype, the *Thousand and One Nights,* marks her story as postmodern—that is, as a tale that flouts its own artifices and disguises. Thus the Arabesque frames and the tales within tales embedded within the frames blend into the pastiche and interlaced fragmentariness that define postmodernism. The gender-bending, morphing, cross-dressing, transgressive identities that mark Gün's characters give the narrative world of her tales an unreality or surreality. It is this forged constructedness that unmasks her world as fabrication, very much in the manner of Shahrazad and her sister, who know that their very survival depends on their resourcefulness as fabricators and forgers of interminably chain-linked tales. Gün's method makes us fully aware that, like Shahrazad and her sister's survival through protracted make-believe, our reality depends on the efficacy and persuasiveness of our fictions. In this sense, Gün succeeds in translating the fast-talking survivalist ruses of another culture into the hip and quick cultural currency minted for our own era on Hollywood sets, in television studios, and on Madison Avenue.

PRONUNCIATIONS:
   Güneli Gün: GUE-nel-lee GUEN
   Shahrazad: SHAH-rah-ZAHD
   Hürü: WHUE-rue

from The Road to Baghdad

Chapter 17. The False Caliph

LIFE IN THE REALM OF FICTIONS

"Sickness is for the body," Shahrazad said, opening the largest of her black Abbasid trunks, "as madness is for the mind. Art is for the fragile sanity between what decays and what remains."

"Does that go for poetry, too?" Hürü said. "I always thought poetry was just one damn thing after another."

"Tonight," Shahrazad said, ignoring her question, "we must understand the hyperbola of the 'False Caliph.' I'm the False Caliph, you are the False Jafar Barmaki, and Camphor gets to play False Mesrur, the Lord High Executioner. Here are your clothes. These were actually worn by the historical Jafar."

"That's right," Hürü said. "Last time I saw him, he wore this cravat. Did you know that it was Jafar Barmaki who invented the necktie? Seems that as a young man, he was quite a dandy."

"Right," Shahrazad said. "Now we must send word to Shahriyar. He, too, must dress up, as the Real Caliph, disguised as a merchant. His righthand man gets to play the Real Barmaki, disguised as the second merchant. And the Chief Justice of the realm, who happens to be black, is the Real Mesrur, also disguised as a merchant."

"But how are those men to know what you have in mind?"

"Ah, that part is easy," Shahrazad said, eyes sparkling. "'The False Caliph' is an odd bit of fiction everybody knows. They all know it, but they don't get it. That's the trouble with the story, you see. It is a parable whose message has been buried under many layers of traditional Harun-er-Rashid lore. I always thought it was ruined by its ending. Tonight we'll recreate the story's true meaning. I'm going to send Shahriyar word to have his Chief Teller retell him the story of the 'False Caliph.' He'll know what to do then."

"Gosh," Hürü said. "Will Shahriyar be game?" Hürü asked.

"Why not? Seeing mine is the only game in town?"

"Somehow," Hürü mumbled, "I had the impression that Shahriyar was a . . . a crashing bore."

"Oh, he is! Yet he's also quite exciting. You see, he, too, wants to understand something about himself."

"Then, give me the story quick," Hürü said, "so I won't be the only dummy in Baghdad."

"Let's see," Shahrazad said, sitting on the trunk. "'The False Caliph' opens with Harun-er-Rashid suffering one of his nocturnal depressions. He calls in Mesrur, and he has Jafar Barmaki, his wise old Chamberlain, summoned out of his bed. Disguised as three merchants, the trio descends on Baghdad. Night life in the streets takes them to the banks of the River Tigris. There, they see an old man sitting in a rowboat. They ask him to take them for a ride.

"The old boatman refuses flat out. Not safe, going pleasure boating on the Tigris anymore, he tells them; the Caliph has taken to cruising downstream in a splendid barge. Every night. Not only that, he's forbidden all other night traffic. The penalty for disobeying is heavy. The Caliph will have your head. 'Here comes the Caliph's barge now!'

"'Good heavens!' cries the disguised Caliph. 'For two dinars, old man, row us under the arches of the Middle Bridge. Let's take a closer look at his Nocturnal Caliph!'

"Well, two dinars! The old boatman takes a chance. He eases his boat under an arch and covers his passengers under a black tarp. Peeking from under, the real royal company take a good look at the splendid barge. At the stem, a man holds a torch made of red gold feeding the flame with Sumatran aloes. The man wears a short cloak of red satin; over one shoulder runs a ribbon of yellow silk embroidered with silver; the turban on his head is made of the finest muslin. At the stern stands another man, in like dress, holding a similar torch.

"In the middle of the barge, two hundred slaves stand at attention on either side of a raised throne of gold. On the throne is a young man, handsome and elegant, who is clad in the garments of the Abbasid Caliphs: black stuff embroidered with gold. In front of him stands a grand personage who seems none other than Grand Vizier Jafar. Behind him looms a black eunuch with a naked sword in hand, no doubt the person of Lord Mesrur.

"The bright pleasure barge with its extravagant lights cruises by. The real Caliph, hidden among the shadows and the black shapes of masonry, watches his double go on his way, enthroned in a blaze of light. Harun is amazed, but being who he is, and so sure of himself, he's not even angry at the young man who apes him. In fact he is immensely excited by the sight of his double.

"'Did you see what I saw?' Harun cries. 'There went the living image of the Caliph! You, Jafar, seemed to stand in front of him. And you, Mesrur, behind.'

"Intrigued, the trio go to watch their doubles again the next night. Harun is no longer bored. This time, they follow the False Caliph to a stately house where a banquet is in progress. They manage to slip in so easily, you wonder if they weren't expected, if this isn't a trap to catch the Real Caliph.

"The trio is given food and drink, but they keep their eyes on the pretentious young man. Presently, under the influence of songs about unrequited love, the False Caliph gets up to rend his clothes to bits. He faints, four times over. On his milk-white skin are deep scars. Somebody's beaten the hell out of the False Caliph.

"Who? And why? The True Caliph must know. The False Caliph tells all. Turns out the False Caliph has been wooed and wed by a lady who wears the family jewels, if you know what I mean. This lady happens to be Jafar Barmaki's half-sister, and she's wildly jealous. During her frequent business trips out of Baghdad, she wants her young husband to stay put in the house. Or else! Being the handsome, elegant young man he is, the False Caliph has attracted the attention of Lady Zubaida, the Caliph's formidable wife. He's been unable to refuse Lady Zubaida's invitation to a party at her private quarters. But, on his return, his wife finds out he's been stepping out. Furious, she has him beaten to within an inch of his life and throws him out on his elegant ear.

"But the False Caliph confesses he's still crazy about his wife. Not only that, he implies he's guessed the real identities of the merchant trio. He says he puts on the dog every night just to impress the people of Baghdad, thereby drawing the Real Caliph into his own story. His object, so he says, is none other than begging Harun-er-Rashid's help. Will the Real Caliph make his wife take him back?

"Well, Harun doesn't resist the course of True Love. He makes the disagreeable Barmaki woman take her pussy of a husband back. You wonder why, don't you? What a let-down! Such an extravagant beginning and a shabby little end.

"That's what we will explore, Hürü girl. Why must Shahrazad put her signature on a seamy little domestic drama? We will wear the Abbasid black and go down the Tigris in splendor tonight!"

"Why?" Hürü said.

"Why, oh, why!" Shahrazad cried impatiently. "Because Shahrazad always wanted to wear the pants and masquerade as the Caliph. That's why! Does that satisfy you?"

"Plenty," Hürü said. "So hand me Jafar's trousers. I'll wear them."

"And tie on this long white beard," Shahrazad said. "The Chamberlain who plays the Real Jafar wears the real thing. A trim white beard. He's my good old Dad."

"Your Dad!" Hürü cried. "Your Dad runs around Baghdad putting on shows? Wow! What a family!"

"Thanks to me!" Shahrazad said. "Without me, they'd all try being consistently themselves all the time. Rigid as hell. What's the fun in being tied down to a single persona?"

"Some of us would like to construct one," Hürü said. "Some of us don't even have a reliable persona yet. Me, for example."

"That's what I like about you," Shahrazad said. "You're still somewhat unpredictable. My husband, too. Just as you think you have him figured out, he says something surprising. Or he'll go do some damn thing."

Baghdad nights were still enchanting. And fraught with danger. Cruising down the Tigris in a blaze of lights wasn't half bad either. On a borrowed barge. And a cast of out-of-work actors. Not only did Hürü get to see Shahriyar, she saw the deep scars that marred Shahrazad's strong back. And she wondered. How could these two be so civilized and yet . . . And what about Shahrazad's Dad? This slim and elegant old man who so reminded Hürü of her own father. Why did he go along with these shenanigans?

Shahriyar looked mild. Tall and red-bearded, not your hooknosed swarthy Arab at all. His skin was tenderly white and his fingers long, cool and clean; he said little and what he said was not idle. He paid Hürü no attention . . . as if his wife's new student didn't exist, or if she did, she didn't matter. He intimidated Hürü, who liked to think of herself as an intrepid person. Perhaps because she knew at once that she bored Shahriyar. He wasn't the image of kindness either, the way he walked—like a big cat, a panther perhaps, with something sinister lurking in his feline strength. He played panther to Shahrazad's wolf. Cat and dog. Hürü liked Shahrazad instinctively, despite the bad press the wolf gets.

Who knows what Big Shahriyar learned from the theatrics. He seemed to have a good time though, almost as good a time as did Big Camphor, who played the black executioner as if she'd known Mesrur personally. When Shahriyar left—after filling his face with the food Camphor had prepared—he was still in character.

"Hah!" cried Shahrazad, trim and vigorous in her skinny black trousers, flowing black silk shirt and black leather boots. "I'm Shahrazad the Termagant,[1] a vociferous and turbulent Arabess whose words are noxious as her farts! No wonder! In poisonous air like that, even a palace is too narrow a house for *two* Would-be Caliphs! Perhaps, now that I've renounced my false bid for the Caliphacy, Shahriyar can get on with the business of becoming the Real Caliph."

"Oh, pooh!" Hürü said.

Before she could say more, a loud knocking at the door stopped Hürü. On the doorstep towered an extremely tall woman, heavily veiled and cloaked. In her hand was a heavy braided leather crop. Obviously she'd been riding some poor horse.

"Welcome home, my Beauty," the False Caliph said, advancing, arms open. The haughty dame swished the riding crop with a dangerous snaky motion. But, familiar as you please, up the stairs she went to the master bedroom. The feline way the strange woman walked, gracefully muscular, reminded Hürü of someone else. Oh, my God! Must be Shahriyar himself, in drag! Playing this time Jafar Barmaki's sadistic sister.

No wonder the cries that emanated from the master bedroom kept Hürü up all night. A couple of animals, she thought. Tearing each other apart.

"I, too, was born in a famous city," Shahrazad said as she breakfasted. "And I, too, was born to a big beautiful woman! Safiye, the big blond Amazon who repeats herself in my family every third generation. Next, Safiye will be born to one of my daughters."

"Oh," Hürü said, "wish I could've seen her! But I must be out of sync with her incarnations."

"Safiye was so successful," Shahrazad said, "she didn't need to stand in her daughters' way, Dunyazad's and mine. But Mom died young. Dad was addicted to books, to the liberal arts, to intelligent company. He loved showing me off. I was a child prodigy. Since Dunyazad wasn't born until I turned nine, I had all the time in the world to imagine the world.

"Soon I outstripped my tutors. I had to dress up as a lad and go down to the city Seminary. I loved college, you know, being one of those lucky kids who bypass the boredom of secondary school. By the time I turned sixteen, believe me, I was the most educated person in all of Baghdad.

"But I'd lost my woman's place, without truly gaining the world of men. For example, who would I marry? Aside from a certain professor of logic, a man in his late sixties, no man pleased me halfway. Besides, who'd marry a girl who was such a royal pain in the ass?

---

1. Furious creature in Christian morality plays and farces; thought to be a Muslim deity.

"No matter. I'd stay a maiden. And become a loving aunt. Dunyazad, that plump darling, had no inclination for anything besides her own sensuous body. Even as a baby, she sat with one hand always toying with the little wedge between her legs. She'd suckle Mom's nipples as if she intended to consume that beautiful lady in her infantile passion. In the schoolroom, Dunyazad only used the feather end of the quill, dreaming hotly, quim wet, lips half open, gasping shamelessly as she came. Bless her voluptuousness, that one had no use for the quill's point.

"I met Shahriyar at the Seminary. He was doing post-graduate work. So was I, still passing myself off as a young man. He challenged me to a verbal duel. Well, I beat the pants off the Crown Prince. He took it like a sport, and soon we became fast friends. But I always evaded physical contest with him, turning his boisterous challenges to jokes. I teased him for pissing farther, for the size of his mantool, for his crapulous nights in the company of whores.

"'A Sissy is what you are!' Shahriyar teased back. 'Your balls have retracted into your head!'

"He was pleased, though. His physical prowess proved an equalizer. One day we were watching some wrestlers in the field. Shahriyar suddenly seized me by the nape, threw me down and locked me in some fancy hold. Not knowing what to do, I tried twisting away. Well, he managed to tear away the front of my suit. As he pinned down my shoulders, he saw my two naked breasts. There could be no moment more inflaming! and we didn't put off the urge either. Right then and there we went at it, wrestlers gaping at us and all. And most tiptoed away, not wanting to embarrass the Crown Prince. But who was embarrassed? We made love until the cows came home. And you know the cows don't come home by themselves. Oh, there was war in our embrace. All night and most of the next morning, too.

"'I wondered,' Shahriyar confessed, finally sitting up, 'if I was turning queer or what . . . the way I felt about you. This sure takes a load off my mind. My balls, too!'

"'We could get married,' I suggested.

"'Why not?' says Shahriyar. 'I always wanted a girl who'd do my reading and writing.'

"What does a woman do when in doubt? She marries. Now that the truth was out, I couldn't even land a job teaching at the Seminary. So why not get married? Landing a job as the Queen wasn't all that bad, either. But marriage wasn't as much fun. Shahriyar didn't much like it, either.

"'A big mistake,' he said, 'marrying a girl who would be king.'

"Was it just me? Or were men and women basically incompatible? I still don't know the answer. When I asked Shahriyar for a parallel existence, I hadn't written anything more inventive than a shopping list. Or more exciting than a term paper. Fear of the unknown beset me.

"'You're leaving,' Shahriyar said sadly. 'Clearing out for good.'

"'I've done some terrible things.'

"'Don't tell me,' he said, placing his forefinger on my lips.

"'You feel sorrow for me,' I said. 'Is that right?'

"'Maybe,' he said. 'But perhaps it's something else. For example, love.'

"And I moved in here. The walls of this hall were lined with my library, the boys settled in boarding school, Camphor retained. Then a huge silence fell over the house. A mute presence inhabited it which was as pervasive and obdurate as Camphor. Giving life to a suspended house didn't quite take my own life out of suspension. I had a good cry. I had two good cries. And I enjoyed both tremendously.

"I was free at last to do as I liked. But what did I really like? Mohammed pre-scribed spinning to women. 'Sitting for an hour employed with the distaff is better for women,' Mohammed said, 'than a year's worship. For every piece of cloth woven of the thread they've spun, women shall receive in Paradise the reward of martyrs.' Nice, eh? But I hadn't had a proper girlhood. I could only spin with words. And my only distaff was the intellect. But what words should I spin? And in what order?

"Somewhere under my hand must be a full storehouse of words—if only I had the serenity to apprehend the treasury. 'Open Sesame' might enrich Ali Baba, but for me the key word didn't crack open a sesame bun. I was sitting in the library, and thinking that I needed a *jinn* or a *jann*—some supernatural power like in the old tale about Aladdin's Lamp.

"'Jann Baath!'"[2] I cried passionately. 'Where the hell are you when you're really needed?'

"No sooner were the words out of my mouth than a creature materialized right out of that bookshelf there. The one devoted to the fables of the ancients. The out-landish creature gained substance right under my eyes. Not only did he look like a real man, he was the spitting image of Shahriyar. Just dressed oddly in a skimpy shirt and even skimpier trousers which showed most of his well-muscled legs, and tan as a sailor, too. Something free and easy about this creature who stood before me. And why not? I had called for the Spirit Reawakened after, Jann Baath.

"'You called?' he said, pleased as a cat who got away with something good. 'Can I really believe my eyes? You are Shahrazad, aren't you? I was on my boat talking to a friend. I had just said, "Even Shahrazad has run out of tales . . ." when you called me by my name. And here I am, at your service.'

"'Jann Baath? That your name?' I said. 'So you're a *jann*. And are you quite sure that you're not a *jinni?*

"'I'm no *jinni*—unless, of course, you consider that our English word for *genius* comes from your Arabic word, *jinn*.'

"'So you admit to being a genius?' I said. 'I'll be damned!' He blushed, high ve-locity and deep crimson. I liked him right off.

"He seemed to be under the impression that we spoke English. I'd never even heard of this language. His tongue was translated into Arabic as his person was trans-lated to Baghdad. But I believed him when he said he came from the Antipodes. As I said, he could have been Shahriyar's twin, but he was also, in some essential way, dif-ferent. Light skinned like my husband but more rosy, as are people who eat too much beef, the translated man's tonsure was smoother than a honeydew melon settled into a soft crescent of wispy red-gold hair. Over his shy smile grew a thatch of manly bris-tle. I like modesty in men, especially in one so tall and, obviously, devilishly clever. We fell to exchanging stories. He said he too was a writer of fictions, like me. Pray tell, what fictions did I write?

"'Your *Thousand and One Nights*,' he said. 'Your work, although not read as much in the particular future I come from, has never been off my desk.'

"'That's nice, dear Jann,' I said. 'But what are the thousand and one nights?'

"'*Alf Laylah Wa Laylah*,' he insisted.

---

2. Transcription of the pronunciation of John Barth's name into a comic pseudo-Oriental form. Güneli Gün was a student of Barth's at the Johns Hopkins University Writing Seminars.

"This Jann Baath really held forth. Turns out he was professorial as they come. He praised, invoked, recited; he apostrophised, philosophized, rhapsodized; he harangued me 'til I finally understood I was meant to write an opus that would survive for all time. Not only that, I already knew all the stories I was to pen. The material existed in the popular domain. I was shocked. How vulgar! Me, Shahrazad? Put over a bunch of tales told to children and dim-witted adults? Never! Hardly a story existed in the bag, I told him, that one might repeat in good company!

"On and on, I scolded the genius. I had one of the best minds of the age, I said; I wasn't about to waste my intellect on a mishmash of tales that evolved among illiterate peasants from the land of the Maghrabis all the way to China. Misapprehended, annexed from one culture to another, the tales were so punky that not even a desert Bedouin could stand the stuff. No psychological verisimilitude, no philosophical grounding, no fresh insights about the way we live now, the stories were empty shells. Besides, they were so often such bad replicas of each other that reading all the tales was like sitting in the barber's chair and having all one's teeth extracted. I congratulated Jann Baath on his patience and generosity. Turns out, however, that the structure of the tales was what intrigued this genie. 'Oriental,' he said, naming the structure. 'Patterns within patterns.'

"'I don't know from Oriental,' I said. 'Oriental as opposed to what? But tell me, what glue holds the patterns together?'

"'Your own life, of course,' Jann Baath said. 'The ultimate ransom: your own life, dear girl.'

"Was I amazed! Couldn't Jann Baath see I was a woman practically his own age, with a tribe of children of my own, and a disastrous marriage behind me? Perhaps he was only perceiving the Shahrazad in his own mind's eye. He lectured the student-princess in his imagination. So touching. So wonderful. I wanted to know more.

"Apparently, this Shahriyar in the story enjoyed a new Moslem virgin every night. And he had her destroyed in the morning. Women being the faithless sows Shahriyar thought they were, he didn't want them putting the horns on him. The carnage of virgins went on until, one night, Shahrazad arrived on her verbal charger.

"At the peril of her own life, Shahrazad told the misogynist king stories every night, but didn't divulge the ending. To hear the end, she had to be spared for another night when, just as she was through telling, she began a new story and stopped again at daybreak just before the climax. The king had to tune in the next night, that is, if he were to get his jollies. So Shahrazad went on for a thousand and one nights, staying her own execution, making babies and gaining time both for herself and for Shahriyar. Shahriyar, too, needed time to get himself domesticated into a loving husband. Not bad! Not bad, at all!

"'So,' I said lightly, 'I get revenge on Shahriyar, after all!'

"'Your motive isn't revenge,' said Jann Baath. 'Don't you see? Although writers often avenge themselves on the villains of their real lives, your motive is to *redeem* Shahriyar. You woo him away from his misogyny, bless your gentle heart. You save him from having to live out his life as the caricature of an Oriental potentate.'

"'And how did I get such a gentle heart?' I said, though my heart wished that I were suddenly granted a heavenly commodity of goodwill.

"'Ah, by writing *as if* you already have a gentle heart!' exclaimed the Jann, his bright eyes twinkling goodnaturedly. 'And, thereby, creating an audience of gentle hearts. That's the magic of art. If art cannot redeem the barbarities of history or spare us the horrors of living and dying, at least it sustains, refreshes, expands, ennobles, and enriches our spirits along the way.'

"'As if,' I said.

"'As if,' repeated Jann Baath.

"And, with that, the said Jann disappeared into the same shelves from which he'd appeared. Did I really see him? Or was he a projection of my mind? Did I invent him as the Good Shahriyar? Shahriyar as I'd like him to be? Or was he supernatural? Maybe he was a real *jann* who provided me with an idea. I don't know. And, ultimately, it doesn't matter.

"Maybe, I thought to myself, just maybe I can produce a work that's out of this world. If I could only reopen our verbal treasurehouse for the cynical and brutalized citizens of Baghdad, I could perhaps alchemize their souls again. Yes, I'd spring the Flying Horses from the storehouse, the Enchanted Princesses, the Love-struck Princes faithful even in adversity. I'd remind the reader of hardboiled merchants who still could navigate wondrous worlds beneath their daily lives. Maybe I, too, could recreate a race of ennobled Arabs.

"After all, the written charm is known to be more potent than the spoken one. Some feel that writing is magic that heals, fixes and protects. Self-knowledge unlocks man's better nature, especially the nature of those occupied with power and responsibility. Of course, I have Shahriyar in mind. My husband, my patron and, of course, my Caliph. I'm crafting this book for his eyes, though he says he cares little for escapist literature and will not read it. Do you realize how much it will cost to reproduce a book this size? I can't even afford publication. So, why do I keep writing?"

"I'll bet," Hürü interrupted, "Abd-es-Samad has something to do with your compulsion. Last time I saw him, he was dying to get hold of your book. I think that old fart has put the hex on you."

"The hell with magicians!" Shahrazad cried. "I don't care who exploits the book. All I want is to write it well. No, Abd-es-Samad is nothing to me."

"You don't know this Abd-es-Samad," Hürü said. "He pinches everything."

"Then he's welcome to everything!" Shahrazad shouted. "After all, who am I? Someone who's never travelled outside Baghdad. An obscure writer. I couldn't even keep house at a mediocre palace where I alternately played the bitter queen, the inept mother and, most lamentably, the failed thinker.

"I am also the thousand-and-one persons I have hallucinated. I am Sinbad the Sailor. Yes, my mind has travelled to that splendid showplace of death called the City of Brass. I've seen kingdoms under the sea, kept company with vagrants, outcasts, criminals and rogues in contexts both dirty and clean, abandoned myself to a hundred love-deaths in Baghdad, to a hundred-and-one infidelities in Cairo. I've put demons and warlocks under control, been flown on *jinn* to China and back. I've been transformed into birds, beasts, into saints, Jews, Christians, into wags, ghouls, merchants both prudent and imprudent, into wastrels, hunchbacks, imps, into enchantresses with menageries of lovers, into kings whose reigns are golden.

"But what's my mettle? My substance? That is precisely what I want to know. I long to exhaust all the shapes of my being. As each tale falls away from me, so does another guise, another need, another dream. Someday the shell called Shahrazad will be so empty, I will see the face of God."

Shahrazad fell silent.

"Wow!" Hürü cried. "Is that how it's done? Can you really see the Face by exhausting all faces?"

━━◆━━

John Barth
b. 1930

Maryland-born John Barth is one of America's best-known postmodern novelists and short-story writers. In his many novels, short stories, and critical essays, Barth has explored postmodernist modes of narration both theoretically and practically. Almost all of his works are intensely self-referential, commenting on their own structure and motifs as they evolve, and often feature frame narratives and characters who are themselves writers or storytellers and discourse at length about their craft. While so much reflection on storytelling might well bog down the telling of the story itself, Barth takes care to integrate it into an energetically evolving plot and is always ready to crack a joke at his own expense. In his retelling of the *Thousand and One Nights,* Scheherazade is able to tell so many stories not because of her extraordinary narrative imagination but because a bald, middle-aged, and bespectacled genie from the future appears at the right moment and retells them to her from the book of the *Thousand and One Nights* that he has already read. This genie is clearly John Barth himself, who thereby becomes one crucial link in the seamless transmission of stories from the past to the future and back.

The reworking of already existing literary materials is one of the hallmarks of Barth's fiction. In his usual comic and bawdy manner, he not only retells the *Thousand and One Nights* but also takes on Greek myths, which serve as the basis for the other stories in *Chimera,* the 1972 collection that includes "Dunyazadiad"—a Greek-style coinage that means "The Tale of Dunyazad," as Barth upends the classic tale by telling it from the perspective of Scheherazade's younger sister. Barth's elaborate reworkings of earlier texts also refer to the enigmatic short stories of Argentinean writer Jorge Luis Borges, and, increasingly, to his own earlier fiction. Barth's 1994 novel *Once Upon a Time: A Floating Opera,* for example, echoes the title of his very first novel, *The Floating Opera* from 1956, and features a character named John Barth whose final work, the text indicates, the readers are holding in their hands.

Barth doubles his texts back upon themselves not only in the way in which they refer to earlier sources, but also through the motif of the university, with its departments of creative writing and literary studies; many of his characters are thoroughly familiar with literary critical vocabulary and don't hesitate to comment on their own lives and relationships in those terms, thereby ultimately collapsing the distinction between fiction and reality. No doubt Barth's own career is obliquely reflected in these characters: After giving up his studies at the Juilliard School and his plan to become a jazz arranger, he completed college and a master's degree (1952) at Johns Hopkins University, then went on to teach at Pennsylvania State University and the State University of New York at Buffalo. In 1973 he finally returned to Johns Hopkins, where he remained until his retirement in 1990. Just as such elements of his biography make their way into his fiction, in Barth's view reality is made up of the stories that we tell; among the wide variety of materials he has worked with, this is one of the most insistently recurring motifs of his fiction.

Dunyazadiad

1

"At this point I interrupted my sister as usual to say, 'You have a way with words, Scheherazade. This is the thousandth night I've sat at the foot of your bed while you and the King made love and you told him stories, and the one in progress holds me like a genie's gaze. I wouldn't dream of breaking in like this, just before the end, except that I hear the first rooster crowing in the east, et cetera, and the King really ought to sleep a bit before daybreak. I wish I had your talent.'

"And as usual Sherry replied, 'You're the ideal audience, Dunyazade. But this is nothing; wait till you hear the ending, tomorrow night! Always assuming this auspicious King doesn't kill me before breakfast, as he's been going to do these thirty-three and a third months.'

"'Hmp,' said Shahryar. 'Don't take your critics for granted; I may get around to it yet. But I agree with your little sister that this is a good one you've got going, with its impostures that become authentic, its ups and downs and flights to other worlds. I don't know how in the world you dream them up.'

"'Artists have their tricks,' Sherry replied. We three said good night then, six goodnights in all. In the morning your brother went off to court, enchanted by Sherry's story. Daddy came to the palace for the thousandth time with a shroud under his arm, expecting to be told to cut his daughter's head off; in most other respects he's as good a vizier[1] as he ever was, but three years of suspense have driven him crackers in this one particular—and turned his hair white, I might add, and made him a widower. Sherry and I, after the first fifty nights or so, were simply relieved when Shahryar would hmp and say, 'By Allah, I won't kill her till I've heard the end of her story'; but it still took Daddy by surprise every morning. He groveled gratitude per usual; the King per usual spent the day in his durbar,[2] bidding and forbidding between man and man, as the saying goes; I climbed in with Sherry as soon as he was gone, and per usual we spent *our* day sleeping in and making love. When we'd had enough of each other's tongues and fingers, we called in the eunuchs, maidservants, mamelukes,[3] pet dogs and monkeys; then we finished off with Sherry's Bag of Tricks: little weighted balls from Baghdad, dildoes from the Ebony Isles and the City of Brass, et cetera. Not to break a certain vow of mine, I made do with a roc-down[4] tickler from Bassorah, but Sherry touched all the bases. Her favorite story is about some pig of an ifrit[5] who steals a girl away on her wedding night, puts her in a treasure-casket locked with seven steel padlocks, puts the casket in a crystal coffer, and puts the coffer on the bottom of the ocean, so that nobody except himself can have her. But whenever he brings the whole rig ashore, unlocks the locks with seven keys, and takes her out and rapes her, he falls asleep afterward on her lap; she slips out from under and cuckolds him with every man who passes by, taking their seal rings as proof; at the end of the story she has five hundred seventy-two seal rings, and the stupid ifrit still thinks he *possesses* her! In the same way, Sherry put a hundred horns a day on your brother's head: that's about a hundred thousand horns by now. And every day she saved till last the Treasure Key, which is what her story starts and ends with.

"Three and a third years ago, when King Shahryar was raping a virgin every night and killing her in the morning, and the people were praying that Allah would dump the whole dynasty, and so many parents had fled the country with their daughters that in all the Islands of India and China there was hardly a young girl fit to fuck, my sister was an undergraduate arts-and-sciences major at Banu Sasan University. Besides being Homecoming Queen, valedictorian-elect, and a four-letter varsity ath-

---

1. A high official, governor, or first minister in some Muslim countries, especially the Ottoman Empire.
2. Royal court.
3. Military slaves of non-Arab origin.

4. A roc is a mythical bird.
5. In Islamic mythology, an evil spirit, usually very strong and devious.

lete, she had a private library of a thousand volumes and the highest average in the history of the campus. Every graduate department in the East was after her with fellowships—but she was so appalled at the state of the nation that she dropped out of school in her last semester to do full-time research on a way to stop Shahryar from killing all our sisters and wrecking the country.

"Political science, which she looked at first, got her nowhere. Shahryar's power was absolute, and by sparing the daughters of his army officers and chief ministers (like our own father) and picking his victims mainly from the families of liberal intellectuals and other minorities, he kept the military and the cabinet loyal enough to rule out a coup d'état. Revolution seemed out of the question, because his woman-hating, spectacular as it was, was reinforced more or less by all our traditions and institutions, and as long as the girls he was murdering were generally upper-caste, there was no popular base for guerrilla war. Finally, since he could count on your help from Samarkand,[6] invasion from outside or plain assassination were bad bets too: Sherry figured your retaliation would be worse than Shahryar's virgin-a-night policy.

"So we gave up poly sci (I fetched her books and sharpened her quills and made tea and alphabetized her index cards) and tried psychology—another blind alley. Once she'd noted that *your* reaction to being cuckolded by your wife was homicidal rage followed by despair and abandonment of your kingdom, and that Shahryar's was the reverse; and established that *that* was owing to the difference in your ages and the order of revelations; and decided that whatever pathology was involved was a function of the culture and your position as absolute monarchs rather than particular hang-ups in your psyches, et cetera—what was there to say?

"She grew daily more desperate; the body-count of deflowered and decapitated Moslem girls was past nine hundred, and Daddy was just about out of candidates. Sherry didn't especially care about herself, you understand—wouldn't have even if she hadn't guessed that the King was sparing her out of respect for his vizier and her own accomplishments. But beyond the general awfulness of the situation, she was particularly concerned for my sake. From the day I was born, when Sherry was about nine, she treasured me as if I were hers; I might as well not have had parents; she and I ate from the same plate, slept in the same bed; no one could separate us; I'll bet we weren't apart for an hour in the first dozen years of my life. But I never had her good looks or her way with the world—and I was the youngest in the family besides. My breasts were growing; already I'd begun to menstruate: any day Daddy might have to sacrifice me to save Sherry.

"So when nothing else worked, as a last resort she turned to her first love, unlikely as it seemed, mythology and folklore, and studied all the riddle/puzzle/secret motifs she could dig up. 'We need a miracle, Doony,' she said (I was braiding her hair and massaging her neck as she went through her notes for the thousandth time), 'and the only genies *I've* ever met were in stories, not in Moormans'-rings and Jews'-lamps. It's in words that the magic is—Abracadabra, Open Sesame, and the rest—but the magic words in one story aren't magical in the next. The real magic is to understand which words work, and when, and for what; the trick is to learn the trick.'

"This last, as our frantic research went on, became her motto, even her obsession. As she neared the end of her supply of lore, and Shahryar his supply of virgins, she

---

6. The city of Samarkand lies in what is today southern Uzbekistan. It was conquered by the Arabs in the 8th century C.E. and flourished under their rule. It became famous as the capital of the Mongol Empire from the 14th to the 17th centuries.

became more and more certain that her principle was correct, and desperate that in the whole world's stock of stories there was none that confirmed it, or showed us how to use it to solve the problem. 'I've read a thousand tales about treasures that nobody can find the key to,' she told me; 'we have the key and can't find the treasure.' I asked her to explain. 'It's all in here,' she declared—I couldn't tell whether she meant her ink-stand or the quill she pointed toward it. I seldom understood her any more; as the crisis grew, she gave up reading for daydreaming, and used her pen less for noting instances of the Magic Key motif in world literature than for doodling the letters of our alphabet at random and idly tickling herself.

"'Little Doony,' she said dreamily, and kissed me: 'pretend this whole situation is the plot of a story we're reading, and you and I and Daddy and the King are all fictional characters. In this story, Scheherazade finds a way to change the King's mind about women and turn him into a gentle, loving husband. It's not hard to imagine such a story, is it? Now, no matter what way she finds—whether it's a magic spell or a magic story with the answer in it or a magic anything—it comes down to particular words in the story we're reading, right? And those words are made from the letters of our alphabet: a couple-dozen squiggles we can draw with this pen. This is the key, Doony! And the treasure, too, if we can only get our hands on it! It's as if—as if the key to the treasure *is* the treasure!'

"As soon as she spoke these last words a genie appeared from nowhere right there in our library-stacks. He didn't resemble anything in Sherry's bedtime stories: for one thing, he wasn't frightening, though he was strange-looking enough: a light-skinned fellow of forty or so, smooth-shaven and bald as a roc's egg. His clothes were simple but outlandish; he was tall and healthy and pleasant enough in appearance, except for queer lenses that he wore in a frame over his eyes. He seemed as startled as we were—you should've seen Sherry drop that pen and pull her skirts together!—but he got over his alarm a lot sooner, and looked from one to the other of us and at a stubby little magic wand he held in his fingers, and smiled a friendly smile.

"'Are you really Scheherazade?' he asked. 'I've never had a dream so clear and lifelike! And you're little Dunyazade—just as I'd imagined both of you! Don't be frightened: I can't tell you what it means to me to see and talk to you like this; even in a dream, it's a dream come true. Can you understand English? I don't have a word of Arabic. O my, I can't believe this is really happening!'

"Sherry and I looked at each other. The Genie didn't seem dangerous; we didn't know those languages he spoke of; every word he said was in *our* language, and when Sherry asked him whether he'd come from her pen or from her words, he seemed to understand the question, though he didn't know the answer. He was a writer of tales, he said—anyhow a *former* writer of tales—in a land on the other side of the world. At one time, we gathered, people in his country had been fond of reading; currently, however, the only readers of artful fiction were critics, other writers, and unwilling students who, left to themselves, preferred music and pictures to words. His own pen (that magic wand, in fact a magic quill with a fountain of ink inside) had just about run dry: but whether he had abandoned fiction or fiction him, Sherry and I couldn't make out when we reconstructed this first conversation later that night, for either in our minds or in his a number of crises seemed confused. Like Shahryar's, the Genie's life was in disorder—but so far from harboring therefore a grudge against woman-kind, he was distractedly in love with a brace of new mistresses, and only recently had been able to choose between them. His career, too, had reached a hiatus which he would have been pleased to call a turning-point if he could have espied any way to turn: he wished neither to repudiate nor to repeat his past performances; he aspired to go beyond them toward a future they were not attuned to and, by some magic, at the same time go back to the original springs of narrative. But how this was to be managed was as unclear to him as the answer to the Shahryar-problem was to us—the more so since he couldn't say how much of his difficulty might be owing to his own limitations, his age and stage and personal vicissitudes; how much to the general decline of letters in his time and place; and how much to the other crises with which his country (and, so he alleged, the very species) was beset—crises as desperate and problematical, he avowed, as ours, and as inimical to the single-mindedness needed to compose great works of art or the serenity to apprehend them.

"So entirely was he caught up in these problems, his work and life and all had come to a standstill. He had taken leave of his friends, his family, and his post (he was a doctor of letters), and withdrawn to a lonely retreat in the marshes, which only the most devoted of his mistresses deigned to visit.

"'My project,' he told us, 'is to learn where to go by discovering where I am by reviewing where I've been—where we've *all* been. There's a kind of snail in the Maryland marshes—perhaps I invented him—that makes his shell as he goes along out of whatever he comes across, cementing it with his own juices, and at the same time makes his path instinctively toward the best available material for his shell; he carries his history on his back, living in it, adding new and larger spirals to it from the present as he grows. That snail's pace has become my pace—but I'm going in circles, following my own trail! I've quit reading and writing; I've lost track of who I am; my name's just a jumble of letters; so's the whole body of literature: strings of letters and empty spaces, like a code that I've lost the key to.' He pushed those odd lenses up on the bridge of his nose with his thumb—a habit that made me giggle—and grinned. 'Well, *almost* the whole body. Speaking of keys, I suspect that's how I got here.'

"By way of answer to Sherry's question then, whether he had sprung from her quill-pen or her words, he declared that his researches, like hers, had led him to an impasse; he felt that a treasure-house of new fiction lay vaguely under his hand, if he could find the key to it. Musing idly on this figure, he had added to the morass of notes he felt himself mired in, a sketch for a story about a man who comes somehow to realize that the key to the treasure he's searching for *is* the treasure. Just exactly how so (and how the story might be told despite all the problems that beset him) he had no chance to consider, for the instant he set on paper the words *The key to the treasure is the treasure,* he found himself with us—for how long, or to what end, or by what means, he had no idea, unless it was that of all the storytellers in the world, his very favorite was Scheherazade.

"'Listen how I chatter on!' he ended happily. 'Do forgive me!'

"My sister, after some thought, ventured the opinion that the astonishing coincidence of her late reveries and his, which had led them as it were simultaneously to the same cryptic formulation, must have something to do with his translation to her library. She looked forward, she said, to experimenting whether a reverse translation could be managed, if the worst came to the worst, to spirit me out of harm's way; as for herself, she had no time or use for idle flights of fancy, however curious, from the gynocide that was ravaging her country: remarkable as it was, she saw no more relevance to her problems than to his in this bit of magic.

"'But we know the answer's right here in our hands!' the Genie exclaimed. 'We're both storytellers: you must sense as strongly as I that it has something to do with the key to the treasure's being the treasure.'

"My sister's nostrils narrowed. 'Twice you've called me a storyteller,' she said; 'yet I've never told a story in my life except to Dunyazade, and her bedtime stories were the ones that everybody tells. The only tale I ever invented myself was this key-to-the-treasure one just now, which I scarcely understand . . .'

"'Good lord!' the Genie cried. 'Do you mean to say that you haven't even *started* your thousand and one nights yet?'

"Sherry shook her head grimly. 'The only thousand nights I know of is the time our pig of a king has been killing the virgin daughters of the Moslems.'

"Our bespectacled visitor then grew so exhilarated that for some time he couldn't speak at all. Presently he seized my sister's hand and dumbfounded us both by declaring his lifelong adoration of her, a declaration that brought blushes to our cheeks. Years ago, he said, when he'd been a penniless student pushing book-carts through the library-stacks of his university to help pay for his education, he'd contracted a passion for Scheherazade upon first reading the tales she beguiled King Shahryar with, and had sustained that passion so powerfully ever since that his love affairs with other, 'real' women seemed to him by comparison unreal, his two-decade marriage but a prolonged infidelity to her, his own fictions mere mimicries, pallid counterfeits of the authentic treasure of her *Thousand and One Nights*.

"'Beguiled the King with!' Sherry said. 'I've thought of that! Daddy believes that Shahryar would really like to quit what he's doing before the country falls apart, but needs an excuse to break his vow without losing face with his younger brother. I'd considered letting him make love to me and then telling him exciting stories, which I'd leave unfinished from one night to the next till he'd come to know me too well to kill me. I even thought of slipping in stories about kings who'd suffered worse hardships than he and his brother without turning vindictive; or lovers who weren't unfaithful; or husbands who loved their wives more than themselves. But it's too fanciful! Who knows which stories would work? Especially in those first few nights! I can see him sparing me for a day or two, maybe, out of relief; but then he'd react against his lapse and go back to his old policy. I gave the idea up.'

"The Genie smiled; even *I* saw what he was thinking. 'But you say you've read the book!' Sherry exclaimed. 'Then you must remember what stories are in it, and in which order!'

"'I don't have to remember,' said the Genie. 'In all the years I've been writing stories, your book has never been off my worktable. I've made use of it a thousand times, if only by just seeing it there.'

"Sherry asked him then whether he himself had perhaps invented the stories she allegedly told, or would tell. 'How could I?' he laughed. 'I won't be born for a dozen centuries yet! You didn't invent them either, for that matter; they're those ancient ones you spoke of, that "everybody tells": Sinbad the Sailor, Aladdin's Lamp, Ali Baba and the Forty Thieves . . .'

"'What others?' Sherry cried. 'In which order? I don't even *know* the Ali Baba story! Do you have the book with you? I'll give you everything I have for it!'

"The Genie replied that inasmuch as he'd been holding her book in his hand and thinking about her when he'd written the magic words, and it had not been translated to her library along with him, he inferred that he could not present her with a copy even if the magic were repeatable. He did however remember clearly what he called the frame-story: how Shahryar's young brother Shah Zaman had discovered his bride's adulteries, killed her, abandoned the kingdom of Samarkand, and come to live with Shahryar in the Islands of India and China; how, discovering that Shahryar's wife was equally unfaithful, the brothers had retreated to the wilderness, encountered the ifrit and the maiden, concluded that all women are deceivers, and returned to their respective kingdoms, vowing to deflower a virgin every night and kill her in the morning; how the Vizier's daughter Scheherazade, to end this massacre, had volunteered herself, much against her father's wishes, and with the aid of her sister Dunyazade—who at the crucial moment between sex and sleep asked for a story, and fed the King's suspense by interrupting the tale at daybreak, just before the climax—stayed Shahryar's hand long enough to win his heart, restore his senses, and save the country from ruin.

"I hugged my sister and begged her to let me help her in just that way. She shook her head: 'Only this Genie has read the stories I'm supposed to tell, and he doesn't remember them. What's more, he's fading already. If the key to the treasure is the treasure, we don't have it in our hands yet.'

"He had indeed begun fading away, almost disappeared; but as soon as Sherry repeated the magic sentence he came back clearly, smiling more eagerly than before, and declared he'd been thinking the same words at the same moment, just when we'd begun to fade and his writing-room to reappear about him. Apparently, then, he and Sherry could conjure the phenomenon at will by imagining simultaneously that the key to the treasure was the treasure: they were, presumably, the only two people in the history of the world who had imagined it. What's more, in that instant when he'd waked, as it were, to find himself back in the marshes of *America,* he'd been able to glance at the open table of contents of Volume One of the *Thousand and One Nights* book and determine that the first story after the frame-story was a compound tale called 'The Merchant and the Genie'—in which, if he remembered correctly, an outraged ifrit delays the death of an innocent merchant until certain sheiks have told their stories.

"Scheherazade thanked him, made a note of the title, and gravely put down her pen. 'You have it in your power to save my sisters and my country,' she said, 'and the King too, before his madness destroys him. All you need to do is supply me from the future with these stories from the past. But perhaps at bottom you share the King's feelings about women.'

"'Not at all!' the Genie said warmly. 'If the key trick really works, I'll be honored to tell your stories to you. All we need to do is agree on a time of day to write the magic words together.'

"I clapped my hands—but Sherry's expression was still cool. 'You're a man,' she said; 'I imagine you expect what every man expects who has the key to any treasure a woman needs. In the nature of the case, I have to let Shahryar take me first; after that I'll cuckold him with you every day at sunset if you'll tell me the story for the night to come. Is that satisfactory?'

"I feared he'd take offense, but he only shook his head. Out of his old love for her, he gently declared, and his gratitude for the profoundest image he knew of the storyteller's situation, he would be pleased beyond words to play any role whatever in Scheherazade's story, without dreaming of further reward. His *own* policy, moreover, which he had lived by for many nights more than a thousand, was to share beds with no woman who did not reciprocate his feelings. Finally, his new young mistress—to whom he had been drawn by certain resemblances to Scheherazade—delighted him utterly, as he hoped he did her; he was no more tempted to infidelity than to incest or pederasty. His adoration of Scheherazade was as strong as ever—even stronger now that he'd met her in the lovely flesh—but it was not possessive; he desired her only as the old Greek poets their Muse, as a source of inspiration.

"Sherry tapped and fiddled with her quill. 'I don't know these poets you speak of,' she said sharply. 'Here in our country, love isn't so exclusive as all that. When I think of Shahryar's harem-full of concubines on the one hand, and the way his wife got even with him on the other, and the plots of most of the stories I know—especially the ones about older men with young mistresses—I can't help wondering whether you're not being a bit naïve, to put it kindly. Especially as I gather you've suffered your share of deceit in the past, and no doubt done your share of deceiving. Even so, it's a refreshing surprise, if a bit of a put-down, that you're not interested in taking sexual advantage of your position. Are you a eunuch?'

"I blushed again, but the Genie assured us, still unoffended, that he was normally equipped, and that his surpassing love for his young lady, while perhaps invincibly innocent, was not naïve. His experience of love gone sour only made him treasure more highly the notion of a love that time would season and improve; no sight on earth more pleased his heart, annealed as it was by his own past passions and defeats, than that rare one of two white-haired spouses who still cherished each other and their life together. If love died, it died; while it lived, let it live forever, et cetera. Some fictions, he asserted, were so much more valuable than fact that in rare instances their beauty made them real. The only Baghdad was the Baghdad of the *Nights,* where carpets flew and genies sprang from magic words; he was ours to command as one of those, and without price. Should one appear to *him* and offer him three wishes, he'd be unable to summon more than two, inasmuch as his first—to have live converse with the storyteller he'd loved best and longest—had already been granted.

"Sherry smiled now and asked him what would be the other two wishes. The second, he replied, would be that he might die before his young friend and he ceased to treasure each other as they did currently in their saltmarsh retreat. The third (what presently stood alone between him and entire contentment) would be that he not die without adding some artful trinket or two, however small, to the general treasury of civilized delights, to which no keys were needed beyond goodwill, attention, and a moderately cultivated sensibility: he meant the treasury of art, which if it could not redeem the barbarities of history or spare us the horrors of living and dying, at least sustained, refreshed, expanded, ennobled, and enriched our spirits along the painful way. Such of his scribblings as were already in print he did not presume to have that grace; should he die before he woke from his present sweet dream of Scheherazade, this third wish would go unfulfilled. But even if neither of these last was ever granted (and surely such boons were rare as treasure keys), he would die happier to have had the first.

"Hearing this, Sherry at last put by her reserve, took the stranger's writing-hand in her own, apologized for her discourtesy, and repeated her invitation, this time warmly: if he would supply her with enough of her stories to reach her goal, she was his in secret whenever he wished after her maiden night with Shahryar. Or (if deception truly had no more savor for him), when the slaughter of her sisters had ceased, let him spirit her somehow to his place and time, and she'd be his slave and concubine forever—assuming, as one was after all realistically obliged to assume, that he and his current love would by then have wearied of each other.

"The Genie laughed and kissed her hand. 'No slaves; no concubines. And my friend and I intend to love each other forever.'

"'That will be a greater wonder than all of Sinbad's together,' Sherry said. 'I pray it may happen, Genie, and your third wish be granted too. For all one knows, you may already have done what you hope to do: time will tell. But if Dunyazade and I can find any way at all to help you with *your* tales-to-come in return for the ones you've pledged to us—and you may be sure we'll search for such a way as steadfastly as we've searched for a way to save our sex—we'll do it though we die for it.'

"She made him promise then to embrace his mistress for her, whom she vowed to love thenceforth as she loved me, and by way of a gift to her—which she prayed might translate as the precious book had not—she took from her earlobe a gold ring worked in the form of a spiral shell, of which his earlier image had reminded her. He accepted it joyfully, vowing to spin from it, if he could, as from a catherine-wheel[7] or whirling galaxy, a golden shower of fiction. Then he kissed us both (the first male lips I'd felt except Father's, and the only such till yours) and vanished, whether by his will or another's we couldn't tell.

"Sherry and I hugged each other excitedly all that night, rehearsing every word that had passed between the Genie and ourselves. I begged her to test the magic for a week before offering herself to the King, to make sure that it—and her colleague from the future—could be relied upon. But even as we laughed and whispered, another of our sisters was being raped and murdered in the palace; Sherry offered herself to Shahryar first thing in the morning, to our father's distress; let the King lead her at nightfall into his fatal bed and fall to toying with her, then pretended to weep for being separated from me for the first time in our lives. Shahryar bid her fetch me in to sit at the foot of the bed; almost in a faint I watched him help her off with the pretty nightie I'd crocheted for her myself, place a white silk cushion under her bottom, and gently open her legs; as I'd never seen a man erect, I groaned despite myself when he opened his robe and I saw what he meant to stick her with: the hair done up in pearls, the shaft like a minaret decorated with arabesques, the head like a cobra's spread to strike. He chuckled at my alarm and climbed atop her; not to see him, Sherry fixed her welling eyes on me, closing them only to cry the cry that must be cried when there befell the mystery concerning which there is no inquiry. A moment later, as the cushion attested her late virginity and tears ran from her eye-corners to her ears, she seized the King's hair, wrapped about his waist her lovely legs, and to insure the success of her fiction, pretended a grand transport of rapture. I could neither bear to watch nor turn my eyes away. When the beast was spent and tossing fitfully (from shame and guilt, I hoped, or unease at Sherry's willingness to die), I gathered my senses as best I could and asked her to tell me a story.

"'With pleasure,' she said, in a tone still so full of shock it broke my heart, 'if this pious and auspicious King will allow it.' Your brother grunted, and Sherry began, shakily, the tale of the Merchant and the Genie, framing in it for good measure the First Sheik's Story as her voice grew stronger. At the right moment I interrupted to praise the story and say I thought I'd heard a rooster crowing in the east; as though I'd been kept in ignorance of the King's policy, I asked whether we mightn't sleep awhile before sunrise and hear the end of the story tomorrow night—along with the one about the Three Apples, which I liked even more. 'O Doony!' Sherry pretended to scold. 'I know a dozen better than that: how about the Ebony Horse, or Julnar the Sea-Born, or the Ensorcelled Prince? But just as there's no young woman in the country worth having that the King hasn't had his fill of already, so I'm sure there's no story he hasn't heard till he's weary of it. I could no more expect to tell him a new story than show him a new way to make love.'

"'I'll be the judge of that,' said Shahryar. So we sweated out the day in each other's arms and at sunset tried the magic key; you can imagine our relief when the

---

7. A rotating type of firework.

Genie appeared, pushed up his eyeglasses with a grin, and recited to us the Second and Third Sheiks' Stories, which he guessed were both to be completed on that crucial second night in order, on the one hand, to demonstrate a kind of narrative inexhaustibility or profligacy (at least a generosity commensurate to that of the sheiks themselves), while, on the other hand, not compounding the suspense of unfinished tales-within-tales at a time when the King's reprieve was still highly tentative. Moreover, that the ifrit will grant the merchant's life on account of the stories ought to be evident enough by daybreak to make, without belaboring, its admonitory point. The spiral earring, he added happily, had come through intact, if anything more beautiful for the translation; his mistress was delighted with it, and would return Sherry's embrace with pleasure, he was confident, as soon as the memory of her more contemporary rivals was removed enough, and she secure enough in his love, for him to tell her the remarkable story of the magic key. Tenderly then he voiced his hope that Scheherazade had not found the loss of her maidenhood wholly repugnant to experience, or myself to witness; if the King was truly to be wooed away from his misogyny, many ardent nights lay ahead, and for the sake of Scheherazade's spirit as well as her strategy it would be well if she could take some pleasure in them.

"'Never!' my sister declared. 'The only pleasure I'll take in that bed is the pleasure of saving my sisters and cuckolding their killer.'

"The Genie shrugged and faded; Shahryar came in, bid us good evening, kissed Sherry many times before caressing her more intimately, then laid her on the bed and worked her over playfully in as many positions as there are tales in the Trickery-of-Women series, till I couldn't tell whether her outcries were of pain, surprise, or—mad as the notion seemed—a kind of pleasure despite herself. As for me, though I was innocent of men, I had read in secret all the manuals of love and erotic stories in Sherry's library, but had thought them the wild imaginings of lonely writers in their dens, a kind of self-tickling with the quill such as Sherry herself had fallen into; for all it was my own sister I saw doing such incredible things in such odd positions, it would be many nights before I fully realized that what I witnessed were not conjured illustrations from those texts, but things truly taking place.

"'On with the story,' Shahryar commanded when they were done. Unsteadily at first, but then in even better voice than the night before, Sherry continued the Merchant-and-Genie story, and I, mortified to find myself still moistening from what I'd seen, almost forgot to interrupt at the appropriate time. Next day, as we embraced each other, Sherry admitted that while she found the King himself as loathsome as ever, the things he did to her were no longer painful, and might even be pleasurable, as would be the things she did to him, were he a bedpartner she could treasure as our Genie treasured his. More exactly, once the alarm of her defloration and her fear of being killed in the morning began to pass, she found abhorrent not Shahryar himself—undeniably a vigorous and handsome man for his forty years, and a skillful lover—but his murderous record with our sex, which no amount of charm and tender caressing could expunge.

"'No amount at all?' our Genie asked when he appeared again, on cue, at sunset. 'Suppose a man had been a kind and gentle fellow until some witch put a spell on him that deranged his mind and made him do atrocious things; then suppose a certain young lady has the power to cure him by loving him despite his madness. She can lift the spell because she recognizes that it *is* a spell, and not his real nature . . .'

"'I hope that's not my tale for tonight,' Sherry said dryly, pointing out that while Shahryar may once upon a time have been a loving husband, even in those days he gave out virgin slave-girls to his friends, kept a houseful of concubines for himself, and cut his wife in half for taking a lover after twenty years of one-sided fidelity. 'And no magic can bring a thousand dead girls back to life, or unrape them. On with the story.'

"'You're a harder critic than your lover,' the Genie complained, and recited the opening frame of the Fisherman and the Genie, the simplicity of which he felt to be a strategic change of pace for the third night—especially since it would lead, on the fourth and fifth, to a series of tales-within-tales-within-tales, a narrative complexity he described admiringly as 'Oriental.'

"So it went, month after month, year after year; at the foot of Shahryar's bed by night and in Scheherazade's by day, I learned more about the arts of making love and telling stories than I had imagined there was to know. It pleased our Genie, for example, that the tale of the Ensorcelled Prince had been framed by that of the Fisherman and the Genie, since the prince himself had been encased (in the black stone palace); also, that the resolution of the story thus enframed resolved as well the tale that framed it. This metaphorical construction he judged more artful than the 'mere plot-function' (that is, preserving our lives and restoring the King's sanity!) which Sherry's Fisherman-tale and the rest had in the story of her *own* life; but that 'mere plot-function,' in turn, was superior to the artless and arbitrary relation between most framed and framing tales. This relation (which to me seemed less important than what the stories were *about*) interested the two of them no end, just as Sherry and Shahryar were fascinated by the pacing of their nightly pleasures or the refinement of their various positions, instead of the degree and quality of their love.

"Sherry kissed me. 'That other either goes without saying,' she said, 'or it doesn't go at all. Making love and telling stories both take more than good technique—but it's only the technique that we can *talk* about.'

"The Genie agreed: 'Heartfelt ineptitude has its appeal, Dunyazade; so does heartless skill. But what you want is passionate virtuosity.' They speculated endlessly on such questions as whether a story might imaginably be framed from inside, as it were, so that the usual relation between container and contained would be reversed and paradoxically reversible—and (for my benefit, I suppose) what human state of affairs such an odd construction might usefully figure. Or whether one might go beyond the usual tale-within-a-tale, beyond even the tales-within-tales-within-tales-within-tales which our Genie had found a few instances of in that literary treasure-house he hoped one day to add to, and conceive a series of, say, *seven* concentric stories-within-stories, so arranged that the climax of the innermost would precipitate that of the next tale out, and that of the next, et cetera, like a string of firecrackers or the chains of orgasms that Shahryar could sometimes set my sister catenating.[8]

"This last comparison—a favorite of theirs—would lead them to a dozen others between narrative and sexual art, whether in spirited disagreement or equally spirited concord. The Genie declared that in his time and place there were scientists of the passions who maintained that language itself, on the one hand, originated in 'infantile pregenital erotic exuberance, polymorphously perverse,' and that conscious attention, on the other, was a 'libidinal hypercathexis'—by which magic phrases they seemed to mean that writing and reading, or telling and listening, were literally ways of making love. Whether this was in fact the case, neither he nor

8. Stringing together.

Sherry cared at all; yet they liked to speak *as if it were* (their favorite words), and accounted thereby for the similarity between conventional dramatic structure—its exposition, rising action, climax, and dénouement[9]—and the rhythm of sexual intercourse from foreplay through coitus to orgasm and release. Therefore also, they believed, the popularity of love (and combat, the darker side of the same rupee) as a theme for narrative, the lovers' embrace as its culmination, and post-coital lassitude as its natural ground: what better time for tales than at day's end, in bed after making love (or around the campfire after battle or adventure, or in the chimney corner after work), to express and heighten the community between the lovers, comrades, co-workers?

"'The longest story in the world—' Sherry observed, 'The Ocean of Story, seven hundred thousand distichs[1]—was told by the god Siva to his consort Parvati as a gift for the way she made love to him one night. It would take a minstrel five hundred evenings to recite it all, but she sat in his lap and listened contentedly till he was done.'

"To this example, which delighted him, the Genie added several unfamiliar to us: a great epic called *Odyssey,* for instance, whose hero returns home after twenty years of war and wandering, makes love to his faithful wife, and recounts all his adventures to her in bed while the gods prolong the night in his behalf; another work called *Decameron,* in which ten courtly lords and ladies, taking refuge in their country houses from an urban pestilence, amuse one another at the end of each day with stories (some borrowed from Sherry herself) as a kind of *substitute* for making love—an artifice in keeping with the artificial nature of their little society. And, of course, that book about Sherry herself which he claimed to be reading from, in his opinion the best illustration of all that the very relation between teller and told was by nature erotic. The teller's role, he felt, regardless of his actual gender, was essentially masculine, the listener's or reader's feminine, and the tale was the medium of their intercourse.

"'That makes me unnatural,' Sherry objected. 'Are you one of those vulgar men who think that women writers are homosexuals?'

"'Not at all,' the Genie assured her. 'You and Shahryar usually make love in Position One before you tell your story, and lovers like to switch positions the second time.' More seriously, he had not meant to suggest that the 'femininity' of readership was a docile or inferior condition: a lighthouse, for example, passively sent out signals that mariners labored actively to receive and interpret; an ardent woman like his mistress was at least as energetic in his embrace as he in embracing her; a good reader of cunning tales worked in her way as busily as their author; et cetera. Narrative, in short—and here they were again in full agreement—was a love-relation, not a rape: its success depended upon the reader's consent and cooperation, which she could withhold or at any moment withdraw; also upon her own combination of experience and talent for the enterprise, and the author's ability to arouse, sustain, and satisfy her interest—an ability on which his figurative life hung as surely as Scheherazade's literal.

"'And like all love-relations,' he added one afternoon, 'it's potentially fertile for both partners, in a way you should approve, for it goes beyond male and female. The reader is likely to find herself pregnant with new images, as you hope Shahryar will become with respect to women; but the storyteller may find himself pregnant too . . .'

9. The outcome or resolution of a plot.
1. Scheherazade is referring to a Sanskrit collection of stories composed by the writer Samadeva in the 11th cen-

tury (many of these stories, like those of *Thousand and One Nights,* derived from older narrative material). A distich is a two-line verse.

"Much of their talk was over my head, but on hearing this last I hugged Sherry tight and prayed to Allah it was not another of their *as if*'s. Sure enough, on the three hundred eighth night her tale was interrupted not by me but by the birth of Ali Shar, whom despite his resemblance to Shahryar I clasped to my bosom from that hour as if I had borne instead of merely helping to deliver him. Likewise on the six hundred twenty-fourth night, when little Gharíb came lustily into the world, and the nine hundred fifty-ninth, birthday of beautiful Jamilah-Melissa. Her second name, which means 'honey-sweet' in the exotic tongues of Genie-land, we chose in honor of our friend's still-beloved mistress, whom he had announced his intention to marry despite Sherry's opinion that while women and men might in some instances come together as human beings, wives and husbands could never. The Genie argued, for his part, that no matter how total, exclusive, and permanent the commitment between two lovers might turn out to be, it lacked the dimensions of spiritual seriousness and public responsibility which only marriage, with its ancient vows and symbols, rites and risks, provided.

"'It can't last,' Sherry said crossly. The Genie put on her finger a gift from his fiancée to her namesake's mother—a gold ring patterned with rams'-horns and conches, replicas of which she and the Genie meant to exchange on their wedding day—and replied, 'Neither did Athens. Neither did Rome. Neither did all of Jamshid's glories. But we must live as if it can and will.'

"'Hmp,' said Sherry, who over the years had picked up a number of your brother's ways, as he had hers. But she gave them her blessing—to which I added mine without reservations or *as if*'s—and turned the ring much in the lamplight when he was gone, trying its look on different hands and fingers and musing as if upon its design.

"Thus we came to the thousandth night, the thousandth morning and afternoon, the thousandth dipping of Sherry's quill and invocation of the magic key. And for the thousand and first time, still smiling, our Genie appeared to us, his own ring on his finger as it had been for some forty evenings now—an altogether brighter-looking spirit than had materialized in the book-stacks so long past. We three embraced as always; he asked after the children's health and the King's, and my sister, as always, after his progress toward that treasury from which he claimed her stories were drawn. Less reticent on this subject than he had been since our first meeting, he declared with pleasure that thanks to the inspiration of Scheherazade and to the thousand comforts of his loving wife, he believed he had found his way out of that slough of the imagination in which he'd felt himself bogged: whatever the merits of the new work, like an ox-cart driver in monsoon season or the skipper of a grounded ship, he had gone forward by going back, to the very roots and springs of story. Using, like Scheherazade herself, for entirely present ends, materials received from narrative antiquity and methods older than the alphabet, in the time since Sherry's defloration he had set down two-thirds of a projected series of three *novellas,* longish tales which would take their sense from one another in several of the ways he and Sherry had discussed, and, if they were successful (here he smiled at me), manage to be seriously, even passionately, *about* some things as well.[2]

"'The two I've finished have to do with mythic heroes, true and false,' he concluded. 'The third I'm just in the middle of. How good or bad they are I can't say yet, but I'm sure they're *right*. You know what I mean, Scheherazade.'

---

2. John Barth's book *Chimera,* from which "Dunyazadiad" is taken, consists of three novellas, the other two based on Greek myths.

"She did; I felt as if I did also, and we happily re-embraced. Then Sherry remarked, apropos of middles, that she'd be winding up the story of Ma'aruf the Cobbler that night and needed at least the beginning of whatever tale was to follow it.

"The Genie shook his head. 'My dear, there are no more. You've told them all.' He seemed cruelly undisturbed by a prospect that made the harem spin before my eyes and brought me near to swooning.

"'No more!' I cried. 'What will she do?'

"'If she doesn't want to risk Shahryar's killing her and turning to you,' he said calmly, 'I guess she'll have to invent something that's not in the book.'

"'I don't invent,' Sherry reminded him. Her voice was no less steady than his, but her expression—when I got hold of my senses enough to see it—was grave. 'I only recount.'

"'Borrow something from that treasury!' I implored him. 'What will the children do without their mother?' The harem began to spin again; I gathered all my courage and said: 'Don't desert us, friend; give Sherry that story you're working on now, and you may do anything you like with me. I'll raise your children if you have any; I'll wash your Melissa's feet. Anything.'

"The Genie smiled and said to Sherry, 'Our little Dunyazade is a woman.' Thanking me then for my offer as courteously as he had once Scheherazade, he declined it, not only for the same reasons that had moved him before, but also because he was confident that the only tales left in the treasury of the sort King Shahryar was likely to be entertained by were the hundred mimicries and retellings of Sherry's own.

"'Then my thousand nights and a night are ended,' Sherry said. 'Don't be ungrateful to our friend, Doony; everything ends.'

"I agreed, but tearfully wished myself—and Ali Shar, Gharíb, and little Melissa, whom all I loved as dearly as I loved my sister—out of a world where the only happy endings were in stories.

"The Genie touched my shoulder. 'Let's not forget,' he said, 'that from my point of view—a tiresome technical one, I'll admit—it is a story that we're coming to the end of. All these tales your sister has told the King are simply the middle of her own story—hers and yours, I mean, and Shahryar's, and his young brother Shah Zaman's.'

"I didn't understand—but Sherry did, and squeezing my other shoulder, asked him quietly whether, that being the tiresome technical case, it followed that a happy ending might be invented for the framing-story.

"'The author of The Thousand and One Nights doesn't invent,' the Genie reminded her; 'he only recounts how, after she finished the tale of Ma'aruf the Cobbler, Scheherazade rose from the King's bed, kissed ground before him, and made bold to ask a favor in return for the thousand and one nights' entertainment. "Ask, Scheherazade," the King answers in the story—whereupon you send Dunyazade to fetch the children in, and plead for your life on their behalf, so that they won't grow up motherless.'

"My heart sprang up; Sherry sat silent. 'I notice you don't ask on behalf of the stories themselves,' the Genie remarked, 'or on behalf of your love for Shahryar and his for you. That's a pretty touch: it leaves him free to grant your wish, if he chooses to, on those other grounds. I also admire your tact in asking only for your life; that gives him the moral initiative to repent his policy and marry you. I don't think I'd have thought of that.'

"'Hmp,' said Sherry.

"'Then there's the nice formal symmetry—'

"'Never *mind* the symmetry!' I cried. 'Does it work or not?' I saw in his expression then that it did, and in Sherry's that this plan was not news to her. I hugged them both, weeping enough for joy to make our ink run, so the Genie said, and begged Sherry to promise me that I could stay with her and the children after their wedding as I had before, and sit at the foot of her bed forever.

"'Not so fast, Doony,' she said. 'I haven't decided yet whether or not I care to end the story that way.'

"'Not care to?' I looked with fresh terror to the Genie. 'Doesn't she *have* to, if it's in the book?'

"He too appeared troubled now, and searched Sherry's face, and admitted that not everything he'd seen of our situation in these visions or dreams of his corresponded exactly to the story as it came to him through the centuries, lands, and languages that separated us in waking hours. In his translation, for example, all three children were male and nameless; and while there was no mention of Scheherazade's *loving* Shahryar by the end of the book, there was surely none of her despising him, or cuckolding him, more or less, with me and the rest. Most significantly, it went without saying that he himself was altogether absent from the plot—which, however, he prayed my sister to end as it ended in his version: with the double marriage of herself to your brother and me to you, and our living happily together until overtaken by the Destroyer of Delights and Severer of Societies, et cetera.

"While I tried to assimilate this astonishing news about myself, Sherry asked with a smile whether by 'his version' the Genie meant that copy of the *Nights* from which he'd been assisting us or the story he himself was in midst of inventing; for she liked to imagine, and profoundly hoped it so, that our connection had not been to her advantage only: that one way or another, she and I and our situation were among those 'ancient narrative materials' which he had found useful for his present purposes. How did *his* version end?

"The Genie closed his eyes for a moment, pushed back his glasses with his thumb, and repeated that he was still in the middle of that third novella in the series, and so far from drafting the climax and dénouement, had yet even to plot them in outline. Turning then to me, to my great surprise he announced that the title of the story was *Dunyazadiad;* that its central character was not my sister but myself, the image of whose circumstances, on my 'wedding-night-to-come,' he found as arresting for taletellers of his particular place and time as was my sister's for the estate of narrative artists in general.

"'All those nights at the foot of that bed, Dunyazade!' he exclaimed. 'You've had the whole literary tradition transmitted to you—and the whole erotic tradition, too! There's no story you haven't heard; there's no way of making love that you haven't seen again and again. I think of you, little sister, a virgin in both respects: All that innocence! All that sophistication! And now it's *your* turn: Shahryar has told young Shah Zaman about his wonderful mistress, how he loves her as much for herself as for her stories—*which he also passes on;* the two brothers marry the two sisters; it's your wedding night, Dunyazade . . . But wait! Look here! Shahryar deflowered and killed a virgin a night for a thousand and one nights before he met Scheherazade; Shah Zaman has been doing the same thing, but it's only now, a thousand nights and a night later, that *he* learns about Scheherazade—that means he's had two thousand and two young women at the least since he killed his wife, and not one has pleased him enough to move him to spend a second night with her, much less spare her life! What are you going to do to entertain *him,* little sister? Make love in exciting new ways? There are none! Tell him stories, like Scheherazade? He's heard them all! Dunyazade, Dunyazade! Who can tell your story?'

"More dead than alive with fright, I clung to my sister, who begged the Genie please to stop alarming me. All apologies, he assured us that what he was describing was not *The Thousand and One Nights* frame-story (which ended happily without mention of these terrors), but his own novella, a pure fiction—to which also he would endeavor with all his heart to find some conclusion in keeping with his affection for me. Sherry further eased my anxiety by adding that she too had given long thought to my position as the Genie described it, and was not without certain plans with respect to our wedding night; these, as a final favor to our friend, she had made written note of in the hope that whether or not they succeeded, he might find them useful for his story; but she would prefer to withhold them from me for the present.

"'You sense as I do, then,' the Genie said thoughtfully, 'that we won't be seeing each other again.'

"Sherry nodded. 'You have other stories to tell. I've told mine.'

"Already he'd begun to fade. 'My best,' he said, 'will be less than your least. And I'll always love you, Scheherazade! Dunyazade, I'm your brother! Good night, sisters! Fare well!'

"We kissed; he disappeared with Sherry's letter; Shahryar sent for us; still shaken, I sat at the bed-foot while he and Sherry did a combination from the latter pages of *Ananga Ranga* and *Kama Sutra*[3] and she finished the tale of Ma'aruf the Cobbler. Then she rose as the Genie had instructed her, kissed ground, begged boon; I fetched in Ali Shar, walking by himself now, Gharíb crawling, Jamilah-Melissa suckling at my milkless breast as if it were her mother's. Sherry made her plea; Shahryar wept, hugged the children, told her he'd pardoned her long since, having found in her the refutation of all his disenchantment, and praised Allah for having appointed her the savior of her sex. Then he sent for Daddy to draft the marriage contract and for you to hear the news of Scheherazade and her stories; when you proposed to marry me, Sherry countered with Part Two of our plan (of whose Part Three I was still ignorant): that in order for her and me never to be parted, you must abandon Samarkand and live with us, sharing your brother's throne and passing yours to our father in reparation for his three-years' anguish. I found you handsomer than Shahryar and more terrifying, and begged my sister to say what lay ahead for me.

"'Why, a fine wedding-feast, silly Doony!' she teased. 'The eunuchs will perfume our Hammam-bath with rose- and willow-flower water, musk-pods, eaglewood, ambergris;[4] we'll wash and clip our hair; they'll dress me like the sun and you the moon, and we'll dance in seven different dresses to excite our bridegrooms. By the end of the wine and music they'll scarcely be able to contain their desire; each of us will kiss the other three good night, twelve good-nights in all, and our husbands will hurry us off toward our separate bridal-chambers—'

"'O Sherry!'

"'*Then,*' she went on, no tease in her voice now, 'on the very threshold of their pleasures I'll stop, kiss ground, and say to my lord and master: "O King of the Sun and the Moon and the Rising Tide, et cetera, thanks for marrying me at last after sleeping with me for a thousand and one nights and begetting three children on me

---

3. Ancient Indian treatises on sexuality.
4. "Hammam" is the Arabic word for "bath" and refers to what is now called a Turkish bath with a steam room.

Ambergris is made out of substances found in the sperm whale and used for perfumes.

and listening while I amused you with proverbs and parables, chronicles and pleas-antries, quips and jests and admonitory instances, stories and anecdotes, dialogues and histories and elegies and satires and Allah alone knows what else! Thanks too for giving my precious little sister to your brute of a brother, and the kingdom of Samarkand to our father, whose own gratitude we'll hope may partially restore his sanity! And thanks above all for kindly ceasing to rape and murder a virgin every night, and for persuading Shah Zaman to cease also! I have no right to ask anything further of you at all, but should be overjoyed to serve your sexual and other interests humbly until the day you tire of me and either have me killed or put me by for other, younger women—and indeed I *am* prepared to do just that, as Dunyazade surely is also for Shah Zaman. Yet in view of your boundless magnanimity Q.E.D., I make bold to ask a final favor." If we're lucky, Shahryar will be so mad to get me into bed that he'll say "Name it"—whereupon I point out to him that a happy occasion is about to bring to pass what a thousand ill ones didn't, your separation from me till morning. Knowing my husband, I expect he'll propose a little something *à quatre*,[5] at which I'll blush appropriately and declare that I'm resigned after all to the notion of losing you for a few hours, and wish merely thirty minutes or so of private conversation with you before you and your bridegroom retire, to tell you a few things that every virgin bride should know. "What on earth is there in that line that she hasn't seen us do a hundred times?" your delicate brother-in-law will inquire. "Seeing isn't doing," I'll reply: "I myself have pretty intensive sexual experience, for example, but of one man only, and would be shy as any virgin with another than yourself; Shah Zaman has the widest carnal acquaintance in the world, I suppose, but no long and deep knowledge of any one woman; among the four of us, only you, King of the Age, et cetera, can boast both sorts of experience, having humped your way through twenty years of marriage, a thousand and one one-nighters, and thirty-three and a third months with me, not to mention odd hours with all the concubines in your stable. But little Dunyazade has no experience at all, except vicariously." That master of the quick re-tort will say "Hmp" and turn the matter over to Shah Zaman, who after bringing to it the full weight of his perspicacity will say, in effect, "Okay. But make it short." They'll withdraw, with the grandest erections you and I have ever shuddered at—and *then* I'll tell you what to do in Part Three. After which we'll kiss good night, go in to our husbands, and do it. Got that?'

    "'Do *what?*' I cried—but she'd say no more till all had fallen out as she de-scribed: our wedding-feast and dance; the retirement toward our chambers; her inter-ruption and request; your permission and stipulation that the conference be brief, inasmuch as you were more excited by me than you'd been by any of the two thou-sand unfortunates whose maidenheads and lives you'd done away with in the five and a half years past. You two withdrew, your robes thrust out before; the moment your bedroom doors closed, Sherry spat in your tracks, took my head between her hands, and said: 'If ever you've listened carefully, little sister, listen now. For all his good in-tentions, our Genie of the Key is either a liar or a fool when he says that any man and woman can treasure each other until death—unless their lifetimes are as brief as our murdered sisters'! Three thousand and three, Doony—dead! What have you and I and all that fiction accomplished, except to spare another thousand from a quick end to their misery? What are they saved for, if not a more protracted violation, at the hands

5. For four.

of fathers, husbands, lovers? For the present, it's our masters' pleasure to soften their policy; the patriarchy isn't changed: I believe it will persist even to our Genie's time and place. Suppose his relation to his precious Melissa were truly as he describes it, and not merely as he wishes and imagines it: it would only be the exception that proves the wretched rule. So here we stand, and there you're about to lie, and spread your legs and take it like the rest of us! Thanks be to Allah you can't be snared as I was in the trap of *novelty,* and think to win some victory for our sex by diverting our persecutors with naughty stunts and stories! There *is* no victory, Doony, only unequal retaliation; it's time we turned from tricks to trickery, tales to lies. Go in to your lusty husband now, as I shall to mine; let him kiss and fondle and undress you, paw and pinch and slaver, lay you on the bed; but when he makes to stick you, slip out from under and whisper in his ear that for all his vast experience of sex, there remains one way of making love, most delicious of all, that both he and Shahryar are innocent of, inasmuch as a Genie revealed it to us only last night when we prayed Allah for a way to please such extraordinary husbands. So marvelous is this Position of the Genie, as we'll call it, that even a man who's gone through virgins like breakfast-eggs will think himself newly laid, et cetera. What's more, it's a position in which the woman does everything, her master nothing—except submit himself to a more excruciating pleasure than he's ever known or dreamed of. No more is required of him than that he spread-eagle himself on the bed and suffer his wrists and ankles to be bound to its posts with silken cords, lest by a spasm of early joy he abort its heavenly culmination, et cetera. Then, little sister, then, when you have him stripped and bound supine and salivating, take from the left pocket of your seventh gown the razor I've hid there, as I shall mine from mine—and geld the monster! Cut his bloody engine off and choke him on it, as I'll do to Shahryar! Then we'll lay our own throats open, to spare ourselves their sex's worse revenge. Adieu, my Doony! May we wake together in a world that knows nothing of *he* and *she!* Good night.'

"I moved my mouth to answer; couldn't; came to you as if entranced; and while you kissed me, found the cold blade in my pocket. I let you undress me as in a dream, touch my body where no man has before, lay me down and mount to take me; as in a dream I heard me bid you stay for a rarer pleasure, coax you into the Position of the Genie, and with this edge in hand and voice, rehearse the history of your present bondage. Your brother's docked; my sister's dead; it's time we joined them."

2

"That's the end of your story?"

Dunyazade nodded.

Shah Zaman looked narrowly at his bride, standing naked beside the bed with her trembling razor, and cleared his throat. "If you really mean to use that, kindly kill me with it first. A good hard slice across the Adam's apple should do the trick."

The girl shuddered, shook her head. As best he could, so bound, the young man shrugged.

"At least answer one question: Why in the world did you tell me this extraordinary tale?"

Her eyes still averted, Dunyazade explained in a dull voice that one aspect of her sister's revenge was this reversal not only of the genders of teller and told (as conceived by the Genie), but of their circumstances, the latter now being at the former's mercy.

"Then have some!" urged the King. "For yourself!" Dunyazade looked up. Despite his position, Shah Zaman smiled like the Genie through his pearly beard and declared that Scheherazade was right to think love ephemeral. But life itself was scarcely less so, and both were sweet for just that reason—sweeter yet when enjoyed as if they might endure. For all the inequity of woman's lot, he went on, thousands of women found love as precious as did their lovers: one needed look no farther than Scheherazade's stories for proof of that. If a condemned man—which is what he counted himself, since once emasculate he'd end his life as soon as he could lay hands on his sword—might be granted a last request, such as even *he* used to grant his nightly victims in the morning, his would be to teach his fair executioner the joys of sex before she unsexed him.

"Nonsense," Dunyazade said crossly. "I've seen all that."

"Seeing's not feeling."

She glared at him. "I'll learn when I choose, then, from a less bloody teacher: someone I love, no matter how foolishly." She turned her head. "If I ever meet such a man. Which I won't." Vexed, she slipped into her gown, holding the razor awkwardly in her left hand while she fastened the hooks.

"What a lucky fellow! You don't love me then, little wife?"

"Of course not! I'll admit you're not the monster I'd imagined—in appearance, I mean. But you're a total stranger to me, and the thought of what you did to all those girls makes me retch. Don't waste your last words in silly flirting; you won't change my mind. You'd do better to prepare yourself to die."

"I'm quite prepared, Dunyazade," Shah Zaman replied calmly. "I have been from the beginning. Why else do you suppose I haven't called my guards in to kill you? I'm sure my brother's long since done for Scheherazade, if she really tried to do what she put you up to doing. Shahryar and I would have been great fools not to anticipate this sort of thing from the very first night, six years ago."

"I don't believe you."

The King shrugged his eyebrows and whistled through his teeth; two husky mamelukes stepped at once from behind a tapestry depicting Jamshid's seven-ringed cup, seized Dunyazade by the wrists, covered her mouth, and took the open razor from her hand.

"Fair or not," Shah Zaman said conversationally as she struggled, "your only power at present is what I choose to give you. And fair or not, I choose to give it." He smiled. "Let her have the razor, my friends, and take the rest of the night off. If you don't believe that I deliberately put myself in your hands from the first, Dunyazade, you can't deny I'm doing so now. All I ask is leave to tell you a story, in exchange for the one you've told me; when I'm finished you may do as you please."

The mamelukes reluctantly let her go, but left the room only when Shah Zaman, still stripped and bound, repeated his order. Dunyazade sat exhausted on a hassock, rubbed her wrists, pinned up her fallen hair, drew the gown more closely about her.

"I'm not impressed," she said. "If I pick up the razor, they'll put an arrow through me."

"That hadn't occurred to me," Shah Zaman admitted. "You'll have to trust me a little, then, as I'm trusting you. Do pick it up. I insist."

"You insist!" Dunyazade said bitterly. She took up the razor, let her hand fall passively beside the hassock, began to weep.

"Let's see, now," mused the King. "How can we give you the absolute advantage? They're very fast, those guards, and loyal; if they really *are* standing by, what I fear is that they'll misconstrue some innocent movement of yours and shoot."

"What difference does it make?" Dunyazade said miserably. "Poor Sherry!"

"I have it! Come sit here beside me. Please, do as I say! Now lay that razor's edge exactly where you were going to put it before; then you can make your move before any marksman can draw and release. You'll have to hold me in your other hand; I've gone limp with alarm."

Dunyazade wept.

"Come," the King insisted: "it's the only way you'll be convinced I'm serious. No, I mean right up against it, so that you could do your trick in half a second. Whew, that gooseflesh isn't faked! What a situation! Now look here: even this advantage gripes you, I suppose, since it was given instead of taken: the male still leading the female, et cetera. No help for that just now. Besides, between any two people, you know—what I mean, it's not the patriarchy that makes you take the passive role with your sister, for example. Never mind that. See me sweat! Now, then: I agree with that Genie of yours in the matter of priorities, and I entreat you not only to permit me to tell you a story, but to make love with me first."

Dunyazade shut her eyes and whipped her head from side to side.

"As you wish," said the King. "I'd never force you, as you'll understand if you'll hear my story. Shall I tell it?"

Dunyazade moved her head indifferently.

"More tightly. Careful with that razor!"

"Can't you make it go down?" the girl asked thickly. "It's obscene. And distracting. I think I'm going to be sick."

"Not more distracting than your little breasts, or your little fingers . . . No, please, I insist you keep hold of your advantage! My story's short, I promise, and I'm at your mercy. So:

"Six years ago I thought myself the happiest man alive. I'd had a royal childhood; my college years were a joy; my career had gone brilliantly; at twenty-five I ruled a kingdom almost as prosperous as Shahryar's at forty. I was popular with my subjects; I kept the government reasonably honest, the various power groups reasonably in hand, et cetera. Like every king I kept a harem of concubines for the sake of my public image, but as a rule they were reserved for state visitors. For myself I wanted nobody except my bride, never mind her name, whom after a whole year of marriage I still loved more than any woman I'd ever known. After a day's work in the durbar, bidding and forbidding et cetera, I'd rush in to dinner, and we'd play all night like two kittens in a basket. No trick of love we didn't turn together; no myth of gods and nymphs we didn't mimic. The harem girls, when I used them, only reminded me of how much I preferred my wife; often as not I'd dismiss them in mid-clip and call her in for the finish.

"When my brother summoned me here to visit that first time, much as I longed to see him it was all I could do to leave my bride behind; we made our first goodbyes; then I was as overjoyed as I imagined she'd be when I discovered that I'd forgotten a diamond necklace I'd meant to present to Shahryar's queen. I rushed back to the palace myself instead of sending after it, so that we could make love once again before I left—and I found her in our bed, riding astride the chief cook! Her last words were 'Next time invite *me*'; I cut them both in two, four halves in all, not to seem a wittol;[6] came here and found my sister-in-law cuckolding my brother with the black-amoor Sa'ad al-Din Saood, who swung from trees, slavered and gibbered, and sported a yard that made mine look like your little finger. Kings no more, Shahryar and I left together by the postern gate, resolved to kill ourselves as the most wretched fools on earth if our misery was particular. One day as we were wandering in the marshes, far from the paths of men, devouring our own souls, we saw what we thought was a water-spout coming up the bay, and climbed a loblolly pine for safety. It turned out to be that famous ifrit of your sister's story: he took the steel coffer out of its casket, unlocked the seven locks with seven keys, fetched out and futtered the girl he'd stolen on her wedding night, and fell asleep in her lap; she signaled us to come down and ordered us both to cuckold the ifrit with her then and there. Who says a man can't be forced? We did our best, and she added our seal rings to the five hundred seventy she'd already collected. We understood then that no woman on earth who wants a rogering will go unrogered, though she be sealed up in a tower of brass.

"So. When I'd first told my brother of my own cuckolding, he'd vowed that in my position he'd not have rested till he'd killed a thousand women: now we went back to his palace; he put to death his queen and all his concubines and their lovers, and we took a solemn oath to rape and kill a virgin a night, so as never again to be deceived. I came home to Samarkand, wondering at the turns of our despair: how a private apocalypse can infect the state and bring about one more general, et cetera. With this latter motive, more than for revenge on womankind, I resolved to hold to our dreadful policy until my kingdom fell to ruin or an outraged populace rose up and slew me.

"But unlike Shahryar, I said nothing at first to my vizier, only told him to fetch me a beautiful virgin for the night. Not knowing that I meant to kill her in the morning, he brought me his own daughter, a girl I knew well and had long admired, Samarkand's equivalent of Scheherazade. I assumed he was pandering to his own advancement, and smiled at the thought of putting them to death together; I soon learned, however, from the woman herself, that it was her own idea to come to me—and her motive, unlike your sister's, was simple love. I undressed and fell to toying with her; she wept; I asked what ailed her: it was not being separated from her sister, but being alone at last with me, the fulfillment of her lifelong dream. I found myself much touched by this and, to my surprise, impotent. Stalling for time, I remarked that such dreams could turn out to be nightmares. She embraced me timidly and replied that she deplored my murdering my wife and her paramour, both of whom she'd known and rather liked, for though in a general way she sympathized with my disenchanted outrage, she believed she understood as well my wife's motives for cuckolding me, which in her view were not all that different, essentially, from the ifrit's maiden's in the story. Despite my anger, she went on bravely to declare that she herself took what she called the Tragic View of Sex and Temperament: to wit, that while perfect equality between men and women was the only defensible value in that line, she was not at all certain it was attainable; even to pursue it ardently, against the grain of things as they were, was in all likelihood to spoil one's chances for happiness in love; *not* to pursue it, on the other hand, once one had seen it clearly to be the ideal, no doubt had the same effect. For herself, though she deplored injustice whether in

6. A dated word for a husband who resigns himself to the unfaithfulness of his wife.

individuals or in institutions, and gently affirmed equality as the goal that lovers lovingly should strive for, however far short of it their histories and temperaments made them fall, yet she knew herself personally to be unsuited for independence, formed by her nature and upbringing to be happy only in the shadow of a man whom she admired and respected more than herself. She was anything but blind to my faults and my own blindness to them, she declared, but so adored me withal that if I could love her even for a night she'd think her life complete, and wish nothing further unless maybe a little Shah Zaman to devote the rest of her years to raising. Or if my disillusionment with women were so extreme (as she seemed uncannily to guess from my expression) that I had brought her to my bed not to marry her or even add her to my harem, but merely to take her virginity and her life, I was welcome to both; she only prayed I might be gentle in their taking.

"This last remark dismayed me the more because it echoed something my late wife had said on our wedding night: that even death at my hands would be sweeter to her than life at another's. How I despised, resented, missed her! As if it were I who was cut in two, I longed to hold her as in nights gone by, yet would have halved her bloody halves if she'd been restored to me. There lay my new woman on the bed, naked and still now; I stood on my knees between hers, weeping so for her predecessor's beauty and deceit, my own blindness and cruelty—and the wretched state of affairs between man and womankind that made love a will-o'-the-wisp, jealousy and boredom and resentment the rule—that I could neither function nor dissemble. I told her of all that had taken place between my departure from Samarkand and my return, the oath I'd sworn with my brother, and my resolve to keep it lest I seem chicken-hearted and a fool.

"'Lest you *seem!*' the girl cried out. 'Harems, homicides—everything for the sake of seeming!' She commanded me then, full of irony for all her fears, to *keep* my vow if I meant to keep it, or else cut out her tongue before I cut off her head; for if I sent her to the block without deflowering her first, she would declare to any present, even if only her executioner, that I was a man in seeming merely, not in fact, and offer her maidenhead as proof. Her courage astonished me as much as her words. 'By Allah,' I vowed to her, 'I won't kill you if I can't get it up for you first.' But that miserable fellow in your left hand, which had never once failed me before, and which stands up now like an idiot soldier in enemy country, as if eager to be cut down, deserted me utterly. I tried every trick I knew, in vain, though my victim willingly complied with my instructions. I could of course have killed her myself, then and there, but I had no wish to seem a hypocrite even for a moment in her eyes; nor, for that matter, to let her die a virgin—nor, I admitted finally to myself, to let her die at all before she was overtaken like the rest of us by the Destroyer of Delights et cetera. For seven nights we tossed and tumbled, fondled and kissed and played, she reaching such heats of unaccustomed joy as to cry out, no longer sarcastically, that if only I would stick her first with my carnal sword, she'd bare her neck without complaint to my steel. On the seventh night, as we lay panting in a sweat of frustration, I gave her my dagger and invited her to do me and Samarkand the kindness of killing me at once, for I'd rather die than seem unable to keep my vow.

"'You *are* unable to keep it,' she told me softly: 'not because you're naturally impotent, but because you're *not* naturally cruel. If you'd tell your brother that after thinking it over you've simply come to a conclusion different from his, you'd be cured as if by magic.' And in fact, as if by magic indeed, what she said was so true that at her very words the weight was lifted from heart and tool together; they rose as one. Gratefully, tenderly, I went into her at last; we cried for joy, came at once, fell asleep in each other's arms.

"No question after that of following Shahryar's lead; on the other hand, I found myself in the morning not yet man enough after all to send word to him of my change of heart and urge him to change his. Neither was I, after all, in love enough with the Vizier's daughter to risk again the estate of marriage, which she herself considered problematical at best.

"'I never expected you to marry me,' she told me when I told her these things, 'though I'd be dishonest if I didn't say I dreamed and prayed you might. All I ever really hoped for was a love affair with you, and a baby to remember it by. Even if I don't have the baby, I've had the affair: you truly loved me last night.'

"I did, and for many nights after—but not enough to make the final step. What your Genie said concerning marriage could have come from my own mouth if I had the gift of words: to anyone of moral imagination who's known it, no other relation between men and women has true seriousness; yet that same imagination kept me from it. And I dreaded the day my brother would get word of my weakness. I grew glum and cross; my mistress, intuitive as ever, guessed the reason at once. 'You can neither keep your vow nor break it,' she told me: 'Perhaps you'd better do both for a while, till you find your way.' I asked her how such a contradiction was possible. 'By the magic words *as if,*' she replied, 'which, to a person satisfied with seeming, are more potent than all the genii in the tales.'

"She then set forth a remarkable proposal: legend had it that far to the west of Samarkand was a country peopled entirely with women, adjoining another wholly male: for two months every spring they mated freely with each other on neutral ground, the women returning home as they found themselves pregnant, giving their male children to the neighboring tribe and raising the girls as members of their own. Whether or not such a community in fact existed, she thought it a desirable alternative to the present state of affairs, and unquestionably preferable to death; since I couldn't treasure her as she treasured me (and not for a moment did she *blame* me for that incapacity), she proposed to establish such an alternative society herself, with my assistance. I was to proclaim my brother's policy as my own, take to bed a virgin every night and declare her executed in the morning; but instead of actually raping and killing them I would tell them of her alternative society and send them secretly from Samarkand, in groups of a hundred or so, to organize and populate it. If, knowing their destiny, they chose to spend their last night in Samarkand making love with me, that was their affair; none, she imagined, would choose death over emigration, and any who found their new way of life not to their liking could return to Samarkand if and when I changed my policy, or migrate elsewhere in the meanwhile. In any case they'd be alive and free; or, if the pioneers were captured and made slaves of by barbarians before the new society was established, they'd be no worse off than the millions of their sisters already in that condition. On the other hand, separate societies of men and women, mingling freely at their own wills as equals on neutral ground, might just make possible a true society of the future in which the separation was no longer necessary. And in the meantime, of course, for better or worse, it would be as if I'd kept my dreadful vow.

"At first hearing, the plan struck me as absurd; after a few nights it seemed less so, perhaps even feasible; by the end of a week of examining passionately with her all the alternatives, it seemed no less unreasonable than they. My angel herself, in keeping with her Tragic View, didn't expect the new society to *work* in the naïve sense: what human institutions ever did? It would have the vices of its virtues; if not nipped in the bud by marauding rapists, it would grow and change and rigidify in forms and values quite different from its founders'—codifying, institutionalizing, and perverting its original spirit. No help for that.

"Was there ever such a woman? I kissed her respectfully, then ardently a final time. After one last love-making in the morning, while my hand lingered on her left breast, she declared calmly her intention, upon arriving at her virgin kingdom, to amputate that same breast for symbolic reasons and urge her companions to do the same, as a kind of initiation rite. 'We'll make up a practical excuse for it,' she said: "'The better to draw our bows," et cetera. But the real point will be that in one aspect we're all woman, in another all warrior. Maybe we'll call ourselves The Breastless Ones.'

"'That seems extreme,' I remarked. She replied that a certain extremism was necessary to the survival of anything radically innovative. Later generations, she assumed, established and effete, would find the ancestral custom barbaric and honor its symbolism, if at all, with a correspondingly symbolic mammectomy[7]—a decorative scar, perhaps, or cosmetic mark. No matter; everything passed.

"So did our connection: with a thousand thanks to her for opening my eyes, a thousand good wishes for the success of her daring enterprise, and many thousands of dinars[8] to support it (which for portability and security she converted into a phial of diamonds and carried intravaginally), I declared her dead, let her father the Vizier in on our secret, and sent her off secretly to one of my country castles on a distant lake, where she prepared for the expedition west-ward while her companions, the ostensible victims of my new policy, accumulated about her. Perhaps a third, apprised of their fate, chose to remain virginal, whether indignantly, ruefully, or gratefully; on the other two-thirds who in whatever spirit elected to go hymenless to the new society, I bestowed similar phials of jewels. Somewhat less than fifty per cent of this number found themselves impregnated by our night together, and so when the first detachment of two hundred pioneers set out across the western wastes, their actual number was about two hundred sixty. Since I pursued this policy for nearly two thousand nights, the number of pilgrims and unborn children sent west from Samarkand must have totaled about twenty-six hundred; corrected for a normal male birth rate of somewhat over fifty per cent, a rather higher than normal rate of spontaneous abortion, and infant as well as maternal mortality owing to the rigors of traveling and of settling a new territory, and ignoring—as one must to retain one's reason—the possibility of mass enslavement, rape, massacre, or natural catastrophe, the number of pioneers to the Country of the Breastless must be at least equal to the number of nights until Shahryar's message concerning your sister arrived from the Islands of India and China.

"Of the success or failure of those founding mothers I know nothing; kept myself ignorant deliberately, lest I learn that I was sending them after all to the Destroyer of Delights and Severer of Societies. The folk of Samarkand never rose against me; nor did my vizier, like Shahryar's, have difficulty enlisting sacrificial virgins; even at the end, though my official toll was twice my brother's, about half the girls were volunteers—from all which, I infer that their actual fate was an open secret. For all I know, my original mistress never truly intended to found her gynocracy;[9] the whole proposal was perhaps a ruse; perhaps they all slipped back into the country with their phials of gems for dowry, married and lived openly under my nose. No matter: night after night I brought them to bed, set forth their options, then either glumly stripped

---

7. Breast amputation.   9. A social system in which the elite are women.
8. Currency of several Arabic countries.

and pronged them or spent the night in chaste sleep and conversation. Tall and short, dark and fair, lean and plump, cold and ardent, bold and timid, clever and stupid, comely and plain—I bedded them all, spoke with them all, possessed them all, but was myself possessed by nothing but despair. Though I took many, with their consent, I wanted none of them. Novelty lost its charm, then even its novelty. Unfamiliarity I came to loathe: the foreign body in the dark, the alien touch and voice, the endless *exposition*. All I craved was someone with whom to get on with the story of my life, which was to say, of our life together: a loving friend; a loving wife; a treasurable wife; a wife, a wife.

"My brother's second message, when it came, seemed a miraculous reprise of that fatal first, six years before: I turned the kingdom over to my vizier and set out at once, resolved to meet this Scheherazade who had so wooed and yarned him back to the ways of life that he meant to wed her. 'Perhaps she has a younger sister,' I said to myself; if she does, I'll make no inquiries, demand no stories, set no conditions, but humbly put my life in her hands, tell her the whole tale of the two thousand and two nights that led me to her, and bid her end that story as she will—whether with the last goodnight of all or (what I can just dimly envision, like dawn in another world) some clear and fine and fresh good morning."

Dunyazade yawned and shivered. "I can't imagine what you're talking about. Am I expected to believe that preposterous business of Breastless Pilgrims and Tragic Views?"

"Yes!" cried Shah Zaman, then let his head fall back to the pillow. "They're too important to be lies. Fictions, maybe—but truer than fact."

Dunyazade covered her eyes with her razor-hand. "What do you expect me to do? Forgive you? Love you?"

"Yes!" the King cried again, his eyes flashing. "Let's end the dark night! All that passion and hate between men and women; all that confusion of inequality and difference! Let's take the truly tragic view of love! Maybe it *is* a fiction, but it's the profoundest and best of all! Treasure me, Dunyazade, as I'll treasure you!"

"For pity's sake stop!"

But Shah Zaman urged ardently: "Let's embrace; let's forbear; let's love as long as we can, Dunyazade—then embrace again, forbear and love again!"

"It won't work."

"Nothing *works!* But the enterprise is noble; it's full of joy and life, and the other ways are deathly. Let's make love like passionate equals!"

"You mean *as if* we were equals," Dunyazade said. "You know we're not. What you want is impossible."

"Despite your heart's feelings?" pressed the King. "Let it be *as if!* Let's make a philosophy of that *as if!*"

Dunyazade wailed: "I want my sister!"

"She may be alive; my brother, too." More quietly, Shah Zaman explained that Shahryar had been made acquainted with his brother's recent history and opinions, and had vowed that should Scheherazade ever attempt his life, he'd manage himself somewhat similarly: that is (as he was twenty years older, and more conservative), not exactly granting his wife the power to kill him, but disarming and declining to kill *her*, and within the bounds of good public relations, permitting her a freedom comparable to his own. The harem was a royal tradition, necessarily public; Scheherazade could take what lovers she would, but of necessity in private. Et cetera.

"Did you really imagine your sister *fooled* Shahryar for a thousand nights with her mamelukes and dildoes?" Shah Zaman laughed. "A man couldn't stay king very long if he didn't even know what was going on in the harem! And why do you suppose he permitted it, if not that he loved her too much, and was too sick of his other policy, to kill her? She changed his mind, all right, but she never fooled him: he used to believe that all women were unfaithful, and that the only way to spare himself the pain of infidelity was to deflower and kill them; now he believes that all *people* are unfaithful, and that the way to spare oneself the pain of infidelity is to love and not to care. He chooses equal promiscuity; I choose equal fidelity. Let's treasure each other, Dunyazade!"

She shook her head angrily, or desperately. "It's absurd. You're only trying to talk your way out of a bad spot."

"Of course I am! And of course it's absurd! Treasure me!"

"I'm exhausted. I should use the razor on both of us, and be done with it."

"Treasure me, Dunyazade!"

"We've talked all night; I hear the cocks; it's getting light."

"Good morning, then! Good morning!"

3

Alf Laylah Wa Laylah, The Book of the Thousand Nights and a Night, is not the story of Scheherazade, but the story of the story of her stories, which in effect begins: "There is a book called *The Thousand and One Nights,* in which it is said that once upon a time a king had two sons, Shahryar and Shah Zaman," et cetera; it ends when a king long after Shahryar discovers in his treasury the thirty volumes of *The Stories of the Thousand Nights and a Night,* at the end of the last of which the royal couples—Shahryar and Scheherazade, Shah Zaman and Dunyazade—emerge from their bridal chambers after the wedding night, greet one another with warm good mornings (eight in all), bestow Samarkand on the brides' long-suffering father, and set down for all posterity *The Thousand Nights and a Night.*

If I could invent a story as beautiful, it should be about little Dunyazade and her bridegroom, who pass a thousand nights in one dark night and in the morning embrace each other; they make love side by side, their faces close, and go out to greet sister and brother in the forenoon of a new life. Dunyazade's story begins in the middle; in the middle of my own, I can't conclude it—but it must end in the night that all good mornings come to. The Arab storytellers understood this; they ended their stories not "happily ever after," but specifically "until there took them the Destroyer of Delights and Desolator of Dwelling-places, and they were translated to the truth of Almighty Allah, and their houses fell waste and their palaces lay in ruins, and the Kings inherited their riches." And no man knows it better than Shah Zaman, to whom therefore the second half of his life will be sweeter than the first.

To be joyous in the full acceptance of this dénouement is surely to possess a treasure, the key to which is the understanding that Key and Treasure are the same. There (with a kiss, little sister) is the sense of our story, Dunyazade: The key to the treasure is the treasure.

Italo Calvino
1923–1985

Displaced even at birth, Italo Calvino was born in Santiago, Cuba, while his Italian parents were on a scientific expedition. His youth was spent in San Remo, Italy, and he attended the University of Turin intermittently between 1941 and 1947. He deserted the Young Fascist ranks into which he was drafted in 1940 and joined the Resistance—an experience that taught him to suspect the seeming stability of human institutions and the unreliable nature of human constancy. After World War II, he worked as a journalist for the Communist periodical *L'Unitá,* and in 1948 he joined the publishing house Einaudi, for which he would work as editor and author until 1984 even as he continued to write for a number of Italian periodicals throughout his career. Like Jorge Luis Borges, whom he admired, Calvino would explore the thresholds between reality and imagination, realism and fantasy, rationality and invention. His novels and tales read much like fables on language. They often read as allegories on the human capacity to find worlds in words and to discover the fragility of the human condition and of what we take to be historical or material reality.

In his work Calvino combines history's caprices with the whimsy of imaginative fancy. His novels enact the unreliable character of memory, history, vision, institutions, and orthodoxies even as they play with scientific theories and methods, as in his works *Cosmicomics* and *Mr. Palomar.* The geographies of the imagination find greater solidity in his works. When he died of a cerebral hemorrhage on 19 September 1985, he was preparing to deliver the Charles Eliot Norton lectures at Harvard University. Those lectures were subsequently published as *Six Memos for the Next Millennium* (1988).

Reading and writing are frequent themes in Calvino's fiction, and he dramatizes the processes of literacy in such novels as *If on a Winter's Night a Traveller* (1979), full of stories about stories within stories. One of his most delightful and suggestive enactments of storytelling is *Invisible Cities* (1971), excerpted here. In this work, Calvino brings together two very different imaginary worlds: Scheherazade's Persian/Arab sea of stories and the partly factual, partly fantastic medieval Travels of Marco Polo. In the late thirteenth century, Polo had traveled to China, where he lived for many years in the court of the cultivated emperor Kublai Khan, son of the Mongol invader Chingiz Khan. Polo served in the Khan's government and apparently undertook several fact-finding missions for the Khan to distant regions. Calvino presents Polo describing a series of magical, mysterious cities, each account given an emblematic heading—"Cities and Eyes," "Cities and the Dead," each of which appears five times in the course of the book; two of these series are given here. As Polo describes these "invisible cities," he becomes a Scheherazadian storyteller who portrays life in an aging empire—modern as much as medieval—and, in the process, engages in a meditation on the sovereign powers of storytelling itself.

from Invisible Cities[1]

CITIES AND MEMORY 1

Leaving there and proceeding for three days toward the east, you reach Diomira, a city with sixty silver domes, bronze statues of all the gods, streets paved with lead, a crystal theater, a golden cock that crows each morning on a tower. All these beauties will already be familiar to the visitor, who has seen them also in other cities. But the special quality of this city for the man who arrives there on a September evening,

---

1. Translated by William Weaver. The first episode begins as though it is part of an already ongoing conversation.

when the days are growing shorter and the multicolored lamps are lighted all at once at the doors of the food stalls and from a terrace a woman's voice cries ooh!, is that he feels envy toward those who now believe they have once before lived an evening identical to this and who think they were happy, that time.

CITIES AND MEMORY 2

When a man rides a long time through wild regions he feels the desire for a city. Finally he comes to Isidora, a city where the buildings have spiral staircases encrusted with spiral seashells, where perfect telescopes and violins are made, where the foreigner hesitating between two women always encounters a third, where cockfights degenerate into bloody brawls among the bettors. He was thinking of all these things when he desired a city. Isidora, therefore, is the city of his dreams: with one difference. The dreamed-of city contained him as a young man; he arrives at Isidora in his old age. In the square there is the wall where the old men sit and watch the young go by; he is seated in a row with them. Desires are already memories.

CITIES AND MEMORY 3

In vain, great-hearted Kublai, shall I attempt to describe Zaira, city of high bastions. I could tell you how many steps make up the streets rising like stairways, and the degree of the arcades' curves, and what kind of zinc scales cover the roofs; but I already know this would be the same as telling you nothing. The city does not consist of this, but of relationships between the measurements of its space and the events of its past: the height of a lamppost and the distance from the ground of a hanged usurper's swaying feet; the line strung from the lamppost to the railing opposite and the festoons that decorate the course of the queen's nuptial procession; the height of that railing and the leap of the adulterer who climbed over it at dawn; the tilt of a guttering and a cat's progress along it as he slips into the same window; the firing range of a gunboat which has suddenly appeared beyond the cape and the bomb that destroys the guttering; the rips in the fish net and the three old men seated on the dock mending nets and telling each other for the hundredth time the story of the gunboat of the usurper, who some say was the queen's illegitimate son, abandoned in his swaddling clothes there on the dock.

As this wave from memories flows in, the city soaks it up like a sponge and expands. A description of Zaira as it is today should contain all Zaira's past. The city, however, does not tell its past, but contains it like the lines of a hand, written in the corners of the streets, the gratings of the windows, the banisters of the steps, the antennae of the lightning rods, the poles of the flags, every segment marked in turn with scratches, indentations, scrolls.

CITIES AND MEMORY 4

Beyond six rivers and three mountain ranges rises Zora, a city that no one, having seen it, can forget. But not because, like other memorable cities, it leaves an unusual image in your recollections. Zora has the quality of remaining in your memory point by point, in its succession of streets, of houses along the streets, and of doors and windows in the houses, though nothing in them possesses a special beauty or rarity. Zora's secret lies in the way your gaze runs over patterns following one another as in a musical score where not a note can be altered or displaced. The man who knows by heart how Zora is made, if he is unable to sleep at night, can imagine he is walking along the streets and he remembers the order by which the copper clock follows the barber's striped awning, then the fountain with the nine jets, the astronomer's glass tower, the melon vendor's kiosk, the statue of the hermit and the lion, the Turkish bath, the café at the corner, the alley that leads to the harbor. This city which cannot be expunged from the mind is like an armature, a honeycomb in whose cells each of us can place the things he wants to remember: names of famous men, virtues, numbers, vegetable and mineral classifications, dates of battles, constellations, parts of speech. Between each idea and each point of the itinerary an affinity or a contrast can be established, serving as an immediate aid to memory. So the world's most learned men are those who have memorized Zora.

But in vain I set out to visit the city: forced to remain motionless and always the same, in order to be more easily remembered, Zora has languished, disintegrated, disappeared. The earth has forgotten her.

Cities and Memory 5

In Maurilia, the traveler is invited to visit the city and, at the same time, to examine some old post cards that show it as it used to be: the same identical square with a hen in the place of the bus station, a bandstand in the place of the overpass, two young ladies with white parasols in the place of the munitions factory. If the traveler does not wish to disappoint the inhabitants, he must praise the postcard city and prefer it to the present one, though he must be careful to contain his regret at the changes within definite limits: admitting that the magnificence and prosperity of the metropolis Maurilia, when compared to the old, provincial Maurilia, cannot compensate for a certain lost grace, which, however, can be appreciated only now in the old post cards, whereas before, when that provincial Maurilia was before one's eyes, one saw absolutely nothing graceful and would see it even less today, if Maurilia had remained unchanged; and in any case the metropolis has the added attraction that, through what it has become, one can look back with nostalgia at what it was.

Beware of saying to them that sometimes different cities follow one another on the same site and under the same name, born and dying without knowing one another, without communication among themselves. At times even the names of the inhabitants remain the same, and their voices' accent, and also the features of the faces; but the gods who live beneath names and above places have gone off without a word and outsiders have settled in their place. It is pointless to ask whether the new ones are better or worse than the old, since there is no connection between them, just as the old post cards do not depict Maurilia as it was, but a different city which, by chance, was called Maurilia, like this one.

Trading Cities 1

Proceeding eighty miles into the northwest wind, you reach the city of Euphemia, where the merchants of seven nations gather at every solstice and equinox. The boat that lands there with a cargo of ginger and cotton will set sail again, its hold filled with pistachio nuts and poppy seeds, and the caravan that has just unloaded sacks of nutmegs and raisins is already cramming its saddlebags with bolts of golden muslin for the return journey. But what drives men to travel up rivers and cross deserts to come here is not only the exchange of wares, which you could find, everywhere the same, in all the bazaars inside and outside the Great Khan's empire, scattered at your feet on the same yellow mats, in the shade of the same awnings protecting them from the flies, offered with the same lying reduction in prices. You do not come to Euphemia only to buy and sell, but also because at night, by the fires all around the market, seated on sacks or barrels or stretched out on piles of carpets, at each word that one man says—such as "wolf," "sister," "hidden treasure," "battle," "scabies," "lovers"—the others tell, each one, his tale of wolves, sisters, treasures, scabies, lovers, battles. And you know that in the long journey ahead of you, when to keep awake against the camel's swaying or the junk's rocking, you start summoning up your memories one by one, your wolf will have become another wolf, your sister a different sister, your battle other battles, on your return from Euphemia, the city where memory is traded at every solstice and at every equinox.

TRADING CITIES 2

In Chloe, a great city, the people who move through the streets are all strangers. At each encounter, they imagine a thousand things about one another; meetings which could take place between them, conversations, surprises, caresses, bites. But no one greets anyone; eyes lock for a second, then dart away, seeking other eyes, never stopping.

A girl comes along, twirling a parasol on her shoulder, and twirling slightly also her rounded hips. A woman in black comes along, showing her full age, her eyes restless beneath her veil, her lips trembling. A tattooed giant comes along; a young man with white hair; a female dwarf; two girls, twins, dressed in coral. Something runs among them, an exchange of glances like lines that connect one figure with another and draw arrows, stars, triangles, until all combinations are used up in a moment, and other characters come on to the scene: a blind man with a cheetah on a leash, a courtesan with an ostrich-plume fan, an ephebe, a Fat Woman. And thus, when some people happen to find themselves together, taking shelter from the rain under an arcade, or crowding beneath an awning of the bazaar, or stopping to listen to the band in the square, meetings, seductions, copulations, orgies are consummated among them without a word exchanged, without a finger touching anything, almost without an eye raised.

A voluptuous vibration constantly stirs Chloe, the most chaste of cities. If men and women began to live their ephemeral dreams, every phantom would become a person with whom to begin a story of pursuits, pretenses, misunderstandings, clashes, oppressions, and the carousel of fantasies would stop.

TRADING CITIES 3

When he enters the territory of which Eutropia is the capital, the traveler sees not one city but many, of equal size and not unlike one another, scattered over a vast, rolling plateau. Eutropia is not one, but all these cities together; only one is inhabited at a time, the others are empty; and this process is carried out in rotation. Now I shall tell you how. On the day when Eutropia's inhabitants feel the grip of weariness and no one can bear any longer his job, his relatives, his house and his life, debts, the people he must greet or who greet him, then the whole citizenry decides to move to the next city, which is there waiting for them, empty and good as new; there each will take up a new job, a different wife, will see another landscape on opening his window, and will spend his time with different pastimes, friends, gossip. So their life is renewed from move to move, among cities whose exposure or declivity or streams or winds make each site somehow different from the others. Since their society is ordered without great distinctions of wealth or authority, the passage from one function to another takes place almost without jolts; variety is guaranteed by the multiple assignments, so that in the span of a lifetime a man rarely returns to a job that has already been his.

Thus the city repeats its life, identical, shifting up and down on its empty chessboard. The inhabitants repeat the same scenes, with the actors changed; they repeat the same speeches with variously combined accents; they open alternate mouths in identical yawns. Alone, among all the cities of the empire, Eutropia remains always the same. Mercury, god of the fickle, to whom the city is sacred, worked this ambiguous miracle.

TRADING CITIES 4

In Ersilia, to establish the relationships that sustain the city's life, the inhabitants stretch strings from the corners of the houses, white or black or gray or black-and-white according to whether they mark a relationship of blood, of trade, authority, agency. When the strings become so numerous that you can no longer pass among them, the inhabitants leave: the houses are dismantled; only the strings and their supports remain.

From a mountainside, camping with their household goods, Ersilia's refugees look at the labyrinth of taut strings and poles that rise in the plain. That is the city of Ersilia still, and they are nothing.

They rebuild Ersilia elsewhere. They weave a similar pattern of strings which they would like to be more complex and at the same time more regular than the other. Then they abandon it and take themselves and their houses still farther away.

Thus, when traveling in the territory of Ersilia, you come upon the ruins of the abandoned cities, without the walls which do not last, without the bones of the dead which the wind rolls away: spiderwebs of intricate relationships seeking a form.

TRADING CITIES 5

In Esmeralda, city of water, a network of canals and a network of streets span and intersect each other. To go from one place to another you have always the choice between land and boat: and since the shortest distance between two points in Esmeralda is not a straight line but a zigzag that ramifies in tortuous optional routes, the ways that open to each passerby are never two, but many, and they increase further for those who alternate a stretch by boat with one on dry land.

And so Esmeralda's inhabitants are spared the boredom of following the same streets every day. And that is not all: the network of routes is not arranged on one level, but follows instead an up-and-down course of steps, landings, cambered bridges, hanging streets. Combining segments of the various routes, elevated or on ground level, each inhabitant can enjoy every day the pleasure of a new itinerary to reach the same places. The most fixed and calm lives in Esmeralda are spent without any repetition.

Secret and adventurous lives, here as elsewhere, are subject to greater restrictions. Esmeralda's cats, thieves, illicit lovers move along higher, discontinuous ways, dropping from a rooftop to a balcony, following gutterings with acrobats' steps. Below, the rats run in the darkness of the sewers, one behind the other's tail, along with conspirators and smugglers: they peep out of manholes and drainpipes, they slip through double bottoms and ditches, from one hiding place to another they drag crusts of cheese, contraband goods, kegs of gunpowder, crossing the city's compactness pierced by the spokes of underground passages.

A map of Esmeralda should include, marked in different colored inks, all these routes, solid and liquid, evident and hidden. It is more difficult to fix on the map the routes of the swallows, who cut the air over the roofs, dropping long invisible parabolas with their still wings, darting to gulp a mosquito, spiraling upward, grazing a pinnacle, dominating from every point of their airy paths all the points of the city.

↦ ≭◆≖ ↤

Assia Djebar
b. 1936

Born Fatima-Zohra Imalhayène in Cherchell, a small coastal town west of Algiers, Algeria, Assia Djebar in 1955 became the first Algerian woman to be admitted to the prestigious École Normale Supérieure de Sèvres, France. In 1956, in support of Algeria's struggle for independence from France, she turned from her studies to writing fiction under the pen name she has used ever since. Perhaps the most internationally visible woman writer in the Arab world, Djebar has been constant in her social commitment on behalf of her native country and its decolonization. Her work speaks forcefully for human rights, especially the rights of women in Arab culture and throughout the world. Her novels and short stories, starting with her first novel, *The Mischief* (1957), have been devoted to giving voice and presence to the silenced and the marginalized. She has also written poetry, plays, and film scripts, and she received a prize from the Venice Film Festival for her 1978 film *La nouba des femmes du Mont Chenoua* ("The Mount Chenoua Band of Women"). Her work has been translated into numerous languages, and she has been the recipient of a number of prestigious international literary prizes.

In her version of the *Thousand and One Nights,* Djebar transposes the romantic tales to the grim realities of timeless wedding rituals that serve as rites of passage for young girls. In juxtaposing the fairy tale with the common practices of city and country alike, and of centuries-old traditions and modern customs, Djebar dramatizes the timelessness of women's subjugation and the rites of the wedding night, which becomes a threshold into womanhood and a passage from innocence to experience—an initiation into the sisterhood of timeless Scheherazades.

PRONUNCIATION:
Assia Djebar: AHS-see-ah djeh-BAHR

from A Sister to Sheherazade[1]
The Sister

The brass bedstead is eventually auctioned, its brass fittings crushed and put out for sale on the pavement by the junk dealer. The voice beneath the bed is once again that of the woman who lurks there through the night to waken the sleeper on the verge of the new day.

---

1. Translated by Dorothy Blair.

Every night a woman prepares to keep watch to prevent the executioner's bloody deed. The listener now is the sister. Her vigil ensures that she will render without fail the promised assistance; she brings the hope of salvation before the new day dawns.

The sister waits beneath the bed. The favourite's sister; and she is there just because she is the sister, so taboo to the polygamist. The story-teller's sister, sister to the woman who has dreams and anticipates her fate, who is hailed as the sultan's bride for a day, and who knows that at sunrise she will be sacrificed and who, with every word she utters, hovers between extinction and the throne.

The master lies in the centre of the bed, with fixed eyes, the man interposed between woman listening to woman. A current flows from the story-teller above to the woman keeping watch below this stage—the setting for love.

The man who has the power of life and death listens. He listens as he carries the weight of the fatal verdict, which he suspends for twelve hours at the most, until the following dusk.

A woman keeps secret watch beneath the bed: a woman prompts the other with a word at the first sign of weakening. Her voice is ready to fly to the rescue, picking up every dropped stitch in the tale, and this woman is the sister.

But first of all she had had to let the sounds and ferment of amorous play flow over her head. The confused murmurs: a *wadi* in spate, even in the heart of the desert. Menacing, roaring, deadly flood waters.

But why does the sister take up her place beneath the bed? . . . The law allows the polygamist to take any concubine, any female slave of whom he is the master, except the sister of the woman whom he tumbles in his bed. Thus, the sister beneath the bed can lie in wait, hearing everything, and for that very reason, shield from death.

She can take up her lodging in the morass of the others' sexual pleasure and keep guard at the same time. Alone, under the draperies of the divan, on which they sport, she lets their silken sensuality slip past, and at the same time forestalls death's advance. Alone, since she is the favourite's sister, her double and the one who can never be her rival. Her duty is to waken; she is also the one who snares the birds.

Up above, the sultan's bride spins her tales; she is fighting for her life. Her sister, beneath the couch, rallies the past victims.

* * *

Nuptials on a Straw Mat

We children could get into the next-door house by climbing on to the low wall and jumping down on to the adjacent terrace. The oldest girl in this family had had a "French-style" wedding: arrayed in a white satin gown, with two little bridesmaids in white tulle, holding a bouquet of orange-blossom—so that white became, not the symbol of virginity, but of entry into the Western world—on the morrow of a union consummated by force, with the brutality of rape.

Then the bride, flanked by the little bridesmaids in their fancy get-up, had posed for the photographer—the only man admitted to mingle with the host of female guests who had left their silken veils folded at the door as they arrived. Attired in low-cut gowns, well-nigh Parisian in elegance, they saw themselves sharing in the new ceremonial. Their comments—including those on the "camera man", for whom this had been quite exciting—had been kept up well into the next few weeks.

The bride had been "given" to a first cousin; but, thanks to a progressive evolution in customs, the second daughter could hope, as she herself said, to be able to marry for love.

This second daughter was a romantic soul. From the age of twelve, when she was taken out of school, to remain a recluse till her marriage, she had read avidly all the love-stories serialized in the fashion magazines to which she subscribed. She had even managed to get hold of several novels by Colette[2]—the *Claudine* series as well as *Chéri*. She spoke in a hushed voice, she did not so much daydream as withdraw completely from the real world . . .

In any case, the local matrons lauded to the skies her skill in embroidery, dress-making and lacemaking. They spoke with equal admiration of her beauty, her modesty (she blushed at the slightest word and never managed to make her tiny voice heard in the many social gatherings), as of her trousseau. Especially of her trousseau!

It combined the local Andalusian tradition and that of the European dream described by the French magazines. According to the former, the bride must arrive in her new home with a score of tunic-dresses in diverse colours, all embroidered with gold thread, and, in addition, everything for the conjugal bed-chamber: a number of mattresses of blond wool, which had been washed in surrounding streams, sterilized and compressed by indefatigable servants; counterpanes, drawn-thread-worked sheets, sequined cushions, hangings for the bed and curtains for the windows; and, lastly, the hand-embroidered toilet-bag for the weekly bath. But, like any European girl, she prepared an abundant wardrobe for herself: silk blouses, embroidered with drawn-thread-work (in Tunisian, Algerian or Moroccan style), short skirts and knitted pullovers. What is more, the second daughter, like her elder sister, had a right to the white gown for the great day—which however she would don only after she had appeared in the outfit consisting of garnet-red tunic, *saroual* with matching waistcoat, sequined sashes and flower-patterned mules. But she was not satisfied to order this immaculate gown by post and then make a few alterations. No, she cut it out herself, she embroidered it herself; last year she had regularly sat up half the night making this "trousseau fit for a princess" with her own fair hands.

And every matron mused: how would she dare ask for the hand of this most beautiful, most sweet-natured, most gifted of virgins, for any of her sons? In fact, every one of these ladies feared the mother's uncompromising pride. It was well known that, in this family where sons had been born only after a brood of girls, the arrogant, strong-willed mother had eventually overshadowed the meek and reticent father.

So, nothing was lacking in preparation for the new nuptials, except the suitor. After the mother had rejected the seventh, the eighth request for her daughter, suddenly the news spread that the affair had been concluded. The second daughter had been "given." To whom? There were already equivocal smiles—not even to any son of theirs or anyone from the capital! Yes, a "foreigner" had been accepted: to be sure, he was said to be a real scholar, a professor of something or other, some said of German, according to others it was mathematics which he had studied in Germany up to a very high level!

That in no way diminished the stigma: the man was not a native of their town, nor even of any other town; he quite simply came from a nearby village. The two mothers had met at the Turkish baths, exchanged flatteries and become friendly. The gossips

---

2. Sidonie Gabrielle Colette (1873–1954), considered by some the first modern feminist author, explored femininity, sexuality, and the tension between the sexes.

added that the two women had much in common, "particularly their faults", shrilly asserted one neighbour. But in any case the match seemed to be serious with the suitor bearing the hallmark of a high official. The girl was lucky after all, that exceptional trousseau was in some way an omen: it augured a life of travel. And may Allah the All-Merciful protect her!

The first disappointment for the sisters—from the eldest who was already married, down to the fourth, a little girl who climbed over the wall to visit us—was the revelation of a custom thought to be obsolete: in the fiancé's native village, the marriage had to be performed according to the austere code of practice which the patron saint of the region had instituted some centuries before. It was known as marrying "according to Sidi Maamar's Bough" . . .

This saintly personage had, in the days of old, preached against the ostentatious luxury of the inhabitants of the then prosperous cities. So he had set out the procedure for wedding ceremonies, down to the smallest detail. His disciples accepted the rule, not only obeying it themselves, but imposing it even more strictly on all their male offspring. If any of their descendants insisted on breaking the "chain" it was noticed that children born of the union were without exception physically or mentally handicapped, unless they turned out to be ne'er-do-wells or jailbirds. This was proof that the saint's curse had remained alive over the centuries, and he was still vigilant down to the present day "when aeroplanes fly and the radio speaks all by itself," as one of the pious ladies commented.

The fiancé's mother had explained. She could not go against the rule: the chain with them passed from father to son; she herself had suffered from such a ceremony "almost funereal, as if she'd been an orphan, still in mourning," she had added . . . Thanks be to God, her daughters and her only son had turned out an honour and the joy of her heart, a light for her mature years, a beacon for old age! So it would be for the new bride; she would suffer one night only—the first—of humility in obedience to the strict custom: in return would come the promise of blessing on her children who would be conceived "beneath the bough of the saint." A girl must be worthy of this opportunity for a husband like her son!

It seemed to us girls, as we listened to the youngest sister's story, that these people of peasant origin were quite amazing! Barbarians, disguised as city-dwellers, giving themselves over to magical practices, to primitive penances.

Certainly, we too acknowledged the saints' presence in our midst, with the matrons calling on them endlessly, at every turn in the conversation. Time and time again, they invoked their memory to heighten every discourse, on every possible subject, with the result that this familiarity seemed, by its very abuse, to be pure rhetoric, a mere stylistic device. As for controlling our day-to-day existence, our feminine love of ostentation, and dictating how our ceremonies should be conducted! No! Our men-folk were literate in Arabic as well as in French! Our sons might not go abroad in search of diplomas and degrees, but what was so grand about this if, meanwhile, the women trembled with fear like ignorant villagers? They might just as well live like the peasants they were and "not mix with their betters," as one of our aunts had concluded peremptorily, with a gesture in the direction of the neighbours.

"Poor girl!" she added. "I'm afraid that they are offering her as the sacrificial lamb to the herdsmen!"

"And what about Sidi Maamar's curse?" another asked.

"Islam is one, Islam is pure and unadorned! It allows you leisure for rejoicing! The law cannot change, it is the same, everywhere from our town to faraway Medina; I don't need any *fqih*[3] or learned doctor from the *Zitouna* to explain it to me!"

But our neighbours had to comply. The girl prepared for her nuptials to take place beneath "Sidi Maamar's bough."

During the weeks before the set date, the women gossiping on the terraces every evening dwelt interminably on the details of the curious protocol.

No embroidered tunic, no jewels, not the slightest adornment for the bride on the wedding day, nor the preceding day nor even during the ritual of the *hammam*[4] two days before: at a pinch they might be permitted to wave candles and intone hymns during the evening ceremony, when the virgin's hands and feet were tinted with henna.

It was soon learned that only a token dowry had been given: one golden twenty-franc coin, which the bride was to save scrupulously and never spend. On the morning when the procession of barouches[5] and cars arrived in our street, bringing the groom's female relatives from their hamlet, muffled up in their veils to escort the bride, there must be no clamour, no jubilant ululation, no music; at the most one old woman could hold a candle and recite some verses from the Quran at the exact moment when the match-makers stepped over the threshold.

These women would drink neither lemonade nor milk of welcome, they would not partake of a single date or the smallest almond cake. They would simply fetch away the virgin for whom they had come. She will have her face completely hidden and her body shrouded in a seamless cloth of wool or linen, so that she can neither see nor be seen by anyone, until her new master, alone with her at night, piously and solemnly removes the veil from her face: thus had the Saint Maamar decreed, four centuries ago.

And the gossipmongers mused at dusk: the bride would be conveyed like an object, gaze turned inwards, face bathed in tears, just fit to be buried! . . . What masochism, whereas fate, already so hard on women, did at least guarantee them the glamour of a wedding day!

This marriage promised to have nothing but misery in store. The gossipers were amazed, they protested that they'd never let a daughter of theirs make such a match, one might as well condemn the innocent maid to the grip of deliberate celibacy! It must be added that none of them was invited, only near relatives, as well as the female members of our family, as we were close neighbours.

I remember that wedding—or more exactly the morning after the wedding night.

The bride's mother had been in tears since the previous evening: no ululation, cakes not distributed (she hadn't been able to resist making them), the absence of professional female musicians from the town, the elegant, varied trousseau which no one had seen! She had decided to get her own back the next day, by displaying the luxury that had been forbidden the day before.

We set out before dawn to drive to that mysterious village: ten or so veiled women from the two adjacent houses piled into the van into which the mother had already loaded the trousseau, baskets filled with foodstuffs and the most delicate pas-

---

3. Scholar.
4. Turkish bath.

5. Four-wheeled carriages.

tries. She would show those villagers, by preparing the wedding banquet herself, how refined her family was and what her daughter meant to her and all towns-women! The wedding celebrations would be up to the usual standards and the ascetic saint with his mortification of the flesh would have to take a back seat and let an older tradition be observed!

I can remember our excitement as we set out, still half-asleep, in the morning twilight, driving in the cold along the corniche, through the bluish mist. I remember our arrival at that house which was—well, what can I say?—just like any in the city— a building occupied by families of teachers from different regions. But, above all, I remember the bride, the moment we caught sight of her.

We entered the smallest room in the house, where mattresses were piled up on the bare tiles. There was total, tense silence, broken only by convulsive sobs coming from a white-shrouded heap huddled up against the wall, while a group of dumb-struck children clustered around, staring at the unidentifiable back. With an abrupt gesture, the mother chased the horde away. Only three women remained, I think, in addition to ourselves, the two little girls who were to be the bridesmaids—decked out in our white lace dresses and the shiny patent-leather shoes which seemed shockingly conspicuous in this setting!

The mother, with her woollen veil draped round her waist, stared for a moment at her daughter, huddled there, shaking with sobs. I have never forgotten the opacity of that silence. There was an enormous mirror facing the door, from which a large white sheet had just been removed and still hung down from one side. I could see the mother's reflection, seeming larger than life, as she stood with her face contorted.

"O my daughter! Grievous blow! Day of joy! day of woe!" she declaimed, rhyming the Arabic words.

She gazed at her own image with a grimace of helpless despair and without even bending down to the bride, whose sobs suddenly ceased, she angrily, violently lacerated her own cheeks. Two female relatives rushed in and forced her outside (was it not a rule of the most basic modesty that mother and daughter should not be left alone the day after the wedding night, as if the intrusion of the man destroyed for ever the protection the mother could give to the virgin?).

"Shame on you!" one of the relatives chided.

"Have a care for your daughter's happiness!" murmured the other.

"Her destiny is only just beginning, do not be such an evil omen!"

The mother allowed herself to be dragged into the vestibule. We two little girls remained with one woman, probably the bride's older sister who had just slipped discreetly into the room, with modest bearing and anxious expression.

She sat down and put her arms round the bride who had resumed her convulsive sobbing after her mother's angry outburst. She crouched down beside her sister, whispering words of comfort, gradually encouraging her to give vent to her pent-up feelings, let her cup of bitterness spill over, say what hidden grievance sparked off this misery. Seated on a mattress, shocked by the mother's violence, I wondered what I should do. I felt ashamed of my incongruous white dress; should I listen, try to make out the cause of the bride's distress, see if it persisted, if? . . . The two sisters huddled together under the same veil, deep in whispered conference. At this precise moment, or perhaps later when the confession was resumed in snatches of conversation with other women in the town, I became aware of what heavy destructive footsteps had crushed the tender shoots in the dream garden.

The union had been consummated—for so the saint's code had decreed—on a simple sheepskin or a rush-mat: two bodies copulating under a blanket. Was it this uncouthness that caused the bride to sob so bitterly in the next day's first pale morning light?

She had to make her appearance in the afternoon, dressed in her finery, the tiara on her brow, but with swollen eyelids, and puffy-faced from the shock to her virginity.

"So," commented her friends, who claimed to be in the secret, "she wept because she didn't like the bridegroom!"

"Didn't like him?"

"He was too small, and probably an insensitive oaf!"

"Insensitive or unaffectionate?"

"What is affection in a man?" sniggered a malicious voice. "Do our masters even know what affection is, since God has made all of us women, young or old, beautiful or ugly, to be like sheep, following at their heels!"

"Shame on you, with your bold, poisonous tongue!"

"What does it matter if the bridegroom is small and boorish?" retorted loudly another buxom woman. "A man is a man! As long as he works to keep his wife and children and walks in the path of God, that alone is luck in marriage!"

"She didn't like him, she didn't like him!" the younger women repeated. They knew that this second daughter was a romantic soul. What had been the use of the trousseau, so meticulously prepared and the "French-style" wedding gown, that she wore only on the second day, after interminable debates? What had her tongue-tied shyness and her purity led to?

I recall these scattered details of that wedding celebration—the copulation on a rush-mat, an unloving bridegroom and a tear-stained bride—but I also remember the bitter prelude, the outburst which some will deem puerile.[6] As if, in our town as elsewhere, whether the marriage is celebrated with the blessing of a long-dead saint or accompanied by shrill cries of jubilation from submissive towns-women, there was no hope in sight thereafter.

➤ END OF PERSPECTIVES: THE 1001 NIGHTS IN THE TWENTIETH CENTURY ➤

Léopold Sédar Senghor
1906–2001

Léopold Sédar Senghor's career has been trailblazing in both poetry and politics, as can easily be seen from the number of his "first-time" achievements: in 1935 he became the first black university graduate in the French education system, passing an extremely competitive examination to become a secondary school teacher; in 1960 he became the first president of the newly independent Republic of Senegal, formerly a French colony; and in 1984 he was the first black person to be inducted into the highly selective *Académie Française,* an institution with enormous cultural prestige and significant power regarding official uses of the French language. The fact that Senghor, an African writer and statesman, was invited to form part of this body indicates just how crucial a role Senghor himself and, more gener-

6. Childish.

ally, African writers and artists now play for the continuing vitality of French language and culture.

Senghor was born in 1906 in the town of Joal, south of the Senegalese capital of Dakar; this location meant that he wasn't initially a French citizen, a privilege that was only accorded automatically to the inhabitants of a few select cities. His father was a prosperous merchant who dealt in livestock and peanuts; the family came from the ethnic group of the Serer and was Roman Catholic, while the majority of the Senegalese population was ethnically Wolof and Muslim by religion. Senghor was sent to a Catholic mission school, where he learned to speak French, and then went on to a seminary, but he decided against pursuing a career in the church and switched to a secular high school. In 1927 he went to the Lycée Louis-le-Grand in Paris on a fellowship for further study. This was where he met Caribbean poet Aimé Césaire, who enrolled there in the early 1930s; together with several other writers, Senghor and Césaire became central figures in the emerging *négritude* movement, which sought to express and emphasize black African values and cultures. After obtaining French citizenship and completing his degree in 1935, Senghor taught at several schools and completed his mandatory military service. He was drafted to fight in World War II, was taken prisoner by the Germans, and spent two years as a prisoner of war before regaining freedom.

Senghor's first volume of poetry, *Shadow Songs*, was published in 1945; in 1948 his *Black Offerings* appeared, and he edited an extremely influential anthology of poetry entitled *Anthology of the New Black and Madagascan Poetry in the French Language*. This collection became famous because of Jean-Paul Sartre's preface "Black Orpheus," which foregrounded what he called the "anti-racist racism" of the poetry. Sartre argued that Senghor sought an African cultural essence that could be juxtaposed with European culture but that in doing so, Senghor nevertheless adopted some white European definitions of blackness; accepting the European notion that Africans were invested more strongly in emotion than in reason, for example, he foregrounded and celebrated such emotion. Neither was his stance toward the colonial power ultimately confrontational: His search for cultural essences led him to seek for universal ground where different cultures could meet. Both of these basic assumptions were rejected by subsequent generations of African intellectuals and writers, who took a more oppositional stance toward Europe and expressed doubt that the difference between black and white cultures could be captured in terms of opposed "essences."

After the war, Senghor was elected on a Socialist ticket as one of two Senegalese deputies to the French National Assembly; in 1948 he founded the Senegalese Democratic Bloc, and in 1956 he became mayor of the city of Thiès. Throughout the 1950s, he was active in promoting political movements that would enhance federations and alliances between African states. When Senegal became a republic in 1960, he was elected president. He survived a coup attempt in 1962 and was reelected several times before he retired from office in 1980. He was considered an extremely effective leader during these two decades, and throughout his political career, he continued to publish poetry: *Ethiopiques* (1956), *Nocturnes* (1961), *Lettres d'hivernage* ("Wintertime Letters," 1972), and *Elégies majeures* ("Major Elegies," 1979). A comprehensive collection of his poetry, *Oeuvre poétique*, appeared in 1990.

Senghor's poetry displays a range of different tones and forms over time, but certain themes regularly recur: the evocation of an African past, the celebration of blackness, the investigation of what it means to be a racial self, and the possibilities for encounters between different cultures. The lyrical beauty of his verse is easier to see and understand than that of Aimé Césaire, whose friendship and literary accomplishments Senghor invokes in "Letter to a Poet." Yet for all their elegant metaphors and polished lyricism, his poems do unsettle their readers through their challenges to clichéd views of racial relationships. Senghor's tribute to the beauty of an African in "Black Woman" stuns the reader with its exquisite images, yet it is also meant as a frontal attack on cultures whose standard of feminine beauty is defined by the "huge, long-legged, golden girls" mentioned in "To New York." By the same token, his celebration of Harlem's vibrant and authentic nightlife is coupled with a rejection of the official image of white New York and the rigidity and artificiality of its attractions. Much of the energy of Senghor's poetry derives from this tension between the seductive beauty of his lyrical idiom and the mordant critiques of white culture it often conveys. Yet this criticism was often perceived as too indirect by younger generations of African poets, who viewed Senghor as excessively conciliatory toward European power and preferred more explicitly African modes of expression. Even these controversial engagements with Senghor's heritage, however, confirm his towering presence in twentieth-century African literature.

Letter to a Poet[1]

TO AIMÉ CÉSAIRE[2]

To my Brother *aimé,* beloved friend, my bluntly fraternal greetings!
Black sea gulls like seafaring boatmen have brought me a taste
Of your tidings mixed with spices and the noisy fragrance of Southern
    Rivers
And Islands. They showed your influence, your distinguished brow,
5   The flower of your delicate lips. They are now your disciples,
A hive of silence, proud as peacocks. You keep their breathless zeal
From fading until moonrise. Is it your perfume of exotic fruits,
Or your wake of light in the fullness of day?
O, the many plum-skin women in the harem of your mind!

10   Still charming beyond the years, embers aglow under the ash
Of your eyelids, is the music we stretched our hands
And hearts to so long ago. Have you forgotten your nobility?
Your talent to praise the Ancestors, the Princes,
And the Gods, neither flower nor drops of dew?
15   You were to offer the Spirits the virgin fruits of your garden
—You ate only the newly harvested millet blossom
And stole not a petal to sweeten your mouth.
At the bottom of the well of my memory, I touch your face
And draw water to refresh my long regret.
20   You recline royally, elbow on a cushion of clear hillside,
Your bed presses the earth, easing the toil of wetland drums
Beating the rhythm of your song, and your verse
Is the breath of the night and the distant sea.
You praised the Ancestors and the legitimate princes.
25   For your rhyme and counterpoint you scooped a star from the heavens.
At your bare feet poor men threw down a mat of their year's wages,
And women their amber hearts and soul-wrenching dance.

My friend, my friend—Oh, you will come back, come back!
I shall await you under the mahogany tree, the message
30   Already sent to the woodcutter's boss. You will come back
For the feast of first fruits when the soft night
In the sloping sun rises steaming from the rooftops

---

1. Translated by Melvin Dixon.   2. See page 644 for Césaire, whose first name, Aimé, means "beloved."

And athletes, befitting your arrival,
Parade their youthfulness, adorned like the beloved.

Nocturne (She Flies She Flies)[1]
For Two Horns and a Balafong[2]

She flies she flies through the white flat lands, and patiently I take my aim
Giddy with desire. She takes her chances to the bush
Passion of thorns and thickets. Then I will bring her to bay in the chain of
  hours
Snuffing the soft panting of her flanks, mottled with shadow
5   And under the foolish Great Noon, I will twist her arms of glass.
The antelope's jubilant death rattle will intoxicate me, new palm wine
And I will drink long long the wild blood that rises to her heart
The milk blood that flows to her mouth, odours of damp earth.

Am I not the son of Dyogoye?[3] Dyogoye the famished Lion.

Black Woman[1]

Nude woman, black woman
Clothed in your color which is life itself, in your form which is beauty!
I grew in your shadow, and the softness of your hands covered my eyes.
Then, in the heat of Summer and Noon, suddenly I discover you, Promised
  Land, from the top of a high parched hill
5   And your beauty strikes me to the heart, like the flash of an eagle.

Nude woman, dark woman
Ripe fruit firm of flesh, somber ecstasies of black wine, mouth that moves
  my mouth to poetry
Prairie of pure horizons, prairie trembling in the East wind's passionate caress
Tom-tom taut over sculptured frame, groaning beneath the Conqueror's
  fingers
10   Your deep contralto voice is the sacred melody of the Beloved.

Nude woman, dark woman
Oil not ruffled by the slightest breath, oil smooth on the athlete's flanks, the
  flanks of the princes of Mali[2]
Heaven-limbed gazelle, the moist drops are stars on the night of your skin
Delights of mind's caprice, reflections of red gold on your rippling skin
15   In the dark shadow of your hair, my anguish brightens with the dawning sun
  of your eyes.

Nude woman, black woman
I sing your disappearing beauty, fixing it in an Eternal shape,
Before an envious Destiny transforms you into ashes to nourish the roots of
  life.

1. Translated by John Reed and Clive Wake.
2. African percussion instrument.
3. An allusion to Senghor's father, Basile Dyogoye
Senghor.

1. Translated by Norman R. Shapiro.
2. A country in West Africa, formerly part of an important
West African empire.

To New York[1]
(for jazz orchestra and trumpet solo)

New York! At first I was bewildered by your beauty,
Those huge, long-legged, golden girls.
So shy, at first, before your blue metallic eyes and icy smile,
So shy. And full of despair at the end of skyscraper streets
5   Raising my owl eyes at the eclipse of the sun.
Your light is sulphurous against the pale towers
Whose heads strike lightning into the sky,
Skyscrapers defying storms with their steel shoulders
And weathered skin of stone.
10   But two weeks on the naked sidewalks of Manhattan—
At the end of the third week the fever
Overtakes you with a jaguar's leap
Two weeks without well water or pasture all birds of the air
Fall suddenly dead under the high, sooty terraces.
15   No laugh from a growing child, his hand in my cool hand.
No mother's breast, but nylon legs. Legs and breasts
Without smell or sweat. No tender word, and no lips,
Only artificial hearts paid for in cold cash
And not one book offering wisdom.
20   The painter's palette yields only coral crystals.
Sleepless nights, O nights of Manhattan!
Stirring with delusions while car horns blare the empty hours
And murky streams carry away hygenic loving
Like rivers overflowing with the corpses of babies.

II

25   Now is the time for signs and reckoning, New York!
Now is the time of manna and hyssop.[2]
You have only to listen to God's trombones, to your heart
Beating to the rhythm of blood, your blood.
I saw Harlem teeming with sounds and ritual colors
30   And outrageous smells—
At teatime in the home of the drugstore-deliveryman
I saw the festival of Night begin at the retreat of day.
And I proclaim Night more truthful than the day.
It is the pure hour when God brings forth
35   Life immemorial in the streets,
All the amphibious elements shining like suns.
Harlem, Harlem! Now I've seen Harlem, Harlem!
A green breeze of corn rising from the pavements

---

1. Translated by Melvin Dixon.

2. Manna is bread provided by God; hyssop is a plant commonly used as medicine.

Plowed by the Dan dancers' bare feet,[3]
40   Hips rippling like silk and spearhead breasts,
Ballets of water lilies and fabulous masks
And mangoes of love rolling from the low houses
To the feet of police horses.
And along sidewalks I saw streams of white rum
45   And streams of black milk in the blue haze of cigars.
And at night I saw cotton flowers snow down
From the sky and the angels' wings and sorcerers' plumes.
Listen, New York! O listen to your bass male voice,
Your vibrant oboe voice, the muted anguish of your tears
50   Falling in great clots of blood,
Listen to the distant beating of your nocturnal heart,
The tom-tom's rhythm and blood, tom-tom blood and tom-tom.

III

New York! I say New York, let black blood flow into your blood.
Let it wash the rust from your steel joints, like an oil of life
55   Let it give your bridges the curve of hips and supple vines.
Now the ancient age returns, unity is restored,
The reconciliation of Lion and Bull and Tree
Idea links to action, the ear to the heart, sign to meaning.
See your rivers stirring with musk alligators
60   And sea cows with mirage eyes. No need to invent the Sirens.[4]
Just open your eyes to the April rainbow
And your ears, especially your ears, to God
Who in one burst of saxophone laughter
Created heaven and earth in six days,
65   And on the seventh slept a deep Negro sleep.

Correspondence[1]

This is the hour of a friendly vigil night
When your nimble presence softens the light.
On paper white as a beach,
My hands search your dream hands to reach.

5   Dear one, we travel by the express train's silent leap.
So many unknown eyelashes peep
On the night of your wide eyes!
So many waving scarves on the horizon skies!

Will I ever again see the bleeding city
10   Where rises the endless lament of minarets?[2]

---

3. The Dan are an ethnic group from the African country
of Liberia; they are famous for their mask dances.
4. In Homer's *Odyssey,* feminine sea creatures who lure

men to their deaths with beautiful songs.
1. Translated by Melvin Dixon.
2. The tower of a mosque.

Aimé Césaire

b. 1913

Poet and politician: These are the two main dimensions of Aimé Césaire's career. Born on the island of Martinique in 1913, he became not only an influential statesman and a prominent thinker on issues of colonialism and postcolonialism but also one of the most important modern Caribbean poets. During his education in Paris in the 1930s, he met and became close friends with French Guinean writer Léon Damas and Senegalese writer Léopold Sédar Senghor, with whom he co-founded a student journal, *L'Etudiant noir*. From this collaboration emerged the crucial concept of *négritude,* which became a fundamental category for rethinking the relation between white European and black African and Caribbean culture: broadly speaking, it refers to the self-confident assertion of black identity and the achievements of black culture, challenging the colonialist and racist hierarchies in terms of which African cultures had previously been defined. On the eve of World War II in 1939, Césaire returned to Martinique to become a school teacher. In 1945 he was elected mayor of Martinique's capital, Fort-de-France, and a member of the French National Assembly. While holding these offices, he helped redefine the political status of France's former colonies, most importantly in cosponsoring the law that transformed them into French overseas departments, a status that gave them significant political and economic rights. He viewed the fight against colonialism as a part of the struggle of the international working class, and he was a member of the French Communist Party from 1945 to 1956; in 1958 he helped to found the Parti Progressiste Martiniquais. In 1983, a year after the French government created "regional councils" in the French overseas departments, he became president of the Martinican council. He retired from electoral politics in 1993.

Césaire's political struggle on behalf of France's former colonies went hand in hand with his literary works, in which colonial oppression and liberation figure as prominent topics. In both his poetry and his plays, he exposes the cultural and ideological strategies that subject black people to white domination, and he outlines counterimages of a rebellious, imaginative, and self-confident black culture. At the same time, his relationship with French culture remained profoundly ambivalent, including elements of both admiration and rejection, though he remained a lifelong Francophone poet (a speaker and writer of French). His first long poem, *Notebook of a Return to the Native Land,* first published in 1939 and revised in various editions over fifteen years, has remained his most lasting achievement. In the *Notebook,* Césaire addresses the situation of the Caribbean in particular and colonized black cultures in general, using a series of different voices and perspectives; while it is tempting to identify his own view with only one or two of these voices, his full understanding of what *négritude* means emerges only from seeing the different perspectives in the poem together.

By turns outcry, lament, prophecy, and manifesto, the *Notebook* deploys a wide range of poetic strategies from allusions to the Bible and Shakespeare all the way to the striking metaphoric juxtapositions of surrealist poetry. Césaire uses these resources to evoke visions of Caribbean misery and beauty, the suffering of African slaves on their journey West, and the self-confidence of blacks rising up against their oppressors. Though the overall thrust of the poem isn't difficult to understand, the details are often quite hard to grasp, as they are in the surrealist poetry that influenced Césaire deeply. But this difficulty itself has a political thrust: By writing poetry that even French readers find challenging, Césaire, as the poetic voice of the colonized, thrusts all the weight, complexity, and beauty of French education and the French language back at his oppressors. This, certainly, is a message that no French reader of the poem could miss.

PRONUNCIATIONS:
 Aimé Césaire: ay-MAY say-ZAIR
  grigri: GREE-gree

Notebook of a Return to the Native Land[1]

At the end of the wee hours . . .

Beat it, I said to him, you cop, you lousy pig, beat it, I detest the flunkies of order and the cockchafers of hope. Beat it, evil grigri,[2] you bedbug of a petty monk. Then I turned toward paradises lost for him and his kin, calmer than the face of a woman telling lies, and there, rocked by the flux of a never exhausted thought I nourished the wind, I unlaced the monsters and heard rise, from the other side of disaster, a river of turtledoves and savanna clover which I carry forever in my depths height-deep as the twentieth floor of the most arrogant houses and as a guard against the putrefying force of crepuscular surroundings, surveyed night and day by a cursed venereal sun.

At the end of the wee hours burgeoning with frail coves, the hungry Antilles, the Antilles pitted with smallpox, the Antilles dynamited by alcohol, stranded in the mud of this bay, in the dust of this town sinisterly stranded.

At the end of the wee hours, the extreme, deceptive desolate bedsore on the wound of the waters; the martyrs who do not bear witness; the flowers of blood that fade and scatter in the empty wind like the screeches of babbling parrots; an aged life mendaciously smiling, its lips opened by vacated agonies; an aged poverty rotting under the sun, silently; an aged silence bursting with tepid pustules, the awful futility of our raison d'être.[3]

At the end of the wee hours, on this very fragile earth thickness exceeded in a humiliating way by its grandiose future—the volcanoes will explode, the naked water will bear away the ripe sun stains and nothing will be left but a tepid bubbling pecked at by sea birds—the beach of dreams and the insane awakenings.

At the end of the wee hours, this town sprawled-flat toppled from its common sense, inert, winded under its geometric weight of an eternally renewed cross, indocile to its fate, mute, vexed no matter what, incapable of growing with the juice of this earth, self-conscious, clipped, reduced, in breach of fauna and flora.

At the end of the wee hours, this town sprawled-flat . . .

And in this inert town, this squalling throng so astonishingly detoured from its cry as this town has been from its movement, from its meaning, not even worried, detoured from its true cry, the only cry you would have wanted to hear because you feel it alone belongs to this town; because you feel it lives in it in some deep refuge and pride of this inert town, this throng detoured from its cry of hunger, of poverty, of revolt, of hatred, this throng so strangely chattering and mute.

1. Translated by Clayton Eshleman and Annette Smith.   3. Reason for being.
2. African amulet.

In this inert town, this strange throng which does not pack, does not mix: clever at discovering the point of disencasement,[4] of flight, of dodging. This throng which does not know how to throng, this throng, clearly so perfectly alone under the sun, like a woman one thought completely occupied with her lyric cadence, who abruptly challenges a hypothetical rain and enjoins it not to fall; or like a rapid sign of the cross without perceptive motive; or like the sudden grave animality of a peasant, urinating standing, her legs parted, stiff.

In this inert town, this desolate throng under the sun, not connected with anything that is expressed, asserted, released in broad earth daylight, its own. Neither with Josephine, Empress of the French, dreaming way up there above the nigger scum. Nor with the liberator fixed in his whitewashed stone liberation.[5] Nor with the conquistador. Nor with this contempt, with this freedom, with this audacity.

At the end of the wee hours, this inert town and its beyond of lepers, of consumption, of famines, of fears squatting in the ravines, fears perched in the trees, fears dug in the ground, fears adrift in the sky, piles of fears and their fumaroles of anguish.

At the end of the wee hours, the morne[6] forgotten, forgetful of leaping.

At the end of the wee hours, the morne in restless, docile hooves—its malarial blood routs the sun with its overheated pulse.

At the end of the wee hours, the restrained conflagration of the morne like a sob gagged on the verge of a bloodthirsty burst, in quest of an ignition that slips away and ignores itself.

At the end of the wee hours, the morne crouching before bulimia on the lookout for tuns and mills,[7] slowly vomiting out its human fatigue, the morne solitary and its blood shed, the morne bandaged in shades, the morne and its ditches of fear, the morne and its great hands of wind.

At the end of the wee hours, the famished morne and no one knows better than this bastard morne why the suicide choked with a little help from his hypoglossal[8] jamming his tongue backward to swallow it; why a woman seems to float belly up on the Capot River (her chiaroscuro body submissively organized at the command of her navel) but she is only a bundle of sonorous water.

And neither the teacher in his classroom, nor the priest at catechism will be able to get a word out of this sleepy little nigger, no matter how energetically they drum on his shorn skull, for starvation has quick-sanded his voice into the swamp of hunger (a word-one-single-word and we-will-forget-about-Queen-Blanche-of-Castille,[9] a-word-one-single-word, you-should-see-this-little-savage-who-doesn't-know-any-of-The-Ten-Commandments).

---

4. Joint where a piece of machinery can be taken apart.
5. French abolitionist Victor Schoelcher (1804–1893), honored with a statue in Martinique's capital.
6. Hill.

7. Casks of rum at the island's sugar mills.
8. Nerve under the tongue.
9. Medieval queen, whose name means "White."

for his voice gets lost in the swamp of hunger,
and there is nothing, really nothing to squeeze out of this little brat,
other than a hunger which can no longer climb to the rigging of his voice
a sluggish flabby hunger,
a hunger buried in the depths of the Hunger of this famished morne.

At the end of the wee hours, the disparate stranding, the exacerbated stench of corruption, the monstrous sodomies of the host and the sacrificing priest, the impassable beakhead frames of prejudice and stupidity, the prostitutions, the hypocrisies, the lubricities, the treasons, the lies, the frauds, the concussions—the panting of a deficient cowardice, the heave-holess enthusiasms of supernumerary sahibs, the greeds, the hysterias, the perversions, the clownings of poverty, the cripplings, the itchings, the hives, the tepid hammocks of degeneracy. Right here the parade of laughable and scrofulous buboes,[1] the forced feedings of very strange microbes, the poisons without known alexins,[2] the sanies of really ancient sores, the unforeseeable fermentations of putrescible species.

At the end of the wee hours, the great motionless night, the stars deader than a caved-in balafo.[3]

the teratical[4] bulb of night, sprouted from our vileness and our renunciations.

And our foolish and crazy stunts to revive the golden splashing of privileged moments, the umbilical cord restored to its ephemeral splendor, the bread, and the wine of complicity, the bread, the wine, the blood of honest weddings.

And this joy of former times making me aware of my present poverty, a bumpy road plunging into a hollow where it scatters a few shacks; an indefatigable road charging at full speed a morne at the top of which it brutally quicksands into a pool of clumsy houses, a road foolishly climbing, recklessly descending, and the carcass of wood, which I call "our house," comically perched on minute cement paws, its coiffure of corrugated iron in the sun like a skin laid out to dry, the main room, the rough floor where the nail heads gleam, the beams of pine and shadow across the ceiling, the spectral straw chairs, the grey lamp light, the glossy flash of cockroaches in a maddening buzz . . . .

At the end of the wee hours, this most essential land restored to my gourmandise,[5] not in diffuse tenderness, but the tormented sensual concentration of the fat tits of the mornes with an occasional palm tree as their hardened sprout, the jerky orgasm of torrents from Trinité to Grand Rivière,[6] the hysterical grandsuck of the sea.

And time passed quickly, very quickly.

After August and mango trees decked out in all their little moons, September begetter of cyclones, October igniter of sugar-cane, November who purrs in the distilleries, there came Christmas.

---

1. Pus-filled swellings.
2. Antidotes. Sanies: oozings.
3. African instrument.

4. Monstrous.
5. Greedy hunger.
6. Towns in Martinique.

It had come in at first, Christmas did, with a tingling of desires, a thirst for new tenderness, a burgeoning of vague dreams, then with a purple rustle of its great joyous wings it had suddenly flown away, and then its abrupt fall out over the village that made the shack life burst like an overripe pomegranate.

Christmas was not like other holidays. It didn't like to gad about the streets, to dance on public squares, to mount the wooden horses, to use the crowd to pinch women, to hurl fireworks in the faces of the tamarind trees. It had agoraphobia,[7] Christmas did. What it wanted was a whole day of bustling, preparing, a cooking and cleaning spree, endless jitters
about-not-having-enough,
about-running-short,
about-getting-bored,

then at evening an unimposing little church, which would benevolently make room for the laughter, the whispers, the secrets, the love talk, the gossip and the guttural cacophony of a plucky singer and also boisterous pals and shameless hussies and shacks up to their guts in succulent goodies, and not stingy, and twenty people can crowd in, and the street is deserted, and the village turns into a bouquet of singing, and you are cozy in there, and you eat good, and you drink hearty and there are blood sausages, one kind only two fingers wide twined in coils, the other broad and stocky, the mild one tasting of wild thyme, the hot one spiced to an incandescence, and steaming coffee and sugared anise and milk punch, and the liquid sun of rums, and all sorts of good things which drive your taste buds wild or distill them to the point of ecstasy or cocoon them with fragrances, and you laugh, and you sing, and the refrains flare on and on like coco-palms:

ALLELUIA
KYRIE ELEISON . . . LEISON . . . LEISON
CHRISTE ELEISON . . . LEISON . . . LEISON.

And not only do the mouths sing, but the hands, the feet, the buttocks, the genitals, and your entire being liquefies into sounds, voices, and rhythm.

At the peak of its ascent, joy bursts like a cloud. The songs don't stop, but now anxious and heavy roll through the valleys of fear, the tunnels of anguish and the fires of hell.

And each one starts pulling the nearest devil by his tail, until fear imperceptibly fades in the fine sand lines of dream, and you really live as in a dream, and you drink and you shout and you sing as in a dream, and doze too as in a dream, with rose petal eyelids, and the day comes velvety as a sapodilla tree, and the liquid manure smell of the cacao trees, and the turkeys which shell their red pustules in the sun, and the obsessive bells, and the rain
the bells . . . the rain . . .
that tinkle, tinkle, tinkle . . .

At the end of the wee hours, this town sprawled-flat . . .

It crawls on its hands without the slightest desire to drill the sky with a stature of protest. The backs of the houses are afraid of the sky truffled with fire, their feet of the

7. Fear of open spaces.

drownings of the soil, they chose to perch shallowly between surprises and treacheries. And yet it advances, the town does. It even grazes every day further out into its tide of tiled corridors, prudish shutters, gluey courtyards, dripping paintwork. And petty hushed-up scandals, petty unvoiced guilts, petty immense hatreds knead the narrow streets into bumps and potholes where the waste-water grins longitudinally through turds . . .

At the end of the wee hours, life prostrate, you don't know how to dispose of your aborted dreams, the river of life desperately torpid in its bed, neither turgid nor low, hesitant to flow, pitifully empty, the impartial heaviness of boredom distributing shade equally on all things, the air stagnant, unbroken by the brightness of a single bird.

At the end of the wee hours, another little house very bad-smelling in a very narrow street, a minuscule house which harbors in its guts of rotten wood dozens of rats and the turbulence of my six brothers and sisters, a cruel little house whose demands panic the ends of our months and my temperamental father gnawed by one persistent ache, I never knew which one, whom an unexpected sorcery could lull to melancholy tenderness or drive to towering flames of anger; and my mother whose legs pedal, pedal, night and day, for our tireless hunger, I was even awakened at night by these tireless legs which pedal the night and the bitter bite in the soft flesh of the night of a Singer[8] that my mother pedals, pedals for our hunger and day and night.

At the end of the wee hours, beyond my father, my mother, the shack chapped with blisters, like a peach tree afflicted with curl, and the thin roof patched with pieces of gasoline cans, which create swamps of rust in the stinking sordid grey straw pulp, and when the wind whistles, these odds and ends make a noise bizarre, first like the crackling of frying, then like a brand dropped into water the smoke of its twigs flying up. And the bed of boards from which my race arose, my whole entire race from this bed of boards, with its kerosene case paws, as if it had elephantiasis,[9] that bed, and its kidskin, and its dry banana leaves, and its rags, yearning for a mattress, my grandmother's bed. (Above the bed, in a jar full of oil a dim light whose flame dances like a fat cockroach . . . on the jar in gold letters: MERCI.)[1]
And this rue Paille, this disgrace,

an appendage repulsive as the private parts of the village which extends right and left, along the colonial highway, the grey surge of its shingled roofs. Here there are only straw roofs, spray browned and wind plucked.

Everybody despises rue Paille. It's there that the village youth go astray. It's there especially that the sea pours forth its garbage, its dead cats and its croaked dogs. For the street opens on to the beach, and the beach alone cannot satisfy the sea's foaming rage.

A blight this beach as well, with its piles of rotting muck, its furtive rumps relieving themselves, and the sand is black, funereal, you've never seen a sand so black, and the scum glides over it yelping, and the sea pummels it like a boxer, or rather the sea is a huge dog licking and biting the shins of the beach, biting them so fiercely that it will end up devouring it, the beach and rue Paille along with it.

---

8. A brand of sewing machine.   1. Thank you (French).
9. A disease that causes extreme enlargement of the legs.

At the end of the wee hours, the wind of long ago—of betrayed trusts, of uncertain evasive duty and that other dawn in Europe—arises . . . .

To go away.
As there are hyena-men and panther-men, I would be a jew-man
a Kaffir-man[2]
a Hindu-man-from-Calcutta
a Harlem-man-who-doesn't-vote

the famine man, the insult-man, the torture man you can grab anytime, beat up,
kill—no joke, kill—without having to account to anyone, without having to make
excuses to anyone
a jew-man
a pogrom-man
a puppy
a beggar
but *can* one kill Remorse, perfect as the stupefied face of an English lady discovering
a Hottentot skull in her soup-tureen?

I would rediscover the secret of great communications and great combustions. I would say storm. I would say river. I would say tornado. I would say leaf. I would say tree. I would be drenched by all rains, moistened by all dews. I would roll like frenetic blood on the slow current of the eye of words turned into mad horses into fresh children into clots into curfew into vestiges of temples into precious stones remote enough to discourage miners. Whoever would not understand me would not understand any better the roaring of a tiger.

And you ghosts rise blue from alchemy from a forest of hunted beasts of twisted machines of a jujube tree of rotten flesh of a basket of oysters of eyes of a network of straps in the beautiful sisal of human skin I would have words vast enough to contain you earth taut earth drunk
earth great vulva raised to the sun
earth great delirium of God's mentula[3]
savage earth arisen from the storerooms of the sea a clump of Cecropia[4] in your mouth earth whose tumultuous face I can only compare to the virgin and mad forest which were it in my power I would show in guise of a face to the undeciphering eyes of men all I would need is a mouthful of jiculi milk[5] to discover in you always as distant as a mirage—a thousand times more native and made golden by a sun that no prism divides—the earth where everything is free and fraternal, my earth.

To go away. My heart was pounding with emphatic generosities. To go away . . .
I would arrive sleek and young in this land of mine and I would say to this land whose

---

2. South African whites' term of insult for blacks.
3. Penis.
4. A kind of tree native to the tropical regions of the Americas.

5. Césaire's variation on the term for a kind of tree. Jiculi milk is a plant-based poison that is believed not to harm wild creatures.

loam is part of my flesh: "I have wandered for a long time and I am coming back to the deserted hideousness of your sores."

I would go to this land of mine and I would say to it. "Embrace me without fear . . . And if all I can do is speak, it is for you I shall speak."

And again I would say:

"My mouth shall be the mouth of those calamities that have no mouth, my voice the freedom of those who break down in the solitary confinement of despair."

And on the way I would say to myself:

"And above all, my body as well as my soul, beware of assuming the sterile attitude of a spectator, for life is not a spectacle, a sea of miseries is not a proscenium, a man screaming is not a dancing bear . . ."

And behold here I am!

Once again this life hobbling before me, what am I saying life, *this death,* this death without sense or piety, this death that so pathetically falls short of greatness, the dazzling pettiness of this death, this death hobbling from pettiness to pettiness; these shovelfuls of petty greeds over the conquistador; these shovelfuls of petty flunkies over the great savage, these shovelfuls of petty souls over the three-souled Carib,[6] and all these deaths futile

absurdities under the splashing of my open conscience

tragic futilities lit up by this single noctiluca[7]

and I alone, sudden stage of these wee hours when the apocalypse of monsters cavorts then, capsized, hushes

warm election of cinders, of ruins and collapses

—One more thing! only one, but please make it only one: I have no right to measure life by my sooty finger span; to reduce myself to this little ellipsoidal nothing trembling four fingers above the line, I a man, to so overturn creation, that I include myself between latitude and longitude!

> At the end of the wee hours,
> the male thirst and the desire stubborn,
> here I am, severed from the cool oases of brotherhood
> this so modest nothing bristles with hard splinters
> this too safe horizon is startled like a jailer.

Your last triumph, tenacious crow of Treason.

What is mine, these few thousand deathbearers who mill in the calabash of an island and mine too, the archipelago arched with an anguished desire to negate itself, as if from maternal anxiety to protect this impossibly delicate tenuity separating one America from another; and these loins which secrete for Europe the hearty liquor of a Gulf Stream, and one of the two slopes of incandescence between which the Equator tightropewalks toward Europe. And my nonfence island, its brave audacity standing at the stern of this Polynesia, before it, Guadeloupe, split in two down its dorsal line and equal in poverty to us, Haiti where negritude rose for the first time and stated that it believed in its humanity and the funny little tail of Florida where the strangulation

---

6. The Caribs were the native people that inhabited the Antilles before the arrival of the Europeans.

7. An organism that is luminescent in the dark.

of a nigger is being completed, and Africa gigantically caterpillaring up to the Hispanic foot of Europe it nakedness where Death scythes widely.

And I say to myself Bordeaux and Nantes and Liverpool and New York and San Francisco

not an inch of this world devoid of my fingerprint
and my calcaneum[8] on the spines of skyscrapers and my filth in the glitter of gems!
Who can boast of being better off than I? Virginia.
Tennessee. Georgia. Alabama
monstrous putrefactions of stymied
revolts
marshes of putrid blood
trumpets absurdly muted
land red, sanguineous, consanguineous land.

What is mine also: a little
cell in the Jura,[9]
a little cell, the snow lines it with white bars
the snow is a jailer mounting
guard before a prison

What is mine
a lonely man imprisoned in
whiteness
a lonely man defying the white
screams of white death
(TOUSSAINT, TOUSSAINT L'OUVERTURE)[1]

a man who mesmerizes
the white hawk of white death
a man alone in the sterile
sea of white sand
a coon grown old standing up to
the waters of the sky

Death traces a shining circle
above this man
death stars softly above his head
death breathes, crazed, in the ripened
cane field of his arms
death gallops in the prison like
a white horse
death gleams in the dark like the
eyes of a cat

8. Heel bone.
9. A range of mountains in France.
1. Toussaint l'Ouverture (1743–1803) was originally a slave. He became one of the leaders of uprisings in the 1790s and the governor of Haiti, but he was arrested by the French shortly afterward; he died imprisoned in the Jura mountains.

death hiccups like water under the Keys
death is a struck bird
death wanes
death flickers
death is a very shy patyura[2]
death expires in a white pool
of silence.
Swellings of night in the four corners
of this dawn
convulsions of congealed death
tenacious fate
screams erect from mute earth
the splendor of this blood will it not burst open?

At the end of the wee hours this land without a stele,[3] these paths without mem-
ory, these winds without a tablet.
So what?
We would tell. Would sing. Would howl.
Full voice, ample voice, you would be our wealth, our spear pointed.
Words?
Ah yes, words!

Reason, I crown you evening wind.
Your name voice of order?
To me the whip's corolla.
Beauty I call you the false claim of the stone.
But ah! my raucous laughter
smuggled in
Ah! my saltpetre treasure!
Because we hate you
and your reason, we claim kinship
with dementia praecox[4] with the flaming madness
of persistent cannibalism

Treasure, let's count:
the madness that remembers
the madness that howls
the madness that sees
the madness that is unleashed
And you know the rest

That 2 and 2 are 5
that the forest miaows
that the tree plucks the maroons[5] from the fire
that the sky strokes its beard
etc. etc. . . .

---

2. Césaire's variation on the French term for a kind of peccary.
3. A column or upright slab of stone that is inscribed or decorated with images.
4. Schizophrenia (literally, premature dementia).
5. Chestnuts; also slang for "runaway slaves."

Who and what are we?
A most worthy question!

From staring too long at trees I have
become a tree and my long tree
feet have dug in the ground large
venom sacs high cities of bone
from brooding too long on the Congo
I have become a Congo resounding with
forests and rivers
where the whip cracks like a great banner
the banner of a prophet
where the water goes
likouala-likouala
where the angerbolt hurls its greenish
axe forcing the boars of
putrefaction to the lovely wild edge
of the nostrils.

At the end of the wee hours the sun which
hacks and spits up its lungs

At the end of the wee hours
a slow gait of sand
a slow gait of gauze
a slow gait of corn kernels
At the end of the wee hours
a full gallop of pollen
a full gallop of a slow gait of
little girls
a full gallop of hummingbirds
a full gallop of daggers to stave in
the earth's breast

customs angels mounting guard over
prohibitions at the gates of foam

I declare my crimes and that there is nothing
to say in my defense.
Dances. Idols. An apostate.[6] I too
I have assassinated God with my laziness with
my words with my gestures
with my obscene songs

I have worn parrot plumes
musk cat skins
I have exhausted the missionaries' patience
insulted the benefactors of mankind.
Defied Tyre. Defied Sidon.

6. A person who has abandoned his or her faith.

Worshipped the Zambezi.[7]
The extent of my perversity overwhelms me!

But why impenetrable jungle are you still hiding the raw zero of my mendacity and from a self-conscious concern for nobility not celebrating the horrible leap of my Pahouin[8] ugliness?

voum rooh oh
voum rooh oh
to charm the snakes to conjure
the dead
voum rooh oh
to compel the rain to turn back
the tidal waves
voum rooh oh
to keep the shade from moving
voum rooh oh that my own skies
may open

—me on a road, a child, chewing
sugar cane root
—a dragged man on a bloodspattered road
a rope around his neck
—standing in the center of a huge circus,
on my black forehead a crown of daturas[9]
voum rooh
to fly off
higher than quivering higher
than the sorceresses toward other stars
ferocious exultation of forests and
mountains uprooted at the hour
when no one expects it
the islands linked for a thousand years!

voum rooh oh
that the promised times may return
and the bird who knew my name
and the woman who had a thousand names
names of fountain sun and tears
and her hair of minnows
and her steps my climates
and her eyes my seasons
and the days without injury
and the nights without offense
and the stars my confidence
and the wind my accomplice

---

7. Tyre and Sidon, cities on the coast of Palestine, were important Phoenician centers of commerce and culture in antiquity. The Zambezi is a river in south-central Africa.

8. A group of peoples in West Africa.
9. Plants with large flowers in the shape of a trumpet that have a narcotic or poisonous effect.

But who misleads my voice? who grates
my voice? Stuffing my throat
with a thousand bamboo fangs. A thousand
sea urchin stakes. It is you dirty end
of the world. Dirty end of the wee hours.
It is you dirty hatred. It is you weight
of the insult and a hundred years of whip
lashes. It is you one hundred years of my
patience, one hundred years of my effort
simply to stay alive
rooh oh
we sing of venomous flowers
flaring in fury-filled prairies;
the skies of love cut with bloodclots;
the epileptic mornings; the white blaze
of abyssal sands, the sinking
of flotsam in nights electrified
with feline smells.

What can I do?

One must begin somewhere.

Begin what?

The only thing in the world
worth beginning:
The End of the world of course.

Torte[1]
oh torte of the terrifying autumn
where the new steel and the perennial concrete
grow
torte oh torte
where the air rusts in great sheets
of evil glee
where the sanious water scars the great
solar cheeks
I hate you
one still sees madras rags around the loins
of women rings in their ears
smiles on their lips babies
at their nipples, these for starters:

ENOUGH OF THIS OUTRAGE!

So here is the great challenge and the satanic
compulsion and the insolent
nostalgic drift of April moons,
of green fires, of yellow fevers!

1. Loaf of local bread.

Vainly in the tepidity of your throat
you ripen for the twentieth time the same indigent
solace that we are
mumblers of words

Words? while we handle
quarters of earth, while we wed
delirious continents, while
we force steaming gates,
words, ah yes, words! but
words of fresh blood, words that are
tidal waves and erysipelas[2]
malarias and lava and brush
fires, and blazes of flesh,
and blazes of cities . . .

Know this:
the only game I play is the millennium
the only game I play is the Great
Fear

Put up with me. I won't put up with you!

Sometimes you see me with a great display of brains
snap up a cloud too red
or a caress of rain, or a prelude
of wind,
don't fool yourself:

I am forcing the vitelline membrane[3] that separates
me from myself,
I am forcing the great waters which girdle me with blood

I and I alone choose
a seat on the last train of the last
surge of the last tidal wave

I and I alone
make contact with the latest
anguish

I and oh, only I
secure the first
drops of virginal milk through a straw!

And now a last boo:
to the sun (not strong enough to inebriate
my very tough head)
to the mealy night with its golden
hatchings of erratic fireflies
to the head of hair trembling at the very

2. Infectious skin diseases.   3. Thin membrane around a fertilized egg in the womb.

top of the cliff
where the wind leaps in bursts of salty
cavalries
I clearly read in my pulse that for me
exoticism is no provender

Leaving Europe utterly twisted with screams
the silent currents of despair
leaving timid Europe which
collects and proudly overrates itself
I summon this egotism beautiful
and bold
and my ploughing reminds me of an implacable cutwater.

So much blood in my memory! In my memory are lagoons. They are covered with
          death's-heads.
They are not covered with water lilies.
In my memory are lagoons. No women's loincloths spread out on their shores.
My memory is encircled with blood. My memory has a belt of corpses!
and machine gun fire of rum barrels brilliantly sprinkling
our ignominious revolts, amorous glances swooning from having
swigged too much ferocious freedom

(niggers-are-all-alike, I-tell-you vices-all-the-vices-believe-you-me
nigger-smell, that's-what-makes-cane-grow
remember-the-old-saying:
beat-a-nigger, and you feed him)
among "rocking chairs" contemplating the voluptuousness of quirts[4]
I circle about, an unappeased filly

Or else quite simply as they like to think of us!
Cheerfully obscene, completely nuts about jazz to cover their extreme boredom
I can boogie-woogie, do the Lindy-hop and tap-dance.
And for a special treat the muting of our cries muffled with wah-wah. Wait . . .
          Everything is as it should be. My good angel grazes the neon. I swallow
          batons. My dignity wallows in puke . . .

          Sun, Angel Sun, curled Angel of the Sun
          for a leap beyond the sweet and greenish
     treading of the waters of abjection!

     But I approached the wrong sorcerer, on this exorcised earth, cast adrift from its pre-
cious malignant purpose, this voice that cries, little by little hoarse, vainly, vainly hoarse,
     and there remains only the accumulated droppings of our lies—and they do
not respond.
What madness to dream up a marvelous caper above the baseness!
Oh Yes the Whites are great warriors hosannah to the master and to the nigger-
gelder!

4. Slave whips.

Victory! Victory, I tell you: the defeated are content!
Joyous stenches and songs of mud!

By a sudden and beneficent inner revolution, I now ignore my repugnant ugliness.

On Midsummer Day, as soon as the first shadows fall on the village of Gros-Morne, hundreds of horse dealers gather on rue "De PROFUNDIS,"[5] a name at least honest enough to announce an onrush from the shoals of Death. And it truly is from Death, from its thousand petty local forms (cravings unsatisfied by Para grass and tipsy bondage to the distilleries) that the astonishing cavalry of impetuous nags surges unfenced toward the great-life. What a galloping! what neighing! what sincere urinating! what prodigious droppings! "A fine horse difficult to mount!"—"A proud mare sensitive to the spur"—"A fearless foal superbly pasterned!"

And the shrewd fellow whose waistcoat displays a proud watch chain, palms off instead of full udders, youthful mettle and genuine contours, either the systematic puffiness from obliging wasps, or the obscene stings from ginger, or the helpful distribution of several gallons of sugared water.

I refuse to pass off my puffiness for authentic glory.
And I laugh at my former childish fantasies.
No, we've never been Amazons of the king of Dahomey, nor princes of Ghana with eight hundred camels, nor wise men in Timbuktu under Askia the Great, nor the architects of Djenne, nor Madhis, nor warriors.[6] We don't feel under our armpit the itch of those who in the old days carried a lance. And since I have sworn to leave nothing out of our history (I who love nothing better than a sheep grazing his own afternoon shadow), I may as well confess that we were at all times pretty mediocre dishwashers, shoeblacks without ambition, at best conscientious sorcerers and the only unquestionable record that we broke was that of endurance under the chicote[7] . . .

And this land screamed for centuries that we are bestial brutes; that the human pulse stops at the gates of the slave compound; that we are walking compost hideously promising tender cane and silky cotton and they would brand us with red-hot irons and we would sleep in our excrement and they would sell us on the town square and an ell of English cloth and salted meat from Ireland cost less than we did, and this land was calm, tranquil, repeating that the spirit of the Lord was in its acts.

We the vomit of slave ships
We the venery of the Calabars[8]
what? Plug up our ears?
We, so drunk on jeers and inhaled fog that we rode the roll to death!
Forgive us fraternal whirlwind!

I hear coming up from the hold the enchained curses, the gasps of the dying, the noise of someone thrown into the sea . . . the baying of a woman in labor . . . the

---

5. Literally, "from the depths": the beginning of Psalm 129, a psalm sung during Christian liturgy to express the suffering of souls exiled from heaven; it is often used as a prayer for the dead.
6. Dahomey and Ghana are countries in West Africa; Timbuktu and Djenné are cities in Mali, also in West Africa. Djenné was once the capital of the Songhaï Em-

pire, which was ruled by Askia the Great from 1493 to 1529. Madhis were Islamic sovereigns in some parts of Africa, especially in the Sudan.
7. A leather whip.
8. The hunting targets of the Coast of Calabars in West Africa, which was notorious for slave trade.

scrape of fingernails seeking throats . . . the flouts of the whip . . . the seethings of vermin amid the weariness . . .

Nothing could ever lift us toward a noble hopeless adventure.
So be it. So be it.
I am of no nationality recognized by the chancelleries.
I defy the craniometer. Homo sum[9] etc.
Let them serve and betray and die
So be it. So be it. It was written in the shape of their pelvis.

And I, and I,
I was singing the hard fist
You must know the extent of my cowardice. One evening on the streetcar facing me, a nigger.

A nigger big as a pongo[1] trying to make himself small on the streetcar bench. He was trying to leave behind, on this grimy bench, his gigantic legs and his trembling famished boxer hands. And everything had left him, was leaving him. His nose which looked like a drifting peninsula and even his negritude discolored as a result of untiring tawing.[2] And the tawer was Poverty. A big unexpected lop-eared bat whose claw marks in his face had scabbed over into crusty islands. Or rather, it was a tireless worker, Poverty was, working on some hideous cartouche.[3] One could easily see how that industrious and malevolent thumb had kneaded bumps into his brow, bored two bizarre parallel tunnels in his nose, overexaggerated his lips, and in a masterpiece of caricature, planed, polished and varnished the tiniest cutest little ear in all creation.

He was a gangly nigger without rhythm or measure.

A nigger whose eyes rolled a bloodshot weariness.

A shameless nigger and his toes sneered in a rather stinking way at the bottom of the yawning lair of his shoes.

Poverty, without any question, had knocked itself out to finish him off.

It had dug the socket, had painted it with a rouge of dust mixed with rheum.

It had stretched an empty space between the solid hinge of the jaw and bone of an old tarnished cheek. Had planted over it the small shiny stakes of a two- or three-day beard. Had panicked his heart, bent his back.

And the whole thing added up perfectly to a hideous nigger, a grouchy nigger, a melancholy nigger, a slouched nigger, his hands joined in prayer on a knobby stick. A nigger shrouded in an old threadbare coat. A comical and ugly nigger, with some women behind me sneering at him.

He was COMICAL AND UGLY,
COMICAL AND UGLY for sure.
I displayed a big complicitous smile . . .
My cowardice rediscovered!
Hail to the three centuries which uphold my civil rights and my minimized blood!
My heroism, what a farce!

---

9. "I am human." Craniometers were instruments used to measure the size and shape of heads, thought to indicate crucial differences between "primitive" and "civilized" races.

1. A large ape.
2. Curing into white leather.
3. A carved ornamental tablet.

This town fits me to a t.

And my soul is lying down. Lying down like this town in its refuse and mud.

This town, my face of mud.

For my face I demand the vivid homage of spit! . . .

So, being what we are, ours the warrior thrust, the triumphant knee, the well-plowed
plains of the future?

Look, I'd rather admit to uninhibited ravings, my heart in my brain like a drunken
knee.

My star now, the funereal menfenil.[4]

And on this former dream my cannibalistic cruelties:

(The bullets in the mouth thick saliva

our heart from daily lowness bursts the continents break the fragile bond of isth-
muses

lands leap in accordance with the fatal division of rivers

and the morne which for centuries kept its scream within itself, it is its turn to draw
and quarter the silence and this people an ever-rebounding spirit

and our limbs vainly disjointed by the most refined tortures

and life even more impetuously jetting from this compost—unexpected as a soursop
amidst the decomposition of jack tree fruit!)

On this dream so old in me my cannibalistic cruelties

I was hiding behind a stupid vanity destiny called me I was hiding behind it and suddenly there was a man on the ground, his feeble defenses scattered,

his sacred maxims trampled underfoot, his pedantic rhetoric oozing air through each
wound.

There is a man on the ground

and his soul is almost naked

and destiny triumphs in watching this soul which defied its metamorphosis in the ancestral slough.

I say that this is right.

My back will victoriously exploit the chalaza of fibers.[5]

I will deck my natural obsequiousness with gratitude

And the silver-braided bullshit of the postillion of Havana, lyrical baboon pimp for
the glamour of slavery, will be more than a match for my enthusiasm.

I say that this is right.

I live for the flattest part of my soul.

For the dullest part of my flesh!

Tepid dawn of ancestral heat and fear

I now tremble with the collective trembling that our docile blood sings in the
madrepore.[6]

And these tadpoles hatched in me by my prodigious ancestry!

Those who invented neither powder nor compass

---

4. A kind of hawk.
5. The flexibility of a whip.

6. A kind of coral.

those who could harness neither steam nor electricity
those who explored neither the seas nor the sky but who know
in its most minute corners the land of suffering
those who have known voyages only through uprootings
those who have been lulled to sleep by so much kneeling
those whom they domesticated and Christianized
those whom they inoculated with degeneracy
tom-toms of empty hands
inane tom-toms of resounding sores
burlesque tom-toms of tabetic treason[7]

       Tepid dawn of ancestral heat and fears
overboard with alien riches
overboard with my genuine falsehoods
But what strange pride suddenly illuminates me!
let the hummingbird come
let the sparrow hawk come
the breach in the horizon
the cynocephalus[8]
let the lotus bearer of the world come
the pearly upheaval of dolphins
cracking the shell of the sea
let a plunge of islands come
let it come from the disappearing of days of dead
flesh in the quicklime of birds of prey
let the ovaries of the water come where the future stirs its testicles
let the wolves come who feed in the untamed openings of the body at the hour when
       my moon and your sun meet at the ecliptic inn

under the reserve of my uvula[9] there is a wallow of boars
under the grey stone of the day there are your eyes which are a shimmering conglom-
       erate of coccinella[1]
in the glance of disorder there is this swallow of mint and broom which melts always
       to be reborn in the tidal wave of your light
Calm and lull oh my voice the child who does not know that the map of spring is al-
       ways to be drawn again
the tall grass will sway gentle ship of hope for the cattle
the long alcoholic sweep of the swell
the stars with the bezels of their rings never in sight will cut the pipes of the glass or-
       gan of evening zinnias
coryanthas
will then pour into the rich extremity of my fatigue
and you star please from your luminous foundation draw lemurian being—of man's
       unfathomable sperm the yet undared form

---

7. Wasted, weak treason.
8. Species of apes with doglike snouts, such as baboons or mandrills.
9. Tissue at the back of the throat.
1. Beetles.

carried like an ore in woman's trembling belly!

oh friendly light
oh fresh source of light
those who have invented neither powder nor compass
those who could harness neither steam nor electricity
those who explored neither the seas nor the sky but those
without whom the earth would not be the earth
gibbosity[2] all the more beneficent as the bare earth even more earth
silo where that which is earthiest about earth ferments and ripens
my negritude is not a stone, its deafness hurled against the clamor of the day
my negritude is not a leukoma[3] of dead liquid over the earth's dead eye
my negritude is neither tower nor cathedral
it takes root in the red flesh of the soil
it takes root in the ardent flesh of the sky
it breaks through the opaque prostration with its upright patience

Eia for the royal Cailcedra![4]
Eia for those who have never invented anything
for those who never explored anything
for those who never conquered anything

but yield, captivated, to the essence of all things
ignorant of surfaces but captivated by the motion of all things
indifferent to conquering, but playing the game of the world
truly the eldest sons of the world
porous to all the breathing of the world
fraternal locus for all the breathing of the world
drainless channel for all the water of the world
spark of the sacred fire of the world
flesh of the world's flesh pulsating with the very motion of the world!
          Tepid dawn of ancestral virtues

Blood! Blood! all our blood aroused by the male heart of the sun
those who know about the femininity of the moon's oily body
the reconciled exultation of antelope and star
those whose survival travels in the germination of grass!
Eia perfect circle of the world, enclosed concordance!

Hear the white world
horribly weary from its immense efforts
its stiff joints crack under the hard stars
hear its blue steel rigidity pierce the mystic flesh
its deceptive victories tout its defeats
hear the grandiose alibis of its pitiful stumblings

2. Bulging.
3. A white scar on the cornea of the eye.

4. An African tree species.

Pity for our omniscient and naive conquerors!

Eia for grief and its udders of reincarnated tears
for those who have never explored anything
for those who have never conquered anything

Eia for joy
Eia for love
Eia for grief and its udders of reincarnated tears

and here at the end of these wee hours is my virile prayer that I hear neither the
laughter nor the screams, my eyes fixed on this town which I prophesy, beautiful,

grant me the savage faith of the sorcerer
grant my hands power to mold
grant my soul the sword's temper
I won't flinch. Make my head into a figurehead
and as for me, my heart, do not make me into a father nor a brother,
nor a son, but into the father, the brother, the son,
nor a husband, but the lover of this unique people.

Make me resist any vanity, but espouse its genius as the fist the extended arm!

Make me a steward of its blood
make me trustee of its resentment
make me into a man for the ending
make me into a man for the beginning
make me into a man of meditation
but also make me into a man of germination

make me into the executor of these lofty works
the time has come to gird one's loins like a brave man—

But in doing so, my heart, preserve me from all hatred
do not make me into that man of hatred for whom I feel only hatred
for entrenched as I am in this unique race
you still know my tyrannical love
you know that it is not from hatred of other races
that I demand a digger for this unique race
that what I want
is for universal hunger
for universal thirst

to summon it to generate,
free at last, from its intimate closeness
the succulence of fruit.

And be the tree of our hands!
it turns, for all, the wounds cut
in its trunk
the soil works for all
and toward the branches a headiness of fragrant precipitation!

But before stepping on the shores of future orchards
grant that I deserve those on their belt of sea
grant me my heart while awaiting the earth
grant me on the ocean sterile
but somewhere caressed by the promise of the clew-line[5]
grant me on this diverse ocean
the obstinacy of the fierce pirogue[6]
and its marine vigor.

See it advance rising and falling on the pulverized wave
see it dance the sacred dance before the greyness of the village
see it trumpet from a vertiginous conch

see the conch gallop up to the uncertainty of the morne

and see twenty times over the paddle
vigorously
plow the water
the pirogue rears under the attack of the swells
deviates for an instant
tries to escape, but the paddle's rough caress turns it,
then it charges, a shudder runs along the wave's spine,
the sea slobbers and rumbles
the pirogue like a sleigh glides onto the sand.

       At the end of these wee hours, my virile prayer:

grant me pirogue muscles on this raging sea
and the irresistible gaiety of the conch of good tidings!
Look, now I am only a man, no degradation, no spit perturbs him, now I am only a
        man who accepts emptied of anger
(nothing left in his heart but immense love, which burns)

I accept . . . I accept . . . totally, without reservation . . .
my race that no ablution of hyssop[7] mixed with lilies could purify
my race pitted with blemishes
my race a ripe grape for drunken feet
my queen of spittle and leprosy
my queen of whips and scrofula
my queen of squasma and chloasma (oh those queens I once loved in the remote gardens of spring against the illumination of all the candles of the chestnut trees!)
I accept. I accept.
and the flogged nigger saying: "Forgive me master"
and the twenty-nine legal blows of the whip
and the four-feet-high cell
and the spiked iron-collar
and the hamstringing of my runaway audacity

---

5. Line fastened to the lower corner of a sail.
6. A dug-out canoe with a sail.

7. A plant that is commonly used as medicine, perfume,
and condiment.

and the fleur de lys flowing from the red iron into the fat of my shoulder
and Monsieur VAULTIER MAYENCOURT'S dog house where I barked
six poodle months
and Monsieur BRAFIN
and Monsieur FOURNIOL
and Monsieur de la MAHAUDIERE[8]
and the yaws
the mastiff
the suicide
the promiscuity
the bootkin
the shackles
the rack
the cippus
the head screw

Look, am I humble enough? Have I enough calluses on my knees? Muscles on my loins?
Grovel in mud. Brace yourself in the thick of the mud. Carry.
Soil of mud. Horizon of mud. Sky of mud.
Dead of the mud, oh names to thaw in the palm of a feverish breathing!

Siméon Piquine, who never knew his father or mother; unheard of in any town hall and who wandered his whole life—seeking a new name.

Grandvorka—of him I only know that he died, crushed one harvest evening, it was his job, apparently, to throw sand under the wheels of the running locomotive, to help it across bad spots.

Michel who used to write me signing a strange name. Lucky Michel address *Condemned District* and you their living brothers Exélie Vêté Congolo Lemké Boussolongo what healer with his thick lips would suck from the depths of the gaping wound the tenacious secret of venom?

what cautious sorcerer would undo from your ankles the viscous tepidity of mortal rings?

Presences it is not on your back that I will make my peace with the world

Islands scars of the water
Islands evidence of wounds
Islands crumbs
Islands unformed
Islands cheap paper shredded upon the water
Islands stumps skewered side by side on the flaming sword of the Sun
Mulish reason you will not stop me from casting on the waters at the mercy of the currents of my thirst

8. The names and details mentioned here are based on historical accounts of slave treatment.

your form, deformed islands,
your end, my defiance.

Annulose islands,[9] single beautiful hull
And I caress you with my oceanic hands. And I turn you
around with the tradewinds of my speech. And I lick you with my seaweed
              tongues.
And I sail you unfreebootable!

O death your mushy marsh!
Shipwreck your hellish debris! I accept!

At the end of the wee hours, lost puddles, wandering scents, beached hurricanes, demasted hulls, old sores, rotted bones, vapors, shackled volcanoes, shallow-rooted dead, bitter cry. I accept!

And my special geography too; the world map made for my own use, not tinted with the arbitrary colors of scholars, but with the geometry of my spilled blood, I accept both the determination of my biology, not a prisoner to a facial angle, to a type of hair, to a well-flattened nose, to a clearly Melanian coloring,[1] and negritude, no longer a cephalic index, or plasma, or soma, but measured by the compass of suffering and the Negro every day more base, more cowardly, more sterile, less profound, more spilled out of himself, more separated from himself, more wily with himself, less immediate to himself,

I accept, I accept it all

and far from the palatial sea that foams beneath the suppurating syzygy[2] of blisters, miraculously lying in the despair of my arms the body of my country, its bones shocked and, in its veins, the blood hesitating like a drop of vegetal milk at the injured point of the bulb . . .

Suddenly now strength and life assail me like a bull and the water of life overwhelms the papilla of the morne, now all the veins and veinlets are bustling with new blood and the enormous breathing lung of cyclones and the fire hoarded in volcanoes and the gigantic seismic pulse which now beats the measure of a living body in my firm conflagration.

And we are standing now, my country and I, hair in the wind, my hand puny in its enormous fist and now the strength is not in us but above us, in a voice that drills the night and the hearing like the penetrance of an apocalyptic wasp. And the voice proclaims that for centuries Europe has force-fed us with lies and bloated us with pestilence,

for it is not true that the work of man is done
that we have no business being on earth
that we parasite the world
that it is enough for us to heel to the world

9. Ring-shaped islands.
1. Dark-skinned.

2. Configuration in which a planet or star forms a straight line with the sun and the earth.

whereas the work has only begun
and man still must overcome all the interdictions wedged in the recesses of his fervor
and no race has a monopoly on beauty, on intelligence, on strength

and there is room for everyone at the convocation of conquest and we know now that
the sun turns around our earth lighting the parcel designated by our will alone and that
every star falls from sky to earth at our omnipotent command.

I now see the meaning of this trial by the sword: my country is the "lance of night" of
my Bambara ancestors.[3] It shrivels and its point desperately retreats toward the haft
when it is sprinkled with chicken blood and it says that its nature requires the blood of
man, his fat, his liver, his heart, not chicken blood.

And I seek for my country not date hearts, but men's hearts which, in order to enter the silver cities through the great trapezoidal gate, beat with warrior blood, and as
my eyes sweep my kilometers of paternal earth I number its sores almost joyfully and
I pile one on top of the other like rare species, and my total is ever lengthened by unexpected mintings of baseness.

And there are those who will never get over not being made in the likeness of God but
of the devil, those who believe that being a nigger is like being a second-class clerk;
waiting for a better deal and upward mobility; those who beat the drum of compromise in front of themselves, those who live in their own dungeon pit; those who drape
themselves in proud pseudomorphosis; those who say to Europe: "You see, I *can* bow
and scrape, like you I pay my respects, in short, I am no different from you; pay no attention to my black skin: the sun did it."

And there is the nigger pimp, the nigger askari,[4] and all the zebras shaking themselves
in various ways to get rid of their stripes in a dew of fresh milk. And in the midst of
all that I say right on! my grandfather dies, I say right on! the old negritude progressively cadavers itself.

No question about it: he was good nigger. The Whites say he was a good nigger, a really good nigger, massa's good ole darky. I say right on!

He was a good nigger, indeed,
poverty had wounded his chest and back and they had stuffed into his brain that a fa-
tality impossible to trap weighed on him; that he had no control over his own fate;
that an evil Lord had for all eternity inscribed Thou Shall Not in his pelvic constitution; that he must be a good nigger; must sincerely believe in his worthlessness, without any perverse curiosity to check out the fatidic[5] hieroglyphs.

He was a very good nigger

and it never occurred to him that he could hoe, burrow, cut anything, anything else really than insipid cane

3. A West African ethnicity.   5. Prophetic.
4. African working as a colonial soldier.

He was a very good nigger.

And they threw stones at him, bits of scrap iron, broken bottles, but neither these stones, nor this scrap iron, nor these bottles . . . O peaceful years of God on this terraqueous[6] clod!

and the whip argued with the bombilation of the flies over the sugary dew of our sores.

I say right on! The old negritude
progressively cadavers itself
the horizon breaks, recoils and expands
and through the shedding of clouds and the flashing of a sign
the slave ship cracks everywhere . . . Its belly convulses and resounds . . . The ghastly tapeworm of its cargo gnaws the fetid guts of the strange suckling of the sea!

And neither the joy of sails filled like a pocket stuffed with doubloons, nor the tricks played on the dangerous stupidity of the frigates of order prevent it from hearing the threat of its intestinal rumblings

In vain to ignore them the captain hangs the biggest loudmouth nigger from the main yard or throws him into the sea, or feeds him to his mastiffs

Reeking of fried onions the nigger scum rediscovers the bitter taste of freedom in its spilled blood

And the nigger scum is on its feet

the seated nigger scum
unexpectedly standing
standing in the hold
standing in the cabins
standing on the deck
standing in the wind
standing under the sun
standing in the blood
   standing
      and
         free
standing and no longer a poor madwoman in her maritime freedom and destitution
gyrating in perfect drift
and there she is:
most unexpectedly standing
standing in the rigging
standing at the tiller
standing at the compass
standing at the map
standing under the stars

6. Earth-and-water.

    standing
        and
            free
and the lustral[7] ship fearlessly advances on the crumbling water.

And now our ignominous plops are rotting away!
by the clanking noon sea
by the burgeoning midnight sun
listen sparrow hawk who holds the keys to the orient
by the disarmed day
by the stony spurt of the rain

listen dogfish that watches over the occident

listen white dog of the north, black serpent of the south that cinches the sky girdle
There still remains one sea to cross
oh still one sea to cross
that I may invent my lungs
that the prince may hold his tongue
that the queen may lay me
still one old man to murder
one madman to deliver
that my soul may shine bark shine
bark bark bark
and the owl my beautiful inquisitive animal angel may hoot.
The master of laughter?
The master of ominous silence?
The master of hope and despair?
The master of laziness? Master of the dance?
    It is I!
and for this reason, Lord,
the frail-necked men
receive and perceive deadly triangular calm[8]

Rally to my side my dances
you bad nigger dances
the carcan-cracker dance
the prison-break dance
the it-is-beautiful-good-and-legitimate-to-be-a-nigger-dance
Rally to my side my dances and let the sun bounce on the racket of my hands

but no the unequal sun is not enough for me
coil, wind, around my new growth
light on my cadenced fingers
to you I surrender my conscience and its fleshy rhythm
to you I surrender the fire in which my weakness smolders
to you I surrender the "chain-gang"
to you the swamps

---

7. Purified.

8. Referring both to the Holy Trinity and to the triangular trade in slaves between Europe, Africa, and the Americas.

to you the nontourist of the triangular circuit
devour wind
to you I surrender my abrupt words
devour and encoil yourself
and self-encoiling embrace me with a more ample shudder
embrace me unto furious us
embrace, embrace US
but after having drawn from us blood
drawn by our own blood!
embrace, my purity mingles only with yours
so then embrace
like a field of even filagos[9]
at dusk
our multicolored purities
and bind, bind me without remorse
bind me with your vast arms to the luminous clay
bind my black vibration to the very navel of the world
bind, bind me, bitter brotherhood
then, strangling me with your lasso of stars
rise,
Dove
rise
rise
rise
I follow you who are imprinted on my ancestral white cornea.
rise sky licker
and the great black hole where a moon ago I wanted to drown it is there I will now fish
    the malevolent tongue of the night in its motionless veerition!!

━━━━◈━━━━

James Baldwin
1924–1987

Like Aimé Césaire, Ernest Hemingway, and other writers before him, James Baldwin found in Paris a vantage point that provided perspective on his upbringing in the Americas. Written largely in France, Baldwin's essays, stories, novels, and plays constitute one of the most searching bodies of work on American race relations, often seen through the prism of sexual and familial conflict. Unlike the Caribbean-born Claude McKay, who figured prominently in the Harlem Renaissance before moving to France (see p. 243), Baldwin was born in Harlem itself, the son of a young, unmarried houseworker in the Harlem ghetto. Three years later she married a Pentecostal preacher, with whom she had eight children. Baldwin grew up having to help raise his younger siblings, while also dealing with his stepfather—"the most bitter man I

---

9. A kind of pine tree that grows in the tropics.   1. A noun derived from the verb "to veer": change of direction.

have ever met," as Baldwin wrote in a long essay, "Notes of a Native Son" (1955). As Baldwin put it, "we had got on badly, partly because we shared, in our different fashions, the vice of stubborn pride."

In Harlem, Baldwin was moved by two very different kinds of artistic experience: his stepfather's eloquent preaching, filled with the cadences of the King James Bible, and the musical cadences of jazz. His stepfather (whom he always referred to as his father) frowned on music halls and dancing, and didn't allow jazz to be played at home, though he kept on his wall a portrait of the great trumpeter Louis Armstrong, whom he had known in New Orleans. Baldwin himself became a storefront preacher as a teenager, but gradually forsook his stepfather's profession and faith, while jazz remained an ongoing influence. After graduating from high school, he spent a few years working odd jobs and living in the artistic, bohemian community of New York's Greenwich Village, then moved to Paris in 1948. There he found jazz being appreciated as a sophisticated art form by avant-garde French writers; the novelist and philosopher Jean-Paul Sartre, for example, had showcased a jazz singer in a crucial scene of his 1938 novel *Nausea*. Baldwin's powerful story "Sonny's Blues," included here, evokes the dangerous beauty of jazz in terms influenced by French existentialism as developed by Sartre and others, which stresses the anguished freedom of those who have abandoned the illusion that the world has a predetermined meaning. Instead, the existentialist must deliberately wrest meaning from "nothingness," much as Baldwin shows the jazz pianist Sonny doing.

Baldwin's own prose employs jazz-like modulations of theme, moving back and forth among interwoven concerns and motifs. Discordant elements pile together, brought into vivid relation, as in the opening paragraph of "Notes of a Native Son":

> On the 29th of July, in 1943, my father died. On the same day, a few hours later, his last child was born. Over a month before this, while all our energies were concentrated in waiting for these events, there had been, in Detroit, one of the bloodiest race riots of the century. A few hours after my father's funeral, while he lay in state in the undertaker's chapel, a race riot broke out in Harlem. On the morning of the 3rd of August, we drove my father to the graveyard through a wilderness of smashed plate glass.

Aimé Césaire used startling juxtapositions of this kind in his surrealist poetry; here, they are rendered in lucid prose, its controlled surface showing both a distanced irony and also a simmering rage and grief. Like the French existentialists, Baldwin was both a cool observer and a deeply engaged activist; he traveled frequently back to the United States in the 1950s and 1960s to work with Martin Luther King, Jr., and other civil rights activists. His best-selling book *The Fire Next Time* (1963) gave a searing indictment of American racial relations, which he cuttingly described as stemming not from "a Negro problem" but from "a white problem."

Even as he found friends and allies on both sides of the Atlantic, Baldwin also encountered resistance, particularly as he began to explore issues of homosexuality in his fiction (a largely taboo theme among many black as well as white activists); seeking distance from both Europe and America, he lived for various periods in the Middle East. He aroused conflict as well with his continual probing of the differences between essay and fiction, breaking with his friend and mentor Richard Wright in 1949 after he criticized Wright's novel *Native Son* as self-righteous and simplistic protest fiction that failed the responsibility to be true to life in its full complexity. In his 1950 essay "Encounter on the Seine," given here, Baldwin can be seen distancing himself from the all-embracing community of *négritude* championed by Césaire and by Léopold Sédar Senghor, as Baldwin suggests that American blacks have to deal with very different historical and present circumstances than those that confront Caribbeans or Africans. This essay too shows Baldwin's ongoing fascination with jazz, and its subtitle, "Black Meets Brown," echoes the title of a major composition by Duke Ellington, *Black, Brown, and Beige*. Ellington was one of the first black jazz artists to have major crossover appeal among white as well as black audiences, and his title asserted a commonality among all shades of color, while also slyly presenting Euro-American "beige" as only a paler form of brown. By contrast, Baldwin explores the disjunctions among "black" and "brown" themselves. In his story "Sonny's Blues" (1957), Baldwin opens up the tensions between brothers in a single family, showing a narrator who has to confront his younger brother's self-destructive lifestyle and—equally baffling to the narrator—his brother's growing ambition to succeed as a jazz pianist. Distributing himself across his characters and across the Atlantic, Baldwin became one of the most cosmopolitan of modern writers, even as he continued to explore the charged territory of his youth in New York.

Encounter on the Seine: Black Meets Brown

In Paris nowadays it is rather more difficult for an American Negro to become a really successful entertainer than it is rumored to have been some thirty years ago. For one thing, champagne has ceased to be drunk out of slippers, and the frivolously colored thousand-franc note is neither as elastic nor as freely spent as it was in the 1920's. The musicians and singers who are here now must work very hard indeed to acquire the polish and style which will land them in the big time. Bearing witness to this eternally tantalizing possibility, performers whose eminence is unchallenged, like Duke Ellington or Louis Armstrong, occasionally pass through. Some of their ambitious followers are in or near the big time already; others are gaining reputations which have yet to be tested in the States. Gordon Heath, who will be remembered for his performances as the embattled soldier in Broadway's *Deep Are the Roots* some seasons back, sings ballads nightly in his own night club on the Rue L'Abbaye; and everyone who comes to Paris these days sooner or later discovers Chez Inez, a night club in the Latin Quarter run by a singer named Inez Cavanaugh, which specializes in fried chicken and jazz. It is at Chez Inez that many an unknown first performs in public, going on thereafter if not always to greater triumphs, at least to other night clubs, and possibly landing a contract to tour the Riviera during the spring and summer.

In general, only the Negro entertainers are able to maintain a useful and unquestioning comradeship with other Negroes. Their nonperforming, colored countrymen are, nearly to a man, incomparably more isolated, and it must be conceded that this isolation is deliberate. It is estimated that there are five hundred American Negroes living in this city, the vast majority of them veterans studying on the G.I. Bill. They are studying everything from the Sorbonne's standard *Cours de Civilisation Française* to abnormal psychology, brain surgery, music, fine arts, and literature. Their isolation from each other is not difficult to understand if one bears in mind the axiom, unquestioned by American landlords, that Negroes are happy only when they are kept together. Those driven to break this pattern by leaving the U.S. ghettos not merely have effected a social and physical leave-taking but also have been precipitated into cruel psychological warfare. It is altogether inevitable that past humiliations should become associated not only with one's traditional oppressors but also with one's traditional kinfolk.

Thus the sight of a face from home is not invariably a source of joy, but can also quite easily become a source of embarrassment or rage. The American Negro in Paris is forced at last to exercise an undemocratic discrimination rarely practiced by Americans, that of judging his people, duck by duck, and distinguishing them one from another. Through this deliberate isolation, through lack of numbers, and above all through his own overwhelming need to be, as it were, forgotten, the American Negro in Paris is very nearly the invisible man.[1]

The wariness with which he regards his colored kin is a natural extension of the wariness with which he regards all of his countrymen. At the beginning, certainly, he cherishes rather exaggerated hopes of the French. His white countrymen, by and large, fail to justify his fears, partly because the social climate does not encourage an outward display of racial bigotry, partly out of their awareness of being ambassadors, and finally, I should think, because they are themselves relieved at being no longer forced to think in terms of color. There remains, nevertheless, in the encounter of white Americans and Negro Americans the high potential of an awkward or an ugly situation.

The white American regards his darker brother through the distorting screen created by a lifetime of conditioning. He is accustomed to regard him either as a needy and deserving martyr or as the soul of rhythm, but he is more than a little intimidated to find this stranger so many miles from home. At first he tends instinctively, whatever his intelligence may belatedly clamor, to take it as a reflection on his personal honor and good-will; and at the same time, with that winning generosity, at once good-natured and uneasy, which characterizes Americans, he would like to establish communication, and sympathy, with his compatriot. "And how do *you* feel about it?" he would like to ask, "it" being anything—the Russians, Betty Grable, the Place de la Concorde. The trouble here is that any "it" so tentatively offered, may suddenly become loaded and vibrant with tension, creating in the air between the two thus met an intolerable atmosphere of danger.

The Negro, on the other hand, via the same conditioning which constricts the outward gesture of the whites, has learned to anticipate: as the mouth opens he divines what the tongue will utter. He has had time, too, long before he came to Paris, to reflect on the absolute and personally expensive futility of taking any one of his countrymen to task for his status in America, or of hoping to convey to them any of his experience. The American Negro and white do not, therefore, discuss the past, except in considerately guarded snatches. Both are quite willing, and indeed quite wise, to remark instead the considerably overrated impressiveness of the Eiffel Tower.

The Eiffel Tower has naturally long since ceased to divert the French, who consider that all Negroes arrive from America, trumpet-laden and twinkle-toed, bearing scars so unutterably painful that all of the glories of the French Republic may not suffice to heal them. This indignant generosity poses problems of its own, which, language and custom being what they are, are not so easily averted.

The European tends to avoid the really monumental confusion which might result from an attempt to apprehend the relationship of the forty-eight states to one another, clinging instead to such information as is afforded by radio, press, and film, to anecdotes considered to be illustrative of American life, and to the myth that we have ourselves perpetuated. The result, in conversation, is rather like seeing one's back yard reproduced with extreme fidelity, but in such a perspective that it becomes a place which one has never seen or visited, which never has existed, and which can never exist. The Negro is forced to say "Yes" to many a difficult question, and yet to deny the conclusions to which his answers seem to point. His past, he now realizes, has not been simply a series of ropes and bonfires and humiliations, but something

---

1. *The Invisible Man* was a science-fiction story by H. G. Wells, made into a 1933 Hollywood movie; later used by Ralph Ellison for his 1952 novel *Invisible Man* about an anonymous black man's struggle in a hostile society.

vastly more complex, which, as he thinks painfully, "It was much worse than that," was also, he irrationally feels, something much better. As it is useless to excoriate his countrymen, it is galling now to be pitied as a victim, to accept this ready sympathy which is limited only by its failure to accept him as an American. He finds himself involved, in another language, in the same old battle: the battle for his own identity. To accept the reality of his being an American becomes a matter involving his integrity and his great hopes, for only by accepting this reality can he hope to make articulate to himself or to others the uniqueness of his experience, and to set free the spirit so long anonymous and caged.

The ambivalence of his status is thrown into relief by his encounters with the Negro students from France's colonies who live in Paris. The French African comes from a region and a way of life which—at least from the American point of view—is exceedingly primitive, and where exploitation takes more naked forms. In Paris, the African Negro's status, conspicuous and subtly inconvenient, is that of a colonial; and he leads here the intangibly precarious life of someone abruptly and recently uprooted. His bitterness is unlike that of his American kinsman in that it is not so treacherously likely to be turned against himself. He has, not so very many miles away, a homeland to which his relationship, no less than his responsibility, is overwhelmingly clear: His country must be given—or it must seize—its freedom. This bitter ambition is shared by his fellow colonials, with whom he has a common language, and whom he has no wish whatever to avoid; without whose sustenance, indeed, he would be almost altogether lost in Paris. They live in groups together, in the same neighborhoods, in student hotels and under conditions which cannot fail to impress the American as almost unendurable.

Yet what the American is seeing is not simply the poverty of the student but the enormous gap between the European and American standards of living. *All* of the students in the Latin Quarter live in ageless, sinister-looking hotels; they are all forced continually to choose between cigarettes and cheese at lunch.

It is true that the poverty and anger which the American Negro sees must be related to Europe and not to America. Yet, as he wishes for a moment that he were home again, where at least the terrain is familiar, there begins to race within him, like the despised beat of the tom-tom, echoes of a past which he has not yet been able to utilize, intimations of a responsibility which he has not yet been able to face. He begins to conjecture how much he has gained and lost during his long sojourn in the American republic. The African before him has endured privation, injustice, medieval cruelty; but the African has not yet endured the utter alienation of himself from his people and his past. His mother did not sing "Sometimes I Feel Like a Motherless Child," and he has not, all his life long, ached for acceptance in a culture which pronounced straight hair and white skin the only acceptable beauty.

They face each other, the Negro and the African, over a gulf of three hundred years—an alienation too vast to be conquered in an evening's good-will, too heavy and too double-edged ever to be trapped in speech. This alienation causes the Negro to recognize that he is a hybrid. Not a physical hybrid merely: in every aspect of his living he betrays the memory of the auction block and the impact of the happy ending. In white Americans he finds reflected—repeated, as it were, in a higher key—his tensions, his terrors, his tenderness. Dimly and for the first time, there begins to fall into perspective the nature of the roles they have played in the lives and history of each other. Now he is bone of their bone, flesh of their flesh;[2] they have loved and hated

2. Like Adam and Eve (Genesis 2:23).

and obsessed and feared each other and his blood is in their soil. Therefore he cannot deny them, nor can they ever be divorced.

The American Negro cannot explain to the African what surely seems in himself to be a want of manliness, of racial pride, a maudlin ability to forgive. It is difficult to make clear that he is not seeking to forfeit his birthright as a black man, but that, on the contrary, it is precisely this birthright which he is struggling to recognize and make articulate. Perhaps it now occurs to him that in this need to establish himself in relation to his past he is most American, that this depthless alienation from oneself and one's people is, in sum, the American experience.

Yet one day he will face his home again; nor can he realistically expect to find overwhelming changes. In America, it is true, the appearance is perpetually changing, each generation greeting with short-lived exultation yet more dazzling additions to our renowned façade. But the ghetto, anxiety, bitterness, and guilt continue to breed their indescribable complex of tensions. What time will bring Americans is at last their own identity. It is on this dangerous voyage and in the same boat that the American Negro will make peace with himself and with the voiceless many thousands gone before him.

Sonny's Blues

I read about it in the paper, in the subway, on my way to work. I read it, and I couldn't believe it, and I read it again. Then perhaps I just stared at it, at the newsprint spelling out his name, spelling out the story. I stared at it in the swinging lights of the subway car, and in the faces and bodies of the people, and in my own face, trapped in the darkness which roared outside.

It was not to be believed and I kept telling myself that, as I walked from the subway station to the high school. And at the same time I couldn't doubt it. I was scared, scared for Sonny. He became real to me again. A great block of ice got settled in my belly and kept melting there slowly all day long, while I taught my classes algebra. It was a special kind of ice. It kept melting, sending trickles of ice water all up and down my veins, but it never got less. Sometimes it hardened and seemed to expand until I felt my guts were going to come spilling out or that I was going to choke or scream. This would always be at a moment when I was remembering some specific thing Sonny had once said or done.

When he was about as old as the boys in my classes his face had been bright and open, there was a lot of copper in it; and he'd had wonderfully direct brown eyes, and great gentleness and privacy. I wondered what he looked like now. He had been picked up, the evening before, in a raid on an apartment downtown, for peddling and using heroin.

I couldn't believe it: but what I mean by that is that I couldn't find any room for it anywhere inside me. I had kept it outside me for a long time. I hadn't wanted to know. I had had suspicions, but I didn't name them, I kept putting them away. I told myself that Sonny was wild, but he wasn't crazy. And he'd always been a good boy, he hadn't ever turned hard or evil or disrespectful, the way kids can, so quick, so quick, especially in Harlem. I didn't want to believe that I'd ever see my brother going down, coming to nothing, all that light in his face gone out, in the condition I'd already seen so many others. Yet it had happened and here I was, talking about algebra to a lot of boys who might, every one of them for all I knew, be popping off needles every time they went to the head.[1] Maybe it did more for them than algebra could.

1. Bathroom.

I was sure that the first time Sonny had ever had horse,[2] he couldn't have been much older than these boys were now. These boys, now, were living as we'd been living then, they were growing up with a rush and their heads bumped abruptly against the low ceiling of their actual possibilities. They were filled with rage. All they really knew were two darknesses, the darkness of their lives, which was now closing in on them, and the darkness of the movies, which had blinded them to that other darkness, and in which they now, vindictively, dreamed, at once more together than they were at any other time, and more alone.

When the last bell rang, the last class ended, I let out my breath. It seemed I'd been holding it for all that time. My clothes were wet—I may have looked as though I'd been sitting in a steam bath, all dressed up, all afternoon. I sat alone in the class-room a long time. I listened to the boys outside, downstairs, shouting and cursing and laughing. Their laughter struck me for perhaps the first time. It was not the joyous laughter which—God knows why—one associates with children. It was mocking and insular, its intent was to denigrate. It was disenchanted, and in this, also, lay the au-thority of their curses. Perhaps I was listening to them because I was thinking about my brother and in them I heard my brother. And myself.

One boy was whistling a tune, at once very complicated and very simple, it seemed to be pouring out of him as though he were a bird, and it sounded very cool and moving through all that harsh, bright air, only just holding its own through all those other sounds.

I stood up and walked over to the window and looked down into courtyard. It was the beginning of the spring and the sap was rising in the boys. A teacher passed through them every now and again, quickly, as though he or she couldn't wait to get out of that courtyard, to get those boys out of their sight and off their minds. I started collecting my stuff. I thought I'd better get home and talk to Isabel.

The courtyard was almost deserted by the time I got downstairs. I saw this boy standing in the shadow of a doorway, looking just like Sonny. I almost called his name. Then I saw that it wasn't Sonny, but somebody we used to know, a boy from around our block. He'd been Sonny's friend. He'd never been mine, having been too young for me, and, anyway, I'd never liked him. And now, even though he was a grown-up man, he still hung around that block, still spent hours on the street corners, was always high and raggy. I used to run into him from time to time and he'd often work around to asking me for a quarter or fifty cents. He always had some real good excuse, too, and I always gave it to him, I don't know why.

But now, abruptly, I hated him. I couldn't stand the way he looked at me, partly like a dog, partly like a cunning child. I wanted to ask him what the hell he was doing in the school courtyard.

He sort of shuffled over to me, and he said, "I see you got the papers. So you already know about it."

"You mean Sonny? Yes, I already know about it. How come they didn't get you?"

He grinned. It made him repulsive and it also brought to mind what he'd looked like as a kid. "I wasn't there. I stay away from them people."

"Good for you." I offered him a cigarette and I watched him through the smoke. "You come all the way down here just to tell me about Sonny?"

"That's right." He was sort of shaking his head and his eyes looked strange, as though they were about to cross. The bright sun deadened his damp dark brown skin

2. Heroin.

and it made his eyes look yellow and showed up the dirt in his kinked hair. He smelled funky. I moved a little away from him and I said, "Well, thanks. But I already know about it and I got to get home."

"I'll walk you a little ways," he said. We started walking. There were a couple of kids still loitering in the courtyard and one of them said goodnight to me and looked strangely at the boy beside me.

"What're you going to do?" he asked me. "I mean, about Sonny?"

"Look. I haven't seen Sonny for over a year, I'm not sure I'm going to do anything. Anyway, what the hell *can* I do?"

"That's right," he said quickly, "ain't nothing you can do. Can't much help old Sonny no more, I guess."

It was what I was thinking and so it seemed to me he had no right to say it.

"I'm surprised at Sonny, though," he went on—he had a funny way of talking, he looked straight ahead as though he were talking to himself—"I thought he was too smart to get hung."[3]

"I guess he thought so too," I said sharply, "and that's how he got hung. And how about you? You're pretty goddamn smart, I bet."

Then he looked directly at me, just for a minute. "I ain't smart," he said. "If I was smart, I'd have reached for a pistol a long time ago."

"Look. Don't tell *me* your sad story, if it was up to me, I'd give you one." Then I felt guilty—guilty, probably, for never having supposed that the poor bastard *had* a story of his own, much less a sad one, and I asked, quickly, "What's going to happen to him now?"

He didn't answer this. He was off by himself some place. "Funny thing," he said, and from his tone we might have been discussing the quickest way to get to Brooklyn, "when I saw the papers this morning, the first thing I asked myself was if I had anything to do with it. I felt sort of responsible."

I began to listen more carefully. The subway station was on the corner, just before us, and I stopped. He stopped, too. We were in front of a bar and he ducked slightly, peering in, but whoever he was looking for didn't seem to be there. The juke box was blasting away with something black and bouncy and I half watched a barmaid as she danced her way from the juke box to her place behind the bar. And I watched her face as she laughingly responded to something someone said to her, still keeping time to the music. When she smiled one saw the little girl, one sensed the doomed, still-struggling woman beneath the battered face of the semi-whore.

"I never *give* Sonny nothing," the boy said finally, "but a long time ago I come to school high and Sonny asked me how it felt." He paused, I couldn't bear to watch him, I watched the barmaid, and I listened to the music which seemed to be causing the pavement to shake. "I told him it felt great." The music stopped, the barmaid paused and watched the juke box until the music began again. "It did."

All this was carrying me some place I didn't want to go. I certainly didn't want to know how it felt. It filled everything, the people, the houses, the music, the dark, quicksilver barmaid, with menace; and this menace was their reality.

"What's going to happen to him now?" I asked again.

"They'll send him away some place and they'll try to cure him." He shook his head. "Maybe he'll even think he's kicked the habit. Then they'll let him loose"—he gestured, throwing his cigarette into the gutter. "That's all."

"What do you mean, that's *all*?"

3. Caught.

But I knew what he meant.

"I *mean,* that's *all.*" He turned his head and looked at me, pulling down the corners of his mouth. "Don't you know what I mean?" he asked, softly.

"How the hell *would* I know what you mean?" I almost whispered it, I don't know why.

"That's right," he said to the air, "how would *he* know what I mean?" He turned toward me again, patient and calm, and yet I somehow felt him shaking, shaking as though he was going to fall apart. I felt that ice in my guts again, the dread I'd felt all afternoon; and again I watched the barmaid, moving about the bar, washing glasses, and singing. "Listen. They'll let him out and then it'll just start all over again. That's what I mean."

"You mean—they'll let him out. And then he'll just start working his way back in again. You mean he'll never kick the habit. Is that what you mean?"

"That's right," he said, cheerfully. "*You* see what I mean."

"Tell me," I said at last, "why does he want to die? He must want to die, he's killing himself, why does he want to die?"

He looked at me in surprise. He licked his lips. "He don't want to die. He wants to live. Don't nobody want to die, ever."

Then I wanted to ask him—too many things. He could not have answered, or if he had, I could not have borne the answers. I started walking. "Well, I guess it's none of my business."

"It's going to be rough on old Sonny," he said. We reached the subway station. "This is your station?" he asked. I nodded. I took one step down. "Damn!" he said, suddenly. I looked up at him. He grinned again. "Damn it if I didn't leave all my money home. You ain't got a dollar on you, have you? Just for a couple of days, is all."

All at once something inside gave and threatened to come pouring out of me. I didn't hate him any more. I felt that in another moment I'd start crying like a child.

"Sure," I said. "Don't sweat." I looked in my wallet and didn't have a dollar, I only had a five. "Here," I said. "That hold you?"

He didn't look at it—he didn't want to look at it. A terrible, closed look came over his face, as though he was keeping the number on the bill a secret from him and me. "Thanks," he said, and now he was dying to see me go. "Don't worry about Sonny. Maybe I'll write him or something."

"Sure," I said. "You do that. So long."

"Be seeing you," he said. I went on down the steps.

And I didn't write Sonny or send him anything for a long time. When I finally did, it was just after my little girl died, he wrote me back a letter which made me feel like a bastard.

Here's what he said:

Dear brother,

    You don't know how much I needed to hear from you. I wanted to write you many a time but I dug how much I must have hurt you and so I didn't write. But now I feel like a man who's been trying to climb up out of some deep, real deep and funky hole and just saw the sun up there, outside. I got to get outside.

    I can't tell you much about how I got here. I mean I don't know how to tell you. I guess I was afraid of something or I was trying to escape from something and you know I have never been very strong in the head (smile). I'm glad Mama and Daddy are dead and can't see what's happened to their son and I swear if I'd known what I was doing I would never have hurt you so, you and a lot of other fine people who were nice to me and who believed in me.

I don't want you to think it had anything to do with me being a musician. It's more than that. Or maybe less than that. I can't get anything straight in my head down here and I try not to think about what's going to happen to me when I get outside again. Sometime I think I'm going to flip and *never* get outside and sometime I think I'll come straight back. I tell you one thing, though, I'd rather blow my brains out than go through this again. But that's what they all say, so they tell me. If I tell you when I'm coming to New York and if you could meet me, I sure would appreciate it. Give my love to Isabel and the kids and I was sure sorry to hear about little Gracie. I wish I could be like Mama and say the Lord's will be done, but I don't know it seems to me that trouble is the one thing that never does get stopped and I don't know what good it does to blame it on the Lord. But maybe it does some good if you believe it.

Your brother,
Sonny

Then I kept in constant touch with him and I sent him whatever I could and I went to meet him when he came back to New York. When I saw him many things I thought I had forgotten came flooding back to me. This was because I had begun, finally, to wonder about Sonny, about the life that Sonny lived inside. This life, whatever it was, had made him older and thinner and it had deepened the distant stillness in which he had always moved. He looked very unlike my baby brother. Yet, when he smiled, when we shook hands, the baby brother I'd never known looked out from the depths of his private life, like an animal waiting to be coaxed into the light.

"How you been keeping?" he asked me.

"All right. And you?"

"Just fine." He was smiling all over his face. "It's good to see you again."

"It's good to see you."

The seven years' difference in our ages lay between us like a chasm: I wondered if these years would ever operate between us as a bridge. I was remembering, and it made it hard to catch my breath, that I had been there when he was born; and I had heard the first words he had ever spoken. When he started to walk, he walked from our mother straight to me. I caught him just before he fell when he took the first steps he ever took in this world.

"How's Isabel?"

"Just fine. She's dying to see you."

"And the boys?"

"They're fine, too. They're anxious to see their uncle."

"Oh, come on. You know they don't remember me."

"Are you kidding? Of course they remember you."

He grinned again. We got into a taxi. We had a lot to say to each other, far too much to know how to begin.

As the taxi began to move, I asked, "You still want to go to India?"

He laughed. "You still remember that. Hell, no. This place is Indian enough for me."

"It used to belong to them," I said.

And he laughed again. "They damn sure knew what they were doing when they got rid of it."

Years ago, when he was around fourteen, he'd been all hipped on the idea of going to India. He read books about people sitting on rocks, naked, in all kinds of weather, but mostly bad, naturally, and walking barefoot through hot coals and arriving at wisdom. I used to say that it sounded to me as though they were getting away from wisdom as fast as they could. I think he sort of looked down on me for that.

"Do you mind," he asked, "if we have the driver drive alongside the park? On the west side—I haven't seen the city in so long."

"Of course not," I said. I was afraid that I might sound as though I was humoring him, but I hoped he wouldn't take it that way.

So we drove along, between the green of the park and the stony, lifeless elegance of hotels and apartment buildings, toward the vivid, killing streets of our childhood. These streets hadn't changed, though housing projects jutted up out of them now like rocks in the middle of the boiling sea. Most of the houses in which we had grown up had vanished, as had the stores from which we had stolen, the basements in which we had first tried sex, the rooftops from which we had hurled tin cans and bricks. But houses exactly like the houses of our past yet dominated the landscape, boys exactly like the boys we once had been found themselves smothering in these houses, came down into the streets for light and air and found themselves encircled by disaster. Some escaped the trap, most didn't. Those who got out always left something of themselves behind, as some animals amputate a leg and leave it in the trap. It might be said, perhaps, that I had escaped, after all, I was a school teacher; or that Sonny had, he hadn't lived in Harlem for years. Yet, as the cab moved uptown through streets which seemed, with a rush, to darken with dark people, and as I covertly studied Sonny's face, it came to me that what we both were seeking through our separate cab windows was that part of ourselves which had been left behind. It's always at the hour of trouble and confrontation that the missing member aches.

We hit 110th Street[4] and started rolling up Lenox Avenue. And I'd known this avenue all my life, but it seemed to me again, as it had seemed on the day I'd first heard about Sonny's trouble, filled with a hidden menace which was its very breath of life.

"We almost there," said Sonny.

"Almost." We were both too nervous to say anything more.

We live in a housing project. It hasn't been up long. A few days after it was up it seemed uninhabitably new, now, of course, it's already rundown. It looks like a parody of the good, clean, faceless life—God knows the people who live in it do their best to make it a parody. The beat-looking grass lying around isn't enough to make their lives green, the hedges will never hold out the streets, and they know it. The big windows fool no one, they aren't big enough to make space out of no space. They don't bother with the windows, they watch the TV screen instead. The playground is most popular with the children who don't play at jacks, or skip rope, or roller skate, or swing, and they can be found in it after dark. We moved in partly because it's not too far from where I teach, and partly for the kids; but it's really just like the houses in which Sonny and I grew up. The same things happen, they'll have the same things to remember. The moment Sonny and I started into the house I had the feeling that I was simply bringing him back into the danger he had almost died trying to escape.

Sonny has never been talkative. So I don't know why I was sure he'd be dying to talk to me when supper was over the first night. Everything went fine, the oldest boy remembered him, and the youngest boy liked him, and Sonny had remembered to bring something for each of them; and Isabel, who is really much nicer than I am,

4. The northern border of Manhattan's Central Park and southern border of Harlem.

more open and giving, had gone to a lot of trouble about dinner and was genuinely glad to see him. And she's always been able to tease Sonny in a way that I haven't. It was nice to see her face so vivid again and to hear her laugh and watch her make Sonny laugh. She wasn't, or, anyway, she didn't seem to be, at all uneasy or embarrassed. She chatted as though there was no subject which had to be avoided and she got Sonny past his first, faint stiffness. And thank God she was there, for I was filled with that icy dread again. Everything I did seemed awkward to me, and everything I said sounded freighted with hidden meaning. I was trying to remember everything I'd heard about dope addiction and I couldn't help watching Sonny for the signs. I wasn't doing it out of malice. I was trying to find out something about my brother. I was dying to hear him tell me he was safe.

"Safe!" my father grunted, whenever Mama suggested trying to move to a neighborhood which might be safer for children. "Safe, hell! Ain't no place safe for kids, nor nobody."

He always went on like this, but he wasn't, ever, really as bad as he sounded, not even on weekends, when he got drunk. As a matter of fact, he was always on the lookout for "something a little better," but he died before he found it. He died suddenly, during a drunken weekend in the middle of the war, when Sonny was fifteen. He and Sonny hadn't ever gotten on too well. And this was partly because Sonny was the apple of his father's eye. It was because he loved Sonny so much and was frightened for him, that he was always fighting with him. It doesn't do any good to fight with Sonny. Sonny just moves back, inside himself, where he can't be reached. But the principal reason that they never hit it off is that they were so much alike. Daddy was big and rough, and loud-talking, just the opposite of Sonny, but they both had—that same privacy.

Mama tried to tell me something about this, just after Daddy died. I was home on leave from the army.

This was the last time I ever saw my mother alive. Just the same, this picture gets all mixed up in my mind with pictures I had of her when she was younger. The way I always see her is the way she used to be on a Sunday afternoon, say, when the old folks were talking after the big Sunday dinner. I always see her wearing pale blue. She'd be sitting on the sofa. And my father would be sitting in the easy chair, not far from her. And the living room would be full of church folks and relatives. There they sit, in chairs all around the living room, and the night is creeping up outside, but nobody knows it yet. You can see the darkness growing against the windowpanes and you hear the street noises every now and again, or maybe the jangling beat of a tambourine from one of the churches close by, but it's real quiet in the room. For a moment nobody's talking, but every face looks darkening, like the sky outside. And my mother rocks a little from the waist, and my father's eyes are closed. Everyone is looking at something a child can't see. For a minute they've forgotten the children. Maybe a kid is lying on the rug, half asleep. Maybe somebody's got a kid in his lap and is absent-mindedly stroking the kid's head. Maybe there's a kid, quiet and big-eyed, curled up in a big chair in the corner. The silence, the darkness coming, and the darkness in the faces frightens the child obscurely. He hopes that the hand which strokes his forehead will never stop—will never die. He hopes that there will never come a time when the old folks won't be sitting around the living room, talking about where they've come from, and what they've seen, and what's happening to them and their kinfolk.

But something deep and watchful in the child knows that this is bound to end, is already ending. In a moment someone will get up and turn on the light. Then the old folks will remember the children and they won't talk any more that day. And when light fills the room, the child is filled with darkness. He knows that every time this happens he's moved just a little closer to that darkness outside. The darkness outside is what the old folks have been talking about. It's what they've come from. It's what they endure. The child knows that they won't talk any more because if he knows too much about what's happened to *them,* he'll know too much too soon, about what's going to happen to *him.*

The last time I talked to my mother, I remember I was restless. I wanted to get out and see Isabel. We weren't married then and we had a lot to straighten out between us.

There Mama sat, in black, by the window. She was humming an old church song, *Lord, you brought me from a long ways off.* Sonny was out somewhere. Mama kept watching the streets.

"I don't know," she said, "if I'll ever see you again, after you go off from here. But I hope you'll remember the things I tried to teach you."

"Don't talk like that," I said, and smiled. "You'll be here a long time yet."

She smiled, too, but she said nothing. She was quiet for a long time. And I said, "Mama, don't you worry about nothing. I'll be writing all the time, and you be getting the checks. . . ."

"I want to talk to you about your brother," she said, suddenly. "If anything happens to me he ain't going to have nobody to look out for him."

"Mama," I said, "ain't nothing going to happen to you *or* Sonny. Sonny's all right. He's a good boy and he's got good sense."

"It ain't a question of his being a good boy," Mama said, "nor of his having good sense. It ain't only the bad ones, nor yet the dumb ones that gets sucked under." She stopped, looking at me. "Your Daddy once had a brother," she said, and she smiled in a way that made me feel she was in pain. "You didn't never know that, did you?"

"No," I said, "I never knew that," and I watched her face.

"Oh, yes," she said, "your Daddy had a brother." She looked out the window again. "I know you never saw your Daddy cry. But *I* did—many a time, through all these years."

I asked her, "What happened to his brother? How come nobody's ever talked about him?"

This was the first time I ever saw my mother look old.

"His brother got killed," she said, "when he was just a little younger than you are now. I knew him. He was a fine boy. He was maybe a little full of the devil, but he didn't mean nobody no harm."

The she stopped and the room was silent, exactly as it had sometimes been on those Sunday afternoons. Mama kept looking out into the streets.

"He used to have job in the mill," she said, "and, like all young folks, he just liked to perform on Saturday nights. Saturday nights, him and your father would drift around to different places, go to dances and things like that, or just sit around with people they knew, and your father's brother would sing, he had a fine voice, and play along with himself on his guitar. Well, this particular Saturday night, him and your father was coming home from some place, and they were both a little drunk and there was a moon that night, it was bright like day. Your father's brother was feeling kind of good, and he was whistling to himself, and he had his guitar slung over his shoulder. They was coming down a hill and beneath them was a road that turned off from the highway. Well, your father's brother, being always kind of frisky, decided to run down that hill, and he did, with that guitar banging and clanging behind him, and he ran across the road, and he was making water behind a tree.

And your father was sort of amused at him and he was still coming down the hill, kind of slow. Then he heard a car motor and that same minute his brother stepped from behind the tree, into the road, in the moonlight. And he started to cross the road. And your father started to run down the hill, he says he don't know why. This car was full of white men. They was all drunk, and when they seen your father's brother, they let out a great whoop and holler and they aimed the car straight at him. They was having fun, they just wanted to scare him, the way they do sometimes, you know. But they was drunk. And I guess the boy, being drunk, too, and scared, kind of lost his head. By the time he jumped it was too late. Your father says he heard his brother scream when the car rolled over him, and he heard the wood of that guitar when it give, and he heard them strings go flying, and he heard them white men shouting, and the car kept on a-going and it ain't stopped till this day. And, time your father got down the hill, his brother weren't nothing but blood and pulp."

Tears were gleaming on my mother's face. There wasn't anything I could say.

"He never mentioned it," she said, "because I never let him mention it before you children. Your Daddy was like a crazy man that night and for many a night thereafter. He says he never in his life seen anything as dark as that road after the lights of that car had gone away. Weren't nothing, weren't nobody on that road, just your Daddy and his brother and that busted guitar. Oh, yes. Your Daddy never did really get right again. Till the day he died he weren't sure but that every white man he saw was the man that killed his brother."

She stopped and took out her handkerchief and dried her eyes and looked at me.

"I ain't telling you all this," she said, "to make you scared or bitter or to make you hate nobody. I'm telling you this because you got a brother. And the world ain't changed."

I guess I didn't want to believe this. I guess she saw this in my face. She turned away from me, toward the window again, searching those streets.

"But I praise my Redeemer," she said at last, "that He called your Daddy home before me. I ain't saying it to throw no flowers at myself, but, I declare, it keeps me from feeling too cast down to know I helped your father get safely through this world. Your father always acted like he was the roughest, strongest man on earth. And everybody took him to be like that. But if he hadn't had *me* there—to see his tears!"

She was crying again. Still, I couldn't move. I said, "Lord, Lord, Mama, I didn't know it was like that."

"Oh, honey," she said, "there's a lot that you don't know. But you are going to find it out." She stood up from the window and came over to me. "You got to hold on to your brother," she said, "and don't let him fall, no matter what it looks like is happening to him and no matter how evil you gets with him. You going to be evil with him many a time. But don't you forget what I told you, you hear?"

"I won't forget," I said. "Don't you worry, I won't forget. I won't let nothing happen to Sonny."

My mother smiled as though she were amused at something she saw in my face. Then, "You may not be able to stop nothing from happening. But you got to let him know you's *there*."

Two days later I was married, and then I was gone. And I had a lot of things on my mind and I pretty well forgot my promise to Mama until I got shipped home on a special furlough for her funeral.

And, after the funeral, with just Sonny and me alone in the empty kitchen, I tried to find out something about him.

"What do you want to do?" I asked him.

"I'm going to be a musician," he said.

For he had graduated, in the time I had been away, from dancing to the juke box to finding out who was playing what, and what they were doing with it, and he had bought himself a set of drums.

"You mean, you want to be a drummer?" I somehow had the feeling that being a drummer might be all right for other people but not for my brother Sonny.

"I don't think," he said, looking at me very gravely, "that I'll ever be a good drummer. But I think I can play the piano."

I frowned. I'd never played the role of the older brother quite so seriously before, had scarcely ever, in fact, *asked* Sonny a damn thing. I sensed myself in the presence of something I didn't really know how to handle, didn't understand. So I made my frown a little deeper as I asked: "What kind of musician do you want to be?"

He grinned. "How many kinds do you think there are?"

"Be *serious*," I said.

He laughed, throwing his head back, and then looked at me. "I *am* serious."

"Well, then, for Christ's sake, stop kidding around and answer a serious question. I mean, do you want to be a concert pianist, you want to play classical music and all that, or—or what?" Long before I finished he was laughing again. "For Christ's *sake*, Sonny!"

He sobered, but with difficulty. "I'm sorry. But you sound so—*scared!*" and he was off again.

"Well, you may think it's funny now, baby, but it's not going to be so funny when you have to make your living at it, let me tell you *that*." I was furious because I knew he was laughing at me and I didn't know why.

"No," he said, very sober now, and afraid, perhaps, that he'd hurt me, "I don't want to be a classical pianist. That isn't what interests me. I mean"—he paused, looking hard at me, as though his eyes would help me to understand, and then gestured helplessly, as though perhaps his hand would help—"I mean, I'll have a lot of studying to do, and I'll have to study *everything,* but, I mean, I want to play *with*—jazz musicians." He stopped. "I want to play jazz," he said.

Well, the word had never before sounded as heavy, as real, as it sounded that afternoon in Sonny's mouth. I just looked at him and I was probably frowning a real frown by this time. I simply couldn't see why on earth he'd want to spend his time hanging around nightclubs, clowning around on bandstands, while people pushed each other around a dance floor. It seemed—beneath him, somehow. I had never thought about it before, had never been forced to, but I suppose I had always put jazz musicians in a class with what Daddy called "good-time people."

"Are you *serious?*"

"Hell, *yes,* I'm serious."

He looked more helpless than ever, and annoyed, and deeply hurt.

I suggested, helpfully: "You mean—like Louis Armstrong?"[5]

His face closed as though I'd struck him. "No. I'm not talking about none of that old-time, down home crap."

---

5. The great jazz trumpeter, who had made his reputation in the 1920s.

"Well, look, Sonny, I'm sorry, don't get mad. I just don't altogether get it, that's all. Name somebody—you know, a jazz musician you admire."

"Bird."

"Who?"

"Bird! Charlie Parker![6] Don't they teach you nothing in the goddamn army?"

I lit a cigarette. I was surprised and then a little amused to discover that I was trembling. "I've been out of touch," I said. "You'll have to be patient with me. Now. Who's this Parker character?"

"He's just one of the greatest jazz musicians alive," said Sonny, sullenly, his hands in his pockets, his back to me. "Maybe *the* greatest," he added, bitterly, "that's probably why *you* never heard of him."

"All right, I said, "I'm ignorant. I'm sorry. I'll go out and buy all the cat's records right away, all right?"

"It don't," said Sonny, with dignity, "make any difference to me. I don't care what you listen to. Don't do me no favors."

I was beginning to realize that I'd never seen him so upset before. With another part of my mind I was thinking that this would probably turn out to be one of those things kids go through and that I shouldn't make it seem important by pushing it too hard. Still, I didn't think it would do any harm to ask: "Doesn't all this take a lot of time? Can you make a living at it?"

He turned back to me and half leaned, half sat, on the kitchen table. "Everything takes time," he said, "and—well, yes, sure, I can make a living at it. But what I don't seem to be able to make you understand is that it's the only thing I want to do."

"Well, Sonny," I said, gently, "you know people can't always do exactly what they *want* to do—"

"*No*, I don't know that," said Sonny, surprising me. "I think people *ought* to do what they want to do, what else are they alive for?"

"You getting to be a big boy," I said desperately, "it's time you started thinking about your future."

"I'm thinking about my future," said Sonny, grimly. "I think about it all the time."

I gave up. I decided, if he didn't change his mind, that we could always talk about it later. "In the meantime," I said, "you got to finish school." We had already decided that he'd have to move in with Isabel and her folks. I knew this wasn't the ideal arrangement because Isabel's folks are inclined to be dicty[7] and they hadn't especially wanted Isabel to marry me. But I didn't know what else to do. "And we have to get you fixed up at Isabel's."

There was a long silence. He moved from the kitchen table to the window. "That's a terrible idea. You know it yourself."

"Do you have a *better* idea?"

He just walked up and down the kitchen for a minute. He was as tall as I was. He had started to shave. I suddenly had the feeling that I didn't know him at all.

He stopped at the kitchen table and picked up my cigarettes. Looking at me with a kind of mocking, amused defiance, he put one between his lips. "You mind?"

"You smoking already?"

6. Jazz saxophonist (1920–1955), famous as an impro-   7. Stuck-up.
viser.

He lit a cigarette and nodded, watching me through the smoke. "I just wanted to see if I'd have the courage to smoke in front of you." He grinned and blew a great cloud of smoke to the ceiling. "It was easy." He looked at my face. "Come on, now. I bet you was smoking at my age, tell the truth."

"I didn't say anything but the truth was on my face, and he laughed. But now there was something very strained in his laugh. "Sure. And I bet that ain't all you was doing."

He was frightening me a little. "Cut the crap," I said. "We already decided that you was going to go and live at Isabel's. Now what's got into you all of a sudden?"

"*You* decided it," he pointed out. "*I* didn't decide nothing." He stopped in front of me, leaning against the stove, arms loosely folded. "Look, brother. I don't want to stay in Harlem no more, I really don't." He was very earnest. He looked at me, then over toward the kitchen window. There was something in his eyes I'd never seen before, some thoughtfulness, some worry all his own. He rubbed the muscle of one arm. "It's time I was getting out of here."

"Where do you want to *go*, Sonny?"

"I want to join the army. Or the navy, I don't care. If I say I'm old enough, they'll believe me."

Then I got mad. It was because I was so scared. "You must be crazy. You god-damn fool, what the hell you want to go and join the *army* for?"

"I just told you. To get out of Harlem."

"Sonny, you haven't even finished *school*. And if you really want to be a musician, how do you expect to study if you're in the *army?*"

He looked at me, trapped, and in anguish. "There's ways. I might be able to work out some kind of deal. Anyway, I'll have the G.I. Bill when I come out."

"*If* you come out." We stared at each other. "Sonny, please. Be reasonable. I know the setup is far from perfect. But we got to do the best we can."

"I ain't learning nothing in school," he said. "Even when I go." He turned away from me and opened the window and threw his cigarette out into the narrow alley. I watched his back. "At least, I ain't learning nothing you'd want me to learn." He slammed the window so hard I thought the glass would fly out, and turned back to me. "And I'm sick of the stink of these garbage cans!"

"Sonny," I said, "I know how you feel. But if you don't finish school now, you're going to be sorry later that you didn't." I grabbed him by the shoulders. "And you only got another year. It ain't so bad. And I'll come back and I swear I'll help you do *whatever* you want to do. Just try to put up with it till I come back. Will you please do that? For me?"

He didn't answer and he wouldn't look at me.

"Sonny. You hear me?"

He pulled away. "I hear you. But you never hear anything *I* say."

I didn't know what to say to that. He looked out of the window and then back at me. "OK," he said, and sighed. "I'll try."

Then I said, trying to cheer him up a little, "They got a piano at Isabel's. You can practice on it."

And as a matter of fact, it did cheer him up for a minute. "That's right," he said to himself. "I forgot that." His face relaxed a little. But the worry, the thoughtfulness, played on it still, the way shadows play on a face which is staring into the fire.

But I thought I'd never hear the end of that piano. At first, Isabel would write me, saying how nice it was that Sonny was so serious about his music and how, as soon as he came in from school, or wherever he had been when he was supposed to be at school, he went straight to that piano and stayed there until suppertime. And, after supper, he went back to that piano and stayed there until everybody went to bed. He was at the piano all day Saturday and all day Sunday. Then he bought a record player and started playing records. He'd play one record over and over again, all day long sometimes, and he'd improvise along with it on the piano. Or he'd play one section of the record, one chord, one change, one progression, then he'd do it on the piano. Then back to the record. Then back to the piano.

Well, I really don't know how they stood it. Isabel finally confessed that it wasn't like living with a person at all, it was like living with sound. And the sound didn't make any sense to her, didn't make any sense to any of them—naturally. They began, in a way, to be afflicted by this presence that was living in their home. It was as though Sonny were some sort of god, or monster. He moved in an atmosphere which wasn't like theirs at all. They fed him and he ate, he washed himself, he walked in and out of their door; he certainly wasn't nasty or unpleasant or rude, Sonny isn't any of those things; but it was as though he were all wrapped up in some cloud, some fire, some vision all his own; and there wasn't any way to reach him.

At the same time, he wasn't really a man yet, he was still a child, and they had to watch out for him in all kinds of ways. They certainly couldn't throw him out. Neither did they dare to make a great scene about that piano because even they dimly sensed, as I sensed, from so many thousands of miles away, that Sonny was at that piano playing for his life.

But he hadn't been going to school. One day a letter came from the school board and Isabel's mother got it—there had, apparently, been other letters but Sonny had torn them up. This day, when Sonny came in, Isabel's mother showed him the letter and asked where he'd been spending his time. And she finally got it out of him that he'd been down in Greenwich Village, with musicians and other characters, in a white girl's apartment. And this scared her and she started to scream at him and what came up, once she began—though she denies it to this day—was what sacrifices they were making to give Sonny a decent home and how little he appreciated it.

Sonny didn't play the piano that day. By evening, Isabel's mother had calmed down but then there was the old man to deal with, and Isabel herself. Isabel says she did her best to be calm but she broke down and started crying. She says she just watched Sonny's face. She could tell, by watching him, what was happening with him. And what was happening was that they penetrated his cloud, they had reached him. Even if their fingers had been a thousand times more gentle than human fingers ever are, he could hardly help feeling that they had stripped him naked and were spitting on that nakedness. For he also had to see that his presence, that music, which was life or death to him, had been torture for them and that they had endured it, not at all for his sake, but only for mine. And Sonny couldn't take that. He can take it a little better today than he could then but he's still not very good at it and, frankly, I don't know anybody who is.

The silence of the next few days must have been louder than the sound of all the music ever played since time began. One morning, before she went to work, Isabel was in his room for something and she suddenly realized that all of his records were gone. And she knew for certain that he was gone. And he was. He went as far as the navy would carry him. He finally sent me a postcard from some place in Greece and that was the first I knew that Sonny was still alive. I didn't see him any more until we were both back in New York and the war had long been over.

He was a man by then, of course, but I wasn't willing to see it. He came by the house from time to time, but we fought almost every time we met. I didn't like the way he carried himself, loose and dreamlike all the time, and I didn't like his friends, and his music seemed to be merely an excuse for the life he led. It sounded just that weird and disordered.

Then we had a fight, a pretty awful fight, and I didn't see him for months. By and by I looked him up, where he was living, in a furnished room in the Village, and I tried to make it up. But there were lots of other people in the room and Sonny just lay on his bed, and he wouldn't come downstairs with me, and he treated these other people as though they were his family and I weren't. So I got mad and then he got mad, and then I told him that he might just as well be dead as live the way he was living. Then he stood up and he told me not to worry about him any more in life, that he *was* dead as far as I was concerned. Then he pushed me to the door and the other people looked on as though nothing were happening, and he slammed the door behind me. I stood in the hallway, staring at the door. I heard somebody laugh in the room and then the tears came to my eyes. I started down the steps, whistling to keep from crying, I kept on whistling to myself, *You going to need me, baby, one of these cold, rainy days.*

I read about Sonny's trouble in the spring. Little Grace died in the fall. She was a beautiful little girl. But she only lived a little over two years. She died of polio and she suffered. She had a slight fever for a couple of days, but it didn't seem like anything and we just kept her in bed. And we would certainly have called the doctor, but the fever dropped, she seemed to be all right. So we thought it had just been a cold. Then, one day, she was up, playing, Isabel was in the kitchen fixing lunch for the two boys when they'd come in from school, and she heard Grace fall down in the living room. When you have a lot of children you don't always start running when one of them falls, unless they start screaming or something. And, this time, Grace was quiet. Yet, Isabel says that when she heard that *thump* and then that silence, something happened in her to make her afraid. And she ran to the living room and there was little Grace on the floor, all twisted up, and the reason she hadn't screamed was that she couldn't get her breath. And when she did scream, it was the worst sound, Isabel says, that she'd ever heard in all her life, and she still hears it sometimes in her dreams. Isabel will sometimes wake me up with a low, moaning, strangled sound and I have to be quick to awaken her and hold her to me and where Isabel is weeping against me seems a mortal wound.

I think I may have written Sonny the very day that little Grace was buried. I was sitting in the living room in the dark, by myself, and I suddenly thought of Sonny. My trouble made his real.

One Saturday afternoon, when Sonny had been living with us, or, anyway, been in our house, for nearly two weeks, I found myself wandering aimlessly about the living room, drinking from a can of beer, and trying to work up the courage to search Sonny's room. He was out, he was usually out whenever I was home, and Isabel had taken the children to see their grandparents. Suddenly I was standing still in front of the living room window, watching Seventh Avenue. The idea of searching Sonny's room made me still. I scarcely dared to admit to myself what I'd be searching for. I didn't know what I'd do if I found it. Or if I didn't.

On the sidewalk across from me, near the entrance to a barbecue joint, some people were holding an old-fashioned revival meeting. The barbecue cook, wearing a dirty white apron, his conked hair reddish and metallic in the pale sun, and a cigarette between his lips, stood in the doorway, watching them. Kids and older people paused in their errands and stood there, along with some older men and a couple of very tough-looking women who watched everything that happened on the avenue, as though they owned it, or were maybe owned by it. Well, they were watching this, too. The revival was being carried on by three sisters in black, and a brother. All they had were their voices and their Bibles and a tambourine. The brother was testifying and while he testi-fied two of the sisters stood together, seeming to say, amen, and the third sister walked around with the tambourine outstretched and a couple of people dropped coins into it. Then the brother's testimony ended and the sister who had been taking up the collection dumped the coins into her palm and transferred them to the pocket of her long black robe. Then she raised both hands, striking the tambourine against the air, and then against one hand, and she started to sing. And the two other sisters and the brother joined in.

It was strange, suddenly, to watch, though I had been seeing these street meetings all my life. So, of course, had everybody else down there. Yet, they paused and watched and listened and I stood still at the window. *"Tis the old ship of Zion,"* they sang, and the sister with the tambourine kept a steady, jangling beat, *"it has rescued many a thousand!"* Not a soul under the sound of their voices was hearing this song for the first time, not one of them had been rescued. Nor had they seen much in the way of rescue work being done around them. Neither did they especially believe in the holiness of the three sisters and the brother, they knew too much about them, knew where they lived, and how. The woman with the tambourine, whose voice dom-inated the air, whose face was bright with joy, was divided by very little from the woman who stood watching her, a cigarette between her heavy, chapped lips, her hair a cuckoo's nest, her face scarred and swollen from many beatings, and her black eyes glittering like coal. Perhaps they both knew this, which was why, when, as rarely, they addressed each other, they addressed each other as Sister. As the singing filled the air the watching, listening faces underwent a change, the eyes focusing on some-thing within; the music seemed to soothe a poison out of them; and time seemed, nearly, to fall away from the sullen, belligerent, battered faces, as though they were fleeing back to their first condition, while dreaming of their last. The barbecue cook half shook his head and smiled, and dropped his cigarette and disappeared into his joint. A man fumbled in his pockets for change and stood holding it in his hand impa-tiently, as though he had just remembered a pressing appointment further up the av-enue. He looked furious. Then I saw Sonny, standing on the edge of the crowd. He was carrying a wide, flat notebook with a green cover, and it made him look, from where I was standing, almost like a schoolboy. The coppery sun brought out the cop-per in his skin, he was very faintly smiling, standing very still. Then the singing stopped, the tambourine turned into a collection plate again. The furious man dropped in his coins and vanished, so did a couple of the women, and Sonny dropped some change in the plate, looking directly at the woman with a little smile. He started across the avenue, toward the house. He has a slow, loping walk, something like the way Harlem hipsters walk, only he's imposed on this his own half-beat. I had never really noticed it before.

I stayed at the window, both relieved and apprehensive. As Sonny disappeared from my sight, they began singing again. And they were still singing when his key turned in the lock.

"Hey," he said.

"Hey, yourself. You want some beer?"

"No. Well, maybe." But he came up to the window and stood behind me, looking out. "What a warm voice," he said.

They were singing *If I could only hear my mother pray again!*

"Yes," I said, "and she can sure beat that tambourine."

"But what a terrible song," he said, and laughed. He dropped his notebook on the sofa and disappeared into the kitchen. "Where's Isabel and the kids?"

"I think they went out to see their grandparents. You hungry?"

"No." He came back into the living room with his can of beer. "You want to come some place with me tonight?"

I sensed, I don't know how, that I couldn't possibly say no. "Sure. Where?"

He sat down on the sofa and picked up his notebook and started leafing through it. "I'm going to sit in with some fellows in a joint in the Village."

"You mean, you're going to play, tonight?"

"That's right." He took a swallow of his beer and moved back to the window. He gave me a sidelong look. "If you can stand it."

"I'll try," I said.

He smiled to himself and we both watched as the meeting across the way broke up. The three sisters and the brother, heads bowed, were singing *God be with you till we meet again.* The faces around them were very quiet. Then the song ended. The small crowd dispersed. We watched the three women and the lone man walk slowly up the avenue.

"When she was singing before," said Sonny, abruptly, "her voice reminded me for a minute of what heroin feels like sometimes—when it's in your veins. It makes you feel sort of warm and cool at the same time. And distant. And—and sure." He sipped his beer, very deliberately not looking at me. I watched his face. "It makes you feel—in control. Sometimes you've got to have that feeling."

"Do you?" I sat down slowly in the easy chair.

"Sometimes." He went back to the sofa and picked up his notebook again. "Some people do."

"In order," I asked, "to play?" And my voice was very ugly, full of contempt and anger.

"Well"—he looked at me with great, troubled eyes, as though, in fact, he hoped his eyes would tell me things he could never otherwise say—"they *think* so. And *if* they think so—!"

"And what do *you* think?" I asked.

He sat on the sofa and put his can of beer on the floor. "I don't know," he said, and I couldn't be sure if he were answering my question or pursuing his thoughts. His face didn't tell me. "It's not so much to *play*. It's to *stand* it, to be able to make it at all. On any level." He frowned and smiled: "In order to keep from shaking to pieces."

"But these friends of yours," I said, "they seem to shake themselves to pieces pretty goddamn fast."

"Maybe." He played with the notebook. And something told me that I should curb my tongue, that Sonny was doing his best to talk, that I should listen. "But of course you only know the ones that've gone to pieces. Some don't—or at least they haven't *yet* and that's just about all *any* of us can say." He paused. "And then there are some who just live, really, in hell, and they know it and they see what's happening and they go right on. I don't know." He sighed, dropped the notebook, folded his arms. "Some guys, you can tell from the way they play, they on something *all* the time. And you can see that, well, it makes something real for them. But of course," he picked up his beer from the floor and sipped it and put the can down again, "they *want* to, too, you've got to see that. Even some of them that say they don't—*some,* not all."

"And what about you?" I asked—I couldn't help it. "What about you? Do *you* want to?"

He stood up and walked to the window and remained silent for a long time. Then he sighed. "Me," he said. Then: "While I was downstairs before, on my way here, listening to that woman sing, it struck me all of a sudden how much suffering she must have had to go through—to sing like that. It's *repulsive* to think you have to suffer that much."

I said: "But there's no way not to suffer—is there, Sonny?"

"I believe not," he said and smiled, "but that's never stopped anyone from trying." He looked at me. "Has it?" I realized, with this mocking look, that there stood between us, forever, beyond the power of time and forgiveness, the fact that I had held silence—so long!—when he had needed human speech to help him. He turned back to the window. "No, there's no way not to suffer. But you try all kinds of ways to keep from drowning in it, to keep on top of it, and to make it seem—well, like *you.* Like you did something, all right, and now you're suffering for it. You know?" I said nothing. "Well you know," he said, impatiently, "why *do* people suffer? Maybe it's better to do something to give it a reason, *any* reason."

"But we just agreed," I said, "that there's no way not to suffer. Isn't it better, then, just to—take it?"

"But nobody just takes it," Sonny cried, "that's what I'm telling you! *Everybody* tries to. You're just hung up on the *way* some people try—it's not *your* way!"

The hair on my face began to itch, my face felt wet. "That's not true," I said, "that's not true. I don't give a damn what other people do, I don't even care how they suffer. I just care how *you* suffer." And he looked at me. "Please believe me," I said, "I don't want to see you—die—trying not to suffer."

"I won't," he said, flatly, "die trying not to suffer. At least, not any faster than anybody else."

"But there's no need," I said, trying to laugh, "is there? in killing yourself."

I wanted to say more, but I couldn't. I wanted to talk about will power and how life could be—well, beautiful. I wanted to say that it was all within; but was it? or rather, wasn't that exactly the trouble? And I wanted to promise that I would never fail him again. But it would all have sounded—empty words and lies.

So I made the promise to myself and prayed that I would keep it.

"It's terrible sometimes, inside," he said, "that's what's the trouble. You walk these streets, black and funky and cold, and there's not really a living ass to talk to, and there's nothing shaking, and there's no way of getting it out—that storm inside. You can't talk it and you can't make love with it, and when you finally try to get with it and play it, you realize *nobody's* listening. So *you've* got to listen. You got to find a way to listen."

And then he walked away from the window and sat on the sofa again, as though all the wind had suddenly been knocked out of him. "Sometimes you'll do *anything* to play, even cut your mother's throat." He laughed and looked at me. "Or your brother's." Then he sobered. "Or your own." Then: "Don't worry. I'm all right now and I think I'll *be* all right. But I can't forget—where I've been. I don't mean just the physical place I've been, I mean where I've *been.* And *what* I've been."

"What have you been, Sonny?" I asked.

He smiled—but sat sideways on the sofa, his elbow resting on the back, his fingers playing with his mouth and chin, not looking at me. "I've been something I didn't recognize, didn't know I could be. Didn't know anybody could be." He stopped, looking inward, looking helplessly young, looking old. "I'm not talking about it now because I feel *guilty* or anything like that—maybe it would be better if I did, I don't know. Anyway, I can't really talk about it. Not to you, not to anybody," and now he turned and faced me. "Sometimes, you know, and it was actually when I was most *out* of the world, I felt that I was in it, that I was *with* it, really, and I could play or I didn't really have to *play,* it just came out of me, it was there. And I don't know how I played, thinking about it now, but I know I did awful things, those times, sometimes, to people. Or it wasn't that I *did* anything to them—it was that they weren't real." He picked up the beer can; it was empty; he rolled it between his palms: "And other times—well, I needed a fix, I needed to find a place to lean, I needed to clear a space to *listen*—and I couldn't find it, and I—went crazy, I did terrible things to *me,* I was terrible *for* me." He began pressing the beer can between his hands, I watched the metal begin to give. It glittered, as he played with it, like a knife, and I was afraid he would cut himself, but I said nothing. "Oh well. I can never tell you. I was all by myself at the bottom of something, stinking and sweating and crying and shaking, and I smelled it, you know? *my* stink, and I thought I'd die if I couldn't get away from it and yet, all the same, I knew that everything I was doing was just locking me in with it. And I didn't know," he paused, still flattening the beer can, "I didn't know, I still *don't* know, something kept telling me that maybe it was good to smell your own stink, but I didn't think that *that* was what I'd been trying to do—and—who can stand it?" and he abruptly dropped the ruined beer can, looking at me with a small, still smile, and then rose, walking to the window as though it were the lodestone rock.[8] I watched his face, he watched the avenue. "I couldn't tell you when Mama died—but the reason I wanted to leave Harlem so bad was to get away from drugs. And then, when I ran away, that's what I was running from—really. When I came back, nothing had changed, *I* hadn't changed, I was just—older." And he stopped, drumming with his fingers on the windowpane. The sun had vanished, soon darkness would fall. I watched his face. "It can come again," he said, almost as though speaking to himself. Then he turned to me. "It can come again," he repeated. "I just want you to know that."

"All right," I said, at last. "So it can come again. All right."

He smiled, but the smile was sorrowful. "I had to try to tell you," he said.

"Yes," I said. "I understand that."

"You're my brother," he said, looking straight at me, and not smiling at all.

"Yes," I repeated, "yes. I understand that."

He turned back to the window, looking out. "All that hatred down there," he said, "all that hatred and misery and love. It's a wonder it doesn't blow the avenue apart."

We went to the only nightclub on a short, dark street, downtown. We squeezed through the narrow, chattering, jam-packed bar to the entrance of the big room, where the bandstand was. And we stood there for a moment, for the lights were very dim in this room and we couldn't see. Then, "Hello, boy," said a voice and an enormous black man, much older than Sonny or myself, erupted out of all that atmospheric lighting and put an arm around Sonny's shoulder. "I been sitting right here," he said, "waiting for you."

He had a big voice, too, and heads in the darkness turned toward us.

Sonny grinned and pulled a little away, and said, "Creole, this is my brother. I told you about him."

---

8. Magnetic rock, guide for sailors at sea.

Creole shook my hand. "I'm glad to meet you, son," he said, and it was clear that he was glad to meet me *there,* for Sonny's sake. And he smiled, "You got a real musician in *your* family," and he took his arm from Sonny's shoulder and slapped him, lightly, affectionately, with the back of his hand.

"Well. Now I've heard it all," said a voice behind us. This was another musician, and a friend of Sonny's, a coal-black, cheerful-looking man, built close to the ground. He immediately began confiding to me, at the top of his lungs, the most terrible things about Sonny, his teeth gleaming like a lighthouse and his laugh coming up out of him like the beginning of an earthquake. And it turned out that everyone at the bar knew Sonny, or almost everyone; some were musicians, working there, or nearby, or not working, some were simply hangers-on, and some were there to hear Sonny play. I was introduced to all of them and they were all very polite to me. Yet, it was clear that, for them, I was only Sonny's brother. Here, I was in Sonny's world. Or rather: his kingdom. Here, it was not even a question that his veins bore royal blood.

They were going to play soon and Creole installed me, by myself, at a table in a dark corner. Then I watched them, Creole, and the little black man, and Sonny, and the others, while they horsed around, standing just below the bandstand. The light from the bandstand spilled just a little short of them and, watching them laughing and gesturing and moving about, I had the feeling that they, nevertheless, were being most careful not to step into that circle of light too suddenly: that if they moved into the light too suddenly, without thinking, they would perish in flame. Then, while I watched, one of them, the small, black man, moved into the light and crossed the bandstand and started fooling around with his drums. Then—being funny and being, also, extremely ceremonious—Creole took Sonny by the arm and led him to the piano. A woman's voice called Sonny's name and a few hands started clapping. And Sonny, also being funny and being ceremonious, and so touched, I think, that he could have cried, but neither hiding it nor showing it, riding it like a man, grinned, and put both hands to his heart and bowed from the waist.

Creole then went to the bass fiddle and a lean, very bright-skinned brown man jumped up on the bandstand and picked up his horn. So there they were, and the atmosphere on the bandstand and in the room began to change and tighten. Someone stepped up to the microphone and announced them. Then there were all kinds of murmurs. Some people at the bar shushed others. The waitress ran around, frantically getting in the last orders, guys and chicks got closer to each other, and the lights on the bandstand, on the quartet, turned to a kind of indigo. Then they all looked different there. Creole looked about him for the last time, as though he were making certain that all his chickens were in the coop, and then he—jumped and struck the fiddle. And there they were.

All I know about music is that not many people ever really hear it. And even then, on the rare occasions when something opens within, and the music enters, what we mainly hear, or hear corroborated, are personal, private, vanishing evocations. But the man who creates the music is hearing something else, is dealing with the roar rising from the void and imposing order on it as it hits the air. What is evoked in him, then, is of another order, more terrible because it has no words, and triumphant, too, for that same reason. And his triumph, when he triumphs, is ours. I just watched Sonny's face. His face was troubled, he was working hard, but he wasn't with it. And I had the feeling that, in a way, everyone on the bandstand was waiting for him, both waiting for him and pushing him along. But as I began to watch Creole, I realized that it was Creole who held them all back. He had them on a short rein. Up there, keeping the beat with his whole body, wailing on the fiddle, with his eyes half closed, he was listening to everything, but he was listening to Sonny. He was having a dialogue with Sonny. He wanted Sonny to leave the shoreline and strike out for the deep water. He was Sonny's witness that deep water and drowning were not the same thing—he had been there, and he knew. And he wanted Sonny to know. He was waiting for Sonny to do the things on the keys which would let Creole know that Sonny was in the water.

And, while Creole listened, Sonny moved, deep within, exactly like someone in torment. I had never before thought of how awful the relationship must be between the musician and his instrument. He has to fill it, this instrument, with the breath of life, his own. He has to make it do what he wants it to do. And a piano is just a piano. It's made out of so much wood and wires and little hammers and big ones, and ivory. While there's only so much you can do with it, the only way to find this out is to try; to try and make it do everything.

And Sonny hadn't been near a piano for over a year. And he wasn't on much better terms with his life, not the life that stretched before him now. He and the piano stammered, started one way, got scared, stopped; started another way, panicked, marked time, started again; then seemed to have found a direction, panicked again, got stuck. And the face I saw on Sonny I'd never seen before. Everything had been burned out of it, and, at the same time, things usually hidden were being burned in, by the fire and fury of the battle which was occurring in him up there.

Yet, watching Creole's face as they neared the end of the first set, I had the feeling that something had happened, something I hadn't heard. Then they finished, there was scattered applause, and then, without an instant's warning, Creole started into something else, it was almost sardonic, it was *Am I Blue*. And, as though he commanded, Sonny began to play. Something began to happen. And Creole let out the reins. The dry, low, black man said something awful on the drums, Creole answered, and the drums talked back. Then the horn insisted, sweet and high, slightly detached perhaps, and Creole listened, commenting now and then, dry, and driving, beautiful and calm and old. Then they all came together again, and Sonny was part of the family again. I could tell this from his face. He seemed to have found, right there beneath his fingers, a damn brand-new piano. It seemed that he couldn't get over it. Then for awhile, just being happy with Sonny, they seemed to be agreeing with him that brand-new pianos certainly were a gas.

Then Creole stepped forward to remind them that what they were playing was the blues. He hit something in all of them, he hit something in me, myself, and the music tightened and deepened, apprehension began to beat the air. Creole began to tell us what the blues were all about. They were not about anything very new. He and his boys up there were keeping it new, at the risk of ruin, destruction, madness, and death, in order to find new ways to make us listen. For, while the tale of how we suffer, and how we are delighted, and how we may triumph is never new, it always must be heard. There isn't any other tale to tell, it's the only light we've got in all this darkness.

And this tale, according to that face, that body, those strong hands on those strings, has another aspect in every country, and a new depth in every generation. Listen, Creole seemed to be saying, listen. Now these are Sonny's blues. He made the little black man on the drums know it, and the bright, brown man on the horn. Creole wasn't trying any longer to get Sonny in the water. He was wishing him Godspeed. Then he stepped back, very slowly, filling the air with the immense suggestion that Sonny speak for himself.

Then they all gathered around Sonny and Sonny played. Every now and again one of them seemed to say, amen. Sonny's fingers filled the air with life, his life. But that life contained so many others. And Sonny went all the way back, he really began with the spare, flat statement of the opening phrase of the song. Then he began to make it his. It was very beautiful because it wasn't hurried and it was no longer a lament. I seemed to hear with what burning he had made it his, with what burning we had yet to make it ours, how we could cease lamenting. Freedom lurked around us and I understood, at last, that he could help us to be free if we would listen, that he would never be free until we did. Yet, there was no battle in his face now. I heard what he had gone through, and would continue to go through until he came to rest in earth. He had made it his: that long line, of which we knew only Mama and Daddy. And he was giving it back, as everything must be given back, so that, passing through death, it can live forever. I saw my mother's face again, and felt, for the first time, how the stones of the road she had walked on must have bruised her feet. I saw the moonlit road where my father's brother died. And it brought something else back to me, and carried me past it, I saw my little girl again and felt Isabel's tears again, and I felt my own tears begin to rise. And I was yet aware that this was only a moment, that the world waited outside, as hungry as a tiger, and that trouble stretched above us, longer than the sky.

Then it was over. Creole and Sonny let out their breath, both soaking wet, and grinning. There was a lot of applause and some of it was real. In the dark, the girl came by and I asked her to take drinks to the bandstand. There was a long pause, while they talked up there in the indigo light and after awhile I saw the girl put a Scotch and milk on top of the piano for Sonny. He didn't seem to notice it, but just before they started playing again, he sipped from it and looked toward me, and nodded. Then he put it back on top of the piano. For me, then, as they began to play again, it glowed and shook above my brother's head like the very cup of trembling.

Gerald Vizenor
b. 1934

Gerald Vizenor refers to himself as a "postindian." His reason for choosing this unusual term is highlighted by the Native American character Son Bear, who observes in Vizenor's screenplay *Harold and the Orange* that "Columbus never discovered anything, and when he never did he invented Indians because we never heard the word before he dropped by by accident." This paradoxical and humorous rejection of a white character's condescension captures the essence of Vizenor's own attempt to unsettle stereotyped assumptions about Native American culture. In his literary works and his essays, Vizenor insists that indigenous cultures in North America encompass a vast range of fundamentally different peoples, languages, and customs, and the category of the "Indian" or "Native American" is an invention of the dominant white culture for its own social and political purposes. But his Native American characters are by no means passive victims of domination; on the contrary, they use cultural resources with ingenuity and skill to craft their own identities and strategies of "survivance" rather than "survival," a word that Vizenor rejects as too passive. Vizenor's model in shaping new self-images is the "trickster," an important figure in many types of Native American mythology, such as the "Coyote Tales" included in Volume E. In Vizenor's work, the trickster is a person who eludes the firm grip of definitive categorizations: both male and female, the trickster takes on many different physical shapes (including those of animals) and often exists on a tenuous borderline between reality and imagination, sometimes becoming a mere shadow or mirror image. More than a sly survivor, the trickster unsettles what the dominant culture means by "reality," showing how it might take on quite different forms in another culture's eyes.

By virtue of his own origin, Gerald Vizenor is ideally placed to explore such cultural border crossings. Born in Minneapolis in 1934, he is the son of an Ojibwa (also called Chippewa or Anishinaabe) Indian and a white mother. Not coincidentally, people of mixed racial backgrounds take on crucial importance in some of his works, such as the short story collection *Landfall Meditation: Crossblood Stories* (1991). The "mixed-blood" or "cross-blood" figure is a symbol to Vizenor of cultural fertility and creativity, not of the shortfalls that the older term "half-breed" implies; the cultural hybridization of mixed-blood heritage promises avenues of escape from petrified thought and outdated social forms. But the particular symbolic value that Vizenor attributes to the mixed-blood character doesn't mean that cultural identity is in some way prescribed by one's genetic origins or that a mixed ethnic heritage provides "natural" access to different cultures. Vizenor's own development as a "Native American" writer is the most striking example of the detours that cultural identification can take. At two crucial moments of his career, he discovered essential dimensions of his Ojibwa heritage through the intermediary of completely unrelated cultures. While he was stationed in northern Japan with the U.S. Army between 1952 and 1955, he got to know haiku, the traditional seventeen-syllable Japanese verse form that often focuses on one moment of interaction between humans and nature. Even in translation, haiku poems struck Vizenor immediately since he saw them as closely connected to the way in which nature is presented in dream songs in Anishinaabe, the language of the Ojibwa. Throughout the 1960s, he published volumes of haiku poetry, and haiku-type descriptions of nature have persisted in his novels and short stories.

In the fall of 1983, Vizenor went to Tianjin University in the People's Republic of China as a visiting professor of English. During his stay, he attended a theater performance that included some scenes from the Chinese opera *The Monkey King,* and once again his encounter with a foreign cultural artifact triggered new insights about his own cultural heritage. The monkey king, in Chinese mythology, is a figure who in some respects parallels the trickster figure of Native American myth. Vizenor was so deeply impressed with the significance of this mythological figure for the contemporary Chinese audience that he used it as the basis of his novel *Griever: An American Monkey King in China* (1987), which won the 1988 American Book Award. From that moment on the trickster figure assumed central importance in both his fiction and nonfiction. The impact of Vizenor's stays in Japan and China on his representations of Native American traditions clearly illustrates his own insight that ethnic origins alone don't shape cultural experience. Instead, cultural experience is the result of a gradual process of conscious or unconscious self-fashioning.

The tensions that can sometimes arise in this self-fashioning are quite visible in Vizenor's career as well as in his writings. In his earlier years he held varied positions as a social worker in Minnesota correctional institutions, a newspaper journalist, a teacher trainer, and a college instructor. He completed college at the University of Minnesota in 1960 and took graduate courses there as well as at Harvard University. As his career unfolded, he became increasingly associated with the academic world, building up a program in Indian studies at Bemidji State University and teaching Native American literature and history at Lake Forest College, the University of Minnesota, the University of California at Santa Cruz, and most recently the University of California at Berkeley. Like many other contemporary Native American writers, Vizenor therefore undertakes his research and writing about predominantly oral cultures and histories at an institution that is deeply committed to the printed word. This tension emerges quite explicitly in his short story "Shadows," whose protagonist condemns printed words as "dead voices" and warns the first-person narrator never to publish her stories; the narrator's writing and our reading of the story therefore clearly violate an oral tradition that, at a more abstract level, both writing and reading are meant to preserve. (Compare the Zaïrean novelist Mbwil Ngal, page 966, whose hero is actually put on trial for the sacrilege of connecting African orality to print.) This paradox underlies all attempts to preserve and transmit oral forms of narrative and poetry by means of print volumes; Vizenor has often undertaken the task of bringing Ojibwa songs and stories to print, both through his novels and short stories and through collections of texts translated from Anishinaabe, such as *Summer in the Spring: Ojibwa Songs and Stories* (1981), and in his book *The People Named the Chippewa: Narrative Histories* (1984). Through his extensive work as a writer, editor, and historian as well as through his political engagement on behalf of Native American communities, Gerald Vizenor has emerged as one of the most important voices in Native American culture at the turn of the millennium.

Ice Tricksters

Uncle Clement told me last night that he knows *almost* everything. Almost, that's his nickname and favorite word in stories, lives with me and my mother in a narrow house on the Leech Lake Chippewa Indian Reservation in northern Minnesota.

Last night, just before dark, we drove into town to meet my cousin at the bus depot and to buy rainbow ice cream in thick brown cones. Almost sat in the back seat of our old car and started his stories the minute we were on the dirt road around the north side of the lake on our way to town. The wheels bounced and raised thick clouds of dust and the car doors shuddered. He told me about the time he almost started an ice cream store when he came back from the army. My mother laughed and turned to the side. The car rattled on the washboard road. She shouted, "I heard that one before!"

"Almost!" he shouted back.

"What almost happened?" I asked. My voice bounced with the car.

"Well, it was winter then," he said. Fine brown dust settled on his head and the shoulders of his overcoat. "Too cold for ice cream in the woods, but the idea came to mind in the summer, almost."

"Almost, you know almost everything about nothing," my mother shouted and then laughed, "or almost nothing about almost everything."

"Pincher, we're almost to the ice cream," he said and brushed me on the head with his right hand. He did that to ignore what my mother said about what he knows. Clouds of dust covered the trees behind us on both sides of the road.

Almost is my great-uncle, and he decides on our nicknames, even the nicknames for my cousins who live in the cities and visit the reservation in the summer. Pincher, the name he gave me, was natural because I pinched my way through childhood. I learned about the world between two fingers. I pinched everything, or *almost* everything, as my uncle would say. I pinched animals, insects, leaves, water, fish, ice cream, the moist air, winter breath, snow, and even words, the words I could see or almost see. I pinched the words and learned how to speak sooner than my cousins. Pinched words are easier to remember. Some words, like government and grammar, are unnatural, never seen and never pinched. Who could pinch a word like grammar?

Almost named me last winter when my grandmother was sick with pneumonia and died on the way to the public health hospital. She had no teeth and covered her mouth when she smiled, almost a child. I sat in the back seat of the car and held her thin brown hand. Even her veins were hidden, it was so cold that night. On the road we pinched summer words over the hard snow and ice. She smiled and said, *papakine, papakine,* over and over. That means cricket or grasshopper in our tribal language and we pinched that word together. We pinched *papakine* in the back seat of our cold car on the way to the hospital. Later she whispered *bisanagami sibi,* the river is still, and then she died. My mother straightened her fingers, but later, at the wake in our house, my grandmother pinched a summer word and we could see that. She was buried in the cold earth with a warm word between her fingers. That's when my uncle gave me my nickname.

Almost never told lies, but he used the word almost to stretch the truth like a tribal trickster, my mother told me. The trickster is a character in stories, an animal, or person, even a tree at times, who pretends the world can be stopped with words, and he frees the world in stories. Almost said the trickster is almost a man and almost a woman, and almost a child, a clown who laughs and plays games with words in stories. The trickster is almost a free spirit. Almost told me about the trickster many times, and I think I almost understand his stories. He brushed my head with his hand and said, "The almost world is a better world, a sweeter dream than the world we are taught to understand in school."

"I understand, almost," I told my uncle.

"People are almost stories, and stories tell almost the whole truth," Almost told me last winter when he gave me my nickname. "Pincher is your nickname and names are stories too, *gega*." The word *gega* means *almost* in the Anishinaabe or Chippewa language.

"Pincher *gega*," I said and then tried to pinch a tribal word I could not yet see clear enough to hold between my fingers. I could almost see *gega*.

Almost, no matter the season, wore a long overcoat. He bounced when he walked, and the thick bottom of the overcoat hit the ground. The sleeves were too short but he never minded that because he could eat and deal cards with no problems. So there he was in line for a rainbow ice cream cone, dressed for winter, or almost winter he would say. My mother wonders if he wears that overcoat for the attention.

"*Gega, gega,*" an old woman called from the end of the line. "You spending some claims money on ice cream or a new coat?" No one ignored his overcoat.

"What's that?" answered Almost. He cupped his ear to listen because he knew the old woman wanted to move closer, ahead in the line. The claims money she mentioned is a measure of everything on the reservation. The federal government promised to settle a treaty over land with tribal people. Almost and thousands of others have been waiting for more than a century to be paid for land that was taken from them. There were rumors at least once a week that federal checks were in the mail, final payment for the broken treaties. When white people talk about a rain dance, tribal people remember the claims dancers who promised a federal check in every mailbox.

"Claims money," she whispered in the front of the line.

"Almost got a check this week," Almost said and smiled.

"Almost is as good as nothing," she said back.

"Pincher gets a bicycle when the claims money comes."

"My husband died waiting for the claims settlement," my mother said. She looked at me and then turned toward the ice cream counter to order. I held back my excitement about a new bicycle because the claims money might never come; no one was ever sure. Almost believed in rumors, and he waited one morning for a check to appear in his mailbox on the reservation. Finally, my mother scolded him for wasting his time on promises made by the government. "You grow old too fast on government promises," she said. "Anyway, the government has nothing to do with bicycles." He smiled at me and we ate our rainbow ice cream cones at the bus depot. That was a joke because the depot is nothing more than a park bench in front of a restaurant. On the back of the bench was a sign that announced an ice sculpture contest to be held in the town park on July Fourth.

"Ice cube sculpture?" asked my mother.

"No blocks big enough around here in summer," I said, thinking about the ice sold to tourists, cubes and small blocks for camp coolers.

"Pig Foot, he cuts ice from the lake in winter and stores it in a cave, buried in straw," my uncle whispered. He looked around, concerned that someone might hear about the ice cave. "Secret *mikwam,* huge blocks, enough for a great sculpture." The word *mikwam* means ice.

"Never mind," my mother said as she licked the ice cream on her fingers. The rainbow turned pink when it melted. The pink ran over her hand and under her rings.

Black Ice was late, but that never bothered her because she liked to ride in the back of buses at night. She sat in the dark and pretended that she could see the people who lived under the distant lights. She lived in a dark apartment building in Saint Paul with her mother and older brother and made the world come alive with light more than with sound or taste. She was on the reservation for more than a month last summer, and we thought her nickname would be Light or Candle or something like that, even though she wore black clothes. Not so. Almost avoided one obvious name and chose another when she attended our grandmother's funeral. Black Ice had never been on the reservation in winter. She slipped and fell seven times on black ice near the church and so she got that as a nickname.

Black Ice was the last person to leave the bus. She held back behind the darkened windows as long as she could. Yes, she was shy, worried about being embarrassed in public. I might be that way too, if we lived in an apartment in the cities, but the only public on the reservation are the summer tourists. She was happier when we bought her a rainbow ice cream cone. She was dressed in black, black everything, even black canvas shoes, no, almost black. The latest television style in the cities. Little did my uncle know that her reservation nickname would describe a modern style of clothes. We sat in the back seat on the way back to our house. We could smell the dust in the dark, in the tunnel of light through the trees. The moon was new that night.

"Almost said he would buy me my first bicycle when he gets his claims money," I told Black Ice. She brushed her clothes; there was too much dust.

"I should've brought my new mountain bike," she said. "I don't use it much though. Too much traffic and you have to worry about it being stolen."

"Should we go canoeing? We have a canoe."

"Did you get a television yet?" asked Black Ice.

"Yes," I boasted, "my mother won a big screen with a dish and everything at a bingo game on the reservation." We never watched much television though.

"Really?"

"Yes, we can get more than a hundred channels."

"On the reservation?"

"Yes, and bingo too."

"Well, here we are, paradise at the end of a dust cloud," my mother announced as she turned down the trail to our house on the lake. The headlights held the eyes of a raccoon, and we could smell a skunk in the distance. Low branches brushed the side of the car; we were home. We sat in the car for a few minutes and listened to the night. The dogs were panting. Mosquitoes, so big we called them the state bird, landed on our arms, bare knuckles, and warm shoulder blades. The water was calm and seemed to hold back a secret dark blue light from the bottom of the lake. One loon called and another answered. One thin wave rippled over the stones on the shore. We ducked mosquitoes and went into the house. We were tired, and too tired in the morning to appreciate the plan to carve a trickster from a block of ice.

Pig Foot lived alone on an island. He came down to the wooden dock to meet us in the morning. We were out on the lake before dawn, my uncle at the back of the canoe in his overcoat. We paddled and he steered us around the point of the island where bald eagles nested.

"Pig Foot?" questioned Black Ice.

"Almost gave him that nickname," I whispered to my cousin as we came closer to the dock. "Watch his little feet; he prances like a pig when he talks. The people in town swear his feet are hard and cloven."

"Are they?"

"No," I whispered as the canoe touched the dock.

"Almost," shouted Pig Foot.

"Almost," said Almost. "Pincher, you know him from the funeral, and this lady is from the city. We named her Black Ice."

"*Makate Mikwam,*" said Pig Foot. "Black ice comes with the white man and roads. No black ice on this island." He tied the canoe to the dock and patted his thighs with his open hands. The words *makate mikwam* mean black ice.

Black Ice looked down at Pig Foot's feet when she stepped out of the canoe. He wore black overshoes, the toes were turned out. She watched him prance on the rough wooden dock when he talked about the weather and mosquitoes. The black flies and mosquitoes on the island, special breeds, were more vicious than anywhere else on the reservation. Pig Foot was pleased that no one camped on the island because of the black flies. Some people accused him of raising mean flies to keep the tourists away. "Not a bad idea, now that I think about it," said Pig Foot. He had a small bunch of black hair on his chin. He pulled the hair when he was nervous and revealed a row of short stained teeth. Black Ice turned toward the sunrise and held her laughter.

"We come to see the ice cave," said Almost. "We need a large block to win the ice sculpture contest in four days."

"What ice cave is that?" asked Pig Foot.

"The almost secret one!" shouted Almost.

"That one, sure enough," said Pig Foot. He mocked my uncle and touched the lapel of his overcoat. "I was wondering about that contest. What does ice have to do with July Fourth?" He walked ahead as he talked, and then every eight steps he would stop and turn to wait for us. But if you were too close you would bump into him when he stopped. Black Ice counted his steps, and when we were near the entrance to the ice cave she imitated his prance, toes turned outward. She pranced seven steps and then waited for him to turn on the eighth.

Pig Foot stopped in silence on the shore where the bank was higher and where several trees leaned over the water. There, in the vines and boulders, we could feel the cool air. A cool breath on the shore.

Pig Foot told us we could never reveal the location of the ice cave, but he said we could tell stories about ice and the great spirit of winter in summer. He said this because most tribal stories should be told in winter, not in summer when evil spirits could be about to listen and do harm to words and names. We agreed to the conditions and followed him over the boulders into the wide cold cave. We could hear our breath, even a heartbeat. Whispers were too loud in the cave.

"Almost the scent of winter on July Fourth," whispered Almost. "In winter we overturn the ice in shallow creeks to smell the rich blue earth, and then in summer we taste the winter in this ice cave, almost."

"Almost, you're a poet, sure enough, but that's straw, not the smell of winter," said Pig Foot. He was hunched over where the cave narrowed at the back. Beneath the mounds of straw were huge blocks of ice, lake ice, blue and silent in the cave. Was that thunder, or the crack of winter ice on the lake? "Just me, dropped a block over the side." In winter he sawed blocks of ice in the bay where it was the thickest and towed the blocks into the cave on an aluminum slide. Pig Foot used the ice to cool his cabin in summer, but Almost warned us that there were other reasons. Pig Foot believes that the world is becoming colder and colder, the ice thicker and thicker. Too much summer in the blood would weaken him, so he rests on a block of ice in the cave several hours a week to stay in condition for the coming of the ice age on the reservation.

"Black Ice, come over here," said Almost. "Stretch out on this block." My cousin brushed the straw from the ice and leaned back on the block. "Almost, almost, now try this one, no this one, almost."

"Almost what?" asked Black Ice.

"Almost a whole trickster," whispered Almost. Then he told us what he had in mind. A trickster, he wanted us to carve a tribal trickster to enter in the ice sculpture contest. "What does a trickster look like?" I asked. Trickster was a word I could not see, there was nothing to pinch. How could I know a trickster between my fingers?

"Almost like a person," he said and brushed the straw from a block as large as me. "Almost in there, we have three days to find the trickster in the ice."

Early the next morning we paddled across the lake to the ice cave to begin our work on the ice trickster. We were dressed for winter. I don't think my mother believed us when we told her about the ice cave. "Almost," she said with a smile, "finally found the right place to wear his overcoat in the summer."

Pig Foot was perched on a block of ice when we arrived. We slid the block that held the trickster to the center of the cave and set to work with an ax and chisels. We rounded out a huge head, moved down the shoulders, and on the second day we freed the nose, ears, and hands of the trickster. I could see him in the dark blue ice; the trickster was almost free. I could almost pinch the word trickster.

Almost directed as we carved the ice on the first and second days, but on the third and final day he surprised us. We were in the cave dressed in winter coats and hats, ready to work, when he told us to make the final touches on our own, to liberate the face of the trickster. Almost and Pig Foot leaned back on a block of ice; we were in charge of who the trickster would become in ice.

Black Ice wanted the trickster to look like a woman. I wanted the ice sculpture to look like a man. The trickster, we decided, would be both, one side a man and the other side a woman. The true trickster, almost a man and almost a woman. In the end the ice trickster had features that looked like our uncle, our grandmother, and other members of our families. The trickster had small feet turned outward, he wore an overcoat, and she pinched her fingers on one hand. He was ready for the contest, she was the ice trickster on July Fourth.

That night we tied sheets around the ice trickster and towed her behind the canoe to the park on the other side of the lake. The ice floated and the trickster melted slower in the water. We rounded the south end of the island and headed to the park near the town, slow and measured like traders on a distant sea. The park lights reflected on the calm water. We tied the ice trickster to the end of the town dock and beached our canoe. We were very excited, but soon we were tired and slept on the grass in the park near the dock. The trickster was a liberator; she would win on Independence Day. Almost, anyway.

"The trickster melted," shouted Almost. He stood on the end of the dock, a sad uncle in his overcoat, holding the rope and empty sheets. At first we thought he had tricked us, we thought the whole thing was a joke, so we laughed. We rolled around on the grass and laughed. Almost was not amused at first. He turned toward the lake to hide his face, but then he broke into wild laughter. He laughed so hard he almost lost his balance in that heavy overcoat. He almost fell into the lake.

"The ice trickster won at last," said Black Ice.

"No, wait, she almost won. No ice trickster would melt that fast in the lake," he said and ordered us to launch the canoe for a search. Overnight the trickster had slipped from the sheets and floated free from the dock, somewhere out in the lake. The ice trickster was free on July Fourth.

We paddled the canoe in circles and searched for hours and hours but we could not find the ice trickster. Later, my mother rented a motorboat and we searched in two circles.

Almost was worried that the registration would close, so he abandoned the search and appealed to the people who organized the ice sculpture competition. They agreed to extend the time, and they even invited other contestants to search for the ice trickster. The lake was crowded with motorboats.

"There she floats," a woman shouted from a fishing boat. We paddled out and towed the trickster back to the dock. Then we hauled her up the bank to the park and a pedestal. We circled the pedestal and admired the ice trickster.

"Almost a trickster," said Almost. We looked over the other entries. There were more birds than animals, more heads than hips or hands, and the other ice sculptures were much smaller. Dwarfs next to the ice trickster. She had melted some overnight in the lake, but he was still head and shoulders above the other entries. The competition was about to close when we learned that there was a height restriction. Almost never read the rules. No entries over three feet and six inches in any direction. The other entries were much smaller. No one found large blocks of ice in town, so they were all within the restrictions. Our trickster was four feet tall, or at least she was that tall when we started out in the ice cave.

"No trickster that started out almost he or she can be too much of either," said Almost. We nodded in agreement, but we were not certain what he meant.

"What now?" asked Black Ice.

"Get a saw," my mother ordered. "We can cut the trickster down a notch or two on the bottom." She held her hand about four inches from the base to see what a shorter trickster would look like.

"Almost short enough," said Almost. "He melted some, she needs to lose four more inches by my calculations. We should have left her in the lake for another hour."

Pig Foot turned the trickster on his side, but when we measured four inches from the bottom he protested. "Not the feet, not my feet, those are my feet on the trickster."

"Not my ear either."

"Not the hands," I pleaded.

"The shins," shouted Black Ice. No one had claimed the shins on the ice trickster, so we measured and sawed four inches from his shins and then carved the knees to fit the little pig feet.

"Almost whole," announced Almost.

"What's a trickster?" asked the three judges who hurried down the line of pedestals before the ice sculptures melted beyond recognition.

"Almost a person," said Black Ice.

"What person?"

"My grandmother," I told the judges. "See how she pinched her fingers. She was a trickster; she pinched a cricket there." Pig Foot was nervous; he pranced around the pedestal.

The judges prowled back and forth, whispered here and there between two pedestals, and then they decided that there would be two winners because they could not decide on one. "The winners are the Boy and His Dog, and that ice trickster, Almost a Person," the judges announced.

The ice trickster won a bicycle, a large camp cooler, a dictionary, and twelve double rainbow cones. The other ice cave sculptors gave me the bicycle because I had never owned one before, and because the claims payment might be a bad promise. We divided the cones as best we could between five people, Almost, Pig Foot, Black Ice, me, and my mother.

Later, we packed what remained of the ice trickster, including the shin part, and took him back to the ice cave, where she lasted for more than a year. She stood in the back of the cave without straw and melted down to the last drop of a trickster. She was almost a whole trickster, almost.

Shadows

Bagese, as you must have heard by now, became a bear last year in the city. She is the same tribal woman who was haunted by stones and mirrors, and she warned me never to publish these stories or reveal the location of her apartment.

She was a wild bear who teased children and enchanted me with her trickster stories. She could be hesitant, the moves of an old woman, but her arms were thick, her hands were hard and wide, and she covered her mouth when she laughed because she was embarrassed that her teeth were gone.

Most of the time she celebrated her descent from the stones and the bears, wore a beaded necklace and blue moccasins that were puckered at the toes, but she would never be considered traditional, or even an urban pretender who treasured the romantic revisions of the tribal past. She was closer to stones, trickster stories, and tribal chance, than the tragedies of a vanishing race.

Bagese reeked of urine, and the marbled sweat on her stout neck had a wicked stench. She wore the same loose dress every time we met, and never washed her hair in more than a year. She was a strain on the nose, but even so she convinced me to believe in bears, and it seemed so natural at the time to hear her say that stones, animals, and birds were liberated at last in the city. She was a bear, and the bears were at war in her stories.

That bear woman warned me more than once, and with wicked humor she hauled me close to her neck and pounded me on the head with her hard hands. I felt like a mongrel, and the smell of her body made me sick to my stomach. She was a bear and teased me in mirrors as she did the children, and at the same time she said that tribal

David P. Bradley (Chippewa), *The Santa Fe Collector,* 1980. Bradley's painting focuses on how Native American identity is mediated through high art, folk art, and the media. "The collector" is herself borrowed from James McNeill Whistler's famous painting of his mother. She is shown indoors among paintings, books, a Native American–style rug, and a TV set. Nature is reduced to a few potted plants and an image on TV, and the collector sits next to a painting of a Native American, while the "real" Native Americans are left outside the window.

stories must be told not recorded, told to listeners but not readers, and she insisted that stories be heard through the ear not the eye. She was very determined about the ear in spite of the obvious inconsistencies. The tribal world was remembered in the ear, but she never said anything about the nose.

I listened, held my breath, and promised not to publish what she told me. I was in her scent and could do nothing less, of course, and she told me stories about the liberation of animals, birds, and insects in the cities. She even encouraged me to tell my own stories, but my stories were lectures, or dead voices, so she told me to imagine in my own way the stories she had told me. I imitated her voice at first, practiced her hesitant manner, and repeated the sounds of her animal characters.

The secret, she told me, was not to pretend, but to see and hear the real stories behind the words, the voices of the animals in me, not the definitions of the words alone. I lectured on tribal philosophies at the university, and what she told me at first might have fallen on deaf ears in the classroom.

The best listeners were shadows, animals, birds, and humans, because their shadows once shared the same stories. She said there were tricksters in our voices and natural sounds, tricksters who remembered the scenes, the wild visions in the shadows of our words. She warned me that even the most honored lectures were dead voices, that shadows were dead in recitations. She said written words were the burial grounds of shadows. The tricksters in the word are seen in the ear not the eye.

She was such an incredible person, a natural contradiction in a cold and chemical civilization, and you will understand later why my promises were broken to remember her stories, the mirrors in her apartment, and the dead voices at the treeline. She became a bear and carved her image on a sacred copper dish the night before she vanished. She seemed to leave her mark, a signature, and that ended the game.

Bagese lived alone in a garden apartment on a busy street near Lake Merritt in Oakland, California. The front windows were below an untrimmed hedge and faced a bus stop. I visited her there many times over a period of two years. We first met on the street, and the other times were in her apartment. She wore the same clothes and never washed her hair or neck once in that time.

The city buses rattled the aluminum dishes in the sink, and overnight bits of paint and plaster were shaken loose from the ceiling and covered the table. The kitchen walls were touched with shadows of mold, the corners held their own natural traces. The ivy in a black plastic pot flourished at the windows, a lonesome brush with morning light, nothing more.

Bagese was born without a last name near a town on the crossroads at the border of the Leech Lake Reservation in Minnesota. She was born long before tribal bingo and remembered the rush of wild rice on the side of an aluminum canoe, the sound of the last cash crop in the autumn of her birth.

She learned as a child to hear the sounds of birds in their seasons. She pretended to be a bluebird, an oriole, and imitated a cardinal. Later, when she was thirteen, thin, silent, and alone, she told me she became a blue heron. She laughed when the herons mocked her moves in the cattails. She was too slow over the shiners in shallow water, and worried that she would never survive with the birds, because the birds were hunted and driven with the animals from the reservation. Their shadows were lost in lesson plans and irrefutable bird guides.

Bagese told me that she was born dead at the treeline, buried in tribal voices. I pretended to understand, but some of her stories were obscure and she never responded to my constant doubts. She was alone, silent most of the time, and never seemed to have any human friends, but she remembered too much of the natural world to ever live in isolation. At first that seemed to be a contradiction, the seclusion of her apartment and the separation of her stories about animals and birds driven to the city.

I was certain that she told no one else these stories, and that I was the only one who listened to her for more than a year. She should have been my discovery at the cages, but as you can see, she must have waited there to catch my ear. How else could she have finished her game?

Later, she convinced me that silence and isolation were learned with the eyes not the ears. She heard wild voices in the shadows, in the dance of leaves, in the pose of a cockroach on the bread board, and she remembered their stories with such pleasure, compassion, and imagination, that even a cockroach could be humbled with pride.

She remembered as a child how she turned to natural voices on the water, how she turned to nature when humans abused the silence, but more than once the loons and mallards mocked her in a canoe. She held an escape distance from the hunters and mechanical winters, practiced the manners of animals and the stories of birds. She learned to hear their shadows and survived on their stories.

I was never sure how to hear the stories she told me. I could see the scenes that she described, but meaning escaped me because the stories never ended. She just paused or stopped, and that was never certain either. She seemed to be more at ease with crows and bears than other birds and animals. There were real bears, remembered bears, bear voices, the bears in the mirrors, and the bears who returned to their shadows in the cities. She declared that the bears at last found a new wilderness in the city.

She told me the bears were tricksters in mirrors and stories in their own seasons, of course, but never more devious than humans. She was hunted with the bears by lonesome men that last autumn on the reservation. Their moves were sudden, mean, and measured in a cold and silent sight at the treeline.

Bagese remembered that one summer she was an otter on the great river, how she turned over and over in the bright water. She was an otter shadow in her stories and pretended that her coat would become a medicine bundle. She carried the sacred stones and the miigis[1] of creation. She told me how inspired she was to give her body to the tribe, to hold that power in ceremonies, to shoot the spirit of the miigis shell that would heal the present. She said the past was stolen, the tribe was invented and recited in dead voices, and the present was hunted and driven with the animals and birds from the treelines. The animals and birds, and their shadows of creation, she insisted, had become outcasts and dreamers in the cities. She heard the dead voices, and became a bear in the mirror.

Bagese Bear assumed a surname when she moved from the treeline to Oakland, California. She said her uncle had been relocated there on a federal program. Sucker, a nickname that described his mouth and the way he inhaled his words, she said, learned how to weld at a government scrapyard on San Francisco Bay. A few years later he returned to the reservation and repaired automobiles with a blowtorch. She listened and remembered his trickster stories about freedom and demons in the city. His stories were shadows and sanctuaries in the winter, and the scenes he described were new tribal creations and relocations.

Bagese has lived in that same apartment at the bus stop for more than fifteen years because it was close to the caged birds at Lake Merritt. I first met her there, at an aviary near the lake. I heard her voice in the distance, a salutation early in the morning, and there she was at a cage with the crows. She held the attention of an elder crow in a real conversation. She even had a way with the wounded golden eagle in a round cage near the crows. I mean, she spoke in such a way that the eagle answered and bounced closer to the bars to hear her stories.

My grandmother carried on with lovebirds and caged canaries, but this was different. These were wild birds caged until their wounds healed, and they listened to her stories. I mean their shadows and her stories were in the same natural time. I thought she was a shaman, but in fact she had taken me into her stories and trickster game.

I followed her to a bench at the narrow end of the lake and asked her what she had told the crows and the golden eagle. She was slow to respond to me, as if the caged birds were a secret. I did not appreciate her natural hesitation at first, but later she told stories of the wanaki trickster game[2] in the same slow, scrupulous manner, with pauses a mean listener would take advantage of at the verbs.

I knew she had me that morning because she hesitated, covered her mouth, and then turned to the side. She seemed to laugh, but the sound was no more than sudden breath.

---

1. The miigis shell, similar to a cowrie shell, is sacred to the Anishinaabe; according to legend, it arose from the water and guided the Anishinaabe on a long journey along the Great Lakes.

2. A game of chance played with seven cards; *wanaki* means "to live somewhere in peace" in the language of the Anishinaabe.

The folds on her neck opened and closed when she turned to the side to avoid my doubts. She would have been more cordial, it was clear, if I had been a caged bird. I mentioned the cages, what a shame it was to cage wild birds, and she turned her head in the other direction. The hesitation was more than the season.

The magnolias spread their bright shadows overnight with petals behind the bench, and the bees rushed the tender wisteria blooms that embraced the arbor near the lake.

"No shame," she whispered.

"That crow heard you."

"So he did, and so did you," she said and turned toward me. She held her hands to her mouth and looked past me, to one side of my head, and then the other.

"Can you see me here?"

"Can you hear, are you a bear?" asked Bagese.

"Hardly, but please, don't let my human appearance hold back your imagination." I moved to catch her eyes, but there was no one there. I was certain that she had bad vision.

"Your animals are dead voices."

"No, not really, my cat complains every morning, but why would you ask me about my pets?" I was suspicious and leaned back on the bench to watch her hands. She laughed, and then she rushed me on the bench and pounded me on the head. Her mouth was uncovered, close to mine for the first time, and her wild tongue bounced from side to side on her gums.

"The animals in your stories," she shouted.

"What stories?"

"The stories you hear in the mirrors," she said and then gestured with her mouth toward the twisted wisteria bound to the arbor behind me. I turned to see the blossoms, and she was gone without a sound. I could not believe what had happened to me. I was the discoverer that morning and she turned me into a child on the bench. She tricked me and touched my sense of innocence.

Bagese has tried to lose me every time we got together, as she had done that first morning on the bench, but elusive or not, the more she hesitated and resisted my interest, the more winsome she became to me. No one ever carried on stories with caged birds the way she did, and no one could be so hard and soft at the same time, or so hesitant with such a wicked tongue. She was an old bear who teased insects with her body odor, and that was no mean distinction in the city.

I followed her that early morning to her apartment two blocks from the lake, but it was not as easy as it might sound. I never thought an old woman could trick me on the street, she could never walk that fast, but somehow she summoned two mongrels to rush me from behind, the perfect diversion. The mongrels barked, and when they retreated, she was gone.

I was certain she lived on the same block as the mongrels, and tried to imagine what she would have in the windows of her apartment. She was not behind the violets or animal figurines. I walked on both sides of the street, studied the buildings, even searched behind several homes, but there were no traces. She never told me her name.

I rested on a bench at a bus stop, and it was there, in a most unusual manner that I found her apartment. The city buses stopped at the corner, and when two students boarded they commented on the crazy bear behind the hedge. The bus roared from the curb, but there was only ivy in the window of the garden apartment. Closer, the interior came alive with mirrors, and a collection of stones, many stones, birds, leaves, flowers, insects, and other mysterious things spread out like a map on the floor. I learned later that she had laid out a wanaki game.

I crouched behind the hedge and waited at the window for a sign that she lived there. I was sure it was her apartment, but no one was there. The bright clouds of an ocean storm came ashore and rushed the eucalyptus trees. The rain came in bursts, cold and hard, and blurred the window.

Something moved in the mirrors, and the mirrors were everywhere, but the images were distant and obscure. The room was a dream scene, sensuous motions in the rain. The mirrors and stones seemed to be alive. I had no idea what the mirrors were reflecting because nothing seemed to be moving in the apartment. I would learn later, of course, that she was a bear in the mirrors, an image that escaped me for several months.

The buses roared, the windows rattled, the storm clouds passed, and at last she appeared in the mirrors. When she saw me at the window she covered her head with her hands and danced in the leaves and stones on the floor. I could not hear, but she must have laughed over my appearance at the window, a clever ruse. I was so determined to find this woman that nothing reminded me of my compulsive and stupid behavior at the time, crouched at her kitchen window like a peeper.

She might have struck me blind, but instead she taught me how to hear and see the animals in stories. Nothing comes around in chance when the best moments are lost to manners and the clock.

"Laundry," she said at the door, and that became my nickname. She laughed and pounded me on the head. "You smell like television soap, the sweet smell of laundry is a dead voice."

Bagese invited me in, of course, and over the threshold there was a transformation of voices in the apartment, nothing in my life has ever been the same since. She told me stories with wild voices that demanded my attention and imagination, stories she warned me to remember but never, never to publish. She cursed the dead voices of civilization, the word demons who hear no stories on the run. She praised chance and tricked the demons with dead pronouns.

The wanaki chance, for instance, was her game of natural meditation, the stories that liberated shadows and the mind. Chance is an invitation to animal voices in a tribal world, and the word "wanaki" means to live somewhere in peace, a chance at peace.

She turned seven cards in the game, one each for the bear, beaver, squirrel, crow, flea, praying mantis, and the last was the trickster figure, a wild card that transformed the player into an otter, a rabbit, a crane, a spider, or even a human. The animals, birds, and insects were pictured in unusual poses on the cards. The bear, for instance, was a flamenco dancer, the crow was a medical doctor, and the praying mantis was the president. The cards and creatures were stories, and she insisted that nothing was ever personal in a game of wanaki chance.

Bagese told me that the poses of the creatures were the common poses of civilization, the stories and shadows of the animals and birds in the mirrors. She compared the wanaki peace cards to tarot cards that depict the vices and virtues of human adventures, but tarot was in the eye and wanaki was in the ear. The fortunes were never the same as animal stories.

She has lived in a wanaki game since she moved to the city. Every morning she selects one of the seven cards and concentrates on the picture of the bird, animal, insect, or wild chance of the trickster. She explained that the players must use the plural pronoun *we* to share in the stories and become the creatures on the cards. That morning she had become the stories of the crow and gathered bits and pieces of nature, fallen leaves and feathers near the lake, and placed them in similar positions in her apartment, which was all part of the wanaki chance. The shape of the lake was obvious once she told me about the game. The objects were laid out as she had found them in the miniature shape of Lake Merritt.

The beaver and squirrel stones were placed in the north on the floor of her apartment, the bear in the east, the flea in the west, the crow and praying mantis in the south, and the last card was the trickster in the center of the wanaki game.

I was more than eager to remind her that the wanaki cards were an obvious contradiction to what she had told me. The pictures on the cards were the same as written words and could not be heard. I was certain she wanted me to ask obvious questions. "So, how can you hear stones and pictures?"

"The bear is painted not printed, and the praying mantis is seen as the president, this is a shadow, a chance not a word," she insisted.

"Written words are pictures."

"Printed books are the habits of dead voices," she said and turned a mirror in my direction to distract me. "The ear not the eyes sees the stories."

"And the eye hears the stories."

"The voices are dead."

"So, the wanaki pictures are dead."

"There are no others, these are my picture stories, no one sees them but hears my stories," she said and then drew one of the seven cards in the game. She held the picture to the mirror and the praying mantis became a bear.

The natural meditation scene was conspicuous, and the dead birds on the miniature bay were a bit much, but she enlivened my ambivalence with stories about a tribal woman who brought dead animals and birds back to life on the reservation.

"She must have been the resurrection shaman."

"You could say that," she responded.

"She could make a fortune at a chemical company."

"She already has on weekends," said Bagese.

"So, why are you playing miniature meditation with leaves and twigs in your apartment when you could bring back the dead and buy your own reservation?"

I never doubted that she had the power and the stories to bring back the dead, even dead voices at a great distance. The moment she appeared as a bear was more than enough power to transform the world, at least in my mind, but the mirrors that haunted her apartment were too much for me to understand.

The return of dead animals and birds was a story that made sense, but the mirrors that haunted her apartment were outside of my imagination and appreciation. These mirrors held images that were never in that room, and there were images that she could see, but not me. I avoided the mirrors for fear that my face would vanish, or that my image would tell me who the animals were in my past. My present memories and insecurities were more than enough for me to understand. The evolution of the animals in me, or as she said, the animal shadows that came to me as stories, would be too much to endure at rush hour, in line at the bank, or in a lecture at the university.

I was not surprised to learn that there seemed to be a hierarchy of mirrors in that apartment. There were round hand mirrors everywhere, beveled mirrors, suspended mirrors, table mirrors, tile mirrors, and framed mirrors covered the walls. She teased me to watch myself in the mirrors, the smaller mirrors. She even positioned a portable mirror to catch me when I sat at the kitchen table. When I refused to look into the mirrors she laughed and pounded me on the head.

I can never be sure, but there seemed to be something sexual about the mirrors in her apartment. There was never any doubt that her lust almost did me in when at last, after seven months of visits, she appeared to me as a bear in the tabernacle mirror. I will never forget that moment in her maw, and since then she has never pounded me on the head.

The Empire tabernacle mirror was mounted with distinction on a partition just inside the door to her apartment. As the door opened, there was the tabernacle. The distinctive decorated glass was the first mirror in her apartment. I have never seen anything like it, not to mention the haunting reflections of the other mirrors. The tabernacle frame was turned and painted black and gold with carved rosettes in the corner blocks. The upper part of the framed mirror was decorated with the creatures pictured on the wanaki cards. The face of the trickster, a bear in a human figure at the center of the scene, was a miniature metallic mirror. I saw her as a bear in that tabernacle mirror. The landscape was painted on the reverse side of the glass, and the main mirror was below the wanaki scene.

Bagese told me stories in the animal, bird, and insect voices of the wanaki game. She teased the trickster in the tabernacle, and pounded the mirrors that leaned too close to the dead voices. Two years later she was gone without a trace. The mirrors were down, the apartment was empty, but the ivy held to the window. I remember her stories as our stories now, and if she heard them told once more, even these published versions, she might return to pound me on the head as promised.

⇒✛ PERSPECTIVES ✛⇐
Indigenous Cultures
in the Twentieth Century

Linguists estimate that of the more than 6,000 languages that were once spoken across the globe, more than half may be extinct by the end of this century. This drastic reduction of linguistic variety points to a broad threat to cultural diversity that especially affects indigenous cultures across many nations. Due to a range of political, economic, social, and cultural forms of domination, members of indigenous cultures have often lost their habitats and culturally significant places and objects, and they have been assimilated into more dominant cultures by force or by choice. Education, military service, mass media, and intermarriage can all contribute to the blurring of cultural boundaries and often to the fading or disappearance of the less dominant culture. In this context of strong pressure on small ethnic communities to give up at least a part of their distinctiveness, writers take on a particularly important role as custodians of knowledge about traditional ways of learning, speaking, and acting and as ambassadors able to mediate between different cultures.

The literary texts assembled in this section all grow out of a consciousness of this role and investigate different aspects of the encounter between indigenous ways of life and modern Western culture. Who is entitled to write the history of such encounters? What is gained and lost when an indigenous person assimilates into the dominant culture? What relevance might a detailed knowledge of the natural world have in an urban habitat? How does one reconcile a traditional sense of connection to the land with trade in real estate? What aspects of an indigenous culture do anthropologists study, and how does their knowledge relate to the self-perceptions of the people they study? How do indigenous and modern forms of wisdom or knowledge compare? These are some of the issues that indigenous writers raise in their poetry and fiction. Questions with specifically literary and artistic dimensions equally arise. How can oral forms of knowledge and narrative claim authority in a world of printed documents and televised images? What role do indigenous artifacts, especially those with sacred meanings, play in a culture where art is a commodity to be bought and sold?

As they reflect on problems such as these, indigenous writers also offer more general assessments of the fate of their cultures. At one end of the spectrum, writers such as Archie Weller and Oodgeroo of the tribe Noonuccal mournfully describe what they perceive as dead-end situations for indigenous peoples: racism, violence, poverty, and loss of trust in the ability of their own cultural heritages to offer solutions for a modern existence drive their protagonists to despair and lead to the erasure of their identities. Other writers take a less pessimistic stance. Native American writer Gerald Vizenor's short stories and Leslie Marmon Silko's free verse portray some of the strengths and talents that indigenous or mixed heritages provide for their characters: flexibility, ingenuity, craftiness, the ability to improvise, knowledge of places and of nature, and mastery of existential as well as of artistic skills all enable these characters to cope with difficult social problems and sometimes to improve their situations. Yet other authors such as Paula Gunn Allen celebrate the resilience of indigenous cultures in the face of adversity or describe the mingling of cultures as a moment of historical gain rather than loss: an opportunity for casting off outdated modes of thought and for creating new, hybrid cultural identities and practices.

But the expressive power of the texts in this section often depends less on such general assessments than on the ways in which they force the reader to confront a specific, unaccustomed perspective. Such alternative views cast common and familiar situations in an entirely new light. Words from unfamiliar languages and references to unknown customs and places are the most visible indicators of different cultural worlds, and challenge the reader to discover their meanings. More profoundly, the characters' interpretations of events and their reactions to them quite often diverge from what a reader who is not familiar with their cultures might have expected, thereby opening up a window onto a new way of understanding the world. The native woman's treatment of the college professor in Vizenor's "Shadows," the Laguna people's view of anthropologists and archeologists in Silko's *Storyteller,* the Native Americans watching John Wayne shoot Indians in a Western in Erdrich's poem, and the narrator's play on a visitor's understanding of the phrase "Indian ruins" in one of Allen's poems all provide such glimpses of an entirely different approach to nature, culture, and history. These encounters with alternative views are often surprising and amusing, but sometimes also deliberately unsettling: They offer the pleasure of discovering the strange in the familiar, but they can also imply very serious criticism of specific social groups, behavior patterns, and values. Many of the writers in this section skillfully maintain this tension between invitation and critique in their portrayal of cultures at the intersection of tradition and modernization; they dare us to leave our accustomed worldviews behind and to familiarize ourselves with a perspective in which our own culture might appear quite different from what we have thought.

⊷ ▆◆▆ ⊶

Oodgeroo of the Tribe Noonuccal
1920–1993

Oodgeroo was born Kathleen Ruska on Stradbroke Island in Queensland, Australia, and was known for most of her life by her married name, Kath Walker. As an Aboriginal Australian, she came to know various forms of racial prejudice early on in her life, among them limited educational and professional possibilities. After finishing school in 1933, she worked as a domestic servant for several white families in order to make a living during a decade hit hard by the Depression. In 1941 she enlisted in the Australian Women's Army Service and was trained as a switchboard operator. She married a childhood friend in 1942, but the marriage fell apart after only a few years, and Oodgeroo was forced to return to domestic service.

In the late 1950s she joined the movement to gain civil rights for Aborigines, who at the time were subject to legislation that gave the Department of Native Affairs ample power to confine Aborigines to reservations, control their movements and access to their wages, withhold permission for marriage, and remove Aboriginal children from their parents' custody. Oodgeroo assumed ever-greater responsibilities in the Aboriginal liberation movement and acquired a reputation as a fiery and charismatic speaker. At the same time, she began to write poetry with the help of a group of aspiring and established authors, the Realist Writers. From the beginning, her strong sense of Aboriginal identity, her political engagement, and her poetic expression were inseparable. "Must we native Old Australians / In our own land rank as aliens?" she asked pointedly in the poem "Aboriginal Charter of Rights" (1963), and called out:

> We want hope, not racialism,
> Brotherhood, not ostracism,
> Black advance, not white ascendance:
> Make us equals, not dependents.

Her collection of poetry *We Are Going,* whose title poem is given below, was published in 1964 in a context of rising confrontation between Aborigines and whites. The first book by an Aboriginal writer ever to be published in Australia, it became a runaway success, selling more than ten thousand copies in seven editions. Other volumes of poetry followed, such as *The Dawn Is at Hand* (1966) and *My People* (1970), as well as a collection of native legends, *Stradbroke Dreamtime* (1972). While some critics dismissed her poetry for its failure to comply with the conventions of formal, metrical, British-style verse, others were galvanized by its rhetorical energy. Oodgeroo's verse, with its insistent rhythms and end rhymes, is particularly effective in oral delivery and is easily memorized and reproduced, factors that no doubt contributed to its popularity.

In 1971, at a time when many of the original organizations for Aboriginal rights disappeared and Oodgeroo suffered from ill health, she retired to her home island and founded Moongalba, a center for Aboriginal culture that over the years put thousands of Aboriginal children in touch with their heritage. It also attracted teachers and foreign academics, while Oodgeroo herself traveled abroad extensively as an ambassador for Aboriginal culture and rights. In 1988 racial tensions broke out anew on the occasion of Australia's bicentennial celebrations. Many Aborigines felt that this celebration of "the birth of a nation" deliberately concealed the dire consequences that the arrival of European settlers had brought about for Australia's indigenous cultures and its natural environment. In protest, Kath Walker renounced her English name and assumed the name of a woman from an Aboriginal legend who is charged with writing out the tribes' stories on paper made from tree bark. This name, Oodgeroo, together with the name of her tribe, stayed with her until her death in 1993, and it is the one by which her contributions to Australian politics and literature are remembered.

Pronunciation:
Noonuccal: NOO-nuckle

We Are Going

For Grannie Coolwell

They came into the little town
A semi-naked band subdued and silent,
All that remained of their tribe.
They came here to the place of their old bora ground[1]
5   Where now the many white men hurry about like ants.
Notice of estate agents reads: "Rubbish May Be Tipped Here."
Now it half covers the traces of the old bora ring.
They sit and are confused, they cannot say their thoughts:
"We are as strangers here now, but the white tribe are the strangers.
10   We belong here, we are of the old ways.
We are the corroboree[2] and the bora ground,
We are the old sacred ceremonies, the laws of the elders.
We are the wonder tales of Dream Time,[3] the tribal legends told.
We are the past, the hunts and the laughing games, the wandering camp fires.
15   We are the lightning-bolt over Gaphembah Hill
Quick and terrible,
And the Thunder after him, that loud fellow.
We are the quiet daybreak paling the dark lagoon.
We are the shadow-ghosts creeping back as the camp fires burn low.
20   We are nature and the past, all the old ways
Gone now and scattered.
The scrubs are gone, the hunting and the laughter.

1. The bora ground or bora ring is the site where, in Aboriginal ritual, the bora, or initiation ceremony, is performed, marking a youth's entry into manhood.
2. An Aboriginal dance ceremony that can be either ritual and sacred or informal and secular in character.

3. A reference to the primordial time and events that, in Aboriginal belief, brought the world into being in its material as well as its spiritual and moral dimensions and whose shaping influence endures.

> *The eagle is gone, the emu and the kangaroo are gone from this place.*
> *The bora ring is gone.*
25 *The corroboree is gone.*
> *And we are going."*

⚜

Archie Weller
b. 1957

In 1980 Australian Archie Weller was released from jail after what he considered a wrongful conviction. Embittered and angry, he sat down to write and in a mere six weeks completed the novel *The Day of the Dog,* which won the Western Australian Week Fiction Award. It was later turned into a prize-winning film, *Blackfellas* (1991). Weller went on to become a well-known author, with collections of well-received short stories and plays as well as another novel, *Land of Golden Clouds* (1998), which ventures into science fiction by describing a far-into-the-future, postnuclear Australia.

Weller is of mixed Aboriginal and white descent, one of his grandmothers being Aboriginal. He grew up on a farm in southwestern Australia and attended Guildford Grammar School, an exclusive private boarding school, for eight years. His professional career has included a wide range of jobs from farm worker, printer, gardener, and dishwasher to hospital aide. In the late 1990s his Aboriginal identity became a cause for controversy as part of a whole series of cases in which the indigenous descent of various Australian writers and artists was put into question; these controversies—also involving a prominent Aboriginal writer named Mudrooroo among others—raised complex questions about what constitutes authentic Aboriginal identity.

Weller's story collection *Going Home* (1986), whose 1979 title story is presented here, focuses on the struggles of younger Aboriginal men caught in between the demands of white and native cultures and often emphasizes how difficult it is for them to escape the dilemmas of this confrontation. Just what it means to be a socially and financially successful Aboriginal in a society dominated by whites is the question at the heart of "Going Home."

Going Home

> I want to go home.
> I want to go home.
> Oh, Lord, I want to go home.

Charlie Pride[1] moans from a cassette, and his voice slips out of the crack the window makes. Out into the world of magpies' soothing carols, and parrots' cheeky whistles, of descending darkness and spirits.

The man doesn't know that world. His is the world of the sleek new Kingswood that speeds down the never-ending highway.

At last he can walk this earth with pride, as his ancestors did many years before him. He had his first exhibition of paintings a month ago. They sold well, and with the proceeds he bought the car.

The slender black hands swing the shiny black wheel around a corner. Blackness forms a unison of power.

For five years he has worked hard and saved and sacrificed. Now, on his twenty-first birthday, he is going home.

---

1. A famous African-American country and western singer (b. 1938).

New car, new clothes, new life.

He plucks a cigarette from the packet beside him, and lights up.

His movements are elegant and delicate. His hair is well-groomed, and his clothes are clean.

Billy Woodward is coming home in all his might, in his shining armour.

Sixteen years old. Last year at school.

His little brother Carlton and his cousin Rennie Davis, down beside the river, on that last night before he went to the college in Perth,[2] when all three had had a good-bye drink, with their girls beside them.

Frogs croaking into the silent hot air and some animal blundering in the bulrushes on the other side of the gentle river. Moonlight on the ruffled water. Nasal voices whispering and giggling. The clink of beer bottles.

That year at college, with all its schoolwork, and learning, and discipline, and uniformity, he stood out alone in the football carnival.

Black hands grab the ball. Black feet kick the ball. Black hopes go soaring with the ball to the pasty white sky.

No one can stop him now. He forgets about the river of his Dreaming[3] and the people of his blood and the girl in his heart.

The year when he was eighteen, he was picked by a top city team as a rover.[4] This was the year that he played for the state, where he was voted best and fairest on the field.

That was a year to remember.

He never went out to the park at Guildford, so he never saw his people: his dark, silent staring people, his rowdy, brawling, drunk people.

He was white now.

Once, in the middle of the night, one of his uncles had crept around to the house he rented and fallen asleep on the verandah. A dirty pitiful carcase, encased in a black greatcoat that had smelt of stale drink and lonely, violent places. A withered black hand had clutched an almost-empty metho[5] bottle.

In the morning, Billy had shouted at the old man and pushed him down the steps, where he stumbled and fell without pride. The old man had limped out of the creaking gate, not understanding.

The white neighbours, wakened by the noise, had peered out of their windows at the staggering old man stumbling down the street and the glowering youth muttering on the verandah. They had smirked in self-righteous knowledge.

Billy had moved on the next day.

William Jacob Woodward passed fifth year with flying colours. All the teachers were proud of him. He went to the West Australian Institute of Technology to further improve his painting, to gain fame that way as well.

He bought clean, bright clothes and cut off his long hair that all the camp[6] girls had loved.

---

2. The capital of western Australia.

3. Dreaming, when spelled with a capital letter, refers to an Aboriginal belief and to a person's identification with a particular place, animal, or plant that has spiritual significance.

4. In Australian National Football, one of three players in a team who don't have fixed positions but follow the ball.

5. Methylated spirits, a basic type of alcoholic drink.

6. An Aboriginal settlement.

Billy Woodward was a handsome youth, with the features of his white grand-father and the quietness of his Aboriginal forebears. He stood tall and proud, with the sensitive lips of a dreamer and a faraway look in his serene amber eyes.

He went to the nightclubs regularly and lost his soul in the throbbing, writhing electrical music as the white tribe danced their corroboree[7] to the good life.

He would sit alone at a darkened corner table, or with a painted-up white girl— but mostly alone. He would drink wine and look around the room at all the happy or desperate people.

He was walking home one night from a nightclub when a middle-aged Aborigi-nal woman stumbled out of a lane.

She grinned up at him like the Gorgon[8] and her hands clutched at his body, like the lights from the nightclub.

"Billy! Ya Billy Woodward, unna?"[9]

"Yes. What of it?" he snapped.

"Ya dunno me? I'm ya Auntie Rose, from down Koodup."

She cackled then. Ugly, oh, so ugly. Yellow and red eyes and broken teeth and a long, crooked, white scar across her temple. Dirty grey hair all awry.

His people.

His eyes clouded over in revulsion. He shoved her away and walked off quickly.

He remembered her face for many days afterwards whenever he tried to paint a picture. He felt ashamed to be related to a thing like that. He was bitter that she was of his blood.

That was his life: painting pictures and playing football and pretending. But his people knew. They always knew.

In his latest game of football he had a young part-Aboriginal opponent who stared at him the whole game with large, scornful black eyes seeing right through him.

After the game, the boy's family picked him up in an old battered station wagon.

Billy, surrounded by all his white friends, saw them from afar off. He saw the children kicking an old football about with yells and shouts of laughter and two lanky boys slumping against the door yarning to their hero, and a buxom girl leaning out the window and an old couple in the back. The three boys, glancing up, spotted debonair Billy. Their smiles faded for an instant and they speared him with their proud black eyes.

So Billy was going home, because he had been reminded of home (with all its carefree joys) at that last match.

It is raining now. The shafts slant down from the sky, in the glare of the headlights. Night-time, when woodarchis[1] come out to kill, leaving no tracks: as though they are cloud shadows passing over the sun.

Grotesque trees twist in the half-light. Black tortured figures, with shaggy heads and pleading arms. Ancestors crying for remembrance. Voices shriek or whisper in tired chants: tired from the countless warnings that have not been heeded.

---

7. An Aboriginal dance ceremony that can be either ritual and sacred or informal and secular in character.
8. In Greek mythology, the gorgons were female figures with snakes for hair and so terrifyingly ugly that those who looked at them turned into stone.
9. "Isn't that so?"
1. Evil spirits, small hairy men with red eyes, some say, or else a feather foot (Weller's note).

They twirl around the man, like the lights of the city he knows. But he cannot understand these trees. They drag him onwards, even when he thinks of turning back and not going on to where he vowed he would never go again.

A shape, immovable and impassive as the tree it is under, steps into the road on the Koodup turnoff.

An Aboriginal man.

Billy slews to a halt, or he will run the man over.

Door opens.

Wind and rain and coloured man get in.

"Ta, mate. It's bloody cold 'ere," the coloured man grates, then stares quizzically at Billy, with sharp black eyes. "Nyoongah,[2] are ya, mate?"

"Yes."

The man sniffs noisily, and rubs a sleeve across his nose.

"Well, I'm Darcy Goodrich, any rate, bud."

He holds out a calloused hand. Yellow-brown, blunt scarred fingers, dirty nails. A lifetime of sorrow is held between the fingers.

Billy takes it limply.

"I'm William Woodward."

"Yeah?" Fathomless eyes scrutinise him again from behind the scraggly black hair that falls over his face.

"Ya goin' anywheres near Koodup, William?"

"Yes."

"Goodoh. This is a nice car ya got 'ere. Ya must 'ave plen'y of boya,[3] unna?"

Silence from Billy.

He would rather not have this cold, wet man beside him, reminding him. He keeps his amber eyes on the lines of the road as they flash under his wheels.

White . . . white . . . white . . .

"Ya got a smoke, William?"

"Certainly. Help yourself."

Black blunt fingers flick open his expensive cigarette case.

"Ya want one too, koordah?"[4]

"Thanks."

"Ya wouldn't be Teddy Woodward's boy, would ya, William?"

"Yes, that's right. How are Mum and Dad—and everyone?"

Suddenly he has to know all about his family and become lost in their sea of brownness.

Darcy's craggy face flickers at him in surprise, then turns, impassive again, to the rain-streaked window. He puffs on his cigarette quietly.

"What, ya don't know?" he says softly. "Ya Dad was drinkin' metho. 'E was blind drunk, an' in the 'orrors, ya know? Well, this truck came out of nowhere when 'e was crossin' the road on a night like this. Never seen 'im. Never stopped or nothin'. Ya brother Carl found 'im next day an' there was nothin' no one could do then. That was a couple of years back now."

Billy would have been nineteen then, at the peak of his football triumph. On one of those bright white nights, when he had celebrated his victories with wine and white women, Billy's father had been wiped off the face of his country—all alone.

---

2. Part-Aboriginal.   4. Brother, friend.
3. Cash.

He can remember his father as a small gentle man who was the best card cheat in the camp. He could make boats out of duck feathers and he and Carlton and Billy had had races by the muddy side of the waterhole, from where his people had come long ago, in the time of the beginning.

The lights of Koodup grin at him as he swings around a bend. Pinpricks of eyes, like a pack of foxes waiting for the blundering black rabbit.

"Tell ya what, buddy. Stop off at the hotel an' buy a carton of stubbies."[5]

"All right, Darcy." Billy smiles and looks closely at the man for the first time. He desperately feels that he needs a friend as he goes back into the open mouth of his previous life. Darcy gives a gap-toothed grin.

"Bet ya can't wait to see ya people again."

His people: ugly Auntie Rose, the metho-drinking Uncle, his dead forgotten father, his wild brother and cousin. Even this silent man. They are all his people.

He can never escape.

The car creeps in beside the red brick hotel.

The two Nyoongahs scurry through the rain and shadows and into the glare of the small hotel bar.

The barman is a long time coming, although the bar is almost empty. Just a few old cockies and young larrikins,[6] right down the other end. Arrogant grey eyes stare at Billy. No feeling there at all.

"A carton of stubbies, please."

"Only if you bastards drink it down at the camp. Constable told me you mob are drinking in town and just causing trouble."

"We'll drink where we bloody like, thanks, mate."

"Will you, you cheeky bastard?" The barman looks at Billy, in surprise. "Well then, you're not gettin' nothin' from me. You can piss off, too, before I call the cops. They'll cool you down, you smart black bastard."

Something hits Billy deep inside with such force that it makes him want to clutch hold of the bar and spew up all his pride.

He is black and the barman is white, and nothing can ever change that.

All the time he had gulped in the wine and joy of the nightclubs and worn neat fashionable clothes and had white women admiring him, played the white man's game with more skill than most of the wadgulas[7] and painted his country in white man colours to be gabbled over by the wadgulas: all this time he has ignored his mumbling, stumbling tribe and thought he was someone better.

Yet when it comes down to it all, he is just a black man.

Darcy sidles up to the fuming barman.

"'Scuse me, Mr 'Owett, but William 'ere just come 'ome, see," he whines like a beaten dog. "We *will* be drinkin' in the camp, ya know."

"Just come home, eh? What was he inside for?"

Billy bites his reply back so it stays in his stomach, hard and hurtful as a gallstone.

"Well all right, Darcy. I'll forget about it this time. Just keep your friend out of my hair."

Good dog, Darcy. Have a bone, Darcy. Or will a carton of stubbies do?

Out into the rain again.

---

5. Short, squat beer bottles.
6. Cockies: small farmers; larrikins: young, rough men or hooligans.

7. Whites. Pronounced "why-jellah" (derived from "white fellow").

They drive away and turn down a track about a kilometre out of town.

Darcy tears off a bottle top, handing the bottle to Billy. He grins.

"Act stupid, buddy, an' ya go a lo—ong way in this town."

Billy takes a long draught of the bitter golden liquid. It pours down his throat and into his mind like a shaft of amber sunlight after a gale. He lets his anger subside.

"What ya reckon, Darcy? I'm twenty-one today."

Darcy thrusts out a hand, beaming.

"Tw'n'y-bloody-one, eh? 'Ow's it feel?"

"No different from yesterday."

Billy clasps the offered hand firmly.

They laugh and clink bottles together in a toast, just as they reach the camp.

Dark and wet, with a howling wind. Rain beating upon the shapeless humpies.[8] Trees thrash around the circle of the clearing in a violent rhythm of sorrow and anger, like great monsters dancing around a carcase.

Darcy indicates a hut clinging to the edge of the clearing.

"That's where ya mum lives."

A rickety shape of nailed-down tin and sheets of iron. Two oatbags, sewn together, form a door. Floundering in a sea of tins and rags and parts of toys or cars. Mud everywhere.

Billy pulls up as close to the door as he can get. He had forgotten what his house really looked like.

"Come on, koordah. Come an' see ya ole mum. Ya might be lucky, too, an' catch ya brother."

Billy can't say anything. He gets slowly out of the car while the dereliction looms up around him.

The rain pricks at him, feeling him over.

He is one of the brotherhood.

A mouth organ's reedy notes slip in and out between the rain. It is at once a profoundly sorrowful yet carefree tune that goes on and on.

Billy's fanfare home.

He follows Darcy, ducking under the bag door. He feels unsure and out of place and terribly alone.

There are six people: two old women, an ancient man, two youths and a young, shy, pregnant woman.

The youth nearest the door glances up with a blank yellowish face, suspicion embedded deep in his black eyes. His long black hair that falls over his shoulders in gentle curls is kept from his face by a red calico headband. Red for the desert sands whence his ancestors came, red for the blood spilt by his ancestors when the white tribe came. Red, the only bright thing in these drab surroundings.

The youth gives a faint smile at Darcy and the beer.

"G'day, Darcy. Siddown 'ere. 'Oo ya mate is?"

"Oo'd ya think, Carl, ya dopy prick? 'E's ya brother come 'ome."

Carlton stares at Billy incredulously, then his smile widens a little and he stands up, extending a slim hand.

They shake hands and stare deep into each other's faces, smiling. Brown-black and brown-yellow. They let their happiness soak silently into each other.

---

8. Makeshift housing built with simple materials.

Then his cousin Rennie, also tall and slender like a young boomer,[9] with bushy red-tinged hair and eager grey eyes, shakes hands. He introduces Billy to his young woman, Phyllis, and reminds him who old China Groves and Florrie Waters (his mother's parents) are.

His mother sits silently at the scarred kitchen table. Her wrinkled brown face has been battered around, and one of her eyes is sightless. The other stares at her son with a bleak pride of her own.

From that womb I came, Billy thinks, like a flower from the ground or a fledgling from the nest. From out of the reserve I flew.

Where is beauty now?

He remembers his mother as a laughing brown woman, with long black hair in plaits, singing soft songs as she cleaned the house or cooked food. Now she is old and stupid in the mourning of her man.

"So ya come back after all. Ya couldn't come back for ya Dad's funeral, but— unna? Ya too good for us mob,[1] I s'pose," she whispers in a thin voice like the mouth organ before he even says hello, then turns her eyes back into her pain.

"It's my birthday, Mum. I wanted to see everybody. No one told me Dad was dead."

Carlton looks up at Billy.

"I make out ya twenty-one, Billy."

"Yes."

"Well, shit, we just gotta 'ave a party." Carlton half-smiles. "We gotta get more drink, but," he adds.

Carlton and Rennie drive off to town in Billy's car. When they leave, Billy feels unsure and alone. His mother just stares at him. Phyllis keeps her eyes glued on the mound of her womb and the grandparents crow to Darcy, camp talk he cannot understand.

The cousins burst through the door with a carton that Carlton drops on the table, then he turns to his brother. His smooth face holds the look of a small child who is about to show his father something he has achieved. His dark lips twitch as they try to keep from smiling.

"'Appy birthday, Billy, ya ole cunt," Carlton says, and produces a shining gold watch from the ragged pocket of his black jeans.

"It even works, Billy," grins Rennie from beside his woman, so Darcy and China laugh.

The laughter swirls around the room like dead leaves from a tree.

They drink. They talk. Darcy goes home and the old people go to bed. His mother has not talked to Billy all night. In the morning he will buy her some pretty curtains for the windows and make a proper door and buy her the best dress in the shop.

They chew on the sweet cud of their past. The memories seep through Billy's skin so he isn't William Woodward the talented football player and artist, but Billy the wild, half-naked boy, with his shock of hair and carefree grin and a covey of girls fluttering around his honey body.

Here they are—all three together again, except now young Rennie is almost a father and Carlton has just come from three months' jail. And Billy? He is nowhere.

At last, Carlton yawns and stretches.

---

9. A large male kangaroo.　　　　1. A community of Aborigines.

"I reckon I'll 'it that bed." Punches his strong brother gently on the shoulder. "See ya t'morrow, Billy, ole kid." He smiles.

Billy camps beside the dying fire. He rolls himself into a bundle of ragged blankets on the floor and stares into the fire. In his mind he can hear his father droning away, telling legends that he half-remembered, and his mother softly singing hymns. Voices and memories and woodsmoke drift around him. He sleeps.

He wakes to the sound of magpies carolling in the still trees. Rolls up off the floor and rubs the sleep from his eyes. Gets up and stacks the blankets in a corner, then creeps out to the door.

Carlton's eyes peep out from the blankets on his bed.

"Where ya goin'?" he whispers.

"Just for a walk."

"Catch ya up, Billy," he smiles sleepily. With his headband off, his long hair falls every way.

Billy gives a salutation and ducks outside.

A watery sun struggles up over the hills and reflects in the orange puddles that dot the camp. Broken glass winks white, like the bones of dead animals. Several children play with a drum, rolling it at each other and trying to balance on it. Several young men stand around looking at Billy's car. He nods at them and they nod back. Billy stumbles over to the ablution block: three bent and rusty showers and a toilet each for men and women. Names and slogans are scribbled on every available space. After washing away the staleness of the beer he heads for the waterhole, where memories of his father linger. He wants—a lot—to remember his father.

He squats there, watching the ripples the light rain makes on the serene green surface. The bird calls from the jumble of green-brown-black bush are sharp and clear, like the echoes of spirits calling to him.

He gets up and wanders back to the humpy. Smoke from fires wisps up into the grey sky.

Just as he slouches to the edge of the clearing, a police van noses its way through the mud and water and rubbish. A pale, hard, supercilious face peers out at him. The van stops.

"Hey, you! Come here!"

The people at the fires watch, from the corner of their eyes, as he idles over.

"That your car?"

Billy nods, staring at the heavy, blue-clothed sergeant. The driver growls, "What's your name, and where'd you get the car?"

"I just told you it's my car. My name's William Jacob Woodward, if it's any business of yours," Billy flares.

The sergeant's door opens with an ominous crack as he slowly gets out. He glances down at black Billy, who suddenly feels small and naked.

"You any relation to Carlton?"

"If you want to know—"

"I want to know, you black prick. I want to know everything about you."

"Yeah, like where you were last night when the store was broken into, as soon as you come home causing trouble in the pub," the driver snarls.

"I wasn't causing trouble, and I wasn't in any robbery. I like the way you come straight down here when there's trouble—"

"If you weren't in the robbery, what's this watch?" the sergeant rumbles triumphantly, and he grabs hold of Billy's hand that has marked so many beautiful marks and painted so many beautiful pictures for the wadgula people. He twists it up behind Billy's back and slams him against the blank blue side of the van. The golden watch dangles between the pink fingers, mocking the stunned man.

"Listen. I was here. You can ask my grandparents or Darcy Goodrich, even," he moans. But inside he knows it is no good.

"Don't give me that, Woodward. You bastards stick together like flies on a dunny[2] wall," the driver sneers.

Nothing matters any more. Not the trees, flinging their scraggly arms wide in freedom. Not the people around their warm fires. Not the drizzle that drips down the back of his shirt onto his skin. Just this thickset, glowering man and the sleek oiled machine with POLICE stencilled on the sides neatly and indestructibly.

"You mongrel black bastard, I'm going to make you—and your fucking brother—jump. You could have killed old Peters last night," the huge man hisses dangerously. Then the driver is beside him, glaring from behind his sunglasses.

"You Woodwards are all the same, thieving boongs.[3] If you think you're such a fighter, beating up old men, you can have a go at the sarge here when we get back to the station."

"Let's get the other one now, Morgan. Mrs. Riley said there were two of them."

He is shoved into the back, with a few jabs to hurry him on his way. Hunches miserably in the jolting iron belly as the van revs over to the humpy. Catches a glimpse of his new Kingswood standing in the filth. Darcy, a frightened Rennie and several others lean against it, watching with lifeless eyes. Billy returns their gaze with the look of a cornered dingo[4] who does not understand how he was trapped yet who knows he is about to die. Catches a glimpse of his brother being pulled from the humpy, sad yet sullen, eyes downcast staring into the mud of his life—mud that no one can ever escape.

He is thrown into the back of the van.

The van starts up with a satisfied roar.

Carlton gives Billy a tired look as though he isn't even there, then gives his strange, faint smile.

"Welcome 'ome, brother," he mutters.

Paula Gunn Allen
b. 1939

Paula Gunn Allen came to know Native American traditions through her mixed-blood ancestry as well as through the academic study of literature and culture. Born in New Mexico to a mother of mixed Laguna Pueblo, Sioux, and Scottish origin and a father of Lebanese-American descent, Allen grew up in a small town close to Laguna Pueblo and Acoma reservations. She studied at the University of Oregon and went on to complete a doctorate in American studies at the University of New Mexico. Profoundly influenced by the mix of Native American oral traditions and Western writing in N. Scott Momaday's *House Made of Dawn,* she has pursued a dual career as a poet and a scholar of Native American literature and culture.

2. Restroom.
3. Aboriginals.

4. Australian wild dog.

In her poetry and in such works as her well-known collection of essays *The Sacred Hoop: Recovering the Feminine in American Indian Traditions* (1986), Allen emphasizes the crucial role of women in Native American tribal traditions and storytelling rituals. While the historial and anthropological evidence for some of her contentions has caused controversy in scholarly circles, her work has been very influential in attracting attention to feminine mythical figures and rituals in Native American culture. Allen's feminist viewpoint emphasizes the conditions of lesbians especially, a perspective that grew out of her own experience of coming out after three marriages and divorces: Her novel *The Woman Who Owned the Shadows* (1983) features a mixed-blood, lesbian protagonist who gradually comes to accept her own racial and sexual identity.

Allen has edited collections of Native American literature, both traditional and contemporary. One of these, *Spider Woman's Granddaughter: Traditional Tales and Contemporary Writing by Native American Women* (1989), won the Before Columbus Foundation American Book Award in 1990. Throughout her career, she has published volumes of poetry such as *Shadow Country* (1982), *Wyrds* (1987), and *Skin and Bones* (1988). As the poems presented here show, Allen not only highlights how women become victims of racial and sexual discrimination but also celebrates the resourcefulness and resilience they have developed in facing their difficult existential condition.

Pocahontas to Her English Husband, John Rolfe[1]

In a way, then, Pocahontas was a kind of traitor to her people. . . .
Perhaps I am being a little too hard on her. The crucial point, it
seems to me, is to remember that Pocahontas was a hostage. Would
she have converted freely to Christianity if she had not been in
captivity? There is no easy answer to this question other than to
note that once she was free to do what she wanted, she avoided her
own people like the plague. . . .
Pocahontas was a white dream—a dream of cultural superiority.

—Charles Larson
American Indian Fiction

Had I not cradled you in my arms,
oh beloved perfidious[2] one,
you would have died.
And how many times did I pluck you
5   from certain death in the wilderness—
my world through which you stumbled
as though blind?
Had I not set you tasks,
your masters far across the sea
10   would have abandoned you—
did abandon you, as many times
they left you

---

1. Pocahontas (c. 1595–1617) was the daughter of Powhatan, a Native American chief, in Virginia at the time of the British colonization. She allegedly saved the life of English Captain John Smith and became an intermediary between Powhatan and the struggling colony at Jamestown. She converted to Christianity and, in 1614, married the successful tobacco planter John Rolfe (1585–1622); their son, Thomas, was born in 1615. In 1616 the family traveled to England, where Pocahontas became very popular in distinguished society and was received at the royal palace in Whitehall. She died in 1617 while preparing to return to America.
2. Treacherous, faithless.

to reap the harvest of their lies.
Still you survived, oh my fair husband,
15   and brought them gold
wrung from a harvest I taught you
to plant. Tobacco.
It is not without irony that by this crop
your descendants die, for other
20   powers than you know
take part in this as in all things.
And indeed I did rescue you—
not once but a thousand thousand times
and in my arms you slept, a foolish child,
25   and under my protecting gaze you played,
chattering nonsense about a God
you had not wit to name. I'm sure
you wondered at my silence, saying I was
a simple wanton, a savage maid,
30   dusky daughter of heathen sires
who cartwheeled naked through the muddy towns
learning the ways of grace only
by your firm guidance, through
your husbandly rule:
35   no doubt, no doubt.
I spoke little, you said.
And you listened less,
but played with your gaudy dreams
and sent ponderous missives to the throne
40   striving thereby to curry favor
with your king.
I saw you well. I
understood your ploys and still
protected you, going so far as to die
45   in your keeping—a wasting,
putrefying Christian death—and you,
deceiver, whiteman, father of my son,
survived, reaping wealth greater
than any you had ever dreamed
50   from what I taught you and
from the wasting of my bones.

Taking a Visitor to See the Ruins

FOR JOE BRUCHAC

He's still telling about the time he came west
and was visiting me. I knew he
wanted to see some of the things

everybody sees when they're in the wilds of New Mexico.
5   So when we'd had our morning coffee
after he'd arrived, I said,

Would you like to go see some old Indian ruins?
His eyes brightened with excitement,
he was thinking, no doubt,

10   of places like the ones he'd known where he came from,
sacred caves filled with falseface masks,
ruins long abandoned, built secure

into the sacred lands; or of pueblos[1]
once home to vanished people but peopled still
15   by their ghosts, connected still with the bone-old land.

Sure, he said. I'd like that a lot.
Come on, I said, and we got in my car,
drove a few blocks east, toward the towering peaks

of the Sandias.[2] We stopped at a tall
20   high-security apartment building made of stone,
went up a walk past the pond and pressed the buzzer.

They answered and we went in,
past the empty pool room, past the empty party room,
up five flights in the elevator, down the abandoned hall.

25   Joe, I said when we'd gotten inside the chic apartment,
I'd like you to meet the old Indian ruins
I promised.

My mother, Mrs. Francis, and my grandmother, Mrs. Gottlieb.[3]
His eyes grew large, and then he laughed
30   looking shocked at the two

women he'd just met. Silent for a second, they laughed too.
And he's still telling the tale of the old
Indian ruins he visited in New Mexico,

the two who still live pueblo style in high-security dwellings
35   way up there where the enemy can't reach them
just like in the olden times.

—✠✦✠—

Leslie Marmon Silko
b. 1948

Leslie Marmon Silko is one of the best-known writers of the Native American Renaissance. Born in New Mexico in 1948 to a family of Laguna, Hispanic, and Anglo-American descent, Leslie Silko grew up on a Laguna Pueblo reservation. She completed a B.A. in English at the University of New Mexico and then briefly enrolled in law school before deciding on a liter-

1. Villages built by the sedentary Native American tribes of the American Southwest. The Pueblo Indians typically constructed multistory dwellings that housed several families. The Laguna, of whose community Allen is a mem-   ber, belong to this group of tribes.
2. A mountain range east of Albuquerque, New Mexico.
3. The names of Paula Gunn Allen's mother and maternal grandmother.

ary career instead. While holding various teaching jobs, she spent two years in Ketchikan, Alaska, where she wrote most of *Ceremony* (1977), a novel that garnered her particularly high praise. *Ceremony* portrays a mixed-blood protagonist who returns as a veteran of World War II only to confront alienation and guilt. His wartime experiences, his mixed cultural origins, and the present-day condition of the Native American community to which he belongs all contribute to his existential crisis, which is symbolic of the broader cultural conflicts often experienced by Native Americans. Silko later published another novel, *Almanac of the Dead* (1991), and several volumes of nonfiction addressing various aspects of contemporary Native American life.

Silko is also an accomplished poet whose lyrical texts blend Native American content with forms that are for the most part derived from modernist Euro-American poetry: free verse, irregular stanzas, and experimentation with the typographical arrangement of printed words. Her early volume of poetry *Laguna Woman* (1974) was particularly successful; in her later work *The Storyteller* (1981), Silko uses prose, free verse, autobiographical material, and photographs in an innovative mix of traditional and contemporary elements. As the title indicates, one of Silko's most insistently recurring concerns is the importance of narrative to cultural identity and continuity and the ways in which oral narrative that springs from a minority culture can perpetuate itself amidst a dominant culture that privileges printed texts and images. Drawing on the Laguna Pueblo tradition, which has been culturally mixed for several centuries, she emphasizes the need for flexible adaptation and ingenuity in the confrontation between different cultures.

from The Storyteller
[THE ARCHEOLOGISTS]

Grandpa Hank had grown up mostly at Paguate
with his Grandma and Grandpa Anaya
although his parents
lived at Laguna.[1]
5   He used to drive an old wagon between Laguna and Paguate
and he used to pretend it was a fancy buggy
one of those light fast buggies.
Later on my great-grandpa bought a buggy
and it was Grandpa Hank's job
10   to drive tourists around the Laguna-Acoma area.
Grandpa Hank said
mostly the tourists came to see Acoma
the "Sky City"[2] which was already famous then.
In 1908 when the Smithsonian Institution
15   excavated the top of *Katsi'ma,* Enchanted Mesa[3]
Grandpa drove some of the archeologists
out there in his buggy.
The archeologists used a small brass cannon
to shoot a line over the top of Enchanted Mesa
20   so they could rig a crude elevator.

---

1. Paguate and Laguna are towns in New Mexico.
2. Acoma pueblo was founded around 1100 C.E., the oldest settlement in the United States that has been continuously inhabited. It is called "Sky City" because it is located atop a high plateau of sandstone that rises about 350 feet above the surrounding valley, at over 7,000 feet above sea level.
3. Enchanted Mesa is a rock monolith several miles east of Acoma pueblo that towers 400 feet above the surrounding landscape. According to legend, its top was once inhabited.

I asked Grandpa
what the archeologists found up there—
I had always been curious about what might be
on top of Enchanted Mesa.
25   "Did they find the bones of that old blind lady
and that baby," I asked him
"You know, the ones they tell about in that old story?"
There is an old story about a blind woman
being stranded on top of enchanted mesa with a tiny baby
30   *the time the sandstone trail to the top collapsed.*

"I didn't see any bones,"
            Grandpa Hank said,
but those Smithsonian people were putting everything
into wooden boxes as fast as they could.
They took everything with them
35   in those wooden boxes
back to Washington D.C."
Then Grandpa said
            "You know
probably all those boxes of things
they took from Enchanted Mesa
40   are still just sitting somewhere
in the basement of some museum."

                    * * *

Toe'osh: A Laguna Coyote Story

FOR SIMON ORTIZ,[4] JULY 1973

In the wintertime
at night
we tell coyote stories
            and drink Spañada[5] by the stove.
5   How coyote got his
ratty old fur coat
            bits of old fur
            the sparrows stuck on him
            with dabs of pitch.
10   That was after he lost his proud original one in a poker game.
Anyhow, things like that
are always happening to him,
that's what he said, anyway.

And it happened to him at Laguna
15   and Chinle
and Lukachukai[6] too, because coyote got too smart for his own good.

---

4. Simon Ortiz is a well-known Native American writer   5. An inexpensive kind of wine.
from the Acoma tribe.   6. Chinle and Likachukai are towns in Arizona.

But the Navajos say he won a contest once.
It was to see who could sleep out in a
snowstorm the longest
20   and coyote waited until chipmunk badger and skunk were all
curled up under the snow
and then he uncovered himself and slept all night
inside
and before morning he got up and went out again
25   and waited until the others got up before he came
in to take the prize.

Some white men came to Acoma and Laguna a hundred years ago
and they fought over Acoma land and Laguna women, and even now
some of their descendants are howling in
30   the hills southeast of Laguna.

Charlie Coyote wanted to be governor
and he said that when he got elected
he would run the other men off
the reservation
35   and keep all the women for himself.

One year
the politicians got fancy
at Laguna.
They went door to door with hams and turkeys
40   and they gave them to anyone who promised
to vote for them.
On election day all the people
stayed home and ate turkey
and laughed.

45   The Trans-Western pipeline vice president came
to discuss right-of-way.
The Lagunas let him wait all day long
because he is a busy and important man.
And late in the afternoon they told him
50   to come back again tomorrow.

They were after the picnic food
that the special dancers left
down below the cliff.
And Toe'osh and his cousins hung themselves
55   down over the cliff
holding each other's tail in their mouth making a coyote chain
until someone in the middle farted
and the guy behind him opened his
mouth to say "What stinks?" and they
60   all went tumbling down, like that.

Howling and roaring
Toe'osh scattered white people

out of bars all over Wisconsin.
He bumped into them at the door
65   until they said
            "Excuse me"
And the way Simon meant it
was for 300 or maybe 400 years.

* * *

[FRANZ BOAS' VISIT]

In 1918 Franz Boas, ethnologist and linguist
passed through Laguna.
His talented protégé
Elsie Clews Parsons
5   stayed behind to collect Laguna texts
from which Boas planned to construct
a grammar of the Laguna language.
Boas, as it turns out
was tone-deaf
10   and the Laguna language is tonal[7]
so it is fortunate he allowed Ms. Parsons
to do the actual collecting of the stories.

Although Boas was never able to construct the Laguna grammar
he did distinguish himself
15   with the languages of Northwest Coast tribes
which are not tonal languages.

In the collection which Parsons made
there is a coyote story
told in Laguna
20   by my great-grandfather.
It is a very simple story
with a little song
which is repeated four times
the meadowlark teasing the she-coyote
25   calling her
            "Coyote long-long-long-long mouth!"
Until Coyote gets so confused and upset
she spits out the water
she was carrying back to her pups.
30   Four times Coyote tries to carry the water back
and four times Meadowlark sings this song
            "Coyote long-long-long-long mouth!"
and Coyote opens her mouth
spilling the water.
35   When she finally gets back to her pups
they are all dead from thirst.

---

7. A tonal language is one in which the same word changes meaning when pronounced with different pitches of voice.

A good deal of controversy surrounded
and still surrounds my great-grandfather and his brother[8]
who both married Laguna women.
40   Ethnologists blame the Marmon brothers
for all kinds of factions and trouble at Laguna
and I am sure much of it is true—
their arrival was bound to complicate
the already complex politics at Laguna.
45   They came on the heels of a Baptist preacher named Gorman
who also must have upset Laguna ceremonialism.

All I know of my great-grandpa Marmon
are the stories my family told
and the old photographs which show him
50   a tall thin old white man
with a white beard
wearing a black suit coat
and derby hat.
He stands with his darker sons
55   and behind the wire-rim glasses he wore
I see in his eyes
he had come to understand this world
differently.
Maybe he chose that particular coyote story
60   to tell Parsons
because for him at Laguna
that was the one thing he had to remember:
          No matter what is said to you by anyone
          you must take care of those most dear to you.

━━━◈━━━

N. Scott Momaday
b. 1934

N. Scott Momaday is considered the most distinguished Native American writer of his generation. His novel *House Made of Dawn* (1968), which won the Pulitzer Prize for Fiction in 1969,
marks the beginning of what literary scholars call the "Native American Renaissance," a
flourishing of Native American literature and art that began in the 1960s. Momaday used sophisticated techniques in integrating materials from the oral traditions of his father's Kiowa
heritage into his fiction and poetry, and his work has influenced a host of younger Native
American writers such as Paula Gunn Allen, Louise Erdrich, and Leslie Marmon Silko. Yet it
would be misguided to understand Momaday only as a Kiowa writer; like several other prominent novelists and poets of the Native American Renaissance, he came to engage Kiowa oral

8. Walter Marmon and his brother Robert, Silko's great-grandfather, came to Laguna from Ohio. During the 1870s, both of
them served as pueblo governors. They were Protestants, and their influence contributed to the destabilization of the combination of Laguna religion and Roman Catholicism that had endured for several centuries. Some sacred sites at Laguna
were destroyed as a consequence.

traditions after intense academic training in literary studies. He was born in Oklahoma in 1934, son of a Kiowa father and a mother of Scottish, French, and Cherokee descent. Due to his parents' teaching positions, Momaday spent much of his youth on Navajo and Pueblo reservations in Arizona and New Mexico. He studied political science at the University of New Mexico at Albuquerque and completed a doctorate in American literature at Stanford University in 1963. He has held teaching positions in California and at the University of Arizona at Tucson.

In his writing, Momaday fuses Native American materials with elements from many other cultures and languages, ranging from mainstream American literature (he met with and was influenced by William Faulkner) to Japanese painting, the French *chanson,* and German Expressionism. In fact, Momaday himself doesn't speak Kiowa: He compiled a collection of Kiowa stories, *The Journey of Tai-me* (1967), with his father's help. The diverse cultural elements he employs are manifest in his *The Names: A Memoir* (1976) and the novel *The Ancient Child* (1989). Momaday's oeuvre also includes volumes of poetry and nature writing, and some of his texts are accompanied by his own drawings and paintings. Since the 1970s, Momaday has also written essays on Native American culture and on environmental issues.

The Way to Rainy Mountain (1969) has sometimes been called Momaday's most innovative work because it fuses different genres in highly original fashion. Each of the text's twenty-four segments includes three elements: Kiowa mythology, historical and anthropological analysis, and autobiographical reflection. Complementing and illuminating each other, these elements offer different perspectives on Kiowa experience and history and result in a text that can't easily be classified as native mythology, novel, autobiography, or history.

from The Way to Rainy Mountain

1

You know, everything had to begin, and this is how it was: the Kiowas came one by one into the world through a hollow log. They were many more than now, but not all of them got out. There was a woman whose body was swollen up with child, and she got stuck in the log. After that, no one could get through, and that is why the Kiowas are a small tribe in number. They looked all around and saw the world. It made them glad to see so many things. They called themselves Kwuda, "coming out."

They called themselves Kwuda and later Tepda, both of which mean "coming out." And later still they took the name Gaigwu, a name which can be taken to indicate something of which the two halves differ from each other in appearance. It was once a custom among Kiowa warriors that they cut their hair on the right side of the head only and on a line level with the lobe of the ear, while on the left they let the hair grow long and wore it in a thick braid wrapped in otter skin. "Kiowa" is indicated in sign language by holding the hand palm up and slightly cupped to the right side of the head and rotating it back and forth from the wrist. "Kiowa" is thought to derive from the softened Comanche form of Gaigwu.

I remember coming out upon the northern Great Plains in the late spring. There were meadows of blue and yellow wildflowers on the slopes, and I could see the still, sunlit plain below, reaching away out of sight. At first there is no discrimination in the eye, nothing but the land itself, whole and impenetrable. But then smallest things begin to stand out of the depths—herds and rivers and groves—and each of these has perfect being in terms of distance and of silence and of age. Yes, I thought, now I see the earth as it really is; never again will I see things as I saw them yesterday or the day before.

2

They were going along, and some were hunting. An antelope was killed and quartered in the meadow. Well, one of the big chiefs came up and took the udders of that animal for himself, but another big chief wanted those udders also, and there was a great quarrel between them. Then, in anger, one of these chiefs gathered all of his followers together and went away. They are called *Azatanhop,* "the udder-angry travelers off." No one knows where they went or what happened to them.

This is one of the oldest memories of the tribe. There have been reports of a people in the Northwest who speak a language that is similar to Kiowa.

In the winter of 1848–49, the buffalo ranged away from easy reach, and food was scarce. There was an antelope drive in the vicinity of Bent's Fort, Colorado. According to ancient custom, antelope medicine was made, and the Kiowas set out on foot and on horse-back—men, women, and children—after game. They formed a great circle, inclosing a large area of the plain, and began to converge upon the center. By this means antelope and other animals were trapped and killed, often with clubs and even with the bare hands. By necessity were the Kiowas reminded of their ancient ways.

One morning on the high plains of Wyoming I saw several pronghorns in the distance. They were moving very slowly at an angle away from me, and they were almost invisible in the tall brown and yellow grass. They ambled along in their own wilderness dimension of time, as if no notion of flight could ever come upon them. But I remembered once having seen a frightened buck on the run, how the white rosette of its rump seemed to hang for the smallest fraction of time at the top of each frantic bound—like a succession of sunbursts against the purple hills.

3

Before there were horses the Kiowas had need of dogs. That was a long time ago, when dogs could talk. There was a man who lived alone; he had been thrown away, and he made his camp here and there on the high ground. Now it was dangerous to be alone, for there were enemies all around. The man spent his arrows hunting food. He had one arrow left, and he shot a bear; but the bear was only wounded and it ran away. The man wondered what to do. Then a dog came up to him and said that many enemies were coming; they were close by and all around. The man could think of no way to save himself. But the dog said: "You know, I have puppies. They are young and weak and they have nothing to eat. If you will take care of my puppies, I will show you how to get away." The dog led the man here and there, around and around, and they came to safety.

A hundred years ago the Comanche Ten Bears remarked upon the great number of horses which the Kiowas owned. "When we first knew you," he said, "you had nothing but dogs and sleds." It was so; the dog is primordial. Perhaps it was dreamed into being.

The principal warrior society of the Kiowas was the Ka-itsenko, "Real Dogs," and it was made up of ten men only, the ten most brave. Each of these men wore a long ceremonial sash and carried a sacred arrow. In time of battle he must by means of this arrow impale the end of his sash to the earth and stand his ground to the death. Tradition has it that the founder of the Ka-itsenko had a dream in which he saw a band of warriors, outfitted after the fashion of the society, being led by a dog. The dog sang the song of the Ka-itsenko, then said to the dreamer: "You are a dog; make a noise like a dog and sing a dog song."

There were always dogs about my grandmother's house. Some of them were nameless and lived a life of their own. They belonged there in a sense that the word "ownership" does not include. The old people paid them scarcely any attention, but they should have been sad, I think, to see them go.

11

A long time ago there were two brothers. It was winter, and the buffalo had wandered far away. Food was very scarce. The two brothers were hungry, and they wondered what to do. One of them got up in the early morning and went out, and he found a lot of fresh meat there on the ground in front of the tipi. He was very happy, and he called his brother outside. "Look," he said. "Something very good has happened, and we have plenty of food." But his brother was afraid and said: "This is too strange a thing. I believe that we had better not eat that meat." But the first brother scolded him and said that he was foolish. Then he went ahead and ate of the meat all by himself. In a little while something awful happened to him; he began to change. When it was all over, he was no longer a man; he was some kind of water beast with little short legs and a long, heavy tail. Then he spoke to his brother and said: "You were right, and you must not eat of that meat. Now I must go and live in the water, but we are brothers, and you ought to come and see me now and then." After that the man went down to the water's edge, sometimes, and called his brother out. He told him how things were with the Kiowas.

During the peyote ritual[1] a fire is kept burning in the center of the tipi, inclosed within a crescent-shaped altar. On top of the altar there is a single, sacred peyote. After the chief priest utters the opening prayer, four peyotes are given to each celebrant, who eats them one after another. Then, in turn, each man sings four sacred songs, and all the while there is the sound of the rattle and the drum—and the fitful, many-colored glare of the fire. The songs go on all through the night, broken only by intervals of prayer, additional distributions of peyote, and, at midnight, a peculiar baptismal ceremony.

Mammedaty was a peyote man, and he was therefore distinguished by these things: a necklace of beans, a beaded staff and rattle, an eagle-bone whistle, and a fan made from the feathers of a water bird. He saw things that other men do not see. Once a heavy rain caused the Washita River to overflow and Rainy Mountain Creek to swell and "back up." Mammedaty went to the creek, near the crossing, to swim. And while he was there, the water began strangely to move against him, slowly at first, then fast, in high, hard waves. There was some awful commotion beneath the surface, and Mammedaty got out of the water and ran away. Later he went back to that place. There was a wide swath in the brush of the bank and the tracks of a huge animal, leading down to the water's edge.

17

Bad women are thrown away. Once there was a handsome young man. He was wild and reckless, and the chief talked to the wind about him. After that, the man went hunting. A great whirlwind passed by, and he was blind. The Kiowas have no need of

---

1. Peyote, or mescal, is a cactus commonly found in the southwestern United States and Mexico; with its strong hallucinogenic effects, it plays an important role in Native American ritual in the Southwest.

a blind man; they left him alone with his wife and child. The winter was coming on and food was scarce. In four days the man's wife grew tired of caring for him. A herd of buffalo came near, and the man knew the sound. He asked his wife to hand him a bow and an arrow. "You must tell me," he said, "when the buffalo are directly in front of me." And in that way he killed a bull, but his wife said that he had missed. He asked for another arrow and killed another bull, but again his wife said that he had missed. Now the man was a hunter, and he knew the sound an arrow makes when it strikes home, but he said nothing. Then his wife helped herself to the meat and ran away with her child. The man was blind; he ate grass and kept himself alive. In seven days a band of Kiowas found him and took him to their camp. There in the firelight a woman was telling a story. She told of how her husband had been killed by enemy warriors. The blind man listened, and he knew her voice. That was a bad woman. At sunrise they threw her away.

In the Kiowa calendars there is graphic proof that the lives of women were hard, whether they were "bad women" or not. Only the captives, who were slaves, held lower status. During the Sun Dance² of 1843, a man stabbed his wife in the breast because she accepted Chief Dohasan's invitation to ride with him in the ceremonial procession. And in the winter of 1851–52, Big Bow stole the wife of a man who was away on a raiding expedition. He brought her to his father's camp and made her wait outside in the bitter cold while he went in to collect his things. But his father knew what was going on, and he held Big Bow and would not let him go. The woman was made to wait in the snow until her feet were frozen.

Mammedaty's grandmother, Kau-au-ointy, was a Mexican captive, taken from her homeland when she was a child of eight or ten years. I never knew her, but I have been to her grave at Rainy Mountain.

KAU-AU-OINTY
BORN 1834
DIED 1929
AT REST

She raised a lot of eyebrows, they say, for she would not play the part of a Kiowa woman. From slavery she rose up to become a figure in the tribe. She owned a great herd of cattle, and she could ride as well as any man. She had blue eyes.

19

On a raid against the Utes,³ one of two brothers was captured. The other, alone and of his own will, stole into the Ute camp and tried to set his brother free, but he too was captured. The chief of the Utes had respect for the man's bravery, and he made a bargain with him. If he could carry his brother on his back and walk upon a row of greased buffalo heads without falling to the ground, both brothers would be given horses and allowed to return in safety to their home. The man bore his brother on his back and walked upon the heads of the buffalo and kept his footing. The Ute chief was true to his word, and the brothers returned to their own people on horseback.

---

2. A common summer ritual among Native American tribes of the plains, during which men danced for several nights. The last Kiowa Sun Dance was held in 1887.

3. A Native American tribe whose territory once covered parts of Colorado, Utah, Arizona, and northern Mexico.

After the fight at Palo Duro Canyon, the Kiowas came in, a few at a time, to surrender at Fort Sill.[4] Their horses and weapons were confiscated, and they were imprisoned. In a field just west of the post, the Indian ponies were destroyed. Nearly 800 horses were killed outright; two thousand more were sold, stolen, given away.

SUMMER 1879

Tsen-pia Kado, "Horse-eating sun dance." It is indicated on the Set-tan calendar[5] by the figure of a horse's head above the medicine lodge. This dance was held on Elm Fork of Red River, and was so called because the buffalo had now become so scarce that the Kiowa, who had gone on their regular hunt the preceding winter, had found so few that they were obliged to kill and eat their ponies during the summer to save themselves from starving. This may be recorded as the date of the disappearance of the buffalo from the Kiowa country. Thenceforth the appearance of even a single animal was a rare event.—Mooney[6]

In New Mexico the land is made of many colors. When I was a boy I rode out over the red and yellow and purple earth to the west of Jemez Pueblo.[7] My horse was a small red roan,[8] fast and easy-riding. I rode among the dunes, along the bases of mesas[9] and cliffs, into canyons and arroyos.[1] I came to know that country, not in the way a traveler knows the landmarks he sees in the distance, but more truly and intimately, in every season, from a thousand points of view. I know the living motion of a horse and the sound of hooves. I know what it is, on a hot day in August or September, to ride into a bank of cold, fresh rain.

21

Mammedaty was the grandson of Guipahgo,[2] and he was well-known on that account. Now and then Mammedaty drove a team and wagon out over the plain. Once, in the early morning, he was on the way to Rainy Mountain. It was summer and the grass was high and meadowlarks were calling all around. You know, the top of the plain is smooth and you can see a long way. There was nothing but the early morning and the land around. Then Mammedaty heard something. Someone whistled to him. He looked up and saw the head of a little boy nearby above the grass. He stopped the horses and got down from the wagon and went to see who was there. There was no one; there was nothing there. He looked for a long time, but there was nothing there.

There is a single photograph of Mammedaty. He is looking past the camera and a little to one side. In his face there is calm and good will, strength and intelligence. His hair is drawn close to the scalp, and his braids are long and wrapped with fur. He wears a kilt, fringed leggings, and beaded moccasins. In his right hand there is a peyote fan. A family characteristic: the veins stand out in his hands, and his hands are small and rather long.

---

4. Allusion to an important battle in the Red River War in Texas in the fall of 1874, which broke down the resistance of the Southern Plains Indians and led to their confinement in reservations. Most of the Kiowa surrendered in February 1875.

5. One of several pictographic calendars kept by the Kiowa, in which the Sun Dance ceremony served as an important reference point for the summer.

6. James Mooney, an anthropologist from the Smithsonian's Bureau of American Ethnology, lived and conducted research on a Kiowa reservation during the 1890s and early 1900s; he published groundbreaking studies of Kiowa culture.

7. Jemez Pueblo in New Mexico is one of the places where Momaday's parents taught in the 1940s.

8. A horse with a bay-colored coat mixed with white hair.

9. High plateaus.

1. Ravines.

2. The Native American name of Lone Wolf, a Kiowa chief who played a crucial role during the transition to reservation life that was forced upon the Kiowas in the 1870s.

Mammedaty saw four things that were truly remarkable. This head of the child was one, and the tracks of the water beast another. Once, when he walked near the pecan grove, he saw three small alligators on a log. No one had ever seen them before and no one ever saw them again. Finally, there was this: something had always bothered Mammedaty, a small aggravation that was never quite out of mind, like a name on the tip of the tongue. He had always wondered how it is that the mound of earth which a mole makes around the opening of its burrow is so fine. It is nearly as fine as powder, and it seems almost to have been sifted. One day Mammedaty was sitting quietly when a mole came out of the earth. Its cheeks were puffed out as if it had been a squirrel packing nuts. It looked all around for a moment, then blew the fine dark earth out of its mouth. And this it did again and again, until there was a ring of black, powdery earth on the ground. That was a strange and meaningful thing to see. It meant that Mammedaty had got possession of a powerful medicine.

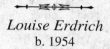

Louise Erdrich
b. 1954

Karen Louise Erdrich, an American novelist and poet of mixed European and Chippewa descent, grew up in North Dakota near the reservation of the Chippewa Turtle Mountain Band, of which she is an enrolled member. Erdrich is most famous for her fiction, which usually describes the interconnected lives of partly Native American and partly white families in the Minnesota–North Dakota region. Her novels *Love Medicine* (1984), *The Beet Queen* (1986), *Tracks* (1988), and *The Bingo Palace* (1994) all share some characters and family background in their exploration of different lives and generations, as well as central themes such as the relationship between biological and affective parentage. Erdrich's gradual expansion and reworking of this fictional family network as well as her expert handling of narrative point of view have often been compared to William Faulkner's portrayal of an imaginary county in the South of the United States. Several of her novels and short stories have won prestigious literary prizes. Erdrich has also published two volumes of poetry, *Jacklight* (1984) and *Baptism of Desire* (1989). "Dear John Wayne" approaches the relationship between Native American and white culture through the role of media—in particular the popular film genre of the Western—in disseminating a certain view of American history. She explores the impact this view might have on the current condition of Native Americans in the United States and how Native Americans themselves approach this portrayal of history.

Dear John Wayne

August and the drive-in picture is packed.
We lounge on the hood of the Pontiac
surrounded by the slow-burning spirals they sell
at the window, to vanquish the hordes of mosquitoes.
5   Nothing works. They break through the smoke screen for blood.

Always the lookout spots the Indians first,
spread north to south, barring progress.
The Sioux or some other Plains bunch
in spectacular columns, ICBM missiles,[1]
10   feathers bristling in the meaningful sunset.

---

1. Intercontinental Ballistic Missile, a rocket designed to hit remote targets.

Grey Cohoe (Navajo, 1944–1991), *Battle of the Butterflies at Tocito,* 1984. Navajo
artist Grey Cohoe combines elements of surrealism, pop art, and the Western in his
Battle of the Butterflies at Tocito. The painting shows a John-Wayne style cowboy figure whose right eye, "the one closest to the Native American figures," is replaced by a
cloudy blur of white color. The dark figures of the Native Americans, lacking faces or
other physical details, reinforce the sense of their invisibility that this non-eye conveys. At the same time, the pop-art-colored marbles in the foreground are juxtaposed
with a shrill explosion of color on the right that seems to tear apart their self-contained
beauty. The immobility of the four male figures in juxtaposition with these images of
childhood treasure and violence convey a sense of foreboding: Tocito, Cohoe's birth-
place in New Mexico, seems barely contained on the brink of a cultural violence that
is for the moment forestalled only by a complete lack of communication.

The drum breaks. There will be no parlance.
Only the arrows whining, a death-cloud of nerves
swarming down on the settlers
who die beautifully, tumbling like dust weeds
15   into the history that brought us all here
together: this wide screen beneath the sign of the bear.

The sky fills, acres of blue squint and eye
that the crowd cheers. His face moves over us,
a thick cloud of vengeance, pitted
20 like the land that was once flesh. Each rut,
each scar makes a promise: *It is
not over, this fight, not as long as you resist.*

Everything we see belongs to us.

A few laughing Indians fall over the hood
25 slipping in the hot spilled butter.
The eye sees a lot, John, but the heart is so blind.
Death makes us owners of nothing.
He smiles, a horizon of teeth
the credits reel over, and then the white fields
30 again blowing in the true-to-life dark.
The dark films over everything.
We get into the car
scratching our mosquito bites, speechless and small
as people are when the movie is done.
35 We are back in our skins.

How can we help but keep hearing his voice,
the flip side of the sound track, still playing:
Come on, boys, we got them
where we want them, drunk, running.
40 *They'll give us what we want, what we need.*
Even his disease was the idea of taking everything.[2]
Those cells, burning, doubling, splitting out of their skins.

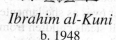

Ibrahim al-Kuni
b. 1948

Ibrahim al-Kuni is arguably the most interesting novelist and short-story writer to emerge from the Arab countries of the Maghrib (North Africa) in the last forty years. He was born in Ghadamis in the Libyan Desert to a Tuareg nomadic family. After completing his primary and secondary education in Libya, he demonstrated an early literary talent and started publishing articles and short stories in Libyan newspapers and weeklies. He established himself very quickly as one of the rising literary stars in Libya and won a scholarship to study literature at the famous Gorky Institute for Literature in Moscow, from which he graduated in 1976. Although he published many stories and two books of essays before going to Moscow, it was during his study of literature there that he found his unique style and discovered the magical reservoir of stories in his culture and memory waiting to be tapped.

Upon his return from Russia he embarked on an ambitious literary project, to write the world of the Tuareg into the forms of the modern novel and the short story. Al-Kuni isn't

2. The actor John Wayne, famous for dozens of Westerns in which he usually played the typical hero of the American frontier, died of cancer in 1979.

unique as a Tuareg literary figure writing in Arabic, for there have been several, but the majority of them are religious scholars specializing in Islamic thought and Qur'anic exegesis. There are also a number of poets writing in one or another of the Tuareg languages or dialects. But al-Kuni's uniqueness springs from the fact that he chose the modern narrative genres.

In works such as *The Oasis* (1984) and *The Stone Goddess* (1992) he portrays the desert differently than his predecessors, for he neither posits it as an alternative to modernity nor treats it with romanticism and nostalgia as a lost paradise. He puts it, for the first time, on the cognitive map of Arab interest, as a fecund world of human experience that provides Arab culture with an added dimension. He presents the desert as a felicitous space: open and intimate, yet mysterious, dangerous, and unknown. Its rich and autonomous world has integrity, inner cohesion, and vitality, neither dependent on its modern counterpart nor viable only as a bygone archetypal world. Its sophisticated ecological system and its universe of integrated yet conflicting races and cultures endow it with a cosmic dimension. By opening up the world of the desert, al-Kuni has provided Arabic literature with a dimension of magic realism in some ways similar to that in Latin American fiction. His novels and short stories of the Tuareg desert confirm the vitality of freedom and the cosmic harmony of the desert life and its alluring charm, as shown in the story selected here.

PRONUNCIATION:
   Ibrahim al-Kuni: EE-bra-HEEM al-KOU-nee

The Golden Bird of Misfortune[1]

> *Abdullah worshiped for four hundred years, then occupied himself*
> *with the singing of a bird on a tree in the garden of his house. He*
> *was repaid for this by God ceasing to love him.*
>
> Farid al-Din al-'Attar al-Nisaburi's
> *The Conference of the Birds*[2]

No sooner had it alighted on a scraggy wild bush than, standing bolt upright in front of the tent, she saw the poor child staring at its fabulously bright feathers. Like someone stung, she leapt up and hurled herself at the boy, encircling him with her arms. The tears coursed down from her eyes as she lamented, "No, no, don't look at it like that! It's a delusion. It's a trick. It steals children from their mothers."

But the child was able to detach himself from his mother's embrace with the litheness of a snake and to follow the extraordinary colored bird with the golden wings, the like of which he had never previously seen. He walked toward it fascinated.

The golden bird did not move, did not heed his approach. It waited for him until he was standing in front of it. The child stretched out his hand until it was almost touching the bird's feathers, which glowed under the rays of dusk, then it adroitly flew down and moved a couple of paces beyond the reach of his hand. The mesmerized child advanced farther, almost grasping hold of it. Again it evaded his hand and ran a few more steps. The child was breathless with curiosity and longing, and the extraordinary bird prepared itself for a long chase.

The mother wailed. "Woe is me! Now the chase has begun. Did I not tell you that it is a bird of ill-omen? It lures away children and draws them into the desert. Come back, child! Come back!"

---

1. Translated by Denys Johnson-Davies.
2. A famous poetic narrative by the Persian poet Farid al-Din al-'Attar (1145–1221), in which a group of birds journey in search of a mythical bird, the Simorgh, whom they want to have as their king.

The boy did not come back. He rushed off behind the golden messenger of enticement, which moved coquettishly, flirtatiously, as it made its escape. The child rushed after it, breathing hard, baffled by his desire to grasp it, to take possession of it. On that day his mother rescued him. Running behind them, she caught hold of him and forcibly took him back.

Night fell and darkness reigned. The father returned and she informed him in alarm of what had occurred. He declared with peremptory roughness, "If the bird comes back, shut the boy in. Tie him to a rope and fasten it to that peg."

The bird did not return on the following day, nor for several days after. It then seized the opportunity of the father being away and the mother having gone to visit a friend in the neighboring hamlet, and it advanced upon its confused victim. In the late afternoon it led him on, crossed with him the southern plains, traversing hills and valleys in an astounding chase. The wonderful golden bird would wait proudly until the child reached it and was about to grasp hold of it, when it would slip away, gracefully move off a pace or two, or three at the most, and then stand waiting as it turned to right and left. Sometimes it would direct toward the child an enigmatic look from its small, slyly lustrous eyes and spread its brilliant wings in womanly enticement until the child drew close and was bending over it, certain that this time he would grab hold of it, when it would again slip away with astonishing agility and forge ahead.

The chase continued.

Darkness advanced and finally covered the everlasting desert, and the bird disappeared.

The child found himself soiled with sweat, urine, and fatigue. He collapsed under a bush and fell asleep. At night he was woken by the howling of wolves and heard the conversation of the djinn in the open air. He recited the Chapter of Unity,[3] which he had learned from his mother, as he watched the stars scattered in the darkness of the skies. The stars entertained him with their secret language, speaking to him of things he did not understand. Finally, he became sleepy again.

In the morning, he wandered for a long time in the desolate waste before they found him in a small wadi, lying under a sparse genista shrub with bloodied feet and cracked lips, exhausted and shattered by fatigue.

After the father had forced her to cease her long weeping and she was able to hold back her tears, the mother said that night, "Have you seen what the bird of ill-omen has done to you? It's Satan. Do you not understand?" She shook him violently as, driven by what had happened, she repeated, "It steals children from their mothers. It's Satan—the accursed Satan."

The father stopped her with a brusque movement, and she went back to her sobbing. They were gathered around the stove before repairing to sleep. The boy fell asleep as he sat there.

They had been blessed with him after they had despaired.

They had made the rounds of all the quacks, sorcerers, and holy men known in the oases of the desert until they had despaired of compassion. Talismans had been of no use, nor had amulets. She had procured the rarest of herbs and people had brought her, from the central parts of the continent,[4] preparations made from snake poisons and the brains of wild beasts.

---

3. A short chapter of the Qur'an used to ward off Satan and evil.

4. A reference to sub-Saharan Africa, where magic, or black magic, is famed for its potency.

When they were close to the climacteric, they had been taken to the frightening Magian fortune-teller, who had become famous through dealing with the heathen company of the djinn in the oasis of Adrar.

Had they not sought him out in the plains of faraway Red Hammada[5] he would not have deigned to meet them. The Magian fortune-teller had ceased to receive people and had gone into isolation a long time ago after a continuous series of battles and encounters organized by the Mustansir dervishes against the companies of believing djinn, who had taken possession of the last of the strongholds of wisdom in the desert, claiming that it was armed with talismans and amulets inspired by texts from the Quran. The group announced that the age of idols had come to an end and that the Magian's profession was an abomination, an act of Satan, so he had suffered persecution and was forced to cease practicing his readings that possessed understanding of the darkness and the unknown. He was likewise shunned by people through fear of the violence of the newly converted groups, so the leading pagan fortune-teller found himself isolated and besieged. He sought refuge in a cave in the mountain of Adrar and lived with his followers, in hiding from the arrogant, unbelieving djinn, who vie in breaking open talismans and sometimes in exchanging insulting names among themselves. Often people heard the eminent fortune-teller guffawing in his cave at the jokes of his loyal followers who had applied themselves tirelessly to keeping him amused so as to ease his loneliness.

He received the two of them at the entrance to the desolate cave that had been hacked out of the mountain top. He addressed them in Hausa.[6] On realizing that they did not understand it, he condescended to talk to them in the Tuareg tongue of Tamahaq.[7] As for the language of the Quran, he uttered not a word of it, and they knew that he was doing this in outrage at the Isawi dervishes, who had swept away his glory in the oasis. His complexion was tanned despite his isolation within the darkness of the cave. He was dressed from tip to toe in black, so that in the darkness he looked like a djinn from the company of unbelievers.

The people of the oasis had come to tremble at his followers, saying that the djinn had become hostile in their behavior ever since the dervishes had entered the Sufi orders and the assemblage of djinn had split into two companies: one that followed the true religion and believed in the dervishes, and one that had remained as they were—unbelieving, idolatrous, and following the fearsome Magian fortune-teller.

Perhaps it was such reports that affected the woman and caused her to tremble at merely seeing this idol sent from the homeland of caves and darkness.

He slaughtered a white chicken at her bare feet and stained her body with blood. He handled her rounded buttocks and toyed with her swelling breasts as he muttered the talismans of ancient idols and tilled her body with his rough fingers daubed with the blood of the snow-white chicken.

The husband followed these rites in a daze. The fortune-teller warned him against uttering any Quranic verses or traditions of the prophets before beginning his pagan recitations in the language of the Hausa and the djinn. He had said, "My helpers do not like that—Quranic verses and biographies of the messengers and prophets are forbidden in my house!"

---

5. The southern part of the Libyan Sahara.
6. The African language of the inhabitants of northern Nigeria.
7. The language of the Tuareg who live in the Libyan

Desert of the Red Hammada. It is also the mother tongue of the writer, who didn't learn Arabic, the language of the Qur'an, until he was nine years old.

Then he scattered a powder like incense in the stove. Clouds of evil-smelling vapor rose up. The woman experienced vertigo, while her husband had a sensation of nausea. Then the bronzed Magian again fingered her body, staining it with the remnants of the blood. Finally he said, "We have finished the first stage. Tomorrow you will go with me and I shall show you the tomb in whose presence you must both sleep for three consecutive nights."

After mumbling some cryptic incantations, he concluded by saying, "It is the oldest grave in the desert. It is the oldest grave in the world—the tomb of tombs and the goal of the universe, a goal before people knew of the goal of the dervishes and the beaters on tambourines."

The tomb was a heap of black stones clinging to the foot of the mountain, below the gloomy cave. The first night passed calmly, and the second, and on the third night she saw her shameful dream, which bashfulness prevented her from recounting to her husband. She saw herself being given in marriage to the King of the Djinn. He penetrated her, unusually, in the morning and made her taste such an experience that she still reels at the memory of its frenzy. The frightening king had used her as no human man had ever used a woman. The two of them crossed the vast wadi, making their way on the stones, and she could not free herself of his blazingly feverish body.

She hid the great secret from her husband without knowing that he too had hidden his secret from her, for on that final night she was groaning and twisting and giving vent to her pain from her excessive, agonized pleasure. Neither of them was able to look the other in the eye for the space of several whole months. The fortune-teller had bestowed on them a pagan spell for the awaited heir apparent and he refused to take payment for his rites.

A few weeks later he saw that she had cravings for certain foods and was devouring white mud.

No sooner was the boy born than she quickly hung the spell round his neck, after securing it in a wrapping of leather and decorating it with magical mosaic colors. When the charm was lost, a year ago on one of their journeys across the desert, the woman was distraught, but the stupid husband calmed her down by saying that he would arrange for her to have a spell from a holy man at the neighboring hamlet, not knowing that the spells of holy men do not replace the charms of the pagan fortune-teller. As soon as the bird of ill-omen came the poor mother remembered her lost charm.

She felt distress and portents of evil.

The golden bird is the messenger of Satan to entice children and steal them away from their mothers. The old women in the desert say that it appears only rarely but when it does, many victims will fall to it, for its appearance is linked to drought and lean years. The old wise women in the deserts of Timbuktu[8] confirm that the secret of its evil omen lies in its golden feathers. Thus, wheresoever the sparkle of the devilish gold flashes, ill-luck makes its appearance, blood flows, and the accursed Satan is at work.

Today the bird has again made its appearance and has lured the wretched boy to his destruction, the mother unaware, for she has gone to the nearby hamlet to borrow a full waterskin.

---

8. The Tuareg land in southern Libya and Northern Mali and Chad.

In the days following its first appearance, precautions were taken. She carried out her husband's order by tying the boy to a peg with rough fiber threads, and she never went out to the pasture or to visit women neighbors in the nearby plains without making sure that the fetters around the bleeding leg of the child were firmly secured. He cried when she was away and would try to escape from the cruel shackle, for the rough rope had carved a bloody collar around his young leg. Secretly at night in her bed, she felt pity for him, but would go back in the morning to secure the rope in her fear for him.

But time is the bane of the memory, the temptation of extinction and forgetfulness. Weeks passed and she grew complacent and relaxed her vigilance. Going away to borrow water, she left the boy loose in the house. The ill-omened bird came after she had gone and abducted the child.

He pursued it in the plains and the wadis; he ascended the heights and went down the hills. The pursuit continued into the late afternoon, and when the time for siesta came the child collapsed, his face set in the dust, panting for breath. The cruel sun was seated on its throne; its rays were released from their hiding-place and burnt the boy with their fire. His tender feet were dyed with blood, his lips were dry, his throat parched of the last drop of saliva.

The bird did not vanish until that moment. It witnessed the shudderings and tremblings of the child, at which it alighted on a wild bush with faded branches and started to spread its fabulous wings and preen them with its amazing beak.

The child regained consciousness before dusk and continued the chase, crawling on hands and knees over the savage stones. He did not turn his gaze to his bleeding limbs and had no sensation of his flesh being lacerated as the stones mangled it, strewing blood on the rocks.

They found the rotting body on the following day under a solitary and desolate lotus tree.

Through the days and nights she wept for him. She mourned him to the desert, the vastness, the wild trees, and the sacred crane. She did not cease moaning until the man took her on a journey to the cave of the fearsome Magian fortune-teller, craving to obtain another boy. There they told her that the detestable fortune-teller had died, and they expressed pride that Adrar had been cleansed for evermore of the filth of idols, but she went to the foot of the mountain where the oldest grave in the world had been erected, and there she lamented as she repeated her misfortune. "Why did You give him to me if You wanted to take him from me? Why?"

The Isawi dervishes answered her question as they swayed ecstatically, beating on tambourines and raising their voices in Sufi panegyrics about divine love, there at the foot of the mountain. "He takes only from those He has liked, and He gives only to those He has loved."[9]

⇥ END OF PERSPECTIVES: INDIGENOUS CULTURES IN THE TWENTIETH CENTURY ⇤

---

9. The final words of the story are a Sufi chant, giving the story a cosmic significance.

Zhang Ailing (Eileen Chang)
1920–1995

A native of Shanghai, Zhang Ailing was born into a distinguished family of statesmen and scholars. She studied at the University of Hong Kong until 1941, when the bombing of Pearl Harbor sent her back to Shanghai. There she embarked on a literary career that was marked by the publication of numerous short stories, essays, and four novels, written in both Chinese and English (using "Eileen" as a Western equivalent for her Chinese name). Having left China for Hong Kong in 1952, she moved to the United States in 1955, where her reclusive life made her known as the "Garbo of Chinese letters." She has been much admired for her contributions to the development of a modern Chinese written vernacular and for a style whose irony and colloquialism captured contemporary urban life in China in all of its frustrations. Written in English, her story "Stale Mates," given here, explores the uncertain situation of young lovers caught between old and new ways of life

PRONUNCIATIONS:
> *Zhang Ailing:* JAHNG eye-LING
> *Zhou:* Joe
> *Zhu:* JOO

Stale Mates

Two men and two girls in a boat sat facing each other on wicker seats under the flat blue awning. Cups of tea stood on the low table between them. They were eating *ling,* water chestnuts about the size and shape of a Cupid's-bow mouth. The shells were dark purplish red and the kernels white.

"*Missu* Zhou is very stylish today," one of the men said. It was also stylish to address girls as "Miss."

Miss Zhou glared at him through her new spectacles and threw a *ling* shell at him. Her glasses had round black rims and perfectly flat lenses, as she was not near-sighted. The year was 1924, when eyeglasses were fashionable. Society girls wore them. Even streetwalkers affected glasses in order to look like girl students.

Each of the men sat with his own girl because the little boat balanced better this way than if the two girls sat side by side. The pale green water looked thick and just a little scummy, and yet had a suggestion of lingering fragrance like a basin of water in which a famous courtesan had washed her painted face.

The girls were around twenty—young for high school in those days when progressive women of all ages flocked to the primary schools. Miss Zhou was much admired for her vivacity and boldness as being typical of the New Woman, while Miss Fan's was the beauty of a still life. She sat smiling a little, her face a slim pointed oval, her long hair done in two round glossy black side knobs. She wore little makeup and no ornaments except a gold fountain pen tucked in her light mauve tunic. Her trumpet sleeves ended flaring just under the elbow.

The young men were Luo and Wen. Luo was tall and thin. His pale turquoise long gown hung well on him in a more literal sense than when the phrase was applied to Westerner's clothes. He taught in the same school as Wen. They both owned land in their home village and taught school in Hangzhou merely as an excuse to live by the West Lake, where every scenic spot was associated with the memory of some poet or reigning beauty.

The four had been meeting almost daily for more than a year. They would go out on the lake, have dinner at one of the restaurants along the shore, and go boating again if there was a moon. Somebody would read Shelley aloud and the girls held hands with each other when they felt moved. Always there were four of them, sometimes six but never two. The men were already married—a universal predicament. Practically everybody was married and had children before ever hearing of love. Wen and Luo had to be content with discussing the girls interminably between themselves, showing each other the girls' carefully worded letters, admiring their calligraphy, analyzing their personalities from the handwriting. Love was such a new experience in China that a little of it went a long way.

They sailed into a patch of yellowing lotus leaves, the large green plates crunching noisily against the boat. Then there was silence. The boatman and his little daughter were resting on their oars, letting the boat drift. Now and then the water made a small swallowing sound as if it had a piece of candy in its mouth.

"Going home this weekend?" Miss Fan asked.

"I suppose I can't get out of it this time," Luo answered smiling. "My mother has been complaining."

She smiled. The mention of his mother did not alter the fact that he was going back to his wife.

Lately Luo had been feeling increasingly guilty about going home, while Miss Fan had allowed her resentment to become more manifest before and after each visit.

"I have made a decision," he said in a low voice, looking at her. Then, when she did not ask him what it was, he said, "Missu Fan, will you wait for me? It might take years."

She had turned away, her head bent. Her hands played with the lower left corner of her slitted blouse, furling and unfurling it.

Actually she did not agree to his getting a divorce until days later. But that evening, when the four of them dined at a restaurant famous for its lake fish, Luo already felt pledged and dedicated. All the wine he drank tasted like the last cup before setting out on a long hard journey on a cold night.

The restaurant was called the Tower Beyond Towers. It leaned over the lake on three sides. Despite the view and its poetic name it was a nonchalantly ugly place with greasy old furniture. The waiter shouted orders to the kitchen in a singsong chant. When the glass dome was lifted from the plate of live shrimp, some of the shrimp jumped across the table, in and out of the sauce dish, and landed on Miss Fan, trailing soya sauce down the front of her blouse. Miss Zhou squealed. In the dingy yellow electric light Miss Fan looked flushed and happy and did not seem to mind at all.

Luo did not go home until the Saturday after that. The journey took two hours by train and wheelbarrow. His wife looked sheepish as her mother-in-law loudly and ostentatiously excused her from various duties because her husband was home. She was wearing a short blue overall with the red satin binding of a silk tunic showing underneath it. She had not been sure that he would be coming.

He spoke to her that night about divorce. She cried all night. It was terrible, almost as if a judge were to sleep in the same bed with a condemned man. Say what he might, he knew he was consigning her to dishonourable widowhood for the rest of her life.

"Which of the Seven Out Rules have I violated?" she kept asking through angry sobs. Ancient scholars had named the seven conditions under which a wife might justifiably be evicted from her husband's house.

His mother flew into a rage on being told. She would not hear of it. Luo went back to Hangzhou and stopped coming home altogether. His mother got his uncle to go up to Hangzhou and talk him out of his foolishness. He in turn managed to persuade a cousin to go and talk to his family. It took infernally long to negotiate through relatives who were, furthermore, unreliable transmitters of harsh words, being peacemakers at heart, especially where matrimony was concerned. To break up a marriage is a cardinal sin that automatically takes ten years off a man's given life span.

Luo got a lawyer to write his wife an alarmingly worded request for divorce. His wife's family, the Zhangs, boiled over with rage. Did he think his wife was an orphan? Not all the Zhangs were dead. True, they could not revenge themselves on the faithless man unless his wife were to hang herself on his lintel. That would place his life and property entirely at their mercy. But it was not for them to recommend such a step to her.

The head of the Luo clan was moved to speak. The old man threatened to invite the Family Law out of its niche and beat the young rascal in the ancestral temple. "Family Law" was a euphemism for the plank used for flogging.

Miss Fan and Luo continued to see each other in the company of Wen and Miss Zhou. Their friends were delighted and exhilarated by the courage of this undertaking—though it did put Wen in a difficult position, even if Miss Zhou was never openly reproachful. It now appeared as though the wistfulness that was part of the beauty of their relationship was not one of those things that couldn't be helped.

Luo was only home once in two years. They were difficult years for both the mother and daughter-in-law. They began to get on each other's nerves. There was an unwritten law that a wife could never be divorced once she had worn mourning white and the ramie scarf of mourning for a parent-in-law. So the old lady got the idea that her daughter-in-law wished for her death. It would certainly settle the divorce problem. But the old lady swore she would see the younger woman out of the house vertically before she made her own exit horizontally.

Outwardly the divorce negotiations had not gained much ground in six years. Miss Fan's family never did approve. Now they kept reminding her that at twenty-six she was becoming an old maid. Soon she would not even qualify for *tianfang*—room filler, a wife to fill up a widower's empty room. It seemed to her family that Luo was only waiting to have her on his own terms. It was doubtful whether he was seriously trying to get a divorce. Possibly alimony was the stumbling block. There were those who said he was actually quite poor. What little he had must have dwindled away through his long absence from home, with his estate left in the hands of an estranged wife. There had been some unpleasantness over the divorce question at the school where he was teaching. If he didn't depend on his job for a living, why didn't he resign?

Miss Zhou told Wen confidentially that Miss Fan had been out to dinner with a pawnbroker, chaperoned by members of her family and a lady matchmaker. Wen was not to tell Luo.

In his indignation Wen told Luo anyway, though of course he added, "It's all her family's doing."

"They didn't tie her up with a rope and drag her to the restaurant, did they?" Luo said sardonically. He promised not to take up the matter with her immediately as that would betray the source of his information.

But that evening Luo drank too much rice wine when they dined at the Tower Beyond Towers which had the lake on three sides. "Congratulations, Missu Fan!" he said. "I hear you are going to invite us to your wedding feast." He drained his cup and strode off angrily.

Miss Fan refused to join them that next day. Luo's letters were returned unopened. A week later Miss Zhou reported that Miss Fan had again been dining with the pawn-broker. Everything was settled; the man had given her a big diamond engagement ring.

Luo's divorce action had reached the point where it began to move through its own momentum. There were signs that his wife's side was now more ready to listen to reason. He would be a laughing-stock for the rest of his life if he were to return to his wife at this stage. So he went ahead with the divorce, giving his wife a generous settlement as he had promised. As soon as the decree was final he got a professional matchmaker to approach the Wangs of the dye works on his behalf. The eldest Wang girl was reported to be the prettiest girl in town.

After an exchange of photographs and due investigation, the Wangs accepted him. Luo sold a great part of his land and bought Miss Wang a diamond ring even bigger than the one Miss Fan was said to have got. He was married after three months.

For some reason, Miss Fan's match did not come off. Maybe the pawnbroker had his doubts about modern girls and had heard something of Miss Fan's long attach-ment to Luo. According to the Fans it was because they had found out that the pawn-broker had falsified his age. Some malicious tongues had it that it was the other way around.

In the natural course of things Luo would have run into Miss Fan sooner or later, living in the same town. But their friends were not content to leave it to chance. Somehow they felt it was important for them to meet again. It could not be that they wanted Luo to savour fully his revenge; they had disapproved of the way he had hit back at her at the expense of his own ideals. Maybe they wanted him to realize the mistake he had made and feel sorry. But perhaps the most likely explanation would be that they just thought it would be sad and beautiful—and therefore a good thing—for the two to meet once again on the lake under the moon.

It was arranged without the knowledge of either of them. One night Luo was out on a boat with Wen—Miss Zhou was now married and not seeing them any more. Some people shouted at them from another boat. It was a couple they used to know. Miss Fan was with them.

When the two boats drew near, Wen stepped over to the other boat, urging Luo to come with him. Luo found himself sitting across the small table from Miss Fan. The tea in the cups shone faintly, in each cup a floating silver disk swaying slightly with the movement of the boat. Her face and white-clad shoulders were blue-rimmed with moonlight. It stunned him how she could look just the same when so much had happened.

They went through the amenities as if there were nothing amiss, but without di-rectly addressing a single remark to each other. No reference was made to Luo's new marriage. The talk was mostly about the government-sponsored West Lake Exhibi-tion and its ugly memorial that dominated the vista along the bank.

"It's an eyesore. Spoils everything," Luo said. "It will never be the same again." Her eyes met his, wavered a little, and looked away.

After going round the lake they landed and separated. The day after, Luo received a letter addressed to him in Miss Fan's handwriting. He tore it open, his heart pounding, and found a sheet of blank paper inside. He knew instantly what she meant. She had wanted to write him but what could she say?

Soon it was no secret among their friends that they were again seeing a lot of each other. Luo again started divorce proceedings. This time he had very few sympathizers. He now looked like a scoundrel where he had once been a pioneer. It was another long struggle. On her part Miss Fan was also engaged in a struggle. Hers was against the forces of the years, against men's very nature which tires so easily. And in her struggle she had nobody to stand by her side as she stood by Luo. She remained quietly pretty. Her coiffure and clothes were masterpieces of subtle compromise between fashion and memory. He never wanted her to look any different from the way she did when he had first known her. Yet he would have been distressed if it had suddenly occurred to him that she looked dated. She fell in with all his moods without being monotonously pliant. She read all the books he gave her and was devoted to Shelley.

He finally had to fight it out in the courts with his wife's family. The Wangs were adamant against divorce. Lawsuits were expensive, especially when judges proved to be tractable. Luo got his divorce at the end of five years. Though in reduced circumstances, he had built a small white house exactly the way Miss Fan and he had planned it, on a site they had chosen long ago. He had closed down his old house in the country after his mother's death. Their new home was on stilts, leaning out of the green hills right over the lake. Climbing roses and wisteria trailed over the moon window.

The newlyweds paid routine visits to relatives. They were usually pressed to stay for dinner and play mahjong. Luo had never known her to be fond of the game. He told his wife it was good of her to comply but there was no need to keep it up all night and promise to come back for more the next day. She answered that people teased her into it, saying she could not bear to be away from her bridegroom a single minute.

She complained of living so far out. When she came back late from her mahjong parties she often had difficulty finding a rickshaw puller willing to take her home. When she was not out playing mahjong she lounged about in soiled old gowns with torn slits and frayed frogs. Half the time she lay in bed cracking watermelon seeds, spitting the shells over the bedclothes and into her slippers on the floor. His hints at taking more interest in her appearance were at first ignored. Then she flared up and said his fussiness was unmanly. "No wonder you never get anywhere."

Luo did his best to keep up a good front. Still he supposed that news of their quarrels got about, because one day a relative mentioned casually to him that Miss Wang had not yet remarried. "Why don't you ask her to come back?"

Luo shook his head sadly. He needed some persuasion, but of course he knew that the Wangs would agree that this was the best way out, much as they hated him. The family's good name would suffer if their daughter took a second husband.

His wife, the former Miss Fan, did not hear of the matter until all arrangements had been made. Despite scenes and threats of suicide, the day Miss Wang returned to him escorted by members of the Wang family she was there to receive them and play hostess at the small informal celebration. She addressed Miss Wang's brother and sister-in-law as "Brother" and "Sister-in-law". She apologized for the dinner. "It's difficult for us to get a good cook, living so far away from the market. Terribly inconvenient. Else I would have made him fetch back your young lady long ago. Of course she ought to come and live here. One can't be staying with parents all the time." Miss Wang did not speak, since she was almost a bride.

No agreement had been reached as to the mode of address between the two women, who were understood to be of equal status. They were merely referred to as "That of the House of Fan" and "That of the House of Wang" behind each other's back.

Not long afterward an elder of Luo's clan spoke to him. "I see no reason why you shouldn't ask your first wife to come back. It would only be fair."

Luo could not think of any valid objection either. He went down to the country where she was living with her family, and brought her back to the rose-covered little house by the lake.

Both of his ex-wives were much richer than he was after the divorce settlements. But they never helped him out, no matter what straits he got into from providing for three women and their squabbling servants and later their children. He could not really blame them, taking everything into consideration. He would not have minded it so much if "That of the House of Fan" did not taunt him continually about the others' lack of feeling for him.

And now that he had lived down the scandal and ridicule, people envied him his *yan fu,* glamorous blessings—extraordinary in an age that was at least nominally monogamous, for it was already 1936—living with three wives in a rose-covered little house by the lake. On the rare occasions when he tried to tell somebody he was unhappy, the listener would guffaw. "Anyhow," the friend would say, "there are four of you—just right for a nice game of mahjong."

—◆—

Mahasweta Devi
b. 1926

When Mahasweta Devi began to write, women were rarely taken seriously as writers. Despite this, Devi has written more than a hundred novels, plays, and short-story collections. Though she grew up under the British Raj, when English was prescribed as the language of education and literature, she persisted in writing in her native Bengali. And though women of Devi's education were expected to concentrate on domestic settings, if they were allowed to write at all, mutinies and rebellions have been her subjects of choice.

She was born in Dhaka, now the capital of Bangladesh, and graduated in 1946 with a B.A. in English from Vishvabharati University in Santiniketan, an alternative school founded by India's Nobel Laureate Rabindranath Tagore. She also earned a master's degree in English literature from Calcutta University (1963) and taught at the college level in Calcutta. Her work is marked by a social activism that dates back to her involvement with the Gananatya Group of artists and writers who took their theatrical performances to the villages and countryside of Bengal in the 1930s and 1940s. She has studied rural societies as an anthropologist and has delved into the history of India. These pursuits have influenced her social activism as well as her fiction and plays. In her first novel, *Jhansi Rani* (1956), she dramatized the historical figure of Rani, Queen of Jhansi, who died leading an Indian rebellion against British rule in 1857. She also narrated in novel form the Barsi Munda tribal revolt of the nineteenth century in what is considered her most famous novel, *Rights Over the Forest* (1977). In a collection of her short stories, *A Womb of Fire* (1978), she has depicted more recent historic uprisings such as the 1960s Marxist rebellion of the Naxalbari peasants in eastern India. In 1984 she resigned from her college teaching post to devote herself full time to social work among the Bengali and Bihar tribes and outcasts. She has continued to write for periodicals and journals on behalf of the tribal communities. In addition to her novels, numerous plays, and twenty collections of short stories, she has also written children's literature and textbooks and has translated a number of literary works from other languages into Bengali. In 1996 she received the Jnanpith Award, India's highest literary prize, and donated the prize money to a tribal welfare society. In 1997 she was awarded the Magsaysay Prize, considered the Asian equivalent of the Nobel Prize, for journalism, literature, and creative communication.

Like many of her novels, Devi's story "Breast-Giver" is a powerful work of social protest focused on a woman's body as object, instrument, and resource that social norms make legitimately exploitable. Literally a cash cow (hired out as a wet nurse for money)—a source of sustenance through her body—the protagonist becomes the embodiment of women, of mother India, and of the colonial territory whose exploitation sustains its imperial masters. (Her name itself evokes the mother of the Hindu god Krishna, hence the mother who breast-feeds the world.) Devi blends political history, mythical legend, traditional tale, and ideological polemic in a narrative that indicts patriarchy, colonialism, and women's exploitation by other women. The translation, by Gayatri Chakravorty Spivak, conveys the vividness of Devi's style (by translating the title for example, literally as "breast-giver" rather than as "wet nurse"). Various English words appear in the Bengali text; these are italicized in Spivak's translation, to mark their foreignness in the Bengali context.

PRONUNCIATIONS:
Haldarkartha: HULL-dur-kur-tah
Harisal: ho-REE-shal
Jashoda: JOH-shoh-da
Kangalicharan: cahn-GAH-lee-chuh-run
Mahasweta Devi: muh-HAH-shwey-ta DAY-vee
Nabin: noh-BEAN

Breast-Giver

1

My aunties they lived in the woods,
in the forest their home they did make
Never did Aunt say here's a sweet dear,
eat sweetie, here's a piece of cake.

Jashoda doesn't remember if her aunt was kind or unkind. It is as if she were Kangalicharan's wife from birth, the mother of twenty children, living or dead, counted on her fingers. Jashoda doesn't remember at all when there was no child in her womb, when she didn't feel faint in morning, when Kangali's body didn't *drill* her body like a geologist in a darkness lit only by an oil-lamp. She never had the time to calculate if she could or could not bear motherhood. Motherhood was always her way of living and keeping alive her world of countless beings. Jashoda was a mother by profession, *professional mother.* Jashoda was not an *amateur* mama like the daughters and wives of the master's house. The world belongs to the professional. In this city, this kingdom, the amateur beggar-pickpocket-hooker has no place. Even the mongrel on the path or side-walk, the greedy crow at the garbage don't make room for the upstart *amateur.* Jashoda had taken motherhood as her profession.

The responsibility was Mr. Haldar's new son-in-law's Studebaker and the sudden desire of the youngest son of the Haldar-house to be a driver. When the boy suddenly got a whim in mind or body, he could not rest unless he had satisfied it instantly. These sudden whims reared up in the loneliness of the afternoon and kept him at slave labour like the khalifa[1] of Bagdad. What he had done so far on that account did not oblige Jashoda to choose motherhood as a profession.

One afternoon the boy, driven by lust, attacked the cook and the cook, since her body was heavy with rice, stolen fishheads, and turnip greens, and her body languid with sloth, lay back, saying, "Yah, do what you like." Thus did the incubus of Bagdad get off the boy's shoulders and he wept repentant tears, mumbling, "Auntie, don't tell." The cook—saying, "What's there to tell?"—went quickly to sleep. She never told anything. She was sufficiently proud that her body had attracted the boy. But the thief thinks of the loot. The boy got worried at the improper supply of fish and fries in his dish. He considered that he'd be fucked if the cook gave him away. Therefore on another afternoon, driven by the Bagdad djinn, he stole his mother's ring, slipped it into the cook's pillowcase, raised a hue and cry, and got the cook kicked out. Another afternoon he lifted the radio set from his father's room and sold it. It was difficult for his parents to find the connection between the hour of the afternoon and the boy's behaviour, since his father had created him in the deepest night by the astrological calendar and the tradition of the Haldars of Harisal. In fact you enter the sixteenth century as you enter the gates of this house. To this day you take your wife by the astrological almanac. But these matters are mere blind alleys. Motherhood did not become Jashoda's profession for these afternoon-whims.

One afternoon, leaving the owner of the shop, Kangalicharan was returning home with a handful of stolen samosas[2] and sweets under his dhoti.[3] Thus he returns daily. He and Jashoda eat rice. Their three offspring return before dark and eat stale samosa and sweets. Kangalicharan stirs the seething vat of milk in the sweet shop and cooks and feeds "food cooked by a good Brahmin" to those pilgrims at the Lion-seated goddess's[4] temple who are proud that they are not themselves "fake Brahmins by sleight of hand". Daily he lifts a bit of flour and such and makes life easier. When he puts food in his belly in the afternoon he feels a filial inclination towards Jashoda, and he goes to sleep after handling her capacious bosom. Coming home in the afternoon, Kangalicharan was thinking of his imminent pleasure and tasting paradise at the thought of his wife's large round breasts. He was picturing himself as a farsighted son of man as he thought that marrying a fresh young thing, not working her over-much, and feeding her well led to pleasure in the afternoon. At such a moment the Halder son, complete with Studebaker, swerving by Kangalicharan, ran over his feet and shins.

Instantly a crowd gathered. It was an accident in front of the house after all, "otherwise I'd have drawn blood," screamed Nabin, the pilgrim-guide. He guides the pilgrims to the Mother goddess of Shakti-power,[5] his temper is hot in the afternoon sun. Hearing him roar, all the Haldars who were at home came out. The Haldar chief started thrashing his son, roaring, "You'll kill a Brahmin,[6] you bastard, you unthinking bull?" The youngest son-in-law breathed relief as he saw that his Studebaker was

1. Ruler.
2. Fried snacks.
3. Loincloth.
4. A warrior goddess.

5. Cosmic energy. Shakti is worshiped as the mother of the cosmos.
6. Member of the highest, priestly caste.

not much damaged and, to prove that he was better human material than the money rich, *culture*-poor in-laws, he said in a voice as fine as the finest muslin, "Shall we let the man die? Shouldn't we take him to the hospital?"—Kangali's boss was also in the crowd at the temple and, seeing the samosas and sweets flung on the roadway was about to say, "Eh Brahmin!! Stealing food?" Now he held his tongue and said, "Do that *sir.*" The youngest son-in-law and the Haldar chief took Kangalicharan quickly to the hospital. The master felt deeply grieved. During the Second War, when he helped the anti-Fascist struggle of the Allies by buying and selling scrap iron—then Kangali was a mere lad. Reverence for Brahmins crawled in Mr. Haldar's veins. If he couldn't get Chatterjeebabu[7] in the morning he would touch the feet of Kangali, young enough to be his son, and put a pinch of dust from his chapped feet on his own tongue. Kangali and Jashoda came to his house on feast days and Jashoda was sent a gift of cloth and vermillion when his daughters-in-law were pregnant. Now he said to Kangali— "Kangali! don't worry son. You won't suffer as long as I'm around." Now it was that he thought that Kangali's feet, being turned to ground meat, he would not be able to taste their dust. He was most unhappy at the thought and he started weeping as he said, "What has the son of a bitch done." He said to the doctor at the hospital, "Do what you can! Don't worry about cash."

But the doctors could not bring the feet back. Kangali returned as a lame Brahmin. Haldarbabu had a pair of crutches made. The very day Kangali returned home on crutches, he learned that food had come to Jashoda from the Haldar house every day. Nabin was third in rank among the pilgrim-guides. He could only claim thirteen percent of the goddess's food[8] and so had an inferiority complex. Inspired by seeing Rama-Krishna[9] in the movies a couple of times, he called the goddess "my crazy one" and by the book of the Kali-worshippers kept his consciousness immersed in local spirits. He said to Kangali, "I put flowers on the crazy one's feet in your name. She said I have a share in Kangali's house, he will get out of the hospital by that fact." Speaking of this to Jashoda, Kangali said, "What? When I wasn't there, you were getting it off with Nabin?" Jashoda then grabbed Kangali's suspicious head between the two hemispheres of the globe and said, "Two maid servants from the big house slept here every day to guard me. Would I look at Nabin? Am I not your faithful wife?"

In fact Kangali heard of his wife's flaming devotion at the big house as well. Jashoda had fasted at the mother's temple, had gone through a female ritual, and had travelled to the outskirts to pray at the feet of the local guru. Finally the Lionseated came to her in a dream as a midwife carrying a *bag* and said, "Don't worry. Your man will return." Kangali was most overwhelmed by this. Haldarbabu said, "See, Kangali? The bastard unbelievers say, the mother gives a dream, why togged as a midwife? I say, she creates as mother, and preserves as midwife."

Then Kangali said, "Sir! How shall I work at the sweetshop any longer. I can't stir the vat with my kerutches.[1] You are god. You are feeding so many people in so many ways. I am not begging. Find me a job."

Haldarbabu said, "Yes Kangali! I've kept you a spot. I'll make you a shop in the corner of my porch. The Lionseated is across the way! Pilgrims come and go. Put up a shop of dry sweets. Now there's a wedding in the house. It's my bastard seventh son's wedding. As long as there's no shop, I'll send you food."

---

7. Honored Chatterjee (a Brahmin name).
8. Alms of food given to the temple is divided by the priests.

9. Bengali mystic (1836–1882) devoted to the goddess Kali and the wild rituals associated with her.
1. Crutches.

Hearing this, Kangali's mind took wing like a rainbug in the rainy season. He came home and told Jashoda, "Remember Kalidasa's poem?[2] You eat because there isn't, wouldn't have got if there was? That's my lot, chuck. Master says he'll put up a shop after his son's wedding. Until then he'll send us food. Would this have happened if I had legs? All is Mother's will, dear!"

Everyone is properly amazed that in this fallen age the wishes and wills of the Lionseated, herself found by a dream-command a hundred and fifty years ago, are circulating around Kangalicharan Patitundo. Haldarbabu's change of heart is also Mother's will. He lives in independent India, the India that makes no distinctions among people, kingdoms, languages, varieties of Brahmins, varieties of Kayasthas[3] and so on. But he made his cash in the British era, when *Divide and Rule* was the policy. Haldarbabu's mentality was constructed then. Therefore he doesn't trust anyone—not a Punjabi-Oriya-Bihari-Gujarati-Marathi-Muslim. At the sight of an unfortunate Bihari child or a starvation-ridden Oriya beggar his flab-protected heart, located under a forty-two inch Gopal brand vest, does not itch with the rash of kindness. He is a successful son of Harisal. When he sees a West Bengali fly he says, "Tchah! at home even the flies were fat—in the bloody West everything is pinched-skinny." All the temple people are struck that such a man is filling with the milk of human kindness toward the West Bengali Kangalicharan. For some time this news is the general talk. Haldarbabu is such a patriot that, if his nephews or grandsons read the lives of the nation's leaders in their schoolbook, he says to his employees, "Nonsense! why do they make 'em read the lives of characters from Dhaka, Mymensingh, Jashore? Harisal is made of the bone of the martyr god. One day it will emerge that the *Vedas* and the *Upanishads* were also written in Harisal."[4] Now his employees tell him, "You have had a *change of heart,* so much kindness for a West Bengali, you'll see there is divine *purpose* behind this." The Boss is delighted. He laughs loudly and says "there is no East or West for a Brahmin. If there's a sacred thread around his neck you have to give him respect even when he's taking a shit."

Thus all around blow the sweet winds of sympathy-compassion-kindness. For a few days, whenever Nabin tries to think of the Lionseated, the heavy-breasted, languid-hipped body of Jashoda floats in his mind's eye. A slow rise spreads in his body at the thought that perhaps she is appearing in his dream as Jashoda, just as she appeared in Jashoda's as a midwife. The fifty percent pilgrim-guide says to him, "Male and female both get this disease. Bind the root of a white forget-me-not in your ear when you take a piss."

Nabin doesn't agree. One day he tells Kangali, "As the Mother's son I won't make a racket with Shaktipower. But I've thought of a plan. There's no problem with making a Hare Krishna racket. I tell you, get a Gopal[5] in your dream. My Aunt brought a stony Gopal from Puri. I give it to you. You announce that you got it in a dream. You'll see there'll be a to-do in no time, money will roll in. Start for money, later you'll get devoted to Gopal."

Kangali says, "Shame, brother! Should one joke with gods?"

"Ah get lost," Nabin scolds. Later it appears that Kangali would have done well to listen to Nabin. For Haldarbabu suddenly dies of heart failure. Shakespeare's *welkin*[6] breaks on Kangali and Jashoda's head.

---

2. Fourth-century C.E. classical Sanskrit poet.
3. The second-highest caste.
4. Bengali.

5. Image of Krishna.
6. Sky, heavens.

2

Haldarbabu truly left Kangali in the lurch. Those wishes of the Lionseated that were manifesting themselves around Kangali *via-media* Haldarbabu disappeared into the blue like the burning promises given by a political party before the election and became magically invisible like the heroine of a fantasy. A European witch's *bodkin*[7] pricks the colored balloon of Kangali and Jashoda's dreams and the pair falls in deep trouble. At home, Gopal, Nepal and Radharani whine interminably for food and abuse their mother. It is very natural for children to cry so for grub. Ever since Kangalicharan's loss of feet they'd eaten the fancy food of the Haldar household. Kangali also longs for food and is shouted at for trying to put his head in Jashoda's chest in the way of Gopal, the Divine Son. Jashoda is fully an Indian woman, whose unreasonable, unreasoning, and unintelligent devotion to her husband and love for her children, whose unnatural renunciation and forgiveness, have been kept alive in the popular consciousness by all Indian women from Sati-Savitri-Sita through Nirupa Roy and Chand Osmani. The creeps of the world understand by seeing such women that the old Indian tradition is still flowing free—they understand that it was with such women in mind that the following aphorisms have been composed—"A female's life hangs on like a turtle's"—"her heart breaks but no word is uttered"—"the woman will burn, her ashes will fly / Only then will we sing her / praise on high." Frankly, Jashoda never once wants to blame her husband for the present misfortune. Her mother-love wells up for Kangali as much as for the children. She wants to become the earth and feed her crippled husband and helpless children with a fulsome harvest. Sages did not write of this motherly feeling of Jashoda's for her husband. They explained female and male as Nature and the Human Principle. But this they did in the days of yore—when they entered this *peninsula* from another land. Such is the power of the Indian soil that all women turn into mothers here and all men remain immersed in the spirit of holy childhood. Each man the Holy Child and each women the Divine Mother. Even those who deny this and wish to slap *current posters* to the effect of the *"eternal she"*—"Mona Lisa"—"La passionaria"—"Simone de Beauvoir," et cetera,[8] over the old ones and look at women that way are, after all, Indian cubs. It is notable that the educated Babus desire all this from women outside the home. When they cross the threshold they want the Divine Mother in the words and conduct of the revolutionary ladies. The *process* is most complicated. Because he understood this the heroines of Saratchandra[9] always fed the hero an extra mouthful of rice. The apparent simplicity of Saratchandra's and other similar writers' writings is actually very complex and to be thought of in the evening, peacefully after a glass of wood-apple juice. There is too much influence of fun and games in the lives of the people who traffic in studies and intellectualism in West Bengal and therefore they should stress the wood-apple correspondingly. We have no idea of the loss we are sustaining because we do not stress the wood-apple-type-herbal remedies correspondingly.

However, it's incorrect to cultivate the habit of repeated incursions into *by-lanes* as we tell Jashoda's life story. The reader's patience, unlike the cracks in Calcutta streets, will not widen by the decade. The real thing is that Jashoda was in a cleft stick. Of course they ate their fill during the Master's funeral days, but after everything was over Jashoda clasped Radharani to her bosom and went over to the big

---

7. Long hairpin.
8. A random mixture of Western women, symbols variously of mystery, freedom, sensuality, and political engagement.
9. Bengali novelist of sentimental fiction (1876–1938).

house. Her aim was to speak to the Mistress and ask for the cook's job in the vegetarian kitchen.[1]

The Mistress really grieved for the Master. But the lawyer let her know that the Master had left her the proprietorship of this house and the right to the rice warehouse. Girding herself with those assurances, she has once again taken the rudder of the family empire. She had really felt the loss of fish and fish-head. Now she sees that the best butter, the best milk sweets from the best shops, heavy cream, and the best variety of bananas can also keep the body going somehow. The Mistress lights up her easychair. A six-months' babe in her lap, her grandson. So far six sons have married. Since the almanac approves of the taking of a wife almost every month of the year, the birth rooms in a row on the ground floor of the Mistress's house are hardly ever empty. The *lady doctor* and Sarala the midwife never leave the house. The Mistress has six daughters. They too breed every year and a half. So there is a constant *epidemic* of blanket-quilt-feeding spoon-bottle-oilcloth-*Johnson's baby powder*-bathing basin.

The Mistress was out of her mind trying to feed the boy. As if relieved to see Jashoda she said, "You come like a god! Give her some milk, dear, I beg you. His mother's sick—such a brat, he won't touch a bottle." Jashoda immediately suckled the boy and pacified him. At the Mistress's special request Jashoda stayed in the house until nine p.m. and suckled the Mistress's grandson again and again. The cook filled a big bowl with rice and curry for her own household. Jashoda said as she suckled the boy, "Mother! The Master said many things. He is gone, so I don't think of them. But Mother! Your Brahmin-son does not have his two feet. I don't think for myself. But thinking of my husband and sons I say, give me any kind of job. Perhaps you'll let me cook in your household?"

"Let me see dear! Let me think and see." The Mistress is not as sold on Brahmins as the Master was. She doesn't accept fully that Kangali lost his feet because of her son's afternoon whims. It was written for Kangali as well, otherwise why was he walking down the road in the blazing sun grinning from ear to ear? She looks in charmed envy at Jashoda's *mammal projections* and says, "The good lord sent you down as the legendary Cow of Fulfillment. Pull the teat and milk flows! The ones I've brought to my house, haven't a quarter of this milk in their nipples!"

Jashoda says, "How true Mother! Gopal was weaned when he was three. This one hadn't come to my belly yet. Still it was like a flood of milk. Where does it come from, Mother? I have no good food, no pampering!"

This produced a lot of talk among the women at night and the menfolk got to hear it too at night. The second son, whose wife was sick and whose son drank Jashoda's milk, was particularly uxorious. The difference between him and his brothers was that the brothers created progeny as soon as the almanac gave a good day, with love or lack of love, with irritation or thinking of the accounts at the works. The second son impregnates his wife at the same *frequency,* but behind it lies deep love. The wife is often pregnant, that is an act of God. But the second son is also interested in that the wife remain beautiful at the same time. He thinks a lot about how to *combine* multiple pregnancies and beauty, but he cannot fathom it. But today, hearing from his wife about Jashoda's surplus milk, the second son said all of a sudden, "Way found."

"Way to what?"

"Uh, the way to save you pain."

1. In devotion to the memory of their dead husbands,   Hindu widows become strict vegetarians.

"How? I'll be out of pain when you burn me. Can a year-breeder's health mend?"

"It will, it will, I've got a divine engine in my hands! You'll breed yearly *and* keep your body."

The couple discussed. The husband entered his Mother's room in the morning and spoke in heavy whispers. At first the Mistress hemmed and hawed, but then she thought to herself and realized that the proposal was worth a million rupees. Daughters-in-law *will* be mothers. When they are mothers, they will suckle their children. Since they will be mothers as long as it's possible—progressive suckling will ruin their shape. Then if the sons look outside, or harass the maidservants, she won't have a voice to object. Going out because they can't get it at home—this is just. If Jashoda becomes the infants' suckling-mother, her daily meals, clothes on feast days, and some monthly pay will be enough. The Mistress is constantly occupied with women's rituals. There Jashoda can act as the fruitful Brahmin wife. Since Jashoda's misfortune is due to her son, that sin too will be lightened.

Jashoda received a portfolio when she heard her proposal. She thought of her breasts as most precious objects. At nights when Kangalicharan started to give her a feel she said, "Look. I'm going to pull our weight with these. Take good care how you use them." Kangalicharan hemmed and hawed that night, of course, but his Gopal frame of mind disappeared instantly when he saw the amounts of grains-oil-vegetables coming from the big house. He was illuminated by the spirit of Brahma the Creator and explained to Jashoda, "You'll have milk in your breasts only if you have a child in your belly. Now you'll have to think of that and suffer. You are a faithful wife, a goddess. You will yourself be pregnant, be filled with a child, rear it at your breast, isn't this why Mother came to you as a midwife?"

Jashoda realized the justice of these words and said, with tears in her eyes, "You are husband, you are guru. If I forget and say no, correct me. Where after all is the pain? Didn't Mistress-Mother breed thirteen? Does it hurt a tree to bear fruit?"

So this rule held. Kangalicharan became a professional father. Jashoda was by *profession* Mother. In fact to look at Jashoda now even the sceptic is convinced of the profundity of that song of the path of devotion. The song is as follows:

> Is a Mother so cheaply made?
> Not just by dropping a babe!

Around the paved courtyard on the ground floor of the Haldar house over a dozen auspicious milch cows live in some state in large rooms. Two Biharis[2] look after them as Mother Cows. There are mountains of rind-bran-hay-grass-molasses. Mrs Haldar believes that the more the cow eats, the more milk she gives. Jashoda's place in the house is now above the Mother Cows. The Mistress's sons become incarnate Brahma and create progeny. Jashoda preserves the progeny.

Mrs. Haldar kept a strict watch on the free flow of her supply of milk. She called Kangalicharan to her presence and said, "Now then, my Brahmin son? You used to stir the vat at the shop, now take up the cooking at home and give her a rest. Two of her own, three here, how can she cook at day's end after suckling five?"

Kangalicharan's intellectual eye was thus opened. Downstairs the two Biharis gave him a bit of chewing tobacco and said, "Mistress Mother said right. We serve the Cow Mother as well—your woman is the Mother of the world."

---

2. Natives of Bihar in Western Bengal.

From now on Kangalicharan took charge of the cooking at home. Made the children his assistants. Gradually he became an expert in cooking plantain curry, lentil soup, and pickled fish, and by constantly feeding Nabin a head-curry with the head of the goat dedicated to the Lionseated he tamed that ferocious cannabis-artist and drunkard. As a result Nabin inserted Kangali into the temple of Shiva the King. Jashoda, eating well-prepared rice and curry every day, became as inflated as the *bank account* of a Public Works Department *officer*. In addition, Mistress-Mother gave her milk gratis. When Jashoda became pregnant, she would send her preserves, conserves, hot and sweet balls.

Thus even the sceptics were persuaded that the Lionseated had appeared to Jashoda as a midwife for this very reason. Otherwise who has ever heard or seen such things as constant pregnancies, giving birth, giving milk like a cow, without a thought, to others' children? Nabin too lost his bad thoughts. Devotional feelings came to him by themselves. Whenever he saw Jashoda he called out "Mother! Mother! Dear Mother!" Faith in the greatness of the Lionseated was rekindled in the area and in the air of the neighbourhood blew the *electrifying* influence of goddess-glory.

Everyone's devotion to Jashoda became so strong that at weddings, showers, namings, and sacred-threadings they invited her and gave her the position of chief fruitful woman. They looked with a comparable eye on Nepal-Gopal-Neno-Boncha-Patal etc. because they were Jashoda's children, and as each grew up, he got a sacred thread and started catching pilgrims for the temple. Kangali did not have to find husbands for Radharani, Altarani, Padmarani and such daughters. Nabin found them husbands with exemplary dispatch and the faithful mother's faithful daughters went off each to run the household of her own Shiva! Jashoda's worth went up in the Haldar house. The husbands are pleased because the wives' knees no longer knock when they riffle the almanac. Since their children are being reared on Jashoda's milk, they can be the Holy Child in bed at will. The wives no longer have an excuse to say "no". The wives are happy. They can keep their figures. They can wear blouses and bras of "European cut". After keeping the fast of Shiva's night by watching all-night picture shows they are no longer obliged to breast-feed their babies. All this was possible because of Jashoda. As a result Jashoda became vocal and, constantly suckling the infants, she opined as she sat in the Mistress's room, "A woman breeds, so here medicine, there bloodpeshur,[3] here doctor's visits. Showoffs! Look at me! I've become a year-breeder! So is my body failing, or is my milk drying? Makes your skin crawl? I hear they are drying their milk with injishuns.[4] Never heard of such things!"

The fathers and uncles of the current young men of the Haladar house used to whistle at the maidservants as soon as hair grew on their upper lips. The young ones were reared by the Milk-Mother's milk, so they looked upon the maid and the cook, their Milk-Mother's friends, as mothers too and started walking around the girls' school. The maids said, "Joshi! You came as The Goddess! You made the air of this house change!" So one day as the youngest son was squatting to watch Jashoda's milking, she said, "There dear, my Lucky! All this because you swiped him in the leg! Whose wish was it then?" "The Lionseated's," said Haldar junior.

He wanted to know how Kangalicharan could be Brahma without feet? This encroached on divine area, and he forgot the question.

All is the Lionseated's will!

_____

3. Blood pressure tests.   4. Injections.

3

Kangali's shins were cut in the fifties, and our narrative has reached the present. In twenty-five years, sorry, in thirty, Jashoda has been confined twenty times. The maternities toward the end were profitless, for a new wind entered the Haldar house somehow. Let's finish the business of the twenty-five or thirty years. At the beginning of the narrative Jashoda was the mother of three sons. Then she became gravid[5] seventeen times. Mrs. Haldar died. She dearly wished that one of her daughters-in-law should have the same good fortune as her mother-in-law. In the family the custom was to have a second wedding if a couple could produce twenty children. But the daughters-in-law called a halt at twelve-thirteen-fourteen. By evil counsel they were able to explain to their husbands and make arrangements at the hospital. All this was the bad result of the new wind. Wise men have never allowed a new wind to enter the house. I've heard from my grandmother that a certain gentleman would come to her house to read the liberal journal *Saturday Letter*. He would never let the tome enter his home. "The moment wife, or mother, or sister reads that paper," he would say, "she'll say 'I'm a woman! Not a mother, not a sister not a wife.'" If asked what the result would be, he'd say, "They would wear shoes while they cooked." It is a perennial rule that the power of the new wind disturbs the peace of the women's quarter.

It was always the sixteenth century in the Haldar household. But at the sudden significant rise in the membership of the house the sons started building new houses and splitting. The most objectionable thing was that in the matter of motherhood, the old lady's granddaughters-in-law had breathed a completely different air before they crossed her threshold. In vain did the Mistress say that there was plenty of money, plenty to eat. The old man had dreamed of filling half Calcutta with Haldars. The granddaughters-in-law were unwilling. Defying the old lady's tongue, they took off to their husbands' places of work. At about this time, the pilgrim-guides of the Lion-seated had a tremendous fight and some unknown person or persons turned the image of the goddess around. The Mistress's heart broke at the thought that the Mother had turned her back. In pain she ate an unreasonable quantity of jackfruit in full summer and died shitting and vomiting.

4

Death liberated the Mistress, but the sting of staying alive is worse than death.

Jashoda was genuinely sorry at the Mistress's death. When an elderly person dies in the neighbourhood, it's Basini who can weep most elaborately. She is an old maid-servant of the house. But Jashoda's meal ticket was offered up with the Mistress. She astounded everyone by weeping even more elaborately.

"Oh blessed Mother!" Basini wept. "Widowed, when you lost your crown, you became the Master and protected everyone! Whose sins sent you away Mother! Ma, when I said, don't eat so much jackfruit, you didn't listen to me at all Mother!"

Jashoda let Basini get her breath and lamented in that pause, "Why should you stay, Mother! You are blessed, why should you stay in this sinful world! The daughters-in-law have moved the throne! When the tree says I won't bear, alas it's a sin! Could you bear so much sin, Mother! Then did the Lionseated turn her back, Mother! You knew the abode of good works had become the abode of sin, it was not for you Mother! Your heart left when the Master left Mother! You held your body only because you thought of the family. O mistresses, O daughters-in-law! take a vermillion print of her footstep! Fortune will be tied to the door if you keep that print! If you touch your forehead to it every morning, pain and disease will stay out!"

Jashoda walked weeping behind the corpse to the burning ghat[6] and said on return, "I saw with my own eyes a chariot descend from heaven, take Mistress Mother from the pyre, and go on up."

After the funeral days were over, the eldest daughter-in-law said to Jashoda, "Brahmin sister! the family is breaking up. Second and Third are moving to the house in Beleghata. Fourth and Fifth are departing to Maniktala-Bagmari. Youngest will depart to our Dakshineswar house."

"Who stays here?"

"I will. But I'll let the downstairs. Now must the family be folded up. You reared everyone on your milk, food was sent every day. The last child was weaned, still Mother sent you food for eight years. She did what pleased her. Her children said nothing. But it's no longer possible."

"What'll happen to me, elder daughter-in-law-sister?"

"If you cook for my household, your board is taken care of. But what'll you do with yours?"

"What?"

"It's for you to say. You are the mother of twelve living children! The daughters are married. I hear the sons call pilgrims, eat temple food, stretch out in the courtyard. Your Brahmin-husband has set himself up in the Shiva temple, I hear. What do you need?"

Jashoda wiped her eyes. "Well! Let me speak to the Brahmin."

Kangalicharan's temple had really caught on. "What will you do in my temple?" he asked.

"What does Nabin's niece do?"

"She looks after the temple household and cooks. You haven't been cooking at home for a long time. Will you be able to push the temple traffic?"

"No meals from the big house. Did that enter your thieving head? What'll you eat?"

"You don't have to worry," said Nabin.

"Why did I have worry for so long? You're bringing it in at the temple, aren't you? You've saved everything and eaten the food that sucked my body."

"Who sat and cooked?"

"The man brings, the woman cooks and serves. My lot is inside out. Then you ate my food, now you'll give me food. Fair's fair."

Kangali said on the beat, "Where did you bring in the food? Could you have gotten the Haldar house? Their door opened for *you* because *my* legs were cut off. The Master had wanted to set *me* up in business. Forgotten everything, you cunt?"

"Who's the cunt, you or me? Living off a wife's carcass, you call that a man?"

The two fought tooth and nail and cursed each other to the death. Finally Kangali said, "I don't want to see your face again. Buzz off!"

"All right."

Jashoda too left angry. In the mean time the various pilgrim-guide factions conspired to turn the image's face forward, otherwise disaster was imminent. As a result, penance rituals were being celebrated with great ceremony at the temple. Jashoda

6. Cremation site.

went to throw herself at the goddess's feet. Her aging, milkless, capacious breasts are breaking in pain. Let the Lionseated understand her pain and tell her the way.

Jashoda lay three days in the courtyard. Perhaps the Lionseated has also breathed the new wind. She did not appear in a dream. Moreover, when, after her three days' fast, Jashoda went back shaking to her place, her youngest came by. "Dad will stay at the temple. He's told Naba and I to ring the bells. We'll get money and holy food every day."

"I see! Where's dad?"

"Lying down. Golapi-auntie is scratching the prickly heat on his back. Asked us to buy candy with some money. So we came to tell you."

Jashoda understood that her usefulness had ended not only in the Haldar house but also for Kangali. She broke her fast in name and went to Nabin to complain. It was Nabin who dragged the Lionseated's image the other way. After he had settled the dispute with the other pilgrim-guides re the overhead income from the goddess Basanti ritual, the goddess Jagadhatri ritual, and the autumn Durga Puja,[7] it was he who once again pushed and pulled the image the right way. He'd poured some liquor into his aching throat, had smoked a bit of cannabis, and was now addressing the local electoral candidate: "No offerings for the Mother from you! Her glory is back. Now we'll see how you win!"

Nabin is the proof of all the miracles that can happen if, even in this decade, one stays under the temple's power. He had turned the goddess's head himself and had himself believed that the Mother was averse because the pilgrim-guides were not organizing like all the want-votes groups. Now, after he had turned the goddess's head he had the idea that the Mother had turned on her own.

Jashoda said, "What are you babbling?"

Nabin said, "I'm speaking of mother's glory."

Jashoda said, "You think I don't know that you turned the image's head yourself?"

Nabin said, "Shut up, Joshi. God gave me ability, and intelligence, and only then could the thing be done through me."

"Mother's glory has disappeared when you put your hands on her."

"Glory disappeared! If so, how come, the fan is turning, and you are sitting under the fan? Was there ever an elettiri[8] fan on the porch ceiling?"

"I accept. But tell me, why did you burn my luck? What did I ever do to you?"

"Why? Kangali isn't dead."

"Why wait for death? He's more than dead to me."

"What's up?"

Jashoda wiped her eyes and said in a heavy voice, "I've carried so many, I was the regular milk-mother at the Master's house. You know everything. I've never left the straight and narrow."

"But of course. You are a portion of the Mother."

"But Mother remains in divine fulfillment. Her 'portion' is about to die for want of food. Haldar-house has lifted its hand from me."

"Why did you have to fight with Kangali? Can a man bear to be insulted on grounds of being supported?"

"Why did you have to plant your niece there?"

---

7. Another goddess and her rituals.   8. Electric.

"That was divine play. Golapi used to throw herself in the temple. Little by little Kangali came to understand that he was the god's companion-incarnate and she *his* companion."

"Companion indeed! I can get my husband from her clutches with one blow of a broom!"

Nabin said, "No! that can't be any more. Kangali is a man in his prime, how can he be pleased with you any more? Besides, Golapi's brother is a real hoodlum, and he is guarding her. Asked *me* to *get out*. If I smoke ten pipes, he smokes twenty. Kicked me in the midriff. I went to speak for you. Kangali said, don't talk to me about her. Doesn't know her man, knows her master's house. The master's house is her household god, let her go there."

"I will."

Then Jashoda returned home, half-crazed by the injustice of the world. But her heart couldn't abide the empty room. Whether it suckled or not, it's hard to sleep without a child at the breast. Motherhood is a great addiction. The addiction doesn't break even when the milk is dry. Forlorn Jashoda went to the Haldaress. She said, "I'll cook and serve, if you want to pay me, if not, not. You must let me stay here. That sonofabitch is living at the temple. What disloyal sons! They are stuck there too. For whom shall I hold my room?"

"So stay. You suckled the children, and you're a Brahmin. So stay. But sister, it'll be hard for you. You'll stay in Basini's room with the others. You mustn't fight with anyone. The master is not in a good mood. His temper is rotten because his third son went to Bombay and married a local girl. He'll be angry if there's noise."

Jashoda's good fortune was her ability to bear children. All this misfortune happened to her as soon as that vanished. Now is the downward time for Jashoda the milk-filled faithful wife who was the object of the reverence of the local houses devoted to the Holy Mother. It is human nature to feel an inappropriate vanity as one rises, yet not to feel the *surrender* of "let me learn to bite the dust since I'm down" as one falls. As a result one makes demands for worthless things in the old way and gets kicked by the weak.

The same thing happened to Jashoda. Basini's crowd used to wash her feet and drink the water. Now Basini said easily, "You'll wash your own dishes. Are you my master, that I'll wash your dishes. You are the master's servant as much as I am."

As Jashoda roared, "Do you know who I am?" she heard the eldest daughter-in-law scold, "This is what I feared. Mother gave her a swelled head. Look here, Brahmin sister! I didn't call you, you begged to stay, don't break the peace."

Jashoda understood that now no one would attend to a word she said. She cooked and served in silence and in the late afternoon she went to the temple porch and started to weep. She couldn't even have a good cry. She heard the music for the evening worship at the temple of Shiva. She wiped her eyes and got up. She said to herself, "Now save me, Mother! Must I finally sit by the roadside with a tin cup? Is that what you want?"

The days would have passed in cooking at the Haldar-house and complaining to the Mother. But that was not enough for Jashoda. Jashoda's body seemed to keel over. Jashoda doesn't understand why nothing pleases her. Everything seems confused inside her head. When she sits down to cook she thinks she's the milk-mother of this house. She's going home in a showy sari with a free meal in her hand. Her breasts feel empty, as if wasted. She had never thought she wouldn't have a child's mouth at her nipple.

Joshi became bemused. She serves nearly all the rice and curry, but forgets to eat. Sometimes she speaks to Shiva the King, "If Mother can't do it, you take me away. I can't pull any more."

Finally it was the sons of the eldest daughter-in-law who said, "Mother! Is the milk-Mother sick? She acts strange."

The eldest daughter-in-law said, "Let's see."

The eldest son said, "Look here! She's a Brahmin's daughter, if anything happens to her, it'll be a sin for us."

The daughter-in-law went to ask. Jashoda had started the rice and then lain down in the kitchen on the spread edge of her sari. The eldest daughter-in-law, looking at her bare body, said, "Brahmin sister! Why does the top of your left tit look so red? God! flaming red!"

"Who knows? It's like a stone pushing inside. Very hard, like a rock."

"What is it?"

"Who knows? I suckled so many, perhaps that's why?"

"Nonsense! One gets breast-stones or pus-in-the-tit if there's milk. Your youngest is ten."

"That one is gone. The one before survived. That one died at birth. Just as well. This sinful world!"

"Well the doctor comes tomorrow to look at my grandson. I'll ask. Doesn't look good to me."

Jashoda said with her eyes closed, "Like a stone tit, with a stone inside. At first the hard ball moved about, now it doesn't move, doesn't budge."

"Let's show the doctor."

"No, sister daughter-in-law, I can't show my body to a male doctor."

At night when the doctor came the eldest daughter-in-law asked him in her son's presence. She said, "No pain, no burning, but she is keeling over."

The doctor said, "Go ask if the *nipple* has shrunk, if the armpit is swollen like a seed."

Hearing "swollen like a seed," the eldest daughter-in-law thought, "How crude!" Then she did her field investigations and said, "She says all that you've said has been happening for some time."

"How old?"

"If you take the eldest son's age she'll be about fifty-five."

The doctor said, "I'll give you medicine."

Going out, he said to the eldest son, "I hear your *cook* has a problem with her *breast.* I think you should take her to the *cancer hospital.* I didn't see her. But from what I heard it could be *cancer* of the *mammary gland."*

Only the other day the eldest son lived in the sixteenth century. He has arrived at the twentieth century very recently. Of his thirteen offspring he has arranged the marriages of the daughters, and the sons have grown up and are growing up at their own speed and in their own way. But even now his grey cells are covered in the darkness of the eighteenth- and the pre-Bengal-Renaissance nineteenth centuries. He still does not take smallpox vaccination and says, "Only the lower classes get smallpox. I don't need to be vaccinated. An upper-caste family, respectful of gods and Brahmins, does not contract that disease."

He pooh-poohed the idea of cancer and said, "Yah! Cancer indeed! That easy! You misheard, all she needs is an ointment. I can't send a Brahmin's daughter to a hospital just on your word."

Jashoda herself also said, "I can't go to hospital. Ask me to croak instead. I didn't go to hospital to breed, and I'll go now? That corpse-burning devil returned a cripple because he went to hospital!"

The elder daughter-in-law said, "I'll get you a herbal ointment. This ointment will surely soothe. The hidden boil will show its tip and burst."

The herbal ointment was a complete failure. Slowly Jashoda gave up eating and lost her strength. She couldn't keep her sari on the left side. Sometimes she felt burning, sometimes pain. Finally the skin broke in many places and sores appeared. Jashoda took to her bed.

Seeing the hang of it, the eldest son was afraid, if at his house a Brahmin died! He called Jashoda's sons and spoke to them harshy, "It's your mother, she fed you so long, and now she is about to die! Take her with you! She has everyone and she should die in a Kayastha household?"

Kangali cried a lot when he heard this story. He came to Jashoda's almost-dark room and said, "Wife! You are a blessed auspicious faithful woman! After I spurned you, within two years the temple dishes were stolen, I suffered from boils in my back, and that snake Golapi tricked Napla, broke the safe, stole everything and opened a shop in Tarakeswar. Come, I'll keep you in state."

Jashoda said, "Light the lamp."

Kangali lit the lamp.

Jashoda showed him her bare left breast, thick with running sores and said, "See these sores? Do you know how these sores smell? What will you do with me now? Why did you come to take me?"

"The Master called."

"Then the master doesn't want to keep me." Jashoda sighed and said, "There is no solution about me. What can you do with me?"

"Whatever, I'll take you tomorrow. Today I clean the room. Tomorrow for sure."

"Are the boys well? Noblay and Gaur used to come, they too have stopped."

"All the bastards are selfish. Sons of my spunk after all. As inhuman as I."

"You'll come tomorrow?"

"Yes—yes—yes."

Jashoda smiled suddenly. A heart-splitting nostalgia-provoking smile.

Jashoda said, "Dear, remember?"

"What, wife?"

"How you played with these tits? You couldn't sleep otherwise? My lap was never empty, if this one left my nipple, there was that one, and then the boys of the Master's house. How I could, I wonder now!"

"I remember everything, wife!"

In this instant Kangali's words are true. Seeing Jashoda's broken, thin, suffering form even Kangali's selfish body and instincts and belly-centred consciousness remembered the past and suffered some empathy. He held Jashoda's hand and said, "You have fever?"

"I get feverish all the time. I think by the strength of the sores."

"Where does this rotten stink come from?"

"From these sores."

Jashoda spoke with her eyes closed. Then she said, "Bring the holy doctor. He cured Gopal's *typhoid* with *homoeopathy*."

"I'll call him. I'll take you tomorrow."

Kangali left. That he went out, the tapping of his crutches, Jashoda couldn't hear. With her eyes shut, with the idea that Kangali was in the room, she said spiritlessly, "If you suckle you're a mother, all lies! Nepal and Gopal don't look at me, and the Master's boys don't spare a peek to ask how I'm doing." The sores on her breast kept mocking her with a hundred mouths, a hundred eyes. Jashoda opened her eyes and said, "Do you hear?"

Then she realized that Kangali had left.

In the night she sent Basini for *Lifebuoy* soap and at dawn she went to take a bath with the soap. Stink, what a stink! If the body of a dead cat or dog rots in the garbage you can get a smell like this. Jashoda had forever scrubbed her breasts carefully with soap and oil, for the master's sons had put the nipples in their mouth. Why did those breasts betray her in the end? Her skin burns with the sting of soap. Still Jashoda washed herself with soap. Her head was ringing, everything seemed dark. There was fire in Jashoda's body, in her head. The black floor was very cool. Jashoda spread her sari and lay down. She could not bear the weight of her breast standing up.

As Jashoda lay down, she lost sense and consciousness with fever. Kangali came at the proper time: but seeing Jashoda he lost his grip. Finally Nabin came and rasped, "Are these people human? She reared all the boys with her milk and they don't call a doctor? I'll call Hari the doctor."

Haribabu took one look at her and said, "Hospital."

Hospitals don't admit people who are so sick. At the efforts and recommendations of the elder son, Jashoda was admitted.

"What's the matter? O Doctorbabu, what's the problem?" Kangali asked, weeping like a boy.

"Cancer."

"You can get cancer in a tit?"

"Otherwise how did she get it?"

"Her own twenty, thirty boys at the master's house—she had a lot of milk—"

"What did you say? How many did she *feed?*"

"About fifty for sure."

"Fif-ty!"

"Yes sir."

"She had twenty children?"

"Yes sir."

"*God!*"

"Sir!"

"What?"

"Is it because she suckled so many—?"

"One can't say why someone gets cancer, one can't say. But when people breast-feed too much—didn't you realize earlier? It didn't get to this in a day."

"She wasn't with me, sir. We quarrelled—"

"I see."

"How do you see her? Will she get well?"

"Get well! See how long she lasts. You've brought her in the last stages. No one survives this stage."

Kangali left weeping. In the late afternoon, harassed by Kangali's lamentations, the eldest son's second son went to the doctor. He was minimally anxious about Jashoda—but his father nagged him and he was financially dependent on his father.

The doctor explained everything to him. It happened not in a day, but over a long time. Why? No one could tell. How does one perceive breast cancer? A hard lump inside the breast toward the top can be removed. Then gradually the lump inside becomes large, hard and like a congealed pressure. The skin is expected to turn orange, as is expected a shrinking of the nipple. The gland in the armpit can be inflamed. When there is *ulceration,* that is to say sores, one can call it the final stages. Fever? From the point of view of seriousness it falls in the second or third category. If there is something like a sore in the body, there can be fever. This is *secondary.*

The second son was confused with all this specialist talk. He said, "Will she live?"

"No."

"How long will she suffer?"

"I don't think too long."

"When there's nothing to be done, how will you treat her?"

"*Painkiller, sedative, antibiotic* for the fever. Her body is very, very *down.*"

"She stopped eating."

"You didn't take her to a doctor?"

"Yes."

"Didn't he tell you?"

"Yes."

"What did he say?"

"That it might be cancer. Asked us to take her to the hospital. She didn't agree."

"Why would she? She'd die!"

The second son came home and said, "When Arun-doctor said she had *cancer,* she might have survived if treated then."

His mother said, "If you know that much then why didn't you take her? Did I stop you?"

Somewhere in the minds of the second son and his mother an unknown sense of guilt and remorse came up like bubbles in the dirty and stagnant water and vanished instantly.

Guilt said—she lived with us, we never took a look at her, when did the disease catch her, we didn't take it seriously at all. She was a silly person, reared so many of us, we didn't look after her. Now, with everyone around her she's dying in hospital, so many children, husband living, when she clung to us, then we had—! What an alive body she had, milk leaped out of her, we never thought she would have this disease.

The disappearance of guilt said—who can undo Fate? It was written that she'd die of *cancer*—who'd stop it? It would have been wrong if she had died here—her husband and sons would have asked, how did she die? We have been saved from that wrongdoing. No one can say anything.

The eldest son assured them, "Now Arun-doctor says no one survives *cancer.* The *cancer* that Brahmin-sister has can lead to cutting of the tit, removing the uterus, even after that people die of *cancer.* See, Father gave us a lot of reverence toward Brahmins—we are alive by father's grace. If Brahmin-sister had died in our house, we would have had to perform the penance-ritual."

Patients much less sick than Jashoda die much sooner. Jashoda astonished the doctors by hanging on for about a month in hospital. At first Kangali, Nabin, and the boys did indeed come and go, but Jashoda remained the same, comatose, cooking with fever, spellbound. The sores on her breast gaped more and more and the breast now looks like an open wound. It is covered by a piece of thin *gauze* soaked in *antiseptic lotion,* but the sharp smell of putrefying flesh is circulating silently in the room's air like incense-smoke. This brought an ebb in the enthusiasm of Kangali and the other visitors. The doctor said as well, "Is she not responding? All for the better. It's hard to bear without consciousness, can anyone bear such death-throes consciously?"

"Does she know that we come and go?"

"Hard to say."

"Does she eat."

"Through tubes."

"Do people live this way?"

"Now you're very—"

The doctor understood that he was unreasonably angry because Jashoda was in this condition. He was angry with Jashoda, with Kangali, with women who don't take the signs of breast-cancer *seriously* enough and finally die in this dreadful and hellish pain. Cancer constantly defeats patient and doctor. One patient's cancer means the patient's death and the defeat of science, and of course of the doctor. One can medicate against the secondary symptom, if eating stops one can *drip glucose* and feed the body, if the lungs become incapable of breathing there is *oxygen*—but the advance of *cancer,* its expansion, spread, and killing, remain unchecked. The word *cancer* is a general signifier, by which in the different parts of the body is meant different *malignant growths.* Its characteristic properties are to destroy the infected area of the body, to spread by *metastasis,* to return after *removal,* to creat *toxaemia.*

Kangali came out without a proper answer to his question. Returning to the temple, he said to Nabin and his sons, "There's no use going any more. She doesn't know us, doesn't open her eyes, doesn't realize anything. The doctor is doing what he can."

Nabin said, "If she dies?"

"They have the *telephone number* of the old Master's eldest son, they'll call."

"Suppose she wants to see you. Kangali, your wife is a blessed auspicious faithful woman! Who would say the mother of so many. To see her body—but she didn't bend, didn't look elsewhere."

Talking thus, Nabin became gloomily silent. In fact, since he'd seen Jashoda's infested breasts, many a philosophic thought and sexological argument have been slowly circling Nabin's drug-and-booze-addled dim head like great rutting snakes emptied of venom. For example, I lusted after her? This is the end of that intoxicating bosom? Ho! Man's body's a zero. To be crazy for that is to be crazy.

Kangali didn't like all this talk. His mind had already *rejected* Jashoda. When he saw Jashoda in the Haldar-house he was truly affected and even after her admission into hospital he was passionately anxious. But now that feeling is growing cold. The moment the doctor said Jashoda wouldn't last, he put her out of mind almost painlessly. His sons are his sons. Their mother had become a distant person for a long time. Mother meant hair in a huge topknot, blindingly white clothes, a strong personality. The person lying in the hospital is someone else, not Mother.

Breast *cancer* makes the brain *comatose,* this was a solution for Jashoda.

Jashoda understood that she had come to hospital, she was in the hospital, and that this desensitizing sleep was a medicated sleep. In her weak, infected, dazed brain she thought, has some son of the Haldar-house become a doctor?

No doubt he sucked her milk and is now repaying the milk-debt? But those boys entered the family business as soon as they left high school! However, why don't the people who are helping her so much free her from the stinking presence of her chest? What a smell, what treachery? Knowing these breasts to be the rice-winner, she had constantly conceived to keep them filled with milk. The breast's job is to hold milk. She kept her breast clean with perfumed soap, she never wore a top, even in youth, because her breasts were so heavy.

When the *sedation* lessens, Jashoda screams, "Ah! Ah! Ah!"—and looks for the nurse and the doctor with passionate bloodshot eyes. When the doctor comes, she mutters with hurt feelings, "You grew so big on my milk, and now you're hurting me so?"

The doctor says, "She sees her milk-sons all over the world."

Again injection and sleepy numbness. Pain, tremendous pain, the cancer is spreading *at the expense of the human host.* Gradually Jashoda's left breast bursts and becomes like the *crater* of a volcano. The smell of putrefaction makes approach difficult.

Finally one night, Jashoda understood that her feet and hands were getting cold. She understood that death was coming. Jashoda couldn't open her eyes, but she understood that some people were looking at her hand. A needle pricked her arm. Painful breathing inside. Has to be. Who is looking? Are these her own people? The people whom she suckled because she carried them, or those she suckled for a living? Jashoda thought, after all, she had suckled the world, could she then die alone? The doctor who sees her every day, the person who will cover her face with a sheet, will put her on a cart, will lower her at the burning ghat, the untouchable who will put her in the furnace, are all her milk-sons. One must become Jashoda if one suckles the world. One has to die friendless, with no one left to put a bit of water in the mouth. Yet someone was supposed to be there at the end. Who was it? It was who? Who was it?

Jashoda died at 11 p.m.

The Haldar-house was called on the phone. The phone didn't ring. The Haldars *disconnected* their phone at night.

Jashoda Devi, Hindu female, lay in the hospital morgue in the usual way, went to the burning ghat in a van, and was burnt. She was cremated by an untouchable.

Jashoda was God manifest, others do and did whatever she thought. Jashoda's death was also the death of God. When a mortal masquerades as God here below, she is forsaken by all and she must always die alone.

⇒ PERSPECTIVES ⇐
Gendered Spaces

Femininity and masculinity are not simple biological concepts but complex social and cultural categories that are experienced through a host of practical and symbolic distinctions. In each culture and at various historical moments, these distinctions can be drawn in dramatically different ways: what type of work men or women are allowed to do, what positions of leadership and social institutions they have access to, how they are educated, what legal rights and procedures they can avail themselves of, what patterns of social and sexual behavior are acceptable for them, how their bodies are allowed to appear in public, and what language is appropriate for them to use—all these are areas in which gender differences make themselves manifest. The meanings and uses of private, public, and sacred spaces are another means through which different societies shape and express gender distinctions; tacit and explicit rules and conventions about who has access to certain spaces, the sorts of behavior and language that are desirable in each, and the symbolic meanings such sites convey all reveal important dimensions of the cultural understanding of gender. The stories in this section explore such relationships between gender and space; while they point to the gender-coded conventions that create and define certain spaces, they also focus on how such rules are subverted, circumvented, or re-appropriated by individuals who, for a variety of reasons, are dissatisfied with them. Spaces of protest, rebellion, or utopian longing emerge along with those that express and safeguard established conventions.

The spaces in these stories are more than neutral settings; they represent forces that the characters need to confront in defining their own selves and shaping their futures. The harem in Fatima Mernissi's story, for example, is far more than a mere location: It is also a way of understanding how families work and what role women should assume in them. Ama Ata Aidoo's "No Sweetness Here" offers a counterpoint to Mernissi's "The Harem Within" by focusing on a woman who is about to undergo a divorce from a polygamous marriage. She has a house of her own to live in, but she will be left with almost no means of subsistence. Both authors focus on the hard realities of women's lives in the developing world, but although Aidoo describes them mostly from without by means of dialogue and the description of concrete events, Mernissi focuses on the view from inside: As her title "The Harem Within" already indicates, some of these realities are psychological rather than physical. In Jamaica Kincaid's hallucinatory story "My Mother," bodies themselves become gendered spaces that transform and transmute as a mother-daughter psychodrama plays out.

Public spaces too can be gendered. Gabriel García Márquez's short story portrays a situation in which material hardship and limited professional possibilities certainly play a role in the background, but the focus of the narrative lies on the public as well as the private surveillance that the girl, Mina, is constantly exposed to: Not only are her absences from church noted and interpreted by others in the village but at home her own grandmother, by virtue of a blindness that has reinforced all her other senses to an almost supernatural degree, notices and knows the meaning of Mina's every move. While the spaces that surround female characters tend to define limits, they can also spell out opportunities—particularly for the male (and bisexual) protagonists of Juan Goytisolo's *Makbara,* the North African bazaar is a site of erotic intersection and multiple possibilities rather than of restrictive conventions.

Noting such differences doesn't imply that the stories always aim to convey a realistic picture of the conditions the characters live in or that they straightforwardly represent the culture that they describe. Goytisolo's "A Reading of the Space in Xemaá-El-Fná" is most obviously not a description of gender relations as they really exist in Arab culture but a fantasy of an ideal social, and erotic space that is translated into a particular cultural place. So while each of the

Ulrike Rosenbach, *To Have No Power Is to Have Power*, 1978. Photo from a public multimedia performance in which the artist is caught in a net in front of screens that display images ranging from classical art all the way to contemporary popular culture.

stories addresses social and cultural conditions that are (or were) only too real, they shouldn't be mistaken for sociological documents: Each one of them, as it reports on the ways in which gender definitions and relations are shaped and reshaped by different spaces, also creates new perspectives and constructions of gender.

⋙⟐⋙

Clarice Lispector
1925–1977

A Brazilian novelist and author of short stories, Clarice Lispector was born in the Ukraine. Her parents immigrated to Brazil shortly after her birth, and she grew up in Recife and Rio de Janeiro. A precocious child, she graduated from secondary school at age twelve and published her first short story in the same year. She entered law school in 1941 and received her law degree three years later at age nineteen, the same year she published her first novel, *Close to the Savage Heart* (1944), a title she took from a phrase in James Joyce's *Portrait of the Artist as a Young Man.* Her first novel won a prestigious prize. She went on to publish nine novels, eight collections of short stories, a number of children's stories, and a translation of Oscar Wilde's

Picture of Dorian Gray. Having married a diplomat, she traveled widely and lived abroad for long periods during her lifetime, including seven years in Washington, D.C., in the 1950s, during which she didn't publish any of her work. She left her husband at the end of this period and returned with her two young children to Rio, where she resumed her publishing career and lived for the rest of her life.

Lispector's work is marked by its anguished intensity and existential search for meaning, often in the most ordinary experiences and fleeting events in her characters' lives. Subtly psychological and at times oppressively claustrophobic in the intimacy of her domestic settings, Lispector penetrates the small changes and seemingly insignificant events that become traumatic and life transforming in the lives of her characters. Her story "Preciousness" shows Lispector's uncanny insight into the crises of adolescence, of female characters especially, and manages to juxtapose these subtleties with the equally human traits of incomprehension and insensitivity. The results are often brutal and, not infrequently, maddening in her characters.

Preciousness

Early in the morning it was always the same thing renewed: to awaken. A thing that was slow, extended, vast. Vastly, she opened her eyes.

She was fifteen years old and she was not pretty. But inside her thinness existed the almost majestic vastness in which she stirred, as in a meditation. And within the mist there was something precious. Which did not extend itself, did not compromise itself nor contaminate itself. Which was intense like a jewel. Herself.

She awakened before the others, since to go to school she would have to catch a bus and a train and this would take her an hour. This would also give her an hour. Of daydreams as acute as a crime. The morning breeze violating the window and her face until her lips became hard and icy cold. Then she was smiling. As if smiling in itself were an objective. All this would happen if she were fortunate enough to "avoid having anyone look at her."

When she got up in the morning—the moment of vastness having passed in which everything unfolded—she hastily dressed, persuaded herself that she had no time to take a bath, and her family, still asleep, would never guess how few she took. Under the burning lamp in the dining room she swallowed her coffee which the maid, scratching herself in the gloom of the kitchen, had reheated. She scarcely touched the bread which the butter failed to soften. With her mouth fresh from fasting, her books under her arm, she finally opened the door and passed quickly from the stale warmth of the house into the cold fruition of the morning. Where she no longer felt any need to hurry. She had to cross a long deserted road before reaching the avenue, from the end of which a bus would emerge swaying in the morning haze, with its headlights still lit. In the June breeze, the mysterious act, authoritarian and perfect, was to raise one's arm— and already from afar the trembling bus began to become distorted, obeying the arrogance of her body, representative of a supreme power; from afar the bus started to become uncertain and slow, slow and advancing, every moment more concrete—until it pulled up before her, belching heat and smoke, smoke and heat. Then she got on, as serious as a missionary, because of the workers on the bus who "might say something to her." Those men who were no longer just boys. But she was also afraid of boys, and afraid of the youngest ones too. Afraid they would "say something to her," would look her up and down. In the seriousness of her closed lips there was a great plea: that they should respect her. More than this. As if she had made some vow, she was obliged to be venerated and while, deep inside, her heart beat with fear, she too venerated herself, she, the custodian of a rhythm. If they watched her, she became rigid and sad.

What spared her was that men did not notice her. Although something inside her, as her sixteen years gradually approached in heat and smoke—something might be intensely surprised—and this might surprise some men. As if someone had touched her on the shoulder. A shadow perhaps. On the ground the enormous shadow of a girl without a man, an uncertain element capable of being crystallized which formed part of the monotonous geometry of the great public ceremonies. As if they had touched her on the shoulder. They watched her yet did not see her. She cast a greater shadow than the reality that existed. In the bus the workmen were silent with their lunch boxes on their laps, sleep still hovering on their faces. She felt ashamed at not trusting them, tired as they were. But until she could forget them, she felt uneasy. The fact is that they "knew." And since she knew too, hence her disquiet. Her father also knew. An old man begging alms knew. Wealth distributed, and silence.

Later, with the gait of a soldier, she crossed—unscathed—the Largo da Lapa, where day had broken. At this point the battle was almost won. On the tram she chose an empty seat, if at all possible, or, if she was lucky, she sat down beside some reassuring woman with a bundle of clothes on her lap, for example—and that was the first truce. Once at school, she would still have to confront the long corridor where her fellow pupils would be standing in conversation, and where the heels of her shoes made a noise that her tense legs were unable to suppress as if she were vainly trying to silence the beating of a heart—those shoes with their own dance rhythm. A vague silence emerged among the boys who perhaps sensed, beneath her pretense, that she was one of the prudes. She passed between the aisles of her fellow pupils growing in stature, and they did not know what to think or say. The noise made by her shoes was ugly. She gave away her own secret with her wooden heels. If the corridor should last a little longer, as if she had forgotten her destiny, she would run with her hands over her ears. She only possessed sturdy shoes. As if they were still the same ones they had solemnly put on her at birth. She crossed the corridor, which seemed as interminable as the silence in a trench and in her expression there was something so ferocious— and proud too because of her shadow—that no one said a word to her. Prohibitive, she forbade them to think.

Until at last she reached the classroom. Where suddenly everything became unimportant and more rapid and light, where her face revealed some freckles, her hair fell over her eyes, and where she was treated like a boy. Where she was intelligent. The astute profession. She appeared to have studied at home. Her curiosity instructed her more than the answers she was given. She divined—feeling in her mouth the bitter taste of heroic pains—she divined the fascinated repulsion her thinking head created in her companions who, once more, did not know what to say about her. Each time more, the great deceiver became more intelligent. She had learned to think. The necessary sacrifice: in this way "no one dared."

At times, while the teacher was speaking, she, intense, nebulous, drew symmetrical lines on her exercise book. If a line, which had to be at the same time both strong and delicate, went outside the imaginary circle where it belonged, everything would collapse: she became self-absorbed and remote, guided by the avidity of her ideal. Sometimes, instead of lines, she drew stars, stars, stars, so many and so high that she came out of this task of foretelling exhausted, lifting her drowsy head.

The return journey home was so full of hunger that impatience and hatred gnawed at her heart. Returning home it seemed another city: in the Largo da Lapa hundreds of people reflected by her hunger seemed to have forgotten, and if they remembered they would bare their teeth. The sun outlined each man with black charcoal. Her own shadow was a black post. At this hour, in which greater caution had to be exercised, she was protected by the kind of ugliness which her hunger accentuated, her features darkened by the adrenaline that darkened the flesh of animals of prey. In the empty house, with the whole family out and about their business, she shouted at the maid who did not even answer. She ate like a centaur. Her face close to her plate, her hair almost in her food.

"Skinny, but you can eat all right," the quick-witted maid was saying.

"Go to blazes," she shouted at her sullenly.

In the empty house, alone with the maid, she no longer walked like a soldier, she no longer needed to exercise caution. But she missed the battle of the streets: the melancholy of freedom, with the horizon still so very remote. She had surrendered to the horizon. But the nostalgia of the present. The lesson of patience, the vow to wait. From which perhaps she might never know how to free herself. The afternoon transforming itself into something interminable and until they all might return home to dinner and she might become to her relief a daughter, there was this heat, her book opened and then closed, an intuition, this heat: she sat down with her head between her hands, feeling desperate. When she was ten, she remembered, a little boy who loved her had thrown a dead rat at her. "Dirty thing!" she had screamed, white with indignation. It had been an experience. She had never told anyone. With her head between her hands, seated. She said fifteen times, "I am well, I am well, I am well," then she realized that she had barely paid attention to the score. Adding to the total, she said once more: "I am well, sixteen." And now she was no longer at the mercy of anyone. Desperate because well and free, she was no longer at anyone's mercy. She had lost her faith. She went to converse with the maid, the ancient priestess. They recognized each other. The two of them barefooted in the kitchen, the smoke rising from the stove. She had lost her faith, but on the border of grace, she sought in the maid only what the latter had already lost, not what she had gained. She pretended to be distracted and, conversing, she avoided conversation. "She imagines that at my age I must know more than I do, in fact, and she is capable of teaching me something," she thought, her head between her hands, defending her ignorance with her body. There were elements missing, but she did not want them from someone who had already forgotten them. The great wait was part of it. And inside that vastness—scheming.

All this, certainly. Prolonged, exhausted, the exasperation. But on the following morning, as an ostrich slowly uncurls its head, she awoke. She awoke to the same intact mystery, and opening her eyes she was the princess of that intact mystery.

As if the factory horn had already whistled, she dressed hastily and downed her coffee in one gulp. She opened the front door. And then she no longer hurried. The great immolation of the streets. Sly, alert, the wife of an apache. A part of the primitive rhythm of a ritual.

It was an even colder and darker morning than the previous ones, and she shivered in her sweater. The white mist left the end of the road invisible. Everything seemed to be enveloped in cotton-wool, one could not even hear the noise of the buses passing along the avenue. She went on walking along the uncertain path of the road. The houses slept behind closed doors. The gardens were hard with frost. In the dark air, not in the sky, but in the middle of the road, there was a star: a great star of ice which had not yet disappeared, hovering uncertainly in the air, humid and formless. Surprised in its delay, it grew round in its hesitation. She looked at the nearby star. She walked alone in the bombarded city.

No, she was not alone. Her eyes glowering with disbelief, at the far end of her street, within the mist, she spied two men. Two youths coming toward her. She looked around her as if she might have mistaken the road or the city. But she had mistaken the minutes; she had left the house before the star and the two men had time to disappear. Her heart contracted with fear.

Her first impulse, confronted with her error, was to retrace her steps and go back into the house until they had passed. "They are going to look at me, I know, there is no one else for them to stare at and they are going to stare at me!" But how could she turn back and escape, if she had been born for difficulties? If her entire slow preparation was to have the unknown outcome to which she, through her devotion, had to adhere, how could she retreat, and then never more forget the shame of having waited in misery behind a door?

And perhaps there might not even be danger. They would not have the courage to say anything because she would pass with a firm gait, her mouth set, moving in her Spanish rhythm.

On heroic legs, she went on walking. As she approached, they also approached— and then they all approached and the road became shorter and shorter. The shoes of the two youths mingled with the noise of her own shoes and it was awful to listen to. It was insistent to listen to. Either their shoes were hollow or the ground was hollow. The stones on the ground gave warning. Everything was hollow and she was listening, powerless to prevent it, the silence of the enclosure communicating with the other streets in the district, and she saw, powerless to prevent it, that the doors' had become more securely locked. Even the star had disappeared. In the new pallor of darkness, the road surrendered to the three of them. She was walking and listening to the men, since she could not see them and since she had to know them. She could hear them and surprised herself with her own courage. It was the gift. And the great vocation for a destiny. She advanced, suffering as she obeyed. If she could succeed in thinking about something else, she would not hear their shoes. Nor what they might be saying. Nor the silence in which their paths would cross.

With brusque rigidity she looked at them. When she least expected it, carrying the vow of secrecy, she saw them rapidly. Were they smiling? No, they were serious.

She should not have seen. Because, by seeing, she for an instant was in danger of becoming an individual, and they also. That was what she seemed to have been warned about: so long as she could preserve a world of classical harmony, so long as she remained impersonal, she would be the daughter of the gods, and assisted by that which must be accomplished. But, having seen that which eyes, upon seeing, diminish, she had put herself in danger of being "herself"—a thing tradition did not protect.

For an instant she hesitated completely, lost for a direction to take. But it was too late to retreat. It would not be too late only if she ran; but to run would mean going completely astray, and losing the rhythm that still sustained her, the rhythm that was her only talisman—given to her on the edge of the world where it was for her being alone—on the edge of the world where all memories had been obliterated, and as an incomprehensible reminder, the blind talisman had remained as the rhythm for her destiny to copy, executing it for the consummation of the whole world. Not her own. If she were to run, that order would be altered. And she would never be pardoned her greatest error: haste. And even when one escapes they run behind one, these are things one knows.

Rigid, like a catechist, without altering for a second the slowness with which she advanced, she continued to advance.

"They are going to look at me, I know!" But she tried, through the instinct of a previous life, not to betray her fear. She divined what fear was unleashing. It was to be rapid and painless. Only for a fraction of a second would their paths cross, rapid, instantaneous, because of the advantage in her favor of her being in movement and of them coming in the opposite direction, which would allow the instant to be reduced to the necessary essential—to the collapse of the first of the seven mysteries so secret that only one knowledge of them remained: the number seven.

"Don't let them say anything, only let them think, I don't mind them thinking."

It would be rapid, and a second after the encounter she would say, in astonishment, striding through other and yet other streets, "It almost didn't hurt." But what in fact followed had no explanation.

What followed were four awkward hands, four awkward hands that did not know what they wanted, four mistaken hands of someone without a vocation, four hands that touched her so unexpectedly that she did the best thing that she could have done in the world of movement: she became paralyzed. They, whose premeditated part was merely that of passing alongside the darkness of her fear, and then the first of the seven mysteries would collapse; they, who would represent but the horizon of a single approaching step, had failed to understand their function and, with the individuality of those who experience fear, they had attacked. It had lasted less than a fraction of a second in that tranquil street. Within a fraction of a second, they touched her as if all seven mysteries belonged to them. Which she preserved in their entirety and became the more a larva and felt seven more years behind.

She did not look at them because her face was turned with serenity toward the void.

But on account of the haste with which they wounded her, she realized that they were more frightened than she was. So terrified that they were no longer there. They were running.

"They were afraid that she might call out for help and that the doors of the houses might open one by one," she reasoned. They did not know that one does not call out for help.

She remained standing, listening in a tranquil frenzy to the sound of their shoes in flight. The pavement was hollow or their shoes were hollow or she herself was hollow. In the hollow sound of their shoes she listened attentively to the fear of both youths. The sound beat clearly on the paving stones as if they were beating incessantly on a door and she were waiting for them to stop. So clear on the bareness of the stone that the tapping of their steps did not seem to grow any more distant: it was there at her feet like a dance of victory. Standing, she had nowhere to sustain herself unless by her hearing.

The sonority did not diminish, their departure was transmitted to her by a scurry of heels ever more precise. Those heels no longer echoed on the pavement, they resounded in the air like castanets, becoming ever more delicate. Then she perceived that for some time now she had heard no further sound. And, carried back by the wind, the silence and an empty road.

Until this moment, she had kept quiet, standing in the middle of the pavement. Then, as if there were several phases of the same immobility, she remained still. A moment later she sighed. And in a new phase she kept still.

She then slowly retreated back toward a wall, hunched up, moving very slowly, as if she had a broken arm, until she was leaning against the wall, where she remained inscribed. And there she remained quite still.

"Not to move is what matters," she thought from afar, "not to move." After a time, she would probably have said to herself, "Now, move your legs a little, very slowly," after which, she sighed and remained quiet, watching. It was still dark.

Then the day broke. Slowly she retrieved her books scattered on the ground. Further ahead lay her open exercise book. When she bent over to pick it up, she saw the large round handwriting which until this morning had been hers.

Then she left. Without knowing how she had filled in the time, unless with steps and more steps, she arrived at the school more than two hours late. Since she had thought about nothing, she did not realize how the time had slipped by. From the presence of the Latin master she discovered with polite surprise that in class they had already started on the third hour.

"What happened to you?" whispered the girl with the satchel at her side.

"Why?"

"Your face is white. Are you feeling unwell?"

"No," she said so clearly that several pupils looked at her. She got up and said in a loud voice, "Excuse me!"

She went to the lavatory. Where, before the great silence of the tiles, she cried out in a high shrill voice, "I am all alone in the world! No one will ever help me, no one will ever love me! I am all alone in the world!"

She was standing there, also missing the third class, on the long lavatory bench in front of several wash basins.

"It doesn't matter, I'll copy the notes later, I'll borrow someone's notes and copy them later at home—I am all alone in the world!"

She interrupted herself, beating her clenched fists several times on the bench.

The noise of four shoes suddenly began like a fine and rapid downpour of rain. A blind noise, nothing was reflected on the shiny bricks. Only the clearness of each shoe which never became entangled even once with another shoe. Like nuts falling. It was only a question of waiting as one waits for them to stop knocking on the door. Then they stopped.

When she went to set her hair in front of the mirror, she looked so ugly.

She possessed so little, and they had touched her.

She was so ugly and precious.

Her face was pale, her features grown refined. Her hands, still stained with ink from the previous day, moistening her hair.

"I must take more care of myself," she thought. She did not know how to. The truth is that each time she knew even less how to. The expression of her nose was that of a snout peeping through a hedge.

She went back to the bench and sat down quietly, with her snout.

"A person is nothing. No," she retorted in weak protest, "don't say that," she thought with kindness and melancholy. "A person is something," she said in kindness.

But, during dinner, life assumed an urgent and hysterical meaning.

"I need some new shoes! Mine make a lot of noise, a woman can't walk on wooden heels, it attracts too much attention! No one gives me anything! No one gives me anything!" And she was so feverish and breathless that no one had the courage to tell her that she would not get them. They only said, "You are not a woman and all shoe heels are made of wood."

Until, just as a person grows fat, she ceased, without knowing through which process, to be precious. There is an obscure law which decrees that the egg be protected until the chicken is born, a bird of fire. And she got her new shoes.

Fatima Mernissi
b. 1940

Fatima Mernissi is a prominent sociologist and the best-known Arab sociological writer in the West. She was born in Fez, Morocco, to a rich, established, traditional family and was raised in the family harem (separate women's quarters). Her father was an open-minded traditionalist, however, and allowed her to continue her education all the way to a doctorate. From a very early age she developed a keen eye for observation and internalized the Moroccan woman's perspective. She started teaching at the most distinguished university in Morocco, l'Université Mohammed-V, in Rabat, and soon became a full professor. She championed the cause of women in Morocco, a country little known previously for its feminist movement. She wrote extensively on women's positions in Arabic culture, including both the popular culture and the official culture of the traditional establishment. Some of her early academic works received considerable attention in France and were then translated into English.

Mernissi's scholarly works include *Islam and Democracy, The Forgotten Queen of Islam, Doing Daily Battle, Beyond the Veil,* and *Women and Islam: An Historical and Theological Enquiry.* In 1981 she created a collective working group called *Women, Families, Children* and launched the journal *Approche* with a French publisher. A few years later in 1997, she directed her attention to the innovative nongovernmental leaders who started a project called "Civic Synergy." Her work with them involves animating writing workshops to enhance communication skills and has inspired her work on a recent book, *Cyber-Islam as a Cosmic Mirror: Sufism and Civic Initiative in Digital Morocco.*

But Mernissi is as much known for her narrative and autobiographical work as she is for her scholarly and academic studies on modern Muslim society and the situation of women in Islam. Her 1994 autobiographical account of her childhood and early youth in Fez, *Dreams of Trespass,* makes fascinating and insightful reading. The success of this autobiographical narrative led her to devote more of her energy to creative writing. Her most recent book is *Chahrazad n'est pas marocaine* (translated as *Scheherazade Goes West*). "The Harem Within," an essay or episode in *Dreams of Trespass,* shows her ability to re-create at once both a personal and a collective past.

PRONUNCIATION:
Fatima Mernissi: FAH-ti-mah mare-NEE-see

The Harem Within

Our harem in Fez was surrounded by high walls and, with the exception of the little square chunk of sky that you could see from the courtyard below, nature did not exist. Of course, if you rushed like an arrow up to the terrace, you could see that the sky was larger than the house, larger than everything, but from the courtyard, nature seemed irrelevant. It had been replaced by geometric and floral designs reproduced on tiles, woodwork, and stucco. The only strikingly beautiful flowers we had in the house were those of the colorful brocades which covered the sofas and those of the embroidered silk drapes that sheltered the doors and windows. You could not, for example, open a shutter to look outside when you wanted to escape. All the windows opened onto the courtyard. There were none facing the street.

Once a year, during springtime, we went on a *nuzha,* or picnic, at my uncle's farm in Oued Fez,[1] ten kilometers from the city. The important adults rode in cars, while the children, divorced aunts, and other relatives were put into two big trucks rented for the occasion. Aunt Habiba and Chama always carried tambourines, and they would make such a hell of a noise along the way that the truck driver would go crazy. "If you ladies don't stop this," he would shout, "I'm going to drive off the road and throw everyone into the valley." But his threats always came to nothing, because his voice would be drowned out by the tambourines and hand clapping.

On picnic day, everyone woke up at dawn and buzzed around the courtyard as if it were a religious festival day with groups of people organizing food here, drinks there, and putting drapes and carpets into bundles everywhere. Chama and Mother took care of the swings. "How can you have a picnic without swings?" they would argue whenever Father suggested they forget about them for once, because it took so much time to hang them from the trees. "Besides," he would add, just to provoke Mother, "swings are fine for children, but when heavy grownups are involved, the poor trees might suffer." While Father talked and waited for Mother to get angry, she would just keep on packing up the swings and the ropes to tie them with, without a single glance in his direction. Chama would sing aloud, "If men can't tie the swings / women will do it / Lallallalla," imitating the high-pitched melody of our national anthem "Maghribuna watanuna" (Our Morocco, Our Homeland).[2] Meanwhile, Samir and I would be feverishly looking for our espadrilles, for there was no help to be had from our mothers, so involved were they in their own projects, and Lalla[3] Mani would be counting the number of glasses and plates "just to evaluate the damage, and see how many will be broken by the end of the day." She could do without the picnic, she often said, especially since as far as tradition was concerned, its origin was dubious. "There's no record of it in the Hadith,"[4] she said, "It might even be counted as a sin on Judgment Day."

We would arrive on the farm in mid-morning, equipped with dozens of carpets and light sofas and *khanouns.*[5] Once the carpets had been unfolded, the light sofas would be spread out, the charcoal fires lit, and the shish kebabs grilled. The teakettles would sing along with the birds. Then, after lunch, some of the women would scatter into the woods and fields, searching for flowers, herbs, and other kinds of plants to use in their beauty treatments. Others would take turns on the swings. Only after sunset would we make the journey back to the house, and the gate would be closed behind us. And for days after that, Mother would feel miserable. "When you spend a whole day among trees," she would say, "waking up with walls as horizons becomes unbearable."

You could not get into our house, except by passing through the main gate controlled by Ahmed the doorkeeper. But you could get out a second way, by using the

---

1. The valley of the river that runs just outside the walled city of Fez.
2. Maghrib is the Arabic name for Morocco, the land of the setting sun, from *gharb* (west) [Mernissi's note].
3. A female term of respect used often in Morocco for older women of middle or upper class. It is also used as a term of reverence for younger royal women instead of the usual term "princess."

4. A compilation of the Prophet Mohammed's deeds and sayings. Recorded and written down after his death, the Hadith is considered to be one of the primary sources of Islam, the first being the Koran, the book revealed directly by Allah to his Prophet [Mernissi's note].
5. Portable charcoal fire containers, the Moroccan equivalent of the barbecue grill. They can be made of pottery or metal [Mernissi's note].

roof-level terrace. You could jump from our terrace to the neighbors' next door, and then go out to the street through their door. Officially, our terrace key was kept in Lalla Mani's possession, with Ahmed turning off the lights to the stairs after sunset. But because the terrace was constantly being used for all kinds of domestic activities throughout the day, from retrieving olives that were stored in big jars up there, to washing and drying clothes, the key was often left with Aunt Habiba, who lived in the room right next to the terrace.

The terrace exit route was seldom watched, for the simple reason that getting from it to the street was a difficult undertaking. You needed to be quite good at three skills: climbing, jumping, and agile landing. Most of the women could climb up and jump fairly well, but not many could land gracefully. So, from time to time, someone would come in with a bandaged ankle, and everyone would know just what she'd been up to. The first time I came down from the terrace with bleeding knees, Mother explained to me that a woman's chief problem in life was figuring out how to land. "Whenever you are about to embark on an adventure," she said, "you have to think about the landing. Not about the takeoff. So whenever you feel like flying, think about how and where you'll end up."

But there was also another, more solemn reason why women like Chama and Mother did not consider escaping from the terrace to be a viable alternative to using the front gate. The terrace route had a clandestine, covert dimension to it, which was repulsive to those who were fighting for the principle of a woman's right to free movement. Confronting Ahmed at the gate was a heroic act. Escaping from the terrace was not, and did not carry with it that inspiring, subversive flame of liberation.

None of this intrigue applied, of course, to Yasmina's farm. The gate had hardly any meaning, because there were no walls. And to be in a harem, I thought, you needed a barrier, a frontier. That summer, when I visited Yasmina, I told her what Chama had said about how harems got started. When I saw that she was listening, I decided to show off all my historical knowledge, and started talking about the Romans and their harems, and how the Arabs became the sultans of the planet thanks to Caliph Harun al-Rashid's one thousand women, and how the Christians tricked the Arabs by changing the rules on them while they were asleep. Yasmina laughed a lot when she heard the story, and said that she was too illiterate to evaluate the historical facts, but that it all sounded very funny and logical too. I then asked her if what Chama had said was true or false, and Yasmina said that I needed to relax about this right-and-wrong business. She said that there were things which could be both, and things which could be neither. "Words are like onions," she said. "The more skins you peel off, the more meanings you encounter. And when you start discovering multiplicities of meanings, then right and wrong becomes irrelevant. All these questions about harems that you and Samir have been asking are all fine and good, but there will always be more to be discovered." And then she added, "I am going to peel one more skin for you now. But remember, it is only one among others."

The word "harem," she said, was a slight variation of the word *haram,* the forbidden, the proscribed. It was the opposite of *halal,* the permissible. Harem was the place where a man sheltered his family, his wife or wives, and children and relatives. It could be a house or a tent, and it referred both to the space and to the people who lived within it. One said "Sidi[6] So-and-So's harem," referring both to his family

---

6. "Sidi" (or "Si" for short) is a term of respect used for older men of certain status or learning.

members and to his physical home. One thing that helped me see this more clearly was when Yasmina explained that Mecca, the holy city, was also called Haram.[7] Mecca was a space where behavior was strictly codified. The moment you stepped inside, you were bound by many laws and regulations. People who entered Mecca had to be pure: they had to perform purification rituals, and refrain from lying, cheating, and doing harmful deeds. The city belonged to Allah and you had to obey his *shari'a,* or sacred law, if you entered his territory. The same thing applied to a harem when it was a house belonging to a man. No other men could enter it without the owner's permission, and when they did, they had to obey his rules. A harem was about private space and the rules regulating it. In addition, Yasmina said, it did not need walls. Once you knew what was forbidden, you carried the harem within. You had it in your head, "inscribed under your forehead and under your skin." That idea of an invisible harem, a law tattooed in the mind, was frightfully unsettling to me. I did not like it at all, and I wanted her to explain more.

The farm, said Yasmina, was a harem, although it did not have walls. "You only need walls, if you have streets!" But if you decided, like Grandfather, to live in the countryside, then you didn't need gates, because you were in the middle of the fields and there were no passersby. Women could go freely out into the fields, because there were no strange men hovering around, peeping at them. Women could walk or ride for hours without seeing a soul. But if by chance they did meet a male peasant along the way, and he saw that they were unveiled, he would cover his head with the hood of his own *djellaba*[8] to show that he was not looking. So in this case, Yasmina said, the harem was in the peasant's head, inscribed somewhere under his forehead. He knew that the women on the farm belonged to Grandfather Tazi, and that he had no right to look at them.

This business of going around with a frontier inside the head disturbed me, and discreetly I put my hand to my forehead to make sure it was smooth, just to see if by any chance I might be harem-free. But then, Yasmina's explanation got even more alarming, because the next thing she said was that any space you entered had its own invisible rules, and you needed to figure them out. "And when I say space," she continued, "It can be any space—a courtyard, a terrace, or a room, or even the street for that matter. Wherever there are human beings, there is a *qa'ida,* or invisible rule. If you stick to the *qa'ida,* nothing bad can happen to you." In Arabic, she reminded me, *qa'ida* meant many different things, all of which shared the same basic premise. A mathematical law or a legal system was a *qa'ida,* and so was the foundation of a building. *Qa'ida* was also a custom, or a behavioral code. *Qa'ida* was everywhere. Then she added something which really scared me: "Unfortunately, most of the time, the *qa'ida* is against women."

"Why?" I asked. "That's not fair, is it?" And I crept closer so as not to miss a word of her answer. The world, Yasmina said, was not concerned about being fair to women. Rules were made in such a manner as to deprive them in some way or another. For example, she said, both men and women worked from dawn until very late at night. But men made money and women did not. That was one of the invisible rules. And when a woman worked hard, and was not making money, she was stuck in a harem, even though she could not see its walls. "Maybe the rules are ruthless be-

7. An Arabic word meaning "sanctuary" and also the sacred domain of any Mosque, and "al-Haram" with the definite article, is the term reserved for the Ka'ba in Mecca.

8. The common hooded dress for men in traditional Morocco.

cause they are not made by women," was Yasmina's final comment. "But why aren't they made by women?" I asked. "The moment women get smart and start asking that very question," she replied, "instead of dutifully cooking and washing dishes all the time, they will find a way to change the rules and turn the whole planet upside down." "How long will that take?" I asked, and Yasmina said, "A long time."

I asked her next if she could tell me how to figure out the invisible rule or *qaʾida*, whenever I stepped into a new space. Were there signals, or something tangible that I could look for? No, she said, unfortunately not, there were no clues, except for the violence after the fact. Because the moment I disobeyed an invisible rule, I would get hurt. However, she noted that many of the things people enjoyed doing most in life, like walking around, discovering the world, singing, dancing, and expressing an opinion, often turned up in the strictly forbidden category. In fact, the *qaʾida*, the invisible rule, often was much worse than walls and gates. With walls and gates, you at least knew what was expected from you.

At those words, I almost wished that all rules would suddenly materialize into frontiers and visible walls right before my very eyes. But then I had another uncomfortable thought. If Yasmina's farm was a harem, in spite of the fact that there were no walls to be seen, then what did *hurriya*, or freedom, mean? I shared this thought with her, and she seemed a little worried, and said that she wished I would play like other kids, and stop worrying about walls, rules, constraints, and the meaning of *hurriya*. "You'll miss out on happiness if you think too much about walls and rules, my dear child," she said. "The ultimate goal of a woman's life is happiness. So don't spend your time looking for walls to bang your head on." To make me laugh, Yasmina would spring up, run to the wall, and pretend to pound her head against it, screaming, "*Aie, aie!* The wall hurts! The wall is my enemy!" I exploded with laughter, relieved to learn that bliss was still within reach, in spite of it all. She looked at me and put her finger to her temple, "You understand what I mean?"

Of course I understood what you meant, Yasmina, and happiness did seem absolutely possible, in spite of harems, both visible and invisible. I would run to hug her, and whisper in her ear as she held me and let me play with her pink pearls. "I love you Yasmina. I really do. Do you think I will be a happy woman?"

"Of course you will be happy!" she would exclaim. "You will be a modern, educated lady. You will realize the nationalists' dream. You will learn foreign languages, have a passport, devour books, and speak like a religious authority. At the very least, you will certainly be better off than your mother. Remember that even I, as illiterate and bound by tradition as I am, have managed to squeeze some happiness out of this damned life. That is why I don't want you to focus on the frontiers and the barriers all the time. I want you to concentrate on fun and laughter and happiness. That is a good project for an ambitious young lady."

Ama Ata Aidoo
b. 1942

The daughter of a tribal chief in Ghana, Ama Ata Aidoo was given an in-depth education. After attending high school in Cape Coast, she studied at the University of Ghana in Legon, where she was among the first graduates when she completed her B.A. in 1964. Already during her studies, she was working on her own writing and collaborated with Efua Sutherland, a Ghanaian playwright. Her first play, *The Dilemma of a Ghost,* was produced the year she graduated. After studying for a short time at Stanford University in the United States on a creative writing fellowship, Aidoo began to teach at the Institute of African Studies at the University of Ghana, and then lectured and taught at various universities in Africa and the United States. She served briefly as Ghana's secretary of education from 1982 to 1983, and subsequently moved to Zimbabwe, where she worked as a writer and for a short time took a position in the Ministry of Education. A novelist and playwright, Aidoo has also published poetry and children's books.

In many of her novels, short stories, and plays, Aidoo takes up African oral storytelling traditions, sometimes insisting that her works be read aloud rather than silently; she often addresses the clash between African and European cultures, West Africa's history of slavery, and particularly the situation of African women, who are doubly oppressed by (neo-)colonial rule and homegrown patriarchal structures. The difficulties of marriage for African women and the situation of those who have traveled abroad or who otherwise develop a sense of the injustices that are inflicted upon African women are also explored in many of Aidoo's other works such as the novel *Our Sister Killjoy* (1977), the play *Anowa* (1970), and *Changes: A Love Story* (1991). "No Sweetness Here," the prize-winning title story from a 1970 collection of Aidoo's short stories, explores precisely this situation through the juxtaposition of a Westernized teacher and the mother of one of her pupils, illuminating the social, cultural, economic, and legal realities of women's lives even in a country that has achieved political independence.

PRONUNCIATION:
   Ama Ata Aidoo: AH-mah ah-TAH EYE-doo

No Sweetness Here

He was beautiful, but that was not important. Beauty does not play such a vital role in a man's life as it does in a woman's, especially if that man is a Fanti.[1] If a man's beauty is so ill-mannered as to be noticeable, people discreetly ignore its existence. Only an immodest girl like me would dare comment on a boy's beauty. "Kwesi is so handsome," I was always telling his mother. "If ever I am transferred from this place, I will kidnap him." I enjoyed teasing the dear woman and she enjoyed being teased about him. She would look scandalised, pleased and alarmed all in one fleeting moment.

'Ei, Chicha.' She called me the Fanticised version of "teacher." "You should not say such things. The boy is not very handsome really." But she knew she was lying. "Besides, Chicha, who cares whether a boy is handsome or not?" Again she knew that at least she cared, for, after all, didn't the boy's wonderful personality throw a warm light on the mother's lively though already waning beauty? Then gingerly, but in a remarkably matter-of-fact tone, she would voice out her gnawing fear. "Please Chicha, I always know you are just making fun of me, but please, promise me you won't take Kwesi away with you." Almost at once her tiny mouth would quiver and she would hide her eyes in her cloth as if ashamed of her great love and her fears. But I understood. "O, Maami, don't cry, you know I don't mean it."

"Chicha I am sorry, and I trust you. Only I can't help fearing, can I? What will I do, Chicha, what would I do, should something happen to my child?" She would raise her pretty eyes, glistening with unshed tears.

"Nothing will happen to him," I would assure her. "He is a good boy. He does not fight and therefore there is no chance of anyone beating him. He is not dull, at least

1. An ethnic group living in Ghana, West Africa.

not too dull which means he does not get more cane-lashes than the rest of his mates. . . ."

"Chicha, I shall willingly submit to your canes if he gets his sums wrong," she would hastily intervene.

"Don't be funny. A little warming-up on a cold morning wouldn't do him any harm. But if you say so, I won't object to hitting that soft flesh of yours." At this, the tension would break and both of us begin laughing. Yet I always went away with the image of her quivering mouth and unshed tears in my mind.

Maami Ama loved her son; and this is a statement silly, as silly as saying Maami Ama is a woman. Which mother would not? At the time of this story, he had just turned ten years old. He was in Primary Class Four and quite tall for his age. His skin was as smooth as shea-butter and as dark as charcoal. His black hair was as soft as his mother's. His eyes were of the kind that always remind one of a long dream on a hot afternoon. It is indecent to dwell on a boy's physical appearance, but then Kwesi's beauty was indecent.

The evening was not yet come. My watch read 4.15 p.m., that ambiguous time of the day, which the Fantis, despite their great ancient astronomic knowledge, have always failed to identify. For the very young and very old, it is certainly evening, for they've stayed at home all day and they begin to persuade themselves that the day is ending. Bored with their own company, they sprawl in the market-place or by their own walls. The children begin to whimper for their mothers, for they are tired with playing "house". Fancying themselves starving, they go back to what was left of their lunch, but really they only pray that mother will come home from the farm soon. The very old certainly do not go back on lunch remains but they do bite back at old conversational topics which were fresh at ten o'clock.

"I say, Kwame, as I was saying this morning, my first wife was a most beautiful woman," old Kofi would say.

"Oh! yes, yes, she was an unusually beautiful girl. I remember her." Old Kwame would nod his head but the truth was he was tired of the story and he was sleepy. "It's high time the young people came back from the farm."

But I was a teacher, and I went the white man's way. School was over. Maami Ama's hut was at one end of the village and the school was at the other. Nevertheless it was not a long walk from the school to her place because Bamso is not really a big village. I had left my books to little Grace Ason to take home for me; so I had only my little clock in my hand and I was walking in a leisurely way. As I passed the old people, they shouted their greetings. Here too it was always the Fanticised form of the English.

"Kudiimin-o,[2] Chicha." Then I would answer, "Kudiimin, Nana." When I greeted first, the response was "Tanchiw", that is "Thank you."

"Chicha, how are you?"

"Nana, I am well."

"And how are the children?"

"Nana, they are well."

"*Yoo,* that is good." When an old man felt inclined to be talkative, especially if he had more than me for audience, he would compliment me on the work I was doing. Then he would go on to the assets of education, especially female education, ending up with quoting Dr. Aggrey.[3]

---

2. Good evening.
3. Dr. James Emmanuel Kwegyir Aggrey (1875–1927) was an intellectual from Ghana who traveled widely in

Africa, Europe, and the United States and passionately promoted the importance of education for Africans.

So this evening too, I was delayed: but it was as well, for when I arrived at the hut, Maami Ama had just arrived from the farm. The door opened, facing the village, and so I could see her. Oh, that picture is still vivid in my mind. She was sitting on a low stool with her load before her. Like all the loads the other women would bring from the farms into their homes, it was colourful with miscellaneous articles. At the very bottom of the wide wooden tray were the cassava and yam tubers, rich muddy brown, the colour of the earth. Next were the plantain, of the green colour of the woods from which they came. Then there were the gay vegetables, the scarlet pepper, garden eggs, golden pawpaw and crimson tomatoes. Over this riot of colours the little woman's eyes were fixed, absorbed, while the tiny hands delicately picked the pepper. I made a scratchy noise at the door. She looked up and smiled. Her smile was a wonderful flashing whiteness.

"Oh Chicha, I have just arrived."

"So I see. *Ayekoo.*"[4]

"*Yaa,* my own. And how are you, my child?"

"Very well, Mother."

"And you?"

"Tanchiw. Do sit down, there's a stool in that corner. Sit down. Mmmm. . . . Life is a battle. What can we do? We are just trying, my daughter."

"Why were you longer at the farm today?"

"After weeding that plot I told you about last week, I thought I would go for one or two yams."

"Ah!" I cried.

"You know tomorrow is Ahobaa. Even if one does not feel happy, one must have some yam for old Ahor."[5]

"Yes. So I understand. The old saviour deserves it. After all it is not often that a man offers himself a sacrifice to the gods to save his people from a pestilence."

"No, Chicha, we Fantis were so lucky."

"But Maami Ama, why do you look so sad? After all, the yams are quite big." She gave me a small grin, looking at the yams she had now packed at the corner.

"Do you think so? Well, they are the best of the lot. My daughter, when life fails you, it fails you totally. One's yams reflect the total sum of one's life. And mine look wretched enough."

"O, Maami, why are you always speaking in this way? Look at Kwesi, how many mothers can boast of such a son? Even though he is only one, consider those who have none at all. Perhaps some woman is sitting at some corner envying you."

She chuckled. "What an unhappy woman she must be who would envy Ama! But thank you, I should be grateful for Kwesi."

After that we were quiet for a while. I always loved to see her moving quietly about her work. Having finished unpacking, she knocked the dirt out of the tray and started making fire to prepare the evening meal. She started humming a religious lyric. She was a Methodist.

> *We are fighting*
> *We are fighting*
> *We are fighting for Canaan, the Heavenly Kingdom above.*

---

4. Hello.

5. Ahobaa is a festival commemorating the end of an epidemic; according to Fante legend, Ahor was killed so that

his sacrifice would free his people from punishment by the gods for their offenses.

I watched her and my eyes became misty, she looked so much like my own mother. Presently, the fire began to smoke. She turned round. "Chicha."

"Maami Ama."

"Do you know that tomorrow I am going to have a formal divorce?"

"Oh!" And I could not help the dismay in my voice.

I had heard, soon after my arrival in the village, that the parents of that most beautiful boy were as good as divorced. I had hoped they would come to a respectful understanding for the boy's sake. Later on when I got to know his mother, I had wished for this, for her own sweet self's sake. But as time went on I had realised this could not be or was not even desirable. Kodjo Fi was a selfish and bullying man, whom no decent woman ought to have married. He got on marvellously with his two other wives but they were three of a feather. Yet I was sorry to hear Maami was going to have a final breach with him.

"Yes, I am," she went on. "I should. What am I going on like this for? What is man struggling after? Seven years is a long time to bear ill-usage from a man coupled with contempt and insults from his wives. What have I done to deserve the abuse of his sisters? And his mother!"

"Does she insult you too?" I exclaimed.

"Why not? Don't you think she would? Considering that I don't buy her the most expensive cloths on the market and I don't give her the best fish from my soup, like her daughters-in-law do."

I laughed. "The mean old witch!"

"Chicha, don't laugh. I am quite sure she wanted to eat Kwesi but I baptised him and she couldn't."

"Oh, don't say that, Maami. I am quite sure they all like you, only you don't know."

"My child, they don't. They hate me."

"But what happened?" I asked the question I had wanted to ask for so long.

"You would ask, Chicha! I don't know. They suddenly began hating me when Kwesi was barely two. Kodjo Fi reduced my housekeeping money and sometimes he refused to give me anything at all. He wouldn't eat my food. At first, I used to ask him why. He always replied, 'It is nothing.' If I had not been such an unlucky woman, his mother and sisters might have taken my side, but for me there was no one. That planting time, although I was his first wife, he allotted to me the smallest, thorniest plot."

"Ei, what did you say about it?"

"What could I say? At that time my mother was alive, though my father was already dead. When I complained to her about the treatment I was getting from my husband, she told me that in marriage, a woman must sometimes be a fool. But I have been a fool for far too long a time."

"Oh!" I frowned.

"Mother has died and left me and I was an only child too. My aunts are very busy looking after the affairs of their own daughters. I've told my uncles several times but they never take me seriously. They feel I am only a discontented woman."

"You?" I asked in surprise.

"Perhaps you would not think so. But there are several who do feel like that in this village."

She paused for a while, while she stared at the floor.

"You don't know, but I've been the topic of gossip for many years. Now, I only want to live on my own looking after my child. I don't think I will ever get any more children. Chicha, our people say a bad marriage kills the soul. Mine is fit for burial."

"Maami, don't grieve."

"My daughter, my mother and father who brought me to this world have left me alone and I've stopped grieving for them. When death summoned them, they were glad to lay down their tools and go to their parents. Yes, they loved me all right but even they had to leave me. Why should I make myself unhappy about a man for whom I ceased to exist a long time ago?"

She went to the big basket, took out some cassava and plantain, and sitting down began peeling them. Remembering she had forgotten the wooden bowl into which she would put the food, she got up to go for it. She looked like an orphan indeed.

"In this case," I continued the conversation, "what will happen to Kwesi?"

"What will happen to him?" she asked in surprise. "This is no problem. They may tell me to give him to his father."

"And would you?"

"No, I wouldn't."

"And would you succeed in keeping him if his father insisted?"

"Well, I would struggle, for my son is his father's child but he belongs to my family."

I sat there listening to these references to the age-old customs of my people of which I had been ignorant. I was surprised. She washed the food, now cut into lumps, and arranged it in the cooking-pot. She added water and put it on the fire. She blew at it and it burst into flames.

"Maami Ama, has not your husband got a right to take Kwesi from you?" I asked her.

"He has, I suppose, but not entirely. Anyway, if the elders who would make the divorce settlement ask me to let him go and stay with his father, I wouldn't refuse."

"You are a brave woman."

"Life has taught me to be brave," she said, looking at me and smiling. "By the way, what is the time?"

I told her, "It is six minutes to six o'clock."

"And Kwesi has not yet come home?" she exclaimed.

"Mama, here I am," a piping voice announced.

"My husband, my brother, my father, my all-in-all, where are you?" And there he was. All at once, for the care-worn village woman, the sun might well have been rising from the east instead of setting behind the coconut palms. Her eyes shone. Kwesi saluted me and then his mother. He was a little shy of me and he ran away to the inner chamber. There was a thud which meant he had thrown his books down.

"Kwesi," his mother called out to him. "I have always told you to put your books down gently. I did not buy them with sand, and you ought to be careful with them."

He returned to where we were. I looked at him. He was very dirty. There was sand in his hair, ears and eyes. His uniform was smeared with mud, crayon and berry-juice. His braces were hanging down on one side. His mother gave an affectionate frown. "Kwesi, you are very dirty, just look at yourself. You are a disgrace to me. Anyone would think your mother does not look after you well." I was very much amused, for I knew she meant this for my ears. Kwesi just stood there, without a care in the world.

"Can't you play without putting sand in your hair?" his mother persisted.

"I am hungry," he announced. I laughed.

"Shame, shame, and your chicha is here. Chicha, you see? He does not fetch me water. He does not fetch me firewood. He does not weed my farm on Saturdays as other schoolboys do for their mothers. He only eats and eats." I looked at him; he fled again into the inner chamber for shame. We both started laughing at him. After a time I got up to go.

"Chicha, I would have liked you to eat before you went away; that's why I am hurrying up with the food." Maami tried to detain me.

"Oh, it does not matter. You know I eat here when I come, but today I must go away. I have the children's books to mark."

"Then I must not keep you away from your work."

"Tomorrow I will come to see you," I promised.

"Yoo, thank you."

"Sleep well, Maami."

"Sleep well, my daughter." I stepped into the open air. The sun was far receding. I walked slowly away. Just before I was out of earshot, Maami shouted after me, "And remember, if Kwesi gets his sums wrong, I will come to school to receive his lashes, if only you would tell me."

"*Yoo,*" I shouted back. Then I went away.

The next day was Ahobaada. It was a day of rejoicing for everyone. In the morning, old family quarrels were being patched up. In Maami Ama's family all became peaceful. Her aunts had—or thought they had—reconciled themselves to the fact that, when Maami Ama's mother was dying, she had instructed her sisters, much to their chagrin, to give all her jewels to her only child. This had been one of the reasons why the aunts and cousins had left Ama so much to her own devices. "After all, she has her mother's goods, what else does she need?" they were often saying. However, today, aunts, cousins and nieces have come to a better understanding. Ahobaa is a season of goodwill! Nevertheless, Ama is going to have a formal divorce today. . . .

It had not been laid down anywhere in the Education Ordinance that schoolchildren were to be given holidays during local festivals. And so no matter how much I sympathised with the kids, I could not give them a holiday, although Ahobaa was such an important occasion for them they naturally felt it a grievance to be forced to go to school while their friends at home were eating too much yam and meat. But they had their revenge on me. They fidgeted the whole day. What was worse, the schoolroom was actually just one big shed. When I left the Class One chicks to look at the older ones, they chattered; when I turned to them, Class Two and Class Three began shouting. Oh, it was a fine situation. In the afternoon, after having gone home to taste the festive dishes, they nearly drove me mad. So I was relieved when it was three o'clock. Feeling no sense of guilt, I turned them all out to play. They rushed out to the field. I packed my books on the table for little Grace to take home. My intention was to go and see the divorce proceedings which had begun at one o'clock and then come back at four to dismiss them. These divorce cases took hours to settle, and I hoped I would hear some of it.

As I walked down between the rows of desks, I hit my leg against one. The books on it tumbled down. As I picked them up I saw they belonged to Kwesi. It was the desk he shared with a little girl. I began thinking about him and the unhappy connection he had with what was going on at that moment down in the village. I remembered every word of the conversation I had had with his mother the previous evening. I became sad at the prospect of a possible separation from the mother who loved him so much and whom he loved. From his infancy they had known only each other, a lonely mother and a lonely son. Through the hot sun, she had carried him on her back as she weeded her cornfield. How could she dare to put him down under a tree in the shade when there was no one to look after him? Other women had their own younger sisters or those of their husbands to help with the baby; but she had had no one. The only face the little one had known was his mother's. And now . . .

"But," I told myself, "I am sure it will be all right with him."

"Will it?" I asked myself.

"Why not? He is a happy child."

"Does that solve the problem?"

"Not all together, but . . ."

"No buts; one should think of the house into which he would be taken now. He may not be a favourite there."

But my other voice told me that a child need not be a favourite to be happy.

I had to bring the one-man argument to an end. I had to hurry. Passing by the field, I saw some of the boys playing football. At the goal at the further end was a headful of hair shining in the afternoon sun. I knew the body to which it belonged. A goalkeeper is a dubious character in infant soccer. He is either a good goalkeeper and that is why he is at the goal, which is usually difficult to know in a child, or he is a bad player. If he is a bad player, he might as well be in the goal as anywhere else. Kwesi loved football, that was certain, and he was always the goalkeeper. Whether he was good or not I had never been able to see. Just as I passed, he caught a ball and his team clapped. I heard him give the little squeaky noise that passed for his laugh. No doubt he was a happy child.

Now I really ran into the village. I immediately made my way to Nana Kum's house, for the case was going on there. There was a great crowd in front of the house. Why were there so many people about? Then I remembered that it being a holiday, everyone was at home. And of course, after the eating and the drinking of palm-wine in the morning and midday, divorce proceedings certainly provide an agreeable diversion, especially when other people are involved and not ourselves.

The courtyard was a long one and as I jostled to where Maami Ama was sitting, pieces of comments floated into my ears. "The elders certainly have settled the case fairly," someone was saying. "But it seemed as if Kodjo Fi had no strong proofs for his arguments," another was saying. "Well, they both have been sensible. If one feels one can't live with a woman, one might as well divorce her. And I hate a woman who cringes to a man," a third said. Finally I reached her side. Around her were her family, her two aunts, Esi and Ama, her two cousins and the two uncles. To the right were the elders who were judging the case; opposite were Kodjo Fi and his family.

"I have come, Maami Ama," I announced myself.

She looked at me. "You ought to have been here earlier, the case has been settled already."

"And how are things?" I inquired.

"I am a divorced woman."

"What were his grounds for wanting to divorce you?"

"He said I had done nothing, he only wanted to . . ."

"Eh! Only the two of you know what went wrong," the younger aunt cried out, reproachfully. "If after his saying that, you had refused to be divorced, he would have had to pay the Ejecting Fee, but now he has got the better of you."

"But aunt," Maami protested, "how could I refuse to be divorced?"

"It's up to you. I know it's your own affair, only I wouldn't like your mother's ghost to think that we haven't looked after you well."

"I agree with you," the elder aunt said.

"Maami Ama, what was your debt?" I asked her.

"It is quite a big sum."

"I hope you too had something to reckon against him?"

"I did. He reckoned the dowry, the ten cloths he gave me, the Knocking Fee. . . ."

All this had been heard by Kodjo Fi and his family and soon they made us aware of it.

"Kodjo," his youngest sister burst out, "you forgot to reckon the Knife Fee."

"No. Yaa, I did not forget," Kodjo Fi told her. "She had no brothers to whom I would give the fee."

"It's all right then," his second sister added.

But the rest of his womenfolk took this to be a signal for more free comments.

"She is a bad woman and I think you are well rid of her," one aunt screamed.

"I think she is a witch," the youngest sister said.

"Oh, that she is. Anyway, only witches have no brothers or sisters. They eat them in the mother's womb long before they are born."

Ama's aunts and cousins had said nothing so far. They were inclined to believe Ama was a witch too. But Maami sat still. When the comments had gone down a bit, she resumed the conversation with me.

"As I was saying, Chicha, he also reckoned the price of the trunk he had given me and all the cost of the medicine he gave me to make me have more children. There was only the Cooking Cost for me to reckon against his."

"Have you got money to pay the debt?" I asked her.

"No, but I am not going to pay it. My uncles will pay it out of the family fund and put the debt down against my name."

"Oh!"

"But you are a fool," Maami Ama's eldest aunt shouted at her.

"I say you are a fool," she insisted.

"But aunt . . ." Maami Ama began to protest.

"Yes! And I hope you are not going to answer back. I was born before your mother and now that she is dead, I'm your mother! Besides, when she was alive I could scold her when she went wrong, and now I say you are a fool. For seven years you have struggled to look after a child. Whether he ate or not was your affair alone. Whether he had any cloth or not did not concern any other person. When Kwesi was a child he had no father. When he nearly died of measles, no grandmother looked in. As for aunts, he began getting them when he started going to school. And now you are allowing them to take him away from you. Now that he is grown enough to be counted among the living, a father knows he has got a son."

"So, so!" Kodjo Fi's mother sneered at her. "What did you think? That Kodjo would give his son as a present to you, eh? The boy belongs to his family, but he must be of some service to his father too."

"Have I called your name?" Ama's aunt asked the old woman.

"You have not called her name but you were speaking against her son." This again was from Kodjo Fi's youngest sister.

"And who are you to answer my mother back?" Ama's two cousins demanded of her.

"Go away. But who are you people?"

"Go away, too, you greedy lot."

"It is you who are greedy, witches."

"You are always calling other people witches. Only a witch can know a witch."

Soon everyone was shouting at everyone else. The people who have come started going home, and only the most curious ones stood by to listen. Maami Ama was murmuring something under her breath which I could not hear. I persuaded her to come with me. All that time no word had passed between her and her ex-husband. As we turned to go, Kodjo Fi's mother shouted at her, "You are hurt. But that is what you deserve. We will get the child. We will! What did you want to do with him?"

Maami Ama turned round to look at her. "What are you putting yourself to so much trouble for? When Nana Kum said the boy ought to go and stay with his father, did I make any objection? He is at the school. Go and fetch him. Tomorrow, you can send your carriers to come and fetch his belongings from my hut." These words were said quietly.

Then I remembered suddenly that I had to hurry to school to dismiss the children. I told Maami Ama to go home but that I would try to see her before night.

This time I did not go by the main street. I took the back door through back streets and lanes. It was past four already. As I hurried along, I heard a loud roaring sound which I took to be echoes of the quarrel, so I went my way. When I reached the school, I did not like what I saw. There was not a single childish soul anywhere. But everyone's books were there. The shed was as untidy as ever. Little Grace had left my books too. Of course I was more than puzzled. "How naughty these children are. How did they dare to disobey me when I had told them to wait here until I came to dismiss them?" It was no use looking around the place. They were not there. "They need discipline," I threatened to the empty shed. I picked up my books and clock. Then I noticed that Kwesi's desk was clean of all his books. Nothing need be queer about this; he had probably taken his home. As I was descending the hill the second time that afternoon, I saw that the whole school was at the other end of the main street. What were the children doing so near Maami Ama's place? I ran towards them.

I was not prepared for what I saw. As if intentionally, the children had formed a circle. When some of them saw me, they all began to tell me what had happened. But I did not hear a word. In the middle of the circle, Kwesi was lying flat on his back. His shirt was off. His right arm was swollen to the size of his head. I simply stood there with my mouth open. From the back yard, Maami Ama screamed, "I am drowning, people of Bamso, come and save me!" Soon the whole village was there.

What is the matter? What has happened? Kwesi has been bitten by a snake. Where? Where? At school. He was playing football. Where? What has happened? Bitten by a snake, a snake, a snake.

Questions and answers were tossed from mouth to mouth in the shocked evening air. Meanwhile, those who knew about snake-bites were giving the names of different cures. Kwesi's father was looking anxiously at his son. That strong powerful man was almost stupid with shock and alarm. Dose upon dose was forced down the reluctant throat but nothing seemed to have any effect. Women paced up and down around the hut, totally oblivious of the fact that they had left their festive meals half prepared. Each one was trying to imagine how she would have felt if Kwesi had been her child, and in imagination they suffered more than the suffering mother. "The gods and spirits of our fathers protect us from calamity!"

After what seemed an unbearably long time, the messenger who had been earlier sent to Surdo, the village next to Bamso, to summon the chief medicine man arrived, followed by the eminent doctor himself. He was renowned for his cure of snake-bites. When he appeared, everyone gave a sigh of relief. They all remembered someone, perhaps a father, brother or husband, he had snatched from the jaws of death. When he gave his potion to the boy, he would be violently sick, and then of course, he would be out of danger. The potion was given. Thirty minutes; an hour; two hours; three, four hours. He had not retched. Before midnight, he was dead. No grown-up in Bamso village slept that night. Kwesi was the first boy to have died since the school was inaugurated some six years previously. "And he was his mother's only child. She has no one now. We do not understand it. Life is not sweet!" This was their verdict.

The morning was very beautiful. It seemed as if every natural object in and around the village had kept vigil too. So they too were tired. I was tired too. I had gone to bed at about five o'clock in the morning and since it was a Saturday I could have a long sleep. At ten o'clock, I was suddenly roused from sleep by shouting. I opened my window but I could not see the speakers. Presently Kweku Sam, one of the young men in the village, came past my window. "Good morning, Chicha." He shouted his greeting to me.

"Good morning, Kweku," I responded. "What is the shouting about?"

"They are quarrelling."

"And what are they quarrelling about now?"

"Each is accusing the other of having been responsible for the boy's death."

"How?"

"Chicha, I don't know. Only women make too much trouble for themselves. It seems as if they are never content to sit quiet but they must always hurl abuse at each other. What has happened is too serious to be a subject for quarrels. Perhaps the village has displeased the gods in some unknown way and that is why they have taken away this boy." He sighed. I could not say anything to that. I could not explain it myself, and if the villagers believed there was something more in Kwesi's death than the ordinary human mind could explain, who was I to argue?

"Is Maami Ama herself there?"

"No, I have not seen her there."

He was quiet and I was quiet.

"Chicha, I think I should go away now. I have just heard that my sister has given birth to a girl."

"So," I smiled to myself. "Give her my congratulations and tell her I will come to see her tomorrow."

"*Yoo.*"

He walked away to greet his new niece. I stood for a long time at the window staring at nothing, while I heard snatches of words and phrases from the quarrel. And these were mingled with weeping. Then I turned from the window. Looking into the little mirror on the wall, I was not surprised to see my whole face bathed in unconscious tears. I did not feel like going to bed. I did not feel like doing anything at all. I toyed with the idea of going to see Maami Ama and then finally decided against it. I could not bear to face her; at least, not yet. So I sat down thinking about him. I went over the most presumptuous daydreams I had indulged in on his account. "I would have taken him away with me in spite of his mother's protests." She was just being absurd. "The child is a boy, and sooner or later, she must learn to live without him. The highest class here is Primary Six and when I am going away, I will take him. I will give him a secondary education. Perhaps, who knows, one day he may win a scholarship to the university." In my daydreams, I had never determined what career he would have followed, but he would be famous, that was certain. Devastatingly handsome, he would be the idol of women and the envy of every man. He would visit Britain, America and all these countries we have heard so much about. He would see all the seven wonders of the world. "Maami shall be happy in the end," I had told my-self. "People will flock to see the mother of such an illustrious man. Although she has not had many children, she will be surrounded by her grandchildren. Of course, away from the village." In all these reveries his father never had a place, but there was I, and there was Maami Ama, and there was his father, and he, that bone of contention, was lost to all three. I saw the highest castles I had built for him come tumbling down, noiselessly and swiftly.

He was buried at four o'clock. I had taken the school-children to where he lay in state. When his different relatives saw the little uniformed figure they all forgot their dif-ferences and burst into loud lamentations. "Chicha, O Chicha, what shall I do now that Kwesi is dead?" His grandmother addressed me. "Kwesi, my Beauty, Kwesi my Master, Kwesi-my-own-Kwesi," one aunt was chanting, "Father Death has done me an ill turn."

"Chicha," the grandmother continued, "my washing days are over, for who will give me water? My eating days are over, for who will give me food?" I stood there, saying nothing. I had let the children sing "Saviour Blessed Saviour". And we had gone to the cemetery with him.

After the funeral, I went to the House of Mourning as one should do after a bur-ial. No one was supposed to weep again for the rest of the day. I sat there listening to visitors who had come from the neighbouring villages.

"This is certainly sad, and it is most strange. School has become like business; those who found it earlier for their children are eating more than the children themselves. To have a schoolboy snatched away like this is unbearable indeed," one woman said.

"Ah, do not speak," his father's youngest sister broke in. "We have lost a treasure."

"My daughter," said the grandmother again, "Kwesi is gone, gone for ever to our forefathers. And what can we do?"

"What can we do indeed? When flour is scattered in the sand, who can sift it? But this is the saddest I've heard, that he was his mother's only one."

"Is that so?" another visitor cried. "I always thought she had other children. What does one do, when one's only water-pot breaks?" she whispered. The question was left hanging in the air. No one dared say anything more.

I went out. I never knew how I got there, but I saw myself approaching Maami Ama's hut. As usual, the door was open. I entered the outer room. She was not there. Only sheep and goats from the village were busy munching at the cassava and the yams. I looked into the inner chamber. She was there. Still clad in the cloth she had worn to the divorce proceedings, she was not sitting, standing or lying down. She was kneeling, and like one drowning who catches at a straw, she was clutching Kwesi's books and school uniform to her breast. "Maami Ama, Maami Ama," I called out to her. She did not move. I left her alone. Having driven the sheep and goats away, I went out, shutting the door behind me. "I must go home now," I spoke to myself once more. The sun was sinking behind the coconut palm. I looked at my watch. It was six o'clock; but this time, I did not run.

━━◆═◆━━━

Hanan Al-Shaykh
b. 1945

A varied life has taken Hanan Al-Shaykh from the south of Lebanon to Beirut, Cairo, and the Arabian Gulf to London and Paris. These moves have provided her with a unique perspective on the life of her own country and of fellow Arab women, enabling her to interweave firsthand experience with a comparative and multicultural outlook. She has written short stories and novels and has been recognized as one of the most talented female writers of her generation. She was born in Beirut in 1945 to a Shi'ite middle-class family from the south of Lebanon and was educated in Beirut and Cairo. She started her career at the age of twenty-one as a journalist for a Beirut newspaper, writing particularly for its women's weekly. A few years after her marriage in 1968, she went to live in London (1975–1977) and Saudi Arabia (1977–1983) before settling in London in 1983.

Her first novel, *Suicide of a Dead Man* (1970), established her unique style of writing, profoundly dislodging the patriarchal system without openly challenging it. Unlike most first novels by Arab women writers that draw on autobiographical experience and are told through the female voice, *Suicide* is narrated by a middle-aged married man probing his life in the light of his obsessive desire for a sixteen-year-old girl. Beneath the apparent reproduction of the dominant power relations, the author conducts her subtle deconstruction of the ethos of patriarchy. Later novels *Satan's Hopper* (1975) and *The Story of Zahra* (1980) feature women seeking freedom and happiness in a changing society.

Her fourth novel, *Women of Sand and Myrrh* (1988), is a fascinating work both thematically and artistically. It is a novel of four women—two Arab, one Lebanese, and one American—who live in an unnamed desert society. Yet the condition in which they live brings elements of similarity and contrast into their lives, which is portrayed as a function of the way women and men perceive one another and themselves. Under the restrictive conditions of the climate and the socially constructed environment, foreign, even Western, women don't fare better than local ones. The title of the novel juxtaposes sand (with its associations of beauty, emptiness, and sterility) and myrrh with its richly exotic connotations of luxurious promises (being the gift offered to Christ in his cradle). The novel is redolent with symbols and allusions. The very structure of the novel, in which each section conveys a sense of independence while also being an integral part of the whole, reflects the degree of sophistication in the author's feminist vision.

This technique is also used in Al-Shaykh's two recent novels, *Beirut Blues* (1992) and *Only in London* (2000). The novels employ a fragmentary structure, corresponding to the devastation of war-torn Lebanon in *Beirut Blues* and the complexity of metropolitan, multiethnic London in *Only in London*. The life of the Arab community in London provides *Only in London* a microcosm of the contradictions of the Arab society that they left behind.

"A Season of Madness" reflects some of the subtle qualities of Al-Shaykh's narrative and demonstrates her sensitive way of subverting patriarchal and traditional orders.

PRONUNCIATIONS:
Fatin: fah-TEEN
Hanan Al-Shaykh: HAN-an all-SHAYKH

A Season of Madness

I fell upon my mother-in-law, biting her nose. I had always hated her nose. The day before I had banged the door in her face and emptied the rubbish bin on her from the balcony as she went to get in the car and drive away. I scattered frangipani blossoms over her and sang to her and put a garland of jasmine around her neck, pulling her toward me and kissing her face and hands and her silk scarf. I took the scarf off her and spread it out on the floor and asked her why we did not hire one of the horse-drawn carriages printed on it. Some of the time she tried to escape from me and other times she composed herself and made some effort to bring me to my senses, then despaired and looked up at the ceiling, pleading with God to tell her what she had done to deserve a mad daughter-in-law. "I only chose her as a wife for my son because she came from one of the best families," she protested.

My response was to kick my legs high in the air, demanding to know why I felt so hot, and praying for ice cubes to cool me down, holding out my skirt to receive them. My husband rushed over and tried to pull my skirt over my bare legs[1] and I struggled and bit his hand. All he said as he steered me toward my room was "Is this really how you want us to live, Fatin?"

The two of them finally pushed me into my room and I sat staring at my reflection in the mirror and laughed at my appearance in disbelief. I heard them commiserating with each other over the state of the house, his bad luck in marrying me, and the children's distress at seeing their mother losing her mind.

His mother suggested taking me to a doctor locally, while he favored sending me back to Lebanon. They debated whether this would provoke too much of a scandal,[2] then he pronounced that I would be a source of shame whichever they did, for I already was, even within those four walls: I wore no protection during my periods; I calculated how many eyelashes I had, using a pencil to separate them; I stuck flowers in the front of my shoes; I threw things away regardless of their value; I had tried to jump out of the window and fly, and run away in a truck transporting ivory, clinging on to the tusks until the driver found me and handed me over to the police.

I stumbled along in my madness, never meeting my real self except when my eyes fell on the watercolors, which the strange light in this African country had inspired me to paint; it was a light that broke the hold of the sun's burning rays for a short time at daybreak and dusk. I often wondered if I should tear these paintings down from the walls, in case they were what made my husband keep hoping that the old Fatin would return. (She was the girl who could not even say yes when she was asked to be his bride because, as well as being shy, she was dazzled by the fact that the offer was coming from a member of a wealthy emigrant family.) What really happened was that I did not think too much about whether to accept or refuse. If I finally said yes, it was probably because I was distracted by his mother's gold bracelet, wondering what logic could possibly lie behind the choice of the charms dangling from it: an acorn, a house, a heart, a mountain, the Lebanese flag and a tortoise.

All I could hear now was my mother-in-law—she who was used to finding an answer to everything—questioning, scolding, complaining because he could not decide what to do about me, while he merely repeated, "God help us," in resigned tones.

I felt more hopeful when the doctor came. He asked them to describe how my condition had worsened and if some incident had sparked it. "The sea," answered my mother-in-law. "It began that time she went to the sea and it poured with rain."

Then he turned to me and asked me my age. "The age of madness," I replied.

This answer ensured that he never addressed me again. He asked them if there was any mental illness in my family. When they both shook their heads, I interrupted and said they were lying: they knew about my aunt; the cause of her madness remained a mystery and she had been moved from one psychiatric unit to another. I described how my mother had made me take her a dish of tabbouleh one day, and how she had pushed me against the wall and forced me to swap clothes with her,

---

1. A woman baring her legs is considered a shameful act   2. Madness is considered a scandal in Arab culture.
in conservative Arab culture.

threatening to kill me if I opened my mouth. She had gone home in my place, slept in my bed, gone to school, played with my friends, married a man living in Africa and had hundreds of children with him. Although she visited Lebanon often, she had never come to visit me in the clinic. I fell silent briefly when I noticed the doctor leaving the room, then renewed my efforts, and screamed and howled and meowed and brayed and struck my face and banged on the window.

The saga continued and I could no longer bear the passing of time. I was worn out by the waiting and the madness. I decided that in order to resolve the situation I would have to develop my madness and become dangerous.

"She's crazy. The doctor's confirmed it," shouted my mother-in-law. "I guessed as much. Even when she was sane, her eyes had signs of it. I'll find you another wife once we've sent her back to her family. Let them pay for her to be treated. The children will be all right at their boarding schools." Then she lowered her voice and said very quietly, "Marriage is like everything else in life—a matter of luck. Who says a worm-eaten apple can't look red and juicy from the outside?"

I listened intently as I floated above the wooden floor, and sank, and tried to rise again. His voice drowned out hers, accusing her of being hard and selfish. He swore he would never marry again, because he was not going to leave me: he could not forget how I used to be when I was well. Marriage was for better or worse. He would have me cured. He loved me, he would never make me look ridiculous by sending me back to my family. He would stand by me. I shook my head, rejecting his compassion, floating farther away. His mother was temporarily infected by my madness and screamed maniacally at him: "I'm telling you she'll kill you. She'll poison you. She'll tear you apart with her teeth. Can't you see she's turned into a crazy bitch? She'll burn you alive, or stick a knife in you while you're asleep."

Encouraged by her reaction, I became more absorbed in my madness, rising and falling, then floating again, borne along by the sweat that was pouring off me. I heard him shouting back at her, pushing her away, and vowing not to abandon me even if I did take a knife to him. She exploded with rage, trying to make him see that he must extricate himself from my power, for I had procured charms from the magicians at the seaside, where I used to go sketching, and had planned out his fate for him.

"I'll never leave her. Never," he interrupted. "I'd give up the world for her."

When I heard this, I directed my energies to calming myself down, and took the last escape route left open to me: I washed my face, tied back my hair, fastened my robe modestly around me as I used to in the past, and went out to them in the filigree sandals that I had not worn since I went mad. I sat facing them, utterly composed, disregarding their eyes, which stood out from their faces with lives of their own, but full of panic. My calmness made them flex their arms and legs, ready to ward off any sudden attacks, or run for their lives.

But I hesitated, not knowing where to start. Should I tell them that I had been content like any wife, firmly convinced that life was marriage, children, running a house, sex from time to time, and secretly retiring inside myself when I wanted to question my feelings, or a certain melody made me happy or sad? I had begun to snatch some time to draw and paint, and eventually another man had come into my life. He used to watch me regularly as I sat facing the sea, trying to transfer the color of it onto the paper in front of me, and would pick up everything I left behind me, even raking up the colored chalk dust with his fingernails, seeing this scavenging as hugely important. I could feel that my life had changed, and everything around me began to have some meaning: the temperature of the seawater lapping around my feet;

his liking for the misshapen nail on my little toe; the glass of fruit juice in his hand; silence interspersed with talk, sleep with anxiety. The time came when he could pass his hand over my face without touching it, and I would feel a great warmth suffusing me and my heart beating faster, and when I stopped being able to force myself to leave these sensations behind as I reluctantly entered the other world which was in full swing at home. Although all aspects of this world—from the salt cellar and pepper pot to the place of my burial when my time was up—ran through everything I did, everything except breathing freely from the heart, I decided to loose the threads from the cocoon of marriage one by one, taking great care to ensure that none snapped or changed color. What I really wanted was for my husband to discover that he had no choice but to leave me.

I began by handing him the soap, pretending to forget that this is said to be a sign of an imminent parting. I kissed his eyes while he slept, disregarding the song that says, "Don't kiss me on my eyes, or tomorrow we'll be separated"; I took care that the toes of his shoes were always pointing toward the front door. Nevertheless, my husband continued to live his life as normal both at home and at work, so I had no choice but to make him revolted by me. Without much effort I turned myself into a human dustbin: I drank milk as if it were water, although I was allergic to it. I encouraged my guts to swell up with it, and with the cabbage, cauliflower and pulses that I also ate in large quantities. I swallowed garlic cloves as if they were pieces of chocolate, crunched onions as if they were sweet-smelling carrots, and then went to bed without brushing my teeth. While I was waiting for my husband to join me, I belched incessantly, releasing the pent-up gases whose odor spread through the surrounding air.

However, I always found my husband at my side when I woke up in the morning. He stayed, despite my acts of rebellion and constant questioning of my life with him. Why did nature not do its job and make him disappear, or rescue me from the pit I was in and cast me out into the world? When nothing changed, and after periods of thought that were agitated, calm, logical and reckless by turns, I decided upon madness.

But I did not disclose all this to them now; I found myself confessing to them in a low voice, articulating very clearly, that I was not mad, but afraid and ashamed because I had fallen in love with another man and wanted a divorce so that I could marry him. I asked them to forgive me for pretending to be mad because my husband's good-heartedness and generous nature had stopped me from telling the truth, which was that I had never loved him all the time I lived with him and had feared that the knowledge of this might fester inside him, a wound refusing to heal. My conscience had eaten away at me on account of my unfaithfulness to him, and I had believed that my contrived madness would prompt him to remove me from his life without any qualms—indeed, he would welcome the prospect. I added that I was determined to ask for a divorce but wanted nothing from them, not even the Beirut apartment, which was in my name. As I said this, I realized that my mother-in-law was the one I feared most.[3] Then I forced myself to look up and confront them. All the time I was giving an honest account of myself I had been staring at the floor. Now I fixed my eyes on their faces to prove to them how strong and brave I was, whatever their reactions might be. I waited for one of them to respond, expecting reproaches, physical blows, retribution of some kind, convincing myself that I would escape from them, regardless of the outcome.

---

3. The mother-in-law is a commonly disliked figure in Arab culture, especially when she is the matriarch of the larger family.

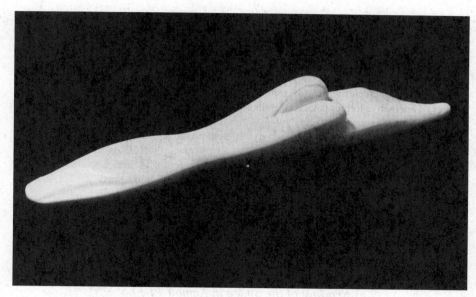

Louise Bourgeois, *Femme Couteau* ("Knife Woman"), 1969–1970. Sculpture in pink marble.

Then his mother was clasping my hand, twisting her mouth into a grimace of pity and murmuring, "She's crazy, poor thing. Nothing can be done for her."

My husband collapsed, burying his face in his hands and repeating sadly, "Poor thing, she's so young. I swear to God, I'll take her anywhere in the world to find a cure for her."

Juan Goytisolo
b. 1931

Born in Barcelona, Spain, Juan Goytisolo grew up under the dictatorship of Francisco Franco, which lasted from the end of the Spanish Civil War in 1939 until Franco's death in 1975. Tired of the rigidity and narrow limits of artistic, intellectual, and sexual expression that he experienced under the Franco regime, Goytisolo emigrated to France in 1957. During extensive travels that led him to the Soviet Union, Cuba, Canada, and the United States, he also came to know North African and Arab culture, which impressed him so deeply that he established a secondary residence in Marrakesh, Morocco. While Goytisolo's earliest novels were written in a realist style, his most famous works—such as *Marks of Identity* (1966), *Count Julian* (1970), and *Juan the Landless* (1975)—are critiques of Spanish society written in a much more experimental narrative mode. *Makbara* (1980) and *Landscapes After the Battle* (1982) are full-fledged postmodernist novels in which experimentation with style and voice works against the emergence of any coherent plot.

"A Reading of the Space in Xemaá-El-Fná" is the last chapter of Goytisolo's novel *Makbara,* named after the place in Arab cemeteries where lovers meet for secret trysts. This chapter stands on its own as the imagining of a space that breaks down all the boundaries and rules that constrain and oppress the protagonists: a place whose significance is at the same time spatial, social, cultural, economic, political, and sexual. While Goytisolo views this utopian space as one where many social boundaries are blurred, he foregrounds the freedom it offers from sexual categorizations and restrictions. Even though it is a public urban site, it allows for intimacies that European cities—here portrayed as cold, restrictive places—would never permit. Clearly, Goytisolo describes an ideal cultural location rather than a real one, but it is significant that he clearly identifies it with Arab culture, crystallized in the spatial form of the bazaar. Seen as an alternative to European conceptions of gender identity, Arab culture here presents itself in a very different guise than in Fatima Mernissi's Moroccan context. Part of this difference derives from Goytisolo's and Mernissi's very different narrative goals. While Mernissi seeks to convey to her audience a sense of the realities of a particular culture, Goytisolo is in search of imaginative counterpoints to realities that he views as in need of change. Literature becomes, for him, the medium in which such alternatives can be successfully imagined.

PRONUNCIATIONS:

> *Juan Goytisolo:* WAHN goy-tih-SO-low
> *Xemaa-el-Fna:* she-mah-AH-ell-f'NAH

from Makbara

A Reading of the Space in Xemaá-El-Fná[1]

in order to make the first contact easier, the Guide Bleu[2] recommends going up to the flower-covered terrace of a café in the late afternoon, as the sun is setting the urban landscape afire and it is possible to watch the city's ubiquitous improvisation of its festival in all its splendor

Fodor, on the other hand, proposes a morning incursion by way of Bab Fteuh, so as to get a firsthand idea of the incredible bric-a-brac for sale in its markets

more prudent, Nagel, Baedeker, Pol suggest a casual, discreet approach, sneaking up on it quietly and unobtrusively from the sidelines and letting oneself be swept along by the crowd until one finds oneself unexpectedly inside

couleur locale breakaway fascinación

and yet

all the guidebooks lie

like a spider, like an octopus, like a centipede slithering away, wriggling and writhing, escaping one's embrace, forbidding possession

there is no way of getting a firm grasp on it

an agora,[3] a theatrical performance, a point of convergence: an open and plural space, a vast common of ideas

peasants, shepherds, soldiers, tradesmen, hucksters who have flocked to it from the bus terminals, the taxi stands, the street stops of jitneys poking drowsily along: coalesced into an idle mass, absorbed in contemplating the daily hustle and bustle, taking refuge in the anonymous freedom and permissiveness of these surroundings: in continuous, capricious movement: an immediate contact between strangers, a forgetting of social constraints, identification in prayer and laughter, the temporary suspension of hierarchies, the joyous equality of bodies

---

1. Translated by Helen Lane. Xemaá-el-Fná is a famous plaza in the Moroccan city of Marrakesh, where vendors, performers, dancers, and musicians congregate every day.
2. The "Guides Bleus" (blue guides) are a French guide-

book series. Fodor, Nagel, Baedeker, and Pol are other well-known European travel guides.
3. A public space that served as a forum or marketplace in ancient Greek cities.

strolling slowly along, without the slavery of a time schedule, following the wayward inspiration of the crowd: a traveler in a constantly moving, vagabond world: attuned now to the rhythm of all the others: in graceful and fruitful nomadism: a slender needle in the middle of the haystack: lost in a maremagnum[4] of odors, sensations, images, multiple acoustic vibrations: the dazzling court of a kingdom of madmen and charlatans: a poverty-stricken utopia of absolute equality and freedom: migrating from group to group, as though wandering from one pasture to another: in the neutral space of chaotic, delirious stereophonic sound: tambourines guitars drums rebecs cries of street vendors speeches suras[5] screams: a fraternal community with no notion of asylums, ghettos, outcasts: lunatics, freaks, monsters set up camp wherever they choose, proudly exhibit stumps and scars, rebuke the passersby with furious gestures: blind savonarolas, crawling beggars, reciters of the Koran, men possessed, energumens:[6] each with his particular obsession riding on his back, shielded in his madness as though it were a conch shell, breasting the tide of an indifferent, mocking, compassionate crowd

the multitude overflows into the traffic along the thoroughfare, surrounds the cars and the jitneys, hems in the little carts of the delivery boys, blockades the flocks of sheep and goats, takes on the appearance of a huge demonstration without a purpose, of a popular army without ranks or hierarchies: bicycles steered by aerialists, packs of donkeys loaded with baskets, buses whose parking maneuvers give rise to feelings of pity, the clumsy movements of a defenseless beached whale: speed, strength, power forced to obey majority rule: the impotence, the futility of horns and engines: the revenge of the spontaneous, the motley, the proliferating on the ordering of all things according to strict classes: a no-man's land where the body is king and the effigy hung on buildings and lampposts a grotesque, faded puppet

survival of the nomad ideal as a utopia: a universe without a government or a leader, the free circulation of persons and goods, land owned and used in common, the tending of flocks, sheer centrifugal force: the abolition of private property and hierarchy, of rigid spatial boundaries, of domination based on sex and age, of the ugly accumulation of wealth: emulating the fruitful freedom of the gypsy who respects no frontiers: encamping in a vast present of quests and adventure: making no distinction between sea and land, navigating across the latter in the lighthearted mood of the fisherman: creating structures to welcome the world-wanderer, free ports for trading and talking together, marketplaces, little bazaars for the exchange of ideas

seafaring nomads or fishermen sailing across sand: palm groves in the middle of the desert: islands of green in an ocher ocean, with a rough, rippling surface: a groundswell that curls the crests of the dunes: tree trunks with the tops lopped off, towering like topmasts: tiny caravans like flotillas struggling to make headway in heavy seas
analogies between desert and ocean: endless space, isolation, silence, the imbricated patterns formed by waves and dunes, boundless, unbridled freedom, brightness, sharp clarity, absolute purity

---

4. Confusion.
5. The rebec is an Arab string instrument; suras are chapters of the Koran.
6. Madmen (Spanish). Girolamo Savonarola (1452–1498) was the prior of San Marco in Florence during the reign of the Medici; after their expulsion, he established dictatorial regime in Florence until the Pope sentenced him to death.

an aleatory relationship with the elements: a common dependency on wind and rain, sun, moon, stars, storms
ancestral caution, experience, wisdom in the face of climactic traps and snares, sudden treacherous changes in the sky
a keen sense of direction, a similar reading of the stars, an acute sensitivity that heads straight for the school of fish or the trickle of water lying ahead
mobility, courage, uncertainty, solidarity when danger threatens, stamina, moderation, spontaneous and fraternal hospitality

a portable business establishment: peddling reduced to its simplest expression: a threadbare carpet or a little straw mat: odd, meager means of livelihood: a little metal box containing a handful of roots, a worn pack of cards, an anatomical plate in color, a treatise on the art of love and aphrodisiac recipes, an old, well-thumbed copy of the Koran: Aladdin's lamp at nightfall, a protective parasol perhaps, open like an umbelliferous mushroom, beneath which a gnome in felt slippers and a peaked cap shelters himself as best he can from the sun's despotism

the proverbial difficulty of listing all the things that space engenders

knicknacks, miscellaneous utensils, odds and ends swept along narrow streets and main arteries by a violent maelstrom: countless objects of every sort and description wherever the eye happens to land: an utterly mad proliferation of useless goods: advertisements and images of consumer products to entice the possible buyer
patiently setting down nouns, adjectives one after the other, parts of speech fighting a losing battle with the perfect simultaneity of the photograph: chasing after the same effect in vain, like a traveler who misses the train and stands on the platform panting grotesquely till he runs out of breath
artifacts, gadgets, products filling the vacuum, materially occupying the entire urban landscape, pouring out in a cloying stream from bazaars and stalls, overwhelming the visual field to the point of nausea

> pyramids of almonds and walnuts, dried henna leaves, Moorish shish kebabs, steaming caldrons of harira, sacks of broad beans, mountains of sticky, filthy dates, carpets, water jugs, mirrors, teakettles, trinkets and baubles, plastic sandals, woolen caps, gaudy lengths of cloth, embroidered sashes, rings, watches with colored dials, faded postcards, magazines, calendars, cheap paperbacks, fat sausages, pensive sheeps' heads, cans of olives, bunches of mint, sugarloaves, blaring transistor radios, kitchen utensils, earthenware pots, couscous bowls, wicker hampers, leather jackets, straw bags from the Sahara, esparto-grass fruit baskets, Berber handcrafts, stone figurines, pipe bowls, sand roses, fly-specked pastries, sweets tinted violent colors, lupine, garden seeds, eggs, crates of fruit, spices, jugs of sour milk, loose cigarettes sold separately, salted peanuts, wooden spoons and ladles, miniature radios, cassettes of Xil Xilala and Noss-el-Ghiwán,[7] tourist folders, passport cases, photographs of Pelé, Um Kalsúm, Farid-el-Atrach, His Majesty the King,[8] a map of the city of Paris, a bizarre Eiffel Tower

---

7. Moroccan music bands.
8. Pelé is a famous Brazilian soccer player; Um Kalsúm is the name of a popular Egyptian singer; Farid-el-Atrach, a singer and actor, was known for his romantic leading roles; His Majesty refers to the King of Morocco.

adding
in homage to Jacques Prévert
to this odd inventory of miscellaneous items
the symbolic presence
of a RATON LAVEUR[9]

the comfortable garments enveloping the Arab body: the freedom of expression offered bodily members by the flowing robes, physiques hinted at by the softness and
suppleness of cloth whose folds set off curves and hollows more suggestively and effectively than if they were nakedly displayed: a clever, elusive game of hide-and-seek
in the communal anonymity of the public square: faces, legs, waists, bosoms delicately outlined behind chaste veils and kerchiefs, severely unadorned caftans, decorous almalafas and fuquías:[1] thighs in helicoidal[2] rotation round the shadowy center
of the target, hips waggling with the rhythmical movement of connecting rods,
breasts under only the very slightest tension quivering joyfully: currents, vibrations,
rushes of blood immediately reflected in parallel and opposite tumescences, concealed beneath the coarse-textured djellabah or the ample, prudent burnoose:[3] in-
guinal cones[4] that transform the fabric into a Bedouin jaima that discreetly shelters
the erect tentpole: in an indiscriminate mingling that lends itself to unavowable secret
pandering, bawdy gusts of wind, subtle maneuvers of pollination: a little market
based on supply and demand in which the bargain is sealed with smiles and signs, and
experts in the field of spontaneous semiology,[5] the prospective participants in the deal
decipher desires and impulses by way of the reading of each other's garments against
the light

amid burnooses, fuquías, jeans made in Korea and Hong Kong, T-shirts bearing the
official seal of Yale, California, Harvard, New York University
it is pointless to ask those wearing them whether they are graduates of these institutions: most likely only a few can even read the letters of the Latin alphabet
the ridiculous prestige of a superannuated system twinkling brightly across a distance
of countless light-years, like the glow of a planet blown to bits long ago, of a falling
star long since dead
the vanity of a culture turned into a gadget, cut off from the roots from which it ought
to be drawing its vital sap, unaware even of its own dramatic non-existence

the conception of wearing apparel as symbol, reference, disguise: the variety and the
splendor of the dress permitted in the brief parenthesis of a holiday celebration: the
temporary shedding of one's ordinary garments and social personality: changing
one's clothes so as to change one's skin: being, for a few short hours, a nabob,[6] a
world traveler, a king: staging a performance for oneself and others
(elderly men dressed in white from head to foot, girls with silver earrings and
bracelets, delicate, transparent almaizales,[7] a profusion of new sashes and slippers,
turbans like gracefully coiled serpents)

---

9. Jacques Prévert (1900–1977), a well-known French
poet, wrote a humorous poem called "Inventory," whose
refrain includes a steadily increasing number of "ratons
laveurs"—i.e., raccoons.
1. Long garments worn in North Africa.
2. Spiral-shaped.

3. Djellabahs and burnooses are loose, hooded cloaks.
4. Cones at the groin.
5. The theory of signs.
6. An important, wealthy, or powerful person.
7. Headdresses worn in North Africa.

a theatrical spectacle: the calls of muezzins[8] in the minarets of the mosques as an accompaniment in the background: shoddy footlights, stage sets, backdrops: joining in the rejoicing of the chorus bidding farewell to the fast of Ramadan[9]

the fierce rivalry of the halca:[1] multiple, simultaneous attractions: the frank abandonment of this or that spectacle by a crowd continually in search of novelty, the infectious excitement of the knot of onlookers gathered together a few steps farther along: the need to raise the voice, argue, polish up the come-on, perfect the gesture, exaggerate the grimace that will capture the attention of the passerby or irresistibly unleash his laughter: capering clowns, agile tumblers, Gnaua drummers and dancers,[2] shrieking monkeys, the pitches of healers and herb-sellers, the sudden bursts of sound from flutes and tambourines as the hat is passed: immobilizing, entertaining, seducing an eternally drifting audience seeking only to be diverted, magnetizing it little by little and attracting it to one's own particular territory, wooing it away from a rival's siren song, and finally extracting from it the shiny dirham[3] that will be the reward for physical strength, perseverance, cleverness, virtuosity

a comic, smiling parody that mirrors in reverse the agitation, the frenzy, the commotion of operations on the New York Stock Exchange during its frequent gales of euphoric optimism or gusts of panic, when the Dow-Jones average suddenly shoots upward or suddenly tumbles amid the frantic shouts of customers, the dizzying shifts in the figures posted on the big board, the frantic clatter of the stock tickers, the rapid-fire gibberish of the professional traders
local color à rebours:[4] the awesome bedlam of whites

sitting on the ground, a simpleminded soul strokes the strings of his rebec, lovingly cradling it like a wet nurse: the crowd censors out his humble, wretched presence, hurries on past him, engrossed in its affairs, allowing him to enjoy a diaphanous transparency, abandoning him to his monotonous, obsessive strumming: lips set in a perpetual smile, a strabismic[5] gaze, a life projected toward an impossible horizon: charitable folk keep him alive and he accepts his destiny with cheerful resignation: coming into this world to rock his instrument to and fro, to play sour notes, to repeat the same gestures endlessly, to occupy day after day a modest gap in the common space of the public square

a veiled woman plays a game of solitaire as she waits for a nibble from a client: an old man draws a graffito in chalk as he recites a sura half to himself: the chorus of beggars chant, over and over without a pause, fisabili-l-lah and smilingly shake their alms boxes: the sun beats down on their heads, chisels and accentuates the lack of expressiveness of their features, sculpts and immobilizes their forced smiles, makes them blink (or is it the swarm of flies that is responsible?) as though they had recovered their sight despite their empty eyesockets, their glass eyes, their hideously scarred eyelids

---

8. The Muslim criers who call the faithful to prayer five times a day from the minaret of a mosque.
9. The 9th month of the Muslim year, during which the faithful fast between dawn and dusk.
1. The performance of the oral storyteller ("halaigú").
2. The Gnaua are descendents of slave brotherhoods in sub-Saharan Africa, famous for their music, hymns, and prayers that mix Arabic and Bambara.
3. Moroccan coin.
4. In reverse.
5. Squinting.

the brotherhood of the Ulad-de-Sidi-Hamad-u-Musa suddenly huddles together to form the great pyramid: youngsters scramble up the stirrups of hands, hoist each other up with rapid gestures, find a firm foothold on the shoulders of the men down below who are bearing their weight, give a helping hand in turn to those who are to mount to the very top: a rigid hierarchy based on weight and age: from the robust adults at the base to the frail child who ingenuously waves to his retinue of admirers from the lofty height of his wondrous throne: the bright colors of short jackets and balloon trousers blaze, and in obedience to a signal from the leader, the hefty acrobats at the bottom slowly shift the axis of the entire pyramid so that it makes one, two, three complete circles in lithe and graceful equilibrium: as meanwhile the audience cheers and applauds and adds a few dirhams to the brotherhood's slim, modest peculum:[6] as they drop off the pyramid, the youngest ones begin their acrobatic exercises to the throbbing beat of a drum: supple aerialists perform their daring turns in a swift, weightless whirlwind: cartwheels, somersaults, perilous leaps, defying Newton's laws, making a mockery of the ponderous earthbound apple, proving the volatile nature of the bodies of children forged in the rigor and austerity of lives without protection or families, left to rely on their own resources from their tenderest years onward: others bend their trunks back, expand their rib cages like accordion bellows, thrust their heads between their legs, put their limbs out of joint, subject themselves to disastrous contortions, appear to fold up by doubling over backward: camp chairs that unexpectedly metamorphose, assume human form once again, and even have the courage to force a weak smile as they catch sight of the admiring glances of the audience

the circular empty space, the resounding vacuum of the Gnaua rite: an area vacated by the insistent beat of a drum in order to present the severe rigor of their immutable spectacle at the proper distance: a group of actors standing in a row, immaculate trousers and blouses, smooth, dark legs, unadorned and quintessentially naked: the dervish who is that day's principal performer bares his gleaming teeth, whirls drunkenly round and round in his bare feet, imitates a Cossack dance,[7] flogging space with the cheery tassel of his fez like a whip: the compelling rhythm of clacking castanets causes him to twirl about even faster and paves the way for the sudden appearance of the oldest member of the group, as skinny as a handful of vine shoots but possessed of a suppleness and vigor that absolutely belie his years: a body language in which muscles are the vocabulary: nerves the morphology: joints the syntax: vibrations, meaning, message convey themselves directly to those watching, affect their sensory organs, run down their skins in the form of a tingling sensation, giving rise to a form of knowledge immediately linked to feeling an auditory and visual pleasure, a bliss of the senses that fills the spectator's soul and lingers on long after the troupe's exit from the scene, like that fleeting mixture of satisfaction and surfeit experienced by one who has just furtively made love

two old men with the look of Hindustani fakirs present a rich, motley sample of their useless handiwork on the threadbare carpet covering the territory they have patiently acquired by usucapion:[8] an odd assortment of improvised flower vases made out of

6. Private property.
7. A dervish is a member of a Sufi religious brotherhood; Cossack dances are associated with a group of people in the former Soviet Union, many of whose members once served in the elite cavalry units of the Russian army.
8. Squatter's rights. Hindustani fakirs: the two old men look like religious beggars or holy men.

bottles, Esso oil cans, tins of Nido milk powder, water jugs, candleholders, each and every one of them topped off with plastic roses insensitive to the round of the seasons, the cruel, continuous assault of the furious sun: the complex structure of their pipes imitates the form of a saxophone, the smell of the incense they are burning is mindful both of a place of worship and a den of kif smokers:[9] dozens of doves flutter about in a flurry of white amid the flower vases, become intoxicated from the fumes of the aromatic resin, alight on the heads of the two old men, peck at birdseed from their gnarled hands, bill and coo at each other, exchange simpering politenesses in the sylvan thickets of their beards, explore, without ever venturing beyond them, the magic limits of the little square of carpet

a strong skull shaved perfectly bare, a thick stubby neck, broad shoulders, coppery skin, thick lips, a Mongol mustache trickling down past his chin, gold-capped teeth
Fantomas
Big Boss
Tarzan
Saruj
Antar
Taras Bulba[1]
he surpasses in both eloquence and height all the halaiquís staging their acts in the square: his imposing presence and stentorian voice attract each day an eager audience, willing captives of his fake arrogance: arms akimbo, legs spread apart, he reels off, like a schoolboy reciting from memory, the geographical itinerary of his adventures, his endless string of nicknames: his explosive, suggestive, mordant way with words skillfully exploits the resources of popular speech: a lingo free of all restraint, inhibition, repression: tales of complicated love affairs, cuckoldry, cunning mingled helter-skelter with verses, obscenities, suras, bursts of laughter, imprecations, insults: yarns involving backsides, cunts, pricks that abruptly end in moral preaching: breaking off between two episodes he goes round the circle gathered about him, warns the women to withdraw, grabs a youngster by the scruff of the neck and gracefully sends him flying with a show of ferocious severity: his fabrications of a Rabelais redivivus[2] at once extol and make a mockery of the perils of sexual pleasure: a florid abundance of allusions, paraphrases, euphemisms adorned with auriferous grins,[3] onomatopoeic outbursts, swift up-and-down movements of his fist with the middle finger of his other hand inserted in it: fornication: Tiznit: fellatio: Tefraút: anal intercourse: Uarzazát:[4] not forgetting the rules of classical oratory, the rhetorical question addressed to his hearers: I ask you: how was young Xuhá[5] able to keep his honor intact the night he slept in a den of sodomites?: the answer: by being clever and foresighted enough to pour thick bean

9. Marijuana smokers.

1. Most of these names refer to the protagonists of famous texts and films ranging from high literature to popular culture and across several centuries. Fantômas is the hero of more than 30 French thrillers written by Pierre Souvestre and Marcel Allain before World War I who commits horrifying but ingenious crimes in an unending series of disguises. In 1913 a series of enormously popular silent films based on the novels appeared. Big Boss is Bruce Lee's antagonist in the movie *The Big Boss* (1971), which started Lee's career as a kung fu film star. Saruj or Saruh is a famous oral storyteller whom Goytisolo greatly admired.

Antar is the poet and warrior hero of the medieval Arabic *Romance of Antar*. Taras Bulba is the protagonist of a novella by Russian author Nikolai Gogol (1809–1852).
2. Goytisolo is comparing the Arabic storyteller to the French Renaissance writer François Rabelais (d. 1553), whose works celebrate bodily excesses in eating, drinking, and sexuality.
3. Literally, grins that contain gold; an allusion to the storyteller's dental work.
4. Tiznit, Tefraút, and Uarzazát are Moroccan towns.
5. Hero of many humorous stories of Arabic folklore.

soup down the seat of his underpants beforehand!: a general smile that transforms it-self into a gesture of prayer, the ritual accompaniment of the well-known invocation if Allah does not give a man strength, my brothers, He makes it up to him by giving him cunning: so let us admire His wisdom and give Him thanks!

the roll of drums in the late afternoon, when the copper-colored sun, behind the Kutubia,[6] heightens and enhances the wondrous sights of the city with postcard splen-dors: the cheerful green of the palm trees in the public park, the bright ocher of pri-vate houses and official buildings, a serene atmosphere of imperturbable blue, the dis-tant ridges of the Atlas range topped with plumes of purest white: a luminosity that stimulates and intoxicates, blends with the frenzy of the dances and the hawkers' cries, predisposes the stranger to enjoy a bit of freedom: deep within the vast area es-tablished for the pleasure and glory of the senses: absorbed in the rewarding idleness of those who roam about at their leisure, footloose and fancy free: with the certainty of being welcomed with open arms by some hospitable tribe or other: of being, in a word, the master of one's body and a possible candidate for the enjoyment and pos-session of that of one's male or female neighbor: awareness of one's own attractive-ness and youth and desire for the other, or vice versa, translated into a coded language of coughs, winks, smiles: offerings on the open market, within the reach of anyone willing or able to give value for value received: far from the irreducible molecular or-der of the great industrialized European city: the hostility of the clock, the pressure of time, rush hours, infinite loneliness shared bumper to bumper: separation into individ-ual cells with nuclei incapable of fusion, isolation in crowds of people packed to-gether like sardines: a tool a robot a cipher a machine: incorporality, keeping one's distance, invisibility, ataraxy:[7] the diametrical opposite of the easy familiarity that recognizes no boundaries: of the realm of adventures and encounters, the language of hips, the telegraphy of gestures, festive semierections: visual and auditory invitations to feel out, to explore, to engage in the furtive chase, to paw with a disembodied hand

a concrete, material, direct fraternity of the group of spectators, physical and sensory contacts in the restless promiscuity of the halca: arms brushing against arms, legs against legs, sporadic touches, cautious approximative maneuvers: antennae directed toward sounding out the intentions of the silent target of this campaign with no fear of slaps in the face or cries of outrage: the prelude to more intensive and daring encir-clement tactics: a discreet, continuous advance of one's own trunk in the direction of the coveted posterior: an opulence that is hidden yet hinted at, thanks to the clinging, pandering cloth that permits one to catch a fleeting glimpse of the topography: the ul-timate goal the careful insertion of one's convexity in the concavity offered with com-plicitous delight or a silent sense of guilt: an accentuation at this point of the recipro-cal motions, meanwhile maintaining the necessary rigor as one anxiously awaits the outcome: with one's hands in one's pockets, lending aid and support to the rigid and eager device that will permit penetration: shared emotions, furtively concealed from the public eye, deliciously disturbing and intense by virtue of their strict secrecy: the awareness of that excitement of the clandestine celebrated by the poets, pleasure min-gled with precaution as when one walks amid sand dunes: an amorous skirmish that through the insurmountable barrier of the cloth inflames and tautens the nerves to a

6. A large mosque in Marrakesh.   7. Calmness, tranquility.

point of impossible fervor: until the enigmatic veiled woman slips out of one's grasp, turns round and disappears on the arm of the spouse to whom she has been unfaithful, without a single backward glance at the anonymous body with which she has nonetheless just coupled

an elderly mime, decked out in a blond wig, throws coins into the air, catches them as they fall, performs magic feats, makes things disappear by sleight of hand, fools the eye, poses for the camera of a tourist couple, demands money from them for the snap-shots they've taken, asks permission to kiss their cheeks, and after barely grazing those of the husband, effusively repeats the operation with the man's better half, to the acclaim of a delighted audience that is familiar with the mime's whole bag of tricks and rewards his mocking impudence with great howls of laughter
two clowns do a modest comic turn in rudimentary disguises: donkey's ears, dialogue bellowed at the top of their lungs, both pretending that the other is stone deaf, blows aimed at each other's padded behinds, withering comments and gratuitous insults having to do with each other's sexual or excretory habits
musicians recite chants destined to invoke the favors of a salih with miraculous powers: sinewy flute players, with swarthy complexions and bushy mustaches, ac-company the movements of a transvestite in a filmy veil, female garments, and an em-broidered sash, whose winks, wagglings, cajoleries, giggles entrance and enchant the spectators who stand rooted to the spot: day laborers, women, little kids, soldiers extend their joined palms in the worshipful gesture of azalá,[8] join in the prayers and ejaculatory petitions, thoroughly enjoying the spectacle as a seeker of alms in a white turban and robe screams at the top of his voice, makes a great show of his emotions, lays on hands, sends old women and young girls on their way with his hasty blessing as he squats on his haunches, feigns beatific fits of ecstasy, writhes theatrically on the ground in convulsions of self-centered piety

installed in the center of the halca, the man proudly empties out his sack as though about to make a careful inventory of its treasures: the reptiles, slowly poking their tiny heads out, tied together by the tail in heterogeneous groups, each strains vainly to escape in a different direction in a demonstration of ineffectual centrifugal force: skinks, lizards, geckos adopting, by reason of their uncoordinated effort to flee, the formless mobility of an organism obeying blind tropisms:[9] their master stuffs them into a wooden cage, and with the gesture of a hardworking seamstress shoving a safety pin into her mouth, places between his lips a lizard missing its tail but still treacherously alive: once he has done so, he stands up, tosses his head back, shakes the braided topknot jutting out of the middle of his shaved skull, and with the reptile still tightly clasped between his lips, proceeds round and round the circle of spectators brandishing the knife with which he operates in vivo:[1] suddenly he stops dead in his tracks, removes the creature from his mouth, holds it tightly in his hand as though about to subject it to another daring vivisection, breaks into a frenetic chant that is half a prayer and half an exorcism: formulas against sickness, the evil eye, accidents, declaimed with closed eyes and abundant fine sprays of saliva: his body suddenly mo-tionless: as the sweat trickles down his face and disappears in his faunlike beard of a splendid goatish male: how to make sure a woman will get the curse?: how to keep an

8. A gesture of prayer.   1. In the live body of the lizard.
9. Movements of a plant in response to external stimuli.

unmarried woman from getting pregnant and dishonoring her family?: simple, perfectly simple: natural medicine, the remedy of the Almighty himself: neither condoms nor the pill nor diaphragms nor jumping off moving trains: lizard-tail extract! the saurians writhe frantically as though foreseeing their hapless fate: the solemn ritual of their captor: swinging his topknot to and fro for a brief moment, tossing the already mutilated specimen into his treasure chest, choosing another victim, stuffing it into his buccal cavity[2] down to its hind legs, taking the ritual number of turns around the circle, returning to the center, stretching out his hands in a prayerful gesture, and lopping off its tail in one energetic bite of his strong teeth, letting a few drops of blood run down the corners of his mouth, spitting out the severed tail, collecting with the movements of a zombie the generous offering of the spectators

seating himself ceremoniously on the ground, revealing one by one the secrets of a battered satchel, tracing a magic circle in chalk around him, reciting a prayer with extended palms, holding up a bunch of medicinal herbs, passing around an anatomical plate illustrating the state of pregnancy
reeling off the list of dangers lying in wait for the female body, announcing his exclusive possession of the infallible panacea, pronouncing the formulas of exorcism guaranteed to make the devil flee, exhibiting a vial filled with a liquid dyed a violent color, shaking its foaming contents until the bottle overflows, slowly pouring the potion into a glass without ever quite filling it to the brim
sprinkling the fine dust of a powerful talisman into it, stirring the mixture thus obtained with an old spoon, adding a copious emission of saliva, raising the philter to the lips of the first troubled woman to fall for his line, laying his hands on her head in benediction as she anxiously swallows it
health, happiness, her husband's love for the modest price of one dirham as the woman goes off with a prayerfully contemplative expression, as though she had just taken communion

to live, literally, by storytelling: a story that, quite simply, is never-ending: a weightless edifice of sound in perpetual de(con)struction: a length of fabric woven by Penelope and unwoven night and day:[3] a sand castle mechanically swept away by the sea
serving up to an audience ever hungry for stories a familiar theme: keeping up the suspense with a sustained effort of imagination: resorting if need be to the tricks and ruses of the mime: shifting the registers of his voice from bass to tenor
the hearers form a semicircle round the peddler of dreams, absorb his phrases with hypnotic attention, abandon themselves wholeheartedly to the spectacle of his richly varied mimetic activity: the onomatopoeia of hoofbeats, the roaring of wild beasts, the screeching voices of the deaf, the falsetto of old men, the deep booming voices of giants, the weeping of women, the whisper of dwarfs: now and again he breaks off his story at the crucial moment and a worried expression comes over the rapt faces of the youngsters hanging on his every word in the flickering light of his oil lamp: the travels and heroic exploits of Antar, the devilish pranks of Aicha Debbana, the tales of Harun-er-Rachid[4] are an invitation to his young audience to participate actively in the recitation: they have the same effect as a psychodrama, forming through a play of

2. The cavity of the mouth.
3. A reference to Homer's *Odyssey* in which Penelope, while awaiting the return of her husband Odysseus from the Trojan War, keeps other suitors off by pretending to weave a shroud during the day that she undoes by night.
4. Famous caliph of Baghdad, celebrated in the *Thousand and One Nights*.

identifications and antagonisms the rudiments of their embryonic sociability: when Xuhá appears at the palace, at once clothed and naked, on foot and on horseback, laughing and weeping, a hearty, spontaneous burst of laughter greets his enterprise and the clever trick he has played on the sultan: an ideal realm in which cunning is rewarded and brute force is punished, the utopia of a just god whose designs are profound and honorable: the necessary antidote for a miserable, barefoot existence, empty bellies, a reality that is cruelly unjust: the hardworking deceiver knows this and eloquently slakes his hearers' thirst for adventure: these little elves in their djellabahs are his only means of livelihood: slowly, with the patience of a spider, he will isolate them from the world: encapsulated in a delicate bubble: his cunning, invisible verbal prison

freeing language, freeing all discourse opposed to the dominant, normal scheme of things: putting an end to the implacable silence decreed by law, superstition, precepts: the authoritative voice of fathers, husbands, leaders, aulic councils of the tribe:[5] a flood of words, violently jerked out of the mouth, like someone pulling out by force a serpent stubbornly holding fast to his viscera: supple, guttural, hoarse, pliable: a language that is born, leaps about, stretches, climbs, becomes spindly: an endless strand of spaghetti, a slender thread, a paper streamer, as in the famous Chaplin sequence:[6] the possibility of telling tales, inventing lies, making up stories, pouring out what is stored up in the brain and the belly, the heart, vagina, testicles: talking and talking, in a torrent of words, for hours and hours on end: vomiting dreams, words, stories till everything has been emptied out: a literature within reach of illiterates, women, the simpleminded, nuts: of all those who have found themselves traditionally deprived of the right to express their fantasies and speak of their troubles: condemned to hold their tongues, to obey, to remain out of sight, to communicate by means of signs and whispers: protected by the semiofficial neutrality of the place: by the immunity of the jester who speaks harsh truths from behind the deceptive mask of laughter: orators without a pulpit or a platform or a lectern: possessed by a sudden fit of frenzy: charlatans, bamboozlers, fast talkers, liars and storytellers each and every one of them

nightfall: when the bazaar closes down and dancers, drummers, rhapsodists, flutists take off, literally, for other parts with their music: the gradual dispersal of the groups of spectators, an anxious and restless crowd, like a hive threatened with destruction: the slow emergence of empty spaces, a complicated web of meetings and chance encounters on the vast dark esplanade: dejected women waiting patiently, squatting on their haunches, for a last-minute act of charity: others seeking their plunder on the sly, arranging a rendezvous by signs: little shops and stalls gathering their goods together and kerosene lamps theatrically lighting new meeting places and points of convergence: lean-to restaurants that can be quickly assembled and disassembled, traveling kitchens, implements and portable stoves ready for the evening meal: the smells of fried food and soup, cumin, mint tea, awakening the appetite of those strolling by and enticing them into sitting down on the side benches of the stall of their choice
a succession of luminous still lifes projected in a magic lantern: the illustrations of some long-ago edition of The Thousand and One Nights, with merchants, alfaquis,[7]

---

5. Ancient social and legal councils.
6. In Charlie Chaplin's film *City Lights* (1931), the hero is eating a plate of spaghetti in a festively decorated restaurant; a paper streamer gets mixed in with the spaghetti, and the protagonist keeps chewing on what appears to be an interminable strand of pasta.
7. Muslim scholars.

craftsmen, shopboys, students of the Koran painted against a background of caldrons of soup, skewers of grilled meat, smoking frying pans, little baskets of fruit, terracotta bowls of olives, plates of bright scarlet salad, depicted with a precision and an eye for minute detail difficult to tone down to achieve an effect of vagueness and distance: a picture of the universe by way of the images of Sheherazade or Aladdin: the entire square condensed within a single book, the reading of which supplants reality

a deserted stage set, rows of shut stalls, remnants of the festival, papers blowing in the wind, excrement and fruit peels, dogs nosing about, beggars sleeping with their forearms resting on their knees and the hoods of their burnooses lowered over their faces a palimpsestic reading:[8] a calligraphy that over the years is erased and then retraced day after day: a precarious combination of signs whose message is uncertain: infinite possibilities of play opening up in the space that is now vacant: blackness, emptiness, the nocturnal silence of the page that is still blank

—— ⟝⟜ ——

Gabriel García Márquez
b. 1928

The publication of Colombian writer Gabriel García Márquez's novel *Cien años de soledad* ("One Hundred Years of Solitude") in 1967 changed the course of twentieth-century fiction. Translated into more than thirty languages, it attracted the attention of a worldwide reading public and started what became known as the "boom" period for Latin American literature in the 1970s and after. García Márquez's international importance was confirmed when he was awarded the Nobel Prize in literature in 1982. One of the characteristic features of García Márquez's novels as well as of other Latin American fiction is "magic realism," a term coined by Cuban novelist Alejo Carpentier in the 1940s: Magical realist fiction blends accounts of ordinary events and historical occurrences with elements of the supernatural and the fantastic but narrates both with the same matter-of-fact tone. It thereby often conveys a very different sense of the boundaries between the real and the unreal, and the physical and spiritual worlds, than European and North American novels. For all that, García Márquez's magic realism still *is* a form of realism—he had worked for many years as a journalist for various Latin American newspapers while also writing fiction and film scripts. His fiction relies on close observation of how people act and communicate in everyday circumstances; his talent in turning such observations into compelling fiction is evident in the novel *Chronicle of a Death Foretold* (1981), which features no obvious "magic realist" elements but describes in minute and suspenseful detail the events leading up to a murder in a small town—a murder everyone except the victim knows will happen. This talent is also obvious in his earlier fiction: The short story "Artificial Roses" (1962) focuses entirely on quite common events and conversations in the life of a young woman and her grandmother, but through the details we catch a glimpse of the deeper relationship between the two women as well as of the girl's disappointment with her lover.

Artificial Roses[1]

Feeling her way in the gloom of dawn, Mina put on the sleeveless dress which the night before she had hung next to the bed, and rummaged in the trunk for the detachable sleeves. Then she looked for them on the nails on the walls, and behind the

---

8. A palimpsest is a text made up of several superimposed layers of writing.   1. Translated by J. S. Bernstein.

doors, trying not to make noise so as not to wake her blind grandmother, who was sleeping in the same room. But when she got used to the darkness, she noticed that the grandmother had got up, and she went into the kitchen to ask her for the sleeves.

"They're in the bathroom," the blind woman said. "I washed them yesterday afternoon."

There they were, hanging from a wire with two wooden clothespins. They were still wet. Mina went back into the kitchen and stretched the sleeves out on the stones of the fireplace. In front of her, the blind woman was stirring the coffee, her dead pupils fixed on the stone border of the veranda, where there was a row of flowerpots with medicinal herbs.

"Don't take my things again," said Mina. "These days, you can't count on the sun."

The blind woman moved her face toward the voice.

"I had forgotten that it was the first Friday,"[2] she said.

After testing with a deep breath to see if the coffee was ready, she took the pot off the fire.

"Put a piece of paper underneath, because these stones are dirty," she said.

Mina ran her index finger along the fireplace stones. They were dirty, but with a crust of hardened soot which would not dirty the sleeves if they were not rubbed against the stones.

"If they get dirty you're responsible," she said.

The blind woman had poured herself a cup of coffee. "You're angry," she said, pulling a chair toward the veranda. "It's a sacrilege to take Communion when one is angry." She sat down to drink her coffee in front of the roses in the patio. When the third call for Mass rang, Mina took the sleeves off the fireplace and they were still wet. But she put them on. Father Angel would not give her Communion with a bare-shouldered dress on. She didn't wash her face. She took off the traces of rouge with a towel, picked up the prayer book and shawl in her room, and went into the street. A quarter of an hour later she was back.

"You'll get there after the reading of the gospel," the blind woman said, seated opposite the roses in the patio.

Mina went directly to the toilet. "I can't go to Mass," she said. "The sleeves are wet, and my whole dress is wrinkled." She felt a knowing look follow her.

"First Friday and you're not going to Mass," exclaimed the blind woman.

Back from the toilet, Mina poured herself a cup of coffee and sat down against the whitewashed doorway, next to the blind woman. But she couldn't drink the coffee.

"You're to blame," she murmured, with a dull rancor, feeling that she was drowning in tears.

"You're crying," the blind woman exclaimed.

She put the watering can next to the pots of oregano and went out into the patio, repeating, "You're crying." Mina put her cup on the ground before sitting up.

"I'm crying from anger," she said. And added, as she passed next to her grandmother, "You must go to confession because you made me miss the first-Friday Communion."

The blind woman remained motionless, waiting for Mina to close the bedroom door. Then she walked to the end of the veranda. She bent over haltingly until she

2. In Roman Catholicism, there is a custom to take Communion on the first Fridays of nine consecutive months with a special devotion to Christ's Sacred Heart. The custom originated in the 17th century and is believed to ensure that those who follow it will not die in sin or without sacraments.

found the untouched cup in one piece on the ground. While she poured the coffee into the earthen pot, she went on:

"God knows I have a clear conscience."

Mina's mother came out of the bedroom.

"Who are you talking to?" she asked.

"To no one," said the blind woman. "I've told you already that I'm going crazy."

Ensconced in her room, Mina unbuttoned her bodice and took out three little keys which she carried on a safety pin. With one of the keys she opened the lower drawer of the armoire and took out a miniature wooden trunk. She opened it with another key. Inside there was a packet of letters written on colored paper, held together by a rubber band. She hid them in her bodice, put the little trunk in its place, and locked the drawer. Then she went to the toilet and threw the letters in.

"I thought you were at church," her mother said when Mina came into the kitchen.

"She couldn't go," the blind woman interrupted. "I forgot that it was first Friday, and I washed the sleeves yesterday afternoon."

"They're still wet," murmured Mina.

"I've had to work hard these days," the blind woman said.

"I have to deliver a hundred and fifty dozen roses for Easter," Mina said.

The sun warmed up early. Before seven Mina set up her artificial-rose shop in the living room: a basket full of petals and wires, a box of crêpe paper, two pairs of scissors, a spool of thread, and a pot of glue. A moment later Trinidad arrived, with a pasteboard box under her arm, and asked her why she hadn't gone to Mass.

"I didn't have any sleeves," said Mina.

"Anyone could have lent some to you," said Trinidad.

She pulled over a chair and sat down next to the basket of petals.

"I was too late," Mina said.

She finished a rose. Then she pulled the basket closer to shirr the petals with the scissors.[3] Trinidad put the pasteboard box on the floor and joined in the work.

Mina looked at the box.

"Did you buy shoes?" she asked.

"They're dead mice," said Trinidad.

Since Trinidad was an expert at shirring petals, Mina spent her time making stems of wire wound with green paper. They worked silently without noticing the sun advance in the living room, which was decorated with idyllic prints and family photographs. When she finished the stems, Mina turned toward Trinidad with a face that seemed to end in something immaterial. Trinidad shirred with admirable neatness, hardly moving the petal tip between her fingers, her legs close together. Mina observed her masculine shoes. Trinidad avoided the look without raising her head, barely drawing her feet backward, and stopped working.

"What's the matter?" she said.

Mina leaned toward her.

"He went away," she said.

Trinidad dropped the scissors in her lap.

"No."

"He went away," Mina repeated.

Trinidad looked at her without blinking. A vertical wrinkle divided her knit brows.

---

3. Pulling the fabric together.

"And now?" she asked.

Mina replied in a steady voice.

"Now nothing."

Trinidad said goodbye before ten.

Freed from the weight of her intimacy, Mina stopped her a moment to throw the dead mice into the toilet. The blind woman was pruning the rosebush.

"I'll bet you don't know what I have in this box," Mina said to her as she passed. She shook the mice.

The blind woman began to pay attention. "Shake it again," she said. Mina repeated the movement, but the blind woman could not identify the objects after listening for a third time with her index finger pressed against the lobe of her ear.

"They are the mice which were caught in the church traps last night," said Mina.

When she came back, she passed next to the blind woman without speaking. But the blind woman followed her. When she got to the living room, Mina was alone next to the closed window, finishing the artificial roses.

"Mina," said the blind woman. "If you want to be happy, don't confess with strangers."

Mina looked at her without speaking. The blind woman sat down in the chair in front of her and tried to help with the work. But Mina stopped her.

"You're nervous," said the blind woman.

"Why didn't you go to Mass?" asked the blind woman.

"You know better than anyone."

"If it had been because of the sleeves, you wouldn't have bothered to leave the house," said the blind woman. "Someone was waiting for you on the way who caused you some disappointment."

Mina passed her hands before her grandmother's eyes, as if cleaning an invisible pane of glass.

"You're a witch," she said.

"You went to the toilet twice this morning," the blind woman said. "You never go more than once."

Mina kept making roses.

"Would you dare show me what you are hiding in the drawer of the armoire?" the blind woman asked.

Unhurriedly, Mina stuck the rose in the window frame, took the three little keys out of her bodice, and put them in the blind woman's hand. She herself closed her fingers.

"Go see with your own eyes," she said.

The blind woman examined the little keys with her finger-tips.

"My eyes cannot see down the toilet."

Mina raised her head and then felt a different sensation: she felt that the blind woman knew that she was looking at her.

"Throw yourself down the toilet if what I do is so interesting to you," she said.

The blind woman ignored the interruption.

"You always stay up writing in bed until early morning," she said.

"You yourself turn out the light," Mina said.

"And immediately you turn on the flashlight," the blind woman said. "I can tell that you're writing by your breathing."

Mina made an effort to stay calm. "Fine," she said without raising her head. "And supposing that's the way it is. What's so special about it?"

"Nothing," replied the blind woman. "Only that it made you miss first-Friday Communion."

With both hands Mina picked up the spool of thread, the scissors, and a fistful of unfinished stems and roses. She put it all in the basket and faced the blind woman. "Would you like me to tell you what I went to do in the toilet, then?" she asked. They both were in suspense until Mina replied to her own question:

"I went to take a shit."

The blind woman threw the three little keys into the basket. "It would be a good excuse," she murmured, going into the kitchen. "You would have convinced me if it weren't the first time in your life I've ever heard you swear." Mina's mother was coming along the corridor in the opposite direction, her arms full of bouquets of thorned flowers.

"What's going on?" she asked.

"I'm crazy," said the blind woman. "But apparently you haven't thought of sending me to the madhouse so long as I don't start throwing stones."

⊶ ⊯◈⊯ ⊷

Jamaica Kincaid
b. 1949

The writer known today as Jamaica Kincaid grew up in circumstances that were unlikely to produce an important writer—or even someone named "Jamaica Kincaid" at all. She was born and raised as Elaine Potter Richardson on the Caribbean island of Antigua, then a British colony, in a working-class family, with a carpenter stepfather and a demanding but emotionally distant mother. She grew up reading voraciously, absorbing many British novels assigned in the Antiguan school system, and she read as much more as she could get on her own, even stealing books from the library. When she finished high school at age seventeen, her mother sent her to the suburbs of New York City to work as an au pair—"as a servant," as Kincaid has described the position. Soon she left the family she'd been sent to and began working at odd jobs in New York, studying for periods at the New School and later at Franconia College in New Hampshire. She never completed a degree, though, but started writing short pieces for *Ingenue* and other magazines, publishing under the name "Jamaica Kincaid" because her family disapproved of her writing.

In the mid-seventies, she began writing for *The New Yorker,* whose legendary editor William Shawn encouraged her developing interests in writing fiction and had a shaping influence on her experimental writing. These stories became Kincaid's prize-winning first collection of stories, *At the Bottom of the River* (1983), which included the story "My Mother." Kincaid has gone on to write extensively about her family and about Antigua; her books include the novels *Annie John* (1985) and *Lucy* (1990), *The Autobiography of My Mother* (1996), and the nonfiction essay *In a Small Place* (1988), which criticizes post–independence Antiguans for carrying on old colonial patterns themselves and turning their island into a glorified tourist trap. Much of Kincaid's fiction deals with mother–daughter relations. Of her mother, Kincaid has said that "all her children are quite happy to have been born, but all of us are quite sure she should never have been a mother." Kincaid's story "My Mother" explores the tense intimacy between the speaker and her mother, expressed in a strongly lyrical, even hallucinatory prose. House and body alike are gendered spaces that metamorphose alarmingly but also creatively, as the daughter negotiates the terms of her dependence and independence in a constantly shifting emotional landscape.

My Mother

Immediately on wishing my mother dead and seeing the pain it caused her, I was sorry and cried so many tears that all the earth around me was drenched. Standing before my mother, I begged her forgiveness, and I begged so earnestly that she took pity on me, kissing my face and placing my head on her bosom to rest. Placing her arms around me, she drew my head closer and closer to her bosom, until finally I suffocated. I lay on her bosom, breathless, for a time uncountable, until one day, for a reason she has kept to herself, she shook me out and stood me under a tree and I started to breathe again. I cast a sharp glance at her and said to myself, "So." Instantly I grew my own bosoms, small mounds at first, leaving a small, soft place between them, where, if ever necessary, I could rest my own head. Between my mother and me now were the tears I had cried, and I gathered up some stones and banked them in so that they formed a small pond. The water in the pond was thick and black and poisonous, so that only unnamable invertebrates could live in it. My mother and I now watched each other carefully, always making sure to shower the other with words and deeds of love and affection.

I was sitting on my mother's bed trying to get a good look at myself. It was a large bed and it stood in the middle of a large, completely dark room. The room was completely dark because all the windows had been boarded up and all the crevices stuffed with black cloth. My mother lit some candles and the room burst into a pink-like, yellow-like glow. Looming over us, much larger than ourselves, were our shadows. We sat mesmerized because our shadows had made a place between themselves, as if they were making room for someone else. Nothing filled up the space between them, and the shadow of my mother sighed. The shadow of my mother danced around the room to a tune that my own shadow sang, and then they stopped. All along, our shadows had grown thick and thin, long and short, had fallen at every angle, as if they were controlled by the light of day. Suddenly my mother got up and blew out the candles and our shadows vanished. I continued to sit on the bed, trying to get a good look at myself.

My mother removed her clothes and covered thoroughly her skin with a thick gold-colored oil, which had recently been rendered in a hot pan from the livers of reptiles with pouched throats. She grew plates of metal-colored scales on her back, and light, when it collided with this surface, would shatter and collapse into tiny points. Her teeth now arranged themselves into rows that reached all the way back to her long white throat. She uncoiled her hair from her head and then removed her hair altogether. Taking her head into her large palms, she flattened it so that her eyes, which were by now ablaze, sat on top of her head and spun like two revolving balls. Then, making two lines on the soles of each foot, she divided her feet into crossroads. Silently, she had instructed me to follow her example, and now I too traveled along on my white underbelly, my tongue darting and flickering in the hot air. "Look," said my mother.

My mother and I were standing on the seabed side by side, my arms laced loosely around her waist, my head resting securely on her shoulder, as if I needed the support. To make sure she believed in my frailness, I sighed occasionally—long soft sighs, the kind of sigh she had long ago taught me could evoke sympathy. In fact, how I really felt was invincible. I was no longer a child but I was not yet a woman. My skin had just blackened and cracked and fallen away and my new impregnable carapace had taken full hold. My nose had flattened; my hair curled in and stood out straight from my head simultaneously; my many rows of teeth in their retractable trays were in place. My mother and I wordlessly made an arrangement—I sent out my beautiful sighs, she received them; I leaned ever more heavily on her for support, she offered her shoulder, which shortly grew to the size of a thick plank. A long time passed, at the end of which I had hoped to see my mother permanently cemented to the seabed. My mother reached out to pass a hand over my head, a pacifying gesture, but I laughed and, with great agility, stepped aside. I let out a horrible roar, then a self-pitying whine. I had grown big, but my mother was bigger, and that would always be so. We walked to the Garden of Fruits and there ate to our hearts' satisfaction. We departed through the southwesterly gate, leaving as always, in our trail, small colonies of worms.

With my mother, I crossed, unwillingly, the valley. We saw a lamb grazing and when it heard our footsteps it paused and looked up at us. The lamb looked cross and miserable. I said to my mother, "The lamb is cross and miserable. So would I be, too, if I had to live in a climate not suited to my nature." My mother and I now entered the cave. It was the dark and cold cave. I felt something growing under my feet and I bent down to eat it. I stayed that way for years, bent over eating whatever I found growing under my feet. Eventually, I grew a special lens that would allow me to see in the darkest of darkness; eventually, I grew a special coat that kept me warm in the coldest of coldness. One day I saw my mother sitting on a rock. She said, "What a strange expression you have on your face. So cross, so miserable, as if you were living in a climate not suited to your nature." Laughing, she vanished. I dug a deep, deep hole. I built a beautiful house, a floorless house, over the deep, deep hole. I put in lattice windows, most favored of windows by my mother, so perfect for looking out at people passing by without her being observed. I painted the house itself yellow, the windows green, colors I knew would please her. Standing just outside the door, I asked her to inspect the house. I said, "Take a look. Tell me if it's to your satisfaction." Laughing out of the corner of a mouth I could not see, she stepped inside. I stood just outside the door, listening carefully, hoping to hear her land with a thud at the bottom of the deep, deep hole. Instead, she walked up and down in every direction, even pounding her heel on the air. Coming outside to greet me, she said, "It is an excellent house. I would be honored to live in it," and then vanished. I filled up the hole and burnt the house to the ground.

My mother has grown to an enormous height. I have grown to an enormous height also, but my mother's height is three times mine. Sometimes I cannot see from her breasts on up, so lost is she in the atmosphere. One day, seeing her sitting on the seashore, her hand reaching out in the deep to caress the belly of a striped fish as he swam through a place where two seas met, I glowed red with anger. For a while then I lived alone on the island where there were eight full moons and I adorned the face of each moon with expressions I had seen on my mother's face. All the expressions favored me. I soon grew tired of living in this way and returned to my mother's side. I remained, though glowing red with anger, and my mother and I built houses on opposite banks of the dead pond. The dead pond lay between us; in it, only small invertebrates with poisonous lances lived. My mother behaved toward them as if she had suddenly found herself in the same room with relatives we had long since risen above.

I cherished their presence and gave them names. Still I missed my mother's close company and cried constantly for her, but at the end of each day when I saw her return to her house, incredible and great deeds in her wake, each of them singing loudly her praises, I glowed and glowed again, red with anger. Eventually, I wore myself out and sank into a deep, deep sleep, the only dreamless sleep I have ever had.

One day my mother packed my things in a grip[1] and, taking me by the hand, walked me to the jetty, placed me on board a boat, in care of the captain. My mother, while caressing my chin and cheeks, said some words of comfort to me because we had never been apart before. She kissed me on the forehead and turned and walked away. I cried so much my chest heaved up and down, my whole body shook at the sight of her back turned toward me, as if I had never seen her back turned toward me before. I started to make plans to get off the boat, but when I saw that the boat was encased in a large green bottle, as if it were about to decorate a mantelpiece, I fell asleep, until I reached my destination, the new island. When the boat stopped, I got off and I saw a woman with feet exactly like mine, especially around the arch of the instep. Even though the face was completely different from what I was used to, I recognized this woman as my mother. We greeted each other at first with great caution and politeness, but as we walked along, our steps became one, and as we talked, our voices became one voice, and we were in complete union in every other way. What peace came over me then, for I could not see where she left off and I began, or where I left off and she began.

My mother and I walk though the rooms of her house. Every crack in the floor holds a significant event: here, an apparently healthy young man suddenly dropped dead; here a young woman defied her father and, while riding her bicycle to the forbidden lover's meeting place, fell down a precipice, remaining a cripple for the rest of a very long life. My mother and I find this a beautiful house. The rooms are large and empty, opening on to each other, waiting for people and things to fill them up. Our white muslin skirts billow up around our ankles, our hair hangs straight down our backs as our arms hang straight at our sides. I fit perfectly in the crook of my mother's arm, on the curve of her back, in the hollow of her stomach. We eat from the same bowl, drink from the same cup; when we sleep, our heads rest on the same pillow. As we walk through the rooms, we merge and separate, merge and separate; soon we shall enter the final stage of our evolution.

The fishermen are coming in from sea; their catch is bountiful, my mother has seen to that. As the waves plop, plop against each other, the fishermen are happy that the sea is calm. My mother points out the fishermen to me, their contentment is a source of my contentment. I am sitting in my mother's enormous lap. Sometimes I sit on a mat she has made for me from her hair. The lime trees are weighed down with limes—I have already perfumed myself with their blossoms. A hummingbird has nested on my stomach, a sign of my fertileness. My mother and I live in a bower made from flowers whose petals are imperishable. There is the silvery blue of the sea, crisscrossed with sharp darts of light, there is the warm rain falling on the clumps of castor bush, there is the small lamb bounding across the pasture, there is the soft

1. Bag.

ground welcoming the soles of my pink feet. It is in this way my mother and I have lived for a long time now.

↦ END OF PERSPECTIVES: GENDERED SPACES ↤

Mariama Bâ
1929–1981

So Long a Letter (*Une si longue lettre,* first published in French in 1979) is an unusual book written by an equally extraordinary author. As its title already indicates, *So Long a Letter* is an epistolary novel—that is, a novel in letter form. But while most epistolary novels include exchanges of many letters by different individuals, Bâ's entire narrative consists of only one long letter written by a Senegalese woman to her female friend. Sent at a crucial turning point in her life, Ramatoulaye's letter recapitulates much of her past, her marriage of twenty-five years, and her lifelong friendship with the addressee, Aissatou. Seeing events consistently from Ramatoulaye's perspective gives the reader a unique opportunity to witness the evolving relationships between men and women in the novel from the inside. Yet the choice of the epistolary format also raises a number of intriguing questions for the reader, precisely because Ramatoulaye's view is the only one we have access to: How reliable is she as a narrator? Can we entirely trust her descriptions of herself and others? We might also wonder how far Ramatoulaye really goes in her revindication of the woman's viewpoint—is she a "feminist," or does her attitude differ from what one would normally associate with such a perspective? As the letter gradually puts into relief Ramatoulaye's and Aissatou's very different reactions to polygamy, two questions arise: Which of the two attitudes is the novel ultimately meant to endorse, and how do dimensions such as religion and social class affect the protagonists' decision making? Bâ skillfully uses the limits of Ramatoulaye's perspective to engage the reader in these questions.

The technical expertise Bâ displays in her construction of the narrative is all the more impressive since *So Long a Letter* was her first novel. It was also the last of her novels to be published during her lifetime: Already fifty-one at the publication of *So Long a Letter* (an unusually advanced age for a first novel), Bâ died in 1981, months before the publication of her second work, *Scarlet Song*. In spite of her extremely short career as a writer, she acquired a reputation as one of Senegal's finest women novelists. Born in Dakar in 1929, she grew up in a traditional Muslim family. Her father was a civil servant who became Senegal's first Minister of Health, but due to her mother's early death, Bâ was raised mostly by her maternal grandparents. Against the grandparents' wishes for a more conventional upbringing, she was sent to a French primary school, completed the Ecole Normale in Rufisque with the highest grades, and obtained a teacher's diploma in 1947. After having taught for twelve years, health reasons forced to her to become a regional school inspector instead, a position she held until her death. Married to and later divorced from Obeye Diop, Senegal's Minister of Information, she raised nine children. As one of the women writers who directly experienced Senegalese independence, she offers her reader unique insights into how this large-scale political transformation affected the more personal contexts of gender, marriage, and family politics.

PRONUNCIATIONS:
Aissatou: ay-sah-tou
Ousmane: ous-MAHN
Ramatoulaye: rah-mah-tou-LAY

So Long a Letter[1]

TO ABIBATOU NIANG, PURE AND CONSTANT,
LUCID AND THOROUGH, WHO SHARES MY FEELINGS.
TO ANNETTE D'ERNEVILLE OF THE WARM HEART AND THE LEVEL HEAD.
TO ALL WOMEN AND MEN OF GOOD WILL.

1

Dear Aissatou,

I have received your letter. By way of reply, I am beginning this diary, my prop in my distress. Our long association has taught me that confiding in others allays pain.

Your presence in my life is by no means fortuitous. Our grandmothers in their compounds were separated by a fence and would exchange messages daily. Our mothers used to argue over who would look after our uncles and aunts. As for us, we wore out wrappers and sandals on the same stony road to the koranic school; we buried our milk teeth in the same holes and begged our fairy godmothers to restore them to us, more splendid than before.

If over the years, and passing through the realities of life, dreams die, I still keep intact my memories, the salt of remembrance.

I conjure you up. The past is reborn, along with its procession of emotions. I close my eyes. Ebb and tide of feeling: heat and dazzlement, the woodfires, the sharp green mango, bitten into in turns, a delicacy in our greedy mouths. I close my eyes. Ebb and tide of images: drops of sweat beading your mother's ochre-coloured face as she emerges from the kitchen, the procession of young wet girls chattering on their way back from the springs.

We walked the same paths from adolescence to maturity, where the past begets the present.

My friend, my friend, my friend. I call on you three times.[2]

Yesterday you were divorced. Today I am a widow.

Modou is dead. How am I to tell you? One does not fix appointments with fate. Fate grasps whom it wants, when it wants. When it moves in the direction of your desires, it brings you plenitude. But more often than not, it unsettles, crosses you. Then one has to endure. I endured the telephone call which disrupted my life.

A taxi quickly hailed! Fast! Fast! Faster still! My throat is dry. There is a rigid lump in my chest. Fast: faster still. At last, the hospital: the mixed smell of suppurations and ether. The hospital—distorted faces, a train of tearful people, known and unknown, witnesses to this awful tragedy. A long corridor, which seems to stretch out endlessly. At the end, a room. In the room, a bed. On the bed, Modou stretched out, cut off from the world of the living by a white sheet in which he is completely enveloped. A trembling hand moves forward and slowly uncovers the body. His hairy chest, at rest forever, is visible through his crumpled blue shirt with thin stripes. This face, set in pain and surprise, is indeed his, the bald forehead, the half-open mouth are indeed his. I want to grasp his hand. But someone pulls me away. I can hear Mawdo, his doctor friend, explaining to me: a heart attack came on suddenly in his office while he was dictating a letter. The secretary had the presence of mind to call me.

---

1. Translated by Modupé Bodé-Thomas.

2. An invocation that indicates the seriousness of the subject to be discussed [Bâ's note].

Mawdo recounts how he arrived too late with the ambulance. I think: the doctor after death. He mimes the massaging of the heart that was undertaken, as well as the futile effort at mouth-to-mouth resuscitation. Again, I think: heart massage, mouth-to-mouth resuscitation, ridiculous weapons against the divine will.

I listen to the words that create around me a new atmosphere in which I move, a stranger and tormented. Death, the tenuous passage between two opposite worlds, one tumultuous, the other still.

Where to lie down? Middle age demands dignity. I hold tightly on to my prayer beads. I tell the beads ardently, remaining standing on legs of jelly. My loins beat as to the rhythm of childbirth.

Cross-sections of my life spring involuntarily from my memory, grandiose verses from the Koran, noble words of consolation fight for my attention.

Joyous miracle of birth, dark miracle of death. Between the two, a life, a destiny, says Mawdo Bâ.

I look intently at Mawdo. He seems to be taller than usual in his white overall. He seems to me thin. His reddened eyes express forty years of friendship. I admire his noble hands, hands of an absolute delicacy, supple hands used to tracking down illness. Those hands, moved by friendship and a rigorous science, could not save his friend.

2

Modou Fall is indeed dead, Aissatou. The uninterrupted procession of men and women who have "learned" of it, the wails and tears all around me, confirm his death. This condition of extreme tension sharpens my suffering and continues till the following day, the day of interment.

What a seething crowd of human beings come from all parts of the country, where the radio has relayed the news.

Women, close relatives, are busy. They must take incense, eau-de-cologne, cotton-wool to the hospital for the washing of the dead one. The seven metres of white muslin, the only clothing Islam allows for the dead, are carefully placed in a new basket. The *Zem-Zem,* the miracle water from the holy places of Islam religiously kept by each family, is not forgotten. Rich, dark wrappers are chosen to cover Modou.

My back propped up by cushions, legs outstretched, my head covered with a black wrapper, I follow the comings and goings of people. Across from me, a new winnowing fan bought for the occasion receives the first alms. The presence of my co-wife beside me irritates me. She has been installed in my house for the funeral, in accordance with tradition. With each passing hour her cheeks become more deeply hollowed, acquire ever more rings, those big and beautiful eyes which open and close on their secrets, perhaps their regrets. At the age of love and freedom from care, this child is dogged by sadness.

While the men, in a long, irregular file of official and private cars, public buses, lorries and mopeds, accompany Modou to his last rest (people were for a long time to talk of the crowd which followed the funeral procession), our sisters-in-law undo our hair. My co-wife and myself are put inside a rough and ready tent made of a wrapper pulled taut above our heads and set up for the occasion. While our sisters-in-law are constructing it, the women present, informed of the work in hand, get up and throw some coins on to the fluttering canopy so as to ward off evil spirits.

This is the moment dreaded by every Senegalese woman, the moment when she sacrifices her possessions as gifts to her family-in-law; and, worse still, beyond her possessions she gives up her personality, her dignity, becoming a thing in the service of the man who has married her, his grandfather, his grandmother, his father, his mother, his brother, his sister, his uncle, his aunt, his male and female cousins, his friends. Her behaviour is conditioned: no sister-in-law will touch the head of any wife who has been stingy, unfaithful or inhospitable.

As for ourselves, we have been deserving, and our sisters-in-law sing a chorus of praises chanted at the top of their voices. Our patience before all trials, the frequency of our gifts find their justification and reward today. Our sisters-in-law give equal consideration to thirty years and five years of married life. With the same ease and the same words, they celebrate twelve maternities and three. I note with outrage this desire to level out, in which Modou's new mother-in-law rejoices.

Having washed their hands in a bowl of water placed at the entrance to the house, the men, back from the cemetery, file past the family grouped around us, the widows. They offer their condolences punctuated with praises of the deceased.

"Modou, friend of the young as of the old. . . ."

"Modou, the lion-hearted, champion of the oppressed. . . ."

"Modou, at ease as much in a suit as in a caftan. . . ."[3]

"Modou, good brother, good husband, good Muslim. . . ."

"May God forgive him. . . ."

"May he regret his earthly stay in his heavenly bliss. . . ."

"May the earth rest lightly on him!"

They are there, his childhood playmates on the football ground, or during bird hunts, when they used catapults. They are there, his classmates. They are there, his companions in the trade union struggles.

The *Siguil ndigale*[4] come one after the other, poignant, while skilled hands distribute to the crowd biscuits, sweets, cola nuts, judiciously mixed, the first offerings to heaven for the peaceful repose of the deceased's soul.

3

On the third day, the same comings and goings of friends, relatives, the poor, the unknown. The name of the deceased, who was popular, has mobilized a buzzing crowd, welcomed in my house that has been stripped of all that could be stolen, all that could be spoilt. Mats of all sorts are spread out everywhere there is space. Metal chairs hired for the occasion take on a blue hue in the sun.

Comforting words from the Koran fill the air; divine words, divine instructions, impressive promises of punishment or joy, exhortations to virtue, warnings against evil, exaltation of humility, of faith. Shivers run through me. My tears flow and my voice joins weakly in the fervent "Amen" which inspires the crowd's ardour at the end of each verse.

The smell of the *lakh*[5] cooling in the calabashes pervades the air, exciting.

Also passed around are large bowls of red or white rice, cooked here or in neighbouring houses. Iced fruit juices, water and curds are served in plastic cups. The men's group eats in silence. Perhaps they remember the stiff body, tied up and lowered by their hands into a gaping hole, quickly covered up again.

In the women's corner, nothing but noise, resonant laughter, loud talk, hand slaps, strident exclamations. Friends who have not seen each other for a long time hug

---

3. A full-length garment with long sleeves.
4. Form of condolence that also expresses hope of moral recovery [Bâ's note].

5. Senegalese food prepared from roughly kneaded millet flour, which is cooked in water and eaten with curds [Bâ's note].

each other noisily. Some discuss the latest material on the market. Others indicate where they got their woven wrappers from. The latest bits of gossip are exchanged. They laugh heartily and roll their eyes and admire the next person's *boubou*,[6] her original way of using henna to blacken hands and feet by drawing geometrical figures on them.

From time to time an exasperated manly voice rings out a warning, recalls the purpose of the gathering: a ceremony for the redemption of a soul. The voice is quickly forgotten and the brouhaha begins all over again, increasing in volume.

In the evening comes the most disconcerting part of this third day's ceremony. More people, more jostling in order to hear and see better. Groups are formed according to relationships, according to blood ties, areas, corporations. Each group displays its own contribution to the costs. In former times this contribution was made in kind: millet, livestock, rice, flour, oil, sugar, milk. Today it is made conspicuously in banknotes, and no one wants to give less than the other. A disturbing display of inner feeling that cannot be evaluated now measured in francs! And again I think how many of the dead would have survived if, before organizing these festive funeral ceremonies, the relative or friend had bought the life-saving prescription or paid for hospitalization.

The takings are carefully recorded. It is a debt to be repaid in similar circumstances. Modou's relatives open an exercise book. Lady Mother-in-Law (Modou's) and her daughter have a notebook. Fatim, my younger sister, carefully records my takings in a note-pad.

As I come from a large family in this town, with acquaintances at all levels of society, as I am a schoolteacher on friendly terms with the pupils' parents, and as I have been Modou's companion for thirty years, I receive the greater share of money and many envelopes. The regard shown me raises me in the eyes of the others and it is Lady Mother-in-Law's turn to be annoyed. Newly admitted into the city's bourgeoisie by her daughter's marriage, she too reaps banknotes. As for her silent, haggard child, she remains a stranger in these circles.

The sudden calls from our sisters-in-law bring her out of her stupor. They reappear after their deliberation. They have contributed the large sum of two hundred thousand francs to "dress" us.[7] Yesterday, they offered us some excellent *thiakry*[8] to quench our thirst. The Fall family's *griot*[9] is proud of her role as go-between, a role handed down from mother to daughter.

"One hundred thousand francs from the father's side."

"One hundred thousand francs from the mother's side."

She counts the notes, blue and pink, one by one, shows them round and concludes: "I have much to say about you Falls, grandchildren of Damel Madiodio, who have inherited royal blood. But one of you is no more. Today is not a happy day. I weep with you for Modou, whom I used to call 'bag of rice', for he would frequently give me a sack of rice. Therefore accept this money, you worthy widows of a worthy man."

The share of each widow must be doubled, as must the gifts of Modou's grandchildren, represented by the offspring of all his male and female cousins.

Thus our family-in-law take away with them a wad of notes, painstakingly topped, and leave us utterly destitute, we who will need material support.

---

6. A long, loose-fitting garment worn by both men and women.
7. It is the duty of the husband's sisters to buy his widow's mourning clothes [Bâ's note].

8. A drink prepared by mixing sugared curds with well-kneaded millet flour; it is cooked in steam [Bâ's note].
9. Black African, of any nationality, who is part-poet, part-musician, part-sorcerer [Bâ's note].

Afterwards comes the procession of old relatives, old acquaintances, *griots,* gold-smiths, *laobés*[1] with their honeyed language. The "goodbyes" following one after the other at an infernal rate are irritating because they are neither simple nor free: they re-quire, depending on the person leaving, sometimes a coin, sometimes a banknote.

Gradually the house empties. The smell of stale sweat and food blend as trails in the air, unpleasant and nauseating. Cola nuts spat out here and there have left red stains: my tiles, kept with such painstaking care, are blackened. Oil stains on the walls, balls of crumpled paper. What a balance sheet for a day!

My horizon lightened, I see an old woman. Who is she? Where is she from? Bent over, the ends of her *boubou* tied behind her, she empties into a plastic bag the left-overs of red rice. Her smiling face tells of the pleasant day she has just had. She wants to take back proof of this to her family, living perhaps in Ouakam, Thiaroye or Pikine.[2]

Standing upright, her eyes meeting my disapproving look, she mutters between teeth reddened by cola nuts: "Lady, death is just as beautiful as life has been."

Alas, it's the same story on the eighth and fortieth days, when those who have "learned" belatedly make up for lost time. Light attire showing off slim waistlines, prominent backsides, the new brassière or the one bought at the second-hand market, chewing sticks wedged between teeth, white or flowered shawls, heavy smell of in-cense and of *gongo,*[3] loud voices, strident laughter. And yet we are told in the Koran that on the third day the dead body swells and fills its tomb; we are told that on the eighth it bursts; and we are also told that on the fortieth day it is stripped. What then is the significance of these joyous, institutionalized festivities that accompany our prayers for God's mercy? Who has come out of self-interest? Who has come to quench his own thirst? Who has come for the sake of mercy? Who has come so that he may remember?

Tonight Binetou, my co-wife, will return to her SICAP villa.[4] At last! Phew!

The visits of condolence continue: the sick, those who have journeyed or have merely arrived late, as well as the lazy, come to fulfil what they consider to be a sa-cred duty. Child-naming ceremonies may be missed but never a funeral. Coins and notes continue to pour on the beckoning fan.

Alone, I live in a monotony broken only by purifying baths, the changing of my mourning clothes every Monday and Friday.

I hope to carry out my duties fully. My heart concurs with the demands of reli-gion. Reared since childhood on their strict precepts, I expect not to fail. The walls that limit my horizon for four months and ten days do not bother me. I have enough memories in me to ruminate upon. And these are what I am afraid of, for they smack of bitterness.

May their evocation not soil the state of purity in which I must live.

Till tomorrow.

4

Aissatou, my friend, perhaps I am boring you by relating what you already know.

I have never observed so much, because I have never been so concerned.

---

1. The carpenter caste of Senegal.
2. Suburbs of Dakar, capital of Senegal [Bâ's note].
3. Sweet-smelling and stimulating powder [Bâ's note].

4. Building society in the Cap-Vert department of Senegal (Dakar and environs), which constructs houses for sale or rent [Bâ's note].

The family meeting held this morning in my sitting-room is at last over. You can easily guess those who were present: Lady Mother-in-Law, her brother and her daughter, Binetou, who is even thinner; old Tamsir, Modou's brother, and the *Imam*[5] from the mosque in his area; Mawdo Bâ; my daughter and her husband Abdou.

The *mirasse* commanded by the Koran requires that a dead person be stripped of his most intimate secrets; thus is exposed to others what was carefully concealed. These exposures crudely explain a man's life. With consternation, I measure the extent of Modou's betrayal. His abandonment of his first family (myself and my children) was the outcome of the choice of a new life. He rejected us. He mapped out his future without taking our existence into account.

His promotion to the rank of technical adviser in the Ministry of Public Works, in exchange for which, according to the spiteful, he checked the trade union revolt, could not control the mire of expenses by which he was engulfed. Dead without a penny saved. Acknowledgement of debts? A pile of them: cloth and gold traders, home-delivery grocers and butchers, car-purchase instalments.

Hold on. The star attraction of this "stripping": the origins of the elegant SICAP villa, four bedrooms, two bathrooms, pink and blue, large sitting-room, a three-room flat, built at his own expense at the bottom of the second courtyard for Lady Mother-in-Law. And furniture from France for his new wife and furniture constructed by local carpenters for Lady Mother-in-Law.

This house and its chic contents were acquired by a bank loan granted on the mortgage of "Villa Fallene", where I live. Although the title deeds of this house bear his name, it is nonetheless our common property, acquired by our joint savings. Insult upon injury!

Moreover, he continued the monthly payments of seventy-five thousand francs to the SICAP. These payments were to go on for about ten years before the house would become his.

Four million francs borrowed with ease because of his privileged position, which had enabled him to pay for Lady Mother-in-Law and her husband to visit Mecca to acquire the titles of *Alhaja* and *Alhaji;* which equally enabled Binetou to exchange her Alfa Romeos at the slightest dent.

Now I understand the terrible significance of Modou's abandonment of our joint bank account. He wanted to be financially independent so as to have enough elbow room.

And then, having withdrawn Binetou from school, he paid her a monthly allowance of fifty thousand francs, just like a salary due to her. The young girl, who was very gifted, wanted to continue her studies, to sit for her *baccalauréat*.[6] So as to establish his rule, Modou, wickedly, determined to remove her from the critical and unsparing world of the young. He therefore gave in to all the conditions of the grasping Lady Mother-in-Law and even signed a paper committing himself to paying the said amount. Lady Mother-in-Law brandished the paper, for she firmly believed that the payments would continue, even after Modou's death, out of the estate.

As for my daughter, Daba, she waved about a bailiff's affidavit, dated the very day of her father's death, that listed all the contents of the SICAP Villa. The list supplied by Lady Mother-in-Law and Binetou made no mention of certain objects and items of furniture, which had mysteriously disappeared or had been fraudulently removed.

---

5. The officiating minister at a mosque.   6. High school graduation examination.

You know that I am excessively sentimental. I was not at all pleased by this display on either side.

5

When I stopped yesterday, I probably left you astonished by my disclosures.

Was it madness, weakness, irresistible love? What inner confusion led Modou Fall to marry Binetou?

To overcome my bitterness, I think of human destiny. Each life has its share of heroism, an obscure heroism, born of abdication, of renunciation and acceptance under the merciless whip of fate.

I think of all the blind people the world over, moving in darkness. I think of all the paralysed the world over, dragging themselves about. I think of all the lepers the world over, wasted by their disease.

Victims of a sad fate which you did not choose, compared with your lamentations, what is my quarrel, cruelly motivated, with a dead man who no longer has any hold over my destiny? Combining your despair, you could have been avengers and made them tremble, all those who are drunk on their wealth; tremble, those upon whom fate has bestowed favours. A horde powerful in its repugnance and revolt, you could have snatched the bread that your hunger craves.

Your stoicism has made you not violent or subversive but true heroes, unknown in the mainstream of history, never upsetting established order, despite your miserable condition.

I repeat, beside your visible deformities, what are moral infirmities from which in any case you are not immune? Thinking of you, I thank God for my eyes which daily embrace heaven and earth. If today moral fatigue makes my limbs stiff, tomorrow it will leave my body. Then, relieved, my legs will carry me slowly and I shall again have around me the iodine and the blue of the sea. The star and white cloud will be mine. The breath of wind will again refresh my face. I will stretch out, turn around, I will vibrate. Oh, health, live in me. Oh, health. . . .

My efforts cannot for long take my mind off my disappointment. I think of the suckling baby, no sooner born than orphaned. I think of the blind man who will never see his child's smile. I think of the cross the one-armed man has to bear. I think. . . . But my despair persists, but my rancour remains, but the waves of an immense sadness break in me!

Madness or weakness? Heartlessness or irresistible love? What inner torment led Modou Fall to marry Binetou?

And to think that I loved this man passionately, to think that I gave him thirty years of my life, to think that twelve times over I carried his child. The addition of a rival to my life was not enough for him. In loving someone else, he burned his past, both morally and materially. He dared to commit such an act of disavowal.

And yet, what didn't he do to make me his wife!

6

Do you remember the morning train that took us for the first time to Ponty-Ville, the teachers' training college in Sebikotane?[7] Ponty-Ville is the countryside still green from the last rains, a celebration of youth right in the middle of nature, banjo music in

---

7. A town about 30 miles from Dakar.

dormitories transformed into dance floors, conversations held along the rows of geraniums or under the thick mango trees.

Modou Fall, the very moment you bowed before me, asking me to dance, I knew you were the one I was waiting for. Tall and athletically built, of course. Olive-coloured skin due to your distant Moorish blood, no question. Virility and fineness of features harmoniously blended, once again, no question. But, above all, you knew how to be tender. You could fathom every thought, every desire. You knew many undefinable things, which glorified you and sealed our relationship.

As we danced, your forehead, hairline already receding, bent over my own. The same happy smile lit up our faces. The pressure of your hand became more tender, more possessive. Everything in me gave in and our relationship endured over the school years and during the holidays, strengthened in me by the discovery of your subtle intelligence, of your embracing sensitivity, of your readiness to help, of your ambition, which suffered no mediocrity. It was this ambition which led you, on leaving school, to prepare on your own for the two examinations of the *baccalauréat.* Then you left for France and, according to your letters, you lived there as a recluse, attaching little importance to the glitter that met your regard; but you grasped the deep sense of a history that has worked so many wonders and of a great culture that overwhelmed you. The milky complexion of the women had no hold on you. Again, quoting from your letters: "On the strictly physical plane, the white woman's advantage over the black woman lies in the variety of her colour, the abundance, length and softness of her hair. There are also the eyes which can be blue, green, often the colour of new honey." You also used to complain of the sombreness of the skies, under which no coconut trees waved their tops. You missed the swinging hips of black women walking along the pavements, this gracious deliberate slowness characteristic of Africa, which charmed your eyes. You were sick at heart at the dogged rhythm of the life of the people and the numbing effect of the cold. You would finish by saying that your studies were your staff, your buttress. You would end with a string of endearments and conclude by reassuring me: "It's you whom I carry within me. You are my protecting black angel. Would I could quickly find you, if only to hold your hand tightly so that I may forget hunger and thirst and loneliness."

And you returned in triumph. With a degree in law! In spite of your voice and your gift of oratory, you preferred obscure work, less well paid but constructive for your country, to the showiness of the lawyer.

Your achievement did not stop there. Your introduction of your friend Mawdo Bâ into our circle was to change the life of my best friend, Aissatou.

I no longer scorn my mother's reserve concerning you, for a mother can instinctively feel where her child's happiness lies. I no longer laugh when I think that she found you too handsome, too polished, too perfect for a man. She often spoke of the wide gap between your two upper incisors: the sign of the primacy of sensuality in the individual. What didn't she do, from then on, to separate us? She could see in you only the eternal khaki suit, the uniform of your school. All she remembered of you were your visits, considered too long. You were idle, she said, therefore with plenty of time to waste. And you would use that time to "stuff" my head, to the disadvantage of more interesting young people.

Because, being the first pioneers of the promotion of African women, there were very few of us. Men would call us scatter-brained. Others labelled us devils. But many wanted to possess us. How many dreams did we nourish hopelessly that could have been fulfilled as lasting happiness and that we abandoned to embrace others, those that have burst miserably like soap bubbles, leaving us empty-handed?

7

Aissatou, I will never forget the white woman who was the first to desire for us an "uncommon" destiny. Together, let us recall our school, green, pink, blue, yellow, a veritable rainbow: green, blue and yellow, the colours of the flowers everywhere in the compound; pink the colour of the dormitories, with the beds impeccably made. Let us hear the walls of our school come to life with the intensity of our study. Let us relive its intoxicating atmosphere at night, while the evening song, our joint prayer, rang out, full of hope. The admission policy, which was based on an entrance examination for the whole of former French West Africa, now broken up into autonomous republics, made possible a fruitful blend of different intellects, characters, manners and customs. Nothing differentiated us, apart from specific racial features, the Fon girl from Dahomey and the Malinke one from Guinea.[8] Friendships were made that have endured the test of time and distance. We were true sisters, destined for the same mission of emancipation.

To lift us out of the bog of tradition, superstition and custom, to make us appreciate a multitude of civilizations without renouncing our own, to raise our vision of the world, cultivate our personalities, strengthen our qualities, to make up for our inadequacies, to develop universal moral values in us: these were the aims of our admirable headmistress. The word "love" had a particular resonance in her. She loved us without patronizing us, with our plaits either standing on end or bent down, with our loose blouses, our wrappers. She knew how to discover and appreciate our qualities.

How I think of her! If the memory of her has triumphed over the ingratitude of time, now that flowers no longer smell as sweetly or as strongly as before, now that age and mature reflection have stripped our dreams of their poetic virtue, it is because the path chosen for our training and our blossoming has not been at all fortuitous. It has accorded with the profound choices made by New Africa for the promotion of the black woman.

Thus, free from frustrating taboos and capable now of discernment, why should I follow my mother's finger pointing at Daouda Dieng, still a bachelor but too mature for my eighteen years. Working as an African doctor at the Polyclinique, he was well-to-do and knew how to use his position to advantage. His villa, perched on a rock on the Corniche[9] facing the sea, was the meeting place for the young elite. Nothing was missing, from the refrigerator, containing its pleasant drinks, to the record player, which exuded sometimes langorous, sometimes frenzied music.

Daouda Dieng also knew how to win hearts. Useful presents for my mother, ranging from a sack of rice, appreciated in that period of war penury, to the frivolous gift for me, daintily wrapped in paper and tied with ribbons. But I preferred the man in the eternal khaki suit. Our marriage was celebrated without dowry, without pomp, under the disapproving looks of my father, before the painful indignation of my frustrated mother, under the sarcasm of my surprised sisters, in our town struck dumb with astonishment.

8

Then came your marriage with Mawdo Bâ, recently graduated from the African School of Medicine and Pharmacy. A controversial marriage. I can still hear the angry rumours in town:

8. The Fon are an ethnic group in the Republic of Benin, which was formerly called Dahomey. The Malinke or Mandinka are represented in several West African countries; Guinea lies to the south of Senegal.
9. Coastal road.

"What, a Toucouleur[1] marrying a goldsmith's daughter? He will never 'make money.'"

"Mawdo's mother is a Dioufene, a *Guelewar* from the Sine.[2] What an insult to her, before her former co-wives." (Mawdo's father was dead.)

"In the desire to marry a "short skirt" come what may, this is what one gets."

"School turns our girls into devils who lure our men away from the right path."

And I haven't recounted all. But Mawdo remained firm. "Marriage is a personal thing," he retorted to anyone who cared to hear.

He emphasized his total commitment to his choice of life partner by visiting your father, not at home but at his place of work. He would return from his outings illuminated, happy to have "moved in the right direction," he would say triumphantly. He would speak of your father as a "creative artist." He admired the man, weakened as he was by the daily dose of carbon dioxide he inhaled working in the acrid atmosphere of the dusty fumes. Gold is his medium, which he melts, pours, twists, flattens, refines, chases. "You should see him," Mawdo would add. "You should see him breathe over the flame." His cheeks would swell with the life from his lungs. This life would animate the flame, sometimes red, sometimes blue, which would rise or curve, wax or wane at his command, depending on what the work demanded. And the gold specks in the showers of red sparks, and the uncouth songs of the apprentices punctuating the strokes of the hammer here, and the pressure of hands on the bellows there would make passers-by turn round.

Aissatou, your father knew all the rites that protect the working of gold, the metal of the djinns. Each profession has its code, known only to the initiated and transmitted from father to son. As soon as your elder brothers left the huts of the circumcised, they moved into this particular world, the whole compound's source of nourishment.

But what about your younger brothers? Their steps were directed towards the white man's school. Hard is the climb up the steep hill of knowledge to the white man's school: kindergarten remains a luxury that only those who are financially sound can offer their young ones. Yet it is necessary, for this is what sharpens and channels the young ones' attention and sensibilities.

Even though the primary schools are rapidly increasing, access to them has not become any easier. They leave out in the streets an impressive number of children because of the lack of places.

Entrance into secondary school is no panacea for the child at an age fraught with the problems of consolidating his personality, with the explosion of puberty, with the discovery of the various pitfalls: drugs, vagrancy, sensuality.

The university has its own large number of despairing rejects.

What will the unsuccessful do? Apprenticeship to traditional crafts seems degrading to whoever has the slightest book-learning. The dream is to become a clerk. The trowel is spurned.

The horde of the jobless swells the flood of delinquency.

Should we have been happy at the desertion of the forges, the workshops, the shoemaker's shops? Should we have rejoiced so wholeheartedly? Were we not beginning to witness the disappearance of an elite of traditional manual workers?

---

1. An ethnic group concentrated in the Senegal River valley in northern Senegal; smaller groups also live in other West-African nations.
2. Princess of the Sine [Bâ's note]. Sine is a region of Senegal, southeast of Dakar, where the *guelewar* are an old aristocracy; the Toucouleur, or Tukulor, the ethnic group to which Mawdo's mother belongs, were historically among the most resistant to the implantation of Islam.

Eternal questions of our eternal debates. We all agreed that much dismantling was needed to introduce modernity within our traditions. Torn between the past and the present, we deplored the "hard sweat" that would be inevitable. We counted the possible losses. But we knew that nothing would be as before. We were full of nostalgia but were resolutely progressive.

9

Mawdo raised you up to his own level, he the son of a princess and you a child from the forges. His mother's rejection did not frighten him.

Our lives developed in parallel. We experienced the tiffs and reconciliations of married life. In our different ways, we suffered the social constraints and heavy burden of custom. I loved Modou. I compromised with his people. I tolerated his sisters, who too often would desert their own homes to encumber my own. They allowed themselves to be fed and petted. They would look on, without reacting, as their children romped around on my chairs. I tolerated their spitting, the phlegm expertly secreted under my carpets.

His mother would stop by again and again while on her outings, always flanked by different friends, just to show off her son's social success but particularly so that they might see, at close quarters, her supremacy in this beautiful house in which she did not live. I would receive her with all the respect due to a queen, and she would leave satisfied, especially if her hand closed over the banknote I had carefully placed there. But hardly would she be out than she would think of the new band of friends she would soon be dazzling.

Modou's father was more understanding. More often than not, he would visit us without sitting down. He would accept a glass of cold water and would leave, after repeating his prayers for the protection of the house.

I knew how to smile at them all, and consented to wasting useful time in futile chatter. My sisters-in-law believed me to be spared the drudgery of housework.

"With your two housemaids!" they would say with emphasis.

Try explaining to them that a working woman is no less responsible for her home. Try explaining to them that nothing is done if you do not step in, that you have to see to everything, do everything all over again: cleaning up, cooking, ironing. There are the children to be washed, the husband to be looked after. The working woman has a dual task, of which both halves, equally arduous, must be reconciled. How does one go about this? Therein lies the skill that makes all the difference to a home.

Some of my sisters-in-law did not envy my way of living at all. They saw me dashing around the house after a hard day at school. They appreciated their comfort, their peace of mind, their moments of leisure and allowed themselves to be looked after by their husbands, who were crushed under their duties.

Others, limited in their way of thinking, envied my comfort and purchasing power. They would go into raptures over the many "gadgets" in my house: gas cooker, vegetable grater, sugar tongs. They forgot the source of this easy life; first up in the morning, last to go to bed, always working.

You, Aissatou, you forsook your family-in-law, tightly shut in with their hurt dignity. You would lament to me: "Your family-in-law respects you. You must treat them well. As for me, they look down on me from the height of their lost nobility. What can I do?"

While Mawdo's mother planned her revenge, we lived: Christmas Eve parties organized by several couples, with the costs shared equally, and held in turns in the different homes. Without self-consciousness, we would revive the dances of yester-year:

the lively beguine, frenzied rumbas, languid tangos. We rediscovered the old beatings of the heart that strengthened our feelings.

We would also leave the stifling city to breathe in the healthy air of seaside suburbs.

We would walk along the Dakar Corniche, one of the most beautiful in West Africa, a sheer work of art wrought by nature. Rounded or pointed rocks, black or ochre-coloured, overlooking the ocean. Greenery, sometimes a veritable hanging garden spread out under the clear sky. We would go on to the road to Ouakam, which also leads to Ngor and further on to Yoff airport. We would recognize on the way the narrow road leading farther on to Almadies beach.

Our favourite spot was Ngor beach, situated near the village of the same name, where old bearded fishermen repaired their nets under the silk-cotton trees. Naked and snotty children played in complete freedom when they were not frolicking about in the sea.

On the fine sand, washed by the waves and swollen with water, naively painted canoes awaited their turn to be launched into the waters. In their hollows small pools of blue water would glisten, full of light from the sky and sun.

What a crowd on public holidays! Numerous families would stroll about, thirsty for space and fresh air. People would undress, without embarrassment, tempted by the benevolent caress of the iodized breeze and the warmth from the sun's rays. The idle would sleep under spread parasols. A few children, spade and bucket in hand, would build and demolish the castles of their imagination.

In the evening the fishermen would return from their laborious outings. Once more, they had escaped the moving snare of the sea. At first simple points on the horizon, the boats would become more distinct from one another as they drew nearer. They would dance in the hollows of the waves, then would lazily let themselves be dragged along. Fishermen would gaily furl their sails and draw in their tackle. While some of them would gather together the wriggling catch, others would wring out their soaked clothes and mop their faces.

Under the wondering gaze of the kids, the live fish would flip up as the long sea snakes would curve themselves inwards. There is nothing more beautiful than a fish just out of water, its eye clear and fresh, with golden or silvery scales and beautiful blueish glints!

Hands would sort out, group, divide. We would buy a good selection at bargain prices for the house.

The sea air would put us in good humour. The pleasure we indulged in and in which all our senses rejoiced would intoxicate both rich and poor with health. Our communion with deep, bottomless and unlimited nature refreshed our souls. Depression and sadness would disappear, suddenly to be replaced by feelings of plenitude and expansiveness.

Reinvigorated, we would set out for home. How jealously we guarded the secret of simple pleasures, health-giving remedy for the daily tensions of life.

Do you remember the picnics we organized at Sangalkam, in the farm Mawdo Bâ inherited from his father? Sangalkam remains the refuge of people from Dakar, those who want a break from the frenzy of the city. The younger set, in particular, has bought land there and built country residences: these green, open spaces are conducive to rest, meditation and the letting off of steam by children. This oasis lies on the road to Rufisque.

Mawdo's mother had looked after the farm before her son's marriage. The memory of her husband had made her attached to this plot of land, where their joint and patient hands had disciplined the vegetation that filled our eyes with admiration.

Yourself, you added the small building at the far end: three small, simple bed-rooms, a bathroom, a kitchen. You grew many flowers in a few corners. You had a hen run built, then a closed pen for sheep.

Coconut trees, with their interlacing leaves, gave protection from the sun. Succulent sapodilla stood next to sweet-smelling pomegranates. Heavy mangoes weighed down the branches. Pawpaws resembling breasts of different shapes hung tempting and inaccessible from the tops of elongated trunks.

Green leaves and browned leaves, new grass and withered grass were strewn all over the ground. Under our feet the ants untiringly built and rebuilt their homes.

How warm the shades over the camp beds! Teams for games were formed one after the other amid cries of victory or lamentations of defeat.

And we stuffed ourselves with fruits within easy reach. And we drank the milk from coconuts. And we told "juicy stories!" And we danced about, roused by the strident notes of a gramophone. And the lamb, seasoned with white pepper, garlic, butter, hot pepper, would be roasting over the wood fire.

And we lived. When we stood in front of our over-crowded classes, we represented a force in the enormous effort to be accomplished in order to overcome ignorance.

Each profession, intellectual or manual, deserves consideration, whether it requires painful physical effort or manual dexterity, wide knowledge or the patience of an ant. Ours, like that of the doctor, does not allow for any mistake. You don't joke with life, and life is both body and mind. To warp a soul is as much a sacrilege as murder. Teachers—at kindergarten level, as at university level—form a noble army accomplishing daily feats, never praised, never decorated. An army forever on the move, forever vigilant. An army without drums, without gleaming uniforms. This army, thwarting traps and snares, everywhere plants the flag of knowledge and morality.

How we loved this priesthood, humble teachers in humble local schools. How faithfully we served our profession, and how we spent ourselves in order to do it honour. Like all apprentices, we had learned how to practise it well at the demonstration school, a few steps away from our own, where experienced teachers taught the novices that we were how to apply, in the lessons we gave, our knowledge of psychology and method. . . . In those children we set in motion waves that, breaking, carried away in their furl a bit of ourselves.

10

Modou rose steadily to the top rank in the trade union organizations. His understanding of people and things endeared him to both employers and workers. He focused his efforts on points that were easily satisfied, that made work lighter and life more pleasant. He sought practical improvements in the workers' conditions. His slogan was: what's the use of taunting with the impossible? Obtaining the "possible" is already a victory.

His point of view was not unanimously accepted, but people relied on his practical realism.

Mawdo could take part in neither trade unionism nor politics, for he hadn't the time. His reputation as a good doctor was growing; he remained the prisoner of his mission in a hospital filled to capacity with the sick, for people were going less and less to the native doctor who specialized in brewing the same concoctions of leaves for different illnesses.

Everybody was reading newspapers and magazines. There was unrest in North Africa.[3]

Did these interminable discussions, during which points of view concurred or clashed, complemented each other or were vanquished, determine the aspect of the New Africa?

The assimilationist dream of the colonist drew into its crucible our mode of thought and way of life. The sun helmet worn over the natural protection of our kinky hair, smoke-filled pipe in the mouth, white shorts just above the calves, very short dresses displaying shapely legs: a whole generation suddenly became aware of the ridiculous situation festering in our midst.

History marched on, inexorably. The debate over the right path to take shook West Africa. Brave men went to prison; others, following in their footsteps, continued the work begun.

It was the privilege of our generation to be the link between two periods in our history, one of domination, the other of independence. We remained young and efficient, for we were the messengers of a new design. With independence achieved, we witnessed the birth of a republic, the birth of an anthem and the implantation of a flag.[4]

I heard people repeat that all the active forces in the country should be mobilized. And we said that over and above the unavoidable opting for such-and-such a party, such-and-such a model of society, what was needed was national unity. Many of us rallied around the dominant party,[5] infusing it with new blood. To be productive in the crowd was better than crossing one's arms and hiding behind imported ideologies.

Modou, a practical man, led his unions into collaboration with the government, demanding for his troops only what was possible. But he cursed the hasty establishment of too many embassies, which he judged to be too costly for our under-developed country. This bleeding of the country for reasons of pure vanity, among other things, such as the frequent invitation of foreigners, was just a waste of money. And, with his wage-earners in mind, he would repeatedly growl, "So many schools, or so much hospital equipment lost! So many monthly wage increases! So many tarred roads!"

You and Mawdo would listen to him. We were scaling the heights, but your mother-in-law, who saw you resplendent beside her son, who saw her son going more and more frequently to your father's workshop, who saw your mother fill out and dress better, your mother-in-law thought more and more of her revenge.

11

I know that I am shaking you, that I am twisting a knife in a wound hardly healed; but what can I do? I cannot help remembering in my forced solitude and reclusion.

Mawdo's mother is Aunty Nabou to us and Seynabou to others. She bore a glorious name in the Sine: Diouf. She is a descendant of Bour-Sine.[6] She lived in the past, unaware of the changing world. She clung to old beliefs. Being strongly attached to her privileged origins, she believed firmly that blood carried with it virtues, and, nodding her head, she would repeat that humble birth would always show in a person's

3. Reference to the war of independence in Algeria, which broke out in 1954 and lasted until Algeria gained independence from France in 1962.
4. Senegal achieved independence from France in 1960.
5. The Union Progressiste Sénégalaise (Senegalese Progressive Party), which had been founded in 1958 by the man who was to become independent Senegal's first president, Léopold Sédar Senghor. Senghor was one of the advocates of "African socialism," based not on European Marxism but on African collectivist traditions.
6. The designation of the king in the Sine region; the implication is that Aunty Nabou descends from a royal line.

bearing. And life had not been kind to Mawdo's mother. Very early, she lost her dear husband; bravely, she brought up her eldest son Mawdo and two other daughters, now married . . . and well married. She devoted herself with the affection of a tigress to her "one and only man," Mawdo Bâ. When she swore by her only son's nose, the symbol of life, she had said everything. Now, her "only man" was moving away from her, through the fault of this cursed daughter of a goldsmith, worse than a *griot* woman. The *griot* brings happiness. But a goldsmith's daughter! . . . she burns everything in her path, like the fire in a forge.

So while we lived without concern, considering your marriage a problem of the past, Mawdo's mother thought day and night of a way to get her revenge on you, the goldsmith's daughter.

One fine day she decided to pay a visit to her younger brother, Farba Diouf, a customary chief in Diakhao.[7] She packed a few well chosen clothes into a suitcase that she borrowed from me, stuffed a basket full of various purchases: provisions and foodstuffs that are dear or rare in the Sine (fruits from France, cheese, preserves), toys for nephews, lengths of material for her brother and his four wives.

She asked Modou for some money, which she carefully folded and put away in her purse. She had her hair done, painted her feet and hands with henna. Thus dressed, adorned, she left.

These days, the road to Rufisque forks at the Diamniadio crossroads: the National 1, to the right, leads, after Mbour, to the Sine-Saloum, while the National 2 goes through Thies and Tivaouane, cradle of Tidjanism,[8] towards Saint-Louis, former capital of Senegal. Aunty Nabou did not enjoy the benefit of these pleasant roads. Jostled in the bus on the bumpy road, she sought refuge in her memories. The dizzying speed of the vehicle, carrying her towards the place of her childhood, did not prevent her from recognizing the familiar countryside. Here, Sindia, and to the left, Popenguine, where the Catholics celebrate Whitsun.

How many generations has this same unchanging countryside seen glide past! Aunty Nabou acknowledged man's vulnerability in the face of the eternity of nature. By its very duration, nature defies time and take its revenge on man.

The baobab trees held out the giant knots of their branches towards the skies; slowly, the cows moved across the road, their mournful stare defying the vehicles; shepherds in baggy trousers, their sticks on their shoulders or in their hands, guided the animals. Men and animals blended, as in a picture risen from the depths of time.

Aunty Nabou closed her eyes every time the bus passed another vehicle. She was especially frightened of the big lorries with their huge loads.

The beautiful Medinatou-Minaouara mosque had not yet been built to the glory of Islam, but in the same pious spirit, men and women prayed by the side of the road. "You have to come away from Dakar to be convinced of the survival of traditions," murmured Aunty Nabou.

On the left, prickly shrubs bordered the Ndiassane forest; monkeys darted out to enjoy the light.

Thiadiaye, Tataguine, Diouroupe, then Ndioudiouf, and finally Fatick, capital of the Sine. Puffing and steaming, the bus branched off to the left. Jolts and still more jolts. Finally Diakhao, the royal Diakhao, Diakhao, cradle and tomb of the Bour-Sine, Diakhao of her ancestors, beloved Diakhao, with the vast compound of its old palace.

The same heaviness tortured her heart on each visit paid to the family domain.

---

7. A town in the Sine region.   8. An African Muslim brotherhood.

First of all, water for ablutions and a mat on which to pray and to meditate before the tomb of the ancestor. And then she let her gaze, marked with sadness and filled with history, roam over the other tombs. Here, the dead and the living lived together in the family compound: each king, returned from his coronation, planted two trees in the yard that marked out his last resting place. Fervently, Aunty Nabou intoned the religious verses, directing them at the tombs of the dead. Her face wore a tragic mask in this place of grandeur, which sang of the past to the sound of the *djou-djoungs,* the royal drums.

She swore that your existence, Aissatou, would never tarnish her noble descent.

Associating in her thoughts antiquated rites and religion, she remembered the milk to be poured into the Sine[9] to appease the invisible spirits. Tomorrow, in the river, she would make her offerings to protect herself from the evil eye, while at the same time attracting the benevolence of the *tours.*[1]

Royally received, she immediately resumed her position as the elder sister of the master of the house. Nobody addressed her without kneeling down. She took her meals alone, having been served with the choicest bits from the pots.

Visitors came from everywhere to honour her, thus reminding her of the truth of the law of blood. For her, they revived the exploits of the ancestor Bour-Sine, the dust of combats and the ardour of thoroughbred horses. . . . And, heady with the heavy scent of burnt incense, she drew force and vigour from the ancestral ashes stirred to the eclectic sound of the *koras.*[2] She summoned her brother.

"I need a child beside me," she said, "to fill my heart. I want this child to be both my legs and my right arm. I am growing old. I will make of this child another me. Since the marriage of my own children, the house has been empty."

She was thinking of you, working out her vengeance, but was very careful not to speak of you, of her hatred for you.

"Let your wish be fulfilled," replied Farba Diouf. "I have never asked you to educate any of my daughters, not wanting to tire you. Yet today's children are difficult to keep in check. Take young Nabou, your namesake. She is yours. I ask only for her bones."

Satisfied, Aunty Nabou packed her suitcase again, filled her basket with all that could be found in the village and is dear in town: dried couscous, roasted groundnut paste, millet, eggs, milk, chicken. Holding young Nabou's hand firmly in her right hand, she took the road back to town.

12

As she handed me back my suitcase, Aunty Nabou introduced young Nabou to me; she also introduced her at the homes of all her friends.

With my help, young Nabou was admitted into the French school. Maturing in her aunt's protective shade, she learned the secret of making delicious sauces, of using an iron and wielding a pestle. Her aunt never missed an opportunity to remind her of her royal origin, and taught her that the first quality in a woman is docility.

After obtaining her primary school certificate, and after a few years in secondary school, the older Nabou advised her niece to sit the entrance examination for the State School of Midwifery: "This school is good. You receive an education there. No garlands for heads. Young, sober girls without earrings, dressed in white, which is the colour of purity. The profession you will learn there is a beautiful one; you will earn your living and you will acquire grace for your entry into paradise by helping at the

---

9. Underground river [Bâ's note].
1. Invisible companions [Bâ's note].

2. Long-necked stringed instruments used in West Africa, somewhat resembling a lute.

birth of new followers of Mohammed, the prophet. To tell the truth, a woman does not need too much education. In fact, I wonder how a woman can earn her living by talking from morning to night."

Thus, young Nabou became a midwife. One fine day, Aunty Nabou called Mawdo and said to him: "My brother Farba has given you young Nabou to be your wife, to thank me for the worthy way in which I have brought her up. I will never get over it if you don't take her as your wife. Shame kills faster than disease."

I knew about it. Modou knew about it. The whole town knew about it. You, Aissatou, suspected nothing and continued to be radiant.

And because his mother had fixed a date for the wedding night, Mawdo finally had the courage to tell you what every woman was whispering: you had a co-wife. "My mother is old. The knocks and disappointments of life have weakened her heart. If I spurn this child, she will die. This is the doctor speaking and not the son. Think of it, her brother's daughter, brought up by her, rejected by her son. What shame before society!"

It was "so as not to see his mother die of shame and chagrin" that Mawdo agreed to go to the rendez-vous of the wedding night. Faced with this rigid mother moulded by the old morality, burning with the fierce ardour of antiquated laws, what could Mawdo Bâ do? He was getting on in years, worn out by his arduous work. And then, did he really want to fight, to make a gesture of resistance? Young Nabou was so tempting. . . .

From then on, you no longer counted. What of the time and the love you had invested in your home? Only trifles, quickly forgotten. Your sons? They counted for very little in this reconciliation between a mother and her "one and only man"; you no longer counted, any more than did your four sons: they could never be equal to young Nabou's sons.

The *griots* spoke of young Nabou's sons, exalting them: "Blood has returned to its source."

Your sons did not count. Mawdo's mother, a princess, could not recognize herself in the sons of a goldsmith's daughter.

In any case, could a goldsmith's daughter have any dignity, any honour? This was tantamount to asking whether you had a heart and flesh. Ah! for some people the honour and chagrin of a goldsmith's daughter count for less, much less, than the honour and chagrin of a *Guelewar*.

Mawdo did not drive you away. He did his duty and wished that you would stay on. Young Nabou would continue to live with his mother; it was you he loved. Every other night he would go to his mother's place to see his other wife, so that his mother "would not die", to "fulfil a duty."

How much greater you proved to be than those who sapped your happiness!

You were advised to compromise: "You don't burn the tree which bears the fruit."

You were threatened through your flesh: "Boys cannot succeed without their father."

You took no notice.

These commonplace truths, which before had lowered the heads of many wives as they raised them in revolt, did not produce the desired miracle; they did not divert you from your decision. You chose to make a break, a one-way journey with your four sons, leaving this letter for Mawdo, in clear view, on the bed that used to be yours. I remember the exact words:

Mawdo,
   Princes master their feelings to fulfil their duties. "Others" bend their heads and, in silence, accept a destiny that oppresses them.

That, briefly put, is the internal ordering of our society, with its absurd divisions. I will not yield to it. I cannot accept what you are offering me today in place of the happiness we once had. You want to draw a line between heartfelt love and physical love. I say that there can be no union of bodies without the heart's acceptance, however little that may be.

If you can procreate without loving, merely to satisfy the pride of your declining mother, then I find you despicable. At that moment you tumbled from the highest rung of respect on which I have always placed you. Your reasoning, which makes a distinction, is unacceptable to me: on one side, me, "your life, your love, your choice," on the other, "young Nabou, to be tolerated for reasons of duty."

Mawdo, man is one: greatness and animal fused together. None of his acts is pure charity. None is pure bestiality.

I am stripping myself of your love, your name. Clothed in my dignity, the only worthy garment, I go my way.

Goodbye,
Aissatou

And you left. You had the surprising courage to take your life into your own hands. You rented a house and set up home there. And instead of looking backwards, you looked resolutely to the future. You set yourself a difficult task; and more than just my presence and my encouragements, books saved you. Having become your refuge, they sustained you.

The power of books, this marvellous invention of astute human intelligence. Various signs associated with sound: different sounds that form the word. Juxtaposition of words from which springs the idea, Thought, History, Science, Life. Sole instrument of interrelationships and of culture, unparalleled means of giving and receiving. Books knit generations together in the same continuing effort that leads to progress. They enabled you to better yourself. What society refused you, they granted: examinations sat and passed took you also to France. The School of Interpreters, from which you graduated, led to your appointment into the Senegalese Embassy in the United States. You make a very good living. You are developing in peace, as your letters tell me, your back resolutely turned on those seeking light enjoyment and easy relationships.

And Mawdo? He renewed his relationship with his family. Those from Diakhao invaded his house: those from Diakhao sustained young Nabou. But—and Mawdo knew it—there was no possible comparison between yourself and young Nabou; you, so beautiful and so gentle, you, whose tenderness for him was so deep and disinterested, you, who knew how to mop your husband's brow, you, who could always find the right words with which to make him relax.

And Mawdo? What didn't he say? "I am completely disorientated. You can't change the habits of a grown man. I look for shirts and trousers in the old places and I touch only emptiness."

I had no pity for Mawdo.

"My house is a suburb of Diakhao. I find it impossible to get any rest there. Everything there is dirty. Young Nabou gives my food and my clothes away to visitors."

I did not listen to Mawdo.

"Somebody told me he'd seen you with Aissatou yesterday. Is it true? Is she around? How is she? What about my sons?"

I did not answer Mawdo.

For Mawdo, and through him all men, remained an enigma to me. Your departure had truly shaken him. His sadness was clearly evident. When he spoke of you, the inflexions in his voice hardened. But his disillusioned air, the bitter criticisms of his home, his wit, which railed at everything, did not in the least prevent the periodic swelling of young Nabou's belly. Two boys had already been born.

When faced with this visible fact, proof of his intimate relations with young Nabou, Mawdo would twist with anger. His look was like a whip: "Look here, don't be an idiot. How can you expect a man to remain a stone when he is constantly in contact with the woman who runs his house?" He added as illustration: "I saw a film in which the survivors of an air crash survived by eating the flesh of the corpses. This fact demonstrates the force of the instincts in man, instincts that dominate him, regardless of his level of intelligence. Slough off this surfeit of dreamy sentimentality. Accept reality in its crude ugliness."

"You can't resist the imperious laws that demand food and clothing for man. These same laws compel the 'male' in other respects. I say 'male' to emphasize the bestiality of instincts. . . . You understand. . . . A wife must understand, once and for all, and must forgive; she must not worry herself about 'betrayals of the flesh.' The important thing is what there is in the heart; that's what unites two beings inside." (He struck his chest, at the point where the heart lies.)

"Driven to the limits of my resistance, I satisfy myself with what is within reach. It's a terrible thing to say. Truth is ugly when one analyses it."

Thus, to justify himself, he reduced young Nabou to a "plate of food." Thus, for the sake of "variety," men are unfaithful to their wives.

I was irritated. He was asking me to understand. But to understand what? The supremacy of instinct? The right to betray? The justification of the desire for variety? I could not be an ally to polygamic instincts. What, then, was I to understand?

How I envied your calmness during your last visit! There you were, rid of the mask of suffering. Your sons were growing up well, contrary to all predictions. You did not care about Mawdo. Yes, indeed, there you were, the past crushed beneath your heel. There you were, an innocent victim of an unjust cause and the courageous pioneer of a new life.

13

My own crisis came three years after your own. But unlike in your own case, the source was not my family-in-law. The problem was rooted in Modou himself, my husband.

My daughter Daba, who was preparing for her *baccalauréat,* often brought some of her classmates home with her. Most of the time it was the same young girl, a bit shy, frail, made noticeably uncomfortable by our style of life. But she was really beautiful in this her adolescent period, in her faded but clean clothes! Her beauty shone, pure. Her shapely contours could not but be noticed.

I sometimes noticed that Modou was interested in the pair. Neither was I worried when I heard him suggest that he should take Binetou home in the car—"because it was getting late," he would say.

Binetou was going through a metamorphosis, however. She was now wearing very expensive off-the-peg dresses. Smilingly, she would explain to my daughter: "Oh, I have a sugar-daddy who pays for them."

Then one day, on her return from school, Daba confided to me that Binetou had a serious problem: "The sugar-daddy of the boutique dresses wants to marry Binetou. Just imagine. Her parents want to withdraw her from school, with only a few months to go before the *bac,* to marry her off to the sugar-daddy."

"Advise her to refuse," I said.

"And if the man in question offers her a villa, Mecca for her parents, a car, a monthly allowance, jewels?"

"None of that is worth the capital of youth."

"I agree with you, mum. I'll tell Binetou not to give in; but her mother is a woman who wants so much to escape from mediocrity and who regrets so much her past beauty, faded in the smoke from the wood fires, that she looks enviously at everything I wear; she complains all day long."

"What is important is Binetou herself. She must not give in."

And then, a few days afterwards, Daba renewed the conversation, with its surprising conclusion.

"Mum! Binetou is heartbroken. She is going to marry her sugar-daddy. Her mother cried so much. She begged her daughter to give her life a happy end, in a proper house, as the man has promised them. So she accepted."

"When is the wedding?"

"This coming Sunday, but there'll be no reception. Binetou cannot bear the mockery of her friends."

And in the evening of this same Sunday on which Binetou was being married off I saw come into my house, all dressed up and solemn, Tamsir, Modou's brother, with Mawdo Bâ and his local *Imam*. Where had they come from, looking so awkward in their starched *boubous?* Doubtless, they had come looking for Modou to carry out an important task that one of them had been charged with. I told them that Modou had been out since morning. They entered laughing, deliberately sniffing the fragrant odour of incense that was floating on the air. I sat in front of them, laughing with them. The *Imam* attacked:

"There is nothing one can do when Allah the almighty puts two people side by side."

"True, true," said the other two in support.

A pause. He took a breath and continued: "There is nothing new in this world."

"True, true," Tamsir and Mawdo chimed in again.

"Some things we may find to be sad are much less so than others. . . ."

I followed the movement of the haughty lips that let fall these axioms, which can precede the announcement of either a happy event or an unhappy one. What was he leading up to with these preliminaries that rather announced a storm? So their visit was obviously planned.

Does one announce bad news dressed up like that in one's Sunday best? Or did they want to inspire confidence with their impeccable dress?

I thought of the absent one. I asked with the cry of a hunted beast: "Modou?"

And the *Imam*, who had finally got hold of a leading thread, held tightly on to it. He went on quickly, as if the words were glowing embers in his mouth: "Yes, Modou Fall, but, happily, he is alive for you, for all of us, thanks be to God. All he has done is to marry a second wife today. We have just come from the mosque in Grand Dakar where the marriage took place."

The thorns thus removed from the way, Tamsir ventured: "Modou sends his thanks. He says it is fate that decides men and things: God intended him to have a second wife, there is nothing he can do about it. He praises you for the quarter of a century of marriage in which you gave him all the happiness a wife owes her husband. His family, especially myself, his elder brother, thank you. You have always held us in respect. You know that we are Modou's blood."

Afterwards there were the same old words, which were intended to relieve the situation: "You are the only one in your house, no matter how big it is, no matter how dear life is. You are the first wife, a mother for Modou, a friend for Modou."

Tamsir's Adam's apple danced about in his throat. He shook his left leg, crossed over his folded right leg. His shoes, white Turkish slippers, were covered with a thin layer of red dust, the colour of the earth in which they had walked. The same dust covered Mawdo's and the *Imam*'s shoes.

Mawdo said nothing. He was reliving his own experience. He was thinking of your letter, your reaction, and you and I were so alike. He was being wary. He kept his head lowered, in the attitude of those who accept defeat before the battle.

I acquiesced under the drops of poison that were burning me: "A quarter of a century of marriage," "a wife unparalleled." I counted backwards to determine where the break in the thread had occurred from which everything had unwound. My mother's words came back to me: "too perfect. . . ." I completed at last my mother's thought with the end of the dictum: ". . . to be honest." I thought of the first two incisors with a wide gap between them, the sign of the primacy of love in the individual. I thought of his absence, all day long. He had simply said: "Don't expect me for lunch." I thought of other absences, quite frequent these days, crudely clarified today yet well hidden yesterday under the guise of trade union meetings. He was also on a strict diet, "to break the stomach's egg," he would say laughingly, this egg that announced old age.

Every night when he went out he would unfold and try on several of his suits before settling on one. The others, impatiently rejected, would slip to the floor. I would have to fold them again and put them back in their places; and this extra work, I discovered, I was doing only to help him in his effort to be elegant in his seduction of another woman.

I forced myself to check my inner agitation. Above all, I must not give my visitors the pleasure of relating my distress. Smile, take the matter lightly, just as they announced it. Thank them for the humane way in which they have accomplished their mission. Send thanks to Modou, "a good father and a good husband," "a husband become a friend." Thank my family-in-law, the *Imam*, Mawdo. Smile. Give them something to drink. See them out, under the swirls of incense that they were sniffing once again. Shake their hands.

How pleased they were, all except Mawdo, who correctly judged the import of the event.

14

Alone at last, able to give free rein to my surprise and to gauge my distress. Ah! yes, I forgot to ask for my rival's name so that I might give a human form to my pain.

My question was soon answered. Acquaintances from Grand Dakar came rushing to my house, bringing the various details of the ceremony. Some of them did so out of true friendship for me; others were spiteful and jealous of the promotion Binetou's mother would gain from the marriage.

"I don't understand." They did not understand either the entrance of Modou, a "personality," into this extremely poor family.

Binetou, a child the same age as my daughter Daba, promoted to the rank of my co-wife, whom I must face up to. Shy Binetou! The old man who bought her the new off-the-peg dresses to replace the old faded ones was none other than Modou. She had innocently confided her secrets to her rival's daughter because she thought that this dream, sprung from a brain growing old, would never become reality. She had told everything: the villa, the monthly allowance, the offer of a future trip to Mecca for her parents. She thought she was stronger than the man she was dealing with. She did not know Modou's strong will, his tenacity before an obstacle, the pride he invests in winning, the resistance that inspires new attempts at each failure.

Daba was furious, her pride wounded. She repeated all the nicknames Binetou had given her father: old man, pot-belly, sugar-daddy! . . . the person who gave her life had been daily ridiculed and he accepted it. An overwhelming anger raged inside Daba. She knew that her best friend was sincere in what she said. But what can a child do, faced with a furious mother shouting about her hunger and her thirst to live?

Binetou, like many others, was a lamb slaughtered on the altar of affluence. Daba's anger increased as she analysed the situation: "Break with him, mother! Send this man away. He has respected neither you nor me. Do what Aunty Aissatou did; break with him. Tell me you'll break with him. I can't see you fighting over a man with a girl my age."

I told myself what every betrayed woman says: if Modou was milk, it was I who had had all the cream. The rest, well, nothing but water with a vague smell of milk.

But the final decision lay with me. With Modou absent all night (was he already consummating his marriage?), the solitude that lends counsel enabled me to grasp the problem.

Leave? Start again at zero, after living twenty-five years with one man, after having borne twelve children? Did I have enough energy to bear alone the weight of this responsibility, which was both moral and material?

Leave! Draw a clean line through the past. Turn over a page on which not everything was bright, certainly, but at least all was clear. What would now be recorded there would hold no love, confidence, grandeur or hope. I had never known the sordid side of marriage. Don't get to know it! Run from it! When one begins to forgive, there is an avalanche of faults that comes crashing down, and the only thing that remains is to forgive again, to keep on forgiving. Leave, escape from betrayal! Sleep without asking myself any questions, without straining my ear at the slightest noise, waiting for a husband I share.

I counted the abandoned or divorced women of my generation whom I knew.

I knew a few whose remaining beauty had been able to capture a worthy man, a man who added fine bearing to a good situation and who was considered "better, a hundred times better than his predecessor." The misery that was the lot of these women was rolled back with the invasion of the new happiness that changed their lives, filled out their cheeks, brightened their eyes. I knew others who had lost all hope of renewal and whom loneliness had very quickly laid underground.

The play of destiny remains impenetrable. The cowries that a female neighbour throws on a fan in front of me do not fill me with optimism, neither when they remain face upwards, showing the black hollow that signifies laughter, nor when the grouping of their white backs seems to say that "the man in the double trousers"[3] is coming towards me, the promise of wealth. "The only thing that separates you from them, man and wealth, is the alms of two white and red cola nuts," adds Farmata, my neighbour.

She insists: "There is a saying that discord here may be luck elsewhere. Why are you afraid to make the break? A woman is like a ball; once a ball is thrown, no one

---

3. A man in Western-style clothes [Bâ's note].

can predict where it will bounce. You have no control over where it rolls, and even less over who gets it. Often it is grabbed by an unexpected hand. . . ."

Instead of listening to the reasoning of my neighbour, a *griot* woman who dreams of the generous tips due to the go-between, I looked at myself in the mirror. My eyes took in the mirror's eloquence. I had lost my slim figure, as well as ease and quickness of movement. My stomach protruded from beneath the wrapper that hid the calves developed by the impressive number of kilometres walked since the beginning of my existence. Suckling had robbed my breasts of their round firmness. I could not delude myself: youth was deserting my body.

Whereas a woman draws from the passing years the force of her devotion, despite the ageing of her companion, a man, on the other hand, restricts his field of tenderness. His egoistic eye looks over his partner's shoulder. He compares what he had with what he no longer has, what he has with what he could have.

I had heard of too many misfortunes not to understand my own. There was your own case, Aissatou, the cases of many other women, despised, relegated or exchanged, who were abandoned like a worn-out or out-dated *boubou*.

To overcome distress when it sits upon you demands strong will. When one thinks that with each passing second one's life is shortened, one must profit intensely from this second; it is the sum of all the lost or harvested seconds that makes for a wasted or a successful life. Brace oneself to check despair and get it into proportion! A nervous breakdown waits around the corner for anyone who lets himself wallow in bitterness. Little by little, it takes over your whole being.

Oh, nervous breakdown! Doctors speak of it in a detached, ironical way, emphasizing that the vital organs are in no way disturbed. You are lucky if they don't tell you that you are wasting their time with the ever-growing list of your illnesses—your head, throat, chest, heart, liver—that no X-ray can confirm. And yet what atrocious suffering is caused by nervous breakdowns!

And I think of Jacqueline, who suffered from one. Jacqueline, the Ivorian, had disobeyed her Protestant parents and had married Samba Diack, a contemporary of Mawdo Bâ's, a doctor like him, who, on leaving the African School of Medicine and Pharmacy, was posted to Abidjan.[4] Jacqueline often came round to see us, since her husband often visited our household. Coming to Senegal, she found herself in a new world, a world with different reactions, temperament and mentality from that in which she had grown up. In addition, her husband's relatives—always the relatives— were cool towards her because she refused to adopt the Muslim religion and went instead to the Protestant church every Sunday.

A black African, she should have been able to fit without difficulty into a black African society, Senegal and the Ivory Coast both having experienced the same colonial power. But Africa is diverse, divided. The same country can change its character and outlook several times over, from north to south or from east to west.

Jacqueline truly wanted to become Senegalese, but the mockery checked all desire in her to co-operate. People called her *gnac*,[5] and she finally understood the meaning of this nickname that revolted her so.

Her husband, making up for lost time, spent his time chasing slender Senegalese women, as he would say with appreciation, and did not bother to hide his adventures, respecting neither his wife nor his children. His lack of precautions brought to

4. Ivorian: a person from the nation of Côte d'Ivoire (Ivory Coast); Abidjan is its capital.

5. Someone who comes from the hinterland; in West African English, "bushman" [Bâ's note].

Jacqueline's knowledge the irrefutable proof of his misconduct: love notes, check stubs bearing the names of the payees, bills from restaurants and for hotel rooms. Jacqueline cried; Samba Diack "lived it up." Jacqueline lost weight: Samba Diack was still living fast. Jacqueline complained of a disturbing lump in her chest, under her left breast; she said she had the impression that a sharp point had pierced her there and was cutting through her flesh right to her very bones. She fretted. Mawdo listened to her heart: nothing wrong there, he would say. He prescribed some tranquillizers. Eagerly, Jacqueline took the tablets, tortured by the insidious pain. The bottle empty, she noticed that the lump remained in the same place; she continued to feel the pain just as acutely as ever.

She consulted a doctor from her own country, who ordered an electrocardiogram and various blood tests. Nothing to be learned from the electric reading of the heart, nothing abnormal found in the blood. He too prescribed tranquillizers, big, effervescent tablets that could not allay poor Jacqueline's distress.

She thought of her parents, of their refusal to consent to her marriage. She wrote them a pathetic letter, in which she begged for their forgiveness. They sent their sincere blessing but could do nothing to lighten the strange weight in her chest.

Jacqueline was taken to Fann Hospital on the road to Ouakam, near the university, where medical students do their internship, as they do at the Aristide Le Dantec Hospital. This hospital did not exist at the time Mawdo Bâ and Samba Diack studied at the School of Medicine and Pharmacy. It has many departments, housed either in separate buildings or in adjoining ones to facilitate communication. These buildings, despite their number and size, do not manage to fill up the hospital's vast grounds. On entering it, Jacqueline thought of those gone mad, confined inside. It was necessary to explain to her that the mad ones were in psychiatric care and that here they were called the mentally sick and in any case, were not violent, the violent ones being confined in the psychiatric hospital at Thiaroye. Jacqueline was in a neurology ward, and those of us who went to visit her learned that the hospital also had departments for treating tuberculosis and infectious diseases.

Jacqueline lay prostrate in her bed. Her beautiful but neglected black hair, through which no comb had been run ever since she began consulting doctor after doctor, formed shaggy tufts on her head. When the scarf protecting it slipped out of place, it would uncover the coating of a mixture of roots that we poured on her, for we tried everything to draw this sister out of her private hell. And it was your mother, Aissatou, who went to consult the native medicine men for us and brought back *safara*[6] from her visits and directions for the sacrifices you quickly carried out.

Jacqueline's thoughts turned to death. She waited for it, frightened and tormented, her hand on her chest, where the tenacious, invisible lump foiled all the ruses, scoffed maliciously at all the tranquillizers. Jacqueline's room-mate was a French Technical Co-operation teacher of literature, posted to the Lycée Faidherbe in Saint-Louis. The only thing she knew of Saint-Louis, she said, was the bridge that spanned the river. A sore throat, an affliction as sudden as it was violent, had prevented her from taking up her duties and had brought her here, where she was waiting to be repatriated.

I observed her often. Old, for her unmarried status. Thin, angular even, without any charm. Her studies must have been her only form of recreation during her youth.

6. Liquid with supernatural powers [Bâ's note].

Sour-tempered, she must have put off any passionate advances. It was perhaps her loneliness that had made her seek for a change. A teaching post in Senegal must have corresponded to her dreams of escape. She had come therefore, but all her frustrated dreams, all her disappointed hopes, all her crushed revolt connived to attack her throat, protected by a navy-blue scarf with white dots, which contrasted with the paleness of her chest. The medication with which her throat was painted gave a blueish tint to her thin lips, pinched over their misery. She had big, luminous, blue eyes, the only light, the only point of beauty, the only heavenly grace in her ungracious face. She tapped against her throat; Jacqueline tapped against her chest. We would laugh at their ways, especially when the patient from the next room came to "chat," as she said, and would uncover her back for the refreshing caress of the air-conditioner. She suffered from sudden flushes, which burned her terribly at this spot.

Strange and varied manifestations of neuro-vegetative dystonia.[7] Doctors, beware, especially if you are neurologists or psychiatrists. Often, the pains you are told of have their roots in moral torment. Vexations suffered and constant frustrations: these are what accumulate somewhere in the body and choke it.

Jacqueline, who enjoyed life, bravely endured blood test after blood test. Another electrocardiogram, another X-ray of the lungs. An electro-encephalogram was carried out, which revealed traces of her suffering. It then became necessary to do a gaseous electro-encephalography. This is extremely painful, always entailing a lumbar puncture. That day, Jacqueline remained confined to bed, looking more pitiful and haggard than ever before.

Samba Diack was kind and touched by his wife's breakdown.

One fine day, after a month of treatment (intravenous injections and tranquillizers), after a month of investigations, during which her French neighbour had returned to her country, the doctor who was head of the Neurology Department asked to see Jacqueline. She found in front of her a man whom maturity and the nobility of his job had made even more attractive, a man who had not been hardened by constant dealing with the most deplorable of miseries, that of mental alienation. With his sharp eyes, accustomed to judging, he looked into those of Jacqueline in order to discover in her soul the source of the distress disrupting her organism. In a soft, reassuring voice, which in itself was balm to this overstrung being, he explained: "Madame Diack, I assure you that there is nothing at all wrong with your head. The X-rays have shown nothing, and neither have the blood tests. The problem is that you are depressed, that is . . . not happy. You wish the conditions of life were different from what they are in reality, and this is what is torturing you. Moreover, you had your babies too soon after each other; the body loses its vital juices, which haven't had the time to be replaced. In short, there is nothing endangering your life.

"You must react, go out, give yourself a reason for living. Take courage. Slowly, you will overcome. We will give you a series of shock treatments with curare[8] to relax you. You can leave afterwards."

The doctor punctuated his words by nodding his head and smiling convincingly, giving Jacqueline much hope. Re-animated, she related the discussion to us and confided that she had left the interview already half-cured. She knew the heart of her illness and would fight against it. She was morally uplifted. She had come a long way, had Jacqueline!

---

7. A slightly dated medical term that refers to states of depression combined with neurological dysfunctions.

8. A substance that is made from South American plants; it is used as a poison as well as for therapeutic purposes.

Why did I recall this friend's ordeal? Was it because of its happy ending? Or merely to delay the formulation of the choice I had made, a choice that my reason rejected but that accorded with the immense tenderness I felt towards Modou Fall?

Yes, I was well aware of where the right solution lay, the dignified solution. And, to my family's great surprise, unanimously disapproved of by my children, who were under Daba's influence, I chose to remain. Modou and Mawdo were surprised, could not understand. . . .

Forewarned, you, my friend, did not try to dissuade me, respectful of my new choice of life.

I cried every day.

From then on, my life changed. I had prepared myself for equal sharing, according to the precepts of Islam concerning polygamic life. I was left with empty hands.

My children, who disagreed with my decision, sulked. In opposition to me, they represented a majority I had to respect.

"You have not finished suffering," predicted Daba.

I lived in a vacuum. And Modou avoided me. Attempts by friends and family to bring him back to the fold proved futile. One of the new couple's neighbours explained to me that the "child" would go "all a-quiver" each time Modou said my name or showed any desire to see his children. He never came again; his new-found happiness gradually swallowed up his memory of us. He forgot about us.

15

Aissatou, my dear friend, I've told you that there can be no possible comparison between you and young Nabou. But I also realize that there can be no possible comparison between young Nabou and Binetou. Young Nabou grew up beside her aunt, who had earmarked her as the spouse of her son Mawdo. Used to seeing him, she let herself be drawn towards him, naturally, without any shock. His greying hair did not offend her; she found his thickening features reassuring. And then she loved and still loves Mawdo, even if their interests are not always the same. School had not left a strong mark on young Nabou, preceded and dominated as it was by the strength of character of Aunty Nabou, who, in her rage for vengeance, had left nothing to chance in the education she gave her niece. It was especially while telling folk tales, late at night under the starlit sky, that Aunty Nabou wielded her power over young Nabou's soul: her expressive voice glorified the retributive violence of the warrior; her expressive voice lamented the anxiety of the Loved One, all submissive. She saluted the courage of the reckless; she stigmatized trickery, laziness, calumny; she demanded care of the orphan and respect for old age. Tales with animal characters, nostalgic songs kept young Nabou breathless. And slowly but surely, through the sheer force of repetition, the virtues and greatness of a race took root in this child.

This kind of oral education, easily assimilated, full of charm, has the power to bring out the best in the adult mind, developed in its contact with it. Softness and generosity, docility and politeness, poise and tact, all these qualities made young Nabou pleasant. Mawdo used to call her "finicky," with a shrug of his shoulders.

And then, young Nabou had a profession. She had no time to worry about her "state of mind." In charge of frequent shifts at the "Repos Mandel" Maternity Home, on the outskirts of the crowded and badly serviced suburban areas, all day and several times over she would go through the same gestures engendering life. Babies passed again and again between her expert hands.

Still image from Sembène Ousmane's film *Xala,* 1975, based on his novel of the same title (1974). Like Bâ's *So Long a Letter, Xala* revolves around polygamy in Senegal. The photograph shows the protagonist, the middle-aged businessman El Hadji Abdou Kader Beye, with his new bride and third wife, the 19-year-old N'Gone. "This third marriage raised him to the rank of traditional nobility; it represented a kind of promotion," the novel's narrator comments.

She would come back from work railing at the lack of beds that led to the discharge, too early in her opinion, of the new mothers; worried about the lack of staff, inadequate instruments, medicines. She would say, with deep concern: "The fragile baby is let loose too quickly into a hygienically unsound social environment."

She thought of the great rate of infant mortality, which nights of care and devotion cannot decrease. She thought: What a thrilling adventure it is to turn a baby into a healthy man. But how many mothers are able to accomplish that feat?

In the midst of life, in the midst of poverty, in the midst of ugliness, young Nabou would often triumph with her knowledge and experience; but she sometimes knew heartrending failure; she remained powerless, faced with the force of death.

Young Nabou, responsible and aware, like you, like me! Even though she is not my friend, we often shared the same problems.

She found life hard and, being a fighter, had not the least inclination for frivolities.

As for Binetou, she had grown up in complete liberty in an environment where survival was of the essence. Her mother was more concerned with putting the pot on the boil than with education. Beautiful, lively, kindhearted, intelligent, Binetou had access to many of her friends' well-off families and was sharply aware of what she was sacrificing by her marriage. A victim, she wanted to be the oppressor. Exiled in the world of adults, which was not her own, she wanted her prison gilded. Demanding, she tormented. Sold, she raised her price daily. What she renounced, those things which before used to be the sap of her life and which she would bitterly enumerate, called for exorbitant compensations, which Modou exhausted himself trying to provide. Echoes of her life would reach me, amplified or muted according to the visitor. The seductive power of mature age, of silvery temples, was unknown to Binetou. And Modou would dye his hair every month. His waistline painfully restrained by old-fashioned trousers, Binetou would never miss a chance of laughing wickedly at him. Modou would leave himself winded trying to imprison youth in its decline, which abandoned him on all sides: the graceless sag of a double chin, the gait hesitant and heavy at the slightest cool breeze. Gracefulness and beauty surrounded him. He was afraid of disappointing, and so that there would be no time for close scrutiny of him, he would create daily celebrations during which the bright young thing would move, an elf with slender arms who with a laugh could make life beautiful or with a pout bring sadness.

People talked of bewitchment. With determination, friends begged me to react: "You are letting someone else pluck the fruits of your labour."

Vehemently, they recommended *marabouts*,[9] sure in their science, who had proved themselves by bringing husbands back to the fold, by separating them from evil women. These charlatans lived far away. Casamance was mentioned, where the Diola and Madjago excel in magic philtres. They suggested Linguère, the country of the Fulba, quick in vengeance through charms as through arms. They also talked of Mali, the country of the Bambara, with faces deeply scarred with tribal marks.[1]

To act as I was urged would have been to call myself into question. I was already reproaching myself for a weakness that had not prevented the degradation of my home. Was I to deny myself because Modou had chosen another path? No, I would not give in to the pressure. My mind and my faith rejected supernatural power. They rejected this easy attraction, which kills any will to fight. I looked reality in the face.

Reality had the face of Lady Mother-in-Law, swallowing up double mouthfuls from the trough offered her. Her hunch about a gilded way of life was being proved right. Her unsteady hut, with zinc walls covered with magazine pages where pin-ups and advertisements were placed side by side, had grown dim in her memory. One motion of her hand in her bathroom and delicious jets of hot water would massage her back. Another in the kitchen and ice cubes would cool the water in her glass. One more and a flame would spring from the gas cooker and she would prepare herself a delicious omelette.

The senior wife hitherto neglected, Lady Mother-in-Law emerged from the shadows and took her unfaithful husband back in tow. She held valuable trump cards: grilled meats, roasted chicken and (why not?) banknotes slipped into the pockets of the *boubou* hanging in the bedroom. She no longer counted the cost of water bought from the Tukulor hawker of the vital liquid drawn from public springs. Having known poverty, she rejoiced in her new-found happiness. Modou fulfilled her expectations. He would thoughtfully send her wads of notes to spend and would offer her, after his trips abroad, jewellery and rich *boubous*. From then on, she joined the category of

---

9. Holy men associated with Islam or traditional African religions; they are credited with supernatural powers.

1. Casamance and Linguère are provinces of Senegal; Mali is a neighboring country. The Diola, Madjago, Fulba, and Bambara are different ethnic groups.

women "with heavy bracelets" lauded by the *griots*. Thrilled, she would listen to the radio transmitting songs dedicated to her.

Her family reserved the best place for her during ceremonies and listened to her advice. When Modou's large car dropped her and she emerged, there would be a rush of outstretched hands into which she placed banknotes.

Reality was also Binetou, who went from night club to night club. She would arrive draped in a long, costly garment, a gold belt, a present from Modou on the birth of their first child, shining round her waist. Her shoes tapped on the ground, announcing her presence. The waiters would move aside and bow respectfully in the hope of a royal tip. With a contemptuous look, she would eye those already seated. With a pout like that of a spoilt child, she would indicate to Modou the table she had chosen. With a wave of her hand, like a magician, she would have various bottles lined up. She was showing off to the young people and wanted to impress them with her form of success. Binetou, incontestably beautiful and desirable! "Bewitching," people admitted. But when the moment of admiration passed, she was the one who lowered her head at the sight of couples graced with nothing but their youth and rich in their happiness alone.

The couples held each other or danced apart depending on the music, sometimes slow and coaxing, sometimes vigorous and wild. When the trumpet blared out, backed by the frenzy of the drums, the young dancers, excited and untiring, would stamp, jump and caper about, shouting their joy. Modou would try to follow suit. The harsh lights betrayed him to the unpitying sarcasm of some of them, who called him a "cradle-snatcher." What did it matter! He had Binetou in his arms. He was happy.

Worn out, Binetou would watch with a disillusioned eye the progress of her friends. The image of her life, which she had murdered, broke her heart.

Sometimes also, despite my disapproval, Daba would go to the night clubs. Dressed simply, she would appear on her fiancé's arm; she would arrive late on purpose so as to sit in full view of her father. It was a grotesque confrontation: on one side, an ill-assorted couple, on the other two well-matched people.

And the evening created an extreme tension that opposed two former friends, a father and his daughter, a son-in-law and his father-in-law.

16

I was surviving. In addition to my former duties, I took over Modou's as well.

The purchase of basic foodstuffs kept me occupied at the end of every month; I made sure that I was never short of tomatoes or of oil, potatoes or onions during those periods when they became rare in the markets; I stored bags of "Siam" rice, much loved by the Senegalese. My brain was taxed by new financial gymnastics.

The last date for payment of electricity bills and of water rates demanded my attention. I was often the only woman in the queue.

Replacing the locks and latches of broken doors, replacing broken windows was a bother, as well as looking for a plumber to deal with blocked sinks. My son Mawdo Fall complained about burnt-out bulbs that needed replacement.

I survived. I overcame my shyness at going alone to cinemas; I would take a seat with less and less embarrassment as the months went by. People stared at the middle-aged lady without a partner. I would feign indifference, while anger hammered against my nerves and the tears I held back welled up behind my eyes.

From the surprised looks, I gauged the slender liberty granted to women.

The early shows at the cinema filled me with delight. They gave me the courage to meet the curious gaze of various people. They did not keep me away for long from my children.

What a great distraction from distress is the cinema! Intellectual films, those with a message, sentimental films, detective films, comedies, thrillers, all these were my companions. I learned from them lessons of greatness, courage and perseverance. They deepened and widened my vision of the world, thanks to their cultural value. The cinema, an inexpensive means of recreation, can thus give healthy pleasure.

I survived. The more I thought about it, the more grateful I became to Modou for having cut off all contact. I had the solution my children wanted—the break without having taken the initiative. The lie had not taken root. Modou was excising me from his life and was proving it by his unequivocal attitude.

What do other husbands do? They wallow in indecision; they force themselves to be present where neither their feelings nor their interests continue to reside. Nothing impresses them in their home: the wife all dressed up, the son full of tenderness, the meal tastefully served. They remain stolid, like marble. They wish only that the hours may pass rapidly. At night, feigning fatigue or illness, they snore deeply. How quick they are to greet the liberating daybreak, which puts an end to their torment!

I was not deceived, therefore. I no longer interested Modou, and I knew it. I was abandoned: a fluttering leaf that no hand dares to pick up, as my grandmother would have said.

I faced up to the situation bravely. I carried out my duties; they filled the time and channelled my thoughts. But my loneliness would emerge at night, burdensome. One does not easily undo the tenuous ties that bind two people together during a journey fraught with hardship. I lived the proof of it, bringing back to life past scenes, past conversations. Our common habits sprang up at their usual times. I missed dreadfully our nightly conversation; I missed our bursts of refreshing or understanding laughter. Like opium, I missed our daily consultations. I pitted myself against shadows. The wanderings of my thoughts chased away all sleep. I side-stepped my pain in a refusal to fight it.

The continuity of radio broadcasts was a great relief. I gave the radio the role of comforter. At night the music lulled my anxiety. I heard the message of old and new songs, which awakened hope. My sadness dissolved.

With all the force I had, I called eagerly to "another man" to replace Modou.

Distressing awakenings succeeded the nights. My love for my children sustained me. They were a pillar; I owed them help and affection.

Did Modou appreciate, in its full measure, the void created by his absence in this house? Did Modou attribute to me more energy than I had to shoulder the responsibility of my children?

I adopted a sprightly tone to rouse my battalion. The coffee warmed the atmosphere, exuding its sweet fragrance. Foaming baths, mutual teasing and laughter. A new day and increased efforts! A new day, and waiting. . . .

Waiting for what? It would not be easy to get my children to accept a new masculine presence. Having condemned their father, could they be tolerant towards another man? Besides, what man would have the courage to face twelve pairs of hostile eyes, which openly tear you apart?

Waiting! But waiting for what? I was not divorced . . . I was abandoned: a fluttering leaf that no hand dares to pick up, as my grandmother would have said.

I survived. I experienced the inadequacy of public transport. My children laughed at themselves in making this harsh discovery. One day, I heard Daba advise them: "Above all, don't let mum know that it is stifling in those buses during the rush hours."

I shed tears of joy and sadness together: joy in being loved by my children, the sadness of a mother who does not have the means to change the course of events.

I told you then, without any ulterior motive, of this painful aspect of our life, while Modou's car drove Lady Mother-in-Law to the four corners of town and while Binetou streaked along the roads in an Alfa Romeo, sometimes white, sometimes red.

I shall never forget your response, you, my sister, nor my joy and my surprise when I was called to the Fiat agency and was told to choose a car which you had paid for, in full. My children gave cries of joy when they learned of the approaching end of their tribulations, which remain the daily lot of a good many other students.

Friendship has splendours that love knows not. It grows stronger when crossed, whereas obstacles kill love. Friendship resists time, which wearies and severs couples. It has heights unknown to love.

You, the goldsmith's daughter, gave me your help while depriving yourself.

And I learned to drive, stifling my fear. The narrow space between the wheel and the seat was mine. The flattened clutch glided in the gears. The brake reduced the forward thrust and, to speed along, I had to step on the accelerator. I did not trust the accelerator. At the slightest pressure from my feet, the car lurched forward. My feet learned to dance over the pedals. Whenever I was discouraged, I would say: Why should Binetou sit behind a wheel and not I? I would tell myself: Don't disappoint Aissatou. I won this battle of nerves and *sang-froid*.[2] I obtained my driving licence and told you about it.

I told you: and now—my children on the backseat of the cream-coloured Fiat 125; thanks to you, my children can look the affluent mother-in-law and the fragile child in the eye in the streets of the town.

Modou surprised, unbelieving, inquired into the source of the car. He never accepted the true story. Like Mawdo's mother, he too believed that a goldsmith's daughter had no heart.

17

I take a deep breath.

I've related at one go your story as well as mine. I've said the essential, for pain, even when it's past, leaves the same marks on the individual when recalled. Your disappointment was mine, as my rejection was yours. Forgive me once again if I have reopened your wound. Mine continues to bleed.

You may tell me: the path of life is not smooth; one is bruised by its sharp edges. I also know that marriage is never smooth. It reflects differences in character and capacity for feeling. In one couple the man may be the victim of a fickle woman or of a woman shut up in her own preoccupations who rejects all dialogue and quashes all moves towards tenderness. In another couple alcoholism is the leprosy that gnaws away at health, wealth and peace. It shows up an individual's disordered state through grotesque spectacles by which his dignity is undermined, in situations where physical blows become solid arguments and the menacing blade of a knife an irresistible call for silence.

2. Self-possession.

With others it is the lure of easy gain that dominates: incorrigible players at the gaming table or seated in the shade of a tree. The heated atmosphere of rooms full of fiendish odours, the distorted faces of tense players. The giddy whirl of playing cards swallows up time, wealth, conscience, and stops only with the last breath of the person accustomed to shuffling them.

I try to spot my faults in the failure of my marriage. I gave freely, gave more than I received. I am one of those who can realize themselves fully and bloom only when they form part of a couple. Even though I understand your stand, even though I respect the choice of liberated women, I have never conceived of happiness outside marriage.

I loved my house. You can testify to the fact that I made it a haven of peace where everything had its place, that I created a harmonious symphony of colours. You know how soft-hearted I am, how much I loved Modou. You can testify to the fact that, mobilized day and night in his service, I anticipated his slightest desire.

I made peace with his family. Despite his desertion of our home, his father and mother and Tamsir, his brother, still continued to visit me often, as did his sisters. My children too grew up without much ado. Their success at school was my pride, just like laurels thrown at the feet of my lord and master.

And Modou was no prisoner. He spent his time as he wished. I well understood his desire to let off steam. He fulfilled himself outside as he wished in his trade union activities.

I am trying to pinpoint any weakness in the way I conducted myself. My social life may have been stormy and perhaps injured Modou's trade union career. Can a man, deceived and flouted by his family, impose himself on others? Can a man whose wife does not do her job well honestly demand a fair reward for labour? Aggression and condescension in a woman arouse contempt and hatred for her husband. If she is gracious, even without appealing to any ideology, she can summon support for any action. In a word, a man's success depends on feminine support.

And I ask myself. I ask myself, why? Why did Modou detach himself? Why did he put Binetou between us?

You, very logically, may reply: "Affections spring from nothing; sometimes a grimace, the carriage of a head can seduce a heart and keep it."

I ask myself questions. The truth is that, despite everything, I remain faithful to the love of my youth. Aissatou, I cry for Modou, and I can do nothing about it.

18

Yesterday I celebrated, as is the custom, the fortieth day of Modou's death. I have forgiven him. May God hear the prayer I say for him every day. I celebrated the fortieth day in meditation. The initiated read the Koran. Their fervent voices rose towards heaven. Modou Fall, may God accept you among his chosen few.

After going through the motions of piety, Tamsir came and sat in my bedroom in the blue armchair that used to be your favourite. Sticking his head outside, he signalled to Mawdo; he also signalled to the *Imam* from the mosque in his area. The *Imam* and Mawdo joined him. This time, Tamsir speaks. There is a striking resemblance between Modou and Tamsir, the same tics donated by the inexplicable law of heredity. Tamsir speaks with great assurance; he touches, once again, on my years of marriage, then he concludes: "When you have 'come out' (that is to say, of mourning), I shall marry you. You suit me as a wife, and further, you will continue to live here, just as if Modou were not dead. Usually it is the younger brother who inherits his elder brother's wife. In this case, it is the opposite. You are my good luck. I shall marry you. I prefer you to the other one, too frivolous, too young. I advised Modou against that marriage."

What a declaration of love, full of conceit, in a house still in mourning. What assurance and calm aplomb! I look Tamsir straight in the eye. I look at Mawdo. I look at the *Imam*. I draw my black shawl closer. I tell my beads. This time I shall speak out.

My voice has known thirty years of silence, thirty years of harassment. It bursts out, violent, sometimes sarcastic, sometimes contemptuous.

"Did you ever have any affection for your brother? Already you want to build a new home for yourself, over a body that is still warm. While we are praying for Modou, you are thinking of future wedding festivities.

"Ah, yes! Your strategy is to get in before any other suitor, to get in before Mawdo, the faithful friend, who has more qualities than you and who also, according to custom, can inherit the wife. You forget that I have a heart, a mind, that I am not an object to be passed from hand to hand. You don't know what marriage means to me: it is an act of faith and of love, the total surrender of oneself to the person one has chosen and who has chosen you." (I emphasized the word "chosen.")

"What of your wives, Tamsir? Your income can meet neither their needs nor those of your numerous children. To help you out with your financial obligations, one of your wives dyes, another sells fruit, the third untiringly turns the handle of her sewing machine. You, the revered lord, you take it easy, obeyed at the crook of a finger. I shall never be the one to complete your collection. My house shall never be for you the coveted oasis: no extra burden; my 'turn' every day;[3] cleanliness and luxury, abundance and calm! No, Tamsir!

"And then there are Daba and her husband, who have demonstrated their financial acumen by buying up all your brother's properties. What promotion for you! Your friends are going to look at you with envy in their eyes."

Mawdo signalled with his hand for me to stop.

"Shut up! Shut up! Stop! Stop!"

But you can't stop once you've let your anger loose. I concluded, more violent than ever: "Tamsir, purge yourself of your dreams of conquest. They have lasted forty days. I shall never be your wife."

The *Imam* prayed God to be his witness.

"Such profane words and still in mourning!" Tamsir got up without a word. He understood fully that he'd been defeated.

Thus I took my revenge for that other day when all three of them had airily informed me of the marriage of Modou Fall and Binetou.

19

Aissatou, even in my mourning clothes I have no peace of mind.

After Tamsir, Daouda Dieng. . . . You remember Daouda Dieng, my former suitor. To his maturity I had preferred inexperience, to his generosity, poverty, to his gravity, spontaneity, to his stability, adventure.

He came to Modou's funeral. In the envelope that he gave Fatim there was a large sum of money. And his look was insistent, saying a great deal—of course.

---

3. The statutory visit that every polygamous man must make to the bedroom of each of his wives in turn [Bâ's note].

Where he is concerned, I believe to be true what he used to tell us jokingly, whenever by chance we met again: one never forgets a first love.

After Tamsir, eliminated that memorable day when I quelled his lust for conquest; after Tamsir, then, Daouda Dieng, a candidate for my hand! Daouda Dieng was my mother's favourite. I can still hear her persuasive voice advise me: a woman must marry the man who loves her but never the one she loves; that is the secret of lasting happiness.

Daouda Dieng had kept himself well, compared with Mawdo and Modou. Just on the threshold of old age, he had resisted the repeated attacks of time and exertion. He was elegantly dressed in a suit of embroidered brocade; he remained the same well-groomed man, meticulous and close-shaved. He wore his social success boldly but without condescension.

Although a deputy at the National Assembly, he remained accessible, with gestures that lent weight to his opinions. His lightly silvered hair gave him unquestionable charm.

For the last three years he had commanded attention in the political race through the sobriety of his actions and the precision of his words. His car, with its distinctive cockade in the national colours, was parked on the opposite pavement.

How much I preferred his emotion to Tamsir's confident arrogance! His trembling lips betrayed him. His look swept over my face. I took refuge in banalities: "How is Aminata (his wife)? And the children? And your clinic? What's it like at the National Assembly?"

My questions came uninterrupted, as much to put him at ease as to renew the dialogue that had for so long been cut off. He replied briefly. But my last question provoked a shrug of the shoulders, to signify "It's all right," said challengingly.

I went on: "It must be all right, that male Assembly!"

I said it teasingly, rolling my eyes round. Eternal woman: even in mourning, you want to make a strike, you want to seduce, you want to arouse interest!

Daouda was no fool. He knew very well that I wanted to relieve him of his embarrassment and to draw back the curtain of silence and constraint that separated us, created by the long years and my former refusal to marry him.

"Still very critical, Ramatoulaye! Why this ironical statement and this provocative epithet when there are women in the Assembly?"

"Four women, Daouda, four out of a hundred deputies. What a ridiculous ratio! Not even one for each province."

Daouda laughed, an open, communicative laugh, which I found stimulating.

We laughed noisily together. I saw again his beautiful set of teeth, capped with the circumflex accent of a black moustache, combed and very sleek. Ah! those teeth, set close together, had won my mother's confidence!

"But you women, you are like mortar shells. You demolish. You destroy. Imagine a large number of women in the Assembly. Why, everything would explode, go up in flames."

And we laughed again.

Wrinkling my brow, I commented: "But we are not incendiaries; rather, we are stimulants!" And I pressed on: "In many fields, and without skirmishes, we have taken advantage of the notable achievements that have reached us from elsewhere, the gains wrested from the lessons of history. We have a right, just as you have, to education, which we ought to be able to pursue to the furthest limits of our intellectual capacities.

We have a right to equal well-paid employment, to equal opportunities. The right to vote is an important weapon. And now the Family Code has been passed, restoring to the most humble of women the dignity that has so often been trampled upon.

"But Daouda, the constraints remain; but Daouda, old beliefs are revived; but Daouda, egoism emerges, scepticism rears its head in the political field. You want to make it a closed shop and you huff and puff about it.

"Nearly twenty years of independence! When will we have the first female minister involved in the decisions concerning the development of our country? And yet the militancy and ability of our women, their disinterested commitment, have already been demonstrated. Women have raised more than one man to power."

Daouda listened to me. But I had the impression that more than my ideas, it was my voice that captivated him.

And I continued: "When will education be decided for children on the basis not of sex but of talent?"

Daouda Dieng was savouring the warmth of the inner dream he was spinning around me. As for me, I was bolting like a horse that has long been tethered and is now free and revelling in space. Ah, the joy of having an interlocutor before you, especially an admirer!

I had remained the same Ramatoulaye . . . a bit of a rebel.

I drew Daouda Dieng along with my ardour. He was an upright man, and each time the situation demanded, he would fight for social justice. It was not love of show or money that had driven him towards politics, but his true love for his fellow man, the urge to redress wrongs and injustice.

"Whom are you addressing, Ramatoulaye? You are echoing my speeches at the National Assembly, where I have been called a 'feminist.' I am not, in fact, the only one to insist on changing the rules of the game and injecting new life into it. Women should no longer be decorative accessories, objects to be moved about, companions to be flattered or calmed with promises. Women are the nation's primary, fundamental root, from which all else grows and blossoms. Women must be encouraged to take a keener interest in the destiny of the country. Even you who are protesting; you preferred your husband, your class, your children to public life. If men alone are active in the parties, why should they think of the women? It is only human to give yourself the larger portion of the cake when you are sharing it out.

"Don't be self-centred in your reaction. Consider the situation of every one of the country's citizens. No one is well-off, not even those of us who are considered to be secure and financially sound, when in fact all our savings go towards the maintenance of an avid electoral clientele which believes itself to be our promoters. Developing a country is not easy. The more responsibility one has, the more one feels it; poverty breaks your heart, but you have no control over it. I am speaking of the whole range of material and moral poverty. Better living requires roads, decent houses, wells, clinics, medicines, seeds. I am one of those who advocated that independence celebrations should be rotated annually among the regions. Any initiative that enables regional investments and transformations is welcome.

"We need money, a mountain of money, which we must get from others by winning their confidence. With just one rainy season and our single crop, Senegal will not go far despite all our determination."

Night fell quickly from the skies, in a hurry to darken men and things. It came through the venetian blinds in the sitting-room. The *muezzin*'s invitation to the *Timiss* prayer was persuasive;⁴ Ousmane stood on tiptoe and flicked on the switch. There was a sudden flood of light.

Daouda, well aware of the constraints of my situation, got up. He lifted Ousmane up towards the lamp, and Ousmane chuckled, arms stretched. He let him down. "Till tomorrow," he said. "I came to discuss something else. You led me into a political discussion. Every discussion is profitable. Till tomorrow," he repeated.

He smiled: neat rows of good teeth. He smiled and opened the door. I heard his footsteps recede. A moment later the humming of his powerful car carried him homewards.

What will he say to Aminata, his wife and cousin, to justify his lateness? . . .

Daouda Dieng did indeed come back the next day. But unfortunately for him, and fortunately for me, my maternal aunts were visiting me and he was prevented from expressing himself freely. He did not dare to stay too long.

20

Today is Friday. I've taken a refreshing bath. I can feel its revitalizing effect, which, through my open pores, soothes me.

The smell of soap surrounds me. Clean clothes replace my crumpled ones. The cleanliness of my body pleases me. I think that as she is the object of attraction for so many eyes, cleanliness is one of the essential qualities of a woman. The most humble of huts is pleasing when it is clean; the most luxurious setting offers no attraction if it is covered in dust.

Those women we call "house"-wives deserve praise. The domestic work they carry out, and which is not paid in hard cash, is essential to the home. Their compensation remains the pile of well ironed, sweet-smelling washing, the shining tiled floor on which the foot glides, the gay kitchen filled with the smell of stews. Their silent action is felt in the least useful detail: over there, a flower in bloom placed in a vase, elsewhere a painting with appropriate colours, hung up in the right place.

The management of the home is an art. We have learned the hard way, and it is still not over. Even deciding on the menus is not easy if one thinks of the number of days there are in a year and of the fact that there are three meals in one day. Managing the family budget requires flexibility, vigilance and prudence in performing the financial gymnastics that send you from one more or less dangerous leap to another, from the first to the last day of the month.

To be a woman! To live the life of a woman!

Ah, Aissatou!

Tonight I am restless. The flavour of life is love. The salt of life is also love.

Daouda came back. An outfit of blue brocade had replaced the grey outfit of the first visit and the chocolate-coloured one of the second.

He began right at the doorway, in the same tone of voice as I had used at our first meeting, without stopping for breath: "How are you? And the children, and your Assembly? And what about Ousmane?" Hearing his name, Ousmane appeared, his mouth and cheeks covered with the chocolate he munched all day long.

Daouda grabbed hold of this little slip of a man, who struggled and kicked his legs about. He let him go with a friendly tap on his buttocks and a picture book in his hands. Ousmane, shouting with joy, ran to show his present to the household. "No

---

4. Muezzin: the Muslim crier who calls the faithful to prayer five times a day from the minaret of a mosque.

visitors? I shall lead the discussion today . . . I from the male Assembly." He laughed maliciously. "Don't think that I criticize just for the fun of it. Our incipient democracy, which is changing the situation of the citizen and for which your party may take much credit, appeals to me. Socialism, which is the heart of your action, is the expression of my deepest aspirations if it is adapted to the realities of our life, as your political secretary claims. The openings it has created are considerable, and Senegal offers a new prospect of liberty regained. I appreciate all that, especially when all around us, to our right and to our left, one-party systems have been imposed. A single party never expresses the unanimous view of the citizens. If all individuals were made in the same mould, it would lead to an appalling collectivism. Differences produce conflicts, which may be beneficial to the development of a country if they occur among true patriots, whose only ambition is the happiness of the citizen.

"But enough of politics, Ramatoulaye. I refuse to go along with you, like the other day. I have had my fill of 'democracy,' 'struggle,' 'freedom' and what have you, all those expressions that float about me daily. Enough, Ramatoulaye. Listen to me, rather. The bush radio has informed me of your refusal to marry Tamsir. Is it true?"

"Yes."

"I, in turn, and for the second time in my life, have come to ask for your hand . . . after you are out of mourning, of course. I have the same feeling for you as I had before. Separation, your marriage, my own, none of these has been able to sap my love for you. Indeed, separation has made it keener; time has consolidated it; my advance in years has purified it. I love you dearly, but with my head. You are a widow with young children. I am head of a family. Each of us has the weight of the 'past' to help us in understanding each other. I open my arms to you for new-found happiness; will you accept?"

I opened my eyes wide, not in astonishment—a woman can always predict a declaration of this kind—but in a kind of stupor. Ah yes, Aissatou, those well-worn words, which have for long been used and are still being used, had taken root in me. Their sweetness, of which I had been deprived for years, intoxicated me: I feel no shame in admitting it to you.

Very reasonably, the deputy concluded: "Don't give me an answer immediately. Think about my proposal. I shall come back tomorrow at the same time."

And, as if embarrassed by his own revelations, Daouda went away, after flashing a smile at me.

My neighbour, Farmata, the *griot* woman, dashed in after him, excited. She was always trying to see into the future with her cowries, and the least agreement of her predictions with reality thrilled her.

"I met the strong, rich man with the 'double trousers' seen in the cowries. He gave me five thousand francs."

She blinked her deep, piercing eyes that were always trying to probe into mysteries.

"I have given the recommended alms of two white and red cola nuts," she confessed to me. "Our destinies are linked. Your shade protects me. You don't fell the tree whose shade protects you. You water it. You watch over it."

Dear Farmata, how far from my thoughts you were! The restlessness with which I was struggling and which you had foreseen did not in the least signify the anguish of love.

21

Tomorrow? What a short time for reflection, for the decisive commitment of a life, especially when that life has known, in the recent past, the bitter tears of disappointment! I still have a vision of the intelligent eye of Daouda Dieng, the pout of the stubborn lips, which contrasted with the gentleness emanating from his profoundly charitable person, who saw only the best in people and ignored the rest. I could read him like an open book in which each sign was a symbol, but an easily interpreted symbol.

My heart no longer beats wildly in the whirl of the spoken words. I am touched by the sincerity of words, but I am not carried away by it; my euphoria, born of the hunger and thirst for tenderness, fades away as the hours dance past.

I cannot put out any flags. The proposed celebration does not tempt me. My heart does not love Daouda Dieng. My mind appreciates the man. But heart and mind often disagree.

How I should have liked to be galvanized in favour of this man, to be able to say yes! It is not that the memory of the deceased lies heavy within me. The dead have only the weight conceded to them or the weight of the good they have done. It is not that the presence of my young children poses a problem; he could have filled the role of the father who had abandoned them. Thirty years later, my own personal refusal is the only thing that conditions me. I have no definable reason. Our currents are opposed. Daouda Dieng's reputation for seriousness has already been established.

A good husband? Yes. Public rumour, so wicked and thirsty for gossip where personalities are concerned, has never mentioned any goings-on of his. His wife and cousin, whom he married five years after my marriage out of his duty as a citizen and not out of love (another male expression to explain a natural action), has borne his children. Wife and children, placed by this dutiful man on a pedestal of respectability, offered him an enviable refuge, the outcome of his own effort.

He never accepted any honour without associating his wife with it. He involved her in his political actions, his numerous travels, the various sponsorships for which he was canvassed and which increased his electoral constituency.

Before leaving, Farmata, the *griot* woman of the cowries, had said: "Your mother was right. Daouda is wonderful. What *guer*[5] gives five thousand francs today! Daouda has neither exchanged his wife nor abandoned his children; if he has come back looking for you, you, an old woman burdened with a family, it is because he loves you; he can look after you and your family. Think about it. Accept."

All the trump cards! But what do these count for in the uncontrollable law of attraction! So as not to hurt him under my roof, I sent Farmata, the *griot* woman of the cowries, with a sealed envelope for him, with the following instructions. "This letter must be given to him personally, away from his wife and children."

For the first time, I was turning to Farmata for help, and this embarrassed me. She was happy, having dreamed of this role right from our youth. But I always acted alone; she was never a participant in my problems, only informed—just like any "vulgar acquaintance," she would complain. She was thrilled, ignorant of the cruel message she was bearing.

Daouda's clinic was not far from the Villa Fallene. There was a stop for the *cars rapides*[6] just a few metres from his doorstep.

This clinic, set up with a bank loan granted by the state to those doctors and pharmacists who expressed the desire for it, enabled Daouda Dieng to continue practising his profession. He had understood that a doctor could not abandon his call: "A doctor's training is slow, long, taxing, and they are not two a penny either; they are more

5. Nobleman [Bâ's note].   6. Express buses.

useful in their profession than anywhere else; if they can combine their job with other activities, so much the better; but what insensitivity, to give up looking after others for something else!" Thus would Daouda explain himself to our mutual friends, such as Mawdo Bâ and Samba Diack, his colleagues.

Farmata, therefore, patiently waited her turn and, once in front of Daouda in the consulting room, she handed the envelope over to him. Daouda read:

> Daouda,
>
> You are chasing after a woman who has remained the same, Daouda, despite the intense ravages of suffering.
>
> You who have loved me, who love me still—I don't doubt it—try to understand me. My conscience is not accommodating enough to enable me to marry you, when only esteem, justified by your many qualities, pulls me towards you. I can offer you nothing else, even though you deserve everything. Esteem is not enough for marriage, whose snares I know from experience. And then the existence of your wife and children further complicates the situation. Abandoned yesterday because of a woman, I cannot lightly bring myself between you and your family.
>
> You think the problem of polygamy is a simple one. Those who are involved in it know the constraints, the lies, the injustices that weigh down their consciences in return for the ephemeral joys of change. I am sure you are motivated by love, a love that existed well before your marriage and that fate has not been able to satisfy. It is with infinite sadness and tear-filled eyes that I offer you my friendship. Dear Daouda, please accept it. It is with great pleasure that I shall continue to welcome you to my house.
>
> Shall I hope to see you again?
>
> Ramatoulaye

Farmata, who had smiled in handing over her letter, told me how her smile soured on her face as Daouda read. Then instinct and observation brought a look of sadness to her face, for Daouda wrinkled his eyebrows, creased his forehead, bit his lips and sighed.

Daouda put down my letter. Calmly, he stuffed an envelope with a wad of blue notes. He scrawled on a piece of paper the terrible words that had separated us before and that he had acquired during his medical course: "All or nothing. Adieu."

Aissatou, Daouda Dieng never came back again.

"Bissimilai! Bissimilai![7] What was it you dared to write and make me messenger of? You have killed a man. His crestfallen face cried it out to me. You have rejected the messenger sent to you by God to reward you for your sufferings. God will punish you for not having followed the path towards peace. You have refused greatness! You shall live in mud. I wish you another Modou to make you shed tears of blood.

"Who do you take yourself for? At fifty, you have dared to break the wolere.[8] You trample upon your luck: Daouda Dieng, a rich man, a deputy, a doctor, of your own age group, with just one wife. He offers you security, love, and you refuse! Many women, of Daba's age even, would wish to be in your place.

"You boast of reasons. You speak of love instead of bread. Madame wants her heart to miss a beat. Why not flowers, just like in the films?

"Bissimilai! Bissimilai! You so withered, you want to choose a husband like an eighteen-year-old girl. Life will spring a surprise on you and then, Ramatoulaye, you will bite your fingers. I don't know what Daouda has written. But there is money in

7. Beginning of the first *sourate* of the Koran, which has passed into general speech; the expression denotes surprise [Bâ's note].
8. Old friendship [Bâ's note].

the envelope. He is a true *samba linguere*[9] from the olden days. May God satisfy, gratify Daouda Dieng. My heart is with him."

Such was Farmata's tirade on her return from her mission. She thoroughly upset me. The truth of this woman, a childhood companion through the long association of our families, could not hold good for me, even in its logic of concern. . . . Once more, I was refusing the easy way because of my ideal. I went back to my loneliness, which a momentary flash had brightened briefly. I wore it again, as one wears a familiar garment. Its cut suited me well. I moved easily in it, despite Farmata. I wanted "something else." And this "something else" was impossible without the full agreement of my heart.

Tamsir and Daouda having been rejected, there were no more barriers between the suitors and me. I then watched filing past and besieging me old men in search of easy revenue, young men in search of adventure to occupy their leisure. My successive refusals gave me in town the reputation of a "lioness" or "mad woman."

Who let loose this greedy pack of hounds after me? For my charms had faded with the many maternities, with time, with the tears. Ah! the inheritance, the fat share acquired by my daughter Daba and her husband and put at my disposal.

They had led the fight for the distribution of Modou's estate. My son-in-law laid down on the table the advance for the SICAP villa and five years' rent.

The SICAP villa went to my daughter, who, with the bailiff's affidavit in hand, listed the contents and bought it.

The story of the Villa Fallene was easy to relate: the land and building represented a bank loan granted ten years ago on the security of our joint salaries. The contents, renewed two years ago, belonged to me, and to support this claim, I produced the receipts. There remained Modou's clothes: those that I recognized because I had chosen and cared for them; and the others . . . from the second part of his life. I found it difficult to imagine him in this get-up of a young wolf. . . . They were distributed to his family.

The jewels and presents given to Lady Mother-in-Law and her daughter were theirs by right.

Lady Mother-in-Law hiccoughed, cried. She was being stripped, and she asked for mercy. She did not want to move out. . . .

But Daba is like all the young, without pity.

"Remember, I was your daughter's best friend. You made her my mother's rival. Remember. For five years you deprived my mother and her twelve children of their breadwinner. Remember. My mother has suffered a great deal. How can a woman sap the happiness of another? You deserve no pity. Pack up. As for Binetou, she is a victim, your victim. I feel sorry for her."

Lady Mother-in-Law sobbed. Binetou? Indifference itself. What did it matter to her what was being said? She was already dead inside . . . ever since her marriage to Modou.

22

I feel an immense fatigue. It begins in my soul and weighs down my body.

Ousmane, my last born, holds out your letter to me. Ousmane is six years old. "It's Aunty Aissatou."

9. A man of repute [Bâ's note].

He has the privilege of bringing me all your letters. How does he recognize them? By their stamp? By their envelope? By the careful writing, characteristic of you? By the scent of lavender emanating from them? Children have clues different from our own. Ousmane enjoys his find. He exults in it.

These caressing words, which relax me, are indeed from you. And you tell me of the "end." I calculate. Tomorrow is indeed the end of my seclusion. And you will be there within reach of my hand, my voice, my eyes.

"End or new beginning?" My eyes will discover the slightest change in you. I have already totalled up my own; my seclusion has withered me. Worries have given me wrinkles; my fat has melted away. I often tap against bone where before there was rounded flesh.

When we meet, the signs on our bodies will not be important. The essential thing is the content of our hearts, which animates us; the essential thing is the quality of the sap that flows through us. You have often proved to me the superiority of friendship over love. Time, distance, as well as mutual memories have consolidated our ties and made our children brothers and sisters. Reunited, will we draw up a detailed account of our faded bloom, or will we sow new seeds for new harvests?

I hear Daba's footsteps. She is back from the Blaise Diagne secondary school, where she has been representing me in answer to a summons. A conflict between my son, Mawdo Fall, and his philosophy teacher. They clash frequently when the time comes to return corrected essays.

As you know, there is a substantial age gap between Daba and Mawdo Fall, the result of two miscarriages.

This clash, which Daba is trying to resolve, is the third within six months in this form. Mawdo Fall has a remarkable gift for literary work. Right from Form One, he has been top of his class in this subject; but this year for every capital letter forgotten, for a few commas omitted, for a misspelt word, his teacher knocks off one or two marks. Because of this, Jean-Claude, a white boy who has always come second, has moved up to first position. The teacher cannot tolerate a black coming first in philosophy. And Mawdo Fall complains.

This always ends in a quarrel and a summons.

Daba was ready to tell the teacher off, and no nonsense. But I calmed her down. Life is an eternal compromise. What is important is the examination paper. . . . This, too, will be at the mercy of the marker. No one will have any say over him. So why fight a teacher for one or two marks that can never change the destiny of a student?

I always tell my children: you are students maintained by your parents. Work hard so as to merit their sacrifices. Cultivate yourselves instead of protesting. When you are adults, if your opinions are to carry weight, they must be based on knowledge backed by diplomas. A diploma is not a myth. It is not everything, true. But it crowns knowledge, work. Tomorrow, you will be able to elect to power anyone of your choice, anyone you find suitable. It is your choice, and not ours, that will direct the country.

Now our society is shaken to its very foundations, torn between the attraction of imported vices and the fierce resistance of old virtues.

The dream of a rapid social climb prompts parents to give their children more knowledge than education. Pollution seeps in through hearts as well as into the air.

"Phased out" or "outdated," perhaps even "old fogies," we belong to the past. But all four of us were made of stern stuff, with upright minds full of intense questionings that stuck within our inner selves, not without pain. Aissatou, no matter how unhappy the outcome of our unions, our husbands were great men. They led the struggle of their lives, even if success eluded their grasp; one does not easily overcome the burdens of a thousand years.

I observe the young. Where are those bright eyes, prompt to react when scorned honour demands redress? Where is the vigorous pride that guides a whole community towards its duty? The appetite to live kills the dignity of living.

You can see that I digress from the problem of Mawdo Fall.

The headmaster of the school certainly understands the Mawdo Fall-teacher conflict. But you try to side with a student against his teacher!

Daba is here beside me, lighthearted, smiling with all her teeth at a mission successfully accomplished.

Daba does not find household work a burden. Her husband cooks rice as well as she does; her husband who claims, when I tell him he "spoils" his wife: "Daba is my wife. She is not my slave, nor my servant."

I sense the tenderness growing between this young couple, an ideal couple, just as I have always imagined. They identify with each other, discuss everything so as to find a compromise.

All the same, I fear for Daba. Life holds many surprises. When I discuss it with her, she shrugs her shoulders: "Marriage is no chain. It is mutual agreement over a life's programme. So if one of the partners is no longer satisfied with the union, why should he remain? It may be Abou (her husband); it may be me. Why not? The wife can take the initiative to make the break."

She reasons everything out, that child. . . . She often tells me: "I don't want to go into politics; it's not that I am not interested in the fate of my country and, most especially, that of woman. But when I look at the fruitless wranglings even within the ranks of the same party, when I see men's greed for power, I prefer not to participate. No, I am not afraid of ideological struggle, but in a political party it is rare for a woman to make an easy break-through. For a long time men will continue to have the power of decision, whereas everyone knows that polity should be the affair of women. No: I prefer my own association, where there is neither rivalry nor schism, neither malice nor jostling for position; there are no posts to be shared, nor positions to be secured. The headship changes every year. Each of us has equal opportunity to advance her ideas. We are given tasks according to our abilities in our activities and organizations that work towards the progress of women. Our funds go towards humanitarian work; we are mobilized by a militancy as useful as any other, but it is a healthy militancy, whose only reward is inner satisfaction."

She reasoned everything out, that child . . . She had her own opinions about everything.

I look at her, Daba, my eldest child, who has helped me so admirably with her brothers and sisters. It is Aissatou, your namesake, who has taken over from her the running of the house.

Aissatou washes the youngest ones: Omar, eight years old, and Ousmane, your friend. The others can manage well enough on their own. Aissatou is helped in her task by Amy and her twin sister Awa, whom she is training.

My twins are so similar that I sometimes confuse them. They are mischievous and play tricks on everybody. Aminata works better than Awa. Physically so similar, why are they so different in character?

The upkeep and education of young children do not pose serious problems; washed, fed, cared for, supervised, my own are growing well—with, of course, the nearly daily battle against sores, colds, headaches, in which I excel, simply from having had to struggle.

It is Mawdo Bâ who comes to my aid during the serious illnesses. Even though I criticize him for his weakness, which broke up your relationship, I praise him very sincerely for the help he gives me. Despite his friend Modou's desertion of our home, I can still wake him up, at no matter what hour.

23

My grown children are causing me a great deal of concern. My worries pale when I recall my grandmother, who found in popular wisdom an appropriate dictum for each event. She liked to repeat: "The mother of a family has no time to travel. But she has time to die." She would lament when, despite her sleepiness, she still had to carry out her share of the duties: "Ah, if only I had a bed on which to lie down."

Mischievously, I would point to the three beds in her room. In irritation, she would say: "You have your life before and not behind you. May God grant that you experience what I have gone through." And here I am today, "going through" just that experience.

I thought a child was born and grew up without any problem. I thought one mapped out a straight path and that he would step lightly down it. I now saw, at first hand, the truth of my grandmother's prophecies: "The fact that children are born of the same parents does not necessarily mean that they will resemble each other."

"Being born of the same parents is just like spending the night in the same bedroom."

To allay the fear of the future that her words might possibly have aroused, my grandmother would offer some solutions: "Different personalities require different forms of discipline. Strictness here, comprehension there. Smacking, which is successful with the very young ones, annoys the older ones. The nerves daily undergo severe trials! But that is the mother's lot."

Courageous grandmother, I drew from your teaching and example the courage that galvanizes one at the times when difficult choices have to be made.

The other night I surprised the trio (as they are popularly known), Arame, Yacine and Dieynaba, smoking in their bedroom. Everything about their manner showed that they were used to it: their way of holding the cigarette between their fingers or raising it gracefully to their lips, of inhaling like connoisseurs. Their nostrils quivered and let out the smoke. And these young ladies inhaled and exhaled while doing their lessons and their homework. They savoured their pleasure greedily, behind the closed door, for I try, as much as possible, to respect their privacy.

People say that Dieynaba, Arame and Yacine take after me. They are bound by their friendship and willingness to help, as well as by a multitude of similarities; they form a block, with the same defensive or distrustful reactions, before my other children; they swop dresses, trousers, tops, being nearly the same size. I have never had to intervene in their conflicts. The trio has a reputation for hard work at school.

But to grant themselves the right to smoke! They were dumbfounded before my anger. The unexpectedness of it gave me a shock. A woman's mouth exhaling the acrid smell of tobacco instead of being fragrant. A woman's teeth blackened with tobacco instead of sparkling with whiteness! Yet their teeth were white. How did they manage the feat?

I considered the wearing of trousers dreadful in view of our build, which is not that of slim Western women. Trousers accentuate the ample figure of the black woman and further emphasize the curve of the small of the back. But I gave in to the rush towards this fashion, which constricted and hampered instead of liberating. Since my daughters wanted to be "with it," I accepted the addition of trousers to their wardrobes.

Suddenly I became afraid of the flow of progress. Did they also drink? Who knows, one vice leads to another. Does it mean that one can't have modernism without a lowering of moral standards?

Was I to blame for having given my daughters a bit of liberty? My grandfather did not allow young people in his house. At ten o'clock at night, with a bell in his hand, he would warn visitors of the closure of the entrance gate. He punctuated the ringing of the bell with the same instruction: "Whoever does not live here should scram."

As for myself, I let my daughters go out from time to time. They went to the cinema without me. They received male and female friends. There were arguments to justify my behaviour. Unquestionably, at a certain age, a boy or girl opens up to love. I wanted my daughters to discover it in a healthy way, without feelings of guilt, secretiveness or degradation. I tried to penetrate their relationships: I created a favourable atmosphere for sensible behaviour and for confidence.

And the result is that under the influence of their circle they have acquired the habit of smoking. And I was left in the dark, I who wanted to control everything. My grandmother's wise words came to mind: "You can feed your stomach as well as you please; it will still provide for itself without your knowing."

I had to do some thinking. There was a need for some reorganization to stop the rot. My grandmother would perhaps have suggested, "For a new generation, a new method."

I did not mind being a "stick-in-the-mud." I was aware of the harmful effects of tobacco, and I could not agree to its use. My conscience rejected it, as it rejected alcohol.

From then on, relentlessly, I was on the lookout for its odour. It played hide-and-seek with my watchfulness. Sly and ironic, it would tease my nostrils and then disappear. Its favourite hiding place was the toilet, especially at night. But it no longer dared to expose itself openly, with jaunty shamelessness.

24

Today I was not able to finish my evening prayer as I wanted to: cries from the street made me jump up from the mat on which I was seated.

Standing on the veranda, I see my sons Alioune and Malick arriving in tears. They are in a pitiable state: torn clothes, bodies covered in dust from a fall, knees bleeding beneath the shorts. There is a large hole in the right sleeve of Malick's sweater; the arm on the same side hangs down limply. One of the boys supporting him explains to me: "A motorcyclist knocked down Malick and Alioune. We were playing football."

A young man with long hair, white glasses, amulets round the neck, moves forward. The grey dust from the road covers his denim outfit. Mauled by the children for whom he has became the target, a red wound on his leg, he is visibly taken aback by so much hostility. In a polite tone and manner, which contrast with his slovenly appearance, he offers his excuses: "I saw the children too late while making a left turn. I thought I would have a clear road, since it is a one-way street. I did not imagine that the children had set up a playing field. In vain, I tried to brake. I hit the stones marking the goal post. When I fell, your two sons also fell, along with three other small boys. I am sorry."

I am pleasantly surprised by the young motorcyclist. I railed, but not against him. I know from experience the difficulty of driving in town, especially in the Medina. The tarred surface is a favourite area for children. Once they have taken possession, nothing else counts. They will dance around the ball like devils. Sometimes the object of their passion is a thick rag ball, all tied up. It doesn't matter! The driver's only recourse is his brakes, his horn, his composure; a small, disorderly opening is made for him, quickly closed up again in the hustle. Behind him the shouts begin again, even louder.

"It's not your fault, young man. My sons are to blame. They slipped away as I was praying. Off you go, young man—or rather, wait a moment while I get you some spirit and cotton-wool for your wound."

Aissatou, your namesake, brings methylated iodine and cotton. She takes care of the stranger and then of Alioune. The little boys of the area disapprove of my reaction. They want the man "at fault" to be punished; I give them a ticking-off. Ah, children! They cause an accident and, in addition, they want to punish.

Malick's hanging arm looks to me as if it is broken. It droops unnaturally. "Quick, Aissatou! Take him to hospital. If you can't find Mawdo, go to Casualty. Quick, go, child." Aissatou dresses quickly and speedily helps Malick to clean up and change.

The dried blood from the wounds leaves dark and repulsive stains on the ground. Cleaning them up, I think of the identical nature of men: the same red blood irrigating the same organs. These organs, situated in the same places, carry out the same functions. The same remedies cure the same illnesses everywhere under the sun, whether the individual be white or black. Everything unites men. Why, then, do they kill each other in ignoble wars for causes that are futile when compared with the massacre of human lives? So many devastating wars! And yet man takes himself to be a superior being. In what way is his intelligence useful to him? His intelligence begets both good and ill, more often ill than good.

I go back to my place on the mat decorated with a picture of a mosque in green, reserved for my use only, just as is the kettle for my ablutions. Alioune, still sniffing, pushes Ousmane aside so as to take his place beside me, looking for consolation, which I refuse him. On the contrary, I seize the opportunity to tell him off: "The road is not a playing field. You got off lightly today. But tomorrow, watch out! You will have some bone broken, like your brother."

Alioune complains: "But there is no playing field in the area. Mothers won't let us play football in the compounds. So what do we do?"

His comment is valid. Officers in charge of town planning must make provision for playing fields when they are developing open spaces.

Some hours later Aissatou and Malick return from the hospital where, once again, Mawdo has taken good care of them. Malick's plastered arm tells me that the drooping arm had indeed been broken. Ah, how dearly children make one pay for the joy of bringing them into the world!

Just as I thought, my friend: it never rains but it pours. This is my luck: once misfortune has me in its grip, it never lets go of me again.

Aissatou, your namesake, is three months pregnant. Farmata, the *griot* woman of the cowries, very cleverly led me to this discovery. Public rumour had spurred her on perhaps, or her keen powers of observation had simply served her well.

Each time she cast her cowries to cut short our discussions (we had diverging points of view on everything), she would breathe a "Hm" of discontent. With heavy sighs, she would point out in the jumble of cowries a young pregnant girl.

I had certainly noticed your namesake's sudden loss of weight, her lack of appetite, the swelling of her breasts: all indications of the child she was carrying. But puberty also transforms adolescents; they grow fatter or thinner, taller. And then, shortly after her father's death, Aissatou had had a violent attack of malaria, checked by Mawdo Bâ. The disappearance of her plumpness dates from this period.

Aissatou refused to regain weight, in order to keep her slender figure. I naturally ascribed her light intake of food and her distaste for certain foodstuffs to this new mania. Now thin, she swam in her trousers and, to my great joy, wore only dresses.

Little Oumar did tell me one day that Aissatou used to vomit in their bathroom every morning while bathing him. But Aissatou, when questioned, denied it, said it was the water mixed with toothpaste that she spat out. Oumar no longer spoke of vomiting. My mind focused on something else.

How could I guess that my daughter, who had calmed my anger during the cigarette affair, was now indulging in an even more dangerous game? Merciless fate had surprised me again—as usual, without any weapons with which to defend myself.

Every day Farmata would insist a bit more on the "young pregnant girl" of her cowries. She would show her to me. The girl's condition was making the woman suffer. She was eloquent: "Look, I say, look! This separate cowry, hollow side turned upwards. Look at this one, adjusting itself to the other, white side up, like a cooking pot and its cover lid. The child is in the belly. It forms one body with its mother. The two groups of cowries are separated: This indicates an unattached woman. But as the cowries are small, they indicate a young girl."

And her hand threw down, again and again, the gossipy cowries. They fell away from each other, collided, overlapped. Their tell-tale chink filled the winnowing fan, and the same group of two cowries always remained separate, to reveal distress. I followed their language dispassionately.

And then, one evening, annoyed by my naiveté, Farmata said boldly: "Question your daughters, Ramatoulaye. A mother must be pessimistic."

Worried by the relentless repetition, anxious, I accepted the proposition. Moving like a gazelle with delicate limbs, she swept into Aissatou's bedroom, afraid that I would change my mind. She came out, a triumphant gleam in her eye. Aissatou followed her, in tears. Farmata sent away Ousmane, who was nestled within my *boubou*, locked the door and declared: "The cowries cannot always be wrong. If they have insisted for so long, it means there is something there. Water and sand have been mixed; they have become mud. Gather up your mud. Aissatou does not deny her condition. I have saved her by exposing the matter. You guessed nothing. She did not dare confide in you. You would never have got out of this situation."

I was dumbfounded. I, so prone to chide, was silent. I was flushed and breathless. I closed my eyes, opened them again. I gnawed at my tongue.

The first question that comes to mind on discovering such a condition is: who? Who is behind this theft, for there has been a theft? Who is behind this injury, for injury it is. Who has dared? Who? Who? Aissatou mentioned a certain Ibrahima Sall who, as she talked, very soon became simply Iba.

Bewildered, I look at my daughter, so well brought up, so tender with me, so ready to help in the house, so efficient in every way, so many fine qualities allied with such behaviour!

Iba is a law student at the university. They met at a friend's birthday celebration. Iba sometimes went to meet her at school when she did not "come down" at lunch time. He had invited her on two occasions to his room in the university halls of residence. She confessed her liking for him! No, Iba had not demanded anything, had not forced her. Everything had happened naturally between them. Iba knew of her condition. He had refused the services of one of his mates who wanted to "help" him. He loved her. Though he was on a scholarship, he had decided to deprive himself for the maintenance of his child.

I learned everything at one go, from a broken voice accompanied by much sniffing but without any regret! Aissatou bent her head. I recognized the unvarnished truth of her story. I recognized her in her whole-hearted gift of herself to this lover who had succeeded in uniting in this heart my image and his own. Aissatou lowered her eyes, conscious of the pain crushing me; I remained silent. My hand supported my tired head. Aissatou lowered her eyes. She heard my inner self give way. She was fully aware of the seriousness of her action, considering my recent widow-hood, following upon my abandonment. After Daba, she was the oldest of the succession of daughters. The oldest should set an example. . . . My teeth gnashed in anger. . . .

Remembering, like a lifebuoy, the tender and consoling attitude of my daughter during my distress, my long years of loneliness, I overcame my emotion. I sought refuge in God, as at every moment of crisis in my life. Who decides death and life? God, the Almighty!

And also, one is a mother in order to understand the inexplicable. One is a mother to lighten the darkness. One is a mother to shield when lightning streaks the night, when thunder shakes the earth, when mud bogs one down. One is a mother in order to love without beginning or end.

To make my being a defensive barrier between my daughter and any obstacle. At this moment of confrontation, I realized how close I was to my child. The umbilical cord took on new life, the indestructible bond beneath the avalanche of storms and the duration of time. I saw her once more, newly sprung from me, kicking about, her tongue pink, her tiny face creased under her silky hair. I could not abandon her, as pride would have me do. Her life and her future were at stake, and these were powerful considerations, overriding all taboos and assuming greater importance in my heart and in my mind. The life that fluttered in her was questioning me. It was eager to blossom. It vibrated, demanding protection.

I was the one who had not been equal to the situation. Glutted with optimism, I had not suspected the crisis of her conscience, the passion of her being, the torment of her thoughts, the miracle she was carrying.

One is a mother so as to face the flood. Was I to threaten, in the face of my daughter's shame, her sincere repentance, her pain, her anguish? Was I?

I took my daughter in my arms. Painfully, I held her tightly, with a force multiplied tenfold by pagan revolt and primitive tenderness. She cried. She choked on sobs.

How could she have lived alone with her secret? I was traumatized by the effort and skill employed by this child to escape my anger whenever she felt faint or whenever she took over from me beside my troublesome youngsters. I felt sick. I felt terribly sick.

I took myself in hand with superhuman effort. The shadows faded away. Courage! The rays of light united to form an appeasing brightness. My decision to help and protect emerged from the tumult. It gained strength as I wiped the tears, as I caressed the burning brow.

Young Aissatou shall have an appointment with the doctor, not later than tomorrow.

Farmata was astonished. She expected wailing: I smiled. She wanted strong reprimands: I consoled. She wished for threats: I forgave.

No doubt about it: she will never know what to expect from me. To give a sinner so much attention was beyond her. She had dreams of sumptuous marriage celebrations for Aissatou, which would compensate her for my own meagre nuptials when she was a young girl, already tied to my steps like a shadow. She used to sing your praises, Aissatou, you who would give her a lot of money at the future wedding of your namesake. The story of the Fiat whetted her appetite and credited you with fabulous wealth. She dreamed of festivities, and here was this girl who had given herself to a penniless student, who would never be grateful to her. She reproached me for my calm: "You have mainly daughters. Adopt an attitude that you can keep up. You will see. If Aissatou can do 'this,' I wonder what your trio of smokers will do. Smother your daughter with caresses, Ramatoulaye. You will see."

I will indeed see when I ask to meet Ibrahima Sall tomorrow. . . .

25

Ibrahima Sall entered my room at the appointed time. His punctuality pleased me.

Tall, simply dressed. Pleasant features, on the whole. But with remarkably beautiful eyes, velvety, tender in the casement of his long eyelashes. One would like to see them in a woman's face . . . the smile as well. I let my gaze rest on the set of his teeth. No treacherous gaps. Without being self-conscious about it, Ibrahima Sall was indeed the embodiment of the romantic young lover. He pleased me, and I noticed his cleanliness with relief: short hair combed, nails cut, shoes polished. He must be an orderly man and therefore without deceit.

It was I who had summoned him, but it was he who started the conversation: "How many times I have wanted to arrange this discussion, to let you know. I know what a daughter means to her mother, and Aissatou has told me so much about you, your closeness to her, that I think I know you already. I am not just looking for excitement. Your daughter is my first love. I want her to be the only one. I regret what has happened. If you agree, I will marry Aissatou. My mother will look after her child. We will continue with our studies."

Here then, concise and well said, was all I wanted to hear. How to reply? Should I agree readily to his propositions? Farmata, who was present during the discussion, was looking out for squalls.

She asked: "You were really the first?"

"Yes," confirmed Iba Sall.

"Then, warn your mother. We or I shall go to see her tomorrow to announce your crime. She had better save a lot of money to compensate my niece. Anyway, couldn't you have waited until you had a good job before running after girls?"

Ibrahima Sall heard the *griot* woman's remarks without showing any irritation. Perhaps he already knew her well enough by name and character to remain politely silent.

My own preoccupations were very different from those of Farmata. We were right in the middle of the school year. What was to be done to prevent my daughter's expulsion from school?

I told Iba Sall of my fears. He too had given some thought to the problem. The child would be born during the holidays. The essential thing was not to panic, just to let the months go past, and for Aissatou to dress in loose clothes. At the beginning of the following school year the baby would be two months old. Aissatou would then join the final-year class. After this final year, marriage.

My daughter's boyfriend had worked it out logically and reminded me of Daba's clearness of mind.

Ibrahima Sall himself ran no risk of being expelled from the university. And even had he still been at school, who would inform the school of his position as father-to-be? There would be no change in him. He would remain "flat" . . . while my daughter's swollen belly would point an accusing finger.

When will there be a lenient law to help erring schoolgirls whose condition is not camouflaged by long holidays?

I added nothing to all this careful planning. At that moment, I felt that my child was being detached from my being, as if I were again bringing her into the world. She was no longer under my protection. She belonged more to her boyfriend. A new family was being born before my very eyes.

I accepted my subordinate role. The ripe fruit must drop away from the tree.

May God smooth the new path of this child's life.

Yet what a path!

26

Aissatou, reassuring habits regain ascendancy.

My heart beats monotonously under my black wrappers. How I like to listen to this slow rhythm! A new substance is trying to graft itself on to the household.

Ibrahima Sall comes every day and gives each of us what he can. He offers Mawdo Fall his logic and clarity in discussions of the topics of his essays. He provides chocolate regularly for Oumar and Ousmane. He is not too proud to play with Malick and Alioune, who have given up the street for my compound.

Malick's arm is still in plaster. Just as long as his leg, which cannot keep away from the ball, does not break in its turn!

But the trio (Arame, Yacine and Dieynaba) refuse to accept this "intrusion." The trio greet him correctly but without enthusiasm. The trio are hostile to his invitations. They begrudge him for having. . . .

Ibrahima Sall urges Aissatou on in her lessons and home-work. He has his girlfriend's success at heart. He does not want to be responsible for any regression whatsoever. Aissatou's marks improve: there's a silver lining in every cloud!

Farmata finds it difficult to accept Ibrahima Sall, whom she describes as "cocksure," "shameless." She never misses an opportunity of hitting out at him: "Has one ever seen a stranger untie a goat in the house?"

Unperturbed, Ibrahima Sall tries to adapt. He seeks out my company, discusses current events with me, sometimes brings me magazines and fruit. His parents, informed some time ago by the vigilant Farmata, also come round to see us and are anxious about Aissatou's health. And reassuring habits regain ascendancy. . . .

I envy you for having had only boys! You don't know the terrors I face in dealing with the problems of my daughters.

I have finally decided to broach the problem of sexual education. Aissatou, your namesake, caught me unawares. From now on, I will take precautions. I address myself to the trio, the twins being still too young.

How I had hesitated earlier! I did not want to give my daughters a free hand by offering them immunity in pleasure. The world is upside-down. Mothers of yore taught chastity. Their voice of authority condemned all extra-marital "wanderings."

Modern mothers favour "forbidden games." They help to limit the damage and, better still, prevent it. They remove any thorn or pebble that might hinder the progress of their children towards the conquest of all forms of liberty! I apply myself painfully to this necessity.

All the same, I insist that my daughters be aware of the value of their bodies. I emphasize the sublime significance of the sexual act, an expression of love. The existence of means of contraception must not lead to an unhindered release of desires and instincts. It is through his self-control, his ability to reason, to choose, his power of attachment, that the individual distinguishes himself from the animal.

Each woman makes of her life what she wants. A profligate life for a woman is incompatible with morality. What does one gain from pleasures? Early ageing, debasement, no doubt about it, I further stressed.

My words fell uneasily on my female audience. Of us all, I was the most vulnerable. For the trio's faces registered no surprise. My chopped sentences aroused no special interest. I had the impression that I was saying the obvious.

Perhaps the trio knew already. . . . A long silence. . . . And the trio disappeared. I let out a sigh of relief. I felt that I had emerged into the light after a long journey through a dark, narrow tunnel.

27

Till tomorrow, my friend.

We will then have time to ourselves, especially as I have obtained an extension of my widow's leave.

I reflect. My new turn of mind is hardly surprising to you. I cannot help unburdening myself to you. I might as well sum up now.

I am not indifferent to the irreversible currents of women's liberation that are lashing the world. This commotion that is shaking up every aspect of our lives reveals and illustrates our abilities.

My heart rejoices each time a woman emerges from the shadows. I know that the field of our gains is unstable, the retention of conquests difficult: social constraints are ever-present, and male egoism resists.

Instruments for some, baits for others, respected or despised, often muzzled, all women have almost the same fate, which religions or unjust legislation have sealed.

My reflections determine my attitude to the problems of life. I analyse the decisions that decide our future. I widen my scope by taking an interest in current world affairs.

I remain persuaded of the inevitable and necessary complementarity of man and woman.

Love, imperfect as it may be in its content and expression, remains the natural link between these two beings.

To love one another! If only each partner could move sincerely towards the other! If each could only melt into the other! If each would only accept the other's successes and failures! If each would only praise the other's qualities instead of listing his faults! If each could only correct bad habits without harping on about them! If each could penetrate the other's most secret haunts to forestall failure and be a support while tending to the evils that are repressed!

The success of the family is born of a couple's harmony, as the harmony of multiple instruments creates a pleasant symphony.

The nation is made up of all the families, rich or poor, united or separated, aware or unaware. The success of a nation therefore depends inevitably on the family.

Why aren't your sons coming with you? Ah, their studies. . . .

So, then, will I see you tomorrow in a tailored suit or a long dress? I've taken a bet with Daba: tailored suit. Used to living far away, you will want—again, I have taken a bet with Daba—table, plate, chair, fork.

More convenient, you will say. But I will not let you have your way. I will spread out a mat. On it there will be the big, steaming bowl into which you will have to accept that other hands dip.

Beneath the shell that has hardened you over the years, beneath your sceptical pout, your easy carriage, perhaps I will feel you vibrate. I would so much like to hear you check or encourage my eagerness, just as before, and, as before, to see you take part in the search for a new way.

I warn you already, I have not given up wanting to refashion my life. Despite everything—disappointments and humiliations—hope still lives on within me. It is from the dirty and nauseating humus that the green plant sprouts into life, and I can feel new buds springing up in me.

The word "happiness" does indeed have meaning, doesn't it? I shall go out in search of it. Too bad for me if once again I have to write you so long a letter. . . .

Ramatoulaye

Chinua Achebe

b. 1930

Chinua Achebe occupies a key position in the history of postcolonial African literature. Until the 1958 publication of his novel *Things Fall Apart,* readers outside Africa encountered Africa in fiction largely through European perspectives. Joseph Conrad's *Heart of Darkness* (page 61) occupied a preeminent position in literature about Africa and its European colonization. Though incisive and critical of the European imperial enterprise in the continent, Conrad's remains a European perspective, and it was Achebe who presented an African reading of Africa to the wider world for the first time in the twentieth century. Some have felt that Achebe's narrative isn't actually African enough. Critics point out that the novel is written in one of the colonists' imperial languages, English, and, starting with the title of the novel (taken from W. B. Yeats), its literary antecedents and narrative strategies are as much European as the story is African. Achebe hasn't shied away from engaging in this discussion among critics and scholars of postcolonialism. As an African author and a Western academic and critic, he clearly is an interested party in more than one sense. As such, he can be seen as a writer who embodies simultaneously the cultures of the colonized and of the colonizer.

It is interesting, and also historically intriguing, that Achebe has viewed himself as an African insider, as attested to by his essay, included here, on the 1962 meeting of African intellectuals at Makarere University College in Uganda. That was an occasion for a "declaration of literary independence" by the African writers who gathered there, many of whom would in fact form the first cohort of postcolonial African authors. It would be some years before it came to light that Achebe along with the other African writers at that defining moment were indeed insiders, but they were also in the process of being turned inside out by the circumstances of the very occasion in which they were defining themselves. They would come to learn that their self-defining moment was in fact a move in a larger ideological and neocolonial chess game played by superpowers in the course of the Cold War. Unbeknownst to most of them, they were being gathered under the auspices of the U.S. Central Intelligence Agency through one of the proxy organizations it operated in Paris called the Society for Cultural Freedom.

Like his writing, Achebe himself is the product of an interesting mixture of educational institutions and religious traditions. Born in Ogidi, eastern Nigeria, an Igbo region, Achebe was
the fifth of six children. His father was a teacher in an evangelical Protestant school of the
Church Missionary Society. He was originally christened "Albert," after the son of England's
Queen Victoria. Upon entering the university, he dropped his English name and kept his indigenous Igbo name, "Chinua." His secondary schooling was in Government College in
Umuahia, which he entered in 1944. He received his university education at University College
of Ibadan, from which he graduated in 1953 with a degree in English, history, and theology.
Upon graduation he traveled throughout Africa and to America and then joined the Nigerian
Broadcasting Company in 1954. Four years later he published his first novel, *Things Fall Apart,*
in which he attempted to portray traditional life before the arrival of the colonizing Europeans.
The work became a classic of African literature with translations into more than fifty languages.
In 1960 he published his second novel, *No Longer at Ease,* followed by *Arrow of God* in 1964.
These novels depict the clash of traditional Igbo life with colonial and missionary incursions by
European powers.

Throughout the 1950s and 1960s Achebe worked in broadcasting, becoming director of
External Services in charge of the Voice of Nigeria in 1961. He cofounded a publishing com-
pany in 1967 and was then appointed a research fellow at the University of Nigeria. Starting
in 1971 he edited the journal *Okike,* which published and promoted new writing in Nigeria.
Nigeria was torn by civil wars from 1966 to 1970, which were chiefly between his own Igbo
people and the non-Igbo; these conflicts forced Achebe and his family to flee to Lagos,
Nigeria's capital. His collection of poems based on his country's internecine strife won the
Commonwealth Poetry Prize in 1972. In the same year Achebe published a collection of short
stories, *Girls at War,* and traveled to the United States to teach at the University of Massa-
chusetts in Amherst. He returned to Nigeria in 1976 to continue his engagement in the political life of his country, and in 1983 he published *The Trouble with Nigeria,* a scathing attack
on the national corruption among Nigeria's leaders. Yet another military coup, the fifth, two
years later became the basis for Achebe's fifth novel, *Anthills of the Savannah* (1987), an indictment of military power and dictatorship. The following year he was partially paralyzed as
a result of a car accident but recovered enough to resume his writing career and to accept a
teaching position at Bard College in New York, where he has taught since. *Things Fall Apart*
has remained his best known and most influential work. Situated between a complex, traditional world and the European invasion and colonization that ensued, the narrative of *Things
Fall Apart* has taken on much greater historical and cultural significance than usually accorded a work of fiction.

The pieces that follow Achebe's novel unfold the complexities of postcolonial cultural exchange, focusing especially on the issue of language. In his essay "The African Writer and the
English Language," Achebe argues that African writers have a sovereign right to make use of
colonial languages like English, which can unite audiences otherwise split among many local
ethnic languages and cultures. Colonialism, Achebe says, gave Africans "a language with
which to talk to one another. If it failed to give them a song, it at least gave them a tongue, for
sighing." Now, a new generation will remake English for new purposes and new audiences.

In the first Resonance that follows Achebe's essay, Kenyan writer Ngugi wa Thiong'o offers
a pointed rejoinder, recalling the same 1962 conference Achebe discusses, but describing it to
very different effect as displaying a neocolonialist blindness to the central role of native African
languages. Ngugi goes on to describe the mixed messages offered him by his own colonial education and his eventual decision to abandon the use of English for fiction, in favor of his native
Gĩkũyũ.

The language debate has been carried out in fiction and poetry as much as in essays, as can
be seen in the two Resonances following Ngugi's essay. First come excerpts form Congolese
wrier Mbwil Ngal's hilarious, satiric novel *Giambatista Viko: or, the Rape of African Discourse,*

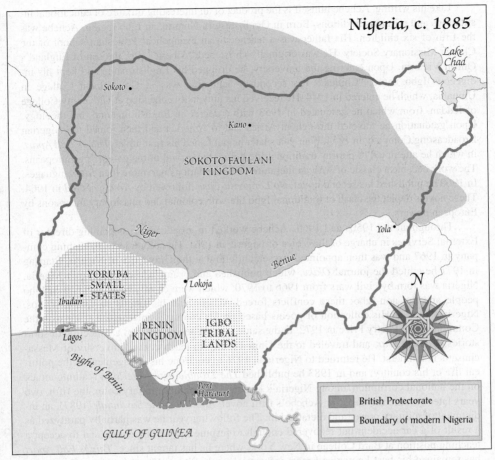

In 1885, British control was confined to Lagos and Niger Delta but would quickly advance up river and into the interior under the direction of the Royal Niger Company. Missionaries such as Mr. Brown and Mr. Smith often preceded colonial administrators.

whose hero—a self–hating African writer and professor—is kidnapped by tribalists who demand that he renounce the French language and its culture. Finally, white South African poet Jeremy Cronin gives a moving reflection on the challenge of representing a landscape marked by so many layers of language—Zulu and other native languages, Dutch-derived Afrikaans, and English. In his great novel, Conrad had carried out a searching exploration of the darkness at the heart of the European exploitation of Africa while hardly giving a single spoken line to an actual African character. In *Things Fall Apart,* and in the vigorous debates it has helped inspire, African writers have responded in many varied voices, in languages newly remade for a new world.

PRONUNCIATIONS:

Chinua Achebe: CHIN-ow-ah ah-CHAY-bay
Mbwil Ngal: m'BWEEL n'GAHL
Ngugi wa-Thiong'o: GOU-gie wah-tee-ON-go

Things Fall Apart

Principal Characters in the Novel[1]

Akueke (ah-KWAY-kay): Daughter of Obierika, whose marriage is negotiated

Anene (ah-NAY-nay): Ekwefi's first husband

Chielo (chee-AY-lah): The current priestess of the oracle

Chika (CHEE-kah): The former priestess of the oracle, during Unoka's time

Ekwefi (eh-KWAY-fee): Okonkwo's second wife; mother of Ezinma

Enoch: A Christian convert; a fanatic, who killed the sacred python and sought confrontation with Igbo traditionalists

Ezeani (ay-tsay-AH-nee): The priest of the earth goddess

Ezeudu (ay-TSEU-du): An important elder; the oldest man in Okonkwo's village

Ezeugo (ay-TSEU-gah): A powerful orator usually chosen as spokesman

Ezinma (ay-TSEEN-mah): Okonkwo's favorite daughter

Ikemefuna (ee-kay-may-FOO-nah): The boy from Mbaino given to Umuofia as compensation for murder

Maduka (MAH-dou-kah): Son of Obierika, a promising young wrestler

Mr. Brown: The first white missionary based in Umuofia

Mr. Kiaga: The Igbo missionary left in charge of the fledgling church in Mbanta

Mr. Smith: The zealous white missionary who replaced Mr. Brown

Ndulue (en-dou-LOO-ay): Husband who died at the same time as his wife

Nwakibie (nwah-key-BEE-ay): a big man in Umuofia, who helped Okonkwo get started in planting yams

Nwoye (NWO-yeh): Okonkwo's oldest son, who converts to Christianity and adopts the name Isaac

Obiageli (ah-bya-GAY-lee): Sister of Nwoye

Obierika (ah-byer-EE-kah): Okonkwo's good friend and confidant

Ogbuefi Udo (ag-BWAY-fee OU-dah): The man whose wife was murdered by the people of Mbaino

Ojiugo (ah-JYOU-go): One of Okonkwo's three wives, mother of Obiageli

Okagbue (ah-KAG-bway): The medicine man who finds and destroys Ezinma's *iyi-uwa*

Okonkwo (ah-CONK-wah): The main character, a strong, proud man

Okoye (ah-CO-yay): A friend of Okonkwo's father, who tries unsuccessfully to get back the money Unoka had borrowed

Ozoemena (ah-tso-ay-MAY-nah): Wife who dies at the same time as her husband

Uchendu (ou-CHEN-dou): Okonkwo's uncle, the senior man of Mbanta where Okonkwo's family lives in exile

Unoka (ou-NO-kah): Okonkwo's late father, an easygoing, rather lazy person

Glossary of Words and Phrases Used in the Text

(Igbo terms are in italics; *o* indicates "aw" sound as in *awful*.)

Afo: One of the four market days

agadi-nwayi: Old woman

---

[1]. Achebe prefaces his novel with this list of characters (pronunciations added) and definitions of the many Igbo terms that appear in the text.

agbala: Woman; also, an insulting term for a man who has taken no title

Agbala: The name of the oracle consulted by the people of Umuofia

Amadiora: The god of thunder and lightning

Ani: The earth goddess

bride-price: Or bridewealth; the gifts transferred from the groom's family to that of the bride, which cement the marriage and legitimize the children

chi: One's personal god, or guardian spirit

Chukwu: The supreme god

cowries: Shells imported from the Indian Ocean, widely used as currency in precolonial Africa

District Commissioner: The British official in charge of a particular African district

efulefu: An empty, worthless man

egwugwu: The masked spirits, representing the ancestral spirits of the village

Eke: One of the four market days

ekwe: A wooden drum

eneke-nti-oba: A kind of bird

eze-agai-nwayi: The teeth of an old woman

foo-foo: Or fufu; pounded yam eaten as part of most meals

harmattan: A cold, dry wind that blows from the North

iba: Fever

Ibo: The older spelling of "Igbo," less commonly used today

Idemili: One of the three most prestigious titles in Igboland

Ifejioku: The god of yams, the men's crop and principal food of the Igbo

Iguedo: Okonkwo's village, one of the nine villages that make up Umuofia

ikenga: A wooden carving that becomes imbued with a man's personal spirit

ilo: The village common, where meetings, ceremonies, and sports competitions take place

inyanga: Showing off; bragging

isa-ifi: A ceremony held to determine faithfulness if a woman had been separated from her fiancé or husband for some time and were then reunited with him

iyi-uwa: A special stone that forms the link between an *ogbanje* and the spirit world. The child would eventually die if the *iyi-uwa* were not discovered and destroyed.

jigida: A string of waist-beads

kite: A bird that appears during the dry season

kola nuts: Offered to guests on special occasions

kotma: "Court man," or court messenger; a corruption of the English term

kwenu: A shout of approval and greeting

maize: Corn

ndichie: The elders, who meet in council and make decisions binding the clan

nna ayi: Our father

nne: Mother

nno: An expression of welcome

nso-ani: Sacrilege

nza: A tiny bird

obi: The living quarters of the head of the family

obodo dike: The land of the brave

ochu: Murder or manslaughter

ogbanje: A changeling; a child who repeatedly dies and returns to its mother to be reborn

Ogbuefi: An honorific used before the name of a man who has taken the *ozo* title
ogene: A kind of gong
ogwu: Supernatural medicine
osu: An outcast; having been dedicated to a god, the *osu* was not allowed to mix
   with the freeborn, or to marry one of them
Oye: One of the four market days
ozo: One of the titles an important Igbo man could aspire to
palm kernels: The core of the fruit of the oil palm tree, which were cracked to
   release the oil
palm-oil: Used in cooking and for preparing food, also a major cash crop exported
   to Europe
palm-wine: A fermented drink prepared from the sap of certain palm trees
plantain: A starchy kind of banana, cooked as food
pottage: A stew
singlets: Men's undershirts
sisal: A kind of cactus plant with fibrous leaves
tufia: A curse or oath
udu: A type of drum made from pottery
uli: A dye used by women for drawing patterns on the skin
umuada: A family gathering of daughters, for which the female kinsfolk return to
   their village of origin
Umuofia: The clan Okonkwo belonged to, made up of nine villages
umunna: A wide group of kinsmen (the masculine form of *umuada*)
Uri: Part of the betrothal ceremony when the dowry or bridewealth is paid

Things Fall Apart

Turning and turning in the widening gyre
The falcon cannot hear the falconer;
Things fall apart; the centre cannot hold;
Mere anarchy is loosed upon the world.

W. B. Yeats, "The Second Coming"[1]

PART 1

Chapter 1

Okonkwo was well known throughout the nine villages and even beyond. His fame rested on solid personal achievements. As a young man of eighteen he had brought honour to his village by throwing Amalinze the Cat. Amalinze was the great wrestler who for seven years was unbeaten, from Umuofia to Mbaino. He was called the Cat because his back would never touch the earth. It was this man that Okonkwo threw in a fight which the old men agreed was one of the fiercest since the founder of their town engaged a spirit of the wild for seven days and seven nights.

---

1. William Butler Yeats's poem "The Second Coming" can be found on page 324. The Irish poet, writing after World War I, refers to Judgment Day and the new age to commence with Christ's second coming as announced in Matthew 24:31–46, a cosmic recommencement that is preceded by apocalyptic calamity and cosmic catastrophe. With the title of his novel, Achebe alludes to the catastrophe in Yeats's poem and refers as well to the undoing of a traditional African order by the calamities of colonization, religious conversion, and imposed political transition from traditional society to a modernized order.

The drums beat and the flutes sang and the spectators held their breath. Amalinze was a wily craftsman, but Okonkwo was as slippery as a fish in water. Every nerve and every muscle stood out on their arms, on their backs and their thighs, and one almost heard them stretching to breaking point. In the end Okonkwo threw the Cat.

That was many years ago, twenty years or more, and during this time Okonkwo's fame had grown like a bush-fire in the harmattan. He was tall and huge, and his bushy eyebrows and wide nose gave him a very severe look. He breathed heavily, and it was said that, when he slept, his wives and children in their out-houses could hear him breathe. When he walked, his heels hardly touched the ground and he seemed to walk on springs, as if he was going to pounce on somebody. And he did pounce on people quite often. He had a slight stammer and whenever he was angry and could not get his words out quickly enough, he would use his fists. He had no patience with unsuccessful men. He had had no patience with his father.

Unoka, for that was his father's name, had died ten years ago. In his day he was lazy and improvident and was quite incapable of thinking about tomorrow. If any money came his way, and it seldom did, he immediately bought gourds of palm-wine, called round his neighbours and made merry. He always said that whenever he saw a dead man's mouth he saw the folly of not eating what one had in one's lifetime. Unoka was, of course, a debtor, and he owed every neighbour some money, from a few cowries to quite substantial amounts.

He was tall but very thin and had a slight stoop. He wore a haggard and mournful look except when he was drinking or playing on his flute. He was very good on his flute, and his happiest moments were the two or three moons after the harvest when the village musicians brought down their instruments, hung above the fireplace. Unoka would play with them, his face beaming with blessedness and peace. Sometimes another village would ask Unoka's band and their dancing *egwugwu* to come and stay with them and teach them their tunes. They would go to such hosts for as long as three or four markets, making music and feasting. Unoka loved the good fare and the good fellowship, and he loved this season of the year, when the rains had stopped and the sun rose every morning with dazzling beauty. And it was not too hot either, because the cold and dry harmattan wind was blowing down from the north. Some years the harmattan was very severe and a dense haze hung on the atmosphere. Old men and children would then sit round log fires, warming their bodies. Unoka loved it all, and he loved the first kites that returned with the dry season, and the children who sang songs of welcome to them. He would remember his own childhood, how he had often wandered around looking for a kite sailing leisurely against the blue sky. As soon as he found one he would sing with his whole being, welcoming it back from its long, long journey, and asking it if it had brought home any lengths of cloth.

That was years ago, when he was young. Unoka, the grown-up, was a failure. He was poor and his wife and children had barely enough to eat. People laughed at him because he was a loafer, and they swore never to lend him any more money because he never paid back. But Unoka was such a man that he always succeeded in borrowing more, and piling up his debts.

One day a neighbour called Okoye came in to see him. He was reclining on a mud bed in his hut playing on the flute. He immediately rose and shook hands with Okoye, who then unrolled the goatskin which he carried under his arm, and sat down. Unoka went into an inner room and soon returned with a small wooden disc containing a kola nut, some alligator pepper and a lump of white chalk.

"I have kola," he announced when he sat down, and passed the disc over to his guest.

"Thank you. He who brings kola brings life. But I think you ought to break it," replied Okoye passing back the disc.

"No, it is for you, I think," and they argued like this for a few moments before Unoka accepted the honour of breaking the kola. Okoye, meanwhile, took the lump of chalk, drew some lines on the floor, and then painted his big toe. As he broke the kola, Unoka prayed to their ancestors for life and health, and for protection against their enemies. When they had eaten they talked about many things: about the heavy rains which were drowning the yams, about the next ancestral feast and about the impending war with the village of Mbaino. Unoka was never happy when it came to wars. He was in fact a coward and could not bear the sight of blood. And so he changed the subject and talked about music, and his face beamed. He could hear in his mind's ear the blood-stirring and intricate rhythms of the *ekwe* and the *udu* and the *ogene,* and he could hear his own flute weaving in and out of them, decorating them with a colourful and plaintive tune. The total effect was gay and brisk, but if one picked out the flute as it went up and down and then broke up into short snatches, one saw that there was sorrow and grief there.

Okoye was also a musician. He played on the *ogene.* But he was not a failure like Unoka. He had a large barn full of yams and he had three wives. And now he was going to take the Idemili title, the third highest in the land. It was a very expensive ceremony and he was gathering all his resources together. That was in fact the reason why he had come to see Unoka. He cleared his throat and began:

"Thank you for the kola. You may have heard of the title I intend to take shortly."

Having spoken plainly so far, Okoye said the next half a dozen sentences in proverbs. Among the Ibo the art of conversation is regarded very highly, and proverbs are the palm-oil with which words are eaten. Okoye was a great talker and he spoke for a long time, skirting round the subject and then hitting it finally. In short, he was asking Unoka to return the two hundred cowries he had borrowed from him more than two years before. As soon as Unoka understood what his friend was driving at, he burst out laughing. He laughed loud and long and his voice rang out clear as the *ogene,* and tears stood in his eyes. His visitor was amazed, and sat speechless. At the end, Unoka was able to give an answer between fresh outbursts of mirth.

"Look at that wall," he said, pointing at the far wall of his hut, which was rubbed with red earth so that it shone. "Look at those lines of chalk;" and Okoye saw groups of short perpendicular lines drawn in chalk. There were five groups, and the smallest group had ten lines. Unoka had a sense of the dramatic and so he allowed a pause, in which he took a pinch of snuff and sneezed noisily, and then he continued: "Each group there represents a debt to someone, and each stroke is one hundred cowries. You see, I owe that man a thousand cowries. But he has not come to wake me up in the morning for it. I shall pay you, but not today. Our elders say that the sun will shine on those who stand before it shines on those who kneel under them. I shall pay my big debts first." And he took another pinch of snuff, as if that was paying the big debts first. Okoye rolled his goatskin and departed.

When Unoka died he had taken no title at all and he was heavily in debt. Any wonder then that his son Okonkwo was ashamed of him? Fortunately, among these people a man was judged according to his worth and not according to the worth of his father. Okonkwo was clearly cut out for great things. He was still young but he had won fame as the greatest wrestler in the nine villages. He was a wealthy farmer and had two barns full of yams, and had just married his third wife. To crown it all he had taken two titles and had shown incredible prowess in two inter-tribal wars. And so although Okonkwo was still young, he was already one of the greatest men of his time. Age was respected among his people, but achievement was revered. As the elders said, if a child washed his hands he could eat with kings. Okonkwo had clearly washed his hands and so he ate with kings and elders. And that was how he came to look after the doomed lad who was sacrificed to the village of Umuofia by their neighbours to avoid war and bloodshed. The ill-fated lad was called Ikemefuna.

Chapter 2

Okonkwo had just blown out the palm-oil lamp and stretched himself on his bamboo bed when he heard the *ogene* of the town-crier piercing the still night air. *Gome, gome, gome, gome,* boomed the hollow metal. Then the crier gave his message, and at the end of it beat his instrument again. And this was the message. Every man of Umuofia was asked to gather at the market-place tomorrow morning. Okonkwo wondered what was amiss, for he knew certainly, that something was amiss. He had discerned a clear overtone of tragedy in the crier's voice, and even now he could still hear it as it grew dimmer and dimmer in the distance.

The night was very quiet. It was always quiet except on moonlight nights. Darkness held a vague terror for these people, even the bravest among them. Children were warned not to whistle at night for fear of evil spirits. Dangerous animals became even more sinister and uncanny in the dark. A snake was never called by its name at night, because it would hear. It was called a string. And so on this particular night as the crier's voice was gradually swallowed up in the distance, silence returned to the world, a vibrant silence made more intense by the universal trill of a million million forest insects.

On a moonlight night it would be different. The happy voices of children playing in open fields would then be heard. And perhaps those not so young would be playing in pairs in less open places, and old men and women would remember their youth. As the Ibo say: "When the moon is shining the cripple becomes hungry for a walk."

But this particular night was dark and silent. And in all the nine villages of Umuofia a town-crier with his *ogene* asked every man to be present tomorrow morning. Okonkwo on his bamboo bed tried to figure out the nature of the emergency—war with a neighbouring clan? That seemed the most likely reason, and he was not afraid of war. He was a man of action, a man of war. Unlike his father he could stand the look of blood. In Umuofia's latest war he was the first to bring home a human head. That was his fifth head; and he was not an old man yet. On great occasions such as the funeral of a village celebrity he drank his palm-wine from his first human head.

In the morning the market-place was full. There must have been about ten thousand men there, all talking in low voices. At last Ogbuefi Ezeugo stood up in the midst of them and bellowed four times, "*Umuofia kwenu,*" and on each occasion he faced a different direction and seemed to push the air with a clenched fist. And ten thousand men answered "*Yaa!*" each time. Then there was perfect silence. Ogbuefi Ezeugo was a powerful orator and was always chosen to speak on such occasions. He moved his hand over his white head and stroked his white beard. He then adjusted his cloth, which was passed under his right arm-pit and tied above his left shoulder.

"*Umuofia kwenu,*" he bellowed a fifth time, and the crowd yelled in answer. And then suddenly like one possessed he shot out his left hand and pointed in the direction of Mbaino, and said through gleaming white teeth firmly clenched: "Those sons of wild animals have dared to murder a daughter of Umuofia." He threw his head down and gnashed his teeth, and allowed a murmur of suppressed anger to sweep the crowd. When he began again, the anger on his face was gone and in its place a sort of smile hovered, more terrible and more sinister than the anger. And in a clear unemotional voice he told Umuofia how their daughter had gone to market at Mbaino and had been killed. That woman, said Ezeugo, was the wife of Ogbuefi Udo, and he pointed to a man who sat near him with a bowed head. The crowd then shouted with anger and thirst for blood.

Many others spoke, and at the end it was decided to follow the normal course of action. An ultimatum was immediately dispatched to Mbaino asking them to choose between war on the one hand, and on the other the offer of a young man and a virgin as compensation.

Umuofia was feared by all its neighbours. It was powerful in war and in magic, and its priests and medicine-men were feared in all the surrounding country. Its most potent war-medicine was as old as the clan itself. Nobody knew how old. But on one point there was general agreement—the active principle in that medicine had been an old woman with one leg. In fact, the medicine itself was called *agadi-nwayi*, or old woman. It had its shrine in the centre of Umuofia, in a cleared spot. And if anybody was so foolhardy as to pass by the shrine after dusk he was sure to see the old woman hopping about.

And so the neighbouring clans who naturally knew of these things feared Umuofia, and would not go to war against it without first trying a peaceful settlement. And in fairness to Umuofia it should be recorded that it never went to war unless its case was clear and just and was accepted as such by its Oracle—the Oracle of the Hills and the Caves. And there were indeed occasions when the Oracle had forbidden Umuofia to wage a war. If the clan had disobeyed the Oracle they would surely have been beaten, because their dreaded *agadi-nwayi* would never fight what the Ibo call *a fight of blame.*

But the war that now threatened was a just war. Even the enemy clan knew that. And so when Okonkwo of Umuofia arrived at Mbaino as the proud and imperious emissary of war, he was treated with great honour and respect, and two days later he returned home with a lad of fifteen and a young virgin. The lad's name was Ikemefuna, whose sad story is still told in Umuofia unto this day.

The elders, or *ndichie,* met to hear a report of Okonkwo's mission. At the end they decided, as everybody knew they would, that the girl should go to Ogbuefi Udo to replace his murdered wife. As for the boy, he belonged to the clan as a whole, and there was no hurry to decide his fate. Okonkwo was, therefore, asked on behalf of the clan to look after him in the interim. And so for three years Ikemefuna lived in Okonkwo's household.

Okonkwo ruled his household with a heavy hand. His wives, especially the youngest, lived in perpetual fear of his fiery temper, and so did his little children. Perhaps down in his heart Okonkwo was not a cruel man. But his whole life was dominated by fear, the fear of failure and of weakness. It was deeper and more intimate than the fear of evil and capricious gods and of magic, the fear of the forest, and the forces of nature, malevolent, red in tooth and claw. Okonkwo's fear was greater than these. It was not external but lay deep within himself. It was the fear of himself, lest he should be found to resemble his father. Even as a little boy he had resented his father's failure and weakness, and even now he still remembered how he had suffered when a playmate had told him that his father was *agbala*. That was how Okonkwo first came to know that *agbala* was not only another name for a woman, it could also mean a man who had taken no title. And so Okonkwo was ruled by one passion—to hate every-thing that his father Unoka had loved. One of those things was gentleness and another was idleness.

During the planting season Okonkwo worked daily on his farms from cock-crow until the chickens went to roost. He was a very strong man and rarely felt fatigue. But his wives and young children were not as strong, and so they suffered. But they dared not complain openly. Okonkwo's first son, Nwoye, was then twelve years old but was already causing his father great anxiety for his incipient laziness. At any rate, that was how it looked to his father, and he sought to correct him by constant nagging and beating. And so Nwoye was developing into a sad-faced youth.

Okonkwo's prosperity was visible in his household. He had a large compound enclosed by a thick wall of red earth. His own hut, or *obi,* stood immediately behind the only gate in the red walls. Each of his three wives had her own hut, which together formed a half moon behind the *obi.* The barn was built against one end of the red walls, and long stacks of yam stood out prosperously in it. At the opposite end of the compound was a shed for the goats, and each wife built a small attachment to her hut for the hens. Near the barn was a small house, the "medicine house" or shrine where Okonkwo kept the wooden symbols of his personal god and of his ancestral spirits. He worshipped them with sacrifices of kola nut, food and palm-wine, and offered prayers to them on behalf of himself, his three wives and eight children.

So when the daughter of Umuofia was killed in Mbaino, Ikemefuna came into Okonkwo's household. When Okonkwo brought him home that day he called his most senior wife and handed him over to her.

"He belongs to the clan," he told her. "So look after him."

"Is he staying long with us?" she asked.

"Do what you are told, woman," Okonkwo thundered, and stammered. "When did you become one of the *ndichie* of Umuofia?"

And so Nwoye's mother took Ikemefuna to her hut and asked no more questions.

As for the boy himself, he was terribly afraid. He could not understand what was happening to him or what he had done. How could he know that his father had taken a hand in killing a daughter of Umuofia? All he knew was that a few men had arrived at their house, conversing with his father in low tones, and at the end he had been taken out and handed over to a stranger. His mother had wept bitterly, but he had been too surprised to weep. And so the stranger had brought him, and a girl, a long, long way from home, through lonely forest paths. He did not know who the girl was, and he never saw her again.

Chapter 3

Okonkwo did not have the start in life which many young men usually had. He did not inherit a barn from his father. There was no barn to inherit. The story was told in Umuofia of how his father, Unoka, had gone to consult the Oracle of the Hills and the Caves to find out why he always had a miserable harvest.

The Oracle was called Agbala, and people came from far and near to consult it. They came when misfortune dogged their steps or when they had a dispute with their neighbours. They came to discover what the future held for them or to consult the spirits of their departed fathers.

The way into the shrine was a round hole at the side of a hill, just a little bigger than the round opening into a hen-house. Worshippers and those who came to seek knowledge from the god crawled on their belly through the hole and found themselves in a dark, endless space in the presence of Agbala. No one had ever beheld Agbala, except his priestess. But no one who had ever crawled into his awful shrine had come out without the fear of his power. His priestess stood by the sacred fire which she built in the heart of the cave and proclaimed the will of the god. The fire did not burn with a flame. The glowing logs only served to light up vaguely the dark figure of the priestess.

Sometimes a man came to consult the spirit of his dead father or relative. It was said that when such a spirit appeared, the man saw it vaguely in the darkness, but never heard its voice. Some people even said that they had heard the spirits flying and flapping their wings against the roof of the cave.

Many years ago when Okonkwo was still a boy his father, Unoka, had gone to consult Agbala. The priestess in those days was a woman called Chika. She was full of the power of her god, and she was greatly feared. Unoka stood before her and began his story.

"Every year," he said sadly, "before I put any crop in the earth, I sacrifice a cock to Ani, the owner of all land. It is the law of our fathers. I also kill a cock at the shrine of Ifejioku, the god of yams. I clear the bush and set fire to it when it is dry. I sow the yams when the first rain has fallen, and stake them when the young tendrils appear. I weed—"

"Hold your peace!" screamed the priestess, her voice terrible as it echoed through the dark void. "You have offended neither the gods nor your fathers. And when a man is at peace with his gods and his ancestors, his harvest will be good or bad according to the strength of his arm. You, Unoka, are known in all the clan for the weakness of your matchet and your hoe. When your neighbours go out with their axe to cut down virgin forests, you sow your yams on exhausted farms that take no labour to clear. They cross seven rivers to make their farms; you stay at home and offer sacrifices to a reluctant soil. Go home and work like a man."

Unoka was an ill-fated man. He had a bad *chi* or personal god, and evil fortune followed him to the grave, or rather to his death, for he had no grave. He died of the swelling which was an abomination to the earth goddess. When a man was afflicted with swelling in the stomach and the limbs he was not allowed to die in the house. He was carried to the Evil Forest and left there to die. There was a story of a very stubborn man who staggered back to his house and had to be carried again to the forest and tied to a tree. The sickness was an abomination to the earth, and so the victim could not be buried in her bowels. He died and rotted away above the earth, and was not given the first or the second burial. Such was Unoka's fate. When they carried him away, he took with him his flute.

With a father like Unoka, Okonkwo did not have the start in life which many young men had. He neither inherited a barn nor a title, nor even a young wife. But in spite of these disadvantages, he had begun even in his father's lifetime to lay the foundations of a prosperous future. It was slow and painful. But he threw himself into it like one possessed. And indeed he was possessed by the fear of his father's contemptible life and shameful death.

There was a wealthy man in Okonkwo's village who had three huge barns, nine wives and thirty children. His name was Nwakibie and he had taken the highest but one title which a man could take in the clan. It was for this man that Okonkwo worked to earn his first seed yams.

He took a pot of palm-wine and a cock of Nwakibie. Two elderly neighbours were sent for, and Nwakibie's two grown-up sons were also present in his *obi*. He presented a kola nut and an alligator pepper, which was passed round for all to see and then returned to him. He broke it, saying: "We shall all live. We pray for life, children, a good harvest and happiness. You will have what is good for you and I will have what is good for me. Let the kite perch and let the eagle perch too. If one says no to the other, let his wing break."

After the kola nut had been eaten Okonkwo brought his palm-wine from the corner of the hut where it had been placed and stood it in the centre of the group. He addressed Nwakibie, calling him "Our father."

"*Nna ayi,*" he said. "I have brought you this little kola. As our people say, a man who pays respect to the great paves the way for his own greatness. I have come to pay you my respects and also to ask a favour. But let us drink the wine first."

Everybody thanked Okonkwo and the neighbours brought out their drinking horns from the goatskin bags they carried. Nwakibie brought down his own horn, which was fastened to the rafters. The younger of his sons, who was also the youngest man in the group, moved to the centre, raised the pot on his left knee and began to pour out the wine. The first cup went to Okonkwo, who must taste his wine before anyone else. Then the group drank, beginning with the eldest man. When everyone had drunk two or three horns, Nwakibie sent for his wives. Some of them were not at home and only four came in.

"Is Anasi not in?" he asked them. They said she was coming. Anasi was the first wife and the others could not drink before her, and so they stood waiting.

Anasi was a middle-aged woman, tall and strongly built. There was authority in her bearing and she looked every inch the ruler of the womenfolk in a large and prosperous family. She wore the anklet of her husband's titles, which the first wife alone could wear.

She walked up to her husband and accepted the horn from him. She then went down on one knee, drank a little and handed back the horn. She rose, called him by his name and went back to her hut. The other wives drank in the same way, in their proper order, and went away.

The men then continued their drinking and talking. Ogbuefi Idigo was talking about the palm-wine tapper, Obiako, who suddenly gave up his trade.

"There must be something behind it," he said, wiping the foam of wine from his moustache with the back of his left hand. "There must be a reason for it. A toad does not run in the daytime for nothing."

"Some people say the Oracle warned him that he would fall off a palm tree and kill himself," said Akukalia.

"Obiako has always been a strange one," said Nwakibie. "I have heard that many years ago, when his father had not been dead very long, he had gone to consult the Oracle. The Oracle said to him, 'Your dead father wants you to sacrifice a goat to him.' Do you know what he told the Oracle? He said, 'Ask my dead father if he ever had a fowl when he was alive.'" Everybody laughed heartily except Okonkwo, who laughed uneasily because as the saying goes, an old woman is always uneasy when dry bones are mentioned in a proverb. Okonkwo remembered his own father.

At last the young man who was pouring out the wine held up half a horn of the thick, white dregs and said, "What we are eating is finished." "We have seen it," the others replied. "Who will drink the dregs?" he asked. "Whoever has a job in hand," said Idigo, looking at Nwakibie's elder son, Igwelo, with a mischievous twinkle in his eye.

Everybody agreed that Igwelo should drink the dregs. He accepted the half-full horn from his brother and drank it. As Idigo had said, Igwelo had a job in hand because he had married his first wife a month or two before. The thick dregs of palm-wine were supposed to be good for men who were going in to their wives.

After the wine had been drunk Okonkwo laid his difficulties before Nwakibie.

"I have come to you for help," he said. "Perhaps you can already guess what it is. I have cleared a farm but have no yams to sow. I know what it is to ask a man to trust another with his yams, especially these days when young men are afraid of hard work. I am not afraid of work. The lizard that jumped from the high iroko tree to the ground said he would praise himself if no one else did. I began to fend for myself at an age when most people still suck at their mothers' breasts. If you give me some yam seeds I shall not fail you."

Nwakibie cleared his throat. "It pleases me to see a young man like you these days when our youth have gone so soft. Many young men have come to me to ask for yams but I have refused because I knew they would just dump them in the earth and leave them to be choked by weeds. When I say no to them they think I am hard-hearted. But it is not so. Eneke the bird says that since men have learnt to shoot with-out missing, he has learnt to fly without perching. I have learnt to be stingy with my yams. But I can trust you. I know it as I look at you. As our fathers said, you can tell a ripe corn by its look. I shall give you twice four hundred yams. Go ahead and prepare your farm."

Okonkwo thanked him again and again and went home feeling happy. He knew that Nwakibie would not refuse him, but he had not expected he would be so gener-ous. He had not hoped to get more than four hundred seeds. He would now have to make a bigger farm. He hoped to get another four hundred yams from one of his fa-ther's friends at Isiuzo.

Share-cropping was a very slow way of building up a barn of one's own. After all the toil one only got a third of the harvest. But for a young man whose father had no yams, there was no other way. And what made it worse in Okonkwo's case was that he had to support his mother and two sisters from his meagre harvest. And supporting his mother also meant supporting his father. She could not be expected to cook and eat while her husband starved. And so at a very early age when he was striving des-perately to build a barn through sharecropping Okonkwo was also fending for his fa-ther's house. It was like pouring grains of corn into a bag full of holes. His mother and sisters worked hard enough, but they grew women's crops, like coco-yams, beans and cassava. Yam, the king of crops, was a man's crop.

The year that Okonkwo took eight hundred seed-yams from Nwakibie was the worst year in living memory. Nothing happened at its proper time; it was either too early or too late. It seemed as if the world had gone mad. The first rains were late, and, when they came, lasted only a brief moment. The blazing sun returned, more fierce than it had ever been known, and scorched all the green that had appeared with the rains. The earth burned like hot coals and roasted all the yams that had been sown. Like all good farmers, Okonkwo had begun to sow with the first rains. He had sown four hundred seeds when the rains dried up and the heat returned. He watched the sky all day for signs of rain-clouds and lay awake all night. In the morning he went back to his farm and saw the withering tendrils. He had tried to protect them from the smouldering earth by making rings of thick sisal leaves around them. But by the end of the day the sisal rings were burnt dry and grey. He changed them every day, and prayed that the rain might fall in the night. But the drought continued for eight market weeks and the yams were killed.

Some farmers had not planted their yams yet. They were the lazy easy-going ones who always put off clearing their farms as long as they could. This year they were the wise ones. They sympathised with their neighbours with much shaking of the head, but inwardly they were happy for what they took to be their own foresight.

Okonkwo planted what was left of his seed-yams when the rains finally returned. He had one consolation. The yams he had sown before the drought were his own, the harvest of the previous year. He still had the eight hundred from Nwakibie and the four hundred from his father's friend. So he would make a fresh start.

But the year had gone mad. Rain fell as it had never fallen before. For days and nights together it poured down in violent torrents, and washed away the yam heaps. Trees were uprooted and deep gorges appeared everywhere. Then the rain became less violent. But it went on from day to day without a pause. The spell of sunshine which always came in the middle of the wet season did not appear. The yams put on luxuriant green leaves, but every farmer knew that without sunshine the tubers would not grow.

That year the harvest was sad, like a funeral, and many farmers wept as they dug up the miserable and rotting yams. One man tied his cloth to a tree branch and hanged himself.

Okonkwo remembered that tragic year with a cold shiver throughout the rest of his life. It always surprised him when he thought of it later that he did not sink under the load of despair. He knew he was a fierce fighter, but that year had been enough to break the heart of a lion.

"Since I survived that year," he always said, "I shall survive anything." He put it down to his inflexible will.

His father, Unoka, who was then an ailing man, had said to him during that terrible harvest month: "Do not despair. I know you will not despair. You have a manly and a proud heart. A proud heart can survive a general failure because such a failure does not prick its pride. It is more difficult and more bitter when a man fails *alone*."

Unoka was like that in his last days. His love of talk had grown with age and sickness. It tried Okonkwo's patience beyond words.

Chapter 4

"Looking at a king's mouth," said an old man, "one would think he never sucked at his mother's breast." He was talking about Okonkwo, who had risen so suddenly from great poverty and misfortune to be one of the lords of the clan. The old man bore no ill-will towards Okonkwo. Indeed he respected him for his industry and success. But he was struck, as most people were, by Okonkwo's brusqueness in dealing with less successful men. Only a week ago a man had contradicted him at a kindred meeting which they held to discuss the next ancestral feast. Without looking at the man Okonkwo had said: "This meeting is for men." The man who had contradicted him had no titles. That was why he had called him a woman. Okonkwo knew how to kill a man's spirit.

Everybody at the kindred meeting took sides with Osugo when Okonkwo called him a woman. The oldest man present said sternly that those whose palm-kernels were cracked for them by a benevolent spirit should not forget to be humble. Okonkwo said he was sorry for what he had said, and the meeting continued.

But it was really not true that Okonkwo's palm-kernels had been cracked for him by a benevolent spirit. He had cracked them himself. Anyone who knew his grim struggle against poverty and misfortune could not say he had been lucky. If ever a man deserved his success, that man was Okonkwo. At an early age he had achieved fame as the greatest wrestler in all the land. That was not luck. At the most one could say that his *chi* or personal god was good. But the Ibo people have a proverb that when a man says yes his *chi* says yes also. Okonkwo said yes very strongly; so his *chi* agreed. And not only his *chi* but his clan too, because it judged a man by the work of his hands. That was why Okonkwo had been chosen by the nine villages to carry a message of war to their enemies unless they agreed to give up a young man and a virgin to atone for the murder of Udo's wife. And such was the deep fear that their enemies had for Umuofia that they treated Okonkwo like a king and brought him a virgin who was given to Udo as wife, and the lad Ikemefuna.

The elders of the clan had decided that Ikemefuna should be in Okonkwo's care for a while. But no one thought it would be as long as three years. They seemed to forget all about him as soon as they had taken the decision.

At first Ikemefuna was very much afraid. Once or twice he tried to run away, but he did not know where to begin. He thought of his mother and his three-year-old sister and wept bitterly. Nwoye's mother was very kind to him and treated him as one of her own children. But all he said was: "When shall I go home?" When Okonkwo heard that he would not eat any food he came into the hut with a big stick in his hand and stood over him while he swallowed his yams, trembling. A few moments later he went behind the hut and began to vomit painfully. Nwoye's mother went to him and placed her hands on his chest and on his back. He was ill for three market weeks, and when he recovered he seemed to have overcome his great fear and sadness.

He was by nature a very lively boy and he gradually became popular in Okonkwo's household, especially with the children. Okonkwo's son, Nwoye, who was two years younger, became quite inseparable from him because he seemed to know everything. He could fashion out flutes from bamboo stems and even from the elephant grass. He knew the names of all the birds and could set clever traps for the little bush rodents. And he knew which trees made the strongest bows.

Even Okonkwo himself became very fond of the boy—inwardly of course. Okonkwo never showed any emotion openly, unless it be the emotion of anger. To show affection was a sign of weakness; the only thing worth demonstrating was strength. He therefore treated Ikemefuna as he treated everybody else—with a heavy hand. But there was no doubt that he liked the boy. Sometimes when he went to big village meetings or communal ancestral feasts he allowed Ikemefuna to accompany him, like a son, carrying his stool and his goatskin bag. And, indeed, Ikemefuna called him father.

Ikemefuna came to Umuofia at the end of the carefree season between harvest and planting. In fact he recovered from his illness only a few days before the Week of Peace began. And that was also the year Okonkwo broke the peace, and was punished, as was the custom, by Ezeani, the priest of the earth goddess.

Okonkwo was provoked to justifiable anger by his youngest wife, who went to plait her hair at her friend's house and did not return early enough to cook the afternoon meal. Okonkwo did not know at first that she was not at home. After waiting in vain for the dish he went to her hut to see what she was doing. There was nobody in the hut and the fireplace was cold.

"Where is Ojiugo?" he asked his second wife, who came out of her hut to draw water from the gigantic pot in the shade of a small tree in the middle of the compound.

"She has gone to plait her hair."

Okonkwo bit his lips as anger welled up within him.

"Where are her children? Did she take them?" he asked with unusual coolness and restraint.

"They are here," answered his first wife, Nwoye's mother. Okonkwo bent down and looked into her hut. Ojiugo's children were eating with the children of his first wife.

"Did she ask you to feed them before she went?"

"Yes," lied Nwoye's mother, trying to minimise Ojiugo's thoughtlessness.

Okonkwo knew she was not speaking the truth. He walked back to his *obi* to wait Ojiugo's return. And when she returned he beat her very heavily. In his anger he had forgotten that it was the Week of Peace. His first two wives ran out in great alarm pleading with him that it was the sacred week. But Okonkwo was not the man to stop beating somebody half-way through, not even for fear of a goddess.

Okonkwo's neighbours heard his wife crying and sent their voices over the compound walls to ask what was the matter. Some of them came over to see for themselves. It was unheard of to beat somebody during the sacred week.

Before it was dusk Ezeani, who was the priest of the earth goddess, Ani, called on Okonkwo in his *obi*. Okonkwo brought out kola nut and placed it before the priest.

"Take away your kola nut. I shall not eat in the house of a man who has no respect for our gods and ancestors."

Okonkwo tried to explain to him what his wife had done, but Ezeani seemed to pay no attention. He held a short staff in his hand which he brought down on the floor to emphasize his points.

"Listen to me," he said when Okonkwo had spoken. "You are not a stranger in Umuofia. You know as well as I do that our forefathers ordained that before we plant any crops in the earth we should observe a week in which a man does not say a harsh word to his neighbour. We live in peace with our fellows to honour our great goddess of the earth without whose blessing our crops will not grow. You have committed a great evil." He brought down his staff heavily on the floor. "You wife was at fault, but even if you came into your *obi* and found her lover on top of her, you would still have committed a great evil to beat her." His staff came down again. "The evil you have done can ruin the whole clan. The earth goddess whom you have insulted may refuse to give us her increase, and we shall all perish." His tone now changed from anger to command. "You will bring to the shrine of Ani tomorrow one she-goat, one hen, a length of cloth and a hundred cowries." He rose and left the hut.

Okonkwo did as the priest said. He also took with him a pot of palm-wine. Inwardly, he was repentant. But he was not the man to go about telling his neighbours that he was in error. And so people said he had no respect for the gods of the clan. His enemies said his good fortune had gone to his head. They called him the little bird *nza* who so far forgot himself after a heavy meal that he challenged his *chi*.

No work was done during the Week of Peace. People called on their neighbours and drank palm-wine. This year they talked of nothing else but the *nso-ani* which Okonkwo had committed. It was the first time for many years that a man had broken the sacred peace. Even the oldest men could only remember one or two other occasions somewhere in the dim past.

Ogbuefi Ezeudu, who was the oldest man in the village, was telling two other men who came to visit him that the punishment for breaking the Peace of Ani had become very mild in their clan.

"It has not always been so," he said. "My father told me that he had been told that in the past a man who broke the peace was dragged on the ground through the village until he died. But after a while this custom was stopped because it spoilt the peace which it was meant to preserve."

"Somebody told me yesterday," said one of the younger men, "that in some clans it is an abomination for a man to die during the Week of Peace."

"It is indeed true," said Ogbuefi Ezeudu. "They have that custom in Obodoani. If a man dies at this time he is not buried but cast into the Evil Forest. It is a bad custom which these people observe because they lack understanding. They throw away large numbers of men and women without burial. And what is the result? Their clan is full of the evil spirits of these unburied dead, hungry to do harm to the living."

After the Week of Peace every man and his family began to clear the bush to make new farms. The cut bush was left to dry and fire was then set to it. As the smoke rose into the sky kites appeared from different directions and hovered over the burning field in silent valediction. The rainy season was approaching when they would go away until the dry season returned.

Okonkwo spent the next few days preparing his seed-yams. He looked at each yam carefully to see whether it was good for sowing. Sometimes he decided that a yam was too big to be sown as one seed and he split it deftly along its length with his sharp knife. His eldest son, Nwoye, and Ikemefuna helped him by fetching the yams in long baskets from the barn and in counting the prepared seeds in groups of four hundred. Sometimes Okonkwo gave them a few yams each to prepare. But he always found fault with their effort, and he said so with much threatening.

"Do you think you are cutting up yams for cooking?" he asked Nwoye. "If you split another yam of this size, I shall break your jaw. You think you are still a child. I began to own a farm at your age. And you," he said to Ikemefuna, "do you not grow yams where you come from?"

Inwardly Okonkwo knew that the boys were still too young to understand fully the difficult art of preparing seed-yams. But he thought that one could not begin too early. Yam stood for manliness, and he who could feed his family on yams from one harvest to another was a very great man indeed. Okonkwo wanted his son to be a great farmer and a great man. He would stamp out the disquieting signs of laziness which he thought he already saw in him.

"I will not have a son who cannot hold up his head in the gathering of the clan. I would sooner strangle him with my own hands. And if you stand staring at me like that," he swore, "Amadiora will break your head for you!"

Some days later, when the land had been moistened by two or three heavy rains, Okonkwo and his family went to the farm with baskets of seed-yams, their hoes and matchets, and the planting began. They made single mounds of earth in straight lines all over the field and sowed the yams in them.

Yam, the king of crops, was a very exacting king. For three or four moons it demanded hard work and constant attention from cockcrow till the chickens went back to roost. The young tendrils were protected from earth-heat with rings of sisal leaves. As the rains became heavier the women planted maize, melons and beans between the yam mounds. The yams were then staked, first with little sticks and later with tall and big tree branches. The women weeded the farm three times at definite periods in the life of the yams, neither early nor late.

And now the rains had really come, so heavy and persistent that even the village rain-maker no longer claimed to be able to intervene. He could not stop the rain now, just as he would not attempt to start it in the heart of the dry season, without serious danger to his own health. The personal dynamism required to counter the forces of these extremes of weather would be far too great for the human frame.

And so nature was not interfered with in the middle of the rainy season. Sometimes it poured down in such thick sheets of water that earth and sky seemed merged in one grey wetness. It was then uncertain whether the low rumbling of Amadiora's thunder came from above or below. At such times, in each of the countless thatched huts of Umuofia, children sat around their mother's cooking fire telling stories, or with their father in his *obi* warming themselves from a log fire, roasting and eating maize. It was a brief resting period between the exacting and arduous planting season and the equally exacting but light-hearted month of harvests.

Ikemefuna had begun to feel like a member of Okonkwo's family. He still thought about his mother and his three-year-old sister, and he had moments of sadness and depression. But he and Nwoye had become so deeply attached to each other that such moments became less frequent and less poignant. Ikemefuna had an endless stock of folk tales. Even those which Nwoye knew already were told with a new freshness and the local flavour of a different clan. Nwoye remembered this period very vividly till the end of his life. He even remembered how he had laughed when Ikemefuna told him that the proper name for a corn-cob with only a few scattered grains was *ezeagadi-nwayi,* or the teeth of an old woman. Nwoye's mind had gone immediately to Nwayieke, who lived near the udala tree. She had about three teeth and was always smoking her pipe.

Gradually the rains became lighter and less frequent, and earth and sky once again became separate. The rain fell in thin, slanting showers through sunshine and quiet breeze. Children no longer stayed indoors but ran about singing:

> "The rain is falling, the sun is shining,
> Alone Nnadi is cooking and eating."

Nwoye always wondered who Nnadi was and why he should live all by himself, cooking and eating. In the end he decided that Nnadi must live in that land of Ikemefuna's favourite story where the ant holds his court in splendour and the sands dance for ever.

Chapter 5

The Feast of the New Yam was approaching and Umuofia was in a festival mood. It was an occasion for giving thanks to Ani, the earth goddess and the source of all fertility. Ani played a greater part in the life of the people than any other deity. She was the ultimate judge of morality and conduct. And what was more, she was in close communion with the departed fathers of the clan whose bodies had been committed to earth.

The Feast of the New Yam was held every year before the harvest began, to honour the earth goddess and the ancestral spirits of the clan. New yams could not be eaten until some had first been offered to these powers. Men and women, young and old, looked forward to the New Yam Festival because it began the season of plenty—the new year. On the last night before the festival, yams of the old year were all disposed of by those who still had them. The new year must begin with tasty, fresh yams and not the shrivelled and fibrous crop of the previous year. All cooking-pots, calabashes and wooden bowls were thoroughly washed, especially the wooden mortar in which yam was pounded. Yam foo-foo and vegetable soup was the chief food in the celebration. So much of it was cooked that, no matter how heavily the family ate or how many friends and relations they invited from neighbouring villages, there was always a huge quantity of food left over at the end of the day. The story was always told of a wealthy man who set before his guests a mount of foo-foo so high that those who sat on one side could not see what was happening on the other, and it was not until late in the evening that one of them saw for the first time his in-law who had arrived during the course of the meal and had fallen to on the opposite side. It was only then that they exchanged greetings and shook hands over what was left of the food.

The New Yam Festival was thus an occasion for joy throughout Umuofia. And every man whose arm was strong, as the Ibo people say, was expected to invite large numbers of guests from far and wide. Okonkwo always asked his wives' relations, and since he now had three wives his guests would make a fairly big crowd.

But somehow Okonkwo could never become as enthusiastic over feasts as most people. He was a good eater and he could drink one or two fairly big gourds of palm-wine. But he was always uncomfortable sitting around for days waiting for a feast or getting over it. He would be very much happier working on his farm.

The festival was now only three days away. Okonkwo's wives had scrubbed the walls and the huts with red earth until they reflected light. They had then drawn patterns on them in white, yellow and dark green. They then set about painting themselves with cam wood and drawing beautiful black patterns on their stomachs and on their backs. The children were also decorated, especially their hair, which was shaved in beautiful patterns. The three women talked excitedly about the relations who had been invited, and the children revelled in the thought of being spoilt by these visitors from mother-land. Ikemefuna was equally excited. The New Yam Festival seemed to him to be a much bigger event here than in his own village, a place which was already becoming remote and vague in his imagination.

And then the storm burst. Okonkwo, who had been walking about aimlessly in his compound in suppressed anger, suddenly found an outlet.

"Who killed this banana tree?" he asked.

A hush fell on the compound immediately.

"Who killed this tree? Or are you all deaf and dumb?"

As a matter of fact the tree was very much alive. Okonkwo's second wife had merely cut a few leaves off it to wrap some food, and she said so. Without further argument Okonkwo gave her a sound beating and left her and her only daughter weeping. Neither of the other wives dared to interfere beyond an occasional and tentative, "It is enough, Okonkwo," pleaded from a reasonable distance.

His anger thus satisfied, Okonkwo decided to go out hunting. He had an old rusty gun made by a clever blacksmith who had come to live in Umuofia long ago. But although Okonkwo was a great man whose prowess was universally acknowledged, he was not a hunter. In fact he had not killed a rat with his gun. And so when he called Ikemefuna to fetch his gun, the wife who had just been beaten murmured something about guns that never shot. Unfortunately for her, Okonkwo heard it and ran madly into his room for the loaded gun, ran out again and aimed at her as she clambered over the dwarf wall of the barn. He pressed the trigger and there was a loud report accompanied by the wail of his wives and children. He threw down the gun and jumped into the barn, and there lay the woman, very much shaken and frightened but quite unhurt. He heaved a heavy sigh and went away with the gun.

In spite of this incident the New Yam Festival was celebrated with great joy in Okonkwo's household. Early that morning as he offered a sacrifice of new yam and palm-oil to his ancestors he asked them to protect him, his children and their mothers in the new year.

As the day wore on his in-laws arrived from three surrounding villages, and each party brought with them a huge pot of palm-wine. And there was eating and drinking till night, when Okonkwo's in-laws began to leave for their homes.

The second day of the new year was the day of the great wrestling match between Okonkwo's village and their neighbours. It was difficult to say which the people enjoyed more—the feasting and fellowship of the first day or the wrestling contest of the second. But there was one woman who had no doubt whatever in her mind. She was Okonkwo's second wife, Ekwefi, whom he nearly shot. There was no festival in all the seasons of the year which gave her as much pleasure as the wrestling match. Many years ago when she was the village beauty Okonkwo had won her heart by throwing the Cat in the greatest contest within living memory. She did not marry him because he was too poor to pay her bride-price. But a few years later she ran away from her husband and came to live with Okonkwo. All this happened many years ago. Now Ekwefi was a woman of forty-five who had suffered a great deal in her time. But her love of wrestling contests was still as strong as it was thirty years ago.

It was not yet noon on the second day of the New Yam Festival. Ekwefi and her only daughter, Ezinma, sat near the fireplace waiting for the water in the pot to boil. The fowl Ekwefi had just killed was in the wooden mortar. The water began to boil, and in one deft movement she lifted the pot from the fire and poured the boiling water on to the fowl. She put back the empty pot on the circular pad in the corner, and looked at her palms, which were black with soot. Ezinma was always surprised that her mother could lift a pot from the fire with her bare hands.

"Ekwefi," she said, "is it true that when people are grown up, fire does not burn them?" Ezinma, unlike most children, called her mother by her name.

"Yes," replied Ekwefi, too busy to argue. Her daughter was only ten years old but she was wiser than her years.

"But Nwoye's mother dropped her pot of hot soup the other day and it broke on the floor."

Ekwefi turned the hen over in the mortar and began to pluck the feathers.

"Ekwefi," said Ezinma, who had joined in plucking the feathers, "my eyelid is twitching."

"It means you are going to cry," said her mother.

"No," Ezinma said, "it is this eyelid, the top one."

"That means you will see something."

"What will I see?" she asked.

"How can I know?" Ekwefi wanted her to work it out herself.

"Oho," said Ezinma at last. "I know what it is—the wrestling match."

At last the hen was plucked clean. Ekwefi tried to pull out the horny beak but it was too hard. She turned round on her low stool and put the beak in the fire for a few moments. She pulled again and it came off.

"Ekwefi!" a voice called from one of the other huts. It was Nwoye's mother, Okonkwo's first wife.

"Is that me?" Ekwefi called back. That was the way people answered calls from outside. They never answered yes for fear it might be an evil spirit calling.

"Will you give Ezinma some fire to bring to me?" Her own children and Ikemefuna had gone to the stream.

Ekwefi put a few live coals into a piece of broken pot and Ezinma carried it across the clean-swept compound to Nwoye's mother.

"Thank you, Nma," she said. She was peeling new yams, and in a basket beside her were green vegetables and beans.

"Let me make the fire for you," Ezinma offered.

"Thank you, Ezigbo," she said. She often called her Ezigbo, which means "the good one."

Ezinma went outside and brought some sticks from a huge bundle of firewood. She broke them into little pieces across the sole of her foot and began to build a fire, blowing it with her breath.

"You will blow your eyes out," said Nwoye's mother, looking up from the yams she was peeling. "Use the fan." She stood up and pulled out the fan which was fastened into one of the rafters. As soon as she got up, the troublesome nanny-goat, which had been dutifully eating yam peelings, dug her teeth into the real thing, scooped out two mouthfuls and fled from the hut to chew the cud in the goats' shed. Nwoye's mother swore at her and settled down again to her peeling. Ezinma's fire was now sending up thick clouds of smoke. She went on fanning it until it burst into flames. Nwoye's mother thanked her and she went back to her mother's hut.

Just then the distant beating of drums began to reach them. It came from the direction of the *ilo,* the village playground. Every village had its own *ilo* which was as old as the village itself and where all the great ceremonies and dances took place. The drums beat the unmistakable wrestling dance—quick, light and gay, and it came floating on the wind.

Okonkwo cleared his throat and moved his feet to the beat of the drums. It filled him with fire as it had always done from his youth. He trembled with the desire to conquer and subdue. It was like the desire for woman.

"We shall be late for the wrestling," said Ezinma to her mother.

"They will not begin until the sun goes down."

"But they are beating the drums."

"Yes. The drums begin at noon but the wrestling waits until the sun begins to sink. Go and see if your father has brought out yams for the afternoon."

"He has. Nwoye's mother is already cooking."

"Go and bring our own, then. We must cook quickly or we shall be late for the wrestling."

Ezinma ran in the direction of the barn and brought back two yams from the dwarf wall.

Ekwefi peeled the yams quickly. The troublesome nanny-goat sniffed about, eating the peelings. She cut the yams into small pieces and began to prepare a pottage, using some of the chicken.

At that moment they heard someone crying just outside their compound. It was very much like Obiageli, Nwoye's sister.

"Is that not Obiageli weeping?" Ekwefi called across the yard to Nwoye's mother.

"Yes," she replied. "She must have broken her water-pot."

The weeping was now quite close and soon the children filed in, carrying on their heads various sizes of pots suitable to their years. Ikemefuna came first with the biggest pot, closely followed by Nwoye and his two younger brothers. Obiageli brought up the rear, her face streaming with tears. In her hand was the cloth pad on which the pot should have rested on her head.

"What happened?" her mother asked, and Obiageli told her mournful story. Her mother consoled her and promised to buy her another pot.

Nwoye's younger brothers were about to tell their mother the true story of the accident when Ikemefuna looked at them sternly and they held their peace. The fact was that Obiageli had been making *inyanga* with her pot. She had balanced it on her head, folded her arms in front of her and began to sway her waist like a grown-up young lady. When the pot fell down and broke she burst out laughing. She only began to weep when they got near the iroko tree outside their compound.

The drums were still beating, persistent and unchanging. Their sound was no longer a separate thing from the living village. It was like the pulsation of its heart. It throbbed in the air, in the sunshine, and even in the trees, and filled the village with excitement.

Ekwefi ladled her husband's share of the pottage into a bowl and covered it. Ezinma took it to him in his *obi*.

Okonkwo was sitting on a goatskin already eating his first wife's meal. Obiageli, who had brought it from her mother's hut, sat on the floor waiting for him to finish. Ezinma placed her mother's dish before him and sat with Obiageli.

"Sit like a woman!" Okonkwo shouted at her. Ezinma brought her two legs together and stretched them in front of her.

"Father, will you go to see the wrestling?" Ezinma asked after a suitable interval.

"Yes," he answered. "Will you go?"

"Yes." And after a pause she said: "Can I bring your chair for you?"

"No, that is a boy's job." Okonkwo was specially fond of Ezinma. She looked very much like her mother, who was once the village beauty. But his fondness only showed on very rare occasions.

"Obiageli broke her pot today," Ezinma said.

"Yes, she has told me about it," Okonkwo said between mouthfuls.

"Father," said Obiageli, "people should not talk when they are eating or pepper may go down the wrong way."

"That is very true. Do you hear that, Ezinma? You are older than Obiageli but she has more sense."

He uncovered his second wife's dish and began to eat from it. Obiageli took the first dish and returned to her mother's hut. And then Nkechi came in, bringing the third dish. Nkechi was the daughter of Okonkwo's third wife.

In the distance the drums continued to beat.

Chapter 6

The whole village turned out on the *ilo*, men, women and children. They stood round in a huge circle leaving the centre of the playground free. The elders and grandees of the village sat on their own stools brought there by their young sons or slaves. Okonkwo was among them. All others stood except those who came early enough to secure places on the few stands which had been built by placing smooth logs on forked pillars.

The wrestlers were not there yet and the drummers held the field. They too sat just in front of the huge circle of spectators, facing the elders. Behind them was the big and ancient silk-cotton tree which was sacred. Spirits of good children lived in that tree waiting to be born. On ordinary days young women who desired children came to sit under its shade.

There were seven drums and they were arranged according to their sizes in a long wooden basket. Three men beat them with sticks, working feverishly from one drum to another. They were possessed by the spirit of the drums.

The young men who kept order on these occasions dashed about, consulting among themselves and with the leaders of the two wrestling teams, who were still outside the circle, behind the crowd. Once in a while two young men carrying palm fronds ran round the circle and kept the crowd back by beating the ground in front of them or, if they were stubborn, their legs and feet.

At last the two teams danced into the circle and the crowd roared and clapped. The drums rose to a frenzy. The people surged forwards. The young men who kept order flew around, waving their palm fronds. Old men nodded to the beat of the drums and remembered the days when they wrestled to its intoxicating rhythm.

The contest began with boys of fifteen or sixteen. There were only three such boys in each team. They were not the real wrestlers; they merely set the scene. Within a short time the first two bouts were over. But the third created a big sensation even among the elders who did not usually show their excitement so openly. It was as quick as the other two, perhaps even quicker. But very few people had ever seen that kind of wrestling before. As soon as the two boys closed in, one of them did something which no one could describe because it had been as quick as a flash. And the other boy was flat on his back. The crowd roared and clapped and for a while drowned the frenzied drums. Okonkwo sprang to his feet and quickly sat down again. Three young men from the victorious boy's team ran forward, carried him shoulder-high and danced through the cheering crowd. Everybody soon knew who the boy was. His name was Maduka, the son of Obierika.

The drummers stopped for a brief rest before the real matches. Their bodies shone with sweat, and they took up fans and began to fan themselves. They also drank water from small pots and ate kola nuts. They became ordinary human beings again, talking and laughing among themselves and with others who stood near them. The air, which had been stretched taut with excitement, relaxed again. It was as if water had been poured on the tightened skin of a drum. Many people looked around, perhaps for the first time, and saw those who stood or sat next to them.

"I did not know it was you," Ekwefi said to the woman who had stood shoulder to shoulder with her since the beginning of the matches.

"I do not blame you," said the woman. "I have never seen such a large crowd of people. Is it true that Okonkwo nearly killed you with his gun?"

"It is true indeed, my dear friend. I cannot yet find a mouth with which to tell the story."

"Your *chi* is very much awake, my friend. And how is my daughter, Ezinma?"

"She has been very well for some time now. Perhaps she has come to stay."

"I think she has. How old is she now?"

"She is about ten years old."

"I think she will stay. They usually stay if they do not die before the age of six."

"I pray she stays," said Ekwefi with a heavy sigh.

The woman with whom she talked was called Chielo. She was the priestess of Agbala, the Oracle of the Hills and the Caves. In ordinary life Chielo was a widow with two children. She was very friendly with Ekwefi and they shared a common shed in the market. She was particularly fond of Ekwefi's only daughter, Ezinma, whom she called "my daughter." Quite often she bought bean-cakes and gave Ekwefi some to take home to Ezinma. Anyone seeing Chielo in ordinary life would hardly believe she was the same person who prophesied when the spirit of Agbala was upon her.

The drummers took up their sticks again and the air shivered and grew tense like a tightened bow.

The two teams were ranged facing each other across the clear space. A young man from one team danced across the centre to the other side and pointed at whomever he wanted to fight. They danced back to the centre together and then closed in.

There were twelve men on each side and the challenge went from one side to the other. Two judges walked around the wrestlers and when they thought they were equally matched, stopped them. Five matches ended in this way. But the really exciting moments were when a man was thrown. The huge voice of the crowd then rose to the sky and in every direction. It was even heard in the surrounding villages.

The last match was between the leaders of the teams. They were among the best wrestlers in all the nine villages. The crowd wondered who would throw the other this year. Some said Okafo was the better man; others said he was not the equal of Ikezue. Last year neither of them had thrown the other even though the judges had allowed the contest to go on longer than was the custom. They had the same style and one saw the other's plans beforehand. It might happen again this year.

Dusk was already approaching when their contest began. The drums went mad and the crowds also. They surged forward as the two young men danced into the circle. The palm fronds were helpless in keeping them back.

Ikezue held out his right hand. Okafo seized it, and they closed in. It was a fierce contest. Ikezue strove to dig in his right heel behind Okafo so as to pitch him backwards in the clever *ege* style. But the one knew what the other was thinking. The crowd had surrounded and swallowed up the drummers, whose frantic rhythm was no longer a mere disembodied sound but the very heart-beat of the people.

The wrestlers were now almost still in each other's grip. The muscles on their arms and their thighs and on their backs stood out and twitched. It looked like an equal match. The two judges were already moving forward to separate them when Ikezue, now desperate, went down quickly on one knee in an attempt to fling his man backwards over his head. It was a sad miscalculation. Quick as the lightning of Amadiora, Okafo raised his right leg and swung it over his rival's head. The crowd burst into a thunderous roar. Okafo was swept off his feet by his supporters and carried home shoulder-high. They sang his praise and the young women clapped their hands:

> *Who will wrestle for our village?*
> *Okafo will wrestle for our village.*
> *Has he thrown a hundred men?*
> *He has thrown four hundred men.*
> *Has he thrown a hundred Cats?*
> *He has thrown four hundred Cats.*
> *Then send him word to fight for us.*

Chapter 7

For three years Ikemefuna lived in Okonkwo's household and the elders of Umuofia seemed to have forgotten about him. He grew rapidly like a yam tendril in the rainy season, and was full of the sap of life. He had become wholly absorbed into his new family. He was like an elder brother to Nwoye, and from the very first seemed to have kindled a new fire in the younger boy. He made him feel grown-up; and they no longer spent the evenings in mother's hut while she cooked, but now sat with Okonkwo in his *obi,* or watched him as he tapped his palm tree for the evening wine. Nothing pleased Nwoye now more than to be sent for by his mother or another of his father's wives to do one of those difficult and masculine tasks in the home, like splitting wood, or pounding food. On receiving such a message through a younger brother or sister, Nwoye would feign annoyance and grumble aloud about women and their troubles.

Okonkwo was inwardly pleased at his son's development, and he knew it was due to Ikemefuna. He wanted Nwoye to grow into a tough young man capable of ruling his father's household when he was dead and gone to join the ancestors. He wanted him to be a prosperous man, having enough in his barn to feed the ancestors with regular sacrifices. And so he was always happy when he heard him grumbling about women. That showed that in time he would be able to control his women-folk. No matter how prosperous a man was, if he was unable to rule his women and his children (and especially his women) he was not really a man. He was like the man in the song who had ten and one wives and not enough soup for his foo-foo.

So Okonkwo encouraged the boys to sit with him in his *obi,* and he told them stories of the land—masculine stories of violence and bloodshed. Nwoye knew that it was right to be masculine and to be violent, but somehow he still preferred the stories that his mother used to tell, and which she no doubt still told to her younger children—stories of the tortoise and his wily ways, and of the bird *eneke-nti-oba* who challenged the whole world to a wrestling contest and was finally thrown by the cat. He remembered the story she often told of the quarrel between Earth and Sky long ago, and how Sky withheld rain for seven years, until crops withered and the dead could not be buried because the hoes broke on the stony Earth. At last Vulture was sent to plead with Sky, and to soften his heart with a song of the suffering of the sons of men. Whenever Nwoye's mother sang this song he felt carried away to the distant scene in the sky where Vulture, Earth's emissary, sang for mercy. At last Sky was moved to pity, and he gave to Vulture rain wrapped in leaves of coco-yam. But as he flew home his long talon pierced the leaves and the rain fell as it had never fallen before. And so heavily did it rain on Vulture that he did not return to deliver his message but flew to a distant land, from where he had espied a fire. And when he got there he found it was a man making a sacrifice. He warmed himself in the fire and ate the entrails.

That was the kind of story that Nwoye loved. But he now knew that they were for foolish women and children, and he knew that his father wanted him to be a man. And so he feigned that he no longer cared for women's stories. And when he did this he saw that his father was pleased, and no longer rebuked him or beat him. So Nwoye and Ikemefuna would listen to Okonkwo's stories about tribal wars or how, years ago, he had stalked his victim, overpowered him and obtained his first human head. And as he told them of the past they sat in darkness or the dim glow of logs, waiting for the women to finish their cooking. When they finished, each brought her bowl of foo-foo and bowl of soup to her husband. An oil lamp was lit and Okonkwo tasted from each bowl, and then passed two shares to Nwoye and Ikemefuna.

In this way the moons and the seasons passed. And then the locusts came. It had not happened for many a long year. The elders said locusts came once in a generation, reappeared every year for seven years and then disappeared for another lifetime. They went back to their caves in a distant land, where they were guarded by a race of stunted men. And then after another lifetime these men opened the caves again and the locusts came to Umuofia.

They came in the cold harmattan season after the harvests had been gathered, and ate up all the wild grass in the fields.

Okonkwo and the two boys were working on the red outer walls of the compound. This was one of the lighter tasks of the after-harvest season. A new cover of thick palm branches and palm leaves was set on the walls to protect them from the next rainy season. Okonkwo worked on the outside of the wall and the boys worked from within. There were little holes from one side to the other in the upper levels of the wall, and through these Okonkwo passed the rope, or *tie-tie,* to the boys and they passed it round the wooden stays and then back to him; and in this way the cover was strengthened on the wall.

The women had gone to the bush to collect firewood, and the little children to visit their playmates in the neighbouring compounds. The harmattan was in the air and seemed to distil a hazy feeling of sleep on the world. Okonkwo and the boys worked in complete silence, which was only broken when a new palm frond was lifted on to the wall or when a busy hen moved dry leaves about in her ceaseless search for food.

And then quite suddenly a shadow fell on the world, and the sun seemed hidden behind a thick cloud. Okonkwo looked up from his work and wondered if it was going to rain at such an unlikely time of the year. But almost immediately a shout of joy broke out in all directions, and Umuofia, which had dozed in the noon-day haze, broke into life and activity.

"Locusts are descending," was joyfully chanted everywhere, and men, women and children left their work or their play and ran into the open to see the unfamiliar sight. The locusts had not come for many, many years, and only the old people had seen them before.

At first, a fairly small swarm came. They were the harbingers sent to survey the land. And then appeared on the horizon a slowly-moving mass like a boundless sheet of black cloud drifting towards Umuofia. Soon it covered half the sky, and the solid mass was now broken by tiny eyes of light like shining star-dust. It was a tremendous sight, full of power and beauty.

Everyone was now about, talking excitedly and praying that the locusts should camp in Umuofia for the night. For although locusts had not visited Umuofia for many years, everybody knew by instinct that they were very good to eat. And at last the locusts did descend. They settled on every tree and on every blade of grass; they settled on the roofs and covered the bare ground. Mighty tree branches broke away under them, and the whole country became the brown-earth colour of the vast, hungry swarm.

Many people went out with baskets trying to catch them, but the elders counselled patience till nightfall. And they were right. The locusts settled in the bushes for the night and their wings became wet with dew. Then all Umuofia turned out in spite of the cold harmattan, and everyone filled his bags and pots with locusts. The next morning they were roasted in clay pots and then spread in the sun until they became dry and brittle. And for many days this rare food was eaten with solid palm-oil.

Okonkwo sat in his *obi* crunching happily with Ikemefuna and Nwoye, and drinking palm-wine copiously, when Ogbuefi Ezeudu came in. Ezeudu was the oldest man in this quarter of Umuofia. He had been a great and fearless warrior in his time, and was now accorded great respect in all the clan. He refused to join in the meal, and asked Okonkwo to have a word with him outside. And so they walked out together, the old man supporting himself with his stick. When they were out of ear-shot, he said to Okonkwo:

"That boy calls you father. Do not bear a hand in his death." Okonkwo was surprised, and was about to say something when the old man continued:

"Yes, Umuofia has decided to kill him. The Oracle of the Hills and the Caves has pronounced it. They will take him outside Umuofia as is the custom, and kill him there. But I want you to have nothing to do with it. He calls you his father."

The next day a group of elders from all the nine villages of Umuofia came to Okonkwo's house early in the morning, and before they began to speak in low tones Nwoye and Ikemefuna were sent out. They did not stay very long, but when they went away Okonkwo sat still for a very long time supporting his chin in his palms. Later in the day he called Ikemefuna and told him that he was to be taken home the next day. Nwoye overheard it and burst into tears, whereupon his father beat him heavily. As for Ikemefuna, he was at a loss. His own home had gradually become very faint and distant. He still missed his mother and his sister and would be very glad to see them. But somehow he knew he was not going to see them. He remembered once when men had talked in low tones with his father; and it seemed now as if it was happening all over again.

Later, Nwoye went to his mother's hut and told her that Ikemufuna was going home. She immediately dropped the pestle with which she was grinding pepper, folded her arms across her breast and sighed, "Poor child."

The next day, the men returned with a pot of wine. They were all fully dressed as if they were going to a big clan meeting or to pay a visit to a neighbouring village. They passed their cloths under the right arm-pit, and hung their goatskin bags and sheathed matchets over their left shoulders. Okonkwo got ready quickly and the party set out with Ikemefuna carrying the pot of wine. A deathly silence descended on Okonkwo's compound. Even the very little children seemed to know. Throughout that day Nwoye sat in his mother's hut and tears stood in his eyes.

At the beginning of their journey the men of Umuofia talked and laughed about the locusts, about their women, and about some effeminate men who had refused to come with them. But as they drew near to the outskirts of Umuofia silence fell upon them too.

The sun rose slowly to the centre of the sky, and the dry, sandy footway began to throw up the heat that lay buried in it. Some birds chirruped in the forests around. The men trod dry leaves on the sand. All else was silent. Then from the distance came the faint beating of the *ekwe*. It rose and faded with the wind—a peaceful dance from a distant clan.

"It is an *ozo* dance," the men said among themselves. But no one was sure where it was coming from. Some said Ezimili, others Abame or Aninta. They argued for a short while and fell into silence again, and the elusive dance rose and fell with the wind. Somewhere a man was taking one of the titles of his clan, with music and dancing and a great feast.

The footway had now become a narrow line in the heart of the forest. The short trees and sparse undergrowth which surrounded the men's village began to give way to giant trees and climbers which perhaps had stood from the beginning of things, untouched by the axe and the bush-fire. The sun breaking through their leaves and branches threw a pattern of light and shade on the sandy footway.

Ikemefuna heard a whisper close behind him and turned round sharply. The man who had whispered now called out aloud, urging the others to hurry up.

"We still have a long way to go," he said. Then he and another man went before Ikemefuna and set a faster pace.

Thus the men of Umuofia pursued their way, armed with sheathed matchets, and Ikemefuna, carrying a pot of palm-wine on his head, walked in their midst. Although he had felt uneasy at first, he was not afraid now. Okonkwo walked behind him. He could hardly imagine that Okonkwo was not his real father. He had never been fond of his real father, and at the end of three years he had become very distant indeed. But his mother and his three-year-old sister . . . of course she would not be three now, but six. Would he recognize her now? She must have grown quite big. How his mother would weep for joy, and thank Okonkwo for having looked after him so well and for bringing him back. She would want to hear everything that had happened to him in all these years. Could he remember them all? He would tell her about Nwoye and his mother, and about the locusts . . . Then quite suddenly a thought came upon him. His mother might be dead. He tried in vain to force the thought out of his mind. Then he tried to settle the matter the way he used to settle such matters when he was a little boy. He still remembered the song:

> Eze elina, elina!
> Sala
> Eze ilikwa ya
> Ikwaba akwa oligholi
> Ebe Danda nechi eze
> Ebe Uzuzu nete egwu
> Sala

He sang it in his mind, and walked to its beat. If the song ended on his right foot, his mother was alive. If it ended on his left, she was dead. No, not dead, but ill. It ended on the right. She was alive and well. He sang the song again, and it ended on the left. But the second time did not count. The first voice gets to Chukwu, or God's house. That was a favourite saying of children. Ikemefuna felt like a child once more. It must be the thought of going home to his mother.

One of the men behind him cleared his throat. Ikemefuna looked back, and the man growled at him to go on and not stand looking back. The way he said it sent cold fear down Ikemefuna's back. His hands trembled vaguely on the black pot he carried. Why had Okonkwo withdrawn to the rear? Ikemefuna felt his legs melting under him. And he was afraid to look back.

As the man who had cleared his throat drew up and raised his matchet, Okonkwo looked away. He heard the blow. The pot fell and broke in the sand. He heard Ikemefuna cry, "My father, they have killed me!" as he ran towards him. Dazed with fear, Okonkwo drew his matchet and cut him down. He was afraid of being thought weak.

As soon as his father walked in, that night, Nwoye knew that Ikemefuna had been killed, and something seemed to give way inside him, like the snapping of a tightened bow. He did not cry. He just hung limp. He had had the same kind of feeling not long ago, during the last harvest season. Every child loved the harvest season. Those who were big enough to carry even a few yams in a tiny basket went with grown-ups to the farm. And if they could not help in digging up the yams, they could gather firewood together for roasting the ones that would be eaten there on the farm. This roasted yam soaked in red palm-oil and eaten in the open farm was sweeter than any meal at home. It was after such a day at the farm during the last harvest that Nwoye had felt for the first time a snapping inside him like the one he now felt. They were returning home with baskets of yams from a distant farm across the stream when they had heard the voice of an infant crying in the thick forest. A sudden hush had fallen on the women, who had been talking, and they had quickened their steps. Nwoye had heard that twins were put in earthenware pots and thrown away in the forest, but he had never yet come across them. A vague chill had descended on him and his head had seemed to swell, like a solitary walker at night who passes an evil spirit on the way. Then something had given way inside him. It descended on him again, this feeling, when his father walked in, that night after killing Ikemefuna.

Chapter 8

Okonkwo did not taste any food for two days after the death of Ikemefuna. He drank palm-wine from morning till night, and his eyes were red and fierce like the eyes of a rat when it was caught by the tail and dashed against the floor. He called his son, Nwoye, to sit with him in his *obi*. But the boy was afraid of him and slipped out of the hut as soon as he noticed him dozing.

He did not sleep at night. He tried not to think about Ikemefuna, but the more he tried the more he thought about him. Once he got up from bed and walked about his compound. But he was so weak that his legs could hardly carry him. He felt like a drunken giant walking with the limbs of a mosquito. Now and then a cold shiver descended on his head and spread down his body.

On the third day he asked his second wife, Ekwefi, to roast some plantains for him. She prepared them the way he liked—with slices of oil-bean and fish.

"You have not eaten for two days," said his daughter Ezinma when she brought the food to him. "So you must finish this." She sat down and stretched her legs in front of her. Okonkwo ate the food absentmindedly. "She should have been a boy," he thought as he looked at his ten-year-old daughter. He passed her a piece of fish.

"Go and bring me some cold water," he said. Ezinma rushed out of the hut, chewing the fish, and soon returned with a bowl of cool water from the earthen pot in her mother's hut.

Okonkwo took the bowl from her and gulped the water down. He ate a few more pieces of plantain and pushed the dish aside.

"Bring me my bag," he asked, and Ezinma brought his goatskin bag from the far end of the hut. He searched in it for his snuff-bottle. It was a deep bag and took almost the whole length of his arm. It contained other things apart from his snuff-bottle. There was a drinking horn in it, and also a drinking gourd, and they knocked against each other as he searched. When he brought out the snuff-bottle he tapped it a few times against his knee-cap before taking out some snuff on the palm of his left hand. Then he remembered that he had not taken out his snuff-spoon. He searched his bag again and brought out a small, flat, ivory spoon, with which he carried the brown snuff to his nostrils.

Ezinma took the dish in one hand and the empty water bowl in the other and went back to her mother's hut. "She should have been a boy," Okonkwo said to himself again. His mind went back to Ikemefuna and he shivered. If only he could find some work to do he would be able to forget. But it was the season of rest between the harvest and the next planting season. The only work that men did at this time was covering the walls of their compound with new palm fronds. And Okonkwo had already done that. He had finished it on the very day the locusts came, when he had worked on one side of the wall and Ikemefuna and Nwoye on the other.

"When did you become a shivering old woman," Okonkwo asked himself, "you are known in all the nine villages for your valour in war. How can a man who has killed five men in battle fall to pieces because he has added a boy to their number? Okonkwo, you have become a woman indeed."

He sprang to his feet, hung his goatskin bag on his shoulder and went to visit his friend, Obierika.

Obierika was sitting outside under the shade of an orange tree making thatches from leaves of the raffia-palm. He exchanged greetings with Okonkwo and led the way into his *obi*.

"I was coming over to see you as soon as I finished that thatch," he said, rubbing off the grains of sand that clung to his thighs.

"Is it well?" Okonkwo asked.

"Yes," replied Obierika. "My daughter's suitor is coming today and I hope we will clinch the matter of the bride-price. I want you to be there."

Just then Obierika's son, Maduka, came into the *obi* from outside, greeted Okonkwo and turned towards the compound.

"Come and shake hands with me," Okonkwo said to the lad. "Your wrestling the other day gave me much happiness." The boy smiled, shock hands with Okonkwo and went into the compound.

"He will do great things," Okonkwo said. "If I had a son like him I should be happy. I am worried about Nwoye. A bowl of pounded yams can throw him in a wrestling match. His two younger brothers are more promising. But I can tell you, Obierika, that my children do not resemble me. Where are the young suckers that will grow when the old banana tree dies? If Ezinma had been a boy I would have been happier. She has the right spirit."

"You worry yourself for nothing," said Obierika. "The children are still very young."

"Nwoye is old enough to impregnate a woman. At his age I was already fending for myself. No, my friend, he is not too young. A chick that will grow into a cock can be spotted the very day it hatches. I have done my best to make Nwoye grow into a man, but there is too much of his mother in him."

"Too much of his grandfather," Obierika thought, but he did not say it. The same thought also came to Okonkwo's mind. But he had long learnt how to lay that ghost. Whenever the thought of his father's weakness and failure troubled him he expelled it by thinking about his own strength and success. And so he did now. His mind went to his latest show of manliness.

"I cannot understand why you refused to come with us to kill that boy," he asked Obierika.

"Because I did not want to," Obierika replied sharply. "I had something better to do."

"You sound as if you question the authority and the decision of the Oracle, who said he should die."

"I do not. Why should I? But the Oracle did not ask me to carry out its decision."

"But someone had to do it. If we were all afraid of blood, it would not be done. And what do you think the Oracle would do then?"

"You know very well, Okonkwo, that I am not afraid of blood; and if anyone tells you that I am, he is telling a lie. And let me tell you one thing, my friend. If I were you I would have stayed at home. What you have done will not please the Earth. It is the kind of action for which the goddess wipes out whole families."

"The Earth cannot punish me for obeying her messenger," Okonkwo said. "A child's fingers are not scalded by a piece of hot yam which its mother puts into its palm." "That is true," Obierika agreed. "But if the Oracle said that my son should be killed I would neither dispute it nor be the one to do it."

They would have gone on arguing had Ofoedu not come in just then. It was clear from his twinkling eyes that he had important news. But it would be impolite to rush him. Obierika offered him a lobe of the kola nut he had broken with Okonkwo. Ofoedu ate slowly and talked about the locusts. When he finished his kola nut he said: "The things that happen these days are very strange."

"What has happened?" asked Okonkwo.

"Do you know Ogbuefi Ndulue?" Ofoedu asked.

"Ogbuefi Ndulue of Ire village," Okonkwo and Obierika said together.

"He died this morning," said Ofoedu.

"That is not strange. He was the oldest man in Ire," said Obierika.

"You are right," Ofoedu agreed. "But you ought to ask why the drum has not been beaten to tell Umuofia of his death."

"Why?" asked Obierika and Okonkwo together.

"That is the strange part of it. You know his first wife who walks with a stick?"

"Yes. She is called Ozoemena."

"That is so," said Ofoedu. "Ozoemena was, as you know, too old to attend Ndulue during his illness. His younger wives did that. When he died this morning, one of these women went to Ozoemena's hut and told her. She rose from her mat, took her stick and walked over to the *obi*. She knelt on her knees and hands at the threshold and called her husband, who was laid on a mat. "Ogbuefi Ndulue," she called, three times, and went back to her hut. When the youngest wife went to call her again to be present at the washing of the body, she found her lying on the mat, dead."

"That is very strange indeed," said Okonkwo. "They will put off Ndulue's funeral until his wife has been buried."

"That is why the drum has not been beaten to tell Umuofia."

"It was always said that Ndulue and Ozoemena had one mind," said Obierika. "I remember when I was a young boy there was a song about them. He could not do anything without telling her."

"I did not know that," said Okonkwo. "I thought he was a strong man in his youth."

"He was indeed," said Ofoedu.

Okonkwo shook his head doubtfully.

"He led Umuofia to war in those days," said Obierika.

Okonkwo was beginning to feel like his old self again. All that he required was something to occupy his mind. If he had killed Ikemefuna during the busy planting season or harvesting it would not have been so bad; his mind would have been centred on his work. Okonkwo was not a man of thought but of action. But in the absence of work, talking was the next best.

Soon after Ofoedu left, Okonkwo took up his goatskin bag to go.

"I must go home to tap my palm trees for the afternoon," he said.

"Who taps your tall trees for you?" asked Obierika.

"Umezulike," replied Okonkwo.

"Sometimes I wish I had not taken the *ozo* title," said Obierika. "It wounds my heart to see these young men killing palm trees in the name of tapping."

"It is so indeed," Okonkwo agreed. "But the law of the land must be obeyed."

"I don't know how we got that law," said Obierika. "In many other clans a man of title is not forbidden to climb the palm tree. Here we say he cannot climb the tall tree but he can tap the short ones standing on the ground. It is like Dimaragana, who would not lend his knife for cutting up dog-meat because the dog was taboo to him, but offered to use his teeth."

"I think it is good that our clan holds the *ozo* title in high esteem," said Okonkwo. "In those other clans you speak of, *ozo* is so low that every beggar takes it."

"I was only speaking in jest," said Obierika. "In Abame and Aninta the title is worth less than two cowries. Every man wears the thread of title on his ankle, and does not lose it even if he steals."

"They have indeed soiled the name of *ozo,*" said Okonkwo as he rose to go.

"It will not be very long now before my in-laws come," said Obierika.

"I shall return very soon," said Okonkwo, looking at the position of the sun.

There were seven men in Obierika's hut when Okonkwo returned. The suitor was a young man of about twenty-five, and with him were his father and uncle. On Obierika's side were his two elder brothers and Maduka, his sixteen-year-old son.

"Ask Akueke's mother to send us some kola nuts," said Obierika to his son. Maduka vanished into the compound like lightning. The conversation at once centred on him, and everybody agreed that he was as sharp as a razor.

"I sometimes think he is too sharp," said Obierika, somewhat indulgently. "He hardly ever walks. He is always in a hurry. If you are sending him on an errand he flies away before he has heard half of the message."

"You were very much like that yourself," said his eldest brother. "As our people say, 'When mother-cow is chewing grass its young ones watch its mouth.' Maduka has been watching your mouth."

As he was speaking the boy returned, followed by Akueke, his half-sister, carrying a wooden dish with three kola nuts and alligator pepper. She gave the dish to her father's eldest brother and then shook hands, very shyly, with her suitor and his relatives. She was about sixteen and just ripe for marriage. Her suitor and his relatives surveyed her young body with expert eyes as if to assure themselves that she was beautiful and ripe.

She wore a coiffure which was done up into a crest in the middle of the head. Cam wood was rubbed lightly into her skin, and all over her body were black patterns drawn with *uli.* She wore a black necklace which hung down in three coils just above her full, succulent breasts. On her arms were red and yellow bangles, and on her waist four or five rows of *jigida,* or waist-beads.

When she had shaken hands, or rather held out her hand to be shaken, she returned to her mother's hut to help with the cooking.

"Remove your *jigida* first," her mother warned as she moved near the fireplace to bring the pestle resting against the wall. "Every day I tell you that *jigida* and fire are not friends. But you will never hear. You grew your ears for decoration, not for hearing. One of these days your *jigida* will catch fire on your waist, and then you will know."

Akueke moved to the other end of the hut and began to remove the waist-beads. It had to be done slowly and carefully, taking each string separately, else it would break and the thousand tiny rings would have to be strung together again. She rubbed each string downwards with her palms until it passed the buttocks and slipped down to the floor around her feet.

The men in the *obi* had already begun to drink the palm-wine which Akueke's suitor had brought. It was a very good wine and powerful, for in spite of the palm fruit hung across the mouth of the pot to restrain the lively liquor, white foam rose and spilled over.

"That wine is the work of a good tapper," said Okonkwo.

The young suitor, whose name was Ibe, smiled broadly and said to his father: "Do you hear that?" He then said to the others: "He will never admit that I am a good tapper."

"He tapped three of my best palm trees to death," said his father, Ukegbu.

"That was about five years ago," said Ibe, who had begun to pour out the wine, "before I learnt how to tap." He filled the first horn and gave it to his father. Then he poured out for the others. Okonkwo brought out his big horn from the goatskin bag, blew into it to remove any dust that might be there, and gave it to Ibe to fill.

As the men drank, they talked about everything except the thing for which they had gathered. It was only after the pot had been emptied that the suitor's father cleared his voice and announced the object of their visit.

Obierika then presented to him a small bundle of short broomsticks. Ukegbu counted them.

"They are thirty?" he asked.

Obierika nodded in agreement.

"We are at last getting somewhere," Ukegbu said, and then turning to his brother and his son he said: "Let us go out and whisper together." The three rose and went outside. When they returned Ukegbu handed the bundle of sticks back to Obierika. He counted them; instead of thirty there were now only fifteen. He passed them over to his eldest brother, Machi, who also counted them and said:

"We had not thought to go below thirty. But as the dog said, 'If I fall down for you and you fall down for me, it is play.' Marriage should be a play and not a fight; so we are falling down again." He then added ten sticks to the fifteen and gave the bundle to Ukegbu.

In this way Akueke's bride-price was finally settled at twenty bags of cowries. It was already dusk when the two parties came to this agreement.

"Go and tell Akueke's mother that we have finished," Obierika said to his son, Maduka. Almost immediately the woman came in with a big bowl of foo-foo. Obierika's second wife followed with a pot of soup, and Maduka brought in a pot of palm-wine.

As the men ate and drank palm-wine they talked about the customs of their neighbours.

"It was only this morning," said Obierika, "that Okonkwo and I were talking about Abame and Aninta, where titled men climb trees and pound foo-foo for their wives."

"All their customs are upside-down. They do not decide bride-price as we do, with sticks. They haggle and bargain as if they were buying a goat or a cow in the market."

"That is very bad," said Obierika's eldest brother. "But what is good in one place is bad in another place. In Umunso they do not bargain at all, not even with broomsticks. The suitor just goes on bringing bags of cowries until his in-laws tell him to stop. It is a bad custom because it always leads to a quarrel."

"The world is large," said Okonkwo. "I have even heard that in some tribes a man's children belong to his wife and her family."

"That cannot be," said Machi. "You might as well say that the woman lies on top of the man when they are making the children."

"It is like the story of white men who, they say, are white like this piece of chalk," said Obierika. He held up a piece of chalk, which every man kept in his *obi* and with which his guests drew lines on the floor before they ate kola nuts. "And these white men, they say, have no toes."[2]

"And have you never seen them?" asked Machi.

"Have you?" asked Obierika.

"One of them passes here frequently," said Machi. "His name is Amadi."

Those who knew Amadi laughed. He was a leper, and the polite name for leprosy was "the white skin."

Chapter 9

For the first time in three nights, Okonkwo slept. He woke up once in the middle of the night and his mind went back to the past three days without making him feel uneasy. He began to wonder why he had felt uneasy at all. It was like a man wondering in broad day-light why a dream had appeared so terrible to him at night. He stretched himself and scratched his thigh where a mosquito had bitten him as he slept. Another one was wailing near his right ear. He slapped the ear and hoped he had killed it. Why do they always go for one's ears? When he was a child his mother had told him a story about it. But it was as silly as all women's stories. Mosquito, she had said, had asked Ear to marry him, whereupon Ear fell on the floor in uncontrollable laughter. "How much longer do you think you will live?" she asked. "You are already a skeleton." Mosquito went away humiliated, and any time he passed her way he told Ear that he was still alive.

Okonkwo turned on his side and went back to sleep. He was roused in the morning by someone banging on his door.

"Who is that?" he growled. He knew it must be Ekwefi. Of his three wives Ekwefi was the only one who would have the audacity to bang on his door.

"Ezinma is dying," came her voice, and all the tragedy and sorrow of her life were packed in those words.

Okonkwo sprang from his bed, pushed back the bolt on his door and ran into Ekwefi's hut.

Ezinma lay shivering on a mat beside a huge fire that her mother had kept burning all night.

"It is *iba*," said Okonkwo as he took his matchet and went into the bush to collect the leaves and grasses and barks of trees that went into making the medicine for *iba*.

Ekwefi knelt beside the sick child, occasionally feeling with her palm the wet, burning forehead.

Ezinma was an only child and the centre of her mother's world. Very often it was Ezinma who had decided what food her mother should prepare. Ekwefi even gave her such delicacies as eggs, which children were rarely allowed to eat because such food tempted them to steal. One day as Ezinma was eating an egg Okonkwo had come in unexpectedly from his hut. He was greatly shocked and swore to beat Ekwefi if she dared to give the child eggs again. But it was impossible to refuse Ezinma anything. After her father's rebuke she developed an even keener appetite for eggs. And she enjoyed above all the secrecy in which she now ate them. Her mother always took her into their bedroom and shut the door.

Ezinma did not call her mother *Nne* like all children. She called her by her name, Ekwefi, as her father and other grown-up people did. The relationship between them

2. Their feet are hidden in shoes.

was not only that of mother and child. There was something in it like the companionship of equals, which was strengthened by such little conspiracies as eating eggs in the bedroom.

Ekwefi had suffered a good deal in her life. She had borne ten children and nine of them had died in infancy; usually before the age of three. As she buried one child after another her sorrow gave way to despair and then to grim resignation. The birth of her children, which should be a woman's crowning glory, became for Ekwefi mere physical agony devoid of promise. The naming ceremony after seven market weeks became an empty ritual. Her deepening despair found expression in the names she gave her children. One of them was a pathetic cry, Onwumbiko—"Death, I implore you." But Death took no notice; Onwumbiko died in his fifteenth month. The next child was a girl, Ozoemena—"May it not happen again." She died in her eleventh month, and two others after her. Ekwefi then became defiant and called her next child Onwuma—"Death may please himself." And he did.

After the death of Ekwefi's second child, Okonkwo had gone to a medicine-man, who was also a diviner of the Afa Oracle, to inquire what was amiss. This man told him that the child was an *ogbanje,* one of those wicked children who, when they died, entered their mother's wombs to be born again.

"When your wife becomes pregnant again," he said, "let her not sleep in her hut. Let her go and stay with her people. In that way she will elude her wicked tormentor and break its evil cycle of birth and death."

Ekwefi did as she was asked. As soon as she became pregnant she went to live with her old mother in another village. It was there that her third child was born and circumcised on the eighth day. She did not return to Okonkwo's compound until three days before the naming ceremony. The child was called Onwumbiko.

Onwumbiko was not given proper burial when he died. Onkonkwo had called in another medicine-man who was famous in the clan for his great knowledge about *ogbanje* children. His name was Okagbue Uyanwa. Okagbue was a very striking figure, tall, with a full beard and a bald head. He was light in complexion and his eyes were red and fiery. He always gnashed his teeth as he listened to those who came to consult him. He asked Okonkwo a few questions about the dead child. All the neighbours and relations who had come to mourn gathered round them.

"On what market-day was it born?" he asked.

"*Oye,*" replied Okonkwo.

"And it died this morning?"

Okonkwo said yes, and only then realised for the first time that the child had died on the same market-day as it had been born. The neighbours and relations also saw the coincidence and said among themselves that it was very significant.

"Where do you sleep with your wife, in your *obi* or in her own hut?" asked the medicine-man.

"In her hut."

"In future call her into your *obi.*"

The medicine-man then ordered that there should be no mourning for the dead child. He brought out a sharp razor from the goatskin bag slung from his left shoulder and began to mutilate the child. Then he took it away to bury in the Evil Forest, holding it by the ankle and dragging it on the ground behind him. After such treatment it would think twice before coming again, unless it was one of the stubborn ones who returned, carrying the stamp of their mutilation—a missing finger or perhaps a dark line where the medicine-man's razor had cut them.

By the time Onwumbiko died Ekwefi had become a very bitter woman. Her husband's first wife had already had three sons, all strong and healthy. When she had borne her third son in succession, Okonkwo had slaughtered a goat for her, as was the custom. Ekwefi had nothing but good wishes for her. But she had grown so bitter about her own *chi* that she could not rejoice with others over their good fortune. And so, on the day that Nwoye's mother celebrated the birth of her three sons with feasting and music, Ekwefi was the only person in the happy company who went about with a cloud on her brow. Her husband's wife took this for malevolence, as husbands' wives were wont to. How could she know that Ekwefi's bitterness did not flow outwards to others but inwards into her own soul; that she did not blame others for their good fortune but her own evil *chi* who denied her any?

At last Ezinma was born, and although ailing she seemed determined to live. At first Ekwefi accepted her, as she had accepted others—with listless resignation. But when she lived on to her fourth, fifth and sixth years, love returned once more to her mother, and, with love, anxiety. She determined to nurse her child to health, and she put all her being into it. She was rewarded by occasional spells of health during which Ezinma bubbled with energy like fresh palm-wine. At such times she seemed beyond danger. But all of a sudden she would go down again. Everybody knew she was an *ogbanje*. These sudden bouts of sickness and health were typical of her kind. But she had lived so long that perhaps she had decided to stay. Some of them did become tired of their evil rounds of birth and death, or took pity on their mothers, and stayed. Ekwefi believed deep inside her that Ezinma had come to stay. She believed because it was that faith alone that gave her own life any kind of meaning. And this faith had been strengthened when a year or so ago a medicine-man had dug up Ezinma's *iyi-uwa*. Everyone knew then that she would live because her bond with the world of *ogbanje* had been broken. Ekwefi was reassured. But such was her anxiety for her daughter that she could not rid herself completely of her fear. And although she believed that the *iyi-uwa* which had been dug up was genuine, she could not ignore the fact that some really evil children sometimes misled people into digging up a specious one.

But Ezinma's *iyi-uwa* had looked real enough. It was a smooth pebble wrapped in a dirty rag. The man who dug it up was the same Okagbue who was famous in all the clan for his knowledge in these matters. Ezinma had not wanted to co-operate with him at first. But that was only to be expected. No *ogbanje* would yield her secrets easily, and most of them never did because they died too young—before they could be asked questions.

"Where did you bury your *iyi-uwa?*" she asked in return.

"You know where it is. You buried it in the ground somewhere so that you can die and return again to torment your mother."

Ezinma looked at her mother, whose eyes, sad and pleading, were fixed on her.

"Answer the question at once," roared Okonkwo, who stood beside her. All the family were there and some of the neighbours too.

"Leave her to me," the medicine-man told Okonkwo in a cool, confident voice. He turned again to Ezinma. "Where did you bury your *iyi-uwa?*"

"Where they bury children," she replied, and the quiet spectators murmured to themselves.

"Come along then and show me the spot," said the medicine-man.

The crowd set out with Ezinma leading the way and Okagbue following closely behind her. Okonkwo came next and Ekwefi followed him. When she came to the main road, Ezinma turned left as if she was going to the stream.

"But you said it was where they bury children?" asked the medicine-man.

"No," said Ezinma, whose feeling of importance was manifest in her sprightly walk. She sometimes broke into a run and stopped again suddenly. The crowd followed her silently. Women and children returning from the stream with pots of water on their heads wondered what was happening until they saw Okagbue and guessed that it must be something to do with *ogbanje*. And they all knew Ekwefi and her daughter very well.

When she got to the big udala tree Ezinma turned left into the bush, and the crowd followed her. Because of her size she made her way through trees and creepers more quickly than her followers. The bush was alive with the tread of feet on dry leaves and sticks and the moving aside of tree branches. Ezinma went deeper and deeper and the crowd went with her. Then she suddenly turned round and began to walk back to the road. Everybody stood to let her pass and then filed after her.

"If you bring us all this way for nothing I shall beat sense into you," Okonkwo threatened.

"I have told you to let her alone. I know how to deal with them," said Okagbue.

Ezinma led the way back to the road, looked left and right and turned right. And so they arrived home again.

"Where did you bury your *iyi-uwa*?" asked Okagbue when Ezinma finally stopped outside her father's *obi*. Okagbue's voice was unchanged. It was quiet and confident.

"It is near that orange tree," Ezinma said.

"And why did you not say so, you wicked daughter of Akalogoli?" Okonkwo swore furiously. The medicine-man ignored him.

"Come and show me the exact spot," he said quietly to Ezinma.

"It is here," she said when they got to the tree.

"Point at the spot with your finger," said Okagbue.

"It is here," said Ezinma touching the ground with her finger. Okonkwo stood by, rumbling like thunder in the rainy season.

"Bring me a hoe," said Okagbue.

When Ekwefi brought the hoe, he had already put aside his goatskin bag and his big cloth and was in his underwear, a long and thin strip of cloth wound round the waist like a belt and then passed between the legs to be fastened to the belt behind. He immediately set to work digging a pit where Ezinma had indicated. The neighbours sat around watching the pit becoming deeper and deeper. The dark top-soil soon gave way to the bright-red earth with which women scrubbed the floor and walls of huts. Okagbue worked tirelessly and in silence, his back shining with perspiration. Okonkwo stood by the pit. He asked Okagbue to come up and rest while he took a hand. But Okagbue said he was not tired yet.

Ekwefi went into her hut to cook yams. Her husband had brought out more yams than usual because the medicine-man had to be fed. Ezinma went with her and helped in preparing the vegetables.

"There is too much green vegetable," she said.

"Don't you see the pot is full of yams?" Ekwefi asked. "And you know how leaves become smaller after cooking."

"Yes," said Ezinma, "that was why the snake-lizard killed his mother."

"Very true," said Ekwefi.

"He gave his mother seven baskets of vegetables to cook and in the end there were only three. And so he killed her," said Ezinma.

"That is not the end of the story."

"Oho," said Ezinma, "I remember now. He brought another seven baskets and cooked them himself. And there were again only three. So he killed himself too."

Outside the *obi* Okagbue and Okonkwo were digging the pit to find where Ezinma had buried her *iyi-uwa*. Neighbours sat around, watching. The pit was now so deep that they no longer saw the digger. They only saw the red earth he threw up mounting higher and higher. Okonkwo's son, Nwoye, stood near the edge of the pit because he wanted to take in all that happened.

Okagbue had again taken over the digging from Okonkwo. He worked, as usual, in silence. The neigbours and Okonkwo's wives were now talking. The children had lost interest and were playing.

Suddenly Okagbue sprang to the surface with the agility of a leopard.

"It is very near now," he said. "I have felt it."

There was immediate excitement and those who were sitting jumped to their feet.

"Call your wife and child," he said to Okonkwo. But Ekwefi and Ezinma had heard the noise and run out to see what it was.

Okagbue went back into the pit, which was now surrounded by spectators. After a few more hoe-fuls of earth he struck the *iyi-uwa*. He raised it carefully with the hoe and threw it to the surface. Some women ran away in fear when it was thrown. But they soon returned and everyone was gazing at the rag from a reasonable distance. Okagbue emerged and without saying a word or even looking at the spectators he went to his goatskin bag, took out two leaves and began to chew them. When he had swallowed them, he took up the rag with his left hand and began to untie it. And then the smooth, shiny pebble fell out. He picked it up.

"Is this yours?" he asked Ezinma.

"Yes," she replied. All the women shouted with joy because Ekwefi's troubles were at last ended.

All this had happened more than a year ago and Ezinma had not been ill since. And then suddenly she had begun to shiver in the night. Ekwefi brought her to the fireplace, spread her mat on the floor and built a fire. But she had got worse and worse. As she knelt by her, feeling with her palm the wet, burning forehead, she prayed a thousand times. Although her husband's wives were saying that it was nothing more than *iba,* she did not hear them.

Okonkwo returned from the bush carrying on his left shoulder a large bundle of grasses and leaves, roots and barks of medicinal trees and shrubs. He went into Ekwefi's hut, put down his load and sat down.

"Get me a pot," he said, "and leave the child alone."

Ekwefi went to bring the pot and Okonkwo selected the best from his bundle, in their due proportion, and cut them up. He put them in the pot and Ekwefi poured in some water.

"Is that enough?" she asked when she had poured in about half of the water in the bowl.

"A little more . . . I said a *little.* Are you deaf?" Okonkwo roared at her.

She set the pot on the fire and Okonkwo took up his matchet to return to his *obi*.

"You must watch the pot carefully," he said as he went, "and don't allow it to boil over. If it does its power will be gone." He went away to his hut and Ekwefi began to tend the medicine pot almost as if it was itself a sick child. Her eyes went constantly from Ezinma to the boiling pot and back to Ezinma.

Okonkwo returned when he felt the medicine had cooked long enough. He looked it over and said it was done.

"Bring a low stool for Ezinma," he said, "and a thick mat."

He took down the pot from the fire and placed it in front of the stool. He then roused Ezinma and placed her on the stool, astride the steaming pot. The thick mat was thrown over both. Ezinma struggled to escape from the choking and overpowering steam, but she was held down. She started to cry.

When the mat was at last removed she was drenched in perspiration. Ekwefi mopped her with a piece of cloth and she lay down on a dry mat and was soon asleep.

Chapter 10

Large crowds began to gather on the village *ilo* as soon as the edge had worn off the sun's heat and it was no longer painful on the body. Most communal ceremonies took place at that time of the day, so that even when it was said that a ceremony would begin "after the midday meal" everyone understood that it would begin a long time later, when the sun's heat had softened.

It was clear from the way the crowd stood or sat that the ceremony was for men. There were many women, but they looked on from the fringe like outsiders. The titled men and elders sat on their stools waiting for the trials to begin. In front of them was a row of stools on which nobody sat. There were nine of them. Two little groups of people stood at a respectable distance beyond the stools. They faced the elders. There were three men in one group and three men and one woman in the other. The woman was Mgbafo and the three men with her were her brothers. In the other group were her husband, Uzowulu, and his relatives. Mgbafo and her brothers were as still as statues into whose faces the artist has moulded defiance. Uzowulu and his relatives, on the other hand, were whispering together. It looked like whispering, but they were really talking at the top of their voices. Everybody in the crowd was talking. It was like the market. From a distance the noise was a deep rumble carried by the wind.

An iron gong sounded, setting up a wave of expectation in the crowd. Everyone looked in the direction of the *egwugwu* house. *Gome, gome, gome, gome* went the gong, and a powerful flute blew a high-pitched blast. Then came the voices of the *egwugwu,* guttural and awesome. The wave struck the women and children and there was a backward stampede. But it was momentary. They were already far enough where they stood and there was room for running away if any of the *egwugwu* should go towards them.

The drum sounded again and the flute blew. The *egwugwu* house was now a pandemonium of quavering voices: *Aru oyim de de de dei!*[3] filled the air as the spirits of the ancestors, just emerged from the earth, greeted themselves in their esoteric language. The *egwugwu* house into which they emerged faced the forest, away from the crowd, who saw only its back with the many-coloured patterns and drawings done by specially chosen women at regular intervals. These women never saw the inside of the hut. No woman ever did. They scrubbed and painted the outside walls under the supervision of men. If they imagined what was inside, they kept their imagination to themselves. No woman ever asked questions about the most powerful and the most secret cult in the clan.

3. Greetings, body of my friend.

Aru oyim de de de dei! flew around the dark, closed hut like tongues of fire. The ancestral spirits of the clan were abroad. The metal gong beat continuously now and the flute, shrill and powerful, floated on the chaos.

And then the *egwugwu* appeared. The women and children sent up a great shout and took to their heels. It was instinctive. A woman fled as soon as an *egwugwu* came in sight. And when, as on that day, nine of the greatest masked spirits in the clan came out together it was a terrifying spectacle. Even Mgbafo took to her heels and had to be restrained by her brothers.

Each of the nine *egwugwu* represented a village of the clan. Their leader was called Evil Forest. Smoke poured out of his head.

The nine villages of Umuofia had grown out of the nine sons of the first father of the clan. Evil Forest represented the village of Umeru, or the children of Eru, who was the eldest of the nine sons.

"*Umuofia kwenu!*" shouted the leading *egwugwu,* pushing the air with his raffia arms. The elders of the clan replied, "*Yao!*"

"*Umuofia kwenu!*"

"*Yaa!*"

"*Umuofia kwenu!*"

"*Yaa!*"

Evil Forest then thrust the pointed end of his rattling staff into the earth. And it began to shake and rattle, like something agitating with a metallic life. He took the first of the empty stools and the eight other *egwugwu* began to sit in order of seniority after him.

Okonkwo's wives, and perhaps other women as well, might have noticed that the second *egwugwu* had the springy walk of Okonkwo. And they might also have noticed that Okonkwo was not among the titled men and elders who sat behind the row of *egwugwu*. But if they thought these things they kept them within themselves. The *egwugwu* with the springy walk was one of the dead fathers of the clan. He looked terrible with the smoked raffia body, a huge wooden face painted white except for the round hollow eyes and the charred teeth that were as big as a man's fingers. On his head were two powerful horns.

When all the *egwugwu* had sat down and the sound of the many tiny bells and rattles on their bodies had subsided, Evil Forest addressed the two groups of people facing them.

"Uzowulu's body, I salute you," he said. Spirits always addressed humans as "bodies." Uzowulu bent down and touched the earth with his right hand as a sign of submission.

"Our father, my hand has touched the ground," he said.

"Uzowulu's body, do you know me?" asked the spirit.

"How can I know you, father? You are beyond our knowledge."

Evil Forest then turned to the other group and addressed the eldest of the three brothers.

"The body of Odukwe, I greet you," he said, and Odukwe bent down and touched the earth. The hearing then began.

Uzowulu stepped forward and presented his case.

"That woman standing there is my wife, Mgbafo. I married her with my money and my yams. I do not owe my in-laws anything. I owe them no yams. I owe them no coco-yams. One morning three of them came to my house, beat me up and took my wife and children away. This happened in the rainy season. I have waited in vain for my wife to return. At last I went to my in-laws and said to them, 'You have taken back your sister. I did not send her away. You yourselves took her. The law of the clan is that you should return her bride-price.' But my wife's brother said they had nothing to tell me. So I have brought the matter to the fathers of the clan. My case is finished. I salute you."

"Your words are good," said the leader of the *egwugwu*. "Let us hear Odukwe. His words may also be good."

Odukwe was short and thick-set. He stepped forward, saluted the spirits and began his story.

"My in-law has told you that we went to his house, beat him up and took our sister and her children away. All that is true. He told you that he came to take back her bride-price and we refused to give it him. That is also true. My in-law, Uzowulu, is a beast. My sister lived with him for nine years. During those years no single day passed in the sky without his beating the woman. We have tried to settle their quarrels time without number and on each occasion Uzowulu was guilty—"

"It is a lie!" Uzowulu shouted.

"Two years ago," continued Odukwe, "when she was pregnant, he beat her until she miscarried."

"It is a lie. She miscarried after she had gone to sleep with her lover."

"Uzowulu's body, I salute you," said Evil Forest, silencing him. "What kind of lover sleeps with a pregnant woman?" There was a loud murmur of approbation from the crowd. Odukwe continued:

"Last year when my sister was recovering from an illness, he beat her again so that if the neighbours had not gone in to save her she would have been killed. We heard of it, and did as you have been told. The law of Umuofia is that if a woman runs away from her husband her bride-price is returned. But in this case she ran away to save her life. Her two children belong to Uzowulu. We do not dispute it, but they are too young to leave their mother. If, on the other hand, Uzowulu should recover from his madness and come in the proper way to beg his wife to return she will do so on the understanding that if he ever beats her again we shall cut off his genitals for him."

The crowd roared with laughter. Evil Forest rose to his feet and order was immediately restored. A steady cloud of smoke rose from his head. He sat down again and called two witnesses. They were both Uzowulu's neighbours, and they agreed about the beating. Evil Forest then stood up, pulled out his staff and thrust it into the earth again. He ran a few steps in the direction of the women; they all fled in terror, only to return to their places almost immediately. The nine *egwugwu* then went away to consult together in their house. They were silent for a long time. Then the metal gong sounded and the flute was blown. The *egwugwu* had emerged once again from their underground home. They saluted one another and then reappeared on the *ilo*.

"*Umuofia kwenu!*" roared Evil Forest, facing the elders and grandees of the clan.

"*Yaa!*" replied the thunderous crowd, then silence descended from the sky and swallowed the noise.

Evil Forest began to speak and all the while he spoke everyone was silent. The eight other *egwugwu* were as still as statues.

"We have heard both sides of the case," said Evil Forest. "Our duty is not to blame this man or to praise that, but to settle the dispute." He turned to Uzowulu's group and allowed a short pause.

"Uzowulu's body, do you know me?"

"How can I know you, father? You are beyond our knowledge," Uzowulu replied.

"I am Evil Forest. I kill a man on the day that his life is sweetest to him."

"That is true," replied Uzowulu.

"Go to your in-laws with a pot of wine and beg your wife to return to you. It is not bravery when a man fights with a woman." He turned to Odukwe, and allowed a brief pause.

"Odukwe's body, I greet you," he said.

"My hand is on the ground," replied Odukwe.

"Do you know me?"

"No man can know you," replied Odukwe.

"I am Evil Forest, I am Dry-meat-that-fills-the-mouth, I am Fire-that-burns-without-faggots. If your in-law brings wine to you, let your sister go with him. I salute you." He pulled his staff from the hard earth and thrust it back.

"*Umuofia kwenu!*" he roared, and the crowd answered.

"I don't know why such a trifle should come before the *egwugwu,*" said one elder to another.

"Don't you know what kind of man Uzowulu is? He will not listen to any other decision," replied the other.

As they spoke two other groups of people had replaced the first before the *egwugwu,* and a great land case began.

Chapter 11

The night was impenetrably dark. The moon had been rising later and later every night until now it was seen only at dawn. And whenever the moon forsook evening and rose at cock-crow the nights were as black as charcoal.

Ezinma and her mother sat on a mat on the floor after their supper of yam foo-foo and bitter leaf soup. A palm-oil lamp gave out yellowish light. Without it, it would have been impossible to eat; one could not have known where one's mouth was in the darkness of that night. There was an oil lamp in all four huts on Okonkwo's compound, and each hut seen from the others looked like a soft eye of yellow half-light set in the solid massiveness of night.

The world was silent except for the shrill cry of insects, which was part of the night, and the sound of wooden mortar and pestle as Nwayieke pounded her foo-foo. Nwayieke lived four compounds away, and she was notorious for her late cooking. Every woman in the neighbourhood knew the sound of Nwayieke's mortar and pestle. It was also part of the night.

Okonkwo had eaten from his wives' dishes and was now reclining with his back against the wall. He searched his bag and brought out his snuff-bottle. He turned it on to his left palm, but nothing came out. He hit the bottle against his knee to shake up the tobacco. That was always the trouble with Okeke's snuff. It very quickly went damp, and there was too much saltpetre in it. Okonkwo had not brought snuff from him for a long time. Idigo was the man who knew how to grind good snuff. But he had recently fallen ill.

Low voices, broken now and again by singing, reached Okonkwo from his wives' huts as each woman and her children told folk stories. Ekwefi and her daughter, Ezinma, sat on a mat on the floor. It was Ekwefi's turn to tell a story.

"Once upon a time," she began, "all the birds were invited to a feast in the sky. They were very happy and began to prepare themselves for the great day. They painted their bodies with red cam wood and drew beautiful patterns on them with *uli*.

"Tortoise saw all these preparations and soon discovered what it all meant. Nothing that happened in the world of the animals ever escaped his notice; he was full of cunning. As soon as he heard of the great feast in the sky his throat began to itch at the very thought. There was a famine in those days and Tortoise had not eaten a good meal for two moons. His body rattled like a piece of dry stick in his empty shell. So he began to plan how he would go to the sky."

"But he had no wings," said Ezinma.

"Be patient," replied her mother. "That is the story. Tortoise had no wings, but he went to the birds and asked to be allowed to go with them.

"'We know you too well,' said the birds when they had heard him. 'You are full of cunning and you are ungrateful. If we allow you to come with us you will soon begin your mischief.'"

"'You do not know me,' said Tortoise. 'I am a changed man. I have learnt that a man who makes trouble for others is also making it for himself.'

"Tortoise had a sweet tongue, and within a short time all the birds agreed that he was a changed man, and they each gave him a feather, with which he made two wings.

"At last the great day came and Tortoise was the first to arrive at the meeting-place. When all the birds had gathered together, they set off in a body. Tortoise was very happy and voluble as he flew among the birds, and he was soon chosen as the man to speak for the party because he was a great orator.

"'There is one important thing which we must not forget,' he said as they flew on their way. 'When people are invited to a great feast like this, they take new names for the occasion. Our hosts in the sky will expect us to honour this age-old custom.'

"None of the birds had heard of this custom but they knew that Tortoise, in spite of his failings in other directions, was a widely-travelled man who knew the customs of different people. And so they each took a new name. When they had all taken, Tortoise also took one. He was to be called *All of you*.

"At last the party arrived in the sky and their hosts were very happy to see them. Tortoise stood up in his many-coloured plumage and thanked them for their invitation. His speech was so eloquent that all the birds were glad they had brought him, and nodded their heads in approval of all he said. Their hosts took him as the king of the birds, especially as he looked somewhat different from the others.

"After kola nuts had been presented and eaten, the people of the sky set before their guests the most delectable dishes Tortoise had ever seen or dreamt of. The soup was brought out hot from the fire and in the very pot in which it had been cooked. It was full of meat and fish. Tortoise began to sniff aloud. There was pounded yam and also yam pottage cooked with palm-oil and fresh fish. There were also pots of palm-wine. When everything had been set before the guests, one of the people of the sky came forward and tasted a little from each pot. He then invited the birds to eat. But Tortoise jumped to his feet and asked: 'For whom have you prepared this feast?'

"'For all of you,' replied the man.

"Tortoise turned to the birds and said: 'You remember that my name is *All of you*. The custom here is to serve the spokesman first and the others later. They will serve you when I have eaten.'

"He began to eat and the birds grumbled angrily. The people of the sky thought it must be their custom to leave all the food for their king. And so Tortoise ate the best part of the food and then drank two pots of palm-wine, so that he was full of food and drink and his body filled out in his shell.

"The birds gathered round to eat what was left and to peck at the bones he had thrown all about the floor. Some of them were too angry to eat. They chose to fly home on an empty stomach. But before they left each took back the feather he had lent to Tortoise. And there he stood in his hard shell full of food and wine but without any wings to fly home. He asked the birds to take a message for his wife, but they all refused. In the end Parrot, who had felt more angry than the others, suddenly changed his mind and agreed to take the message.

"'Tell my wife,' said Tortoise, 'to bring out all the soft things in my house and cover the compound with them so that I can jump down from the sky without very great danger.'

"Parrot promised to deliver the message, and then flew away. But when he reached Tortoise's house he told his wife to bring out all the hard things in the house. And so she brought out her husband's hoes, matchets, spears, guns and even his cannon. Tortoise looked down from the sky and saw his wife bringing things out, but it was too far to see what they were. When all seemed ready he let himself go. He fell and fell and fell until he began to fear that he would never stop falling. And then like the sound of his cannon he crashed on the compound."

"Did he die?" asked Ezinma.

"No," replied Ekwefi. "His shell broke into pieces. But there was a great medicine-man in the neigbourhood. Tortoise's wife sent for him and he gathered all the bits of shell and stuck them together. That is why Tortoise's shell is not smooth."

"There is no song in the story," Ezinma pointed out.

"No," said Ekwefi. "I shall think of another one with a song. But it is your turn now."

"Once upon a time," Ezinma began, "Tortoise and Cat went to wrestle against Yams—no, that is not the beginning. Once upon a time there was a great famine in the land of animals. Everybody was lean except Cat, who was fat and whose body shone as if oil was rubbed on it . . ."

She broke off because at that very moment a loud and high-pitched voice broke the outer silence of the night. It was Chielo, the priestess of Agbala, prophesying. There was nothing new in that. Once in a while Chielo was possessed by the spirit of her god and she began to prophesy. But tonight she was addressing her prophecy and greetings to Okonkwo, and so everyone in his family listened. The folk stories stopped.

"*Agbala do-o-o-o! Agbala ekeneo-o-o-o,*"[4] came the voice like a sharp knife cutting through the night. "*Okonkwo! Agbala ekene gio-o-o-o! Agbala cholu ifu ada ya Ezinmao-o-o-o!*"[5]

At the mention of Ezinma's name Ekwefi jerked her head sharply like a animal that had sniffed death in the air. Her heart jumped painfully within her.

The priestess had now reached Okonkwo's compound and was talking with him outside his hut. She was saying again and again that Agbala wanted to see his daughter, Ezinma. Okonkwo pleaded with her to come back in the morning because Ezinma was now asleep. But Chielo ignored what he was trying to say and went on shouting that Agbala wanted to see his daughter. Her voice was as clear as metal, and Okonkwo's women and children heard from their huts all that she said. Okonkwo was still pleading that the girl had been ill of late and was asleep. Ekwefi quickly took her to their bedroom and placed her on their high bamboo bed.

The priestess suddenly screamed. "Beware, Okonkwo!" she warned. "Beware of exchanging words with Agbala. Does a man speak when a god speaks? Beware!"

---

4. Agbala greets you. Agbala wants something.   5. Agbala greets you. Agbala wants to see his daughter, Ezinma.

She walked through Okonkwo's hut into the circular compound and went straight towards Ekwefi's hut. Okonkwo came after her.

"Ekwefi," she called, "Agbala greets you. Where is my daughter, Ezinma? Agbala wants to see her."

Ekwefi came out from her hut carrying her oil lamp in her left hand. There was a light wind blowing, so she cupped her right hand to shelter the flame. Nwoye's mother, also carrying an oil lamp, emerged from her hut. Her children stood in the darkness outside their hut watching the strange event. Okonkwo's youngest wife also came out and joined the others.

"Where does Agbala want to see her?" Ekwefi asked.

"Where else but in his house in the hills and the caves?" replied the priestess.

"I will come with you, too," Ekwefi said firmly.

"*Tufia-a!*"[6] the priestess cursed, her voice cracking like the angry bark of thunder in the dry season. "How dare you, woman, to go before the mighty Agbala of your own accord? Beware, woman, lest he strike you in his anger. Bring me my daughter."

Ekwefi went into her hut and came out again with Ezinma.

"Come, my daughter," said the priestess. "I shall carry you on my back. A baby on its mother's back does not know that the way is long."

Ezinma began to cry. She was used to Chielo calling her "my daughter." But it was a different Chielo she now saw in the yellow half-light.

"Don't cry, my daughter," said the priestess, "lest Agbala be angry with you."

"Don't cry," said Ekwefi, "she will bring you back very soon. I shall give you some fish to eat." She went into the hut again and brought down the smoke-black basket in which she kept her dried fish and other ingredients for cooking soup. She broke a piece in two and gave it to Ezinma, who clung to her.

"Don't be afraid," said Ekwefi, stroking her head, which was shaved in places, leaving a regular pattern of hair. They went outside again. The priestess bent down on one knee and Ezinma climbed on her back, her left palm closed on her fish and her eyes gleaming with tears.

"*Agbala do-o-o-o! Agbala ekeneo-o-o-o! . . .*" Chielo began once again to chant greetings to her god. She turned round sharply and walked through Okonkwo's hut, bending very low at the eaves. Ezinma was crying loudly now, calling on her mother. The two voices disappeared into the thick darkness.

A strange and sudden weakness descended on Ekwefi as she stood gazing in the direction of the voices like a hen whose only chick has been carried away by a kite. Ezinma's voice soon faded away and only Chielo was heard moving farther and farther into the distance.

"Why do you stand there as though she had been kidnapped?" asked Okonkwo as he went back to his hut.

"She will bring her back soon," Nwoye's mother said.

But Ekwefi did not hear these consolations. She stood for a while, and then, all of a sudden, made up her mind. She hurried through Okonkwo's hut and went outside.

"Where are you going?" he asked.

"I am following Chielo," she replied and disappeared in the darkness. Okonkwo cleared his throat, and brought out his snuff-bottle from the goatskin bag by his side.

6. Spit!

The priestess's voice was already growing faint in the distance. Ekwefi hurried to the main footpath and turned left in the direction of the voice. Her eyes were useless to her in the darkness. But she picked her way easily on the sandy footpath hedged on either side by branches and damp leaves. She began to run, holding her breasts with her hands to stop them flapping noisily against her body. She hit her left foot against an outcropped root, and terror seized her. It was an ill omen. She ran faster. But Chielo's voice was still a long way away. Had she been running too? How could she go so fast with Ezinma on her back? Although the night was cool, Ekwefi was beginning to feel hot from her running. She continually ran into the luxuriant weeds and creepers that walled in the path. Once she tripped up and fell. Only then did she realise, with a start, that Chielo had stopped her chanting. Her heart beat violently and she stood still. Then Chielo's renewed outburst came from only a few paces ahead. But Ekwefi could not see her. She shut her eyes for a while and opened them again in an effort to see. But it was useless. She could not see beyond her nose.

There were no stars in the sky because there was a rain-cloud. Fireflies went about with their tiny green lamps, which only made the darkness more profound. Between Chielo's outbursts the night was alive with the shrill tremor of forest insects woven into the darkness.

"*Agbala do-o-o-o! . . . Agbala ekeneo-o-o-o! . . .*" Ekwefi trudged behind, neither getting too near nor keeping too far back. She thought they must be going towards the sacred cave. Now that she walked slowly she had time to think. What would she do when they got to the cave? She would not dare to enter. She would wait at the mouth, all alone in that fearful place. She thought of all the terrors of the night. She remembered the night, long ago, when she had seen *Ogbuagali-odu,* one of those evil essences loosed upon the world by the potent "medicines" which the tribe had made in the distant past against its enemies but had now forgotten how to control. Ekwefi had been returning from the stream with her mother on a dark night like this when they saw its glow as it flew in their direction. They had thrown their water-pots and lain by the roadside expecting the sinister light to descend on them and kill them. That was the only time Ekwefi ever saw *Ogbuagali-odu.* But although it had happened so long ago, her blood still ran cold whenever she remembered that night.

The priestess's voice came at longer intervals now, but its vigour was undiminished. The air was cool and damp with dew. Ezinma sneezed. Ekwefi muttered, "Life to you." At the same time the priestess also said, "Life to you, my daughter." Ezinma's voice from the darkness warmed her mother's heart. She trudged slowly along.

And then the priestess screamed. "Somebody is walking behind me!" she said. "Whether you are spirit or man, may Agbala shave your head with a blunt razor! May he twist your neck until you see your heels!"

Ekwefi stood rooted to the spot. One mind said to her: "Woman, go home before Agbala does you harm." But she could not. She stood until Chielo had increased the distance between them and she began to follow again. She had already walked so long that she began to feel a slight numbness in the limbs and in the head. Then it occurred to her that they could not have been heading for the cave. They must have by-passed it long ago; they must be going towards Umuachi, the farthest village in the clan. Chielo's voice now came after long intervals.

It seemed to Ekwefi that the night had become a little lighter. The cloud had lifted and a few stars were out. The moon must be preparing to rise, its sullenness over. When the moon rose later in the night, people said it was refusing food, as a sullen husband refuses his wife's food when they have quarrelled.

"*Agbala do-o-o-o! Umuachi! Agbala ekene unuo-o-o!*" It was just as Ekwefi had thought. The priestess was now saluting the village of Umuachi. It was unbelievable, the distance they had covered. As they emerged into the open village from the narrow forest track the darkness was softened and it became possible to see the vague shape of trees. Ekwefi screwed her eyes up in an effort to see her daughter and the priestess, but whenever she thought she saw their shape it immediately dissolved like a melting lump of darkness. She walked numbly along.

Chielo's voice was now rising continuously, as when she first set out. Ekwefi had a feeling of spacious openness, and she guessed they must be on the village *ilo*, or playground. And she realised too with something like a jerk that Chielo was no longer moving forward. She was, in fact, returning. Ekwefi quickly moved away from her line of retreat. Chielo passed by, and they began to go back the way they had come.

It was a long and weary journey and Ekwefi felt like a sleepwalker most of the way. The moon was definitely rising, and although it had not yet appeared on the sky its light had already melted down the darkness. Ekwefi could now discern the figure of the priestess and her burden. She slowed down her pace so as to increase the distance between them. She was afraid of what might happen if Chielo suddenly turned round and saw her.

She had prayed for the moon to rise. But now she found the half-light of the incipient moon more terrifying than the darkness. The world was now peopled with vague, fantastic figures that dissolved under her steady gaze and then formed again in new shapes. At one stage Ekwefi was so afraid that she nearly called out to Chielo for companionship and human sympathy. What she had seen was the shape of a man climbing a palm tree, his head pointing to the earth and his legs skywards. But at that very moment Chielo's voice rose again in her possessed chanting, and Ekwefi recoiled, because there was no humanity there. It was not the same Chielo who sat with her in the market and sometimes bought bean-cakes for Ezinma, whom she called her daughter. It was a different woman—the priestess of Agbala, the Oracle of the Hills and Caves. Ekwefi trudged along between two fears. The sound of her benumbed steps seemed to come from some other person walking behind her. Her arms were folded across her bare breasts. Dew fell heavily and the air was cold. She could no longer think, not even about the terrors of night. She just jogged along in a half-sleep only waking to full life when Chielo sang.

At last they took a turning and began to head for the caves. From then on, Chielo never ceased in her chanting. She greeted her god in a multitude of names—the owner of the future, the messenger of earth, the god who cut a man down when his life was sweetest to him. Ekwefi was also awakened and her benumbed fears revived.

The moon was now up and she could see Chielo and Ezinma clearly. How a woman could carry a child of that size so easily and for so long was a miracle. But Ekwefi was not thinking about that. Chielo was not a woman that night.

"*Agbala do-o-o-o! Agbala ekeneo-o-o! Chi negbu madu ubosi ndu ya nato ya uto daluo-o-o! . . .*"[7]

Ekwefi could already see the hills looming in the moonlight. They formed a circular ring with a break at one point through which the foot-track led to the centre of the circle.

As soon as the priestess stepped into this ring of hills her voice was not only doubled in strength but was thrown back on all sides. It was indeed the shrine of a great

7. Agbala wants! Agbala greets! Spirit who kills one on the day his life is so pleasant he gives thanks!

god. Ekwefi picked her way carefully and quietly. She was already beginning to doubt the wisdom of her coming. Nothing would happen to Ezinma, she thought. And if anything happened to her could she stop it? She would not dare to enter the underground caves. Her coming was quite useless, she thought.

As these things went through her mind she did not realise how close they were to the cave mouth. And so when the priestess with Ezinma on her back disappeared through a hole hardly big enough to pass a hen, Ekwefi broke into a run as though to stop them. As she stood gazing at the circular darkness which had swallowed them, tears gushed from her eyes, and she swore within her that if she heard Ezinma cry she would rush into the cave to defend her against all the gods in the world. She would die with her.

Having sworn that oath, she sat down on a stony ledge and waited. Her fear had vanished. She could hear the priestess's voice, all its metal taken out of it by the vast emptiness of the cave. She buried her face in her lap and waited.

She did not know how long she waited. It must have been a very long time. Her back was turned on the footpath that led out of the hills. She must have heard a noise behind her and turned round sharply. A man stood there with a matchet in his hand. Ekwefi uttered a scream and sprang to her feet.

"Don't be foolish," said Okonkwo's voice. "I thought you were going into the shrine with Chielo," he mocked.

Ekwefi did not answer. Tears of gratitude filled her eyes. She knew her daughter was safe.

"Go home and sleep," said Okonkwo. "I shall wait here."

"I shall wait too. It is almost dawn. The first cock has crowed."

As they stood there together, Ekwefi's mind went back to the days when they were young. She had married Anene because Okonkwo was too poor then to marry. Two years after her marriage to Anene she could bear it no longer and she ran away to Okonkwo. It had been early in the morning. The moon was shining. She was going to the stream to fetch water. Okonkwo's house was on the way to the stream. She went in and knocked at his door and he came out. Even in those days he was not a man of many words. He just carried her into his bed and in the darkness began to feel around her waist for the loose end of her cloth.

Chapter 12

On the following morning the entire neighbourhood wore a festive air because Okonkwo's friend, Obierika, was celebrating his daughter's *uri*. It was the day on which her suitor (having already paid the greater part of her bride-price) would bring palm-wine not only to her parents and immediate relatives but to the wide and extensive group of kinsmen called *umunna*. Everybody had been invited—men, women and children. But it was really a woman's ceremony and the central figures were the bride and her mother.

As soon as day broke, breakfast was hastily eaten and women and children began to gather at Obierika's compound to help the bride's mother in her difficult but happy task of cooking for a whole village.

Okonkwo's family was astir like any other family in the neighbourhood. Nwoye's mother and Okonkwo's youngest wife were ready to set out for Obierika's compound with all their children. Nwoye's mother carried a basket of coco-yams, a cake of salt and smoked fish which she would present to Obierika's wife. Okonkwo's youngest wife, Ojiugo, also had a basket of plantains and coco-yams and a small pot of palm-oil. Their children carried pots of water.

Ekwefi was tired and sleepy from the exhausting experiences of the previous night. It was not very long since they had returned. The priestess, with Ezinma sleeping on her back, had crawled out of the shrine on her belly like a snake. She had not as much as looked at Okonkwo and Ekwefi or shown any surprise at finding them at the mouth of the cave. She looked straight ahead of her and walked back to the village. Okonkwo and his wife followed at a respectful distance. They thought the priestess might be going to her house, but she went to Okonkwo's compound, passed through his *obi* and into Ekwefi's hut and walked into her bedroom. She placed Ezinma carefully on the bed and went away without saying a word to anybody.

Ezinma was still sleeping when everyone else was astir, and Ekwefi asked Nwoye's mother and Ojiugo to explain to Obierika's wife that she would be late. She had got ready her basket of coco-yams and fish, but she must wait for Ezinma to wake.

"You need some sleep yourself," said Nwoye's mother. "You look very tired."

As they spoke Ezinma emerged from the hut, rubbing her eyes and stretching her spare frame. She saw the other children with their water-pots and remembered that they were going to fetch water for Obierika's wife. She went back to the hut and brought her pot.

"Have you slept enough?" asked her mother.

"Yes," she replied. "Let us go."

"Not before you have had your breakfast," said Ekwefi. And she went into her hut to warm the vegetable soup she had cooked last night.

"We shall be going," said Nwoye's mother. "I will tell Obierika's wife that you are coming later." And so they all went to help Obierika's wife—Nwoye's mother and her four children and Ojiugo with her two.

As they trooped through Okonkwo's *obi* he asked: "Who will prepare my afternoon meal?"

"I shall return to do it," said Ojiugo.

Okonkwo was also feeling tired and sleepy, for although nobody else knew it, he had not slept at all last night. He had felt very anxious but did not show it. When Ekwefi had followed the priestess, he had allowed what he regarded as a reasonable and manly interval to pass and then gone with his matchet to the shrine, where he thought they must be. It was only when he had got there that it had occurred to him that the priestess might have chosen to go round the villages first. Okonkwo had returned home and sat waiting. When he thought he had waited long enough he again returned to the shrine. But the Hills and the Caves were as silent as death. It was only on his fourth trip that he had found Ekwefi, and by then he had become gravely worried.

Obierika's compound was as busy as an ant-hill. Temporary cooking tripods were erected on every available space by bringing together three blocks of sun-dried earth and making a fire in their midst. Cooking pots went up and down the tripods, and foo-foo was pounded in a hundred wooden mortars. Some of the women cooked the yams and the cassava, the others prepared vegetable soup. Young men pounded the foo-foo or split firewood. The children made endless trips to the stream.

Three young men helped Obierika to slaughter the two goats with which the soup was made. They were very fat goats, but the fattest of all was tethered to a peg near the wall of the compound. It was as big as a small cow. Obierika had sent one of his relatives all the way to Umuike to buy that goat. It was the one he would present alive to his in-laws.

"The market of Umuike is a wonderful place," said the young man who had been sent by Obierika to buy the giant goat. "There are so many people on it that if you threw up a grain of sand it would not find a way to fall to earth again."

"It is the result of a great medicine," said Obierika. "The people of Umuike wanted their market to grow and swallow up the markets of their neighbours. So they made a powerful medicine. Every market-day, before the first cock-crow, this medicine stands on the market-ground in the shape of an old woman with a fan. With this magic fan she beckons to the market all the neighbouring clans. She beckons in front of her and behind her, to her right and to her left."

"And so everybody comes," said another man, "honest men and thieves. They can steal your cloth from off your waist in that market."

"Yes," said Obierika. "I warned Nwankwo to keep a sharp eye and a sharp ear. There was once a man who went to sell a goat. He led it on a thick rope which he tied round his wrist. But as he walked through the market he realised that people were pointing at him as they do to a madman. He could not understand it until he looked back and saw that what he led at the end of the tether was not a goat but a heavy log of wood."

"Do you think a thief can do that kind of thing single-handed?" asked Nwankwo.

"No," said Obierika. "They use medicine."

When they had cut the goats' throats and collected the blood in a bowl, they held them over an open fire to burn off the hair, and the smell of burning hair blended with the smell of cooking. Then they washed them and cut them up for the women who prepared the soup.

All this ant-hill activity was going smoothly when a sudden interruption came. It was a cry in the distance: *Oji odu achu iiiji-o-o!* (*The one that uses its tail to drive flies away!*) Every woman immediately abandoned whatever she was doing and rushed out in the direction of the cry.

"We cannot all rush out like that, leaving what we are cooking to burn in the fire," shouted Chielo, the priestess. "Three or four of us should stay behind."

"It is true," said another woman. "We will allow three or four women to stay behind."

Five women stayed behind to look after the cooking-pots, and all the rest rushed away to see the cow that had been let loose. When they saw it they drove it back to its owner, who at once paid the heavy fine which the village imposed on anyone whose cow was let loose on his neighbours' crops. When the women had exacted the penalty they checked among themselves to see if any woman had failed to come out when the cry had been raised.

"Where is Mgbogo?" asked one of them.

"She is ill in bed," said Mgbogo's next-door neighbour. "She has *iba*."

"The only other person is Udenkwo," said another woman, "and her child is not twenty-eight days yet."

Those women whom Obierika's wife had not asked to help her with the cooking returned to their homes, and the rest went back, in a body, to Obierika's compound.

"Whose cow is it?" asked the women who had been allowed to stay behind.

"It was my husband's," said Ezelagbo. "One of the young children had opened the gate of the cow-shed."

Early in the afternoon the first two pots of palm-wine arrived from Obierika's in-laws. They were duly presented to the women, who drank a cup or two each, to help them in their cooking. Some of it also went to the bride and her attendant maidens, who were putting the last delicate touches of razor to her coiffure and cam wood on her smooth skin.

When the heat of the sun began to soften, Obierika's son, Maduka, took a long broom and swept the ground in front of his father's *obi*. And as if they had been waiting for that, Obierika's relatives and friends began to arrive, every man with his goatskin bag hung on one shoulder and a rolled goatskin mat under his arm. Some of them were accompanied by their sons bearing carved wooden stools. Okonkwo was one of them. They sat in a half circle and began to talk of many things. It would not be long before the suitors came.

Okonkwo brought out his snuff-bottle and offered it to Ogbuefi Ezenwa, who sat next to him. Ezenwa took it, tapped it on his knee-cap, rubbed his left palm on his body to dry it before tipping a little snuff into it. His actions were deliberate, and he spoke as he performed them.

"I hope our in-laws will bring many pots of wine. Although they come from a village that is known for being close-fisted, they ought to know that Akueke is the bride for a king."

"They dare not bring fewer than thirty pots," said Okonkwo. "I shall tell them my mind if they do."

At that moment Obierika's son, Maduka, led out the giant goat from the inner compound, for his father's relatives to see. They all admired it and said that that was the way things should be done. The goat was then led back to the inner compound.

Very soon after, the in-laws began to arrive. Young men and boys in single file, each carrying a pot of wine, came first. Obierika's relatives counted the pots as they came. Twenty, twenty-five. There was a long break, and the hosts looked at each other as if to say, "I told you." Then more pots came. Thirty, thirty-five, forty, forty-five. The hosts nodded in approval and seemed to say, "Now they are behaving like men." Altogether there were fifty pots of wine. After the pot-bearers came Ibe, the suitor, and the elders of his family. They sat in a half-moon, thus completing a circle with their hosts. The pots of wine stood in their midst. Then the bride, her mother and half a dozen other women and girls emerged from the inner compound, and went round the circle shaking hands with all. The bride's mother led the way, followed by the bride and the other women. The married women wore their best cloths and the girls wore red and black waist-beads and anklets of brass.

When the women retired, Obierika presented kola nuts to his in-laws. His eldest brother broke the first one. "Life to all of us," he said as he broke it. "And let there be friendship between your family and ours."

The crowd answered: *Ee-e-e!*"

"We are giving you our daughter today. She will be a good wife to you. She will bear you nine sons like the mother of our town."

"*Ee-e-e!*"

The oldest man in the camp of the visitors replied: "It will be good for you and it will be good for us."

"*Ee-e-e!*"

"This is not the first time my people have come to marry your daughter. My mother was one of you."

"*Ee-e-e!*"

"And this will not be the last, because you understand us and we understand you. You are a great family."

"Ee-e-e!"

"Prosperous men and great warriors." He looked in the direction of Okonkwo. "Your daughter will bear us sons like you."

"Ee-e-e!"

The kola was eaten and the drinking of palm-wine began. Groups of four or five men sat round with a pot in their midst. As the evening wore on, food was presented to the guests. There were huge bowls of foo-foo and steaming pots of soup. There were also pots of yam pottage. It was a great feast.

As night fell, burning torches were set on wooden tripods and the young men raised a song. The elders sat in a circle and the singers went round singing each man's praise as they came before him. They had something to say for every man. Some were great farmers, some were orators who spoke for the clan; Okonkwo was the greatest wrestler and warrior alive. When they had gone round the circle they settled down in the centre, and girls came from the inner compound to dance. At first the bride was not among them. But when she finally appeared holding a cock in her right hand, a loud cheer rose from the crowd. All the other dancers made way for her. She presented the cock to the musicians and began to dance. Her brass anklets rattled as she danced and her body gleamed with cam wood in the soft yellow light. The musicians with their wood, clay and metal instruments went from song to song. And they were all gay. They sang the latest song in the village:

> *If I hold her hand*
> *She says, "Don't touch!"*
> *If I hold her foot*
> *She says, "Don't touch!"*
> *But when I hold her waist-beads*
> *She pretends not to know.*

The night was already far spent when the guests rose to go, taking their bride home to spend seven market weeks with her suitor's family. They sang songs as they went, and on their way they paid short courtesy visits to prominent men like Okonkwo, before they finally left for their village. Okonkwo made a present of two cocks to them.

Chapter 13

Go-di-di-go-go-di-go. Di-go-go-di-go. It was the *ekwe* talking to the clan. One of the things every man learned was the language of the hollowed-out instrument. Diim! Diim! Diim! boomed the cannon at intervals.

The first cock had not crowed, and Umuofia was still swallowed up in sleep and silence when the *ekwe* began to talk, and the cannon shattered the silence. Men stirred on their bamboo beds and listened anxiously. Somebody was dead. The cannon seemed to rend the sky. Di-go-go-di-go-di-di-go-go floated in the message-laden night air. The faint and distant wailing of women settled like a sediment of sorrow on the earth. Now and again a full-chested lamentation rose above the wailing whenever a man came into the place of death. He raised his voice once or twice in manly sorrow and then sat down with the other men listening to the endless wailing of the women and the esoteric language of the *ekwe*. Now and again the cannon boomed. The wailing of the women would not be heard beyond the village, but the *ekwe* carried the news to all the nine villages and even beyond. It began by naming the clan: *Umuofia obodo dike* "the land of the brave." *Umuofia obodo dike! Umuofia obodo dike!* It said this over and over again, and as it dwelt on it, anxiety mounted in every heart that heaved on a bamboo bed that night. Then it went nearer and named the village: *Iguedo of the yellow grinding-stone!* It was Okonkwo's village. Again and again Iguedo was called and men waited breathlessly in all the nine villages. At last the man was named and people sighed "E-u-u, Ezeudu is dead." A cold shiver ran down Okonkwo's back as he remembered the last time the old man had visited him. "That boy calls you father," he had said. "Bear no hand in his death."

Ezeudu was a great man, and so all the clan was at his funeral. The ancient drums of death beat, guns and cannon were fired, and men dashed about in frenzy, cutting down every tree or animal they saw, jumping over walls and dancing on the roof. It was a warrior's funeral, and from morning till night warriors came and went in their age-groups. They all wore smoked raffia skirts and their bodies were painted with chalk and charcoal. Now and again an ancestral spirit or *egwugwu* appeared from the underworld, speaking in a tremulous, unearthly voice and completely covered in raffia. Some of them were very violent, and there had been a mad rush for shelter earlier in the day when one appeared with a sharp matchet and was only prevented from doing serious harm by two men who restrained him with the help of a strong rope tied round his waist. Sometimes he turned round and chased those men, and they ran for their lives. But they always returned to the long rope he trailed behind. He sang, in a terrifying voice, that Ekwenzu, or Evil Spirit, had entered his eye.

But the most dreaded of all was yet to come. He was always alone and was shaped like a coffin. A sickly odour hung in the air wherever he went, and flies went with him. Even the greatest medicine-men took shelter when he was near. Many years ago another *egwugwu* had dared to stand his ground before him and had been transfixed to the spot for two days. This one had only one hand and with it carried a basket full of water.

But some of the *egwugwu* were quite harmless. One of them was so old and infirm that he leaned heavily on a stick. He walked unsteadily to the place where the corpse was laid, gazed at it a while and went away again—to the underworld.

The land of the living was not far removed from the domain of the ancestors. There was coming and going between them, especially at festivals and also when an old man died, because an old man was very close to the ancestors. A man's life from birth to death was a series of transition rites which brought him nearer and nearer to his ancestors.

Ezeudu had been the oldest man in the village, and at his death there were only three men in the whole clan who were older, and four or five others in his own age-group. Whenever one of these ancient men appeared in the crowd to dance unsteadily the funeral steps of the tribe, younger men gave way and the tumult subsided.

It was a great funeral, such as befitted a noble warrior. As the evening drew near, the shouting and the firing of guns, the beating of drums and the brandishing and clanging of matchets increased.

Ezeudu had taken three titles in his life. It was a rare achievement. There were only four titles in the clan, and only one or two men in any generation ever achieved the fourth and highest. When they did, they became the lords of the land. Because he had taken titles, Ezeudu was to be buried after dark with only a glowing brand to light the sacred ceremony.

But before this quiet and final rite, the tumult increased tenfold. Drums beat violently and men leaped up and down in a frenzy. Guns were fired on all sides and sparks flew out as matchets clanged together in warriors' salutes. The air was full of dust and the smell of gunpowder. It was then that the one-handed spirit came, carrying a basket full of water. People made way for him on all sides and the noise subsided. Even the smell of gunpowder was swallowed in the sickly smell that now filled the air. He danced a few steps to the funeral drums and then went to see the corpse.

"Ezeudu!" he called in his gutteral voice. "If you had been poor in your last life I would have asked you to be rich when you come again. But you were rich. If you had been a coward, I would have asked you to bring courage. But you were a fearless warrior. If you had died young, I would have asked you to get life. But you lived long. So I shall ask you to come again the way you came before. If your death was the death of nature, go in peace. But if a man caused it, do not allow him a moment's rest." He danced a few more steps and went away.

The drums and the dancing began again and reached fever-heat. Darkness was around the corner, and the burial was near. Guns fired the last salute and the cannon rent the sky. And then from the centre of the delirious fury came a cry of agony and shouts of horror. It was as if a spell had been cast. All was silent. In the centre of the crowd a boy lay in a pool of blood. It was the dead man's sixteen-year-old son, who with his brothers and half-brothers had been dancing the traditional farewell to their father. Okonkwo's gun had exploded and a piece of iron had pierced the boy's heart.

The confusion that followed was without parallel in the tradition of Umuofia. Violent deaths were frequent, but nothing like this had ever happened.

The only course open to Okonkwo was to flee from the clan. It was a crime against the earth goddess to kill a clansman, and a man who committed it must flee from the land. The crime was of two kinds, male and female. Okonkwo had committed the female, because it had been inadvertent. He could return to the clan after seven years.

That night he collected his most valuable belongings into headloads. His wives wept bitterly and their children wept with them without knowing why. Obierika and half a dozen other friends came to help and to console him. They each made nine or ten trips carrying Okonkwo's yams to store in Obierika's barn. And before the cock crowed Okonkwo and his family were fleeing to his motherland. It was a little village called Mbanta, just beyond the borders of Mbaino.

As soon as the day broke, a large crowd of men from Ezeudu's quarter stormed Okonkwo's compound, dressed in garbs of war. They set fire to his houses, demolished his red walls, killed his animals and destroyed his barn. It was the justice of the earth goddess, and they were merely her messengers. They had no hatred in their hearts against Okonkwo. His greatest friend, Obierika, was among them. They were merely cleansing the land which Okonkwo had polluted with the blood of a clansman.

Obierika was a man who thought about things. When the will of the goddess had been done, he sat down in his *obi* and mourned his friend's calamity. Why should a man suffer so greviously for an offence he had committed inadvertently? But although he thought for a long time he found no answer. He was merely led into greater complexities. He remembered his wife's twin children, whom he had thrown away. What crime had they committed? The Earth had decreed that they were an offence on the land and must be destroyed. And if the clan did not exact punishment for an offence against the great goddess, her wrath was loosed on all the land and not just on the offender. As the elders said, if one finger brought oil it soiled the others.

PART 2

Chapter 14

Okonkwo was well received by his mother's kinsmen in Mbanta. The old man who received him was his mother's younger brother, who was now the eldest surviving member of that family. His name was Uchendu, and it was he who had received Okonkwo's mother twenty and ten years before when she had been brought home from Umuofia to be buried with her people. Okonkwo was only a boy then and Uchendu still remembered him crying the traditional farewell: "Mother, mother, mother is going."

That was many years ago. Today Okonkwo was not bringing his mother home to be buried with her people. He was taking his family of three wives and eleven children to seek refuge in his motherland. As soon as Uchendu saw him with his sad and weary company he guessed what had happened, and asked no questions. It was not until the following day that Okonkwo told him the full story. The old man listened silently to the end and then said with some relief: "It is a female *ochu*." And he arranged the requisite rites and sacrifices.

Okonkwo was given a plot of ground on which to build his compound, and two or three pieces of land on which to farm during the coming planting season. With the help of his mother's kinsmen he built himself an *obi* and three huts for his wives. He then installed his personal god and the symbols of his departed fathers. Each of Uchendu's five sons contributed three hundred seed-yams to enable their cousin to plant a farm, for as soon as the first rain came farming would begin.

At last the rain came. It was sudden and tremendous. For two or three moons the sun had been gathering strength till it seemed to breathe a breath of fire on the earth. All the grass had long been scorched brown, and the sand felt like live coals to the feet. Evergreen trees wore a dusty coat of brown. The birds were silenced in the forests, and the world lay panting under the live, vibrating heat. And then came the clap of thunder. It was an angry, metallic and thirsty clap, unlike the deep and liquid rumbling of the rainy season. A mighty wind arose and filled the air with dust. Palm trees swayed as the wind combed their leaves into flying crests like strange and fantastic coiffure.

When the rain finally came, it was in large, solid drops of frozen water which the people called "the nuts of the water of heaven." They were hard and painful on the body as they fell, yet young people ran about happily picking up the cold nuts and throwing them into their mouths to melt.

The earth quickly came to life and the birds in the forests fluttered around and chirped merrily. A vague scent of life and green vegetation was diffused in the air. As the rain began to fall more soberly and in smaller liquid drops, children sought for shelter, and all were happy, refreshed and thankful.

Okonkwo and his family worked very hard to plant a new farm. But it was like beginning life anew without the vigour and enthusiasm of youth, like learning to become left-handed in old age. Work no longer had for him the pleasure it used to have, and when there was no work to do he sat in a silent half-sleep.

His life had been ruled by a great passion—to become one of the lords of the clan. That had been his life-spring. And he had all but achieved it. Then everything had been broken. He had been cast out of his clan like a fish on to a dry, sandy beach, panting. Clearly his personal god or *chi* was not made for great things. A man could not rise beyond the destiny of his *chi*. The saying of the elders was not true—that if a man said yea his *chi* also affirmed. Here was a man whose *chi* said nay despite his own affirmation.

The old man, Uchendu, saw clearly that Okonkwo had yielded to despair and he was greatly troubled. He would speak to him after the *isa-ifi* ceremony.

The youngest of Uchendu's five sons, Amikwu, was marrying a new wife. The bride-price had been paid and all but the last ceremony had been performed. Amikwu and his people had taken palm-wine to the bride's kinsmen about two moons before Okonkwo's arrival in Mbanta. And so it was time for the final ceremony of confession.

The daughters of the family were all there, some of them having come a long way from their homes in distant villages. Uchendu's eldest daughter had come from Obodo, nearly half a day's journey away. The daughters of Uchendu's brothers were also there. It was a full gathering of *umuada,* in the same way as they would meet if a death occurred in the family. There were twenty-two of them.

They sat in a big circle on the ground and the bride sat in the centre with a hen in her right hand. Uchendu sat by her, holding the ancestral staff of the family. All the other men stood outside the circle, watching. Their wives watched also. It was evening and the sun was setting.

Uchendu's eldest daughter, Njide, asked the questions.

"Remember that if you do not answer truthfully you will suffer or even die at child-birth," she began. "How many men have lain with you since my brother first expressed the desire to marry you?"

"None," she replied simply.

"Answer truthfully," urged the other women.

"None?" asked Njide.

"None," she answered.

"Swear on this staff of my fathers," said Uchendu.

"I swear," said the bride.

Uchendu took the hen from her, slit its throat with a sharp knife and allowed some of the blood to fall on his ancestral staff.

From that day Amikwu took the young bride to his hut and she became his wife. The daughters of the family did not return to their homes immediately but spent two or three days with their kinsmen.

On the second day Uchendu called together his sons and daughters and his nephew, Okonkwo. The men brought their goatskin mats, with which they sat on the floor, and the women sat on a sisal mat spread on a raised bank of earth. Uchendu pulled gently at his grey beard and gnashed his teeth. Then he began to speak, quietly and deliberately, picking his words with great care:

"It is Okonkwo that I primarily wish to speak to," he began. "But I want all of you to note what I am going to say. I am an old man and you are all children. I know more about the world than any of you. If there is any one among you who thinks he knows more let him speak up." He paused, but no one spoke.

"Why is Okonkwo with us today? This is not his clan. We are only his mother's kinsmen. He does not belong here. He is an exile, condemned for seven years to live in a strange land. And so he is bowed with grief. But there is just one question I would like to ask him. Can you tell me, Okonkwo, why it is that one of the commonest names we give our children is Nneka, or 'Mother is Supreme?' We all know that a man is the head of the family and his wives do his bidding. A child belongs to its father and his family and not to its mother and her family. A man belongs to his fatherland and not to his motherland. And yet we say Nneka—'Mother is Supreme.' Why is that?"

There was silence. "I want Okonkwo to answer me," said Uchendu.

"I do not know the answer," Okonkwo replied.

"You do not know the answer? So you see that you are a child. You have many wives and many children—more children than I have. You are a great man in your clan. But you are still a child, *my* child. Listen to me and I shall tell you. But there is one more question I shall ask. Why is it that when a woman dies she is taken home to be buried with her own kinsmen? She is not buried with her husband's kinsmen. Why is that? Your mother was brought home to me and buried with my people. Why was that?"

Okonkwo shook his head.

"He does not know that either," said Uchendu, "and yet he is full of sorrow because he has come to live in his motherland for a few years." He laughed a mirthless laughter, and turned to his sons and daughters. "What about you? Can you answer my question?"

They all shook their heads.

"Then listen to me," he said and cleared his throat. "It's true that a child belongs to its father. But when a father beats his child, it seeks sympathy in its mother's hut. A man belongs to his fatherland when things are good and life is sweet. But when there is sorrow and bitterness he finds refuge in his motherland. Your mother is there to protect you. She is buried there. And that is why we say that mother is supreme. Is it right that you, Okonkwo, should bring your mother a heavy face and refuse to be comforted? Be careful or you may displease the dead. Your duty is to comfort your wives and children and take them back to your fatherland after seven years. But if you allow sorrow to weigh you down and kill you, they will all die in exile." He paused for a long while. "These are now your kinsmen." He waved at his sons and daughters. "You think you are the greatest sufferer in the world. Do you know that men are sometimes banished for life? Do you know that men sometimes lose all their yams and even their children? I had six wives once. I have none now except that young girl who knows not her right from her left. Do you know how many children I have buried—children I begot in my youth and strength? Twenty-two. I did not hang myself, and I am still alive. If you think you are the greatest sufferer in the world ask my daughter, Akueni, how many twins she has borne and thrown away. Have you not heard the song they sing when a woman dies?

> For whom is it well, for whom is it well?
> There is no one for whom it is well.

"I have no more to say to you."

Chapter 15

It was in the second year of Okonkwo's exile that his friend, Obierika, came to visit him. He brought with him two young men, each of them carrying a heavy bag on his head. Okonkwo helped them put down their loads. It was clear that the bags were full of cowries.

Okonkwo was very happy to receive his friend. His wives and children were very happy too, and so were his cousins and their wives when he sent for them and told them who his guest was.

"You must take him to salute our father," said one of the cousins.

"Yes," replied Okonkwo. "We are going directly." But before they went he whispered something to his first wife. She nodded, and soon the children were chasing one of their cocks.

Uchendu had been told by one of his grandchildren that three strangers had come to Okonkwo's house. He was therefore waiting to receive them. He held out his hands to them when they came into his *obi,* and after they had shaken hands he asked Okonkwo who they were.

"This is Obierika, my great friend. I have already spoken to you about him."

"Yes," said the old man, turning to Obierika. "My son has told me about you, and I am happy you have come to see us. I knew your father, Iweka. He was a great man. He had many friends here and came to see them quite often. Those were good days when a man had friends in distant clans. Your generation does not know that. You stay at home, afraid of your next-door neighbour. Even a man's motherland is strange to him nowadays." He looked at Okonkwo. "I am an old man and I like to talk. That is all I am good for now." He got up painfully, went into an inner room and came back with a kola nut.

"Who are the young men with you?" he asked as he sat down again on his goatskin. Okonkwo told him.

"Ah," he said. "Welcome, my sons." He presented the kola nut to them, and when they had seen it and thanked him, he broke it and they ate.

"Go into that room," he aid to Okonkwo, pointing with his finger. "You will find a pot of wine there."

Okonkwo brought the wine and they began to drink. It was a day old, and very strong.

"Yes," said Uchendu after a long silence. "People travelled more in those days. There is not a single clan in these parts that I do not know very well. Aninta, Umuazu, Ikeocha, Elumelu, Abame—I know them all."

"Have you heard," asked Obierika, "that Abame is no more?"

"How is that?" asked Uchendu and Okonkwo together.

"Abame has been wiped out," said Obierika. "It is a strange and terrible story. If I had not seen the few survivors with my own eyes and heard their story with my own ears, I would not have believed. Was it not on an Eke day that they fled into Umuofia?" he asked his two companions, and they nodded their heads.

"Three moons ago," said Obierika, "on an Eke market-day a little band of fugitives came into our town. Most of them were sons of our land whose mothers had been buried with us. But there were some too who came because they had friends in our town, and others who could think of nowhere else open to escape. And so they fled into Umuofia with a woeful story." He drank his palm-wine, and Okonkwo filled his horn again. He continued:

"During the last planting season a white man had appeared in their clan."

"An albino," suggested Okonkwo.

"He was not an albino. He was quite different." He sipped his wine. "And he was riding an iron horse.[1] The first people who saw him ran away, but he stood beckoning to them. In the end the fearless ones were near and even touched him. The elders consulted their Oracle and it told them that the strange man would break their clan and spread destruction among them." Obierika again drank a little of his wine. "And so they killed the white man and tied his iron horse to their sacred tree because it looked as if it would run away to call the man's friends. I forgot to tell you another thing which the Oracle said. It said that other white men were on their way. They were locusts, it said, and that first man was their harbinger sent to explore the terrain. And so they killed him."

---

1. Bicycle.

"What did the white man say before they killed him?" asked Uchendu.

"He said nothing," answered one of Obierika's companions.

"He said something, only they did not understand him," said Obierika. "He seemed to speak through his nose."

"One of the men told me," said Obierika's other companion, "that he repeated over and over again a word that resembled Mbaino. Perhaps he had been going to Mbaino and had lost his way."

"Anyway," resumed Obierika, "they killed him and tied up his iron horse. This was before the planting season began. For a long time nothing happened. The rains had come and yams had been sown. The iron horse was still tied to the sacred silk-cotton tree. And then one morning three white men led by a band of ordinary men like us came to the clan. They saw the iron horse and went away again. Most of the men and women of Abame had gone to their farms. Only a few of them saw these white men and their followers. For many market weeks nothing else happened. They have a big market in Abame on every other Afo day and, as you know, the whole clan gathers there. That was the day it happened. The three white men and a very large number of other men surrounded the market. They must have used a powerful medicine to make themselves invisible until the market was full. And they began to shoot. Everybody was killed, except the old and the sick who were at home and a handful of men and women whose *chi* were wide awake and brought them out of that market." He paused.

"Their clan is now completely empty. Even the sacred fish in their mysterious lake have fled and the lake has turned the colour of blood. A great evil has come upon their land as the Oracle had warned."

There was a long silence. Uchendu ground his teeth audibly. Then he burst out:

"Never kill a man who says nothing. Those men of Abame were fools. What did they know about the man?" He ground his teeth again and told a story to illustrate his point. "Mother Kite once sent her daughter to bring food. She went, and brought back a duckling. 'You have done very well,' said Mother Kite to her daughter, 'but tell me, what did the mother of this duckling say when you swooped and carried its child away?' 'It said nothing,' replied the young kite. 'It just walked away.' 'You must return the duckling,' said the Mother Kite. 'There is something ominous behind the silence.' And so Daughter Kite returned the duckling and took a chick instead. 'What did the mother of this chick do?' asked the old kite. 'It cried and raved and cursed me,' said the young kite. 'Then we can eat the chick,' said her mother. 'There is nothing to fear from someone who shouts.' Those men of Abame were fools."

"They were fools," said Okonkwo after a pause. "They had been warned that danger was ahead. They should have armed themselves with their guns and their matchets even when they went to market."

"They have paid for their foolishness," said Obierika. "But I am greatly afraid. We have heard stories about white men who made the powerful guns and the strong drinks and took slaves away across the seas, but no one thought the stories were true."

"There is no story that is not true," said Uchendu. "The world has no end, and what is good among one people is an abomination with others. We have albinos among us. Do you not think that they came to our clan by mistake, that they have strayed from their ways to a land where everybody is like them?"

Okonkwo's first wife soon finished her cooking and set before their guests a big meal of pounded yams and bitter-leaf soup. Okonkwo's son, Nwoye, brought in a pot of sweet wine tapped from the raffia palm.

"You are a big man now," Obierika said to Nwoye. "Your friend Anene asked me to greet you."

"Is he well?" asked Nwoye.

"We are all well," said Obierika.

Ezinma brought them a bowl of water with which to wash their hands. After that they began to eat and to drink the wine.

"When did you set out from home?" asked Okonkwo.

"We had meant to set out from my house before cock-crow," said Obierika. "But Nweke did not appear until it was quite light. Never make an early morning appointment with a man who has just married a new wife." They all laughed.

"Has Nweke married a wife?" asked Okonkwo.

"He has married Okadigbo's second daughter," said Obierika.

"That is very good," said Okonkwo. "I do not blame you for not hearing the cock crow."

When they had eaten, Obierika pointed at the two heavy bags.

"That is the money from your yams," he said. "I sold the big ones as soon as you left. Later on I sold some of the seed-yams and gave out others to share-croppers. I shall do that every year until you return. But I thought you would need the money now and so I brought it. Who knows what may happen tomorrow? Perhaps green men will come to our clan and shoot us."

"God will not permit it," said Okonkwo. "I do not know how to thank you."

"I can tell you," said Obierika. "Kill one of your sons for me."

"That will not be enough," said Okonkwo.

"Then kill yourself," said Obierika.

"Forgive me," said Okonkwo, smiling. "I shall not talk about thanking you any more."

Chapter 16

When nearly two years later Obierika paid another visit to his friend in exile the circumstances were less happy. The missionaries had come to Umuofia. They had built their church there, won a handful of converts and were already sending evangelists to the surrounding towns and villages. That was a source of great sorrow to the leaders of the clan; but many of them believed that the strange faith and the white man's god would not last. None of his converts was a man whose word was heeded in the assembly of the people. None of them was a man of title. They were mostly the kind of people that were called *efulefu*, worthless, empty men. The imagery of an *efulefu* in the language of the clan was a man who sold his matchet and wore the sheath to battle. Chielo, the priestess of Agbala, called the converts the excrement of the clan, and the new faith was a mad dog that had come to eat it up.

What moved Obierika to visit Okonkwo was the sudden appearance of the latter's son, Nwoye, among the missionaries in Umuofia.

"What are you doing here?" Obierika had asked when after many difficulties the missionaries had allowed him to speak to the boy.

"I am one of them," replied Nwoye.

"How is your father?" Obierika asked, not knowing what else to say.

"I don't know. He is not my father," said Nwoye, unhappily.

And so Obierika went to Mbanta to see his friend. And he found that Okonkwo did not wish to speak about Nwoye. It was only from Nwoye's mother that he heard scraps of the story.

The arrival of the missionaries had caused a considerable stir in the village of Mbanta. There were six of them and one was a white man. Every man and woman came out to see the white man. Stories about these strange men had grown since one of them had been killed in Abame and his iron horse tied to the sacred silk-cotton tree. And so everybody came to see the white man. It was the time of the year when everybody was at home. The harvest was over.

When they had all gathered, the white man began to speak to them. He spoke through an interpreter who was an Ibo man, though his dialect was different and harsh to the ears of Mbanta. Many people laughed at his dialect and the way he used words strangely. Instead of saying "myself" he always said "my buttocks." But he was a man of commanding presence and the clansmen listened to him. He said he was one of them, as they could see from his colour and his language. The other four black men were also their brothers, although one of them did not speak Ibo. The white man was also their brother because they were all sons of God. And he told them about this new God, the Creator of all the world and all the men and women. He told them that they worshipped false gods, gods of wood and stone. A deep murmur went through the crowd when he said this. He told them that the true God lived on high and that all men when they died went before Him for judgment. Evil men and all the heathen who in their blindness bowed to wood and stone were thrown into a fire that burned like palm-oil. But good men who worshipped the true God lived for ever in His happy kingdom. "We have been sent by this great God to ask you to leave your wicked ways and false gods and turn to Him so that you may be saved when you die," he said.

"Your buttocks understand our language," said someone lightheartedly and the crowd laughed.

"What did he say?" the white man asked his interpreter. But before he could answer, another man asked a question: "Where is the white man's horse?" he asked. The Ibo evangelists consulted among themselves and decided that the man probably meant bicycle. They told the white man and he smiled benevolently.

"Tell them," he said, "that I shall bring many iron horses when we have settled down among them. Some of them will even ride the iron horse themselves." This was interpreted to them but very few of them heard. They were talking excitedly among themselves because the white man had said he was going to live among them. They had not thought about that.

At this point an old man said he had a question. "Which is this god of yours," he asked, "the goddess of the earth, the god of the sky, Amadiora of the thunderbolt, or what?"

The interpreter spoke to the white man and he immediately gave his answer. "All the gods you have named are not gods at all. They are gods of deceit who will tell you to kill your fellows and destroy innocent children. There is only one true God and He has made the earth, the sky, you and me and all of us."

"If we leave our gods and follow your god," asked another man, "who will protect us from the anger of our neglected gods and ancestors?"

"Your gods are not alive and cannot do you any harm," replied the white man. "They are pieces of wood and stone."

When this was interpreted to the men of Mbanta they broke into derisive laughter. These men must be mad, they said to themselves. How else could they say that Ani and Amadior were harmless? And Idemili and Ogwugwu too? And some of them began to go away.

Then the missionaries burst into song. It was one of those gay and rollicking tunes of evangelism which had the power of plucking at silent and dusty chords in the heart of an Ibo man. The interpreter explained each verse to the audience, some of whom now stood enthralled. It was a story of brothers who lived in darkness and in fear, ignorant of the love of God. It told of one sheep out on the hills, away from the gates of God and from the tender shepherd's care.

After the singing the interpreter spoke about the Son of God whose name was Jesu Kristi. Okonkwo, who only stayed in the hope that it might come to chasing the men out of the village or whipping them, now said:

"You told us with your own mouth that there was only one god. Now you talk about his son. He must have a wife, then." The crowd agreed.

"I did not say He had a wife," said the interpreter, somewhat lamely.

"Your buttocks said he had a son," said the joker. "So he must have a wife and all of them must have buttocks."

The missionary ignored him and went on to talk about the Holy Trinity. At the end of it Okonkwo was fully convinced that the man was mad. Hs shrugged his shoulders and went away to tap his afternoon palm-wine.

But there was a young lad who had been captivated. His name was Nwoye, Okonkwo's first son. It was not the mad logic of the Trinity that captivated him. He did not understand it. It was the poetry of the new religion, something felt in the marrow. The hymn about brothers who sat in darkness and in fear seemed to answer a vague and persistent question that haunted his young soul—the question of the twins crying in the bush and the question of Ikemefuna who was killed. He felt a relief within as the hymn poured into his parched soul. The words of the hymn were like the drops of frozen rain melting on the dry plate of the panting earth. Nwoye's callow mind was greatly puzzled.

Chapter 17

The missionaries spent their first four or five nights in the market-place, and went into the village in the morning to preach the gospel. They asked who the king of the village was, but the villagers told them that there was no king. "We have men of high title and the chief priests and the elders," they said.

It was not very easy getting the men of high title and the elders together after the excitement of the first day. But the missionaries persevered, and in the end they were received by the rulers of Mbanta. They asked for a plot of land to build their church.

Every clan and village had its "evil forest." In it were buried all those who died of the really evil diseases, like leprosy and smallpox. It was also the dumping ground for the potent fetishes of great medicine-men when they died. An "evil forest" was, therefore, alive with sinister forces and powers of darkness. It was such a forest that the rulers of Mbanta gave to the missionaries. They did not really want them in their clan, and so they made them that offer which nobody in his right senses would accept.

"They want a piece of land to build their shrine," said Uchendu to his peers when they consulted among themselves. "We shall give them a piece of land." He paused, and there was a murmur of surprise and disagreement. "Let us give them a portion of the Evil Forest. They boast about victory over death. Let us give them a real battlefield in which to show their victory." They laughed and agreed, and sent for the missionaries, whom they had asked to leave them for a while so that they might "whisper together." They offered them as much of the Evil Forest as they cared to take. And to their greatest amazement the missionaries thanked them and burst into song.

"They do not understand," said some of the elders. "But they will understand when they go to their plot of land tomorrow morning." And they dispersed.

The next morning the crazy men actually began to clear a part of the forest and to build their house. The inhabitants of Mbanta expected them all to be dead within four days. The first day passed and the second and third and fourth, and none of them died. Everyone was puzzled. And then it became known that the white man's fetish had unbelievable power. It was said that he wore glasses on his eyes so that he could see and talk to evil spirits. Not long after, he won his first three converts.

Although Nwoye had been attracted to the new faith from the very first day, he kept it secret. He dared not go too near the missionaries for fear of his father. But whenever they came to preach in the open market-place or the village playground, Nwoye was there. And he was already beginning to know some of the simple stories they told.

"We have now built a church," said Mr. Kiaga, the interpreter, who was now in charge of the infant congregation. The white man had gone back to Umuofia, where he built his headquarters and from where he paid regular visits to Mr. Kiaga's congregation at Mbanta.

"We have now built a church," said Mr. Kiaga, "and we want you all to come in every seventh day to worship the true God."

On the following Sunday, Nwoye passed and re-passed the little red-earth and thatch building without summoning enough courage to enter. He heard the voice of singing and although it came from a handful of men it was loud and confident. Their church stood on a circular clearing that looked like the open mouth of the Evil Forest. Was it waiting to snap its teeth together? After passing and re-passing by the church, Nwoye returned home.

It was well known among the people of Mbanta that their gods and ancestors were sometimes long-suffering and would deliberately allow a man to go on defying them. But even in such cases they set their limit at seven market weeks or twenty-eight days. Beyond that limit no man was suffered to go. And so excitement mounted in the village as the seventh week approached since the impudent missionaries built their church in the Evil Forest. The villagers were so certain about the doom that awaited these men that one or two converts thought it wise to suspend their allegiance to the new faith.

At last the day came by which all the missionaries should have died. But they were still alive, building a new red-earth and thatch house for their teacher, Mr. Kiaga. That week they won a handful more converts. And for the first time they had a woman. Her name was Nneka, the wife of Amadi, who was a prosperous farmer. She was very heavy with child.

Nneka had had four previous pregnancies and childbirths. But each time she had borne twins, and they had been immediately thrown away. Her husband and his family were already becoming highly critical of such a woman and were not unduly perturbed when they found she had fled to join the Christians. It was a good riddance.

One morning Okonkwo's cousin, Amikwu, was passing by the church on his way from the neighbouring village, when he saw Nwoye among the Christians. He was greatly surprised, and when he got home he went straight to Okonkwo's hut and told him what he had seen. The women began to talk excitedly, but Okonkwo sat unmoved.

It was late afternoon before Nwoye returned. He went into the *obi* and saluted his father, but he did not answer. Nwoye turned round to walk into the inner compound when his father, suddenly overcome with fury, sprang to his feet and gripped him by the neck.

"Where have you been?" he stammered.

Nwoye struggled to free himself from the choking grip.

"Answer me," roared Okonkwo, "before I kill you!" He seized a heavy stick that lay on the dwarf wall and hit him two or three savage blows.

"Answer me!" he roared again. Nwoye stood looking at him and did not say a word. The women were screaming outside, afraid to go in.

"Leave that boy at once!" said a voice in the outer compound. It was Okonkwo's uncle Uchendu. "Are you mad?"

Okonkwo did not answer. But he left hold of Nwoye, who walked away and never returned.

He went back to the church and told Mr. Kiaga that he had decided to go to Umuofia, where the white missionary had set up a school to teach young Christians to read and write.

Mr. Kiaga's joy was very great. "Blessed is he who forsakes his father and his mother for my sake," he intoned. "Those that hear my words are my father and my mother."

Nwoye did not fully understand. But he was happy to leave his father. He would return later to his mother and his brothers and sisters and convert them to the new faith.

As Okonkwo sat in his hut that night, gazing into a log fire, he thought over the matter. A sudden fury rose within him and he felt a strong desire to take up his matchet, go to the church and wipe out the entire vile and miscreant gang. But on further thought he told himself that Nwoye was not worth fighting for. Why, he cried in his heart, should he, Okonkwo, of all people be cursed with such a son? He saw clearly in it the finger of his personal god or *chi*. For how else could he explain his great misfortune and exile and now his despicable son's behaviour? Now that he had time to think of it, his son's crime stood out in stark enormity. To abandon the gods of one's father and go about with a lot of effeminate men clucking like old hens was the very depth of abomination. Suppose when he died all his male children decided to follow Nwoye's steps and abandon their ancestors? Okonkwo felt a cold shudder run through him at the terrible prospect, like the prospect of annihilation. He saw himself and his father crowding round their ancestral shrine waiting in vain for worship and sacrifice and finding nothing but ashes of bygone days, and his children the while praying to the white man's god. If such a thing were ever to happen, he, Okonkwo, would wipe them off the face of the earth.

Okonkwo was popularly called the "Roaring Flame." As he looked into the log fire he recalled the name. He was a flaming fire. How then could he have begotten a son like Nwoye, degenerate and effeminate? Perhaps he was not his son. No! he could not be. His wife had played him false. He would teach her! But Nwoye resembled his grandfather, Unoka, who was Okonkwo's father. He pushed the thought out of his mind. He, Okonkwo, was called a flaming fire. How could he have begotten a woman for a son? At Nwoye's age Okonkwo had already become famous throughout Umuofia for his wrestling and his fearlessness.

He sighed heavily, and as if in sympathy the smouldering log also sighed. And immediately Okonkwo's eyes were opened and he saw the whole matter clearly. Living fire begets cold, impotent ash. He sighed again, deeply.

Chapter 18

The young church in Mbanta had a few crises early in its life. At first the clan had assumed that it would not survive. But it had gone on living and gradually becoming stronger. The clan was worried, but not overmuch. If a gang of *efulefu* decided to live in the Evil Forest it was their own affair. When one came to think of it, the Evil Forest was a fit home for such undesirable people. It was true they were rescuing twins from the bush, but they never brought them into the village. As far as the villagers were concerned, the twins still remained where they had been thrown away. Surely the earth goddess would not visit the sins of the missionaries on the innocent villagers?

But on one occasion the missionaries had tried to overstep the bounds. Three converts had gone into the village and boasted openly that all the gods were dead and impotent and that they were prepared to defy them by burning all their shrines.

"Go and burn your mothers' genitals," said one of the priests. The men were seized and beaten until they streamed with blood. After that nothing happened for a long time between the church and the clan.

But stories were already gaining ground that the white man had not only brought a religion but also a government. It was said that they had built a place of judgement in Umuofia to protect the followers of their religion. It was even said that they had hanged one man who killed a missionary.

Although such stories were now often told they looked like fairy-tales in Mbanta and did not as yet affect the relationship between the new church and the clan. There was no question of killing a missionary here, for Mr. Kiaga, despite his madness, was quite harmless. As for his converts, no one could kill them without having to flee from the clan, for in spite of their worthlessness they still belonged to the clan. And so nobody gave serious thought to the stories about the white man's government or the consequences of killing the Christians. If they became more troublesome than they already were they would simply be driven out of the clan.

And the little church was at that moment too deeply absorbed in its own troubles to annoy the clan. It all began over the question of admitting outcasts.

These outcasts, or *osu*, seeing that the new religion welcomed twins and such abominations, thought that it was possible that they would also be received. And so one Sunday two of them went into the church. There was an immediate stir; but so great was the work the new religion had done among the converts that they did not immediately leave the church when the outcasts came in. Those who found themselves nearest to them merely moved to another seat. It was a miracle. But it only lasted till the end of the service. The whole church raised a protest and were about to drive these people out, when Mr. Kiaga stopped them and began to explain.

"Before God," he said, "there is no slave or free. We are all children of God and we must receive these our brothers."

"You do not understand," said one of the converts. "What will the heathen say of us when they hear that we receive *osu* into our midst? They will laugh."

"Let them laugh," said Mr. Kiaga. "God will laugh at them on the judgment day. Why do the nations rage and the peoples imagine a vain thing? He that sitteth in the heavens shall laugh. The Lord shall have them in derision."

"You do not understand," the convert maintained. "You are our teacher, and you can teach us the things of the new faith. But this is a matter which we know." And he told him what an *osu* was.

He was a person dedicated to a god, a thing set apart—a taboo for ever, and his children after him. He could neither marry nor be married by the free-born. He was in fact an outcast, living in a special area of the village, close to the Great Shrine. Wherever he went he carried with him the mark of his forbidden caste—long, tangled and dirty hair. A razor was taboo to him. An *osu* could not attend an assembly of the free-born, and they, in turn, could not shelter under his roof. He could not take any of the four titles of the clan, and when he died he was buried by his kind in the Evil Forest. How could such a man be a follower of Christ?

"He needs Christ more than you and I," said Mr. Kiaga.

"Then I shall go back to the clan," said the convert. And he went. Mr. Kiaga stood firm, and it was his firmness that saved the young church. The wavering converts drew inspiration and confidence from his unshakable faith. He ordered the outcasts to shave off their long, tangled hair. At first they were afraid they might die.

"Unless you shave off the mark of your heathen belief I will not admit you into the church," said Mr. Kiaga. "You fear that you will die. Why should that be? How are you different from other men who shave their hair? The same God created you and them. But they have cast you out like lepers. It is against the will of God, who has promised everlasting life to all who believe in His holy name. The heathen say you will die if you do this or that, and you are afraid. They also said I would die if I built my church on this ground. Am I dead? They said I would die if I took care of twins. I am still alive. The heathen speak nothing but falsehood. Only the word of our God is true."

The two outcasts shaved off their hair, and soon they were among the strongest adherents of the new faith. And what was more, nearly all the *osu* in Mbanta followed their example. It was in fact one of them who in his zeal brought the church into serious conflict with the clan a year later by killing the sacred python, the emanation of the god of water.

The royal python was the most revered animal in Mbanta and all the surrounding clans. It was addressed as "Our Father," and was allowed to go wherever it chose, even into people's beds. It ate rats in the house and sometimes swallowed hens' eggs. If a clansman killed a royal python accidentally, he made sacrifices of atonement and performed an expensive burial ceremony such as was done for a great man. No punishment was prescribed for a man who killed the python knowingly. Nobody thought that such a thing could ever happen.

Perhaps it never did happen. That was the way the clan at first looked at it. No one had actually seen the man do it. The story had arisen among the Christians themselves.

But, all the same, the rulers and elders of Mbanta assembled to decide on their action. Many of them spoke at great length and in fury. The spirit of war was upon them. Okonkwo, who had begun to play a part in the affairs of his motherland, said that until the abominable gang was chased out of the village with whips there would be no peace.

But there were many others who saw the situation differently, and it was their counsel that prevailed in the end.

"It is not our custom to fight for our gods," said one of them. "Let us not presume to do so now. If a man kills the sacred python in the secrecy of his hut, the matter lies between him and the god. We did not see it. If we put ourselves between the god and his victim we may receive blows intended for the offender. When a man blasphemes what do we do? Do we go and stop his mouth? No. We put our fingers into our ears to stop us hearing. That is a wise action."

"Let us not reason like cowards," said Okonkwo. "If a man comes into my hut and defaecates on the floor, what do I do? Do I shut my eyes? No! I take a stick and break his head. That is what a man does. These people are daily pouring filth over us, and Okeke says we should pretend not to see." Okonkwo made a sound full of disgust. This was a womanly clan, he thought. Such a thing could never happen in his fatherland, Umuofia.

"Okonkwo has spoken the truth," said another man. "We should do something. But let us ostracise these men. We would then not be held accountable for their abominations."

Everybody in the assembly spoke, and in the end it was decided to ostracise the Christians. Okonkwo ground his teeth in disgust.

That night a bell-man went through the length and breadth of Mbanta proclaiming that the adherents of the new faith were thenceforth excluded from the life and privileges of the clan.

The Christians had grown in number and were now a small community of men, women and children, self-assured and confident. Mr. Brown, the white missionary, paid regular visits to them. "When I think that it is only eighteen months since the Seed was first sown among you," he said, "I marvel at what the Lord hath wrought."

It was Wednesday in Holy week and Mr. Kiaga had asked the women to bring red earth and white chalk and water to scrub the church for Easter, and the women had formed themselves into three groups for this purpose. They set out early that morning, some of them with their water-pots to the stream, another group with hoes and baskets to the village red-earth pit, and the others to the chalk quarry.

Mr. Kiaga was praying in the church when he heard the women talking excitedly. He rounded off his prayer and went to see what it was all about. The women had come to the church with empty water-pots. They said that some young men had chased them away from the stream with whips. Soon after, the women who had gone for red earth returned with empty baskets. Some of them had been heavily whipped. The chalk women also returned to tell a similar story.

"What does it all mean?" asked Mr. Kiaga, who was greatly perplexed.

"The village has outlawed us," said one of the women. "The bell-man announced it last night. But it is not our custom to debar anyone from the stream or the quarry."

Another woman said, "They want to ruin us. They will not allow us into the markets. They have said so."

Mr. Kiaga was going to send into the village for his men-converts when he saw them coming on their own. Of course they had all heard the bell-man, but they had never in all their lives heard of women being debarred from the stream.

"Come along," they said to the women. "We will go with you to meet those cowards." Some of them had big sticks and some even matchets.

But Mr. Kiaga restrained them. He wanted first to know why they had been outlawed.

"They say that Okoli killed the sacred python," said one man.

"It is false," said another. "Okoli told me himself that it was false."

Okoli was not there to answer. He had fallen ill on the previous night. Before the day was over he was dead. His death showed that the gods were still able to fight their own battles. The clan saw no reason then for molesting the Christians.

Chapter 19

The last big rains of the year were falling. It was the time for treading red earth with which to build walls. It was not done earlier because the rains were too heavy and would have washed away the heap of trodden earth; and it could not be done later because harvesting would soon set in, and after that the dry season.

It was going to be Okonkwo's last harvest in Mbanta. The seven wasted and weary years were at last dragging to a close. Although he had prospered in his motherland Okonkwo knew that he would have prospered even more in Umuofia, in the land of his fathers where men were bold and warlike. In these seven years he would have climbed to the utmost heights. And so he regretted every day of his exile. His mother's kinsmen had been very kind to him, and he was grateful. But that did not alter the facts. He had called the first child born to him in exile Nneka—"Mother is Supreme"—out of politeness to his mother's kinsmen. But two years later when a son was born he called him Nwofia—"Begotten in the Wilderness."

As soon as he entered his last year in exile Okonkwo sent money to Obierika to build him two huts in his old compound where he and his family would live until he built more huts and the outside wall of his compound. He could not ask another man to build his own *obi* for him, nor the walls of his compound. Those things a man built for himself or inherited from his father.

As the last heavy rains of the year began to fall, Obierika sent word that the two huts had been built and Okonkwo began to prepare for his return, after the rains. He would have liked to return earlier and build his compound that year before the rains stopped, but in doing so he would have taken something from the full penalty of seven years. And that could not be. So he waited impatiently for the dry season to come.

It came slowly. The rain became lighter and lighter until it fell in slanting showers. Sometimes the sun shone through the rain and a light breeze blew. It was a gay and airy kind of rain. The rainbow began to appear, and sometimes two rainbows, like a mother and her daughter, the one young and beautiful, and the other an old and faint shadow. The rainbow was called the python of the sky.

Okonkwo called his three wives and told them to get things together for a great feast. "I must thank my mother's kinsmen before I go," he said.

Ekwefi still had some cassava left on her farm from the previous year. Neither of the other wives had. It was not that they had been lazy, but that they had many children to feed. It was therefore understood that Ekwefi would provide cassava for the feast. Nwoye's mother and Ojiugo would provide the other things like smoked fish, palm-oil and pepper for the soup. Okonkwo would take care of meat and yams.

Ekwefi rose early on the following morning and went to her farm with her daughter, Ezinma, and Ojiugo's daughter, Obiageli, to harvest cassava tubers. Each of them carried a long cane basket, a matchet for cutting down the soft cassava stem, and a little hoe for digging out the tuber. Fortunately, a light rain had fallen during the night and the soil would not be very hard.

"It will not take us long to harvest as much as we like," said Ekwefi.

"But the leaves will be wet," said Ezinma. Her basket was balanced on her head, and her arms folded across her breasts. She felt cold. "I dislike cold water dropping on my back. We should have waited for the sun to rise and dry the leaves."

Obiageli called her 'Salt' because she said that she disliked water. "Are you afraid you may dissolve?"

The harvesting was easy, as Ekwefi had said. Ezinma shook every tree violently with a long stick before she bent down to cut the stem and dig out the tuber. Sometimes it was not necessary to dig. They just pulled the stump and earth rose, roots snapped below, and the tuber was pulled out.

When they had harvested a sizeable heap they carried it down in two trips to the steam, where every woman had a shallow well for fermenting her cassava.

"It should be ready in four days or even three," said Obiageli. "They are young tubers."

"They are not all that young," said Ekwefi. "I planted the farm nearly two years ago. It is a poor soil and that is why the tubers are so small."

Okonkwo never did things by halves. When his wife Ekwefi protested that two goats were sufficient for the feast he told her that it was not her affair.

"I am calling a feast because I have the wherewithal. I cannot live on the bank of a river and wash my hands with spittle. My mother's people have been good to me and I must show my gratitude."

And so three goats were slaughtered and a number of fowls. It was like a wedding feast. There was foo-foo and yam pottage, egusi[2] soup and bitter-leaf soup and pots and pots of palm-wine.

All the *umunna* were invited to the feast, all the descendants of Okolo, who had lived about two hundred years before. The oldest member of this extensive family was Okonkwo's uncle, Uchendu. The kola nut was given to him to break, and he prayed to the ancestors. He asked them for health and children. "We do not ask for wealth because he that has health and children will also have wealth. We do not pray to have more money but to have more kinsmen. We are better than animals because we have kinsmen. An animal rubs its aching flank against a tree, a man asks his kinsman to scratch him." He prayed especially for Okonkwo and his family. He then broke the kola nut and threw one of the lobes on the ground for the ancestors.

As the broken kola nuts were passed round, Okonkwo's wives and children and those who came to help them with the cooking began to bring out the food. His sons brought out the pots of palm-wine. There was so much food and drink that many kinsmen whistled in surprise. When all was laid out, Okonkwo rose to speak.

"I beg you to accept this little kola," he said. "It is not to pay you back for all you did for me in these seven years. A child cannot pay for its mother's milk. I have only called you together because it is good for kinsmen to meet."

Yam pottage was served first because it was lighter than foo-foo and because yam always came first. Then the foo-foo was served. Some kinsmen ate it with egusi soup and others with bitter-leaf soup. The meat was then shared so that every member of the *umunna* had a portion. Every man rose in order of years and took a share. Even the few kinsmen who had not been able to come had their shares taken out for them in due turn.

As the palm-wine was drunk one of the oldest members of the *umunna* rose to thank Okonkwo:

"If I say that we did not expect such a big feast I will be suggesting that we did not know how open-handed our son, Okonkwo is. We all know him, and we expected a big feast. But it turned out to be even bigger than we expected. Thank you. May all you took out return again tenfold. It is good in these days when the younger generation consider themselves wiser than their sires to see a man doing things in the grand, old way. A man who calls his kinsmen to a feast does not do so to save them from starving. They all have food in their own homes. When we gather together in the moonlit village ground it is not because of the moon. Every man can see it in his own compound. We come together because it is good for kinsmen to do so. You may ask

---

2. Melon seed.

why I am saying all this. I say it because I fear for the younger generation, for you people." He waved his arm where most of the young men sat. "As for me, I have only a short while to live, and so have Uchendu and Unachukwu and Emefo. But I fear for you young people because you do not understand how strong is the bond of kinship. You do not know what it is to speak with one voice. And what is the result? An abominable religion has settled among you. A man can now leave his father and his brothers. He can curse the gods of his fathers and his ancestors, like a hunter's dog that suddenly goes mad and turns on his master. I fear for you; I fear for the clan." He turned again to Okonkwo and said, "Thank you for calling us together."

PART 3

Chapter 20

Seven years was a long time to be away from one's clan. A man's place was not always there, waiting for him. As soon as he left, someone else rose and filled it. The clan was like a lizard; if it lost its tail it soon grew another.

Okonkwo knew these things. He knew that he had lost his place among the nine masked spirits who administered justice in the clan. He had lost the chance to lead his warlike clan against the new religion, which, he was told, had gained ground. He had lost the years in which he might have taken the highest titles in the clan. But some of these losses were not irreparable. He was determined that his return should be marked by his people. He would return with a flourish, and regain the seven wasted years.

Even in his first year in exile he had begun to plan for his return. The first thing he would do would be to rebuild his compound on a more magnificent scale. He would build a bigger barn than he had before and he would build huts for two new wives. Then he would show his wealth by initiating his sons in the *ozo* society. Only the really great men in the clan were able to do this. Okonkwo saw clearly the high esteem in which he would be held, and he saw himself taking the highest title in the land.

As the years of exile passed one by one it seemed to him that his *chi* might now be making amends for the past disaster. His yams grew abundantly, not only in his motherland but also in Umuofia, where his friend gave them out year by year to share-croppers.

Then the tragedy of his first son had occurred. At first it appeared as if it might prove too great for his spirit. But it was a resilient spirit, and in the end Okonkwo overcame his sorrow. He had five other sons and he would bring them up in the way of the clan.

He sent for the five sons and they came and sat in his *obi*. The youngest of them was four years old.

"You have all seen the great abomination of your brother. Now he is no longer my son or your brother. I will only have a son who is a man, who will hold his head up among my people. If any one of you prefers to be a woman, let him follow Nwoye now while I am alive so that I can curse him. If you turn against me when I am dead I will visit you and break your neck."

Okonkwo was very lucky in his daughters. He never stopped regretting that Ezinma was a girl. Of all his children she alone understood his every mood. A bond of sympathy had grown between them as the years had passed.

Ezinma grew up in her father's exile and became one of the most beautiful girls in Mbanta. She was called Crystal of Beauty, as her mother had been called in her youth. The young ailing girl who had caused her mother so much heartache had been transformed, almost overnight, into a healthy, buoyant maiden. She had, it was true, her moments of depression when she would snap at everybody like an angry dog. These moods descended on her suddenly and for no apparent reason. But they were very rare and short-lived. As long as they lasted, she could bear no other person but her father.

Many young men and prosperous middle-aged men of Mbanta came to marry her. But she refused them all, because her father had called her one evening and said to her: "There are many good and prosperous people here, but I shall be happy if you marry in Umuofia when we return home."

That was all he had said. But Ezinma had seen clearly all the thought and hidden meaning behind the few words. And she had agreed.

"Your half-sister, Obiageli, will not understand me," Okonkwo said. "But you can explain to her."

Although they were almost the same age. Ezinma wielded a strong influence over her half-sister. She explained to her why they should not marry yet, and she agreed also. And so the two of them refused every offer of marriage in Mbanta.

"I wish she were a boy," Okonkwo thought within himself. She understood things so perfectly. Who else among his children could have read his thought so well? With two beautiful grown-up daughters his return to Umuofia would attract considerable attention. His future sons-in-law would be men of authority in the clan. The poor and unknown would not dare to come forth.

Umuofia had indeed changed during the seven years Okonkwo had been in exile. The church had come and led many astray. Not only the low-born and the outcast but sometimes a worthy man had joined it. Such a man was Ogbuefi Ugonna,[1] who had taken two titles, and who like a madman had cut the anklet of his titles and cast it away to join the Christians. The white missionary was very proud of him and he was one of the first men in Umuofia to receive the sacrament of Holy Communion, or Holy Feast as it was called in Ibo. Ogbuefi Ugonna had thought of the Feast in terms of eating and drinking, only more holy than the village variety. He had therefore put his drinking-horn into his goatskin bag for the occasion.

But apart from the church, the white men had also brought a government. They had built a court where the District Commissioner judged cases in ignorance. He had court messengers who brought men to him for trial. Many of these messengers came from Umuru on the bank of the Great River, where the white men first came many years before and where they had built the centre of their religion and trade and government. These court messengers were greatly hated in Umuofia because they were foreigners and also arrogant and high-handed. They were called *kotma*, and because of their ash-coloured shorts they earned the additional name of Ashy-Buttocks. They guarded the prison, which was full of men who had offended against the white man's law. Some of these prisoners had thrown away their twins and some had molested the Christians. They were beaten in the prison by the *kotma* and made to work every morning clearing the government compound and fetching wood for the white Commissioner and the court messengers. Some of these prisoners were men of title who should be above such mean occupation. They were grieved by the indignity and mourned for their neglected farms. As they cut grass in the morning the younger men sang in time with the strokes of their matchets:

1. Father's honor, lit. "with an eagle feather."

> Kotma *of the ash buttocks,*
> *He is fit to be a slave*
> *The white man has no sense,*
> *He is fit to be a slave*

The court messengers did not like to be called Ashy-Buttocks, and they beat the men. But the song spread in Umuofia.

Okonkwo's head was bowed in sadness as Obierika told him these things.

"Perhaps I have been away too long," Okonkwo said, almost to himself. "But I cannot understand these things you tell me. What is it that has happened to our people? Why have they lost the power to fight?"

"Have you not heard how the white man wiped out Abame?" asked Obierika.

"I have heard," said Okonkwo. "But I have also heard that Abame people were weak and foolish. Why did they not fight back? Had they no guns and matchets? We would be cowards to compare ourselves with the men of Abame. Their fathers had never dared to stand before our ancestors. We must fight these men and drive them from the land."

"It is already too late," said Obierika sadly. "Our own men and our sons have joined the ranks of the stranger. They have joined his religion and they help to uphold his government. If we should try to drive out the white men in Umuofia we should find it easy. There are only two of them. But what of our own people who are following their way and have been given power? They would go to Umuru and bring the soldiers, and we would be like Abame." He paused for a long time and then said: "I told you on my last visit to Mbanta how they hanged Aneto."

"What has happened to that piece of land in dispute?" asked Okonkwo.

"The white man's court has decided that it should belong to Nnama's family, who had given much money to the white man's messengers and interpreter."

"Does the white man understand our custom about land?"

"How can he when he does not even speak our tongue? But he says that our customs are bad; and our own brothers who have taken up his religion also say that our customs are bad. How do you think we can fight when our own brothers have turned against us? The white man is very clever. He came quietly and peaceably with his religion. We were amused at his foolishness and allowed him to stay. Now he has won our brothers, and our clan can no longer act like one. He has put a knife on the things that held us together and we have fallen apart."

"How did they get hold of Aneto to hang him?" asked Okonkwo.

"When he killed Oduche in the fight over the land, he fled to Aninta to escape the wrath of the earth. This was about eight days after the fight, because Oduche had not died immediately from his wounds. It was on the seventh day that he died. But everybody knew that he was going to die and Aneto got his belongings together in readiness to flee. But the Christians had told the white man about the accident, and he sent his *kotma* to catch Aneto. He was imprisoned with all the leaders of his family. In the end Oduche died and Aneto was taken to Umuru and hanged. The other people were released, but even now they have not found the mouth with which to tell of their suffering."

The two men sat in silence for a long while afterwards.

Chapter 21

There were many men and women in Umuofia who did not feel as strongly as Okonkwo about the new dispensation. The white man had indeed brought a lunatic religion, but he had also built a trading store and for the first time palm-oil and kernel became things of great price, and much money flowed into Umuofia.

And even in the matter of religion there was a growing feeling that there might be something in it after all, something vaguely akin to method in the overwhelming madness.

This growing feeling was due to Mr. Brown, the white missionary, who was very firm in restraining his flock from provoking the wrath of the clan. One member in particular was very difficult to restrain. His name was Enoch and his father was the priest of the snake cult. The story went around that Enoch had killed and eaten the sacred python, and that his father had cursed him.

Mr. Brown preached against such excess of zeal. Everything was possible, he told his energetic flock, but everything was not expedient. And so Mr. Brown came to be respected even by the clan, because he trod softly on its faith. He made friends with some of the great men of the clan and on one of his frequent visits to the neighbouring villages he had been presented with a carved elephant tusk, which was a sign of dignity and rank. One of the great men in that village was called Akunna and he had given one of his sons to be taught the white man's knowledge in Mr. Brown's school.

Whenever Mr. Brown went to that village he spent long hours with Akunna in his *obi* talking through an interpreter about religion. Neither of them succeeded in converting the other but they learnt more about their different beliefs.

"You say that there is one supreme God who made heaven and earth," said Akunna on one of Mr. Brown's visits. "We also believe in Him and call Him Chukwu. He made all the world and the other gods."

"There are no other gods," said Mr. Brown. "Chukwu is the only God and all others are false. You carve a piece of wood—like that one" (he pointed at the rafters from which Akunna's carved *Ikenga* hung), "and you call it a god. But it is still a piece of wood."

"Yes," said Akunna. "It is indeed a piece of wood. The tree from which it came was made by Chukwu, as indeed all minor gods were. But He made them for His messengers so that we could approach Him through them. It is like yourself. You are the head of your church."

"No," protested Mr. Brown. "The head of my church is God Himself."

"I know," said Akunna, "but there must be a head in this world among men. Somebody like yourself must be the head here."

"The head of my church in that sense is in England."

"That is exactly what I am saying. The head of your church is in your country. He has sent you here as his messenger. And you have also appointed your own messengers and servants. Or let me take another example, the District Commissioner. He is sent by your king."

"They have a queen," said the interpreter on his own account.

"Your queen sends her messenger, the District Commissioner. He finds that he cannot do the work alone and so he appoints *kotma* to help him. It is the same with God, or Chukwu. He appoints the smaller gods to help Him because His work is too great for one person."

"You should not think of him as a person," said Mr. Brown. "It is because you do so that you imagine He must need helpers. And the worst thing about it is that you give all the worship to the false gods you have created."

"That is not so. We make sacrifices to the little gods, but when they fail and there is no one else to turn to we go to Chukwu. It is right to do so. We approach a great man through his servants. But when his servants fail to help us, then we go to the last source of hope. We appear to pay greater attention to the little gods but that is not so. We worry them more because we are afraid to worry their Master. Our fathers knew that Chukwu was the Overlord and that is why many of them gave their children the name Chukwuka—'Chukwu is Supreme.'"

"You said one interesting thing," said Mr. Brown. "You are afraid of Chukwu. In my religion Chukwu is a loving Father and need not be feared by those who do His will."

"But we must fear Him when we are not doing His will," said Akunna. "And who is to tell His will? It is too great to be known."

In this way Mr. Brown learnt a good deal about the religion of the clan and he came to the conclusion that a frontal attack on it would not succeed. And so he built a school and a little hospital in Umuofia. He went from family to family begging people to send their children to his school. But at first they only sent their slaves or sometimes their lazy children. Mr. Brown begged and argued and prophesied. He said that the leaders of the land in the future would be men and women who had learnt to read and write. If Umuofia failed to send her children to the school, strangers would come from other places to rule them. They could already see that happening in the Native Court, where the D. C. was surrounded by strangers who spoke his tongue. Most of these strangers came from the distant town of Umuru on the bank of the Great River where the white man first went.

In the end Mr. Brown's arguments began to have an effect. More people came to learn in his school, and he encouraged them with gifts of singlets[2] and towels. They were not all young, these people who came to learn. Some of them were thirty years old or more. They worked on their farms in the morning and went to school in the afternoon. And it was not long before the people began to say that the white man's medicine was quick in working. Mr. Brown's school produced quick results. A few months in it were enough to make one a court messenger or even a court clerk. Those who stayed longer became teachers; and from Umuofia labourers went forth into the Lord's vineyard. New churches were established in the surrounding villages and a few schools with them. From the very beginning religion and education went hand in hand.

Mr. Brown's mission grew from strength to strength, and because of its link with the new administration it earned a new social prestige. But Mr. Brown himself was breaking down in health. At first he ignored the warning signs. But in the end he had to leave his flock, sad and broken.

It was in the first rainy season after Okonkwo's return to Umuofia that Mr. Brown left for home. As soon as he had learnt of Okonkwo's return five months earlier, the missionary had immediately paid him a visit. He had just sent Okonkwo's son, Nwoye, who was now called Isaac,[3] to the new training college for teachers in Umuru. And he had hoped that Okonkwo would be happy to hear of it. But Okonkwo had driven him away with the threat that if he came into his compound again, he would be carried out of it.

Okonkwo's return to his native land was not as memorable as he had wished. It was true his two beautiful daughters aroused great interest among suitors and marriage negotiations were soon in progress, but, beyond that, Umuofia did not appear to have taken any special notice of the warrior's return. The clan had undergone such profound change during his exile that it was barely recognizable. The new religion

---

2. T-shirts.   3. Son of Abraham, Genesis 22.

and government and the trading stores were very much in the people's eyes and minds. There were still many who saw these new institutions as evil, but even they talked and thought about little else, and certainly not about Okonkwo's return.

And it was the wrong year too. If Okonkwo had immediately initiated his two sons into the *ozo* society as he had planned he would have caused a stir. But the initiation rite was performed once in three years in Umuofia, and he had to wait for nearly two years for the next round of ceremonies.

Okonkwo was deeply grieved. And it was not just a personal grief. He mourned for the clan, which he saw breaking up and falling apart, and he mourned for the warlike men of Umuofia, who had so unaccountably become soft like women.

Chapter 22

Mr. Brown's successor was the Reverend James Smith, and he was a different kind of man. He condemned openly Mr. Brown's policy of compromise and accommodation. He saw things as black and white. And black was evil. He saw the world as a battlefield in which the children of light were locked in mortal conflict with the sons of darkness. He spoke in his sermons about sheep and goats and about wheat and tares. He believed in slaying the prophets of Baal.

Mr. Smith was greatly distressed by the ignorance which many of his flock showed even in such things as the Trinity and the Sacraments. It only showed that they were seeds sown on a rocky soil. Mr. Brown had thought of nothing but numbers. He should have known that the kingdom of God did not depend on large crowds. Our Lord Himself stressed the importance of fewness. Narrow is the way and few the number. To fill the Lord's holy temple with an idolatrous crowd clamouring for signs was a folly of everlasting consequence. Our Lord used the whip only once in His Life—to drive the crowd away from His church.

Within a few weeks of his arrival in Umuofia Mr. Smith suspended a young woman from the church for pouring new wine into old bottles. This woman had allowed her heathen husband to mutilate her dead child. The child had been declared an *ogbanje,* plaguing its mother by dying and entering her womb to be born again. Four times this child had run its evil round. And so it was mutilated to discourage it from returning.

Mr. Smith was filled with wrath when he heard of this. He disbelieved the story which even some of the most faithful confirmed, the story of really evil children who were not deterred by mutilation, but came back with all the scars. He replied that such stories were spread in the world by the Devil to lead men astray. Those who believed such stories were unworthy of the Lord's table.

There was a saying in Umuofia that as a man danced so the drums were beaten for him. Mr. Smith danced a furious step and so the drums went mad. The overzealous converts who had smarted under Mr. Brown's restraining hand now flourished in full favour. One of them was Enoch, the son of the snake-priest who was believed to have killed and eaten the sacred python. Enoch's devotion to the new faith had seemed so much greater than Mr. Brown's that the villagers called him The Outsider who wept louder than the bereaved.

Enoch was short and slight of build, and always seemed in great haste. His feet were short and broad, and when he stood or walked his heels came together and his feet opened outwards as if they had quarrelled and meant to go in different directions. Such was the excessive energy bottled up in Enoch's small body that it was always erupting in quarrels and fights. On Sundays he always imagined that the sermon was preached for the benefit of his enemies. And if he happened to sit near one of them he would occasionally turn to give him a meaningful look, as if to say, "I told you so." It was Enoch who touched off the great conflict between church and clan in Umuofia which had been gathering since Mr. Brown left.

It happened during the annual ceremony which was held in honour of the earth deity. At such times the ancestors of the clan who had been committed to Mother Earth at their death emerged again as *egwugwu* through tiny ant-holes.

One of the greatest crimes a man could commit was to unmask an *egwugwu* in public, or to say or do anything which might reduce its immortal prestige in the eyes of the uninitiated. And this was what Enoch did.

The annual worship of the earth goddess fell on a Sunday, and the masked spirits were abroad. The Christian women who had been to church could not therefore go home. Some of their men had gone out to beg the *egwugwu* to retire for a short while for the women to pass. They agreed and were already retiring, when Enoch boasted aloud that they would not dare to touch a Christian. Whereupon they all came back and one of them gave Enoch a good stroke of the cane, which was always carried. Enoch fell on him and tore off his mask. The other *egwugwu* immediately surrounded their desecrated companion, to shield him from the profane gaze of women and children, and led him away. Enoch had killed an ancestral spirit, and Umuofia was thrown into confusion.

That night the Mother of the Spirits walked the length and breadth of the clan, weeping for her murdered son. It was a terrible night. Not even the oldest man in Umuofia had ever heard such a strange and fearful sound, and it was never to be heard again. It seemed as if the very soul of the tribe wept for a great evil that was coming— its own death.

On the next day all the masked *egwugwu* of Umuofia assembled in the market-place. They came from all the quarters of the clan and even from the neighbouring villages. The dreadful Otakagu came from Imo, and Ekwensu, dangling a white cock, arrived from Uli. It was a terrible gathering. The eerie voices of countless spirits, the bells that clattered behind some of them, and the clash of matchets as they ran forwards and backwards and saluted one another, sent tremors of fear into every heart. For the first time in living memory the sacred bullroarer was heard in broad daylight.

From the market-place the furious band made for Enoch's compound. Some of the elders of the clan went with them, wearing heavy protections of charms and amulets. These were men whose arms were strong in *ogwu*, or medicine. As for the ordinary men and women, they listened from the safety of their huts.

The leaders of the Christians had met together at Mr. Smith's parsonage on the previous night. As they deliberated they could hear the Mother of Spirits wailing for her son. The chilling sound affected Mr. Smith, and for the first time he seemed to be afraid.

"What are they planning to do?" he asked. No one knew, because such a thing had never happened before. Mr. Smith would have sent for the District Commissioner and his court messengers, but they had gone on tour on the previous day.

"One thing is clear," said Mr. Smith. "We cannot offer physical resistance to them. Our strength lies in the Lord." They knelt down together and prayed to God for delivery.

"O Lord save Thy people," cried Mr. Smith.

"And bless Thine inheritance," replied the men.

They decided that Enoch should be hidden in the parsonage for a day or two. Enoch himself was greatly disappointed when he heard this, for he had hoped that a holy war was imminent; and there were a few other Christians who thought like him. But wisdom prevailed in the camp of the faithful and many lives were thus saved.

The band of *egwugwu* moved like a furious whirlwind to Enoch's compound and with matchet and fire reduced it to a desolate heap. And from there they made for the church, intoxicated with destruction.

Mr. Smith was in his church when he heard the masked spirits coming. He walked quietly to the door which commanded the approach to the church compound, and stood there. But when the first three or four *egwugwu* appeared on the church compound he nearly bolted. He overcame this impulse and instead of running away he went down the two steps that led up to the church and walked towards the approaching spirits.

They surged forward, and a long stretch of the bamboo fence with which the church compound was surrounded gave way before them. Discordant bells clanged, matchets clashed and the air was full of dust and weird sounds. Mr. Smith heard a sound of footsteps behind him. He turned round and saw Okeke, his interpreter. Okeke had not been on the best of terms with his master since he had strongly condemned Enoch's behaviour at the meeting of the leaders of the church during the night. Okeke had gone as far as to say that Enoch should not be hidden in the parsonage, because he would only draw the wrath of the clan on the pastor. Mr. Smith had rebuked him in very strong language, and had not sought his advice that morning. But now, as he came up and stood by him confronting the angry spirits, Mr. Smith looked at him and smiled. It was a wan smile, but there was deep gratitude there.

For a brief moment the onrush of the *egwugwu* was checked by the unexpected composure of the two men. But it was only a momentary check, like the tense silence between blasts of thunder. The second onrush was greater than the first. It swallowed up the two men. Then an unmistakable voice rose above the tumult and there was immediate silence. Space was made around the two men, and Ajofia began to speak.

Ajofia was the leading *egwugwu* of Umuofia. He was the head and spokesman of the nine ancestors who administered justice in the clan. His voice was unmistakable and so he was able to bring immediate peace to the agitated spirits. He then addressed Mr. Smith, and as he spoke clouds of smoke rose from his head.

"The body of the white man, I salute you," he said, using the language in which immortals spoke to men.

"The body of the white man, do you know me?" he asked.

Mr. Smith looked at his interpreter, but Okeke, who was a native of distant Umuru, was also at a loss.

Ajofia laughed in his gutteral voice. It was like the laugh of rusty metal. "They are strangers," he said, "and they are ignorant. But let that pass." He turned round to his comrades and saluted them, calling them the fathers of Umuofia. He dug his rattling spear into the ground and it shook with metallic life. Then he turned once more to the missionary and his interpreter.

"Tell the white man that we will not do him any harm," he said to the interpreter. "Tell him to go back to his house and leave us alone. We liked his brother who was with us before. He was foolish, but we liked him, and for his sake we shall not harm his brother. But this shrine which he built must be destroyed. We shall no longer allow it in our midst. It has bred untold abominations and we have come to put an end to it." He turned to his comrades, "Fathers of Umuofia, I salute you;" and they replied with one gutteral voice. He turned again to the missionary. "You can stay with us if you like our ways. You can worship your own god. It is good that a man should worship the gods and the spirits of his fathers. Go back to your house so that you may not be hurt. Our anger is great but we have held it down so that we can talk to you."

Mr. Smith said to his interpreter: "Tell them to go away from here. This is the house of God and I will not live to see it desecrated."

Okeke interpreted wisely to the spirits and leaders of Umuofia: "The white man says he is happy you have come to him with your grievances, like friends. He will be happy if you leave the matter in his hands."

"We cannot leave the matter in his hands because he does not understand our customs, just as we do not understand his. We say he is foolish because he does not know our ways, and perhaps he says we are foolish because we do not know his. Let him go away."

Mr. Smith stood his ground. But he could not save his church. When the *egwugwu* went away the red-earth church which Mr. Brown had built was a pile of earth and ashes. And for the moment the spirit of the clan was pacified.

Chapter 23

For the first time in many years Okonkwo had a feeling that was akin to happiness. The times which had altered so unaccountably during his exile seemed to be coming round again. The clan which had turned false on him appeared to be making amends.

He had spoken violently to his clansmen when they had met in the market-place to decide on their action. And they had listened to him with respect. It was like the good old days again, when a warrior was a warrior. Although they had not agreed to kill the missionary or drive away the Christians, they had agreed to do something substantial. And they had done it. Okonkwo was almost happy again.

For two days after the destruction of the church, nothing happened. Every man in Umuofia went about armed with a gun or a matchet. They would not be caught unawares, like the men of Abame.

Then the District Commissioner returned from his tour. Mr. Smith went immediately to him and they had a long discussion. The men of Umuofia did not take any notice of this, and if they did, they thought it was not important. The missionary often went to see his brother white man. There was nothing strange in that.

Three days later the District Commissioner sent his sweet-tongued messenger to the leaders of Umuofia asking them to meet him in his headquarters. That also was not strange. He often asked them to hold such palavers, as he called them. Okonkwo was among the six leaders he invited.

Okonkwo warned the others to be fully armed. "An Umuofia man does not refuse a call," he said. "He may refuse to do what he is asked; he does not refuse to be asked. But the times have changed, and we must be fully prepared."

And so the six men went to see the District Commissioner, armed with their matchets. They did not carry guns, for that would be unseemly. They were led into the court-house where the District Commissioner sat. He received them politely. They unslung their goatskin bags and their sheathed matchets, put them on the floor, and sat down.

"I have asked you to come," began the Commissioner, "because of what happened during my absence. I have been told a few things but I cannot believe them until I have heard your own side. Let us talk about it like friends and find a way of ensuring that it does not happen again."

Ogbuefi Ekwueme rose to his feet and began to tell the story.

"Wait a minute," said the Commissioner. "I want to bring in my men so that they too can hear your grievances and take warning. Many of them come from distant places and although they speak your tongue they are ignorant of your customs. James! Go and bring in the men." His interpreter left the court-room and soon returned with twelve men. They sat together with the men of Umuofia, and Ogbuefi Ekwueme began again to tell the story of how Enoch murdered an *egwugwu*.

It happened so quickly that the six men did not see it coming. There was only a brief scuffle, too brief even to allow the drawing of a sheathed matchet. The six men were handcuffed and led into the guardroom.

"We shall not do you any harm," said the District Commissioner to them later, "if only you agree to co-operate with us. We have brought a peaceful administration to you and your people so that you may be happy. If any man ill-treats you we shall come to your rescue. But we will not allow you to ill-treat others. We have a court of law where we judge cases and administer justice just as it is done in my own country under a great queen. I have brought you here because you joined together to molest others, to burn people's houses and their place of worship. That must not happen in the dominion of our queen, the most powerful ruler in the world. I have decided that you will pay a fine of two hundred bags of cowries. You will be released as soon as you agree to this and undertake to collect that fine from your people. What do you say to that?"

The six men remained sullen and silent and the Commissioner left them for a while. He told the court messengers, when he left the guardroom, to treat the men with respect because they were the leaders of Umuofia. They said, "Yes, sir," and saluted.

As soon as the District Commissioner left, the head messenger, who was also the prisoners' barber, took down his razor and shaved off all the hair on the men's heads. They were still handcuffed, and they just sat and moped.

"Who is the chief among you?" the court messenger asked in jest. "We see that every pauper wears the anklet of title in Umuofia. Does it cost as much as ten cowries?"

The six men ate nothing throughout that day and the next. They were not even given any water to drink, and they could not go out to urinate or go into the bush when they were pressed. At night the messengers came in to taunt them and to knock their shaven heads together.

Even when the men were left alone they found no words to speak to one another. It was only on the third day, when they could no longer bear the hunger and the insults, that they began to talk about giving in.

"We should have killed the white man if you had listened to me," Okonkwo snarled.

"We could have been in Umuru now waiting to be hanged," someone said to him.

"Who wants to kill the white man?" asked a messenger who had just rushed in. Nobody spoke.

"You are not satisfied with your crime, but you must kill the white man on top of it." He carried a strong stick, and he hit each man a few blows on the head and back. Okonkwo was choked with hate.

As soon as the six men were locked up, court messengers went into Umuofia to tell the people that their leaders would not be released unless they paid a fine of two hundred and fifty bags of cowries.

"Unless you pay the fine immediately," said their headman, "we will take your leaders to Umuru before the big white man, and hang them."

This story spread quickly through the villages, and was added to as it went. Some said that the men had already been taken to Umuru and would be hanged on the following day. Some said that their families would also be hanged. Others said that soldiers were already on their way to shoot the people of Umuofia as they had done in Abame.

It was the time of the full moon. But that night the voice of children was not heard. The village *ilo* where they always gathered for a moon-play was empty. The women of Iguedo did not meet in their secret enclosure to learn a new dance to be displayed later to the village. Young men who were always abroad in the moonlight kept their huts that night. Their manly voices were not heard on the village paths as they went to visit their friends and lovers. Umuofia was like a startled animal with ears erect, sniffing the silent, ominous air and not knowing which way to run.

The silence was broken by the village crier beating his sonorous *ogene*. He called every man in Umuofia, from the Akakanma age-group upwards, to a meeting in the market-place after the morning meal. He went from one end of the village to the other and walked all its breadth. He did not leave out any of the main footpaths.

Okonkwo's compound was like a deserted homestead. It was as if cold water had been poured on it. His family was all there, but everyone spoke in whispers. His daughter Ezinma had broken her twenty-eight day visit to the family of her future husband, and returned home when she heard that her father had been imprisoned, and was going to be hanged. As soon as she got home she went to Obierika to ask what the men of Umuofia were going to do about it. But Obierika had not been home since morning. His wives thought he had gone to a secret meeting. Ezinma was satisfied that something was being done.

On the morning after the village crier's appeal the men of Umuofia met in the market-place and decided to collect without delay two hundred and fifty bags of cowries to appease the white man. They did not know that fifty bags would go to the court messengers, who had increased the fine for that purpose.

Chapter 24

Okonkwo and his fellow prisoners were set free as soon as the fine was paid. The District Commissioner spoke to them again about the great queen, and about peace and good government. But the men did not listen. They just sat and looked at him and at his interpreter. In the end they were given back their bags and sheathed matchets and told to go home. They rose and left the court-house. They neither spoke to anyone nor among themselves.

The court-house, like the church, was built a little way outside the village. The footpath that linked them was a very busy one because it also led to the stream, beyond the court. It was open and sandy. Footpaths were open and sandy in the dry season. But when the rains came the bush grew thick on either side and closed in on the path. It was now dry season.

As they made their way to the village the six men met women and children going to the stream with their waterpots. But the men wore such heavy and fearsome looks that the women and children did not say "*nno*" or "welcome" to them, but edged out of the way to let them pass. In the village little groups of men joined them until they became a sizeable company. They walked silently. As each of the six men got to his compound, he turned in, taking some of the crowd with him. The village was astir in a silent, suppressed way.

Ezinma had prepared some food for her father as soon as news spread that the six men would be released. She took it to him in his *obi*. He ate absent-mindedly. He had no appetite; he only ate to please her. His male relations and friends had gathered in his *obi,* and Obierika was urging him to eat. Nobody else spoke, but they noticed the long stripes on Okonkwo's back where the warder's whip had cut into his flesh.

The village crier was abroad again in the night. He beat his iron gong and announced that another meeting would be held in the morning. Everyone knew that Umuofia was at last going to speak its mind about the things that were happening.

Okonkwo slept very little that night. The bitterness in his heart was now mixed with a kind of child-like excitement. Before he had gone to bed he had brought down his war dress, which he had not touched since his return from exile. He had shaken out his smoked raffia skirt and examined his tall feather head-gear and his shield. They were all satisfactory, he had thought.

As he lay on his bamboo bed he thought about the treatment he had received in the white man's court, and he swore vengeance. If Umuofia decided on war, all would be well. But if they chose to be cowards he would go out and avenge himself. He thought about wars in the past. The noblest, he thought, was the war against Isike. In those days Okudo was still alive. Okudo sang a war song in a way that no other man could. He was not a fighter, but his voice turned every man into a lion.

"Worthy men are no more," Okonkwo sighed as he remembered those days. "Isike will never forget how we slaughtered them in that war. We killed twelve of their men and they killed only two of ours. Before the end of the fourth market week they were suing for peace. Those were days when men were men."

As he thought of these things he heard the sound of the iron gong in the distance. He listened carefully, and could just hear the crier's voice. But it was very faint. He turned on his bed and his back hurt him. He ground his teeth. The crier was drawing nearer and nearer until he passed by Okonkwo's compound.

"The greatest obstacle in Umuofia," Okonkwo thought bitterly, "is that coward, Egonwanne. His sweet tongue can change fire into cold ash. When he speaks he moves our men to impotence. If they had ignored his womanish wisdom five years ago, we would not have come to this." He ground his teeth. "Tomorrow he will tell them that our fathers never fought a 'war of blame.' If they listen to him I shall leave them and plan my own revenge."

The crier's voice had once more become faint, and the distance had taken the harsh edge off his iron gong. Okonkwo turned from one side to the other and derived a kind of pleasure from the pain his back gave him. "Let Egonwanne talk about a 'war of blame' tomorrow and I shall show him my back and head." He ground his teeth.

The market-place began to fill as soon as the sun rose. Obierika was waiting in his *obi* when Okonkwo came along and called him. He hung his goatskin bag and his sheathed matchet on his shoulder and went out to join him. Obierika's hut was close to the road and he saw every man who passed to the market-place. He had exchanged greetings with many who had already passed that morning.

When Okonkwo and Obierika got to the meeting-place there were already so many people that if one threw up a grain of sand it would not find its way to the earth again. And many more people were coming from every quarter of the nine villages. It warmed Okonkwo's heart to see such strength of numbers. But he was looking for one man in particular, the man whose tongue he dreaded and despised so much.

"Can you see him?" he asked Obierika.

"Who?"

"Egonwanne," he said, his eyes roving from one corner of the huge market-place to the other. Most of the men were seated on goatskins on the ground. A few of them sat on wooden stools they had brought with them.

"No," said Obierika, casting his eyes over the crowd. "Yes, there he is, under the silk-cotton tree. Are you afraid he would convince us not to fight?"

"Afraid? I do not care what he does to *you*. I despise him and those who listen to him. I shall fight alone if I choose."

They spoke at the top of their voices because everybody was talking, and it was like the sound of a great market.

"I shall wait till he has spoken," Okonkwo thought. "Then I shall speak."

"But how do you know he will speak against war?" Obierika asked after a while.

"Because I know he is a coward," said Okonkwo. Obierika did not hear the rest of what he said because at that moment somebody touched his shoulder from behind and he turned round to shake hands and exchange greetings with five or six friends. Okonkwo did not turn around even though he knew the voices. He was in no mood to exchange greetings. But one of the men touched him and asked about the people of his compound.

"They are well," he replied without interest.

The first man to speak to Umuofia that morning was Okika, one of the six who had been imprisoned. Okika was a great man and an orator. But he did not have the booming voice which a first speaker must use to establish silence in the assembly of the clan. Onyeka had such a voice; and so he was asked to salute Umuofia before Okika began to speak.

"*Umuofia kwenu!*" he bellowed, raising his left arm and pushing the air with his open hand.

"*Yaa!*" roared Umuofia.

"*Umuofia kwenu!*" he bellowed again, and again and again, facing a new direction each time. And the crowd answered, "*Yaa!*"

There was immediate silence as though cold water had been poured on a roaring flame.

Okika sprang to his feet and also saluted his clansmen four times. Then he began to speak:

"You all know why we are here, when we ought to be building our barns or mending our huts, when we should be putting our compounds in order. My father used to say to me: 'Whenever you see a toad jumping in broad daylight, then know that something is after its life.' When I saw you all pouring into this meeting from all the quarters of our clan so early in the morning, I knew that something was after our life." He paused for a brief moment and then began again:

"All our gods are weeping. Idemili is weeping. Ogwugwu is weeping. Agbala is weeping, and all the others. Our dead fathers are weeping because of the shameful sacrilege they are suffering and the abomination we have all seen with our eyes." He stopped again to steady his trembling voice.

"This is a great gathering. No clan can boast of greater numbers or greater valour. But are we all here? I ask you: Are all the sons of Umuofia with us here?" A deep murmur swept through the crowd.

"They are not," he said. "They have broken the clan and gone their several ways. We who are here this morning have remained true to our fathers, but our brothers have deserted us and joined a stranger to soil their fatherland. If we fight the stranger we shall hit our brothers and perhaps shed the blood of a clansman. But we must do it. Our fathers never dreamt of such a thing, they never killed their brothers. But a white man never came to them. So we must do what our fathers would never have done. Eneke the bird was asked why he was always on the wing and he replied: 'Men have learnt to shoot without missing their mark and I have learnt to fly without perching on a twig.' We must root out this evil. And if our brothers take the side of evil we must root them out too. And we must do it *now*. We must bale this water now that it is only ankle-deep . . ."

At this point here was a sudden stir in the crowd and every eye was turned in one direction. There was a sharp bend in the road that led from the market-place to the white man's court, and to the stream beyond it. And so no one had seen the approach of the five court messengers until they had come round the bend, a few paces from the edge of the crowd. Okonkwo was sitting at the edge.

He sprang to his feet as soon as he saw who it was. He confronted the head messenger, trembling with hate, unable to utter a word. The man was fearless and stood his ground, his four men lined up behind him.

In that brief moment the world seemed to stand still, waiting. There was utter silence. The men of Umuofia were merged into the mute backcloth of trees and giant creepers, waiting.

The spell was broken by the head messenger. "Let me pass!" he ordered.

"What do you want here?"

"The white man whose power you know too well has ordered this meeting to stop."

In a flash Okonkwo drew his matchet. The messenger crouched to avoid the blow. It was useless. Okonkwo's matchet descended twice and the man's head lay beside his uniformed body.

The waiting backcloth jumped into tumultuous life and the meeting was stopped. Okonkwo stood looking at the dead man. He knew that Umuofia would not go to war. He knew because they had let the other messengers escape. They had broken into tumult instead of action. He discerned fright in that tumult. He heard voices asking: "Why did he do it?"

He wiped his matchet on the sand and went away.

Chapter 25

When the District Commissioner arrived at Okonkwo's compound at the head of an armed band of soldiers and court messengers he found a small crowd of men sitting wearily in the *obi*. He commanded them to come outside, and they obeyed without a murmur.

"Which among you is called Okonkwo?" he asked through his interpreter.

"He is not here," replied Obierika.

"Where is he?"

"He is not here!"

The Commissioner became angry and red in the face. He warned the men that unless they produced Okonkwo forthwith he would lock them all up. The men murmured among themselves, and Obierika spoke again.

"We can take you where he is, and perhaps your men will help us."

The Commissioner did not understand what Obierika meant when he said, "Perhaps your men will help us." One of the most infuriating habits of these people was their love of superfluous words, he thought.

Obierika with five or six others led the way. The Commissioner and his men followed, their firearms held at the ready. He had warned Obierika that if he and his men played any monkey tricks they would be shot. And so they went.

There was a small bush behind Okonkwo's compound. The only opening into this bush from the compound was a little round hole in the red-earth wall through which fowls went in and out in their endless search for food. The hole would not let a man through. It was to this bush that Obierika led the Commissioner and his men. They skirted round the compound, keeping close to the wall. The only sound they made was with their feet as they crushed dry leaves.

Then they came to the tree from which Okonkwo's body was dangling, and they stopped dead.

"Perhaps your men can help us bring him down and bury him," said Obierika. "We have sent for strangers from another village to do it for us, but they may be a long time coming."

The District Commissioner changed instantaneously. The resolute administrator in him gave way to the student of primitive customs.

"Why can't you take him down yourselves?" he asked.

"It is against our custom," said one of the men. "It is an abomination for a man to take his own life. It is an offence against the Earth, and a man who commits it will not be buried by his clansmen. His body is evil, and only strangers may touch it. That is why we ask your people to bring him down, because you are strangers."

"Will you bury him like any other man?" asked the Commissioner.

"We cannot bury him. Only strangers can. We shall pay your men to do it. When he has been buried we will then do our duty by him. We shall make sacrifices to cleanse the desecrated land."

Obierika, who had been gazing steadily at his friend's dangling body, turned suddenly to the District Commissioner and said ferociously: "That man was one of the greatest men in Umuofia. You drove him to kill himself; and now he will be buried like a dog . . ." He could not say any more. His voice trembled and choked his words.

"Shut up!" shouted one of the messengers, quite unnecessarily.

"Take down the body," the Commissioner ordered his chief messenger, "and bring it and all these people to court."

"Yes, sah," the messenger said, saluting.

The Commissioner went away, taking three or four of the soldiers with him. In the many years in which he had toiled to bring civilization to different parts of Africa he had learnt a number of things. One of them was that a District Commissioner must never attend to such undignified details as cutting down a dead man from the tree. Such attention would give the natives a poor opinion of him. In the book which he planned to write he would stress that point. As he walked back to the court he thought about that book. Every day brought him some new material. The story of this man who had killed a messenger and hanged himself would make interesting reading. One could almost write a whole chapter on him. Perhaps not a whole chapter but a reasonable paragraph, at any rate. There was so much else to include, and one must be firm in cutting out details. He had already chosen the title of the book, after much thought: *The Pacification of the Primitive Tribes of the Lower Niger.*

from The African Writer and the English Language

In June 1962, there was a writers' gathering at Makerere, impressively styled: "A Conference of African Writers of English Expression."[1] Despite this sonorous and rather solemn title, it turned out to be a very lively affair and a very exciting and useful experience for many of us. But there was something which we tried to do and failed—that was to define "African literature" satisfactorily.

Was it literature produced *in* Africa or *about* Africa? Could African literature be on any subject, or must it have an African theme? Should it embrace the whole continent or south of the Sahara, or just *Black* Africa? And then the question of language. Should it be in indigenous African languages or should it include Arabic, English, French, Portuguese, Afrikaans, et cetera?

In the end we gave up trying to find an answer, partly—I should admit—on my own instigation. Perhaps we should not have given up so easily. It seems to me from some of the things I have since heard and read that we may have given the impression of not knowing what we were doing, or worse, not daring to look too closely at it.

A Nigerian critic, Obi Wali, writing in *Transition 10,* said: "Perhaps the most important achievement of the conference . . . is that African literature as now defined and understood leads nowhere."

I am sure that Obi Wali must have felt triumphantly vindicated when he saw the report of a different kind of conference held later at Fourah Bay to discuss African literature and the University curriculum. This conference produced a tentative definition of African literature as follows: "Creative writing in which an African setting is authentically handled or to which experiences originating in Africa are integral." We are told specifically that Conrad's *Heart of Darkness* qualifies as African literature while Graham Greene's *Heart of the Matter* fails because it could have been set anywhere outside Africa.

A number of interesting speculations issue from this definition which admittedly is only an interim formulation designed to produce an indisputably desirable end, namely, to introduce African students to literature set in their environment. But I could not help being amused by the curious circumstance in which Conrad, a Pole, writing in English could produce African literature while Peter Abrahams would be ineligible should he write a novel based on his experiences in the West Indies.

What all this suggests to me is that you cannot cram African literature into a small, neat definition. I do not see African literature as one unit but as a group of associated units—in fact the sum total of all the *national* and *ethnic* literatures of Africa.

A national literature is one that takes the whole nation for its province and has a realized or potential audience throughout its territory. In other words a literature that is written in the *national* language. An ethnic literature is one which is available only to one ethnic group within the nation. If you take Nigeria as an example, the national literature, as I see it, is the literature written in English; and the ethnic literatures are in Hausa, Ibo, Yoruba, Efik, Edo, Ijaw, etc., etc.

Any attempt to define African literature in terms which overlook the complexities of the African scene at the material time is doomed to failure. After the elimination of white rule shall have been completed, the single most important fact in Africa

---

1. The conference took place at Makerere University College, in Kampala, Uganda, a colonial overseas extension of the University of London. The many African writers referred to by Achebe in this essay formed the first wave of African intellectuals and authors in postcolonial Africa.

in the second half of the twentieth century will appear to be the rise of individual nation-states. I believe that African literature will follow the same pattern.

What we tend to do today is to think of African literature as a newborn infant. But in fact what we have is a whole generation of newborn infants. Of course, if you only look cursorily, one infant is pretty much like another; but in reality each is already set on its own separate journey. Of course, you may group them together on the basis of anything you choose—the color of their hair, for instance. Or you may group them together on the basis of the language they will speak or the religion of their fathers. Those would all be valid distinctions; but they could not begin to account fully for each individual person carrying, as it were, his own little, unique lodestar of genes.

Those who in talking about African literature want to exclude North Africa because it belongs to a different tradition surely do not suggest that Black Africa is anything like homogeneous. What does Shabaan Robert have in common with Christopher Okigbo or Awoonor-Williams? Or Mongo Beti of Cameroun and Paris with Nzekwu of Nigeria? What does the champagne-drinking upper-class Creole society described by Easmon of Sierra Leone have in common with the rural folk and fishermen of J. P. Clark's plays? Of course, some of these differences could be accounted for on individual rather than national grounds, but a good deal of it is also environmental.

I have indicated somewhat offhandedly that the national literature of Nigeria and of many other countries of Africa is, or will be, written in English. This may sound like a controversial statement, but it isn't. All I have done has been to look at the reality of present-day Africa. This "reality" may change as a result of deliberate, e.g., political, action. If it does, an entirely new situation will arise, and there will be plenty of time to examine it. At present it may be more profitable to look at the scene as it is.

What are the factors which have conspired to place English in the position of national language in many parts of Africa? Quite simply the reason is that these nations were created in the first place by the intervention of the British which, I hasten to add, is not saying that the peoples comprising these nations were invented by the British.

The country which we know as Nigeria today began not so very long ago as the arbitrary creation of the British. It is true, as William Fagg says in his excellent new book, *Nigerian Images,* that this arbitrary action has proved as lucky in terms of African art history as any enterprise of the fortunate Princes of Serendip.[2] And I believe that in political and economic terms too this arbitrary creation called Nigeria holds out great prospects. Yet the fact remains that Nigeria was created by the British—for their own ends. Let us give the devil his due: colonialism in Africa disrupted many things, but it did create big political units where there were small, scattered ones before. Nigeria had hundreds of autonomous communities ranging in size from the vast Fulani Empire founded by Usman dan Fodio in the north to tiny village entities in the east. Today it is one country.

Of course there are areas of Africa where colonialism divided up a single ethnic group among two or even three powers. But on the whole it did bring together many peoples that had hitherto gone their several ways. And it gave them a language with which to talk to one another. If it failed to give them a song, it at least gave them a tongue, for sighing. There are not many countries in Africa today where you could

2. A name for Ceylon, used in a Persian fairy tale about three constantly lucky princes there.

abolish the language of the erstwhile colonial powers and still retain the facility for mutual communication. Therefore those African writers who have chosen to write in English or French are not unpatriotic smart alecks with an eye on the main chance—outside their own countries. They are by-products of the same process that made the new nation-states of Africa.

You can take this argument a stage further to include other countries of Africa. The only reason why we can even talk about African unity is that when we get together we can have a manageable number of languages to talk in—English, French, Arabic.

The other day I had a visit from Joseph Kariuki of Kenya. Although I had read some of his poems and he had read my novels, we had not met before. But it didn't seem to matter. In fact I had met him through his poems, especially through his love poem, *Come Away My Love,* in which he captures in so few words the trials and tensions of an African in love with a white girl in Britain:

> Come away, my love, from streets
> Where unkind eyes divide
> And shop windows reflect our difference.

By contrast, when in 1960 I was traveling in East Africa and went to the home of the late Shabaan Robert, the Swahili poet of Tanganyika, things had been different. We spent some time talking about writing, but there was no real contact. I knew from all accounts that I was talking to an important writer, but of the nature of his work I had no idea. He gave me two books of his poems which I treasure but cannot read—until I have learned Swahili.

And there are scores of languages I would want to learn if it were possible. Where am I to find the time to learn the half dozen or so Nigerian languages, each of which can sustain a literature? I am afraid it cannot be done. These languages will just have to develop as tributaries to feed the one central language enjoying nationwide currency. Today, for good or ill, that language is English. Tomorrow it may be something else, although I very much doubt it.

Those of us who have inherited the English language may not be in a position to appreciate the value of the inheritance. Or we may go on resenting it because it came as part of a package deal which included many other items of doubtful value and the positive atrocity of racial arrogance and prejudice which may yet set the world on fire. But let us not in rejecting the evil throw out the good with it.

Some time last year I was traveling in Brazil meeting Brazilian writers and artists. A number of the writers I spoke to were concerned about the restrictions imposed on them by their use of the Portuguese language. I remember a woman poet saying she had given serious thought to writing in French! And yet their problem is not half as difficult as ours. Portuguese may not have the universal currency of English or French but at least it is the national language of Brazil with her eighty million or so people, to say nothing of the people of Portugal, Angola, Mozambique, etc.

Of Brazilian authors I have only read, in translation, one novel by Jorge Amado, who is not only Brazil's leading novelist but one of the most important writers in the world. From that one novel, *Gabriella,* I was able to glimpse something of the exciting Afro-Latin culture which is the pride of Brazil and is quite unlike any other culture. Jorge Amado is only one of the many writers Brazil has produced. At their national writers' festival there were literally hundreds of them. But the work of the vast majority will be closed to the rest of the world forever, including no doubt the work of some excellent writers. There is certainly a great advantage to writing in a world language.

I think I have said enough to give an indication of my thinking on the importance of the world language which history has forced down our throats. Now let us look at some of the most serious handicaps. And let me say straightaway that one of the most serious handicaps is *not* the one people talk about most often, namely, that it is impossible for anyone ever to use a second language as effectively as his first. This assertion is compounded of half truth and half bogus mystique. Of course, it is true that the vast majority of people are happier with their first language than with any other. But then the majority of people are not writers. We do have enough examples of writers who have performed the feat of writing effectively in a second language. And I am not thinking of the obvious names like Conrad. It would be more germane to our subject to choose African examples.

The first name that comes to my mind is Olauda Equiano, better known as Gustavus Vassa, the African. Equiano was an Ibo, I believe from the village of Iseke in the Orlu division of Eastern Nigeria. He was sold as a slave at a very early age and transported to America. Later he bought his freedom and lived in England. In 1789 he published his life story, a beautifully written document which, among other things, set down for the Europe of his time something of the life and habit of his people in Africa, in an attempt to counteract the lies and slander invented by some Europeans to justify the slave trade.

Coming nearer to our times, we may recall the attempts in the first quarter of this century by West African nationalists to come together and press for a greater say in the management of their own affairs. One of the most eloquent of that band was the Honorable Casely Hayford of the Gold Coast. His presidential address to the National Congress of British West Africa in 1925 was memorable not only for its sound common sense but as a fine example of elegant prose. The governor of Nigeria at the time was compelled to take notice and he did so in characteristic style: he called Hayford's Congress "a self-selected and self-appointed congregation of educated African gentlemen." We may derive some amusement from the fact that British colonial administrators learned very little in the following quarter of a century. But at least they *did* learn in the end—which is more than one can say for some others.

It is when we come to what is commonly called creative literature that most doubt seems to arise. Obi Wali, whose article "Dead End of African Literature" I referred to, has this to say: ". . . until these writers and their Western midwives accept the fact that any true African literature must be written in African languages, they would be merely pursuing a dead end, which can only lead to sterility, uncreativity and frustration."

But far from leading to sterility, the work of many new African writers is full of the most exciting possibilities.

Take this from Christopher Okigbo's *Limits:*

> Suddenly becoming talkative like weaverbird
> Summoned at offside of dream remembered
> Between sleep and waking
> I hand up my egg-shells
> To you of palm grove,
> Upon whose bamboo towers hang
> Dripping with yesterupwine
> A tiger mask and nude spear. . . .

> Queen of the damp half light,
> I have had my cleansing.
> Emigrant with air-borne nose,
> The he-goat-on-heat.

Or take the poem, *Night Rain,* in which J. P. Clark captures so well the fear and wonder felt by a child as rain clamors on the thatch roof at night and his mother, walking about in the dark, moves her simple belongings

> Out of the run of water
> That like ants filing out of the wood
> Will scatter and gain possession
> Of the floor. . . .

I think that the picture of water spreading on the floor "like ants filing out of the wood" is beautiful. Of course if you had never made fire with faggots, you may miss it. But Clark's inspiration derives from the same source which gave birth to the saying that a man who brings home ant-ridden faggots must be ready for the visit of lizards.

I do not see any signs of sterility anywhere here. What I do see is a new voice coming out of Africa, speaking of African experience in a world-wide language. So my answer to the question *Can an African ever learn English well enough to be able to use it effectively in creative writing?* is certainly yes. If on the other hand you ask: *Can he ever learn to use it like a native speaker?* I should say, I hope not. It is neither necessary nor desirable for him to be able to do so. The price a world language must be prepared to pay is submission to many different kinds of use. The African writer should aim to use English in a way that brings out his message best without altering the language to the extent that its value as a medium of international exchange will be lost. He should aim at fashioning out an English which is at once universal and able to carry his peculiar experience. I have in mind here the writer who has something new, something different to say. The nondescript writer has little to tell us, anyway, so he might as well tell it in conventional language and get it over with. If I may use an extravagant simile, he is like a man offering a small, nondescript routine sacrifice for which a chick, or less, will do. A serious writer must look for an animal whose blood can match the power of his offering.

In this respect Amos Tutola is a natural. A good instinct has turned his apparent limitation in language into a weapon of great strength—a half-strange dialect that serves him perfectly in the evocation of his bizarre world. His last book, and to my mind, his finest, is proof enough that one can make even an imperfectly learned second language do amazing things. In this book, *The Feather Woman of the Jungle,* Tutola's superb storytelling is at last cast in the episodic form which he handles best instead of being painfully stretched on the rack of the novel.

From a natural to a conscious artist: myself, in fact. Allow me to quote a small example from *Arrow of God,* which may give some idea of how I approach the use of English. The Chief Priest in the story is telling one of his sons why it is necessary to send him to church:

> I want one of my sons to join these people and be my eyes there. If there is nothing in it you will come back. But if there is something there you will bring home my share. The world is like a Mask, dancing. If you want to see it well you do not stand in one place. My spirit tells me that those who do not befriend the white man today will be saying *had we known* tomorrow.

Now supposing I had put it another way. Like this for instance:

I am sending you as my representative among these people—just to be on the safe side in case the new religion develops. One has to move with the times or else one is left behind. I have a hunch that those who fail to come to terms with the white man may well regret their lack of foresight.

The material is the same. But the form of the one is *in character* and the other is not. It is largely a matter of instinct, but judgment comes into it too.

You read quite often nowadays of the problems of the African writer having first to think in his mother tongue and then to translate what he has thought into English. If it were such a simple, mechanical process, I would agree that it was pointless—the kind of eccentric pursuit you might expect to see in a modern Academy of Lagado;[3] and such a process could not possibly produce some of the exciting poetry and prose which is already appearing.

One final point remains for me to make. The real question is not whether Africans *could* write in English but whether they *ought to*. Is it right that a man should abandon his mother tongue for someone else's? It looks like a dreadful betrayal and produces a guilty feeling.

But for me there is no other choice. I have been given this language and I intend to use it. I hope, though, that there always will be men, like the late Chief Fagunwa, who will choose to write in their native tongue and insure that our ethnic literature will flourish side by side with the national ones. For those of us who opt for English, there is much work ahead and much excitement.

Writing in the London *Observer* recently, James Baldwin said:

> My quarrel with the English language has been that the language reflected none of my experience. But now I began to see the matter another way. . . . Perhaps the language was not my own because I had never attempted to use it, had only learned to imitate it. If this were so, then it might be made to bear the burden of my experience if I could find the stamina to challenge it, and me, to such a test.

I recognize, of course, that Baldwin's problem is not exactly mine, but I feel that the English language will be able to carry the weight of my African experience. But it will have to be a new English, still in full communion with its ancestral home but altered to suit its new African surroundings.

∞

RESONANCES

Ngugi wa Thiong'o: from *The Language of African Literature*[1]

The language of African literature cannot be discussed meaningfully outside the context of those social forces which have made it both an issue demanding our attention and a problem calling for a resolution.

---

3. A group of scientists producing pointless, trivial experiments in Jonathan Swift's *Gulliver's Travles*.
1. The Kenyan novelist, playwright, and essayist Ngugi wa Thiong'o (b. 1938) began his career writing novels of disillusionment and family conflict and then turned increasingly to political themes, dramatizing Kenya's struggle for independence from Britain in his novel *A Grain of Wheat*. Following independence in 1963, Kenya's leaders suppressed opposition parties and established dictatorial

rule. Ngugi was jailed for a year after publishing *Petals of Blood* (1977), a satirical indictment of Kenya's post-independence leadership; he subsequently took up teaching positions in the United States. The 1986 essay excerpted here, published in book form in *Decolonizing the Mind*, discusses the politics of language and his own decision to begin writing in his native Gĩkũyũ after many years of writing fiction in English.

On the one hand is imperialism in its colonial and neo-colonial phases continuously press-ganging the African hand to the plough to turn the soil over, and putting blinkers on him to make him view the path ahead only as determined for him by the master armed with the bible and the sword. In other words, imperialism continues to control the economy, politics, and cultures of Africa. But on the other, and pitted against it, are the ceaseless struggles of African people to liberate their economy, politics and culture from that Euro-American-based stranglehold to usher a new era of true communal self-regulation and self-determination. It is an ever-continuing struggle to seize back their creative initiative in history through a real control of all the means of communal self-definition in time and space. The choice of language and the use to which language is put is central to a people's definition of themselves in relation to their natural and social environment, indeed in relation to the entire universe. Hence language has always been at the heart of the two contending social forces in the Africa of the twentieth century.

* * *

In 1962 I was invited to that historic meeting of African writers at Makerere University College, Kampala, Uganda. The list of participants contained most of the names which have now become the subject of scholarly dissertations in universities all over the world. The title? "A Conference of *African Writers of English Expression.*"

I was then a student of *English* at Makerere, an overseas college of the University of London. The main attraction for me was the certain possibility of meeting Chinua Achebe. I had with me a rough typescript of a novel in progress, *Weep Not, Child,* and I wanted him to read it. In the previous year, 1961, I had completed *The River Between,* my first-ever attempt at a novel, and entered it for a writing competition organised by the East African Literature Bureau. I was keeping in step with the tradition of Peter Abrahams with his output of novels and autobiographies from *Path of Thunder* to *Tell Freedom* and followed by Chinua Achebe with his publication of *Things Fall Apart* in 1959. Or there were their counterparts in French colonies, the generation of Sédar Senghor and David Diop included in the 1947/48 Paris edition of *Anthologie de la nouvelle poésie nègre et malgache de langue française.*[2] They all wrote in European languages as was the case with all the participants in that momentous encounter on Makerere hill in Kampala in 1962.

The title, "A Conference of African Writers of English Expression," automatically excluded those who wrote in African languages. Now on looking back from the self-questioning heights of 1986, I can see this contained absurd anomalies. I, a student, could qualify for the meeting on the basis of only two published short stories, "The Fig Tree (Mũgumo)" in a student journal, *Penpoint,* and "The Return" in a new journal, *Transition.* But neither Shabaan Robert, then the greatest living East African poet with several works of poetry and prose to his credit in Kiswahili, nor Chief Fagunwa, the great Nigerian writer with several published titles in Yoruba, could possibly qualify.

The discussions on the novel, the short story, poetry, and drama were based on extracts from works in English and hence they excluded the main body of work in Swahili, Zulu, Yoruba, Arabic, Amharic and other African languages. Yet, despite

2. *Anthology of the New Negro and Madagascan Poetry in French,* edited by the poet (and future president of Senegal) Léopold Sédar Senghor (see page 638). With an introduction by Jean-Paul Sartre, the anthology was intended to put Francophone African poetry on the French literary map. Senghor's friend and collaborator Birago (David) Diop (1906–1992) wrote vivid stories in French based on West-African folktale traditions.

this exclusion of writers and literature in African languages, no sooner were the introductory preliminaries over than this Conference of "African Writers of English Expression' sat down to the first item on the agenda: "What is African Literature?"

The debate which followed was animated: Was it literature about Africa or about the African experience? Was it literature written by Africans? What about a non-African who wrote about Africa: did his work qualify as African literature? What if an African set his work in Greenland: did that qualify as African literature? Or were African languages the criteria? OK: what about Arabic, was it not foreign to Africa? What about French and English, which had become African languages? What if an European wrote about Europe in an African language? If . . . if . . . if . . . this or that, except the issue: the domination of our languages and cultures by those of imperialist Europe: in any case there was no Fagunwa or Shabaan Robert or any writer in African languages to bring the conference down from the realms of evasive abstractions. The question was never seriously asked: did what we wrote qualify as African literature? The whole area of literature and audience, and hence of language as a determinant of both the national and class audience, did not really figure: the debate was more about the subject matter and the racial origins and geographical habitation of the writer.

English, like French and Portuguese, was assumed to be the natural language of literary and even political mediation between African people in the same nation and between nations in Africa and other continents. In some instances these European languages were seen as having a capacity to unite African peoples against divisive tendencies inherent in the multiplicity of African languages within the same geographic state. Thus Ezekiel Mphahlele[3] later could write, in a letter to *Transition* number 11, that English and French have become the common language with which to present a nationalist front against white oppressors, and even "where the whiteman has already retreated, as in the independent states, these two languages are still a unifying force." In the literary sphere they were often seen as coming to save African languages against themselves. Writing a foreword to Birago Diop's book *Contes d'Amadou Koumba* Sédar Senghor commends him for using French to rescue the spirit and style of old African fables and tales. "However while rendering them into French he renews them with an art which, while it respects the genius of the French language, that language of gentleness and honesty, preserves at the same time all the virtues of the negro-african languages." English, French and Portuguese had come to our rescue and we accepted the unsolicited gift with gratitude. Thus in 1964, Chinua Achebe, in a speech entitled "The African Writer and the English Language," said:

> Is it right that a man should abandon his mother tongue for someone else's? It looks like a
> dreadful betrayal and produces a guilty feeling. But for me there is no other choice. I have
> been given the language and I intend to use it.

See the paradox: the possibility of using mother-tongues provokes a tone of levity in phrases like "a dreadful betrayal" and "a guilty feeling;" but that of foreign languages produces a categorical positive embrace, what Achebe himself, ten years later, was to describe as this "fatalistic logic of the unassailable position of English in our literature."

The fact is that all of us who opted for European languages—the conference participants and the generation that followed them—accepted that fatalistic logic to a greater or lesser degree. * * *

---

3. Black South African novelist and opponent of apartheid, who settled in Kenya after emigrating from South Africa in 1957.

How did we arrive at this acceptance of "the fatalistic logic of the unassailable position of English in our literature," in our culture and in our politics? What was the route from the Berlin of 1884 via the Makerere of 1962 to what is still the prevailing and dominant logic a hundred years later? How did we, as African writers, come to be so feeble towards the claims of our languages on us and so aggressive in our claims on other languages, particularly the languages of our colonization?

Berlin of 1884 was effected through the sword and the bullet.[4] But the night of the sword and the bullet was followed by the morning of the chalk and the blackboard. The physical violence of the battlefield was followed by the psychological violence of the classroom. But where the former was visibly brutal, the latter was visibly gentle, a process best described in Cheikh Hamidou Kane's novel *Ambiguous Adventure* where he talks of the methods of the colonial phase of imperialism as consisting of knowing how to kill with efficiency and to heal with the same art.

> On the Black Continent, one began to understand that their real power resided not at all in the cannons of the first morning but in what followed the cannons. Therefore behind the cannons was the new school. The new school had the nature of both the cannon and the magnet. From the cannon it took the efficiency of a fighting weapon. But better than the cannon it made the conquest permanent. The cannon forces the body and the school fascinates the soul.

In my view language was the most important vehicle through which that power fascinated and held the soul prisoner. The bullet was the means of the physical subjugation. Language was the means of the spiritual subjugation. Let me illustrate this by drawing upon experiences in my own education, particularly in language and literature.

I was born into a large peasant family: father, four wives and about twenty-eight children. I also belonged, as we all did in those days, to a wider extended family and to the community as a whole.

We spoke Gĩkũyũ as we worked in the fields. We spoke Gĩkũyũ in and outside the home. I can vividly recall those evenings of storytelling around the fireside. It was mostly the grown-ups telling the children but everybody was interested and involved. We children would re-tell the stories the following day to other children who worked in the fields picking the pyrethrum flowers, tea-leaves or coffee beans of our European and African landlords.

The stories, with mostly animals as the main characters, were all told in Gĩkũyũ. Hare, being small, weak but full of innovative wit and cunning, was our hero. We identified with him as he struggled against the brutes of prey like lion, leopard, hyena. His victories were our victories and we learnt that the apparently weak can outwit the strong. We followed the animals in their struggle against hostile nature—drought, rain, sun, wind—a confrontation often forcing them to search for forms of co-operation. But we were also interested in their struggles amongst themselves, and particularly between the beasts and the victims of prey. These twin struggles, against nature and other animals, reflected real-life struggles in the human world.

Not that we neglected stories with human beings as the main characters. There were two types of characters in such human-centred narratives: the species of truly human beings with qualities of courage, kindness, mercy, hatred of evil, concern for

---

4. At the Berlin Conference of 1884–1885, the major European powers ratified the colonial division of Africa, including Britain's hold on Kenya and Belgium's claim to the Congo.

others; and a man-eat-man two-mouthed species with qualities of greed, selfishness, individualism and hatred of what was good for the larger co-operative community. Co-operation as the ultimate good in a community was a constant theme. It could unite human beings with animals against ogres and beasts of prey, as in the story of how dove, after being fed with castor-oil seeds, was sent to fetch a smith working far away from home and whose pregnant wife was being threatened by these man-eating two-mouthed ogres.

There were good and bad story-tellers. A good one could tell the same story over and over again, and it would always be fresh to us, the listeners. He or she could tell a story told by someone else and make it more alive and dramatic. The differences really were in the use of words and images and the inflexion of voices to effect different tones.

We therefore learnt to value words for their meaning and nuances. Language was not a mere string of words. It had a suggestive power well beyond the immediate and lexical meaning. Our appreciation of the suggestive magical power of language was reinforced by the games we played with words through riddles, proverbs, transpositions of syllables, or through nonsensical but musically arranged words. So we learnt the music of our language on top of the content. The language, through images and symbols, gave us a view of the world, but it had a beauty of its own. The home and the field were then our pre-primary school but what is important, for this discussion, is that the language of our evening teach-ins, and the language of our immediate and wider community, and the language of our work in the fields were one.

And then I went to school, a colonial school, and this harmony was broken. The language of my education was no longer the language of my culture. I first went to Kamaandura, missionary run, and then to another called Maanguuũ run by nationalists grouped around the Gĩkũyũ Independent and Karinga Schools Association. Our language of education was still Gĩkũyũ. The very first time I was ever given an ovation for my writing was over a composition in Gĩkũyũ. So for my first four years there was still harmony between the language of my formal education and that of the Limuru peasant community.

It was after the declaration of a state of emergency over Kenya in 1952[5] that all the schools run by patriotic nationalists were taken over by the colonial regime and were placed under District Education Boards chaired by Englishmen. English became the language of my formal education. In Kenya, English became more than a language: it was *the* language, and all the others had to bow before it in deference.

Thus one of the most humiliating experiences was to be caught speaking Gĩkũyũ in the vicinity of the school. The culprit was given corporal punishment—three to five strokes of the cane on bare buttocks—or was made to carry a metal plate around the neck with inscriptions such as I AM STUPID or I AM A DONKEY. Sometimes the culprits were fined money they could hardly afford. And how did the teachers catch the culprits? A button was initially given to one pupil who was supposed to hand it over to whoever was caught speaking his mother tongue. Whoever had the button at the end of the day would sing who had given it to him and the ensuing process would bring out all the culprits of the day. Thus children were turned into witch-hunters and in the process were being taught the lucrative value of being a traitor to one's immediate community.

5. The start of armed struggle against British rule.

The attitude to English was the exact opposite: any achievement in spoken or written English was highly rewarded; prizes, prestige, applause; the ticket to higher realms. English became the measure of intelligence and ability in the arts, the sciences, and all the other branches of learning. English became *the* main determinant of a child's progress up the ladder of formal education.

As you may know, the colonial system of education in addition to its apartheid racial demarcation had the structure of a pyramid: a broad primary base, a narrowing secondary middle, and an even narrower university apex. Selections from primary into secondary were through an examination, in my time called Kenya African Preliminary Examination, in which one had to pass six subjects ranging from Maths to Nature Study and Kiswahili. All the papers were written in English. Nobody could pass the exam who failed the English language paper no matter how brilliantly he had done in the other subjects. I remember one boy in my class of 1954 who had distinctions in all subjects except English, which he had failed. He was made to fail the entire exam. He went on to become a turn boy in a bus company. I who had only passes but a credit in English got a place at the Alliance High School, one of the most elitist institutions for Africans in colonial Kenya. The requirements for a place at the University, Makerere University College, were broadly the same: nobody could go on to wear the undergraduate red gown, no matter how brilliantly they had performed in all the other subjects unless they had a credit—not even a simple pass!—in English. Thus the most coveted place in the pyramid and in the system was only available to the holder of an English language credit card. English was the official vehicle and the magic formula to colonial elitedom.

Literary education was now determined by the dominant language while also reinforcing that dominance. Orature (oral literature) in Kenyan languages stopped. In primary school I now read simplified Dickens and Stevenson alongside Rider Haggard.[6] Jim Hawkins, Oliver Twist, Tom Brown—not Hare, Leopard and Lion—were now my daily companions in the world of imagination. In secondary school, Scott and G. B. Shaw vied with more Rider Haggard, John Buchan, Alan Paton, Captain W. E. Johns. At Makerere I read English: from Chaucer to T. S. Eliot with a touch of Graham Greene.

Thus language and literature were taking us further and further from ourselves to other selves, from our world to other worlds.

* * *

But African languages refused to die. They would not simply go the way of Latin to become the fossils for linguistic archaeology to dig up, classify, and argue about the international conferences.

These languages, these national heritages of Africa, were kept alive by the peasantry. The peasantry saw no contradiction between speaking their own mother-tongues and belonging to a larger national or continental geography. They saw no necessary antagonistic contradiction between belonging to their immediate nationality, to their multinational state along the Berlin-drawn boundaries, and to Africa as a whole. These people happily spoke Wolof, Hausa, Yoruba, Ibo, Arabic, Amharic, Kiswahili, Gĩkũyũ, Luo, Luhya, Shona, Ndebele, Kimbundu, Zulu or Lingala without this fact tearing the multinational states apart. During the anti-colonial struggle they showed an unlimited capacity

---

6. All Victorian novelists. H. Rider Haggard was particularly known for *She* (1887) and other novels of colonial adventure in "the Dark Continent."

to unite around whatever leader or party best and most consistently articulated an anti-imperialist position. If anything it was the petty-bourgeoisie, particularly the compradors,[7] with their French and English and Portuguese, with their petty rivalries, their ethnic chauvinism, which encouraged these vertical divisions to the point of war at times. No, the peasantry had no complexes about their languages and the cultures they carried!

In fact when the peasantry and the working class were compelled by necessity or history to adopt the language of the master, they Africanised it without any of the respect for its ancestry shown by Senghor and Achebe, so totally as to have created new African languages, like Krio in Sierra Leone or Pidgin in Nigeria, that owed their identities to the syntax and rhythms of African languages. All these languages were kept alive in the daily speech, in the ceremonies, in political struggles, above all in the rich store of orature—proverbs, stories, poems, and riddles.

The peasantry and the urban working class threw up singers. These sang the old songs or composed new ones incorporating the new experiences in industries and urban life and in working-class struggle and organisations. These singers pushed the languages to new limits, renewing and reinvigorating them by coining new words and new expressions, and in generally expanding their capacity to incorporate new happenings in Africa and the world. * * *

The question is this: we as African writers have always complained about the neo-colonial economic and political relationship to Euro-America. Right. But by our continuing to write in foreign languages, paying homage to them, are we not on the cultural level continuing that neo-colonial slavish and cringing spirit? What is the difference between a politician who says Africa cannot do without imperialism and the writer who says Africa cannot do without European languages?

While we were busy haranguing the ruling circles in a language which automatically excluded the participation of the peasantry and the working class in the debate, imperialist culture and African reactionary forces had a field day: the Christian bible is available in unlimited quantities in even the tiniest African language. The comprador ruling cliques are also quite happy to have the peasantry and the working class all to themselves: distortions, dictatorial directives, decrees, museum-type fossils paraded as African culture, feudalistic ideologies, superstitions, lies, all these backward elements and more are communicated to the African masses in their own languages without any challenges from those with alternative visions of tomorrow who have deliberately cocooned themselves in English, French, and Portuguese. It is ironic that the most reactionary African politician, the one who believes in selling Africa to Europe, is often a master of African languages; that the most zealous of European missionaries who believed in rescuing Africa from itself, even from the paganism of its languages, were nevertheless masters of African languages, which they often reduced to writing. The European missionary believed too much in his mission of conquest not to communicate it in the languages most readily available to the people: the African writer believes too much in "African literature" to write it in those ethnic, divisive and under-developed languages of the peasantry!

The added irony is that what they have produced, despite any claims to the contrary, is not African literature. The editors of the Pelican Guides to English literature in their latest volume were right to include a discussion of this literature as part of twentieth-century English literature, just as the French Academy was right to honour Senghor for

---

7. Buyers (Portuguese), native agents for foreign powers, in charge of local workers.

his genuine and talented contribution to French literature and language. What we have created is another hybrid tradition, a tradition in transition, a minority tradition that can only be termed as Afro-European literature; that is, the literature written by Africans in European languages. It has produced many writers and works of genuine talent: Chinua Achebe, Wole Soyinka, Ayi Kwei Armah, Sembene Ousmane, Agostino Neto, Sédar Senghor and many others. Who can deny their talent? The light in the products of their fertile imaginations has certainly illuminated important aspects of the African being in its continuous struggle against the political and economic consequences of Berlin and after. However we cannot have our cake and eat it! Their work belongs to an Afro-European literary tradition which is likely to last for as long as Africa is under this rule of European capital in a neo-colonial set-up. So Afro-European literature can be defined as literature written by Africans in European languages in the era of imperialism.

But some are coming round to the inescapable conclusion articulated by Obi Wali with such polemical vigour twenty years ago: African literature can only be written in African languages, that is, the languages of the African peasantry and working class, the major alliance of classes in each of our nationalities and the agency for the coming inevitable revolutionary break with neo-colonialism.

I started writing in Gĩkũyũ language in 1977 after seventeen years of involvement in Afro-European literature, in my case Afro-English literature. It was then that I collaborated with Ngũgĩ wa Mĩriĩ in the drafting of the playscript, *Ngaahika Ndeenda* (the English translation was *I Will Marry When I Want*). I have since published a novel in Gĩkũyũ, *Caitaani Mũtharabainĩ* (English translation: *Devil on the Cross*) and completed a musical drama, *Maitũ Njugĩra*, (English translation: *Mother Sing for Me*); three books for children, *Njamba Nene na Mbaathi i Mathagu, Bathitoora ya Njamba Nene, Njamba Nene na Cibũ Kĩng'ang'i,* as well as another novel manuscript: *Matigari Ma Njirũũngi*. Wherever I have gone, particularly in Europe, I have been confronted with the question: why are you now writing in Gĩkũyũ? Why do you now write in an African language? In some academic quarters I have been confronted with the rebuke, "Why have you abandoned us?" It was almost as if, in choosing to write in Gĩkũyũ, I was doing something abnormal. But Gĩkũyũ is my mother tongue! The very fact that what common sense dictates in the literary practice of other cultures is being questioned in an African writer is a measure of how far imperialism has distorted the view of African realities. It has turned reality upside down: the abnormal is viewed as normal and the normal is viewed as abnormal. * * *

We African writers are bound by our calling to do for our languages what Spencer, Milton and Shakespeare did for English; what Pushkin and Tolstoy did for Russian; indeed what all writers in world history have done for their languages by meeting the challenge of creating a literature in them, which process later opens the languages for philosophy, science, technology and all the other areas of human creative endeavours.

But writing in our languages per se—although a necessary first step in the correct direction—will not itself bring about the renaissance in African cultures if that literature does not carry the content of our people's anti-imperialist struggles to liberate their productive forces from foreign control; the content of the need for unity among the workers and peasants of all the nationalities in their struggle to control the wealth they produce and to free it from internal and external parasites.

In other words writers in African languages should reconnect themselves to the revolutionary traditions of an organised peasantry and working class in Africa in their struggle to defeat imperialism and create a higher system of democracy and socialism in alliance with all the other peoples of the world. Unity in that struggle would ensure unity in our multi-lingual diversity. It would also reveal the real links that bind the people of Africa to the peoples of Asia, South America, Europe, Australia and New Zealand, Canada and the U.S.A.

But it is precisely when writers open out African languages to the real links in the struggles of peasants and workers that they will meet their biggest challenge. For to the comprador-ruling regimes, their real enemy is an awakened peasantry and working class. A writer who tries to communicate the message of revolutionary unity and hope in the languages of the people becomes a subversive character. It is then that writing in African languages becomes a subversive or treasonable offence with such a writer facing possibilities of prison, exile or even death. For him there are no "national" accolades, no new year honours, only abuse and slander and innumerable lies from the mouths of the armed power of a ruling minority—ruling, that is, on behalf of U.S.-led imperialism—and who see in democracy a real threat. A democratic participation of the people in the shaping of their own lives or in discussing their own lives in languages that allow for mutual comprehension is seen as being dangerous to the good government of a country and its institutions. African languages addressing themselves to the lives of the people become the enemy of a neo-colonial state.

Mbwil a M. Ngal: from *Giambatista Viko:*
or, The Rape of African Discourse[1]

[*Giambatista Viko, essayist and professor at an unnamed institute of African studies, has been struggling to write a major novel so that he can become "the Napoleon of African letters" and be invited to conferences in Europe. In the following passage, he shares with his disciple Niaiseux ("Simpleton") his difficulties and his ambitions for his novel.*]

"Giving birth to any kind of literature has become painful for me. My fame as some kind of black sun spreads around the planet, but my reputation as a writer isn't building up. Only a discourse internal to Africa can liberate my own, enmeshed as it is in one of those sophisms that only the Westerners can master. A subterranean life exists within us. Freudianism taught this to the West; but the primitives themselves have never forgotten it. From time immemorial, the interior life of individuals, as of society, has been ruled by this entreaty from below that Europe is only now beginning to rediscover."

"Master, I've always said you were born too soon, a century ahead of our times. To tame our African discourse in order to liberate the West's paralyzed, repressed discourse—that seems truly inspired!"

"But consider! No ambiguity! I am of a race that cannot be assimilated to ordinary African writers. We have nothing in common but biology. My place is in Paris, in Geneva. It's only an accident of history that had me born in Africa. To use a resource is not to assimilate. Picasso, Juan Gris, Lipchitz surrounded themselves with

---

1. Translated by David Damrosch. Born in 1933 in Zaire (now the Democratic People's Republic of the Congo), Ngal studied at a Jesuit college there before obtaining a doctorate in Fribourg, Switzerland, with a thesis on the Francophone Caribbean poet Aimé Césaire. He then taught in Europe, Africa, and Canada. His 1975 novel *Giambatista Viko* concerns an ambitious, irascible, Paris-oriented Central African intellectual who is arrested and put on trial after he tries to steal the secrets of African oral culture for use in a novel. Viko's name recalls that of the Italian philosopher Giambattista Vico, whose *Scienza Nuova* ("New Science," 1725) argued that all language began in poetry, the natural medium of primitive people's speech.

Negro masks solely in order to define their own aesthetic intentions;[2] an Apollinaire exerted his own will by turning to fetishes from Guinea and Africa.[3] Let those misunderstand who wish. A means is a means. Don't lose sight of that.

"To give birth to a novel! In effect that means to take up a Western discourse. To develop a story within a visual space. In the spatial-temporal dimension. A yoke that strangely limits the writer's freedom: the possibilities of the discourse itself. 'The power of these diminished words loses the efficacity it enjoys in the magic universe of orality. A spoken word gives power over the thing named; the clay image represents the enemy you kill by piercing it with a needle.' It would take a *Scienza Nuova* to rediscover the spiritual forces that our technological universe has lost, and which have been preserved by the oral societies dismissively called primitive. The power, the ability to decipher the language buried in the depths of symbolism; to decode the enemy's malevolent intentions. The secrets discovered constitute the great epiphanies of the divine beneath the veil of their surroundings—the viewer's essential domain."

"Your childhood was immersed in this universe!"

"Yet we've been torn away far too soon, plunged into the world of the written. We need to rediscover what we've lost. An acoustic space, or rather, an audio-visual one. That of the storyteller! What undefined riches! What freedom in the story's unfolding! None of the novel's rigidity! Novelistic space? Veritable circle of hell! I dream of a novel on the model of the folktale. * * * As far as I'm concerned, my choice is clear. More precisely, I don't have one at all. A humanist culture—Greco-Roman—seasoned with the erudition that everyone grants me! Where would you have me find a place for it? I believe neither in cross-breeding nor in the integration of cultures. Juxtaposition? Perhaps! But who could marry Cartesian logic to Bantu logic? * * * I need a style that will combine many contradictory tendencies: the incantatory, the learned, the moving, the oracular. Sometimes flashing out, glittering, sometimes taken apart. Abrupt opacities here, profound transparencies there. An internal, obsessional discourse, dissolved in an indescribable jumble of times and confusion of perspectives. Punctuation? Don't even mention it!"

[*Viko's plans are interrupted when militant Africanists take over the institute where he works, accusing him of plagiarism, of sexual indiscretions with a visiting Italian structuralist, and above all of trying to forcibly violate native oral culture by reducing it to French prose. Viko and Niaiseux are put in a dungeon cell, where they are visited by a tribal elder.*]

A key grates in the lock. The door opens. A man enters, dressed in a goat skin, biceps ringed with silver bracelets. Pearl headdress, crowned with parrot feathers. He is followed by a young man in an elegant suit. The door closes behind them. Yet the room remains light, even though the door is closed; the source of the light is invisible.

In a flash of insight I perceive the reason for our confinement. My audacities at the office are now having their effects. But I don't breathe a word to Niaiseux.

The man turns to the youth and speaks at length. The young man translates:

"Dogs and sons of dogs! My dignity, my honor forbid me to address you directly. Your crime is immeasurable. You will pay for it with the last drop of your blood. But

---

2. The Cubist artists Pablo Picasso, Juan Gris, and Jacques Lipchitz all used African images in their art; see Color Plate 3 for an example by Picasso.

3. Guillaume Apollinaire (1880–1918) introduced Cubist techniques and African themes into his poetry.

do not dream of being thought of as martyrs; you won't have that honor. The fundamental reason that keeps me from addressing you directly is that our universes—speech and writing—have nothing in common. You have impiously set an abyss between yourselves and us. You have chosen the universe of the book—the space of inscription—abandoning that which nourished your childhood, fed your dreams, and furnished your subconscious. You have tried to drain away this lake of symbols, images, the core that welds together our community's cultural cohesion. For you we are total strangers.

"We have followed your alienation with heavy heart. But we knew that you would never go too far, that a nostalgia would bring you back to our shores. The sacred riches of the orality you have so disdainfully rejected always leave the guilty ones with an odor that pursues them like a gnawing remorse. The gravity of your impiety resides in your attempt to desacralize orality. You have wanted to reappropriate the freedom, the space, the time of the storyteller; to introduce them into novelistic discourse. An atheist's attempt, destitute of faith! Not even stopping at this degree of criminality, you have had the presumption to become initiated in our rites, hoping thus to arrive at your goal. In so doing, you plan to subvert orality and Western discourse alike. You would give birth to hybrid characters, heros, texts! This is why this sacrilege cannot go unpunished."

[*A show trial follows, in which a series of prosecutors harangue Viko and Niaiseux, urging the death penalty, not allowing them to reply. Then "the youngest counselor present" speaks up, urging a degree of clemency.*]

"In undertaking this trial, our intention has not been to construct a Great Wall of China around our continent, to prevent our intellectuals from engaging in dialogue with colleagues elsewhere. The greatest malady that Africa suffers today is the new ideology—found almost everywhere—that seeks a pronounced unanimity. 'Idem velle, idem nolle.'[4] Pluralism has become a crime. I ask myself this question: Progress, or regression? * * * Let me make myself clear. Far be it from me to approve what this young man has done. But I would like to draw our attention to a current ideology, the Africanist ideology that wants African realities to be unique, original. What one of our comrades has just called 'an assault on our security' is nothing more than 'an assault on our specificity,' on our withdrawal within ourselves. But let us not forget that a 'specificity' prepares its own asphyxiation to the degree that it receives no oxygen from outside. Cultures survive only by opening up to other cultures that can liberate them from their tendency to collective narcissism."

[*At the close of this speech, the judge renders his verdict, stopping short of a sentence of death.*]

"You are in our hands today, and we will not simply let you leave. You are condemned to perform the Return to the Native Land.[5] Will you pass the remainder of your days among us? You will come to know, one by one, the joys of living one place today, another the next, until you have made the rounds of our villages eighty-seven times eighty-seven times."

Sustained applause. Everyone cries out, "Wisdom has spoken!"

---

4. Wanting the same things, and not wanting the same things.

5. Unwittingly, the judge echoes the title of Aimé Césaire's long poem, composed in Paris, *Notebook of a Return to the Native Land* (see page 645).

* * *

So I've been condemned. Rejected. Torn away from one society and hurled into another! What fate is this? Reintegration, or eternal banishment? Isn't every condemnation a rejection of human society? They meant to get me back, but haven't they lost me for good? * * * Condemned to wandering—me, GIAMBATISTA! Why did they even bother to mitigate their criminal plan? Wouldn't an outright execution have been better? From village to village—that's to say, from oblivion to oblivion! No sooner will I leave one village behind than another will loom up on the horizon of oblivion. . . . I have been condemned to the Gulag Archipelago of oblivion.[6] * * *

Instinctively I rub my eyes, adjust my glasses, take a deep breath. I look around. I am alone. Alone. The Assembly has dispersed, and I didn't notice. Alone on center stage!

Jeremy Cronin: To learn how to speak[1]

To learn how to speak
With the voices of the land,
To parse the speech in its rivers,
To catch in the inarticulate grunt,
5   Stammer, call, cry, babble, tongue's knot
A sense of the stoneness of these stones
From which all words are cut.
To trace with the tongue wagon-trails
Saying the suffix of their aches in -kuil, -pan, -fontein,[2]
10   In watery names that confirm
The dryness of their ways.
To visit the places of occlusion, or the lick
in a vlei-bank dawn.
To bury my mouth in the pit of your arm,
15   In that planetarium,
Pectoral beginning to the nub of time
Down there close to the water-table, to feel
The full moon as it drums
At the back of my throat
20   Its cow-skinned vowel.
To write a poem with words like:
I'm telling you,
Stompie, stickfast, golovan,
Songololo, just boombang, just
25   To understand the least inflections,

---

6. The Gulag Archipelago was the nickname of a chain of Siberian prisons used in Soviet Russia for political prisoners.
1. South African poet and activist politician Jeremy Cronin was born in 1949, son of an officer in the South African navy and an office worker. He studied philosophy at the University of Cape Town and then in Paris. He became a lecturer at Cape Town until he was arrested in 1976 by the Apartheid government, charged with planning terrorist activities with fellow members of the African National Congress. He began writing poetry during his seven-year jail term, and received wide acclaim for his collection *Inside,* published after his release in 1983. Cronin has continued to write poetry while serving as a leader of the South African Communist Party and a member of the post-Apartheid South African parliament.
2. Endings for place-names, all indicating the presence of water.

To voice without swallowing
Syllables born in tin shacks, or catch
The 5.15 ikwata bust fife°   *quarter past five*
Chwannisberg° train, to reach   *Johannesburg*
30   The low chant of the mine gang's
Mineral glow of our people's unbreakable resolve.

To learn how to speak
With the voices of this land.

∞

⊷ ⧎⬦⧎ ⊶

Wole Soyinka

b. 1934

Wole Soyinka has persistently fused experimental forms of Western writing with African literary and cultural traditions. His writings again and again take on issues of great political importance for contemporary West Africa: colonialism and its aftermath, various forms of African totalitarian rule, the clash between tribal traditions and modern institutions, and the role of
teachers, priests, and intellectuals in African society. His political engagement has repeatedly
forced him to flee his home country, Nigeria, only to return from exile when circumstances allowed it. As a consequence, his career now spans not only five decades but also three continents, and in 1986 he became the first African writer to be awarded the Nobel Prize in literature.

Soyinka—whose full name is Akinwande Oluwole Soyinka—was born in Abeokuta,
western Nigeria. His family is Yoruba, an ethnicity whose symbols and traditions are often addressed in his literary works. He attended college in Ibadan, Nigeria, from 1952 to 1954 and
then went on to the University of Leeds in England, where he received his bachelor's degree in
English literature in 1957. He began to work toward a master's degree but abandoned graduate
school for the theater, becoming a play reader for the Royal Court Theatre in London. After
completing two early plays, he returned to Nigeria in 1960 and wrote *Dance of the Forests,* a
play commissioned for the Nigerian independence celebration, and founded his own theater
company, the 1960 Masks (later renamed Orisun Theater). Throughout the 1960s, he wrote
more plays as well as a novel, *The Interpreters* (1965). But he also repeatedly entered into conflict with the government; these confrontations came to a head in 1967 when civil war broke
out as the eastern region of Biafra unilaterally declared independence from Nigeria: Soyinka
was arrested and held in solitary confinement for more than two years for allegedly assisting
the Biafran rebels and was only freed after an international media campaign on his behalf. His
prison notes, *A Man Died,* as well as a volume of poetry he wrote during his incarceration, *A
Shuttle in the Crypt,* were published in 1972.

Soyinka spent the early 1970s in Europe in voluntary exile, teaching at Cambridge and
Sheffield and writing and staging plays and novels. In 1981 Soyinka published an eloquent
autobiographical work, *Aké: The Years of Childhood.* His most important critical book,
Myth, Literature, and the African World, appeared in 1989. Though the Nobel Prize in 1986
had confirmed Soyinka's status as an internationally recognized playwright, it didn't prevent
further government oppression. He had returned to live in Nigeria, but in 1994 he had to flee
his country once again after the government confiscated his passport and began to persecute
people selling works by or about him. Spending most of his exile in the United States, he

taught at Harvard and Emory universities and published *The Open Sore of a Continent: A Personal Narrative of the Nigerian Crisis* (1996), which directly addressed the events in his homeland. In 1997 the Abacha regime issued a charge of treason against him; these charges were dropped, however, after Sani Abacha's death in 1998, and Soyinka once again returned to Nigeria.

In 1999 he published *The Burden of Memory, the Muse of Forgiveness,* a book that deals with Africa and also with the concept of *négritude* as developed by Léopold Sédar Senghor (see page 638) and Aimé Césaire (page 644). While Soyinka concedes that *négritude* was an important tool in the struggle for the liberation of blacks, he views it as a defensive concept that still at bottom accepts the fundamental distinctions between blacks and whites, Africans and Europeans that colonialist ideology had drawn even as it reverses the values attached to these distinctions. "A tiger does not proclaim his tigritude," as Soyinka once pointedly summed up his critique; his artistic and political goal is to reclaim African history, culture, and identity in their own right rather than as parts of a value scheme that pits them against European identity.

These concerns are prominent in Soyinka's most famous play, *Death and the King's Horseman* (1975), which brilliantly translates into drama the legal and ethical conflict between European colonial government structures and those of Yoruba tradition. Soyinka does this by staging a confrontation between the mandates of a deceased Yoruba king and those of a very much alive British prince. Yet this conflict also points to much deeper differences in the two cultures' understandings of what life and death are and how the dead and the living should relate to each other. This confrontation is also visible in the way the play fuses Western techniques—above all, the genre of the tragedy—with Yoruba ritual forms. The complex fusions of African and European forms, themes, and myths in his plays are one step toward a reconceptualization of African identity.

PRONUNCIATIONS:
 Elesin: eh-leh-SHEEN
 Iyaloja: ee-yah-LOW-jah
 Olunde: oh-LOON-dey
 Wole Soyinka: WOE-lay sho-YEEN-kah

Death and the King's Horseman
Author's Note

This play is based on events which took place in Oyo, ancient Yoruba city of Nigeria, in 1946. That year, the lives of Elesin (Olori Elesin), his son, and the Colonial District Officer intertwined with the disastrous results set out in the play. The changes I have made are in matters of detail, sequence and of course characterisation. The action has also been set back two or three years to while the war was still on, for minor reasons of dramaturgy.

The factual account still exists in the archives of the British Colonial Administration. It has already inspired a fine play in Yoruba (Oba Wàjà) by Duro Ladipo. It has also misbegotten a film by some German television company.

The bane of themes of this genre is that they are no sooner employed creatively than they acquire the facile tag of "clash of cultures," a prejudicial label which, quite apart from its frequent misapplication, presupposes a potential equality *in every given situation* of the alien culture and the indigenous, on the actual soil of the latter. (In the area of misapplication, the overseas prize for illiteracy and mental conditioning undoubtedly goes to the blurb-writer for the American edition of my novel *Season of*

Anomy who unblushingly declares that this work portrays the "clash between old values and new ways, between western methods and African traditions"!) It is thanks to this kind of perverse mentality that I find it necessary to caution the would-be producer of this play against a sadly familiar reductionist tendency, and to direct his vision instead to the far more difficult and risky task of eliciting the play's threnodic essence.[1]

One of the more obvious alternative structures of the play would be to make the District Officer the victim of a cruel dilemma. This is not to my taste and it is not by chance that I have avoided dialogue or situation which would encourage this. No attempt should be made in production to suggest it. The Colonial Factor is an incident, a catalytic incident merely. The confrontation in the play is largely metaphysical, contained in the human vehicle which is Elesin and the universe of the Yoruba mind—the world of the living, the dead and the unborn, and the numinous passage which links all: transition. *Death and the King's Horseman* can be fully realised only through an evocation of music from the abyss of transition.

W.S.

Characters

PRAISE-SINGER	
ELESIN	Horseman of the King
IYALOJA	"Mother" of the market
SIMON PILKINGS	District Officer
JANE PILKINGS	His wife
SERGEANT AMUSA	
JOSEPH	Houseboy to the Pilkingses
BRIDE	
H.R.H. THE PRINCE	
THE RESIDENT	
AIDE-DE-CAMP[2]	
OLUNDE	Eldest son of Elesin
DRUMMERS, WOMEN, YOUNG GIRLS, DANCERS AT THE BALL	

The play should run without an interval. For rapid scene changes, one adjustable outline set is very appropriate.

I

A passage through a market in its closing stages. The stalls are being emptied, mats folded. A few women pass through on their way home, loaded with baskets. On a cloth-stand, bolts of cloth are taken down, display pieces folded and piled on a tray. Elesin Oba enters along a passage before the market, pursued by his drummers and praise-singers. He is a man of enormous vitality, speaks, dances and sings with that infectious enjoyment of life which accompanies all his actions.

PRAISE-SINGER: Elesin o! Elesin Oba! Howu! What tryst is this the cockerel goes to keep with such haste that he must leave his tail behind?

ELESIN [*slows down a bit, laughing*]: A tryst where the cockerel needs no adornment.

---

1. Mournful. A threnody is a song of lamentation for the dead.

2. Military assistant.

PRAISE-SINGER: O-oh, you hear that my companions? That's the way the world goes. Because the man approaches a brand-new bride he forgets the long faithful mother of his children.

ELESIN: When the horse sniffs the stable does he not strain at the bridle? The market is the long-suffering home of my spirit and the women are packing up to go. That Esu-harassed day[3] slipped into the stewpot while we feasted. We ate it up with the rest of the meat. I have neglected my women.

PRAISE-SINGER: We know all that. Still it's no reason for shedding your tail on this day of all days. I know the women will cover you in damask and *alari*[4] but when the wind blows cold from behind, that's when the fowl knows his true friends.

ELESIN: Olohun-iyo![5]

PRAISE-SINGER: Are you sure there will be one like me on the other side?

ELESIN: Olohun-iyo!

PRAISE-SINGER: Far be it for me to belittle the dwellers of that place but, a man is either born to his art or he isn't. And I don't know for certain that you'll meet my father, so who is going to sing these deeds in accents that will pierce the deafness of the ancient ones. I have prepared my going—just tell me: Olohun-iyo, I need you on this journey and I shall be behind you.

ELESIN: You're like a jealous wife. Stay close to me, but only on this side. My fame, my honour are legacies to the living; stay behind and let the world sip its honey from your lips.

PRAISE-SINGER: Your name will be like the sweet berry a child places under his tongue to sweeten the passage of food. The world will never spit it out.

ELESIN: Come then. This market is my roost. When I come among the women I am a chicken with a hundred mothers. I become a monarch whose palace is built with tenderness and beauty.

PRAISE-SINGER: They love to spoil you but beware. The hands of women also weaken the unwary.

ELESIN: This night I'll lay my head upon their lap and go to sleep. This night I'll touch feet with their feet in a dance that is no longer of this earth. But the smell of their flesh, their sweat, the smell of indigo on their cloth, this is the last air I wish to breathe as I go to meet my great forebears.

PRAISE-SINGER: In their time the world was never tilted from its groove, it shall not be in yours.

ELESIN: The gods have said No.

PRAISE-SINGER: In their time the great wars came and went, the little wars came and went; the white slavers came and went, they took away the heart of our race, they bore away the mind and muscle of our race. The city fell and was rebuilt, the city fell and our people trudged through mountain and forest to found a new home but—Elesin Oba do you hear me?

ELESIN: I hear your voice Olohun-iyo.

PRAISE-SINGER: Our world was never wrenched from its true course.

ELESIN: The gods have said No.

PRAISE-SINGER: There is only one home to the life of a river-mussel; there is only one home to the life of a tortoise; there is only one shell to the soul of man: there is

---

3. Esu-Elegbara is the trickster figure in Yoruba culture.   5. A name for the Praise-singer.
4. A rich, woven cloth, brightly coloured [Soyinka's note].

only one world to the spirit of our race. If that world leaves its course and smashes on boulders of the great void, whose world will give us shelter?

ELESIN: It did not in the time of my forebears, it shall not in mine.

PRAISE-SINGER: The cockerel must not be seen without his feathers.

ELESIN: Nor will the Not-I bird be much longer without his nest.

PRAISE-SINGER [*stopped in his lyric stride*]: The Not-I bird, Elesin?

ELESIN: I said, the Not-I bird.

PRAISE-SINGER: All respect to our elders but, is there really such a bird?

ELESIN: What! Could it be that he failed to knock on your door?

PRAISE-SINGER [*smiling*]: Elesin's riddles are not merely the nut in the kernel that breaks human teeth; he also buries the kernel in hot embers and dares a man's fingers to draw it out.

ELESIN: I am sure he called on you, Olohun-iyo. Did you hide in the loft and push out the servant to tell him you were out?

[*Elesin executes a brief, half-taunting dance. The drummer moves in and draws a rhythm out of his steps. Elesin dances towards the market-place as he chants the story of the Not-I bird, his voice changing dexterously to mimic his characters. He performs like a born raconteur, infecting his retinue with his humour and energy. More women arrive during his recital, including Iyaloja.*]

> Death came calling.
> Who does not know his rasp of reeds?
> A twilight whisper in the leaves before
> The great araba falls?[6] Did you hear it?
> Not I! swears the farmer. He snaps
> His fingers round his head, abandons
> A hard-worn harvest and begins
> A rapid dialogue with his legs.
>
> "Not I," shouts the fearless hunter, "but—
> It's getting dark, and this night-lamp
> Has leaked out all its oil. I think
> It's best to go home and resume my hunt
> Another day." But now he pauses, suddenly
> Lets out a wail: "Oh foolish mouth, calling
> Down a curse on your own head! Your lamp
> Has leaked out all its oil, has it?"
> Forwards or backwards now he dare not move.
> To search for leaves and make etutu[7]
> On that spot? Or race home to the safety
> Of his hearth? Ten market-days have passed
> My friends, and still he's rooted there
> Rigid as the plinth of Orayan.
>
> The mouth of the courtesan barely
> Opened wide enough to take a ha'penny robo[8]
> When she wailed: "Not I." All dressed she was
> To call upon my friend the Chief Tax Officer.

---

6. The Araba tree is believed to be the seat of deities.
7. Placatory rites or medicine [Soyinka's note].

8. A delicacy made from crushed melon seeds, fried in tiny balls [Soyinka's note].

But now she sends her go-between instead:
"Tell him I'm ill: my period has come suddenly
But not—I hope—my time."

Why is the pupil crying?
His hapless head was made to taste
The knuckles of my friend the Mallam:
"If you were then reciting the Koran
Would you have ears for idle noises
Darkening the trees, you child of ill omen?"
He shuts down school before its time
Runs home and rings himself with amulets.

And take my good kinsman Ifawomi.
His hands were like a carver's, strong
And true. I saw them
Tremble like wet wings of a fowl
One day he cast his time-smoothed opele[9]
Across the divination board. And all because
The suppliant looked him in the eye and asked,
"Did you hear that whisper in the leaves?"
"Not I," was his reply; "perhaps I'm growing deaf—
Good-day." And Ifa[1] spoke no more that day
The priest locked fast his doors,
Sealed up his leaking roof—but wait!
This sudden care was not for Fawomi
But for Osanyin, courier-bird of Ifa's
Heart of wisdom. I did not know a kite
Was hovering in the sky
And Ifa now a twittering chicken in
The brood of Fawomi the Mother Hen.

Ah, but I must not forget my evening
Courier from the abundant palm, whose groan
Became Not I, as he constipated down
A wayside bush. He wonders if Elegbara
Has tricked his buttocks to discharge
Against a sacred grove. Hear him
Mutter spells to ward off penalties
For an abomination he did not intend.
If any here
Stumbles on a gourd of wine, fermenting
Near the road, and nearby hears a stream
Of spells issuing from a crouching form.
Brother to a sigidi,[2] bring home my wine,
Tell my tapper I have ejected
Fear from home and farm. Assure him,
All is well.

---

9. String of beads used in Ifa divination [Soyinka's note]. This form of divination is commonly used in traditional Yoruba religion to solve everyday problems, to obtain advice in major life changes (birth, death, marriage), or to discover a person's destiny.

1. A reference to the Yoruba deity Orúnmila who speaks through Ifa divination.
2. A squat, carved figure, endowed with the powers of an incubus [Soyinka's note].

PRAISE-SINGER: In your time we do not doubt the peace of farmstead and home, the peace of road and hearth, we do not doubt the peace of the forest.

ELESIN:
There was fear in the forest too.
Not-I was lately heard even in the lair
Of beasts. The hyena cackled loud Not I,
The civet twitched his fiery tail and glared:
Not I. Not-I became the answering-name
Of the restless bird, that little one
Whom Death found nesting in the leaves
When whisper of his coming ran
Before him on the wind. Not-I
Has long abandoned home. This same dawn
I heard him twitter in the gods' abode.
Ah, companions of this living world
What a thing this is, that even those
We call immortal
Should fear to die.

IYALOJA:
But you, husband of multitudes?

ELESIN:
I, when that Not-I bird perched
Upon my roof, bade him seek his nest again,
Safe, without care or fear. I unrolled
My welcome mat for him to see. Not-I
Flew happily away, you'll hear his voice
No more in this lifetime—You all know
What I am.

PRAISE-SINGER:
That rock which turns its open lodes
Into the path of lightning. A gay
Thoroughbred whose stride disdains
To falter though an adder reared
Suddenly in his path.

ELESIN:
My rein is loosened.
I am master of my Fate. When the hour comes
Watch me dance along the narrowing path
Glazed by the soles of my great precursors.
My soul is eager. I shall not turn aside.

WOMEN:
You will not delay?

ELESIN:
Where the storm pleases, and when, it directs
The giants of the forest. When friendship summons
Is when the true comrade goes.

WOMEN:
Nothing will hold you back?

ELESIN:
Nothing. What! Has no one told you yet?
I go to keep my friend and master company.
Who says the mouth does not believe in
"No, I have chewed all that before?" I say I have.
The world is not a constant honey-pot.
Where I found little I made do with little.
Where there was plenty I gorged myself.

> My master's hands and mine have always
> Dipped together and, home or sacred feast,
> The bowl was beaten bronze, the meats
> So succulent our teeth accused us of neglect.
> We shared the choicest of the season's
> Harvest of yams. How my friend would read
> Desire in my eyes before I knew the cause—
> However rare, however precious, it was mine.

WOMEN: *The town, the very land was yours.*

ELESIN: *The world was mine. Our joint hands*
Raised houseposts of trust that withstood
The siege of envy and the termites of time.
But the twilight hour brings bats and rodents—
Shall I yield them cause to foul the rafters?

PRAISE-SINGER: *Elesin Oba! Are you not that man who*
Looked out of doors that stormy day
The god of luck limped by, drenched
To the very lice that held
His rags together? You took pity upon
His sores and wished him fortune.
Fortune was footloose this dawn, he replied,
Till you trapped him in a heartfelt wish
That now returns to you. Elesin Oba!
I say you are that man who
Chanced upon the calabash of honour
You thought it was palm wine and
Drained its contents to the final drop.

ELESIN: *Life has an end. A life that will outlive*
Fame and friendship begs another name.
What elder takes his tongue to his plate,
Licks it clean of every crumb? He will encounter
Silence when he calls on children to fulfill
The smallest errand! Life is honour.
It ends when honour ends.

WOMEN: *We know you for a man of honour.*

ELESIN: Stop! Enough of that!

WOMEN [*puzzled, they whisper among themselves, turning mostly to Iyaloja*]: What is it? Did we say something to give offence? Have we slighted him in some way?

ELESIN: Enough of that sound I say. Let me hear no more in that vein. I've heard enough.

IYALOJA: We must have said something wrong. [*Comes forward a little.*] Elesin Oba, we ask forgiveness before you speak.

ELESIN: I am bitterly offended.

IYALOJA: Our unworthiness has betrayed us. All we can do is ask your forgiveness. Correct us like a kind father.

ELESIN: This day of all days . . .

IYALOJA: It does not bear thinking. If we offend you now we have mortified the gods. We offend heaven itself. Father of us all, tell us where we went astray. [*She kneels, the other women follow.*]

ELESIN:

> *Are you not ashamed? Even a tear-veiled*
> *Eye preserves its function of sight.*
> *Because my mind was raised to horizons*
> *Even the boldest man lowers his gaze*
> *In thinking of, must my body here*
> *Be taken for a vagrant's?*

IYALOJA: Horseman of the King, I am more baffled than ever.

PRAISE-SINGER: The strictest father unbends his brow when the child is penitent, Elesin. When time is short, we do not spend it prolonging the riddle. Their shoulders are bowed with the weight of fear lest they have marred your day beyond repair. Speak now in plain words and let us pursue the ailment to the home of remedies.

ELESIN:

> *Words are cheap. "We know you for*
> *A man of honour." Well tell me, is this how*
> *A man of honour should be seen?*
> *Are these not the same clothes in which*
> *I came among you a full half-hour ago?*

[*He roars with laughter and the women, relieved, rise and rush into stalls to fetch rich cloths.*]

WOMAN: The gods are kind. A fault soon remedied is soon forgiven. Elesin Oba, even as we match our words with deed, let your heart forgive us completely.

ELESIN:

> *You who are breath and giver of my being*
> *How shall I dare refuse you forgiveness*
> *Even if the offence were real.*

IYALOJA [*dancing round him. Sings*]:

> *He forgives us. He forgives us.*
> *What a fearful thing it is when*
> *The voyager sets forth*
> *But a curse remains behind.*

WOMEN:

> *For a while we truly feared*
> *Our hands had wrenched the world adrift*
> *In emptiness.*

IYALOJA:

> *Richly, richly, robe him richly*
> *The cloth of honour is alari*
> *Sanyan³ is the band of friendship*
> *Boa-skin makes slippers of esteem*

WOMEN:

> *For a while we truly feared*
> *Our hands had wrenched the world adrift*
> *In emptiness.*

PRAISE-SINGER:

> *He who must, must voyage forth*
> *The world will not roll backwards*
> *It is he who must, with one*
> *Great gesture overtake the world.*

---

3. A richly valued woven cloth [Soyinka's note].

WOMEN:	*For a while we truly feared*
	Our hands had wrenched the world
	In emptiness.
PRAISE-SINGER:	*The gourd you bear is not for shirking.*
	The gourd is not for setting down
	At the first crossroad or wayside grove.
	Only one river may know its contents
WOMEN:	*We shall all meet at the great market*
	We shall all meet at the great market
	He who goes early takes the best bargains
	But we shall meet, and resume our banter.

[*Elesin stands resplendent in rich clothes, cap, shawl, etc. His sash is of a bright red* alari *cloth. The women dance round him. Suddenly, his attention is caught by an object off-stage.*]

ELESIN:	*The world I know is good.*
WOMEN:	*We know you'll leave it so.*
ELESIN:	*The world I know is the bounty*
	Of hives after bees have swarmed.
	No goodness teems with such open hands
	Even in the dreams of deities.
WOMEN:	*And we know you'll leave it so.*
ELESIN:	*I was born to keep it so. A hive*
	Is never known to wander. An anthill
	Does not desert its roots. We cannot see
	The still great womb of the world—
	No man beholds his mother's womb—
	Yet who denies it's there? Coiled
	To the navel of the world is that
	Endless cord that links us all
	To the great origin. If I lose my way
	The trailing cord will bring me to the roots.
WOMEN:	*The world is in your hands.*

[*The earlier distraction, a beautiful young girl, comes along the passage through which Elesin first made his entry.*]

ELESIN:	*I embrace it. And let me tell you, women—*
	I like this farewell that the world designed,
	Unless my eyes deceive me, unless
	We are already parted, the world and I,
	And all that breeds desire is lodged
	Among our tireless ancestors. Tell me friends,
	Am I still earthed in that beloved market
	Of my youth? Or could it be my will
	Has outleapt the conscious act and I have come
	Among the great departed?

PRAISE-SINGER: Elesin-Oba why do your eyes roll like a bush-rat who sees his fate like his father's spirit, mirrored in the eye of a snake? And all these questions! You're standing on the same earth you've always stood upon. This voice you hear is mine, Oluhun-iyo, not that of an acolyte in heaven.

ELESIN:
> How can that be? In all my life
> As Horseman of the King, the juiciest
> Fruit on every tree was mine. I saw,
> I touched, I wooed, rarely was the answer No.
> The honour of my place, the veneration I
> Received in the eye of man or woman
> Prospered my suit and
> Played havoc with my sleeping hours.
> And they tell me my eyes were a hawk
> In perpetual hunger. Split an iroko tree
> In two, hide a woman's beauty in its heartwood
> And seal it up again—Elesin, journeying by,
> Would make his camp beside that tree
> Of all the shades in the forest.

PRAISE-SINGER: Who would deny your reputation, snake-on-the-loose in dark passages of the market! Bed-bug who wages war on the mat and receives the thanks of the vanquished! When caught with his bride's own sister he protested—but I was only prostrating myself to her as becomes a grateful in-law. Hunter who carries his powder-horn on the hips and fires crouching or standing! Warrior who never makes that excuse of the whining coward—but how can I go to battle without my trousers?—trouserless or shirtless it's all one to him. Oka-rearing-from-a-camouflage-of-leaves, before he strikes the victim is already prone! Once they told him, Howu, a stallion does not feed on the grass beneath him: he replied, true, but surely he can roll on it!

WOMEN: Ba-a-a-ba O!

PRAISE-SINGER: Ah, but listen yet. You know there is the leaf-knibbling grub and there is the cola-chewing beetle; the leaf-nibbling grub lives on the leaf, the cola-chewing beetle lives in the colanut. Don't we know what our man feeds on when we find him cocooned in a woman's wrapper?

ELESIN:
> Enough, enough, you all have cause
> To know me well. But, if you say this earth
> Is still the same as gave birth to those songs,
> Tell me who was that goddess through whose lips
> I saw the ivory pebbles of Oya's river-bed.
> Iyaloja, who is she? I saw her enter
> Your stall; all your daughters I know well.
> No, not even Ogun-of-the-farm[4] toiling
> Dawn till dusk on his tuber patch
> Not even Ogun with the finest hoe he ever
> Forged at the anvil could have shaped
> That rise of buttocks, not though he had
> The richest earth between his fingers.

---

4. Yoruba deity of iron, the forge, and war.

> Her wrapper was no disguise
> For thighs whose ripples shamed the river's
> Coils around the hills of Ilesi. Her eyes
> Were new-laid eggs glowing in the dark.
> Her skin . . .

IYALOJA: Elesin Oba . . .

ELESIN: What! Where do you all say I am?

IYALOJA: Still among the living.

ELESIN:
> And that radiance which so suddenly
> Lit up this market I could boast
> I knew so well?

IYALOJA: Has one step already in her husband's home. She is betrothed.

ELESIN [*irritated*]: Why do you tell me that?

[*Iyaloja falls silent. The women shuffle uneasily.*]

IYALOJA: Not because we dare give you offence Elesin. Today is your day and the whole world is yours. Still, even those who leave town to make a new dwelling elsewhere like to be remembered by what they leave behind.

ELESIN:
> Who does not seek to be remembered?
> Memory is Master of Death, the chink
> In his armour of conceit. I shall leave
> That which makes my going the sheerest
> Dream of an afternoon. Should voyagers
> Not travel light? Let the considerate traveller
> Shed, of his excessive load, all
> That may benefit the living.

WOMEN [*relieved*]: Ah Elesin Oba, we knew you for a man of honour.

ELESIN: Then honour me. I deserve a bed of honour to lie upon.

IYALOJA: The best is yours. We know you for a man of honour. You are not one who eats and leaves nothing on his plate for children. Did you not say it yourself? Not one who blights the happiness of others for a moment's pleasure.

ELESIN:
> Who speaks of pleasure? O women, listen!
> Pleasure palls. Our acts should have meaning.
> The sap of the plantain never dries.
> You have seen the young shoot swelling
> Even as the parent stalk begins to wither.
> Women, let my going be likened to
> The twilight hour of the plantain.

WOMEN: What does he mean Iyaloja? This language is the language of our elders, we do not fully grasp it.

IYALOJA: I dare not understand you yet Elesin.

ELESIN:
> All you who stand before the spirit that dares
> The opening of the last door of passage,
> Dare to rid my going of regrets! My wish
> Transcends the blotting out of thought
> In one mere moment's tremor of the senses.

Do me credit. And do me honour.
I am girded for the route beyond
Burdens of waste and longing.
Then let me travel light. Let
Seed that will not serve the stomach
On the way remain behind. Let it take root
In the earth of my choice, in this earth
I leave behind.

IYALOJA [*turns to women*]: The voice I hear is already touched by the waiting fingers of our departed. I dare not refuse.

WOMAN: But Iyaloja . . .

IYALOJA: The matter is no longer in our hands.

WOMAN: But she is betrothed to your own son. Tell him.

IYALOJA: My son's wish is mine. I did the asking for him, the loss can be remedied. But who will remedy the blight of closed hands on the day when all should be openness and light? Tell him, you say! You wish that I burden him with knowledge that will sour his wish and lay regrets on the last moments of his mind. You pray to him who is your intercessor to the other world—don't set this world adrift in your own time; would you rather it was my hand whose sacrilege wrenched it loose?

WOMAN: Not many men will brave the curse of a dispossessed husband.

IYALOJA: Only the curses of the departed are to be feared. The claims of one whose foot is on the threshold of their abode surpasses even the claims of blood. It is impiety even to place hindrances in their ways.

ELESIN: *What do my mothers say? Shall I step*
                          Burdened into the unknown?

IYALOJA: Not we, but the very earth says No. The sap in the plantain does not dry. Let grain that will not feed the voyager at his passage drop here and take root as he steps beyond this earth and us. Oh you who fill the home from hearth to threshold with the voices of children, you who now bestride the hidden gulf and pause to draw the right foot across and into the resting-home of the great forebears, it is good that your loins be drained into the earth we know, that your last strength be ploughed back into the womb that gave you being.

PRAISE-SINGER: Iyaloja, mother of multitudes in the teeming market of the world, how your wisdom transfigures you!

IYALOJA [*smiling broadly, completely reconciled*]: Elesin, even at the narrow end of the passage I know you will look back and sigh a last regret for the flesh that flashed past your spirit in flight. You always had a restless eye. Your choice has my blessing. [*To the women.*] Take the good news to our daughter and make her ready. [*Some women go off.*]

ELESIN: Your eyes were clouded at first.

IYALOJA: Not for long. It is those who stand at the gateway of the great change to whose cry we must pay heed. And then, think of this—it makes the mind tremble. The fruit of such a union is rare. It will be neither of this world nor of the next. Nor of the one behind us. As if the timelessness of the ancestor world and the unborn have joined spirits to wring an issue of the elusive being of passage . . . Elesin!

ELESIN: I am here. What is it?

IYALOJA: Did you hear all I said just now?

ELESIN: Yes.

IYALOJA: The living must eat and drink. When the moment comes, don't turn the food to rodents' droppings in their mouth. Don't let them taste the ashes of the world when they step out at dawn to breathe the morning dew.

ELESIN: This doubt is unworthy of you Iyaloja.

IYALOJA: Eating the awusa nut is not so difficult as drinking water afterwards.

ELESIN:
> *The waters of the bitter stream are honey to a man*
> *Whose tongue has savoured all.*

IYALOJA: No one knows when the ants desert their home; they leave the mound intact. The swallow is never seen to peck holes in its nest when it is time to move with the season. There are always throngs of humanity behind the leave-taker. The rain should not come through the roof for them, the wind must not blow through the walls at night.

ELESIN: I refuse to take offence.

IYALOJA: You wish to travel light. Well, the earth is yours. But be sure the seed you leave in it attracts no curse.

ELESIN: You really mistake my person Iyaloja.

IYALOJA: I said nothing. Now we must go prepare your bridal chamber. Then these same hands will lay your shrouds.

ELESIN [*exasperated*]: Must you be so blunt? [*Recovers.*] Well, weave your shrouds, but let the fingers of my bride seal my eyelids with earth and wash my body.

IYALOJA: Prepare yourself Elesin.

[*She gets up to leave. At that moment the women return, leading the Bride. Elesin's face glows with pleasure. He flicks the sleeves of his agbada[5] with renewed confidence and steps forward to meet the group. As the girl kneels before Iyaloja, lights fade out on the scene.*]

II

The verandah of the District Officer's bungalow. A tango is playing from an old hand-cranked gramophone and, glimpsed through the wide windows and doors which open onto the fore-stage verandah are the shapes of Simon Pilkings and his wife, Jane, tangoing in and out of shadows in the living-room. They are wearing what is immediately apparent as some form of fancy-dress. The dance goes on for some moments and then the figure of a "Native Administration" policeman emerges and climbs up the steps onto the verandah. He peeps through and observes the dancing couple, reacting with what is obviously a long-standing bewilderment. He stiffens suddenly, his expression changes to one of disbelief and horror. In his excitement he upsets a flowerpot and attracts the attention of the couple. They stop dancing.

PILKINGS: Is there anyone out there?

JANE: I'll turn off the gramophone.

PILKINGS [*approaching the verandah*]: I'm sure I heard something fall over. [*The constable retreats slowly, open-mouthed as Pilkings approaches the verandah.*] Oh it's you Amusa. Why didn't you just knock instead of knocking things over?

---

5. An embroidered robe with wide sleeves, usually worn by kings or chiefs on formal occasions such as weddings or funerals.

AMUSA [*stammers badly and points a shaky finger at his dress*]: Mista Pirinkin . . . Mista Pirinkin . . .

PILKINGS: What is the matter with you?

JANE [*emerging*]: Who is it dear? Oh, Amusa . . .

PILKINGS: Yes it's Amusa, and acting most strangely.

AMUSA [*his attention now transferred to Mrs. Pilkings*]: Mammadam . . . you too!

PILKINGS: What the hell is the matter with you man!

JANE: Your costume darling. Our fancy dress.

PILKINGS: Oh hell, I'd forgotten all about that. [*Lifts the face mask over his head showing his face. His wife follows suit.*]

JANE: I think you've shocked his big pagan heart bless him.

PILKINGS: Nonsense, he's a Moslem. Come on Amusa, you don't believe in all this nonsense do you? I thought you were a good Moslem.

AMUSA: Mista Pirinkin, I beg you sir, what you think you do with that dress? It belong to dead cult, not for human being.

PILKINGS: Oh Amusa, what a let down you are. I swear by you at the club you know—thank God for Amusa, he doesn't believe in any mumbo-jumbo. And now look at you!

AMUSA: Mista Pirinkin, I beg you, take it off. Is not good for man like you to touch that cloth.

PILKINGS: Well, I've got it on. And what's more Jane and I have bet on it we're taking first prize at the ball. Now, if you can just pull yourself together and tell me what you wanted to see me about . . .

AMUSA: Sir, I cannot talk this matter to you in that dress. I no fit.

PILKINGS: What's that rubbish again?

JANE: He is dead earnest too Simon. I think you'll have to handle this delicately.

PILKINGS: Delicately my . . .! Look here Amusa, I think this little joke has gone far enough hm? Let's have some sense. You seem to forget that you are a police officer in the service of His Majesty's Government. I order you to report your business at once or face disciplinary action.

AMUSA: Sir, it is a matter of death. How can man talk against death to person in uniform of death? Is like talking against government to person in uniform of police. Please sir, I go and come back.

PILKINGS [*roars*]: Now! [*Amusa switches his gaze to the ceiling suddenly, remains mute.*]

JANE: Oh Amusa, what is there to be scared of in the costume? You saw it confiscated last month from those *egungun*[1] men who were creating trouble in town. You helped arrest the cult leaders yourself—if the juju[2] didn't harm you at the time how could it possibly harm you now? And merely by looking at it?

AMUSA [*without looking down*]: Madam, I arrest the ring-leaders who make trouble but me I no touch *egungun*. That *egungun* inself, I no touch. And I no abuse 'am. I arrest ring-leader but I treat *egungun* with respect.

PILKINGS: It's hopeless. We'll merely end up missing the best part of the ball. When they get this way there is nothing you can do. It's simply hammering against a brick wall. Write your report or whatever it is on that pad Amusa and take yourself out of here. Come on Jane. We only upset his delicate sensibilities by remaining here.

---

1. Ancestral masquerade [Soyinka's note].   2. African cult practices (related to voodoo).

[*Amusa waits for them to leave, then writes in the notebook, somewhat labori-ously. Drumming from the direction of the town wells up. Amusa listens, makes a movement as if he wants to recall Pilkings but changes his mind. Completes his note and goes. A few moments later Pilkings emerges, picks up the pad and reads.*]

PILKINGS: Jane!

JANE [*from the bedroom*]: Coming darling. Nearly ready.

PILKINGS: Never mind being ready, just listen to this.

JANE: What is it?

PILKINGS: Amusa's report. Listen. "I have to report that it come to my information that one prominent chief, namely, the Elesin Oba, is to commit death tonight as a result of native custom. Because this is criminal offence I await further instruction at charge office. Sergeant Amusa."

[*Jane comes out onto the verandah while he is reading.*]

JANE: Did I hear you say commit death?

PILKINGS: Obviously he means murder.

JANE: You mean a ritual murder?

PILKINGS: Must be. You think you've stamped it all out but it's always lurking under the surface somewhere.

JANE: Oh. Does it mean we are not getting to the ball at all?

PILKINGS: No-o. I'll have the man arrested. Everyone remotely involved. In any case there may be nothing to it. Just rumours.

JANE: Really? I thought you found Amusa's rumours generally reliable.

PILKINGS: That's true enough. But who knows what may have been giving him the scare lately. Look at his conduct tonight.

JANE [*laughing*]: You have to admit he had his own peculiar logic. [*Deepens her voice.*] How can man talk against death to person in uniform of death? [*Laughs.*] Anyway, you can't go into the police station dressed like that.

PILKINGS: I'll send Joseph with instructions. Damn it, what a confounded nuisance!

JANE: But don't you think you should talk first to the man, Simon?

PILKINGS: Do you want to go to the ball or not?

JANE: Darling, why are you getting rattled? I was only trying to be intelligent. It seems hardly fair just to lock up a man—and a chief at that—simply on the er . . . what is that legal word again?—uncorroborated word of a sergeant.

PILKINGS: Well, that's easily decided. Joseph!

JOSEPH [*from within*]: Yes master.

PILKINGS: You're quite right of course, I am getting rattled. Probably the effect of those bloody drums. Do you hear how they go on and on?

JANE: I wondered when you'd notice. Do you suppose it has something to do with this affair?

PILKINGS: Who knows? They always find an excuse for making a noise . . . [*Thoughtfully.*] Even so . . .

JANE: Yes Simon?

PILKINGS: It's different Jane. I don't think I've heard this particular—sound—before. Something unsettling about it.

JANE: I thought all bush drumming sounded the same.

PILKINGS: Don't tease me now Jane. This may be serious.

JANE: I'm sorry. [*Gets up and throws her arms around his neck. Kisses him. The houseboy enters, retreats and knocks.*]

PILKINGS [*wearily*]: Oh, come in Joseph! I don't know where you pick up all these elephantine notions of tact. Come over here.

JOSEPH: Sir?

PILKINGS: Joseph, are you a christian or not?

JOSEPH: Yessir.

PILKINGS: Does seeing me in this outfit bother you?

JOSEPH: No sir, it has no power.

PILKINGS: Thank God for some sanity at last. Now Joseph, answer me on the honour of a christian—what is supposed to be going on in town tonight?

JOSEPH: Tonight sir? You mean that chief who is going to kill himself?

PILKINGS: What?

JANE: What do you mean, kill himself?

PILKINGS: You do mean he is going to kill somebody don't you?

JOSEPH: No master. He will not kill anybody and no one will kill him. He will simply die.

JANE: But why Joseph?

JOSEPH: It is native law and custom. The King die last month. Tonight is his burial. But before they can bury him, the Elesin must die so as to accompany him to heaven.

PILKINGS: I seem to be fated to clash more often with that man than with any of the other chiefs.

JOSEPH: He is the King's Chief Horseman.

PILKINGS [*in a resigned way*]: I know.

JANE: Simon, what's the matter?

PILKINGS: It would have to be him!

JANE: Who is he?

PILKINGS: Don't you remember? He's that chief with whom I had a scrap some three or four years ago. I helped his son get to a medical school in England, remember? He fought tooth and nail to prevent it.

JANE: Oh now I remember. He was that very sensitive young man. What was his name again?

PILKINGS: Olunde. Haven't replied to his last letter come to think of it. The old pagan wanted him to stay and carry on some family tradition or the other. Honestly I couldn't understand the fuss he made. I literally had to help the boy escape from close confinement and load him onto the next boat. A most intelligent boy, really bright.

JANE: I rather thought he was much too sensitive you know. The kind of person you feel should be a poet munching rose petals in Bloomsbury.

PILKINGS: Well, he's going to make a first-class doctor. His mind is set on that. And as long as he wants my help he is welcome to it.

JANE [*after a pause*]: Simon.

PILKINGS: Yes?

JANE: This boy, he was his eldest son wasn't he?

PILKINGS: I'm not sure. Who could tell with that old ram?

JANE: Do you know, Joseph?

JOSEPH: Oh yes madam. He was the eldest son. That's why Elesin cursed master good and proper. The eldest son is not supposed to travel away from the land.

JANE [*giggling*]: Is that true Simon? Did he really curse you good and proper?

PILKINGS: By all accounts I should be dead by now.

JOSEPH: Oh no, master is white man. And good christian. Black man juju can't touch master.

JANE: If he was his eldest, it means that he would be the Elesin to the next king. It's a family thing isn't it Joseph?

JOSEPH: Yes madam. And if this Elesin had died before the King, his eldest son must take his place.

JANE: That would explain why the old chief was so mad you took the boy away.

PILKINGS: Well it makes me all the more happy I did.

JANE: I wonder if he knew.

PILKINGS: Who? Oh, you mean Olunde?

JANE: Yes. Was that why he was so determined to get away? I wouldn't stay if I knew I was trapped in such a horrible custom.

PILKINGS [*thoughtfully*]: No, I don't think he knew. At least he gave no indication. But you couldn't really tell with him. He was rather close you know, quite unlike most of them. Didn't give much away, not even to me.

JANE: Aren't they all rather close, Simon?

PILKINGS: These natives here? Good gracious. They'll open their mouths and yap with you about their family secrets before you can stop them. Only the other day . . .

JANE: But Simon, do they really give anything away? I mean, anything that really counts. This affair for instance, we didn't know they still practised that custom did we?

PILKINGS: Ye-e-es, I suppose you're right there. Sly, devious bastards.

JOSEPH [*stiffly*]: Can I go now master? I have to clean the kitchen.

PILKINGS: What? Oh, you can go. Forgot you were still here.

[*Joseph goes.*]

JANE: Simon, you really must watch your language. Bastard isn't just a simple swear-word in these parts, you know.

PILKINGS: Look, just when did you become a social anthropologist, that's what I'd like to know.

JANE: I'm not claiming to know anything. I just happen to have overheard quarrels among the servants. That's how I know they consider it a smear.

PILKINGS: I thought the extended family system took care of all that. Elastic family, no bastards.

JANE [*shrugs*]: Have it your own way.

[*Awkward silence. The drumming increases in volume. Jane gets up suddenly, restless.*]

That drumming Simon, do you think it might really be connected with this ritual? It's been going on all evening.

PILKINGS: Let's ask our native guide. Joseph! Just a minute Joseph. [*Joseph re-enters.*] What's the drumming about?

JOSEPH: I don't know master.

PILKINGS: What do you mean you don't know? It's only two years since your conversion. Don't tell me all that holy water nonsense also wiped out your tribal memory.

JOSEPH [*visibly shocked*]: Master!

JANE: Now you've done it.

PILKINGS: What have I done now?

JANE: Never mind. Listen Joseph, just tell me this. Is that drumming connected with dying or anything of that nature?

JOSEPH: Madam, this is what I am trying to say: I am not sure. It sounds like the death of a great chief and then, it sounds like the wedding of a great chief. It really mix me up.

PILKINGS: Oh get back to the kitchen. A fat lot of help you are.

JOSEPH: Yes master. [*Goes.*]

JANE: Simon . . .

PILKINGS: Alright, alright. I'm in no mood for preaching.

JANE: It isn't my preaching you have to worry about, it's the preaching of the missionaries who preceded you here. When they make converts they really convert them. Calling holy water nonsense to our Joseph is really like insulting the Virgin Mary before a Roman Catholic. He's going to hand in his notice tomorrow you mark my word.

PILKINGS: Now you're being ridiculous.

JANE: Am I? What are you willing to bet that tomorrow we are going to be without a steward-boy? Did you see his face?

PILKINGS: I am more concerned about whether or not we will be one native chief short by tomorrow. Christ! Just listen to those drums. [*He strides up and down, undecided.*]

JANE [*getting up*]: I'll change and make up some supper.

PILKINGS: What's that?

JANE: Simon, it's obvious we have to miss this ball.

PILKINGS: Nonsense. It's the first bit of real fun the European club has managed to organise for over a year, I'm damned if I'm going to miss it. And it is a rather special occasion. Doesn't happen every day.

JANE: You know this business has to be stopped Simon. And you are the only man who can do it.

PILKINGS: I don't have to stop anything. If they want to throw themselves off the top of a cliff or poison themselves for the sake of some barbaric custom what is that to me? If it were ritual murder or something like that I'd be duty-bound to do something. I can't keep an eye on all the potential suicides in this province. And as for that man—believe me it's good riddance.

JANE [*laughs*]: I know you better than that Simon. You are going to have to do something to stop it—after you've finished blustering.

PILKINGS [*shouts after her*]: And suppose after all it's only a wedding. I'd look a proper fool if I interrupted a chief on his honeymoon, wouldn't I? [*Resumes his angry stride, slows down.*] Ah well, who can tell what those chiefs actually do on their honeymoon anyway? [*He takes up the pad and scribbles rapidly on it.*] Joseph! Joseph! Joseph! [*Some moments later Joseph puts in a sulky appearance.*] Did you hear me call you? Why the hell didn't you answer?

JOSEPH: I didn't hear master.

PILKINGS: You didn't hear me! How come you are here then?

JOSEPH [*stubbornly*]: I didn't hear master.

PILKINGS [*controls himself with an effort*]: We'll talk about it in the morning. I want you to take this note directly to Sergeant Amusa. You'll find him at the charge office. Get on your bicycle and race there with it. I expect you back in twenty minutes exactly. Twenty minutes, is that clear?

JOSEPH: Yes master. [*Going.*]

PILKINGS: Oh er . . . Joseph.

JOSEPH: Yes master?

PILKINGS [*between gritted teeth*]: Er . . . forget what I said just now. The holy water is not nonsense. I was talking nonsense.

JOSEPH: Yes master. [*Goes.*]

JANE [*pokes her head round the door*]: Have you found him?

PILKINGS: Found who?

JANE: Joseph. Weren't you shouting for him?

PILKINGS: Oh yes, he turned up finally.

JANE: You sounded desperate. What was it all about?

PILKINGS: Oh nothing. I just wanted to apologise to him. Assure him that the holy water isn't really nonsense.

JANE: Oh? And how did he take it?

PILKINGS: Who the hell gives a damn! I had a sudden vision of our Very Reverend Macfarlane drafting another letter of complaint to the Resident about my unchristian language towards his parishioners.

JANE: Oh I think he's given up on you by now.

PILKINGS: Don't be too sure. And anyway, I wanted to make sure Joseph didn't "lose" my note on the way. He looked sufficiently full of the holy crusade to do some such thing.

JANE: If you've finished exaggerating, come and have something to eat.

PILKINGS: No, put it all away. We can still get to the ball.

JANE: Simon . . .

PILKINGS: Get your costume back on. Nothing to worry about. I've instructed Amusa to arrest the man and lock him up.

JANE: But that station is hardly secure Simon. He'll soon get his friends to help him escape.

PILKINGS: A-ah, that's where I have out-thought you. I'm not having him put in the station cell. Amusa will bring him right here and lock him up in my study. And he'll stay with him till we get back. No one will dare come here to incite him to anything.

JANE: How clever of you darling. I'll get ready.

PILKINGS: Hey.

JANE: Yes darling.

PILKINGS: I have a surprise for you. I was going to keep it until we actually got to the ball.

JANE: What is it?

PILKINGS: You know the Prince is on a tour of the colonies don't you? Well, he docked in the capital only this morning but he is already at the Residency. He is going to grace the ball with his presence later tonight.

JANE: Simon! Not really.

PILKINGS: Yes he is. He's been invited to give away the prizes and he has agreed. You must admit old Engleton is the best Club Secretary we ever had. Quick off the mark that lad.

JANE: But how thrilling.

PILKINGS: The other provincials are going to be damned envious.

JANE: I wonder what he'll come as.

PILKINGS: Oh I don't know. As a coat-of-arms perhaps. Anyway it won't be anything to touch this.

JANE: Well that's lucky. If we are to be presented I won't have to start looking for a pair of gloves. It's all sewn on.

PILKINGS [laughing]: Quite right. Trust a woman to think of that. Come on, let's get going.

JANE [rushing off]: Won't be a second. [Stops.] Now I see why you've been so edgy all evening. I thought you weren't handling this affair with your usual brilliance— to begin with that is.

PILKINGS [his mood is much improved]: Shut up woman and get your things on.

JANE: Alright boss, coming.

> [*Pilkings suddenly begins to hum the tango to which they were dancing before. Starts to execute a few practice steps. Lights fade.*]

III

A swelling, agitated hum of women's voices rises immediately in the background. The lights come on and we see the frontage of a converted cloth stall in the market. The floor leading up to the entrance is covered in rich velvets and woven cloth. The women come on stage, borne backwards by the determined progress of Sergeant Amusa and his two constables who already have their batons out and use them as a pressure against the women. At the edge of the cloth-covered floor however the women take a determined stand and block all further progress of the men. They begin to tease them mercilessly.

AMUSA: I am tell you women for last time to commot my road. I am here on official business.

WOMAN: Official business you white man's eunuch? Official business is taking place where you want to go and it's a business you wouldn't understand.

WOMAN [*makes a quick tug at the constable's baton*]: That doesn't fool anyone you know. It's the one you carry under your government knickers that counts. [She bends low as if to peep under the baggy shorts. The embarrassed constable quickly puts his knees together. The women roar.]

WOMAN: You mean there is nothing there at all?

WOMAN: Oh there was something. You know that handbell which the whiteman uses to summon his servants . . .?

AMUSA [*he manages to preserve some dignity throughout*]: I hope you women know that interfering with officer in execution of his duty is criminal offence.

WOMAN: Interfere? He says we're interfering with him. You foolish man we're telling you there's nothing there to interfere with.

AMUSA: I am order you now to clear the road.

WOMAN: What road? The one your father built?

WOMAN: You are a Policeman not so? Then you know what they call trespassing in court. Or—[*Pointing to the cloth-lined steps.*]—do you think that kind of road is built for every kind of feet.

WOMAN: Go back and tell the white man who sent you to come himself.

AMUSA: If I go I will come back with reinforcement. And we will all return carrying weapons.

WOMAN: Oh, now I understand. Before they can put on those knickers the white man first cuts off their weapons.

WOMAN: What a cheek! You mean you come here to show power to women and you don't even have a weapon.

AMUSA [*shouting above the laughter*]: For the last time I warn you women to clear the road.

WOMAN: To where?

AMUSA: To that hut. I know he dey dere.

WOMAN: Who?

AMUSA: The chief who call himself Elesin Oba.

WOMAN: You ignorant man. It is not he who calls himself Elesin Oba, it is his blood that says it. As it called out to his father before him and will to his son after him. And that is in spite of everything your white man can do.

WOMAN: Is it not the same ocean that washes this land and the white man's land? Tell your white man he can hide our son away as long as he likes. When the time comes for him, the same ocean will bring him back.

AMUSA: The government say dat kin' ting must stop.

WOMAN: Who will stop it? You? Tonight our husband and father will prove himself greater than the laws of strangers.

AMUSA: I tell you nobody go prove anyting tonight or anytime. Is ignorant and criminal to prove dat kin' prove.

IYALOJA [*entering, from the hut. She is accompanied by a group of young girls who have been attending the Bride*]: What is it Amusa? Why do you come here to disturb the happiness of others.

AMUSA: Madame Iyaloja, I glad you come. You know me. I no like trouble but duty is duty. I am here to arrest Elesin for criminal intent. Tell these women to stop obstructing me in the performance of my duty.

IYALOJA: And you? What gives you the right to obstruct our leader of men in the performance of his duty.

AMUSA: What kin' duty be dat one Iyaloja.

IYALOJA: What kin' duty? What kin' duty does a man have to his new bride?

AMUSA [*bewildered, looks at the women and at the entrance to the hut*]: Iyaloja, is it wedding you call dis kin' ting?

IYALOJA: You have wives haven't you? Whatever the white man has done to you he hasn't stopped you having wives. And if he has, at least he is married. If you don't know what a marriage is, go and ask him to tell you.

AMUSA: This no to wedding.

IYALOJA: And ask him at the same time what he would have done if anyone had come to disturb him on his wedding night.

AMUSA: Iyaloja, I say dis no to wedding.

IYALOJA: You want to look inside the bridal chamber? You want to see for yourself how a man cuts the virgin knot?

AMUSA: Madam . . .

woman: Perhaps his wives are still waiting for him to learn.

AMUSA: Iyaloja, make you tell dese women make den no insult me again. If I hear dat kin' indult once more . . .

GIRL [*pushing her way through*]: You will do what?

GIRL: He's out of his mind. It's our mothers you're talking to, do you know that? Not to any illiterate villager you can bully and terrorise. How dare you intrude here anyway?

GIRL: What a cheek, what impertinence!

GIRL: You've treated them too gently. Now let them see what it is to tamper with the mothers of this market.

GIRLS: Your betters dare not enter the market when the women say no!

GIRL: Haven't you learnt that yet, you jester in khaki and starch?

IYALOJA: Daughters . . .

GIRL: No no Iyaloja, leave us to deal with him. He no longer knows his mother, we'll teach him.

[*With a sudden movement they snatch the batons of the two constables. They begin to hem them in.*]

GIRL: What next? We have your batons? What next? What are you going to do?

[*With equally swift movements they knock off their hats.*]

GIRL: Move if you dare. We have your hats, what will you do about it? Didn't the white man teach you to take off your hats before women?

IYALOJA: It's a wedding night. It's a night of joy for us. Peace . . .

GIRL: Not for him. Who asked him here?

GIRL: Does he dare go to the Residency without an invitation?

GIRL: Not even where the servants eat the left-overs.

GIRLS [*in turn. In an "English" accent*]: Well well it's Mister Amusa. Were you invited? [*Play-acting to one another. The older women encourage them with their titters.*]

—Your invitation card please?

—Who are you? Have we been introduced?

—And who did you say you were?

—Sorry, I didn't quite catch your name.

—May I take your hat?

—If you insist. May I take yours? [*Exchanging the policemen's hats.*]

—How very kind of you.

—Not at all. Won't you sit down?

—After you.

—Oh no.

—I insist.

—You're most gracious.

—And how do you find the place?

—The natives are alright.

—Friendly?

—Tractable.

—Not a teeny-weeny bit restless?

—Well, a teeny-weeny bit restless.

—One might even say, difficult?

—Indeed one might be tempted to say, difficult.

—But you do manage to cope?

—Yes indeed I do. I have a rather faithful ox called Amusa.

—He's loyal?

—Absolutely.

—Lay down his life for you what?

—Without a moment's thought.

—Had one like that once. Trust him with my life.

—Mostly of course they are liars.

—Never known a native tell the truth.

—Does it get rather close around here?

—It's mild for this time of the year.

—But the rains may still come.

—They are late this year aren't they?

—They are keeping African time.

—Ha ha ha ha

—Ha ha ha ha

—The humidity is what gets me.

—It used to be whisky.

—Ha ha ha ha

—Ha ha ha ha

—What's your handicap old chap?

—Is there racing by golly?

—Splendid golf course, you'll like it.

—I'm beginning to like it already.

—And a European club, exclusive.

—You've kept the flag flying.

—We do our best for the old country.

—It's a pleasure to serve.

—Another whisky old chap?

—You are indeed too too kind.

—Not at all sir. Where is that boy? [*With a sudden bellow.*]
Sergeant!

AMUSA [*snaps to attention*]: Yessir!

[*The women collapse with laughter.*]

GIRL: Take your men out of here.

AMUSA [*realising the trick, he rages from loss of face*]: I'm give you warning . . .

GIRL: Alright then. Off with his knickers! [*They surge slowly forward.*]

IYALOJA: Daughters, please.

AMUSA [*squaring himself for defence*]: The first woman wey touch me . . .

IYALOJA: My children, I beg of you . . .

GIRL: Then tell him to leave this market. This is the home of our mothers. We don't
    want the eater of white left-overs at the feast their hands have prepared.

IYALOJA: You heard them Amusa. You had better go.

GIRLS: Now!

AMUSA [*commencing his retreat*]: We dey go now, but make you no say we no
    warn you.

GIRL: Now!

GIRL: Before we read the riot act—you should know all about that.

AMUSA: Make we go. [*They depart, more precipitately.*]

[*The women strike their palms across in the gesture of wonder.*]

WOMEN: Do they teach you all that at school?

WOMAN: And to think I nearly kept Apinke away from the place.

WOMAN: Did you hear them? Did you see how they mimicked the white man?

WOMAN: The voices exactly. Hey, there are wonders in this world!

IYALOJA: Well, our elders have said it: Dada may be weak, but he has a younger sib-
    ling who is truly fearless.

WOMAN: The next time the white man shows his face in this market I will set Wuraola
    on his tail.

[*A woman bursts into song and dance of euphoria—"Tani l'awa o l'ogbeja?
Kayi! A l'ogbeja. Omo Kekere l'ogbeja."*[1] *The rest of the women join in, some placing the girls on their back like infants, other dancing round them. The dance becomes*

---

1. "Who says we haven't a defender? Silence! We have our defenders. Little children are our champions." [Soyinka's note]

general, mounting in excitement. Elesin appears, in wrapper only. In his hands a white velvet cloth folded loosely as if it held some delicate object. He cries out.]

ELESIN: Oh you mothers of beautiful brides! [*The dancing stops. They turn and see him, and the object in his hands. Iyaloja approaches and gently takes the cloth from him.*] Take it. It is no mere virgin stain, but the union of life and the seeds of passage. My vital flow, the last from this flesh is intermingled with the promise of future life. All is prepared. Listen! [*A steady drum-beat from the distance.*] Yes. It is nearly time. The King's dog has been killed. The King's favourite horse is about to follow his master. My brother chiefs know their task and perform it well. [*He listens again.*]

[*The Bride emerges, stands shyly by the door. He turns to her.*]

Our marriage is not yet wholly fulfilled. When earth and passage wed, the consummation is complete only when there are grains of earth on the eyelids of passage. Stay by me till then. My faithful drummers, do me your last service. This is where I have chosen to do my leave-taking, in this heart of life, this hive which contains the swarm of the world in its small compass. This is where I have known love and laughter away from the palace. Even the richest food cloys when eaten days on end; in the market, nothing ever cloys. Listen. [*They listen to the drums.*] They have begun to seek out the heart of the King's favourite horse. Soon it will ride in its bolt of raffia with the dog at its feet. Together they will ride on the shoulders of the King's grooms through the pulse centres of the town. They know it is here I shall await them. I have told them. [*His eyes appear to cloud. He passes his hand over them as if to clear his sight. He gives a faint smile.*] It promises well; just then I felt my spirit's eagerness. The kite makes for wide spaces and the wind creeps up behind its tail; can the kite say less than—thank you, the quicker the better? But wait a while my spirit. Wait. Wait for the coming of the courier of the King. Do you know friends, the horse is born to this one destiny, to bear the burden that is man upon its back. Except for this night, this night alone when the spotless stallion will ride in triumph on the back of man. In the time of my father I witnessed the strange sight. Perhaps tonight also I shall see it for the last time. If they arrive before the drums beat for me, I shall tell him to let the Alafin[2] know I follow swiftly. If they come after the drums have sounded, why then, all is well for I have gone ahead. Our spirits shall fall in step along the great passage. [*He listens to the drums. He seems again to be falling into a state of semi-hypnosis; his eyes scan the sky but it is in a kind of daze. His voice is a little breathless.*] The moon has fed, a glow from its full stomach fills the sky and air, but I cannot tell where is that gateway through which I must pass. My faithful friends, let our feet touch together this last time, lead me into the other market with sounds that cover my skin with down yet make my limbs strike earth like a thoroughbred. Dear mothers, let me dance into the passage even as I have lived beneath your roofs. [*He comes down progressively among them. They make way for him, the drummers playing. His dance is one of solemn, regal motions, each gesture of the body is made with a solemn finality. The women join him, their steps a somewhat more fluid version of his. Beneath the Praise-Singer's exhortations the women dirge "Alẹ lẹ lẹ, awo mi lọ."*]

PRAISE-SINGER: *Elesin Alafin, can you hear my voice?*

2. A traditional Yoruba leader.

ELESIN:	*Faintly, my friend, faintly.*
PRAISE-SINGER:	*Elesin Alafin, can you hear my call?*
ELESIN:	*Faintly my king, faintly.*
PRAISE-SINGER:	*Is your memory sound Elesin?* *Shall my voice be a blade of grass and* *Tickle the armpit of the past?*
ELESIN:	*My memory needs no prodding but* *What do you wish to say to me?*
PRAISE-SINGER:	*Only what has been spoken. Only what concerns* *The dying wish of the father of all.*
ELESIN:	*It is buried like seed-yam in my mind* *This is the season of quick rains, the harvest* *Is this moment due for gathering.*
PRAISE-SINGER:	*If you cannot come, I said, swear* *You'll tell my favourite horse. I shall* *Ride on through the gates alone.*
ELESIN:	*Elesin's message will be read* *Only when his loyal heart no longer beats.*
PRAISE-SINGER:	*If you cannot come Elesin, tell my dog.* *I cannot stay the keeper too long* *At the gate.*
ELESIN:	*A dog does not outrun the hand* *That feeds it meat. A horse that throws its rider* *Slows down to a stop. Elesin Alafin* *Trusts no beasts with messages between* *A king and his companion.*
PRAISE-SINGER:	*If you get lost my dog will track* *The hidden path to me.*
ELESIN:	*The seven-way crossroads confuses* *Only the stranger. The Horseman of the King* *Was born in the recesses of the house.*
PRAISE-SINGER:	*I know the wickedness of men. If there is* *Weight on the loose end of your sash, such weight* *As no mere man can shift; if your sash is earthed* *By evil minds who mean to part us at the last ...*
ELESIN:	*My sash is of the deep purple alari;* *It is no tethering-rope. The elephant* *Trails no tethering-rope; that king* *Is not yet crowned who will peg an elephant—* *Not even you my friend and King.*
PRAISE-SINGER:	*And yet this fear will not depart from me* *The darkness of this new abode is deep—* *Will your human eyes suffice?*

ELESIN:
> *In a night which falls before our eyes*
> *However deep, we do not miss our way.*

PRAISE-SINGER:
> *Shall I now not acknowledge I have stood*
> *Where wonders met their end? The elephant deserves*
> *Better than that we say "I have caught*
> *A glimpse of something." If we see the tamer*
> *Of the forest let us say plainly, we have seen*
> *An elephant.*

ELESIN [*his voice is drowsy*]:
> *I have freed myself of earth and now*
> *It's getting dark. Strange voices guide my feet.*

PRAISE-SINGER:
> *The river is never so high that the eyes*
> *Of a fish are covered. The night is not so dark*
> *That the albino fails to find his way. A child*
> *Returning homewards craves no leading by the hand.*
> *Gracefully does the mask regain his grove at the end of day . . .*
> *Gracefully. Gracefully does the mask dance*
> *Homeward at the end of day, gracefully . . .*

[*Elesin's trance appears to be deepening, his steps heavier.*]

IYALOJA:
> *It is the death of war that kills the valiant,*
> *Death of water is how the swimmer goes*
> *It is the death of markets that kills the trader*
> *And death of indecision takes the idle away*
> *The trade of the cutlass blunts its edge*
> *And the beautiful die the death of beauty.*
> *It takes an Elesin to die the death of death . . .*
> *Only Elesin . . . dies the unknowable death of death . . .*
> *Gracefully, gracefully does the horseman regain*
> *The stables at the end of day, gracefully . . .*

PRAISE-SINGER: How shall I tell what my eyes have seen? The Horseman gallops on before the courier, how shall I tell what my eyes have seen? He says a dog may be confused by new scents of beings he never dreamt of, so he must precede the dog to heaven. He says a horse may stumble on strange boulders and be lamed, so he races on before the horse to heaven. It is best, he says, to trust no messenger who may falter at the outer gate; oh how shall I tell what my ears have heard? But do you hear me still Elesin, do you hear your faithful one?

[*Elesin in his motions appears to feel for a direction of sound, subtly, but he only sinks deeper into his trance-dance.*]

Elesin Alafin, I no longer sense your flesh. The drums are changing now but you have gone far ahead of the world. It is not yet noon in heaven; let those who claim it is begin their own journey home. So why must you rush like an impatient Bride: why do you race to desert your Olohun-iyo?

[*Elesin is now sunk fully deep in his trance, there is no longer sign of any awareness of his surroundings.*]

Does the deep voice of *gbedu*[3] cover you then, like the passage of royal elephants? Those drums that brook no rivals, have they blocked the passage to your ears that my voice passes into wind, a mere leaf floating in the night? Is your flesh lightened Elesin, is that lump of earth I slid between your slippers to keep you longer slowly sifting from your feet? Are the drums on the other side now tuning skin to skin with ours in *osugbo?*[4] Are there sounds there I cannot hear, do footsteps surround you which pound the earth like *gbedu,* roll like thunder round the dome of the world? Is the darkness gathering in your head Elesin? Is there now a streak of light at the end of the passage, a light I dare not look upon? Does it reveal whose voices we often heard, whose touches we often felt, whose wisdoms come suddenly into the mind when the wisest have shaken their heads and murmured: It cannot be done? Elesin Alafin, don't think I do not know why your lips are heavy, why your limbs are drowsy as palm oil in the cold of harmattan.[5] I would call you back but when the elephant heads for the jungle, the tail is too small a handhold for the hunter that would pull him back. The sun that heads for the sea no longer heeds the prayers of the farmer. When the river begins to taste the salt of the ocean, we no longer know what deity to call on, the river-god or Olokun.[6] No arrow flies back to the string, the child does not return through the same passage that gave it birth. Elesin Oba, can you hear me at all? Your eyelids are glazed like a courtesan's, is it that you see the dark groom and master of life? And will you see my father? Will you tell him that I stayed with you to the last? Will my voice ring in your ears awhile, will you remember Olohun-iyo even if the music on the other side sur- passes his mortal craft? But will they know you over there? Have they eyes to gauge your worth, have they the heart to love you, will they know what thorough- bred prances towards them in caparisons of honour? If they do not Elesin, if any there cuts your yam with a small knife, or pours you wine in a small calabash, turn back and return to welcoming hands. If the world were not greater than the wishes of Olohun-iyo, I would not let you go . . .

[*He appears to break down. Elesin dances on, completely in a trance. The dirge wells up louder and stronger. Elesin's dance does not lose its elasticity but his ges- tures become, if possible, even more weighty. Lights fade slowly on the scene.*]

I V

A Masque. The front side of the stage is part of a wide corridor around the great hall of the Residency extending beyond vision into the rear and wings. It is redo- lent of the tawdry decadence of a far-flung but key imperial frontier. The couples in a variety of fancy-dress are ranged around the walls, gazing in the same direc- tion. The guest-of-honour is about to make an appearance. A portion of the local police brass band with its white conductor is just visible. At last, the entrance of Royalty. The band plays "Rule Britannia", badly, beginning long before he is visi- ble. The couples bow and curtsey as he passes by them. Both he and his compan- ions are dressed in seventeenth-century European costume. Following behind are the Resident and his partner similarly attired. As they gain the end of the hall where the orchestra dais begins the music comes to an end. The Prince bows to the

---

3. A deep-timbred royal drum [Soyinka's note].
4. Secret "executive" cult of the Yoruba; its meeting place [Soyinka's note].

5. Winter trade wind that blows from the northeast or east in the southern Sahara.
6. Deity of the ocean and of prosperity.

guests. The band strikes up a Viennese waltz and the Prince formally opens the floor. Several bars later the Resident and his companion follow suit. Others follow in appropriate pecking order. The orchestra's waltz rendition is not of the highest musical standard.

Some time later the Prince dances again into view and is settled into a corner by the Resident who then proceeds to select couples as they dance past for introduction, sometimes threading his way through the dancers to tap the lucky couple on the shoulder. Desperate efforts from many to ensure that they are recognised in spite of, perhaps, their costume. The ritual of introductions soon takes in Pilkings and his wife. The Prince is quite fascinated by their costume and they demonstrate the adaptations they have made to it, pulling down the mask to demonstrate how the egungun normally appears, then showing the various press-button controls they have innovated for the face flaps, the sleeves, etc. They demonstrate the dance steps and the guttural sounds made by the egungun, harass other dancers in the hall, Mrs. Pilkings playing the "restrainer" to Pilkings' manic darts. Everyone is highly entertained, the Royal Party especially who lead the applause.

At this point a liveried footman comes in with a note on a salver and is intercepted almost absent-mindedly by the Resident who takes the note and reads it. After polite coughs he succeeds in excusing the Pilkingses from the Prince and takes them aside. The Prince considerately offers the Resident's wife his hand and dancing is resumed.

On their way out the Resident gives an order to his Aide-de-camp. They come into the side corridor where the Resident hands the note to Pilkings.

RESIDENT: As you see it says "emergency" on the outside. I took the liberty of opening it because His Highness was obviously enjoying the entertainment. I didn't want to interrupt unless really necessary.

PILKINGS: Yes, yes of course sir.

RESIDENT: Is it really as bad as it says? What's it all about?

PILKINGS: Some strange custom they have sir. It seems because the King is dead some important chief has to commit suicide.

RESIDENT: The King? Isn't it the same one who died nearly a month ago?

PILKINGS: Yes sir.

RESIDENT: Haven't they buried him yet?

PILKINGS: They take their time about these things sir. The pre-burial ceremonies last nearly thirty days. It seems tonight is the final night.

RESIDENT: But what has it got to do with the market women? Why are they rioting? We've waived that troublesome tax haven't we?

PILKINGS: We don't quite know that they are exactly rioting yet sir. Sergeant Amusa is sometimes prone to exaggerations.

RESIDENT: He sounds desperate enough. That comes out even in his rather quaint grammar. Where is the man anyway? I asked my aide-de-camp to bring him here.

PILKINGS: They are probably looking in the wrong verandah. I'll fetch him myself.

RESIDENT: No no you stay here. Let your wife go and look for them. Do you mind my dear . . .?

JANE: Certainly not, your Excellency. [*Goes.*]

RESIDENT: You should have kept me informed Pilkings. You realise how disastrous it would have been if things had erupted while His Highness was here.

PILKINGS: I wasn't aware of the whole business until tonight sir.

RESIDENT: Nose to the ground Pilkings, nose to the ground. If we all let these little things slip past us where would the empire be eh? Tell me that. Where would we all be?

PILKINGS [*low voice*]: Sleeping peacefully at home I bet.

RESIDENT: What did you say Pilkings?

PILKINGS: It won't happen again sir.

RESIDENT: It mustn't Pilkings. It mustn't. Where is that damned sergeant? I ought to get back to His Highness as quickly as possible and offer him some plausible explanation for my rather abrupt conduct. Can you think of one Pilkings?

PILKINGS: You could tell him the truth sir.

RESIDENT: I could? No no no no Pilkings, that would never do. What! Go and tell him there is a riot just two miles away from him? This is supposed to be a secure colony of His Majesty, Pilkings.

PILKINGS: Yes sir.

RESIDENT: Ah, there they are. No, these are not our native police. Are these the ring-leaders of the riot?

PILKINGS: Sir, these are my police officers.

RESIDENT: Oh, I beg your pardon officers. You do look a little . . . I say, isn't there something missing in their uniform? I think they used to have some rather colour-ful sashes. If I remember rightly I recommended them myself in my young days in the service. A bit of colour always appeals to the natives, yes, I remember putting that in my report. Well well well, where are we? Make your report man.

PILKINGS [*moves close to Amusa, between his teeth*]: And let's have no more supersti-tious nonsense from you Amusa or I'll throw you in the guardroom for a month and feed you pork!

RESIDENT: What's that? What has pork to do with it?

PILKINGS: Sir, I was just warning him to be brief. I'm sure you are most anxious to hear his report.

RESIDENT: Yes yes yes of course. Come on man, speak up. Hey, didn't we give them some colourful fez hats with all those wavy things, yes, pink tassels . . .

PILKINGS: Sir, I think if he was permitted to make his report we might find that he lost his hat in the riot.

RESIDENT: Ah yes indeed. I'd better tell His Highness that. Lost his hat in the riot, ha ha. He'll probably say well, as long as he didn't lose his head. [*Chuckles to him-self.*] Don't forget to send me a report first thing in the morning young Pilkings.

PILKINGS: No sir.

RESIDENT: And whatever you do, don't let things get out of hand. Keep a cool head and—nose to the ground Pilkings. [*Wanders off in the general direction of the hall.*]

PILKINGS: Yes sir.

AIDE-DE-CAMP: Would you be needing me sir?

PILKINGS: No thanks Bob. I think His Excellency's need of you is greater than ours.

AIDE-DE-CAMP: We have a detachment of soldiers from the capital sir. They accompa-nied His Highness up here.

PILKINGS: I doubt if it will come to that but, thanks, I'll bear it in mind. Oh, could you send an orderly with my cloak.

AIDE-DE-CAMP: Very good sir. [*Goes.*]

PILKINGS: Now Sergeant.

AMUSA: Sir . . . [*Makes an effort, stops dead. Eyes to the ceiling.*]

PILKINGS: Oh, not again.

AMUSA: I cannot against death to dead cult. This dress get power of dead.

PILKINGS: Alright, let's go. You are relieved of all further duty Amusa. Report to me first thing in the morning.

JANE: Shall I come Simon?

PILKINGS: No, there's no need for that. If I can get back later I will. Otherwise get Bob to bring you home.

JANE: Be careful Simon . . . I mean, be clever.

PILKINGS: Sure I will. You two, come with me. [*As he turns to go, the clock in the Residency begins to chime. Pilkings looks at his watch then turns, horror-stricken, to stare at his wife. The same thought clearly occurs to her. He swallows hard. An orderly brings his cloak.*] It's midnight. I had no idea it was that late.

JANE: But surely . . . they don't count the hours the way we do. The moon, or something . . .

PILKINGS: I am . . . not so sure.

[*He turns and breaks into a sudden run. The two constables follow, also at a run. Amusa, who has kept his eyes on the ceiling throughout waits until the last of the footsteps has faded out of hearing. He salutes suddenly, but without once looking in the direction of the woman.*]

AMUSA: Goodnight madam.

JANE: Oh. [*She hesitates.*] Amusa . . . [*He goes off without seeming to have heard.*] Poor Simon . . . [*A figure emerges from the shadows, a young black man dressed in a sober western suit. He peeps into the hall, trying to make out the figures of the dancers.*] Who is that?

OLUNDE [*emerging into the light*]: I didn't mean to startle you madam. I am looking for the District Officer.

JANE: Wait a minute . . . don't I know you? Yes, you are Olunde, the young man who . . .

OLUNDE: Mrs. Pilkings! How fortunate. I came here to look for your husband.

JANE: Olunde! Let's look at you. What a fine young man you've become. Grand but solemn. Good God, when did you return? Simon never said a word. But you do look well Olunde. Really!

OLUNDE: You are . . . well, you look quite well yourself Mrs. Pilkings. From what little I can see of you.

JANE: Oh, this. It's caused quite a stir I assure you, and not all of it very pleasant. You are not shocked I hope?

OLUNDE: Why should I be? But don't you find it rather hot in there? Your skin must find it difficult to breathe.

JANE: Well, it is a little hot I must confess, but it's all in a good cause.

OLUNDE: What cause Mrs. Pilkings?

JANE: All this. The ball. And His Highness being here in person and all that.

OLUNDE [*mildly*]: And that is the good cause for which you desecrate an ancestral mask?

JANE: Oh, so you are shocked after all. How disappointing.

OLUNDE: No I am not shocked Mrs. Pilkings. You forget that I have now spent four years among your people. I discovered that you have no respect for what you do not understand.

JANE: Oh. So you've returned with a chip on your shoulder. That's a pity Olunde. I am sorry.

[*An uncomfortable silence follows.*]

I take it then that you did not find your stay in England altogether edifying.

OLUNDE: I don't say that. I found your people quite admirable in many ways, their conduct and courage in this war for instance.

JANE: Ah yes the war. Here of course it is all rather remote. From time to time we have a black-out drill just to remind us that there is a war on. And the rare convoy passes through on its way somewhere or on manoeuvres. Mind you there is the occasional bit of excitement like that ship that was blown up in the harbour.

OLUNDE: Here? Do you mean through enemy action?

JANE: Oh no, the war hasn't come that close. The captain did it himself. I don't quite understand it really. Simon tried to explain. The ship had to be blown up because it had become dangerous to the other ships, even to the city itself. Hundreds of the coastal population would have died.

OLUNDE: Maybe it was loaded with ammunition and had caught fire. Or some of those lethal gases they've been experimenting on.

JANE: Something like that. The captain blew himself up with it. Deliberately. Simon said someone had to remain on board to light the fuse.

OLUNDE: It must have been a very short fuse.

JANE [*shrugs*]: I don't know much about it. Only that there was no other way to save lives. No time to devise anything else. The captain took the decision and carried it out.

OLUNDE: Yes . . . I quite believe it. I met men like that in England.

JANE: Oh just look at me! Fancy welcoming you back with such morbid news. Stale too. It was at least six months ago.

OLUNDE: I don't find it morbid at all. I find it rather inspiring. It is an affirmative commentary on life.

JANE: What is?

OLUNDE: That captain's self-sacrifice.

JANE: Nonsense. Life should never be thrown deliberately away.

OLUNDE: And the innocent people round the harbour?

JANE: Oh, how does one know? The whole thing was probably exaggerated anyway.

OLUNDE: That was a risk the captain couldn't take. But please Mrs. Pilkings, do you think you could find your husband for me? I have to talk to him.

JANE: Simon? Oh. [*As she recollects for the first time the full significance of Olunde's presence.*] Simon is . . . there is a little problem in town. He was sent for. But . . . when did you arrive? Does Simon know you're here?

OLUNDE [*suddenly earnest*]: I need your help Mrs. Pilkings. I've always found you somewhat more understanding than your husband. Please find him for me and when you do, you must help me talk to him.

JANE: I'm afraid I don't quite . . . . follow you. Have you seen my husband already?

OLUNDE: I went to your house. Your houseboy told me you were here. [*He smiles.*] He even told me how I would recognise you and Mr Pilkings.

JANE: Then you must know what my husband is trying to do for you.

OLUNDE: For me?

JANE: For you. For your people. And to think he didn't even know you were coming back! But how do you happen to be here? Only this evening we were talking about you. We thought you were still four thousand miles away.

OLUNDE: I was sent a cable.

JANE: A cable? Who did? Simon? The business of your father didn't begin till tonight.

OLUNDE: A relation sent it weeks ago, and it said nothing about my father. All it said was, Our King is dead. But I knew I had to return home at once so as to bury my father. I understood that.

JANE: Well, thank God you don't have to go through that agony. Simon is going to stop it.

OLUNDE: That's why I want to see him. He's wasting his time. And since he has been so helpful to me I don't want him to incur the enmity of our people. Especially over nothing.

JANE [sits down open-mouthed]: You . . . you Olunde!

OLUNDE: Mrs. Pilkings, I came home to bury my father. As soon as I heard the news I booked my passage home. In fact we were fortunate. We travelled in the same convoy as your Prince, so we had excellent protection.

JANE: But you don't think your father is also entitled to whatever protection is available to him?

OLUNDE: How can I make you understand? He *has* protection. No one can undertake what he does tonight without the deepest protection the mind can conceive. What can you offer him in place of his peace of mind, in place of the honour and veneration of his own people? What would you think of your Prince if he had refused to accept the risk of losing his life on this voyage? This . . . showing-the-flag tour of colonial possessions.

JANE: I see. So it isn't just medicine you studied in England.

OLUNDE: Yet another error into which your people fall. You believe that everything which appears to make sense was learnt from you.

JANE: Not so fast Olunde. You have learnt to argue I can tell that, but I never said you made sense. However cleverly you try to put it, it is still a barbaric custom. It is even worse—it's feudal! The king dies and a chieftain must be buried with him. How feudalistic can you get!

OLUNDE [waves his hand towards the background. The Prince is dancing past again—to a different step—and all the guests are bowing and curtseying as he passes]: And this? Even in the midst of a devastating war, look at that. What name would you give to that?

JANE: Therapy, British style. The preservation of sanity in the midst of chaos.

OLUNDE: Others would call it decadence. However, it doesn't really interest me. You white races know how to survive; I've seen proof of that. By all logical and natural laws this war should end with all the white races wiping out one another, wiping out their so-called civilisation for all time and reverting to a state of primitivism the like of which has so far only existed in your imagination when you thought of us. I thought all that at the beginning. Then I slowly realised that your greatest art is the art of survival. But at least have the humility to let others survive in their own way.

JANE: Through ritual suicide?

OLUNDE: Is that worse than mass suicide? Mrs. Pilkings, what do you call what those young men are sent to do by their generals in this war? Of course you have also mastered the art of calling things by names which don't remotely describe them.

JANE: You talk! You people with your long-winded, roundabout way of making conversation.

OLUNDE: Mrs. Pilkings, whatever we do, we never suggest that a thing is the opposite of what it really is. In your newsreels I heard defeats, thorough, murderous defeats described as strategic victories. No wait, it wasn't just on your newsreels. Don't forget I was attached to hospitals all the time. Hordes of your wounded passed through those wards. I spoke to them. I spent long evenings by their bedside while they spoke terrible truths of the realities of that war. I know now how history is made.

JANE: But surely, in a war of this nature, for the morale of the nation you must expect . . .

OLUNDE: That a disaster beyond human reckoning be spoken of as a triumph? No. I mean, is there no mourning in the home of the bereaved that such blasphemy is permitted?

JANE [after a moment's pause]: Perhaps I can understand you now. The time we picked for you was not really one for seeing us at our best.

OLUNDE: Don't think it was just the war. Before that even started I had plenty of time to study your people. I saw nothing, finally, that gave you the right to pass judgement on other peoples and their ways. Nothing at all.

JANE [hesitantly]: Was it the . . . . colour thing? I know there is some discrimination.

OLUNDE: Don't make it so simple, Mrs. Pilkings. You make it sound as if when I left, I took nothing at all with me.

JANE: Yes . . . and to tell the truth, only this evening, Simon and I agreed that we never really knew what you left with.

OLUNDE: Neither did I. But I found out over there. I am grateful to your country for that. And I will never give it up.

JANE: Olunde, please, . . . promise me something. Whatever you do, don't throw away what you have started to do. You want to be a doctor. My husband and I believe you will make an excellent one, sympathetic and competent. Don't let anything make you throw away your training.

OLUNDE [genuinely surprised]: Of course not. What a strange idea. I intend to return and complete my training. Once the burial of my father is over.

JANE: Oh, please . . .!

OLUNDE: Listen! Come outside. You can't hear anything against that music.

JANE: What is it?

OLUNDE: The drums. Can you hear the change? Listen.

[The drums come over, still distant but more distinct. There is a change of rhythm, it rises to a crescendo and then, suddenly, it is cut off. After a silence, a new beat begins, slow and resonant.]

There. It's all over.

JANE: You mean he's . . .

OLUNDE: Yes Mrs. Pilkings, my father is dead. His will-power has always been enormous; I know he is dead.

JANE [screams]: How can you be so callous! So unfeeling! You announce your father's own death like a surgeon looking down on some strange . . . stranger's body! You're just a savage like all the rest.

AIDE-DE-CAMP [rushing out]: Mrs. Pilkings. Mrs. Pilkings. [She breaks down, sobbing.] Are you alright, Mrs. Pilkings?

OLUNDE: She'll be alright. [Turns to go.]

AIDE-DE-CAMP: Who are you? And who the hell asked your opinion?

OLUNDE: You're quite right, nobody. [*Going.*]

AIDE-DE-CAMP: What the hell! Did you hear me ask you who you were?

OLUNDE: I have business to attend to.

AIDE-DE-CAMP: I'll give you business in a moment you impudent nigger. Answer my
  question!

OLUNDE: I have a funeral to arrange. Excuse me. [*Going.*]

AIDE-DE-CAMP: I said stop! Orderly!

JANE: No no, don't do that, I'm alright. And for heaven's sake don't act so foolishly.
  He's a family friend.

AIDE-DE-CAMP: Well he'd better learn to answer civil questions when he's asked
  them. These natives put a suit on and they get high opinions of themselves.

OLUNDE: Can I go now?

JANE: No no don't go. I must talk to you. I'm sorry about what I said.

OLUNDE: It's nothing Mrs. Pilkings. And I'm really anxious to go. I couldn't see my
  father before, it's forbidden for me, his heir and successor to set eyes on him from
  the moment of the king's death. But now . . . I would like to touch his body while
  it is still warm.

JANE: You will. I promise I shan't keep you long. Only, I couldn't possibly let you go
  like that. Bob, please excuse us.

AIDE-DE-CAMP: If you're sure . . .

JANE: Of course I'm sure. Something happened to upset me just then, but I'm alright
  now. Really.

[*The Aide-de-camp goes, somewhat reluctantly.*]

OLUNDE: I mustn't stay long.

JANE: Please, I promise not to keep you. It's just that . . . oh you saw yourself what
  happens to one in this place. The Resident's man thought he was being helpful,
  that's the way we all react. But I can't go in among that crowd just now and if I
  stay by myself somebody will come looking for me. Please, just say something for
  a few moments and then you can go. Just so I can recover myself.

OLUNDE: What do you want me to say?

JANE: Your calm acceptance for instance, can you explain that? It was so unnatural. I
  don't understand that at all. I feel a need to understand all I can.

OLUNDE: But you explained it yourself. My medical training perhaps. I have seen
  death too often. And the soldiers who returned from the front, they died on our
  hands all the time.

JANE: No. It has to be more than that. I feel it has to do with the many things we don't
  really grasp about your people. At least you can explain.

OLUNDE: All these things are part of it. And anyway, my father has been dead in my
  mind for nearly a month. Ever since I learnt of the King's death. I've lived with my
  bereavement so long now that I cannot think of him alive. On that journey on the
  boat, I kept my mind on my duties as the one who must perform the rites over his
  body. I went through it all again and again in my mind as he himself had taught
  me. I didn't want to do anything wrong, something which might jeopardise the
  welfare of my people.

JANE: But he had disowned you. When you left he swore publicly you were no longer
  his son.

OLUNDE: I told you, he was a man of tremendous will. Sometimes that's another way
  of saying stubborn. But among our people, you don't disown a child just like that.

Even if I had died before him I would still be buried like his eldest son. But it's time for me to go.

JANE: Thank you. I feel calmer. Don't let me keep you from your duties.

OLUNDE: Goodnight Mrs. Pilkings.

JANE: Welcome home. [*She holds out her hand. As he takes it footsteps are heard approaching the drive. A short while later a woman's sobbing is also heard.*]

PILKINGS [*off*]: Keep them here till I get back. [*He strides into view, reacts at the sight of Olunde but turns to his wife.*] Thank goodness you're still here.

JANE: Simon, what happened?

PILKINGS: Later Jane, please. Is Bob still here?

JANE: Yes, I think so. I'm sure he must be.

PILKINGS: Try and get him out here as quietly as you can. Tell him it's urgent.

JANE: Of course. Oh Simon, you remember . . .

PILKINGS: Yes yes. I can see who it is. Get Bob out here. [*She runs off.*] At first I thought I was seeing a ghost.

OLUNDE: Mr. Pilkings, I appreciate what you tried to do. I want you to believe that. I can only tell you it would have been a terrible calamity if you'd succeeded.

PILKINGS [*opens his mouth several times, shuts it*]: You . . . said what?

OLUNDE: A calamity for us, the entire people.

PILKINGS [*sighs*]: I see. Hm.

OLUNDE: And now I must go. I must see him before he turns cold.

PILKINGS: Oh ah . . . em . . . but this is a shock to see you. I mean er thinking all this while you were in England and thanking God for that.

OLUNDE: I came on the mail boat. We travelled in the Prince's convoy.

PILKINGS: Ah yes, a-ah, hm . . . er well . . .

OLUNDE: Goodnight. I can see you are shocked by the whole business. But you must know by now there are things you cannot understand—or help.

PILKINGS: Yes. Just a minute. There are armed policemen that way and they have instructions to let no one pass. I suggest you wait a little. I'll er . . . yes, I'll give you an escort.

OLUNDE: That's very kind of you. But do you think it could be quickly arranged.

PILKINGS: Of course. In fact, yes, what I'll do is send Bob over with some men to the er . . . place. You can go with them. Here he comes now. Excuse me a minute.

AIDE-DE-CAMP: Anything wrong sir?

PILKINGS [*takes him to one side*]: Listen Bob, that cellar in the disused annexe of the Residency, you know, where the slaves were stored before being taken down to the coast . . .

AIDE-DE-CAMP: Oh yes, we use it as a storeroom for broken furniture.

PILKINGS: But it's still got the bars on it?

AIDE-DE-CAMP: Oh yes, they are quite intact.

PILKINGS: Get the keys please. I'll explain later. And I want a strong guard over the Residency tonight.

AIDE-DE-CAMP: We have that already. The detachment from the coast . . .

PILKINGS: No, I don't want them at the gates of the Residency. I want you to deploy them at the bottom of the hill, a long way from the main hall so they can deal with any situation long before the sound carries to the house.

AIDE-DE-CAMP: Yes of course.

PILKINGS: I don't want His Highness alarmed.

AIDE-DE-CAMP: You think the riot will spread here?

PILKINGS: It's unlikely but I don't want to take a chance. I made them believe I was going to lock the man up in my house, which was what I had planned to do in the first place. They are probably assailing it by now. I took a roundabout route here so I don't think there is any danger at all. At least not before dawn. Nobody is to leave the premises of course—the native employees I mean. They'll soon smell something is up and they can't keep their mouths shut.

AIDE-DE-CAMP: I'll give instructions at once.

PILKINGS: I'll take the prisoner down myself. Two policemen will stay with him throughout the night. Inside the cell.

AIDE-DE-CAMP: Right sir. [Salutes and goes off at the double.]

PILKINGS: Jane. Bob is coming back in a moment with a detachment. Until he gets back please stay with Olunde. [He makes an extra warning gesture with his eyes.]

OLUNDE: Please Mr. Pilkings . . .

PILKINGS: I hate to be stuffy old son, but we have a crisis on our hands. It has to do with your father's affair if you must know. And it happens also at a time when we have His Highness here. I am responsible for security so you'll simply have to do as I say. I hope that's understood. [Marches off quickly, in the direction from which he made his first appearance.]

OLUNDE: What's going on? All this can't be just because he failed to stop my father killing himself.

JANE: I honestly don't know. Could it have sparked off a riot?

OLUNDE: No. If he'd succeeded that would be more likely to start the riot. Perhaps there were other factors involved. Was there a chieftancy dispute?

JANE: None that I know of.

ELESIN [an animal bellow from off]: Leave me alone! Is it not enough that you have covered me in shame! White man, take your hand from my body!

[Olunde stands frozen on the spot. Jane understanding at last, tries to move him.]

JANE: Let's go in. It's getting chilly out here.

PILKINGS [off]: Carry him.

ELESIN: Give me back the name you have taken away from me you ghost from the land of the nameless!

PILKINGS: Carry him! I can't have a disturbance here. Quickly! stuff up his mouth.

JANE: Oh God! Let's go in. Please Olunde. [Olunde does not move.]

ELESIN: Take your albino's hand from me you . . . .

[Sounds of a struggle. His voice chokes as he is gagged.]

OLUNDE [quietly]: That was my father's voice.

JANE: Oh you poor orphan, what have you come home to?

[There is a sudden explosion of rage from off-stage and powerful steps come running up the drive.]

PILKINGS: You bloody fools, after him!

[Immediately Elesin, in handcuffs, comes pounding in the direction of Jane and Olunde, followed some moments afterwards by Pilkings and the constables. Elesin confronted by the seeming statue of his son, stops dead. Olunde stares above his head into the distance. The constables try to grab him. Jane screams at them.]

JANE: Leave him alone! Simon, tell them to leave him alone.

PILKINGS: All right, stand aside you. [*Shrugs.*] Maybe just as well. It might help to calm him down.

[*For several moments they hold the same position. Elesin moves a few steps forward, almost as if he's still in doubt.*]

ELESIN: Olunde? [*He moves his head, inspecting him from side to side.*] Olunde! [*He collapses slowly at Olunde's feet.*] Oh son, don't let the sight of your father turn you blind!

OLUNDE [*he moves for the first time since he heard his voice, brings his head slowly down to look on him*]: I have no father, eater of left-overs.

[*He walks slowly down the way his father had run. Light fades out on Elesin, sobbing into the ground.*]

V

A wide iron-barred gate stretches almost the whole width of the cell in which Elesin is imprisoned. His wrists are encased in thick iron bracelets, chained together; he stands against the bars, looking out. Seated on the ground to one side on the outside is his recent bride, her eyes bent perpetually to the ground. Figures of the two guards can be seen deeper inside the cell, alert to every movement Elesin makes. Pilkings now in a police officer's uniform enters noiselessly, observes him for a while. Then he coughs ostentatiously and approaches. Leans against the bars near a corner, his back to Elesin. He is obviously trying to fall in mood with him. Some moments' silence.

PILKINGS: You seem fascinated by the moon.

ELESIN [*after a pause*]: Yes, ghostly one. Your twin-brother up there engages my thoughts.

PILKINGS: It is a beautiful night.

ELESIN: Is that so?

PILKINGS: The light on the leaves, the peace of the night . . .

ELESIN: The night is not at peace, District Officer.

PILKINGS: No? I would have said it was. You know, quiet . . .

ELESIN: And does quiet mean peace for you?

PILKINGS: Well, nearly the same thing. Naturally there is a subtle difference . . .

ELESIN: The night is not at peace ghostly one. The world is not at peace. You have shattered the peace of the world for ever. There is no sleep in the world tonight.

PILKINGS: It is still a good bargain if the world should lose one night's sleep as the price of saving a man's life.

ELESIN: You did not save my life District Officer. You destroyed it.

PILKINGS: Now come on . . .

ELESIN: And not merely my life but the lives of many. The end of the night's work is not over. Neither this year nor the next will see it. If I wished you well, I would pray that you do not stay long enough on our land to see the disaster you have brought upon us.

PILKINGS: Well, I did my duty as I saw it. I have no regrets.

ELESIN: No. The regrets of life always come later.

[*Some moments' pause.*]

You are waiting for dawn white man. I hear you saying to yourself: only so many hours until dawn and then the danger is over. All I must do is keep him alive tonight. You don't quite understand it all but you know that tonight is when what ought to be must be brought about. I shall ease your mind even more, ghostly one. It is not an entire night but a moment of the night, and that moment is past. The moon was my messenger and guide. When it reached a certain gateway in the sky, it touched that moment for which my whole life has been spent in blessings. Even I do not know the gateway. I have stood here and scanned the sky for a glimpse of that door but, I cannot see it. Human eyes are useless for a search of this nature. But in the house of *osugbo,* those who keep watch through the spirit recognised the moment, they sent word to me through the voice of our sacred drums to prepare myself. I heard them and I shed all thoughts of earth. I began to follow the moon to the abode of gods . . . servant of the white king, that was when you entered my chosen place of departure on feet of desecration.

PILKINGS: I'm sorry, but we all see our duty differently.

ELESIN: I no longer blame you. You stole from me my first-born, sent him to your country so you could turn him into something in your own image. Did you plan it all beforehand? There are moments when it seems part of a larger plan. He who must follow my footsteps is taken from me, sent across the ocean. Then, in my turn, I am stopped from fulfilling my destiny. Did you think it all out before, this plan to push our world from its course and sever the cord that links us to the great origin?

PILKINGS: You don't really believe that. Anyway, if that was my intention with your son, I appear to have failed.

ELESIN: You did not fail in the main thing ghostly one. We know the roof covers the rafters, the cloth covers blemishes; who would have known that the white skin covered our future, preventing us from seeing the death our enemies had prepared for us. The world is set adrift and its inhabitants are lost. Around them, there is nothing but emptiness.

PILKINGS: Your son does not take so gloomy a view.

ELESIN: Are you dreaming now white man? Were you not present at my reunion of shame? Did you not see when the world reversed itself and the father fell before his son, asking forgiveness?

PILKINGS: That was in the heat of the moment. I spoke to him and . . . if you want to know, he wishes he could cut out his tongue for uttering the words he did.

ELESIN: No. What he said must never be unsaid. The contempt of my own son rescued something of my shame at your hands. You may have stopped me in my duty but I know now that I did give birth to a son. Once I mistrusted him for seeking the companionship of those my spirit knew as enemies of our race. Now I understand. One should seek to obtain the secrets of his enemies. He will avenge my shame, white one. His spirit will destroy you and yours.

PILKINGS: That kind of talk is hardly called for. If you don't want my consolation . . .

ELESIN: No white man, I do not want your consolation.

PILKINGS: As you wish. Your son anyway, sends his consolation. He asks your forgiveness. When I asked him not to despise you his reply was: I cannot judge him, and if I cannot judge him, I cannot despise him. He wants to come to you to say goodbye and to receive your blessing.

ELESIN: Goodbye? Is he returning to your land?

PILKINGS: Don't you think that's the most sensible thing for him to do? I advised him to leave at once, before dawn, and he agrees that is the right course of action.

ELESIN: Yes, it is best. And even if I did not think so, I have lost the father's place of honour. My voice is broken.

Obioro Udechukwu (Nigeria),
Silent Faces at Crossroads,
1967.

PILKINGS: Your son honours you. If he didn't he would not ask your blessing.

ELESIN: No. Even a thoroughbred is not without pity for the turf he strikes with his hoof. When is he coming?

PILKINGS: As soon as the town is a little quieter. I advised it.

ELESIN: Yes white man, I am sure you advised it. You advise all our lives although on the authority of what gods, I do not know.

PILKINGS [*opens his mouth to reply, then appears to change his mind. Turns to go. Hesitates and stops again*]: Before I leave you, may I ask just one thing of you?

ELESIN: I am listening.

PILKINGS: I wish to ask you to search the quiet of your heart and tell me—do you not find great contradictions in the wisdom of your own race?

ELESIN: Make yourself clear, white one.

PILKINGS: I have lived among you long enough to learn a saying or two. One came to my mind tonight when I stepped into the market and saw what was going on. You were surrounded by those who egged you on with song and praises. I thought, are these not the same people who say: the elder grimly approaches heaven and you ask him to bear your greetings yonder; do you really think he makes the journey willingly? After that, I did not hesitate.

[*A pause. Elesin sighs. Before he can speak a sound of running feet is heard.*]

JANE [*off*]: Simon! Simon!
PILKINGS: What on earth . . .! [*Runs off.*]

[*Elesin turns to his new wife, gazes on her for some moments.*]

ELESIN: My young bride, did you hear the ghostly one? You sit and sob in your silent heart but say nothing to all this. First I blamed the white man, then I blamed my gods for deserting me. Now I feel I want to blame you for the mystery of the sapping of my will. But blame is a strange peace offering for a man to bring a world he has deeply wronged, and to its innocent dwellers. Oh little mother, I have taken countless women in my life but you were more than a desire of the flesh. I needed you as the abyss across which my body must be drawn, I filled it with earth and dropped my seed in it at the moment of preparedness for my crossing. You were the final gift of the living to their emissary to the land of the ancestors, and perhaps your warmth and youth brought new insights of this world to me and turned my feet leaden on this side of the abyss. For I confess to you, daughter, my weakness came not merely from the abomination of the white man who came violently into my fading presence, there was also a weight of longing on my earth-held limbs. I would have shaken it off, already my foot had begun to lift but then, the white ghost entered and all was defiled.

[*Approaching voices of Pilkings and his wife.*]

JANE: Oh Simon, you will let her in won't you?
PILKINGS: I really wish you'd stop interfering.

[*They come in view. Jane is in a dressing-gown. Pilkings is holding a note to which he refers from time to time.*]

JANE: Good gracious, I didn't initiate this. I was sleeping quietly, or trying to anyway, when the servant brought it. It's not my fault if one can't sleep undisturbed even in the Residency.
PILKINGS: He'd have done the same if we were sleeping at home so don't sidetrack the issue. He knows he can get round you or he wouldn't send you the petition in the first place.
JANE: Be fair Simon. After all he was thinking of your own interests. He is grateful you know, you seem to forget that. He feels he owes you something.
PILKINGS: I just wish they'd leave this man alone tonight, that's all.
JANE: Trust him Simon. He's pledged his word it will all go peacefully.
PILKINGS: Yes, and that's the other thing. I don't like being threatened.
JANE: Threatened? [*Takes the note.*] I didn't spot any threat.
PILKINGS: It's there. Veiled, but it's there. The only way to prevent serious rioting tomorrow—what a cheek!
JANE: I don't think he's threatening you Simon.

PILKINGS: He's picked up the idiom alright. Wouldn't surprise me if he's been mixing with commies or anarchists over there. The phrasing sounds too good to be true. Damn! If only the Prince hadn't picked this time for his visit.

JANE: Well, even so Simon, what have you got to lose? You don't want a riot on your hands, not with the Prince here.

PILKINGS [going up to Elesin]: Let's see what he has to say. Chief Elesin, there is yet another person who wants to see you. As she is not a next-of-kin I don't really feel obliged to let her in. But your son sent a note with her, so it's up to you.

ELESIN: I know who that must be. So she found out your hiding-place. Well, it was not difficult. My stench of shame is so strong, it requires no hunter's dog to follow it.

PILKINGS: If you don't want to see her, just say so and I'll send her packing.

ELESIN: Why should I not want to see her? Let her come. I have no more holes in my rag of shame. All is laid bare.

PILKINGS: I'll bring her in. [Goes off.]

JANE [hesitates, then goes to Elesin]: Please, try and understand. Everything my husband did was for the best.

ELESIN [he gives her a long strange stare, as if he is trying to understand who she is]: You are the wife of the District Officer?

JANE: Yes. My name is Jane.

ELESIN: That is my wife sitting down there. You notice how still and silent she sits? My business is with your husband.

[Pilkings returns with Iyaloja.]

PILKINGS: Here she is. Now first I want your word of honour that you will try nothing foolish.

ELESIN: Honour? White one, did you say you wanted my word of honour?

PILKINGS: I know you to be an honourable man. Give me your word of honour you will receive nothing from her.

ELESIN: But I am sure you have searched her clothing as you would never dare touch your own mother. And there are these two lizards of yours who roll their eyes even when I scratch.

PILKINGS: And I shall be sitting on that tree trunk watching even how you blink. Just the same I want your word that you will not let her pass anything to you.

ELESIN: You have my honour already. It is locked up in that desk in which you will put away your report of this night's events. Even the honour of my people you have taken already; it is tied together with those papers of treachery which make you masters in this land.

PILKINGS: Alright. I am trying to make things easy but if you must bring in politics we'll have to do it the hard way. Madam, I want you to remain along this line and move no nearer to that cell door. Guards! [They spring to attention.] If she moves beyond this point, blow your whistle. Come on Jane. [They go off.]

IYALOJA: How boldly the lizard struts before the pigeon when it was the eagle itself he promised us he would confront.

ELESIN: I don't ask you to take pity on me Iyaloja. You have a message for me or you would not have come. Even if it is the curses of the world, I shall listen.

IYALOJA: You made so bold with the servant of the white king who took your side against death. I must tell your brother chiefs when I return how bravely you waged war against him. Especially with words.

ELESIN: I more than deserve your scorn.

IYALOJA [*with sudden anger*]: I warned you, if you must leave a seed behind, be sure
it is not tainted with the curses of the world. Who are you to open a new life when
you dared not open the door to a new existence? I say who are you to make so
bold? [*The Bride sobs and Iyaloja notices her. Her contempt noticeably increases
as she turns back to Elesin.*] Oh you self-vaunted stem of the plantain, how hollow
it all proves. The pith is gone in the parent stem, so how will it prove with the new
shoot? How will it go with that earth that bears it? Who are you to bring this abomination on us!

ELESIN: My powers deserted me. My charms, my spells, even my voice lacked
strength when I made to summon the powers that would lead me over the last measure of earth into the land of the fleshless. You saw it, Iyaloja. You saw me struggle to retrieve my will from the power of the stranger whose shadow fell across the
doorway and left me floundering and blundering in a maze I had never before encountered. My senses were numbed when the touch of cold iron came upon my
wrists. I could do nothing to save myself.

IYALOJA: You have betrayed us. We fed you sweetmeats such as we hoped awaited
you on the other side. But you said No, I must eat the world's left-overs. We said
you were the hunter who brought the quarry down; to you belonged the vital por-
tions of the game. No, you said, I am the hunter's dog and I shall eat the entrails of
the game and the faeces of the hunter. We said you were the hunter returning home
in triumph, a slain buffalo pressing down on his neck; you said wait, I first must
turn up this cricket hole with my toes. We said yours was the doorway at which we
first spy the tapper when he comes down from the tree, yours was the blessing of
the twilight wine, the purl[7] that brings night spirits out of doors to steal their portion before the light of day. We said yours was the body of wine whose burden
shakes the tapper like a sudden gust on his perch. You said, No, I am content to
lick the dregs from each calabash when the drinkers are done. We said, the dew on
earth's surface was for you to wash your feet along the slopes of honour. You said
No, I shall step in the vomit of cats and the droppings of mice; I shall fight them
for the left-overs of the world.

ELESIN: Enough Iyaloja, enough.

IYALOJA: We called you leader and oh, how you led us on. What we have no intention
of eating should not be held to the nose.

ELESIN: Enough, enough. My shame is heavy enough.

IYALOJA: Wait. I came with a burden.

ELESIN: You have more than discharged it.

IYALOJA: I wish I could pity you.

ELESIN: I need neither your pity nor the pity of the world. I need understanding. Even
I need to understand. You were present at my defeat. You were part of the beginnings. You brought about the renewal of my tie to earth, you helped in the binding
of the cord.

IYALOJA: I gave you warning. The river which fills up before our eyes does not sweep
us away in its flood.

ELESIN: What were warnings beside the moist contact of living earth between my fingers? What were warnings beside the renewal of famished embers lodged eternally in the heart of man. But even that, even if it overwhelmed one with a

---

7. Palm wine froth.

thousandfold temptations to linger a little while, a man could overcome it. It is when the alien hand pollutes the source of will, when a stranger force of violence shatters the mind's calm resolution, this is when a man is made to commit the awful treachery of relief, commit in his thought the unspeakable blasphemy of seeing the hand of the gods in this alien rupture of his world. I know it was this thought that killed me, sapped my powers and turned me into an infant in the hands of unnamable strangers. I made to utter my spells anew but my tongue merely rattled in my mouth. I fingered hidden charms and the contact was damp; there was no spark left to sever the life-strings that should stretch from every finger-tip. My will was squelched in the spittle of an alien race, and all because I had committed this blasphemy of thought—that there might be the hand of the gods in a stranger's intervention.

IYALOJA: Explain it how you will, I hope it brings you peace of mind. The bush-rat fled his rightful cause, reached the market and set up a lamentation. "Please save me!"—are these fitting words to hear from an ancestral mask? "There's a wild beast at my heels" is not becoming language from a hunter.

ELESIN: May the world forgive me.

IYALOJA: I came with a burden I said. It approaches the gates which are so well guarded by those jackals whose spittle will from this day on be your food and drink. But first, tell me, you who were once Elesin Oba, tell me, you who know so well the cycle of the plantain: is it the parent shoot which withers to give sap to the younger or, does your wisdom see it running the other way?

ELESIN: I don't see your meaning Iyaloja?

IYALOJA: Did I ask you for a meaning? I asked a question. Whose trunk withers to give sap to the other? The parent shoot or the younger?

ELESIN: The parent.

IYALOJA: Ah. So you do know that. There are sights in this world which say different Elesin. There are some who choose to reverse this cycle of our being. Oh you emptied bark that the world once saluted for a pith-laden being, shall I tell you what the gods have claimed of you?

[In her agitation she steps beyond the line indicated by Pilkings and the air is rent by piercing whistles. The two Guards also leap forward and place safe-guarding hands on Elesin. Iyaloja stops, astonished. Pilkings comes racing in, followed by Jane.]

PILKINGS: What is it? Did they try something?

GUARD: She stepped beyond the line.

ELESIN [in a broken voice]: Let her alone. She meant no harm.

IYALOJA: Oh Elesin, see what you've become. Once you had no need to open your mouth in explanation because evil-smelling goats, itchy of hand and foot had lost their senses. And it was a brave man indeed who dared lay hands on you because Iyaloja stepped from one side of the earth onto another. Now look at the spectacle of your life. I grieve for you.

PILKINGS: I think you'd better leave. I doubt you have done him much good by coming here. I shall make sure you are not allowed to see him again. In any case we are moving him to a different place before dawn, so don't bother to come back.

IYALOJA: We foresaw that. Hence the burden I trudged here to lay beside your gates.

PILKINGS: What was that you said?

IYALOJA: Didn't our son explain? Ask that one. He knows what it is. At least we hope the man we once knew as Elesin remembers the lesser oaths he need not break.

PILKINGS: Do you know what she is talking about?

ELESIN: Go to the gates, ghostly one. Whatever you find there, bring it to me.

IYALOJA: Not yet. It drags behind me on the slow, weary feet of women. Slow as it is
Elesin, it has long overtaken you. It rides ahead of your laggard will.

PILKINGS: What is she saying now? Christ! Must your people forever speak in riddles?

ELESIN: It will come white man, it will come. Tell your men at the gates to let it through.

PILKINGS [*dubiously*]: I'll have to see what it is.

IYALOJA: You will. [*Passionately.*] But this is one oath he cannot shirk. White one,
you have a king here, a visitor from your land. We know of his presence here. Tell
me, were he to die would you leave his spirit roaming restlessly on the surface of
earth? Would you bury him here among those you consider less than human? In
your land have you no ceremonies of the dead?

PILKINGS: Yes. But we don't make our chiefs commit suicide to keep him company.

IYALOJA: Child, I have not come to help your understanding. [*Points to Elesin.*] This
is the man whose weakened understanding holds us in bondage to you. But ask him
if you wish. He knows the meaning of a king's passage; he was not born yesterday.
He knows the peril to the race when our dead father, who goes as intermediary,
waits and waits and knows he is betrayed. He knows when the narrow gate was
opened and he knows it will not stay for laggards who drag their feet in dung and
vomit, whose lips are reeking of the left-overs of lesser men. He knows he has condemned our king to wander in the void of evil with beings who are enemies of life.

PILKINGS: Yes er . . . but look here . . .

IYALOJA: What we ask is little enough. Let him release our King so he can ride on
homewards alone. The messenger is on his way on the backs of women. Let him
send word through the heart that is folded up within the bolt. It is the least of all his
oaths, it is the easiest fulfilled.

[*The Aide-de-camp runs in.*]

PILKINGS: Bob?

AIDE-DE-CAMP: Sir, there's a group of women chanting up the hill.

PILKINGS [*rounding on Iyaloja*]: If you people want trouble . . .

JANE: Simon, I think that's what Olunde referred to in his letter.

PILKINGS: He knows damned well I can't have a crowd here! Damn it, I explained the
delicacy of my position to him. I think it's about time I got him out of town. Bob,
send a car and two or three soldiers to bring him in. I think the sooner he takes his
leave of his father and gets out the better.

IYALOJA: Save your labour white one. If it is the father of your prisoner you want,
Olunde, he who until this night we knew as Elesin's son, he comes soon himself to
take his leave. He has sent the women ahead, so let them in.

[*Pilkings remains undecided.*]

AIDE-DE-CAMP: What do we do about the invasion? We can still stop them far from here.

PILKINGS: What do they look like?

AIDE-DE-CAMP: They're not many. And they seem quite peaceful.

PILKINGS: No men?

AIDE-DE-CAMP: Mm, two or three at the most.

JANE: Honestly, Simon, I'd trust Olunde. I don't think he'll deceive you about their
intentions.

PILKINGS: He'd better not. Alright, let them in Bob. Warn them to control themselves. Then hurry Olunde here. Make sure he brings his baggage because I'm not returning him into town.

AIDE-DE-CAMP: Very good sir. [*Goes.*]

PILKINGS [*to Iyaloja*]: I hope you understand that if anything goes wrong it will be on your head. My men have orders to shoot at the first sign of trouble.

IYALOJA: To prevent one death you will actually make other deaths? Ah, great is the wisdom of the white race. But have no fear. Your Prince will sleep peacefully. So at long last will ours. We will disturb you no further, servant of the white king. Just let Elesin fulfill his oath and we will retire home and pay homage to our King.

JANE: I believe her Simon, don't you?

PILKINGS: Maybe.

ELESIN: Have no fear ghostly one. I have a message to send my King and then you have nothing more to fear.

IYALOJA: Olunde would have done it. The chiefs asked him to speak the words but he said no, not while you lived.

ELESIN: Even from the depths to which my spirit has sunk, I find some joy that this little has been left to me.

[*The women enter, intoning the dirge "Alẹ lẹ lẹ" and swaying from side to side. On their shoulders is borne a longish object roughly like a cylindrical bolt, covered in cloth. They set it down on the spot where Iyaloja had stood earlier, and form a semi-circle round it. The Praise-Singer and Drummer stand on the inside of the semi-circle but the drum is not used at all. The Drummer intones under the Praise-Singer's invocations.*]

PILKINGS [*as they enter*]: What is *that?*

IYALOJA: The burden you have made white one, but we bring it in peace.

PILKINGS: I said *what* is it?

ELESIN: White man, you must let me out. I have a duty to perform.

PILKINGS: I most certainly will not.

ELESIN: There lies the courier of my King. Let me out so I can perform what is demanded of me.

PILKINGS: You'll do what you need to do from inside there or not at all. I've gone as far as I intend to with this business.

ELESIN: The worshipper who lights a candle in your church to bear a message to his god bows his head and speaks in a whisper to the flame. Have I not seen it ghostly one? His voice does not ring out to the world. Mine are no words for anyone's ears. They are not words even for the bearers of this load. They are words I must speak secretly, even as my father whispered them in my ears and I in the ears of my first-born. I cannot shout them to the wind and the open night-sky.

JANE: Simon . . .

PILKINGS: Don't interfere. Please!

IYALOJA: They have slain the favourite horse of the king and slain his dog. They have borne them from pulse to pulse centre of the land receiving prayers for their king. But the rider has chosen to stay behind. Is it too much to ask that he speak his heart to heart of the waiting courier? [*Pilkings turns his back on her.*] So be it. Elesin Oba, you see how even the mere leavings are denied you. [*She gestures to the Praise-Singer.*]

PRAISE-SINGER: Elesin Oba! I call you by that name only this last time. Remember when I said, if you cannot come, tell my horse. [*Pause.*] What? I cannot hear you? I said, if you cannot come, whisper in the ears of my horse. Is your tongue severed from the roots Elesin? I can hear no response. I said, if there are boulders you cannot climb, mount my horse's back, this spotless black stallion, he'll bring you over them. [*Pauses.*] Elesin Oba, once you had a tongue that darted like a drummer's stick. I said, if you get lost my dog will track a path to me. My memory fails me but I think you replied: My feet have found the path, Alafin.

[*The dirge rises and falls.*]

I said at the last, if evil hands hold you back, just tell my horse there is weight on the hem of your smock. I dare not wait too long.

[*The dirge rises and falls.*]

There lies the swiftest ever messenger of a king, so set me free with the errand of your heart. There lie the head and heart of the favourite of the gods, whisper in his ears. Oh my companion, if you had followed when you should, we would not say that the horse preceded its rider. If you had followed when it was time, we would not say the dog has raced beyond and left his master behind. If you had raised your will to cut the thread of life at the summons of the drums, we would not say your mere shadow fell across the gateway and took its owner's place at the banquet. But the hunter, laden with a slain buffalo, stayed to root in the cricket's hole with his toes. What now is left? If there is a dearth of bats, the pigeon must serve us for the offering. Speak the words over your shadow which must now serve in your place.

ELESIN: I cannot approach. Take off the cloth. I shall speak my message from heart to heart of silence.

IYALOJA [*moves forward and removes the covering*]: Your courier Elesin, cast your eyes on the favoured companion of the King.

[*Rolled up in the mat, his head and feet showing at either end is the body of Olunde.*]

There lies the honour of your household and of our race. Because he could not bear to let honour fly out of doors, he stopped it with his life. The son has proved the father Elesin, and there is nothing left in your mouth to gnash but infant gums.

PRAISE-SINGER: Elesin, we placed the reins of the world in your hands yet you watched it plunge over the edge of the bitter precipice. You sat with folded arms while evil strangers tilted the world from its course and crashed it beyond the edge of emptiness—you muttered, there is little that one man can do, you left us floundering in a blind future. Your heir has taken the burden on himself. What the end will be, we are not gods to tell. But this young shoot has poured its sap into the parent stalk, and we know this is not the way of life. Our world is tumbling in the void of strangers, Elesin.

[*Elesin has stood rock-still, his knuckles taut on the bars, his eyes glued to the body of his son. The stillness seizes and paralyses everyone, including Pilkings who has turned to look. Suddenly Elesin flings one arm round his neck, once, and with the loop of the chain, strangles himself in a swift, decisive pull. The guards rush forward to stop him but they are only in time to let his body down. Pilkings has leapt to the door at the same time and struggles with the lock. He rushes within, fumbles with the handcuffs and unlocks them, raises the body to a sitting position while he tries to give resuscitation. The women continue their dirge, unmoved by the sudden event.*]

IYALOJA: Why do you strain yourself? Why do you labour at tasks for which no one, not even the man lying there would give you thanks? He is gone at last into the passage but oh, how late it all is. His son will feast on the meat and throw him bones. The passage is clogged with droppings from the King's stallion; he will arrive all stained in dung.

PILKINGS [*in a tired voice*]: Was this what you wanted?

IYALOJA: No child, it is what you brought to be, you who play with strangers' lives, who even usurp the vestments of our dead, yet believe that the stain of death will not cling to you. The gods demanded only the old expired plantain but you cut down the sap-laden shoot to feed your pride. There is your board, filled to overflowing. Feast on it. [*She screams at him suddenly, seeing that Pilkings is about to close Elesin's staring eyes.*] Let him alone! However sunk he was in debt he is no pauper's carrion abandoned on the road. Since when have strangers donned clothes of indigo[8] before the bereaved cries out his loss?

[*She turns to the Bride who has remained motionless throughout.*]

Child.

[*The girl takes up a little earth, walks calmly into the cell and closes Elesin's eyes. She then pours some earth over each eyelid and comes out again.*]

Now forget the dead, forget even the living. Turn your mind only to the unborn.

[*She goes off, accompanied by the Bride. The dirge rises in volume and the women continue their sway. Lights fade to a black-out.*]

---

8. The color of mourning.

═┼ PERSPECTIVES ┼═
Postcolonial Conditions

One of the developments that most significantly changed the political face of the globe in the twentieth century was decolonization, that is, the transition of large areas of the world from colonies of mostly European powers to independent nation-states. While this transition occurred gradually in some cases, it was abrupt in others; it took place peacefully at times and at others was achieved by means of violent and sometimes protracted conflict with the colonial power. But the achievement of political independence didn't mean that the economic, social, and cultural forms of domination that accompanied colonialism simply came to an end, some of them left profound marks on the colonized society, while others perpetuated themselves in different guises. "Postcolonial" conditions, then, aren't simply the social and cultural configurations that followed chronologically after the end of colonialism but those that are directly or indirectly shaped by the colonial past and that extend or resist its legacies.

These legacies can take a wide range of forms. Materially, they can manifest themselves in economic and financial dependencies on the former metropolis that limit the autonomy political independence seemed to promise. The government can be controlled by elites from among the former colonized whose economic interests are tied up with those of the colonizers. Politically, the end of colonialism sometimes leaves behind structures of social, ethnic, and racial discrimination that persist even when the authorities who originally enforced them have been displaced. At other times, the presence of a colonial power helped to suppress latent conflicts between different social groups in the colonized country that violently erupt when that power wanes. Poets, playwrights, and novelists who write in the aftermath of colonialism explore these and related conflicts, often focusing on the problems of identity and community that arise from colonial domination and its aftermath.

The most prominent of these identity conflicts arises with the question of how to negotiate the balance between the cultural heritage the colonized claim as originally their own and the one that was brought to them by the colonizer. For those whose lives are shaped by colonialism and postcolonialism, these legacies often don't form two distinct blocks that can be easily separated from each other but instead present themselves as an interwoven spectrum of possibilities and conflicts. At the simplest level, the desire to emulate or appropriate what is admirable about the colonizer's culture may conflict with the wish to give pride of place to one's own cultural heritage. Each of these tendencies can be put to very complex uses. For example, one might want to lay claim to certain aspects of the colonizers' culture (such as an emphasis on scientific rationality or freedom of expression) precisely to turn them against the colonizer's own oppression of the colonized; or, inversely, appropriating certain aspects of the colonizer's culture (for instance, certain conceptions of femininity and the role of women) might become a way of pointing out injustices in one's own culture.

Claiming one's own cultural heritage can be an equally complex undertaking since that heritage may turn out to consist not just of one but of several different and possibly conflicting traditions. "Claiming one's own," in this context, may well imply privileging some of these traditions and silencing others—much as the colonizer had done before—or realizing that the cultural unity by means of which one wanted to resist the colonizer is itself a construct rather than a natural given. Yet again, laying claim to one's own culture in a colonial or postcolonial context may turn out to be problematic because some of the colonized themselves no longer wholeheartedly embrace all of its values. Confronting these problems leads the writers in this section again and again to question who they are, what the nature of their homeland and their native culture is, and how the relationship of an individual to his or her culture should be defined in a context of uneven power distribution.

How can women resist colonial oppression and at the same time the gender discrimination their own culture may impose on them? How could whites living in apartheid South Africa resist the racial discrimination that benefited them socially and economically? Does a Western education undermine non-Western cultural identities? These are some of the questions that postcolonial writers ask. Some of the issues they raise, however, are of a more specifically linguistic and literary nature. What language should the postcolonial writer use? Using the colonizer's language may open up a wide audience, but it may also reinforce its dominance; on the other hand, using the language of the colonized may prevent wide public recognition, but it may also help to show its literary powers of expression. What audience is the postcolonial literary text aimed at? How can mostly oral literary traditions be translated into print? What literary forms and conventions are best suited to express the predicaments of the postcolonial situation? How can a non-Western writer appropriate the Western literary tradition and yet resist its claims of superiority over native traditions? In their wrestling with questions such as these, postcolonial writers turn literary texts into a battleground for cultural struggles that are deeply entangled with conflicts over political power and autonomy; they offer the reader literary insights and formal innovations that these very struggles make possible.

Nadine Gordimer
b. 1923

Nadine Gordimer is South Africa's best-known novelist and one of the most prominent intellectuals to have spoken out against apartheid in the twentieth century. Over more than five decades, in both her fiction and her nonfiction, she has reflected on the political, economic, social, and cultural consequences of racial separatism in South Africa. Unlike many other South African intellectuals who found it impossible to continue living under apartheid, Gordimer has traveled extensively throughout Africa, Europe, and the United States but has always maintained residence in the country to fight its injustices from within.

Gordimer was born in Springs, Transvaal, to Jewish immigrant parents in 1923 and studied briefly at the University of Witwatersrand in Johannesburg without completing a degree. She wrote stories even when she was a teenager and published her first collection, *Face to Face*, in 1949. From 1948 on she lived in Johannesburg, and she taught and lectured at various American universities in the 1960s and 1970s. Her novels and short stories have won numerous prizes, most notably the Nobel Prize in 1991; *Burger's Daughter*, however, was banned by the South African government after the Soweto uprising in 1976, in which black resistance to apartheid broke out in public. In her more recent novels such as *None to Accompany Me* (1994) and *The House Gun* (1998), Gordimer has explored the new problems of postapartheid society.

In novels such as *The Lying Days* (1953), *Occasion for Loving* (1963), *The Late Bourgeois World* (1966), and *Burger's Daughter* (1979), Gordimer explores the moral, political, and psychological options that are open to whites living in a segregated society. Their search for a moral code that would allow them to come to terms with this situation often leads them to dead ends and limitations rather than solutions. Her 1952 story "The Defeated" approaches problems of social segregation obliquely, through a poor Jewish immigrant couple whose daughter moves up into the wealthiest segment of white South African society. The situation of the parents, left behind in poverty and squalor without hope of escape, resembles that of the black mine workers to whom their little store caters. The story illustrates how Gordimer explores the consequences of apartheid and material inequality in the daily lives and experiences of both black and white, liberal and conservative characters.

The Defeated

My mother did not want me to go near the Concession stores[1] because they smelled, and were dirty, and the natives spat tuberculosis germs into the dust. She said it was no place for little girls.

But I used to go down there sometimes, in the afternoon, when static four o'clock held the houses of our Mine, and the sun washed over them like the waves of the sea over sand castles. I felt that life was going on down there at the Concession stores: noise, and movement, and—yes, bad smells, even—and so I would wander down the naked road, with the hot sun uncomfortably drying the membrane inside my nose, seeing the irregular line of narrow white shops lying away ahead like a jumble of shoe boxes.

The signs of life that I craved were very soon evident: rich and careless of its vitality, it overflowed from the crowded pavement of the stores, and the surrounding veld[2] was littered with sucked-out oranges and tatters of dirty paper, and worn into the shabby barrenness peculiar to earth much trampled upon by the feet of men. A fat, one-legged native, with the patient detachment of the business man who knows himself indispensable, sat on the bald veld beside the path that led from the Compound, his stock of walking-sticks standing up, handles tied together, points splayed out fan-wise, his pyramids of bright, thin-skinned oranges waiting. Sometimes he had mealies as well—those big, hard, full-grown ears with rows of yellowish tombstones instead of little pearly teeth—and a brazier made from a paraffin tin to roast them by. Propped against the chipped pillars of the pavement, there were always other vendors, making their small way in lucky beans, herbs, bracelets beaten from copper wire, knitted caps in wonderful colours—blooming like great hairy petunias, or bursting suns, from the needles of old, old native women—and, of course, oranges. Everywhere there were oranges; the pushing, ambling crowds filling the pavement ate them as they stared at the windows, the gossips, sitting with their blankets drawn close and their feet in the gutter, sucked at them, the Concession store cats sniffed at the skins where they lay, hollow-cheeked, discarded in every doorway.

Quite often I had to flick the white pith from where it had landed, on my shoe or even my dress, spat negligently by some absorbed orange-eater contemplating a shirt through breath-smudged plate glass. The wild, wondering, dirty men came up from the darkness of the mine and they lay themselves out to the sun on the veld, and to their mouths they put the round fruit of the sun; and it was the expression of their need.

I would saunter along the shopwindows amongst them, and for me there was a quickening of glamour about the place: the air was thicker with their incense-like body smell, and the sudden rank shock of their stronger sweat, as a bare armpit lifted over my head. The clamour of their voices—always shouting, but so merry, so angry!—and the size of their laughter, and the open-mouthed startle with which they greeted every fresh sight: I felt vaguely the spell of the books I had read, returning; markets in Persia, bazaars in Cairo . . . Nevertheless, I was careful not to let them brush too closely past me, lest some unnameable *something* crawl from their dusty blankets or torn cotton trousers on to my clean self, and I did not like the way they

---

1. Stores catering to the native workers near South African mines. The stores described in the story, as Gordimer has indicated, resemble those in the mining town where she grew up.
2. Open grassland.

spat, with that terrible gurgle in the throat, into the gutter, or, worse still, blew their noses loudly between finger and thumb, and flung the excrement horribly to the air.

And neither did I like the heavy, sickening, greasy carrion-breath that poured from the mouth of the Hotela la Bantu, where the natives hunched intent at zinc-topped forms, eating steaming no-colour chunks of horror that bore no relation to meat as I knew it. The down on my arms prickled in revulsion from the pulpy entrails hanging in dreadful enticement at the window, and the blood-embroidered sawdust spilling out of the doorway.

I know that I wondered how the storekeepers' wives, who sat on soap boxes out-side the doorways of the shops on either side of the eating-house, could stand the breath of that maw. How they could sit, like lizards in the sun; and all the time they breathed in the breath of the eating-house: took it deep into the recesses of their be-ings, whilst my throat closed against it in disgust.

It was down there one burning afternoon that I met Mrs. Saiyetovitz. She was one of the storekeepers' wives, and I had seen her many times before, sitting before the deep, blanket-hung cave of her husband's store, where a pile of tinsel-covered wooden trunks shimmered and flashed a pink or green eye out of the gloom into the outside—wearing her creased alpaca[3] apron, her fat insteps leaning over her down-at-heel shoes. Sometimes she knitted, and sometimes she just sat. On this day there was a small girl hanging about her, drawing on the shopwindow with a sticky forefinger. When the child turned to look at me, I recognized her as one of the girls from "our school"; a girl from my class, as a matter of fact, called Miriam Saiyetovitz. Yes, that was her name: I remembered it because it was ugly—I was always sorry for girls with ugly names.

Miriam was a tousled, black-haired little girl, who wore a red bow in her hair. Now she recognized me, and we stood looking at one another; all at once the spare line of the name "Miriam Saiyetovitz," that was like the scrolled pattern of an iron gate with only the sky behind it, shifted its perspective in my mind, so that now be-tween the cold curly M's and the implacable A's of that gate's framework, I saw a house, a complication of buildings and flowers and figures walking, where before there was nothing but the sky. Miriam Saiyetovitz—and this: behind her name and her school self, the hot and buzzing world of the stores. And I smiled at her, very friendly.

So she knew we had decided to recognize one another and she sauntered over to talk to me. I stood with her in the doorway of her father's store, and I, too, wrote my name and drew cats composed of two capital O's and a sausage tail, with the point of my hot and sticky finger on the window. Of course, she did not exactly introduce me to her mother—children never do introduce their mothers; they merely let it be known, by referring to the woman in question offhand, in the course of play, or going up to speak to her in such a way that the relationship becomes obvious. Miriam went up to her mother and said diffidently: "Ma, I know this girl from school—she's in class with me, can we have some red lemonade?"

And the woman lifted her head from where she sat, wide-legged, so that you couldn't help seeing the knee-elastic of her striped pink silk bloomers, holding over the cotton tops of her stockings, and said, peering, "Take it! Take it! Go, have it!"

---

3. A glossy fabric simulating the skin of the South American alpaca, an animal similar to a llama.

Because I did not then know her, I thought that she was angry, she spoke with such impatience; but soon I knew that it was only her eager generosity that made her fling permission almost fiercely at Miriam whenever the child made some request. Mrs. Saiyetovitz's glance wavered over to me, but she did not seem to be seeing me very clearly: indeed, she could not, for her small, pale, pale eyes narrowed into her big, simple, heavy face were half-blind, and she had always to peer at everything, and never quite see.

I saw that she was very ugly.

Ugly, with the blunt ugliness of a toad; the ugliness of seeming not entirely at home in any element—as if the earth were the wrong place, too heavy and magnetic for a creature already so blunt; and the water would be no better: too subtle and contour-swayed for a creature so graceless. And yet her ugliness was without repellence. When I grew older I often wondered why; she should have been repellent, one should have turned from her, but one did not. She was only ugly. She had the short, stunted yet heavy bones of generations of oppression in the Ghettos of Europe; breasts, stomach, hips crowded sadly, no height, wide strong shoulders, and a round back. Her head settled right down between her shoulders without even the grace of a neck, and her dun flat hair was cut at the level of her ears. Her features were not essentially Semitic; there was nothing so *definite* as that about her: she had no distinction whatever.

Miriam reappeared from the shades of the store, carrying two bottles of red lemonade. A Shangaan[4] emerged at the same time, clutching a newspaper parcel and puzzling over his handful of change, not looking where he was going. Miriam swept past him, the dusty African with his odd, troglodyte[5] unsureness, and his hair plastered into savage whorls with red clay. With one swift movement she knocked the tin caps off the bottles against the scratched frame of the shopwindow, and handed my lemonade to me. "Where did you get it so quickly?" I asked, surprised. She jerked her head back toward the store: "In the kitchen," she said—and applied herself to the bottle.

And so I knew that the Saiyetovitzes lived there, behind the Concession store.

Saturday afternoons were the busiest. Mrs. Saiyetovitz's box stood vacant outside and she helped her husband in the shop. Saturday afternoon was usually my afternoon for going down there, too; my mother and father went out to golf, and I was left with the tick of the clock, the purring monologue of our cat, and the doves gurgling in the empty garden.

On Saturdays every doorway was crowded; a continual shifting stream snaked up and down the pavements; flies tangled overhead, the air smelled hotter, and from the doorway of every store the high, wailing blare and repetition of native songs, played on the gramophone, swung out upon the air and met in discord with the tune of the record being played next door.

Miriam's mother's brother was the proprietor of the Hotela la Bantu, and another uncle had the bicycle shop two doors down. Sometimes she had a message to deliver at the bicycle shop, and I would go in with her. Spare wheels hung across the ceiling, there was a battered wooden counter with a pile of puncture repair outfits, a sewing-machine or two for sale, and, in the window, bells and pumps and mascots cut out of tin, painted yellow and red for the adornment of handlebars. We were invariably offered a lemonade by the uncle, and we invariably accepted. At home I was not al-

4. A member of one of the Tsonga-speaking peoples of   5. Cave dweller.
South Africa.

lowed to drink lemonades unlimited; they might "spoil my dinner"; but Miriam drank them whenever she pleased.

Wriggling in and out amongst the grey-dusty bodies of the natives—their silky brown skin dies in the damp fug underground: after a few months down the mine, it reflects only weariness—Miriam looked with her own calm, quick self-possession upon the setting in which she found herself. Like someone sitting in a swarm of ants; and letting them swarm, letting them crawl all over and about her. Not lifting a hand to flick them off. Not crying out against them in disgust; nor explaining, saying, well, I *like* ants. Just sitting there and letting them swarm, and looking out of herself as if to say: What ants? What ants are you talking about? I giggled and shuddered in excitement at the sight of the dried bats and cobwebby snake-skins rotting in the bleary little window of the medicine shop, but Miriam tugged at my dress and said, "Oh, come on—" I exclaimed at the purple and red shirts lying amongst the dead flies in the wonderful confusion of Saiyetovitz's store window, but Miriam was telling me about her music exam in September, and only frowned at the interruption. I was approaching the confusion of adolescence, and sometimes an uncomfortable, terrible, fascinating curiosity—like a headless worm which lay shamefully hidden in the earth of my soul—crawled out into my consciousness at the sight of the animal obviousness of the natives' male bodies in their scanty covering; but the flash of my guilt at these moments met no answer in Miriam, although she was the same age as I.

If the sight of a boy interrupting his conversation to step out a yard or two on to the veld to relieve himself filled me with embarrassment and real disgust, so that I wanted to go and look at flowers—it seemed that Miriam did not see.

It was quite a long time before she took me into her father's store.

For months it remained a vague, dark, dust-moted world beyond the blanket-hung doorway, into which she was swallowed up and appeared again, whilst I waited outside, with the boys who looked and looked and looked at the windows. Then one day, as she was entering, she paused, and said suddenly and calmly: "Aren't you coming . . .?" Without a word, I followed her in.

It was cool in the store; and the coolness was a surprise. Out of the sun-baked pavement—and into the store that was cool, like a cellar! Light danced only furtively along the folds of the blankets that hung from the ceiling: crackling silent and secret little fires in the curly woollen furze. The blankets were dark sombre hangings, in proud colours, bold and primal. They hung like dark stalactites in the cave, still and heavy, communing only their own colours back to themselves. They brooded over the shop; and over Mr. Saiyetovitz there beneath, treading the worn cement with his disgruntled, dispossessed air of doing his best, but . . . I had glimpsed him before. He lurked within the depths of his store like a beast in its lair, and now and then I had seen the glimmer of his pale, pasty face with the wide upper lip under which the lower closed glumly and puffily.

John Saiyetovitz (his name wasn't John at all, really—it was Yanka, but when he arrived at Cape Town, long ago, the Immigration authorities were tired of attempting to understand and spell the unfamiliar names of the immigrants pouring off the boat, and by the time they'd got the "Saiyetovitz" spelt right, they couldn't be bothered puzzling over the "Yanka", so they scrawled "John" on his papers, and John he was)—John Saiyetovitz was a gentle man, with an almost hangdog gentleness, but when he was trading with the natives, strange blasts of power seemed to blow up in his soul. Africans are the slowest buyers in the world; to them, buying is a ritual, a slow and solemn undertaking. They must go carefully; they nervously scent pitfalls on every side. And confronted with a selection of different kinds of the one thing they want, they are as confused as a child before a plate of pastries; fingering, hesitating, this or that . . .? On a busy Saturday they must be allowed to stand about the shop endlessly, looking up and about, pausing to shake their heads and give a profound "ow!"; sauntering off; going to press their noses against the window again; coming back. And Mr. Saiyetovitz—always the same, unshaven and collarless—lugging a blanket down from the shelves, flinging it upon the counter—and another, and then another, and standing, arms hanging, sullen and smouldering before the blank-faced purchaser. The boy with his helpless stance, and his eyes rolling up in the agony of decision, filling the shop with the sickly odour of his anxious sweat, and clutching his precious guitar.

Waiting, waiting.

And then Mr. Saiyetovitz swooping away in a gesture of rage and denial; don't care, sick-to-death. And the boy anxious, edging forward to feel the cloth again, and the whole business starting up all over again; more blankets, different colours, down from the shelf and hooked from the ceiling—stalactites crumpled to woollen heaps to wonder over. Mr. Saiyetovitz throwing them down, moving in jerks of rage now, and then roughly bullying the boy into a decision. Shouting at him, bundling his purchase into his arms, snatching the money, gesturing him cowed out of the store.

Mr. Saiyetovitz treated the natives honestly, but with bad grace. He forced them to feel their ignorance, their inadequacy, and their submission to the white man's world of money. He spiritually maltreated them, and bitterly drove his nail into the coffin of their confidence.

With me, he was shy, he smiled widely and his hand went to the stud swinging loose at the neck of his half-buttoned shirt, and drew as if in apology over the stubbled landscape of his jaw. He always called me "little girl" and he liked to talk to me in the way that he thought children like to be talked to, but I found it very difficult to make a show of reply, because his English was so broken and fragmentary. So I used to stand there, and say yes, Mr. Saiyetovitz, and smile back and say thank you! to anything that sounded like a question, because the question usually was did I want a lemonade? and of course, I usually did.

The first time Miriam ever came to my home was the day of my birthday party.

Our relationship at school had continued unchanged, just as before; she had her friends and I had mine, but outside of school there was the curious plane of intimacy on which we had, as it were, surprised one another wandering, and so which was shared peculiarly by us.

I had put Miriam's name down on my guest list; she was invited; and she came. She wore a blue taffeta dress which Mrs. Saiyetovitz had made for her (on the old Singer[6] on the counter in the shop, I guessed) and it was quite nice if a bit too frilly. My home was pretty and well-furnished and full of flowers and personal touches of my mother's hands; there was space, and everything shone. Miriam did not open her eyes at it; I saw her finger a bowl of baby-skinned pink roses in the passing, but all afternoon she looked out indifferently as she did at home.

The following Saturday at the store we were discussing the party. Miriam was telling Mrs. Saiyetovitz about my presents, and I was standing by in pleasurable embarrassment at my own importance.

6. A brand of sewing machine.

"Well, please God, Miri," said Mrs. Saiyetovitz at the finish, "you'll also have a party for your birday in April . . . Ve'll be in d'house, and everyting'll be nice, just like you want."—They were leaving the rooms behind the shop—the mournful green plush curtains glooming the archway between the bedroom and the living-room; the tarnished samovar;[7] the black beetles in the little kitchen; Miriam's old black piano with the candlesticks, wheezing in the draughty passage; the damp puddly yard piled with empty packing-cases and eggshells and banana skins; the hovering smell of fish frying. They were going to live in a little house in the township nearby.

But when April came, Miriam took ten of her friends to the Saturday afternoon bioscope[8] in celebration of her birthday. "And to Costas Café afterwards for ice-cream," she stated to her mother, looking out over her head. I think Mrs. Saiyetovitz was disappointed about the party, but she reasoned then, as always, that as her daughter went to school and was educated and could speak English, whilst she herself knew nothing, wasn't clever at all, the little daughter must know best what was right and what was *nice*.

I know now what of course I did not know then: that Miriam Saiyetovitz and I were intelligent little girls into whose brains there never had, and never would, come the freak and wonderful flash that is brilliance. Ours were alabaster intellects: clear, perfect, light; no streaks of dark, unknown granite splitting to reveal secret veins of brightness, like thin gold, between stratum and stratum. We were fitted to be good schoolteachers, secretaries, organizers; we did everything well, nothing badly, and nothing remarkably. But to the Saiyetovitzes, Miriam's brain blazed like the sun, warming their humbleness.

In the year-by-year passage through school, our classmates thinned out one by one; the way seedlings come up in a bunch to a certain stage in their development, and then by some inexplicable process of natural selection, one or two continue to grow and branch up into the air, whilst the others wither or remain small and weedy. The other girls left to go and learn shorthand-and-typewriting: weeded out by the necessity of earning a living. Or moved, and went to other schools: transplanted to some ground of their own. Miriam and I remained, growing straight and steadily . . .

During our matriculation year a sense of wonder and impending change came upon us both; the excitement of coming to an end that is also a beginning. We felt this in one another, and so were drawn together in new earnestness. Miriam came to study with me in the garden at my house, and oftener than ever, I slipped down to the Concession stores to exchange a book or discuss work with her. For although they now had a house, the Saiyetovitzes still lived, in the wider sense of the word, at the store. When Miriam and I discussed our schoolwork, the Saiyetovitzes crept about, very quiet, talking to one another only in hoarse, respectful whispers.

It was during this year, when the wonder of our own capacity to learn was reaching out and catching into light like a veld fire within us, that we began to talk of the University. And, all at once, we talked of nothing else. I spoke to my father of it, and he was agreeable, although my mother thought a girl could do better with her time. But so long as my father was willing to send me, I knew I should go. Ah yes, said Miriam. She liked my father very much; I knew that. In fact she said to me once—it

---

7. A metal urn used to boil water for tea, especially in Russia.   8. Movie theater.

was a strange thing to say, and almost emotionally, she said it, and at a strange time, because we were on the bus going into the town to buy a new winter coat which she had wanted very badly and talked about longingly for days, and her father had just given her the money to get it—she said to me: You know, I think your father's just right—I mean, if you had to choose somebody, a certain kind of person for a father, well, your father'd be just the kind you'd want.

When she broached the subject of University to her parents, they were agreeable for her to go, too. Indeed, they wanted her to go almost more than she herself did. But they worried a great deal about the money side of it; every time I went down to the store there'd be a discussion of ways and means, Saiyetovitz slowly munching his bread and garlic polony[9] lunch, and worrying. Miriam didn't worry about it; they'll find the money, she said. She was a tall girl, now, with beautiful breasts, and a large, dark-featured face that had a certain capable elegance, although her father's glum mouth was unmistakable and on her upper lip faint dark down foreshadowed a heavy middle age. Her parents were peasants; but she was the powerful young Jewess. Beside her, I felt pale in my Scotch gingery-fairness: lightly drawn upon the mind's eye, whilst she was painted in oils.

We both matriculated; not so well as we thought we should, but well enough; and we went to the University. And there, too, we did well enough. We had both decided upon the same course: teaching. In the end, it had seemed the only thing to do. Neither of us had any particular bent.

It must have been a hard struggle for the Saiyetovitzes to keep Miriam at the University, buy her clothes, and pay for her board and lodging in Johannesburg.[1] There is a great deal of money to be made out of native trade concessions purchased from the government; and it doesn't require education or trained commercial astuteness to make it—in fact, trading of this sort seems to flourish in response to something very different: what is needed is instinctive peasant craftiness such as can only be found in the uneducated, in those who have scratched up their own resources. Storekeepers with this quality of peasant craft made money all about Mr. Saiyetovitz, bought houses and motor-cars and banded their wives' retired hands with diamonds in mark of their new idleness. But Mr. Saiyetovitz was a peasant without the peasant's craft; without that flaw in his simplicity that might have given him cheques and deeds of transfer to sign, even if he were unable to read the print on the documents . . . Without this craft, the peasant has only one thing left to him: hard work, dirty work, with the sweet, sickly body-smell of the black men about him all day. Saiyetovitz made no money: only worked hard and long, standing in his damp shirt amidst the clamour of the stores and the death-smell from the eating-house always in his nose.

Meanwhile, Miriam fined down into a lady. She developed a half-bored, half-intolerant shrug of the shoulders in place of the childish sharpness that had been filed jagged by the rub-rub of rough life and harsh contrasts. She became soft-voiced, where she had been loud and gay. She watched and conformed; and soon took on the attitude of liberal-mindedness that sets the doors of the mind slackly open, so that any idea may walk in and out again, leaving very little impression: she could appreciate Bach and Stravinsky,[2] and spend a long evening listening to swing music in the dark of somebody's flat.

---

9. Bologna sausage.
1. South Africa's most important city economically and
financially.
2. A 20th-century Russian composer.

Race and creed had never meant very much to Miriam and me, but at the University she sifted naturally toward the young Jews who were passing easily and enthusiastically, with their people's extraordinary aptitude for creative and scientific work, through Medical School. They liked her; she was invited to their homes for tennis parties, swimming on Sundays, and dances, and she seemed as unimpressed by the luxury of their ten-thousand-pound houses as she had been by the contrast of our clean, pleasant little home, long ago, when she herself was living behind the Concession store.

She usually spent part of the vacations with friends in Johannesburg; I missed her—wandering about the Mine on my own, out of touch, now, with the girls I had left behind in the backwater of the small town. During the second half of one July vacation—she had spent the first two weeks in Johannesburg—she asked me if she could come and spend Sunday at my home, and in the afternoon, one of the medical students arrived at our house in his small car. He had come from Johannesburg; Miriam had evidently told him she would be with us. I gathered her parents did not know of the young man's visit, and I did not speak of it before them.

So the four years of our training passed. Miriam Saiyetovitz and I had dropped like two leaves, side by side into the same current, and been carried downstream together: now the current met a swirl of dead logs, reeds, and the force of other waters, and broke up, divided its drive and its one direction. The leaves floated clear; divergent from one another. Miriam got a teaching post in Johannesburg, but I was sent to a small school in the Northern Transvaal.[3] We met seldom during the first six months of our adult life: Miriam went to Cape Town during the vacation, and I flew to Rhodesia with the first profits of my independence.[4] Then came the war,[5] and I, glad to escape so soon the profession I had once anticipated with such enthusiasm, joined the nursing service and went away for the long, strange interlude of four years. Whilst I was with a field hospital in Italy, I heard that Miriam had married—a Dr. Somebody-or-other; my informant wasn't sure of the name. I guessed it must be one of the boys whom she had known as students. I sent a cable of congratulation, to the Saiyetovitzes' address.

And then, one day I came back to the small mining town and found it there, the same; like a face that has been waiting a long time. My Mother, and my Dad, the big wheels of the shaft turning, the trees folding their wings about the Mine houses; and our house, with the green, square lawn and the cat watching the doves. For the first few weeks I faltered about the old life, feeling my way in a dream so like the old reality that it hurt.

There was a feel about an afternoon that made my limbs tingle with familiarity . . . What . . .? And then, lying on our lawn under the hot sky, I knew: just the sort of glaring summer afternoon that used to send me down to the Concession stores, feeling isolated in the heat. Instantly, I thought of the Saiyetovitzes, and I wanted to go and see them, see if they were still there; what Miriam was doing; where she was, now.

Down at the stores it was the same as ever, only dirtier, smaller, more chipped and smeared—the way reality often is in contrast with the image carried long in the mind. As I stepped so strangely on that old pocked pavement, with the skeleton cats

---

3. Formerly a province of South Africa.
4. Cape Town is South Africa's capital, Rhodesia (now
Zimbabwe) is a country to the north of South Africa.
5. World War II.

and the orange peel and the gobs of spit, my heart tightened with the thought of the Saiyetovitzes. I was in a kind of excitement to see the store again. And there it was; and excitement sank out at the evidence of the monotony of "things". Blankets swung a little in the doorway. Flies crawled amongst the shirts and shoes posed in the window, the hot, wet, sickening fatty smell came over from the eating-house. I met it with the old revulsion: it was like breathing inside someone's stomach. And in the store, amongst the wicked glitter of the tin trunks, beneath the secret whispering of the blankets, the old Saiyetovitzes sat glumly, with patience, waiting . . . As animals wait in a cage; for nothing.

In their delight at seeing me again, I saw that they were older, sadder; that they had somehow given themselves into the weight of their own humbleness, they were without a pinnacle on which to fix their eyes. Whatever place it was that they looked upon now, it was flat.

Mr. Saiyetovitz's mouth had creased in further to the dead folds of his chin; his hair straggled to the rims of his ears. As he spoke to me, I noticed that his hands lay, with a curious helpless indifference, curled on the counter. Mrs. Saiyetovitz shuffled off at once to the back of the shop to make a cup of tea for me, and carried it in, slopping over into the saucer. She was uglier than ever, now, her back hunched up to meet her head, her old thick legs spiralled in crêpe bandages because of varicose veins. And blinder too, I could see: that inquiring look of the blind or deaf smiling unsure at you from her face.

The talk turned almost at once to Miriam, and as they answered my questions about her, I saw them go inert. Yes, she was married; had married a doctor—a flicker of pride in the old man at this. She lived in Johannesburg. Her husband was doing very well. There was a photograph of her home, in one of the more expensive suburbs; a large, white modern house, with flower borders and a fishpond. And there was Miri's little boy, sitting on his swing; and a studio portrait of him, taken with his mother.

There was the face of Miriam Saiyetovitz, confident, carefully made-up and framed in a good hairdresser's version of her dark hair, smiling queenly over the face of her child. One hand lay on the child's shoulder, a smooth hand, wearing large, plain, expensive diamond rings. Her bosom was proud and rounded now—a little too heavy, a little over-ripe in the climate of ease.

I could see in her face that she had forgotten a lot of things.

When his wife had gone into the back of the shop to refill my teacup, old Saiyetovitz went silent, looking at the hand that lay before him on the counter, the fingers twitching a little under the gaze.

It doesn't come out like you think, he said, it doesn't come out like you think.

He looked up at me with a comforting smile.

And then he told me that they had seen Miriam's little boy only three times since he was born. Miriam they saw hardly at all; her husband never. Once or twice a year she came out from Johannesburg to visit them, staying an hour on a Sunday afternoon, and then driving herself back to town again. She had not invited her parents to her home at any time; they had been there only once, on the occasion of the birth of their grandson.

Mrs. Saiyetovitz came back into the store: she seemed to know of what we had been speaking. She sat down on a shot-purple tin trunk and folded her arms over her breast. Ah yes, she breathed, ah yes . . .

I stood there in Miriam's guilt before the Saiyetovitzes, and they were silent, in the accusation of the humble.

But in a little while a Swazi[6] in a tobacco-coloured blanket sauntered dreamily into the shop, and Mr. Saiyetovitz rose heavy with defeat.

Through the eddy of dust in the lonely interior and the wavering fear round the head of the native and the bright hot dance of the jazz blankets and the dreadful submission of Mrs. Saiyetovitz's conquered voice in my ear, I heard his voice strike like a snake at my faith: angry and browbeating, sullen and final, lashing weakness at the weak.

Mr. Saiyetovitz and the native.

Defeated, and without understanding in their defeat.

━━━ ✦ ━━━

Fadwa Tuqan
b. 1917

Fadwa Tuqan is arguably the most prominent Palestinian woman poet and one of the most remarkable writers in the Arab world; she is also a self-taught intellectual who made a conscious effort to master the English language. She was born in Nablus, Palestine, in 1917 to a family from the Palestinian landed aristocracy though her maternal grandmother was of Turkish descent. She was the seventh in a family of ten, and her elder brother Ibrahim was a well-known poet. Her early childhood took place at a turbulent time for Palestine, when Ottoman rule was coming to an end and the British mandate over Palestine began. She went to primary school in Nablus, but her attendance ended abruptly when she was twelve. Her elder brother learned that she was followed by a young boy who once dared to give her a rose. The family decided that she should leave school and stay at home. From that moment on she became aware of the restrictive force of traditional morality and quickly discovered that her large, even palatial, home was a form of prison. Ibrahim felt guilty for hindering her education at a time when she started to show talent for writing poetry, and became her private tutor for structured literary readings. He also instructed her in the art of writing poetry and was the first to read her poems and guide her first steps in the world of poetry.

From a very early age she understood and loathed the hypocrisy of patriarchal double standards and satirized them in her early poems. She started publishing poetry under a pen name. The family was proud of having a son who would choose to become a poet but ashamed to have a daughter aspiring to play a role beyond the traditional one expected from a well-brought-up woman. Hence her poetry was marked from the very beginning by a strong sense of irony and social concern.

The premature death of her brother and mentor Ibrahim in 1941 at age 36 was a blow to her, both personally and in terms of her literary career. He was an outspoken nationalist and the poetic voice of the struggle to liberate Palestine from the British mandate and the Zionists' aspiration to create their Jewish home in Palestine. His death devastated her, and like the classical woman poet al-Khansa, she excelled in writing elegies for her brother, expressing her grief and shock. They were published in the leading literary journal of the Arab world at the time, *al-Risla,* when she was still in her early twenties. A few years later, death knocked on her door again when her father died in 1948, the same year as the disastrous loss of Palestine. Hardened

6. Member of a racially mixed group of people living in Swaziland.

by these catastrophic losses she gained more control over her own destiny and started to play her public role in full.

Her first collection, *My Brother Ibrahim*, appeared in 1946. This was followed by *Alone with Days* (1952), *I Found It* (1956), and *Give Us Love* (1960). The last two collections established her as a leader of the new poetic movement of the 1950s and gained her recognition in the wider Arab world. When the rest of her country fell under Israeli occupation in 1967, she devoted her poetry to resistance against the occupation and to awakening the national Palestinian consciousness. Her post-1967 collections, particularly *Before the Closed Door* (1968), *Alone on the Top of the World* (1973), and *Nightmares and Daymares* (1974), contain very provocative poems. Moshe Dayan, the late Israeli minister of defense, once said that each poem she wrote created ten Palestinian resistance fighters. While the occupation continued and its nightmares intensified, Tuqan continued to write poetry in a subversive vein but with more sophisticated and subtle structures. Her collections *Political Poems* (1980) and *Tamuz and the Other Things* (1987) contain some of her finest poems to date. In 1985 she published her autobiography, *Mountainous Journey, Hard Journey,* which received high critical acclaim and several prizes.

She had started by writing poetry more traditional in its form and themes, but with the emergence of the innovative movement of the 1950s, she changed her approach and developed a lyrical and contemplative voice that was freed from traditional prosody and employed multiple voices, creating a collective canvas in freely varied stanzas. She has written narrative and dramatic poems as well as lyrical and nationalistic odes using myth, dialogue, interior monologue, and flashbacks. With polyphony came the question of time in the poem, and she developed a multilayered patterning in which the poem deals with juxtaposed events in order to reveal a certain unity of time and the underlying essence of a strong sense of national identity.

PRONUNCIATION:

Fadwa Tuqan: FAHD-wah too-QAHN

In the Aging City[1]

City streets and pavements receive me
with other people, the human tide rushes
me on. I move in this current, but only on
the surface, remaining by myself.
5   The tide overflows to sweep
these sidewalks and streets.
Faces, faces, faces rolling on,
dry and grim, they move on the surface,
remaining without human touch.
10   Here is nearness without being near.
Here is the no-presence in presence.
Here is nothing but the presence of absence!

Traffic light reddens; the tide holds back.
Bats flash across memory:
15   *a tank passes, as I crossed in the Nablus marketplace,*
I moved out of its way.
How well I've learned not to disturb
The path of traffic! How well I've memorized
traffic laws!

---

1. Translated by Patricia Alanah Byrne and Naomi Shihab Nye.

20   *now here I am, in the London slave market*
     where they sold my parents and people . . .[2]
     Here I stand, a part of the profitable deal,
     carrying the brunt of the sin—
     Mine was that I am a plant
25   *grown by the mountains of Palestine.*
     Ah! Those who died yesterday are at rest now.
     (I suspect that their corpses cursed me
     as I gave way for a tank to pass,
     then moved on in the stream.)
30   *Aisha's letter is on my desk,*
     Nablus is quiet, life flowing on
     Like river water . . .
     The prison seal is an eloquent silence
     (A guard tells her the trees have fallen,
35   *the woods are not set ablaze anymore.*
     But Aisha insists the forest is thick,
     Trees standing like fortresses. She dreams
     of the forest she left blazing with fire
     five years ago. She heard the thunder
40   *of the wind in her dream, tells the guard:*
     "I don't believe you, you're one of them,
     and you remain the Prophets of the Lie."[3]
     Then she crouches in the darkness of prison, dreaming.
     Shaded by her standing trees she is joyous at the sound
45   *of the far forest rattling with swords of flame.*
     And Aisha dreams and dreams.)

     The traffic light clicks green, the tide drives on.
     My memory flits away, bats fall into a deep well.
     A shadow changes direction, follows me,
50   sends out a bridge.
             —Are you a stranger like I am?
     Two drops separate from the tide,
     sit removed in a corner of the park.
             —Do you like Osborne?[4]
55   —Who doesn't?
             —England's elderly and its officers
                setting with the sun of Suez . . .[5]
             —Who do you think will plant tomorrow's tree
                for this country?
60   —The hippie youth.

---

2. A reference to the Balfour Declaration, which paved the way for the establishment of the state of Israel; it is seen by the Arabs and the Palestinians as unfairly offering their country to other people.
3. A reference to the Zionists, who claimed that Palestine was a land without people for people without land.
4. John Osborne (1929–1994), the British playwright who started the movement known as "the angry young men."
5. A reference to the Suez crisis of 1956, when Britain, France, and Israel invaded Egypt and were forced by both the United States and the Soviet Union to retreat. This was a blow for England's postwar attempts to retain the remains of its empire, on which it used to be said that the sun never set.

—You are sour, very sour.
The hippic tide passes by,
sweeping the city.
London keeps beat with
65   the toll of Big Ben.
            —Around the-corner
                there's a pub and an elegant hotel
                with central heating—will you come?
            —Impossible!
70   A London lady passes, complaining to her dog
of arthritis and a pinched sciatic nerve.
            —Impossible!
            —Aren't you a modern woman?
            —I've grown beyond the days of rashness;
75   sorrow has made me a hundred years old. Impossible!
I remove his arm from my shoulders.
            —I'm besieged by loneliness.
            —We're all besieged by loneliness;
                we're all alone, play along with life alone,
80   suffer alone, and die by ourselves.
                You will remain alone here, even if a hundred
                women embrace you!
City streets and sidewalks swallow us with others,
a human tide sweeping us away in waves of faces.
85   We remain on the surface, touching nothing.

In The Flux

That evening
faces faded around us
The room was drowned in fog
Nothing lived
5   but the shining blue of your eyes
and the call in that
shining blue
where my heart
sailed, a ship
10   driven by the tide
            The tide carried
            us onto a sea
            without shores
            stretching
15   limitless current
            and flow
            waves telling the endless
            story of life
            now abridged in one glance
20   and the earth drowned in the rushing
            flood of winds and rain

That evening
my garden awoke
The fingers of the wind
25   unhinged its fences
Grasses swayed, flowers bursting,
fruits ripening
in the blissful dance of wind and rain
Faces faded, all else was a fog
30   that evening
nothing existed
but the blue shining light in your eyes
and the call in the shining blue
where my heart sailed
35   like a ship driven by the tide.

Face Lost in the Wilderness

Do not fill postcards with memories.
Between my heart and the luxury of passion
stretches a desert where ropes of fire
blaze and smolder, where snakes
5   coil and recoil, swallowing blossoms
with poison and flame.

No! Don't ask me to remember. Love's memory
is dark, the dream clouded;
love is a lost phantom
10   in a wilderness night.
Friend, the night has slain the moon.
In the mirror of my heart you can find no shelter,
only my country's disfigured face,
her face, lovely and mutilated,
15   her precious face . . .

How did the world revolve in this way?
Our love was young. Did it grow in this horror?
In the night of defeat, black waters
covered my land, blood on the walls
20   was the only bouquet.
I hallucinated: "Open your breast,
open your mother's breast for an embrace
priceless are the offerings!"
The jungle beast was toasting in the
25   tavern of crime; winds of misfortune
howled in the four corners.
He was with me that day.
I didn't realize morning
would remove him.
30   Our smiles cheated sorrow
as I raved: "Beloved stranger!

Why did my country become a gateway
to hell? Since when are apples bitter?
When did moonlight stop bathing orchards?
35   My people used to plant fields and love life
Joyfully they dipped their bread in oil
Fruits and flowers tinted the land
with magnificent hues—
will the seasons ever again
40   give their gifts to my people?"
Sorrow—Jerusalem's night is silence and smoke.
They imposed a curfew; now nothing beats in the
heart of the City but their bloodied heels
under which Jerusalem trembles
45   like a raped girl.[1]
Two shadows from a balcony
stared down at the City's night.
In the corner a suitcase of clothes,
souvenirs from the Holy Land—
50   his blue eyes stretched like sad lakes.
He loved Jerusalem. She was his mystical lover.
On and on I ranted, "Ah, love! Why did God abandon
my country? Imprisoning light, leaving us
in seas of darkness?"
55   The world was a mythical dragon standing
at her gate. "Who will ever solve this mystery,
beloved, the secret of these words?"

Now twenty moons have passed,
twenty moons, and my life continues.
60   Your absence too continues. Only one memory remaining:
The face of my stricken country filling my heart.

And my life continues—
the wind merges me with my people
on the terrible road of rocks and thorns.
65   But behind the river, dark forests of spears
sway and swell; the roaring storm
unravels mystery; giving to dragon-silence
the power of words.
A rush and din, flame and sparks
70   lighting the road—
one group after another
falls embracing, in one lofty death.[2]
The night, no matter how long, will continue
to give birth to star after star

---

1. The last three lines of this verse refer to the military occupation of the old Arab city of Jerusalem.

2. A reference to many Palestinians killed by the military
forces of the Israeli occupation of the Palestinian land
since 1967.

75   and my life continues,
          my life continues.

Mahmoud Darwish
b. 1941

Mahmoud Darwish is arguably the most important Arab poet writing today. He has succeeded in achieving wide popularity throughout the Arab world while showing constant concern for innovation and poetic experimentation in language and form. From the early years of his poetic career, Darwish was destined to devote his poetic talent to the cause of Palestine. Indeed, Darwish's childhood in an Israeli-controlled area of Palestine enhanced his sense of being an Arab and a Palestinian despite his Hebrew-language education. He was born in the village of al-Birwa in Palestine in 1941 and educated in his village's primary school and then in Nazareth Secondary School. He was seven when the state of Israel was created and his village was completely destroyed. His father, a wealthy farmer and landowner, was dispossessed and forced to work as a laborer in a quarry to sustain his family of eight children. In 1961 when his village became part of the newly created Israel and, like most Palestinians, he lost his civil rights, he joined the Rakah Israeli Communist Party, the only Israeli political party that accepted Arabs at the time. He worked for the Arabic newspaper of the party and its literary journal, where he published his early poems.

Darwish's first poem, which he read at his school's annual party when he was only fourteen, put him in direct confrontation with Israeli military rule. It was a heartfelt cry from an Arab child to his Jewish peer at school about the simple things denied to an Arab boy and allowed to his Jewish counterpart. The following day, he was summoned to the office of the military ruler of the area and threatened that if he persisted in writing poetry, his father would be prevented from working at the local quarry. At the age of nineteen, he published his first collection of poetry, *Sparrows without Wings* (1960). The following year he was arrested for writing poetry and given his first taste of Israeli prison.

The conflict between the poet and his jailers continued. In 1965 he published his second collection, *Olive Branches,* and was arrested for the second time. In 1966 he published his third collection, *A Lover from Palestine,* and was imprisoned once again. In 1967 he published his fourth collection, *The End of Night,* and was jailed for yet a fourth time. His life became a series of poems and cells, and when he was out of prison his freedom of movement and expression were curtailed, and he was subjected to long periods of house arrest. In his *Diaries of Ordinary Grief* (1973), he talks about life under house arrest as a pattern in which he has his days and "they" have control over his nights, for he wasn't allowed to leave his house between sunset and sunrise. The more the Israeli authorities feared his words, the more he became aware of the power of poetry and of the importance of the Arabic language as an expression of his identity.

In 1970 the pattern of poems and prison was broken when he published his collection *Sparrows Die in Galilee* and left immediately for Moscow to complete his education, which was denied him in Israel. Having completed his one-year course in Moscow, he dreaded going back to the old pattern of poetry and prison and decided to join other Palestinians who left their homeland. In 1971 he moved to Egypt and a year later to Beirut, where he stayed until the Israeli invasion of Lebanon in 1982. In his words, he "joined Ulysses in his search for Ithaca," and developed his poetry as the voice of the Palestinian consciousness on the one hand and as the expression of the aspirations of the oppressed on the other. In his *Diaries,* he states, "He who turned me into a refugee changed me into a bomb," and he has continued to explode in strong poetry ever since. Since 1971 he has published twenty more collections of poetry and two prose works, *Something about Home* (1971) and *A Memory for Oblivion* (1986).

Darwish's rich output of poetry can be divided into three different phases. In the Israeli phase (1960–1971), his poetry is marked by its lyrical iconography of simple Palestinian objects redolent with significance and symbolism. The Beirut phase (1972–1982) witnessed the cynical maturity of the poet and the dissipation of the simple optimism of revolutionary innocence, for this is the phase of inter-Arab conflicts, with more Palestinians being killed by Arabs than by Israelis. Like Eliot's "Unreal city" of *The Waste Land,* Darwish's Beirut amalgamates the spirit of the Arab city and the ethos of hell and is entangled in mythological and intertextual allusions. The third, post-Beirut phase (since 1982) oscillates between long dramatic poems and tense short ones in which he invokes the biblical lyric of lament and turns it against itself so that it ceases to sound euphonious and lyrical. The psalmlike poems depict an abandoned people in Babylonian exile and captivity, and pierce like shrapnel. His long poems, with their epic quality, crystallize the sense of physical dislocation, political chaos, and failure of Arab politics, especially since the Israeli invasion of Lebanon in 1982 and the ongoing, unresolved uprisings that have followed. These poems renew some fundamental aspects of literary modernism's pervasive negativity and pessimism; toward the end of this phase, the poet becomes increasingly aware of the apathy of his reader in a world of endless conflict.

The poems selected here are from the last two phases. The Resonance that accompanies them shows the contemporary Kashmiri-American poet Agha Shahid Ali responding to Darwish and building on his themes of art and exile.

PRONUNCIATION:
   Mahmoud Darwish: mah-MOOD dahr-WEESH

A Poem Which Is Not Green, from My Country[1]

In my country
where Sinbad's sail never swayed in the wind
dreamingly bearing its basket of *jihad°* yarns   *holy war*
& tales of the heroes
5   & of that sun beyond the gorges
where it wandered through no single night of the nights of Scheherazade
where no dawn broke over it
          nor stretched to it white bountiful hands . . .
In my country
10   are the graveyards of light & of luminous flowers,
the well-spring of grief.
The colours of our letter are persecuted.
Trussed it cries out.
They stifled it.
15   They squeezed its spark from it.
They robbed it of the borders of kindness.
They crushed it till it began to burn
& then burst.
Our letter became a wound where dusk is swimming.
20   In silence it is breaking into bud the flowers & bunches of basil!

---

1. Translated by Ian Wedde and Fawwaz Tuqan.

& in my country appointments with dawn are calling out
to the swallows lost behind the horizons of my country
where they cast off neglected their poems
    when the long night of lovers' separation lost them.
25   The swallow may be silent but never forgets its song.
      It will sing it will cry out
when my country's olive trees blossom
when the sky's rains wash away
the spots of consumption the thorns of fate!
30   In my country
they opened the wound & then said: It must be sutured!
They silenced it anaesthetized it
wrapped it with fog
taught it silence & the early autumn of torture.
35   & it was awakened by silence & said:
In my country: in the country of mankind: in every country
the wound grows silent but never heals.
The wound believed in its future.
    Is there anything without future?
40   Where the wound is watered by the blood of songs
in gardens where the colour of life is dry
& the larks sing
& the swallows which returned sing
having come back to life . . .

Diary of a Palestinian Wound[1]
Rubaiyat° for Fadwa Tuqan   *quatrains*

1

We're free not to remember because Carmel's within us
& on our eyelashes grows the grass of the Province of Galilee.[2]
Don't say: I wish we were running to it like the river /
don't say this.
5   We exist in the flesh of our country & it in us.

2

Before June we weren't like little doves
which is why our love wasn't crushed among the chains.
O Sister we've *existed* for twenty years.
We haven't been writing poetry but struggling.

3

10   That shadow cast in your eyes
is a devil / a god:
it came with the month of June to bandage
foreheads with the sun /
it's the colour of a martyr

---

1. Translated by Ian Wedde and Fawwaz Tuqan.   2. Carmel and Galilee are famously beautiful areas now under Israeli control.

10   it's the taste of a prayer.
It can kill or resurrect
    & in either case: ah!

                4

Night falling in your eyes
was a drop of the long night's end in my heart
20   & what gathers us at this hour in this place
is the way back from an age of wilting.

                5

Your voice tonight's a knife & a wound & a bandage
& torpor which crept from the victims' silence /
Where are my people? They quit the tent of exile & returned
25   yet again as captives.

                6

Love-words didn't rust but the beloved
collapses into captivity /   O Beloved you loaded me
with balconies torn loose by wind / porches of houses & guilts.
Once my heart could hold nothing but your eyes
30   & now it's enriched with the homeland.

                7

& we knew what makes the lark's voice
a dagger flashing in the invader's face
& we knew what makes the silence of the cemetery
a festival & gardens of life!

                8

35   While you sang I saw balconies
migrating from the walls & the square /
    falling back to the mountain's waist.
We weren't listening to music nor peering at the colours of words.
There were a million heroes in the room.

                9

40   Because of his face
    a summer & an unnatural pulse have broken into my blood.
I came home abashed /
    the house collapsed upon a martyr's gash.
It was the Christmas manger
45   it was hope
& I was gleaning a festival from the memory of it.

                10

His eyes were dew & fire
    & if I drew near his face it sang
& I evaporated on its arm: a moment of silence & a prayer.
50   Oh call it "a martyr" if you wish.
It's more beautiful than we are.
It left its hovel a youth then returned in its own time
the face of a god!

                11

This land which sucks the skin of martyrs
55   promises wheat & stars to the Summer

so worship it: we are salt & water in its bowels
& in its embrace a wound which is fighting!

12

I was created tearful O Sister & now fire's in my eye
& I shook myself loose of complaints at the Caliph's door.
60   All those who died & those who will die at the day's gate
embraced me   made a bomb of me.

13

The loved ones' house is deserted & Jaffa[3]
has been translated to its very marrow
& whoever was searching for me
65   found nothing but its forehead!
Leave all this death to me O Sister
        leave this vagrancy.
Look! I'm braiding it into a star above its catastrophe.

14

O brave-faced wound
70   my homeland isn't a suitcase
& I'm not a traveller.
I am the lover & the land is the beloved.

15

If I lingered over memories there would grow
on my forehead the grass of regret
75   & I'd grieve for something distant
& if I surrendered to desire
I'd adopt the legends of slaves
but I prefer to make a pebble of my voice
& a melody of the rock.

16

80   My forehead doesn't carry the shadow
        & I can't see my own
& I spit in the wound which fails
to set fire to the night with foreheads.
Save your tears for the festival: we'll cry
85   from nothing but joy.
Come   let's call sudden death in the square
a wedding & a life!

17

& I was reared on the wound & never told my mother
what makes her a tent in the night.
90   I preserved my well-spring & my address & my name
& so observed a million stars in her names.

18

My banner is black & the harbour is a coffin & my back is a bridge.
O Autumn of the age crumbling within us

3. Palestinian city absorbed into the new Israeli city of Tel Aviv.

O Spring of the world reborn within us
95 my rose is red & the harbour is open & my heart is a tree.
                                19
My language is the sound of rippling water in the river of storms.
The sun's & the grain's mirrors are in a battlefield.
No doubt my verse was sometimes askew
but (why deny it?) I was terrific
100 when I traded the dictionary for my heart!
                                20
There had to be enemies for us to find we were twins.
There had to be wind for us to live in the trunks of oaks.
& if the crucified lord hadn't come of age on the throne of the cross
he'd have remained a child whose wound was forfeit: a coward.
                                21
105 I have a word for you /
I haven't said it yet
        because the shadow on the balcony occupies the moon.
My country's an epic /
I was a musician in that epic
110   & I've become a chord!
                                22
The archaeologist's busy analysing stones.
He's looking for his eyes in the rubble of legends
to prove I'm a transient on the road /
lacking eyes & language in civilization's book!
115 Meanwhile I slowly plant my trees & sing about my love.
                                23
The summer cloud which is carried on the back of defeat
pegged out the offspring of Sultans on the lines of mirages.
I am dead & newborn in the night of the crime.
See! see how I cleave to the soil!
                                24
120 It's time for me to trade word for deed.
It's time for me to prove my love to earth & lark
because in this age bludgeon devours guitar
& the mirror shows me diminished
since there came this tree in my eye.

Sirhan Drinks His Coffee in the Cafeteria[1]

They arrive.
Our doors are the sea.
The rain surprised us.
No God but God.
5 The rain surprised us, and the bullets.
The earth here is a carpet,
And they continue to arrive.

---

1. Translated by Rana Kabbani.

You do not know the day.
You cannot tell the colour,
10   Nor the taste. Nor the voice.
You do not know the shape.
Sirhan is born, and Sirhan grows.
He drinks the wine and raves,
He draws his killer and he tears the picture,
15   He kills him when he sees his final shape.

Sirhan writes upon his jacket's sleeve
And memory takes a bird's beak
And eats the wheat of Galilee.

What was love?
20   Hands that were expressive,
Chains and prisons being formed,
Exiles being born.
We wrap around your name.
We were a people now we are of stone.
25   You were a country now you are of smoke.
Old chains are bracelets of blown roses
Old chains are maidenhead and passion
In this new exile.

Sirhan lies when he says he drank your milk.
30   Sirhan grew up in the kitchens of a ship
Which never touched your shores.

What is your name?
I've forgotten.
What is your father's name?
35   I've forgotten.
And your mother's?
I've forgotten.
Did you sleep last night?
I slept for an eternity.
40   Did you dream?
I dreamt.
He cried suddenly:
Why did you drink the oil you smuggled
From the wounds of Christ?

45   We saw his fingers begging.
We saw him measuring the sky with chains.
Lands that change their people,
Stars that spread like pebbles.
He sang:
50   Our generation passed and died.
The killers bred in us the victims grew in us
Blood like water.
Mothers who married enemies.

We called out, "wheat!"
55   The echo came back "war"
We called out, "home!"
The echo came back "war"
We called out, "Jaffa!"
The echo came back "war"
60   From that day on we measured skies with chains.

Sirhan laughs in the kitchens of the ship.
He holds a tourist and is lost.
All lands are far that lead to Nazareth.
All lands are far except for Nazareth.

65   Songs speak to him, and holidays make him lonely.
The smell of coffee is geography.
They exiled you.
They murdered you.
Your father hid behind the texts
70   And watched them come.
The smell of coffee is a tender hand.
The smell of coffee is a voice that takes you.
The smell of coffee is a sound that gurgles
Like the water in the alleys when it rains.

75   Sirhan knows more than one language
Or one woman. He has a pass to leave the ocean
He has another pass to enter it.
He is a drop of blood looking for its wound.
The smell of coffee is geography.
80   He drinks his coffee and he dreams.

You were born here. Yet you live there.
Your city does not sleep. It has no lasting names.
Houses change inhabitants,
Windows leave their places as they enter memory.
85   Sirhan draws a shape then cancels it.
He does not read the papers, so how does sorrow
Reach him?

What is Jerusalem but a stance for speeches,
But a step to hungry power?
90   What is Jerusalem but cigarettes and liquor?
Yet it is my country.
You would not find a difference
Between its curved fields
And my palm.
95   You could not find the difference
Between the night that sleeps in memory
And the night upon the Carmel.

He tears the clouds apart
And throws them at the winds.

100   I ate. I drank. I slept. I dreamt.
        I learnt a vowel.
        He writes: ص ط ض ظ ع ط
        And they disappear before him,
        The dins of oceans in them,
105   The din of silence in them.
        Letters to distinguish us from others.
        We stone them with our diphthongs.
        Shall we fight?
        What matter,
110   Since the Arab revolution
        Remains preserved in anthems,
        In flags and at the bank.
        In your wounds' name they speak their speech.
        Christ becomes a dealer
115   Who signs away his merchandise of cloth.
        No sky for you except this tent:
        It burns, you burn.

        We come to you as prisoners or corpses.
        Sirhan a prisoner of the peace and war.
120   He reads the details of his fate
        On the wall behind the stripper's legs:
        Your war is two wars,
        Your war is two wars.

        Sirhan!
125   Did you kill?
        Sirhan is silent.
        He drinks his coffee and he dreams.
        He draws a map without a border in it.
        He measures earth with chains.
130   He draws a picture of his killer,
        He rips it up,
        Then kills it when it takes a final shape.

Birds Die in Galilee[1]

        We will meet in a while,
        In a year,
        In two years,
        In sixteen.
5   She threw into her camera
        Twenty gardens
        And the birds of Galilee.

        She could not know that we gave her,
        Death and I, the secrets of love

1. Translated by Rana Kabbani.

10 At the custom's gate.
So she must leave what makes wheat
The lashes of the earth,
What makes volcanoes
Another name for jasmine.

15 Nothing tired me at night
Except her silence
When it spread out like a street.
Be what you must, Rita,
Make the silence an axe
20 Or a frame for stars
Or a place for a tree in labour.

Flocks of birds fell like paper
Into the wells
And when I lifted the blue wings
25 I saw a growing grave.
I am the man on whose skin
Chains have carved a country.

RESONANCE

Agha Shahid Ali: Ghazal[1]

Where should we go after the last frontiers,
where should the birds fly after the last sky?

—MAHMOUD DARWISH

In Jerusalem a dead phone's dialed by exiles.
You learn your strange fate: You were exiled by exiles.

One opens the heart to list unborn galaxies.
Don't shut that folder when Earth is filed by exiles.

5 Before Night passes over the wheat of Egypt,
let stones be leavened, the bread torn wild by exiles.

Crucified Mansoor[2] was alone with the Alone:
God's loneliness—Just His—compiled by exiles.

By the Hudson lies Kashmir, brought from Palestine—
10 It shawls the piano, Bach beguiled by exiles.

1. A *ghazal* is a traditional Urdu or Persian love poem, in couplets with a recurring rhyme at the end of each couplet. The greatest modern practitioner of the ghazal form in English has been Agha Shahid Ali. Born in New Delhi in 1949, Ali was raised a Muslim in the northern Indian region of Kashmir, site of prolonged, ongoing conflicts between Hindu nationalists and Muslim separatists. After completing college in India, he emigrated to the United States, where he earned a Ph.D. and an M.F.A. in the 1980s. Before his death in 2001 he directed several creative writing programs and published seven volumes of poetry. Ali wrote many *ghazals* in English, using the classical form to reflect on contemporary romantic, social, and political conflicts, as in this poem, which moves from Darwish to consider a wide range of social and political exiles. 2. Mansoor al-Hallaj, the great Muslim mystic martyr who was crucified in Baghdad for saying "I am the Truth" [Ali's note].

Tell me who's tonight the Physician of Sick Pearls?
Only you as you sit, Desert child, by exiles.

Match Majnoon[3] (he kneels to pray on a wine-stained rug)
or prayer will be nothing, distempered mild by exiles.

15 "Even things that are true can be proved." Even they?
Swear not by Art but, dear Oscar Wilde, by exiles.[4]

Don't weep, we'll drown out the Call to Prayer, O Saqi[5]—
I'll raise my glass before wine is defiled by exiles.

Was—after the last sky—this the fashion of fire:
20 Autumn's mist pressed to ashes styled by exiles?

If my enemy's alone and his arms are empty,
give him my heart silk-wrapped like a child by exiles.

Will you, Belovéd Stranger,[6] ever witness Shahid—
two destinies at last reconciled by exiles?

Faiz Ahmad Faiz
1911–1984

Faiz Ahmad Faiz is the best-known poet to emerge from Pakistan since Muhammad Iqbal (1873–1938), the national poet of Pakistan. Although Faiz's first language was Punjabi, he gained fame with his poems written in Urdu. He combines in his poetry the themes of love and beauty within the political ideals of a vision of a better world. He is credited with revolutionizing traditionally romantic Urdu poetry, infusing it with a new spirit, fresh imagery, and symbolic power. When he speaks of the beloved in his poetry, she transcends the traditional woman who is the object of adoration and extends her significance to that of muse, the country, and often the very idea of revolution.

Faiz was born in Sialkot in Punjab, then a part of India under British rule. His family was well-to-do landowners, and his father was a prominent lawyer who was interested in literature and who counted among his friends several important literary figures including Muhammad Iqbal. This provided the young Faiz with a vibrant literary environment in which he spent his formative years. He started his education via the traditional route of memorizing the Qur'an at the age of four, and then learned Urdu, Persian, and Arabic. He completed his secondary education in English at the Mission School in Sialkot and went on to Government College, Lahore, to study Arabic. After obtaining master's degrees in both Arabic and English, he worked as a teacher of English in Amritsar and then in Lahore until 1942.

---

3. Literally "possessed" or "mad" because he sacrificed everything for love [Ali's note].
4. A line from Oscar Wilde's controversial preface to his 1891 novel *The Picture of Dorian Gray* in which Wilde claimed that art has no moral value beyond its own perfection. Following his trial on sodomy charges—where he was pilloried as an amoral aesthete—Wilde was sen-tenced to two years of hard labor, then went into exile in France.
5. One who pours wine [Ali's note].
6. Either God or the poet's beloved; as in the *ghazals* of the 19th-century poet Ghalib (see Volume E), whom Ali greatly admired, it may be either or both.

It was at this point that he fell under the influence of the leftist Progressive Movement and started writing poetry. During World War II, Faiz served in the Indian army in Delhi, but after the partition of India and the creation of the Islamic republic of Pakistan in 1947, he left the Indian army and moved to Pakistan with his family. In 1948 Faiz became editor of the leftist English-language daily, the Pakistani *Times*. He also worked as managing editor of the Urdu daily *Imroz* and was actively involved in organizing trade unions. His radical politics and opposition to the government and military dictators led to his imprisonment from 1951 to 1955. Later he was forced to go into exile at different times in his career. In 1959 the very government that had imprisoned him appointed him Secretary to the Pakistan Arts Council, a position he held until 1963 when he was awarded the Lenin Peace Prize by the Soviet Union. He then spent a year in London. On his return, he settled down in Karachi, where he was appointed Principal of Abdullah Haroon College. In the 1965 war between India and Pakistan, he worked in the Department of Information, but after the war he was forced into exile again, which he spent in Lebanon, Moscow, and London. He returned to Pakistan in the late 1970s and died in Lahore in 1984.

Faiz first became well known for volumes of poetry published in the early 1950s based on his prison experiences. His description of his life behind prison walls has an introspective tone and vivid imagery that radically changed the nature of Urdu poetry. His poem "Solitary Confinement," included here, is a good example of the poetry of this period. His political poems have been translated into English under the appropriate title *The Rebel's Silhouette*. In these poems and in later love poems, Faiz fused classic traditional forms of Urdu poetry with new symbols, imagery, and visions derived from Western literature and political and philosophical ideas.

PRONUNCIATION:
Faiz Ahmad Faiz: fah-YEASE AH-mahd fah-YEASE

Blockout[1]
India-Pakistan War: 1965

Since our lights were extinguished
I have been searching for a way to see;
my eyes are lost, God knows where.

You who know me, tell me who I am,
5   who is a friend, and who an enemy.
A murderous river has been unleashed[2]
into my veins; hatred beats in it.

Be patient; a flash of lightning will come
from another horizon like the white hand
10 of Moses with my eyes, my lost diamonds.

Only wait a while; the river will find its shores.
My new heart, purified in the acid-bath of poison,
will sail into a harbor.

---

1. Translated by Naomi Lazard.

2. A reference to the senseless war in which Indians were fighting Indians.

On that day, my dear one,
15 I will take up my work again, the songs to beauty,
     my epistles of love.

No Sign of Blood

Nowhere, nowhere is there any trace of blood.
Neither on the hands of the assassin,
                    nor under his fingernails,
not a spot on his sleeve, no stain on the walls.
5 No red on the tip of his dagger,
no dye on the point of his bayonet.
There is no sign of blood anywhere.
This invisible blood was not given in the service of kings
for a reward of bounty, nor as a religious sacrifice
10   to obtain absolution.
It was not spilled on any battlefield for the sake of honor,
celebrated later in script on some banner.
The orphaned blood of murdered parents screamed out
                    for justice;
15 no one had time or patience to listen to its cries.
There was no plaintiff, no witness;
                    therefore no indictment.
It was the blood of those whose homes are made of dust,
blood that in the end became the nourishment for dust.

Solitary Confinement

On the distant horizon a wave of light
begins to play; in my sleep I live
in the city of loss. My eyelids
flutter in their restless dream
5 as morning moves forward
over the loneliness, the country without borders.

A wave of light is dancing
over that distant horizon.
The merest refrain, the ghost of perfume,
10 the beloved face glimpsed for a moment,
torment me with hope, the final disturbance.
They arrive and leave,
travelers who have no time to stay.

I fill the cup of my heart
15 with my morning's drink, today's gall
mixed with yesterday's bitterness.
I make a toast to my friends everywhere,
here in my homeland and across the world:

"Let us drink, my dear ones, to human beauty,
20 to the loveliness of earth."

Reza Baraheni
b. 1935

One of the finest living Iranian poets, Reza Baraheni is the author of more than fifty books—novels, short stories, and criticism, in addition to poetry. Born in Tabriz, Iran, to an Azerbaijani Turkish family, Baraheni earned his doctorate in literary studies from the University of Istanbul, Turkey, in 1963. He was appointed to a professorship at Teheran University, where he served for a number of years until his outspoken views on human rights and the rights of diverse nationalities in Iran led to his repeated imprisonment. Many of his writings grow out of his commitment to human rights and social justice and his direct experiences in that struggle, including the poems in his book *God's Shadow: Prison Poems,* based on his 102 days of solitary confinement and torture under the regime of the Shah in 1973.

He lived in exile thereafter until the Islamic Revolution and the Shah's overthrow in 1979. Baraheni then returned to Iran but continued to campaign on behalf of human rights and to press the right of writers and intellectuals to criticize their own government. These activities led the Ayatollah Khomeini's government in turn to expel him from the University of Teheran in 1982 and to revoke his right to publish his work. This didn't stop him, though, from becoming a coauthor in 1994 of the "Declaration of 134 Iranian Writers," which called on the Iranian government to end censorship and respect intellectual freedom. Following an attempt on his life in 1996, he was able to escape into exile once again.

Like much of his work, the poems included here are based on his prison experience. They document the intricate dimension of political engagement and individual tragedies that ensue when religious belief becomes officialized as government policy and when human beings disappear, or are made to disappear into causes larger than their daily struggles for survival. As a poet of social protest and genuine commitment, Baraheni is heavily invested in human solidarity and the capacity of individuals to overcome their transformation into instruments and victims of the state or official dogma. His poetry tells a cautionary tale of what happens to cultures and people's humanity when overarching concerns of the state and its internal security apparatuses override the predicaments of individuals and the ambiguities of human interconnections.

The Unrecognized

how soon our friends desert us
our intimates are shot
our truest friends get prison for life
our best friends are incarcerated for years and months
5   and the barest acquaintances
    are those
      who pretend they don't know
        the man who's just been released

we have taken an oath
10   to live without recognition
and be as distant from each other as the stars

the man who is coming toward me
    has a face familiar as the sun
once he held his soup bowl to my lips
15   why shouldn't I kiss him?
once the man who just went past

cringed by me under the blows
    of Hosseini's mace
        why shouldn't I shake his hand?

20   and once the girl who just walked away
        raised her scream beyond prison walls
           she had been raped
                why shouldn't I kiss her hand?

how soon our friends desert us
25   our intimates are shot
our truest friends get prison for life
our best friends are incarcerated for years and months
and the barest acquaintances
    are those
30   who pretend they don't know
           the man who's just been released

we have taken an oath
    to live without recognition
and be as distant with each other as the stars

Answers to an Interrogation

mother's face resembles a Tibetan miniature
found in Tashkent[1]
and sold in Chicago

father, who, having bequeathed his soul
5   to us, is dead and gone,
resembled a Georgian[2] Moslem
who might have traveled the Mediterranean, a pilgrim to Mecca[3]

if you don't believe me
he's resting in the Vadiyosslam of Qum[4]
10   dig him out
and read the lines on his face
—that is, if you can read hieroglyphs—
and if you can distinguish hieroglyphs from cancer

once my older brother worked in a factory
15   then he had to wear glasses
he looked like a little James Joyce sneaking out of Ireland
his wife wanted to kill him
after twenty years locked in battle
he was at last separated from his old sow[5]
20   who was not unlike you distinguished men of the SAVAK[6]
with this slight difference—she wanted to tear out his testicles with her teeth

1. Capital city of the Republic of Uzbekistan.
2. From the Georgian Republic in the Caucasus.
3. Saudi Arabian city of pilgrimage for all devout Muslims.
4. Sacred city in west-central Iran.

5. Irish novelist James Joyce's hero Stephen Dedalus described Ireland as "a sow that eats her farrow."
6. The secret police of the Shah of Iran.

sometimes sister tries to act Florence Nightingale[7]
at other times, Che Guevara's[8] sister
—if Che has a sister—
25   with this difference, her brother's body has not been stretched on a platform
        by a colonel yet
but, believe me, her weeping is most sincere

if you want to know something about my younger brother
I should say that he is leftist in two ways
first, he is left-handed
30   and second, his left testicle hangs lower than his right
he has contracted mumps twice measles thrice scarlet fever four times
        chicken pox five
and gonorrhea two thousand five hundred times
once for every glorious year of the history of Iran's
        King of Kings°   *the Shah*

of the character of my wife let it suffice to say
35   that she only lies to you
for the present, my daughter has an absent face
and my son—if, of course, he is born a son—
in the very first decade of his life, God willing,
will witness the fall of this magnificent kingdom of yours
40   and he will not even put you in prison
because you will be dead by suicide
or your friends will have put you out of your misery
—or God knows to what dark hell you will have run away

other than these, I have no family
45   What is the next question, please?

Farough Faroghzad
1935–1967

Farough Faroghzad was born in Teheran to a middle-class family. Her formal education ended with the ninth grade, after which she was sent to a technical school to study sewing and painting. She married at age seventeen and thereafter was expected to devote her life to the home and to her family. But Faroghzad was as unconventional socially as her poetry is revolutionary in the Persian tradition. Divorcing her husband two years after her marriage and relinquishing custody of their son, to whom the poem included here is addressed, she devoted herself to a life of art, literature, and filmmaking. Her 1962 film about a leper colony, *The House Is Black,* was internationally acclaimed and won a number of prizes. Her poetic use of colloquial language, the unveiled treatment of women's plight in Iranian society, and the autobiographical candor of her writing initiated a new era for men and women in Iranian culture. Considered a feminist

---

7. Considered the founder of modern nursing, Nightingale was became famous for her nursing service during the Crimean War (1853–1856).

8. Argentine revolutionary who fought with Fidel Castro to establish the Cuban Revolution. He served in Castro's government and was killed in an armed struggle in Bolivia in 1967.

poet, she wore that mantle proudly, but she progressively assumed a woman's poetic voice that dealt with many issues facing both women and men in modern society. Her most significant books of poetry (*The Captive, The Wall,* and *Rebellion*) were written in the mid-1950s. Iran's most famous woman writer, she is considered the country's founder of feminist literature. At the time of her premature death in an automobile accident, her poems and films were already recognized as a political force in a country undergoing profound social and cultural changes.

PRONUNCIATION:
   Farough Faroghzad: fah-ROUKH fah-rokh-ZAHD

A Poem for You[1]

TO MY SON KÁMYÁR, IN HOPE OF THE FUTURE

This poem I write for you
in a parching summer's sunset
I've gone half this path so ill-begun
in this old grave of sorrow I can't forget

5   This is my lullaby's last phrase
at your sleeping cradle's foot
May the wild call of this outcry
echo in the skies of your youth

May my wandering shadow
10   be kept from your shadow far away
And should someone come to stand one day
between us, let it be God alone, I pray

I lean my pain-wracked forehead
against a dark door
15   I press my cold, weak fingers
with hope at this open door

It was I who laughed at futile slurs,
the one that was branded by shame
I shall be what I'm called to be, I said
20   But oh, the misery that "woman" is my name

When your innocent eyes peruse
this tangled book with no beginning,
at the heart of every song you'll see
the deeprooted revolt of ages blossoming

25   There are no stars shining here
The angels here are weeping, every one
Here the flower of the amaryllis
is worth less than the desert thorn

Demons of lying, shame, and sheer bad faith
30   squat in all the crossroads here

1. Translated by Jascha Kessler.

I see in these dark skies no light
of awakening's bright morning sphere

May my eyes well up
with drops of dew once more
35 I shall tear my veil away
from Mary's virgin face so pure!

I've abandoned the shore of a spotless name
In my breast there's the star of the storm—
the gloomy space of my cell, alas,
40 where my anger burns in its whirling room

I lean my pain-wracked forehead
against a dark door
I press my cold, weak fingers
with hope at this open door

45 I know it will not be an easy fight
with this gaggle of pious hypocrites
O my sweet little child, how long it's lain sunk,
my city and yours, in one of Satan's pits

That day shall come when your longing eyes
50 will read this song of my pain over and over
You will look for me here in my words
and say to yourself, *She* was my mother

+ ≍♦≍ +

Derek Walcott
b. 1930

Born and raised on the Caribbean island of Saint Lucia, a British colony until 1967, Derek Walcott has both experienced and written about the often-troubled transition from colonial to post-colonial conditions. Imperial colonial trade in human labor had brought some of his ancestors to the island: Both of his grandmothers were descended from slaves. Walcott's heritage, like that of many, was mixed: His father, Warwick Walcott, was of English descent on his father's side, and Walcott has written of the irony that his father should have been named after War-wickshire, Shakespeare's home county.

Walcott's education in colonial Saint Lucia was thoroughly British. "The writers of my generation were natural assimilators," Walcott has written in his introduction to *Dream on Monkey Mountain and Other Plays.* "We knew the literatures of Empires, Greek, Roman, British, through their essential classics; and both the patois of the street and the language of the classroom had the elation of discovery." Walcott won a British government scholarship to a college in Jamaica, where he earned a degree in English in 1953. After several years as a school-teacher, he won a fellowship to study theater in New York, then moved to Trinidad and founded the Little Carib Theater Workshop. From that time on, he has written plays fusing Caribbean and European elements while also developing skills as a watercolorist and an extra-ordinary lyric and narrative poet. He has continued to cross physical borders over the years, di-viding his time between his home in Trinidad and a teaching post at Boston University.

Walcott's poems create a landscape of historical and personal memory, overlaying em-pires, centuries, continents, and stages of his own life, most notably in his 1990 verse novel

Omeros, which rewrites Homer's epics—and James Joyce's *Ulysses*—as a Caribbean story of imperial and romantic conflict and a multiple search for the past. (A selection from *Omeros* appears in Volume A as a Resonance for Homer's *Odyssey.*) He was awarded the Nobel Prize in literature two years after its publication. The first two poems given here illustrate two major sides of Walcott's response to colonial and postcolonial conditions. His important early poem "A Far Cry from Africa" (1962) expresses the divisions of history and self that arise from so mixed a heritage, while in "Volcano" (1976) he pays affectionate, ironic homage to his modernist predecessors Conrad and Joyce—artistic exiles both and prime models for the transmutation of colonial experience into lasting art. These poems are followed by "The Fortunate Traveller," a harrowing account of postcolonial border-crossing, self-seeking charity work, and moral corruption.

A Far Cry from Africa

A wind is ruffling the tawny pelt
Of Africa. Kikuyu,[1] quick as flies,
Batten° upon the bloodstreams of the veldt.°   fasten / open country
Corpses are scattered through a paradise.
5   Only the worm, colonel of carrion, cries:
"Waste no compassion on these separate dead!"
Statistics justify and scholars seize
The salients of colonial policy.
What is that to the white child hacked in bed?
10 To savages, expendable as Jews?

Threshed out by beaters, the long rushes break
In a white dust of ibises[2] whose cries
Have wheeled since civilization's dawn
From the parched river or beast-teeming plain.
15 The violence of beast on beast is read
As natural law, but upright man
Seeks his divinity by inflicting pain.
Delirious as these worried beasts, his wars
Dance to the tightened carcass of a drum,
20 While he calls courage still that native dread
Of the white peace contracted by the dead.

Again brutish necessity wipes its hands
Upon the napkin of a dirty cause, again
A waste of our compassion, as with Spain,[3]
25 The gorilla wrestles with the superman.
I who am poisoned with the blood of both,
Where shall I turn, divided to the vein?
I who have cursed
The drunken officer of British rule, how choose
30 Between this Africa and the English tongue I love?
Betray them both, or give back what they give?

---

1. Indigenous people of Kenya.
2. Wading birds resembling storks.
3. In 1936–1939, many in the international community supported the constitutional government of Spain against

a coup led by fascist General Francisco Franco. Franco's forces won, and he ruled as a dictator until his death in 1975.

How can I face such slaughter and be cool?
How can I turn from Africa and live?

Volcano

Joyce was afraid of thunder,
but lions roared at his funeral
from the Zurich zoo.
Was it Zurich or Trieste?[1]
5   No matter. These are legends, as much
As the death of Joyce is a legend,
or the strong rumor that Conrad
is dead, and that *Victory* is ironic.[2]
On the edge of the night-horizon
10   from this beach house on the cliffs
there are now, till dawn,
two glares from the miles-out-
at-sea derricks; they are like
the glow of the cigar
15   and the glow of the volcano
at *Victory*'s end.
One could abandon writing
for the slow-burning signals
of the great, to be, instead,
20   their ideal reader, ruminative,
voracious, making the love of masterpieces
superior to attempting
to repeat or outdo them,
and be the greatest reader in the world.
25   At least it requires awe,
which has been lost to our time;
so many people have seen everything,
so many people can predict,
so many refuse to enter the silence
30   of victory, the indolence
that burns at the core,
so many are no more than
erect ash, like the cigar,
so many take thunder for granted.
35   How common is the lightning,
how lost the leviathans
we no longer look for!
There were giants in those days.
In those days they made good cigars.
40   I must read more carefully.

---

1. Early in his career James Joyce lived in Trieste, where
he began *Ulysses*; he died in Zurich in 1941.
2. *Victory* is a 1915 novel by Joseph Conrad concerning a

European man's unsuccessful attempt to flee from the
corruption of modern civilization by settling on a deserted
island in Malaysia.

The Fortunate Traveller[1]

for Susan Sontag

And I heard a voice in the midst of the four beasts say,
A measure of wheat for a penny,
and three measures of barley for a penny;
and see thou hurt not the oil and the wine.

Revelation 6:6[2]

1

It was in winter. Steeples, spires
congealed like holy candles. Rotting snow
flaked from Europe's ceiling. A compact man,
I crossed the canal in a grey overcoat,
5   on one lapel a crimson buttonhole
for the cold ecstasy of the assassin.
In the square coffin manacled to my wrist:
small countries pleaded through the mesh of graphs,
in treble-spaced, Xeroxed forms to the World Bank
10   on which I had scrawled the one word, MERCY;

I sat on a cold bench
under some skeletal lindens.
Two other gentlemen, black skins gone grey
as their identical, belted overcoats,
15   crossed the white river.
They spoke the stilted French
of their dark river,
whose hooked worm, multiplying its pale sickle,
could thin the harvest of the winter streets.
20   "Then we can depend on you to get us those tractors?"
"I gave my word."
"May my country ask you why you are doing this, sir?"
Silence.
"You know if you betray us, you cannot hide?"
25   A tug. Smoke trailing its dark cry.

At the window in Haiti, I remember
a gecko° pressed against the hotel glass,   lizard
with white palms, concentrating head.
With a child's hands. Mercy, monsieur. Mercy.
30   Famine sighs like a scythe
across the field of statistics and the desert
is a moving mouth. In the hold of this earth
10,000,000 shoreless souls are drifting.
Somalia: 765,000, their skeletons will go under the tidal sand.
35   "We'll meet you in Bristol to conclude the agreement?"

---

1. Walcott's title invokes Thomas Nashe's tale *The Un-*
fortunate Traveller (1594). Susan Sontag (b. 1933) is an
American cultural critic and novelist.

2. One of the Four Horsemen of the Apocalypse is decree-
ing the famine and inflation that accompany wars as the
end of the world approaches.

Steeples like tribal lances, through congealing fog
the cries of wounded church bells wrapped in cotton,
grey mist enfolding the conspirator
like a sealed envelope next to its heart.

40   No one will look up now to see the jet
fade like a weevil through a cloud of flour.
One flies first-class, one is so fortunate.
Like a telescope reversed, the traveller's eye
swiftly screws down the individual sorrow
45   to an oval nest of antic numerals,
and the iris, interlocking with this globe,
condenses it to zero, then a cloud.
Beetle-black taxi from Heathrow[3] to my flat.
We are roaches,
50   riddling the state cabinets, entering the dark holes
of power, carapaced in topcoats,
scuttling around columns, signalling for taxis,
with frantic antennae, to other huddles with roaches;
we infect with optimism, and when
55   the cabinets crack, we are the first
to scuttle, radiating separately
back to Geneva, Bonn, Washington, London.

Under the dripping planes of Hampstead Heath,
I read her letter again, watching the drizzle
60   disfigure its pleading like mascara. Margo,
I cannot bear to watch the nations cry.
Then the phone: "We will pay you in Bristol."
Days in fetid bedclothes swallowing cold tea,
the phone stifled by the pillow. The telly
65   a blue storm with soundless snow.
I'd light the gas and see a tiger's tongue.
I was rehearsing the ecstasies of starvation
for what I had to do. *And have not charity.*[4]

I found my pity, desperately researching
70   the origins of history, from reed-built communes
by sacred lakes, turning with the first sprocketed
water-driven wheels. I smelled imagination
among bestial hides by the gleam of fat,
seeking in all races a common ingenuity.
75   I envisaged an Africa flooded with such light
as alchemized the first fields of emmer wheat and barley,
when we savages dyed our pale dead with ochre,
and bordered our temples
with the ceremonial vulva of the conch
80   in the grey epoch of the obsidian adze.

3. London's primary airport.
4. Quoting St. Paul: "Though I speak with the tongues of men and of angels, and have not charity, I am become as sounding brass, or a tinkling cymbal" (1 Corinthians 13:1).

I sowed the Sahara with rippling cereals,
my charity fertilized these aridities.

What was my field? Late sixteenth century.
My field was a dank acre. A Sussex don,
85   I taught the Jacobean anxieties: *The White Devil.*[5]
Flamineo's torch startles the brooding yews.
The drawn end comes in strides. I loved my Duchess,
the white flame of her soul blown out between
the smoking cypresses. Then I saw children pounce
90   on green meat with a rat's ferocity.

I called them up and took the train to Bristol,
my blood the Severn's[6] dregs and silver.
On Severn's estuary the pieces flash,
Iscariot's salary,[7] patron saint of spies.
95   I thought, who cares how many million starve?
Their rising souls will lighten the world's weight
and level its gull-glittering waterline;
we left at sunset down the estuary.

England recedes. The forked white gull
100   screeches, circling back.
Even the birds are pulled back by their orbit,
even mercy has its magnetic field.
                              Back in the cabin,
I uncap the whisky, the porthole
105   mists with glaucoma. By the time I'm pissed,°   *drunk*
England, England will be
that pale serrated indigo on the sea-line.
"You are so fortunate, you get to see the world—"
Indeed, indeed, sirs, I have seen the world.
110   Spray splashes the portholes and vision blurs.

Leaning on the hot rail, watching the hot sea,
I saw them far off, kneeling on hot sand
in the pious genuflections of the locust,
as Ponce's armoured knees crush Florida
115   to the funereal fragrance of white lilies.

                              2

Now I have come to where the phantoms live,
I have no fear of phantoms, but of the real.
The Sabbath benedictions of the islands.
Treble clef of the snail on the scored leaf,
120   the Tantum Ergo[8] of black choristers
soars through the organ pipes of coconuts.
Across the dirty beach surpliced with lace,
they pass a brown lagoon behind the priest,

---

5. Revenge tragedy (c. 1612) by John Webster.
6. A river running through Wales and England.
7. For betraying Jesus Christ, Judas Iscariot was paid 30

pieces of silver by the Roman authorities.
8. A hymn sung after the Blessed Sacrament has been exposed in the mass.

125 pale and unshaven in his frayed soutane,°   *black robe*
    into the concrete church at Canaries;
    as Albert Schweitzer[9] moves to the harmonium
    of morning, and to the pluming chimneys,
    the groundswell lifts *Lebensraum, Lebensraum.*[1]

    Black faces sprinkled with continual dew—
130 dew on the speckled croton,[2] dew
    on the hard leaf of the knotted plum tree,
    dew on the elephant ears of the dasheen.[3]
    Through Kurtz's teeth, white skull in elephant grass,
    the imperial fiction sings. Sunday
135 wrinkles downriver from the Heart of Darkness.
    The heart of darkness is not Africa.
    The heart of darkness is the core of fire
    in the white center of the holocaust.
    The heart of darkness is the rubber claw
140 selecting a scalpel in antiseptic light,
    the hills of children's shoes outside the chimneys,
    the tinkling nickel instruments on the white altar;
    Jacob, in his last card, sent me these verses:
    "Think of a God who doesn't lose His sleep
145 if trees burst into tears or glaciers weep.
    So, aping His indifference, I write now,
    not Anno Domini: After Dachau."[4]

                              3
    The night maid brings a lamp and draws the blinds.
    I stay out on the verandah with the stars.
150 Breakfast congealed to supper on its plate.

    There is no sea as restless as my mind.
    The promontories snore. They snore like whales.
    Cetus, the whale, was Christ.
    The ember dies, the sky smokes like an ash heap.
155 Reeds wash their hands of guilt and the lagoon
    is stained. Louder, since it rained,
    a gauze of sand flies hisses from the marsh.

    Since God is dead,[5] and these are not His stars,
    but man-lit, sulphurous, sanctuary lamps,
160 it's in the heart of darkness of this earth
    that backward tribes keep vigil of His Body,
    in deya, lampion,[6] and this bedside lamp.
    Keep the news from their blissful ignorance.
    Like lice, like lice, the hungry of this earth
165 swarm to the tree of life. If those who starve

---

9. German physician, missionary, and musician in Africa;
winner of the Nobel Peace Prize in 1952.
1. Space to live in; the term is especially associated with
Nazi Germany's territorial expansion.
2. A tropical plant.

3. The taro plant of tropical Asia.
4. Site of the notorious Nazi concentration camp.
5. So the German philosopher Friedrich Nietzsche declared in his 1882 text *The Gay Science.*
6. A small oil lamp with tinted glass.

like these rain-flies who shed glazed wings in light
grew from sharp shoulder blades their brittle vans
and soared towards that tree, how it would seethe—
ah, Justice! But fires

170 drench them like vermin, quotas
prevent them, and they remain
compassionate fodder for the travel book,
its paragraphs like windows from a train,
for everywhere that earth shows its rib cage

175 and the moon goggles with the eyes of children,
we turn away to read. Rimbaud[7] learned that.
                                    Rimbaud, at dusk,
idling his wrist in water past temples
the plumed dates still protect in Roman file,

180 knew that we cared less for one human face
than for the scrolls in Alexandria's ashes,
that the bright water could not dye his hand
any more than poetry. The dhow's[8] silhouette
moved through the blinding coinage of the river

185 that, endlessly, until we pay one debt,
shrouds, every night, an ordinary secret.

                    4
The drawn sword comes in strides.
It stretches for the length of the empty beach;
the fishermen's huts shut their eyes tight.

190 A frisson° shakes the palm trees.   *excited shiver*
and sweats on the traveller's tree.
They've found out my sanctuary. Philippe, last night:
"It had two gentlemen in the village yesterday, sir,
asking for you while you was in town.

195 I tell them you was in town. They send to tell you,
there is no hurry. They will be coming back."

In loaves of cloud, *and have not charity,*
the weevil will make a sahara of Kansas,
the ant shall eat Russia.

200 Their soft teeth shall make, *and have not charity,*
the harvest's desolation,
and the brown globe crack like a begging bowl,
and though you fire oceans of surplus grain,
and have not charity,

205 still, through thin stalks,
the smoking stubble, stalks
grasshopper: third horseman,
the leather-helmed locust.[9]

---

7. Arthur Rimbaud (1854-1891), French poet. After abandoning poetry at the age of 20, he traveled in Egypt and
the Sudan, later settling in Ethiopia as a trader and arms
dealer.

8. A sailing vessel used by Arabs.
9. The locust, eater of crops, is here identified with the
horseman of the Apocalypse quoted in the poem's epigraph.

➻ ≡✦≒ ➻
Salman Rushdie
b. 1947

Born in Bombay on the day India achieved independence from Britain, Salman Rushdie was raised in largely Muslim Pakistan after the subcontinent was divided later that year. He later settled in England and achieved international fame with his 1981 novel *Midnight's Children,* a sprawling, fantasy-filled comedy of Indian history and individual romance, drawing upon both a multitude of Indian tales and the heritage of British novelists from Laurence Sterne to E. M. Forster. *Midnight's Children* won England's prestigious Booker Prize that year and was later judged the best novel of all the winners in the award's first twenty-five years.

Rushdie's fortunes took a very different turn after he published his 1988 novel *Satanic Verses,* which treated the history of Islam with sometimes sardonic irony. The book was taken by many Muslims as a blasphemous affront, and in 1989 Iran's religious and political leader, the Ayatollah Khomeini, issued a *fatwa,* or religious decree, ordering Rushdie's death. Rushdie had to go into hiding, somewhat reluctantly protected by the government of Britain's Margaret Thatcher, whose policies he had satirized as well. Following Khomeini's death, subsequent Iranian leaders have suggested that the decree would not be enforced; Rushdie eventually settled in the United States and resumed making public appearances.

Rushdie has continued to cross borders in his work as well as in his life; the story given here, "Chekov and Zulu," comes from his 1994 collection *East, West.* At first sight, the title may seem to link a classic European writer with an African tribalist, but in fact the names derive from two of the supporting characters in the television and movie series *Star Trek.* The story plays throughout on the overlays and the gaps between visual and verbal media, popular and classical culture, high tech and low humor. Rushdie's unheroic heroes fancy themselves characters aboard the starship *Enterprise,* blasted somehow into a conflict in the Middle Earth of J. R. R. Tolkien. They use this doubled frame of reference to try and make sense of the cultural dislocations and the growing political violence they experience as they move between England and India. Told in a riot of Indian-inflected English and using a wide array of cultural references, Rushdie's story moves from social comedy to a surprising and chilling conclusion.

Chekov and Zulu

1

On 4th November, 1984, Zulu disappeared in Birmingham, and India House sent his old schoolfriend Chekov to Wembley[1] to see the wife.

"Adaabarz, Mrs. Zulu. Permission to enter?"

"Of course come in, Dipty sahib, why such formality?"

"Sorry to disturb you on a Sunday, Mrs. Zulu, but Zulu-tho hasn't been in touch this morning?"

"With me? Since when he contacts me on official trip? Why to hit a telephone call when he is probably enjoying?"

"Whoops, sore point, excuse *me.* Always been the foot-in-it blunderbuss type."

"At least sit, take tea-shee."

---

1. Birmingham is a city in West Midlands, central England; Wembley is a London suburb.

"Fixed the place up damn fine, Mrs. Zulu, wah-wah.[2] Tasteful decor, in spades, I must say. So much cut-glass! That bounder Zulu must be getting too much pay, more than yours truly, clever dog."

"No, how is it possible? Acting Dipty's tankha[3] must be far in excess of Security Chief."

"No suspicion intended, ji.[4] Only to say what a bargain-hunter you must be."

"Some problem but there is, na?"

"Beg pardon?"

"Arré,[5] Jaisingh! Where have you been sleeping? Acting Dipty Sahib is thirsting for his tea. And biscuits and jalebis, can you not keep two things in your head? Jump, now, guest is waiting."

"Truly, Mrs. Zulu, please go to no trouble."

"No trouble is there, Diptyji, only this chap has become lazy since coming from home. Days off, TV in room, even pay in pounds sterling, he expects all. So far we brought him but no gratitude, what to tell you, noth-*thing*."

"Ah, Jaisingh; why not? Excellent jalebi, Mrs. Z. Thanking you."

Assembled on top of the television and on shelf units around it was the missing man's collection of *Star Trek* memorabilia: Captain Kirk and Spock dolls, spaceship models—a Klingon Bird of Prey, a Romulan vessel, a space station, and of course the Starship *Enterprise*. In pride of place were large figurines of two of the series's supporting cast.

"These old Doon School nicknames," Chekov exclaimed heartily. "They stay put like stuck records. Dumpy, Stumpy, Grumpy, Humpy. They take over from our names. As in our case our intrepid cosmonaut aliases."

"I don't like. This 'Mrs. Zulu' I am landed with! It sounds like a blackie."

"Wear the name with pride, begum[6] sahib. We're old comrades-in-arms, your husband and I; since boyhood days, perhaps he was good enough to mention? Intrepid diplonauts. Our umpteen-year mission to explore new worlds and new civilisations. See there, our alter egos standing on your TV, the Asiatic-looking Russky and the Chink. Not the leaders, as you'll appreciate, but the ultimate professional servants. 'Course laid in!' 'Hailing frequencies open!' 'Warp factor three!' What would that strutting Captain have been without his top-level staffers? Likewise with the good ship Hindustan.[7] We are servants also, you see, just like your fierce Jaisingh here. Never more important than in a moment like the present sad crisis, when an even keel must be maintained, jalebis must be served and tea poured, no matter what. We do not lead, but we enable. Without us, no course can be laid, no hailing frequency opened. No factors can be warped."

"Is he in difficulties, then, your Zulu? As if it wasn't bad enough, this terrible time."

On the wall behind the TV was a framed photograph of Indira Gandhi,[8] with a garland hung around it. She had been dead since Wednesday. Pictures of her cremation had been on the TV for hours. The flower-petals, the garish, unbearable flames.

"Hard to believe it. Indiraji! Words fail one. She was our mother. Hai, hai! Cut down in her prime."

---

2. Excellent.
3. Wages.
4. Term of respect added to ends of sentences or words.
5. Exclamation of surprise.

6. High-ranking Muslim woman.
7. Persian name for India.
8. Indian prime minister between 1966–1977 and 1980–1984; assassinated in 1984.

"And on radio-TV, such-such stories are coming about Delhi goings-on. So many killings, Dipty Sahib. So many of our decent Sikh[9] people done to death, as if all were guilty for the crimes of one-two badmash guards."

"The Sikh community has always been thought loyal to the nation," Chekov reflected. "Backbone of the Army, to say nothing of the Delhi taxi service. Super-citizens, one might say, seemingly wedded to the national idea. But such ideas are being questioned now, you must admit; there are those who would point to the comb, bangle, dagger et cetera as signs of the enemy within."

"Who would dare say such a thing about us? Such an evil thing."

"I know. I know. But you take Zulu. The ticklish thing is, he's not on any official business that we know of. He's dropped off the map, begum sahib. AWOL[1] ever since the assassination. No contact for two days plus."

"O God."

"There is a view forming back at HQ that he may have been associated with the gang. Who have in all probability long-established links with the community over here."

"O God."

"Naturally I am fighting strenuously against the proponents of this view. But his absence is damning, you must see. We have no fear of these tinpot Khalistan wallahs.[2] But they have a ruthless streak. And with Zulu's inside knowledge and security background . . . They have threatened further attacks, as you know. As you must know. As some would say you must know all too well."

"O God."

"It is possible," Chekov said, eating his jalebi, "that Zulu has boldly gone where no Indian diplonaut has gone before."

The wife wept. "Even the stupid name you could never get right. It was with S. 'Sulu.' So-so many episodes I have been made to see, you think I don't know? Kirk Spock McCoy Scott Uhura Chekov *Sulu.*"

"But Zulu is a better name for what some might allege to be a wild man," Chekov said. "For a suspected savage. For a putative traitor. Thank you for excellent tea."

2

In August, Zulu, a shy, burly giant, had met Chekov off the plane from Delhi. Chekov at thirty-three was a small, slim, dapper man in grey flannels, stiff-collared shirt and a double-breasted navy blue blazer with brass buttons. He had bat's-wing eyebrows and a prominent and pugnacious jaw, so that his cultivated tones and habitual soft-spokenness came as something of a surprise, disarming those who had been led by the eyebrows and chin to expect an altogether more aggressive personality. He was a high flyer, with one small embassy already notched up. The Acting Number Two job in London, while strictly temporary, was his latest plum.

"What-ho, Zools! Years, yaar,[3] years," Chekov said, thumping his palm into the other man's chest. "So," he added, "I see you've become a hairy fairy." The young Zulu had been a modern Sikh in the matter of hair—sporting a fine moustache at eighteen, but beardless, with a haircut instead of long tresses wound tightly under a turban. Now, however, he had reverted to tradition.

9. Community in the Punjab whose religion attempts to combine Hinduism and Islam.
1. Absent without leave.

2. Sikh military who call for a separate Sikh state called Khalistan; *wallah* means boy or man.
3. Friend, buddy.

"Hullo, ji," Zulu greeted him cautiously. "So then is it OK to utilise the old modes of address?"

"Utilise away! Wouldn't hear of anything else," Chekov said, handing Zulu his bags and baggage tags. "Spirit of the *Enterprise* and all that jazz."

In his public life the most urbane of men, Chekov when letting his hair down in private enjoyed getting interculturally hot under the collar. Soon after his taking up his new post he sat with Zulu one lunchtime on a bench in Embankment Gardens and jerked his head in the direction of various passers-by.

"Crooks," he said, *sotto voce*.[4]

"Where?" shouted Zulu, leaping athletically to his feet. "Should I pursue?"

Heads turned. Chekov grabbed the hem of Zulu's jacket and pulled him back on to the bench. "Don't be such a hero," he admonished fondly. "I meant all of them, generally; thieves, every last one. God, I love London! Theatre, ballet, opera, restaurants! The Pavilion at Lord's on the Saturday of the Test Match![5] The royal ducks on the royal pond in royal St. James's Park! Decent tailors, a decent mixed grill when you want it, decent magazines to read! I see the remnants of greatness and I don't mind telling you I am impressed. The Athenaeum, Buck House, the lions in Trafalgar Square. *Damn* impressive. I went to a meeting with the junior Minister at the F. & C.O. and realised I was in the old India Office. All that John Company black teak, those tuskers rampant on the old bookcases. Gave me quite a turn. I applaud them for their success: hurrah! But then I look at my own home, and I see that it has been plundered by burglars. I can't deny there is a residue of distress."

"I am sorry to hear of your loss," Zulu said, knitting his brows. "But surely the culpables are not in the vicinity."

"Zulu, Zulu, a figure of speech, my simpleton warrior prince. Their museums are full of our treasures, I meant. Their fortunes and cities, built on the loot they took. So on, so forth. One forgives, of course; that is our national nature. One need not forget."

Zulu pointed at a tramp, sleeping on the next bench in a ragged hat and coat. "Did he steal from us, too?" he asked.

"Never forget," said Chekov, wagging a finger, "that the British working class collaborated for its own gain in the colonial project. Manchester cotton workers, for instance, supported the destruction of our cotton industry. As diplomats we must never draw attention to such facts; but facts, nevertheless, they remain."

"But a beggarman is not in the working class," objected Zulu, reasonably. "Surely this fellow at least is not our oppressor."

"Zulu," Chekov said in exasperation, "don't be so bleddy difficult."

Chekov and Zulu went boating on the Serpentine, and Chekov got back on his hobby-horse. "They have stolen us," he said, reclining boatered and champagned on striped cushions while mighty Zulu rowed. "And now we are stealing ourselves back. It is an Elgin marbles[6] situation."

"You should be more content," said Zulu, shipping oars and gulping cola. "You should be less hungry, less cross. See how much you have! It is enough. Sit back and enjoy. I have less, and it suffices for me. The sun is shining. The colonial period is a closed book."

---

4. Softly.
5. A cricket match played between international all-star teams.
6. A group of sculptures removed from the Acropolis in Athens by Lord Elgin in 1801–1803 and purchased by the British Museum in 1816. Recent opinion polls have suggested that over 90 percent of the British public support the return of the marbles to Greece, though a 1996 resolution in the Parliament was tabled.

"If you don't want that sandwich, hand it over," said Chekov. "With my natural radicalism I should not have been a diplomat. I should have been a terrorist."

"But then we would have been enemies, on opposite sides," protested Zulu, and suddenly there were real tears in his eyes. "Do you care nothing for our friendship? For my responsibilities in life?"

Chekov was abashed. "Quite right, Zools old boy. Too bleddy true. You can't imagine how delighted I was when I learned we would be able to join forces like this in London. Nothing like the friendships of one's boyhood, eh? Nothing in the world can take their place. Now listen, you great lummox, no more of that long face. I won't permit it. Great big chap like you shouldn't look like he's about to blub. Blood brothers, old friend, what do you say? All for one and one for all."

"Blood brothers," said Zulu, smiling a shy smile.

"Onward, then," nodded Chekov, settling back on his cushions. "Impulse power only."

The day Mrs. Gandhi was murdered by her Sikh bodyguards, Zulu and Chekov played squash in a private court in St. John's Wood. In the locker-room after showering, prematurely-greying Chekov still panted heavily with a towel round his softening waist, reluctant to expose his exhaustion-shrivelled purple penis to view; Zulu stood proudly naked, thick-cocked, tossing his fine head of long black hair, caressing and combing it with womanly sensuality, and at last twisting it swiftly into a knot.

"Too good, Zulu yaar. Fataakh! Fataakh! What shots! Too bleddy good for me."

"You desk-pilots, ji. You lose your edge. Once you were ready for anything."

"Yeah, yeah, I'm over the hill. But you were only one year junior."

"I have led a purer life, ji—action, not words."

"You understand we will have to blacken your name," Chekov said softly.

Zulu turned slowly in Charles Atlas pose in front of a full-length mirror.

"It has to look like a maverick stunt. If anything goes wrong, deniability is essential. Even your wife must not suspect the truth."

Spreading his arms and legs, Zulu made his body a giant X, stretching himself to the limit. Then he came to attention. Chekov sounded a little frayed.

"Zools? What do you say?"

"Is the transporter ready?"

"Come on, yaar, don't arse around."

"Respectfully, Mister Chekov, sir, it's my arse. Now then: is the transporter ready?"

"Transporter ready. Aye."

"Then, energise."

Chekov's memorandum, classified top-secret, eyes-only, and addressed to "JTK" (James T. Kirk):

> *My strong recommendation is that Operation Startrek be aborted. To send a Federation employee of Klingon origin unarmed into a Klingon cell to spy is the crudest form of loyalty test. The operative in question has never shown ideological deviation of any sort and deserves better, even in the present climate of mayhem, hysteria and fear. If he fails to persuade the Klingons of his* bona fides *he can expect to be treated with extreme prejudice. These are not hostage takers.*
>
> *The entire undertaking is misconceived. The locally settled Klingon population is not the central problem. Even should we succeed, such intelligence as can be gleaned about more important principals back home will no doubt be of dubious accuracy and limited value. We should advise Star Fleet Headquarters to engage urgently with the grievances*

and aspirations of the Klingon people. Unless these are dealt with fair and square there cannot be a lasting peace.

The reply from JTK:

Your closeness to the relevant individual excuses what is otherwise an explosively communalist document. It is not for you to define the national interest nor to determine what undercover operations are to be undertaken. It is for you to enable such operations to occur and to provide back-up as and when required to do so. As a personal favour to you and in the name of my long friendship with your eminent Papaji I have destroyed your last without keeping a copy and suggest you do the same. Also destroy this.

Chekov asked Zulu to drive him up to Stratford for a performance of *Coriolanus.*[7]

"How many kiddiwinks by now? Three?"

"Four," said Zulu. "All boys."

"By the grace of God. She must be a good woman."

"I have a full heart," said Zulu, with sudden feeling. "A full house, a full belly, a full bed."

"Lucky so and so," said Chekov. "Always were warm-blooded. I, by contrast, am not. Reptiles, certain species of dinosaur, and me. I am in the wife market, by the way, if you know any suitable candidates. Bachelordom being, after a certain point, an obstacle on the career path."

Zulu was driving strangely. In the slow lane of the motorway, as they approached an exit lane, he accelerated towards a hundred miles an hour. Once the exit was behind them, he slowed. Chekov noticed that he varied his speed and lane constantly. "Doesn't the old rattletrap have cruise control?" he asked. "Because, sport, this kind of performance would not do on the bridge of the flagship of the United Federation of Planets."

"Anti-surveillance," said Zulu. "Dry-cleaning." Chekov, alarmed, looked out of the back window.

"Have we been rumbled, then?"

"Nothing to worry about," grinned Zulu. "Better safe than sorry is all. Always anticipate the worst-case scenario."

Chekov settled back in his seat. "You liked toys and games," he said. Zulu had been a crack rifle shot, the school's champion wrestler, and an expert fencer. "Every Speech Day," Zulu said, "I would sit in the hall and clap, while you went up for all the work prizes. English Prize, History Prize, Latin Prize, Form Prize. Clap, clap, clap, term after term, year after year. But on Sports Day I got my cups. And now also I have my area of expertise."

"Quite a reputation you're building up, if what I hear is anything to go by."

There was a silence. England passed by at speed.

"Do you like Tolkien?" Zulu asked.

"I wouldn't have put you down as a big reader," said Chekov, startled. "No offence."

"J. R. R. Tolkien," said Zulu. *"The Lord of the Rings."*[8]

---

7. Shakespeare's bloodiest tragedy; its themes are civil unrest and revolt.

8. Tolkien's triology (1954–1955), written during and just after World War II, concerns a war for control of Middle Earth, in which men, elves, dwarves, and a few British-like hobbits band together to defeat the evil eastern empire of Sauron.

"Can't say I've read the gentleman. Heard of him, of course. Elves and pixies. Not your sort of thing at all, I'd have thought."

"It is about a war to the finish between Good and Evil," said Zulu intently. "And while this great war is being fought there is one part of the world, the Shire, in which nobody even knows it's going on. The hobbits who live there work and squabble and make merry and they have no fucking clue about the forces that threaten them, and those that save their tiny skins." His face was red with vehemence.

"Meaning me, I suppose," Chekov said.

"I am a soldier in that war," said Zulu. "If you sit in an office you don't have one small idea of what the real world is like. The world of action, ji. The world of deeds, of things that are done and maybe undone too. The world of life and death."

"Only in the worst case," Chekov demurred.

"Do I tell you how to apply your smooth-tongued musca-polish to people's behinds?" stormed Zulu. "Then do not tell me how to ply my trade."

Soldiers going into battle pump themselves up, Chekov knew. This chest-beating was to be expected, it must not be misunderstood. "When will you vamoose?" he quietly asked.

"Chekov ji, you won't see me go."

Stratford approached. "Did you know, ji," Zulu offered, "that the map of Tolkien's Middle-earth fits quite well over central England and Wales? Maybe all fairylands are right here, in our midst."

"You're a deep one, old Zools," said Chekov. "Full of revelations today."

Chekov had a few people over for dinner at his modern-style official residence in a private road in Hampstead: a Very Big Businessman he was wooing, journalists he liked, prominent India-lovers, noted Non-Resident Indians. The policy was business as usual. The dreadful event must not be seen to have derailed the ship of State: whose new captain, Chekov mused, was a former pilot himself. As if a Sulu, a Chekov had been suddenly promoted to the skipper's seat.

Damned difficult doing all this without a lady wife to act as hostess, he grumbled inwardly. The best golden plates with the many-headed lion at the centre, the finest crystal, the menu, the wines. Personnel had been seconded from India House to help him out, but it wasn't the same. The secrets of good evenings, like God, were in the details. Chekov meddled and fretted.

The evening went off well. Over brandy, Chekov even dared to introduce a blacker note. "England has always been a breeding ground for our revolutionists," he said. "What would Pandit Nehru[9] have been without Harrow?[1] Or Gandhiji without his formative experiences here? Even the Pakistan idea was dreamt up by young radicals at college in what we then were asked to think of as the Mother Country. Now that England's status has declined, I suppose it is logical that the quality of the revolutionists she breeds has likewise fallen. The Kashmiris![2] Not a hope in hell. And as for these Khalistan types, let them not think that their evil deed has brought their dream a day closer. On the contrary. On the contrary. We will root them out and smash them to—what's the right word?—to *smithereens*."

To his surprise he had begun speaking loudly and had risen to his feet. He sat down hard and laughed. The moment passed.

9. Jawaharlal Nehru, first prime minister of the Republic of India (1947–1964), father of Indira Gandhi.
1. An exclusive English preparatory school.

2. Residents of Kashmir, a territory in dispute between India and Pakistan since 1947.

"The funny thing about this blasted nickname of mine," he said quickly to his dinner-table neighbour, the septuagenarian Very Big Businessman's improbably young and attractive wife, "is that back then we never saw one episode of the TV series. No TV to see it on, you see. The whole thing was just a legend wafting its way from the US and UK to our lovely hill-station of Dehra Dun.

"After a while we got a couple of cheap paperback novelisations and passed them round as if they were naughty books like *Lady C* or some such. Lots of us tried the names on for size but only two of them stuck; probably because they seemed to go together, and the two of us got on pretty well, even though he was younger. A lovely boy. So just like Laurel and Hardy we were Chekov and Zulu."

"Love and marriage," said the woman.

"Beg pardon?"

"*You* know," she said. "Go together like is it milk and porridge. Or a car and garage, that's right. I love old songs. La-la-la-something-brother, you can't have fun without I think it's your mother."[3]

"Yes, now I do recall," said Chekov.

3

Three months later Zulu telephoned his wife.

"O my God where have you vanished are you dead?"

"Listen please my bivi. Listen carefully my wife, my only love."

"Yes. OK. I am calm. Line is bad, but."

"Call Chekov and say condition red."

"Arré! What is wrong with your condition?"

"Please. Condition red."

"Yes. OK. Red."

"Say the Klingons may be smelling things."

"Clingers-on may be smelly things. Means what?"

"My darling, I beg you."

"I have it all right here only. With this pencil I have written it, both."

"Tell him, get Scotty to lock on to my signal and beam me up at once."

"What rubbish! Even now you can't leave off that stupid game."

"Bivi. It is urgent. *Beam me up.*"

Chekov dropped everything and drove. He went via the dry-cleaners as instructed; he drove round roundabouts twice, jumped red lights, deliberately took a wrong turning, stopped and turned round, made as many right turns as possible to see if anything followed him across the stream of traffic, and, on the motorway, mimicked Zulu's techniques. When he was as certain as he could be that he was clean, he headed for the rendezvous point. "Roll over Len Deighton," he thought, "and tell le Carré the news."[4]

He turned off the motorway and pulled into a lay-by. A man stepped out of the trees, looking newly bathed and smartly dressed, with a sheepish smile on his face. It was Zulu.

3. She is mangling the lyrics of Sammy Cahn's 1955 song *Love and Marriage:* "Love and marriage, love and marriage / Go together like a horse and carriage / This I tell you brother / You can't have one without the other."

4. Len Deighton and John le Carré are two writers of spy novels. The line refers to the popular song lyric, "Roll over, Beethoven."

Chekov jumped out of the car and embraced his friend, kissing him on both cheeks. Zulu's bristly beard pricked his lips. "I expected you'd have an arm missing, or blood pouring from a gunshot wound, or some black eyes at least," he said. "Instead here you are dressed for the theatre, minus only an opera cloak and cane."

"Mission accomplished," said Zulu, patting his breast pocket. "All present and correct."

"Then what was that 'condition red' bakvaas?"

"The worst-case scenario," said Zulu, "does not always materialise."

In the car, Chekov scanned the names, places, dates in Zulu's brown envelope. The information was better than anyone had expected. From this anonymous Midlands lay-by a light was shining on certain remote villages and urban back-alleys in Punjab.[5] There would be a round-up, and, for some big badmashes at least, there would no longer be shadows in which to hide.

He gave a little, impressed whistle.

Zulu in the passenger seat inclined his head. "Better move off now," he said. "Don't tempt fate."

They drove south through Middle-earth.

Not long after they came off the motorway, Zulu said, "By the way, I quit."

Chekov stopped the car. The two towers of Wembley Stadium were visible through a gap in the houses to the left.

"What's this? Did those extremists manage to turn your head or what?"

"Chekov, ji, don't be a fool. Who needs extremists when there are the killings in Delhi? Hundreds, maybe thousands. Sikh men scalped and burned alive in front of their families. Boy-children, too."

"We know this."

"Then, ji, we also know who was behind it."

"There is not a shred of evidence," Chekov repeated the policy line.

"There are eyewitnesses and photographs," said Zulu. "We know this."

"There are those who think," said Chekov slowly, "that after Indiraji the Sikhs deserved what they got."

Zulu stiffened.

"You know me better than that, I hope," said Chekov. "Zulu, for God's sake, come on. All our bleddy lives."

"No Congress workers have been indicted," said Zulu. "In spite of all the evidence of complicity. Therefore, I resign. You should quit, too."

"If you have gone so damn radical," cried Chekov, "why hand over these lists at all? Why go only half the bleddy hog?"

"I am a security wallah," said Zulu, opening the car door. "Terrorists of all sorts are my foes. But not, apparently, in certain circumstances, yours."

"Zulu, get in, damn it," Chekov shouted. "Don't you care for your career? A wife and four kiddiwinks to support. What about your old chums? Are you going to turn your back on me?"

But Zulu was already too far away.

Chekov and Zulu never met again. Zulu settled in Bombay and as the demand for private-sector protection increased in that cash-rich boom-town, so his Zulu Shield and Zulu Spear companies prospered and grew. He had three more children, all of them boys, and remains happily married to this day.

---

5. Province divided between India and Pakistan.

As for Chekov, he never did take a wife. In spite of this supposed handicap, however, he did well in his chosen profession. His rapid rise continued. But one day in
May 1991 he was, by chance, a member of the entourage accompanying Mr. Rajiv
Gandhi[6] to the South Indian village of Sriperumbudur, where Rajiv was to address an
election rally. Security was lax, intentionally so. In the previous election, Rajivji felt,
the demands of security had placed an alienating barrier between himself and the
electorate. On this occasion, he decreed, the voters must be allowed to feel close.

After the speeches, the Rajiv group descended from the podium. Chekov, who
was just a few feet behind Rajiv, saw a small Tamil[7] woman come forward, smiling.
She shook Rajiv's hand and did not let go. Chekov understood what she was smiling
about, and the knowledge was so powerful that it stopped time itself.

Because time had stopped, Chekov was able to make a number of private observations. "These Tamil revolutionists are not England-returned," he noted. "So, finally, we have learned to produce the goods at home, and no longer need to import.
Bang goes that old dinner-party standby; so to speak." And, less dryly: "The tragedy
is not how one dies," he thought. "It is how one has lived."

The scene around him vanished, dissolving in a pool of light, and was replaced
by the bridge of the Starship *Enterprise*. All the leading figures were in their appointed places. Zulu sat beside Chekov at the front.

"Shields no longer operative," Zulu was saying. On the main screen, they could
see the Klingon Bird of Prey uncloaking, preparing to strike.

"One direct hit and we're done for," cried Dr. McCoy. "For God's sake, Jim, get
us out of here!"

"Illogical," said First Officer Spock. "The degradation of our dilithium crystal
drive means that warp speed is unavailable. At impulse power only, we would make a
poor attempt indeed to flee the Bird of Prey. Our only logical course is unconditional
surrender."

"Surrender to a Klingon!" shouted McCoy. "Damn it, you cold-blooded, pointy-
eared adding-machine, don't you know how they treat their prisoners?"

"Phaser banks completely depleted," said Zulu. "Offensive capability nil."

"Should I attempt to contact the Klingon captain, sir?" Chekov inquired. "They
could fire at any moment."

"Thank you, Mr. Chekov," said Captain Kirk. "I'm afraid that won't be necessary. On this occasion, the worst-case scenario is the one we are obliged to play out.
Hold your position. Steady as she goes."

"The Bird of Prey has fired, sir," said Zulu.

Chekov took Zulu's hand and held it firmly, victoriously, as the speeding balls of
deadly light approached.

⇒⊢ END OF PERSPECTIVES: POSTCOLONIAL CONDITIONS ⊣⇐

---

6. Indian prime minister 1984–1989, assassinated in May
1991, son of Indira Gandhi.

7. A people of South India and Sri Lanka. The government
of India had been aiding the Sri Lankan government in sup-
pressing violent protests by Tamil separatists in Sri Lanka.

⇜ PERSPECTIVES ⇝
Literature, Technology, and Media

The emergence of new media, from radio early in the twentieth century to the Internet today, has decisively shaped the forms and cultural functions of contemporary literature. Early in the century, media such as radio and film were beginning to assume an important role in the cultural life of Western and some non-Western societies, but they didn't yet represent a challenge to literature as an art form. In the second half of the twentieth century, this configuration changed fundamentally. Many of the storytelling functions that narrative fiction had fulfilled, as well as some of the dramatic enactments of theatrical performance, were transferred to film and television—media that have turned out to be more popular and more easily accessible than literature not only in technologically advanced societies but sometimes especially in those cultures where print literacy is not yet universal. Similarly, some of the meanings that had been associated with lyrical poetry—the expression of personal feelings, the foregrounding of rhythm and sound in language, the play on linguistic ambiguities—shifted from printed verse to the lyrics of pop music for the younger generations of many societies around the globe. These changes do not, of course, imply that live theater and print literature disappeared; on the contrary, some of literature's forms flourished in quite unprecedented fashion. But the themes, forms, and functions of literary texts have gradually changed to reflect the technological reconfiguration of media.

It is not only new and highly technological media, however, that are reshaping our idea of literature. As literary and cultural scholars have taken a more inclusive view of literary forms around the globe, oral literature (or "orature," as it is now more properly called) has begun to occupy a more central position. While the study of myths and folktales had always formed part of literary as well as anthropological studies, their study had most often remained an area of specialization for a chosen few. With the realization that orature still plays a central role in many cultures and offers a rich array of diverse genres and rhetorical forms, the study of oral forms and traditions has gained much wider attention. This altered perspective on orature was also fostered by the discovery that literature in mostly print-oriented cultures might be partially shifting to other media: The transition from oral to printed storytelling may be compared with that from printed to televised or filmic storytelling. Peruvian writer Mario Vargas Llosa explores precisely this juxtaposition in his novel *The Storyteller* by describing how the protagonist, a novelist who begins to work for a television show, searches for an old friend who turns out to have become a "native" oral storyteller.

Like Vargas Llosa, all the writers in this section reflect on the experience of new media, though they foreground quite different dimensions of this encounter. Vargas Llosa and Abdelrahman Munif focus on the confrontation between premodern cultures and imported modern media technologies: the introduction of print literature among native tribes of Peru and of the radio among the Arab peoples living around the Persian Gulf, respectively. In the works of Christa Wolf, Murakami Haruki, and William Gibson, by contrast, people live in a world already filled with the paraphernalia of Western-style modernity, including technological devices. Yet for these modern protagonists, the confrontation with a technological medium—whether it be television, the computer, or the world of international digital connections—means far more than the encounter with a mere instrument; for all of them, information media are becoming a genuine environment, an intangible realm in which they must, for better or for worse, live part of their lives. And for all of the major characters, whether they live in premodern, modern, or postmodern surroundings, what is ultimately at stake are questions of individual and collective identities. How are our thinking, indeed our very perception of the world, reshaped by new media? How do these media transform social relationships, from the most intimate ones to those of an entire community? How do they redistribute power between different members and groups in a community? All of the texts presented here ask these questions, though they answer them in quite different ways. While some of the writers deplore the implications and effects of new media technologies in the circumstances they describe, others discover exhilaration and new possibilities.

The texts in this section also have differing approaches to a "realistic" portrayal of the world. Vargas Llosa, Munif, and Wolf reflect in relatively transparent fashion on events that either did take place or could have; Murakami's fantastic mode and Gibson's futuristic narrative remind us that all of the descriptions of different media we encounter in this section come to us through the particular medium of print; in addition, narrative fiction follows sets of rules and conventions that are all its own and that don't always obey the mandates of realism. These stories invite us to explore this intriguing tension between the literary text as a particular use of the print medium and the possibilities of fictional and nonfictional discourse in other media.

◦━❖☰━◦

Mario Vargas Llosa
b. 1936

Mario Vargas Llosa published his first book, a collection of short stories entitled *The Leaders,* in 1959 when he was twenty-three. This was also the year of the Cuban Revolution, a key event in the history and culture of Latin America that was to mark the literary career of Vargas Llosa and his contemporaries. Born in Arequipa, Peru, Vargas Llosa was taken to Cochabamba, Bolivia, by his mother within a year of his birth after his parents separated. He was raised in Bolivia until age nine, when his mother moved back to his native Peru. He attended the Leoncio Prado Military Academy (1950–1952), which serves as the setting of his irreverent first novel, *The Time of the Hero* (1962), copies of which were ceremonially burned in the Academy's parade grounds. In 1955, while still a teenager, he married Julia Urquidi, his uncle's ex-wife, a marriage experience he turned into one of his most hilarious novels and a national soap opera, *Aunt Julia and the Script Writer* (1977). The marriage foundered, and the novel resulted in a lawsuit by Aunt Julia.

An author of strong social commitment and bold political opinions, Vargas Llosa has always had an ambivalent relationship with his native Peru, culminating in his unsuccessful run for its presidency in 1990. He subsequently moved to Spain and renounced his Peruvian citizenship in favor of Spanish nationality. He was elected to the Royal Academy of the Language, the highest honor for Spanish writers. A perennial candidate for the Nobel Prize, Vargas Llosa is considered one of the most important Latin American novelists of the twentieth century. The long list of prestigious international literary prizes garnered by his fiction attests to his historical significance to the literary renaissance of Latin America in the second half of the last century.

Vargas Llosa was greatly influenced by the nineteenth-century masters of European fiction, especially French realist Gustav Flaubert, on whose masterpiece *Madame Bovary* Vargas Llosa wrote an extensive critical study, *The Perpetual Orgy* (1975). His doctoral dissertation on the Colombian novelist Gabriel García Márquez was published in 1971. Vargas Llosa is a critically sophisticated writer who has reflected much on his craft, and *The Storyteller* represents a period in his work that explores the metanarrative possibilities of fiction constructed around fiction-making institutions and rituals. In the excerpt from the novel included here, Vargas Llosa juxtaposes modes of story making that in turn define their corresponding cultures. Thus he plays on the counterpoint between Christian missionaries in the Amazonian jungle and indigenous shamans; between the Summer School of Linguistics, which actually did operate for many years in the region, and the Machiguengas Indians' language rites and taboos; and between the Irish *seanchaí,* the tellers of ancient legends, and the *habladores,* or storytellers, of this Amazonian Indian tribe, all forgers of language and taletellers whose perpetual retelling perpetually reconstitutes their worlds. Unlike earlier narrative novelists who attempted to locate the authentic source of cultures or their mythic sources, Vargas Llosa dramatizes the improvisational nature of cultural formations and the language acts that make, unmake, and remake cultures, including the myths of their origins.

PRONUNCIATIONS:

Alejandro Pérez: ahl-ay-HAN-droh PAY-rez
habladores: ah-blah-DOOR-ace
Machiguenga: mah-chee-GWEN-gah
Martín: mar-TEEN
Vargas Llosa: VAR-gahs YO-sah

from The Storyteller[1]

For six months in 1981, I was responsible for a program on Peruvian television called the Tower of Babel. The owner of the channel, Genaro Delgado, had lured me into this venture by flashing before my eyes three shiny glass beads: the need to raise the standard of the channel's programs, which had fallen to an absolute low of stupidity and vulgarity during the preceding twelve years of state ownership imposed by the military dictatorship; the excitement of experimenting with a means of communication which, in a country such as Peru, was the only one able to reach, simultaneously, a number of very different audiences; and a good salary.

It really was an extraordinary experience, though also the most tiring and most exasperating one that has ever come my way. "If you organize your time well and devote just half your day to the program, that'll be enough," Genaro had predicted. "And you'll be able to go on with your writing in the afternoon." But in this case, as in so many others, theory was one thing and practice another. The truth was that I devoted every single morning, afternoon, and evening of those months to the Tower of Babel, and most important, the many hours when I didn't seem to be actually working but was nonetheless busy worrying about what had gone wrong on the previous program and trying to anticipate what would go worse still on the next one.

There were four of us who got out the Tower of Babel programs: Luis Llosa, the producer and director of photography; Moshé dan Furgang, the editor; Alejandro Pérez, the cameraman; and myself. I had brought Lucho[2] and Moshé to the channel. They both had film experience—they had each made shorts—but neither they nor I had worked in television before. The title of the program was indicative of its intent: to show something of everything, to create a kaleidoscope of subjects. We naïvely hoped to prove that a cultural program need not be soporific, esoteric, or pedantic, but could be entertaining and not over any viewer's head, since "culture" was not synonymous with science, literature, or any other specialized field, but a way of looking at things, an approach capable of tackling anything of human interest. The idea was that during our hour-long program each week—which often stretched to an hour and a half—we would touch on two or three themes as different as possible, so that the audience would see that a cultural program had as much to offer as, let us say, soccer or boxing, or salsa and humor, and that political reporting or a documentary on the Indian tribes of Amazonia could be entertaining as well as instructive.

When Lucho and Moshé and I drew up lists of subjects, people, and locales that the Tower of Babel could use and planned the most lively way of presenting them,

---

1. Translated by Helen Lane.   2. Luis (nickname).

everything went like a charm. We were full of ideas and eager to discover the creative possibilities of the most popular medium of communication of our time.

What we discovered in practice, however, was our dependence on material factors in an underdeveloped country, the subtle way in which they subvert the best intentions and thwart the most diligent efforts. I can say, without exaggeration, that most of the time that Lucho, Moshé, and I put in on the Tower of Babel was spent not on creative work, on trying to improve the program intellectually and artistically, but was wasted in an attempt to solve problems that at first sight seemed trivial and unworthy of our notice. What to do, for instance, to get the channel's vans to pick us up at the agreed time so as not to miss appointments, planes, interviews? The answer was for us to go personally to the drivers' homes and wake them up, go with them to the channel's offices to collect the recording equipment and from there to the airport or wherever. But as a solution it cost us hours of sleep and didn't always work. It could turn out that, on top of everything else, the blessed van's battery had gone dead, or higher-ups had neglected to authorize the replacement of an oil pan, an exhaust pipe, a tire ripped to shreds the day before on the murderous potholes along the Avenida Arequipa.

From the very first program, I noticed that the images on the screen were marred by strange smudges. What were those dirty half-moons anyway? Alejandro Pérez explained that they were due to defective camera filters. They were worn out and needed replacing. Okay then, replace them. But how to go about getting this done? We tried everything short of murder, and nothing worked. We sent memos to Maintenance, we begged, we got on the phone, we argued face-to-face with engineers, technicians, department heads, and I believe we even took the problem to the owner-director of the channel. They all agreed with us, they were all indignant, they all issued strict orders that the filters be replaced. They may well have been. But the grayish half-moons disfigured all our programs, from first to last. Sometimes, when I tune in on a television program, I can still see those intrusive shadows and think—with a touch of melancholy: Ah, Alejandro's camera.

I don't know who it was who decided that Alejandro Pérez would work with us. It turned out to be a good idea, for when allowances have been made for the "underdevelopment handicap"—which he accepted philosophically, never turning a hair—Alejandro is a very skillful cameraman. His talent is purely intuitive, an innate sense of composition, movement, angle, distance. Alejandro became a cameraman by accident. He'd started out as a house painter, come to Lima from Huánuco, and someone had given him the idea that he might earn himself a little extra money by helping to load the cameras in the stadium on days when a soccer match was being televised. From having to load them so often he learned how to handle them. One day he stood in for an absent cameraman, then another day for another, and almost before he knew it, he turned out to be the channel's star cameraman.

At first his habitual silence made me nervous. Lucho was the only one who managed to talk to him. Or, at any rate, they understood each other subliminally, for in all those six months I can't remember ever hearing Alejandro utter a complete sentence, with subject, verb, and predicate. Only short grunts of approval or dismay, and an exclamation that I feared like the plague, because it meant that, once again, we had been defeated by all-powerful, omnipresent imponderables: "It's fucked up again!" How many times did the sound equipment, the film, the reflector, the monitor "fuck up"? Everything could "fuck up" innumerable times: every one of the things we worked with possessed that fundamental property, perhaps the only one toward which all of them, always, gave proof of a dog-like loyalty. How often did minutely planned projects, interviews obtained after exhausting negotiations, go all to hell because close-mouthed Alejandro came out with his fateful grunt: "It's fucked up again!"

I remember especially well what happened to us in Puerto Maldonado, a town in Amazonia where we had gone to make a documentary short on the death of the poet and guerrilla fighter Javier Heraud.[3] Alaín Elías, Heraud's comrade and the leader of the guerrilla detachment that had been scattered or captured the day Heraud was killed, had agreed to recount, in front of the camera, everything that had happened on that occasion. His testimony was interesting and moving—Alaín had been in the canoe with Javier Heraud when the latter had been shot to death, and he himself had been wounded in the shootout. We had decided to round the documentary out with views of the locale where the incident had taken place and, if possible, with accounts from the inhabitants of Puerto Maldonado who could recall the events of twenty years before.

Even Moshé—who ordinarily stayed behind in Lima to keep up with the editing of the programs—went off to the jungle with Lucho, Alejandro Pérez, and me. In Puerto Maldonado several witnesses agreed to be interviewed. Our great find was a member of the police force who had participated, first off, in the initial incident in the center of town that had revealed the presence of the guerrilleros in Puerto Maldonado to the authorities—an encounter in which a civil guard had been killed—and then later, in the manhunt for Javier Heraud and the shoot-out. The man had since retired from the police force and was working on a farm. Persuading the ex-policeman to allow himself to be interviewed had been extremely difficult, since he was filled with apprehension and reluctant to talk. We finally convinced him and even managed to get permission to interview him in the police station from which the patrols had set out on that day long ago.

At the very moment we started interviewing the ex-policeman, Alejandro's reflectors began to burst like carnival balloons. And when they had all exploded—so that there would be no doubt that the household gods of Amazonia were against the Tower of Babel—the battery of our portable generator quit and the recording equipment went dead. Fucked up again. And one of the first fruits of the program as well. We returned to Lima empty-handed.

Am I exaggerating things so that they stand out more clearly? Perhaps. But I don't think I'm stretching things much. I could tell dozens of stories like this one. And many others to illustrate what is perhaps the very symbol of underdevelopment: the divorce between theory and practice, decisions and facts. During those six months we suffered from this irreducible distance at every stage of our work. There were schedules that gave each of the various producers their fair share of time in the cutting rooms and the sound studios. But in point of fact it was not the schedules but the cunning and the clever maneuvering of each producer or technician that determined who would have more or less time for editing and recording, and who could count on the best equipment.

Of course we very soon caught on to the stratagems, ruses, wiles, or charm that had to be used, not to obtain special privileges, but merely to do a more or less decent job of what we were being paid to do. We were not above such tricks ourselves, but all of them had the disadvantage of taking up precious time that we ought to have de-

3. Peruvian poet and Communist revolutionary (1942–1963).

voted to purely creative work. Since I've been through this experience, my admiration is boundless whenever I happen to see a program on television that is well edited and recorded, lively and original. For I know that behind it there is much more than talent and determination: there is witchcraft, miracle. Some weeks, after viewing the program on the monitor one last time, looking for the perfect finishing touch, we would say to each other: "Good, it came out exactly right in the end." But despite that, on the television screen that Sunday, the sound would fade away altogether, the image leap out of focus, and completely blank frames appear . . . What had "fucked up" this time? The technician on duty was drunk or asleep, he'd pressed the wrong button or run the film backward . . . Television is a risky business for perfectionists; it is responsible for countless cases of insomnia, tachycardia, ulcers, heart attacks . . .

In spite of all this, and by and large, those six months were exciting and intense. I remember how moved I was interviewing Borges[4] in his apartment in downtown Buenos Aires, where his mother's room was kept exactly the way she left it the day she died (an old lady's purple dress laid out on the bed); he apparently never forgave me for having said that his home was a modest one, with a leaky roof. I remember being moved, too, by the portraits of writers painted by Ernesto Sábato,[5] which he allowed us to film in his little house in Santos Lugares, where we went to visit him. Ever since I'd lived in Spain in the early seventies, I had wanted to interview Corín Tellado,[6] whose sentimental romances, radio soap operas, photo-novels, and television melodramas are devoured by countless thousands in Spain and Hispano-America. She agreed to appear on the Tower of Babel and I spent an afternoon with her, on the outskirts of Gijón, in Asturias—she showed me the basement of the house she was occupying, with thousands of novelettes stowed away on bookshelves: she finishes one every two days, each exactly a hundred pages long. She was living there in seclusion because at the time she had been the victim of attempted extortion, though whether a political group or common criminals were behind it was not clear.

From the houses of writers we took our cameras to the stadiums—we did a program on one of the best Brazilian soccer clubs, the Flamengo, and interviewed Zico, the star of the moment, in Rio de Janeiro. We went to Panama, where we visited amateur and professional boxing rings, trying to discover how and why this small Central American country had been the cradle of so many Latin American and world champions in nearly every weight class. In Brazil, we managed to get our cameras into the exclusive clinic of trim, athletic Dr. Pitanguí, whose scalpels made all the women in the world who could pay for his services young and beautiful; and in Santiago de Chile we spoke with Pinochet's Chicago Boys[7] and with his Christian Democratic opponents, who, in the midst of extreme repression, were resisting dictatorship.

We went to Nicaragua on the second anniversary of the revolution, to report on the Sandinistas and their adversaries; and to the University of California at Berkeley, where the great poet, Czeslaw Milosz, a recent winner of the Nobel Prize for Literature, worked in a tiny office in the Department of Slavonic Languages. We went to Coclecito, Panama, where we visited General Omar Torrijos[8] at his home there; though theoretically no longer active in government, he was still the lord and master

---

4. The great Argentinian writer (see page 529).
5. Argentine novelist and public intellectual (b. 1911).
6. One of the most widely read authors of the 20th century, she was born in the city of Gijón, in northern Spain in 1926. She has published over 5,000 novels and soap operas.

7. "Free-market" economists from the University of Chicago hired by Augusto Pinochet, Chilean dictator (1973–1990), to rescue the country's economy.
8. Author and military ruler of Panama between 1968 and 1978.

of the country. We spent the entire day with him, and although he was most affable with me, I was not left as agreeably impressed by him as were other writers who had been his guests. He struck me as the typical Latin American caudillo of unhappy memory, the providential "strongman," authoritative and macho, adulated by civil and military courtiers, who filed through the place all day, flattering him with sickening servility. The most exciting person in the general's Coclecito house was one of his mistresses, a curvaceous blonde we came upon reclining in a hammock. She was just another piece of furniture, for the general neither spoke to her nor introduced her to the guests who came and went . . .

Two days after our return to Lima from Panama, Lucho Llosa, Alejandro Pérez, and I felt a cold shiver run down our spines. Torrijos had just died in a fatal crash of the little plane in which he had sent us back to Panama City from Coclecito. The pilot was the same one we had flown with.

I fainted in Puerto Rico, just a day after recording a short program on the marvelous restoration of old San Juan, guided by Ricardo Alegría, who had been the moving spirit of the project. I was suffering from dehydration as a result of stomach poisoning, contracted in the chicha[9] bars of a north Peruvian village, Catacaos, where we had gone to do a program on straw-hat weaving, a craft the inhabitants have been practicing for centuries; on the secrets of the tondero, a regional dance; and on its picanterías,[1] where fine chicha and highly spiced stews are served (these latter responsible, naturally, for my case of poisoning). Words cannot express my thanks to all the Puerto Rican friends who virtually terrorized the kind doctors of San Jorge Hospital into curing me in time for the Tower of Babel to appear on the air at the usual hour that Sunday.

The program ran regularly every week, and considering the conditions under which we worked, this was quite a feat. I wrote the scripts in vans or planes, went from airport to sound studio to cutting room, and from there to catch another plane to travel hundreds of miles to be in another town or country, often for less time than it had taken me to get there. During those six months, I skipped sleeping, eating, reading, and, naturally, writing. As the channel's budget was limited, I arranged for several of my trips abroad to coincide with invitations to attend literary congresses or give lectures, thus relieving the channel of having to pay my travel and per-diem expenses. The trouble with this arrangement was that it forced me to become a psychic quick-change artist, shifting within seconds from a lecturer to a journalist, from an author with a microphone placed before him to an interviewer who took his revenge by interviewing his interviewers.

Though we did a fair number of programs on the current scene in other countries, most of them dealt with Peruvian subjects. Popular dances and fiestas, university problems, pre-Hispanic archaeological sites, an old ice-cream vendor whose tricycle had cruised the streets of Miraflores[2] for half a century, the story of a Piura[3] bordello, the sub-world of prisons. We discovered how wide an audience the Tower of Babel was reaching when we started getting requests and considerable pressure from various personalities and institutions who wanted us to take notice of them. The most unexpected was perhaps the PIP, the Peruvian Secret Police. A colonel appeared in my office one day, suggesting that I devote a Tower of Babel broadcast to the PIP to cel-

9. Homemade corn liquor.
1. Spicy hors d'oeuvres.

2. Upscale district of the Peruvian capital, Lima.
3. North Peruvian city and province.

ebrate some anniversary or other; to make the program more exciting, the PIP would stage a mock arrest of cocaine smugglers, complete with a shoot-out . . .

One of the calls I received, when the six-month period I had agreed to work for the channel was nearly over, came from a friend I hadn't seen for ages: Rosita Corpancho. There was her warm voice with its drawling Loretano[4] accent, just as in my university years. There, too, intact or perhaps even increased, was her enthusiastic devotion to the Summer Institute of Linguistics. Surely I remembered the Institute? Of course, Rosita . . . Well, the Institute was about to celebrate its I-don't-know-how-many-years in Peru, and what was more, it would soon be packing its bags, having decided that its mission in Amazonia had ended. Would it be possible, perhaps, for the Tower of Babel . . .? I interrupted her to say that, yes, I would be pleased to do a documentary on the work of the linguist-missionaries. And would take advantage of the trip to the jungle to do a program on some of the lesser-known tribes, something we'd had in mind from the beginning. Rosita was delighted and told me she would coordinate everything with the Institute so that we could get about readily in the jungle. Had I any particular tribe in mind? Without hesitation I answered: "The Machiguengas."

Ever since my unsuccessful attempts in the early sixties at writing about the Machiguenga storytellers, the subject had never been far from my mind. It returned every now and then, like an old love, not quite dead coals yet, whose embers would suddenly burst into flame. I had gone on taking notes and scribbling rough drafts that I invariably tore up. And reading, every time I could lay my hands on them, the papers and articles about Machiguengas that kept appearing here and there in scientific journals. The lack of interest in the tribe was giving way to curiosity on several counts. The French anthropologist France-Marie Casevitz-Renard, and another, an American, Johnson Allen, had spent long periods among them and had described their organization, their work methods, their kinship structure, their symbolism, their sense of time. A Swiss ethnologist, Gerhard Baer, who had also lived among them, had made a thorough study of their religion, and Father Joaquín Barriales had begun publishing, in Spanish translation, his large collection of Machiguenga myths and songs. A number of Peruvian anthropologists, classmates of Mascarita's, notably Camino Díez Canseco and Víctor J. Guevara, had studied the tribe's customs and beliefs.

But never in any of these contemporary works had I found any information whatsoever about storytellers. Oddly enough, all reference to them broke off around the fifties. Had the function of storyteller been dying out and finally disappeared at the very time that the Schneils had discovered it? In the reports that the Dominican missionaries—Fathers Pío Aza, Vicente de Cenitagoya, and Andrés Ferrero—wrote about them in the thirties and forties, there were frequent allusions to storytellers. And even earlier, among nineteenth-century travelers as well. One of the first references occurs in the book written by Paul Marcoy, the explorer. On the banks of the Urubamba he came across an "orateur," whom the French traveler witnessed literally hypnotizing an audience of Antis for hours on end. "Do you think those Antis were Machiguengas?" the anthropologist Luis Román asked me, showing me the reference. I was certain they were. Why did modern anthropologists never mention storytellers? It was a question I asked myself each time one of these studies or field observations came to my attention, and I saw, once again, that no mention was made, even in passing, of those wandering tellers of tales, who seemed to me to be the most exquisite

---

4. From the northeastern Amazonian province of Peru.

and precious exemplars of that people, numbering a mere handful, and who, in any event, had forged that curious emotional link between the Machiguengas and my own vocation (not to say, quite simply, my own life).

Why, in the course of all those years, had I been unable to write my story about storytellers? The answer I used to offer myself, each time I threw the half-finished manuscript of that elusive story into the wastebasket, was the difficulty of inventing, in Spanish and within a logically consistent intellectual framework, a literary form that would suggest, with any reasonable degree of credibility, how a primitive man with a magico-religious mentality would go about telling a story. All my attempts led each time to the impasse of a style that struck me as glaringly false, as implausible as the various ways in which philosophers and novelists of the Enlightenment had put words into the mouths of their exotic characters in the eighteenth century, when the theme of the "noble savage" was fashionable in Europe. Despite these failures, per-haps because of them, the temptation was still there, and every now and then, revived by some fortuitous circumstance, it took on new life, and the murmurous, fleeting, rude, and untamed silhouette of the storyteller invaded my house and my dreams. How could I fail to have been moved at the thought of seeing the Machiguengas face-to-face at last?

Since that trip in mid-1958 when I discovered the Peruvian jungle, I had returned to Amazonia several times: to Iquitos, to San Martín, to the Alto Marañón, to Madre de Dios, to Tingo María. But I had not been back to Pucallpa. In the twenty-three years that had gone by, that tiny, dusty village that I remembered as being full of dark, gloomy houses and evangelical churches, had been through an industrial and com-mercial "boom," followed by a depression, and now, as Lucho Llosa, Alejandro Pérez, and I landed there one September afternoon in 1981 to film what was to be the next-to-last program of the Tower of Babel, it was in the first stages of another "boom," though for bad reasons this time: trafficking in cocaine. The rush of heat and the burning light, in whose embrace people and things stand out so sharply (unlike Lima, where even bright sunlight has a grayish cast), are something that always has the effect on me of an emulsive draft of enthusiasm.

But that morning brought the discovery that it was the Schneils whom the Insti-tute had sent to meet us at the Pucallpa airport, and that impressed me even more than the heat and the beautiful landscape of Amazonia. The Schneils in person. They had come to the end of their quarter of a century in the Amazon, the whole of it spent working with the Machiguengas. They were surprised that I remembered them—I have the feeling they didn't remember me at all—and could still recall so many de-tails of what they had told me back then, during our two conversations at the Yarina-cocha base. As we bounced this way and that in the jeep on our way to the Institute, they showed me photographs of their children, young people, some already through college, living in the States. Did they all speak Machiguenga? Of course, it was the family's second language, even before Spanish. I was pleased to learn that the Schneils would be our guides and interpreters in the villages we visited.

Lake Yarina was still a picture postcard, and dusk there more beautiful than ever. The bungalows of the Institute had proliferated along the lakeshore. The minute we climbed out of the jeep, Lucho, Alejandro, and I set to work. We agreed that as soon as night fell, to serve as an introduction to our trip to the forests of the Alto Urubamba, the Schneils would brief us on the places and people we would be seeing up there.

Other than the Schneils, not one of the linguists whom I had met on my previous journey was still in Yarinacocha. Some had gone back to the States; others were doing fieldwork in other jungle regions around the world; and some had died, as had Dr. Townsend, the founder of the Institute. But the linguists whom we met and interviewed, who acted as our guides as we photographed the place from various angles, appeared to be the identical twins of the ones I remembered. The men had close-cropped hair and the athletic, healthy appearance of people who exercise daily, eat according to the instructions of a dietician, don't smoke, and take neither coffee nor alcohol, and the women, encased in dresses as plain as they were decent, without a speck of makeup or a shadow of coquetry, exuded an over-whelming air of efficiency. Men and women alike had the cheerful, imperturbable look of people who believe, who are doing what they believe in, and who know for certain that the truth is on their side: the sort of people who have always fascinated and terrified me.

As long as the light and the caprices of Alejandro Pérez's equipment permitted, we went on collecting material for the program on the Institute: a seminar of bilingual teachers from various villages that was taking place at the time; the elementary readers and grammar books compiled by the linguists; their personal testimony and an overall view of the small town that the Yarinacocha base of operations had become, with its school, its hospital, its sports field, its library, its churches, its communications center, and its airport.

As darkness fell, after a combined work session and meal during which we rounded off our plans for the part of the program devoted to the Institute, we began mapping out the part we would be recording during the following days: the Machiguengas. In Lima I had unearthed and consulted all the documents concerning them that I had been accumulating over the years. But it was chiefly a conversation with the Schneils—once again at their house, once again over tea and cookies prepared by Mrs. Schneil—that provided us with firsthand information on the state of the community that they knew inside out, since it had been their home for the past twenty-five years.

Things had changed considerably for the Machiguengas of the Alto Urubamba[5] and Madre de Dios[6] since the day when Edwin Schneil, stark-naked, had approached that family and it had not fled. Had things changed for the better? The Schneils were firmly convinced that they had. For the moment, the dispersion that had characterized Machiguenga life had largely come to an end—and this was true of the ones on the other side of the Pongo de Mainique as well. The diaspora—little groups scattered here and there with virtually no contact between them, each one fighting desperately for survival—was over; had it continued, it would have meant, purely and simply, the disintegration of the community, the disappearance of its language, and the assimilation of its members by other groups and cultures. After many efforts on the part of the authorities, Catholic missionaries, anthropologists, ethnologists, and the Institute itself, the Machiguengas had begun to accept the idea of forming villages, of coming together in places suitable for working the soil, breeding animals, and developing trade relations with the rest of Peru. Things were evolving rapidly. There were already six settlements, some of them very recent. We would be visiting two of them, New World and New Light.

Of the five thousand surviving Machiguengas—an approximate figure—nearly half were now living in those settlements. One of them, moreover, was half Machiguenga and half Campa (Ashaninka), and thus far the cohabitation of members

---

5. Central Peruvian mountain region and river.   6. East-central Peruvian province and river.

of the two tribes had not given rise to the slightest problem. The Schneils were optimistic and believed that the remaining Machiguengas—including the most elusive of all, the ones known as Kogapakori, would gradually abandon their refuges in the heart of the forest and form new settlements when they saw the advantages that living in community brought to their brothers: a less uncertain life and the possibility of being helped in case of emergency. With heartfelt enthusiasm the Schneils told us of the concrete steps that had already been taken in the villages to integrate them into national life. Schools and agricultural cooperatives, for instance. Both in New World and in New Light there were bilingual schools, with native teachers. We would be seeing them.

Did this mean that the Machiguengas were slowly ceasing to be that primitive people, shut in on itself, pessimistic and defeated, that they had described to me in 1958? To a certain extent, yes. They were less reluctant—the ones who lived in communities, at any rate—to try out novelties, to progress; they had more love of life, perhaps. But as far as their isolation was concerned, one couldn't talk thus far of any real change. Because, even though we could reach their villages in two or three hours in the Institute planes, a journey by river to one of these settlements from any sizable Amazonian town was a matter of days and sometimes weeks. So the idea of their becoming an integral part of Peru was perhaps a little less remote than in the past, but was certainly not a reality as yet.

Would we be able to interview any Machiguengas in Spanish? Yes, a few, though not many. The cacique or governor of New Light, for example, spoke Spanish fluently. What? Did the Machiguengas have caciques now? Hadn't one of the distinctive features of the tribe been the absence of any sort of hierarchic political organization, with leaders and subordinates? Yes, certainly. Before. But that anarchic system typical of them was explained by their dispersion: now that they were gathered together in villages, they needed authorities. The administrator or chief of New Light was a young man and a splendid community leader, a graduate of the Mazamari Bible School. A Protestant pastor, in other words? Well, yes, you might call him that. Had the Bible been translated into Machiguenga yet? Of course, and they had been the translators. In New World and New Light we would be able to film copies of the New Testament in Machiguenga.

I remembered Mascarita and our last conversation in the seedy café on the Avenida España. I heard once again his prophecies and his fulminations. From what the Schneils told us, Saúl's fears, that evening, were becoming a reality. Like other tribes, the Machiguengas were in the very midst of the process of acculturation: the Bible, bilingual schools, an evangelical leader, private property, the value of money, trade, Western clothes, no doubt . . . Was all this a good thing? Had it brought them real advantages as individuals, as people, as the Schneils so emphatically maintained? Or were they, rather, from the free and sovereign "savages" they had been, beginning to turn into "zombies," caricatures of Westerners, as Mascarita had put it? Would a visit of just a couple of days be long enough for me to find out? No, of course it wouldn't.

In the Yarinacocha bungalow that night, I lay awake for a long time thinking. Through the fly screen on the window, I could see a stretch of lake traversed by a golden wake, but the moon, which I imagined as being full and bright, was hidden from me by a clump of trees. Was it a good or a bad omen that Kashiri, that male astral body, sometimes malevolent, sometimes benevolent, of Machiguenga mythology, was concealing his stained face from me? Twenty-three years had passed since I had first slept in one of these bungalows. In all those years it was not only I who had changed, lived through a thousand experiences, grown older. Those Machiguengas, whom I knew, if at all, from only two brief accounts by this American couple, a conversation in Madrid with a Dominican, and a few ethnological studies, had also undergone great changes. Quite evidently, they no longer fitted the images of them that my imagination had invented. They were no longer that handful of tragic, indomitable beings, that society broken up into tiny families, fleeing, always fleeing, from the whites, from the mestizos, from the mountain people, and from other tribes, awaiting and stoically accepting their inevitable extinction as individuals and as a group, yet never giving up their language, their gods, their customs. An irrepressible sadness came over me at the thought that this society scattered in the depths of the damp and boundless forests, for whom a few tellers of tales acted as circulating sap, was doomed to disappear.

How many times in those twenty-three years had I thought of the Machiguengas? How many times had I tried to understand them, intuitively, to write about them; how many plans had I made to journey to their lands? Because of them, all the people or institutions everywhere in the world that might resemble or in any way be associated with the Machiguenga storytellers had held an immediate fascination for me. The wandering troubadours of the Bahia pampas, for instance, who, to the basso continuo of their guitars, weave together medieval romances of chivalry and local gossip in the dusty villages of northeastern Brazil. Seeing one of them that afternoon, in the market square of Uaúa, was enough for me to glimpse, superimposed on the figure of the caboclo,[7] in a leather vest and hat, recounting and singing, to an amused audience, the story of Princess Magalona and the twelve peers of France, the greenish-yellow skin, decorated with symmetrical red stripes and dark spots, of the half-naked storyteller who, far, far from there, on a little beach hidden beneath the jungle foliage of Madre de Dios, was telling an attentive family squatting on their heels about the breathing contest between Tasurinchi and Kientibakori that was the origin of all the good and bad beings in the world.

But even more than the Bahian troubadour, it was the Irish *seanchaí*[8] who had reminded me, so forcefully, of the Machiguenga storytellers. *Seanchaí:* "teller of ancient stories," "the one who knows things," as someone in a Dublin bar had offhandedly translated the word into English. How to explain, if it was not because of the Machiguengas, the rush of emotion, the sudden quickening of my heartbeat that impelled me to intrude, to ask questions, and later on to pester and infuriate Irish friends and acquaintances until they finally sat me down in front of a *seanchaí?* A living relic of the ancient bards of Hibernia, like those ancestors of his whose faint outline blends, in the night of time, with the Celtic myths and legends that are the intellectual foundations of Ireland, the *seanchaí* still recounts, in our own day, old legends, epic deeds, terrible loves, and disturbing miracles, in the smoky warmth of pubs; at festive gatherings where the magic of his words calls forth a sudden silence; in friendly houses, next to the hearth, as outside the rain falls or the storm rages. He can be a tavern-keeper, a truck driver, a parson, a beggar, someone mysteriously touched by the magic wand of wisdom and the art of reciting, of remembering, of reinventing and enriching tales told and retold down through the centuries; a messenger from the times of myth and magic, older than history, to whom Irishmen of today listen spellbound

---

7. Brazilian backwoodsman of mixed race.   8. Traditional Irish storyteller.

for hours on end. I always knew that the intense emotion I felt on that trip to Ireland, thanks to the *seanchaí,* was metaphorical, a way of hearing, through him, the story-teller, and of living the illusion that, sitting there squeezed in among his listeners, I was part of a Machiguenga audience.

And at last, tomorrow, in this unexpected way, guided by the Schneils them-selves, I was going to meet the Machiguengas. So life has its novelistic side, does it? Indeed it does! "I've already told you I want to end with a zoom shot, Alejandro you cunt," Lucho Llosa raved in the next bed, tossing and turning under the mosquito net.

We left at dawn in two of the Institute's single-engine Cessnas, carrying three passengers each. Despite his adolescent face, the pilot of the little plane I was in had already spent several years with the linguist-missionaries, and before piloting planes for them in Amazonia, he had done the same thing in the jungles of Central America and Borneo. The morning was bright and clear and from the air we could easily make out all the meanders of the Ucayali and then of the Urubamba—the little islands, the spluttering launches with outboard motors or pequepeques, the canoes, the channels, the rapids and tributaries—and the tiny villages that at rare intervals showed up as a clearing of huts and reddish earth in the endless green plain. We flew over the penal colony of Sepa, and over the Dominican mission of Sepahua, then left the Alto Urubamba to follow the winding course of the Mipaya, a muddy snake on whose banks, around ten in the morning, we spotted our first destination: New World.

The name Mipaya has historical echoes. Beneath the tangle of vegetation, rubber camps proliferated a century ago. After the terrible death toll that the tribe suffered in the years of the tree-bleeding, the ruined rubber tappers, once the boom was over, tried to clear plantations in the region during the twenties, recruiting their labor by the old system of hunting Indians. It was then that there occurred, here on the shores of the Mipaya, the only instance of Machiguenga resistance known to history. When a planter of the region came to carry off the young men and women of the tribe, the Machiguengas received him with a rain of arrows and killed or wounded several Vira-cochas[9] before being exterminated. The jungle had covered over the scene of the vio-lence with its thick undergrowth of tree trunks, branches, and dead leaves, and not a trace remained of that infamy. Before landing, the pilot circled around the twenty or so conical-roofed huts several times, so that the Machiguengas of New World would remove their children from the one street of the settlement, which served as the land-ing strip. The Schneils had flown in the same Cessna as I, and the minute they climbed out of the plane, a hundred or so villagers surrounded them, showing signs of great excitement and joy, jostling each other to touch and pat them, all talking at the same time in a rhythmic tongue full of harsh sounds and extreme tonal shifts. Save for the schoolmistress dressed in a skirt and blouse and wearing sandals, all the Machiguengas were barefoot, the men in skimpy loincloths or cushmas, the women in yellow or gray cotton tunics of the sort worn by many tribes. Only a few old women wore pampanillas, a thin shawl tucked in at the waist, leaving their breasts bare. Nearly all of them, men and women, had red or black tattoos.

So there they were. Those were the Machiguengas.

I had no time to be carried away by emotion. To make the most of the light, we started work immediately, and fortunately no catastrophe kept us from filming the huts—all of them exactly the same: a simple platform of tree trunks supported on pil-

---

9. Originally, creator of gods for the Incas. Here it refers to Incan or modern metropolitan colonists or strongmen.

ings, with thin walls of cane that reached only halfway up on each side, and a tuft of palm leaves for a roof; the interiors were austere, no more than a place for storing rolled-up mats, baskets, fishing nets, bows and arrows, small quantities of cassava and maize, and a few hollow gourds containing liquids—or from interviewing the schoolmistress, the only one who could express herself in Spanish, though with difficulty. She also looked after the village store, to which a motor launch brought provisions twice a month. My attempts to get any information about storytellers out of her were of no avail. Could she understand who it was I was asking her about? Apparently not. She looked at me with a surprised, slightly anxious expression, as though begging me to express myself in an intelligible way again.

Although we could not talk with them directly but only through the Schneils, the other Machiguengas were obliging enough and we were able to record some dances and songs and film an old woman delicately painting geometric designs on her face with annatto dye. We took shots of the crops sprouting in the fields, the poultry runs, the school, where the teacher insisted that we listen to the national anthem in Machiguenga. The face of one of the children was eaten away by a form of leprosy known as uta, which the Machiguengas attribute to the sting of a pink firefly whose abdomen is speckled with gleaming little dots of light. From the natural, uninhibited way in which the boy acted, running about among the other children, he did not seem, at first sight, to be the object of either discrimination or mockery because of his disfigurement.

As evening set in and we were loading our equipment for the flight to the village—New Light—where we were to spend the night, we learned that New World would probably have to change its location soon. What had happened? One of those chance geographical occurrences that are the daily bread of life in the jungle. During the last rainy season the Mipaya had radically changed its course because of heavy floods and was now so far distant from New World that when the waters were down to their winter level the inhabitants had to go a very long way to reach its shores. So they were looking for another spot, less subject to unforeseeable mischances, in order to re-settle. That would not be difficult for people who had spent their lives on the move—their settlements were evidently born under an atavistic sign of eternal wandering, of a peripatetic destiny—and besides, their huts of tree trunks, cane, and palm leaves were far easier to take down and put up again than were the little houses of civilization.

They explained to us that the twenty-minute flight from New World to New Light was misleading, since it took at least a week to go from one to the other on foot through the jungle, or a couple of days by canoe.

New Light was the oldest of the Machiguenga villages—it had just celebrated its second birthday—and had a little more than twice the number of huts and inhabitants as in New World. Here too, only Martín, the village chief and head administrator, who was the teacher of the bilingual school, was dressed in a shirt, trousers, and shoes, and wore his hair cut in Western style. He was quite young, short, deadly serious, and spoke fast, fluent, syncopated Spanish, dropping a good many word endings. The welcome the Machiguengas of New Light gave the Schneils was as exuberant and noisy as the one in the previous village; all the rest of the day and during a good part of the night we saw groups and individuals patiently waiting for others to take their leave of them so that they could approach and start a crackling conversation full of gestures and grimaces.

In New Light, too, we recorded dances, songs, drum solos, the school, the shop, seed-sowing, looms, tattoos, and an interview with the head of the village, who had been through Bible school at Mazamari; he was young and very thin, with hair cropped almost to his skull, and ceremonious gestures. He was a disciple well versed in the teachings of his masters, for he preferred talking about the Word of God, the Bible, and the Holy Spirit to talking about the Machiguengas. He had a sullen way of beating about the bush and resorting to endless vague biblical verbiage whenever he didn't care to answer a question. I tried twice to draw him out on the subject of story-tellers, and each time, looking at me without understanding, he explained all over again that the book he had on his knee was the word of God and of his apostles in the Machiguenga language.

Our work finished, we went to swim in a gorge of the Mipaya, some fifteen min-utes' walk from the village, guided by the two Institute pilots. Twilight was coming on, the most mysterious and most beautiful hour of the day in Amazonia, as long as there isn't a cloudburst. The place was a real find, a branch of the Mipaya deflected by a natural barrier of rocks, forming a sort of cove where one could swim in warm, quiet waters, or, if one preferred, expose oneself to the full force of the current, pro-tected by the portcullis of rocks. Even silent Alejandro started splashing and laughing, madly happy in this Amazonian Jacuzzi.

When we got back to New Light, young Martín (his manners were exquisite and his gestures genuinely elegant) invited me to drink lemon verbena tea with him in his hut next to the school and the village store. He had a radio transmitter, his means of communication with the headquarters of the Institute at Yarinacocha. There were just the two of us in the room, which was as meticulously neat and clean as Martín him-self. Lucho Llosa and Alejandro Pérez had gone to help the pilots unload the ham-mocks and mosquito nets we were to sleep in. The light was failing fast and the dark shadows were deepening around us. The entire jungle had set up a rhythmical chirring, as always at this hour, reminding me that, beneath its green tangle, myriads of insects dominated the world. Soon the sky would be full of stars.

Did the Machiguengas really believe that the stars were the beams of light from the crowns of spirits? Martín nodded impassively. That shooting stars were the fiery arrows of those little child-gods, the ananeriites, and the morning dew their urine? This time Martín laughed. Yes, that was their belief. And now that the Machiguengas had stopped walking, so as to put down roots in villages, would the sun fall? Surely not: God would take care of keeping it in place. He looked at me for a moment with an amused expression: how had I found out about these beliefs? I told him that I'd been interested in the Machiguengas for nearly a quarter of a century and that from the first I'd made a point of reading everything that was written about them. I told him why. As I spoke, his face, friendly and smiling to begin with, grew stern and distrust-ful. He listened to me grimly, not a muscle of his face moving.

"So, you see, my questions about storytellers aren't just vulgar curiosity but something much more serious. They're very important to me. Perhaps as important as to the Machiguengas, Martín." He remained silent and motionless, with a watchful gleam in the depth of his eyes. "Why didn't you want to tell me anything about them? The schoolmistress at New World wouldn't tell me anything about them, either. Why all this mystery about the habladores, Martín?"

He assured me he didn't understand what I was talking about. What was all this business about "habladores"? He'd never heard a word about them, either in this village or in any other of the community. There might be habladores in other tribes perhaps, but not among the Machiguengas. He was telling me this when the Schneils came in. We hadn't drunk up all that lemon verbena, the most fragrant in all Amazonia, had we? Martín changed the subject, and I thought it best not to pursue the matter.

But an hour later, after we'd taken our leave of Martín and I'd put up my hammock and mosquito net in the hut they'd loaned us, I went out with the Schneils to enjoy the cool evening air, and as we walked in the open surrounded by the dwellings of New Light, the subject came irresistibly to my lips once again.

"In the few hours I've been with the Machiguengas, there are many things I haven't been able to figure out yet," I said. "I have realized one thing, however. Something important."

The sky was a forest of stars and a dark patch of clouds hid the moon, its presence visible only as a diffuse brightness. A fire had been made at one end of New Light, and fleeting silhouettes suddenly stole around it. All the huts were dark except for the one they'd lent to us, some fifty meters away, which was lit by the greenish light of a portable kerosene lamp. The Schneils waited for me to go on. We were walking slowly over soft ground where tall grass grew. Even though I was wearing boots, I had begun to feel mosquitoes biting my ankles and insteps.

"And what is that?" Mrs. Schneil finally asked.

"That all this is quite relative," I went on impetuously. "I mean, baptizing this place New Light and calling the village chief Martín. The New Testament in Machiguenga; sending the Indians to Bible school and making pastors out of them; the violent transition from a nomadic life to a sedentary one; accelerated Westernization and Christianization. So-called modernization. I've realized that it's just outward show. Even though they've started trading and using money, the weight of their own traditions exerts a much stronger pull on them than all that."

I stopped. Was I offending them? I myself didn't know what conclusion to draw from this whole hasty process of reasoning.

"Yes, of course." Edwin Schneil coughed, somewhat disconcerted. "Naturally. Hundreds of years of beliefs and customs don't disappear overnight. It'll take time. What's important is that they've begun to change. Today's Machiguengas are no longer what they were when we arrived, I assure you."

"I've realized that there are depths in them they won't yet allow to be touched," I interrupted him. "I asked the schoolmistress in New World, and Martín as well, about habladores. And they both reacted in exactly the same way; denying that they existed, pretending they didn't even know what I was talking about. It means that even in the most Westernized Machiguengas, such as the schoolmistress and Martín, there's an inviolable inner loyalty to their own beliefs. There are certain taboos they're not prepared to give up. That's why they keep them so thoroughly hidden from outsiders."

There was a long silence in which the chirring of the invisible night insects seemed to grow deafening. Was he going to ask me who habladores were? Would the Schneils also tell me, as the schoolmistress and the village chief-pastor had, that they'd never heard of them? I thought for a moment that habladores didn't exist: that I'd invented them and then housed them in false memories so as to make them real.

"Ah, habladores!" Mrs. Schneil exclaimed at last. And the Machiguenga word or sentence crackled like dead leaves. It seemed to me that it came to greet me, across time, from the bungalow on the shores of Yarinacocha where I had heard it for the first time when I was little more than an adolescent.

"Ah," Edwin Schneil repeated, mimicking the crackling sound twice in a faintly uneasy tone of voice. "Habladores. *Speakers.* Yes, of course, that's one possible translation."

"And how is it that you know about them?" Mrs. Schneil said, turning her head just slightly in my direction.

"Through you. Through the two of you," I murmured.

I sensed that they opened their eyes wide in the darkness and exchanged a look, not understanding. I explained that since that night in their bungalow on the shores of Lake Yarina when they had told me about them, the Machiguenga habladores had lived with me, intriguing me, disturbing me, that since then I had tried a thousand times to imagine them as they wandered through the forest, collecting and repeating stories, fables, gossip, tales they'd invented, from one little Machiguenga island to another in this Amazonian sea in which they drifted, borne on the current of adversity. I told them that, for some reason I found hard to pin down, the existence of those story-tellers, finding out what they were doing and what importance it had in the life of their people, had been, for twenty-three years, a great stimulus for my own work, a source of inspiration and an example I would have liked to emulate. I realized how excited my voice sounded, and fell silent.

By a sort of unspoken agreement, we had halted alongside a pile of tree trunks and branches heaped up in the center of the clearing as though ready to be set alight for a bonfire. We had sat down or leaned back against the logs. Kashiri[1] could now be seen, a yellow-orange crescent, surrounded by his vast harem of sparkling fireflies. There were a lot of mosquitoes as well as clouds of gnats, and we waved our hands back and forth to shoo them away from our faces.

"How really odd. Who would ever have thought that you'd remember a thing like that? And, stranger still, that it would take on such importance in your life?" Edwin Schneil said at last, just to say something. He seemed perplexed and a little flustered. "I didn't even remember our having touched, back then, on the subject of—story-tellers? No, speakers—is that the right word? How odd, how very odd."

"It doesn't surprise me at all that Martín and the schoolmistress of New World didn't want to tell you anything about them," Mrs. Schneil broke in after a moment. "It's a subject no Machiguenga likes to talk about. It's something very private, very secret. Not even with the two of us, who've known them for such a long time now, who've seen so many of them born. I don't understand it. Because they tell you everything, about their beliefs, their ayahuasca rites, the witch doctors. They don't keep anything to themselves. Except anything having to do with the habladores. It's the one thing they always shy away from. Edwin and I have often wondered why there's that taboo."

"Yes, it's a strange thing," Edwin Schneil agreed. "It's hard to understand, because they're very communicative and never object to answering any question they're asked. They're the best informants in the world; ask any anthropologist who's been around here. Maybe they don't want to talk about them or have people meet them, because the habladores are the repositories of their family secrets. They know all the Machiguengas' private affairs. What's that proverb? You don't wash dirty linen in public. Perhaps the taboo about habladores has to do with some feeling of that sort."

In the darkness, Mrs. Schneil laughed. "Well, that's a theory that doesn't convince me," she said. "Because the Machiguengas aren't at all secretive about their personal concerns. If you only knew how often they've left me flabbergasted and red in the face from what they tell me . . . ."

---

1. The moon.

"But, in any case, I can assure you you're wrong if you think it's a religious taboo," Edwin Schneil declared. "It isn't. The habladores aren't sorcerers or priests, like the seripigari or the machikanari. They're tellers of tales, that's all."

"I know that," I said. "You explained that to me the first time. And that's precisely what moves me. That the Machiguengas consider mere storytellers so important that they have to keep their existence a secret."

Every so often a silent shadow passed by, crackled briefly, and the Schneils crackled back what must have been the equivalent of a "Good night," and the shadow disappeared into the darkness. Not a sound came from the huts. Was the whole village already fast asleep?

"And in all these years, you've never heard an hablador?" I asked.

"I've never been that lucky," Mrs. Schneil said. "Up until now they've never offered me that opportunity. But Edwin's had the chance."

"Twice, even." He laughed. "Though in a quarter of a century that's not very often, is it? I hope what I'm going to say won't disappoint you. But I do believe I wouldn't want to repeat the experience."

The first time had been by sheer happenstance, ten years or more before. The Schneils had been living in a small Machiguenga settlement on the Tikompinía for several months, when one morning, leaving his wife in the village, Edwin had gone off to visit another family of the community a few hours upriver by canoe, taking with him a young boy to help him paddle. On reaching their destination, they found that instead of the five or six Machiguengas who lived there, whom Edwin knew, there were at least twenty people gathered together, a number of them from distant hamlets. Oldsters and young children, men and women were squatting in a half circle, facing a man sitting cross-legged in front of them, declaiming. He was a storyteller. Nobody objected to Edwin Schneil and the lad sitting down to listen. And the storyteller did not interrupt his monologue when they joined the audience.

"He was a man getting on in years and spoke so fast that I had trouble following him. He must have been speaking for a good while already. But he didn't seem tired; quite the contrary. The performance went on for several hours more. Every now and then they'd hand him a gourdful of masato and he'd take a swallow to clear his throat. No, I'd never seen that storyteller before. Quite old, at first sight, but as you know, one ages quickly here in the jungle. An old man, among the Machiguengas, can mean one no more than thirty. He was a short man, with a powerful build, very expressive. You or I or anyone else who talked on and on for that many hours would be hoarse-voiced and worn out. But he wasn't. He went on and on, putting everything he had into it. It was his job, after all, and I don't doubt he did it well."

What did he talk about? It was impossible to remember. What a hodgepodge! A bit of everything, anything that came into his head. What he'd done the day before, and the four worlds of the Machiguenga cosmos; his travels, magic herbs, people he'd known; the gods, the little gods, and fabulous creatures of the tribe's pantheon. Animals he'd seen and celestial geography, a maze of rivers with names nobody could possibly remember. Edwin Schneil had had to concentrate to follow the torrent of words that leapt from a cassava crop to the armies of demons of Kientibakori, the spirit of evil, and from there to births, marriages, and deaths in different families or the iniquities of the time of the tree-bleeding, as they called the rubber boom. Very soon Edwin Schneil found himself less interested in the storyteller than in the fascinated, rapt attention with which the Machiguengas listened to him, greeting his jokes with great roars of laughter or sharing his sadness. Their eyes avid, their mouths agape, not one pause, not a single inflection of what the man said was lost on them.

I listened to the linguist the way the Machiguengas had listened to the storyteller. Yes, they did exist, and were like the ones in my dreams.

"To tell the truth, I remember very little of what he said," Edwin Schneil added. "I'm just giving you a few examples. What a mishmash! I can remember his telling about the initiation ceremony of a young shaman, with ayahuasca,[2] under the guidance of a seripigari.[3] He recounted the visions he'd had. Strange, incoherent ones, like certain modern poems. He also spoke of the properties of a little bird, the chobíburiti; if you crush the small bones of its wing and bury them in the floor of the hut, that assures peace in the family."

"We tried his formula and it really didn't work all that well," Mrs. Schneil joked. "Would you say it did, Edwin?"

He laughed.

"The storytellers are their entertainment. They're their films and their television," he added after a pause, serious once more. "Their books, their circuses, all the diversions we civilized people have. They have only one diversion in the world. The storytellers are nothing more than that."

"Nothing less than that," I corrected him gently.

"What's that you say?" he put in, disconcerted. "Well, yes. But forgive me for pressing one point. I don't think there's anything religious behind it. That's why all this mystery, the secrecy they surround them with, is so odd."

"If something matters greatly to you, you surround it with mystery," it occurred to me to say.

"There's no doubt about that," Mrs. Schneil agreed. "The habladores matter a great deal to them. But we haven't discovered why."

Another silent shadow passed by and crackled, and the Schneils crackled back. I asked Edwin whether he'd talked with the old storyteller that time.

"I had practically no time to. I was exhausted when he'd finished talking. All my bones ached, and I fell asleep immediately. I'd sat for four or five hours, remember, without changing position, after having paddled against the current nearly all day. And listened to that chittering of anecdotes. I was all tuckered out. I fell asleep, and when I woke up, the storyteller had gone. And since the Machiguengas don't like to talk about them, I never heard anything more about him."

There he was. In the murmurous darkness of New Light all around me I could see him: skin somewhere between copper and greenish, gathered by the years into innumerable folds; cheekbones, nose, and forehead decorated with lines and circles meant to protect him from the claws and fangs of wild beasts, the harshness of the elements, the enemy's magic and his darts; squat of build, with short muscular legs and a small loincloth around his waist; and no doubt carrying a bow and a quiver of arrows. There he was, walking amid the bushes and the tree trunks, barely visible in the dense undergrowth, walking, walking, after speaking for ten hours, toward his next audience, to go on with his storytelling. How had he begun? Was it a hereditary occupation? Was he specially chosen? Was it something forced upon him by others?

Mrs. Schneil's voice erased the image. "Tell him about the other storyteller," she said. "The one who was so aggressive. The albino. I'm sure that will interest him."

---

2. Hallucinogen.   3. Fermented yucca juice; also a shaman.

"Well, I don't know whether he was really an albino." Edwin Schneil laughed in the darkness. "Among ourselves, we also called him the gringo."

This time it hadn't been by chance. Edwin Schneil was staying in a settlement by the Timpía with a family of old acquaintances, when other families from around about began arriving unexpectedly, in a state of great excitement. Edwin became aware of great palavers[4] going on; they pointed at him, then went off to argue. He guessed the reason for their alarm and told them not to worry; he would leave at once. But when the family he was staying with insisted, the others all agreed that he could stay. However, when the person they were waiting for appeared, another long and violent argument ensued, because the storyteller, gesticulating wildly, rudely insisted that the stranger leave, while his hosts were determined that he should stay. Edwin Schneil decided to take his leave of them, telling them he didn't want to be the cause of dissension. He bundled up his things and left. He was on his way down the path toward another settlement when the Machiguengas he'd been staying with caught up with him. He could come back, he could stay. They'd persuaded the storyteller.

"In fact, nobody was really convinced that I should stay, least of all the storyteller," he added. "He wasn't at all pleased at my being there. He made his feeling of hostility clear to me by not looking at me even once. That's the Machiguenga way: using your hatred to make someone invisible. But we and that family on the Timpía had a very close relationship, a spiritual kinship. We called each other 'father' and 'son' . . ."

"Is the law of hospitality a very powerful one among the Machiguengas?"

"The law of kinship, rather," Mrs. Schneil answered. "If 'relatives' go to stay with their kin, they're treated like princes. It doesn't happen often, because of the great distances that separate them. That's why they called Edwin back and resigned themselves to his hearing the storyteller. They didn't want to offend a 'kinsman.'"

"They'd have done better to be less hospitable and let me leave." Edwin Schneil sighed. "My bones still ache and my mouth even more, I've yawned so much remembering that night."

It was twilight and the sun had not yet set when the storyteller began talking, and he went on with his stories all night long, without once stopping. When at last he fell silent, the light was gilding the tops of the trees and it was nearly midmorning. Edwin Schneil's legs were so cramped, his body so full of aches and pains, that they had to help him stand up, take a few steps, learn to walk again.

"I've never felt so awful in my life," he muttered. "I was half dead from fatigue and physical discomfort. An entire night fighting off sleep and muscle cramp. If I'd gotten up, they would have been very offended. I only followed his tales for the first hour, or perhaps two. After that, all I could do was to keep trying not to fall asleep. And hard as I tried, I couldn't keep my head from nodding from one side to the other like the clapper of a bell."

He laughed softly, lost in his memories.

"Edwin still has nightmares remembering that night's vigil, swallowing his yawns and massaging his legs." Mrs. Schneil laughed.

"And the storyteller?" I asked.

4. Verbal exchanges.

"He had a huge birthmark," Edwin Schneil said. He paused, searching his memories or looking for words to describe them. "And hair redder than mine. A strange person. What the Machiguengas call a serigórompi. Meaning an eccentric; someone different from the rest. Because of that carrot-colored hair of his, we called him the albino or the gringo among ourselves."

The mosquitoes were drilling into my ankles. I could feel their bites and almost see them piercing my skin, which would now swell into horribly painful little blisters. It was the price I had to pay every time I came to the jungle. Amazonia had never failed to exact it of me.

"A huge birthmark?" I stammered, scarcely able to get the words out. "Do you mean uta? An ulcer eating his face away, like that little boy we saw this morning in New World . . ."

"No, no. A birthmark. An enormous dark birthmark," Edwin Schneil interrupted, raising his hand. "It covered the whole right side of his face. An impressive sight, I assure you. I'd never seen a man with one like it, never. Neither among the Machiguengas nor anywhere else. And I haven't seen its like since, either."

I could feel the mosquitoes biting me on all the parts of my body that had no protection: face, neck, arms, hands. The clouds that had hidden the moon were gone and there was Kashiri, clear and bright and not yet full, looking at us. A shiver ran down my body from head to foot.

"He had red hair?" I murmured very slowly. My mouth was dry, but my hands were sweating.

"Redder than mine." He laughed. "A real gringo, I swear. Though perhaps an albino, after all. I didn't have much time to get a close look at him. I've told you what a state I was in after that storytelling session. As though I'd been anesthetized. And when I came to, he was gone, of course. So he wouldn't have to talk to me or bear the sight of my face any longer."

"How old would you say he was?" I managed to get out, with immense fatigue, as though I'd been the one who'd been talking all night long.

Edwin Schneil shrugged. "Who knows?" He sighed. "You've doubtless realized how hard it is to tell how old they are. They themselves don't know. They don't calculate their age the same way we do, and what's more, they all reach that average age very quickly. What you might call Machiguenga age. But certainly younger than I am. About your age, or perhaps a bit younger."

I pretended to cough two or three times to conceal how unnerved I was. I suddenly felt a fierce, intolerable desire to smoke. It was as though every pore in my body had suddenly opened, demanding to inhale a thousand and one puffs of smoke. Five years before, I had smoked what I thought would be my last cigarette; I was convinced that I'd freed myself from tobacco forever; for a long time now, the very smell of cigarette smoke had irritated me, and here, out of the blue, in the darkness of New Light, an overwhelming urge to smoke had arisen from who knows what mysterious depths.

"Did he speak well?" I heard myself ask softly.

"Speak well?" Edwin Schneil asked. "He spoke on and on, without stopping, without pausing, without punctuation marks." He laughed, deliberately exaggerating. "The way storytellers talk. Spilling out all the things that ever were and ever will be. He was what he was, in a word: a teller of tales, and a real chatterbox."

"I mean Machiguenga," I said. "Did he speak it well? Couldn't he . . ."

"Go on," Schneil said.

"Nothing," I said. "A nonsensical idea. Nothing, nothing."

Though I was under the impression that my attention was concentrated on the gnats and mosquitoes biting me and my longing to smoke, I must have asked Edwin Schneil, as in a dream, with a strange ache in my jaws and tongue, as though I were exhausted from using them too much, how long ago all this had been—"Oh, it must have been three and a half years or so ago," he replied—and whether he had heard him again, or seen him, or had news of him, and listened as he answered no to all three questions, as I knew he would: it was a subject the Machiguengas didn't like to talk about.

When I said good night to the Schneils—they were sleeping at Martín's—and went off to the hut where my hammock was, I woke up Lucho Llosa to ask him for a cigarette. "Since when have you smoked?" he said in surprise as he handed me one with hands fumbling from sleep.

I didn't light it. I held it between my fingers at my lips, going through the motions of smoking, all through that long night, while I swung gently in the hammock, listening to the quiet breathing of Lucho, Alejandro, and the pilots, hearing the chirring of the forest, feeling the seconds go by, one by one, slow, solemn, improbable, filled with wonder.

We returned to Yarinacocha very early. Halfway there, we were forced to land because we were overtaken by a storm. In the small Campa village on the banks of the Urubamba where we took refuge, there was an American missionary who might have been a character out of Faulkner—single-minded, fearlessly stubborn, and frighteningly heroic. He had lived in this remote corner of the world for years with his wife and several small children. In my memory I can still see him standing in the torrential rain, energetically leading hymns with both arms and singing in his throaty voice to set a good example, under a flimsy shelter that threatened to collapse at any moment beneath the tremendous downpour. The twenty or so Campas barely moved their lips and gave the impression that they were making no sound, yet kept their eyes riveted on him with the same rapt fascination with which the Machiguengas doubtless contemplated their storytellers.

When we resumed our flight, the Schneils asked me whether I wasn't feeling well. Yes, perfectly well, I replied, though rather tired, since I hadn't slept very much. We stayed in Yarinacocha just long enough to climb into the jeep that would take us to Pucallpa to catch the Fawcett flight to Lima. In the plane Lucho asked me: "Why the long face? What went wrong this time?" I was on the point of explaining why I wasn't saying a word and looked more or less stunned, but when I opened my mouth I realized I wouldn't be able to. It couldn't be summed up in a mere anecdote; it was too unreal and too literary to be plausible, and too serious to joke about as though it were just an amusing incident.

I now knew the reason for the taboo. Did I? Yes. Could it be possible? Yes, it could. That was why they avoided talking about them, that was why they had jealously hidden them from anthropologists, linguists, Dominican missionaries over the last twenty years. That was why they did not appear in the writings of modern ethnologists on the Machiguengas. They were not protecting the institution or the idea of the storyteller in the abstract. They were protecting him. No doubt because he had asked them to. So as not to arouse the Viracochas' curiosity about this strange graft onto the tribe. And they had gone on doing as he asked for so many years now, providing him refuge by way of a taboo which had spread to the entire institution, to the hablador in the abstract. If that was how it had been, they had a great deal of respect for him. If that was how it was, in their eyes he was one of them.

We began editing the program that same night at the channel after going home to shower and change, and I to a pharmacy for ointment and antihistamines for the insect bites. We decided that the program would be in the form of a travelogue, intercutting commentaries and recollections with the interviews we'd done in Yarinacocha and the Alto Urubamba. As he edited the material, Moshé grumbled at us as usual for not having taken certain shots some other way, or for having taken others the way we had. It was then that I remembered that he, too, was Jewish.

"How do you get along with the Chosen People here in Peru?"

"Like a monkey with a mirror, of course," he said. "Why? Do you want to get yourself circumcised?"

"I wonder if you'd do me a favor. Would you have any way of finding out where a family of the community that went to Israel is now?"

"Are we going to do a Tower of Babel on kibbutzim?" Lucho said. "In that case, we'll have to do one on the Palestinian refugees. But how can we? Doesn't the program end next week?"

"The Zuratas. The father, Don Salomón, had a little grocery store in Breña. The son, Saúl, was a friend of mine. They went to Israel in the early seventies, it seems. If you could find out their address there, you'd be doing me a favor."

"I'll see what I can do," Moshé answered. "I imagine they keep a register of such things in the community."

The program on the Institute of Linguistics and the Machiguengas turned out to be longer than we'd foreseen. When we gave it to Control they informed us that on that particular Sunday they'd sold space for a definite time slot, so that if we didn't cut the program ourselves to exactly one hour, the operator would do it any old way he pleased when he put it on the air. Thoroughly pissed off, we had to cut it in a rush, as time was running short. We were already editing the final Tower of Babel for the following Sunday. We'd decided that it would be an anthology of the twenty-four previous programs. But as usual we had to change our plans. For the very start of the program, I'd tried to persuade Doris Gibson to let herself be interviewed and help us compile a short biography of her life as a founder and director of magazines, a businesswoman, a fighter against dictatorship and also its victim—on one famous occasion she'd hauled off and slapped the policemen who had come to seize copies of *Caretas*[5]—and above all, a woman who, in a society that in those days was far more macho and prejudiced than it is now, had been able to make a career for herself and achieve success in fields that were considered male monopolies. At the same time, Doris had been one of the most beautiful women in Lima, courted by millionaires, and the muse of famous painters and poets. The impetuous Doris, who is nonetheless very shy, had turned me down, because, she said, the cameras intimidated her. But that last week she had changed her mind and sent word that she was willing to appear on the program.

I interviewed her, and that interview, together with the anthology, saw the end of the Tower of Babel. Faithful to its destiny, the final program, which Moshé, Lucho, Alejandro, and I watched at my house, sitting around a tableful of Chinese food and ice-cold beer, fell victim to technical imponderables. For one of those mysterious reasons—celestial sabotage—which were the daily bread of the channel, unexpected jazz numbers appeared out of nowhere just as the broadcast began and provided back-

5. A popular magazine.

ground music to all of Doris's stories about General Odría's[6] dictatorship, police seizures of *Caretas,* and Sérvulo Gutiérrez's paintings.

After the program was over and we were drinking to its death and non-resurrection, the phone rang. It was Doris, asking me whether it wouldn't have been more appropriate to have backed her interview with Arequipan yaravíes (she is, among other things, a fiercely loyal Arequipeña) rather than that outlandish jazz. After Lucho, Moshé, and Alejandro had had a good laugh at the explanations I had invented to justify the use of jazz on the program, Moshé said: "By the way, before I forget, I found out what you asked me to."

More than a week had gone by and I hadn't reminded him, because I could guess the answer and was a little unnerved at the prospect of having my suspicions confirmed.

"It seems they never did go to Israel," he said. "Where did you get the idea they'd left the country?"

"You mean the Zuratas?" I asked, knowing very well what he was talking about.

"Don Salomón, at least, didn't go. He died here. He's buried in the Jewish cemetery in Lima, the one on the Avenida Colonial." Moshé took a scrap of paper out of his pocket and read: "October 23, 1960. That's the day they buried him, if you need further details. My grandfather knew him and attended his funeral. As for his son, your friend, he may have gone to Israel, but I couldn't find out for sure. None of the people I asked knew anything about him."

But I do, I thought. I know everything.

"Did he have a big birthmark on his face?" Moshé asked. "My grandfather even remembers that. Did they call him the Phantom of the Opera?"[7]

"An enormous one. We called him Mascarita."

Christa Wolf
b. 1929

Christa Wolf is one of the best-known but also one of the most controversial writers to have emerged from the German Democratic Republic. A novelist, essayist, and literary critic, she evolved from a passionate advocate of socialism into one of its critics; after a long writing career that had brought her alternating waves of rejection and acclaim from East German authorities at some moments and from the West German literary establishment at others, she became the center of full-fledged controversy during the 1990s. The first furious debate arose with the publication of her book of short stories *What Remains,* whose title story examines in partly autobiographical fashion her own surveillance at the hand of the East German secret service. This story, which is highly critical of the GDR political establishment, had been written years earlier, but it was not published until 1990, a year after German reunification; Wolf's critics accused her of opportunism and cowardice in delaying its publication until after the regime she criticized had fallen. Controversy erupted again in 1993, when increased access to secret service archives revealed that Wolf had actually worked as an "informal collaborator" for the East German secret police from 1959 to 1962. Not only was Wolf's individual career at stake in the acrimonious debates over her political engagement but a host of issues was also raised regarding the role of intellectuals and writers in the former GDR. These highly publicized discussions

---

6. Military ruler of Peru from 1948 to 1956.
7. Musical noted for its masked characters. The protago-

nist Mascarita ("Little Mask") gets his nickname because of the birthmark covering half his face.

brought to a climax the long and distinguished career of a writer who has always been engaged with the political questions of her time and whose literary works highlight all the major turning points in the historical development of the GDR.

After studying German literature at the universities of Jena and Leipzig from 1949 to 1953, Wolf published her first book in 1961. But her first breakthrough came with *Divided Heaven* in 1963, a novel that won her great acclaim in East Germany due to the protagonist's decision not to follow her lover to West Germany; this decision was interpreted as a rejection of West German culture and society. In *The Quest for Christa T.,* however, the novel that followed five years later, the protagonist is quite critical of life in a socialist society, and this led to attacks on Wolf by the East German Writers' Congress and praise from West German reviewers. In many subsequent novels and short stories, Wolf has explored Germany's Nazist past and its post–World War II division, the origins of violence and war, and modern society's engagement with technology. The novel *Accident: A Day's News* forms part of these investigations of modern technology. It was written in only four months during the summer of 1986, right after the major accident at the nuclear power plant in Chernobyl in the Ukraine, then still part of the Soviet system with which the East German government was allied. Her novel juxtaposes the lethal consequences of radioactive fallout with the beneficial effects of modern surgery. It focuses particularly on how the Chernobyl disaster was reported on East German radio and television; through the protagonist's reactions to this coverage and her subsequent reading of Joseph Conrad's novella *Heart of Darkness,* Wolf explores what truth literature might have to convey in an age dominated by mass media, which are themselves part of a broad range of extremely powerful new technologies.

from Accident: A Day's News[1]

I was in Kiev[2] only once in my life, in May it was. I remember white houses. Sloping streets. Lots of green, blossoms. The monument to the dead of World War II on the hill above the Dnieper. Hazy images lost amid similar remembrances of other cities. Hazy as well the memory of a love which must have been fresh back then. Someday, soon, everything will have become memory for me. Someday, perhaps already in three, in four weeks—may the time pass quickly—the memory of this day will have gone out of focus as well. Unforgettable: looking out over the Dnieper, mighty Eastern river. The bend of the river. The plain beyond. And the sky. A sky such as this, pure blue.

"*. . . Aghast, the mothers search the sky for the inventions of learned men . . .*"[3] Now we have reached that point. But they can search for a long time, they won't see anything. It is only the suspicion gnawing within them that colors the innocent sky such a poisonous shade. The malignant sky. So the mothers sit down by the radio and attempt to learn the new words. Becquerel.[4] Explanations—by scientists who, unimpeded by any sense of awe as to what holds nature together there at its innermost core,[5] wish not only to know but also to implement. Half-life is what the mothers learn today. Iodine 131. Cesium.[6] Explanations by other scientists who contradict what the first ones said; who are furious and helpless. Now all of that was drizzling down upon us together with the carriers of radioactive substances, such as rain,

---

1. Translated by Heike Schwarzbauer and Rick Takvorian.
2. Capital of the Ukraine, the Soviet Republic where the Chernobyl accident occurred in 1986.
3. A quotation from Bertolt Brecht's poem "1940."
4. A measure of radioactivity.
5. Echoing Faust's ambition in Goethe's *Faust:* "I'll learn

what holds the world together / There at its innermost core."
6. Iodine-131 and cesium-137 are common elements in radioactive fallout. The half-life of a radioactive element is the interval in which half of its atomic nuclei decay.

but you, brother, and may the steady hand of your surgeon preserve your eyesight, will no more get to see it than we will. Calling it "cloud" is merely an indication of our inability to keep pace linguistically with the progress of science. Incessantly gathering information and comparing the new with the previously recorded, our perception apparatus—whose headquarters, I have been told, along with those of the language center, are in the left hemisphere of the brain, where the advanced cognitive functions of the human convene—usually selects that name to designate a new phenomenon which shows the highest number of shared characteristics with those material manifestations which it has known since time immemorial. That's how you would explain the process to me. That is approximately how you explained it to me only recently, when you demonstrated the program stored in your personal computer. I saw how you relished its obedience when you called up the program. You see. It understood. Now it's searching for PH I. Do you see that? READY. So now I press this key. Now it's calculating for us how an arbitrary emission spreads out from its source when that source is twenty meters above the earth's surface. So, let's take a chimney. And the emission can be, for instance, sulfurous smoke. There. And so that you can take it all in at one glance: blipblipblipblipblip: the corresponding graph. That is the advantage of this system, it also does diagrams. Now you can see the curve: quite a sharp rise up to about two hundred meters and then, here, the peak: at a given chimney height of twenty meters, the maximum concentration of pollution would be expected to lie along a circle with a radius of approximately two hundred meters from the source of emission. And, of course, the higher the chimney, the farther the emission area from the source. What shall we say. How about a chimney thirty meters high. The key. READY. Blipblipblipblip: the figures. Now the graph key again. There you go. The peak has moved noticeably. Which was to be expected. So, dear brother, if you had your computer by your bedside you could calculate the drift of our cloud—provided you had the initial data, such as divergence, height of the reactor, wind velocity, to feed into your computer. But you don't . . . .

How strange that *a-tom* in Greek means the same as *in-dividuum* in Latin: unsplittable. The inventors of these words knew neither nuclear fission nor schizophrenia. Whence the modern compulsion to split into ever smaller parts, to split off entire parts of the personality from that ancient being once thought indivisible . . . .

* * *

That evening they showed for the first time, on several TV channels, the silhouette of the accident reactor, an image which I expect will engrave itself in our consciousness just like that of the atomic mushroom cloud. They put some gentlemen in front of the cameras who, solely on account of their nicely tailored gray or bluish-gray suits, the matching ties, the matching haircuts, their prudent choice of words and the whole official capacity of their posture, radiated a soothing effect—quite in contrast to the handful of young, bearded, sweater-clad individuals who, on account of their agitated talk and manic gesticulations, aroused the suspicion that they had unlawfully commandeered the microphones, and I had to think of the people of the country, the silent, hardworking people of both countries[7] whose gazes unite in the evening on the TV screen, and I realized: They will take those in sweaters less seriously than those in their suits made to measure, with their measured opinions and their measured conduct; they want to sit back in their armchairs after a hard day's

7. The people of the two Germanies, the German Democratic Republic and the Federal Republic of Germany.

work like me and have their beer—wine in my case, what of it—and they want to be presented with something that makes them happy, a complicated murder plot, for example, but nothing which affects them too much, and that is the normal behavior we have been taught, so that it would be unjust to reproach them for this behavior merely because it contributes to our deaths. I, too, sensed a strong inclination toward this normal behavior in myself, my wine was well chilled and gave off a greenish glow when I held the glass up to the lamp, and I felt good in my chair, in this room and in the old house; you too, brother, would get well, and why shouldn't a whole mass of other problems find an amicable solution. So everything could have stayed the way it was for a while longer as far as I was concerned, and I, too, was listening to the TV gentlemen in this secret hope. On the one channel they were more preoccupied with the cloud, which now also belonged to our large TV family in a small way, the ragamuffin child, so to speak, and if I understood correctly, our cloud must have split in two at some point, or it drifted off in one direction and back in the other; in any case, Northern and Southern Europe were reprimanded for their regrettable levels of radioactivity, but what could I do for the farmers who swore wildly into the camera because no one could tell them who was going to pay for the plowed-under lettuce; their money was their problem. My problem, on the other hand, was whether we, in an emergency such as this, had to consider ourselves part of Northern Europe, which we otherwise do, flippantly and, actually, out of vanity, or whether we do not, more precisely, belong to Central Europe. In the meantime, the gentlemen in the suits had enumerated to one another all those safety factors which exclude the possibility of a reactor accident and repeated to each other, and to us as well, all the reasons that seemingly make the so-called peaceful utilization of the atom indispensable—that was their word—and if one of them could not immediately come up with some argument, then another came to his aid; it was like a good lesson at school, and I was listening so attentively that after a few minutes I, for my part, was ready to whisper the answers to them, and I did it experimentally and was nearly always right. But then the moderator, who was interested in spreading a calm, composed atmosphere, thought he could safely pin down one of the two gentlemen to the statement that, even in this particularly progressive realm of science and technology, one could make absolutely faultless prognoses about the safety of the plants in question. But of course! I wanted to come to the aid of the interviewee, but that was hasty of me; for now the moderator and I were forced to learn, to our painful surprise, that this guy—despite his general willingness to be accommodating—was not about to be pinned down to this statement. Well, we heard him say, there was no such thing as an absolutely faultless prognosis in such a young branch of technology. As always with new technological developments, one would have to take certain risks into account until one fully mastered this technology as well. That was a law that also applied to the peaceful utilization of nuclear energy.

Now I should have grown cold. Now I should have been shocked or outraged. No such thing. I knew very well that they knew it. Only, I had not expected that they would also say it—be it only this one time. The text for a letter went through my mind in which I—imploringly, how else—was to communicate to someone that the risk of nuclear technology was not comparable to any other risk and that one absolutely had to renounce this technology if there was even the slightest element of uncertainty. I could not think of a real address for the letter in my mind, so I swore out loud and switched channels. I usually do not have the willpower, particularly not that evening, to switch off the TV. You can call this addiction, brother heart, and have done so with slight rebuke; I won't argue. To each his own button, as the rats have theirs, to each his weak point, through which the blessings of civilization can penetrate.

I had a choice of two films, both of which I already knew. In the older black-and-white movie, the actor playing Ingrid Bergman's husband attempted to drive her, his wife, crazy with flickering gaslights and other such primitive apparitions.[8] In the other one, an aging officer in the English secret service, who is actually already retired, succeeds, with the help of his good old psychological methods, in exposing an agent from the other side in the heart of his own headquarters. In tasteful shades of brown, with time-tested actors. I kept pressing the channel button and saw about half of each film. The least of my worries that evening was whether this continual flicking back and forth between channels makes for good mental training, or whether it weakens the powers of concentration. I was feeling superior to the agents of both world systems because they did not know and would not—for a long time, perhaps too long—catch on to the fact that their profession had become redundant. One, two, three radioactive clouds from one, two, three reactors in different parts of the world and the governments would be forced to change their policies out of the instinct for self-preservation, and proceed to downright press their secrets upon the other side. But, naturally, I did not delude myself into thinking that it had already registered this evening with the employers of these nice agents that this radioactive cloud had the capacity of letting one's adversary—or *adversaries*—vanish into thin air. That the sacrifice of doing without the enemy was not the least of the sacrifices which it categorically demanded of us. However, I wondered whether the simple instinct for self-preservation can remain intact at all in people who concentrate long enough on the destruction of the adversary . . .

I went to telephone one more time. In the evening as well the nurse—the night nurse by now—had made reassuring remarks to my sister-in-law concerning you, brother. No, you had in fact woken up, had been thirsty and been given a drink. How grateful I was to the nurse who had quenched your thirst. We reassured each other, talked a little about how we had spent this day, did not mention and did not want to know that you were feeling very poorly, that you were sick to your stomach and horrible pains had set in. I urged my sister-in-law, saying that it would be all right, to take a pill that night, to get some sleep for once. We still could not and would not say to each other all that we had imagined; which films had been running in our heads, in different versions, among them the one where the operation failed. We channeled all those flickering images to those areas of our brain where forgetting takes place . . .

I switched off the TV, locked the front, then the back door, did the supper dishes, put the cold cuts in the refrigerator. And discovered the parade of ants moving across the kitchen floor past the refrigerator, in a straight line, up the cupboard, heading with great determination across the marble surface for the tray with the jam jars. At last I knew how the ants got into the jam. So I had to liberate cupboard and kitchen floor from the ants, wiping them away, drowning them, crushing them, and sweeping them up and plugging, with a cottonball drenched in vinegar, the small hole in the rotten door frame out of which came marching the uninterrupted column. That would do for a few days. Then, luckily just in time, I remembered to fill buckets and pots with water, since, according to a public notice at the store, the water was going to be cut off for a few hours the following morning because of work at the pump house.

---

8. *Gaslight* (1944), directed by George Cukor and featuring Charles Boyer in the male lead role.

In the bathroom I forced myself to go through the same motions as every night, although I was so tired that I wanted only to sleep. Was I losing more hair than usual? What were the first symptoms, anyway? I still had to find a book in which to read a few pages to help me fall asleep. I suppose it was thanks to my tiredness that I took from the shelf the thin book by an author who had been urgently recommended to me for a long time but whom I still had not read because of my aversion to seafaring stories: Joseph Conrad. *Heart of Darkness.*[9] I savored the first seconds of relief in bed, adjusted the position of the lamp above me, and, in a detached manner, read the first page, which, as expected, is about a ship. A seaworthy yawl by the name of *Nelly* which lies at the Thames estuary, waiting for the turn of the tide. Oh, well. I tried to picture the Thames estuary as I had once seen it, but the inner image was immediately pushed aside by a description of the evening light across the water which left me wide awake. "The day was ending in a serenity of still and exquisite brilliance"—this is how it starts. I read it twice. But then the narrator, whose name is Marlow, suddenly spoke the following sentence right to my face: "And this also has been one of the dark places of the earth." Finally, after all this time, I once again felt that thump against my heart which I feel only when a writer speaks to me from the depths of self-experience.

And this also has been one of the dark places of the earth. This also. And also this. I listened to the sounds of the night coming in through the open window, the quiet wind, the sleepy bark of a dog, and, for the first time this year, the frogs. I read on in tense expectation, and after only a few sentences I came to realize: yes, this Marlow knows what he is talking about. He has seen and understood it all, a hundred years prior to this, "our time," and here I lie and listen to him, frightened and delighted, speaking of the wilderness, of the deep darkness of the unknown continent, Africa, and of the secrets in the hearts of its inhabitants, to whom there is no path for the white conquerors. "Mind, none of us would feel exactly like this. What saves us is efficiency—the devotion to efficiency . . ." Ivory. Ivory, any amount of it, wrested from the wilderness and the savages, at any price and by any means, imaginable and unimaginable. Who can ever forget the old black man who gets beaten. Who the forest of death. Who the native village, its inhabitants scattered in mad terror: "What became of the hens I don't know either. I should think the cause of progress got them, anyhow." I groaned, for several reasons, among them in admiration for this writer. How he knew. How alone he must have been. And, on top of everything else, how can I bear to live with these six black men, forged together by chains. "They were called criminals, and the outraged law, like the bursting shells, had to come to them, an insoluble mystery from the sea." I could not read any further, not that evening. Leafing through, I picked out individual phrases, there they were: "Truth—truth stripped of its cloak of time." I would read on tomorrow, perhaps also find out which devices he used to such effect. How he managed to free himself from concepts such as "device," "effect"—the hardest thing of all. Enough for today. That writer, he knew the meaning of sorrow. He set out right into the heart of the blind spot of that culture to which he also belonged, and not in thought alone. Fearlessly into the heart of darkness. And he saw the light which must have led him too, on his way like a "running blaze on a plain, like a flash of lightning in the clouds."

We live in the flicker—may it last as long as the old earth keeps rolling.

So does this person speak to me. So shy, I could hardly expect to find words such as "hate" and "love" in his works. "Greed" I found, often. Greed, greed, greed . . .

9. See page 61.

Before falling asleep I saw that apparatus in intensive-care units which they call an "IV." Are you on an IV, brother? Are you asleep? Then a voice read me to sleep with the passage from the fairy tale in which the true queen is turned into a duck. Now that night the kitchen-boy saw a duck come swimming up the drain, and it said: How now, lord king, art asleep or waking . . .[1]

Late at night I was startled by a voice and by a crying. The voice had called from far away: A faultless monster! The crying came from me, as I noticed after quite some time. I was sitting in bed crying. My face was flooded with tears. Just then, very close to me, in my dream, a giant, nauseatingly putrescent moon had swiftly sunk down below the horizon. A large photograph of my dead mother had been fastened to the dark night sky. I screamed.

How difficult it would be, brother, to take leave of this earth.

◆━━◆ ⚏◆⚏ ◆━━◆

Abdelrahman Munif
b. 1933

Abdelrahman Munif is one of the major Arab writers of the last three decades. He was born in 1933 in Amman, Jordan, the son of a Saudi father and an Iraqi mother, and spent large periods of his life in Jordan, Iraq, Syria, and Lebanon. He studied in Amman, Baghdad, Cairo, and Yugoslavia. This firsthand experience of many Arab countries was the result of a varied career, for he started as a law student and political activist in the Baath Party and then graduated with a degree in economics and became an oil specialist and journalist. Unlike many writers of his generation, he started writing late in his life: His first novel, *The Trees and the Assassination of Marzuq* (1973), appeared when he was forty years old. This wide experience coupled with the late start gave his writing Pan-Arab relevance and maturity.

The appearance of his first novel in 1973, the year of the October War with Israel and an oil boom, coincided with the rejuvenation of the Arabic novel and the exploration of untrodden paths of human experience. The change in literary sensibility toward modernistic writing that took root in the previous decade liberated Arabic literature from the constraints of single-voiced narration. Writers began to embrace the sophistication of polyphonic narrative with its pluralist perspectives and density of voices contending to shed doubt on each other's account of the plot. New novels suppressed their subject matter or submerged it in an elaborate labyrinth of narrative strategies. In addition, the concept of the individual hero and central plot gave way to an elaborate network of relationships in which all characters attain equal importance.

These changes are fully evident in Munif's novels, which abandon the outmoded concept of the individual hero and take their protagonists from the marginalized and violated. He tries to establish his unique fictional space, which is capable of capturing the contradictory nature of the Arab world. Like Hardy's Wessex or Faulkner's Yoknapatawpha, Munif created his imaginary desert town, Thebes, in his first novel and elaborated on it in a series of novels. In this imaginary place, which stands as a metaphor for the enire Arab world, Munif portrays a stagnant environment in which a number of impossibly romantic characters struggle to attain simple dreams.

Munif's most comprehensive metaphor of the Arab condition and its metamorphosis is his quintet *Cities of Salt* with its five parts: *Wilderness* (1984), *Farrow* (1985), *Variations on Night and Day* (1989), *The Uprooted* (1989), and *The Desert of Darkness* (1989). It is the epic contemporary Arabic novel *par excellence* and the contemporary heir of the archetypal Arab narrative of *The Thousand and One Nights*. Unlike Nagib Mahfouz's *Trilogy* with its Cairene world

---

1. A fairy tale by the brothers Grimm entitled "The Three Little Men in the Wood."

and family saga, Munif's quintet is a work of historical, cultural, and moral transformation of Arabia. The structure of the novel is akin to that of *The Thousand and One Nights* in which stories generate other stories in an endless sequence whose main character is time. On the surface, it tells the story of the collective transformation of a Bedouin society from a state of tribal existence into oil boom consumerism and modern state apparatus. The constant violations of tribal ethics and rebellion against its taboos are coupled with an inherent respect for them, a condition that enhances tension and sustains the nightmare. But beneath this surface one sees the dynamics of the impact of modernity on traditionalism, the development of an oppressive state machine, the inner mechanism of American control over the Arabian Peninsula, and the disintegration of the old cultural and moral ethos of Arabia. The excerpt given here highlights the disruptive role played by a new and enticing imported technology.

PRONUNCIATIONS:
> *Abdelrahman Munif:* ahbd-al-RACH-mahn mou-NEEF
> *Rezaie:* retz-EYE-ay

from Cities of Salt[1]

"The world is endless, Your Highness," said Rezaie quickly, "and no matter how far a man travels or how many places he visits, there are still places he must go, that must be visited. Even if everything in this world had an end and a limit, man's yearning to know and discover would still be endless and limitless."

He paused and shook his head, remembering all the places and things he had seen in his travels, and when he noticed the emir listening closely to all that he said, he went on in a different tone. "Your Highness, we should go somewhere together, travel in this world and get to know it."

The emir's laughter rang out, and he turned to his deputy.

"What do you say, Abu Rashwan?"

"Traveling by sea isn't very pleasant at first," said Hassan Rezaie, "but once you get used to it, there's nothing to compare to it."

"I prefer dry ground," replied the emir. He looked at his deputy and said ambiguously, "This seashore, here, in front of us, is killing us. What do you say we see what's beyond it?"

"The high seas are very different from these shoals, Your Excellency," said Hassan Rezaie enthusiastically. "The open sea is a different world!"

"The shallows are better." The emir laughed. "The shallows are safe and near home."

While they were speaking, three of Hassan Rezaie's seamen came into the tent, three of the employees who worked for him on board ship. Sweat ran down their burned red faces, which were the color of old copper. Two of them were carrying a medium-sized sack, containing something very heavy and valuable to judge from the way they carried it and placed it on the ground. The third carried a square black object that look like coal.

In silence, amid rapt attention, Hassan Rezaie got up confidently, took a short knife from his pocket and opened the sack. He asked one of his men to pull out what was inside. He did so very carefully, and Rezaie looked at the emir as he placed the gleaming box with one cloth side—it looked like wool—in front of him, but he re-

1. Translated by Peter Theroux.

mained silent. The emir had never seen anything like it before, and could not guess its purpose. When the ropes, or what looked like ropes, growing from the rear side of the box were connected to the black cube beside it, and Hassan Rezaie announced that everything was in place, he rubbed his hands, smiled broadly and sat beside the box, and looked at the emir and the others before proceeding to the next step. They were utterly silent and seemed a little afraid and curious. Rezaie cleared his throat. "This is a gift I have brought you from far away, Your Highness, and it will bring the whole world to you and bring you to the farthest point of the world, as you sit there."

The emir's eyes opened wide and he nodded continuously to show that he understood and grasped perfectly everything Rezaie was saying. He did not say a word but waited to see what would happen next.

"This machine, Your Excellency, is very sensitive and precise," said Rezaie in a different tone. "No one but yourself may touch it."[2]

The emir looked even more surprised and somewhat afraid, and his men looked at each other.

"Now, we begin," said Rezaie, smiling confidently and rubbing his hands.

He moved his hand to one side of the box and waited a moment, his eyes trained on its middle, his face very close, as if whispering to it. A green light went on in the machine's middle, and the emir looked at the others, and though he tried to be calm his looks were looks of fear and alarm. Rezaie turned some of the knobs on the box, and suddenly sharp voices burst from no one knew where. Everyone present started violently, and a number of the men retreated a few steps, and one man hid behind some others. The emir shifted in his seated position and looked at the others as if to ask them to be strong and prepared for anything. Rezaie moved the knobs more energetically than before. The green light grew brighter, then almost faded away, with a piercing squeak. He touched a knob again, and there was a burst of music. The sound of the music was clear, as if it came from within the tent. The men looked at each other, mildly shocked, and the emir crept toward the box, smiling. Rezaie adjusted the sound and turned it up until it filled the tent.

With pleasure mixed with terror the men listened to the music in silence. After a few minutes, with a quick and crafty movement no one saw, Hassan Rezaie stopped the music. A long, profound silence fell, so palpable that a man could have stroked it with his hands.

Rezaie spoke. "That was music, Your Highness, that was just one station, and there are so many others!"

With the same hidden deftness Hassan Rezaie moved his hand, and there was a distant sound. It rose and fell, and the green light on the box glowed and faded, and when the light glowed, the men heard a voice clearly.

"—And when a king of the land of Serendip dies, he is tied to the rear of a low cart, on his back, with the hair of his head brushing the soil of the earth, as a woman with a broom sweeps the dirt onto his head, crying, 'O people, yesterday this was your king. He owned you and held you in his power, and now he is as you see. He has left the world, and King of Death has taken his soul. Do not be fooled by life, ye who come after,' and so on for three days. He is then bedecked in sandalwood, camphor and saffron, and cremated. His ashes are scattered in the wind."[3]

---

2. The magical radio is treated here as an idol, not to be touched by anyone except the emir himself.

3. A quotation from one of the texts of Ibn al-Sirafi, a medieval Arab geographer.

This is what the men heard. They looked at each other, unable to believe what they had heard. The voice intermingled with other voices and the green light went out, and then they heard nothing.

They look uncomprehendingly at one another: How could this box speak and make music? Who was playing the instruments? Where did he sit? How could he eat and sleep, and how did that tiny space hold him? The speaker sounded like Ibn Naffeh or an eloquent imam! Was he playing the music, too, or was that someone else?

"One . . . two . . . and now three," said Hassan Rezaie delightedly.

Once more he moved his hand on the box, and it began to sing.

> O ship about to depart!
> I have among your happy riders a dear friend
> My eyes were bathed in tears when we said farewell
> My heart wept as I heard the news
> The sun has sunk beneath the horizon
> My soul sighed, I drew my last breath
> When my love embraced me and we said farewell
> My fate fled with him when the sails unfurled . . .

When the song ended, a voice said, "This is the Near East Broadcasting Service." The emir moved closer to Hassan Rezaie and spoke like a child who cannot hide his pleasure and delight. "Now let me do it! Just show me how."

"Let it rest. It has to rest!"

"Just once! Then it can rest."

The emir crept nearer, as a child who knows what fire is creeps nearer to it. Patiently, carefully, he placed his hand where Hassan Rezaie indicated and did as he was told. When the box emitted loud music he started and drew his hand away, and when the music rose to fill the tent he retreated slightly and looked into the men's silent faces. They watched his every movement warily, as if he were conveying to them that he knew more than they did, as if he knew what they didn't. After a few minutes of nodding happily, as if he had conjured up this music from an unknown place, as no one else could do, and after a short silence, Hassan Rezaie spoke uneasily. "Your Highness, it has to rest."

Quietly, expertly, he moved his hands on the box, first on one side, then on the other, then disconnected the ropes from the black stone and put them back. When he was done he rubbed his hands and looked at their faces, especially the emir's, asking them wordlessly what they thought of what they'd seen and heard. Their faces were impassive and uncomprehending, but the emir's head was nodding as if jogged by a strong wind.

"The world around us is a strange one, full of secrets," said the emir. "Almighty God 'teacheth man that which he knew not.' The important thing is for him to keep his intentions holy and open his heart so that Almighty God may inspire and teach him."

The emir's words seemed obscure and meaningless. He addressed his deputy. "The spyglass shows you a hair from a long distance. The yellow steel crate runs like a gazelle and doesn't get tired. This box talks, sings and prays!"

After a moment he spoke in an awed tone. "'Glory be to God, who teacheth man that which he knew not.'"[4]

---

4. A quotation from the Qur'an.

News of the emir's wonderful new gadget spread faster than any item of news ever had. Even the "steel crate," as they called it, though some others called it "the jinn's steed"[5] and talked about it for days although very few of them had actually seen it, and even then from a great distance—even the jinn's steed in American Harran didn't excite nearly as much curiosity, wonder and fear as the new machine did. No one could describe it or say anything specific about it. When the emir sent some of his men to the coffeehouse and the market to invite some of the people to visit him, without giving any reason for the visit or saying what would happen afterward, everyone began to talk about "the new wonder," and three or four of the men said that they had heard a voice, during the day, which seemed to fall from the sky or spring from the earth. One of them said that one day he had heard a voice calling him, but when he turned around there was no one there. Some of them talked to the emir's men, to understand from them anything about the device, but no matter how the emir's men tried to describe it or give them some kind of idea of what it was, they failed. Those who asked about it in the coffeehouse and market did not really know what to ask, and the answers they got only deepened the mystery. The answers were very brief and cryptic: "Something people had never heard of before." "Seeing it is nothing to hearing it." One of the emir's men, named Shihab, whose duty it was to extend the emir's invitation to Ibn Naffeh, Seif and Dabbasi, had to hurry away to extricate himself from the crowd.

"Tomorrow, people of Harran, when you see it," he told them, "you'll go crazy!"

Everyone had been invited by about two hours before sundown, but some of those who had not been invited could not stifle their curiosity or wait to hear what the others would report, so they determined to go and stand nearby; when they got a chance they would find some pretext to push their way in to see the wonderful device and then tell the rest of the Harranis what they had seen before anyone else could.

The emir was profoundly agitated that whole afternoon. He did not sleep and did not leave his tent, and his eyes never left his new gadget. He stood and paced around it to look at it contemplatively close up and from all sides, and he probed it with his fingers to explore its solidity. For hour after hour he devised ways of taking over the operation of the thing for himself, without any help from Hassan Rezaie, and planning the right moment in which to ask him to teach him all the moves—how to begin and where, the second and third steps, until he knew all the operations—so he asked Rezaie to come with the rest of his guests for the demonstration of the wonderful thing. All the townsfolk of Harran would be amazed; they would feel that this was the first day of their lives, or at least the most important. They would shout like children, joyful, afraid and awestruck—how could they not, when he, the emir, was still full of wonder and astonishment at this device that no one had ever seen or heard of?

At one point the emir gave orders for his majlis to be prepared earlier than usual. He was a little afraid that it would not be possible to move the device outdoors.

"I forgot to ask you," he said to Hassan Rezaie nervously. "Today, our majlis in the desert, here, right nearby. Can we take the thing out with us?"[6]

Rezaie assured him that it would be easily accomplished, that he could move it there or anywhere else he pleased, only it had to be done very carefully: the thing must not be shaken or set down too hard, and nothing must be placed on top of it. The emir was delighted to hear this and imagined many places and things.

---

5. The first Arabic term for "car" in Arabia, attributing its great power to the jinn.   6. The word "radio" came much later than the radio itself.

"Now I want you to teach me to use it," he said in a friendly, confidential tone. "Tell me everything."

"It is your right, Your Highness, to know everything, to try out everything," said Hassan, grinning broadly. "For today I'm here to offer any help you need, and tomorrow I may not be."

The emir could not have been more pleased. The man was giving him all his secrets, strengthening his position among others, setting him above them all. He spoke again in the same tone of friendly confidentiality. "God bless you—may He make many more like you."

Hassan Rezaie began to explain to the emir the nature and importance of the machine. He spoke long and copiously. He said that other countries attached great significance to the radio and spent a great deal of money on it. Like a mirror, it reflected the power and standing of a country. It was found in the houses of the rich, who used it to discover what was happening in the world, to learn all the news and events. When the news was over the entertainment began: music, singing, useful lectures, stories, poems and much else besides.

The emir could not understand or follow a great deal of what Hassan Rezaie told him, but he remembered the word *radio,* which kept recurring. He was burning for the man to finish talking so that they could both get the machine working, so that when the men arrived he would not need any assistance or instructions.

"Actions are better than words," he told Rezaie jokingly. "Now let's say, 'In the name of God' and begin."

Without waiting any further he crept close to the radio and sat by it, waiting for Rezaie. He caressed it with a loving hand, as a man pets the face of a loved child, and tapped it gently with his forefinger, as if this was a sign to begin.

Hassan Rezaie began with the same speed and light dexterity. Perhaps he began too quickly for the emir, or perhaps the emir could not grasp everything, for he spoke up almost immediately. "Easy, easy! Take your time!"

"Just as you say, my lord!" Rezaie smiled. He had mastered this form of address to a degree that was unusual in Harran, but it pleased the emir and made him feel important. This way of speaking had caught his attention from Rezaie's first visit, and he realized that he liked it. When he heard him say "my lord" this time, he thought to himself: "People in other places are far more polite than we are; they know everything, especially how to address a man as befits his station."

"Once again, slowly," said Hassan Rezaie.

"Yes, yes, once again, slowly!" replied the emir. "Take your time!"

Before long the sound of the radio filled the huge tent and the surrounding desert; it could even be heard in the tent reserved for the women. Rezaie lowered the volume.

"Now, Your Highness," he said confidently, "you can do it all yourself!"

The emir went to work, but he was anxious and afraid of making a mistake. To make it as easy as possible for the emir, Rezaie said, "The best way, Your Highness, is to count." He paused a moment and nodded as if he had hit upon the ideal way to teach the process, and showed him how.

"One, two, three, and this is four."

He put his hand on the battery, the first step, then on the switch, which was step two, pointed to the dial, which was three, and step four was the volume control. He did it somewhat rapidly, which moved the emir to comment, "Counting is a good way, but it's not how the bedouin pray!"

Rezaie laughed though he did not understand what the emir meant, and when its meaning—"fast or incomplete"—was explained to him, he laughed harder. He spoke as if teaching a child. "One . . . this is one. Good?"

When the emir nodded to show that he understood, he pointed to the switch. "After one is two. This is two."

The emir nodded vigorously, and Hassan asked, "Shall we go on?"

"Trust in God," said the emir regally.

"This is three, Your Highness, and it's the hardest step."

The emir nodded to show that he understood and could handle the difficulty.

"And this is four. It's easy. If you want it loud, so that all Harran can hear it, turn it to the right, and if you want none but yourself to hear it, turn it to the left."

After several tries, during which Hassan Rezaie gave him additional instructions, especially as regarded the battery and the tuning dial, the emir looked pleased.

"This is the last time," he said, "and then we'll let it rest, so that the rest of them can be amazed when they come and hear it." He laughed loudly. "By God, I'll let it roar to the stars until morning!"

The majlis was prepared earlier than usual. The emir's men moved the radio under his supervision, and he gave them sharp orders before and as they moved it. When he was sure that everything was ready, and in order to impart a sense of thrill and importance to the operation, he draped his cloak over the radio to cover it completely.

The emir tried to act and speak naturally, even simply, with his men, and though it felt strange, because he was not used to doing so, he adopted a friendly, fatherly tone, but his inner tension drove him to unusual activity, rapid pacing and a mood that bordered on fright. This was a new experience for him, and although he felt confident and self-assured, there were lingering doubts: "What if the thing just dies, or I make a mistake turning it on or running it? What if I make a mistake counting or confuse the switches, as Hassan Rezaie called them?" He would feel shame if he failed, and if Hassan Rezaie then came to move him aside and take his place and did not fail, but did it easily, Rezaie would look at him out of the corner of his eye, and the others would watch and smile. If that happened, wouldn't he seem, at least to himself, wanting or stupid? His anxiety mounted and he grew more tense. He now wanted to have one last try: "We should try it out once in its new location." But what would Hassan Rezaie say?

Shortly before sundown the men arrived. First came Dabbasi, who was expected to come early, before any others, because he had not seen the emir in several days, and because he felt a vague sense of guilt. Perhaps this was because of Ibn Rashed's death, or perhaps because it had been so long since he'd visited the emir, or perhaps because of his general feeling of futility. In any case he did feel guilty and had not been overly excited by what all the people were saying in Abu As'ad's coffeehouse about the emir's new gadget. He had said more than once, in the coffeehouse, "If you were to travel and see the whole world, people of Harran, you would never believe it was the world you were seeing." He said nothing more, and no one knew what he meant.

Abdullah al-Saad and Muhammad al-Seif arrived together, and al-Zawawi and Ibn Naffeh arrived together, conversing volubly as they hiked up the north hill—about the corruption that was spreading in the world, and the evil that was now so common, the terrible ruin that afflicted the world, and the approaching day of judgment. They talked about what the emir was doing, what was happening in Harran under his very nose, and his contemptible silence in the face of all the trouble. They could not explain his silence or his indulgence toward the Americans; it was more than they could understand, and they could not overlook or tolerate it. And the emir's surprising new gadget—Ibn Naffeh spoke loudly enough for everyone to hear. "We've already seen enough and more, Abu Mohsen. He's like that black man who saw his mother's cunt and went crazy—he wants to drive everyone else crazy, but he won't succeed."

When the sun sank behind the western hills, leaving nothing behind but steadily darkening orange rays, all those the emir had invited were at last present, including three workers, one of whom was Ibn Zamel. Daham al-Muzil was the last to arrive; he had been rushing and stumbled into the tent covered with sweat. The emir looked around to see that all those whom he had invited were present, noticing two or three uninvited Harranis—what did they want?—then rose to speak.

"It is much pleasanter outdoors, my friends."

The men all stood. There was a certain rustling clamor as they stood, but no sound of spoken words. The emir walked a step or two ahead of the rest and seemed confident, but he still had some doubts. He signaled with his hand for Hassan Rezaie to remain close to him, to come nearer, and the man replied with a courtly but spontaneous gesture. Ibn Naffeh's eyes never left Hassan Rezaie for a moment; he had ignored all others to concentrate on him from the moment he arrived. Hassan Rezaie smiled whenever his eyes met Ibn Naffeh's, but Ibn Naffeh did not return the courtesy and never averted his eyes. When he saw the way the emir treated Rezaie he said to himself: "No one knows whether God or Satan brought this man here, but like they say, if a disease comes from the stomach, where does the cure come from? This bastard, this devil, has got into the emir's armpit, and must be the curse of his ancestors and ours."

As soon as the men were seated, all gazing with intense curiosity at the marvel that sat to the emir's left, under his cloak, the emir spoke in a slightly trembling voice. "The world has changed, my friends; it is no longer as it was. It is smaller. It came to the prophet Adam; he did not have to go to it."

None of the men understood what the emir was saying; in fact his speech made them feel even stranger. He went on more confidently. "A man doesn't believe until he's seen with his own eyes, until he has tried something for himself." He turned to Hassan Rezaie and smiled, as though they shared a secret, and said, "When they have seen with their own eyes, they will believe."

He pounced like a cat to pull the cloak aside.

"Do you all see this?" he asked theatrically, pointing.

The men nodded to show that they saw the device.

"It roams the whole world in the twinkling of an eye, and tells you everything."

The men sat silently. The emir rubbed his hands, exactly as Hassan Rezaie had done when he'd worked the radio.

"What you see talks, then it weeps, then it prays!"

He paused to look at the radio, then at the men, and nodded.

"And now we place our trust in God, and begin."

In a barely audible voice the emir began: "One." He touched the battery, waited a moment, and added, "Two." He sat before the radio, his back to the others, and when the green light appeared he leaned over to work the tuning dial, and when he found a station—he was sure, because he heard a few words, and saw the green light flash brightly—he turned to the men.

"Listen—listen," he said in a husky voice. He turned up the volume.

"They were told that Ibn al-Khattab wept when the treasures of Chosroes were revealed to him," they heard, "and he said, 'This was never shown to any nation without bringing them to despair.'"

The sound faded away as soon as this was heard, and it was followed by a loud, continuous buzz. The men looked at each other and at the device that the emir was impatiently working at; they stared and their jaws were slack. The buzzing died away.

"I do not fear poverty for you, rather I fear that you will submit to the world as did they who came before you, that it will make you dissent and fight one another as it did them. The Prophet, peace and blessings be upon him, said, 'Be in this world as a stranger or a traveler passing through.'"

The emir watched every face to see their reactions, and when he saw them looking at one another in silence, and then glancing perplexedly at the radio, he rubbed his hands and laughed.

"That's one." He turned the volume all the way down and said, "You have seen with your own eyes and heard with your own ears. Now listen again."

He leaned over again until he was almost reclining and spun the tuning dial with his ear glued to the radio. He heard a sound, then turned up the volume and laughed. "This is two."

The sound of music surged out to fill the air. He looked at them, nodded and laughed, and turned the sound even higher so that it roared more loudly than before. The men trembled and held their breath, and their hearts pounded. They did not dare look into one another's faces but stole looks here and there from the corners of their eyes. Each was terrified that men would spring out of the box to kill them all. The emir was plainly delighted, and he exchanged long looks with Hassan Rezaie, and they winked at each other when they saw the powerful effect the radio was having; the emir now wished that he had invited all the townspeople of Harran instead of these few—"If all of them had come, we would really be seeing a marvel"—but he gave up this thought, "because secrets are for adults, only for those who understand." After the music there were a few garbled words, and lightly, as Hassan Rezaie had done, the emir switched off the sound.

"That was two, but there're a lot more."

He reclined as he had done before, turning the knob and watching the green light, and when it emitted an even sound he sat up again.

"Now, three."

"It is related that there was a certain seabird, said to be a tern, who dwelt on the seashore with his wife, and when it was time to hatch their young the female told him, 'Let us seek out an inaccessible place in which to hatch, for I fear that the Lord of the Sea will make the water rise to take our chicks.' He told her, 'Hatch them where you are, for we have water and flowers nearby us.' She said, 'O heedless one, think again, for I fear that the Lord of the Sea will take our chicks.' He told her, 'Hatch them where you are, for he will not do that.' She said, 'How sure you are, do you not remember his threats against you? Do you not know yourself and your power?' But he refused to obey her, and when she insisted and he did not listen, she said to him, 'He who will not heed counsel will suffer the same fate as the tortoise who heeded not the two ducks.' And the male said, 'How did that come about?'

"The female said, 'It is related that there was a pond with pasture, in which there dwelt two ducks, and in the pond was a tortoise. Now the tortoise and the ducks loved one another. It befell that the water in the pond diminished, and the ducks came to the tortoise to bid her farewell. They said, "Peace upon you, for we are leaving this place because of the want of water." She replied, "There is a want of water, and I know, for like a ship I can live only in the water, but since you two can live anywhere, take me with you." They told her, "Yes," and she asked, "How can you carry me?" They said, "We will each grasp one end of a stick; bite it in the middle, and we will fly you through the air. Hold fast with your mouth, and beware! If you hear the people talk, say nothing." So they took her and flew into the sky, and when the people saw, they said, "Wonderful indeed, a tortoise flying between two ducks!" and when she heard that she said, "May God blind you, O people!" And when she opened her mouth to speak, she fell to the ground and died.'

"The male said, 'I hear your fable, but fear not the Lord of the Sea.' When the water rose, they fled with their young, and the female said, 'I knew this would befall.' Said the male, 'I will take my revenge,' and he betook himself to the council of birds, and told them, 'You are my brothers and my trusted friends—help me.' They said, 'What do you want us to do?' He said, 'Let us go to the rest of the birds and tell them what we have suffered from the Lord of the Sea. We shall say, "You are birds as we are—help us."' The council of birds told him, 'The griffin is our mistress and our queen, let us go and seek her counsel. She will appear to us and we will recount to her what you suffered from the Lord of the Sea, and we will petition her to avenge us upon him with her power and authority.' They then went with the tern and sought her aid, and she appeared to hear their tale, and they asked her to fly with them to combat the Lord of the Sea, and she consented. When the Lord of the Sea learned that the griffin was seeking him with the other birds, he was afraid to fight, a powerless king; so the tern's young made peace with him and the griffin flew away!"

The emir was delighted and anxious at the same time. The men were perfectly silent as they listened, their tongues tied, awestruck. He found their rigid, silent aspect almost comic, but when the story went on and on and the stories intermingled, and he missed some of the words as he turned and watched them, he became afraid that the device was tired. No sooner had the men heard the last words of the tale, and their faces relaxed, than the emir pounced like a cat on the radio, and some of them heard him say, "Four, three, two, one!"

When the radio was switched off, he returned wearily to his place and sat. He took a deep breath and looked at the sky, and he spoke when he perceived the heavy silence that hung over the group. "As you have seen, my friends, 'God teacheth man that which he knew not.'"

Each of the men had a great deal he might have said. Those who had traveled and seen the world wanted to do nothing but talk; true, Dabbasi had seen a radio before: he had seen one in Egypt at the house of Ibn al-Barih, but it did not strike him as particularly incredible, "because everything in Egypt is incredible." That was how he usually summed up his impressions of Egypt, with no attempt to supply details. Abdullah al-Saad leaned over to Muhammad al-Seif and whispered, "Our friend Ibn al-Naqib in Basra has one, and I've seen it!" The others, who had never been anywhere farther than Ujra, were deeply confused and afraid, and most of them wished that the emir would cover the radio up again and put it away, because "anything can happen in this world." Most of them were not ready to hear any explanation or comment, because the strange device could talk, sing, tell stories and perhaps do many other things as well, in spite of its tiny size. The people inside it might be strange enchanted creatures, probably badly deformed as well. The only one to dare ask a question was Ibn Naffeh, though he was apprehensive and a little afraid.

"Who made this calamity?" he asked Hassan Rezaie.

Rezaie was a little irritated at the hostile stares Ibn Naffeh had directed at him the whole evening, and he answered him brusquely. "Man invented it."

"Tell me—tell me: the Germans or the Americans?"

"This radio was made in Holland."

"Holland?"

"Yes. It was manufactured in Holland."

"Do they know Arabic there? Do they pray and fast and say 'There is no god but God'?"

Dabbasi spoke up, feeling that Ibn Naffeh was becoming more hostile toward Rezaie.

"If Abu Misfer agrees, let's ask our friend to buy one for us and bring it to us on one of his visits to Harran, and if he likes we'll pay for it right now!"

Ibn Naffeh was horrified.

"And put it in our houses, Dabbasi?"

"Trust in God, man, be patient!" Dabbasi smiled.

"And put it in our houses, to attract wolves to our sheep?"

"By God, Ibn Naffeh," said the emir, "you don't like anything not from the Nejd. You don't like anything at all—you say that everything is sacrilegious." He softened his tone and addressed the whole gathering. "My friends, you all heard with your own ears what it said about the Prophet, peace and blessings be upon him, and what it said about Ibn al-Khattab, and others."

Ibn Naffeh got up angrily.

"My friends, be wary of the green of new manure."[7] He paused a moment and added sarcastically, "It has one eye, like Satan, a green eye, and that is what the Prophet repudiated and called the green of new manure."

He added, in a threatening tone, "Tomorrow it will drag you to Hell."

The men who sat in Abu As'ad's coffeehouse that night, watching and waiting, said they had heard unusual noises coming from the north hill; the noises, they said, could be heard, though indistinctly, when night fell and the sea waves calmed. Abdu Muhammad, who spent more time than usual in the coffeehouse that evening, said that he heard the melodies of songs he knew, and that the melodies flowed to him directly from the north hill. Othman al-Asqi, who was deaf in one ear, decided to go to the emir's gathering uninvited, because he could not stifle the curiosity that gripped him when he heard everyone talking about the wonderful device, though some of the men wittily suggested that he had gone only to get a free meal.

Al-Asqi was the first to arrive at the coffeehouse after the visit to the emir and the demonstration of the new marvel. For a long time he was silent, shaking his head and hands in wonderment. When they asked him to describe the radio, he waved his hand to indicate that he could not, because what he had seen could not be explained or described. When he tried, after a great deal of patient insistence from the others, and much hesitation on his part, he said that the emir possessed something truly marvelous: a box, but not like any box. Like a tea chest, smaller or perhaps a little bigger—he was not exactly sure—but when you hit it on the head it shouted and began to talk. It had only one eye, a green eye, the color of spring grass; and if you hit it again, gently, it made pipe and drum music. If you hit it yet again, on the side, it went mute and died.

7. A misquotation from the Prophet Muhammad warning of the seduction of things.

Abu As'ad asked him loudly, and with hand gestures, if the box had round black knobs, like the round loaves that Abdu Muhammad baked, only smaller, and if it had a large funnel like a fat funnel or larger, and if a tall, thin protuberance had to be adjusted before it spoke. After Abu As'ad explained, with the help of several of those present shouting into al-Asqi's ear, Othman said it was nothing like that, that he had not seen the things that Abu As'ad described since he had sat as far as possible from the thing. Abu As'ad asked him if it had small switches and a glass pane in the middle with a moving needle, and al-Asqi said it did have something like that. Abu As'ad leaned forward in his chair.

"Why didn't you say so before, old man!" he said patiently, then shook his head, laughing, and shouted, "That's a radio, my friends!" He turned to Othman. "A radio! Right?"

Othman curled his lip and shrugged to show that he did not know.

"Al-Asqi was watching and listening with his stomach," said one man, who longed to know what a radio was. He was seated at a distance and had been closely following the discussion and gestures.

"If Harran had electricity we would all have had radios long ago," said Abu As'ad, who felt that he knew a great deal more than the others.

He went on to explain to all of them everything he knew about radios, and how they were found everywhere in Beirut, Aleppo and Damascus, and many other places he had lived in or visited. He said that the homes of the rich and eminent were never without a radio, and pointed out that the Nadim Coffeehouse in Beirut's Sahet al-Bourj had both a radio and a gramophone. Then he explained to the men what a gramophone was, how records which resembled thin loaves of bread emitted songs, never tiring of spinning around night and day. People came in throngs from far-distant places to the Nadim Coffeehouse only to hear the songs, and the coffeehouse manager, Wajih Halabi, played songs at the listeners' requests. Abu As'ad kept repeating the word *listeners*. He repeated that as soon as Harran got electricity, the first radio would be installed in the Friends Coffeehouse. He shook his finger in mock warning, however.

"Listen! When we get it, no one may touch it but me!" He paused, then laughed. "And another thing: I can't have you all saying, every minute, 'Abu As'ad, turn this on' and 'Abu As'ad, shut that off.'"

That night, they all said later, Harran did not sleep. The emir's soiree lasted longer than anyone expected or wanted. The sound of the radio, like the song of a distant camel driver in the early evening, grew progressively louder and stronger and everyone heard it. When Hassan Rezaie said with exaggerated politeness that he would like to go home, but that he would be at the emir's disposal at any hour of the morning His Highness desired, the emir announced that the evening was concluded. When they all left, the emir accompanied them for a good distance—longer than he usually did for his guests—and bid them good night, and they all said that the sound of the radio followed them as if the thing were walking behind them, even after they got to the bottom of the hill and reached the market. The sound was clearly audible, and they all laughed when al-Zawawi fell into a ditch in the road.

"That thing opened our ears, Abu Mohsen, but it blinded our eyes!"

The emir lingered after his guests left and turned up the volume of the radio several times, nodding happily in time to the music. He moved it from one place to another, first into his tent and then to the area behind it where he slept; there he was heard talking loudly about the wonderful gadget. He turned the radio up even louder, and the delighted and frightened voices of the women joined in—everyone in the coffeehouse heard. The sound of the radio rose and fell. Abu As'ad was gathering up the chairs in the coffeehouse and talking to his last two customers.

"God willing, within a month we'll have a radio, and we'll hear the songs reaching the sky!"

Ibn Naffeh, who left early and went straight home to Arab Harran, refused to say anything about the radio, and the sound of his praying was heard until late that night, and because of that, or the distance, no one in Arab Hassan could hear the radio. When the others and those who lived in the western hills left the emir's, they all talked about the radio but none of them could describe or explain it.

Before dawn the next day, the emir was seen asking Massoud and another man to move the radio. He went with them all the way and lifted the tent flap himself so that they could move it in easily. Some of the more malicious townspeople said that the emir spent several sleepless days by the radio with his loaded rifle, ready for any surprise that might come from the thing. Ibn Seif said that on one of his visits to the emir he saw two men lifting the radio high into the air while the emir examined the bottom of it with his telescope. When he saw nothing, he moved closer and struck it with the palm of his hand as if knocking on a door. Hearing no sound from within, he crept around it in a circle to look at it from all angles with the telescope, rapping it with his knuckles and palms.

In the mosque, market and workers' camp there was talk of nothing but the new wonder, and everyone longed to see or hear it. The emir, who was completely preoccupied by the radio and let none of his men touch it or go near it in his absence, had entered a new phase of his life. It began by coincidence, when he heard some songs which affected him deeply, and which he and many others remembered for a long time to come.

Murakami Haruki
b. 1949

The novels and short stories of Murakami Haruki—whose name is here given in the usual Japanese order, with the family name preceding the given name—are enormously popular among young readers in Japan and have won the author numerous literary prizes. Increasingly, his works are also becoming best-sellers around the globe among readers who find themselves attracted to Murakami's mix of reflections on specifically Japanese situations and his abundant references to a popular culture of mostly American origin that is shared by young people today across a wide variety of regions, languages, and nations. Murakami himself forms part of the generation of Japanese growing up after World War II who first experienced the full impact of this imported pop culture. Born near Kobe, Japan, in 1949, he studied screenwriting and Greek drama in Tokyo from 1968 until the completion of his bachelor's degree in 1975 and witnessed the upheaval of violent student protests firsthand during this time. From 1974 to 1981 he ran a Tokyo jazz bar together with his wife, thereby establishing another conduit between American and Japanese culture. His first novel, *Hear the Wind Sing,* was published in 1979, and since 1981 he has dedicated himself full time to writing.

The insistently, almost aggressively contemporary idiom of Murakami's fiction has sometimes alienated older Japanese readers, who prefer the more timeless topics and formal diction of a Tanizaki Junichiro or Kawabata Yasunari. Murakami captures elements of late-twentieth-century culture in his themes as well as his language; references to recent technology, Western pop music, and brand-name consumer products come up frequently in his texts, as do changing sexual relations, divorce, and alienation from the professional and social worlds. Some of Murakami's novels are quite realistic, such as *Norwegian Wood* (1987), an account of student life in the 1960s (its title is taken from a Beatles' song), or *The Wind-up Bird Chronicle* (1994), which deals with the violent confrontations between Chinese and Japanese in World War II. But many others combine late-twentieth-century realism, the hard-boiled detective novel (Raymond Chandler being one of Murakami's models), and science fiction: *A Wild Sheep Chase* (1982) and *Hard-Boiled Wonderland and the End of the World* (1985) are good examples of this signature style. The short story "TV People" also belongs to this kind of writing. As is often the case in Murakami's idiosyncratic narrative worlds, it is difficult to know which of the strange incidents the protagonist experiences are part of an objective reality and which ones are figments of his private imagination; neither is it easy to decide just where the boundary between these two realms lies in a world of television and glossy magazines. In this universe that seems part Kafka and part cyberpunk, what is clearly at stake is the protagonist's encounter with television—a medium that has fundamentally transformed late-twentieth-century culture.

TV People[1]

It was Sunday evening when the TV People showed up.

The season, spring. At least, I think it was spring. In any case, it wasn't particularly hot as seasons go, not particularly chilly.

To be honest, the season's not so important. What matters is that it's a Sunday evening.

I don't like Sunday evenings. Or, rather, I don't like everything that goes with them—that Sunday-evening state of affairs. Without fail, come Sunday evening my head starts to ache. In varying intensity each time. Maybe a third to a half of an inch into my temples, the soft flesh throbs—as if invisible threads lead out and someone far off is yanking at the other ends. Not that it hurts so much. It ought to hurt, but strangely, it doesn't—it's like long needles probing anesthetized areas.

And I hear things. Not sounds, but thick slabs of silence being dragged through the dark. *KRZSHAAAAL KKRZSHAAAAAL KKKKRMMMS.* Those are the initial indications. First, the aching. Then, a slight distortion of my vision. Tides of confusion wash through, premonitions tugging at memories, memories tugging at premonitions. A finely honed razor moon floats white in the sky, roots of doubt burrow into the earth. People walk extra loud down the hall just to get me. *KRRSPUMK DUWB KRRSPUMK DUWB KRRSPUMK DUWB.*

All the more reason for the TV People to single out Sunday evening as the time to come around. Like melancholy moods, or the secretive, quiet fall of rain, they steal into the gloom of that appointed time.

Let me explain how the TV People look.

The TV People are slightly smaller than you or me. Not obviously smaller—*slightly* smaller. About, say, 20 or 30%. Every part of their bodies is uniformly smaller. So rather than "small," the more terminologically correct expression might be "reduced."

In fact, if you see TV People somewhere, you might not notice at first that they're small. But even if you don't, they'll probably strike you as somehow strange.

Unsettling, maybe. You're sure to think something's odd, and then you'll take another look. There's nothing unnatural about them at first glance, but that's what's so
unnatural. Their smallness is completely different from that of children and dwarfs.
When we see children, we *feel* they're small, but this sense of recognition comes
mostly from the misproportioned awkwardness of their bodies. They are small,
granted, but not uniformly so. The hands are small, but the head is big. Typically, that
is. No, the smallness of TV People is something else entirely. TV People look as if
they were reduced by photocopy, everything mechanically calibrated. Say their height
has been reduced by a factor of 0.7, then their shoulder width is also in 0.7 reduction;
ditto (0.7 reduction) for the feet, head, ears, and fingers. Like plastic models, only a
little smaller than the real thing.

Or like perspective demos. Figures that look far away even close up. Something
out of a trompe-l'oeil painting where the surface warps and buckles. An illusion
where the hand fails to touch objects close by, yet brushes what is out of reach.

That's TV People.

That's TV People.

That's TV People.

There were three of them altogether.

They don't knock or ring the doorbell. Don't say hello. They just sneak right in. I
don't even hear a footstep. One opens the door, the other two carry in a TV. Not a
very big TV. Your ordinary Sony color TV. The door was locked, I think, but I can't
be certain. Maybe I forgot to lock it. It really wasn't foremost in my thoughts at the
time, so who knows? Still, I think the door was locked.

When they come in, I'm lying on the sofa, gazing up at the ceiling. Nobody at
home but me. That afternoon, the wife has gone out with the girls—some close
friends from her high-school days—getting together to talk, then eating dinner out.
"Can you grab your own supper?" the wife said before leaving. "There's vegetables
in the fridge and all sorts of frozen foods. That much you can handle for yourself,
can't you? And before the sun goes down, remember to take in the laundry, okay?"

"Sure thing," I said. Doesn't faze me a bit. Rice, right? Laundry, right? Nothing
to it. Take care of it, simple as *SLUPPP KRRRTZ!*

"Did you say something, dear?" she asked.

"No, nothing," I said.

All afternoon I take it easy and loll around on the sofa. I have nothing better to
do. I read a bit—that new novel by García Márquez[2]—and listen to some music. I
have myself a beer. Still, I'm unable to give my mind to any of this. I consider going
back to bed, but I can't even pull myself together enough to do that. So I wind up lying on the sofa, staring at the ceiling.

The way my Sunday afternoons go, I end up doing a little bit of various things,
none very well. It's a struggle to concentrate on any one thing. This particular day,
everything seems to be going right. I think, Today I'll read this book, listen to these
records, answer these letters. Today, for sure, I'll clean out my desk drawers, run errands, wash the car for once. But two o'clock rolls around, three o'clock rolls around,
gradually dusk comes on, and all my plans are blown. I haven't done a thing; I've
been lying around on the sofa the whole day, same as always. The clock ticks in my

2. Colombian novelist who won the Nobel Prize in literature in 1982.

Nam June Paik, *Global Encoder*, 1994 (video sculpture, 122 × 84 × 55 inches).

ears. *TRPP Q SCHAOUS TRPP Q SCHAOUS.* The sound erodes everything around me, little by little, like dripping rain. *TRPP Q SCHAOUS TRPP Q SCHAOUS.* Little by little, Sunday afternoon wears down, shrinking in scale. Just like the TV People themselves.

The TV people ignore me from the very outset. All three of them have this look that says the likes of me don't exist. They open the door and carry in their TV. The two put the set on the sideboard, the other one plugs it in. There's a mantel clock and a stack of magazines on the sideboard. The clock was a wedding gift, big and heavy— big and heavy as time itself—with a loud sound, too. *TRPP Q SCHAOUS TRPP Q SCHAOUS.* All through the house you can hear it. The TV People move it off the sideboard, down onto the floor. The wife's going to raise hell, I think. She hates it when things get randomly shifted about. If everything isn't in its proper place, she gets really sore. What's worse, with the clock there on the floor, I'm bound to trip over it in the middle of the night. I'm forever getting up to go to the toilet at two in the morning, bleary-eyed and stumbling over something.

Next, the TV People move the magazines to the table. All of them women's magazines. (I hardly ever read magazines; I read books—personally, I wouldn't mind if every last magazine in the world went out of business.) *Elle* and *Marie Claire* and *Home Ideas,* magazines of that ilk. Neatly stacked on the sideboard. The wife doesn't like me touching her magazines—change the order of the stack, and I never hear the end of it—so I don't go near them. Never once flipped through them. But the TV People couldn't care less: They move them right out of the way, they show no concern, they sweep the whole lot off the sideboard, they mix up the order. *Marie Claire* is on top of *Croissant; Home Ideas* is underneath *An-An.* Unforgivable. And worse, they're scattering the bookmarks onto the floor. They've lost her place, pages with important information. I have no idea what information or how important—might have been for work, might have been personal—but whatever, it was important to the wife, and she'll let me know about it. "What's the meaning of this? I go out for a nice time with friends, and when I come back, the house is a shambles!" I can just hear it, line for line. Oh, great, I think, shaking my head.

Everything gets removed from the sideboard to make room for the television. The TV People plug it into a wall socket, then switch it on. Then there is a tinkling noise, and the screen lights up. A moment later, the picture floats into view. They change the channels by remote control. But all the channels are blank—probably, I think, because they haven't connected the set to an antenna. There has to be an antenna outlet somewhere in the apartment. I seem to remember the superintendent telling us where it was when we moved into this condominium. All you had to do was connect it. But I can't remember where it is. We don't own a television, so I've completely forgotten.

Yet somehow the TV People don't seem bothered that they aren't picking up any broadcast. They give no sign of looking for the antenna outlet. Blank screen, no image—makes no difference to them. Having pushed the button and had the power come on, they've completed what they came to do.

The TV is brand-new. It's not in its box, but one look tells you it's new. The instruction manual and guarantee are in a plastic bag taped to the side; the power cable shines, sleek as a freshly caught fish.

All three TV People look at the blank screen from here and there around the room. One of them comes over next to me and verifies that you can see the TV screen from where I'm sitting. The TV is facing straight toward me, at an optimum viewing distance. They seem satisfied. One operation down, says their air of accomplishment. One of the TV People (the one who'd come over next to me) places the remote control on the table.

The TV People speak not a word. Their movements come off in perfect order, hence they don't need to speak. Each of the three executes his prescribed function with maximum efficiency. A professional job. Neat and clean. Their work is done in no time. As an afterthought, one of the TV People picks the clock up from the floor and casts a quick glance around the room to see if there isn't a more appropriate place to put it, but he doesn't find any and sets it back down. *TRPP Q SCHAOUS TRPP Q SCHAOUS.* It goes on ticking weightily on the floor. Our apartment is rather small, and a lot of floor space tends to be taken up with my books and the wife's reference materials. I am bound to trip on that clock. I heave a sigh. No mistake, stub my toes for sure. You can bet on it.

All three TV People wear dark-blue jackets. Of who-knows-what fabric, but slick. Under them, they wear jeans and tennis shoes. Clothes and shoes all proportionately reduced in size. I watch their activities for the longest time, until I start to think maybe it's *my* proportions that are off. Almost as if I were riding backward on a roller coaster, wearing strong prescription glasses. The view is dizzying, the scale all screwed up. I'm thrown off balance, my customary world is no longer absolute. That's the way the TV People make you feel.

Up to the very last, the TV People don't say a word. The three of them check the screen one more time, confirm that there are no problems, then switch it off by remote control. The glow contracts to a point and flickers off with a tinkling noise. The screen returns to its expressionless, gray, natural state. The world outside is getting dark. I hear someone calling out to someone else. Anonymous footsteps pass by down the hall, intentionally loud as ever. *KRRSPUMK DUWB KRRSPUMK DUWB.* A Sunday evening.

The TV People give the room another whirlwind inspection, open the door, and leave. Once again, they pay no attention to me whatsoever. They act as if I don't exist.

From the time the TV People come into the apartment to the moment they leave, I don't budge. Don't say a word. I remain motionless, stretched out on the sofa, surveying the whole operation. I know what you're going to say: That's unnatural. Total strangers—not one but three—walk unannounced right into your apartment, plunk down a TV set, and you just sit there staring at them, dumbfounded. Kind of odd, don't you think?

I know, I know. But for whatever reason, I don't speak up, I simply observe the proceedings. Because they ignore me so totally. And if you were in my position, I imagine you'd do the same. Not to excuse myself, but *you* have people right in front of you denying your very presence like that, then see if you don't doubt whether you actually exist. I look at my hands half expecting to see clear through them. I'm devastated, powerless, in a trance. My body, my mind are vanishing fast. I can't bring myself to move. It's all I can do to watch the three TV People deposit their television in my apartment and leave. I can't open my mouth for fear of what my voice might sound like.

The TV People exit and leave me alone. My sense of reality comes back to me. These hands are once again my hands. It's only then I notice that the dusk has been swallowed by darkness. I turn on the light. Then I close my eyes. Yes, that's a TV set sitting there. Meanwhile, the clock keeps ticking away the minutes. *TRPP Q SCHAOUS TRPP Q SCHAOUS.*

Curiously, the wife makes no mention of the appearance of the television set in the apartment. No reaction at all. Zero. It's as if she doesn't even see it. Creepy. Because, as I said before, she's extremely fussy about the order and arrangement of furniture and other things. If someone dares to move anything in the apartment, even by a hair, she'll jump on it in an instant. That's her ascendancy. She knits her brows, then gets things back the way they were.

Not me. If an issue of *Home Ideas* gets put under an *An-An,* or a ballpoint pen finds its way into the pencil stand, you don't see me go to pieces. I don't even notice. This is her problem; I'd wear myself out living like her. Sometimes she flies into a rage. She tells me she can't abide my carelessness. Yes, I say, and sometimes I can't stand carelessness about universal gravitation and π and $E = mc^2$, either. I mean it. But when I say things like this, she clams up, taking them as a personal insult. I never mean it that way; I just say what I feel.

That night, when she comes home, first thing she does is look around the apartment. I've readied a full explanation—how the TV People came and mixed everything up. It'll be difficult to convince her, but I intend to tell her the whole truth.

She doesn't say a thing, just gives the place the once-over. There's a TV on the sideboard, the magazines are out of order on the table, the mantel clock is on the floor, and the wife doesn't even comment. There's nothing for me to explain.

"You get your own supper okay?" she asks me, undressing.

"No, I didn't eat," I tell her.

"Why not?"

"I wasn't really hungry," I say.

The wife pauses, half-undressed, and thinks this over. She gives me a long look. Should she press the subject or not? The clock breaks up the protracted, ponderous silence. *TRPP Q SCHAOUS TRPP Q SCHAOUS.* I pretend not to hear; I won't let it in my ears. But the sound is simply too heavy, too loud to shut out. She, too, seems to be listening to it. Then she shakes her head and says, "Shall I whip up something quick?"

"Well, maybe," I say. I don't really feel much like eating, but I won't turn down the offer.

The wife changes into around-the-house wear and goes to the kitchen to fix zosui and tamago-yaki[3] while filling me in on her friends. Who'd done what, who'd said what, who'd changed her hairstyle and looked so much younger, who'd broken up with her boyfriend. I know most of her friends, so I pour myself a beer and follow along, inserting attentive uh-huhs at proper intervals. Though, in fact, I hardly hear a thing she says. I'm thinking about the TV People. That, and why she didn't remark on the sudden appearance of the television. No way she couldn't have noticed. Very odd. Weird, even. Something is wrong here. But what to do about it?

The food is ready, so I sit at the dining-room table and eat. Rice, egg, salt plum. When I've finished, the wife clears away the dishes. I have another beer, and she has a beer, too. I glance at the sideboard, and there's the TV set, with the power off, the remote-control unit sitting on the table. I get up from the table, reach for the remote control, and switch it on. The screen glows and I hear it tinkling. Still no picture. Only the same blank tube. I press the button to raise the volume, but all that does is increase the white-noise roar. I watch the snowstorm for twenty, thirty seconds, then switch it off. Light and sound vanish in an instant. Meanwhile, the wife has seated herself on the carpet and is flipping through *Elle,* oblivious of the fact that the TV has just been turned on and off.

I replace the remote control on the table and sit down on the sofa again, thinking I'll go on reading that long García Márquez novel. I always read after dinner. I might set the book down after thirty minutes, or I might read for two hours, but the thing is to read every day. Today, though, I can't get myself to read more than a page and a half. I can't concentrate; my thoughts keep returning to the TV set. I look up and see it, right in front of me.

I wake at half past two in the morning to find the TV still there. I get out of bed half hoping the thing has disappeared. No such luck. I go to the toilet, then plop down on the sofa and put my feet up on the table. I take the remote control in hand and try turning on the TV. No new developments in that department, either; only a rerun of the same glow and noise. Nothing else. I look at it a while, then switch it off.

---

3. A rice stew cooked with a thick broth and a rolled omelette.

I go back to bed and try to sleep. I'm dead tired, but sleep isn't coming. I shut my eyes and I see them. The TV People carrying the TV set, the TV People moving the clock out of the way, the TV People transferring magazines to the table, the TV People plugging the power cable into the wall socket, the TV People checking the screen, the TV People opening the door and silently exiting. They've stayed on in my head. They're in there walking around. I get back out of bed, go to the kitchen, and pour a double brandy into a coffee cup. I down the brandy and head over to the sofa for another session with Márquez. I open the pages, yet somehow the words won't sink in. The writing is opaque.

Very well, then, I throw García Márquez aside and pick up *Elle*. Reading *Elle* from time to time can't hurt anyone. But there isn't anything in *Elle* that catches my fancy. New hairstyles and elegant white silk blouses and eateries that serve good beef stew and what to wear to the opera, articles like that. Do I care? I throw *Elle* aside. Which leaves me the television on the sideboard to look at.

I end up staying awake until dawn, not doing a thing. At six o'clock, I make myself some coffee. I don't have anything else to do, so I go ahead and fix ham sandwiches before the wife gets up.

"You're up awful early," she says drowsily.

"Mmm," I mumble.

After a nearly wordless breakfast, we leave home together and go our separate ways to our respective offices. The wife works at a small publishing house. Edits a natural-food and life-style magazine. "Shiitake Mushrooms Prevent Gout," "The Future of Organic Farming," you know the kind of magazine. Never sells very well, but hardly costs anything to produce; kept afloat by a handful of zealots. Me, I work in the advertising department of an electrical-appliance manufacturer. I dream up ads for toasters and washing machines and microwave ovens.

In my office building, I pass one of the TV People on the stairs. If I'm not mistaken, it's one of the three who brought the TV the day before—probably the one who first opened the door, who didn't actually carry the set. Their singular lack of distinguishing features makes it next to impossible to tell them apart, so I can't swear to it, but I'd say I'm eight to nine out of ten on the mark. He's wearing the same blue jacket he had on the previous day, and he's not carrying anything in his hands. He's merely walking down the stairs. I'm walking up. I dislike elevators, so I generally take the stairs. My office is on the ninth floor, so this is no mean feat. When I'm in a rush, I get all sweaty by the time I reach the top. Even so, getting sweaty has got to be better than taking the elevator, as far as I'm concerned. Everyone jokes about it: doesn't own a TV or a VCR, doesn't take elevators, must be a modern-day Luddite.[4] Maybe a childhood trauma leading to arrested development. Let them think what they like. They're the ones who are screwed up, if you ask me.

In any case, there I am, climbing the stairs as always; I'm the only one on the stairs—almost nobody else uses them—when between the fourth and fifth floors I pass one of the TV People coming down. It happens so suddenly I don't know what to do. Maybe I should say something?

But I don't say anything. I don't know what to say, and he's unapproachable. He leaves no opening; he descends the stairs so functionally, at one set tempo, with such

---

4. An opponent of modern technology.

regulated precision. Plus, he utterly ignores my presence, same as the day before. I don't even enter his field of vision. He slips by before I can think what to do. In that instant, the field of gravity warps.

At work, the day is solid with meetings from the morning on. Important meetings on sales campaigns for a new product line. Several employees read reports. Blackboards fill with figures, bar graphs proliferate on computer screens. Heated discussions. I participate, although my contribution to the meetings is not that critical because I'm not directly involved with the project. So between meetings I keep puzzling things over. I voice an opinion only once. Isn't much of an opinion, either— something perfectly obvious to any observer—but I couldn't very well go without saying anything, after all. I may not be terribly ambitious when it comes to work, but so long as I'm receiving a salary I have to demonstrate responsibility. I summarize the various opinions up to that point and even make a joke to lighten the atmosphere. Half covering for my daydreaming about the TV People. Several people laugh. After that one utterance, however, I only pretend to review the materials; I'm thinking about the TV People. If they talk up a name for the new microwave oven, I certainly am not aware of it. My mind is all TV People. What the hell was the meaning of that TV set? And why haul the TV all the way to my apartment in the first place? Why hasn't the wife remarked on its appearance? Why have the TV People made inroads into my company?

The meetings are endless. At noon, there's a short break for lunch. Too short to go out and eat. Instead, everyone gets sandwiches and coffee. The conference room is a haze of cigarette smoke, so I eat at my own desk. While I'm eating, the section chief comes around. To be perfectly frank, I don't like the guy. For no reason I can put my finger on: There's nothing you can fault him on, no single target for attack. He has an air of breeding. Moreover, he's not stupid. He has good taste in neckties, he doesn't wave his own flag or lord it over his inferiors. He even looks out for me, invites me out for the occasional meal. But there's just something about the guy that doesn't sit well with me. Maybe it's his habit of coming into body contact with people he's talking to. Men or women, at some point in the course of the conversation he'll reach out a hand and touch. Not in any suggestive way, mind you. No, his manner is brisk, his bearing perfectly casual. I wouldn't be surprised if some people don't even notice, it's so natural. Still—I don't know why—it does bother me. So whenever I see him, almost instinctively I brace myself. Call it petty, it gets to me.

He leans over, placing a hand on my shoulder. "About your statement at the meeting just now. Very nice," says the section chief warmly. "Very simply put, very pivotal. I was impressed. Points well taken. The whole room buzzed at that statement of yours. The timing was perfect, too. Yessir, you keep 'em coming like that."

And he glides off. Probably to lunch. I thank him straight out, but the honest truth is I'm taken aback. I mean, I don't remember a thing of what I said at the meeting. Why does the section chief have to come all the way over to my desk to praise me for *that?* There have to be more brilliant examples of *Homo loquens*[5] around here. Strange. I go on eating my lunch, uncomprehending. Then I think about the wife. Wonder what she's up to right now. Out to lunch? Maybe I ought to give her a call, exchange a few words, anything. I dial the first three digits, have second thoughts, hang up. I have no reason to be calling her. My world may be crumbling, out of balance, but is that a reason to ring up her office? What can I say about all this, anyway?

5. The speaking human (Latin).

Besides, I hate calling her at work. I set down the receiver, let out a sigh, and finish off my coffee. Then I toss the Styrofoam cup into the wastebasket.

At one of the afternoon meetings, I see TV People again. This time, their number has increased by two. Just as on the previous day, they come traipsing across the conference room, carrying a Sony color TV. A model one size bigger. Uh-oh. Sony's the rival camp. If, for whatever reason, any competitor's product gets brought into our offices, there's hell to pay, barring when other manufacturers' products are brought in for test comparisons, of course. But then we take pains to remove the company logo—just to make sure no outside eyes happen upon it. Little do the TV People care: The Sony mark is emblazoned for all to see. They open the door and march right into the conference room, flashing it in our direction. Then they parade the thing around the room, scanning the place for somewhere to set it down, until at last, not finding any location, they carry it backward out the door. The others in the room show no reaction to the TV People. And they can't have missed them. No, they've definitely seen them. And the proof is they even got out of the way, clearing a path for the TV People to carry their television through. Still, that's as far as it went: a reaction no more alarmed than when the nearby coffee shop delivered. They'd made it a ground rule not to acknowledge the presence of the TV People. The others all knew they were there; they just acted as if they weren't.

None of it makes any sense. Does everybody know about the TV People? Am I alone in the dark? Maybe the wife knew about the TV People all along, too. Probably. I'll bet that's why she wasn't surprised by the television and why she didn't mention it. That's the only possible explanation. Yet this confuses me even more. Who or what, then, are the TV People? And why are they always carrying around TV sets?

One colleague leaves his seat to go to the toilet, and I get up to follow. This is a guy who entered the company around the same time I did. We're on good terms. Sometimes we go out for a drink together after work. I don't do that with most people. I'm standing next to him at the urinals. He's the first to complain. "Oh, joy! Looks like we're in for more of the same, straight through to evening. I swear! Meetings, meetings, meetings, going to drag on forever."

"You can say that again," I say. We wash our hands. He compliments me on the morning meeting's statement. I thank him.

"Oh, by the way, those guys who came in with the TV just now . . ." I launch forth, then cut off.

He doesn't say anything. He turns off the faucet, pulls two paper towels from the dispenser, and wipes his hands. He doesn't even shoot a glance in my direction. How long can he keep drying his hands? Eventually, he crumples up his towels and throws them away. Maybe he didn't hear me. Or maybe he's pretending not to hear. I can't tell. But from the sudden strain in the atmosphere, I know enough not to ask. I shut up, wipe my hands, and walk down the corridor to the conference room. The rest of the afternoon's meetings, he avoids my eyes.

When I get home from work, the apartment is dark. Outside, dark clouds have swept in. It's beginning to rain. The apartment smells like rain. Night is coming on. No sign of the wife. I loosen my tie, smooth out the wrinkles, and hang it up. I brush off my suit. I toss my shirt into the washing machine. My hair smells like cigarette smoke, so I take a shower and shave. Story of my life: I go to endless meetings, get smoked to death, then the wife gets on my case about it. The very first thing she did after we were married was make me stop smoking. Four years ago, that was.

Out of the shower, I sit on the sofa with a beer, drying my hair with a towel. The TV People's television is still sitting on the sideboard. I pick up the remote control from the table and push the "on" switch. Again and again I press, but nothing happens. The screen stays dark. I check the plug; it's in the socket, all right. I unplug it, then plug it back in. Still no go. No matter how often I press the "on" switch, the screen does not glow. Just to be sure, I pry open the back cover of the remote-control unit, remove the batteries, and check them with my handy electrical-contact tester. The batteries are fine. At this point, I give up, throw the remote control aside, and slosh down more beer.

Why should it upset me? Supposing the TV did come on, what then? It would glow and crackle with white noise. Who cares, if that's all that'd come on?

I care. Last night it worked. And I haven't laid a finger on it since. Doesn't make sense.

I try the remote control one more time. I press slowly with my finger. But the result is the same. No response whatsoever. The screen is dead. Cold.

Dead cold.

I pull another beer out of the fridge and eat some potato salad from a plastic tub. It's past six o'clock. I read the whole evening paper. If anything, it's more boring than usual. Almost no article worth reading, nothing but inconsequential news items. But I keep reading, for lack of anything better to do. Until I finish the paper. What next? To avoid pursuing that thought any further, I dally over the newspaper. Hmm, how about answering letters? A cousin of mine has sent us a wedding invitation, which I have to turn down. The day of the wedding, the wife and I are going to be off on a trip. To Okinawa.[6] We've been planning it for ages; we're both taking time off from work. We can't very well go changing our plans now. God only knows when we'll get the next chance to spend a long holiday together. And to clinch it all, I'm not even that close to my cousin; haven't seen her in almost ten years. Still, I can't leave replying to the last minute. She has to know how many people are coming, how many settings to plan for the banquet. Oh, forget it. I can't bring myself to write, not now. My heart isn't in it.

I pick up the newspaper again and read the same articles over again. Maybe I ought to start preparing dinner. But the wife might be working late and could come home having eaten. Which would mean wasting one portion. And if I am going to eat alone, I can make do with leftovers; no reason to make something up special. If she hasn't eaten, we can go out and eat together.

Odd, though. Whenever either of us knows he or she is going to be later than six, we always call in. That's the rule. Leave a message on the answering machine if necessary. That way, the other can coordinate: go ahead and eat alone, or set something out for the late arriver, or hit the sack. The nature of my work sometimes keeps me out late, and she often has meetings, or proofs to dispatch, before coming home. Neither of us has a regular nine-to-five job. When both of us are busy, we can go three days without a word to each other. Those are the breaks—just one of those things that nobody planned. Hence we always keep certain rules, so as not to place unrealistic burdens on each other. If it looks as though we're going to be late, we call in and let the other one know. I sometimes forget, but she, never once.

Still, there's no message on the answering machine.

I toss the newspaper, stretch out on the sofa, and shut my eyes.

6. One of the islands that make up the nation of Japan.

I dream about a meeting. I'm standing up, delivering a statement I myself don't understand. I open my mouth and talk. If I don't, I'm a dead man. I have to keep talking. Have to keep coming out with endless blah-blah-blah. Everyone around me is dead. Dead and turned to stone. A roomful of stone statues. A wind is blowing. The windows are all broken; gusts of air are coming in. And the TV People are here. Three of them. Like the first time. They're carrying a Sony color TV. And on the screen are the TV People. I'm running out of words; little by little I can feel my fingertips growing stiffer. Gradually turning to stone.

I open my eyes to find the room aglow. The color of corridors at the Aquarium. The television is on. Outside, everything is dark. The TV screen is flickering in the gloom, static crackling. I sit up on the sofa, and press my temples with my fingertips. The flesh of my fingers is still soft; my mouth tastes like beer. I swallow. I'm dried out; the saliva catches in my throat. As always, the waking world pales after an all-too-real dream. But no, this is real. Nobody's turned to stone. What time is it getting to be? I look for the clock on the floor. *TRPP Q SCHAOUS TRPP Q SCHAOUS.* A little before eight.

Yet, just as in the dream, one of the TV People is on the television screen. The same guy I passed on the stairs to the office. No mistake. The one who first opened the door to the apartment. I'm 100% sure. He stands there—against a bright, fluorescent white background, the tail end of a dream infiltrating my conscious reality—staring at me. I shut, then reopen my eyes, hoping he'll have slipped back to never-never land. But he doesn't disappear. Far from it. He gets bigger. His face fills the whole screen, getting closer and closer.

The next thing I know, he's stepping through the screen. Hands gripping the frame, lifting himself up and over, one foot after the other, like climbing out of a window, leaving a white TV screen glowing behind him.

He rubs his left hand in the palm of his right, slowly acclimating himself to the world outside the television. On and on, reduced right-hand fingers rubbing reduced left-hand fingers, no hurry. He has that all-the-time-in-the-world nonchalance. Like a veteran TV-show host. Then he looks me in the face.

"We're making an airplane," says my TV People visitant. His voice has no perspective to it. A curious, paper-thin voice.

He speaks, and the screen is all machinery. Very professional fade-in. Just like on the news. First, there's an opening shot of a large factory interior, then it cuts to a close-up of the work space, camera center. Two TV People are hard at work on some machine, tightening bolts with wrenches, adjusting gauges. The picture of concentration. The machine, however, is unlike anything I've ever seen: an upright cylinder except that it narrows toward the top, with streamlined protrusions along its surface. Looks more like some kind of gigantic orange juicer than an airplane. No wings, no seats.

"Doesn't look like an airplane," I say. Doesn't sound like my voice, either. Strangely brittle, as if the nutrients had been strained out through a thick filter. Have I grown so old all of a sudden?

"That's probably because we haven't painted it yet," he says. "Tomorrow we'll have it the right color. Then you'll see it's an airplane."

"The color's not the problem. It's the shape. That's not an airplane."

"Well, if it's not an airplane, what is it?" he asks me. If he doesn't know, and I don't know, then what *is* it? "So, that's why it's got to be the color." The TV People rep puts it to me gently. "Paint it the right color, and it'll be an airplane."

I don't feel like arguing. What difference does it make? Orange juicer or airplane—flying orange juicer?—what do I care? Still, where's the wife while all this is happening? Why doesn't she come home? I massage my temples again. The clock ticks on. *TRPP Q SCHAOUS TRPP Q SCHAOUS.* The remote control lies on the table, and next to it the stack of women's magazines. The telephone is silent, the room illuminated by the dim glow of the television.

The two TV People on the screen keep working away. The image is much clearer than before. You can read the numbers on the dials, hear the faint rumble of machinery. *TAABZHRAYBGG TAABZHRAYBGG ARP ARRP TAABZHRAYBGG.* This bass line is punctuated periodically by a sharp, metallic grating. *AREEEENBT AREEEENBT.* And various other noises are interspersed through the remaining aural space; I can't hear anything clearly over them. Still, the two TV People labor on for all they're worth. That, apparently, is the subject of this program. I go on watching the two of them as they work on and on. Their colleague outside the TV set also looks on in silence. At them. At that *thing*—for the life of me, it does not look like an airplane—that insane machine all black and grimy, floating in a field of white light.

The TV People rep speaks up. "Shame about your wife."

I look him in the face. Maybe I didn't hear him right. Staring at him is like peering into the glowing tube itself.

"Shame about your wife," the TV People rep repeats in exactly the same absent tone.

"How's that?" I ask.

"How's that? It's gone too far," says the TV People rep in a voice like a plastic-card hotel key. Flat, uninflected, it slices into me as if it were sliding through a thin slit. "It's gone too far: She's out there."

"It's gone too far: She's out there," I repeat in my head. Very plain, and without reality. I can't grasp the context. Cause has effect by the tail and is about to swallow it whole. I get up and go to the kitchen. I open the refrigerator, take a deep breath, reach for a can of beer, and go back to the sofa. The TV People rep stands in place in front of the television, right elbow resting on the set, and watches me extract the pull-tab. I don't really want to drink beer at this moment; I just need to do something. I drink one sip, but the beer doesn't taste good. I hold the can in my hand dumbly until it becomes so heavy I have to set it down on the table.

Then I think about the TV People rep's revelation, about the wife's failure to materialize. He's saying she's gone. That she isn't coming home. I can't bring myself to believe it's over. Sure, we're not the perfect couple. In four years, we've had our spats; we have our little problems. But we always talk them out. There are things we've resolved and things we haven't. Most of what we couldn't resolve we let ride. Okay, so we have our ups and downs as a couple. I admit it. But is this cause for despair? C'mon, show me a couple who don't have problems. Besides, it's only a little past eight. There must be some reason she can't get to a phone. Any number of possible reasons. For instance . . . I can't think of a single one. I'm hopelessly confused.

I fall back deep into the sofa.

How on earth is that airplane—if it is an airplane—supposed to fly? What propels it? Where are the windows? Which is the front, which is the back?

I'm dead tired. Exhausted. I still have to write that letter, though, to beg off from my cousin's invitation. My work schedule does not afford me the pleasure of attending. Regrettable. Congratulations, all the same.

The two TV People in the television continue building their airplane, oblivious of me. They toil away; they don't stop for anything. They have an infinite amount of work to get through before the machine is complete. No sooner have they finished one operation than they're busy with another. They have no assembly instructions, no plans, but they know precisely what to do and what comes next. The camera ably follows their deft motions. Clear-cut, easy-to-follow camera work. Highly credible, convincing images. No doubt other TV People (Nos. 4 and 5?) are manning the camera and control panel.

Strange as it may sound, the more I watch the flawless form of the TV People as they go about their work, the more the thing starts to look like an airplane. At least, it'd no longer surprise me if it actually flew. What does it matter which is front or back? With all the exacting detail work they're putting in, it *has* to be an airplane. Even if it doesn't appear so—to them, it's an airplane. Just as the little guy said, "If it's not an airplane, then what is it?"

The TV People rep hasn't so much as twitched in all this time. Right elbow still propped up on the TV set, he's watching me. I'm being watched. The TV People factory crew keeps working. Busy, busy, busy. The clock ticks on. *TRPP Q SCHAOUS TRPP Q SCHAOUS.* The room has grown dark, stifling. Someone's footsteps echo down the hall.

Well, it suddenly occurs to me, maybe so. Maybe the wife *is* out there. She's gone somewhere far away. By whatever means of transport, she's gone somewhere far out of my reach. Maybe our relationship has suffered irreversible damage. Maybe it's a total loss. Only I haven't noticed. All sorts of thoughts unravel inside me, then the frayed ends come together again. "Maybe so," I say out loud. My voice echoes, hollow.

"Tomorrow, when we paint it, you'll see better," he resumes. "All it needs is a touch of color to make it an airplane."

I look at the palms of my hands. They have shrunk slightly. Ever so slightly. Power of suggestion? Maybe the light's playing tricks on me. Maybe my sense of perspective has been thrown off. Yet, my palms really do look shriveled. Hey now, wait just a minute! Let me speak. There's something I should say. I must say. I'll dry up and turn to stone if I don't. Like the others.

"The phone will ring soon," the TV People rep says. Then, after a measured pause, he adds, "In another five minutes."

I look at the telephone; I think about the telephone cord. Endless lengths of phone cable linking one telephone to another. Maybe somewhere, at some terminal of that awesome megacircuit, is my wife. Far, far away, out of my reach. I can feel her pulse. Another five minutes, I tell myself. *Which way is front, which way is back?* I stand up and try to say something, but no sooner have I got to my feet than the words slip away.

━┿━

William Gibson
b. 1948

In the 1980s William Gibson became famous in the United States and around the world for coining the word "cyberspace." In Gibson's science fiction, this term refers to a particular type of virtual-reality interface that allows computer users to navigate global electronic networks as if they were a kind of urban space. But the word soon acquired a variety of popular and technical uses and became a general shorthand for the increasingly important experience of global connectivity through computer networks. In novels such as Gibson's *Neuromancer* (1984), which became an instant science fiction classic and widely popularized the term, cyberspace forms part of a bleak near-future scenario in which corporations dominate a world of devastated natural and urban landscapes. The protagonists, whose minds and bodies have often been dramatically altered by innovative surgery, genetic engineering, or drug use, are generally far from the centers of power and operate on the borderlines of legality as they enter cyberspace to find hidden bits of information, steal corporate secrets, or carry out the orders of Artificial Intelligences. Even though they cultivate a rebel-outlaw image in language and appearance, in reality these protagonists are often mere pawns in power games that they only partially understand. But moving about in cyberspace becomes a means of fulfilling their profound Romantic longing to break loose from bodily existence and merge with a more transcendent realm. A whole subgenre of science fiction has portrayed this type of future world in fiction and film, with *Blade Runner* as the most famous example. This genre became known as "cyberpunk" and enjoyed enormous popularity as a new form of counterculture in the 1980s and early 1990s.

Gibson, the author most centrally identified with cyberpunk, was born in South Carolina in 1948 but emigrated to Canada in 1968 after having been rejected by his draft board. He lived first in Toronto and later in Vancouver; from the vantage point of Canada's West Coast, Gibson was well placed to observe the cultural impact of Japan's rise to economic power, which caused considerable anxiety as well as admiration in North America and Europe, and plays a crucial role in Gibson's imagination of the future. The runaway success of his novels and the notoriety associated with being the "inventor" of cyberspace came as a surprise to Gibson, whose self-characterizations tend to be much more modest than those of his admirers. The short story "Burning Chrome," first published in *Omni* magazine in 1982, was the text in which the term "cyberspace" first appeared and became the title story of a short story-collection four years later. It exhibits many of the features that make Gibson's vision of the future seductive as well as problematic: the *film noir* chic of its bars and streets, the high-tech glamour of machinery that has become an integral part of the human body, and the metaphysical longings that find their expression in technical expertise. Yet "Burning Chrome" also exemplifies some of the more unsettling aspects of cyberpunk: the protagonists' disturbing combination of technological sophistication with social and emotional immaturity, the relentless romanticization of serious social problems, and the unquestioning acceptance of violence and crime. Beyond their topical appeal at the time the Internet emerged as a new medium, Gibson's novels and short stories raise far-reaching questions regarding future forms of interaction between humans and machines and their social and psychological implications.

Burning Chrome

It was hot, the night we burned Chrome. Out in the malls and plazas, moths were batting themselves to death against the neon, but in Bobby's loft the only light came from a monitor screen and the green and red LEDs on the face of the matrix simulator. I knew every chip in Bobby's simulator by heart; it looked like your workaday Ono-Sendai VII, the "Cyberspace Seven," but I'd rebuilt it so many times that you'd have had a hard time finding a square millimeter of factory circuitry in all that silicon.

We waited side by side in front of the simulator console, watching the time display in the screen's lower left corner.

"Go for it," I said, when it was time, but Bobby was already there, leaning forward to drive the Russian program into its slot with the heel of his hand. He did it with the tight grace of a kid slamming change into an arcade game, sure of winning and ready to pull down a string of free games.

A silver tide of phosphenes boiled across my field of vision as the matrix began to unfold in my head, a 3-D chessboard, infinite and perfectly transparent. The Russian program seemed to lurch as we entered the grid. If anyone else had been jacked into that part of the matrix, he might have seen a surf of flickering shadow roll out of the little yellow pyramid that represented our computer. The program was a mimetic weapon, designed to absorb local color and present itself as a crash-priority override in whatever context it encountered.

"Congratulations," I heard Bobby say. "We just became an Eastern Seaboard Fission Authority inspection probe. . . ." That meant we were clearing fiberoptic lines with the cybernetic equivalent of a fire siren, but in the simulation matrix we seemed to rush straight for Chrome's data base. I couldn't see it yet, but I already knew those walls were waiting. Walls of shadow, walls of ice.

Chrome: her pretty childface smooth as steel, with eyes that would have been at home on the bottom of some deep Atlantic trench, cold gray eyes that lived under terrible pressure. They said she cooked her own cancers for people who crossed her, rococo custom variations that took years to kill you. They said a lot of things about Chrome, none of them at all reassuring.

So I blotted her out with a picture of Rikki. Rikki kneeling in a shaft of dusty sunlight that slanted into the loft through a grid of steel and glass: her faded camouflage fatigues, her translucent rose sandals, the good line of her bare back as she rummaged through a nylon gear bag. She looks up, and a half-blond curl falls to tickle her nose. Smiling, buttoning an old shirt of Bobby's, frayed khaki cotton drawn across her breasts.

She smiles.

"Son of a bitch," said Bobby, "we just told Chrome we're an IRS audit and three Supreme Court subpoenas. . . . Hang on to your ass, Jack. . . ."

So long, Rikki. Maybe now I see you never.

And dark, so dark, in the halls of Chrome's ice.

Bobby was a cowboy, and ice was the nature of his game, *ice* from ICE, Intrusion Countermeasures Electronics. The matrix is an abstract representation of the relationships between data systems. Legitimate programmers jack into their employers' sector of the matrix and find themselves surrounded by bright geometries representing the corporate data.

Towers and fields of it ranged in the colorless nonspace of the simulation matrix, the electronic consensus-hallucination that facilitates the handling and exchange of massive quantities of data. Legitimate programmers never see the walls of ice they work behind, the walls of shadow that screen their operations from others, from industrial-espionage artists and hustlers like Bobby Quine.

Bobby was a cowboy. Bobby was a cracksman, a burglar, casing mankind's extended electronic nervous system, rustling data and credit in the crowded matrix, monochrome nonspace where the only stars are dense concentrations of information, and high above it all burn corporate galaxies and the cold spiral arms of military systems.

Bobby was another one of those young-old faces you see drinking in the Gentleman Loser, the chic bar for computer cowboys, rustlers, cybernetic second-story men. We were partners.

Bobby Quine and Automatic Jack. Bobby's the thin, pale dude with the dark glasses, and Jack's the mean-looking guy with the myoelectric arm.[1] Bobby's software and Jack's hard; Bobby punches console and Jack runs down all the little things that can give you an edge. Or, anyway, that's what the scene watchers in the Gentle-

---

1. Gibson combines the commonly used prefix "myo-," referring to muscle tissue, with "electric" to indicate the fusion of organic and mechanic components in Automatic Jack's arm.

man Loser would've told you, before Bobby decided to burn Chrome. But they also might've told you that Bobby was losing his edge, slowing down. He was twenty-eight, Bobby, and that's old for a console cowboy.

Both of us were good at what we did, but somehow that one big score just wouldn't come down for us. I knew where to go for the right gear, and Bobby had all his licks down pat. He'd sit back with a white terry sweatband across his forehead and whip moves on those keyboards faster than you could follow, punching his way through some of the fanciest ice in the business, but that was when something happened that managed to get him totally wired, and that didn't happen often. Not highly motivated, Bobby, and I was the kind of guy who's happy to have the rent covered and a clean shirt to wear.

But Bobby had this thing for girls, like they were his private tarot or something, the way he'd get himself moving. We never talked about it, but when it started to look like he was losing his touch that summer, he started to spend more time in the Gentleman Loser. He'd sit at a table by the open doors and watch the crowd slide by, nights when the bugs were at the neon and the air smelled of perfume and fast food. You could see his sunglasses scanning those faces as they passed, and he must have decided that Rikki's was the one he was waiting for, the wild card and the luck changer. The new one.

I went to New York to check out the market, to see what was available in hot software.

The Finn's place has a defective hologram in the window, METRO HOLOGRAFIX, over a display of dead flies wearing fur coats of gray dust. The scrap's waist-high, inside, drifts of it rising to meet walls that are barely visible behind nameless junk, behind sagging pressboard shelves stacked with old skin magazines and yellow-spined years of *National Geographic*.

"You need a gun," said the Finn. He looks like a recombo DNA project aimed at tailoring people for high-speed burrowing. "You're in luck. I got the new Smith and Wesson, the four-oh-eight Tactical. Got this xenon projector slung under the barrel, see, batteries in the grip, throw you a twelve-inch high-noon circle in the pitch dark at fifty yards. The light source is so narrow, it's almost impossible to spot. It's just like voodoo in a nightfight."

I let my arm clunk down on the table and started the fingers drumming; the servos in the hand began whining like overworked mosquitoes. I knew that the Finn really hated the sound.

"You looking to pawn that?" He prodded the Duralumin wrist joint with the chewed shaft of a felt-tip pen. "Maybe get yourself something a little quieter?"

I kept it up. "I don't need any guns, Finn."

"Okay," he said, "okay," and I quit drumming. "I only got this one item, and I don't even know what it is." He looked unhappy. "I got it off these bridge-and-tunnel kids from Jersey last week."

"So when'd you ever buy anything you didn't know what it was, Finn?"

"Wise ass." And he passed me a transparent mailer with something in it that looked like an audio cassette through the bubble padding. "They had a passport," he said. "They had credit cards and a watch. And that."

"They had the contents of somebody's pockets, you mean."

He nodded. "The passport was Belgian. It was also bogus, looked to me, so I put it in the furnace. Put the cards in with it. The watch was okay, a Porsche, nice watch."

It was obviously some kind of plug-in military program. Out of the mailer, it looked like the magazine of a small assault rifle, coated with nonreflective black plastic. The edges and corners showed bright metal; it had been knocking around for a while.

"I'll give you a bargain on it, Jack. For old times' sake."

I had to smile at that. Getting a bargain from the Finn was like God repealing the law of gravity when you have to carry a heavy suitcase down ten blocks of airport corridor.

"Looks Russian to me," I said. "Probably the emergency sewage controls for some Leningrad suburb. Just what I need."

"You know," said the Finn. "I got a pair of shoes older than you are. Sometimes I think you got about as much class as those yahoos from Jersey. What do you want me to tell you, it's the keys to the Kremlin? You figure out what the goddamn thing is. Me, I just sell the stuff."

I bought it.

Bodiless, we swerve into Chrome's castle of ice. And we're fast, fast. It feels like we're surfing the crest of the invading program, hanging ten above the seething glitch systems as they mutate. We're sentient patches of oil swept along down corridors of shadow.

Somewhere we have bodies, very far away, in a crowded loft roofed with steel and glass. Somewhere we have microseconds, maybe time left to pull out.

We've crashed her gates disguised as an audit and three subpoenas, but her defenses are specifically geared to cope with that kind of official intrusion. Her most sophisticated ice is structured to fend off warrants, writs, subpoenas. When we breached the first gate, the bulk of her data vanished behind core-command ice, these walls we see as leagues of corridor, mazes of shadow. Five separate landlines spurted May Day signals to law firms, but the virus had already taken over the parameter ice. The glitch systems gobble the distress calls as our mimetic subprograms scan anything that hasn't been blanked by core command.

The Russian program lifts a Tokyo number from the unscreened data, choosing it for frequency of calls, average length of calls, the speed with which Chrome returned those calls.

"Okay," says Bobby, "we're an incoming scrambler call from a pal of hers in Japan. That should help."

Ride 'em, cowboy.

Bobby read his future in women; his girls were omens, changes in the weather, and he'd sit all night in the Gentleman Loser, waiting for the season to lay a new face down in front of him like a card.

I was working late in the loft one night, shaving down a chip, my arm off and the little waldo jacked straight into the stump.

Bobby came in with a girl I hadn't seen before, and usually I feel a little funny if a stranger sees me working that way, with those leads clipped to the hard carbon studs that stick out of my stump. She came right over and looked at the magnified image on the screen, then saw the waldo moving under its vacuum-sealed dust cover. She didn't say anything, just watched. Right away I had a good feeling about her; it's like that sometimes.

"Automatic Jack, Rikki. My associate."

He laughed, put his arm around her waist, something in his tone letting me know that I'd be spending the night in a dingy room in a hotel.

"Hi," she said. Tall, nineteen or maybe twenty, and she definitely had the goods. With just those few freckles across the bridge of her nose, and eyes somewhere between dark amber and French coffee. Tight black jeans rolled to midcalf and a narrow plastic belt that matched the rose-colored sandals.

But now when I see her sometimes when I'm trying to sleep, I see her somewhere out on the edge of all this sprawl of cities and smoke, and it's like she's a hologram stuck behind my eyes, in a bright dress she must've worn once, when I knew her, something that doesn't quite reach her knees. Bare legs long and straight. Brown hair, streaked with blond, hoods her face, blown in a wind from somewhere, and I see her wave goodbye.

Bobby was making a show of rooting through a stack of audio cassettes. "I'm on my way, cowboy," I said, unclipping the waldo. She watched attentively as I put my arm back on.

"Can you fix things?" she asked.

"Anything, anything you want, Automatic Jack'll fix it." I snapped my Duralumin fingers for her.

She took a little simstim deck from her belt and showed me the broken hinge on the cassette cover.

"Tomorrow," I said, "no problem."

And my oh my, I said to myself, sleep pulling me down the six flights to the street, *what'll Bobby's luck be like with a fortune cookie like that? If his system worked, we'd be striking it rich any night now.* In the street I grinned and yawned and waved for a cab.

Chrome's castle is dissolving, sheets of ice shadow flickering and fading, eaten by the glitch systems that spin out from the Russian program, tumbling away from our central logic thrust and infecting the fabric of the ice itself. The glitch systems are cybernetic virus analogs, self-replicating and voracious. They mutate constantly, in unison, subverting and absorbing Chrome's defenses.

Have we already paralyzed her, or is a bell ringing somewhere, a red light blinking? Does she know?

Rikki Wildside, Bobby called her, and for those first few weeks it must have seemed to her that she had it all, the whole teeming show spread out for her, sharp and bright under the neon. She was new to the scene, and she had all the miles of malls and plazas to prowl, all the shops and clubs, and Bobby to explain the wild side, the tricky wiring on the dark underside of things, all the players and their names and their games. He made her feel at home.

"What happened to your arm?" she asked me one night in the Gentleman Loser, the three of us drinking at a small table in a corner.

"Hang-gliding," I said, "accident."

"Hang-gliding over a wheatfield," said Bobby, "place called Kiev.[2] Our Jack's just hanging there in the dark, under a Nightwing parafoil, with fifty kilos of radar jammed between his legs, and some Russian asshole accidentally burns his arm off with a laser."

I don't remember how I changed the subject, but I did.

2. The capital of the Ukraine, which, at the time this story was written, still formed part of the Soviet Union.

I was still telling myself that it wasn't Rikki who was getting to me, but what Bobby was doing with her. I'd known him for a long time, since the end of the war, and I knew he used women as counters in a game, Bobby Quine versus fortune, versus time and the night of cities. And Rikki had turned up just when he needed something to get him going, something to aim for. So he'd set her up as a symbol for everything he wanted and couldn't have, everything he'd had and couldn't keep.

I didn't like having to listen to him tell me how much he loved her, and knowing he believed it only made it worse. He was a past master at the hard fall and the rapid recovery, and I'd seen it happen a dozen times before. He might as well have had NEXT printed across his sunglasses in green Day-Glo capitals, ready to flash out at the first interesting face that flowed past the tables in the Gentleman Loser.

I knew what he did to them. He turned them into emblems, sigils[3] on the map of his hustler's life, navigation beacons he could follow through a sea of bars and neon. What else did he have to steer by? He didn't love money, in and of itself, not enough to follow its lights. He wouldn't work for power over other people; he hated the responsibility it brings. He had some basic pride in his skill, but that was never enough to keep him pushing.

So he made do with women.

When Rikki showed up, he needed one in the worst way. He was fading fast, and smart money was already whispering that the edge was off his game. He needed that one big score, and soon, because he didn't know any other kind of life, and all his clocks were set for hustler's time, calibrated in risk and adrenaline and that supernal dawn calm that comes when every move's proved right and a sweet lump of someone else's credit clicks into your own account.

It was time for him to make his bundle and get out; so Rikki got set up higher and farther away than any of the others ever had, even though—and I felt like screaming it at him—she was right there, alive, totally real, human, hungry, resilient, bored, beautiful, excited, all the things she was. . . .

Then he went out one afternoon, about a week before I made the trip to New York to see Finn. Went out and left us there in the loft, waiting for a thunderstorm. Half the skylight was shadowed by a dome they'd never finished, and the other half showed sky, black and blue with clouds. I was standing by the bench, looking up at that sky, stupid with the hot afternoon, the humidity, and she touched me, touched my shoulder, the half-inch border of taut pink scar that the arm doesn't cover. Anybody else ever touched me there, they went on to the shoulder, the neck. . . .

But she didn't do that. Her nails were lacquered black, not pointed, but tapered oblongs, the lacquer only a shade darker than the carbon-fiber laminate that sheathes my arm. And her hand went down the arm, black nails tracing a weld in the laminate, down to the black anodized elbow joint, out to the wrist, her hand soft-knuckled as a child's, fingers spreading to lock over mine, her palm against the perforated Duralumin.

Her other palm came up to brush across the feedback pads, and it rained all afternoon, raindrops drumming on the steel and soot-stained glass above Bobby's bed.

Ice walls flick away like supersonic butterflies made of shade. Beyond them, the matrix's illusion of infinite space. It's like watching a tape of a prefab building going up; only the tape's reversed and run at high speed, and these walls are torn wings.

---

3. Signs or images to which magic power is attributed.

Trying to remind myself that this place and the gulfs beyond are only representations, that we aren't "in" Chrome's computer, but interfaced with it, while the matrix simulator in Bobby's loft generates this illusion . . . The core data begin to emerge, exposed, vulnerable. . . . This is the far side of ice, the view of the matrix I've never seen before, the view that fifteen million legitimate console operators see daily and take for granted.

The core data tower around us like vertical freight trains, color-coded for access. Bright primaries, impossibly bright in that transparent void, linked by countless horizontals in nursery blues and pinks.

But ice still shadows something at the center of it all: the heart of all Chrome's expensive darkness, the very heart . . .

It was late afternoon when I got back from my shopping expedition to New York. Not much sun through the skylight, but an ice pattern glowed on Bobby's monitor screen, a 2-D graphic representation of someone's computer defenses, lines of neon woven like an Art Deco prayer rug. I turned the console off, and the screen went completely dark.

Rikki's things were spread across my workbench, nylon bags spilling clothes and makeup, a pair of bright red cowboy boots, audio cassettes, glossy Japanese magazines about simstim stars. I stacked it all under the bench and then took my arm off, forgetting that the program I'd brought from the Finn was in the right-hand pocket of my jacket, so that I had to fumble it out left-handed and then get it into the padded jaws of the jeweler's vise.

The waldo looks like an old audio turntable, the kind that played disc records, with the vise set up under a transparent dust cover. The arm itself is just over a centimeter long, swinging out on what would've been the tone arm on one of those turntables. But I don't look at that when I've clipped the leads to my stump; I look at the scope, because that's my arm there in black and white, magnification 40 ×.

I ran a tool check and picked up the laser. It felt a little heavy; so I scaled my weight-sensor input down to a quarter-kilo per gram and got to work. At 40 × the side of the program looked like a trailer truck.

It took eight hours to crack: three hours with the waldo and the laser and four dozen taps, two hours on the phone to a contact in Colorado, and three hours to run down a lexicon disc that could translate eight-year-old technical Russian.

Then Cyrillic alphanumerics started reeling down the monitor, twisting themselves into English halfway down. There were a lot of gaps, where the lexicon ran up against specialized military acronyms in the readout I'd bought from my man in Colorado, but it did give me some idea of what I'd bought from the Finn.

I felt like a punk who'd gone out to buy a switch-blade and come home with a small neutron bomb.

Screwed again, I thought. *What good's a neutron bomb in a streetfight?* The thing under the dust cover was right out of my league. I didn't even know where to unload it, where to look for a buyer. Someone had, but he was dead, someone with a Porsche watch and a fake Belgian passport, but I'd never tried to move in those circles. The Finn's muggers from the 'burbs had knocked over someone who had some highly arcane connections.

The program in the jeweler's vise was a Russian military icebreaker, a killer-virus program.

It was dawn when Bobby came in alone. I'd fallen asleep with a bag of takeout sandwiches in my lap.

"You want to eat?" I asked him, not really awake, holding out my sandwiches. I'd been dreaming of the program, of its waves of hungry glitch systems and mimetic subprograms; in the dream it was an animal of some kind, shapeless and flowing.

He brushed the bag aside on his way to the console, punched a function key. The screen lit with the intricate pattern I'd seen there that afternoon. I rubbed sleep from my eyes with my left hand, one thing I can't do with my right. I'd fallen asleep trying to decide whether to tell him about the program. Maybe I should try to sell it alone, keep the money, go somewhere new, ask Rikki to go with me.

"Whose is it?" I asked.

He stood there in a black cotton jump suit, an old leather jacket thrown over his shoulders like a cape. He hadn't shaved for a few days, and his face looked thinner than usual.

"It's Chrome's," he said.

My arm convulsed, started clicking, fear translated to the myoelectrics through the carbon studs. I spilled the sandwiches; limp sprouts, and bright yellow dairy-produce slices on the unswept wooden floor.

"You're stone crazy," I said.

"No," he said, "you think she rumbled it? No way. We'd be dead already. I locked on to her through a triple-blind rental system in Mombasa[4] and an Algerian comsat. She knew somebody was having a look-see, but she couldn't trace it."

If Chrome had traced the pass Bobby had made at her ice, we were good as dead. But he was probably right, or she'd have had me blown away on my way back from New York. "Why her, Bobby? Just give me one reason. . . ."

Chrome: I'd seen her maybe half a dozen times in the Gentleman Loser. Maybe she was slumming, or checking out the human condition, a condition she didn't exactly aspire to. A sweet little heart-shaped face framing the nastiest pair of eyes you ever saw. She'd looked fourteen for as long as anyone could remember, hyped out of anything like a normal metabolism on some massive program of serums and hormones. She was as ugly a customer as the street ever produced, but she didn't belong to the street anymore. She was one of the Boys, Chrome, a member in good standing of the local Mob subsidiary. Word was, she'd gotten started as a dealer, back when synthetic pituitary hormones were still proscribed. But she hadn't had to move hormones for a long time. Now she owned the House of Blue Lights.

"You're flat-out crazy, Quine. You give me one sane reason for having that stuff on your screen. You ought to dump it, and I mean *now*. . . ."

"Talk in the Loser," he said, shrugging out of the leather jacket. "Black Myron and Crow Jane. Jane, she's up on all the sex lines, claims she knows where the money goes. So she's arguing with Myron that Chrome's the controlling interest in the Blue Lights, not just some figurehead for the Boys."

"'The Boys,' Bobby," I said. "That's the operative word there. You still capable of seeing that? We don't mess with the Boys, remember? That's why we're still walking around."

"That's why we're still poor, partner." He settled back into the swivel chair in front of the console, unzipped his jump suit, and scratched his skinny white chest. "But maybe not for much longer."

4. A city in southern Kenya.

"I think maybe this partnership just got itself permanently dissolved."

Then he grinned at me. The grin was truly crazy, feral and focused, and I knew that right then he really didn't give a shit about dying.

"Look," I said, "I've got some money left, you know? Why don't you take it and get the tube to Miami, catch a hopper to Montego Bay. You need a rest, man. You've got to get your act together."

"My act, Jack," he said, punching something on the keyboard, "never has been this together before." The neon prayer rug on the screen shivered and woke as an animation program cut in, ice lines weaving with hypnotic frequency, a living mandala.[5] Bobby kept punching, and the movement slowed; the pattern resolved itself, grew slightly less complex, became an alternation between two distant configurations. A first-class piece of work, and I hadn't thought he was still that good. "Now," he said, "there, see it? Wait. There. There again. And there. Easy to miss. That's it. Cuts in every hour and twenty minutes with a squirt transmission to their comsat. We could live for a year on what she pays them weekly in negative interest."

"Whose comsat?"

"Zürich. Her bankers. That's her bankbook, Jack. That's where the money goes. Crow Jane was right."

I stood there. My arm forgot to click.

"So how'd you do in New York, partner? You get anything that'll help me cut ice? We're going to need whatever we can get."

I kept my eyes on his, forced myself not to look in the direction of the waldo, the jeweler's vise. The Russian program was there, under the dust cover.

Wild cards, luck changers.

"Where's Rikki?" I asked him, crossing to the console, pretending to study the alternating patterns on the screen.

"Friends of hers," he shrugged, "kids, they're all into simstim." He smiled absently. "I'm going to do it for her, man."

"I'm going out to think about this, Bobby. You want me to come back, you keep your hands off the board."

"I'm doing it for her," he said as the door closed behind me. "You know I am."

And down now, down, the program a roller coaster through this fraying maze of shadow walls, gray cathedral spaces between the bright towers. Headlong speed.

Black ice. Don't think about it. Black ice.

Too many stories in the Gentleman Loser; black ice is a part of the mythology. Ice that kills. Illegal, but then aren't we all? Some kind of neural-feedback weapon, and you connect with it only once. Like some hideous Word that eats the mind from the inside out. Like an epileptic spasm that goes on and on until there's nothing left at all . . .

And we're diving for the floor of Chrome's shadow castle.

Trying to brace myself for the sudden stopping of breath, a sickness and final slackening of the nerves. Fear of that cold Word waiting, down there in the dark.

I went out and looked for Rikki, found her in a café with a boy with Sendai eyes, half-healed suture lines radiating from his bruised sockets. She had a glossy brochure

5. A symbolic representation of the universe used in Buddhist ritual.

spread open on the table, Tally Isham smiling up from a dozen photographs, the Girl with the Zeiss Ikon Eyes.

Her little simstim deck was one of the things I'd stacked under my bench the night before, the one I'd fixed for her the day after I'd first seen her. She spent hours jacked into that unit, the contact band across her forehead like a gray plastic tiara. Tally Isham was her favorite, and with the contact band on, she was gone, off somewhere in the recorded sensorium of simstim's biggest star. Simulated stimuli: the world—all the interesting parts, anyway—as perceived by Tally Isham. Tally raced a black Fokker ground-effect plane across Arizona mesa tops. Tally dived the Truk Island preserves. Tally partied with the superrich on private Greek islands, heartbreaking purity of those tiny white seaports at dawn.

Actually she looked a lot like Tally, same coloring and cheekbones. I thought Rikki's mouth was stronger. More sass. She didn't want to *be* Tally Isham, but she coveted the job. That was her ambition, to be in simstim. Bobby just laughed it off. She talked to me about it, though. "How'd I look with a pair of these?" she'd ask, holding a full-page headshot, Tally Isham's blue Zeiss Ikons lined up with her own amber-brown. She'd had her corneas done twice, but she still wasn't 20–20; so she wanted Ikons. Brand of the stars. Very expensive.

"You still window-shopping for eyes?" I asked as I sat down.

"Tiger just got some," she said. She looked tired, I thought.

Tiger was so pleased with his Sendais that he couldn't help smiling, but I doubted whether he'd have smiled otherwise. He had the kind of uniform good looks you get after your seventh trip to the surgical boutique; he'd probably spend the rest of his life looking vaguely like each new season's media front-runner; not too obvious a copy, but nothing too original, either.

"Sendai, right?" I smiled back.

He nodded. I watched as he tried to take me in with his idea of a professional simstim glance. He was pretending that he was recording. I thought he spent too long on my arm. "They'll be great on peripherals when the muscles heal," he said, and I saw how carefully he reached for his double espresso. Sendai eyes are notorious for depth-perception defects and warranty hassles, among other things.

"Tiger's leaving for Hollywood tomorrow."

"Then maybe Chiba City, right?" I smiled at him. He didn't smile back. "Got an offer, Tiger? Know an agent?"

"Just checking it out," he said quietly. Then he got up and left. He said a quick goodbye to Rikki, but not to me.

"That kid's optic nerves may start to deteriorate inside six months. You know that, Rikki? Those Sendais are illegal in England, Denmark, lots of places. You can't replace nerves."

"Hey, Jack, no lectures." She stole one of my croissants and nibbled at the top of one of its horns.

"I thought I was your adviser, kid."

"Yeah. Well, Tiger's not too swift, but everybody knows about Sendais. They're all he can afford. So he's taking a chance. If he gets work, he can replace them."

"With these?" I tapped the Zeiss Ikon brochure. "Lot of money, Rikki. You know better than to take a gamble like that."

She nodded. "I want Ikons."

"If you're going up to Bobby's, tell him to sit tight until he hears from me."

"Sure. It's business?"

"Business," I said. But it was craziness.

I drank my coffee, and she ate both my croissants. Then I walked her down to Bobby's. I made fifteen calls, each one from a different pay phone.

Business. Bad craziness.

All in all, it took us six weeks to set the burn up, six weeks of Bobby telling me how much he loved her. I worked even harder, trying to get away from that.

Most of it was phone calls. My fifteen initial and very oblique inquiries each seemed to breed fifteen more. I was looking for a certain service Bobby and I both imagined as a requisite part of the world's clandestine economy, but which probably never had more than five customers at a time. It would be one that never advertised.

We were looking for the world's heaviest fence, for a non-aligned money laundry capable of dry-cleaning a megabuck online cash transfer and then forgetting about it.

All those calls were a waste, finally, because it was the Finn who put me on to what we needed. I'd gone up to New York to buy a new blackbox rig, because we were going broke paying for all those calls.

I put the problem to him as hypothetically as possible.

"Macao,"[6] he said.

"Macao?"

"The Long Hum family. Stockbrokers."

He even had the number. You want a fence, ask another fence.

The Long Hum people were so oblique that they made my idea of a subtle approach look like a tactical nuke-out. Bobby had to make two shuttle runs to Hong Kong to get the deal straight. We were running out of capital, and fast. I still don't know why I decided to go along with it in the first place; I was scared of Chrome, and I'd never been all that hot to get rich.

I tried telling myself that it was a good idea to burn the House of Blue Lights because the place was a creep joint, but I just couldn't buy it. I didn't like the Blue Lights, because I'd spent a supremely depressing evening there once, but that was no excuse for going after Chrome. Actually I halfway assumed we were going to die in the attempt. Even with that killer program, the odds weren't exactly in our favor.

Bobby was lost in writing the set of commands we were going to plug into the dead center of Chrome's computer. That was going to be my job, because Bobby was going to have his hands full trying to keep the Russian program from going straight for the kill. It was too complex for us to rewrite, and so he was going to try to hold it back for the two seconds I needed.

I made a deal with a streetfighter named Miles. He was going to follow Rikki the night of the burn, keep her in sight, and phone me at a certain time. If I wasn't there, or didn't answer in just a certain way, I'd told him to grab her and put her on the first tube out. I gave him an envelope to give her, money and a note.

Bobby really hadn't thought about that, much, how things would go for her if we blew it. He just kept telling me he loved her, where they were going to go together, how they'd spend the money.

"Buy her a pair of Ikons first, man. That's what she wants. She's serious about that simstim scene."

"Hey," he said, looking up from the keyboard, "she won't need to work. We're going to make it, Jack. She's my luck. She won't ever have to work again."

6. A small area at the tip of a peninsula on the Chinese mainland that is administered by Portugal.

"Your luck," I said. I wasn't happy. I couldn't remember when I had been happy. "You seen your luck around lately?"

He hadn't, but neither had I. We'd both been too busy.

I missed her. Missing her reminded me of my one night in the House of Blue Lights, because I'd gone there out of missing someone else. I'd gotten drunk to begin with, then I'd started hitting Vasopressin inhalers. If your main squeeze has just decided to walk out on you, booze and Vasopressin are the ultimate in masochistic pharmacology; the juice makes you maudlin and the Vasopressin makes you remember, I mean really remember. Clinically they use the stuff to counter senile amnesia, but the street finds its own uses for things. So I'd bought myself an ultraintense replay of a bad affair; trouble is, you get the bad with the good. Go gunning for transports of animal ecstasy and you get what you said, too, and what she said to that, how she walked away and never looked back.

I don't remember deciding to go to the Blue Lights, or how I got there, hushed corridors and this really tacky decorative waterfall trickling somewhere, or maybe just a hologram of one. I had a lot of money that night; somebody had given Bobby a big roll for opening a three-second window in someone else's ice.

I don't think the crew on the door liked my looks, but I guess my money was okay.

I had more to drink there when I'd done what I went there for. Then I made some crack to the barman about closet necrophiliacs, and that didn't go down too well. Then this very large character insisted on calling me War Hero, which I didn't like. I think I showed him some tricks with the arm, before the lights went out, and I woke up two days later in a basic sleeping module somewhere else. A cheap place, not even room to hang yourself. And I sat there on that narrow foam slab and cried.

Some things are worse than being alone. But the thing they sell in the House of Blue Lights is so popular that it's almost legal.

At the heart of darkness, the still center, the glitch systems shred the dark with whirlwinds of light, translucent razors spinning away from us; we hang in the center of a silent slow-motion explosion, ice fragments falling away forever, and Bobby's voice comes in across light-years of electronic void illusion—

"Burn the bitch down. I can't hold the thing back—"

The Russian program, rising through towers of data, blotting out the playroom colors. And I plug Bobby's homemade command package into the center of Chrome's cold heart. The squirt transmission cuts in, a pulse of condensed information that shoots straight up, past the thickening tower of darkness, the Russian program, while Bobby struggles to control that crucial second. An unformed arm of shadow twitches from the towering dark, too late.

We've done it.

The matrix folds itself around me like an origami trick.

And the loft smells of sweat and burning circuitry.

I thought I heard Chrome scream, a raw metal sound, but I couldn't have.

Bobby was laughing, tears in his eyes. The elapsed-time figure in the corner of the monitor read 07:24:05. The burn had taken a little under eight minutes.

And I saw that the Russian program had melted in its slot.

We'd given the bulk of Chrome's Zürich account to a dozen world charities. There was too much there to move, and we knew we had to break her, burn her straight down, or she might come after us. We took less than ten percent for ourselves and shot it through the Long Hum setup in Macao. They took sixty percent of that for themselves and kicked what was left back to us through the most convoluted sector of the Hong Kong exchange. It took an hour before our money started to reach the two accounts we'd opened in Zürich.

I watched zeros pile up behind a meaningless figure on the monitor. I was rich.

Then the phone rang. It was Miles. I almost blew the code phrase.

"Hey, Jack, man, I dunno—what's it all about, with this girl of yours? Kinda funny thing here . . ."

"What? Tell me."

"I been on her, like you said, tight but out of sight. She goes to the Loser, hangs out, then she gets a tube. Goes to the House of Blue Lights—"

"She what?"

"Side door. *Employees* only. No way I could get past their security."

"Is she there now?"

"No, man, I just lost her. It's insane down here, like the Blue Lights just shut down, looks like for good, seven kinds of alarms going off, everybody running, the heat out in riot gear. . . . Now there's all this stuff going on, insurance guys, real-estate types, vans with municipal plates. . . ."

"Miles, where'd she go?"

"Lost her, Jack."

"Look, Miles, you keep the money in the envelope, right?"

"You serious? Hey, I'm real sorry. I—"

I hung up.

"Wait'll we tell her," Bobby was saying, rubbing a towel across his bare chest.

"You tell her yourself, cowboy. I'm going for a walk."

So I went out into the night and the neon and let the crowd pull me along, walking blind, willing myself to be just a segment of that mass organism, just one more drifting chip of consciousness under the geodesics.[7] I didn't think, just put one foot in front of another, but after a while I did think, and it all made sense. She'd needed the money.

I thought about Chrome, too. That we'd killed her, murdered her, as surely as if we'd slit her throat. The night that carried me along through the malls and plazas would be hunting her now, and she had nowhere to go. How many enemies would she have in this crowd alone? How many would move, now they weren't held back by fear of her money? We'd taken her for everything she had. She was back on the street again. I doubted she'd live till dawn.

Finally I remembered the café, the one where I'd met Tiger.

Her sunglasses told the whole story, huge black shades with a telltale smudge of fleshtone paintstick in the corner of one lens. "Hi, Rikki," I said, and I was ready when she took them off.

Blue, Tally Isham blue. The clear trademark blue they're famous for, ZEISS IKON ringing each iris in tiny capitals, the letters suspended there like flecks of gold.

"They're beautiful," I said. Paintstick covered the bruising. No scars with work that good. "You made some money."

"Yeah, I did." Then she shivered. "But I won't make any more, not that way."

"I think that place is out of business."

"Oh." Nothing moved in her face then. The new blue eyes were still and very deep.

---

7. Geodesic domes were invented by American engineer Buckminster Fuller; they are used to enclose an area and insulate it against the exterior climate. In the 1960s they were popular as an alternative technology. In several of Gibson's texts, urban spaces are enclosed in geodesic domes.

"It doesn't matter. Bobby's waiting for you. We just pulled down a big score."

"No. I've got to go. I guess he won't understand, but I've got to go."

I nodded, watching the arm swing up to take her hand; it didn't seem to be part of me at all, but she held on to it like it was.

"I've got a one-way ticket to Hollywood. Tiger knows some people I can stay with. Maybe I'll even get to Chiba City."

She was right about Bobby. I went back with her. He didn't understand. But she'd already served her purpose, for Bobby, and I wanted to tell her not to hurt for him, because I could see that she did. He wouldn't even come out into the hallway after she had packed her bags. I put the bags down and kissed her and messed up the paintstick, and something came up inside me the way the killer program had risen above Chrome's data. A sudden stopping of the breath, in a place where no word is. But she had a plane to catch.

Bobby was slumped in the swivel chair in front of his monitor, looking at his string of zeros. He had his shades on, and I knew he'd be in the Gentleman Loser by nightfall, checking out the weather, anxious for a sign, someone to tell him what his new life would be like. I couldn't see it being very different. More comfortable, but he'd always be waiting for that next card to fall.

I tried not to imagine her in the House of Blue Lights, working three-hour shifts in an approximation of REM sleep,[8] while her body and a bundle of conditioned reflexes took care of business. The customers never got to complain that she was faking it, because those were real orgasms. But she felt them, if she felt them at all, as faint silver flares somewhere out on the edge of sleep. Yeah, it's so popular, it's almost legal. The customers are torn between needing someone and wanting to be alone at the same time, which has probably always been the name of that particular game, even before we had the neuroelectronics to enable them to have it both ways.

I picked up the phone and punched the number for her airline. I gave them her real name, her flight number. "She's changing that," I said, "to Chiba City. That right. Japan." I thumbed my credit card into the slot and punched my ID code. "First class." Distant hum as they scanned my credit records. "Make that a return ticket."

But I guess she cashed the return fare, or else didn't need it, because she hasn't come back. And sometimes late at night I'll pass a window with posters of simstim stars, all those beautiful, identical eyes staring back at me out of faces that are nearly as identical, and sometimes the eyes are hers, but none of the faces are, none of them ever are, and I see her far out on the edge of all this sprawl of night and cities, and then she waves goodbye.

⇒ END OF PERSPECTIVES: LITERATURE, TECHNOLOGY, AND MEDIA ⇐

---

8. Rapid eye movement sleep, the phase of deep sleep during which dreams are most likely to occur.

BIBLIOGRAPHY
The Twentieth Century

General Background • Benedict Anderson, *Imagined Communities: Reflections on the Origin and Spread of Nationalism*, 1991. • Michael Bell, *Myth and the Making of Modernity: The Problem of Grounding in Early Twentieth-Century Literature*, 1998. • Hans Bertens, *The Idea of the Postmodern: A History*, 1995. • James Clifford, *The Predicament of Culture: Twentieth-Century Ethnography, Literature, and Art*, 1988. • Fredric Jameson, *Postmodernism, or, The Cultural Logic of Late Capitalism*, 1991. • Brian McHale, *Postmodernist Fiction*, 1993. • Michael North, *The Dialect of Modernism: Race, Language, and Twentieth-Century Literature*, 1994. • Kenneth Richardson, *Twentieth Century Writing: A Reader's Guide to Contemporary Literature*, 1971. • Steven Serafin, *Encyclopedia of World Literature in the 20th Century*, 1999. • Randall Stevenson, *Modernist Fiction: An Introduction*, 1992. • Philip Malcolm Waller Thody, *Twentieth-Century Literature: Critical Issues and Themes*, 1996. • Tzvetan Todorov, *Literature and Its Theorists: A Personal View of Twentieth-Century Criticism*, 1987.

Crosscurrents: The Art of the Manifesto • Cinzia Sartini Blum, *The Other Modernism: F. T. Marinetti's Futurist Fiction of Power*, 1996. • Robert Vincent Daniels, *Trotsky, Stalin, and Socialism*, 1991. • Dennis Keene, *Yokomitsu Riichi, Modernist*, 1980. • Wolfgang Lubitz, *Trotsky Bibliography: An International Classified List of Publications About Leon Trotsky and Trotskyism, 1905–1998*, 1999. • Marianne Martin, *Futurist Art and Theory*, 1968. • Maurice Nadeau, *The History of Surrealism*, 1965. • Marjorie Perloff, *The Futurist Movement: Avant-garde, Avant-guerre, and the Language of Rupture*, 1986. • Julijana Ranc, *Trotzki und die Literaten: Literaturkritik eines Aussenseiters*, 1997. • Kirsten Strom, *Making History: Surrealism and the Invention of a Political Culture*, 2002. • Ian D. Thatcher, *Trotsky*, 2003. • Tristan Tzara, *Sept manifestes Dada, lampisteries (Seven Dada Manifestos and Lampisteries)*, 1977. • Dmitrii Antonovich Volkogonov, *Trotsky: The Eternal Revolutionary*, 1996.

Perspectives: Cosmopolitan Exiles • Donald Davie, *Czeslaw Milosz and the Insufficiency of Lyric*, 1999. • Gerard Delanty, *Citizenship in a Global Age: Society, Culture, Politics*, 2000. • Jacques Derrida, *On Cosmopolitanism and Forgiveness*, 2001. • Vinay Dharwadker, *Cosmopolitan Geographies: New Locations in Literature and Culture*, 2001. • Nigel Dower, *Global Citizenship: A Critical Introduction*, 2002. • Derek Benjamin Heater, *World Citizenship: Cosmopolitan Thinking and Its Opponents*, 2002. • Carsten Holbraad, *Internationalism and Nationalism in European Political Thought*, 2003. • Mark Lilla, *The Reckless Mind: Intellectuals in Politics*, 2001. • Leonard Nathan and Arthur Quinn, *The Poet's Work: An Introduction to Czeslaw Milosz*, 1991. • Martin Tucker, ed., *Literary Exile in the Twentieth Century*, 1991. • Andrew Vincent, *Nationalism and Particularity*, 2002.

Perspectives: Echoes of War • Glenda Abramson, *The Experienced Soul: Studies in Amichai*, 1997. • Glenda Abramson, *The Writing of Yehuda Amichai: A Thematic Approach*, 1989. • Karen Achberger, *Understanding Ingeborg Bachmann*, 1995. • Sven Backman, *Tradition Transformed: Studies in the Poetry of Wilfred Owen*, 1979. • Lisa de Serbine Bahrawy, *The Voice of History: An Exegesis of Selected Short Stories from Ingeborg Bachmann's "Das dreißigste Jahr" and "Simultan" from the Perspective of Austrian History*, 1989. • Stanislaw Baranczak, *A Fugitive from Utopia: The Poetry of Zbigniew Herbert*, 1987. • David Bevan, *Literature and War*, 1990. • Adrian Caesar, *Taking It Like a Man: Suffering, Sexuality, and the War Poets: Brooke, Sassoon, Owen, Graves*, 1993. • Joseph Cohen, *Voices of Israel: Essays on and Interviews with Yehuda Amichai, A.B. Yehoshua, T. Carmi, Aharon Applefeld, and Amos Oz*, 1990. • David Craig, *Extreme Situations: Literature and Crisis from the Great War to the Atom Bomb*, 1979. • Gary Day and Brian Docherty, eds., *British Poetry, 1900–50: Aspects of Tradition*, 1995. • Adrian Del Caro, *The Early Poetry of Paul Celan: In the Beginning Was the Word*, 1997. • Modris Ekstein, *Rites of Spring: The Great War and the Birth of the Modern Age*, 1989. • John Felstiner, *Paul Celan: Poet, Survivor, Jew*, 1995. • Gloria G. Fromm, "Saving Rupert Brooke," *The New Criterion* vol. 6, 1987, 71–77, • Paul Fussell, *The Great War and Modern Memory*, 1975. • Desmond Graham, *The Truth of War: Owen, Rosenberg, and Blunden*, 1984. • Keith Hale, ed., *Friends and Apostoles: The Correspondence of Rupert Brooke and James Strachey, 1905–1914*, 1998. • Shelley Hornstein and Florence Jacobowitz, eds. *Image and Remembrance: Representation and the Holocaust*, 2003. ● Charles S. Kraszewski, *Essays on the Dramatic Works of Polish Poet Zbigniew Herbert*, 2003. ● Dominick LaCapra, *History and Memory After Auschwitz*, 1998. ● Philippe Lacoue-Labarthe, *Poetry as Experience*, 1999. ● Arthur E. Lane, *An Adequate Response: The War Poetry of Wilfred Owen and Siegfried Sassoon*, 1983. ● William E. Laskowski, *Rupert Brooke*, 1994. ● Elizabeth A. Marsland, *The Nation's Cause: French, English, and German Poetry of the First World War*, 1991. ● Margot Norris, "Writing War in the Twentieth Century: An Introduction." *Writing War in the Twentieth Century*, 2000. ● Harold Owen, *Journey from Obscurity; Wilfred Owen, 1893–1918*, 1963–1965. ● Rennie Parker, *The Georgian Poets: Abercrombie, Brooke, Drinkwater, Gibson and Thomas*, 1999. ● Robert B. Pearsall, *Rupert Brooke: The Man and the Poet*, 1974. ● Steve Rabson, *Righteous Cause or Tragic Folly: Changing Views of War in Modern Japanese Poetry*, 1998. ● Jay Rubin, *Injurious to Public Morals: Writers and the Meiji State*, 1984. ● Clarise Samuels, *Holocaust Visions: Surrealism and Existentialism in the Poetry of Paul Celan*, 1993. ● Stuart Sillars, *Structure and Dissolution in English Writing, 1910–1920*, 1999. ● James Tatum, *The Mourner's Song: War and Remembrance from "The Iliad" to Vietnam*, 2003. ● Makoto Ueda, *Modern Japanese Poets and the Nature of Literature*, 1983.

Perspectives: Gendered Spaces ● Simone A. James Alexander, *Mother Imagery in the Novels of Afro-Caribbean Women*, 2001. ● Gloria Anzaldúa, *Borderlands: The New Mextiza / La frontera*, 1999. ● Ada Uzoamaka Azodo and Gay Alden Wilentz, eds. *Emerging Perspectives on Ama Ata Aidoo*, 1999. ● Gaston Bachelard, *The Poetics of Space*, trans. Maria Jolas, 1994. ● Alison Blunt and Gillian Rose, eds., *Writing Women and Space: Colonial and Postcolonial Geographies*, 1994. ● Michel de Certeau, *The Practice of Everday Life*, 1984. ● Bradley Epps, *Significant Violence: Oppression and Resistance in the Later Narrative of Juan Goytisolo*, 1996. ● Moira Ferguson, *Jamaica Kincaid: Where the Land Meets the Body*, 1994. ● Leigh Gilmore, *Limits of Autobiography: Trauma and Testimony*, 2001. ● Michael Keith and Steve Pile, eds., *Place and the Politics of Identity*, 1993. ● Henri Lefebvre, *The Production of Space*, 1991. ● Antonia MacDonald-Smythe, *Making Homes in the West-Indies: Constructions of Subjectivity in the Writings of Michelle Cliff and Jamaica Kincaid*, 2001. ● Doreen Massey, *Space, Place, and Gender*, 1994. ● George R. McMurray, *Gabriel García Márquez*, 1977. ● Fatima Mernissi, *The Harem Within*, 1994. ● Harley D.

Oberhelman, *Gabriel García Márquez: A Study of the Short Fiction*, 1991. ● Vincent O. Odamtten, *The Art of Ama Ata Aidoo: Polylectics and Reading Against Neocolonialism*, 1994. ● Lizabeth Paravisini-Gebert, *Jamaica Kincaid: A Critical Companion*, 1999. ● Randolph D. Pope, *Understanding Juan Goytisolo*, 1995. ● Elizabeth K. Teather, *Embodied Geographies: Spaces, Bodies and Rites of Passage*, 1999. ● Raymond L. Williams, *Gabriel García Márquez*, 1984. ● Virginia Woolf, *A Room of One's Own*, 1989.

Perspectives: Indigenous Cultures in the Twentieth Century ● Chadwick Allen, *Blood Narrative: Indigenous Identity in American Indian and Maori Literary and Activist Texts*, 2002. ● Paula Gunn Allen, *Off the Reservation: Reflections on Boundary-busting, Border-crossing Loose Canons*, 1998. ● Budd L. Hall, Dorothy Goldin Rosenberg, and George Jerry Sefa Dei, eds., *Indigenous Knowledges in Global Contexts: Multiple Readings of Our World*, 2000. ● N. Scott Momaday, *The Man Made of Words: Essays, Stories, Passages*, 1997. ● Patricia Monture-Angus and Renée Hulan, eds. *Native North America: Critical and Cultural Perspectives*, 1999. ● Mudrooroo Narogin, *Indigenous Literature of Australia: Milli Milli Wangka*, 1997. ● Jennifer Sabbioni, Kay Schaffer, and Sidonie Smith, eds., *Indigenous Australian Voices: A Reader*, 1998. ● Lorena Laura Stookey, *Louise Erdrich: A Critical Companion*, 1999. ● Jace Weaver, *That the People Might Live: Native American Literatures and Native American Community*, 1997.

Perspectives: Literature, Technology, and Media ● M. M. Badawi, "Two Novelists from Iraq: Jabra and Munif," *Journal of Arabic Literature*, vol. 23, 1992, 140–154. ● Sven Birkerts, *The Gutenberg Elegies: The Fate of Reading in an Electronic Age*, 1994. ● Issa J. Boullata, "Social Change in Munif's Cities of Salt," *Edebiyât: Journal of Middle Eastern Literatures*, vol. 8, 1998, 191–216. ● Sara Castro-Klaren, *Understanding Mario Vargas Llosa*, 1990. ● Efrain Kristal, *Temptation of the Word: The Novels of Mario Vargas Llosa*, 1998. ● Anna K. Kuhn, *Christa Wolf's Utopian Vision: From Marxism to Feminism*, 1988. ● James Lull, *Media, Communication, Culture: A Global Approach*, 1995. ● Marshall McLuhan, *Understanding Media: The Extensions of Man*, 1994. ● Jean O'Bryan-Knight, *The Story of the Storyteller*, 1995. ● Walter J. Ong, *Orality and Literacy: The Technologizing of the Word*, 1982. ● Neil Postman, *Amusing Ourselves to Death: Public Discourse in an Age of Show Business*, 1985. ● Margit Resch, *Understanding Christa Wolf: Returning Home to a Foreign Land*, 1997.

• Muhammad Siddiq, "The Contemporary Arabic Novel in Perspective," *World Literature Today: A Literary Quarterly of the University of Oklahoma,* vol. 60, 1986, 206–211. • Bruce Sterling, "Preface," in *Mirrorshades: The Cyberpunk Anthology,* ed. Bruce Sterling, 1988. • Matthew Strecher, *Dances with Sheep: The Quest for Identity in the Fiction of Murakami Haruki,* 2002.

Perspectives: Modernism and Revolution in Russia • Vladimir E. Alexandrov, *Andrei Bely, the Major Symbolist Fiction,* 1985. • Steven Broyde, *Osip Mandel'stam and His Age: A Commentary on the Themes of War and Revoution in the Poetry 1913–1923,* 2000. • Sheila Fitzpatrick, *The Russian Revolution,* 2001. • Gregory Freidin, *Coat of Many Colors: Osip Mandelstam and His Mythologies of Self-Presentation,* 1988. • Roger Keys, *Reluctant Modernist: Andrei Bely and the Development of Russian Fiction, 1902–1914,* 1996. • Robert Mann, *Andrei Bely's Petersburg and the Cult of Dionysus,* 1987. • Martin A. Miller, *The Russian Revolution: The Essential Readings,* 2001. • Ryszard Przybylski, *Essay on the Poetry of Osip Mandelstam: God's Grateful Guest,* 1987. • Edward E. Roslof, *Red Priests: Renovationism, Russian Orthodoxy, and Revolution, 1905–1946,* 2002. • Leonard Bertram Schapiro, *The Russian Revolutions of 1917: The Origins of Modern Communism,* 1984. • Stephen A. Smith, *The Russian Revolution: A Very Short Introduction,* 2002. • Ronald Grigor Suny, *A State of Nations: Empire and Nation-Making in the Age of Lenin and Stalin,* 2001.

Perspectives: Modernist Memory • Allyson Booth, *Postcards from the Trenches,* 1996. • Johanna Drucker, *Theorizing Memory: Visual Art and the Critical Tradition,* 1996. • John N. Duvall, *Productive Postmodernism: Consuming Histories and Cultural Studies,* 2002. • Paul Fussell, *The Great War and Modern Memory,* 1994. • Frank Lentricchia, *Modernist Quartet,* 1994. • James Longenbach, *Modernist Poetics of History: Pound, Eliot, and the Sense of the Past,* 1987. • Roger Luckburst and Peter Marks, eds., *Literature and the Contemporary: Fictions and Theories of the Present,* 1999. • Gail McDonald, *Learning to Be Modern: Pound, Eliot, and the American University,* 1993. • Sanford Schwartz, *The Matrix of Modernism: Pound, Eliot, and Early Twentieth-Century Thought,* 1985.

Perspectives: The 1001 Nights in the Twentieth Century • Peter L. Caracciolo, *The Arabian Nights in English Literature: Studies in the Reception of "The Thousand and One Nights" into British Culture,* 1988. • Mia Irene Gerhardt, *The Art of Story-Telling: A Literary Study of "The Thousand and One Nights,"* 1963. • Richard G. Hovannisian, *"The Thousand and One Nights" in Arabic Literature and Society,* 1997. • Edward William Lane, *Arabian Society in the Middle-Ages: Studies from "The Thousand and One Nights,"* 1987. • Sandra Naddaff, *Arabesque: Narrative Structure and the Aesthetics of Repetition in "The 1001 Nights,"* 1991. • Eva Sallis, *Sheherazade Through the Looking Glass: The Metamorphosis of "The Thousand and One Nights,"* 1999.

Perspectives: Poetry About Poetry • Jared Becker, *Eugenio Montale,* 1986. • Herbert Bergman, "Ezra Pound and Walt Whitman," *American Literature,* vol. 27, 1955, 56–61. • Gian-Paolo Biasin, *Il vento di Debussy: la poesia di Montale nella cultura del Novecento,* 1985. • Ettore Bonora, *Lettura di Montale,* 1980. • George Bornstein, ed., *Ezra Pound among the Poets,* 1985. • Clodagh J. Brook, *Expression of the Inexpressible in Eugenio Montale's Poetry: Metaphor, Negation, and Silence,* 2002. • Glauco Cambon, *Eugenio Montale's Poetry: A Dream in Reason's Presence,* 1982. • Detlev Gohrbandt and Bruno von Lutz, eds., *Seeing and Saying: Self-Referentiality in British and American Literature,* 1998. • Saime Y. Goksu and Edward Timms, *Romantic Communist: The Life and Work of Nazm Hikmet,* 1999. • Dietrich Gronau, *Nazim Hikmet,* 1991. • Claire Huffman, *Montale and the Occasions of Poetry,* 1983. • Hugh Kenner, *The Pound Era,* 1971. • H. Martin, ed., *Contemporary Chinese Literature,* 1986. • Bonnie S. McDougall and K. Louie, *The Literature of China in the Twentieth Century,* 1997. • Rebecca J. West, *Eugenio Montale: Poet on the Edge,* 1981. • Anna Whiteside and Michael Issacharoff, eds., *On Referring in Literature,* 1987. • M. Yeh, *Modern Chinese Poetry,* 1991.

Perspectives: Postcolonial Conditions • Fawzia Afzal-Khan, *Cultural Imperialism and the Indo-English Novel: Genre and Ideology in R. K. Narayan, Anita Desai, Kamala Markandaya, and Salman Rushdie,* 1993. • Munir Akash, ed., *Mahmoud Darwish: The Adam of Two Edens,* 2002. • Bill Ashcroft, Gareth Griffiths, and Helen Tiffin, eds., *The Post-Colonial Studies Reader,* 1995. • Bill Ashcroft, ed., *The Empire Writes Back: Theory and Practice in Post-Colonial Literatures,* 1989. • Mita Banerjee, *Chutneyfication of History: Salman Rushdie, Michael Ondaatje, Bharati Mukherjee and the Postcolonial Debate,* 2002. • *Mahmoud Darwish: Unfortunately, It Was Paradise: Selected Poems,* ed., Munir Akash, 2003. • Frantz Fanon, *Black Skin, White Masks,* 1991. • Frantz Fanon, *The Wretched of the Earth,* 1991. • Nadine Gordimer, *The Essential Gesture: Writing, Politics, and*

Places, 1989. ● Gareth Griffiths, *African Literatures in English: East and West,* 2000. ● Dominic Head, *Nadine Gordimer,* 1994. ● Michael C. Hillmann, *Forugh Farrokhzad: A Quarter-Century Later,* 1988. ● Michael C. Hillmann, *A Lonely Woman: Forugh Farrokhzad and Her Poetry,* 1987. ● Nico Israel, *Outlandish: Writing Between Exile and Diaspora,* 2000. ● Bruce Alvin King, ed., *New National and Post-Colonial Literatures: An Introduction,* 1996. ● Aneete Mansson, *Passage to a New Wor(l)d: Exile and Restoration in Mahmoud Darwish's Writings,* 2003. ● Anne McClintock, Aamir Mufti, Ella Shohat, and Social Text Collective, eds., *Dangerous Liaisons: Gender, Nations, and Postcolonial Perspectives,* 1997. ● Albert Memmi, *The Colonizer and the Colonized,* 1991. ● Padmini Mongia, *Contemporary Postcolonial Theory: A Reader,* 1996. ● Ngugi wa Thiong'o, *Decolonising the Mind: The Politics of Language in African Literature,* 1986. ● Lulu Norman, trans., "Mahmoud Darwish on Translating Poetry: The Place of the Universal," *Banipal: Magazine of Modern Arab Literature,* vol. 8, 2000, 25–27. ● Edward Said, *Orientalism,* 1979. ● Edward Said, *Culture and Imperialism,* 1998. ● Barbara Temple-Thurston, *Nadine Gordimer Revisited,* 1999.

Chinua Achebe ● Benedict-Chiaka Njoki, *The Four Novels of Chinua Achebe: A Critical Study,* 1984. ● Ezenwa-Ohaeto, *Chinua Achebe: A Biography,* 1997. ● Simon Gikandi, *Reading Chinua Achebe: Language and Ideology in Fiction,* 1991. ● Ode Ogede, *Achebe and the Politics of Representation: Form Against Itself, From Colonial Conquest and Occupation to Post-independence Disillusionment,* 2001. ● Umelo-Pjinmah, *Chinua Achebe: New Perspectives,* 1991.

Anna Akhmatova ● György Dalos, *The Guest from the Future: Anna Akhmatova and Isaiah Berlin,* 1999. ● T. Patera, *A Concordance to the Poetry of Anna Akhmatova,* 1995. ● Robert Porter, *Seven Soviet Poets,* 2000. ● Roberta Reeder, *Anna Akhmatova: Poet and Prophet,* 1995. ● David N. Wells, *Anna Akhmatova: Her Poetry,* 1996.

Akutagawa Ryunosuke ● David Boyd, "Rashomon: From Akutagawa to Kurosawa," *Literature/Film Quarterly,* vol. 15, 1987, 155–158. ● A. A. Gerow, "The Self Seen as Other: Akutagawa and Film," *Literature/Film Quarterly,* vol. 23, 1995, 197–203. ● Hendrik van Gorn and Ulla Musarra-Schroeder, eds., *Genres as Repositories of Cultural Memory,* 2000. ● Dennis Washburn and Alan Transman, eds., *Studies in Modern Japanese Literature,* 1997. ● Valerie Wayne and Cornelia Moore, eds., *Translations/Transformations: Gender and Culture in Film and Literature East and West: Selected Conference Papers,* 1993.

Mariama Bâ ● Rashidah Ismaili Abubakr, "The Emergence of Mariama Bâ," in *Essays on African Writing,* Vol. 1: *A Re-Evaluation,* Abdulrazak Gurnah, 1993, 24–37. ● Laurie Edson, "Mariama Bâ and the Politics of the Family," *Studies in Twentieth Century Literature,* vol. 17, 1993, 13–25. ● Siga Fatima Jagne, "Mariama Bâ (1929–1981)," in *Postcolonial African Writers: A Bio-Bibliographical Critical Source Book,* ed. Pushpa Naidu Parekh and Siga Fatima Jagne, 1998. ● Adele King, "The Personal and the Political in the Work of Mariama Bâ," *Studies in Twentieth Century Literature,* vol. 18, 1994, 177–188. ● Laura Charlotte Kempen, *Mariama Bâ, Rigoberta Menchu, and Postcolonial Feminism,* 2001. ● Ann McElaney-Johnson, "Epistolary Friendship: La prise de parole in Mariama Bâ's *Une si longue lettre,*" *Research in African Literatures,* vol. 30, 1999, 110–121. ● Emelia Oko, "Eros, Psyche, and Society: Narrative Continuity in Mariama Bâ's *So Long a Letter* and *Scarlet Song,*" in *Feminism and Black Women's Creative Writing: Theory, Practice, and Criticism,* ed. Aduke Adebayo, 1996. ● Angelita Reyes, "The Epistolary Voice and Voices of Indigenous Feminism in Mariama Bâ's *Une si longue lettre,*" *Moving Beyond Boundaries,* Vol. 2: *Black Women's Diasporas,* ed. Carole Boyce Davies, 1994. ● János Riesz, "Mariama Bâ's *Une si longue lettre:* An Erziehungsroman," *Research in African Literatures,* vol. 22, 1991, 27–42. ● Eva Rueschmann, "Female Self-Definition and the African Community in Mariama Bâ's Epistolary Novel *So Long a Letter,*" in *International Women's Writing: New Landscapes of Identity,* ed. Anne E. Brown and Marjanne E. Goozé, 1995. ● Charles Ponnuthurai Sarvan, "Feminism and African Fiction: The Novels of Mariama Bâ," *Modern Fiction Studies,* vol. 34, 1988, 453–464. ● Nahem Yousaf, "The 'Public' versus the 'Private' in Mariama Bâ's Novels," *Journal of Commonwealth Literature,* vol. 30, 1995, 85–98.

James Baldwin ● Harold Bloom, ed., *James Baldwin,* 1986. ● David D. Britt, *Image of the White Man in the Fiction of Langston Hughes, Richard Wright, James Baldwin and Ralph Ellison,* 1968. ● Cyraina E. Johnson-Roullier, *Reading on the Edge: Exiles, Modernities, and Cultural Transformation in Proust, Joyce, and Baldwin,* 2000. ● R. Jothiprakash, *Commitment as a Theme in African American Literature: A Study of James Baldwin and Ralph Ellison,* 1994. ● Keneth Kinnamon, *James Baldwin: A Collection of Critical Essays,* 1974. ● Pat

Lockie, *Analysis of Black/White Relations in the Works of James Baldwin*, 1971. ● Stanley Macebuh, *James Baldwin: A Critical Study*, 1973. ● Dwight A. McBride, ed., *James Baldwin Now*, 1999. ● D. Quentin Miller, ed., *Reviewing James Baldwin: Things Not Seen*, 2000. ● Manasse Mugabo, *Quest for Identity in James Baldwin's Fiction*, 1987. ● Therman B. O'Daniel, ed., *James Baldwin, a Critical Evaluation*, 1977. ● Horace A. Porter, *Stealing the Fire: The Art and Protest of James Baldwin*, 1989. ● Louis H. Pratt, *James Baldwin*, 1978. ● Fred L. Standley and Nancy V. Burt, eds., *Critical Essays on James Baldwin*, 1988.

Samuel Beckett ● Arthur N. Athanason, *Endgame: The Ashbin Play*, 1993. ● Deirdre Bair, *Samuel Beckett: A Biography*, 1978. ● Harold Bloom, ed., *Samuel Beckett's "Endgame,"* 1988. ● Anthony Cronin, *Samuel Beckett: The Last Modernist*, 1996. ● Bell Gale Chevigny, ed., *Twentieth-Century Interpretations of "Endgame": A Collection of Critical Essays*, 1969. ● Martin Esslin, *The Theatre of the Absurd*, 2001. ● Sean Golden, "Familiars in a Ruinstrewn Land: *Endgame* as Political Allegory," *Contemporary Literature*, vol. 22, 1981, 425–455. ● James Knowlson, *Damned to Fame: The Life of Samuel Beckett*, 1996. ● Patrick A. McCarthy, ed., *Critical Essays on Samuel Beckett*, 1986. ● John Pilling, ed., *The Cambridge Companion to Beckett*, 1994. ● Richard Keller Simon, "Dialectical Laughter: A Study of *Endgame*," *Modern Drama*, vol. 25, 1982, 505–513.

Jorge Luis Borges ● Lisa Block de Behar, *Borges, the Passion of an Endless Quotation*, 2003. ● Gene H. Bell-Villada, *Borges and His Fiction: A Guide to His Mind and Art*, 1999. ● Norman Thomas Di Giovanni, *Lesson of the Master: Borges and His Work*, 2003. ● Djelal Kadir, *Questing Fictions: Latin America's Family Romance*, 1986. ● Martín Lafforgue, *AntiBorges*, 1999. ● Selden Rodman and Jorge Luis Borges, *Tongues of Fallen Angels: Conversations with Jorge Luis Borges (and Others)*, 1974. ● Florence L. Yudin, *Nightglow: Borges' Poetics of Blindness*, 1997.

Bertolt Brecht ● Walter Benjamin, *Understanding Brecht*, 1973. ● Peter Brooker, *Bertolt Brecht: Dialectics, Poetry, Politics*, 1988. ● Martin Esslin, *Brecht, a Choice of Evils: A Critical Study of the Man, His Work, and His Opinions*, 1980. ● Ronald D. Gray, *Brecht the Dramatist*, 1976. ● Ronald Hayman, *Brecht: A Biography*, 1983. ● Werner Hecht, ed., *Brechts Theorie des Theaters*, 1986. ● Fredric Jameson, *Brecht and Method*, 1998. ● Carol Martin and Henry Bial, eds., *Brecht Sourcebook*, 2000. ● Siegfried Mews, ed., *Critical Essays on Bertolt Brecht*, 1989. ● Siegfried Mews and Herbert Knust, eds., *Essays on Brecht: Theater and Politics*, 1974. ● Ronald Speirs, *Bertolt Brecht*, 1987. ● Peter Thomson and Glendyr Sacks, eds., *The Cambridge Companion to Brecht*, 1994. ● Klaus Volker, *Brecht: A Biography*, 1978.

André Breton ● Mary Ann Caws, *André Breton*, 1996. ● Suzanne Guerlac, *Literary Polemics: Bataille, Sartre, Valéry, Breton*, 1997. ● Octavio Paz, *Estrella de tres puntas: André Breton y el surrealismo*, 1996. ● Gina McDaniel Tarver, *Issues of Otherness and Identity in the Works of Izquierdo, Kahlo, Artaud, and Breton*, 1996. ● Alain Virmaux, *André Breton: le pôle magnétique*, 1998. ● André Vielwahr, *S'affranchir des contradictions: André Breton de 1925 à 1930*, 1998.

Italo Calvino ● Joann Cannon, *Postmodern Italian Fiction: The Crisis of Reason in Calvino, Eco, Sciascia, Malerba*, 1989. ● Jorge J. E. Gracia, *Literary Philosophers: Borges, Calvino, Eco*, 2002. ● Angela M. Jeannet, *Under the Radiant Sun and the Crescent Moon: Italo Calvino's Storytelling*, 2000. ● Constance Markey, *Italo Calvino: A Journey Toward Postmodernism*, 1999. ● Domenico Scarpa, *Italo Calvino*, 1999.

Alejo Carpentier ● Simon Gikandi, *Writing in Limbo: Modernism and Caribbean Literature*, 1992. ● Roberto González Echevarría, *Alejo Carpentier: The Pilgrim at Home*, 1977. ● Sally Harvey, *Carpentier's Proustian Fiction: The Influence of Marcel Proust on Alejo Carpentier*, 1994. ● Frank Janney and Alejo Carpentier, *Alejo Carpentier and His Early Works*, 1981. ● Djelal Kadir, *Questing Fictions: Latin America's Family Romance*, 1986.

Constantine Cavafy ● Gregory Jusdanis, *The Poetics of Cavafy: Textuality, Eroticism, History*, 1987. ● Edmund Keeley, *Cavafy's Alexandria*, 1996. ● Jane Lagoudis Pinchin, *Alexandria Still: Forster, Durrell, and Cavafy*, 1977. ● Christopher Robinson, *C. P. Cavafy*, 1988.

Aimé Césaire ● A. James Arnold, *Modernism and Négritude: The Poetry and Poetics of Aimé Césaire*, 1981. ● Maryse Condé, *Cahier d'un retour au pays natal: Césaire: analyse critique*, 1978. ● Gregson Davis, *Aimé Césaire*, 1997. ● Lilyan Kesteloot, *Aimé Césaire: L'homme et l'oeuvre*, 1993. ● Janis L. Pallister, *Aimé Césaire*, 1991. ● Michael Richardson, ed., *Refusal of the Shadow: Surrealism and the Caribbean*, trans. Krzysztof Fijalkowski and Michael Richardson, 1996. ● Ronnie Leah Scharfman, *Engagement and the Language of the Subject in the Poetry of Aimé Césaire*, 1987.

Joseph Conrad ● John Batchelor, *The Life of Joseph Conrad: A Critical Biography,* 1993. ● Ted Billy ed., *Critical Essays on Joseph Conrad,* 1987. ● Harold Bloom, ed., *Joseph Conrad's "Heart of Darkness,"* 1987. ● Keith Carabine, ed., *Joseph Conrad: Critical Assessments,* 4 vols., 1992. ● Ford Madox Ford, *Joseph Conrad: A Personal Remembrance,* 1989. ● Christopher L. GoGwilt, *The Invention of the West: Joseph Conrad and the Double-Mapping of Europe and Empire,* 1995. ● Nico Israel, *Outlandish: Writing Between Exile and Diaspora,* 2000. ● Fredric Jameson, *The Political Unconscious: Narrative as a Socially Symbolic Act,* 1981. ● Fredric R. Karl and Laurence Davies, eds., *The Collected Letters of Joseph Conrad,* 1983. ● Owen Knowles and Gene Moore, eds., *The Oxford Reader's Companion to Conrad,* 2000. ● Martin Ray, ed., *Joseph Conrad: Interviews and Recollections,* 1990. ● Edward W. Said, *The World, the Text, and the Critic,* 1966. ● Norman Sherry, ed., *Conrad: The Critical Heritage,* 1973. ● Ian Watt, *Joseph Conrad: A Critical Biography,* 1979. ● Mark A. Wollaeger, *Joseph Conrad and the Fictions of Skepticism,* 1990.

Oswald de Andrade ● Afranio Coutinho, *An Introduction to Literature in Brazil,* 1969. ● Christopher Dunn, *Brutality Garden: Tropicália and the Emergence of a Brazilian Counterculture,* 2001. ● Maria Eugênia de Gama Alves Boaventura, *Oswald de Andrade,* 1986. ● Lucia Helena, *Totens e tabus da modernidade brasileira: símbolo e alegoria na obra de Oswald de Andrade,* 1985. ● Maggie Kilgour, *From Communion to Cannibalism: An Anatomy of Metaphors of Incorporation,* 1990. ● Frank Lestringant, *Cannibals: The Discovery and Representation of the Cannibal from Columbus to Jules Verne,* 1997.

Mahasweta Devi ● Tarun K. Saint, *Bruised Memories: Communal Violence and the Writer,* 2002. ● E. Satyanarayana, *Plays of Mahasweta Devi,* 2000. ● Gayatri C. Spivak, "Moving Devi," in *Other Asias,* 2004.

Assia Djebar ● Gordon Bigelow, "Revolution and Modernity: Assia Djébar's *Les Enfants du Nouveau Monde,*" *Research in African Literatures,* vol. 34, 2003, 13–27. ● Miriam Cooke, *Women Claim Islam: Creating Islamic Feminism Through Literature,* 2001. ● Anne Donadey, *Recasting Postcolonialism: Women Writing Between Worlds,* 2001. ● Ann Donadey, *Polyphonic and Palimpsestic Discourse in the Works of Assia Djebar and Leila Sebbar,* 1993. ● Rafika Merini, *Two Major Francophone Women Writers: Assia Djébar and Leila Sebba: A Thematic Study of Their Works,* 1999. ● Nada Elia, *Trances, Dances, and Vociferations: Agency and Resistance in Africana Women's Narratives,* 2001. ● Elizabeth Warnock, ed., *Remembering Childhood in the Middle East: Memoirs from a Century of Change,* 2002.

Carlos Drummond de Andrade ● Fernando Py, *Bibliografia comentada de Carlos Drummond de Andrade (1918–1930),* 1980. ● Donaldo Schüler, *A dramaticidade na poesia de Drummond,* 1979. ● Ricardo da Silveira Lobo Sternberg, *The Unquiet Self: Self and Society in the Poetry of Carlos Drummond de Andrade,* 1986. ● Mirella Vieira Lima, *Confidência mineira: o amor na poesia de Carlos Drummond de Andrade,* 1995.

T. S. Eliot ● Peter Ackroyd, *T. S. Eliot: A Life,* 1984. ● Harold Bloom, ed., *T. S. Eliot's "The Waste Land,"* 1986. ● Jewel Spears Brooker and Joseph Bentley, *Reading "The Wasteland": Modernism and the Limits of Interpretation,* 1990. ● Valerie Eliot, ed., *"The Waste Land": Fascimile and Transcript of the Original Drafts Including the Annotations of Ezra Pound,* 1971. ● Maud Ellman, *The Poetics of Impersonality: T. S. Eliot and Ezra Pound,* 1987. ● Nancy K. Gish, *"The Waste Land": A Poem of Memory and Desire,* 1988. ● Louis Menand, *Discovering Modernism: T. S. Eliot and His Context,* 1986. ● Anthony David Moody, ed., *The Cambridge Companion to T. S. Eliot,* 1994. ● Jeffrey M. Perl, *Skepticism and Modern Enmity: Before and After Eliot,* 1989. ● John Paul Riquelme, *Harmony of Dissonances: T. S. Eliot, Romanticism and Imagination,* 1990. ● Stanley Sultan, *Eliot, Joyce, and Company,* 1987.

Federico García Lorca ● Martha Nandorfy, *The Poetics of Apocalypse: Federico García Lorca's "Poet in New York",* 2003. ● Andrés Soria Olmedo, *Federico García Lorca,* 2000. ● Gareth D. Walters, *Canciones and the Early Poetry of Lorca: A Study in Critical Methodology and Poetic Maturity,* 2002. ● Sarah Wright, *The Trickster-Function in the Theatre of García Lorca,* 2000.

Gabriel García Márquez ● R. Thomas Berner, *The Literature of Journalism: Text and Context,* 1999. ● J. G. Cobo Borda, *Repertorio crítico sobre Gabriel García Márquez,* 1995. ● Robin W. Fiddian, *García Márquez,* 1995. ● Nelly S. Gonzalez, *Bibliographic Guide to Gabriel García Márquez, 1986–1992,* 1994. ● Djelal Kadir, *The Other Writing: Postcolonial Essays in Latin America's Writing Culture,* 1993. ● Rubén Pelayo, *Gabriel García Márquez: A Critical Companion,* 2001.

Emil Habiby ● Roger Allen, *The Arabic Novel: A Historical and Critical Introduction,* 1982.

• Allen Douglas and Fedwa Malti-Douglas, "Literature and Politics: A Conversation with Emile Habiby," in *The Arabic Novel Since 1950: Critical Essays, Interviews, and Bibliography*, ed. Issa J. Boullata, 1992. • Bruno Kreisky Forum for International Dialogue, *David Grossman/Emile Habiby: A Discussion About Israel Today—Intellectual Mainstreams in Arab and Jewish Communities: Development Towards Fundamentalism on Both Sides*, 1993. • Trevor Le Gassick, *Middle East Journal*, 1980.

James Joyce • Derek Attridge, ed., *The Cambridge Companion to James Joyce*, 1990. • Vincent Cheng, *Joyce, Race and Empire*, 1995. • Kevin J. H. Dettmar, *The Illicit Joyce of Postmodernism: Reading Against the Grain*, 1996. • Richard Ellman, *James Joyce*, 1982. • Herbert S. Gorman, *James Joyce*, 1948. • Clive Hart and David Hayman, eds., *James Joyce's "Ulysses": Critical Essays*, 1974. • Hugh Kenner, *Joyce's Voices*, 1978. • R. B. Kershner, *Joyce, Bakhtin, and Popular Literature: Chronicles of Disorder*, 1989. • Patrick McGee, *Joyce Beyond Marx*, 2001. • Dominic Manganiello, *Joyce's Politics*, 1980. • E. H. Mikhail, *James Joyce: Interviews and Recollections*, 1990. • Margot Norris, *Joyce's Web: The Social Unraveling of Modernism*, 1992. • Marty T. Reynolds, ed., *James Joyce: A Collection of Critical Essays*, 1993. • Fritz Senn, *Joyce's Dislocutions*, 1984. • Joseph Valente, ed., *Quare Joyce*, 1998.

Franz Kafka • Theodor W. Adorno, "Notes on Kafka," in *Prisms*, trans. Samuel and Shierry Weber, 1967. • Harold Bloom, ed., *Franz Kafka's "The Metamorphosis"*, 1988. • Max Brod, *Franz Kafka: A Biography*, 1960. • Stanley Corngold, "Kafka's *The Metamorphosis*: Metamorphosis of the Metaphor," in *Franz Kafka: The Metamorphosis: Translation, Backgrounds and Contexts, Criticism*, trans. and ed. Stanley Corngold, 1996. • Stanley Corngold, *The Commentators' Despair: The Interpretation of Kafka's "Metamorphosis,"* 1971. • Gilles Deleuze and Félix Guattari, *Kafka: Toward a Minor Literature*, trans. Dana Polan, 1986. • Vladimir Nabokov, "Franz Kafka (1883–1924): 'The Metamorphosis (1915),' " in *Lectures on Literature*, ed. Fredson Bowers, 1980. • Johannes Pfeiffer, "The Metamorphosis," trans. Ronald Gray, in *Kafka: A Collection of Critical Essays*, ed. Ronald Gray, 1962. • Heinz Politzer, *Franz Kafka: Parable and Paradox*, 1962. • Allen Thiher, *Franz Kafka: A Study of the Short Fiction*, 1990. • Klaus Wagenbach, *Franz Kafka: Pictures of a Life*, 1984.

Primo Levi • Carole Angier, *The Double Bond: The Life of Primo Levi*, 2002. • Gillian Banner, *Holocaust Literature: Schulz, Levi, Spiegelman and the Memory of the Offence*, 1999. • Robert S. C. Gordon, *Primo Levi's Ordinary Virtues: From Testimony to Ethics*, 2002. • Frederic D. Homer, *Primo Levi and the Politics of Survival*, 2001. • Paolo Momigliano Levi, *Primo Levi: testimone e scrittore di storia*, 1999.

Clarice Lispector • Hélène Cixous, *Readings: The Poetics of Blanchot, Joyce, Kafka, Kleist, Lispector, and Tsvetayeva*, ed. and trans. Verena Andermatt Conley, 1986. • Hélène Cixous, Verena Andermatt, eds., *Reading with Clarice Lispector (Theory and History of Literature Series)*, trans. Verena A. Conley, 1990. • Earl E. Fitz, *Sexuality and Being in the Poststructuralist Universe of Clarice Lispector: The Différance of Desire*, 2001. • Maria José Somerlate Barbosa, *Clarice Lispector: Spinning the Webs of Passion*, 1997.

Lu Xun • Lee Ou-Fan Lee, ed., *Lu Xun and His Legacy*, 1985. • Kang Liu and Xiaobing Tang, eds., *Politics, Ideology, and Literary Discourse in Modern China: Theoretical Interventions and Cultural Critique*, 1993. • Wolfgang Kubin, ed., *Symbols of Anguish: In Search of Melancholy in China*, 2001. • Hua Meng and Sukehiro Hirakawa, eds., *Images of Westerners in Chinese and Japanese Literature*, 2000. • Barbara Stoler Miller, ed., *Masterworks of Asian Literature in Comparative Perspective: A Guide for Teaching*, 1994.

Naguib Mahfouz • Salih J. Altoma, "Naguib Mahfouz: A Profile," *International Fiction Review*, vol. 17, 1990, 128–132. • Michael Beard and Adnan Haydar, eds., *Naguib Mahfouz: From Regional Fame to Global Recognition*, 1993. • Miriam Cooke, "Naguib Mahfouz, Men, and the Egyptian Underworld," in *Fictions of Masculinity: Crossing Cultures, Crossing Sexualities*, ed. Peter F. Murphy, 1994. • Rasheed El-Enany, *Naguib Mahfouz: The Pursuit of Meaning*, 1993. • Hoda Gindi, ed., *Images of Egypt in Twentieth Century Literature*, 1991. • Haim Gordon, *Naguib Mahfouz's Egypt: Existential Themes in His Writings*, 1990. • John C. Hawley, ed., *The Postcolonial Crescent: Islam's Impact on Contemporary Literature*, 1998. • Trevor Le Gassick, ed., *Critical Perspectives on Naguib Mahfouz*, 1991. • Naguib Mahfouz, *The Nobel Lecture*, trans. Mohammed Salmawy, 1998. • Amin Malak, "The Private and the Universal: The Fiction of Naguib Mahfouz," *Toronto South Asian Review*, vol. 11, 1992, 1-8. • Samia Mehrez, *Egyptian Writers Between History and Fiction: Essays on Naguib*

Mahfouz, Sonallah Ibrahim, and Gamal al-Ghitani, 1994. • Matti Moosa, *The Early Novels of Naguib Mahfouz: Images of Modern Egypt,* 1994. • Nedal Al-Mousa, "The Nature and Uses of the Fantastic in the Fictional World of Naguib Mahfouz," *Journal of Arabic Literature,* vol. 23, 1992, 36–48. • Sasson Somekh, "The Essence of Naguib Mahfouz," *Tel Aviv Review,* vol. 2, 1989–1990, 244–257.

Filippo Tommaso Marinetti • Gino Agnese, *Marinetti: una Vita Esplosiva,* 1990. • Ex Libris (Firm), *Futurism: Italian & Russian,* 1985. • James Joll, *Three Intellectuals in Politics,* 1965. • Luciano De Maria, *Marinetti e i Futuristi,* 1994. • Michael Webster, *Reading Visual Poetry After Futurism: Marinetti, Apollinaire, Schwitters, Cummings,* 1995.

Vladimir Mayakovsky • Edward James Brown, *Mayakovsky: A Poet in the Revolution,* 1973. • Ann Charters and Samuel B. Charters, *I Love: The Story of Vladimir Mayakovsky and Lili Brik,* 1979. • Ilya Kutik, *Ode and the Odic: Essays on Mandelstam, Pasternak, Tsvetaeva and Mayakovksy,* 1994. • Juliette R. Stapanian, *Mayakovsky's Cubo-Futurist Vision,* 1986.

Mishima Yukio • Guy Amirthanayagam, *Writers in East-West Encounter: New Cultural Bearings,* 1982. • Owen Heathcote, "Masochism, Sadism, and Homotextuality: The Examples of Yukio Mishima and Eric Jourdan," *Paragraph: A Journal of Modern Critical Theory,* vol. 17, 1994, 174–189. • Nancy G. Hume, ed., *Japanese Aesthetics and Culture: A Reader,* 1995. • Donald H. Mengay, *Body/Talk: Mishima, Masturbation, and Self-Performativity,* in *Genealogy and Literature,* ed. Lee Quinby, 1995. • Susan J. Napier, *Escape from the Wasteland: Romanticism and Realism in the Fiction of Mishima Yukio and Oe Kenzaburo,* 1991. • Ian Nish and Charles Dunn, eds., *European Studies on Japan,* 1979. • Noriko Thunman, *Forbidden Colors: Essays on Body and Mind in the Novels of Mishima Yukio,* 1999. • Peter Wolfe, *Yukio Mishima,* 1989.

Vladimir Nabokov • Vladimir E. Alexandrov, ed., *Nabokov's Otherworld,* 1991. • Brian Boyd, *Vladimir Nabokov: The American Years,* 1991. • Asher Z. Milbauer, *Transcending Exile: Conrad, Nabokov, I. B. Singer,* 1985. • Charles Nicol and Gennady Barabtarlo, eds., *Small Alpine Form: Studies in Nabokov's Short Fiction,* 1993. • Hana Pichova, *The Art of Memory in Exile: Vladimir Nabokov and Milan Kundera,* 2002.

V. S. Naipaul • Dagmar Barnouw, *Naipaul's Strangers,* 2003. • Wimal Dissanayake, *Self and Colonial Desire: Travel Writings of V. S. Naipaul,* 1993. • Helen Hayward, *The Enigma of V. S. Naipaul: Sources and Contexts,* 2002. • Feroza F. Jussawalla, *Conversations with V. S. Naipaul,* 1997. • Judith Levy, *V. S. Naipaul: Displacement and Autobiography,* 1995. • Timothy Weiss, *On the Margins: The Art of Exile in V. S. Naipaul,* 1992.

Pablo Neruda • Marjorie Agosín, *Pablo Neruda,* 1986. • Salvatore Bizzarro, *Pablo Neruda: All Poets the Poet,* 1979. • René de Costa, *The Poetry of Pablo Neruda,* 1979. • Manuel Duran, *Earth Tones: The Poetry of Pablo Neruda,* 1981. • David Goodnough, *Pablo Neruda: Nobel Prize-Winning Poet,* 1998. • Teresa Longo, *Pablo Neruda and the U.S. Culture Industry,* 2002. • Enrico Mario Santi, *Pablo Neruda: The Poetics of Prophecy,* 1982. • Volodia Teitelboim, *Neruda: An Intimate Biography,* trans. Beverly J. De Long-Tonelli, 1991.

Boris Pasternak • Lazar Fleishman, *Poetry and Revolution: Boris Pasternak's "My Sister Life,"* 1999. • David C. Gillespie, *The Twentieth-Century Russian Novel: An Introduction,* 1996. • Ilya Kutik, *The Ode and the Odic: Essays on Mandelstam, Pasternak, Tsvetaeva and Mayakovksy,* 1994. • Robert Porter, *Seven Soviet Poets,* 2000. • Larissa Rudova, *Understanding Boris Pasternak,* 1997. • Larissa Rudova, *Pasternak's Short Fiction and the Cultural Vanguard,* 1994. • Munir Sendich, *Boris Pasternak: A Reference Guide,* 1994. • Efraim Sicher, *Jews in Russian Literature After the October Revolution: Writers and Artists Between Hope and Apostasy,* 1995. • Justin Weir, *The Author as Hero: Self and Tradition in Bulgakov, Pasternak, and Nabokov,* 2002.

Octavio Paz • J. Agustín and B. Pastén, *Octavio Paz: crítico practicante en busca de una poética,* 1999. • Yvon Grenier, *From Art to Politics: Octavio Paz and the Pursuit of Freedom,* 2001. • Mario Pinho, *Volver al ser: un acercamiento a la poética de Octavio Paz,* 1997. • José Quiroga, *Understanding Octavio Paz,* 1998. • Xavier Rodríguez Ledesma, *El pensamiento político de Octavio Paz: las trampas de la ideología,* 1996.

Fernando Pessoa • George Monteiro, *Fernando Pessoa and Nineteenth-Century Anglo-American Literature,* 2000. • Irene Ramalho Santos and Maria Irene Santos, *Atlantic Poets: Fernando Pessoa's Turn in Anglo-American Modernism,* 2002. • Darlene J. Sadlier, *Introduction to Fernando Pessoa: Modernism and the Paradoxes of Authorship,* 1999. • Darlene J. Sadlier, *An Introduction to Fernando Pessoa, Literary Modernist,* 1998.

• Antonio Tabucchi, *Dreams of Dreams: And, The Last Three Days of Fernando Pessoa*, 1999.

Premchand • Madan Gopal, *Munshi Premchand: A Literary Biography*, 1965. • Usha Saksena, "Western Influence on Premchand," *Yearbook of Comparative and General Literature*, vol. 11, 1962, 129–132. • Barbara Stoler Miller, ed., *Masterworks of Asian Literature in Comparative Perspective: A Guide for Teaching*, 1994. • Robert O. Swan, *Munshi Premchand of Lamhi Village*, 1969. • Norman H. Zide, Colin P. Masica, K. C. Bahl, and A. C. Chandola, *A Premchand Reader*, 1962.

Rainer Maria Rilke • Ralph Freedman, *Life of a Poet: Rainer Maria Rilke*, 1996. • William H. Gass, *Reading Rilke: Reflections on the Problems of Translation*, 1999. • J. F. Hendry, *The Sacred Threshold: A Life of Rainer Maria Rilke*, 1983. • Sigrid Kellenter, *Das Sonett bei Rilke*, 1982. • Kathleen L. Komar, *Transcending Angels: Rainer Maria Rilke's "Duino Elegies,"* 1987. • Erika A. Metzger and Michael M. Metzger, eds., *A Companion to the Works of Rainer Maria Rilke*, 2001. • Roger Paulin and Peter Hutchinson, eds., *Rilke's Duino Elegies: Cambridge Readings*, 1996. • Donald Prater, *A Ringing Glass: The Life of Rainer Maria Rilke*, 1986. • Rainer Maria Rilke, *Rilkes Duineser Elegien*, ed. Ulrich Fülleborn and Manfred Engel, 3 vols., 1980–1982.

Diego Rivera • Linda Bank Downs, *Diego Rivera: The Detroit Industry Murals*, 1999. • Pete Hamill, *Diego Rivera*, 1999. • Anthony W. Lee, *Painting on the Left: Diego Rivera, Radical Politics, and San Francisco's Public Murals*, 1999. • Patrick Marnham, *Dreaming with His Eyes Open: A Life of Diego Rivera*, 1998.

Salman Rushdie • M. Keith Booker, ed., *Critical Essays on Salman Rushdie*, 1999. • Timothy Brennan, *Salman Rushdie and the Third World: Myths of the Nation*, 1989. • Roger Y. Clark, *Stranger Gods: Salman Rushdie's Other Worlds*, 2001. • Catherine Cundy, *Salman Rushdie*, 1996. • Damian Grant, *Salman Rushdie*, 1999. • James Harrison, *Salman Rushdie*, 1992. • Sabrina Hassumani, *Salman Rushdie: A Postmodern Reading of His Major Works*, 2002. • Jaina C. Sanga, *Salman Rushdie's Postcolonial Metaphors: Migration, Translation, Hybridity, Blasphemy, and Globalization*, 2001.

Léopold Sédar Senghor • Sylvia Washington Ba, *The Concept of Négritude in the Poetry of Léopold Sédar Senghor*, 1973. • Lilyan Kesteloot, *Comprendre les poèmes de Léopold Sédar Senghor*, 1986. • Sebastian Okechukwu Mezu, *The Poetry of Léopold Sédar Senghor*, 1973. • Wole Soyinka, "L. S. Senghor and Négritude: J'accuse, mais je pardonne," *The Burden of Memory, the Muse of Forgiveness*, 1999. • Janice S. Spleth, ed., *Critical Perspectives on Léopold Sédar Senghor*, 1993. • Janice S. Spleth, *Léopold Sédar Senghor*, 1985. • Janet G. Vaillant, *Black, French, and African: A Life of Léopold Sédar Senghor*, 1990.

Wole Soyinka • A. O. Dasylva, *Understanding Wole Soyinka: Death and the King's Horseman*, 1996. • James Gibbs, ed., *Critical Perspectives on Wole Soyinka*, 1980. • Adewale Maja-Pearce, ed., *Wole Soyinka: An Appraisal*, 1994. • Oyin Ogunba, ed., *Soyinka: A Collection of Critical Essays*, 1994. • Wole Soyinka, *Art, Dialogue, and Outrage: Essays on Literature and Culture*, 1993. • Wole Soyinka, *The Burden of Memory, the Muse of Forgiveness*, 1999. • Wole Soyinka, *Myth, Literature, and the African World*, 1990.

Wallace Stevens • Bart Eeckhout, *Wallace Stevens and the Limits of Reading and Writing*, 2002. • Lisa Malinowski Steinman, *Made in America: Science, Technology, and American Modernist Poets*, 1987. • Charles M. Murphy, *Wallace Stevens: A Spiritual Poet in a Secular Age*, 1997. • Justin Quinn, *Gathered Beneath the Storm: Wallace Stevens, Nature and Community*, 2002. • Louis A. Renza, *Edgar Allan Poe, Wallace Stevens, and the Poetics of American Privacy*, 2002. • Richard P. Rogers, *Wallace Stevens: Man Made Out of Words*, 1988. • Holly Stevens, *Souvenirs and Prophecies: The Young Wallace Stevens*, 1976. • Helen Vendler, *Wallace Stevens: Words Chosen Out of Desire*, 1986.

Marina Tsvetaeva • Hélène Cixous, *Readings: The Poetics of Blanchot, Joyce, Kafka, Kleist, Lispector, and Tsvetayeva*, ed. and trans. Verena Andermatt Conley, 1986. • Lily Feiler, *Marina Tsvetaeva: The Double Beat of Heaven and Hell*, 1994. • Simon Karlinsky, *Marina Tsvetaeva: The Woman, Her World, and Her Poetry*, 1985. • Simon Karlinsky, *Marina Cvetaeva: Her Life and Art*, 1966. • Ilya Kutik, *The Ode and the Odic: Essays on Mandelstam, Pasternak, Tsvetaeva and Mayakovksy*, 1994. • Michael Makin, *Marina Tsvetaeva: The Poetics of Appropriation*, 1993.

César Vallejo • Stephen M. Hart, *César Vallejo: A Critical Bibliography of Research*, 2002. • Tace Hedrick, *Mestizo Modern: Race, Nation, and Identity in Cesar Vallejo, Gabriela Mistral, Frida Kahlo, and Diego Rivera*, 2003.

• Bernard McGuirk, *Latin American Literature: Symptoms, Risks, and Strategies of Post-structuralist Criticism*, 1997. • Adam Sharman, *The Poetry and Poetics of César Vallejo: The Fourth Angle of the Circle*, 1997.

Mario Vargas Llosa • M. Keith Booker, *Vargas Llosa Among the Postmodernists*, 1994. • Sara Castro-Klaren, *Understanding Mario Vargas Llosa*, 1990. • Djelal Kadir, *The Other Writing: Postcolonial Essays in Latin America's Writing Culture*, 1993. • Braulio Muñoz, *A Storyteller: Mario Vargas Llosa Between Civilization and Barbarism*, 2000. • Emil Volek, *Literatura hispanoamericana entre la modernidad y la postmodernidad*, 1994.

Gerald Vizenor • Kimberly M. Blaeser, *Gerald Vizenor: Writing in Oral Tradition*, 1996. • Arnold Krupat, *The Turn to the Native: Studies in Criticism and Culture*, 1996. • Robert A. Lee, ed., *Loosening the Seams: Interpretations of Gerald Vizenor*, 2000. • Gerald Vizenor, *Manifest Manners: Postindian Warriors of Survivance*, 1994. • Gerald Vizenor, *Narrative Chance: Postmodern Discourse on Native American Indian Literatures*, 1993. • Gerald Vizenor, *The People Named the Chippewa: Narrative Histories*, 1984.

William Butler Yeats • Harold Bloom, *Yeats*, 1970. • Terence Brown, *The Life of W. B. Yeats: A Critical Biography*, 1999. • Elizabeth B. Cullingford, *Gender and History in Yeats's Love Poetry*, 1993. • Una Mary Ellis-Fermor, *The Irish Dramatic Movement*, 1954. • Richard Ellman, *Yeats, the Man and the Masks*, 1948. • Richard J. Finneran, *Critical Essays on W. B. Yeats*, 1986. • Maud Gonne, *The Gonne-Yeats Letters 1893–1938*, ed. Anna MacBride White and A. Norman Jeffares, 1993. • Vicki Mahaffrey, *States of Desire: Wilde, Yeats, Joyce, and the Irish Experiment*, 1998. • Lucy McDiarmid, *Saving Civilization: Yeats, Eliot, and Auden Between the Wars*, 1984. • E. H. Mikhail, ed., *W. B. Yeats: Interviews and Recollections*, 2 vols., 1977. • David Pierce, *Yeats's Worlds: Ireland, England and the Poetic Imagination*, 1995. • Jahan Ramazani, *The Hybrid Muse: Postcolonial Poetry in English*, 2001. • M. L. Rosenthal, *Running to Paradise: Yeats's Poetic Art*, 1994.

• Jon Stallworthy, *Between the Lines: Yeats's Poetry in the Making*, 1963. • John Eugene Unterecker, *A Reader's Guide to William Butler Yeats*, 1959.

Derek Walcott • Robert D. Hamner, ed., *Critical Perspectives on Derek Walcott*, 1993. • Bruce King, *Derek Walcott: A Caribbean Life*, 2000. • José Luis Martínez-Dueñas Espejo and José María Pérez Fernández, eds., *Approaches to the Poetics of Derek Walcott*, 2001. • Michael Parker and Roger Starkey, eds., *Postcolonial Literatures: Achebe, Ngugi, Desai, Walcott*, 1995. • Rei Terada, *Derek Walcott's Poetry: American Mimicry*, 1992.

Virginia Woolf • Quentin Bell, *Virginia Woolf: A Biography*, 1972. • Alison Booth, *Greatness Engendered: George Eliot and Virginia Woolf*, 1992. • Thomas C. Carmagno, *The Flight of the Mind: Virginia Woolf's Art and Manic-Depressive Illness*, 1992. • Pamela L. Caughie, *Virginia Woolf and the Postmodern Tradition: Literature in Quest and Question of Itself*, 1991. • Margaret Homans, ed., *Virginia Woolf: A Collection of Critical Essays (Twentieth Century Views)*, 1992. • Mark Hussey, *Virginia Woolf, A to Z: A Comprehensive Reference for Students, Teachers, and Common Readers to Her Work, and Critical Reception*, 1996. • Douglas Mao, *Solid Objects: Modernism and the Test of Production*, 1998. • John Mepham, *Virginia Woolf: A Literary Life*, 1991. • Panthea Reid, *Archives and Art and Affection: A Life of Virginia Woolf*, 1988. • S. P. Rosenbaum, ed., *Virginia Woolf / Women and Fiction: The Manuscript Versions of A Room of One's Own*, 1992. • Sue Roe and Susan Sellers, eds., *The Cambridge Companion to Virginia Woolf*, 2000. • Bonnie Kime Scott, *Refiguring Modernism*, 2 vols., 1995. • Peter Stansky, *On or About December 1910: Early Bloomsbury and Its Intimate World*, 1996. • J. H. Stape, ed., *Virginia Woolf: Interviews and Recollections*, 1995. • Alex Zwerdling, *Virginia Woolf and Real Life*, 1987.

Zhang Ailing • C. T. Hsia, *A History of Modern Chinese Fiction*, 1961. • David Der-Wei Wang, introduction to Zhang Ailing, *The Rice-Sprout Song*, 1988.

CREDITS

1150

Wolf, Christa: Excerpt from "A Day's News" from *Accident / A Day's News* by Christa Wolf, translated by Heike Schwarzbauer. Translation copyright © 1989 by Farrar, Straus & Giroux, LLC. Reprinted by permission of Farrar, Straus & Giroux, LLC.

Woolf, Virginia: Excerpts from *A Room of One's Own* by Virginia Woolf. Copyright © 1929 by Harcourt, Inc., and renewed 1957 by Leonard Woolf. Reprinted by permission of the publisher.

Woolf, Virginia: "Mrs. Dalloway in Bond Street" and "The Lady in the Looking Glass: A Reflection" from *The Complete Shorter Fiction of Virginia Woolf* by Virginia Woolf, published by Hogarth Press. Used by permission of the executors of the Virginia Woolf Estate and The Random House Group Limited.

Yeats, William Butler: "Byzantium" and "Under Ben Bulben." Reprinted by permission of Scribner, a division of Simon & Schuster, Inc., from *The Poems of W. B. Yeats: A New Edition,* edited by Richard J. Finneran. Copyright © 1933 by Macmillan Publishing Company, copyright renewed © 1961 by Bertha Georgie Yeats.

Yeats, William Butler: "The Lake Isle of Innisfree," "Who Goes with Fergus?" and "No Second Troy" reprinted with the permission of Scribner, an imprint of Simon & Schuster Adult Publishing Group, from *The Collected Works of W. B. Yeats: Volume I, The Poems,* Revised, edited by Richard J. Finneran. New York: Scribner 1996.

Yeats, William Butler: "The Wild Swans at Coole" reprinted with the permission of Scribner, an imprint of Simon & Schuster Adult Publishing Group, from *The Collected Works of W. B. Yeats: Volume I, The Poems,* Revised, edited by Richard J. Finneran. Copyright © 1919 by The Macmillan Company; copyright renewed 1947 by Bertha Georgie Yeats.

Yeats, William Butler: "Easter 1916" and "The Second Coming" reprinted with the permission of Scribner, an imprint of Simon & Schuster Adult Publishing Group, from *The Collected Works of W. B. Yeats: Volume I, The Poems,* Revised, edited by Richard J. Finneran. Copyright © 1924 by The Macmillan Company; copyright renewed 1952 by Bertha Georgie Yeats.

Yeats, William Butler: "Sailing to Byzantium" reprinted with the permission of Scribner, an imprint of Simon & Schuster Adult Publishing Group, from *The Collected Works of W. B. Yeats: Volume I, The Poems,* Revised, edited by Richard J. Finneran. Copyright © 1928 by The Macmillan Company; copyright renewed 1956 by Georgie Yeats.

Yokomitsu Riichi: "Sensation and New Sensation," from *Yokomitsu Riichi: Modernist,* edited by Dennis Keene. Copyright © 1980 Columbia University Press. Reprinted by permission of the publisher.

Yosano Akiko: "Oh my little brother, I weep for you . . ."; from *Injurious to Public Morals: Writers and the Meiji State,* edited and translated by Jay Rubin. Copyright © 1984 by the University of Washington Press. Reprinted by permission of the publisher.

Zhang Ailing (Eileen Chang): "Stale Mates" from *Traces of Love and Other Stories* by Eileen Chang, edited by Eva Hung. Copyright © 2000 by The Chinese University of Hong Kong. Reprinted by permission of The Chinese University of Hong Kong.

ILLUSTRATION CREDITS

Cover image: Detail from *Dream of a Sunday Afternoon in the Alameda,* 1947–1948, mural, Hotel del Prado, by Diego Rivera (1866–1957). 4.8 × 15m, 15-¾ × 49-¼ ft. Copyright © Schalkwijk/Art Resource, New York. Inside front cover image: Courtesy of NASA. Page xxvi: Digital Image © The Museum of Modern Art/Licensed by SCALA/Art Resource, New York. The Museum of Modern Art, New York. Acquired through the Lillie P. Bliss Bequest (231.1948). Page 3: David Alfaro Siqueiros (1896–1974) © VAGA, NY. *Echo of a Scream,* 1937. Gift of Edward M. Warburg. Digital Image © The Museum of Modern Art/Licensed by SCALA/Art Resource, New York. The Museum of Modern Art, New York. Page 11: Figure, "Global shrinkage: the effect of changing transport technologies on real distance," from *The Future of the Future* by John McHale. (New York: Braziller, 1969). Page 305: Collection Cinéma/Photos12.com. Page 353: M. C. Escher's "Drawing Hands" © 2003 Cordon Art— The Netherlands. All rights reserved. Page 446: Copyright © 2005 Estate of Pablo Picasso/Artists Rights Society (ARS), New York. Page 705: David Bradley. Page 738: *Battle of the Butterflies at Tocito,* c. 1984, by Grey Cohoe. Navajo, 1944–1991. Acrylic on canvas. Museum purchase. The Philbrook Museum of Art, Tulsa, Oklahoma (1992.4). Page 770: Copyright © Ulrike Rosenbach, 1977. Page 797: Emily and Jerry Speigel Collection, courtesy Cheim & Read, New York. © Louise Bourgeois/Licensed by VAGA, New York. Photo: Alan Finkelman. Page 844: Still photograph courtesy The British Film Institute. Page 1009: Obiora Udechukwu *Silent Faces at a Crossroads,* oil on masonite. Collection and photo: The Artist. Page 1114: Nam June Paik, *Global Encoder.* Photo courtesy Nam June Paik and Carl Solway Gallery, Cincinnati, Ohio. Photo by Chris Gomien and Tom Allison.

FONTS CREDIT

The EuroSlavic, AfroRoman, Macron, TransIndic, Semitic Transliterator, and ANSEL fonts used to publish this work are available from Linguist's Software, Inc., P.O. Box 580, Edmonds, WA 98020-0580 USA, tel (425) 775-1130, www.linguistsoftware.com.

INDEX